Twentieth-Century Literary Criticism

Twentieth-Century Literary Criticism

**Excerpts from Criticism of the
Works of Novelists, Poets, Playwrights,
Short Story Writers, and Other Creative Writers
Who Lived between 1900 and 1960,
from the First Published Critical Appraisals
to Current Evaluations**

Sharon K. Hall
Editor

Dennis Poupard
Associate Editor

**Gale Research Company
Book Tower
Detroit, Michigan 48226**

STAFF

Sharon K. Hall, *Editor*

Dennis Poupard, *Associate Editor*

Thomas Ligotti, James E. Person, Jr., *Senior Assistant Editors*

Earlene M. Alber, Marsha Mackenzie Check, Kathleen Gensley, Thomas Gunton,
Marie Lazzari, Mark W. Scott, Anna C. Wallbillich, Denise Wiloch, *Assistant Editors*

Phyllis Carmel Mendelson, *Contributing Editor*

Carolyn Bancroft, *Production Supervisor*
Lizbeth A. Purdy, *Production Coordinator*

Robert J. Elster, *Research Coordinator*
Carol Angela Thomas, *Research Assistant*

Linda M. Pugliese, *Manuscript Coordinator*
Donna DiNello, *Manuscript Assistant*

Cherie D. Abbey, Elizabeth Babini, Frank James Borovsky, Laura L. Britton,
Ann K. Crowley, Lee Ann Ferency, Jeanne A. Gough, Denise B. Grove, Serita Lanette Lockard,
Gloria Anne Williams, Robyn Vernell Young, *Editorial Assistants*

L. Elizabeth Hardin, *Permissions Supervisor*
Filomena Sgambati, *Assistant Permissions Coordinator*
Anna Maria DiNello, Janice M. Mach, Mary P. McGrane, Patricia A. Seefelt, *Permissions Assistants*

Copyright © 1982 by Gale Research Company

Library of Congress Catalog Card Number 76-46132

ISBN 0-8103-0180-6
ISSN 0276-8178

CONTENTS

PREFACE

It is impossible to overvalue the importance of literature in the intellectual, emotional, and spiritual evolution of humanity. Literature is that which both lifts us out of everyday life and helps us to better understand it. Through the fictive life of an Emma Bovary, a Lambert Strether, a Leopold Bloom, our perceptions of the human condition are enlarged, and we are enriched.

Literary criticism is a collective term for several kinds of critical writing: criticism may be normative, descriptive, textual, interpretive, appreciative, generic. It takes many forms: the traditional essay, the aphorism, the book or play review, even the parodic poem. Perhaps the single unifying feature of literary criticism lies in its purpose: to help us to better understand what we read.

The Scope of the Book

The usefulness of Gale's *Contemporary Literary Criticism (CLC),* which excerpts criticism of current creative writing, suggested an equivalent need among literature students and teachers interested in authors of the period 1900 to 1960. The great poets, novelists, short story writers, and playwrights of this period are by far the most popular writers for study in high school and college literature courses. Moreover, since contemporary critics continue to analyze the work of this period—both in its own right and in relation to today's tastes and standards—a vast amount of relevant critical material confronts the student.

Thus, *Twentieth-Century Literary Criticism (TCLC)* presents significant passages from published criticism on authors who died between 1900 and 1960. Because of the difference in time span under consideration *(CLC* considers authors living from 1960 to the present), there is no duplication between *CLC* and *TCLC.*

Each volume of *TCLC* is carefully designed to present a list of authors who represent a variety of genres and nationalities. The length of an author's section is intended to be representative of the amount of critical attention he or she has received in the English language. Articles and books that have not been translated into English are excluded. An attempt has been made to identify and include excerpts from the seminal essays on each author's work. Additionally, as space permits, especially insightful essays of a more limited scope are included. Thus *TCLC* is designed to serve as an introduction for the student of twentieth-century literature to the authors of that period and to the most significant commentators on these authors.

Each *TCLC* author section represents the scope of critical response to that author's work: some early criticism is presented to indicate initial reactions, later criticism is selected to represent any rise or fall in an author's reputation, and current retrospective analyses provide students with a modern view. Since a *TCLC* author section is intended to be a definitive overview, the editors include between 30 and 40 authors in each 600-page volume (compared to approximately 100 authors in a *CLC* volume of similar size) in order to devote more attention to each author. Because of the great quantity of critical material available on many authors, and because of the resurgence of criticism generated by events such as an author's centennial or anniversary celebration, the republication of an author's works, or publication of a newly translated work or volume of letters, an author may appear more than once.

The Organization of the Book

An author section consists of the following elements: author heading, bio-critical introduction, principal works, excerpts of criticism (each followed by a citation), and, beginning with Volume 3, an annotated bibliography of additional reading.

- The *author heading* consists of the author's full name, followed by birth and death dates. The unbracketed portion of the name denotes the form under which the author most commonly wrote. If an author wrote consistently under a pseudonym, the pseudonym will be listed in the author heading and the real name given in parentheses on the first line of the bio-critical introduction. Also located at the beginning of the bio-critical introduction are any name variations under which an author wrote, including transliterated forms for authors whose languages use nonroman alphabets. Uncertainty as to a birth or death date is indicated by a question mark.

- The *bio-critical introduction* contains biographical and other background information about an author that will elucidate his or her creative output.

- The *list of principal works* is chronological by date of first publication and identifies genres. In those instances where the first publication was other than English language, the title and date of the first English-language edition are given in brackets. Unless otherwise indicated, dramas are dated by first performance, not first publication.

- *Criticism* is arranged chronologically in each author section to provide a perspective on any changes in critical evaluation over the years. For purposes of easier identification, the critic's name and the publication date of the essay are given at the beginning of each piece of criticism.

- A complete *bibliographical citation* designed to facilitate location of the original essay or book by the interested reader accompanies each piece of criticism. An asterisk (*) at the end of a citation indicates the essay is on more than one author.

- The *annotated bibliography* appearing at the end of each author section suggests further reading on the author. In some cases it includes essays for which the editors could not obtain reprint rights. An asterisk (*) at the end of a citation indicates the essay is on more than one author.

Each volume of *TCLC* includes a cumulative index to critics. Under each critic's name is listed the author(s) on which the critic has written and the volume and page where the criticism may be found. *TCLC* also includes a cumulative index to authors with the volume number in which the author appears in boldface after his or her name.

Acknowledgments

No work of this scope can be accomplished without the cooperation of many people. The editors especially wish to thank the copyright holders of the excerpts included in this volume, the permission managers of many book and magazine publishing companies for assisting us in locating copyright holders, and the staffs of the Detroit Public Library, University of Michigan Library, and Wayne State University Library for making their resources available to us. We are also grateful to Fred S. Stein for his assistance with copyright research and Louise Kertesz for her editorial assistance.

Suggestions Are Welcome

Several features have been added to *TCLC* since its original publication in response to various suggestions:

- Since Volume 2—An *Appendix* which lists the sources from which material in the volume is reprinted.

- Since Volume 3—An *Annotated Bibliography* for additional reading.

- Since Volume 4—*Portraits* of the authors.

- Since Volume 6—A *Nationality Index* for easy access to authors by nationality.

If readers wish to suggest authors they would like to have covered in future volumes, or if they have other suggestions, they are cordially invited to write the editor.

AUTHORS TO APPEAR
IN FUTURE VOLUMES

Ady, Endre 1877-1919
Agate, James 1877-1947
Agustini, Delmira 1886-1914
Aldrich, Thomas Bailey
  1836-1907
Annensy, Innokenty
  Fyodorovich 1856-1909
Anstey, Frederick 1856-1934
Arlen, Michael 1895-1956
Barea, Arturo 1897-1957
Baring, Maurice 1874-1945
Baroja, Pio 1872-1956
Barry, Philip 1896-1949
Bass, Eduard 1888-1946
Baum, L(yman) Frank
  1856-1919
Belloc, Hilaire 1870-1953
Benét, Stephen Vincent
  1898-1943
Benét, William Rose 1886-1950
Benson, E(dward) F(rederic)
  1867-1940
Benson, Stella 1892-1933
Beresford, J(ohn) D(avys)
  1873-1947
Besant, Annie(Wood) 1847-1933
Bethell, Mary Ursula 1874-1945
Biely, Andrei 1880-1934
Binyon, Laurence 1869-1943
Bjørnson, Bjørnstjerne
  1832-1910
Blackmore, R(ichard) D(odd-
  ridge) 1825-1900
Blasco Ibanez, Vicente
  1867-1928
Bojer, Johan 1872-1959
Bosman, Herman Charles
  1905-1951
Bottomley, Gordon 1874-1948
Bourne, George 1863-1927
Brandes, Georg (Morris Cohen)
  1842-1927
Broch, Herman 1886-1951
Bromfield, Louis 1896-1956
Buchan, John 1870-1953
Byrne, Donn (Brian Oswald
  Donn-Byre) 1889-1928
Caine, Hall 1853-1931
Campana, Dina 1885-1932
Cannan, Gilbert 1884-1955
Carman, (William) Bliss
  1861-1929
Chapman, John Jay 1862-1933

Churchill, Winston 1871-1947
Corelli, Marie 1855-1924
Corvo, Baron (Frederick William
  Rolfe) 1860-1913
Crane, Stephen 1871-1900
Crawford, F. Marion 1854-1909
Croce, Benedetto 1866-1952
Crowley, Aleister 1875-1947
Davidson, John 1857-1909
Day, Clarence 1874-1935
Delafield, E.M. (Edme Elizabeth
  Monica de la Pasture)
  1890-1943
DeMorgan, William 1839-1917
Doblin, Alfred 1878-1957
Douglas, Lloyd C(assel)
  1877-1951
Douglas, (George) Norman
  1868-1952
Doyle, Sir Arthur Conan
  1859-1930
Dreiser, Theodore 1871-1945
Drinkwater, John 1882-1937
Duun, Olav 1876-1939
Eluard, Paul 1895-1952
Fadeyev, Alexandr 1901-1956
Franklin, (Stella Maria)
  Miles (Lampe) 1879-1954
Feydeau, Georges 1862-1921
Field, Michael (Katharine Harris
  Bradley 1846-1914 and Edith
  Emma Cooper 1862-1913)
Field, Rachel 1894-1942
Flecker, James Elroy 1884-1915
France, Anatole (Anatole
  Thibault) 1844-1924
Freeman, John 1880-1929
Gale, Zona 1874-1938
Giacosa, Giuseppe 1847-1906
Glyn, Elinor 1864-1943
Gogarty, Oliver St. John
  1878-1957
Golding, Louis 1895-1958
Gorky, Maxim 1868-1936
Gosse, Edmund 1849-1928
Gould, Gerald 1885-1936
Grahame, Kenneth 1859-1932
Gray, John 1866-1934
Guiraldes, Ricardo 1886-1927
Gumilyov, Nikolay 1886-1921
Gwynne, Stephen Lucius
  1864-1950
Haggard, H(enry) Rider
  1856-1925

Hale, Edward Everett 1822-1909
Hall, (Marguerite) Radclyffe
  1806-1943
Harris, Frank 1856-1931
Hearn, Lafcadio 1850-1904
Henley, William Ernest
  1849-1903
Hergesheimer, Joseph 1880-1954
Hernandez, Miguel 1910-1942
Herrick, Robert 1868-1938
Hewlett, Maurice 1861-1923
Heyse, Paul (Johann Ludwig
  von) 1830-1914
Heyward, DuBose 1885-1940
Hichens, Robert 1864-1950
Hilton, James 1900-1954
Holtby, Winifred 1898-1935
Hope, Anthony 1863-1933
Housman, Laurence 1865-1959
Howard, Robert E(rvin) 1906-1936
Howard, Sidney 1891-1939
Howells, William Dean
  1837-1920
Hudson, Stephen 1868-1944
Hudson, W(illiam) H(enry)
  1841-1922
Huysmans, Joris-Karl 1848-1907
Ivanov, Vyacheslav Ivanovich
  1866-1949
Jacobs, W(illiam) W(ymark)
  1863-1943
James, Will 1892-1942
Jerome, Jerome K(lapka)
  1859-1927
Jones, Henry Arthur 1851-1929
Kipling, Rudyard 1865-1936
Kornbluth, Cyril M. 1923-1958
Kuzmin, Mikhail Alekseyevich
  1875-1936
Lang, Andrew 1844-1912
Lawson, Henry 1867-1922
Leverson, Ada 1862-1933
Lewisohn, Ludwig 1883-1955
Lindsay, (Nicholas) Vachel
  1879-1931
London, Jack 1876-1916
Lonsdale, Frederick 1881-1954
Louÿs, Pierre 1870-1925
Lowndes, Marie Belloc
  1868-1947
Lucas, E(dward) V(errall)
  1868-1938
Lynd, Robert 1879-1949

MacArthur, Charles
  1895-1956
Macaulay, Rose 1881-1958
McKay, Claude 1889-1948
Mais, Roger 1905-1955
Manning, Frederic
  1887-1935
Marinetti, Filippo Tommaso
  1876-1944
Marquis, Don(ald) Robert Perry
  1878-1937
Marriott, Charles 1869-1957
Martin du Gard, Roger
  1881-1958
Mencken, H(enry) L(ouis)
  1880-1956
Meredith, George 1828-1909
Mew, Charlotte (Mary)
  1870-1928
Mistral, Frédéric 1830-1914
Mitchell, Margaret
  1900-1949
Monro, Harold 1879-1932
Moore, George 1852-1933
Moore, Thomas Sturge
  1870-1944
Morgan, Charles 1894-1958
Morgenstern, Christian 1871-1914
Morley, Christopher
  1890-1957
Murray, (George) Gilbert
  1866-1957
Nervo, Amado 1870-1919
Nietzsche, Friedrich
  1844-1900
Norris, Frank 1870-1902
Noyes, Alfred 1880-1958
Olbracht, Ivan (Kemil
  Zeman) 1882-1952
Pinero, Arthur Wing
  1855-1934
Pontoppidan, Henrik
  1857-1943
Porter, Eleanor H(odgman)
  1868-1920
Porter, Gene(va) Stratton
  1886-1924
Powys, T(heodore) F(rancis)
  1875-1953
Proust, Marcel 1871-1922
Quiller-Couch, Arthur
  1863-1944
Rappoport, Solomon
  1863-1944

Authors to Appear in Future Volumes

Reid, Forrest 1876-1947
Riley, James Whitcomb 1849-1916
Rinehart, Mary Roberts 1876-1958
Roberts, Sir Charles (George Douglas) 1860-1943
Roberts, Elizabeth Madox 1886-1941
Rogers, Will(iam Penn Adair) 1879-1935
Rölvaag, O(le) E(dvart) 1876-1931
Rolland, Romain 1866-1944
Roussel, Raymond 1877-1933
Runyon, (Alfred) Damon 1884-1946
Sabatini, Rafael 1875-1950
Saltus, Edgar (Evertson) 1855-1921

Santayana, George 1863-1952
Schreiner, Olive (Emilie Albertina) 1855-1920
Seeger, Alan 1888-1916
Service, Robert 1874-1958
Seton, Ernest Thompson 1860-1946
Shiel, M(atthew) P(hipps) 1865-1947
Slater, Francis Carey 1875-1958
Sologub, Fyodor 1863-1927
Squire, J(ohn) C(ollings) 1884-1958
Sternheim, Carl 1878-1942
Stockton, Frank R. 1834-1902
Stoker, Bram 1847-1912
Supervielle, Jules 1884-1960
Swinburne, Algernon Charles 1837-1909

Symons, Arthur 1865-1945
Tabb, John Bannister 1845-1909
Tarkington, Booth 1869-1946
Teilhard de Chardin, Pierre 1881-1955
Tey, Josephine (Elizabeth Mackintosh) 1897-1952
Tsvetaeva, Marina 1892-1941
Turner, W(alter) J(ames) R(edfern) 1889-1946
Vachell, Horace Annesley 1861-1955
Van Dine, S.S. (Willard H. Wright) 1888-1939
Van Doren, Carl 1885-1950
Vazov, Ivan 1850-1921
Wallace, Edgar 1874-1932

Wallace, Lewis 1827-1905
Webb, Mary 1881-1927
Webster, Jean 1876-1916
Wedeking, (Benjamin) Frank(lin) 1864-1918
Welch, Denton 1917-1948
Wells, Carolyn 1869-1942
Werfel, Franz 1890-1945
Wister, Owen 1860-1938
Witkiewicz, Stanisław Ignacy 1885-1939
Wren, P(ercival) C(hristopher) 1885-1941
Wylie, Elinor (Morton Hoyt) 1885-1928
Wylie, Francis Brett 1844-1954
Zamyatin, Yevgeny Ivanovich 1884-1937
Zangwill, Israel 1864-1926

Readers are cordially invited to suggest additional authors to the editors.

Alain-Fournier

1886-1914

(Born Henri Alain Fournier) French novelist, poet, short story writer, essayist, and playwright.

In his short life Fournier completed only a single novel, but it is one which readers and critics continue to admire as a minor classic. *Le grand Meaulnes (The Wanderer)* is regarded as a remarkably successful embodiment of neoromanticism, "the most delicate rendering so far achieved in literature of the romantic adolescent consciousness," according to critic Robert Gibson. The novel treats perennial themes in the opposition between idealism and reality, imagination and intellect, childhood dreams and adolescent disillusionment. It is primarily a modern version of the traditional tale of the quest, the search for some lost or unseen ideal. In Fournier's novel this ideal takes the form of lost love and the "country without a name."

Fournier was born at La Chapelle d'Angillon, a pastoral region in central France which served as the inspiration for the idyllic and haunting countryside of Saint-Agathe in *The Wanderer*. He attended secondary school in Paris at the Lycée Lakanal. There he met Jacques Rivière, future editor of the *Nouvelle Revue Française*, where *Le grand Meaulnes* originally appeared. In the lengthy published correspondence of the two friends, Fournier's artistic and psychological development can be followed. The most crucial episode of Fournier's emotional life was a few brief meetings in Paris with a young woman, Yvonne de Quiévrecourt, who did not return his profound affection. They were separated, and Fournier devoted years to finding her again, an ordeal paralleled by Meaulnes's search for Yvonne de Galais in *The Wanderer*. When Fournier later discovered that de Quiévrecourt was married and a mother the sense of loss he felt remained with him the rest of his life.

The Wanderer is distinguished by its simple style which nonetheless achieves an atmosphere of rich detail and a subtle fusion of reality and dreams. These qualities can in part be attributed to the influence on Fournier of the English Pre-Raphaelite artists and French symbolist poets such as Francis Jammes. "Evocative" is the word commonly used to describe the sensory texture and magical aura of childhood that characterizes the novel and expresses the personality of its narrator, Seurel. Critical interpretations often view Seurel as only one aspect of an ideal protagonist formed by three persons: the memory-haunted narrator Seurel, the quixotic Augustin Meaulnes, and the enigmatic Frantz de Galais. The adventures of the trio as they search for lost loves and lost time make up a plot that some critics have found contrived and unrealistic. Likewise the opposition between the sacred and profane loves embodied by the innocent Yvonne and the sexually experienced Valentine Blondeaux adds to the effect of an implausibly neat storyline. However, the frequent comparisons of Fournier's novel with medieval quest narratives and traditional fairy tales argue for the position that it was never the author's intention to write a strictly realistic work. Fournier himself stated that his novel would be "a constant imperceptible shifting back and forth between dream and reality." Most critical readings take this

Courtesy of French Cultural Services

ambition into account and find that the resulting ambiguity lends the tale an elusive quality which defies analysis.

Fournier's early short stories and poems, written between 1905 and 1911 and collected in *Miracles*, share much the same nostalgic themes and mood as *The Wanderer*. But as critic Karen D. Levy points out, the play fragment *La maison dans la forêt* and the unfinished novel *Colombe Blanchet* suggest that Fournier's later work would have taken a quite different direction, one of less fantastic idealism. Whatever might have been the nature of his mature works, Fournier's death in action during the First World War determined that *The Wanderer* alone would survive as his artistic testament.

PRINCIPAL WORKS

Le grand Meaulnes (novel) 1913
  [*The Wanderer*, 1928; published in England as *The Lost Domain*, 1959]
Miracles (poetry, sketches, short stories, unfinished drama, and unfinished novel) 1924
Jacques Rivière et Alain-Fournier: Correspondence, 1905-1914 (letters) 1926

HAVELOCK ELLIS (essay date 1928)

Le Grand Meaulnes holds us, not as a brilliant achievement of rural romance such as George Sand accomplished in *La Mare au Diable,* nor as a fantastic fairy-tale allegory such as Theodore Powys has presented in *Mr. Weston's Good Wine.* Alain-Fournier put forth no magnificent effort. He remained true to his early maxim of the unity of life and art. It is possible to say that there is nothing in *Le Grand Meaulnes* from one end to the other but the trivial details of real life as its author had known life. Only they had fallen slowly from childhood on to a peculiarly sensitive and vibrant organism and when at last they were transformed into art a miracle was achieved and the water had become wine.

We realise the fidelity to his own life of the episodes and the atmosphere in Fournier's novel when we read [his] correspondence. Not only is he himself in the narrative all through, so that, as he once remarks, he hardly knew whether he was Meaulnes or young Seurel or Frantz or the writer of the book, but we may note how in the smallest details he seeks to come as close as he can to his own personal life. . . . The sounds and sights and odours that sank into the sensitive spirit of the real youth—all the traits of this remote and lonely spot of old France—live again transposed in the novel. Nor must we conclude that Alain-Fournier was merely a regional novelist. His outlook was too wide for this; his alert intelligence and emotional sensibility were equally alive in the totally different atmosphere of cities. (pp. xvi-xvii)

[Jacques] Rivière has somewhere remarked that it is not easy to describe the method of Fournier in words that might not equally apply to the method of Maeterlinck's early plays. The methods are, however, totally different. Maeterlinck's structures were of romantic material, heightened by the skilful use of silence, even (to use the phrase of Villiers) a *crescendo* of silences. Fournier's structure was severely realistic in every detail, and it was the interstices of the structure itself that were subtly interpenetrated with dream-life. Rivière, always a severe critic of his friend, told him in early life that he was inclined to be sentimental, and to find everything 'touching.' That certainly was the danger for Fournier; but he was saved by his own acute self-criticism, in spite of his profound contempt of the intellect, and, above all, by his instinct as artist. All his life he was haunted by dreams, but it was his good fortune to be instinctively aware that, as Paul Valéry has put it, 'to tell one's dreams one must be infinitely awake.' (p. xviii)

In every poet—in the heart of everyone who shares in the poet's spirit—there is a certain restless homesickness of the soul for which each seeks to find his own expression. Alain-Fournier was inspired by his own life, and if we seek in prose an expression of this nostalgia of the soul we can perhaps nowhere find it so well expressed as in a book which may now be counted among the permanent human possessions, *Le Grand Meaulnes.* (p. xix)

Havelock Ellis, in his introduction to The Wanderer *by Alain Fournier, translated by Françoise Delisle (translation copyright 1928 by Houghton Mifflin Company; copyright © renewed 1956 by Françoise Lafitte-Cyon; reprinted by permission of Houghton Mifflin Company), Houghton, 1928, pp. iii-xix.*

THE TIMES LITERARY SUPPLEMENT (essay date 1929)

"Le Grand Meaulnes" will appeal much more to one kind of reader than to another. Without the fascinating evidence of the four volumes of the correspondence between Fournier and Rivière—published last year—the strangely adoring and spellbound atmosphere of the novel is likely to seem a mere convention of literary romanticism to some people. Romantic the book certainly is—it is in essence a fairy-tale—but it records a process of poetic experience in which the dream is indistinguishable from actuality, and which bathes commonplace scenes in a radiant and miraculous light. "Behind every moment of life I seek the life of my Paradise; behind every landscape I feel the landscape of my Paradise." These words of Fournier's . . . apply equally well to the facts of his life and to the scheme of his novel. . . .

[It] is the magic which suffuses the incidents of the story, the wandering gleam upon it, which makes it so remarkable an experiment in fiction. Outwardly there is only the story of Augustin Meaulnes, a schoolboy of seventeen, who ran away from school one afternoon in a peasant's cart, lost himself in the pursuit of a schoolboy prank, and discovered the girl Yvonne de Galais in an old forsaken château during the course of a fantastic fête in honour of her brother's engagement. After an absence of four days the boy returned to his school, thenceforth to dream upon the mystery and to plan his way back to the scene of his adventure. Here is no allegory of unearthly beauty and human ecstasy, no cautionary tale of a search for perfection. The writing, though it bears the impress of an uncannily vivid sensibility, is simple and straightforward in the extreme; at no point does it strain after effect. But the naturalistic manner of the narrative does not deceive a reader with a sympathetic turn of fancy. The whole conception of the novel is lit by a sort of poetry of regret for lost innocence and vanished enchantment. The "lost land" of Augustin Meaulnes is actually the country from which, as Fournier said, he was exiled, but it is transformed by the dreaming passion with which he evoked it into the unattainable region inhabited by Yvonne de Galais. . . .

A summary of this kind is a long way from being fair to the novel; inevitably it threatens to make nonsense of its poetic symbolism. The book must be read with something of the concentration one gives to symbolist poetry if one is to appreciate its peculiar and haunting quality. Perhaps the most astonishing thing in it is the effect of the miraculous in the most realistic passages; the schoolboy adventure is equally coherent on the naturalistic plane and on the plane of pure fantasy. . . . But "**Le Grand Meaulnes**" is not in the least romantic in structure; in one respect it is a painstakingly faithful picture of rural life. For the rest, it is a grand gesture in the style of absolute self-expression, akin in this respect to the poetry of Rimbaud.

"Alain-Fournier," in The Times Literary Supplement *(© Times Newspapers Ltd. (London) 1929; reproduced from* The Times Literary Supplement *by permission), No. 1424, May 16, 1929, p. 390.*

DAVID PAUL (essay date 1947)

In both [Alain-Fournier and Andrew Marvell] there is a balance of passion and delicacy, of nostalgia and clarity which denotes a rare, if retiring spirit. The affinity denotes something else. Though Alain-Fournier was, as he said himself, 'profondément paysan'—and of the French soil—there is a quality in his work which is almost unique in French writing. The French mind, even the mind of a La Fontaine, tends to dwell exclusively in the world of experience. Alain-Fournier is one among the very few of his countrymen who could have been perfectly at home in the worlds of innocence of Blake and Shakespeare, of [Henry] Vaughan and [Thomas] Traherne. With Wordsworth and Traherne in particular he has this in common, that his whole work is dominated by the memory, and the continuance of sensations which were most deeply felt in childhood.

The landscape of a happy childhood is at once familiar and mysterious. Every object, every person, every movement and gesture possesses value, grace and significance; a value and a grace which belong, like the details in a picture, to the scheme of which they are a part; a significance which can be felt, like that of music, but not explained. (pp. 440-41)

In the solitary novel which he left behind, before disappearing on the German front in 1914, Alain-Fournier has left perhaps the last version of the world of childhood which can be compared with those of Wordsworth or Traherne. That alone, of course, does not indicate or explain the novel's significance as a whole. *Le Grand Meaulnes* was conceived in childhood, intensely felt and brooded over in adolescence, and at last written in the author's middle twenties, apparently with the dictated ease which sometimes follows long premeditation. On the surface it is, as the author called it, simply a 'novel of adventure and discovery.' But the surface is the least part of it, and though the surface seems transparent, it cannot disclose the dimension in which the adventures take place, or the nature of the discoveries. The novel contains its own interior illumination, and little light can be thrown on it from without. But some help in penetrating its recesses is afforded by Alain-Fournier's other writings, and most of all by his long correspondence with his closest friend, the critic Jacques Rivière. (p. 442)

The characters of the two friends are the kind of opposites which chime: Alain-Fournier, brusque, vigorous, occasionally impassive and given to bouts of silence, afflicted at times with inarticulacy like a toothache, qualifying or confirming Rivière's enthusiasms, reading more with a view to assimilating his own than with the critic's impersonal appraisal of what he read; Rivière, feminine, nervous, excitable, an exhaustive and acutely intelligent reader, subject throughout his early twenties to a series of prostrating and agonised admirations—almost like a series of illnesses—for one literary figure after another— the ascendants and declines of Maeterlinck, Barrès, Claudel and Gide, follow each other like breakers in a heavy sea; Fournier 'refusing to formulate himself'; Riviere perpetually searching for a formula, like a quick-change artist ransacking a jumbled wardrobe. . . . All the crises and monotonies of both lives are reflected, the plans and sudden reversals, the examinations failed, the agonies of military service, the literary dreams and projects, the essays and free-verse poems tremblingly submitted to select reviews, the rejections, the condolences, the excitement of a letter elicited from Claudel in China and the resultant religious crisis, an introduction to Gide. As the years pass a change gathers over the letters. They contract under the pressure of outside events, become nerveless and off-hand. Their reflective quality is rippled over by the continual current of events and emergencies. The legendary expansive leisure of the earlier years is gone.

It is the earlier part of the correspondence which therefore offers the greater interest; and Alain-Fournier's letters, inevitably, are today of greater significance than those of his friend. While Rivière gravitates excitedly from one idea to another, Fournier, having early divined the world of his own art, gravitates steadily towards that alone, so that the sense of his letters is

more deeply continuous. The earlier letters, at least, can be justly compared with those of Keats. The disadvantage of such a comparison lies with the French writer. He did not lead so retired an existence. He had to contend with all the distractions of good health, of finding a way of earning a living, of military service . . . and finally of daily journalism in Paris. In spite of all, his letters have something of the leisured penetration, the wisdom and the charity of Keats. (pp. 442-43)

Alain-Fournier was neither a precocious nor a prematurely sophisticated writer, and it is natural that the early letters should speak with the voice of adolescence. Few writers have felt or evoked with such eloquence the nameless, overpowering impulses of youth, but the intensity never wanders into vagueness, and rarely into sentimentality. On the contrary it tends always to transfer itself to something seen—a landscape glimpsed from the train, a Paris backwater, a family of gipsies, with their caravans—to concentrate its quality, not on an abstraction, but on some exterior object, often an unexpected one. . . .

Even the most youthful of the letters cannot be qualified as those of a belated romantic. Alain-Fournier's impulse was always direct and never literary. He was possessed by an interior passion which, after concentrating a moment on the objects and persons round him, shot past them into infinity. His relationship with Yvonne de Galais—whose name he quite simply gave to the heroine of his novel—can only be compared, if to anything, to Dante's relationship with Beatrice. (p. 444)

At a first reading, *Le Grand Meaulnes* is as clear and as defiant of explanation as would be the surface of a lake reflecting a sky which one cannot see. At a further reading it may be more deeply felt, but it becomes no easier of explanation. Its meaning is of the kind which one feels in certain pictures, more particularly in those of Watteau and Giorgione. Giorgione has been called an abstruse and allegorical painter, but both terms miss the mark. No amount of abstruse speculation or allegorical ingenuity will even begin to elucidate such a picture as the Pastoral Concert, in the Louvre. Every detail of the picture— the white urn-shaped woman turning to dip a jug in the cistern, the two dark-faced musicians leaning secretively towards each other, the woman playing the flute, the sun-soaked background—is weighted with a value beyond its purely aesthetic, functional significance. No appeal to allegory or the pastoral convention will explain it either. The whole picture is intent with a meaning beyond meaning in any explicable sense of the term. It is precisely this kind of symbolism which provides the unknown and immeasurable dimension throughout *Le Grand Meaulnes*—until it unfortunately fails and vanishes a little before the close. It might seem that no quality could be less calculable, and in a way this is true. Yet the letters show how constantly, how critically and how consciously (in so far as consciousness can help the artist) this quality was sensed and searched for by Alain-Fournier for years before the novel was written. (pp. 445-46)

The function of Alain-Fournier's work was, of course, 'escapist,' just as all art is escapist in some sense of the term. He was seeking to escape into his own reality. Unlike the romantic, who constructs or invents it, he was trying to discover it. He has something, but only a little, in common with Gérard de Nerval. There is a delicate but strong foundation of ordered and conscious purpose, of self-critical shrewdness in his work which is not to be found in the writings of that rare, but undeniably deranged visionary. (pp. 446-47)

His novel, when he at last succeeded in bringing it into words, was the growth not simply of ten years but of a lifetime, and it proved to be rooted in life as firmly as a flower is rooted in the soil. It fulfilled a function which is very rarely appreciated or carried out by the novelist. It is true that every novel contains a kind of symbolism, but it is too often of the kind which Alain-Fournier appraised and rejected in Ibsen—and a similar criticism might be applied to the novels of Kafka. Or else it is of the inchoate, unconscious and obsessive kind which dominates Dickens and many lesser novelists. For the novelist in general, symbolism either does not exist, or else it possesses a fascination which dominates his work, reducing every other element to a mechanism which will serve its ends—it becomes as deadly as a didactic purpose. Between the two extremes, *Le Grand Meaulnes* seems almost to stand alone. It is difficult to think of any other novel with which it can be classed. (p. 447)

> David Paul, "The Mysterious Landscape: A Study of Alain-Fournier," in The Cornhill Magazine (© John Murray 1947; reprinted by permission of John Murray (Publishers) Ltd.), Vol. 162, No. 972, Autumn, 1947, pp. 440-49.

DONALD SCHIER (essay date 1952)

Le Grand Meaulnes has always struck me as being far from a masterpiece and, indeed, as a poor book. . . .

Most novels, if they are to have any claim to serious consideration as works of art, must be about credible events that happen to apparently real people. Not that the novel must necessarily be "realistic" in the narrow sense; but it must be convincing. . . . [In *Le Grand Meaulnes*], Fournier intended to re-create and then to transfigure certain aspects of reality, and it is my argument that he has failed. Not only are his people the merest puppets . . . but the action of the novel is so wildly improbable that one cannot take it seriously. (p. 129)

Stripped of its stylistic draperies, the plot of *Le Grand Meaulnes* is . . . a creaking collection of old tricks. The coincidences which are responsible for the Valentine episode are of a kind which no serious novelist since Dickens has dared to use. The oath sworn by Seurel and Meaulnes (which cannot fail to remind one of *Tom Sawyer*) is preposterous enough when one considers the age of Meaulnes and Frantz; but Frantz's whistle on the day of the wedding, like a thin, shrill echo from *Hernani*, reduces the fantastic to the absurd.

The rusty squeaks of the plot machinery are aggravated by the unsoundness of Fournier's primary assumption. This is that in late adolescence one idealizes the simplicity and purity of childhood and seeks to return to it, impelled by the last, glimmering memories of "the clouds of glory." Thus Meaulnes finds in the Domain a land of heart's desire not only because of Yvonne, but because the guests were, by Frantz's wish, children and old people, the two pure extremes of impure life. Similarly Frantz, after the failure of his attempt at suicide, seeks in vagabondage both the uncomplicated joys of childhood and the lost Valentine.

Now I submit that this is an entirely artificial conception. Youths of eighteen or so do not ordinarily idealize childhood, and they are quick to feel insulted at being still considered children at that age. . . . Since the whole book is based on the notion that Meaulnes and Frantz trail their clouds of glory proudly, the reader is faced at the outset with an improbability great enough to invalidate the feeling of psychological consistency upon which even fantasy must rest. Peter Pan as a little boy may be acceptable if worst comes to worst; but a Peter Pan who, like Frantz, has tried to blow his brains out over the

desertion of his beloved, or who, like Meaulnes, has taken a mistress in the absence of his Beatrice, is merely preposterous. (p. 130)

[Although] Fournier's characters were not conceived as real people, they are forced, through Fournier's intention to join the real to the dream world, to act from time to time in the context of ordinary existence. Thus Fournier's plan for the book was doomed from the start. (p. 131)

Meaulnes at his most Byronic is credible and human beside Frantz de Galais. A youth with the airs of a little boy even when he has become a frayed and haggard mountebank, a brother so abysmally self-centered that he does not hesitate to take from his sister her husband of less than one day, Frantz de Galais is little short of a monster. In him the catch-penny melodrama of the book comes to a sharp focus. His vagabondage, the oath, his general air of being both helpless and an evil genius, in all this one can see only the last degradation of the Romantic hero. It is with a real sense of shock that one leaves him at the end of the book established in improbable domesticity with the errant Valentine.

In Fournier's favor it must be said that the realistic aspects of the novel, the descriptions of landscapes, for example, and the *lycée*, of Seurel's mother and the village of Sainte-Agathe are excellent. They are, as one learns from reading the letters to Rivière, Fournier's own memories translated into fiction. In them one does often perceive a high degree of literary skill. The nameless melancholy of adolescence, the wistful, dreamy atmosphere conjured up in the pictures of gloomy winter days in the bare rooms and courtyard of the *lycée*, these have real charm. Yet in themselves they are not enough to force one to admit that Fournier has succeeded in joining the real to the dream world, especially since the most poetic of these evocations, for instance Seurel's revery during a school outing in the woods, deal rather with remembered reality than with the fantasy world of the Domain.

Henri Gillet, an admirer of Fournier, says that on the day when the latter decided to write simply and directly a story which could be his own, he found his road to Damascus. Yet it must certainly be clear from what has been said here that whatever else *Le Grand Meaulnes* may be, it is not a simple story simply told. The plot has manifold complications; the characters, because they are neither convincingly real nor satisfactorily unreal are merely incredible; and Fournier's intention of showing both the child's world and the adult's only results in making the problems of love and birth and death in the latter hang upon the arbitrary willfulness proper to the former. (p. 132)

> Donald Schier, "'Le grand Meaulnes'," in The Modern Language Journal, Vol. XXXVI, No. 3, March, 1952, pp. 129-32.

ROBERT CHAMPIGNY (essay date 1954)

A hero cannot present himself as such in the first person. The hero of Alain-Fournier's novel is Meaulnes; the narrator, Seurel. As far as possible, Fournier avoids letting his hero express himself directly. In the first part of the novel, Meaulnes relates his discovery of the "nameless country" to Seurel. But it is Seurel, the confidant, who relays the story to the reader. . . . Numerous details and comments in the story prevent us from forgetting that we are in direct contact with Seurel, not Meaulnes. The last chapters of the novel, which deal in retrospect with Meaulnes's affair with Valentine, reveal the same preoccupation of the author. At first, we are given a direct account of Meaulnes's diary. . . . The directness of the method is already much weakened by the fact that we are presented with written, not spoken, words, and with past events. But even this approach is considered too direct by Fournier; for the rest of the account . . . Seurel again assumes the role of narrator. . . . Fournier felt that even at this point in his novel the indirect method had to be maintained. (pp. 1-2)

It is true that the indirect method permits the worst kind of hero worship. The hero whose deeds are related by a dull, silly, awe-stricken narrator seems to be magnified in his heroism. This criticism, however, does not seem to apply to *Le Grand Meaulnes.*

First of all, Fournier does not expect the reader to take Seurel's point of view for granted. . . . Fournier has given the reader enough pointers to intimate that Seurel's conception of Meaulnes is inadequate. Meaulnes himself has to realize that he is not a sublimated Seurel. This realization is of central interest. . . . It is not through Seurel that Meaulnes is a hero, but in spite of Seurel.

Two questions then arise: Why did Fournier try to deceive his readers? Why did he use an inadequate narrator? The answers are that the choice of a narrator was an artistic necessity and that the choice of this particular narrator was required by Fournier's loyalty to experience. (pp. 2-3)

The novel is no gratuitous creation; it springs from the memory of Fournier and is based on the reality that he experienced. Fournier chose Seurel as narrator because he had lived most of his childhood and adolescence as Seurel. (p. 6)

Fournier stands between Seurel and Meaulnes. Seurel believes that the marvelous lies in the thing-in-itself, in what is beyond perception. Fournier has lost this faith: the secret box has been opened and found empty. The marvelous is not an objective secret; it is a subjective mystery. Meaulnes, not Seurel, is able to grasp this mystery as such. The poet can try to reveal it directly, not the novelist. (p. 8)

Thought, for Fournier, is not limited to the faculty which permits man to attain scientific or pseudoscientific truth. It is the total psychological activity which permits him to progress toward a personal truth, that is, an adequate interpretation of his experience. Dream enters into this definition of thought, especially since Fournier has taken care to define it as a "vision of the past." He is always afraid of losing the substance of his experience through an abstract interpretation. . . . (p. 11)

Even in *Le Grand Meaulnes* Fournier will leave the task of conceptual interpretation to the critic. The correspondence between Rivière and Fournier is doubly interesting from this point of view, because Rivière was attracted by what repelled Fournier: abstraction and myth.

Rivière reproaches Fournier for what he calls his passivity. As a matter of fact, Fournier was passive ethically. . . . He let the coming of the event take care of itself. But he was remarkably active aesthetically. Unlike Rivière, Fournier did not always read with good will. Rivière gave himself over to Claudel completely. In Claudel, as Rivière himself remarked, Fournier took only what was agreeable to his own experience, to his own aesthetic choice.

Ethical passivity, aesthetic activity: His double allegiance to art and experience may be compared to the method of the researcher. Like the researcher, Fournier needs both hypothesis

and fact. From 1905 to 1911, Fournier's experience becomes experiment. His early experience . . . gives rise to an aesthetic project, or hypothesis. But he is careful not to let his imagination run wild; he is careful not to lose contact with the contents of experience. The hypothesis will determine future experiments, not in their absolute happening, but in their possible meaning, in relation to the aesthetic project. Experiment brings new material to the hypothesis and informs it gradually, but the hypothesis, on the other hand, predetermines in a certain way the meaning of the experiment. In order to find something, one has to know what one is looking for, though in an open, questioning way.

This boldness and this caution, this will-to-art and this loyalty to experience are illustrated in Fournier's letters to Rivière. From time to time, Fournier restates and reshapes his hypothesis. The hypothesis, in its final form, is no other than Meaulnes himself. What the experiments must isolate is Meaulnes so that the shadow may become a portrait. (pp. 11-12)

> *Robert Champigny, in his* Portrait of a Symbolist Hero: An Existential Study Based on the Work of Alain-Fournier *(copyright 1954 by Indiana University Press), Indiana University Press, 1954, 164 p.*

MARCIA C. STUBBS (essay date 1958)

Le Grand Meaulnes seems to glide through a sequence of dreamlike events. The tone is muted, at times mysterious, continually evoking what Fournier once described to his friend, Jacques Rivière, as "the strange lost paradise which I inhabit." But conscious of the barriers the symbolists had erected between themselves and their readers with their shadowy, abstracted characters, Fournier was careful to make his characters credible people. They are, for the most part, young boys. They feel the fears, hopes, doubts and joys of youth. Woven in and out of their extraordinary adventures are the rather prosaic duties and pleasures of the schoolboy. They study with familiar impatience, and with a violence peculiar to youth, participate in school yard games or oppose each other in arguments. And the world in which they live is as credible as they. Fournier pays very minute attention to details. (p. 121)

Fournier's technique emphasizes experience; his purpose is to affirm the reality of the experiences he describes, however strange they may seem. Through the objectivity of the details he brings the reader close to the events so that he may enter into them without difficulty. There are no private symbols and the senses perform as usual. Through the strangeness and the mystery he increases our consciousness of the world we have entered. (p. 122)

Le Grand Meaulnes is the story of a romantic search for a beautiful girl met briefly at a strange festival, an attempt on the part of an individual to order all experience to the attainment of a single desire, to achieve tranquillity out of restlessness, to fulfill expectations of happiness roused by a chance encounter. Chance encounter? No, not so. When the hero, Meaulnes, realizes that he has begun his journey without premeditation he is filled with a profound joy, when he enters the drive of the forsaken manor, "a strange contentment urged him on, a perfect and almost intoxicating peace, the assurance that his goal had been reached and that he had now nothing but happiness to expect." . . . The assurance of peace, the experience of happiness, the dream of fulfillment are no more chance occurrences to Meaulnes, or to Fournier, than was the meeting with Beatrice to Dante, or the promises of heaven to the Christian whose will is bent on eternal rest.

And Meaulnes, during his adventure, is pure will. In accepting the schoolboy we also, and at once, participate in his dedicated search. (pp. 122-23)

Fournier molds a tragic and consequently moving story. The conflict is simple in its scope. It is subjective in so far as it concerns the receptivity of the hero to the forces he is destined to encounter in and about him. But it is not "psychological." If Fournier moved away from symbolism with the personal discovery that "there is no art and no truth but of the particular" it was not to employ his art examining "the ephemeral, the mechanism, the mask social and inconstant," the province of "naturalism" or "realism" in art, but in service of what he called, for lack of a better word, "dreams." "There are errors of dreams, false trails, changes of direction, and it is all this that lives, that excites, snags, loosens, and throws into disorder. The rest of the character is more or less of a mechanism—social or animal—and is not interesting." *Le Grand Meaulnes* is not concerned with a divided will, or personalities in conflict with each other, or man in "society" or the opposition of social forces. The stresses that give rise to conflict all come from one direction.

Looking only at Meaulnes' search, the conflict, the failure to achieve his objective rises in part, ironically, from the intensity of his desires and the perfection of his memory. When Frantz is reunited with Valentine his simple adventure ends and he is apparently at rest. It is almost as if time stood still from the moment of their separation to the moment of their marriage, that the intervening history, the "errors of their dreams" are illusions merely. Not so with Meaulnes. Marriage to Yvonne increases his torment. The end of his search appears now within his grasp but he can not yet claim it. For he had met Yvonne at a fête intended to celebrate the marriage of Frantz, a celebration interrupted by Valentine's "scruples, fear, lack of faith," and in the course of his wanderings, his attempt to find once more the lost manor and the beautiful girl, he has met Frantz and committed himself to a vow to restore the conditions of the meeting. It is the vow that dooms Meaulnes. . . . (p. 124)

That Fournier's hero is engaged in a mission is, I think, a more accurate word-description than search or wandering. Meaulnes' experience at the festival was, in a sense, a religious conversion. In one instant he had seen his paradise, and from that instant the rest of his life takes form. The vow, that Seurel comes to think of as "childish," is, for Meaulnes, a sacred rite. There is no question, for him, of the authority of Frantz' quest; they are as fellow communicants to the same mystery. Mission, too, suggests the passion, the religious fervor with which Meaulnes pursues his ideal. And the end of his search *is* ideal. Meaulnes tells Yvonne on their wedding night, "I am not worthy of you," and at one point, though reluctant to disbelieve in the promise, despairs of completing his mission in this world. (p. 125)

If Meaulnes is on a mission the crucial characterization is Yvonne de Galais, for it is the purpose of his search that gives it validity and that transforms *Le Grand Meaulnes* from a melancholy evocation of childhood, as it has often been regarded, to the affirmation Fournier wanted to record. . . . The fragile beauty, the spiritual grace of Yvonne, her quiet wisdom, even her dress, so simple as to seem at first eccentric, justify Meaulnes' joy in meeting her and his agony when he despairs of finding her again. But what of the terror he feels at their approaching marriage, and his deliberate flight?

It is clear that Fournier intended Meaulnes' flight as a renunciation of human happiness, and his terror as a revelation of the power he had innocently encountered. (pp. 125-26)

The purpose of the hero's search in *Le Grand Meaulnes,* which comprehends both approach and flight, joy and terror, becomes clear when Yvonne first appears at the crisis of his adventure, the mysterious fête, but it had been conceived long before, revealed in a dream "a vision that he had had when a child, and of which he had never spoken to anyone." A purpose that is clearly divine in nature, and that receives its earthly affirmation when Meaulnes and Yvonne meet. "Who are you? What are you doing here? I don't know you. And yet it seems to me that I do know you," Yvonne's glance seemed to say. "Oh, saith the heavenly Christian, I know both whither I go and to whom. I have gone this way many a time before."

Yvonne, attracting Meaulnes to perfection by her presence, embodies the feminine ideal, chaste but maternal, emerging from France's Christian past that Fournier had celebrated in **"Le Corps de la Femme."** But she does not appear to the other characters, nor to the reader, as an allegorical personage or symbol. Though suggesting another world out of space and time, she does not merely represent it; she brings it clearly within the bounds of this world. . . . She appears within the action surrounded by light, but she casts real shadows too, reminding us less perhaps of a medieval illumination than of the wholly natural appearances in myths and legends of gods and goddesses to the mortals and half-mortals of their choice. Nor does *Le Grand Meaulnes* "instruct" in the manner of an allegory. Though rising from the first to the high ground of the Grail tradition, it springs not so much from a system of thought or body of truth logically employed as from an intuition, a particular way of perceiving the nature of reality. Rendered as a narrative of what might have been, and in fact largely was, an actual experience, with all of its sensuous details immediately present, *Le Grand Meaulnes* catches us off guard as a myth does, and engaging us step by step, leads us to an imaginative participation of the senses in a drama of the spirit. (pp. 126-27)

For Fournier there were no coincidences and no machines, and the suggestion of a power beyond human power, both permeating and directing experience, is present in his novel in more than the obvious sequence of events. It subtly penetrates the entire tone of the prose. At every turn in the story a dream perhaps, a vision, an inexplicable feeling, a sudden decision, enters the consciousness of each character to suggest some unknown power urging him on, some unseen hand coloring his experience, some quality of his search that sets it apart from all other earthly events. The insistence upon mystery, strangeness, ineffability and purpose is repeated in the casual but recurrent use of delicate, illusive images—sand, rain, wind, changes of weather; and in a diction that is not exactly archaic but odd, as if secretly engaged. (p. 128)

But if it is providence that transforms Meaulnes' simple desire for an afternoon adventure into a mission, if it is a power benevolent and divine that guides him to the land promised in a vision, one must think again about his failure, and account for the evil in *Le Grand Meaulnes,* the evil that kills Yvonne, reduces Meaulnes to despair and leaves Seurel troubled and unhappy. . . . The hero's search is repeatedly arrested at points where success seems most certain, the vision torments more than it consoles him, and the outcome is not rest but resignation to perpetual striving. (p. 129)

Meaulnes' acceptance of the present is dictated by his desires for the future; his desires for the future are identical with his memory of the past. But the time that is measured, not by men's souls, but by the change of seasons and mutations of landscape is, in the world as Fournier understood it, an irreversible process moving in a definite direction. There can be no return for Meaulnes, either to his memory . . . or from it.

The tragedy of Meaulnes' failure [to fulfill his mission] is not merely the pathos of mutability. It is a tragedy of a mission doomed by its very conception. It is not simply marriage to Yvonne that lies at the end of his search. It is the attainment to that felicity of which Yvonne de Galais is both part and symbol. Meaulnes' memory remains absolute. Yvonne does not change in time. And for Meaulnes, these are sufficient for the desperate hope that nothing need have changed, the belief that he can recapture the experience at the festival. (pp. 131-32)

And perhaps it was, after all, a sinful hope, this panic wish by which Meaulnes is driven. He promises himself, knowing better, a heaven on earth. He begins his search in complete innocence of heart, and is filled with a "deep joy of having at last run away without premeditation." But in his conscious, deliberate attempts to regain his paradise he becomes unwilling to accept anything but the past come to life again. . . . The result is not only cruelty to Valentine and death to Yvonne, but violence to his own will. He loses his pilgrim spirit. (p. 133)

Marcia C. Stubbs, "The Pilgrim Spirit," in Accent *(copyright, 1958, by* Accent*), Vol. 18, No. 2, Spring, 1958, pp. 121-33.*

FREDERICK W. LOCKE   (essay date 1959)

The basic structure of the *Le Grand Meaulnes* involves a fundamental pattern which may be illustrated by means of a story. It is the story of a young man who one day leaving his mother to go out into the great world, comes to the court of a famous king and into the company of renowned knights. There through his prowess he is accepted and for a short time lives happily. One day, however, he hears of a high adventure, and leaves his new home, the great king and all his companions, to go in search of a wondrous treasure. He discovers a castle more beautiful than anything he had ever imagined and has there an adventure which no other knight had ever participated in. But, because of his failure to ask a proper question while in the castle he awakes the next morning to find himself back in the drab world of everyday reality. His one desire thereafter is to find this castle again and to achieve the adventure he had begun. (pp. 138-39)

This story is the *Conte del Graal* of Chrétien de Troyes, and its hero is Percival, the first of the questers for the object called *graal*. The *Conte del Graal* is an excellent paradigm of a motif that reaches as far back as the Gilgamesh Epic, and is as near to us as the *Ulysses* of James Joyce. It is the motif of a Quest, a voyage of discovery, into unknown lands. But what is still more to the point is that this motif wherever it is found reveals a pattern. This pattern may be summarized. When the Quest begins the hero is in his home, living an ordinary life with his family or as the sole support of his mother. One may recall Jack the Giant Killer. Almost immediately the hero leaves his home and sets out on adventures which involve opposition, struggle, usually a decisive battle with a monster, the overcoming of opposition, and finally the discovery of a new home

or a return to the first home with wealth and its attendant happiness.

How is this pattern seen in *Le Grand Meaulnes*? It is by paying close attention to the images that one arrives at the underlying structure. While these images are concrete expressions of temporal and spatial moments in the novel, they are also capable of opening out on to more significant dimensions. . . .

The element of "escape" is provided by the atmosphere of the earlier part of the novel where the reader is presented with the dull and deadening life of a small French village. . . .

Against this background of drab bourgeois life stands the imaginative world of Meaulnes and his friends, the land of fairy in the heads of young boys, the paradigm of the real and circumambient *pays inconnu* of the novel's greater dimension. (p. 139)

It is from this bourgeois *mis en scène* that Meaulnes runs away, though there is no hint that it is an escape he is making, merely a truancy. And so he may have thought himself that day when unknown to anyone he had gone to Fromentin's farm and had the mare harnessed and made his escape to pick up the grandparents of François Seurel before anyone would be the wiser. At the last moment one of the grooms had become suspicious, but it was too late. Meaulnes had escaped. He had escaped from the bourgeois, limited world of Sainte-Agathe's into . . . into what kind of world? He had done what the hero does. He is called Admiral Meaulnes by his comrades.

Meaulnes' breakthrough into the *pays inncconnu* which lies behind the dull world of the everyday takes the measure of his companion, François Seurel, who is unable to escape and who will, in one sense, never escape. . . . The playground . . . is slowly seen as a symbol of escape. From the beginning, when the Seurel family had come to St. Agathe's and Millie, François' mother was inspecting the property to see what renovations would be needed, François stood alone "on the gravel of that *strange playground*, waiting for her, prying shyly around the well and under the cart shed." The image of the playground sustains the image of adolescence and both point to the world outside and to the end of youth and play. When Meaulnes first met François he had asked him "Aren't you coming into the playground?" In re-reading the novel we may, if François Seurel could not, hear the echo of that question: "From time to time above the stillness of the wintry afternoon had arisen the faraway call of a farm girl or of a lad hailing a comrade from one clump of firs to another, and each time that long call over the desolate hills had made me shudder as if it were the voice of Meaulnes inviting me to follow him from afar." (pp. 140-41)

At the end of the novel Meaulnes leaves all homes, a vagabond searching the face of the earth, the Wanderer, as the English translation of the novel calls him.

Who is Meaulnes? Do we really know him from the account of Seurel, or indeed from his own accounts and letters? Who is Frantz, for that matter? Who is the narrator, who is François Seurel? Each is who he is on the terms of the narrative, but each is someone else at the same time.

Perhaps only a second reading will reveal to a reader the kind of characterization that confronts him. In this second reading he may note that Meaulnes and François have a way of getting confused. Before Meaulnes is introduced to the reader his footsteps are heard in the room above the parlor: "A little while ago," said Millie in a low voice, "I heard that noise in the room downstairs; I thought it was you François, come back. . . . No one answered. We stood, the three of us, with beating hearts; then the attic door which led to the kitchen was heard to open; some one came down, crossed the kitchen and appeared in the dim entrance of the dining room.

"Why it is you, Augustin," said the visitor [Meaulnes' mother]. And then again they are so different. Meaulnes is a strapping boy, a leader, while Seurel is a cripple, nervous and wretched. "I can still see myself chasing the nimble schoolboys in the alleys around our house hopping wretchedly on one leg." It is this crippled condition of Seurel that later on accounts for the fact that Meaulnes acts as François' horse in the game of knights which the boys play in the playground. But there is more to it than that. Seurel is progressively seen as another aspect of Meaulnes, a crippled Meaulnes, a less courageous Meaulnes. After Admiral Meaulnes escaped from Sainte-Agathe's, M. Seurel told François to go anyway to get his grandparents. Meaulnes did not know the way to Vierzon. "He will lose himself at the Cross Roads. He will not meet the train at three." But only he who faces the possibility of losing himself at the Cross Roads can have an adventure. Like Oedipus, for instance. Seurel will have his adventure through Meaulnes. Meaulnes will even be instrumental in bringing Yvonne to him so he can fall in love with her. For there is a third love story in the novel, that of François Seurel for Yvonne, and its projection after her death for her daughter. At the end Seurel had said: "Admiral Meaulnes had left with me one joy; I felt that he had come back to take it away from me." In her death the revelation of Seurel's love for Yvonne is complete and almost unbearable. (p. 144)

Seurel does not return to a new home, to that home of the pattern I proposed, to that last movement of the Quest motif. . . . Sainte-Agathe will never be the same for Seurel, living as he will have to with the memory of Meaulnes' story, with his love for the girl from the château. And had not the château itself been destroyed for Meaulnes when he came to live there with his bride? The reality had not fulfilled the dream, and the glory of the Lost Land faded with his achievement of the adventure.

The adventure of Frantz alone was successful, for he was the only one to return of all those who had set out on the Quest. And it would seem at the end that Frantz alone fulfills the pattern I have proposed; Frantz, the least heroic of that band of adventurers. But actually Frantz, the fantastic youth, brings the narrative full circle, back to that bourgeois life of broken dreams with which the novel began. For he too is Meaulnes; that aspect of Meaulnes, at least, which could never grow up. It is Frantz who is the symbol of adolescence in the novel. We actually see the end of the youth of Meaulnes and indirectly that of Seurel. The tragedy of Frantz, however, is hidden from us, and the misery of the boy and girl who enter the little house is hidden from us. But we know, who have read the diary of Meaulnes, what Frantz will find out; for he will discover that Valentine is Yvonne, and like Yvonne, she too will not fill his heart, and will perish. For she too is from a Lost Land. She is that other dimension of Yvonne which Meaulnes discovered and which is revealed to us through the diary. (pp. 145-46)

The pattern I have proposed exists through the only modern means at the disposal of the artist to sustain it: irony. There can be no final movement, but for reasons other than those which account for the incompletion of Chrétien's tale. After all, the pattern is complete in Dante and in the 13th century *Quête du Grall*. *Le Grand Meaulnes* is the story of a *recherche*

de l'Absolu. . . . This desire and pursuit of the whole lies behind the pattern of the Quest which I have outlined, and in it is reflected the quest of adolescence and its end. For it is a Quest for the Absolute, for the ultimate meaning of man's life, for a way out of the fragmentation of the Wasteland: a search for wholeness. But unfortunately all the images of the Absolute have a way of slipping and sliding. As Boethius remarked, an image of the real Good is something that cannot bring us to Beatitude. And he was echoed by Dante when the Italian poet spoke of "those false images which never fully keep their promises." (p. 146)

Frederick W. Locke, "'Le grand Meaulnes': The Desire and Pursuit of the Whole," in Renascence (© copyright, 1959, Marquette University Press), Vol. XI, No. 3, Spring, 1959, pp. 135-46.*

ALAN PRYCE-JONES (essay date 1959)

There is nothing, I believe, in the whole of romantic fiction to exceed the first hundred pages [of *Le Grand Meaulnes*]. So long as the mystery holds, so long as the coiled surprises and wavering colours of a dream deliver none of their reality, *Le Grand Meaulnes* is almost flawless. Later, when the visionary air of these pages is dissipated in explanation, and the haunted events which set the tale in motion are resolved into romance on a different plane, some disappointment is inevitable. After all, Alain-Fournier was a very young man when he wrote his novel. An exquisite setting of the scene was fully within his range; the working-out of the action was not. But there are enough moments of wonder throughout the book to remind us that had he been given time he might have assumed fully the leadership which some of his contemporaries were already willing to accord him.

For what is so fascinating about his book is that it manages to adjust an extreme romanticism of vision to the simplest and most lucid of classical means. Fournier was by no means a dreamer. As his letters to Jacques Rivière show, he had and used an excellent, and an anxious, intellect. But he also possessed the rarest gift of the good novelist: his intellect and his imagination ran in double harness. And he could put them both to the service of a vision which (it is reasonable to think) the years would only have clarified and emboldened.

From its opening words, *Le Grand Meaulnes* sets the key of simplicity in which the whole tale is cast 'He appeared in our house on a Sunday in November 189..' There is no deviation from this key, no inflation of style to match the curious events which follow. But it would be wrong to suppose that the book is in any way simple. On the contrary, it catches at the peculiar mixture of assertive colour and rigidity which ran through much of French art in each sphere in the first decade of this century, from the palette of Matisse to the harmonic structure of Debussy.

For one thing, the point of view of the narrator is an extremely subtle one. He is hardly more than a child, brought up in a remote part of France in the conventional surroundings of a schoolhouse. It is the unquestioned custom of his milieu to go to Mass on Sunday mornings and to Vespers in the evening; he himself is in no active sense a rebel against convention; he states no iconoclastic point of view. Yet somehow, Alain-Fournier brings in just a touch of *The Turn of the Screw*. There is evil about: not enough to satisfy Henry James, but enough to lend a tang to what might otherwise have been no more than a fairy-story. (pp. xi-xiii)

The fairy-story atmosphere is seldom quite dispelled, but it is reinforced by keen knowledge of the rules of life. When they are broken—and the turns of the plot depend on one breakage after another—people suffer not in terms of fantasy, but with all the pain of flesh and blood.

The triumph of Alain-Fournier is to have kept so much balance between the two aspects of his novel. The fairy-story never dissolves into a picture of ordinary life, the leaden touch of reality never wholly dispels the marvel of a dream. This is chiefly due to the fact that although each detail is sharply seen—high-lit as in sleep—there is never any lingering for the sake of effect. We are hardly given time to make the acquaintance of each personage before the dream engulfs him. Thus the schoolmaster, the narrator's father, scarcely has a personality at all. His school is more important than himself; and in our anxiety to sniff the smell of chalk, to hear the bang of the desks, we hardly have time to notice that it is one of the most eccentrically run schools in all literature. In other words, the personage of M. Seurel is reduced to the mere spine upon which a whole skeleton of school life is hung. And this is perfectly right; for if we had time to be interested in M. Seurel we should have been distracted from more important matters. (pp. xiii-xiv)

[The story] will probably be found too symmetrical. Meaulnes loves Yvonne, Frantz love Valentine, and finally, to turn the screw a little farther, Meaulnes persuades himself that, for lack of Yvonne's presence, he can force himself to love Valentine when she no longer can bring herself to return the love of Frantz. The spiral is too neat; and when Valentine, after being driven on to the streets (though Alain-Fournier is too delicate to insist on this), is brought back to Frantz by Meaulnes at the end of the book there is a curious lack of inevitability about the conclusion. The genius of Alain-Fournier was for posing questions, not for finding answers. And so it is that the opening section of his novel so far transcends anything which follows, in spite of the satisfactions offered to curiosity and the constant fillips given to the imagination of an empathetic reader. (pp. xvi-xvii)

The existence of Yvonne de Galais is like that of the blue flower to Novalis: it assumes that somewhere—but always out of reach—there exists a happiness which ravishes the soul. This is, to say the least, an unfashionable view in modern fiction, and the significant thing about it is that it should have been held by Alain-Fournier, who was far from being a sugary or evasive character. What he has done is to write perhaps the last novel of idyllic love which is likely to have universal appeal. (p. xvii)

> *Alan Pryce-Jones, "Introduction" (© Oxford University Press 1959; reprinted by permission of Oxford University Press), in* The Lost Domain: "Le grand Meaulnes" *by Alain-Fournier, translated by Frank Davison, Oxford University Press, Oxford, 1959 (and reprinted by Oxford University Press, 1974), pp. xi-xix.*

STEPHEN ULLMANN   (essay date 1960)

Alain-Fournier worked for seven years on *Le Grand Meaulnes*, and during that long period, his style underwent some significant changes. Between 1907 and 1911, he also wrote several sketches and short stories, some of which were printed in magazines. These juvenile works, which were published many years later by Rivière under the title *Miracles*, are too slight to give

a coherent picture of the evolution of Alain-Fournier's style. They do, however, show quite clearly that he was given at first to a highly literary form of writing, overloaded with ornamental metaphors and comparisons. It is well-nigh impossible to recognize the future author of *Le Grand Meaulnes* in pseudo-Symbolist passages like [those in *La Partie de plaisir*], where the plethora of ill-assorted imagery defeats its own ends. . . .

A typically Symbolist feature of this early imagery is its synaesthetic bias. (p. 100)

The style of these early works is vitiated not only by the sheer weight and incongruity of the images, but also by their artificiality. The analogies are often far-fetched and unconvincing, as for example in [*Madeleine*]. . . .

Even the *Miracle des trois dames,* which was published in August 1910 and is more mature in technique, is not immune from these vices. . . .

Barely a month after the appearance of this story, Alain-Fournier announced to Rivière his 'road to Damascus', the great change in his style. This is very noticeable in the two short stories which he wrote between that date and the publication of *Le Grand Meaulnes*. The accumulations of incongruous analogies have disappeared, and the images themselves are more appropriate and more discreet. Occasionally, there is still a false note. . . . But there are also some apt and expressive comparisons. (p. 101)

These prose pieces were mere exercises, temporary escapes from the sustained effort which went into the writing of the novel. *Le Grand Meaulnes* marks the terminal point of the stylistic development of which one catches some glimpses in the early works. Its muted tones and delicate harmonies, its avoidance of decorative details and reliance on suggestive nuances form an atmosphere in which imagery can play a useful and even an important role, but which puts certain limits on its scope. One critic has described this style as 'extraordinairement lyrique, riche en images, évocateur, métaphorique, musical'. This is only partly true. The metaphorical element is certainly substantial—one image on every three pages, and the pages are small—but the imagery as a whole is discreet and unobtrusive. There is much originality in the images themselves, and some of them possess that quality of 'irressaisissable fraîcheur' which Gide admired in the first part of the novel, at the same time they are mostly short and simple, adding a fleeting note to the narrative without holding it up or diverting attention from it. The most important aspect of the imagery is, however, its structural role, the notable part it plays in the total effect of the book. (p. 102)

> *Stephen Ullmann, "The Symbol of the Sea in 'Le grand Meaulnes'," in his* The Image in the Modern French Novel: Gide, Alain-Fournier, Proust, Camus *(copyright © 1960 by Cambridge University Press), Cambridge, 1960, pp. 99-123.*

MARTIN TURNELL   (essay date 1966)

Le Grand Meaulnes is a unique novel. It has been more widely, more intensely, and more passionately studied than the work of almost any of the other famous one-book novelists. It has been variously interpreted as a religious allegory, as a "morality," as a fantasy, and as a modern version of the medieval "quests." It is plainly more than a straightforward love story with a disastrous ending, but it is difficult to believe that it can be described as a "Christian" novel in any useful or positive sense. The other elements that I have mentioned are undoubtedly there. The dominant theme is the theme of the "quest," but we shall find that this in itself is far from resolving all the problems of interpretation. (pp. 479-80)

Meaulnes and Seurel are "doubles" in the sense that they are both partial portraits of the artist, both projections of tendencies which belonged not merely to the novelist, but to other members of the family on his father's side: a sober, down-to-earth realism and a spirit of adventure. Seurel is the countryman attached to the soil: the representative of the everyday world, the voice of sanity, a mixture of Greek chorus and confidant from French classical tragedy, trying to control Meaulnes' more reckless impulses and to preserve an equilibrium. One of the most striking features of his style as narrator is its concreteness: the presentation of the sights and sounds of the countryside, the way in which a gesture is caught and fixed, whether it is a countrywoman battling against the wind and the rain or a peasant standing speechless, fingering his hat and wondering what to do next. This is in no sense a matter of background; it is an essential element in the pattern of the book which places in perspective Meaulnes' adventures, his extraordinary experience during his first visit to "the mysterious domain," and what can only be called his quest for an earthly paradise.

Nor is that all. We find in the novel what the French call a *dédoublement,* which means that we are looking at life simultaneously under two different and usually conflicting aspects. It is the story of a great adventure in which we move at times in an enchanted world, but we are conscious all the time of a sense of fragility, an underlying menace. Once a peak has been passed the atmosphere becomes more and more threatening as the magic is gradually dissipated by a sense of disenchantment, the fading of dreams and hopes, the sudden plunge from an earthly paradise into something like an earthly hell. François Seurel is the instrument by which the sense of disenchantment seeps in.

The word "quest" is never used in the novel: the word "adventure" occurs constantly. It is clear, however, that the main theme is a number of related "quests" in which the protagonists, with one exception, are frustrated by every kind of mistake and misunderstanding, with the result that they are continually setting out on a false trail which carries them away from their goal.

The novel opens with a simple matter-of-fact statement of Meaulnes' arrival at Sainte-Agathe without actually mentioning his name: "He arrived at our place one Sunday in November 189. . . ." . . . (pp. 481-82)

There follows a deliberately prosaic account of the Seurels' occupation as teachers and of the school buildings. The novel is one in which images are more important than events. Although Alain-Fournier's writing is an example of the plain style and the images are comparatively few in number, the pattern is formed by a series of inter-related images, particularly images of the sea and shipwreck, which are strategically placed. The first comes on the second page, immediately after the description of the school buildings: . . . ". . . such is the brief account of the house where I spent the most painful and the most-loved days of my life—the house from which set out and to which returned, like waves breaking on a barren rock, our adventures." (p. 482)

The order of the words deserves attention. "Painful" and "most-loved" suggest at once a blend of contrary feelings, with the accent on pain, and the extremes between which the emotional

life of the characters moves. It is underlined by the double movement of the waves surging forward only to fling themselves back on the barren rock. For this is, indeed, what happens to the adventurers setting out full of hope, then returning frustrated and disillusioned to their starting point. The construction of the sentence with the crucial word thrust to the end clearly places immense emphasis on "adventures." (p. 483)

When Meaulnes enters the scene he appears as a large youth with his hair cropped like a peasant's. There is, indeed, more in him of the countryman—the practical countryman versed in country lore—than in François Seurel. As soon as he arrives he proceeds to explore the buildings; he unearths some of last year's fireworks and lets them off, which points already to his independence and his individualism. The ominous nature of the "presence" is emphasized at the beginning of Chapter II: "But some one came who took me away from all these peaceable childish pleasures. Some one who blew out the candle which lighted up for me the gentle motherly face bent over the evening meal. Some one who put out the lamp around which our happy family gathered."

The contrasted images of "home" and "world," "interior" and "exterior," with their suggestions of "refuge" and "adventure," "security" and "danger," are as much a part of the pattern of the book as the marine images. Meaulnes is seen here as the intruder, the stranger who coming in from outside, from the world beyond the village, disrupts the peace and security symbolized by the home with the gentle motherly face and the inmates gathered round the lamp.

The quest does not begin as a quest. It begins, as we have seen, as a schoolboy prank when Meaulnes decides secretly that he will drive to the station to meet the narrator's grandparents instead of the narrator himself and one of his schoolfellows who have been chosen by Seurel because they know the way. (pp. 483-84)

The sense of impending disaster or "shipwreck" underlies all these early chapters, but it is a disaster which is both feared and desired.

Although the "adventure" begins as a schoolboy prank, the difficulties and physical hardships that Meaulnes encounters when he loses his way have obvious affinities with the "ordeals" of the knights in medieval stories. The discovery that he has missed his way is brought home to Meaulnes when the penetrating cold awakens him from a doze and he notices that "the landscape had changed." We are told: "Anyone but Meaulnes would have at once retraced his steps. It was the only way of not going still further astray." He obstinately pushes on. "He felt growing within him an exasperated desire to achieve something and get somewhere in spite of all the obstacles." (p. 484)

Meaulnes spends a cold night in a hut and next day pushes on: "Without hurrying he continued on his way. At the corner of a wood there emerged from between two white posts a lane which Meaulnes entered. After a few steps he stopped, filled with surprise, disturbed by a feeling that he could not explain. He went on, however, with the same tired gait; the icy wind made his lips sore and there were moments when he felt stifled. And yet he was filled with an extraordinary sense of contentment, a perfect and almost intoxicating feeling of peace, the certainty that his goal was reached and that now only happiness awaited him."

This is Meaulnes' first sight of "the mysterious domain." It is also the first occasion on which we hear of a "goal." It is the beginning of the euphoria which culminates in the meeting with Yvonne de Galais—the central incident in the novel . . . and continues (as we shall see) after Meaulnes' return to Sainte-Agathe. It is a psychological experience which brings about a profound change in Meaulnes, but it takes place in the setting of a children's fancy-dress party, or possibly a children's carnival. (We are expressly told that everything had been planned in accordance with the wishes of the infant guests.)

This is the stage at which we first become vividly aware of the *dédoublement*. The sense of enchantment is psychological, but the psychological effect is considerably enhanced by material factors. The period clothes of the guests, the period décors of the room where Meaulnes sleeps, the grotesque figure of the clown who lights the lanterns—he recalls somehow the "bad" fairies in a fairy tale—make us feel that we are indeed entering a mysterious domain, but in a curious way the link with the everyday world is never completely severed. It is a carnival, a temporary departure from the everyday world into a world of make-believe. Strange things may happen, but the presence of the children and the fact that Meaulnes wears his school uniform under the period attire can hardly be unintentional. They emphasize that the break *is* temporary, that underneath Meaulnes remains a schoolboy, that he will have to take off the fancy dress and return to reality, that in some respects he himself is little more than a child. (pp. 485-86)

[When Meaulnes sees Yvonne he] has had a glimpse of something which is, or appears to be, outside everyday experience: a vision of beauty, perfection, simplicity, and above all, of purity. He is aware afterwards that something irrevocable has happened to him, that he is a changed man. . . . (p. 487)

Frantz, whose return brings the fête to an abrupt end, is at once a sinister and a pathetic figure, not so much a disruptive as a destructive element. The moment he appears the menacing undertone of the book becomes much more pronounced. The vision—the precarious sense of enchantment—disintegrates, leaving only the tawdry trappings: a scene of "désarroi et dévastation." The carefree atmosphere has vanished; instead of hearing their chatter and their laughter, we see the "figures inquiètes" of the children huddled silently together in the vehicles that are taking them home. It is a foretaste of what is to come. At the unsuccessful picnic at which Meaulnes next meets Yvonne we shall learn that her father has lost his money, that part of the property has been sold, and that some of the buildings have been demolished by the purchasers—facts on which Meaulnes will dwell with a strange masochistic glee. (pp. 487-88)

It is significant that, in spite of her beauty, Yvonne de Galais is now very much a part of the everyday world, that there seems to Meaulnes to have been a reversal of their roles. This and the physical destruction of the supposedly "mysterious domain" explains in part Meaulnes' disillusionment and his extraordinary behavior. For at this point the curve of the book dips steeply. Meaulnes appears determined to wreck everything. He presses the unhappy girl with questions about the destruction of the domain which to her are simply embarrassing questions about a purely family misfortune: "And every time the girl, who was in agonies, had to repeat that everything had disappeared: the old house, so strange and complicated, demolished; the big pool, dried up and filled in; the children with their charming costumes, gone away."

It is the fading of a dream: the house where it all happened gone; the pool in which Meaulnes had once admired his reflection "dried up and filled in." (p. 491)

It is not until after the wedding and Meaulnes' abandonment of his wife that we learn from a diary which François discovers in the home what he had been doing between leaving school and the picnic.

The adventure began, "the mysterious domain" was discovered, through a schoolboy taking a wrong turning. Another wrong turning or false trail provided by Frantz plunges him into a very different adventure. . . .

[In the hope of meeting Yvonne again Meaulnes] goes to the address in Paris given him by Frantz and day after day stations himself outside the house where Yvonne sometimes stays. . . . It is there that, without knowing it, he meets Frantz's ex-fiancée, Valentine, who may well have come there in the hope of finding Frantz. . . . Frantz was not her first love and there is a suggestion that in the past she had not earned her living so innocently and might cease to do so again in the future. Meaulnes and Valentine gradually form an attachment for one another. The novelist is careful to emphasize that, compared with Yvonne, Valentine is not "innocent" or "pure." (p. 492)

We are conscious all the time of the profound differences between Yvonne and Valentine. For Valentine . . . is far from being like Yvonne a model of goodness and beauty. It is difficult, surely, to avoid the feeling that the two somehow represent Sacred and Profane Love. (p. 493)

The outcome [of the novel] is that the only successful "quest" is that of Frantz who, with the assistance of Meaulnes, finds Valentine, marries her, and returns with her to the security of the cottage known as "Frantz's house." Meaulnes has won only to lose again. François gets nothing: his is the grim task of reversing the situation of the happy bridegroom carrying the bride into the married home by carrying the dead Yvonne downstairs in his arms because the house is too narrow for the coffin to be brought upstairs into the chamber of death. (pp. 494-95)

There has been a great deal of speculation about the ultimate "meaning" of the novel. (p. 495)

[My own feeling is that the] image of the "quest" is manifestly central. It has affinities with the medieval "quests," but also, explicitly, with the Romantic "adventure," with the prince searching for the sleeping beauty or the captive princess. There are associations with the Romantic Movement and the Symbolists which are evident in the figure of Yvonne de Galais, who derives both from the Romantic heroine and the Symbolists' *princesse lointaine*, and in the images of an earthly Paradise to which Meaulnes gives a capital letter. Finally, it is a novel if not about childhood, certainly about adolescence, which reminds us that the "lost paradise" of the Romantics was sometimes a childhood paradise like Baudelaire's "vert paradis des amours enfantines."

So far as the main protagonist is concerned, the "quest," like the medieval quests, is a failure. It ends not in happiness or some permanent illumination, but is a prelude to other "quests" or "adventures" which will probably end in failure or disaster. . . . Meaulnes, as surely as the Grail knights, was seeking "the secret mystery of life"; seeking it through union with a woman who is much more the descendant of the Romantic heroine than of Dante's Beatrice. He is convinced that he underwent some form of "initiation" at the fête, but the sequel shows that the initiation was a failure, either because it was an illusion or because he had no vocation for discovering "the secret mystery of life." There is no certain answer to the question. In spite of Meaulnes' conviction that he attained a special degree of "perfection and purity" during the fête, the fact that Yvonne de Galais turned out to be an "ordinary" girl suggests that it was an illusion. On the other hand, the attraction he feels for Valentine suggests an absence of vocation. For Meaulnes is the "huntsman" and "peasant" who would have been well matched with Valentine if she had not belonged to another and he had not had his experience at the fête, which may in fact have incapacitated him for ordinary life. Yvonne is a symbol of purity. Valentine is the reverse, the representative of the material, one might almost say the sinful, everyday life. She marries Frantz, but she has also contributed to Meaulnes' disenchantment. After his contact with her, he sees Yvonne with very different eyes. . . . In a general way the novel is a critique of Romanticism; it shows the fading of the Romantic dream which ends, in life as well as in books, in disillusionment.

There remains the element of childhood. When François Seurel is trying to persuade Meaulnes not to abandon his bride—it is one of the moments when his role most strongly suggests the Greek chorus or the confidant—he speaks of "the terrible temptation of smashing on the spot the marvel that he had won."

Childhood, as the poets have insisted, is a time when we may catch a fleeting glimpse of another and mysterious world beyond our own which is closed to us for ever once childhood has really ended. But childhood is also the time of senseless destruction when we are capable of throwing away our chances, our certainty of happiness, from the same impulse that drives us to smash our toys. Whatever the nature of Meaulnes' *faute* and the sense of guilt that makes him fly to Frantz's assistance at the expense of his own happiness and that of his bride, there is an element of willful destruction behind the tragedy of *Le Grand Meaulnes*. (pp. 496-97)

> Martin Turnell, *"Alain-Fournier and 'Le grand Meaulnes'"* (copyright, 1966, by Martin Turnell), in The Southern Review, Vol. 2, No. 3, Summer, 1966, pp. 477-98.

CATHERINE SAVAGE BROSMAN (essay date 1971)

The psychological and poetic value of the estate image is shared by numerous . . . dwellings described in [*Le Grand Meaulnes*], which are more than just settings for the action. In this study I shall explore the functions of the house image as they illuminate Meaulnes' story, contrast them with the uses of linear images, and propose an evaluation which can contribute to a reading of the novel.

Whether it is the school buildings of the Seurel family, Meaulnes' mother's house, Frantz's house, the uncle's shop, or "les Sablonnières," the estate in the "pays sans nom," the dwellings of the novel are evoked in considerable detail, with emphasis on their apertures, their wings, and their heights. These descriptions, revealing Alain-Fournier's spatial imagination, become correlatives of the characters' relationships to others and themselves and means of making discoveries about themselves. (pp. 499-500)

Les Sablonnières and other houses in the novel are multivalent. They are simultaneously places of origin, places from which one escapes, places of return or refuge, and sites of death. For the main characters, particularly the hero, centripetal forces are constantly in opposition to centrifugal ones. A dialectic of in-out, with passageways emphasized and the narrative angle

of vision switching back and forth, is established. This is suggested in an early scene when François, in his *curtained* bed, watches Meaulnes prowl back and forth from his *open* bed to the end of the room, with its perpetually *open* door. . . . Various openings, contrasted with places of retreat, will reappear at les Sablonnières. . . .

Thus, grills and walls suggest imprisonment, whereas windows and doors are often seen as means of escape (as when Meaulnes dreams in front of the open door at the carter's. . . . The attraction of entrances is heightened by the observation that Seurel's mother has had several doors closed off to make the schoolhouse inhabitable. M. Guiomar speaks of "claustrophilie" in this connection. In the evening, the inside of the house is warm, protective—or so it seems to Seurel in particular, who, it will turn out, will persist as an adult in identifying his destiny with a house whereas Meaulnes will ultimately prefer the road. The feeling of security which the house can offer indicates its function as a maternal image.

A locked door and a hiding place can also mean adventure: Meaulnes closes himself away from the other schoolboys to study the atlas which may lead him back to the mysterious estate. . . . The closed door suggests moreover his solitary destiny. Later, Meaulnes flees to the attic to consider additional possibilities of departure. Windows and doors (often associated with fire and light imagery which suggests promise and security) are thus ambivalent, since the emotional value switches between inside and outside. This ambivalence points to the hesitation in Meaulnes' own behavior. (pp. 500-01)

One of the strengths of Alain-Fournier's art is the direct expression, without analysis, of . . . fundamental memories and fixations. . . . The first image we had of Meaulnes was that of a phantom prowling in the attic. His first expressed fantasy, before the discovery of the domain, is the revival of a childhood revery in which he found himself in a "longue pièce verte," with a soft light and a young girl, sewing. . . . This spatial projection of his revery and its association with magic and love serve as an intimation of the forthcoming discovery of the domain and of its relationship to the past.

Later, it is in the vast annex room where Meaulnes first sleeps at les Sablonnières that he hears the sounds announcing the wedding celebration and his own forthcoming meeting with Yvonne. Like Meaulnes, Frantz, who was to marry that day but instead comes to the room alone, has climbed in through the window—a penetration more furtive and more possessive than the conventional one; then, despairing, he leaves by the same means to take up the life of a wanderer (as Meaulnes will later do). And, just as Meaulnes slept in the sheepfold the night before finding the domain, he, too, sleeps on the night of his departure in an ancient closed carriage, his house on wheels. This foreshadows Frantz's life in the bohemians' carriage. Thus, for both Meaulnes and Frantz (his friend, brother-in-law, and double) initiation, aspirations, rejection and endings are experienced spatially. Their life is rounded not only by a sleep but by a progress from room to room. (p. 502)

The functioning of the house as a maternal image has been noted; the hero's predilections for withdrawal, as well as the emotional value which Seurel attaches to chambers in his narrative, are certainly open to Freudian interpretation. The dark, secret place can symbolize the return to the womb. This maternal association is borne out by Meaulnes' dreams at the domain, in which he visualizes himself as a child with his mother . . . or at a *fête*. It need not be stressed, either, that

Seurel, Yvonne, Valentine, and Frantz all see themselves and Meaulnes as children. . . . But Meaulnes, unlike the others, is to outgrow childhood. And the normalization of his attitude toward the mother-image is suggested by the substitution, in his daydreams, of the girl at the piano for his mother. . . . To the notion of an Oedipal drive, one can add, as an interpretation of Meaulnes' dialectic of house and road, the existentialist notion of an attitude toward one's own being in time. This view can be supported by further analysis.

When Meaulnes, having lost his way, is approaching the domain, indications of barriers, birds of ill-omen, barrenness, and an indeterminate lapse of time show that this is no ordinary wandering, but a mysterious adventure. . . . Meaulnes is in the dream country of the Romantics. Repeated details stress that the house does not belong to the present. . . . Clearly, this is travel in time as well as in space: both time and space may represent an interior voyage. The estate, I propose, is a fragment of the oneiric past, of which Meaulnes, "le Prince d'Aquitaine à la tour abolie," has dreamed, or where, if one takes the most extreme interpretation, reincarnation, one may say that he has lived previously.

He has already tried explicitly to project the dreams related to his past onto the future, in spatial terms. . . . The discovery of the domain is the crystallization of this effort to objectify a past fantasy. What Meaulnes is tempted to do in the realm of the past is not simply find again the comfort of the womb, but make an existential choice for being in the past. This would mean choosing a certain self and playing that role exclusively. In this perspective, distance is psychological, and refuge is ultimately in himself.

The author alludes expressly to a choice of selves for his hero when the latter, just before his meeting with Yvonne, sees himself in the pond as another person. (pp. 503-04)

The romantic hero thus has within himself a double: one who characteristically stands on the threshold (there are several striking instances), who looks outward rather than inward, who goes forward on paths rather than backwards, and who cannot be content with the temptation of reliving in a static manner the pseudo-past of his adventure at les Sablonnières and the more fundamental desires to which it referred. After the disappointments of the vain search, and the experience with Valentine which echoes his original adventure ironically and pathetically, this self chooses a linear, rather than a circular, trajectory. He has recognized that experience is, by its nature, unrepeatable. He later tells François that never again can he reach the purity, the perfection he had at the time of the escape to the domain. . . . That is, he cannot go back, even by a circular path. Curiously, even during the marvelous adventure he had a feeling of what guilt might be—and of pardon. . . . This foreknowledge of a "fall" points to the intuitive, psychological drama which the whole adventure acts out. Man—if Meaulnes, entering the adult world, can be taken as an example—is projected forward, becoming, not being. Only in death would childhood perfection—that is, a coincidence of himself with his ideal—be possible again. (p. 505)

Alain-Fournier's novel can be read, then, as a dialectic between closed and open, retreat and escape, alcove and road; between the house of a story-book past and the open door of the future, of creative possibility. At the opening of the narrative—fifteen years at least after the events—François sees his destiny and Meaulnes', which are of course still associated, as irreparably past and as failure. For him, the loss of the schoolhouse, which

"no longer belongs to us" and to which he will certainly never return, means the end of possibility. The tone of his comments reveals his conviction that their trajectory has been only one of destruction, and the intention of his narrative is to show the failure of their common enterprise, his own failure. . . . But, escaping from François' categorization of him, Meaulnes has moved on. . . . Having established Frantz and Valentine in their house—for they have remained children and will act out Frantz's adolescent dream, magically realized—he will, at least as Seurel imagines him, leave the ruined manor for a new life ahead. (p. 507)

Catherine Savage Brosman, "Alain-Fournier's Domain: A New Look," in The French Review *(copyright 1971 by the American Association of Teachers of French), Vol. XLIV, No. 3, February, 1971, pp. 499-507.*

GEORGE WOODCOCK   (essay date 1974)

Despite the longing for a perishable youth which he shared with them, Alain-Fournier differed profoundly from most of his contemporary novelists of adolescence in France, and particularly from the most celebrated of them, Raymond Radiguet and Jean Cocteau. They remained always within adolescence; it was an impasse which they could not grow beyond. Radiguet escaped from it into death; Cocteau, an arrested Terrible Child, pursued the Game into the Academy itself. Alain-Fournier, on the other hand, wrote—when he was ripe for writing with purpose—from outside adolescence, and what he sought in youth was something of which the young are rarely aware. (p. 348)

It is not adolescence for its own sake that Alain-Fournier evokes in *Le Grand Meaulnes,* but adolescence as the point when we become aware of the value of childhood lost. No novelist—except perhaps Proust—has been nearer to Wordsworth; the *Ode: Intimations of Immortality* (from *Recollections of Early Childhood*) makes an excellent preface to *Le Grand Meaulnes,* for in Alain-Fournier's story we are constantly made aware that "Heaven lies about us in our infancy." As the child grows up, that Heaven recedes, yet men remain aware of it; and in the end Alain-Fournier suggests that, just as in the world childhood always exists, so also does the Heaven it so ephemerally suggests.

For, unlike the adolescent world of the novels of Radiguet and Cocteau, Alain-Fournier's is not one of absolute individual isolation; man finds his way and his salvation through others, and the child which Yvonne de Galais bears to Augustin Meaulnes becomes a messenger from the ever-lost and ever-recovered paradise. To Cocteau and Radiguet adolescence was the end of every hope, as to André Gide it is the beginning of every possibility; to Alain-Fournier it is a point in the great process of life at which, losing childhood, man gets an inkling of its true meaning and begins the search that may end by bringing him to a realization of the spiritual reality that lies behind the repetitious cycle of birth and childhood, manhood and death. (pp. 348-49)

[Alain-Fournier makes] his novel a statement of the significance of adolescence as the period when a man first realizes with peculiar agony his entry into the "shades of the prison-house." He referred often to *Le Grand Meaulnes* as an adventure story; but it is so only in the same way as Conrad's novels are adventure stories. The real adventure is a spiritual one. . . . (p. 352)

It is in [the] context of childhood passing that we must see the great adventure, which happens to Meaulnes alone when he sets off in a cart to meet Seurel's grandparents at the nearest railway station, loses his way, and eventually reaches the isolated manor in whose decaying buildings a strange feast is going on. It is a kind of innocent saturnalia, where the numerous fancy-dressed children are the hosts and masters, and where make-believe shimmers constantly in and out of reality. Each detail is described with naturalistic precision, yet the total effect is fantasy; the behaviour of the people whom Meaulnes encounters seems to him entirely irrational because he knows nothing of the reason why all these children and peasants have gathered together. Even the weather contributes to the feeling of fantasy; in mid-winter the air is as warm as in April, and the birds sing as if spring had already arrived. It is in this phantasmagoric setting that Meaulnes meets Yvonne de Galais and walks with her beside the lake, immediately, completely and for ever in love. Afterwards the wind blows cold, the desperate Frantz de Galais arrives without the bride whose wedding with him everyone has gathered to celebrate, and, seized by some strange mass impulse, the guests depart into the night and carry Meaulnes with them. For him it has been a vision of pure joy, in which the house and its guests, and the wonderful girl and sad Frantz, are so closely linked that they cannot ever be remembered apart. He has seen a magic microcosm of the world of poetic reality which exists in that ephemeral moment of intense awareness as childhood comes to an end. (p. 353)

It is not difficult to detect in this story Alain-Fournier's almost Wordsworthian sense of the meaning of childhood. Somewhere, beyond childhood, lies the real lost land, to which "death alone will give us the key"; when Yvonne's child is born, Seurel is conscious of "someone from a strange country now present in the room with us." In our lives we can only encounter imperfect images of the lost land. Even the party at the manor is made incomplete by the absence of Valentine and the despair of Frantz; only in Meaulnes' irradiating vision, bred out of ignorance of the celebration's true nature, does it seem a paradise. And when Meaulnes finally meets Yvonne again he knows that the dream Yvonne and the real Yvonne are different, however beautiful the latter may be. The difference is given almost macabre emphasis when, after her death, Seurel carries her body down the narrow stairs of the old house. (p. 354)

Yet we are left to wonder if this corpse that lies so heavily is the real Yvonne de Galais, for already Seurel has been conscious of her as a person whose eyes "already contemplate only an inner world." This inner world which Yvonne contemplates before her death is perhaps the same "unknown world" as that of which Seurel is conscious when he first sees the child. Certainly it is in the underlying continuity of this invisible land that the major theme of Alain-Fournier's novel seems to lie. It is true that the lost land never appears—objectively at least—in all its perfection, but its signs are always there; the most unlikely people have knowledge of it—Delouche and Uncle Florentin—and it perhaps exists also in those vestiges of childhood that cling like the rags of glory to almost all the characters of *Le Grand Meaulnes*. Frantz, for instance, grows into manhood without ever truly emerging from childhood. Valentine attracts Meaulnes because there is "something poverty-stricken and childish about her." Seurel, when he is with Yvonne, is "happy like a little child." Yvonne herself, though sometimes "almost maternal" in the impression she makes, can at times look like a "poor distracted child." Even

M. Seurel has "the rather childish curiosity of a schoolmaster," and there is something peculiarly juvenile in the whimsicality and defencelessness of old M. de Galais. In these ways the lost land lingers in many people, but only exceptionally does the vision of that land appear in all its transfigured beauty as it does to Meaulnes. Many other people whom we encounter in the novel turn out to have attended the party at the manor, yet none of them—not even Yvonne or Frantz or M. de Galais who arranged the party—saw in it what Meaulnes saw, a vision projected out of the exaltation of his own spirit, as he makes clear when he tells Seurel: "But I am convinced, now, that when I discovered the nameless manor, I was at the height of what stands for perfection and pure motive in anyone's heart, a height I shall never reach again. In death alone, as I once wrote to you, I may hope to find again the beauty of that day."

Here, of course, we have a repetition of the idea implicit in the medieval romances—that the vision of the Grail will be given only to those who have lived in purity. Meaulnes saw his vision in that fleeting period when innocence may perhaps be thought of as co-existing with the birth of experience.

Yet, as Wordsworth realized—and Blake also—experience brings its own less glorious knowledge. Meaulnes, transgressing, abandons his purity. But he atones, losing much as he does so, but gaining in spiritual stature from the way he lives through experience, so that in the end we see him reunited with childhood, in the living person of his own daughter. Seurel, watching him, can now imagine him "setting out with her for new adventures." He is a man renewed.

Thus the continuity is established, and *Le Grand Meaulnes*, despite its sadness and its frustration, despite the death that leaves of Yvonne only a taste of earth as her hair touches Seurel's lips, ends as a triumphant novel, declaring, as Proust declared, that paradises need never be wholly lost. By breaking down the sense of adolescent isolation, by showing each man's condition as infinitely reflected, Alain-Fournier succeeded in presenting adolescence neither as the beginning of understanding which it appears to Gide, nor as the end of life that it appears to Cocteau, but rather as the time at which the clues to the great continuity of human existence can be revealed in all their suggestive power. (pp. 354-56)

> *George Woodcock, "Alain-Fournier and the Lost Land," in* Queen's Quarterly, *Vol. 81, No. 3, Autumn, 1974, pp. 348-56.*

ELAINE D. CANCALON (essay date 1975)

[Our] purpose is to discuss the influence of fairy-tale structures and motifs on the composition of *Le Grand Meaulnes*. . . . However, our contention is not that Alain-Fournier consciously constructed *Le Grand Meaulnes* on a schema of fairy-tale motifs, but that certain widely known themes had a profound influence on the development of his conception of the novel, and that the underlying significance of these themes became one of the bases for the novel's structure. The universality of the motifs to be discussed would seem to indicate that (as in myths, dreams and games) they represent the symbolic expression of fundamental human needs, aspirations and behaviour. If this is so, then their presence in *Le Grand Meaulnes* places the novel among the important works of our time, which, through their representative structure, provide an insight into the workings of the human psyche. (p. 2)

Through their use of magic, fairy tales express one of the basic aspirations of mankind, and the very quest which we have discussed as the main tenet of symbolism: a search which uses real experience but which manages to transcend its physical limitations. Everyday objects are endowed with magic power enabling heroes and heroines to achieve wondrous feats, to be transported over vast distances in time and space, and to transform or multiply their identity at will. Although nothing specifically miraculous occurs in *Le Grand Meaulnes,* the novel possesses several qualities which endow it with the atmosphere and tone of the world of the fairy tale and enable it to act as a bridge between the author and that "other world" which he seeks. A real object such as the vest which Augustin brings back from the château, acts as a springboard making it possible for him to transcend time and space so that he again believes himself to be participating in the celebration. (p. 4)

By prolonging and enclosing in a cloud of imprecision some of the principal scenes in the novel, Alain-Fournier creates a feeling of mystery which would seem to indicate that the episodes and characters are participants in a world beyond that of everyday appearance. . . .

Meaulnes' experience occurs in a universe which cannot be explained and analyzed rationally. Some force (like the pervasive power in fairy tales) is at work which transfigures an ordinary wedding ceremony, transforming it into an episode from the world of make-believe. (p. 5)

Just as Meaulnes' initial appearance and his entry into the château are veiled in suspense, so Mademoiselle de Galais is first presented hidden behind a literal cloak of mystery. . . .

Her facial expressions and her half-finished sentences intimate that much of what is important must be left unsaid. By continually hinting at some undisclosed secret, Yvonne evokes the feeling of an exterior force (fate, perhaps) which controls her life and Meaulnes'. This constant suggestion transforms the surface realism of the novel into a network of symbols linking reality with an ideal but ill-defined world. (p. 6)

The surface realism of the novel is belied . . . by the occurrence of many unlikely or coincidental episodes. If these episodes were interpreted as the mere narration of real events they would have to be criticized for their improbable nature. Can one grant, for example, the probability that Valentine, having abandoned Frantz, would find her way precisely to the home of François' aunt, and that this aunt should happen to live in the same town as Meaulnes' mother (a coincidence which thus enables François to learn part of Valentine's story)? However, this episode and others like it should not be accepted at face value; their importance lies elsewhere. Their illogical nature, like the magic in fairy tales, reveals the desire (transmitted from the author to his characters) to transcend the possibilities of straightforward representation. The novel is neither a simple recording of actual events, nor a creation of pure fantasy, but an attempt to express symbolically, through the transformation of childhood experiences, certain universal psychological conflicts: the rejection of life's mediocrity, the search for absolute values, the impossibility of total happiness. (p. 7)

In an article entitled "A Psychoanalytic Study of the Fairy Tale," E. K. Schwartz points to the fact that fairy tales are often an illustration and expression of problems involved in the process of growing up. . . . The development which occurs in *Le Grand Meaulnes* is also concerned with the process of growing up as it is remembered by the adult. Although the novel does not begin with the birth of the hero, there are several references to significant early childhood experiences. François remembers the many times he and his family were forced to move to a new location and the sensations connected with those moves; Meaulnes' mother reveals Augustin's adventurous nature and recounts the accident which took his brother's life; and Yvonne describes several incidents in Frantz's childhood, especially those connected with "la maison de Frantz." Of greater importance than these details however, is the basic theme which, as in many fairy tales, embraces the conflicts and struggles encountered in the transition between adolescence and maturity.

The method which Alain-Fournier uses to illuminate this theme is, interestingly enough, also borrowed from the structural devices of the fairy tale and is known as "trebling": "The 'sacred' number three is most common in all fairy tales of all lands (and in the Bible). Persons and things appear in threes. . . . In *Le Grand Meaulnes* the basic problem of becoming an adult is illustrated by a triple personification of the major character: Frantz represents the desire to retain the absolute world of the child, François, the willingness to accept and adapt to the compromises of adulthood, Meaulnes, the adolescent vacillation between these two extremes. Whereas in fairy tales the conflict is always resolved (the young man conquers all obstacles—symbols of his own contradictions—and finally gains his bride, thus assuming the responsibilities of maturity) in *Le Grand Meaulnes* the hero never manages to construct a hierarchy of desires and so emerge as a unified, functional psyche.

Frantz's refusal to relinquish his childhood, and Meaulnes' hesitation to do so, are related to our previous discussion concerning the role of magic and absolutes. By attempting to make the ideal liberty of youth endure, Frantz refuses the relative values of adult life and lives as in a fairy tale where dream and reality are one, because there are no limitations placed on human possibilities. By creating Frantz, Alain-Fournier gives total expression to a cherished dream: the rediscovery of an Eden-like innocence and unity untainted by the practical teachings of actuality. He thus recreates, through the world of the novel, not the actual experiences of the young Henri Fournier, but the dreams of youth transfigured by adult memories and desires. (pp. 8-9)

> *Elaine D. Cancalon, in her introduction to her* Fairy-Tale Structures and Motifs in "Le grand Meaulnes" *(© Herbert Lang & Co. Ltd., Peter Lang Ltd., 1975), Herbert Lang, Peter Lang, 1975, pp. 1-12.*

ROBERT GIBSON (essay date 1975)

Quite how much the reputation of *Le Grand Meaulnes* owes to extra-literary considerations would be difficult to establish with accuracy. Undoubtedly, part of the success it achieved in the France of the 1920s must have been due to the by then mythical figure of Fournier himself, the French equivalent of Rupert Brooke—or, in a later age, of Sidney Keys, Richard Hillary, Keith Douglas or Alun Lewis—the young writer of genius struck down in his prime with most of his promise unfulfilled. . . .

For the many readers of this persuasion, *Le Grand Meaulnes* could not have been more welcome because it was—and remains still—the most delicate rendering so far achieved in literature of the romantic adolescent consciousness: with the enchanted Lost Domain to escape to in the opening part of the novel, and a highly idealistic set of moral values propounded throughout, it could not fail to win over a vast reading public appalled or bemused by the restlessness of their shell-shocked era. The 'escapist' element and the noble moral values have since combined to make it an irresistibly 'safe' and at the same time, thoroughly enjoyable set-book for senior schoolchildren right to the present.

To concede all this, however, is not the whole explanation of the success *Le Grand Meaulnes* has achieved: for a variety of further reasons, it has won the lasting affection of a considerable number of more sophisticated readers too. . . . (p. 284)

[But far] too often critics singled out the dream-like qualities of the first part of the novel and ignored or wrote off the rest. (p. 285)

One can readily understand why Part One of *Le Grand Meaulnes* has been singled out for particular praise because it is here that Fournier's narrative technique is most exquisitely effective. The reader's attention is caught and held with the quite masterly opening chapter which sets the scene with admirable economy of means and, with its clear suggestions of the disruptive effects of Meaulnes' arrival, hints powerfully at the momentous events still to come. Suspense is sustained by the deft building up of atmosphere and by the employing of a narrator who is himself involved in the action and is not, therefore, omniscient. Although, from the very outset, Seurel at once establishes that he is recording events years after they have happened and is all along aware of the final outcome, he re-creates events in the order and manner in which he originally perceived them. The reader is, therefore, made to see through Seurel's eyes. . . . (p. 286)

The dream-like atmosphere of the party is largely created by rapidly juxtaposing scenes which are realistic enough in themselves but seem to have no connection with one another. . . . (pp. 286-87)

It is easy to appreciate why all of this should have captivated so many readers: it is exquisitely fashioned, our world is starved of magic, and this is high romance in the spirit of *Thomas the Rhymer* or *La Belle dame sans merci,* of what Coleridge captured in *Kubla Khan.* . . . (p. 287)

'What then?' indeed: mutilators of the text of *Le Grand Meaulnes* would do well to ponder, because Fournier's aura of enchantment is not left undisturbed. Frantz de Galais makes his petulant entrance, in an atmosphere of gloom and storm, and peremptorily decrees that the party must end. From this point on, the party is taken over by tipsy adults and 'in the park, which for two days, had been full of so much grace and so much wonder, this marked the beginning of the disruption and the desolation.' Meaulnes hears snatches of two folk songs on the stormy night air: the first clearly hints of licentiousness . . . while the refrain of the second is a farewell to love. . . . That re-iterated message of finality in the second song is, though Meaulnes does not appreciate it at the time, directly applicable to him: the party is indeed at an end, for him, and the gaily-coloured lanterns will never be lit for him again.

In bestowing the most enthusiastic of their praises upon this first part of *Le Grand Meaulnes,* Fournier's critics are committing the error of . . . isolating the magic and ignoring the tragic qualities of the novel. In fact, Fournier created the enchanted world of Part One of *Le Grand Meaulnes* only in order to destroy it utterly in Part Three, and this point is hammered home with an insistence one would have thought should have been obvious when, after years of hopeless searching, Meaulnes at last rediscovers the Lost Domain. A grand picnic is organ-

ised, with the express purpose of reuniting him with Yvonne de Galais, and, without mounting bitterness, Meaulnes proceeds to call the roll of all his most cherished memories of the fancy dress party that has never ceased to haunt his dreams. Change and decay is all around: the old manor house has been demolished, the lake has been filled in, the yacht on which he sailed with Yvonne has been sold to pay off family debts, the romantic bric-à-brac of his bedroom has been thrown away; he pretends not to notice that some of the children who once danced so delightfully, now grown older, are viciously ill-treating a donkey. . . . (pp. 287-88)

Meaulnes is profoundly ill at ease in [Yvonne's] presence. He is only too well aware that he has forfeited whatever rights he may ever have had to the lost domain. . . . If the theme of Part One of the novel is the Earthly Paradise, the theme of Part Three is no less certainly Paradise Lost, and it is entirely consistent with this theme that Meaulnes should approach his wedding so full of guilt and foreboding and that Yvonne de Galais, like every other vestige of the first enchanted party, should finally be destroyed. In the light of this, it simply passes all credence that critics could ever have labelled *Le Grand Meaulnes* a *conte bleu* to reassure 'the wistfully inclined'. . . . (pp. 288-89)

The transition between the enchantments of Part One of the novel and the desolation of Part [Three] is effected by a section in which the dominant note is frustration. Meaulnes tries repeatedly to find his way back to the Lost Domain, all his efforts are thwarted, and when he finally leaves, with heavy heart, for Paris, his defeat is emphatically underlined by images of gloom and depression. . . . In this section of *Le Grand Meaulnes,* as indeed throughout the whole novel and his earlier stories and poems, Fournier's great artistic strength is in his ability to convey mood through the selection of telling evocative detail. He is rather less impressive in analysing motivation and in working out the mechanics of his plot.

The first point in the novel where most readers begin to experience difficulty in suspending their disbelief is in Part Two, back in the everyday world of the village school of Sainte-Agathe after the discovery and the loss of the Domain without a Name in which they are normally perfectly ready to believe. Why, most readers ask—if not as they read, then certainly as they reflect afterwards—why does Meaulnes take so long to recognise Frantz de Galais once he has become a temporary fellow-pupil? (p. 289)

In fact, there is a perfectly plausible explanation for Meaulnes' slow reactions, and this is that in spite of all his protestations, he does not, even at this early stage, really want to return to the Lost Domain. The readiness with which he more than once allows Seurel to dissuade him from setting out in search of Yvonne, and his barely credible lack of insistence on speaking there and then with Frantz as soon as he has discovered his true identity, strongly suggest that he really prefers his *princesse* to be *lointaine* and the prolongation of desire to its fulfilment. It could well be that like Saint-Exupéry, who in a later context, sadly recognised that he could not recapture his lost childhood Eden, he has realised that 'One can never again re-enter that infinite world, because it is the *party* and not the park that one would have to reconstitute'. The reader's difficulty is that none of this is made explicit in the novel itself: it all has to be inferred, and not every reader is willing or able to take the trouble to do so.

The second major point of difficulty and controversy in the novel concerns the reasons for Meaulnes' reluctance to meet

Yvonne again once the lost domain has been found, and his abrupt departure the day after his wedding. His motives for hesitating have now changed: whereas in Part Two, he made ineffectual efforts to rediscover the Domain largely because of his fear of being disappointed, now in Part Three, he is wholly inhibited by his guilty conscience. It is in his handling of this section of the novel that Fournier's technical immaturity is most manifest, and it is hard to resist the conclusion that material which was potentially rich in human and dramatic interest has not been exploited to the maximum advantage. (pp. 290-91)

How, then, should *Le Grand Meaulnes* be approached? To try to see it through the eyes of childhood as some of its greatest admirers have recommended, is to imply, quite erroneously, that it is a children's book and is, in any event, to demand what, for most readers, is simply impossible. While it may not be fruitful to pursue too far the analogy between *Le Grand Meaulnes* and the Grail legend, the ideal way to view the novel might nevertheless be, as several critics have suggested, as a modern-dress version of the medieval tale of chivalry: in the best of these, there are to be found the same blend of love, dream, adventure and high endeavour, and the evoking of both character and scene by quick deft touches. (p. 294)

Stimulating though the most recent contributions to Fournier studies have been, they have all, no doubt because of their particular terms of reference, missed one point about *Le Grand Meaulnes* which is of paramount importance and since, in my view, it has never received adequate attention, I propose to examine this now by way of conclusion. What is at issue is the extent to which the dominant mood and distinctive 'flavour' of *Le Grand Meaulnes* is determined by the *persona* of the story-teller, François Seurel.

Seurel's attitude towards the narrative is quite remarkably possessive, and the other characters in the novel are allowed very few opportunities indeed to address themselves directly to the reader: the account of Meaulnes' first discovery of the mysterious domain is provided not by Meaulnes himself but by Seurel and, at the end of the novel, after transcribing only a few pages of Meaulnes' secret notebook, Seurel states that because the handwriting is barely legible, 'it's necessary for me to take over at this point and reconstruct the whole of this part of his story'. In Part Three of the novel, Meaulnes is replaced or, at the very least, seriously rivalled as the character of central interest by Seurel himself. . . . Seurel, then, is almost omnipresent throughout the novel, his voice is the first and last that the reader hears, and he is obliged to listen to it almost throughout.

All of this might be beside the point if Seurel were a thoroughly colourless personality, or a mere lens through which the reader is allowed to view events, but is he? Many critics have assumed that he has indeed no character of his own, and of these, Mr Alan Pryce-Jones is thoroughly typical [see excerpt above]. . . . Seurel does indeed have 'some special quality' and it determines the idiosyncratic atmosphere of the whole novel: the aura of mysteriousness with which he surrounds everyday scenes reveals both his powers of keen observation and his capacity for wonderment; the belief that the countryside around him stretches out to infinity expresses his childlike sense of space; his sense that Nature is brooding, resentful and vaguely menacing is the corollary of his great love of domestic calm and cosiness, and with the recurrent evocations of the cold and windswept landscape can be contrasted a striking number of references to secure and enclosed havens—the schoolhouse

kitchen and the blacksmith's shop at Sainte-Agathe, the farm and the barn where Meaulnes takes shelter on his way to the Lost Domain, the old manorhouse itself, Frantz's little house in the woods—which, cold and draughty though some of them may be, hold out the promise of peace and seclusion amidst the surrounding desolation. To Seurel, they are all places of particular delectation and this is made manifest in the language he employs to describe them: it is never flat and prosaic, it is consistently warm and evocative.

The key traits of his personality are in fact insinuated into the reader's consciousness in the very first chapter of the novel before Meaulnes has even made his appearance, let alone begun to 'work his vast activity', and they are also, in part, subtly explained. Thus his basic timidity and acute uneasiness can be accounted for by the legacy of his crippled knee, and by the effect of his mother's seemingly permanent anxiety: the opening paragraphs are fairly riddled with words like 'despair', 'anxiously', 'fearfully' and 'disquiet'. Seurel is to express the *malaise* of the opening throughout the novel, in his fear of happiness, and the premonitions of impending disaster he feels when cycling to tell Meaulnes that he has found Yvonne, or in the course of the picnic staged in their honour or as he lurks outside the newly-weds' cottage on the very evening after the marriage.

It is in the opening chapter also that Seurel's capacity for hero-worship and romantic exaggeration is demonstrated. Because he himself is so timorous and over-protected, he immediately falls under Meaulnes' spell. (pp. 297-99)

Meaulnes is certainly involved in some highly dramatic situations, but part of the heroic aura which continuously surrounds him is just as certainly fashioned by Seurel. (p. 299)

What is also established in the opening chapter is that Seurel's feelings for Meaulnes are very mixed indeed. If he hero-worships Meaulnes for the glamour and excitement he brings to Sainte-Agathe, he also profoundly resents the dramatic break that Meaulnes obliges him to make with his established way of life. (p. 300)

[In the course of the action] Seurel has lost everything he holds most dear—his childhood peace, his youthful dreams, Yvonne de Galais, Yvonne's nameless daughter and Meaulnes himself—and in the fifteen years which have elapsed since all these momentous events occurred, he seems to have found no adequate consolation. Much of the intervening time seems to have been spent in brooding and, not surprisingly, when the time comes for his tale to be told, it is anything but colourless or matter-of-fact; it is, on the contrary, positively shot through with nostalgia, Seurel's own distinctive mood. He feels eternally disinherited, feels it compulsively to such an extent that his imprint on the whole book is quite indelible; indeed, his personality is so stamped across the narrative that the whole book could, perfectly appropriately, be re-entitled *Le Petit Seurel*.

Of all the characters in *Le Grand Meaulnes*, Seurel has by far the most in common with Fournier himself: they both consistently glorify the past to the detriment of the present, they are both hypersensitively attuned to the beauty, the mystery and, occasionally, the menace, of natural landscape, and they are both inconsolable for lost childhood, lost love and lost innocence; they are both, in a word, thorough-going nostalgicians. But they have something else in common more important than any of these: they are both *artists*. Each has to learn the artist's bitter lesson that before he can begin to re-create his Paradise, he must first lose it utterly; for each, it is the feeling of total loss which inspires the urge to restore, the need for revenge over circumstance and for victory over Time.

In life, Fournier's hopes of earthly happiness withered beneath that glacial and insistent question of Yvonne de Quiévrecourt: *A quoi bon? A quoi bon?* What's the point of persisting like this when it's quite impossible? *Le Grand Meaulnes* provides the triumphant answer: the point is the creation of an imperishable masterpiece. (pp. 303-04)

> *Robert Gibson, in his* The Land without a Name: Alain-Fournier and His World *(copyright © 1975 by Robert Gibson), Paul Elek, 1975, 328 p.*

KAREN D. LEVY (essay date 1978)

Like [*Le Grand Meaulnes*], many of the poems and vignettes written between 1905 and 1911 and collected in *Miracles* emphasize [Alain-Fournier's] preoccupation with an idealized past, with painfully fragile young girls, or with various kinds of unhappy love situations. Lines such as "O Taille-Mince" from **"Dans le chemin qui s'enfonce"** or "Je ne sais plus où Elle est . . . Où est-elle?" from **"Et maintenant que c'est la pluie"** recall descriptions of the heroine in *Le Grand Meaulnes* and echo Fournier's anguished comments in his correspondence concerning the whereabouts of Mlle de Quiévrecourt. And the vignettes entitled **"Le Miracle des trois dames"** and **"Portrait"** also depict the same kind of disillusioning or impossible love as sections of *Le Grand Meaulnes*. . . .

What Fournier did not envisage, however, was that with the completion of the book early in the year 1913 he would in a very real sense be free of at least a good portion of the weight of the past. For the first time he would be able to consider another kind of love based not on absence but on sharing and reciprocity. (p. 306)

The manuscripts he was working on at the time of his death in 1914, and the letters to his family during the last year of his life reveal this important change in attitude. Both the fragment of the play *La Maison dans la forêt* and the novel *Colombe Blanchet* deal with situations where the protagonists attain fulfillment through reciprocal love and the prospect of a future together. In the former work, only one scene of which was actually written, the major character goes through disillusioning experiences, but he is eventually able to accept the love which Clément Borgal describes as "cette rédemption qu'il n'espérait plus." A young peasant youth named Harold, who in many ways resembles both Meaulnes and Frantz, is betrayed by his frivolous Parisian mistress. And this unfaithfulness causes him to lash out violently against "toutes celles qui sont dans les villes à fleureter, à mentir, à tromper." After undergoing a period of bitter frustration coupled with guilt, however, he recovers from his initial disillusionment. Thanks to Eléonore, a beautiful, free-spirited girl living in the wing of an abandoned convent, Harold gradually regains his equilibrium. And he is able to accept a new kind of open love which assumes the role of an earthly salvation. The realization of his dream of a reciprocal relationship seems assured, and he affirms his belief in the future. . . . (p. 307)

In the projected novel *Colombe Blanchet* we find a similar kind of evolution. The major character, a provincial teacher named Jean-Gilles Autissier, is first attracted to the passionate Laurence and then to his student, the innocent Colombe Blanchet. But he eventually realizes that neither Laurence's sensuality nor Colombe's childlike chastity can give him the lasting peace he desires, and he eventually turns to a third character, Colombe's older sister Emilie, "la savante." She alone has suffered like him and can both restore his sense of equilibrium and provide the balanced kind of relationship he needs. It is precisely this last and newest heroine who most interested Fournier. . . . [It was particularly Emilie] who captured Fournier's attention as the expression of a possible love and whom the hero in the projected novel was planning to marry. (p. 308)

After living with a love that fed on absence, Fournier's last projected works and letters reveal how he finally realized that today and tomorrow are more important than yesterday. This significant insight would have been impossible if he had loved only the mythical Yvonne, who was at once part of the past and a creation of Fournier's own imagination. And it is precisely this last and all too often ignored aspect of his development that adds great depth and richness to his literary image. (p. 310)

> *Karen D. Levy, "Alain-Fournier and the Surrealist Quest for Unity," in* Romance Notes, *Vol. XVIII, No. 3, Spring, 1978, pp. 301-10.*

ADDITIONAL BIBLIOGRAPHY

Chase, Cleveland B. "A Memorable Novel in *The Wanderer.*" *The New York Times Book Review* (9 December 1928): 9, 14.
  States that despite its "dream-like, almost fairy-tale structure" *The Wanderer* gives the sense of the "reality of human ideals and aspirations."

De Lutri, Joseph R. "Rimbaud and Fournier: The End of the Quest." *Romance Notes* XVIII, No. 2 (Winter 1977): 153-56.
  Compares *Le grand Meaulnes* with Rimbaud's *Aube,* finding that each expresses a tension between childhood and adolescence.

Dunn, G. I. Introduction to *Le grand Meaulnes,* by Alain Fournier, pp. iv-viii. London: Oxford University Press, 1936.
  Biographical sketch.

Gross, Ruth V. "The Narrator as Demon in Grass and Alain-Fournier." *Modern Fiction Studies* 25, No. 4 (Winter 1979-80): 625-34.
  Compares *Le grand Meaulnes* with Günter Grass's *Katz und Maus,* the two books having the similar structure of a first person narrator obsessed with the hero of the story.

Jones, Marian Giles. *A Critical Commentary on Alain-Fournier's "Le Grand Meaulnes."* London: Macmillan; New York: St Martin's Press, 1968, 80 p.
  Introductory study for students.

March, Harold M. "The 'Other Landscape' of Alain-Fournier." *PMLA* LVI, No. 1 (March 1941): 266-79.
  Traces the evolution of Fournier's thought.

Sussex, R. T. "The Alain-Fournier Tradition: A Recollection." *Meanjin Quarterly* 32, No. 2 (June 1973): 209-12.
  Recollection of a visit with Isabelle Rivière, Jacques Rivière's wife and Fournier's sister.

(Eugen) Bertolt (Friedrich) Brecht

1898-1956

German dramatist, poet, critic, novelist, and short story writer.

Brecht's imagination, artistic genius, and profound grasp of the nature of drama establish him as a chief innovator of modern theatrical techniques. The concept of "epic theater" and use of "alienation effects" are the best known features of his dramatic theory. Brecht effectively exploited an exquisite stage-sense to promote his political and humanistic concerns for the improvement of society, using theater to arouse the social conscience of his audience. The "epic" style of drama is, according to Brecht, intended to appeal "less to the feelings than to the spectator's reason." This is achieved through various "alienation effects" which undermine the lifelike illusion of traditional theater and demand that the audience consider the intellectual issues presented by the play rather than being emotionally engaged by its characters. For example, an actor may begin commenting on the play itself, creating viewer detachment from artificial character roles: the resulting estrangement should cause the spectator to apprehend hackneyed ideas and situations in a new way.

Brecht was born in the Bavarian town of Augsburg, where his family lived the middle-class existence he came to despise in favor of the Marxist ideal of a proletarian society. While still a teenager he had some poetry published. He studied medicine at the Ludwig Maximillian University in Munich and served in a military hospital toward the end of the First World War. His first play, *Baal,* was written at this time, though not produced for several years. Like Brecht's other early plays and poetry, *Baal* displays the influence of German expressionism. *Trommeln in der Nacht (Drums in the Night),* his first play to be produced, and *Im Dickicht der Städte (In the Jungle of Cities)* also exemplify the sordid themes and mood of this literary movement. *Drums in the Night* earned Brecht the Kleist Prize and gained him national recognition.

After his expressionist period, Brecht wrote his first work of "epic theater" in the play *Mann ist Mann (A Man's a Man).* This is also one of a series of "didactic plays," works in which Brecht expressed his new-found committment to the philosophy of communism. Less overtly dogmatic, and one of the playwright's most popular productions, is *Die Dreigroschenoper (The Threepenny Opera),* which also formed the basis of Brecht's only novel. One of several collaborations with composer Kurt Weill, *The Threepenny Opera* is an extravaganza of humor, bitterness, and social statement. Brecht based this drama on John Gay's *The Beggar's Opera.* Throughout his career Brecht adapted the works of other authors, transforming them with modern and highly original interpretations. His literary erudition allowed him to combine a wide range of influences in his work, including Spanish, Oriental, and Elizabethan drama, popular songs, folk literature, and films. This remarkable variety of sources creates in Brecht's plays a lively conglomeration of styles and moods, from the farcical and grotesque to the sternly antitragic.

In 1933 Brecht's Marxist politics forced him to leave fascist Germany and go into self-imposed exile in Scandinavia and the United States. Later the Nazi government annulled the

Courtesy of German Information Center

playwright's citizenship. While in exile Brecht became an anti-Nazi propagandist, writing for a German-language periodical published in Moscow and composing the drama *Furcht und Elend des dritten Reiches (Fear and Misery of the Third Reich).* During this time Brecht also wrote what are critically regarded as his greatest works.

His genius for artistic invention and his desire to motivate social concerns in the playgoer combine in Brecht's mature dramas to form a rich and varied view of existence. Through the crisis of its scientist hero, *Leben des Galilei (Galileo)* reexamines Brecht's recurrent theme of the obstacles to social progress. Yet despite its focus on philosophical issues, critics find in this play a strong main character who, along with the protagonist of *Mutter Courage und ihre Kinder (Mother Courage and Her Children),* enlists the spectator's feelings as well as reason. In his mature works Brecht transcended the single-minded message of his earlier didactic pieces and achieved a more complex viewpoint than that permitted by the official policies and doctrines of communism. About *Der gute Mensch von Sezuan (The Good Woman of Setzuan)* critic Raymond Williams remarks that "Brecht is as far as possible, in this play, from the method of special pleading which insists on the spectator or reader seeing the world through the actions and tensions of a single mind.''

Brecht's ability to express his political and philosophical views in fresh and formally ingenious ways is also observable in his poetry, which he produced throughout his career. In both poetry and drama he attains one of the most controlled and completely realized aesthetic visions in literature. During the last part of his life Brecht returned to Berlin and formed his own company, the Berliner Ensemble, enabling him to implement his dramatic theories and gaining him the admiration of devotees of dramatic art.

(See also *TCLC*, Vol. 1.)

PRINCIPAL WORKS

Trommeln in der Nacht   (drama)   1922
   [*Drums in the Night*, 1966]
Baal   (drama)   1923
   [*Baal*, 1964]
Im Dickicht der Städte   (drama)   1923
   [*In the Jungle of Cities*, 1957]
Das Leben Eduards des Zweiten von England   (drama)
   1924
   [*Edward II*, 1966]
Mann ist Mann   (drama)   1926
   [*A Man's a Man*, 1957]
Die Hauspostille   (poetry)   1927
   [*A Manual of Piety*, 1966]
Die Dreigroschenoper   (drama)   1928
   [*The Threepenny Opera*, 1949]
Aufstieg und Fall der Stadt Mahogonny   (drama)   1930
   [*The Rise and Fall of the Town of Mahogonny*, 1960]
Der Jasager   (drama)   1930
   [*He Who Said Yes/He Who Said No*, 1946]
Die Massnahme   (drama)   1930
   [*The Measures Taken*, 1956]
Die heilige Johanna der Schlachthöfe   (drama)   1932
   [*St. Joan of the Stockyards*, 1956]
Die Mutter   (drama)   1932
   [*The Mother*, 1956]
Dreigroschenroman   (novel)   1933
   [*A Penny for the Poor*, 1937; *Threepenny Novel*, 1956]
Fünf Schwierigkeiten beim Schreiben der Wahrheit
   (essays)   1934
   [*Writing the Truth: Five Difficulties*, 1948]
Lieder, Gedichte, Chöre   (poetry)   1934
Furcht und Elend des dritten Reiches   (drama)   1938
   [*Fear and Misery of the Third Reich*, 1942]
Der gute Mensch von Sezuan   (drama)   1943
   [*The Good Woman of Setzuan*, 1941]
Leben des Galilei   (drama)   1943
   [*Galileo*, 1947]
Die Ausnahme und die Regel   (drama)   1947
   [*The Exception and the Rule*, 1954]
Herr Puntila und sein Knecht Matti   (drama)   1948
   [*Puntila*, 1954]
Kalendergeschichten   (short stories and poetry)   1948
   [*Tales from the Calendar*, 1961]
Der Kaukasische Kreidekreis   (drama)   1948
   [*The Caucasian Chalk Circle*, 1948]
Kleines Organon für das Theatre   (essays)   1949
   [*Little Organ for the Theatre*, 1951]
Mutter Courage und ihre Kinder   (drama)   1949
   [*Mother Courage and Her Children*, 1949]

Der aufhaltsame Aifstieg des Arturo Ui   (drama)   1958
   [*The Rise of Arture Ui*, 1957]
Poems   (poetry)   1976

EMERSON ROBERT LOOMIS   (essay date 1960)

The enigma of Bertolt Brecht continues to trouble the world long after the world has ceased to trouble him. A key to a better understanding of Brecht is to be found in his little known work *Die sieben Todsünden*. . . . This play is significant because in it Brecht dealt specifically with what was a major problem for him—the question of whether truth can be expressed as a generalized abstraction or is only to be found in the concretely subjective.

This problem became a matter of especial concern to Brecht because of the experiences of his formative years in the period of World War I and its aftermath. Like that of many other of his generation, his faith in existing social systems was shattered. It appears that even the philosophy of Marxism was not entirely satisfactory to him. On the other hand, his experiences had given him such a conviction of the fallibility of human nature that a purely subjective interpretation of life seemed unreliable to him. *Die sieben Todsünden* is essentially a presentation of the paradoxes inherent in both the universal and concrete approaches to truth. Brecht's ambiguous solution to the problem is a statement of the paradoxical nature of the human condition itself. (p. 51)

The principal characters are the two sisters, both named Anna. It is obvious from their initial appearance—they enter the stage under a single cloak as if Siamese twins—and from the statements of Anna I that they represent opposing parts of the same personality. As will be seen, Anna I stands for the abstract and Anna II for the concrete approach to truth. The analytical Anna I sings her story while the emotional Anna II tells hers through dance. Both Anna I and Anna II take part in the skit-like pantomimes which illustrate the seven deadly sins. The role of Anna's family—father, two brothers, and even mother—is sung by a male quartet. Their function is to provide a running commentary on the actions of Anna I-Anna II. There are other minor characters who appear in the various pantomimes. (pp. 51-2)

As in a typical Brechtian play, the "plot," if it may be so called, consists of a sequence of loosely connected events which have a cumulative effect. . . .

Brecht's dilemma is dramatized in the problem facing Anna I-Anna II. Before examining this problem, it is well to understand Anna I-Anna II. She represents everyman; such no doubt is the way in which Brecht consciously intended her. But also, in a manner in which he was probably not aware, she stands for Brecht himself. Significantly she represents two aspects of a divided personality. (p. 52)

Anna I represents the conscious aspect of an individual. She is rational, cool-headed, and analytical. As Brecht presents Anna I, her practicality amounts to expediency. She makes choices on the basis of short-term goals, with an analysis of each situation. These choices lead to a definite major goal, which in the play is a material one. She acts on the assumption that there is a fixed system of morality which is valid for all individuals. In short, she believes in objective, universal values.

On the other hand, Anna II represents the subconscious aspect of an individual. She is emotional, hot-headed, and instinctive. As Brecht presents her, her "natural" behavior results in folly from a worldly viewpoint, but suggests personal integrity. She makes choices on the basis of an organic reaction to each situation. Her only major goal is to be herself. She follows no fixed system of morality. In short, Anna II believes only in subjective, human values.

The Family represents society—capitalistic society—but the principle could apply to communistic society as well. Their outlook is that of Anna I. The particular system which they endorse is one based on economic necessity—whatever makes money is right. . . . The Family (and thus society) has confidence in Anna I, but none in Anna II. They expect Anna I to control Anna II. Yet ironically it is Anna II who produces the achievements on which they all depend.

It is the Family which poses the problem to Anna I-Anna II. Characteristically Brecht states the problem in economic terms. The problem specifically is how to live, that is, how to make money. (pp. 52-3)

The working out of the problem confronts Anna I-Anna II with seven crises. In each case, the opposing tendencies of Anna I and Anna II clash, but Anna I always forces Anna II to submit to her decision. By the end of the process, Anna I-Anna II is the product of these choices. (p. 53)

The conflict between Anna I and Anna II is settled in the last and climactic section, that on Envy. Here Anna II rebels against the domination of Anna I in an effort to assert her own desires. She wishes to live like those people who follow their own inclinations regardless of the consequences. Anna I brands this as the sin of Envy. She urges Anna II not to envy such people because, although their instinctive behavior may for a time yield them a good life, they are doomed to disappointment since they have no definite goals. . . . That the instinctive person does indeed in the end come to face Nothingness, symbolized by the closed door, is indicated by Brecht when Anna II tries to re-enter the torn doors through which she had earlier danced. At each door, a dark figure stands, preventing her from entering. (pp. 54-5)

The theme of the work is ostensibly that it is impossible to be good in an evil world. Virtue becomes vice and vice becomes virtue. The Family's rigid system of morality, based on economic expediency, turns the seven actions, which, when judged independently, appear virtues, into sins. It is evident here and from Brecht's other writings that the particular system which makes this situation possible is capitalism. The Family's morality is the bourgeois morality which Brecht so scorned. Certainly there is much in this type of morality which deserves criticism. And it is the validity of his treatment of the difference between the appearance and the reality of capitalism which accounts for much of the popularity of his works.

What may be overlooked is that the logic by which Brecht condemns capitalism also condemns communism, or any other rigid system, as well. What is most damnable in Anna I is that she feels a compulsion to relate everything to a fixed, absolute standard. All actions must contribute to a predetermined goal. The end not only justifies the means, but determines what they are. Actions cannot be judged subjectively according to the unique situation. Thus Anna II's actions would just as certainly

be regarded as sins under communism as under capitalism. (p. 55)

He can give no positive solution because he never found one, perhaps because there is none. But he offers every man the challenge to become a seeker too. (pp. 55-6)

Emerson Robert Loomis, "A Reinterpretation of Bertolt Brecht," in The University of Kansas City Review, *(University of Kansas City, 1960), Vol. XXVII, No. 1, October, 1960, pp. 51-6.*

HEINZ POLITZER (essay date 1962)

What is the epic theater? First and most important, it is, as Eric Bentley noted, a "misnomer." It is certainly non-Aristotelian in so far as it upsets the sequence of time which Aristotle presupposed as one of the constituents of tragedy. As the early Brecht stated in the notes to ***Mahagonny***, "narrative" is to replace "plot." Instead of being "a part of the whole," each scene is to be "an entity in itself," moving in "jerks" rather than in the "evolutionary necessity by which one follows from the other" (*evolutionäre Zwangsläufigkeit*). But the negation of Aristotle's sequence of time does not yet turn the dramatic theater into an epic one. If Aristotle defined the epic as a narrative form in which "many events simultaneously transacted can be represented," he did not exclude coherence and consistency. The epic, Aristotle notes, "should have for its subject a single action, whole and complete, with a beginning, a middle and an end." Yet this is precisely what Brecht attacked when, in the notes to ***The Round Heads and the Pointed Heads*** . . . , he demanded that "certain incidents in the play should be treated as self-contained scenes and raised—by means of inscriptions, music, and sound effects, and the actor's way of playing—above the level of the everyday, the obvious, the expected." It is here that he mentions the *Verfremdungseffekt*, or Alienation Effect, which propels the spectator from a merely passive—or, as Brecht was fond of saying "culinary"—attitude into one of genuine participation. Instead of resting comfortably in his seat, the spectator is expected to take a stand, both literally and figuratively. Or, as Brecht put it, by the "culinary" theater "the audience is entangled in the action on stage," a process which is bound to "exhaust their power of action." The epic theater, on the other hand, arouses their power of action and "extorts decisions from them."

It cannot be denied that some of the shock techniques of his Alienation Effect have contributed greatly to the success of his plays. . . . He uses boards and streamers across the stage to indicate the time and place of the action, to give summaries of the action which is to follow (thus eliminating the "culinary" element of suspense), to contradict the action on stage (thus forcing the spectator to think for himself), or to address the audience in the way a street orator addresses a crowd. The dramatic action is suddenly and illogically interrupted by shrill songs, very often only tenuously relevant to the plot itself. Cruel gags alternate with practical jokes, which are occasionally rather sophisticated. The mechanics of the stage remain visible and function as a play outside the play.

These tricks, which follow one another in rapid succession, do not allow the spectator a moment of respite. They spread an air of excitement such as children might experience when they visit a circus. They seldom fail to impress even the connoisseur, who recognizes them as important steps in the liberation of modern theater from the limitations of realistic stagecraft. Brecht's most exciting Alienation Effect, however, lies in the human sphere. He likes to present characters who are alienated from themselves and from one another. His figures often seem to move in a vacuum where the most unexpected must be expected. Man is shown as "an animal with a peculiar smell"; his words belie his feelings, his deeds belie his words. The dialogue proceeds erratically, the figures bluff each other as well as the audience. In this world without human mercy, even the good is possible—as an Alienation Effect.

Although Brecht claimed to be "the Einstein of the new stage form" (thereby comparing, by implication, his non-Aristotelian drama to Einstein's non-Euclidean geometry), he was far from being the originator of a new dramaturgy. One has only to remember the epic elements in Strindberg's dream and ghost plays where the balanced construction of the realistic stage is already willfully and consciously disrupted. (pp. 100-02)

Nor was Brecht's activism foreign to the writers of the expressionist generation, who rose up in arms against their fathers and charged them with the guilt of World War I and social injustice. They too countered the passive enjoyment of art with the active demand for social Utopia. (p. 102)

Along with Strindberg and O'Neill, Pirandello and Antonin Artaud, Brecht belongs to those who have reconquered the reality of imagination for the contemporary drama. What I question is merely the relevance of his political thinking to his aesthetic theory. Being the most dynamic dramatist Germany had produced since the days of Grabbe and Büchner, he could hardly be satisfied with coming to rest in as closed a system as Marxism is, in spite of its dialectics. More likely, the Marxist superstructure of his theory may have served him as a last camouflage.

The trouble with Brecht is that he was so cunning that he succeeded in outwitting even the most cunning among his critics, right or left. He was a cryptic man and a champion in the art of leaving unwelcome questions open. When his work is at its best, it is just as inscrutable as he was. As a result, *The Caucasian Chalk Circle* . . . , his last major effort, has been hailed as both "the outstanding example of the technique of the 'epic' drama" and a "Parable for the Theater," which, at least on the surface, are somewhat contradictory classifications. Yet both descriptions are very much to the point.

The *Chalk Circle* is epic theater primarily because it consists of three loosely connected parts: the prologue, the story of Grusha the kitchen maid, and the story of Azdak the village recorder. The prologue is set in Soviet Russia and occurs, as Bentley points out, "at a date later than the year when Brecht started work on the play." Russian peasants who return to a village destroyed by the Germans are engaged in a discussion bordering on a quarrel: one group claims the valley as a homestead, the other plans to irrigate it and to use it for vineyards and orchards. The latter group wins out. To celebrate the reconciliation, the play of the *Chalk Circle* proper is performed. (pp. 106-07)

The prologue itself pays lip service to the state, and even to Stalin, since it is set in Stalin's homeland, Georgia; but the drama, in its playfulness, defies the limitations of state-controlled art. Or was Brecht secretly poking fun at the very idea that someone would be so Philistine as to think that one could redistribute songs—and construct plays—like tractors? Did he wish to regain his independence and dignity as a writer simply by asking a silly question? If he did, then this line would indeed rank among the most cunning of his Alienation Effects. Tongue in cheek, he would have justified the prologue where he treats literature as one treats tractors, and he would have pointed to the play, where he produces literature in the only possible way—namely, as literature. Then, the play would have succeeded as obviously as the prologue failed, and yet he would have done nothing more than pose a question. (p. 109)

Was Brecht the playwright superior to Brecht the theoretician in that he granted his audiences complete freedom, the freedom to say "Yes" or "No"? It almost seems so, for his questions became more and more unanswerable the more his stature as a dramatist grew. To side with the progressive peasants in the prologue to the *Chalk Circle* demanded no important decision, especially when one heeded the party line. But it took all of Brecht's skill and inventiveness as a dramatist to make us side with Azdak and Grusha at the end of the parabolic part of the play, and even so we answered only with a very tentative "Yes." One could almost say that the later Brecht singled out the plays which he wanted to survive by basing them on questions that were difficult to answer, if they could be answered at all. (pp. 110-11)

Deeply convinced of man's inhumanity, Brecht harangued his audiences through his Alienation Effects, urging them to *become* human. . . . Inasmuch as this dynamic shows man to be "on trial" and "in the process" of becoming, Brecht's epic theater is a legitimate offspring of the expressionist revolution of the twenties and of European theatrical history in general. Since his aesthetic theory is a mechanism, both of offense and defense, it may well be recognized for what it is: the intellectual mimicry behind which a creative mind hid from outward persecution and inward doubts.

This creation at times leaves its "epicality" behind to grow into theater, great theater, pure and simple. Whether the greatness of these individual scenes will bestow lasting life upon them, only history can tell; and it is harder in Brecht's case than in many another to predict the outcome of time's selective processes. Brecht himself threw in his lot with Marxism, as if he were banking on its ultimate victory. But so far it has been the free West which has welcomed this writer, discussed him, learned from him, and performed his plays. Paradoxically, Brecht's survival may depend on the survival of the West which he, by all ordinary standards, had tried so hard to prevent. (pp. 113-14)

Heinz Politzer, "How Epic Is Bertolt Brecht's Epic Theater?" in Modern Language Quarterly *(© 1962 University of Washington), Vol. XXIII, No. 2, June, 1962, pp. 99-114.*

GERHARD SZCZESNY (essay date 1966)

To think of Bertolt Brecht as an "intellectual" (with all the connotations the term has come to convey in our civilization) is a grievous mistake. If Brecht rebelled against the bourgeois world, it was not because it allowed too little but because it allowed too much play for idiosyncratic freedom. He sought the safety of absolute conformism. He was the prototype of the antiliberal thinker. His particular intelligence did not demand independence of judgment in radical logic and upright honesty but reflected a talent for random conceits, that is, for finding a surprising angle in every subject or disposing of it through noncommittal "wisdom." Brecht thought in situations and therefore in aphorisms. His philosophy of life consisted of a motley array of recipes for tricking reality. Trickery is an indispensable skill for one intent upon reaching his life's goals without baring their true nature. A man who has made it his concern to hide his identity must at all times keep friend and foe guessing as to his true intentions. His utterances must permit multiple interpretations, his comportment must be hermetic.

If there is among the German writers of the past fifty years one whose life and work require that we apply to them exacting standards, then his name is Bertolt Brecht. We owe it to him that we do not separate the playwright from the student of stagecraft nor these from the Marxist moralist. If we survey, in terms of this global perspective, the part of Brecht's existence which he did allow the world to see, we find that the play the staging of which he undertook with unequaled care was his own life. Brecht did not simply live and work, he undertook to act out a meticulously constructed model case. Throughout his life it was his preoccupation to set up and work out with industrious devotion the scenery, the properties, the situations and the texts for the stage epic, *The Life and the Works of the Great Teacher Bertolt Brecht*. His *Galileo* failed when his concern was no longer to show *The Life of Galileo* but to make of this play a scene in *The Life of Bertolt Brecht*.

Unfortunately, poor Mr. Bertolt Brecht was not at all cut out for the heroic role which he had maneuvered himself into having to play. Sometime in the course of the last few months before his death he uttered the now famous words preserved for us by his friend, the Protestant clergyman Karl Kleinschmidt: "Do not write that you admire me. Write that it was troublesome to have me around and that I propose to remain troublesome after my death." The dramatic grandeur of an uncompromising identification with the concept of a radical renewal of the world finally boiled down to the hope of being remembered as "troublesome." For a dyed-in-the-wool Marxist, a singularly modest wish. But this Bertolt Brecht was no dyed-in-the-wool revolutionary. . . . When and where Brecht's plays are good, they survey the world in critical melancholy, being demonstrations of life as it is and will be and by no means appeals to the audience to mount the barricades after leaving the theater. . . . Bravery fared poorly under the tutelage of this master of camouflage. Freedom, to him, was merely another word for bourgeois-capitalist anarchy, and humanity and humaneness were vaguely abstract catch-all appellations of a distant and utopian goddess in whose name every concrete inhuman act committed against a concrete individual human being could be justified.

It is worth mentioning that Brecht never really understood or, perhaps, did not wish to understand the true intent of Marx. Even though there is nowhere in Marx's writings a description of the state mankind was to attain after the emancipation of the individual from all "self-alienation," the ultimate goal is nonetheless explicitly referred to. It was precisely the removal of all vestiges of human self-alienation and the total abolition of governmental authority. The demand for world reforms was prompted by the vision of conditions of life that would permit the concrete individual human being to live out in full his full individuality. "Everyone in accordance with his capabilities; to everyone in accordance with his needs."

Man in his state of bondage to external circumstances was a transitional phenomenon. With Brecht the ultimate goal as seen by Marx does not come into view. It must not, for through it the free development of the human person—categorically denied by Brecht—would appear raised to the status of a supreme ideal.

If there is at all a critical and positive tendency in Brecht's plays, its aim is the replacement of the societal enforcement of the individual's social role under capitalism by the societal enforcement of the individual's social role under communism. The vision of the individual achieving full self-identity does not appear and in fact is explicitly rejected in the theory of the theater of alienation with its protests against identification and empathy. Brecht makes the transitional phase of alienation a definitive stage or ideal. Man is not only now, and deplorably so, "the sum of the prevailing societal conditions," but he will apparently always remain thus. Herbert Lüthy stated correctly that Brecht never evolved "a poetic vision, a concept of endeavor and pursuit, or even a personal formulation with respect to the content of his doctrine. Whenever he tries to define what he teaches, he reiterates, without change and in tinny monotony, the one shelf-worn formula which Marx, doubtless aware that it could as well mean everything as nothing, managed to get along in his theses on Feuerbach: 'to change the world.'"

Brecht never was an enlightener. He always was a sentimental romantic reactionary. He was against the full development of the human individual "in accordance with his needs." (pp. 2-4)

Brecht was a great lyrical and dramatic talent. The full potential of this talent did not come to fruition because Brecht did not succeed in establishing an unprejudiced relationship to himself and to reality. It is tragic, to be sure, that this resulted of necessity in his becoming a second-rate playwright, but still more disastrous in its consequences is the fact that Brecht, past master of trickery, succeeded in outlasting himself in the pose of the Great Teacher. It is because of this that Brecht stands as a justification, as a guide in self-transfiguration to all those who—like him—find no way out of the entanglement of juvenile confusion and then see a solution to all problems in the escape into the Mammoth System. Since we may be certain that several generations to come will continue to seek salvation from the crisis of selfhood and identity in the advocacy of a totalitarian order, it is necessary to destroy the myth of the enlightened man of progress Bertolt Brecht.

Brecht was not a Voltaire or a Diderot; he was not a Lessing or a Büchner. We may apply to him what Sigmund Freud said about Dostoevski: "He missed the chance to become a teacher and liberator of men and sided instead with their jailers. The cultural future of mankind will owe him little."

Brecht sided with the would-be jailers of mankind, pretending to be a teacher and liberator of men. (pp. 5-6)

Gerhard Szczesny, in his The Case against Bertolt Brecht, with Arguments Drawn from His "Life of Galileo," *translated by Alexander Gode (translation copyright © 1969 by Frederick Ungar Publishing Co., Inc.; originally published as* Das Leben des Galilei und der Fall Bertolt Brecht, *Verlag Ullstein GMBH, 1966), Ungar, 1969, 126 p.*

WILLIAM H. GASS   (essay date 1976)

Brecht regularly wrote plays which were too artful, too original, too *just*, to be acceptable to the narrowly political mind which invariably expects the poet to condemn other wars than his, other lies than his, other necessary disciplinary actions, expediencies, confinements, interrogations, tortures, murders, than his—and never wars, lies, secrecy, or tyranny in general.

In play after play, even the most dogmatic and didactic (*The Mother* or *The Measures Taken*, for example, *The Trial of*

Lucullus), the text undermines its intended message, and the party growls its displeasure, admonishes and threatens. One part of Brecht wanted to sell out to discipline, order, and utility, to replace religion with politics, to take a belief like a Teddy bear to bed; another part wanted to compose great plays and have them properly performed. And while that first half tried to submerge us all in the collective, the other continued rather shrewdly to define the special divided self that was Brecht. (p. 196)

> *William H. Gass, "Sartre on Theater" (originally published as "Theatrical Sartre," in* The New York Times Book Review, *October 14, 1976), in his* The World Within the Word *(copyright © 1977 by William H. Gass; reprinted by permission of Alfred A. Knopf, Inc.), Knopf, 1978, pp. 177-202.**

KLAUS VÖLKER (essay date 1976)

The comedy *Man is Man* [*(Mann ist Mann)*] summarizes Brecht's general outlook and theories on the theatre in the mid-nineteen-twenties. The problem of human alienation, which was the subject of *In the Jungle of the Cities* [*(Im Dickicht der Städte)*] and which appeared to be insoluble, is now relegated to a secondary place and seen cynically as the price of technical development. Brecht adopts an affirmative attitude towards man's surrender of his personality, the elimination of individuality. The individual is exchangeable, he no longer has any unmistakable characteristics: *Man is Man*.

In the preface to his play, written in 1927, the author distinguishes between an old and a new class of people, between an age in decline and an age in the ascendant. The members of the former, he declares, are no longer capable of expressing life productively, they no longer develop 'appetites'. They can no longer create art or assimilate it. Brecht sees huge cities and technology as the last great achievements of the old class, though they will be unable to stop its downfall. In these statements one seems to see the Marxist idea that the social entity alters human consciousness: 'The great buildings of New York City and the great electrical inventions alone have not yet given humanity a greater feeling of triumph. Because now, at this very moment, a new type of human being, more important than these, is emerging, and the whole interest of the world is focused on its development'.

Brecht had great hopes of this 'new' human being of the machine age, and was firmly convinced that, by surrendering his personality, he could only add to his essential human nature, and that only in the mass would he acquire significance and strength. 'This new type of human being will not correspond to the picture formed of him by the old type of human being. I believe that he will not permit himself to be changed by the machines but will change them, and that whatever he looks like he will above all look like a human being.' Brecht overlooks the fact that under capitalism mechanization intensifies exploitation, because it increases still further the worker's dependence on the means of production, which do not belong to him, just as he overlooks the 'crippling' of the individual caused by machine work, to which Marx refers: 'The very abatement of his work becomes a means of torture, since the machine does not relieve the worker of his work but the work of its meaning'. By eliminating his personality man is made still harder to recognize as man, weaker and easier to manipulate. Only in a socialist society which encourages man's individual talents, and allows his personality to evolve within the collec-tive, instead of being abolished by it, is the development of this new type of human being conceivable.

Galy Gay, the main character in *Man is Man*, is not a socially positive hero. His 'reassembly', his transformation from a stevedore to a 'human fighting machine', from a character to a collective being, tells us, not that he has become a human being, but that he has been brain-washed. Brecht sees the proceedings mainly as an 'amusement', which everyone is to interpret in his own way. His own view is that Galy Gay gains as a human being through his transformation, but he can understand someone else taking a different view, 'to which I am the last person to take exception'. In spite of this, however, the play does not admit of two opposing interpretations. (pp. 118-19)

[Brecht's] didactic plays were written more for a theatre of the future in a Socialist state, where the audience were to be no longer merely spectators but active participators. For the present these texts were of use mainly to the actors, who studied them for their own benefit; their effect on the outside world was revolutionary only in so far as the bourgeois state showed no interest in sponsoring the performance of such exercises. Side by side with the didactic plays Brecht was working at the big dramatic form which he considered essential if the crucial subjects of the day were to be presented in the theatre. This new form of drama had to be adequate to the 'enormity' of present-day subject-matter. In all the dramatic plans he worked out in this connection he sought a way of tracing the supposedly impenetrable laws of capitalism back to simple economic antecedents. As a model he had in mind the battles on the wheat exchange or the exchange operations of the meat kings in Chicago. In the course of his roundabout attempts to clarify Marxist theory and economic processes there finally emerged, out of the material for various projected plays, the play *St. Joan of the Stockyards* [*Die Heilige Johanna der Schlachthöfe*]. . . .

The action of St. Joan is made up of the threads of three stories: the story of the Salvation Army lieutenant Joan Dark, the story of the meat king Mauler, and the story of the workers in the Chicago stockyards. The three stories, actuated by the same contradictions, are related to the classic periodicity of the trade cycle spoken of by Marx in *Das Kapital*. The underlying idea of Marx's work, 'to reveal the economic law of movement of modern society', is the common denominator of what originally were three different, simultaneously developed, projects for plays. (p. 152)

The structure of [*St. Joan of the Stockyards*] follows the phases of the recurrent cycle which, according to Marx, runs through modern industry: scenes 1-4 denote the end of prosperity, scenes 5-8 illustrate overproduction, scene 9 presents the crisis, scenes 10 and 11 correspond to stagnation. In the final apotheosis (scene 12) the restoration of the cycle is acclaimed and its conformity with natural law confirmed by the capitalists. Each phase is introduced by a letter, containing economic advice, that Mauler has received from friends in New York. These messages, which spark off the 'movement', contrast with the letter Joan fails to pass on. A successful general strike would have brought about a radical change, the mechanism of the capitalist reproductive process would have been disrupted. The failure of the general strike enables the stockyard bosses to overcome the crisis into which they had been plunged by Mauler's greed for gain. Through wastage of the factors of production—cattle are destroyed to keep prices up—the balance between production capacity and consumption capacity is restored.

If the central points of the story correspond to the phases of the trade cycle, seen in terms of its content it is essentially a counterpart to Schiller's romantic tragedy *Die Jungfrau von Orleans (The Maid of Orleans)*. Starting from his thesis that classical dramatic art and verse forms are incompatible with the complexity of modern subject-matter, Brecht still makes it possible to present the world economic crisis on the stage and to speak of money in iambics. He uses quotations and situations from Schiller 'for the purpose of parodic contrast'. He disposes of classical drama by complying with it. Joan's apotheosis at the hands of the capitalists not only parodies Schiller, it also parodies Faust's deliverance as presented by Goethe at the end of his tragedy. For *St. Joan of the Stockyards* is intended to show 'Faustian man as he is today'. Brecht offers a picture of what the bourgeoisie alone is still prepared to understand by self-realization: successful business management. Mauler is not a 'mere incarnation of capital', he corresponds perfectly to Marx's description of the modernized capitalist, who begins to feel a 'human compassion' for his own Adam and therefore experiences a Faustian conflict 'between the urge to amass and the urge to enjoy'. (pp. 156-57)

> *Klaus Völker, in his* Brecht: A Biography, *translated by John Nowell (translation copyright © 1978 by The Seabury Press, Inc.; used by permission of The Continuum Publishing Corporation; originally published as* Bertolt Brecht: Eine Biographie, *Carl Hanser Verlag, 1976), The Seabury Press, 1978, 412 p.*

RONALD D. GRAY (essay date 1976)

Brecht's first plays were written in the chaos of post-war Germany. When he returned to civilian life in 1919, after serving briefly in a military hospital, two literary movements seemed to the *avant-garde* to matter most, Expressionism and Dadaism, and he responded to them at the same time as he rejected them. (p. 16)

[Brecht's *Baal*] is not Expressionistic either in style or purport. It has no staccato rhythms, stabbing spotlights, crazily angular sets, no 'telegraphese', which was the name given to the short, sharp mode of speech some Expressionists favoured, and it is not unintentionally comic, or melodramatic. It does share with the Expressionists, though not in their mood, a concern with a new kind of individual. Baal, not so very aptly named after the heathen god who devoured small children, is at once a lyric poet, a practical joker, a homosexual, every man's dream of a potent lover, a helper of elderly women, and the only really outspoken character in the play. He is also, conveniently for him, without conscience or self-awareness. He might be called a Dionysus. He might be said to express 'a passionate acceptance of the world in all its sordid grandeur'. In fact, that is what he does not do. It was the Expressionists who used that kind of language. *Baal* has more subtlety. (p. 17)

Brecht establishes his play by the way he uses words, more than by any other means. Any dramatist who could write as he did ought to have won attention by that fact alone. There are lyrical passages, for instance, in which he gropes for words at a level where the sound carries as much of his meaning as the literal sense, and this poetic concern, not always so much in evidence later on, occasionally overrides everything else. . . . (p. 18)

In structure, *Baal* is episodic, like the later plays. The scenes are loosely strung together, in no compelling sequence. (p. 19)

The common theme that does unite the scenes up to a point is that a complete realisation of his personality is essential for Baal, and must involve evil as well as good actions—a post-Nietzschean idea. (p. 20)

Of the other early plays which rapidly followed, all take some cognisance of society, whether to accept or reject its claims. *Drums in the Night* is mainly concerned with the reactions of a returned prisoner of war to the abortive left-wing uprisings of late 1918 and early 1919, and is surprisingly different from *Baal,* in taking so much notice of contemporary events. Yet it takes notice only to reject any responsibility for them, or so it appears. (p. 22)

There is a presage of later developments in the insistence that what the audience is seeing is a play. When Kragler rejects Spartacus he knocks down the moon, which is really a Chinese lantern, and the moon 'falls into the river, which has no water in it'. There is a rough reminder here, that the events on stage are not the revolution anyway. (p. 23)

Closer to the later 'alienation' for which Brecht became known is the scene in which a heated argument in a restaurant is interrupted by a waiter, who then retells the whole thing over again for the benefit of a new arrival. By this means, Brecht introduces a pause which can be reflective, as he did later in a variety of ways. Events seen a second time, or narrated as though they had happened before, take on a different look. There is something ironical in the mere fact of the repetition, and absurdities show up which might otherwise not have been apparent. Whether they lead, as the 'alienation' theory later maintained, to any further thought by the audience, let alone to Marxist solutions, is another question. For the moment, all that matters is Brecht's presumably intuitive use of this device, at a time when he can scarcely have thought out its implications.

The New Man and Revolution were the themes of the first two plays. For the third, *In the Cities' Jungle,* Brecht echoed yet another contemporary theme, Dada, or the vogue for nonsense with serious implications. Though the play has none of the special hallmarks of Dadaism—*'bruitisme'*, or the cultivation of noise, 'simultaneity', or the coincidence of incongruities and dissonances as in real life—it has the same rejection of logic, psychology and verisimilitude as not only Dadaists but Futurists, Vorticists and the French followers of [Guillaume] Apollinaire and [Alfred] Jarry cultivated. It is grotesque, and incomprehensible, giving a fantastic caricature of American capitalism, and making no attempt to interest the spectator. (pp. 23-4)

If there was little political matter in these plays, it was largely because Brecht was still questioning himself, still trying to understand himself, and experimenting with all the new ideas in vogue. For the most part they were Romantic in implication: surprisingly often Brecht comes to an uncommitted standpoint, closer to Buddhism than to Marxism, though expressed in his usual laconic way, rather than ecstatically. He drifts, changes like a cloud. . . . (p. 26)

Homosexual themes are prominent not only in *Baal* and *In the Cities' Jungle,* but also in his next play, *The Life of Edward II, King of England,* adapted from Marlowe, and largely concerned with the downfall of a ruthless king on account of his sexual fascination for a worthless favourite, Piers Gaveston. . . . All through these early plays, Brecht is partly dramatising a personal sense that femininity is lax and despicable, that hardness and even harshness is demanded of a man, and possibly some sexual attraction to men might account for the sudden predilections for violence shown by his characters, as in *The Good Woman of Setzuan* where the heroine feels obliged to adopt the mask of a man in order to exercise the harshness she believes to be necessary. Certainly, homosexuality and violence are prominent themes of *Edward II*, though here Brecht's personal concerns are also reflected in Mortimer—a single character instead of the two in Marlowe's play—here presented as an intellectual revolutionary whose chief care is the welfare of working people. (p. 28)

[Brecht was] engaged on a dual path. In one sense he was aiming at complete self-realisation, even if this involved what had till that time been accounted inhumanity. In another he was beginning to experiment with the belief that social change requires such inhumanity. The exploration of what humanity means was the theme of his next play. (p. 30)

[*A Man's a Man*] is the fantastic account of an extremely adaptable character, Galy Gay, who is beguiled by three British soldiers (inspired by Kipling's *Soldiers Three*) into taking the place of a comrade in the Indian Army. Step by step, he is transformed from a peaceable citizen into a ferocious warrior, armed to the teeth and thirsting for blood. The play presents a case of brain-washing, achieved by means of a subtle undermining of the sense of personal identity, with the difference that it is carried out not by trained interrogators but by the hirelings of imperialism, and that the mood of the whole is one of prolonged extravaganza and farce. Bitter farce: as the title indicates, men are men, a man is a man, and any one man can be turned into another and still remain 'man'; once the full potentialities of 'man' are realised, they can be channelled in any direction. Shaw attempted with great success a more light-hearted treatment of a similar theme in *Pygmalion*. Brecht was unwittingly foreshadowing transformations that were to change all Germany within a few years. (pp. 30-1)

Brecht's concern with the condition of the poor appears only dimly in the earlier plays. In the *Threepenny Opera* it found an opportunity to express itself more vigorously, for one of the main themes of [John] Gay's *Beggar's Opera,* from which it was adapted, was poverty. Yet here also, the cynical mood of the day did not allow of a direct appeal to charitable sentiments. Brecht took over the eighteenth-century text, modified it considerably, was helped considerably by Kurt Weill's music, but aimed at his audience's heads rather than at their hearts. The opera was conceived in terms of parody: it went with the current in so far as it appeared to give the public what it wanted, but it did so in such outrageous fashion as to make it deliberately unpalatable. Brecht, in the usual forthright mood of exaggeration which made him paint the faces of soldiers in *Edward II* chalkwhite, to represent fear as their only emotion, went the whole hog with the conventions in this work also. It was one more instance, and for the time being almost the last, of the violent caricature which was meant to force the audience into demanding a contrary. (pp. 33-4)

On the other hand, there is a note of compassion running through the opera which contrasts with all that has been said of it and of Brecht's work so far. (p. 35)

The brief glimpse of what human nature might be, in contrast to what it is, that appeared in *A Man's a Man*, becomes a longer look. It still does not, however, provide insight into the theme of the opera as a whole, which retains a dual aspect, partly amoral, partly charitable. . . . (p. 37)

Not merely is it difficult to relate his characters to the prototypes they are meant to satirise; Brecht's still 'all-embracing' attitude allows him to move at will from one standpoint to another completely contradictory one: at one moment he seems to aim at arousing a general compassion for the condition of all men, at another he allows his characters to advocate extreme brutality, and the oscillation from one to the other renders every reaction uncertain. It is not surprising that his audiences, for whom he had meant to write a 'report' on the kind of entertainment they liked to see, seized on those aspects which took their fancy and ignored the rest. There was grist in the text for everybody's mill. (pp. 37-8)

The didactic plays [including *The Measures Taken, St. Joan of the Stockyards,* and *The Mother*] contribute less than the plays of the 1920s to Brecht's reputation. (p. 64)

[Brecht's] portrayal of social conditions, even in those plays where social criticism is intended, is wildly exaggerated: the America of *Mahagonny* and *St. Joan of the Stockyards* and the England of *The Threepenny Opera* are unrecognisable, and it is only in *Drums in the Night* (and later *Fear and Misery of the Third Reich*) that Brecht gives anything like a picture of conditions in Germany. For the most part, the early plays contain no scenes where human beings enter into any relationship with one another, except in such a parodistic form as the friendship between Macheath and Tiger Brown. The audience is often invited to draw conclusions from what it sees before it, while what it sees is presented in such a form that conclusions are either undrawable or contrary to those pronounced on stage. And when Brecht deliberately turns to the advocacy of reason in his plays, he shows little regard for rationality.

It is a strange mixture, this unadorned forthrightness and lack of sentiment on the one hand, this frankness and originality, receptivity and unshrinking penetration, and on the other hand this seemingly wilful blindness, unwillingness to reason, prejudice, occasional hysteria, and preference for parody and adaptation. Brecht's openness, his 'all-embracing' attitude, was critical only on the impulse of the moment, and his dramatic unities were the largely fortuitous assemblies of these impulses, able to exist side-by-side because they left out of account the continuum of the outside world. Yet the early plays do show also the ability to observe and take account of the rest of humanity. The language of the working men in *Baal*, unlike that in *The Mother* and *St. Joan,* is full of idiomatic turns of phrase. The note of concern about the direction to be taken by human nature enters in *A Man's a Man,* and grows louder in *The Threepenny Opera,* for all that it takes so abrupt a modification into inhumanity in the propagandist plays. . . . Moreover, Brecht had shown repeatedly his ability to make use of the theatre: he was no armchair dramatist but one who constantly envisaged effects in terms of theatrical performance. In *Señora Carrar's Rifles,* a priest raises his hands above his head in a reverent gesture of resignation: he is held in the act by a word, and sits there, a dramatic image of a man 'surrendering'. In *The Measures Taken,* the young agitator removes his mask to declare his true identity, and the physical revelation of his human personality comes as a shock which almost in itself undoes the inhuman doctrine of the play. These, with many other devices reveal Brecht as the man of the theatre he was: a brilliant innovator, a fertile mind, an iconoclast, a man with innumerable facets, but still a dramatist more capable of momentary effects than integrated wholes. (pp. 65-6)

From early days, Brecht was evolving not only plays, but theories of what he was doing and the effect he expected to produce. . . .

The 'V-Effekt', or 'alienation technique'—'V' standing for 'Verfremdung'—is at its simplest a means of making the events on the stage seem strange, unfamiliar. (p. 67)

The action was commented upon or announced by intervening or accompanying projections, a practice which Brecht continued in all his productions, although it has been felt at times to be an affectation. He also used a low curtain masking only half the height of the stage, behind which the movements of actors and stage-hands could easily be seen. In *Puntila* a mountain is made out of chairs. In [*The Horatians and the Curiatians*] the sun is represented by a spotlight carried across the rear of the stage by a technician. . . . [On the whole] the later productions forwent many of the more surprising features of the earlier practice. In the twenties, Brecht was still concerned to avoid anything beautiful, lyrical, or directly moving. He denied emotion, as he denied beauty, as an indulgence that could not be afforded while suffering still existed. Only rational thought would serve to change the human situation as he saw it.

The 'V effect' was not, however, merely a matter of production technique. The style of acting also required a radical change. . . . Brecht required his actors to maintain the same distance from the characters they were portraying as the audience was expected to adopt. . . . The basic function of the actor is thus to 'show', just as a person in conversation may break off in order to demonstrate in pantomime a part of his story. (pp. 67-8)

Brecht frequently abandons the complexities of exposition. Characters do not sustain the Ibsen-like illusion that they are unaware of the audience's presence and must reveal themselves and their relationships by carefully dropped hints which must still preserve the appearance of being natural ingredients of their conversation. In *The Mother*, Pelagea Wlassowa begins the play by directly addressing the audience, explaining who she is, and what her problems are. The same simple opening is found in *The Threepenny Opera* and *The Good Woman of Setzuan*. Alternatively, the audience is placed in possession of the necessary facts of the situation by a narrator who sits at one side of the stage throughout, as in *The Caucasian Chalk Circle,* or the story of the next scene is written on hanging boards. And in most of the plays the action is interrupted by songs which summarise, comment on, or predict the action. In all these ways it becomes inevitable that whatever method of acting or production is used, some element of alienation will make itself felt. (pp. 70-1)

The kind of theatre which these devices would produce was called by Brecht 'epic' theatre, in contrast to the earlier, 'bourgeois' theatre, which was 'dramatic'. The word 'epic' here, translating the German 'episch', is unfortunate. 'Episch' has, in this context, none of the associations with heroism and greatness that 'epic' often has, as in 'an epic tale'; it is merely a literary category, and in German this category includes not only narrative poetry, but also novels, and is often used to distinguish these from the lyric and the drama. In speaking of an 'epic' theatre, Brecht meant to imply a theatre which would not be exciting, 'dramatic', full of tensions and conflicts, but slower-paced, reflective, giving time to reflect and compare. (pp. 71-2)

None of the specifically anti-Nazi plays represents [Brecht's] best work. Yet since they bulk largest in the whole of the anti-Nazi theatre of the period, they are worth attention. *Round Heads and Pointed Heads* . . . is the least satisfying. Like *St. Joan of the Stockyards,* it uses a rough-and-ready blank verse, of a quasi-Shakespearean kind, in order to mock the pretensions of the speakers. But there is more than imitation of Shakespearean forms. On this occasion Brecht took over the main outline of a Shakespeare play, and adapted it to a political purpose, his principal idea being, perhaps, to show that what for Shakespeare was a moral problem was in Brecht's day and age an economic one. (p. 93)

[*The Resistible Rise of Arturo Ui*] is without any doubt the most striking and effective of his explicitly anti-Nazi plays. . . . The deflating of Hitler's pretensions to greatness—and of any tendency in Germany to go on speaking of him as a great man—by linking his career in detailed parallels with the life of a Chicago gangster was a genial idea. Its biggest success is in the scene where the murder by Hitler of Ernst Röhm and his associates is parodied by a mass-slaughter in a garage in front of the headlights of a Ford saloon, an incident that seems to come straight out of a life of Al Capone. Equally telling in an opposite spirit is the scene, based also on Hitler's life, in which Ui receives instruction from a Shakespearean actor on how to make political speeches. (pp. 96-7)

While propagandist and anti-Nazi works were among the first fruits of Brecht's exile, he turned after a while to writing the plays which did most to establish his reputation abroad, *The Life of Galileo, Mother Courage, The Good Woman of Setzuan, Herr Puntila and his Man Matti. (The Caucasian Chalk Circle,* belonging with these in style, was written later. . . .) These were works of a quite different kind. It is possible, though not logically necessary, to read out of them the corollary that only Communism can cure the ills they represent. Their general sphere of interest and concern is not, however, directly political, but rather one of general humanity. They are plays in which the spectator is implicitly invited to consider the behaviour of human beings, to understand, sometimes to sympathise, sometimes to be revolted, and always to ask himself how he might have acted in similar circumstances. There are no incomprehensible farragos or flippant shocks for shock's sake such as occur from time to time in the plays of the twenties, nor are there any choruses ramming home the 'message', as there are in the plays of the early thirties. No one is counselled to do evil so that good may come. Instead, there is an in many ways humane theatre, tolerant, offering comprehension rather than persuasion; though still rigging the balances at times, ranging in mood from tender lyricism to agony of mind, from admiration for the most insignificant details of ordinary living to a buffooning zest in wine, women, and song, from sharp compassion with the miseries of the poor to a not wholly unsympathetic portrayal of the pleasures of the rich. It is the 'human comedy' that Brecht seems most of all bent on showing in these works, and the Communist implications are at most a side-issue. (p. 109)

Galileo's dilemma has been seen, its causes traced, and sympathy for him aroused. But, as Brecht knew, . . . the ability to adapt to circumstances has been far too prevalent in Central European countries for centuries past. The issue of Galileo's cowardice thus takes on a sharp contemporary edge: Galileo, the play affirms, stands at the threshold of a new age, as we seem to do ourselves since 1945. If he recants, the cause of science will suffer a setback, for science depends on a relentless honesty, and cannot be associated with hypocrisy. . . . Brecht sought to stress individual rather than vicarious responsibility. In his habitually exaggerating fashion Brecht does imply . . . that a whole epoch of European history turns on one man's failure.

The confrontation of these two attitudes makes good dramatic material, despite the fundamental intellectual weakness of the play, and it provides notable moments of conflict and tension. (pp. 112-13)

[One] weakness, however, does not appear remediable. In his last long speech Galileo reviews the position of science as he now leaves it, crippled for centuries by his recantation. His own failure, he declares, has been that he sought to accumulate knowledge for the sake of knowledge, without regard to the primary aim of science, the easing of human existence. (p. 113)

But this failure is asserted in a long and intricate monologue which relies entirely on verbal argument, amounting to a lecture from the stage lasting for several minutes. This is bad drama, by any criterion, and it is made to look worse by the irrationality of Galileo's case. He argues, against the historical evidence, that his single failure will reduce scientists from his time on to a race of dwarfs, subservient to the wishes of monarchs and governments. Considering that the first dwarf to appear after Galileo was Newton, born in the year Galileo died, and that even Italian science, which might have been thought most likely to suffer under Papal obdurateness, went on to produce Malpighi, Volta, and Galvani within the next hundred years, it is clear that one defection cannot halt so widespread a human activity. (p. 114)

Thus, as in much of Brecht's work, the theatricality is largely vitiated by the lack of any realistically thought-out content. (p. 115)

Yet *Galileo* remains one of the riper plays. It is riper in one sense, as many East Europeans know, in that it shows with great imagination the alternating self-condemnations and self-reassertions of all who live deviously under a stifling regime. . . . But it is riper in other ways. The fairness with which Galileo's opponents, the cardinals, are treated (not the Aristotelian scientists, who are grotesquely caricatured), and the hearing which is given to the unanswered arguments of the little monk, who asks what simple Christian believers are to make of their harsh lives if they are deprived of the rich comforts of religion, are signs of the complexity which raises *Galileo* above the purely propagandist works. The effect of the play is incalculable—while it is possible to come out of the theatre feeling that an intense demand for heroic courage has been made, it is also possible to see what is gained by taking an adaptive course. The new unwillingness to impose or suggest single answers was the essential mark of the Brecht who emerged in the late 1930s. (pp. 115-16)

Mother Courage is decidedly one of the best things Brecht wrote, and it is significant of it, as an example of 'epic' or 'narrative' theatre, that it is not the story or the political implications, not a connected theme, which remains most strongly in the memory, but a series of isolated moments. (p. 121)

The character of Mother Courage herself is one of the most attractive features. She is adept at turning every situation to her own advantage, conforming with and adapting herself to it in a way that recalls . . . Galileo. She has the vitality of Puntila without his drunkenness or lapses into sobriety, and at the same time she contributes a laconic cynicism of her own, a cunning and ingenuity which are essential for her sheer existence. As a rule she knows exactly how far she can go and how far she can let others go. When the recruiting sergeant threatens to take away her son, she pulls a knife on him, but it is clear that she means the threat as a move in the game, which will not be countered: there is shrewdness in her attitude, not heroism. . . .

Yet when the structure of the play as a whole is considered, it becomes apparent that these qualities do little to bind it together. In its total effect, it is oddly without impact, a series of moments and *coups de théâtre* without coherence. (p. 126)

The impelling power in the play is the sense of waste—not of tragedy. . . . Brecht did not want a sense of tragedy; he was angry with the first-night audience who wept in traditional mood over the bereaved mother, and he included a sardonic chorus offstage, chanting a raucous injunction to her to look alive, as she humped the empty wagon round the stage in the final scene. The mood is akin to the mood in which he had Kattrin beat her drum—a ferocious insistence on the idiocy of the destruction, spoken by a Thersites in the wings, biting in its almost cynical desperation, which is only not cynical, in the last resort, because it is desperate.

But there is no cure offered. All that Brecht gives—as in all the maturer plays—is the intolerable awareness of how things are, not a Marxist or any other solution. He may have thought, it is true, that he had shown sufficient of the causes of war to justify him in maintaining he had written something other than a tragedy. If, on the other hand, we find his analysis too flimsy, we are left with an irremediable awareness of a tragic situation. The difference between this kind of tragic situation and those of earlier centuries is that . . . it does not provide us with a cheap seat in the gods, but kicks us in the shins. That is the peculiarly twentieth-century quality of it, and a reason why it attracts audiences unattuned to its political philosophy. (pp. 135-36)

[*Squire Puntilla and His Man Matti*] is more of an 'epic' play in its structure than almost any other of Brecht's works, a possible exception being *Mother Courage*. There is no argument, no problem, but rather a loose sequence of scenes, and almost no plot; at one point all thought of 'dramatic' interest, in the traditional sense, is abandoned while four women sit by the roadside to exchange stories and reminiscences. . . .

Not having the wartime background of *Mother Courage*, *Puntila* relies on comic incidents to sustain interest. . . . It is boisterous humour, unintellectual—there is no religious satire . . . or any political point to any of Puntila's larking, but it establishes the relaxed mood of the whole work, and its prime aim of entertaining. (p. 137)

Brecht's political influence in the world at large probably consists more in the general idea that his plays convey a Marxist message, rather than in the actual conveying of one. (p. 163)

[Like] almost all modern dramatists of revolt, Brecht does not, in [Robert] Brustein's phrase 'offer any substitute ideas or ideals'. Clearly, he intends a transformation of the world, in which poverty and exploitation no longer exist, but there is no more clarity about it than that. (p. 170)

> *Ronald D. Gray, in his* Brecht the Dramatist *(© Cambridge University Press 1976), Cambridge University Press, 1976, 232 p.*

TERRENCE DES PRES (essay date 1980)

To most of us Brecht's poetry is new. We know him by his plays, and if we come to the poetry from Brechtian theater we shall be, if not misled, then surprised. The two careers ran broadly parallel, but in view of the poems the famous cynicism of the plays looks less savage, less brazenly hard. The whole of Brecht's enormous output, thanks to the poetry now available, needs reading in a different light, not only of genius politically inspired, but of an art directed always to care for how people live. (p. 5)

Graceful and charming Brecht's poetry is not. He detested decorum and polish, any sort of evident refinement, preferring instead the rough vigor of the street and lowbrow forms like the ballad, the popular song, or just "straight-talk." This turn toward the rude and lowly, as Brecht said of his early poetry, was less "a protest against the smoothness and harmony of conventional poetry" than "an attempt to show human dealings as contradictory, fiercely fought over, full of violence." Such poetry, given its sinewy flex and spring, might possibly be called supple. . . .

His poetry does not charm, invite, or tease out of thought. It would be heard, not overheard, and does not bank on its status as Art. Its import is in its occasion and it does not, therefore, claim to be transcendent or self-contained, but rather insists upon its place in history, its provisional nature as utterance *in situ*. Most modern poetry posits *a* world, whereas Brecht's responds to *the* world, in particular to events and conditions which determine—to the benefit of some and the harm of many—people's lives. His position is therefore political. In relation to poetry the term "political" may simply refer to poems which bear witness or, going a step further, to poems which confront and defend or, going all the way, to poems which directly speak for and against. The last kind disturbs us most, and that is the kind Brecht principally wrote. He therefore stands as the extreme example of an art which we in America prefer to believe cannot exist in superior form: political poetry, verse openly didactic, aesthetic energy taking a stand. (p. 6)

[There] is no denying that Brecht wrote some great poetry, and no denying its political bent. Brecht disliked poets who write solely of inner experience. He did not value poetic vision which cultivates itself only, nor did he think that the poet's main job is to feel and perceive in rarefied ways. Poets ought to *say* something, and what they say should be worth hearing even in a world where global politics—the threat of nuclear wipeout, the terrorist who strikes anyone anywhere—increasingly penetrates private life. History is too much with us, and if we would believe Max Frisch, looking upon the ruins of Europe after the Second World War, Brecht's poetry is of the kind we need: the kind that "can stand up against the world in which it is spoken."

By that standard, almost all poetry being written in America fails, or embarrasses, or leaves us lamenting that nobody takes poetry seriously anymore. Times change, so do we, and the poetry of self—the Emersonian mandate—has lost its authority. Our times are not as dark as Brecht's, but they are far from happy and no one, I presume, would predict improvement. Brecht's Marxist vision and his didactic altitude may not be ours but his example still instructs and is potentially liberating, especially if we admit that our lives are more and more knocked about by political forces and that poems worth having are those which can "stand up against" the prevailing climate of violence. (p. 7)

In **"Place of Refuge"** the time is 1937, the place is a fisherman's cottage outside the Danish city of Svendborg. Soon Hitler would invade Denmark, forcing Brecht to use one of the "four doors to escape by." (From there he would go to Sweden, then Finland, then across Russia to the Pacific, and finally to the United States where he would stay until the end of the war.) Much of Brecht's early poetry invents its imagery,

in the manner of Rimbaud. But midway his imagery begins to come from the actual situation of which the poem itself is a part. No doubt a paint-peeled oar lay on the picturesque roof. But oar-on-thatch is an image of disorder, of things out of place, and we understand that destructive winds might come. The mail also comes, so do the boats, and in the poem's context these images of things approaching take on sinister tones. The children may play, but not safely. Mail will cause as much pain as gladness. And business as usual—ferries crossing the water—is not to be trusted.

Like many of Brecht's poems, this one is based on personal circumstances, but like his poetry in general, it is not really personal. Of his work he once said: "maybe the poems in question describe me, but that was not what they were written for. It's not a matter of 'getting acquainted with the poet' but of getting acquainted with the world, and with the people in whose company he is trying to enjoy it and change it." To become acquainted with the world, in this case, is to discover that no place is safe, no refuge secure. Political forces drive us into an exile which, like the poet's retreat, cannot be counted on, neither in life nor in art. (pp. 8-9)

Parody of liturgical forms is one of Brecht's favorite devices; implemented by the ironies of cliché and doggerel, the result is clawlike indeed. Brecht's [**"Spring 1938"**] . . . would be a sentimental rerun of the theme of rebirth, were it not for the political references. But now rebirth cannot be counted on; our defenses, like our stock of traditional themes, are pathetically inadequate. Yet there are only the old themes. Brecht gives them new life by allowing politics to intrude; and in consequence, a mythical experience, punctured by history, loses *and* gains in primitive force. Anyone with children, reading the papers, listening for signals of war, knows how poignant that silence is, when with nothing but a miserable sack, a son and father try to save a dying tree. Slight in itself, the poem is like a stone around the neck. It stood up against the time in which it was written, it stands up now. (p. 10)

Brecht declared himself a Marxist in 1929, and critics often speak of his "conversion" as if there were two Brechts, the rampaging satirist and then the somber ideologue. Over-simple at best, the distinction is misleading and in the end serves no purpose. Over time, of course, the poetry shows change: it turns less often to rhyme and fixed forms; expansiveness gives way to concentration; more poems are rooted in fact, and Brecht's splendid didactic mode moves from ironic depiction to straightforward statement as its central vehicle. But what never changes is Brecht's bedrock loyalty to victims—to losers, outcasts, whole strata of society who from birth were doomed to wretchedness. The disposition, not the system, came first. Many early poems take a plural point of view or address collective experience. Images of mass death occur with upsetting frequency. And Brecht's dominant early form, the narrative, is handled with the dedication and authority proper to a poet whose concern would always be with action, with the ways men and women determine, or have forced upon them, basic conditions of life. Which is to say that Brecht's relation to the world was political from the start. (p. 11)

[For Brecht] might the aesthetic point of view be used against itself? And at what cost?

One solution, for Brecht, was satire as savage as history itself. Another was reliance on didactic forms, which draw their strength from the conviction that life can be changed. A third strategy was to avoid metaphor, especially insofar as metaphor creates the illusion of transcendence—of being "above" *X* by seeing it in terms of *Y*. Of his *Svendborg Poems* Brecht said: "From the bourgeois point of view there has been a staggering impoverishment. Isn't it all a great deal more one-sided, less 'organic,' cooler, more self-conscious (in a bad sense)?" Onesided like an ax, cool like metal at night, and thus a poetry which sometimes seems disrespectful of the reader's sensibilities, at other times insisting on a distance between reader and poem, a sort of aesthetic estrangement. Brecht's famous concept of *Verfremdungseffekt* or "alienation effect" applies not only to his theory of theater, but to the central grain of his poetry as well. He will not grant emotional solace, nor catharsis either. The appeal, here, is more to the mind than the heart. We are not to indulge but to see, and to see we must not feel too much at home. (pp. 17-18)

The didactic element is constant in Brecht. He thought of himself as a teacher, and the point of his work, as he often said, was to make people see. There have of course been great didactic poets, Virgil and Lucretius among them, but for sheer formal inventiveness and for aesthetic effects as powerful as any "pure" poet might hope to create, Brecht's poetry seems to me the supreme example of successful didactic art. The didactic mode served as Brecht's most durable device for bringing poetry and politics into fruitful union, and if, as Walter Benjamin has argued, the important artist not only uses a mode but also transforms and extends it, then Brecht's importance is obvious. Satire is inherently didactic, but the lyric is not, and that Brecht could be didactic *and* lyrical enlarges our idea of poetry in general. And finally, Brecht used the didactic stance to solve perhaps his biggest problem: in radical contrast to the Soviet brand of Marxism, which pretends to speak *for* oppressed peoples, Brecht would go no further than to speak *to* them, propounding no authorities or programs but only insisting that victims everywhere should see themselves in the full sadness of their plight and see also that if politics is part of the human condition, very much of the human condition is a matter of politics.

And yet there is something else, subtler, more delicate, about Brecht's use of didactic forms. They allow him to remain impersonal, they rule out small-talk and self-pity, and where deep emotion arises the didactic stance becomes a technique for restraint, for expression of feeling about world events without splashing the event or the feeling all over the page. (pp. 21-2)

Brecht's poetry embraces a political vision, beautiful in its ideals, which did not survive its totalitarian perversion. The historical failure of Marxism has had enormous consequences for all of us, but for people directly involved the outcome was shattering. Recurring anti-Soviet sentiment and outbreaks of bitterness in Brecht's late poetry reveal the suffering of a man coming to see—as a generation of decent men and women came painfully to see—that the great moment had passed, that the magnificent dream of human liberation would go unrealized. But if political defeat is the end in actual politics, in poetry the case is strangely otherwise. Brecht's vision was betrayed by history but his poetry does not therefore suffer forfeit or become irrelevant. On the contrary, it gains in retroactive depth, taking on dignity and an import which did not exist when the poems were written but which exists now because of the way events turned out.

Political poetry—at least the kind committed to a cause—possesses a destiny, and when destiny ends in defeat, the result is not failure but tragedy. For this reason Brecht's poetry, as

we read it now, bears within it a tragic sense of life which the poet himself could not detect. (pp. 24-5)

Terrence Des Pres, "Poetry in Dark Times" (reprinted by permission of the author and Georges Borchardt, Inc.; copyright © 1981 Terrence Des Pres), in Parnassus: Poetry in Review, *Vol. 8, No. 2, Spring/Summer/Fall/Winter, 1980, pp. 5-28.*

ERIC BENTLEY (essay date 1981)

Baal is neither a Strindbergian dream play nor a Pirandellian "play in the making." What was in part a theory for the older men is here wholly a practice, a state of being, a fact of life. . . . Baal is a "stripped" character—is man stripped of character. There is a paradox about the Victorian Man of Character, the Independent Individual of the age of individualism, which is that he was formed by that age and belonged utterly to that society. Conversely, the rejection of the individual that comes with the twentieth century, and especially after World War I, is a rejection of the society around him, and even of society as such. Baal is the asocial man.

It would be natural enough to call him amoral, and his actions stamp him as what Freud called polymorphous perverse: sensuality is acceptable to him in itself, and he does not limit himself to the "outlets" which society approves. However, if this were the beginning and end of Baal the play that bears his name would simply be a tract favoring the noble savage, a return to an innocent paganism. Nothing could be further from the text. The image of an innocent paganism is present in it; but this is by no means the image of the play as a whole. Baal beholds the innocence, the amorality, of nature all around us, but he beholds it from a distance and with longing and envy. The *sky* would be an ideal mistress indeed, but how far off it is, how unreachable! Between us and primal innocence stands the world, which includes that very society of men which one would reject. (p. 124)

Though all drama tends to be about guilt, one might expect that a drama without individuals, without respect for society—a drama without ego or superego, one might be tempted to put it—would be an exception, would be "beyond guilt." One has read here and there that to give up the individual is to give up the whole notion of responsibility. But it is not so, unless one is uttering a tautology: to give up the individual is to give up *individual* responsibility. Responsibility and guilt remain, and only seem the more unwieldy, the more oppressive, for not being neatly tied to this person and that action.

Brecht does make Baal seem cut off from the meaning of his own actions: from his killing of Ekart and his virtual killing of Johanna Reiher. Only with difficulty, looking back on the play, can one say to oneself: *It is a play about a murderer.* And yet by any humane standard murder is only one among Baal's several offenses and amid his consistent offensiveness. The immediate reason for this difficulty is to be found in Brecht's special perspective. He lends Baal a quality of innocence, but it is an innocence on the other side of guilt. Our minds, which are used to thinking here of a duality (guilt-innocence), have to stretch themselves a little to think in terms of three instead of two: innocence, guilt, and innocence. This innocence is the subject of much of Brecht's writing in this period. It could even be said that around 1919-21 his favorite subject was the innocence that can accrue to extremely vicious, even extremely criminal, people. It is as if one were to speak of regained innocence in an old whore. (p. 125)

If at moments we think that Brecht takes Baal's crimes too lightly—murder, after all, is murder—we quickly realize that in saying, "Baal is no worse than the rest of us," he is not taking a high view of Baal but a low view of the rest of us. He is saying that we are ourselves no better than murderers. We may even be worse than Baal, in that we have missed the romance with the sky and the dream of the little meadow. We may be Baal minus the poetry.

And—what is partly the same thing—minus the pleasure. For though Baal's pleasures are finally poisoned by guilt and ended by aggression, they were not impure at the source. On the contrary, the search for pleasure is the one truly affirmative element in the play, and the reason why the poetry of the play retains a directly and even ingenuously romantic aura. (p. 127)

Baal is an ambiguous, ambivalent figure: part monster—but partly, too, the martyr of a poetic hedonism. And the positive element is more prominent than the negative because it is Baal's special contribution—his monstrousness he has in common with a monstrous world. . . .

Yet if, in the figure of Baal, the more sympathetic element prevails over the less, in the play of *Baal* the poetry of life is overwhelmed by the prose, the beauty by the horror. If, as I believe, a good play amounts finally to a particular vision of life seen as a whole, then this play is a vision of life as an inferno, and the occasional faint gleam of beauty only makes the ugliness look more intensely black. Baal will let no one persuade him he has lost all chance of pleasure. But self is something he lost so long ago that its discovery is never on the cards. One might better put it that he never had a self. Whereas in Ibsen the self is threatened, and in Pirandello it is *said* not to exist, in Brecht both the Ibsenite self and the Pirandellian discussion are so far in the past that they are totally forgotten. There remains the horror: Lowell's "horror of the lost self." And this horror belongs even more to the play than to the protagonist. (p. 128)

> *Eric Bentley, "Baal" (originally published in a slightly different form as "Bertolt Brecht's First Play," in* The Kenyon Review, *Vol. XXVI, No. 1, Winter, 1964), in his* The Brecht Commentaries: 1943-1980 *(reprinted by permission of Grove Press, Inc.; copyright © 1964, 1981 by Eric Bentley), Grove Press, 1981, pp. 122-31.*

ADDITIONAL BIBLIOGRAPHY

Bathrick, David. *The Dialectic of the Early Brecht: An Interpretive Study of "Trommeln in der Nacht."* Stuttgart: Akademischer Verlag Hans-Dieter Heinz, 1975, 147 p.
  Traces "the genesis of *Trommeln in der Nacht* for what it reveals about the author's changing political and aesthetic views."

Demetz, Peter, ed. *Brecht: A Collection of Critical Essays*. Englewood Cliffs, N.J.: Prentice-Hall, 1962, 186 p.
  Includes important commentaries by Eric Bentley, Walter H. Sokel, Hanna Arendt, and Martin Esslin, among others.

Ewen, Frederic. *Bertolt Brecht: His Life, His Art, and His Times*. New York: Citadel Press, 1967, 573 p.
  Major critical biography in English.

Lyons, Charles R. *Bertolt Brecht: The Despair and the Polemic*. Carbondale, Edwardsville: Southern Illinois University Press, 1968, 165 p.
  Study of the major dramas.

Rudnitsky, K. "The Lessons Learned from Brecht." *Theatre Research International* VI, No. 1 (Winter 1980-81): 62-72.
  Discussion of Brecht and Russian stagecraft, observing that "the warmth and sensitivity characteristic of the Russian school of acting were alien to the strict rationalism and austere logic of the composition of Brecht's dramas."

Volker, Klaus. *Brecht Chronicle*. Translated by Fred Wieck. New York: The Seabury Press, 1975, 209 p.
  Chronology of important dates in Brecht's life, including a record of his theatrical productions.

Weisstein, Ulrich. "From the Dramatic Novel to the Epic Theater: A Study of the Contemporary Background of Brecht's Theory and Practice." *The Germanic Review* XXXVIII, No. 3 (May 1963): 257-71.
  Influence of Erwin Piscator and Lion Feuchtwanger on Brecht's dramas.

Willett, John. *The Theatre of Bertolt Brecht: A Study from Eight Aspects*. London: Methuen & Co., 1959, 272 p.
  Chapters on eight aspects of Brecht's drama: the subject matter, the language, the theatrical influences, the music, theatrical practice, the theory, politics, and the plays in English translation. Willett also includes plot outlines of each play.

Ivan (Alexeyevich) Bunin

1870-1953

Russian short story writer, novelist, poet, journalist, and memoirist.

Bunin's fiction vividly evokes the life of the provincial gentry in pre-revolutionary Russia. He was Russia's first winner of the Nobel Prize in literature, and is best known for his short story "Gospodin iz San Frantsisko" ("The Gentleman from San Francisco") and the novel *Derevnya (The Village)*.

As a boy, Bunin received a thorough education in world literature and developed an early interest in writing. This interest was nurtured by his family—disinherited but proud, tradition-bound aristocrats, whose influence on Bunin's work can be seen in his consistent preoccupation with time and history. Childhood memories of life among the gentry and peasantry during the czarist empire's final decades provide the raw material for much of Bunin's fiction. Indeed, his themes, language, and style—a unique conjunction of realistic detachment and romantic subjectivity—reflect the traditions of late nineteenth-century Russian literature.

As a young man Bunin's talent was directed to poetry, and his first volume, *Stikhotvoreniya*, appeared in 1891. The verse he published for the next decade attracted a small readership, but it was not until *Listopad*, in 1901, that Bunin was recognized as an important poet. *Listopad*, like all his verse, is written in the Parnassian style, distinguishing Bunin among his *fin de siècle* contemporaries as the only prominent Russian poet to eschew Aleksandr Blok's and Andrei Bely's new symbolist trend. Bunin won the Russian Academy's Pushkin Prize three times for his poetry as well as his translations of Longfellow, Byron, and Tennyson.

Although his first short stories had appeared in 1892 and his subsequent fiction drew a growing readership, it was not until the publication of *The Village* in 1910 that Bunin received national attention. Critics and followers were divided over the author's intent in the book; some saw the novel as a hate-filled attack on Russia, others saw it as an indictment of the nations' political system, and still others a bleak but objective portrayal of Russian life. The sadness, barbarity, and complexity of the rural gentry was explored again in *Sukhodol (Dry Valley)* and *Ioann Rydalets*, the former regarded by some critics as one of Russian literature's greatest hymns to the nation's vanished way of life. These works marked the beginning of Bunin's artistic maturity, bringing him recognition by Russia's major authors as the country's foremost living prose writer. Bunin's classical treatment of Russian life is often compared with the work of Tolstoy, Lermontov, Chekhov, and Turgenev. His prose is distinguished by the meticulous descriptive skill with which he evokes the colors, textures, aromas, tastes, and sounds of life, while presenting the dark side of the human condition.

During the years just before World War I, Bunin traveled in southern Europe and the Middle East, returning to Russia to write short stories set in foreign lands. In these stories Bunin examines death for the first time, achieving particular success with "The Gentleman from San Francisco," which presents the ultimate uselessness of wealth. Because he opposed the Bolshevik revolution, Bunin left Russia in 1920 and settled in

France, where he lived until his death. His stories were still set in Russia, but his themes expanded to accommodate the author's examinations of the temporality of life, love, and beauty, particularly in his collection *Roza Iyerikhona*. Outstanding works of Bunin's first decade of exile include *Grammatika lyubvi (Grammar of Love)*, *Zhizn' arsen'yeva (The Well of Days)* and *Mitina lyubov' (Mitya's Love)*, the latter being part of a novelized autobiography. In 1933 Bunin received worldwide recognition when he was awarded the Nobel Prize. His newly acquired fame was short-lived, however, and the books he published thereafter attracted little attention, although *Tyomnyye allei (Dark Avenues and Other Stories)* has since received critical appreciation. The stories written in Bunin's last years are often brief sketches, sometimes but a page long, each capturing the essence of a mood or thought.

Bunin's was a tragic vision of life, but one that affirmed with hope the purpose of humanity. His art is concerned with timeless facets of existence rather than contemporary issues, and for this he has been criticized. Nevertheless, Bunin did create a precise prose style, objective though slightly nostalgic, that is unique in Russian literature.

PRINCIPAL WORKS

Stikhotvoreniya (poetry) 1891
Listopad (poetry) 1901
Derevnya (novel) 1910
  [*The Village*, 1923]
Sukhodol (short stories) 1912
  [*Dry Valley* published in *The Elaghin Affair and Other
  Stories*, 1935]
Ioann Rydalets (short stories and poetry) 1913
Gospodin iz San-Frantsisko (short stories) 1916
  [*The Gentleman from San Francisco and Other Stories*,
  1922]
Roza Iyerikhona (short stories and poetry) 1924
Mitina lyubov' (novel) 1925
  [*Mitya's Love*, 1926]
Sny Changa (short stories) 1927
  [*The Dreams of Chang and Other Stories*, 1935]
Solnechnyy udar (short stories) 1927
Grammatika lyubvi (short stories) 1929
  [*Grammar of Love*, 1935]
Zhizn' arsen'yeva (novel) 1930
  [*The Well of Days*, 1933]
Tyomnyye allei (short stories) 1943
  [*Dark Avenues and Other Stories*, 1949]
Vospominaniya (memoirs) 1950
  [*Memories and Portraits*, 1951]
Sobraniye sochineniy. 9 vols. (novels, short stories,
  memoirs, and poetry) 1965-67

J. MIDDLETON MURRY (essay date 1922)

[When the admirable translation] of **"The Gentleman from San Francisco"** appeared last autumn in "The Dial," our feeling was that a new planet had swum into our ken. The story was splendidly *written*, which is another way of saying that the author's imaginative realization of his subject had been not only complete but single. It seemed that he had had, as it were, an apocalyptic vision of his matter as a whole, and that he had transcribed it with a swift intensity which suggested a great reserve of power. Moreover, there was something new in the quality of the vision itself. The ruthlessness with which Bunin stripped the nakedness of modern civilization was comprehensive and synoptic, not petulantly and spasmodically cynical as are so many modern writers with the same theme. Bunin's story was at once swift and majestic, penetrating and powerful; not a scrap, but a finished and ordered work of art.

It is, indeed, a masterpiece, without a doubt one of the finest short stories—it is not so *very* short—of modern times. But the expectations which it aroused are not satisfied by the two volumes of Bunin's prose which have since been made accessible to the Western reader. [**"The Gentleman from San Francisco, and Other Stories"** and **"Le Village"**] are interesting, and assuredly they were worth translating, but they are not on the same level. After Tchehov, Bunin's other short stories are disappointing. The comparison is inevitable. The subjects and the treatment suggest Tchehov, perhaps even derive from Tchehov, but we feel that Tchehov, simply because he was an almost infallible artist, would have handled them differently. If Tchehov had never existed they might have been good Bunin stories; coming after him, they are slightly inferior Tchehov stories.

They are perceptibly mechanized; they lack the beautiful organic completeness, the rhythmic finality, of the master. They are works of his "school."

The decline may be felt in Bunin's novel, **"The Village."** Here again, had there been no Tchehov, we should doubtless consider it a remarkable achievement; and, indeed, as a study of Russian peasant life it is externally far more comprehensive than anything Tchehov wrote. But though it is more comprehensive, it is less universal than "The Ravine" or "The Steppe." Having read it we know far more of Russian village life than we learn from Tchehov; but we seem to know far less of life. For **"The Village,"** though it has some relation to Tchehov's work, nevertheless is marked by a reversion to the methods of the Western "realists." This gives it an unusual documentary value; its absolute literary value is much less certain. Still, it is a book which should certainly be translated into English.

A knowledge of it would give to the mysterious word "Russia" a solid content which it seldom possesses on Western lips. For the West "Russia" has meant so many different and disappointing things; a steam-roller, the Johannine spirit, Tolstoy and Dostoevsky, the Soviet Government, and many things besides. **"The Village"** supplies a content nearer to the reality. And that, we imagine, was largely Bunin's aim. . . .

The village, Bunin says here, is Russia; and the village is to be found in most of the towns also. He has the simplest reason on his side, for he is writing of a country which (as we continually forget) contains well over a hundred millions of illiterate peasants. There is no doubt, then, that he intends the fate of the two peasant brothers, Tikhon and Kouzma, to be symbolical. Tikhon is a peasant-merchant who manages to buy out the squire; yet he is so full of fears for his property that he can never leave it, and all through his gross, unenlightened life, he dreams of the city which he never visits. Kouzma, self-educated, sensitive, and ineffectual, becomes a clerk in the town, and then finds himself dragged back to the village, where he slowly sinks into apathy again. But the men are less important than the *milieu*. The picture of life in a Russian village is drawn with a convincing monotony; it sinks into our souls like a fine mist. Sameness, brutality, naïvety, filth—the cycle returns for ever. It is no wonder that this novel (or "poem," as Bunin prefers to call it) created a sensation when it appeared in Russia in 1909. . . . Though completely free from the neuroticism of the period, it is none the less in complete accord with the despondency which gripped Russian literature between the two revolutions. And it is perhaps not fanciful to trace a psychological connection between **"The Village"** and **"The Gentleman from San Francisco."** On the evidence of **"The Village,"** and of certain short stories . . . , we conceive Bunin as one convinced that Russia's only hope lay in "civilization." . . . All the single-minded and honest spirits who came after the two great visionaries, Tolstoy and Dostoevsky, have cried like Goethe: "More light." Tchehov and Gorky are at one in this; and to me, like Bunin, whose depressing knowledge of the Russian reality is not lightened by a literary genius so powerful as theirs, we imagine the necessity of "civilization" was still more desperate. Then came the war, revealing the rottenness of the civilization on which his hopes had leaned, and by the very extremity of his despair Bunin was inspired. That is, we admit, only a theory; but we need a theory to account for the striking difference between **"The Gentleman from San Francisco"** and Bunin's other writings, between work that is of the first order and work that is respectable. The masterly symbolism of the great liner "Atlantis," which brings the millionaire and his family to the sham summer of a Naples winter and takes him back again, squeezed into a tarpaulin package at the bottom of the hold; the apocalyptic revelation of a ''civilization'' which cannot attain to life and has no place for death; the narrative which sweeps, like one of the Atlantic billows amid which it passes, with a restrained and rhythmical fury from mockery to mockery—there is no visible parallel to these magnificent qualities in the rest of Bunin's prose-work which has been made known to us. Our expectations have been frustrated, but we are not disappointed. When a writer has given us one of the greatest short stories of our age, and perhaps the only great story which is truly modern in the sense that it gives a synthesis of existence under aspects which never existed before the end of the nineteenth century, we have no right to ask more. Bunin has earned a place in the literature of the world. Is there another Russian writer since Gorky of whom so much can be truly said?

> *J. Middleton Murry, ''Ivan Bunin,'' in* The Nation
> & The Athenaeum, *Vol. XXXI, No. 13, June 24,*
> *1922, p. 444.*

J.W. KRUTCH (essay date 1922)

[The vividness and reality of Ivan Bunin's stories in **''The Gentleman from San Francisco and Other Stories''**] are of a sort which one has come to expect almost as a matter of course from Russian fiction. All Bunin's tales have the gloomy intensity characteristic of his race . . . ; some betray that no less characteristic fondness for the violent and the outré which is born of too prolonged brooding upon the darker aspects of his soul; but the best and longest, **''The Gentleman from San Francisco,''** reveals . . . a simple incident with poignancy and power. In it an American millionaire sets out after a life of labor to see the world and he returns after a few weeks upon the same ship, occupying this time a coffin instead of his sumptuous cabin. It gets its effect from a remarkable picture of the complicated machinery at the center of all the complex luxury of modern travel and the irony of the millionaire's return lying unregarded in the lower regions along with the vast engines and the army of workers who a few weeks before had seemed to throb and labor only for him. Now another group of equally petty and transient beings lords it upon the deck above. In the presence of writers like [Bunin and Miss Katherine Mansfield] whose work is so simple and yet so indisputably touched with genius, criticism must admit with some embarrassment its inability to explain the secret. It is easy enough to say that, sticking close to actuality, [he has] left out all that is strained or exaggerated, but the secret cannot be anything so simple as an omission. Nor is it principally that [he has] seen or felt more keenly than others. . . . Those writers who like Bunin . . . seek only to reproduce the flavor of ordinary life are great in proportion as they are able to keep their work from being like the poetry of the unfortunate Mendoza in [Shaw's] ''Man and Superman'': ''Divine poetry to me, doggerel to all the rest of the world.'' (p. 100)

> *J.W. Krutch, ''The Unfortunate Mendoza,'' in* The
> Nation, *Vol. 115, No. 2977, July 26, 1922, pp. 99-*
> *100.*

IVAN BUNIN (essay date 1923)

Twelve years ago I published my novel **''The Village''**. This was the first of a whole series of works which depicted the Russian character without adornment, the Russian soul, its

peculiar complexity, its depths, both bright and dark, though almost invariably tragic. (p. 9)

Some critics have called me cruel and gloomy. I do not think that this definition is fair and accurate. But of course, I have derived much honey and still more bitterness from my wanderings throughout the world, and my observations of human life. I had felt a vague fear for the fate of Russia, when I was depicting her. Is it my fault that reality, the reality in which Russia has been living for more than five years now, has justified my apprehensions beyond all measure; that those pictures of mine which had once upon a time appeared black, and wide of the truth, even in the eyes of Russian people, have become *prophetic*, as some call them now? ''Woe unto thee, Babylon!''—those terible words of the Apocalypse kept persistently ringing in my soul when I wrote **''The Brothers''** and conceived **''The Gentleman from San Francisco,''** only a few months before the War, when I had a presentiment of all its horror, and of the abysses which have since been laid bare in our present-day civilization. Is it my fault, that here again my presentiments have not deceived me?

However, does it mean that my soul is filled only with darkness and despair? Not at all. (pp. 11-12)

> *Ivan Bunin, ''Autobiographical Note,'' in his* The
> Village, *translated by Isabel F. Hapgood (copyright*
> © *1923, copyright renewed* © *1951, Alfred A. Knopf,*
> *Inc.; reprinted by permission of Alfred A. Knopf,*
> *Inc.), Knopf, 1923 (and reprinted by Knopf, 1933),*
> *pp. 7-12.*

GLEB STRUVE (essay date 1933)

Like Turgenev, Bunin began his literary career by writing verse; as with Turgenev, later his prose output definitely overshadowed his poetry. Yet in one thing he is unlike Turgenev: though he owes the place which he occupies in contemporary Russian literature to his prose work, he never stopped writing verse and—what is more—he is a genuine poet. Poetry is to him something more than a preliminary school, a useful training and discipline, as it was to Turgenev; it is an indispensable part of his artistic self-expression; and some of his best verse—both of the earlier and of the later period—is not inferior in quality to the best of his prose. (p. 423)

Bunin's poetry has often been characterised as purely descriptive and even less lyrical than his prose. This statement is much too sweeping to be accepted at its face value. There is a great deal of the descriptive in Bunin's verse, especially in his earlier work; endowed with an exceptionally keen visual sense, Bunin is often tempted to give full play to it, both in his poems and in his stories, and sometimes it is apt to oust all other elements from his poems; but in some of them, without ever becoming effusive or losing his sense of measure and of the supremacy of the logical element in words (in this he is a true ''classicist,'' an heir to Pushkin's tradition in Russian poetry), he reaches a great poignancy of sustained lyrical expression. His craftsmanship, his purely verbal mastery, seldom fail him. In this Bunin showed himself akin to the Symbolists and to the whole of the modern school of poetry, though in substance he was quite alien and even hostile to them; and though keeping aloof from the advanced literary movements of the beginning of the 20th century, he yet shared in its revival of poetical craftsmanship . . . . (pp. 423-24)

Numerically speaking, short stories represent Bunin's most important contribution to literature. Of these there are six volumes dating from the pre-revolutionary period, and four published since the Revolution outside Russia. It is also, perhaps, in the domain of the short story that lie Bunin's greatest and most perfect achievements: such stories as *The Gentleman from San Francisco, The Dreams of Chang, The Sunstroke, Ida, Ignat, A Goodly Life*—I choose on purpose stories written in different veins and dating from different periods—may be placed on a level with the best stories of Turgenev and Chekhov. Bunin's language is a marvel of richness and simplicity. (p. 424)

Bunin possesses also a great power of descriptive suggestion. In his stories there is that atmospheric quality which enables him to discard the plot, the outward incident, and to create a story out of nothing. A short tale of his called *The Snowman* is a good example of such stories created out of nothing. A man sitting late at night in his study in a snowbound, still country-house, hears one of his little nephews cry—he goes to the nursery to find out what is the matter and discovers that it is the snowman outside the window that disturbs the boy, whenever he wakes up, by his mysterious nocturnal appearance. He goes out, destroys the snowman and wanders for a while in the courtyard. The description of that walk, with which the story ends, epitomises its whole atmosphere. (pp. 424-25)

There is perhaps more behind this story than in it; its effect is suggestive, evocative, and this is characteristic of the manner of many of Bunin's stories. It is wrong to regard him as an out-and-out realist indulging in "superfluous details"; Bunin's realism is of poetical quality, and his details are seldom superfluous; they are always subordinated to the whole and play their appointed part.

On the face of it Bunin may seem cold, dispassionate; his coldness, his "metallic" qualities have often been referred to by critics. Yet, the secret of his art lies precisely in his capacity of stirring within us profound and troubled emotions, of striking deep chords, while keeping cold and unperturbed on the surface. Nothing could be more wrong than to regard Bunin as a soothing, quieting author. Himself at bottom unquiet, he is capable of acting disquietingly upon us—and this without resorting to any crude means, to any cheap verbosity, in a delicately suggestive way. (p. 425)

Bunin's all-Russian fame came upon the publication of his first long work—*The Village*. It is not a novel in the conventional accepted sense of the word, and it is not for nothing that Bunin gave it the sub-heading of "a poem." It is a large fresco, a dyptich, picturing Russian village life during the first revolution (1904-05). . . . In *The Village* there is no plot, almost no development; it is a picture of life in a Russian village, painted in dark, sombre colours—the author lays bare before our eyes, on one hand the cruelty and brutality, on the other, the lack of civilisation and the poverty of the Russian peasant. . . . But, of course, *The Village* was never meant as a complete and exhaustive picture of the Russian peasantry. Cruelty and beastliness were not the only things Bunin saw in it—witness several of his other stories with their rich and varied gallery of peasant types; witness the story entitled *The Saint*, and to quote his own words reflecting the "ineffable beauty" (as Bunin says) of the Russian soul. From the literary point of view *The Village* is, though not a perfect, a powerful and significant work; despite its apparent formlessness, it reveals a great constructive ability; despite all absence of plot and movement—a great inner force and impetus. The style, the language show the same force and firmness—a peculiar blend of realism and poetry. There are scenes where the grotesque and the uncanny intermingle in a kind of Goyesque [vision].

In 1912 appeared the second of Bunin's longer works—*Sukhodol*. It is much shorter than *The Village*. In it the social strain in Bunin's work once more found its expression, though in a different aspect from that of *The Village*. From contemporary Russia we are taken back to the days before the emancipation of peasants, and instead of the peasantry attention is centred on the gentry. There appears the motif that could be met with before in some of Bunin's stories—the motif of the impoverishment and physical and moral decay of the country gentry. In Bunin's attitude to it there is a mixture of nostalgic love and regret with a sense of doom. . . . Again, there is no plot; the temporal plane of the story is constantly shifted. Again the same blend of realism and poetry, still more effective than in *The Village,* because more concentrated, undiluted by reflections. In this work of Bunin, despite all its sombreness, there is a haunting, poignant beauty, a musical unity wherein the desolate natural surroundings, the disintegrating framework of social relations, the eccentric characters, and the romantic loveliness of the heroine are fused into a single musical note. For sheer terseness and concentrated power, *Sukhodol* and *Mitya's Love* are perhaps the highest summits of Bunin's work.

The years 1910-1916 were the most productive in Bunin's creative life. A year after *Sukhodol,* he published a book of stories and verse called *John the Weeper,* and in the following year—*The Cup of Life.* Two more years—and he gave us *The Gentleman from San Francisco.* Very simple in construction as all Bunin's stories, it has no plot in the real sense, though there is a story. Its theme is that of *Ecclesiastes,* and a motto from *Ecclesiastes*—"Vanity of vanities; all is vanity"—would have perhaps suited it better than the motto from the *Apocalypse* Bunin chose for it. Its theme is precisely the vanity of all earthly things and the subjection of man to ever-watchful and watching death. The effect of this story is due to the extreme ecomony with which Bunin uses his artistic resources; to the detachment with which the story is told—that detachment has a biblical quality, and it is not the first time we meet in Bunin with biblical qualities of style or with a biblical spirit. (pp. 426-28)

In 1924 Bunin wrote a longish short story, a *nouvelle* called *Mitya's Love* . . . . It stands somewhat apart among Bunin's other works for its more sustained, concentrated psychological interest. It is a simple, straightforward tale of first love and disillusionment leading to a tragic conclusion—the suicide of the young hero. There are only two characters in it that matter, the two partners in the love duel, Mitya and Katya, or even, I should say, there is only one character that interests the author, namely, Mitya, whose tragic love story is unfolded with the inevitability of doom—Katya we see only through Mitya's eyes. It is difficult to define wherein lies the spell of this book with its hackneyed, old-fashioned theme. There is in it a musical quality, an inner rhythm which produces a unique effect. The way in which the description of the awakening of nature in spring and of its gradual transition to summer, is worked into the fabric of the story and made to accompany the amorous torments of Mitya's soul, as he is alternately tossed between joyous expectation and despair, is very striking. The clarity and simplicity of Bunin's language here reaches its highest summit.

In *Mitya's Love* meet the two favourite themes of Bunin—love and death, their deep fundamental mystery.

Love is also the subject of the title-story of Bunin's next book— *The Sunstroke*. . . . (p. 428)

Bunin's last book of stories, entitled *God's Tree,* appeared in 1931. With the exception of the title-story, which adds a new portrait to Bunin's earlier gallery of curious peasant characters—a man with a peculiar philosophy of resignation and indifference to good and evil—with the exception also of some purely lyrical meditations, most of the stories in this book are inordinately short; they are rather poems in prose than stories, and often practically untranslatable, their interest lying in some peculiarity of the Russian language around which they evolve. One Russian critic has rightly remarked that the real hero of this book of Bunin is the Russian language. Some of the stories are short lyrico-philosophical meditations, like Turgenev's *Senilia* or Logan Pearsall Smith's *Trivia*.

I now come to the most significant, if not the most perfect, of Bunin's later works—to his *Life of Arseniev*. . . . It is not a novel in the usual sense of the word, but rather a novelised autobiography. Though written as the life-story of a fictitious character and though quite probably not strictly autobiographical in all its details, there can be no doubt of the autobiographical nature of its groundwork. Yet it is primarily a work of art, and as such may be ranked alongside Aksakov's *Years of Childhood of Bagrov-Grandson* and Tolstoy's *Childhood, Boyhood and Youth*. *The Life of Arseniev* is a more consciously artistic, a better-organized autobiography than either of the above-mentioned classical autobiographies, and at the same time it is more intensely introspective. Though it has some excellently drawn secondary characters (one of the best being Baskakov, little Arseniev's tutor), its interest . . . is focussed on its hero. It is really a story of the formation of a man's personality from his early childhood to his youth, till he is about seventeen years old, a story told with a singleness of purpose and outlook, and reflecting the author's personality.

All the main elements of Bunin's art and outlook—artistic descriptions, lyrico-philosophical meditations and social analysis—are to be found in the *Life of Arseniev*. Parallel with the gradual unfolding and development of a human consciousness, of its awareness of the world, we are shown the outward surroundings amid which this unfolding takes place (descriptions of nature hold a large place in the book, but are closely related to the inner workings of the hero's soul) and the social and historical background of Russian life at the time. The dominant note of this social aspect of the book is once more the decay and impoverishment of the country gentry: it may be said that in the *Life of Arseniev* Bunin has portrayed the further destinies of the Sukhodol family (though his tone has grown milder, his attitude gentler, less accusatory) and the final detachment of its last representative—in the person of the young Arseniev—from his native soil, his *déclassement*, his first attempts to take roots in a new milieu, that of the urban progressive intelligentsia. As a whole the book produces no such effect of musical unity as *Sukhodol* or *Mitya's Love*, but some chapters of it belong to the best things Bunin ever wrote and all of the early part is written with unerring mastery—the early childhood, the description of the first trip to town, the first contact with religion, with death (there are several deaths in the book and, as is often the case with Bunin, they form its most hauntingly beautiful pages), the first experience of love in both its romantic and its fleshly aspects. (pp. 429-30)

Bunin does not aim at creating and embodying new worlds instilled with a life of their own, existing as it were outside their authors, invested by them with an independent and spontaneous existence, in which the author participates only as creator, from the outside so to speak. Bunin does not transform the reality and thereupon exclude himself from it; he is never absent from his works. In this sense Bunin is a "subjective"

writer, as was to some extent—though not in his novels—Turgenev, who often remained primarily a poet. The element of plot, of narrative interest, of movement is either absent or plays but a subordinate part in the great majority of Bunin's stories. It is likewise—or even to a still greater extent—absent from his bigger works. Neither *The Village* nor *Sukhodol,* as I have said, are novels. As for the *Life of Arseniev,* it is totally lacking in any element of invention, it is not fiction in the strict sense of the word. With the exception perhaps of Bely's autobiographical novels, it is the most introspective, subjective work in Russian literature.

Yet in another sense Bunin is an objective writer. His eyes are not only turned inwards, though he never tires of contemplating and studying himself, but are open wide to the whole world. Nature has endowed Bunin with keen senses. His vision, his sense of colours is something extraordinary. (p. 431)

Colour epithets in Bunin's works strike one, indeed, by their richness and variety. One Russian critic has counted, in one of Bunin's Near Eastern travelling sketches, the adjectives denoting only *shades* of colour, and he found twenty-six of them. Bunin's objectivity shows itself also in the care with which he embodies his keen visual sensations and perceptions in his phrases, trying to give them the maximum of exact, concrete, objectivated verbal expressions—Bunin's descriptions strike us by their visual, materialised concreteness. (pp. 431-32)

It would be in vain were we to look in Bunin for a minute psychological analysis, for an endeavour to penetrate deep into other people's souls. The analytical methods of a Dostoyevsky are entirely alien to him. In those of his stories which are something more than mere lyrical compositions, in which there is some semblance of action, of development, some *dramatis personæ,* the number of the latter is more often than not reduced to a strict minimum, and they are shown to us outwardly, with the aid of a few external traits, of a few suggestive details, or of the surrounding atmosphere. Whenever Bunin goes somewhat deeper in his psychological analysis, whenever he sharpens his psychological lancet, he ususally does so with regard to one only of his characters—showing us the others through the eyes of that one. He never shares his psychological attention between all his characters. (pp. 432-33)

In Bunin's later works the number of characters is very often reduced to two. To such stories *à deux* belong some of his best tales, especially those of which love is the subject, in the first place *Mitya's Love*. In his striving for the maximum of simplicity and lucidity Bunin eliminates all that is superfluous, achieving an almost algebraical bareness and transparency of construction. It is therefore entirely wrong to represent Bunin, as some of his Russian critics do, as erring on the side of superfluous minutiae, of overdone realism. In *Mitya's Love* Bunin again adopts the method of filtering one of his characters through the prism of another, even though the story is not told in that other's name. We do not see Katya from the outside, we see her only as a projection of Mitya's mind. The same story over again in *The Sunstroke;* the figure of the hero's travelling companion, barring a purely external portrait drawn with a few light pen-strokes, is left on purpose in the shadow, as if veiled by a cloud of mystery. The attention is focussed on the hero and his emotions, on his own sunny pervasion with love. (p. 433)

[This] method of Bunin's may find an explanation in his characteristic conviction of the fundamental impenetrability and inconceivableness of another man's soul. In an extremely short story, instinct with uncanny atmosphere and relating or rather just alluding to a meaningless murder of an old French-woman in a lonesome, desolate country house by two unknown individuals, Bunin lets escape him this highly significant remark: "The most terrible thing in this world is man with his soul."

Here we come to what, to my mind, is the real essence, the philosophical and psychological *leitmotiv* of Bunin's work, and which may be described as a marvelling perplexity before the mysteries of the world. What do we know, what do we understand?—this query seems to be ever present on Bunin's lips. (p. 434)

Inconceivable are things happening in this world and, confronted with them, helpless is our poor human reason. This sentiment is akin to that which underlies some of Turgenev's stories in the fantastic vein, but with Bunin it is more powerfully rooted, more genuine, I should say. In the later stories it is sounded more and more frequently, more and more persistently. In the story called *An Unknown Friend* . . . Bunin expresses this philosophy of bewilderment, of marvelling perplexity, through the mouthpiece of his heroine, a woman writing letters (that are never answered) to a writer whom she does not know but whose work she admires. "We know nothing," she exclaims in one of her letters. "Everything is marvellous, everything incomprehensible in this world." "We do not even understand our own dreams, the creations of our own imagination." Yet the inconceivability is only one aspect of this attitude; marvelling—what the French call *emerveillement*—is its inevitable complement. This is what distinguishes Bunin from Turgenev who, in the last period of his life, also had that bewildered attitude towards the world, and with whom it led to a thoroughly pessimistic outlook. Bunin is by no means a pessimist. "At bottom"—says the same woman in *An Unknown Friend*—"everything in this world is lovely. . . ." In his foreword to the English translation of *The Village*, replying to the charge of pessimism, Bunin denied it and quoted the 42nd Psalm: "As the hart panteth after the water brooks, so panteth my soul after thee, O God!" And this quotation characterises most appropriately the whole attitude of Bunin.

It is in the story entitled *The Cicadas* that we find the fullest expression of Bunin's philosophy. Strictly speaking, it is not a story; it is a lyrico-philosophical soliloquy, somehow reminding one of some passages in Virginia Woolf's novel *The Waves*, a soliloquy inspired by the stillness and solitude of a southern night broken only by the incessant chirping of the cicadas and by the dull, primeval rumbling of the sea. But for the exceptional quality of its verbal texture, this poem in prose of about a dozen pages might appear tiresome. I will nevertheless translate a few extracts from it, for, in a way, I see in it the key to the whole work of Bunin.

". . . It does not matter—Bunin soliloquises—of what exactly I thought—what matters is my thinking, an act quite inconceivable to me, and what matters still more and is still more inconceivable—is my thinking about that thinking and about my not understanding anything either in myself or in the world, and yet understanding my own not-understanding, understanding my bewilderment in the middle of this night and this magical murmuring, whether living or dead, whether meaningless or telling me something most intimate and most necessary—I know not which."

"Man alone marvels at his own existence. And in this lies his main difference from other creatures who are still in paradise, in not thinking of themselves. But then men, too, differ between themselves—by the extent, the degree of that marvelling. Why did God mark me off so particularly by the fatal sign of wonderment, of 'reasoning,' why does it grow and grow within me? Do the myriads of cicadas filling with their nocturnal lovesong the whole universe around me, do they reason? No, they are in paradise, in the blissful dream of life, and I have already awaked and am wakeful. The world is in them and they are in it, whereas I seem to look at it from outside." (pp. 434-35)

Gleb Struve, "The Art of Ivan Bunin," in The Slavonic Review *(reprinted by permission of the University of London), Vol. XI, No. 32, January, 1933, pp. 423-36.*

CLEANTH BROOKS, JOHN THIBAUT PURSER, and ROBERT PENN WARREN   (essay date 1952)

["**The Gentleman from San Francisco**"] seems merely to unfold a process, to give a simple chronicle, a chronicle with elaborate details and descriptive digressions but merely a simple chronicle after all. . . . [Behind] this simple chronicle there is a conflict, the conflict between those who rule the world and those who are ruled. The story, then, is about the oppressors and the oppressed, about justice. Having said this, let us . . . see how this theme is developed and to what it leads.

There is, first, the story of the Gentleman himself, the proud man who is struck down in the moment of his pride. He is the central character. But we know astonishingly little about him: he is proud, he is self-indulgent, he is contemptuous of others, especially those of inferior economic and social station, he is a complete materialist without even "a mustard seed of what is called mysticism in his heart." We do not even know his name. . . . In other words, Bunin seems to imply, his individuality, his name, is not important. It is not important because the Gentleman as a person is not important; he is important only as a type, as a member of a class, the class who "taken together, now rule the world, as incomprehensibly and, essentially, as cruelly" as the Roman Emperor Tiberius did. This namelessness, then, points us beyond the individual to the real concern of the story, the development of an idea.

In support of this we find the method of the story. Bunin takes the tone of a historian, as it were, as if he were giving an account long afterwards of the way life had been at a certain period. He says, for example: "The class of people to which he belonged was in the habit . . ." Furthermore, observe the great detail devoted to the life of that class, the class upon which, Bunin ironically says, "depend all the blessings of civilization: the cut of dress suits, the stability of thrones, the declaration of wars, the prosperity of hotels."

Once we have accepted the development of a theme, an idea, as the main concern of this story, we understand, too, the significance of many digressions involving minor characters, the hired lovers on the ship, the Asiatic prince and the Gentleman's daughter, the valet Luigi, the boatman Lorenzo, the cab driver, the Emperor Tiberius, the Abruzzi pipers, the hotel proprietor on Capri. A few of these characters belong to the class that rules the world, but most of them belong to the class that, in one way or another, serves the Gentleman and his kind.

We may now notice what at first glance may appear a peculiar fact in a story which has an important element of protest against social injustice: the fact that we do not have a simple arrangement of the rulers as bad and the ruled as good. The daughter of the Gentleman, though she belongs to the class of the rulers and though her notion of love has been corrupted, is yet presented with a certain sympathy: she has some sensitivity, some awareness of her isolation, as we understand from her reaction when her father tells about his dream. On the other hand, most of the characters of the class of the ruled, for example, Lorenzo, the cabman, and the valet Luigi are presented as corrupted in one way or another. Lorenzo has been spoiled and turned into an idler and reveller by admiration for his picturesque good looks. The cabman is a drunkard and gambler. Luigi has been so embittered by his condition that his satiric humor appears even after the Gentleman's death. The general point here seems to be that the unjust system spreads corruption downward as well as upward, that the stain spreads in all directions, and that injustice has persisted from the ancient to the modern world.

Let us lay aside for the moment the theme of social justice. We can see that many of the elements in the story do not seem to be accommodated to it. For instance, the various references to love, the Gentleman's relations with prostitutes, the young couple who are hired to pose as lovers on the liner, the love of the daughter for the Asiatic prince, the figure of the Virgin on the road to Monte Solare. We have here a scale from a degraded form of human love up to Divine love. In between the two extremes there are the hired lovers and the daughter. They imply the same thing: even in the corrupted world people want to believe in love, to have at least the illusion of love. The hired lovers provide a romantic atmosphere by their pretended devotion. The daughter, though she is drawn to the prince merely by social snobbery (personally he is described as very unattractive), must convert this into the emotion of love. Bunin says: "Beautiful were the tender, complex feelings which her meeting with the ungainly man aroused in her—the man in whose veins flowed unusual blood, for after all, it does not matter what in particular stirs up a maiden's soul: money, or fame, or nobility of birth." Bunin has put the matter ironically—"it does not matter." But it does matter, Bunin is implying, that the human being, even when the victim of his system, when accepting the false values of money, fame, and birth, must still try to maintain the illusion of love. That is, over against the injustice of the world there is the idea of love, culminating in Divine love.

A second set of elements that does not seem to be readily accounted for by the theme of injustice is the symbolism of the ship and the captain. It is true that the ship first appears as an easily interpreted symbol for society—the Gentleman and his kind take their ease in the dining room or bar, while the stokers sweat before the furnaces and the lookouts freeze in the crow's nest. But we begin to sense that more is meant. The darkness and the storm are outside the ship, but people ignore that terror for they "trust" the captain, who is presented as a "pagan idol." We can begin now to read the symbolism. The modern world worships its "pagan idol," the technician, the scientist, the administrator, the man who has apparently conquered nature and made irrelevant any concern with the mysteries of life and death. But we see that death does strike down the Gentleman—even though "men still wonder most at death and most absolutely refuse to believe in it." The mystery of death remains despite the skills of all the pagan idols. And even the pagan idol himself who reigns over the ship would be afraid of the darkness and mystery of the sea if he did not have the comfort of the wireless. But let us notice that the wireless is put down as a mystery, a thing "in the last account incomprehensible to him," and notice that the wireless shack is described as a kind of shrine or temple: ". . . the large armored cabin, which now and then filled with mysterious

rumbling sounds and with the dry creaking of blue fires . . ." So in the end the idol, the man who is supposed to know the solution to all problems and who is supposed to bring all to safety, must trust a "mystery."

Before we try to relate this idea to the theme of justice, we may look at the last paragraph of the story, the scene where the Devil leans on Gibraltar and watches the great ship disappear in the dark and storm toward America. What is the Devil doing in this story? There are several details to be observed before we frame an answer. Gibraltar is defined as the "gateway of two worlds," the Old World and the New World, Europe and America. The ship is bigger than the Devil and leaves him behind, staring after it. The ship is a "giant created by the arrogance of the New Man with the old heart."

To put these details together into a pattern, we may begin by taking the Devil as the embodiment of Evil, a quite conventional and usual equation. Then we may say that the Devil is left behind in the Old World because the New World doesn't believe in Evil. The spirit of modernism, that is, takes it that all difficulties are merely difficulties of adjustment of one kind or another. If there is injustice in society, simply change the system. Moral problems, by such reasoning, are not really moral problems, they are problems in "conditioning." The chief concern is not with right and wrong, good and evil, but with what will work. To sum up this point, the modern spirit, which in the story is taken as characteristically American, ignores Evil; it thinks that it can solve all problems by the application of technical skills. Therefore the ship, the symbol of the achievement of the modern spirit, is "bigger" than the Devil.

Now for the second point. The ship is a "giant created by the arrogance of the New Man with the old heart." To interpret, we must say that the New Man, with all his skills has not solved the final problem, the problem of the heart. There can be no justice by merely changing systems, by tinkering machines, either literal machines or social machines. The problem is, in the end, a problem of a change of heart, a birth of moral awareness, a spiritual redemption. . . . With this idea, which is the central and final theme of the story, we can now see how the elements concerning love and the elements concerning the captain as idol are related to the rest of the story. Love may be taken as the redeeming power, the beneficent mystery as opposed to the terrible mystery of death. Then the captain— *i.e.*, the technician, the scientist, the administrator, the being whom all men trust—must himself finally trust a mystery. There is always the mystery of nature and man's fate, for there are always love and death; there is the mystery of the human heart.

We must not conclude this interpretation without a word of caution. We must not be too ready to read the story as an attack on the achievements of the modern spirit. We might even go so far as to say that the story is not an attack at all, but a warning, rather, against a misinterpretation of the modern spirit, an oversimplification of it. The story provides, as it were, a perspective on a problem, and not an absolute and dogmatic solution for it. (pp. 174-77)

Cleanth Brooks, John Thibaut Purser, and Robert Penn Warren, in their discussion of "The Gentleman from San Francisco" by Ivan Bunin, in An Approach to Literature, *edited by Cleanth Brooks, John Thibaut Purser, and Robert Penn Warren (© 1952, renewed 1980; adapted by permission of Prentice-Hall, Inc.,*

Englewood Cliffs, N.J.), third edition, Appleton-Century-Crofts, 1952, pp. 174-77.

RENATO POGGIOLI (essay date 1953)

Within the macrocosm of the universe and within the microcosm of man's experience, Bunin contemplates, like Flaubert, only the workings of cruel and blind forces. His interest in the morbid and pathological in nature and life expresses itself with a kind of unimpassioned and objective detachment, which spurns the pathetic involvement so characteristic of the Russian decadents, and spurns even more the otherworldly longings of the Russian symbolists. . . .

Bunin's mastery is fully revealed even by his poetry, which is far less original than his prose. Without sharing the minority opinion that Bunin's verse is superior to his fiction, one could still say that his craft as a poet, which he has almost ceased practicing for the last quarter of a century, proves even better than his artistry as a prose writer the uniqueness of Bunin's position among the Russian men of letters of his time. As is the case with his stories, the themes of his poems, almost always very short and traditional in form and content, are primarily scenes of Russian life and nature, although here also there appear not too infrequently foreign backgrounds and exotic subjects, sometimes even classical motifs. The impersonality of the tone, the plastic rigor of the style, the lucid order of the structure sharply distinguish Bunin's verse from the suggestive and musical diction, from the pathos and subjectivity of the Russian poetry of the same period. There is less of a decadent strain in his verse than in his prose, and no trace of symbolistic mist. His poems may seem to anticipate the neoclassical and neo-Parnassian revival of such poets as [Mikhail] Kuzmin and [Nikolai] Gumilev, but Bunin's taste is more simple and solemn, less decorative and illustrative than theirs. (p. 135)

Perhaps [Bunin's] poetic keyboard is too narrow and the strings of his lyre are too few: his music is so monotonous as to seem almost monochordal. The range of his poetry is limited on the one hand by obvious and transparent allegories built around a single situation or anecdote, and on the other by timeless and crystal-clear representations of the ever changing seasons of nature or of man's soul. In brief, the limitations of Bunin's lyrics are the same as those of any verse predominantly narrative or evocative in character. Yet his descriptive poetry is more self-contained than those purple passages, in the form of detailed landscapes or of exuberant natural spectacles, which often mar and unbalance his otherwise masterful narrative works. (p. 136)

That Bunin is also a poet is a fact never to be forgotten by the reader of his prose, perhaps even less by the reader of his novels than by the reader of his tales. That the author himself was aware of the poetic quality of his most ambitious undertakings as a writer of fiction is shown by the subtitle "a poem," which he gave to the two novels of his maturity, beginning with *The Village*. . . . One must remember, however, that the Russian word *poema* indicates the epic poem or a poetic narrative of vast proportions; hence the use of that label ought to imply that the poetic quality of the novels so designated resides more in the imaginative design of the whole than in matters of diction and texture. (p. 144)

The composition of *The Village* is based on the usual devices of juxtaposition, parallelism, and symmetry. The quality of its inspiration and style, the almost pre-established harmony of its plan, and finally, its division into three equal, complementary parts, may justify the comparing of this novel to what is called a triptych in the field of the visual arts. The structure is highly contrived, and conveys, therefore, rather than a sense of easy and graceful proportions, an effect of both restraint and constraint.

The first part describes the striving and struggling life of Tikhon Ilich, a "rugged individualist" of peasant origin, who has become an innkeeper and whose sole aim in life is to acquire property and to amass money. (p. 146)

The second part is centered in the life of his brother Kuzma during the years of their long feud. Kuzma is a self-taught peasant, a tramp and an outcast, a naïve idealist always unable to realize his dreams of a better life for himself, for other human beings, or for the Russian people; and who wanders everywhere, hopeless and helpless, searching vainly for happiness, and often merely for luck. The third part describes Kuzma's activities and experiences after his reconciliation with Tikhon, who entrusts him with the task of overseeing a piece of land he has acquired. The novel ends with the marriage of the "Young One," the mistress of Tikhon, with one of his dependents—a marriage which is wanted by her former lover, and which his brother vainly tries to prevent.

The victory in the practical and moral struggle between the two brothers falls, therefore, to the only one who really willed it, and this shows that there is no dramatic contrast between the protagonist and the antagonist. Yet this unbrotherly couple is a relatively new replica of an old psychological opposition, frequently treated in Russian literature, and generally conceived in terms of a friendly contrast, in a relationship of duality rather than of dualism—the opposition between the practical and the unpractical man, the active and the passive one, between the realist and the idealist, the doer and the dreamer. . . .

[Bunin's impartiality in this story] is the impartiality of skepticism and cynicism, or at least the impartiality of an artist's mind looking at human reality from a distance or from above.

For this very reason, Tikhon and Kuzma, who avoid the dangers of becoming mere types, remain as characters so fixed in their own idiosyncrasies that they really fail to merge and to meet. They are contrasted statically, rather than dynamically, and this is why their opposition is more formal than substantial and there is no drama in their conflict. (p. 147)

On the other hand, it must be recognized that the aim of Bunin's novel was to create exactly such an effect. . . . [Each] of Bunin's brothers claims to be an authentic representative of Russian humanity. Paradoxically, it is Kuzma, in whom Bunin rehearses some of the most obvious traits of Russian literary psychology and who is such an evident replica, in modern surroundings and in peasant dress, of the stock figure of the "superfluous man," who claims to be a norm and an exception at the same time, when he describes himself as "a strange type of Russian."

Yet the same thing can be said of the more complex and contradictory figure of Tikhon, who often wavers between a matter-of-fact view of man's lot and an almost mystical boredom with the business of living. . . . Of both one could say what Bunin says of one of them and of Russian psychology in general: "All colors in one soul!"

The greatest shortcoming of *The Village* may be seen in the fact, rather uncommon in Bunin's work, that the two principal characters, especially the antagonist, are unduly given to self-analysis and introspection, that they think, and even talk, too much. (p. 148)

Tikhon and Kuzma resemble each other in other ways, too. Bunin makes this similarity evident through the use of various devices: by the symbolical analogy between Tikhon's sterility and Kuzma's lack of will; by the parallelism between Tikhon's willful and Kuzma's wishful selfishness; by balancing the former's sins of commission with the latter's sins of omission. For these reasons the two brothers stand in this novel not opposite, but beside each other; like figures in a primitive painting, they look straight ahead, not around themselves. Nor is the power of this composite portrait too much weakened by the excessive emphasis of the author on the thoughts or words of his models, which after all are merely added, like the lettering of an ancient picture.

Yet those two figures do not stand alone; as a matter of fact, they act as caryatids supporting a greater structure. Around or against them stands the entire village, which, especially in the third part, becomes the real protagonist of the story, a collective actor rather than a passive chorus. The last panel of the triptych assumes, therefore, the shape of a poliptych of its own. The minor figures, who in the first two parts had occupied the background, now invade the foreground of the picture. Their very presence, by contrast, revitalizes the two protagonists, who end by standing out in a clear-cut separation from the compositional mass.

The secondary characters are less polished and finished, looking more like torsos than like complete statues, yet they are no less solid or perfect. While the protagonists are always designated by their patronymics, the peasants are distinguished only by their Christian names, like Denis and Yakov; or by nicknames, like Odnodvorka; or merely by descriptive labels, like the "Young One" and the "She-Goat." This makes for both picturesqueness and anonymity, and the elemental simplicity of their traits renders them common and peculiar at the same time. Thus, paradoxically, they become almost more real as artistic persons than Tikhon and Kuzma, whose portraits are more detailed and who have more developed personalities. In comparison with the two brothers, the peasants seem to be at the same time more particular and general, more national and universal. For the creative imagination of Bunin, what appears to be less glamorous and interesting on the plane of life may become more suggestive and significant on the plane of art.

The artistic result of *The Village* is achieved, as we have already said, by a skillful and exact craftsmanship which avoids any kind of idealization and sentimentality. Of these peasants and their lot, as of the two protagonists and their life, one could really say what Balashkin says of the contents of his notebook: "They are materials worthy of the devil." Bunin's novel is an attempt to evoke the inferno of peasant Russia: a real inferno, ruled by the Tempter himself, not the bizarre hell of Gogol's fancy, visited by a host of little demons who are merely mischievous and mean. And it is the firmness of the hand which had been able to draw such a picture that led his friend, Boris Zaytsev, to call Bunin "an Antonio Pollaiuolo of our time."

In *The Village* there is no sense of change, no sense of time. The action takes place in a timeless present, without future or hope, without past or memory. For this very reason, that novel is far more representative and typical of Bunin and his creation than *Dry Valley,* which, from any standpoint, is the opposite of *The Village,* an exception or a paradox among the works of this writer and, without any doubt, his supreme masterpiece.

It is really strange that Bunin gave the same subtitle, "A Poem," to two pieces so different in intent, in spirit, and in scope. Here, consciously or not, the subtitle seems to indicate a quality of lyrical nostalgia and suggestiveness, and the very fact that this novelette is extremely short (less than a hundred pages) may allow the reader to interpret the label to mean "a prose poem."

That quality and this definition imply quite clearly that the static style and the sculptural structure of *The Village* have been replaced by an inspiration which is musical in spirit and form. While we compared *The Village* to a triptych or a poliptych, to a visual or plastic composition, *Dry Valley* might be more properly likened to a symphony. *The Village* aims, perhaps unsuccessfully, at achieving that kind of artistic ideal which Nietzsche defined as Apollonian, while *Dry Valley* follows instead a Dionysian impulse. Since Nietzsche had based his esthetic mythology on the philosophy of Schopenhauer, we may state, with the help of the ideas of that thinker, that *Dry Valley* expresses, as only wordless music can, the cosmic will to live through man's death. In truth, the real theme of this tale is the curse of living and dying within the prison of time, a mood which is not conveyed in words but in sighs and tunes. The story itself is told not in speech but in weeping and song, while all the surrounding world seems to weep and sing with it. Here the poet is never afraid of what is called the "pathetic fallacy." Human grief infects creation itself, and in the pauses of the voice of the poet, when the tale is broken by a spell of oblivion or silence, it seems that we can hear the "tears of things."

Yet, even more than *The Village, Dry Valley* may appear at first sight to be a work intentionally or initially written in the realistic tradition, nay, in the very stream of naturalism. Like so many typical naturalistic novels, a genre within which we may include a few works which anticipated or readapted that form, *Dry Valley* is the story of the ruin of a family and it describes all phases and aspects of that ruin: the steady economic decline, the slow physiological and psychological degeneration, the gradual process of degradation of the ethos and the will, the dissipation of the last resources, and the final annihilation of the house or the clan. (pp. 149-51)

Yet *Dry Valley* recalls also a more purely Russian series of literary works, which, from the title of a famous narrative of Sergey Aksakov, perhaps the earliest of its kind, one could call "family chronicles." . . . (p. 151)

The narrator does not recollect the events themselves, but the reminiscences and reports of his old nurse Natalia, who, when he and his sister were in their childhood, used to retell the story of the old times.

The narration takes, therefore, the dual shape of direct and indirect speech, being spoken in both the third and the first person. The ruin of the family is thus projected in three layers of time, and in three different psychological perspectives: the perspective of Natalia, and the perspectives of the narrator both as a child and as an adult. Through these different perspectives we see the unfolding of the crisis, its climax, and its aftermath, but without following either the sequence of time or the chain of events. The various ages and generations merge together continuously, in a series of flashbacks, touched off by a spontaneous association of impressions and moods. Yet even this confusion of the chronology has a logic of its own, and it is the logic of the heart.

That the perspective of the nurse is the most important of the three is evident from every point of view. Her central position as a narrator and witness is symbolized by the fact that her name is continually repeated in the story, almost as frequently as the name of Dry Valley, while the person speaking in the first person remains nameless. As a sign of collective anonymity the narrator uses even more frequently the formula "my sister and I," while Natalia's remarks, when reported in the form of direct speech, are dominated by the plural "we."

This lack of the sense of any clear-cut individual distinction between the various members of the family and their household is poetic and natural, since **Dry Valley** is probably the only narrative of its kind where there is no differentiation between landowners and peasants, between masters and serfs. They may belong to different classes or ranks, but all of them belong even more to the same human breed. . . . And all members of the family and the household base their reciprocal kinship on something higher than the tie of dependence and blood, that is, on their common bond with the land. This is why the real protagonist of the story is neither Natalia nor the Khrushchev clan, but the village and the country of Dry Valley. And its antagonist, who in the end will win, is time itself.

This feeling of attachment to an ancestral land is all the more powerful because it is not the human, perhaps all too human, feeling of the landlord or laborer who loves the earth because of the money or sweat he has shed on it and the wheat or wealth it produces for him. No, the Khrushchevs and their retainers are neither tillers nor exploiters of the soil nourishing them, for they live on it not like human beings, but like plants and trees, and thus are condemned to die as soon as that soil dries up, or they are uprooted from it. (pp. 151-52)

If the family and its mode of existence seem still to survive, it is merely because, thanks to Natalia's narrations as recalled by her former wards, their memory is not yet completely dead. The Khrushchevs and Dry Valley are still floating on the waters of time, into which they will finally sink, a long time after their shipwreck. The future will submerge everything into nothingness, both a past which was only an illusion and a present which is but a shadow. After all, nothing ever happened in Dry Valley, at least in the sense of events which are the effect of human action or of human will. Like the changes of the weather and the cycles of the seasons, every occurrence is there passively accepted, in joy or in sorrow, with patience or resignation.

In the present even less happens; there is only a continuous attempt to recapture the vision and the feeling of "the time lost," to revive "the remembrance of things past." And if there is a sense of absolute and final despair in the soul of the last of the Khrushchevs, it is not so much the awareness that the well of life is completely dried up on their land as the inexorable certainty that sooner or later no one will be left to shed tears on the abandoned ruins and the desert earth. This hopeless feeling that even the last memories will fade away forever, that no heart will survive where the religion of memory could be rekindled again, gives **Dry Valley** a sense of tragic pathos which no work of Bunin ever attained either before or after. (p. 153)

Practically every one of the characters, Natalia even oftener than any other, is frequently defined by the narrator as a "Dry Valley soul." The most typical characteristic of the "Dry Valley soul" is an attitude of awe before life and the world, a naïve belief that every small incident or happening is a miracle or a curse, a wonder or a sign. . . .

In other words, Dry Valley, its "souls," and the very story of their sufferings, are obsessed by superstition and fatalism.

Yet this character of theirs is not treated by Bunin in a positivistic vein, or according to any kind of naturalistic determinism. Nor does he handle this theme with mystical participation or consent; superstition and fatalism are for him merely the human and poetic expression of the primitive sense of the immanent presence of the supernatural in man's life and within nature herself. It is a religious feeling, albeit not a spiritual one, since it does not postulate, even in the characters' minds, that creation is ruled by a benign hand, by a divine providence, or by a cosmic design. Rather it presupposes the existence of superhuman forces, obscure in character and evil in intent, which bring ruin into life and chaos into the world. (p. 154)

But **Dry Valley** is neither a "horror story" nor a "tale of wonder," but an ordinary narrative, filled with the sense of habit rather than with strangeness and surprise, written in an atmosphere which is more hypnotic than magnetic, fabulous because of its imaginative richness, not because of any flight of fancy. Its sense of fatality does not reside in the complexity of the passions or the exceptional destiny of its characters, but in the things themselves and in their very substance, which is the substance of the earth. This is why that fatality is not allegorized, but expressed simply and directly, beginning with the title of the story, which is also the name of its locale. That name is repeated continuously, as if it were a refrain or a spell, and all its suggestion is based on the etymological allusion conveyed by it, by the poetic irony suggesting that Dry Valley is also a "valley of tears." (pp. 154-55)

[The] descriptive passages play a far different role from the panoramas or dioramas which so often overcharge Bunin's work. Here the spectacles or manifestations of nature are dramatis personae, not stage sets. Each one of the different and yet harmonic visions of the village and the country around it, each one of the numberless evocations of a peculiar season or hour in nature or time, is a unique note in this poetic symphony that changes colors and words into music. Here the landscapes are really states of mind, and psychic moods. . . .

Probably **Dry Valley** is the only really symbolist novel ever written in Russia—a paradoxical feat, since its author was disdainful of symbolism and almost a Parnassian in temperament. Yet this short novel is a symbolist work from several points of view, especially in its highly subjective and yet almost impersonal mood. It is symbolist because its suggestiveness is based on intuition and insight, not on abstraction and allegory, and because it reduces the verbal art of the poet, generally conceived in plastic and figurative terms, to the "condition of music." It is thus that this story strangely ends as a kind of tragic pastoral. (p. 155)

Renato Poggioli, "The Art of Ivan Bunin" (originally published in Harvard Slavic Studies, *Vol. 1, Spring, 1953), in his* The Phoenix and the Spider: A Book of Essays about Some Russian Writers and Their View of the Self *(copyright © 1957 by the President and Fellows of Harvard College; excerpted by permission), Cambridge, Mass.: Harvard University Press, 1957, pp. 131-57.*

MARC SLONIM (essay date 1953)

In general love (or, to be more precise, remembrance of love) was one of Bunin's main themes, particularly in his later years. All his love stories are sad and invariably have a tragic ending: Mitya kills himself [in **'Mitya's Love'**]; the mistress of the writer (in **'Henry'**) is murdered by her former lover when she is on the threshold of a new and happy life; . . . the poor young girl who decides to become a prostitute and falls in love with the first man she sleep with dies from tuberculosis (**'Three Rubles'**). All these endings may seem surprising and brusque, as if the author did not know what to do with his characters and hence sentenced them to premature deaths. But these endings are perfectly consistent with Bunin's romantic conception of love, which he combines with a cynical awareness of its coarse physical reality—and he resorts to the same method Turgenev used.

Love is an illuminating inspiration, a brief and tense moment, as Blok put it—and therefore it cannot endure. It is like dawn or lightning. Men aspire to a durable happiness for which they are not born. We want it for life—and we get it for a night, like the hero of **'Sunstroke,'** who spent a few hours with a woman he met aboard a ship, and suddenly realized after her departure that he loved her passionately, yet had failed to learn her name and address. Whenever we attempt to make love permanent, it either turns into the boredom of habit or takes its vengeance by bringing about catastrophes. Bunin's lovers remember only moments of tension, the intoxication, the blissful dizziness, the pungent bite of passion. Like the Romantics, Bunin believes that only fleeting moments are beautiful, and cherishes only what is fated to die soon.

The themes of love and death disclose the essence of Bunin's art. Like Turgenev he sees in love a supreme revelation of the enchantment of life, to which he is extremely sensitive.

The remarkable acuteness and the hard brilliancy of his style correspond to his sensorial and sensual precision. He is, above all, the writer of visual deaths, of forms, lines, and colors, and he renders with pagan joy all earthy, bodily traits, all concrete signs of nature and men. His exactness and completeness remind one of Tolstoy's manner; there is, however, neither Devil nor God in Bunin's world. Everything is external and concrete, and everything is devoid of meaning, subject to evanescence and decay, even though the sky may be sapphire, the sun shine triumphantly, flowers smell enchantingly, and women be adorable. This may seem too simple and naïve a description, yet it is Bunin's attitude. He is allured by the loveliness of nature and appalled by its aloofness; he is bewitched and frightened by the splendor of the world. He emphasizes both the magnificence of the universe and the insignificance of man. This contrast underlies all his philosophy—if such a term may be applied to a writer of his kind. In **'The Star of Love'** the hero kisses the neck of his horse, 'to sense the coarse smell, to feel the earthly flesh—without which it would be too frightening to exist in this world.' The feeling that flesh represents life with all its fascination, beauty, and madness is counterbalanced in Bunin by an oceanic or cosmic feeling. The night and the sea and the stars make him sense Nature, the Great Mother, who absorbs and dissolves everything and from whom all things are reborn. This is the way of all flesh, the wheel of life—and only the stupid children of man try to resist it, grow rebellious, and refuse to accept the truth (**'Mara'** and, above all, **'Cicadas'**).

This almost Hindu outlook (he stressed it in his biography of Tolstoy, as well as in his books on the Near East) is, nevertheless, contradictory to his fear of death. Its shadow is always cast over his stories, and the horror of the nothingness to which all who live are sentenced envelops Bunin's work in a shroud of anxiety and gloom. Nothing is worth concern or attachment, for everything will turn to dust; chance is the only law of life; there is no value or meaning to labor, politics, or knowledge—

the highest aspirations, the loftiest hopes are shadows and fade like flowers, or are as futile as butterflies.

Poet of sensations, instinctual drives, and recollections, Bunin seldom enters into psychological analysis or portrait-painting; in general, he wants to present rather than to explain. He produces characteristics rather than characters, and all his heroes are sketchy, almost without form. One can read a dozen of Bunin's tales without once getting a complete picture of a type, of a character. Yet at the same time the bodily features of each individual, his sensations, his fluctuating emotions are depicted with surprising accuracy—and we remember the way the young lover rode on horseback on a starry night in spring, or how the herbs smelled in the manor garden when the beloved sat on the bench, or how her father drank his tea from a tumbler in a silver glass holder. The concrete traits of this visible, measurable world are described in plastic relief and with delight. This delight in sounds, colors, volume, feelings, sensations is matched by a poignant feeling of decay—and therein lies the peculiarity of Bunin's manner. The flux of sensations and desires, all the illusions and dreams of man, which are in constant change, are projected against a static setting of nature. This prose also possesses a finality: whatever he describes is caught and imprisoned in a plastic, almost sculptural image; his prose is precise and solid in its contours. This is why his art evokes so frequently the similes of chiseling, of cameos and carved gems, and why, in a poem that gives his artistic credo, he speaks of inscribing a sonnet with a steel dagger on the glacier of a mountain peak.

His craftsmanship, his verbal perfection, has a slightly chilly quality. Bunin lacks compassion or immediate interest in human beings: a purely aesthetic fascination of recollection and an icy awareness of death prevail in all his work. He never departs from a haughty, aristocratic contempt for all the trivialities of existence, all struggle or endeavor, which he rejects as utterly futile. Both in his memoirs and in his essays on contemporary topics (including Communism) he displays such a spiteful attitude toward his contemporaries, such an urge to point out the defects and foibles of his former friends, that these irate, malevolent pages stand out as particularly destructive. In general, the great formal beauty of Bunin's writings is not matched by any corresponding moral or intellectual greatness—he is without warmth, generosity, humaneness—and this marks his work with the tarnish of sterility. This scarcity of human feeling also sets limitations to his role in Russian letters: he can be considered only as an epigone of the great masters. (pp. 170-72)

Marc Slonim, "1905 and Its Aftermath," in his Modern Russian Literature: From Chekhov to the Present *(copyright 1953 by Oxford University Press, Inc.; renewed 1981 by Tatiana Slonim; reprinted by permission of the publisher), Oxford University Press, New York, 1953, pp. 153-83.**

SEYMOUR L. GROSS (essay date 1960)

"The Gentleman from San Francisco," like some of Hawthorne's finest tales, has a deceptively unambiguous surface. Superficially, it is the story of a middle-aged wealthy American businessman, who, after years of accumulating money (at the expense of overworked and underpaid Chinese laborers), goes off on a pleasure trip around the world as "a reward for years of toil." He is vain, proud and completely indifferent to the needs and demands of other human beings: he sees them only as mechanisms for the increase of his own comfort and well-being. Everywhere he goes he is treated with sham respect and deference; but when he is suddenly struck down with a heart attack, his cardboard world collapses: his family is uncere-moniously shunted off by an irritated and offended hotel pro-prietor (death is bad for business), and his body is cynically dumped into an empty soda-water box and shipped back to America in the hold of the same ship which had so luxuriously transported him to the Old World.

This brief resumé of what "happens" in **"The Gentleman from San Francisco"** (and the simplistic moral which it invites) is, of course, absurd, for it totally ignores dozens of details: countless natural descriptions; the ubiquitous bells, gongs, and sirens; the hired lovers, the Asiatic prince, the "pagan" cap-tain; the vignettes of Tiberius Caesar, Lorenzo, and the two pipers from Abruzzi. . . . [Commentators] have not failed to recognize that these details—which actually constitute the bulk of the story—must be accounted for in any coherent explanation of the story. But they have had only partial success because they have tried to relate them to some baldly stated moral theme rather than to the story's overarching symbolic structure. That is, they have proceeded from the assumption that the story is an allegorical presentation of the *idea* that twentieth-century civilization has been corrupted by an unjust system, rather than from the assumption that it is a dramatization, full of sorrow and pity, of the *way* modern man has crippled his capacity for sentient response to this "evil and beautiful world." (pp. 153-54)

We may best come at the meaning of **"The Gentleman from San Francisco"** by first concerning ourselves with the description of the two Abruzzi mountaineers who are making a pil-grimage to the statue of the Holy Virgin on Monte Solare. This passage, following as it does the degradation of the Gentleman and the vignettes of the "brutal and filthy" Tiberius and the "care-free reveller" Lorenzo, is not only the one ecstatic mo-ment in a world of boredom, vanity, and cruelty, but is, I believe, the symbolic center of the story as well. (p. 155)

We must be careful not to take this passage merely as a contrast between peasant simplicity and urban corruption, such as is to be found in, say [Ignazio] Silone's *Bread and Wine*. It is not a paean sung to the peasantry who shall inherit the earth from what Brooks, Purser, and Warren call the "arrogant, rapacious, self-indulgent, and brutal capitalism" of the Gentleman and the class he represents [see excerpt above]. . . . To do so would be to give the story a "socialist" bias which it does not have. Bunin never subscribed to (or, as in the case of the modern Communist, gave lip service to) any sentimental disjunction of virtue according to class, as any reader of his bitter portrayal of peasant life, *The Village*, can attest to. . . . The full and joyous response of the two Abruzzi pipers is potentially pos-sible for all men . . . if they can but sense their "pitiful In-dividuality" in the face of the mystery and majesty of the "All-Oneness" of the universe, and respond to it with "that ultimate, all-embracing thing which is called love, the yearning to en-compass within one's heart all the universe, seen and unseen."

In this passage of the two pipers the force which triggers the release of this sentient vitality—love—is Christianity, and, indeed, the whole story takes its peculiar ironic tone as well as various details from the Revelation of St. John, especially Chapter 18, which, as Bunin has told us, was on his mind when he conceived **"The Gentleman from San Francisco"** and from which he chose "Alas, alas, that great city Babylon, that mighty city" as the epigraph for his story. This does not mean, however, that Bunin has excommunicated all beliefs save that

which finds salvation in the Christian God. . . . The sin is not so exclusively Christian in Bunin's view, although, to be sure, it manifests itself in Christian terms in **"The Gentleman from San Francisco,"** probably because the story is set in Italy. . . . [Man's] self-imprisoning cruelty (such as Tiberius's) and his joyless vanity (such as Lorenzo's) are the perverted result of his having turned away from *all* "godhood," away from the mysterious "unseen" world, without which the "seen" world becomes no more than a deadening lump of clay on which men such as the Gentleman from San Francisco sting themselves into a living death with such futile and self-defeating gestures towards happiness as sumptuous dinners ("the crown of the day"), exquisite champagnes, and dreams of illicit lovemaking with "young Neopolitan girls." (pp. 155-57)

In contrast, the two pipers of Abruzzi live . . . the "life of infantile immediacy, sentient with . . . all existence, and death, and the divine majesty of the universe." Unfettered by a wor-ship of their own "self-hood," they are able to enter into a beatific communion with all of nature ("the sun and the morn-ing"), man ("all who suffer in this evil and beautiful world"), and God (the "thrice-blessed Son"). For them, the world is, despite the presence of evil, dazzlingly gorgeous; life is hard but free; and death is preciously mysterious, for without it, as Bunin said on many occasions, life would become insipid and incomplete.

When the life of the Gentleman from San Francisco is seen against this vision of Grace, practically every detail in the story becomes ironically significant. For just as in *The Divine Com-edy* (to which Bunin alludes in the story), where the vision of Paradise is intensified by memories of the infernal and pur-gatorial regions, so too in Bunin's story does the passage of the two pipers gain its intensity from its ironic juxtaposition with the lonely and imprisoned lives of all the other people in the story, whose existences are symbolized by "a lonely parrot babbl[ing] something in its expressionless manner, stirring in its cage, and trying to fall asleep with its paw clutching the upper perch in a most absurd manner."

The initial irony in the story is to be found in its title, not solely because, as has been pointed out, the Gentleman remains forever, like Chaucer's merchant, a nameless figure, but be-cause Bunin has him come from San Francisco. I feel certain that Bunin chose that city as the origin of the Gentleman not only "because California represented, at the turn of the cen-tury, the raw, energetic materialism of the New World" [as M. B. McNamee has suggested], but also because it is the city of St. Francis. It is both terrible and sad, a rueful commentary on the modern world, that a life so esthetically and spiritually desiccated could originate in the city named for a man who had achieved, like the pipers, a perfect communion with nature, man, and God. And as free as this trilateral communion has made the pipers and St. Francis, so has the lack of it incar-cerated the spirit of the Gentleman in a prison of its own devising.

The freedom which the Gentleman's wealth has given him is, in reality, an illusion. His life is a joyless round of activities (which somehow never quite come off) prescribed and pros-cribed by the segment of society to which he belongs. . . . He has thrown away his life working "unweariedly" only because he wanted to "come up to the level of those whom he had once taken as his model." And "the stream of life's pleasures" which he is about to enter into and for which he has worked so hard is, as it turns out, a narrowly restricting artificial canal, the passage down which is determined by the faceless forces of "itinerary," "day's program," and "set routine," which decide what man is "expected to relish," where he is "supposed to stroll," when it is "customary to take tea." . . . It is significant that when the Gentleman, sitting alone in his hotel room looking at his gouty hands, dimly senses the futility of his life, it is the "voice of the second gong sounded throughout the house, as in a heathen temple," which shatters his meditation and sends him down to his lonely death in the library of a foreign hotel. The costume of this world is similarly binding, restricting, stifling: dancing shoes "encase" the feet, collars choke the throat, tight waistcoats squeeze the belly. But when the Gentleman is dying, the servants, in an intuitively symbolic gesture, tear off his tie, collar, waistcoat, "and even—for no visible reason—the dancing shoes from his black silk-covered feet." These artificial trappings of an artificial life are inappropriate for the most natural act of the Gentleman's life—death. (pp. 157-59)

Bunin's strategy in weaving these images of imprisonment—the social regimen, the imperious gongs, the suffocating apparel—is to throw the lives of the Gentleman and his class into ironic perspective: they who think themselves so powerful and free are, in actuality, impotent and enslaved. . . . Like the couple hired by the ship company "to play at love," these people cannot live; they can only play at living—and the script is as cold as death. And all the while the two pipers of Abruzzi are rapturously alive with their yearning to encompass the whole universe, the seen and the unseen: nature, man, and God.

The natural world is for the Gentleman a hostile force, both because he can see it only in terms of itself and because he cannot ultimately control it. (p. 159)

The world of **"The Gentleman from San Francisco"** is excitingly alive with the sights, sounds, and smells of the physical world, but the Gentleman himself is too calloused to respond to them. For him the world is made up only of endless rain, intolerable mud, and the foul smell of rotting fish—it is a world of seasickness, headaches, and irritation. It is a world from which he tries to insulate himself with "visits to lifelessly clean museums," with the sounds of rustling silks, and with the fragrant odors of perfumes and exquisitely prepared delicacies. (pp. 159-60)

More crucial than his insulation from nature is the Gentleman's isolation from the rest of humanity, from all those who find joy and suffering in this evil and beautiful world. . . . [The] Gentleman's life never intersects in any significant way with any other life. From the beginning until the end of his life (and even beyond when he lies alone in the hold of the ship), the Gentleman lives a lonely, detached, solitary existence. He remains contemptuously aloof from the urchins in the streets of the cities he visits, walks by servants . . . "as if not noticing them," and "coldly eyes" his fellow tourists, hiding himself from them behind a newspaper. (p. 160)

Yet there is in this isolation, as Bunin makes clear, something pathetically ironic: This hard man of facts, this paragon of materialistic self-sufficiency, needs love and the feeling of being important to other human beings, but can find both only in the projections of his fantasies and in the illusions of his self-deception. Having lost the sun, he must believe in the warmth of the electric light. So it is that he convinces himself of "the complete sincerity and goodwill of those who so painstakingly fed him [and] served him day and night, anticipating his slightest desire. . . . But the saddest line in the story is the first: "The Gentleman from San Francisco—neither at Naples nor on Capri could anyone recall his name. . . ."

In such an ego-bound world love cannot exist, except in a distorted and artificial form. (p. 161)

The frozen prison of insulation and isolation which modern man has erected about himself is, in Bunin's view, the result of his having become insensitive to the mystery of the universe, . . . and without which, communion with man and nature is impossible. In contrast to the piper's mystical response to the religious dimension of life, the Gentleman's life is completely devoid of any sense of something larger than himself: "there was not a mustard seed of what is called mysticism in his heart." . . . In such a world-view, life flattens out: all things are somehow like all other things. Over and over in the story Bunin employs what might be called the ironic catalogue—a coordinate grouping of unequals to indicate how the purely naturalistic view is cursed with the inability to distinguish among the levels of reality. . . . (pp. 161-62)

Even though the *sense* of mystery has evaporated from life, modern man, ultimately, has no defence against the mystery itself. Whirl as he will "amid the splendor of lights, silks, diamonds, and bare feminine shoulders," down below him, in the maw of the ship, in a tarred soda-water box, is the decaying flesh of the Gentleman from San Francisco. An intimate sense of death, such as the pipers have, makes life richer, more poignantly felt; but for the Gentleman and those who dance upon his grave, death, which they "most absolutely refuse to believe in," can come only as a meaningless, unreasonable blow from out of nowhere. For them it can only be a period put at the end of a sentence that has neither sound nor fury nor signifies anything. (p. 163)

Seymour L. Gross, "Nature, Man, and God in Bunin's 'The Gentleman from San Francisco'," in Modern Fiction Studies *(© 1960 by Purdue Research Foundation, West Lafayette, Indiana 47907, U.S.A.), Vol. VI, No. 2, Summer, 1960, pp. 153-63.*

HUGH NISSENSON   (essay date 1971)

[Ivan Bunin] is perhaps best known in this country for **"The Gentleman From San Francisco."** It's curious to realize that **"Velga,"** written for children and unencumbered by ideology, is a much greater story.

It's a fable: a legendary explanation of the cry of the sea gull. It derives from folk lore; a record of prehistory, recapitulated in the development of every child, when shapes do not hold, and humans and animals exchange identities. In that universe, nothing seems sure—neither life nor love. Velga is a young girl who lives near a fishing village on the northern sea. . . . She is in love with the fisherman, Irald, but he loves her sister, Sneggar. . . .

Irald is lost in a storm. The frantic Velga consults a soothsayer who tells her, "You will spend two days and two nights in anguish and fear on the sea. . . . When you try to set foot on the island where Irald is languishing, you will turn into a sea gull. And he will not know that you died for him." Velga goes to save him, and the prophecy is fulfilled.

Thus, Bunin dramatized that tragic moment in the evolution of human consciousness when murderous hostility is internalized and transfigured into joyous self-sacrifice. In doing so, he created a masterpiece.

Hugh Nissenson, "For Young Readers: 'Velga'," in The New York Times Book Review *(© 1971 by The*

New York Times Company; reprinted by permission),
January 31, 1971, p. 26.

RICHARD N. PORTER (essay date 1977)

There was no writer for whom Bunin had greater affection than for Chekhov; and despite Bunin's denial there was no writer from whom he seems to have profited more. Bunin's narrative technique is much like Chekhov's; some of their stories might almost have been written by either one of them. There are, however, important differences between the writers, especially in theme. Chekhov's "The Lady with the Dog" and Bunin's **"A Sunstroke"** have much in common, are frequently mentioned in connection with each other, and lend themselves to comparison. By discerning what features of the stories are alike and unlike one can learn much about the overall similarities and differences of the authors. (p. 51)

In both stories, a man of the world meets an attractive young married woman who happens to be vacationing alone. In both stories, he seduces her easily. In both stories, the man enjoys himself but does not expect the affair to last and is relieved when the woman goes. In both stories, the man surprises himself by missing the woman intensely and discovers that he has experienced something new, that he has never before felt so strongly about a woman. In both stories, the emphasis is on the reaction to the affair rather than on the affair itself.

In an article on Chekhov's place in the development of Russian literature, Dmitrij Tschižewskij suggests that much of Chekhov's work was poorly received by some Russian critics because they were evaluating him as a realist whereas actually he was a literary impressionist. (p. 52)

Whether or not one wishes to call Chekhov an impressionist, his work does differ from that of many Russian realists in that it favors the nuance and discrete detail over clarity of outline and prefers to suggest themes rather than to state them. The same can be said of Bunin. In his writing generally and in **"A Sunstroke"** in particular, impressionistic features stand out even more than in Chekhov. Bunin makes little effort to develop a plot as such and has the ability, as Struve says, "to create a story out of nothing" [see excerpt above]. As in **"A Sunstroke,"** he often declines to give his characters names, and one knows little about them. He cultivates a vagueness of outline and concentrates on a few poignant or lyric moments. Although his early prose shows the influence of Gorky and the Znanie circle and deals in part with social issues, his approach to these issues is more universal than it is partisan. In his émigré period, Bunin dropped all topical references, treated various aspects of love, and suggested his themes by nuance and detail. In economy and the emphasis of a few poignant moments, **"A Sunstroke"** is more typical of Chekhov than is "The Lady with the Dog." (pp. 52-3)

Despite the similarities of **"A Sunstroke"** and "The Lady with the Dog," they are not entirely alike. The most striking differences are the greater concentration of the Bunin story, its strict focus on the man's reaction, and its termination of the affair after a single night. The stories are also proportioned differently. "The Lady with the Dog" is sixteen pages long: the first half is set in the Crimea, the second half in Moscow and S. **"A Sunstroke"** is eight pages long; but within the first two pages the young woman has gone, and she does not reappear. The stories are constructed differently for good reasons. To some extent, Chekhov and Bunin are talking about the same thing; to some extent, they are not. (p. 53)

In a key passage [in "The Lady with the Dog"], Gurov observes that everything that really matters in his life must be kept hidden from the world, and everything that does not matter goes on in the open. Our habit of keeping important things secret is an aspect of isolation, a theme that runs through all Chekhov's work. In "The Lady with the Dog," the theme has a double application. Gurov and Anna are not really in touch with each other, except in a physical sense, and are essentially isolated. And their affair, which has come to matter to both of them for different reasons, must be kept secret from the world, must be isolated. Chekhov is saying again that no one really knows what goes on within anyone else. Ultimately, we are all set apart from one another, out of touch about things that matter.

Unlike Chekhov in "The Lady with the Dog," Bunin does not bother in **"A Sunstroke"** to motivate his characters psychologically. When the story begins, his lovers are already attracted to each other; and later they are willing to ascribe their attraction to a kind of sunstroke, an appropriate figure that involves, like their affair, surprise, heat, and prostration. Although we read only a few lines of what the young woman has to say, she appears vivacious enough. Apparently, the two lovers are in fine harmony on their single night together, not restrained as they might have been in a story by Chekhov. Isolation is not the problem in **"A Sunstroke."** What bothers the lieutenant is that he cannot have the young woman back, not that he could not get across his feelings to her or that he cannot tell others about his emotion. Bunin is concerned with a different theme, that of transience, and it is in theme that his story mainly differs from Chekhov's.

Most commentators on Bunin's later work have noted that in his stories love does not go on for long. As a rule, something soon comes between his lovers. Perhaps one of them dies. The joy of love is brief; the regret that follows is keen. Insofar as both Gurov and the young lieutenant originally underestimate the importance of their affair, the themes of their stories are alike. In Chekhov, however, the theme of their transience is subordinate to the theme of isolation. In Bunin it is everything.

Transience is what chiefly occupies Bunin, especially in his émigré work. The two most conspicuous results of transience are separation and death, and these subjects engage him almost exclusively after he has passed through his Gorky phase. For that matter, transience and transition are at least subthemes of works such as *The Village* and *Dry Valley*. **"A Sunstroke"** is devoted entirely to the effect of transience on love. The affair does not begin to take on importance for the lieutenant until he realizes that it is over. . . . In what sense does he feel that he has aged ten years once he is back on the boat? Obviously, he is emotionally drained; but he has also made the sad discovery that value and loss are inextricably connected, that one cares most for what cannot be recovered. The realization brings on despair.

Bunin has been accused of exhausting the subject of love and loss and of repeating himself, especially in the collection *Dark Paths*. Whether or not one agrees is largely a matter of taste and of how one likes Bunin's kind of writing. At any rate, for an author whose theme is transience, love is a convenient subject. Nothing else, besides death, elicits such strong emotions as love; and love is a more versatile subject than death since one can also deal with the aftermath of love. (pp. 55-6)

Richard N. Porter, "Bunin's 'A Sunstroke' and Chekhov's 'The Lady with the Dog'," in South Atlantic Bulletin *(copyright © 1977 by South Atlantic*

*Modern Language Association), Vol. XLII, No. 4, November, 1977, pp. 51-6.**

JAMES B. WOODWARD   (essay date 1980)

Bunin's stories of the twenties not only offer further evidence of the remarkable inspirational power of his distinctive approach to the theme of love; they also confirm that in emigration his art continued to develop. The same comment may justifiably be made on his stories of the next two decades. The theme of love continues to predominate, and no major change may be detected in the principal ingredients of his tales, but the spirit of experimentation continues to reveal itself in this last period in an intensified pursuit of brevity. The beginning of this final stage in the evolution of his art is marked by the cycle of forty-one "miniatures" entitled **Short Tales** that he wrote in 1930. Varying in length from a few lines to three pages, they reflect a common aesthetic purpose: to achieve an indissoluble fusion of form and meaning in a multifaceted revelation of the mystery of life and human nature. As usual, meaning is primarily conveyed in these tales not by sequential or cumulative description, but by the diffuse reverberations that are triggered off by the relation of the parts to the whole—by the galvanizing effect on the whole of individual words, phrases, or details. The innovation is the increased power of these reverberations that results from the extreme compression.

The method is clearly illustrated by **"The Eve"**, which consists of two short paragraphs and a one-sentence coda. The setting is urban, and the vantage point of the narrator is that of a passenger in a cab on its way to the local station. The first paragraph lists the sights that catch his eye on the journey. . . . In the second paragraph attention is switched to the interior of the train boarded by the narrator—to the broad shoulders, cropped hair, gold spectacles, and evident self-confidence of a traveler in the same compartment and to the array of handsome suitcases he is constantly checking. The final sentence reads: "But it was already the autumn of 1916." . . . The effect of this statement is to prompt a reassessment of every detail—not only of the contrast between the bourgeois and the doglike tramp [observed from the cab] but also of the [peasants'] "terrible boots" that are implicitly transformed into potential instruments of social change.

In this tale, therefore, the final statement retroactively fuses a succession of disparate details into a coherent, meaningful whole, and this procedure is the one most commonly adopted in the cycle. Occasionally, however, the pattern is reversed. A single example will suffice—**"The Calf's Head"**, which ends with a description of the splitting of a calf's head by a butcher's chopper. There is no direct comment on the act. It acquires its force and meaning solely from its juxtaposition with the preceding reactions to the butcher's shop and its contents of a mother and child whose dinners the head will eventually provide—from the contrast between the child's awe and wonder at the sight of the suspended carcasses and the mother's single-minded devotion to haranguing the butcher. Implicitly apprehended from these two contrasting viewpoints, the mutilation of the head is suggestive, on the one hand, of the horror and sensuous delight with which man is "naturally" accustomed to react to the primitive brutality of life and, on the other, of the weakening of man's sentient responsiveness to the wonder of existence that comes to him with "maturity". . . . The contrast between the implied reactions highlights the degeneracy of modern man.

The impression conveyed by the **Short Tales** is that they were conceived as a series of experiments in which Bunin sought to test the expressive potentialities of the narrative technique he had evolved over the previous two decades. More particularly, in the context of the development of his art, they may be seen as a preparation for his last volume of stories, **Dark Avenues** [**Tyomnyye allei**] in which the same pursuit of brevity is repeatedly in evidence. (pp. 207-09)

The theme of the volume is briefly summarized in Bunin's own reference to it as "a book about love." Since only one of the forty tales—**"Vengeance"** ["**Mest**"] . . .—has an ending that can positively be termed happy, it might perhaps be thought that "a book about tragic love," as suggested by the epithet in the title, would be a more fitting description. The qualification, however, would not only be inappropriate; it would be seriously misleading, for love in these tales is almost invariably a source of joy, an initiation into an unsuspected intensity of experience that transforms all preconceived notions of life and its meaning. "Is there really such a thing as unhappy love?" asks the heroine of **"Natalie"** . . . and almost every tale prompts a negative reply. The recurrent source of tragedy is not love but life as Bunin conceived it, and "a book about life" would perhaps be the most apt definition of the volume. Love ends tragically because the life of man is itself tragic—such is the repeated implication of these unusual stories in which Bunin's tendency to absolve his characters of all responsibility for the motivation of events is displayed more starkly than ever before.

The story **"In Paris"** . . . , for example, portrays two lonely, middle-aged Russian émigrés who meet in a Paris restaurant—a former general and a waitress. They arrange to meet, go to the cinema, and after making love in his apartment decide to live together. Both are rejuvenated by the relationship. "I feel," exclaims the general, "as if I were twenty years old." . . . The next short paragraph reads: "On the third day of Easter he died in a carriage of an underground train. While reading a newspaper he suddenly threw back his head against the back of the seat and rolled his eyes." . . . The reader is given no warning of this climax. It is totally unprepared by the preceding development of the tale, and in this respect it differs sharply from the climax of **"The Gentleman from San Francisco."** Death in this context does not denote the confrontation of a degenerate with reality; it is simply a stark manifestation of the blind, indiscriminate cruelty of life, just as the chance meeting in the restaurant is a manifestation of its indiscriminate beneficence.

"In Paris" is an exceptional work in the cycle only in the sense that it is unequivocally set in the "present"—in the Paris of the Russian émigrés. In general, the "present" is avoided by Bunin, and the reason has already been suggested. Since his theme imposed no constraints of time and place, it was natural that he should pluck his characters and settings from the land and period that had never ceased to dominate his thoughts. In a remarkable variety of prerevolutionary settings—the houses of provincial gentry, the smallholdings of peasants, metropolitan hotels and provincial inns, Volga steamers, the bohemian quarter of Odessa—the same kind of drama is reenacted by an equally remarkable variety of prerevolutionary character types. In almost every story we encounter the same sequence of ecstatic joy and sudden disaster, the same spectacle of human dependence on the whims of fate, and again the punished are usually innocent of all sin. And it is noticeable that even when guilt does exist, the catastrophe that follows is completely unrelated to it.

The point is illustrated by **"Natalie,"** the hero of which, Meshchersky, bears a certain superficial resemblance, as M. Iof'yev has observed, to Sanin in Turgenev's *Spring Waters* [*Veshniye vody*]. . . . Though deeply in love with Natalie, Meshchersky allows himself to be seduced by the charms of his cousin Sonya and is ultimately caught with her by Natalie in a compromising situation. But the heroine's indignant departure does not mark the end of the story. Had it done so, the entire emphasis would have fallen, as it does in Turgenev's tale, on the hero's weakness of will and personal responsibility for the course of events. The story continues, in fact, for another twelve pages, in which hero and heroine, after having been parted for three years, are finally brought together again and Meshchersky's sins are forgiven. Yet no sooner have they declared their undying love for one another than the story ends with the cold, factual statement: "In December she died in premature childbirth on Lake Geneva". . . . Thus a dénouement that would have been fully motivated is replaced by one that is simply appended, and it is precisely this lack of motivation, which is Bunin's aesthetic correlative of irremediable human impotence, that strikes the note of horror.

The stories of **Dark Avenues** resemble Bunin's love stories of the twenties in many obvious respects. It is already apparent that love is again repeatedly depicted as a blinding "flash," as a kind of "sunstroke" yielding to sudden and agonizing "eclipse." Again the heroines are usually seen through the eyes of the heroes, and the latter generally retain the ability to articulate their emotions that differentiates Bunin's lovers of the twenties from their prerevolutionary predecessors. It is equally clear, however, that in these later stories the contrasts are dramatically sharpened, and it is here perhaps that the effects of his experiments in the **Short Tales** are most noticeable. The psychological dramas of "rebels" now recede from view to be replaced by man's wholly conscious and uncomprehending experience of life's polar extremes, the heights of bliss and the depths of despair; the middle ground between the extremes is now completely excluded. The characters, who are often nameless, seem to have no existence outside their pursuit of love and the relationships that reward their efforts. . . . Prised from the routine of their normal lives, the heroes of these tales exist only to experience the most fundamental contrasts of the human condition as magnified in the experience of love.

The concentration of attention on these critical experiences is most commonly effected with the aid of a more extensive use than ever before of the simple expedient that had served Bunin so well in the past—the motif of travel. With few exceptions, the heroes of these stories are portrayed in motion. . . . The common feature of almost all Bunin's protagonists is that their contact with the relatively stable and predictable reality of their individual private worlds is temporarily severed, and their dependence on the vagaries of fate is correspondingly enhanced. Regardless of differences of personality and temperament, they are transformed by the very situations in which they find or place themselves into helpless recipients of life's blessings and blows.

The motif of travel, therefore, enables Bunin to eliminate everything that is irrelevant to his central concern. His heroes simply travel, love, and die or suffer torment. Almost all of them complete the same three-stage course. Yet despite the repetitiveness, even those who are left nameless are endowed with a distinct, recognizable identity, for the element of generalization inherent in the repetitive plot does not produce a schematic type of narrative in which everything is pared down to an algebraic transparency. On the contrary, all the familiar elements of Bunin's mature narrative technique are continually in evidence—not least his habit of placing his heroes in settings that veritably bombard their senses with the most varied stimuli and the superficially digressive but subtly suggestive style of writing in which his poetic genius had always most brilliantly displayed itself. (pp. 213-14)

The story in the cycle that is perhaps most illustrative of this "extravagance" is **"Rusya"** which, although it is a third-person narrative, consists mainly of the hero's recollections of a romantic episode that occurred in his youth. His memory is suddenly jolted when the train on which he is traveling with his wife stops at a small country station not far from the house where the episode took place during his service there as a young tutor. The temporal distance thus established between the time of narration and the events of the narrative determines and motivates the distinctive features of the work's style, in particular, the combination of vague, "poetic" impressions and individual striking details that have embedded themselves in the narrator's memory.

Through the mists of time the setting of his romance with Rusya, his pupil's sister, emerges in his recollections as a green, hot, steamy, almost tropical locality situated near a swamp. Introduced from the very beginning by a reference to the "damp smell of a swamp" that enters the train's windows . . . , the setting plainly alludes to the heat of passion and evokes the conception of love as a fever that takes complete possession of body and soul. The atmosphere created by the proximity of the swamp is sustained throughout the story by colorful descriptions of the ceaseless, seething activity of nature and by the repetition of a small number of individual concrete details that acquire the force of motifs. . . . The explanation of the "extravagance," in short, is apparent almost from the outset. Dispensing with explicit statements, Bunin contrives to create simply by means of repetition and accumulation the atmosphere of tension between the lovers and their environment that augurs the outcome, and, as the narrative unfolds, the active participation of nature in the drama is progressively intensified, finally expressing itself in the irruption into the house of a sinister black cock at the precise moment when the hero and heroine are enjoying their first embrace. . . . In this tale nature as a whole appears to be endowed with a malicious intelligence and almost to be in league with Rusya's mother, who savagely brings the romance to an end.

It should be added, however, that the sense of foreboding is created not only by the extravagant descriptions of nature. . . . [In] **"Light Breathing"** Bunin achieved a similar effect by a different means—by introducing, through the reference to the schoolboy Shenshin, the suggestion of an ending that, though tragic, contrasts with the actual ending. The same device is used in **"Rusya."** When the hero's wife asks him early in the tale why he did not marry the girl, he replies solemnly: "Well, because I shot myself and she stabbed herself with a dagger." . . . The jest makes little impression, but it clearly refers to a dénouement in which the affair may well have culminated. In **"Light Breathing"** the actual dénouement is even more tragic than the "decoy"; the fact that in **"Rusya"** the reverse is the case in no way diminishes the effectiveness of the device as a means of reinforcing the atmosphere that pervades the work. (pp. 215-17)

In this kind of work the form of the narrator's tale is obviously determined by his personal involvement in the events, and the elements of the tale are ordered and the accents placed in accordance with his emotional responses to each recollected experience. At the same time, it is clear that the pace at which the narrative flows may itself be determined by his reactions and thus add substantially to our understanding of his state of mind. It is difficult to think of any Russian writer who has been more attentive than Bunin to the opportunities afforded by the first-person narrative form for oblique psychological characterization of this kind, and the alternations of "economy" and "extravagance" in the tales of *Dark Avenues* may frequently be attributed to the use he makes of them. (p. 218)

James B. Woodward, "The Last Volume," in his Ivan Bunin: A Study of His Fiction *(© 1980 by The University of North Carolina Press), University of North Carolina Press, 1980, pp. 207-26.*

JULIAN W. CONNOLLY (essay date 1981)

Although Ivan Bunin's critics are nearly unanimous in their appreciation of his rich, evocative language and his keen powers of observation, there has been less agreement over the *depth* of his work; indeed, one critic, Fedor Stepun, has stated that Bunin's work completely lacks "organizing ideas." Recent critics have attempted to counter this opinion by pointing to certain broad, philosophical trends in Bunin's prose, but a comprehensive analysis of his complex world-view has yet to appear.

Of the many philosophical currents that can be identified in Bunin's writings, one of the most intriguing is the influence of Buddhism, particularly in the 1910s and 1920. Several critics have noted Bunin's interest in the culture and philosophy of Buddhism, but no one has yet examined it in detail, despite the fact that it was not just a passing phase, but rather a serious process of discovery and assimilation that had a lasting influence on his work and thought. . . .

One can point to several factors that perhaps account for Bunin's striking receptivity to Buddhism. All his writings from such early sketches as **"Nakhutore"** (**"On the Farm"** . . .) down to the late stories of *Temnye allei* (*Dark Avenues* . . .) are concerned with the evanescence of earthly life and its pleasures. Significantly, the teachings of Buddhism address this very issue and offer an explanation of how the love of life causes suffering. Certain of the ideals of self-conduct espoused by Buddhism—humility, simplicity, self-effacement, and patient faith—are depicted as virtues in Bunin's work, too. . . . (p. 11)

Bunin's most direct contact with Buddhist culture occurred during his visit to Ceylon in March 1911. The two-week voyage, as recorded in the sketch **"Vody mnogie"** (**"Many Waters"**), was for Bunin a time of concentrated reflection on life and the meaning of existence. The narrator of **"Many Waters"** cannot reconcile the profound feelings of joy he experiences when he contemplates the beauty of this world with the anguish he feels at the transience of all that is "so close, accustomed, and dear." (p. 12)

The problem of man's attachment to life raised by Bunin in **"Many Waters"** is one of the central issues in Buddhist philosophy. According to the "Four Noble Truths," which were revealed by the Buddha in his first sermon after attaining enlightenment, all human pain is the result of some kind of desire—desire for love, wealth, immortality, etc. Since such desires can never be realized or fulfilled permanently, frustration

and pain inevitably arise within those who experience them. The only way to end suffering, then, is to renounce desire itself, not merely the desire for fame, fortune, or love, but ultimately the desire to live as well. Only in this way can one find peace.

The very simplicity of this conception perhaps helped to crystallize Bunin's own vague reflections on the pain that arises from one's love of life. In a series of short stories beginning with **"Brothers,"** Bunin examines the problem of human desire and demonstrates that man's pursuit of wealth and pleasure leads only to loss, frustration, and suffering.

Most critics have interpreted **"Brothers"** either as an exposé of colonialist exploitation or as a testament to "the absurdity" of life, giving insufficient attention to the explicit Buddhist elements in the tale: the epigraph to the story, "Look at the brothers killing each other. I wish to speak of grief," which is taken from an early Buddhist text, the Sutta-Nipāta; the quotations from the Buddha and his disciples; and the repeated references to the "Exalted One" and "Mara" (the Buddhist god who represents the temptations of earthly life). Yet these elements are essential for an understanding of the story. In broad terms, **"Brothers"** illustrates the vanity of human desire and the suffering that results from an attachment to the things of this world.

In the first part of the story Bunin depicts a young rickshaw driver in Colombo who discovers that his fiancée has become the mistress of a European steamship agent. Faced with the loss of the one thing that he holds dear in life, he purchases a poisonous snake and kills himself with its venom. In this story one may discern Bunin's misgivings about European imperialism, of course, but the story contains a more profound message. The rickshaw driver suffers not only from his exertions on behalf of his European masters, but also from his attachment to life and to love—and this second source of suffering is perhaps the greater. (pp. 13-14)

In the second part of **"Brothers"** Bunin records the reflections of the Englishman who had been the rickshaw driver's last passenger. He ascribes his dissatisfaction and boredom to the fact that he has lived a life of material pleasure and self-indulgence. He has come to realize that, unlike the Buddha, who understood the significance of the "Self" ("Lichnost") in the cosmos, "we exalt our Self above the heavens, we want to concentrate the entire world within it. . . ." . . .

This perception embraces the entire spectrum of human desire, from the rickshaw driver's simple aspirations to the Englishman's hedonism. Both kinds of desire reflect the individual's attempt to possess happiness; the only difference is one of degree. Of course, as the Four Noble Truths indicate, all such attempts are doomed, and neither the rickshaw driver nor the Englishman can succeed in his quest. Thus these two men, so different in station and background, are indeed "brothers." Bunin's title, which had at first seemed ironic given the external relationship between the two men, points to a profound and meaningful kinship between them. (p. 15)

In place of self-assertion Buddhism advocates self-denial and the renunciation of desire. Humility and simplicity had long been virtues in Bunin's work, but perhaps his study of Buddhism gave fresh impetus to this ideal. In 1919 he wrote the short sketch **"Gotami,"** in which he depicts a woman who surrenders to the will of others in preparation for the great sorrows that "would direct her onto the one true path, into the milieu of the Brotherhood of the Yellow Vestments." . . . The narrator continues, "Blessed are they who are humble in their hearts, they who have dissolved the Chain. In an abode of great joy do we live, we who love nothing in this world and who are like a bird, which carries with itself only its wings." . . . Here, Bunin's narrator himself seems to have heeded the call to renounce the world and its temptations. The entire sketch has a strong Eastern flavour, not only in the setting—the foothills of the Himalayas—but also in the imagery and in the heroine's name, which is taken from that of the Buddha's clan.

In **"Brothers"** and **"Gotami"** Bunin depicted the two poles of human behaviour discussed in the teachings of Buddhism. At one end is the futile life of striving and desire characteristic of the majority of men, and at the other the life of renunciation and submission that is practised by only a few. Having examined both types in isolation, Bunin now became interested in the latent tension *between* the two. In his fiction of the early and mid-1920s he began to explore the destinies of those individuals who recognize the futility of desire and yet continue to feel its seductive power. Gradually, this conflict becomes a major thematic centre in his work, and he constructs around it a complex network of ideas and images drawn from both Buddhist and Western thought. (p. 16)

One of the narrator's central concerns is to identify and characterize a certain rare group of individuals (among whom he numbers himself), who are capable of feeling extraordinary empathy with the experiences of peoples from other lands and other times. These remarkable individuals find such a gift both a blessing and a curse: on the one hand their enjoyment of the diversity of life is heightened; on the other they remain painfully aware of its futility. (pp. 17-18)

The inner conflict that Bunin depicts in theoretical terms in **"Night"** is transformed in such works as **"Delo korneta Elagina"** (**"The Elagin Affair"** . . .) into a matter of life and death. The heroine of this story, Mariia Sosnovskaia, suffers clearly from a similar psychological split. Sosnovskaia loves life and its pleasures, even though she knows that her longing for love and happiness cannot be fulfilled. (p. 18)

"The Elagin Affair" illustrates the Buddhist concept of the contradiction between one's desires for the pleasures of life and one's recognition of their futility, even though it contains no direct reference to Buddhism. In this story, as in most of his later work, Bunin can dispense with the exotic imagery and settings of his more overtly "Buddhist" works because he has absorbed the teachings of Buddhism and incorporated them in his own artistic vision. (p. 19)

Julian W. Connolly, "Desire and Renunciation: Buddhist Elements in the Prose of Ivan Bunin," in Canadian Slavonic Papers *(copyright © 1981 by Canadian Slavonic Papers), Vol. XXIII, No. 1, March, 1981, pp. 11-20.*

ADDITIONAL BIBLIOGRAPHY

Bedford, C. H. "The Fulfilment of Ivan Bunin." *Canadian Slavonic Papers* 1 (1956): 31-44.
> An examination of *The Well of Days* which finds that it presents an accurate picture of provincial Russia while illuminating the early life and thought of Bunin himself.

Colin, Andrew Guershoon. "Ivan Bunin in Retrospect." *The Slavonic and East European Review* XXXIV, No. 82 (December 1955): 156-73.
> A biographical and critical essay, which discusses Bunin as a classical Russian author in the tradition of Lermontov, Pushkin, and Alexey Tolstoy.

Croisé, Jacques. "Ivan Bunin: 1870-1953." *The Russian Review* 13, No. 2 (April 1954): 146-51.
> Presents the essence of Bunin's beliefs and outlook.

Kryzytski, Serge. *The Works of Ivan Bunin.* Slavistic Printings and Reprintings, edited by C. H. van Schooneveld, vol. 101. The Hague, Paris: Mouton, 1971, 283 p.
> An intensive study of Bunin's canon.

Lavrin, Janko. "Bunin and Kuprin." In his *A Panorama of Russian Literature,* pp. 207-13. London: University of London Press, 1973.*
> A short overview of Bunin's work.

Nabokov, Vladimir. "Chapter XIV." In his *Conclusive Evidence: A Memoir,* pp. 204-23. New York: Harper & Brothers, Publishers, 1951.*
> Impressions of Bunin drawn from memories of a conversation at a Paris café. Nabokov claims always to have preferred Bunin's poetry to his prose.

Poggioli, Renato. "The Decadents." In his *The Poets of Russia:* 1890-1930, pp. 89-115. Cambridge: Harvard University Press, 1960.*
> A brief biographical and critical essay, encapsulating much of Poggioli's longer and earlier work, "The Art of Ivan Bunin." [See excerpt in entry above.]

Richards, D. J. "Memory and Time Past: A Theme in the Works of Ivan Bunin." *Forum for Modern Language Studies* VII, No. 2 (April 1971): 158-69.
> Examines the importance of the past to Bunin's vision of life.

Strelsky, Nikander. "Bunin: Eclectic of the Future." *The South Atlantic Quarterly* XXV, No. 3 (July 1936): 273-83.
> Scrutinizes Bunin's work in light of his winning the Nobel Prize in literature.

James Branch Cabell

1879-1958

(Also wrote under the name Branch Cabell) American novelist, short story writer, critic, essayist, autobiographer, and dramatist.

Cabell's work belongs to a tradition of fantasy literature that includes Spenser's *The Faerie Queene* and Swift's *Gulliver's Travels*. His most enduring achievement is *The Biography of the Life of Manuel*, a twenty-volume opus which combines novels, novellas, short stories, and criticism. This fictional epic chronicles the fortunes of Manuel and his descendants from medieval France to twentieth-century Virginia, blending mythical lands and beings with historical reality. The "biography" extends beyond the life of its initial hero who, as is explained in *The High Place*, remains "here upon earth to animate the bodies of his children and of their children after them." Manuel is at once an individual and the symbol of a family of characters who evolve according to Cabell's philosophy of human life.

Born to a distinguished Richmond, Virginia, family, Cabell absorbed Southern traditions and values. This heritage contributes to his fiction its codes of chivalry and woman-worship, which are alternately exalted and violated. Cabell graduated from the College of William and Mary, where as an upperclassman he taught French and Greek, later working for newspapers in New York and Richmond. An enthusiasm for genealogy led him to publish several books on his family background, and this interest is reflected in the genealogical design of *The Biography of Manuel*.

Beyond Life, the book written to introduce the *Biography*, outlines the literary and philosophic concepts which serve as its foundation. Cabell adhered to a special definition of romance, one that allowed him to portray glorified adventures beyond mundane reality without falsifying what he saw as the harsh truths of existence: the suffering of life, the emptiness of death, and a permanent alienation at the core of even the most intimate human relations. For Cabell the romantic view of life meant following a system of "dynamic illusions," the codes of self-deception—such as reason, religion, or love—by which individuals and societies are sustained.

Cabell's romantic vision is a union of three basic attitudes toward life—the chivalric, the gallant, and the poetic, all of which are attempts to impose arbitrary values on an indifferent universe. Each work in the *Biography* is designed to dramatize one of these attitudes. The chivalric attitude considers life a trial of the individual: a contest in which certain ideals, including personal honor and public glory, must be valiantly won. This contest can be seen in the heroic quest of Manuel in *Figures of the Earth* and *The Silver Stallion*, with a particular chivalric aspect, that of woman-worship, developed in *Domnei*. The gallant attitude approaches life as a series of pleasures and excitements, a view exemplified by the protagonists of *The High Place* and *Jurgen*. In fact, the use of eroticism in *Jurgen* caused the book's suppression by vice authorities. More cynical than their chivalric predecessors, the heroes of the gallant novels search for fulfillment of their most extreme desires but end with a disillusioning confrontation with reality. Finally,

Culver Pictures

the poetic attitude perceives life as material for artistic creation, the author-heroes of *Something about Eve* and *The Cream of the Jest* taking this path. This approach represents yet another scheme for introducing order and perfection into a chaotic world, seeking to harmonize it with human imagination.

The works after the *Biography* are divided between fiction and nonfiction, with an occasional mixture of the two, as in *These Restless Heads*. Cabell's most important later criticism appears in *Some of Us*, a defense of several contemporary writers—including Elinor Wylie, Ellen Glasgow, and Joseph Hergesheimer—against the trend of neo-humanist criticism which demanded that art deal with moral and social issues. Regarded as the best of the later fiction is the trilogy *Smirt, Smith, Smire*, dreamworld narratives which critics have often compared to Joyce's *Finnegans Wake*.

Critical reception of Cabell has been unusually erratic. His works have inspired extremes of derogation and praise, from Oscar Cargill's calling him "the most tedious person who has achieved high repute as a *literatus* in America," to Vernon L. Parrington's pronouncement that "Mr. Cabell is creating great literature." Cabell's work is said to epitomize the sophisticated cynicism of the 1920s, and his popularity was at its height during that era, declining drastically in the 1930s. Since that time Cabell's works have continued to generate interest among a select audience of admirers, as is evidenced in the pages of *Kalki* and *The Cabellian*, journals devoted to him. Combining extremes of lavish romance and degraded reality, idealistic fantasy and jaded disillusionment, Cabell is one of the outstanding oddities in American fiction.

(See also *Dictionary of Literary Biography*, Vol. 9: *American Novelists, 1910-1945.*)

PRINCIPAL WORKS

The Eagle's Shadow   (novel)   1904
The Line of Love   (short stories)   1905
Gallantry   (short stories)   1907
Chivalry   (short stories)   1909
The Cords of Vanity   (novel)   1909
*The Soul of Melicent***   (novel)   1913
The Rivet in Grandfather's Neck   (novel)   1915
The Certain Hour   (short stories)   1916
From the Hidden Way   (poetry)   1916
The Cream of the Jest   (novel)   1917
Beyond Life   (criticism)   1919
Jurgen   (novel)   1919
Figures of Earth   (novel)   1921
The High Place   (novel)   1923
Straws and Prayer-Books   (criticism)   1924
The Music from Behind the Moon   (novella)   1926
The Silver Stallion   (novel)   1926
Something about Eve   (novel)   1927
The White Robe   (novella)   1928
The Way of Ecben   (novella)   1929
Some of Us   (criticism)   1930
These Restless Heads   (short stories and autobiography)   1932
Ladies and Gentleman   (fictional letters)   1934
Smirt   (novel)   1934
Smith   (novel)   1935
Smire   (novel)   1937
The King Was in His Counting House   (novel)   1938
Hamlet Had an Uncle   (novel)   1940
The First Gentleman of America   (novel)   1942; published in England as *The First American Gentleman*, 1942
The Devil's Own Dear Son   (novel)   1950
As I Remember It   (autobiography)   1955

*These volumes were published as *The Works of James Branch Cabell* in 1927-30; they are collectively referred to as *The Biography of the Life of Manuel.*

**This work was retitled *Domnei* in a revised edition published in 1920.

THE ATHENAEUM   (essay date 1904)

[In 'The Eagle's Shadow'] Mr. Cabell strives to attain ease and grace in that vein of light comedy of which Mr. Henry Harland is for the moment the most popular master, but the best that can be said for him is that he does not fail very egregiously. He has occasionally happy turns of phrase, his epigrams are now and then tolerable, and his dialogue is, on the whole, amusing. But his attempts at elegance are often rather awkward

and his familiarity inept, and the essence of a reader's enjoyment in writing of this kind is that he should feel secure of the author's good taste and lightness of touch. The narrative itself, in spite of an infusion of exciting incident, is of course subordinate to the manner of narration; we know from the beginning that merit and wealth, each being much in love with the other, are bound to come together eventually, and our curiosity as to how this is to be accomplished is never very keen. The plot, however, is entertainingly enough developed, and there is an air of good spirits about the whole thing that is not without attraction. The atmosphere is distinctly American.

> "New Novels: 'The Eagle's Shadow'," *in* The Athenaeum, *No. 4025, December 17, 1904, p. 838.*

JAMES BRANCH CABELL   (essay date 1919)

[It] was a year ago last March that I temporarily put aside my *Something about Eve* to write for Mencken the short story he requested and seemed to merit. I evolved then very much the same "**Some Ladies and Jurgen**" in imagination as eventually appeared in the *Smart Set:* wherein the devil offers Jurgen the three symbolic ladies Guenevere and Cleopatra and Helen, and the poet prefers, upon the whole, his prosaic wife. But as I wrote it out, I scented possibilities—how much more effective, for instance, it would be if Jurgen had previously known and loved and lost these women. Of course, that meant, to me, a dizain, with four tales already suggested: it would be out of space and time, of necessity, if Jurgen were to encounter these three who lived centuries apart. So, with my story still unwritten, I begin to plan the dizain, of ten short stories to be disposed of severally for much fine gold. Ah, but the Cleopatra episode! here I foresee myself heading straight for an imitation of *Aphrodite* and Louÿs' notion of life in Alexandria. Well, then, let us substitute the goddess herself in place of the Cleopatra who symbolizes her, and call the goddess—no, not Aphrodite, the Grecianisms must be reserved for the Helen part. I consider her other names, and am instantly captivated by the umlaut in Anaïtis. So my second heroine becomes Anaïtis, a moon goddess. But her lovers are solar legends— Why, to be sure, for does not Guenevere typify the spring, Anaïtis summer, and Helen in her Leukê avatar the autumn? I perceive that Jurgen is a solar legend, and inevitably spends the winter under-ground. There is the Hell episode postulated, then. So I make out my calendar, and find it 37 days short, since obviously the year must be rounded out. Where was Jurgen between 22 March and 30 April? The question answers itself, and I spy the chance to use that fine idea that has been in my mind for fifteen years or more, as to how Heaven was created.

I am getting on now, with my dizain lacking only three episodes—since the half-written magazine story has obviously split into an opening and an ending of a book. (That is, I thus far think it the ending.) And now I am wondering if there is not a chance at last for that other fine idea I could not ever find a place to work into—the going back to a definite moment in one's past—For what?—obviously for a woman, since Jurgen has by this time taken form as a person—What woman, though?—why, clearly the woman who in his youth represented the never quite attainable Helen. And she was Count Emmerich's second sister, whose existence I had postulated in *The Jest*, with the intention of using her in due time. I christen her Varvara, in general consonance with my Russian Koshchei, who I am beginning to perceive must be more than a mere devil if the book is to ascend—Yes, he must be the Demiurge, and God his creation—Then Koshchei must be rather stupid, and not be bothering himself about Jurgen at all. I need another supernatural agent, some one more near to purely human affairs, to direct Jurgen's wanderings. My mind being already on Russian mythology, and the regaining of a lost day being involved, the Léshy who control the days present themselves, and I select Sereda for Jurgen to wheedle out of, of course, one of the Wednesdays when he was young. Another episode.

But this Varvara (no, nobody will be certain as to the pronunciation of Varvara: call her Dorothy)—will disappoint him, a little anyhow, if he goes back to the actual girl. Really to go back, he must return to the girl as she seemed to him, and himself be young again—But the point is already in my mind that, while Jurgen is to keep the youth that would come back to him with the replevined Wednesday, so far as his body goes, his mind is to remain middle-aged. So I grope to the ironic scheme of letting him seem to his ideal girl as he actually is, and be to her unrecognizable—Then he must, somehow, get rid of his false youth before his interview with Koshchei in the cave: that makes me the tenth episode—No, I still lack the machinery for getting him to the Garden: a centaur appears the handiest method of combining transportation and conversation. (pp. 127-28)

That is about how the outline of the book came to me: and at this stage I went back to the *Smart Set* story and actually wrote it. Thereafter I set about writing my ten episodes (and found them resolutely determined not to be short stories, on any terms); and rewrote them; and put in here and there just anything which occurred to me, and changed this and altered that; and groped to that loathsome last chapter as the tale's inevitable ending. (p. 128)

> *James Branch Cabell, in an extract from his letter to Burton Rascoe, on August 10, 1919, in* Between Friends: Letters of James Branch Cabell and Others, *edited by Padriac Colum and Margaret Freeman Cabell (copyright 1962 by Harcourt Brace Jovanovich, Inc.; reprinted by permission of Margaret Freeman Cabell), Harcourt, 1962, pp. 127-28.*

CONRAD AIKEN   (essay date 1919)

[*Jurgen* is] a *roman de la vie cérébrale*—a novel to make one think of *Marius,* or *Sixtine,* or *A Night in the Luxembourg,* or *Penguin Island,* or Arthur Machen's *Hill of Dreams.* It is above all a novel to make one think of Anatole France, and of the monstrous debt that Mr. Cabell owes him. . . . To which, one might mischievously ask, does he owe the more—to Machen or to France? For Mr. Cabell has drawn heavily on both—on Machen for his *Beyond Life,* which is little more than an elaboration of *Hieroglyphics,* more weightily, but less charmingly written, and for portions of *The Cream of the Jest;* on France for other portions of *The Cream of the Jest* and for *Jurgen.* I do not mean to say that Mr. Cabell is a plagiarist; but it is obvious that he battens rather on literature than on life, and takes in consequence a hue therefrom. His favorite, almost his only protagonist, has always been the man of letters, and Mr. Cabell's sport has been the observation, half tender, half derisive, of this creature's antics in pursuit of the unattainable. His favorite setting has been the country and period of the troubadours. And his style has become, almost automatically, an affair of hollow elaborate punctilios—full of mock romanticisms, courtly rhetoric, mincing and somewhat fatiguing circumlocutions.

These tastes have combined in one or two instances to produce work of some distinction. *The Soul of Melicent,* one of Mr. Cabell's earlier novels, is delicious—so delicate a fusion of romance and extravaganza, so adroitly woven of ethical inversions, that one is perpetually in a pleasant state of uncertainty as to the author's intention. To *The Cream of the Jest,* also, one must pay one's respects—a well-elaborated study of schizophrenia, of the dual life of a man of letters, partly real, partly imaginary—and which is imaginary? . . . One drifts imperceptibly over the threshold. But in these, as in all of Mr. Cabell's work, one finds oneself at the end, in possession of a considerable sense of irritation. This is due partly to the aggressive monotony of the style, for one wearies, and rightly, of so much studied affectation, of these so often repeated dryly-ornate conventions of speech. But the style is not wholly the cause of one's irritation . . . it is rather itself merely a symptom of the cause, which underlies and is responsible for it, as it is responsible also for the choice of theme. This cause is Mr. Cabell's bitter-bright temperament, a temperament which compels him at the same time to seek the "romantic" and to disclaim it: he marries his illusions, as it were, only to divorce them, and what wedlock there is, is brief and bitter. Incapable of surrendering to his own fictions, he must perpetually put in the cynical comment, the dry curl of the lip, mortally afraid lest anyone catch him taking things too seriously. This might be a virtue in a philosopher, but in a novelist it is an ailment. Consequently, Mr. Cabell is forever touching things only to see them wither, a sight which, unhappily, his readers are thus doomed to share. To his readers, I am afraid, Mr. Cabell's recent work has too invidiously the flavor of Dead Sea fruit.

This is particularly true of *Jurgen.* As soon as one has foreseen the plan of *Jurgen,* one is *parti pris*—one cannot help sympathizing with an author who, in this era of the sciolistically psychological novel, of shallow realisms and valetudinarian introspections, undertakes a novel on wider premises and with the attempt, at least, of a wider view. But one's sympathies are sharply chilled. Mr. Cabell's ambition is, if the point be permissible, an acquired rather than a natural one, and while his curiosity is possibly adequate to the undertaking, his intellect, his emotivity, his tastes, are not. He has had, unhappily, a bad attack of Anatole France. His attempts at light irony are clumsy and obvious, his attempts at wit are for the most part little more than boyish *double-entendres* dealing with sex. *Jurgen* has its moments of charm, but in large measure it is merely a recital of the erotic exploits of its hero, each exploit precisely like the last, each reduced by the author to the lowest common denominators of animalism. Granted that Mr. Cabell wishes to show himself a cynic in this regard, to emphasize the motive power in human conduct of this impulse—a theme not wholly new—he has shown himself only the more, dealing with it thus, as lacking imagination and art. One perceives the force and adroitness of his curiosity, the wealth of his erudition on matters profane: if one were adolescent one might enjoy them. As it is, the book for all its ambitiousness comes very near to being repellent, no less for the pseudo-romantic smartness of the style than for its phosphorescent contents. It is, distinctly, a prize for the Freudians! . . . One hopes faintly that, having thus ingloriously purged himself, Mr. Cabell will turn to new work with a clearer temper. (pp. 146-48)

> *Conrad Aiken, "James Branch Cabell and Joseph Hergesheimer" (originally published as "Letters from America, II: Two American Novelists," in* The Athenaeum, *No. 4676, December 12, 1919), in his* Collected Criticism *(copyright © 1935, 1939, 1940, 1942, 1951, 1958 by Conrad Aiken; reprinted by permis-*

sion of Brandt & Brandt Literary Agents, Inc.), Oxford University Press, New York, 1968, pp. 143-48.*

HUGH WALPOLE (essay date 1920)

Let it be said at once that Cabell's art will always be a sign for hostilities. Not only will he remain, in all probability, forever alien to the general public, but he will also, I suspect, be to the end of time a cause for division among cultivated and experienced readers.

His style is also at once a battleground. It is the easiest thing in the world to denounce it as affected, perverse, unnatural, and forced. It would be at once an artificial style were it not entirely natural to the man. Anyone who reads the books in their chronological sequence will perceive the first diffident testing of it in such early works as **"Chivalry"** and **"Gallantry"**; then the acquiescence in it, as though the writer said to himself—"Well, this is what I am—I will rebel against it no longer"; and the final triumphant perfection of it in **"Beyond Life"** and **"Jurgen."** (p. 6)

In both **"Chivalry"** and **"Gallantry"** there is a note of irony far indeed from the innocent sentimentalities of his romantic competitors, but it is, as yet, irony very slightly enforced. **"Chivalry"** need not detain us. . . .

"Gallantry" is a more serious affair. (p. 7)

"Gallantry" is in its inception a string of stories about the Jacobean period in England and France. It has all the right furniture; the masculine heroine scorning the effeminate hero, the eavesdropping behind screens, the duel in the woods, the magnanimous man of iron, the flippant exquisite, the last moment's rescue. Cabell uses these with a delightful gusto, but they are old tricks, and some of them are allowed a too frequent repetition. Nevertheless, here for the first time some of the author's peculiar gifts are apparent. The stories are quite definitely independent, with the very slightest links connecting them, and yet, in these links and in the abundant and amusingly mock serious politics scattered about the pages, there is Cabell's first hint to the reader that he is building something more than a merely imposing erection. If the reader will follow all the stories in the volume in their given sequence, he will gradually perceive that a world of politics and permanent history is passing before him, and behind this world there is a deeper world still, a world that has no boundary of material time, a background against which the figures of the mythology of Greece and Rome and Egypt and the Middle Ages, of the eighteenth century and the twentieth, mingle with equal sight and equal blindness.

The two chief masculine figures of these tales, the Duke of Ormskirk and the dastardly Vanringham, demonstrate the first placing upon the stage of Cabell's two dominant actors. These figures are recurrent through all the later books, and I have heard it urged in adverse criticism that the author is monotonous in his use of them. I believe the exact opposite to be the truer judgment. The author, as is apparent in his later inclusion of all his novels under the single term "Biography," is engaged in the history of the human soul. His books, the reader gradually perceives, are simply varying chapters of the Wandering Jew. He may appear as Ormskirk or Vanringham, as Wycherley or Pope or Sheridan, as Jurgen or Falstaff, as the modern Charteris or Felix Kennaston; behind the ephemeral body the features of the longing, searching, questing soul are the same. There is here, as I think there has never so deliberately been in the work

of any single novelist before, the history of an eternal, ceaseless quest. (pp. 7-8)

Hugh Walpole, in his The Art of James Branch Cabell *(reprinted by permission of the Estate of Hugh Walpole), R. M. McBride & Co., 1920 (and reprinted as a chapter in* James Branch Cabell: Three Essays, *by Carl Van Doren, H. L. Mencken, and Hugh Walpole, Kennikat Press, 1967, pp. 3-16).*

VERNON LOUIS PARRINGTON (essay date 1921)

As whimsical as Bernard Shaw, as provocative as Chesterton, [James Branch Cabell] is more incomprehensible than either to all readers who do not choose to like what they have not always liked. Professing to be a romancer, and defending the glory of romance with inimitable witchery of phrase, he writes no romance that lovers of convention can understand. The lovely fabrics of his tales of Poictesme are all shimmer and sheen, woven of magic and veiling mysteries, instead of the correct taffeta and grosgrain; and the brilliant stuff of his tales of gallantry is fashioned of wit and poetry, instead of the customary wigs and sword play. . . . One needs to walk warily in dealing with Mr. Cabell, or the jest of which he is such a master will turn sardonically upon the critic. In all his thinking vague hinterlands lie behind the commonplace, cryptic meanings lurk behind the obvious; and the credulous, easy-going reader finds himself puzzled, and at last floundering quite hopelessly in a land of bogs and marsh-lights. And yet was ever another writer born to us Americans so insistent upon being understood? He has elaborated his views of life and art at length, and repeated them in successive volumes over nearly a score of years; and finally in what may have been a mood of sheer disgust at the stupidity of those who buy books, he reëlaborated his philosophy and wrote it out in good set terms within the covers of a single volume. *Beyond Life* is an essay altogether remarkable for its haunting beauty of phrase, its honest agnosticism, its brooding irony. It is enough to turn one cynic to consider that so noble a book should have called forth from a reputable gentleman, presumably of good taste and sound judgment, the comment that it "contains cheap and shallow pessimistic observations on human limitations."

That *Beyond Life* . . . , with other of Mr. Cabell's books, contains "observations on the limitations of human nature," is quite obvious; for Mr. Cabell deals in comedy, and what is to become of comedy if it shall not observe those limitations and laugh at them? That it is even pessimistic may likewise be argued with some plausibility; but to assert that it is cheap and shallow is preposterous. An inquisitive mind, deeply concerned with ultimate values, cannot be cheap and shallow. And yet the fault of such widespread misinterpretation may lie in part at Mr. Cabell's own doorstep. An inveterate jester, his sallies often carry implications far beyond the obvious; his strange whimsies spring from depths of thought and emotion beyond the understanding of the careless. His attitude towards life is an odd mixture of the modern and the medieval: there is a medieval simplicity and frankness, a naïve wonder at the mystery that underlies the common, an incorrigible idealism; and this medieval attitude is drenched in modern agnosticism. He passes easily from a broad Chaucerian humor that laughs frankly at the relations of men and women, to a mystical idealization of those relations; and the problem of reconciling the humor and the ideal becomes a serious business with him. He hates the cant and dishonesty of our *bourgeois* existence, and he refuses to take seriously the host of petty concerns that most of us are very serious about. If he were less the artist he would join the disaffected and turn to rend this foolish world; but the spirit of comedy saves him and he contents himself with a jest. But the Cabellian jest uncovers depths of meditation that reveal the philosopher and the poet. In his own large meaning of the word Mr. Cabell is an economist. He is greatly dissatisfied with the "futile body-wasting," which under the "dynamic illusion known as common sense" passes for life, and is concerned to discover what abiding increment a man may get from his body during its brief existence as an entity. His mind is haunted with a sense of realities that lie beneath the surface appearances, and that insist on trickling from his pen in strange comments. It is a careless reader who is deceived or put off the scent by his whimsical vocabulary, who insists on conventional meanings for words which Mr. Cabell chooses to use otherwise than conventional persons use them. Romance and realism—words with which he plays constantly and upon which he hangs his philosophy—do not signify the spurious romance of childish minds, or the shoddy realism of practical minds. If one must insist upon translating his vocabulary into ordinary terms, let us understand that to Mr. Cabell romance and realism mean idealism and conventionalism; and to the profound distinction between these two attitudes towards life, he dedicates his work. (pp. 335-37)

[Mr. Cabell's work] arrives at tolerance for all human shortcomings; it embraces high and low in its sympathies; it achieves urbanity as a final goal. It is the stuff of which great literature is made. And Mr. Cabell is creating great literature. A self-reliant intellectual, rich in the spoils of all literatures, one of the great masters of English prose, the supreme comic spirit thus far granted us, he stands apart from the throng of lesser American novelists, as Mark Twain stood apart, individual and incomparable. (p. 345)

> *Vernon Louis Parrington, "The Incomparable Mr. Cabell" (originally published under a different title in* The Pacific Review, *December, 1921), in his* Main Currents in American Thought, an Interpretation of American Literature from the Beginnings to 1920: The Beginnings of Critical Realism in America, 1860-1920, Vol. 3 *(copyright 1930 by Harcourt Brace Jovanovich, Inc.; copyright 1958 by Vernon L. Parrington, Jr., Louise P. Tucker, Elizabeth P. Thomas; reprinted by permission of the publisher), Harcourt, 1958, pp. 85-92.* *

CARL VAN DOREN (essay date 1922)

Although most novelists with any historical or scholarly hankerings are satisfied to invent here a scene and there a plot and elsewhere an authority, James Branch Cabell has invented a whole province for his imagination to dwell in. He calls it Poictesme and sets it on the map of medieval Europe, but it has no more unity of time and place than has the multitudinous land of *The Faerie Queene*. Around the reigns of Dom Manuel, Count and Redeemer of Poictesme, epic hero of *Figures of Earth*, father of the heroine in *The Soul of Melicent* (later renamed *Domnei*), father of that Dorothy la Desirée whom Jurgen loved (with some other women), father also of that Count Emmerich who succeeded Manuel as ruler at Bellegarde and Storisende—around the reigns of Manuel and Emmerich the various sagas of Mr. Cabell principally revolve. Scandinavia, however, conveniently impinges upon their province, with Constantinople and Barbary, Massilia, Aquitaine, Navarre, Portugal, Rome, England, Paris, Alexandria, Arcadia, Olympus, Asgard, and the Jerusalems Old and New. As many ages of history likewise converge upon Poictesme in its ostensible thirteenth or fourteenth century, from the most mythological times only a little this side of Creation to the most contemporary America of Felix Kennaston who lives at comfortable Lichfield with two motors and with money in four banks but in his mind habitually bridges the gap by imagined excursions into Poictesme and the domains adjacent. (pp. 104-05)

Mr. Cabell has a profound creed of comedy rooted in that romance which is his regular habit. Romance, indeed, first exercised his imagination, in the early years of the century when in many minds he was associated with the decorative Howard Pyle and allowed his pen to move at the languid gait then characteristic of a dozen inferior romancers. Only gradually did his texture grow firmer, his tapestry richer; only gradually did his gaiety strengthen into irony. Although that irony was the progenitor of the comic spirit which now in his maturity dominates him, it has never shaken off the romantic elements which originally nourished it. Rather, romance and irony have grown up in his work side by side. His Poictesme is no less beautiful for having come to be a country of disillusion; nor has his increasing sense of the futility of desire robbed him of his old sense that desire is a glory while it lasts.

He allows John Charteris in *Beyond Life*—for the most part Mr. Cabell's mouthpiece—to set forth the doctrine that romance is the real demiurge, "the first and loveliest daughter of human vanity," whereby mankind is duped—and exalted. (pp. 105-06)

The difference between Mr. Cabell and the popular romancers who in all ages clutter the scene and for whom he has nothing but amused contempt is that they are unconscious dupes of the demiurge whereas he, aware of its ways and its devices, employs it almost as if it were some hippogriff bridled by him in Elysian pastures and respectfully entertained in a snug Virginian stable. His attitude toward romance suggests a cheerful despair: he despairs of ever finding anything truer than romance and so contents himself with Poictesme and its tributaries. The favorite themes of romance being relatively few, he has not troubled greatly to increase them; war and love in the main he finds enough.

Besides these, however, he has always been deeply occupied with one other theme—the plight of the poet in the world. . . . In the amazing fantasy *The Cream of the Jest* Mr. Cabell has embodied the visions of the romancer Felix Kennaston so substantially that Kennaston's diurnal walks in Lichfield seem hardly as real as those nightly ventures which under the guise of Horvendile he makes into the glowing land he has created. Nor are the two universes separated by any tight wall which the fancy must leap over: they flow with exquisite caprice one into another, as indeed they always do in the consciousness of a poet who, like Kennaston or Mr. Cabell, broods continually over the problem how best to perform his function: "to write perfectly of beautiful happenings." (pp. 107-08)

If the poets and warriors who make up the list of Mr. Cabell's heroes devote their lives almost wholly to love, it is for the reason that no other emotion interests him so much or seems to him to furnish so many beautiful happenings about which to write perfectly. Love, like art, is a species of creation, and the moods which attend it, though illusions, are miracles none the less. Of the two aspects of love which especially attract Mr. Cabell he has given the larger share of his attention to the extravagant worship of women ("domnei") developed out of chivalry—the worship which began by ascribing to the beloved the qualities of purity and perfection, of beauty and holiness, and ended by practically identifying her with the divine. This supernal folly reaches its apogee in **Domnei,** in the careers of Perion and Melicent who are so uplifted by ineffable desire that their souls ceaselessly reach out to each other though obstacles large as continents intervene. (pp. 108-09)

Love in **Jurgen** inclines toward another aspect of the passion which Mr. Cabell has studied somewhat less than the chivalrous—the aspect of gallantry. "I have read," says John Charteris, "that the secret of gallantry is to accept the pleasures of life leisurely, and its inconveniences with a shrug; as well as that, among other requisites, the gallant person will always consider the world with a smile of toleration, and his own doings with a smile of honest amusement, and Heaven with a smile which is not distrustful—being thoroughly persuaded that God is kindlier than the genteel would regard as rational." These are the accents, set to slightly different rhythms, of a Congreve; and if there is anything as remarkable about Mr. Cabell as the fact that he has represented the chivalrous and the gallant attitudes toward love with nearly equal sympathy, it is the fact that in an era of militant naturalism and of renascent moralism he has blithely adhered to an affection for unconcerned worldliness and has airily played Congreve in the midst of all the clamorous, serious, disquisitive bassoons of the national orchestra. (pp. 110-11)

> *Carl Van Doren, "James Branch Cabell," in his* Contemporary American Novelists: 1900-1920 *(reprinted with permission of the Estate of Carl Van Doren;* © *1922 by Macmillan Publishing Co., Inc.; copyright renewed* © *1949 by Carl Van Doren), Macmillan, 1922, pp. 104-13.*

ALEISTER CROWLEY (essay date 1923)

We have had Homer and others to combine the affairs of gods and men in a single epos; we have had Balzac and others to combine the affairs of various families. But Cabell has done far more than either of these types of artist. He has taken the ideal forces of the Universe, and shown their relations with mankind over a period of many centuries, from the legendary demigods of Poictesme to the inhabitants of present-day Virginia. He has set no limit to his canvas; and while every detail is exact and brilliant, it retains its proper subordination to the complete Idea. (p. 907)

He has done exactly what the Buddha did long since; he has investigated the Universe in detail and as a whole, and he has come to the same conclusion, "Everything is sorrow." But, like Buddha once more, he has failed to perceive that Sorrow is itself an illusion. Nothing is worth having, nothing is worth keeping, nothing is worth trying for: true, but only in part. Every being must come ultimately to Nothing, for there is nothing for it to attain. Every curve is closed. Every equation must cancel out to zero. Yet every being has only to rid itself of Desire, to follow out its own natural course without hankering after false ideals: so soon as it learns how to do this, sorrow disappears. "Do what thou wilt shall be the whole of the Law." Sorrow arises from our failure to understand ourselves, to calculate our proper orbit, to acquiesce in our true destiny. Once we realize our relation to the Universe, the sum of things becomes part of our own Selfhood. We cease to interfere in the necessary order of Illusions, and the collisions which have hurt us in the past no longer occur. It is true that the total is Nothing; but what we call Ourselves is merely a

symbolic manifestation of Nothing as a system of equal and opposite forces. The true Self is enabled to become conscious of itself by this method. . . . (p. 909)

In **Jurgen** and **Figures of Earth,** especially, I am confident that there is an unfathomable well of Truth of which I have yet drunk but a few sparkling cupfulls. From personal correspondence, indeed, I feel certain that Cabell himself has written "as he was inspired by the Holy Ghost" more subtly and stupendously than his own intelligence is aware. It may be that so colossal a conception as his can never be wholly comprehended by the conscious mind. Certain characters, for instance, such as Manuel's wife, Horvendile, Ahasuerus, Anaitis, Freydis and Beda—the last especially when identified with Mimir—baffle by their simplicity and profundity. One cannot bring into clear consciousness why they really are. Again, one feels the organic necessity of the sequence of certain events without being able to satisfy one's philosophical reason about them. Yet again, there are problems connected with the plane of being on which various characters manifest which leave one eagerly dubious.

In Cabell's technique there are two principal features of exceptional interest and significance. One is the insidious introduction of rhythmical, riming and antistrophic forms. These give an almost uncanny quality to the texture of the tapestry; besides their beauty and their power to exalt the soul, they possess a magical faculty of conveying fine shades of meaning and of enlightening the mind by suggesting allusions to history, literature or philosophy which enrich the explicit expression in an indescribably effective manner.

The other feature is the employment of repetitions. Some apparently casual phrase is made to recur throughout a volume in such a way as to alter the values of the episodes in which it occurs with the most magical effect. It is impossible to explain exactly how the miracle is worked; one can only say that the theme is rendered coherent and ineluctable. The use of the "leit-motif" by Wagner is a very crude prototype of Cabell's device.

Throughout the epos, there is an almost constant consciousness of the relativity of time and space, of their subjectivity. They are perceived from without, as being merely conditions through the postulation of which existence makes itself manifest. We are led to realize that the events of the past and the future are presented to us in sequence for the sake of convenience; they are contributions to our knowledge of a self which is independent of them. One's first love-affair and one's death merely help one to form a mental concept of one's self, just as one's head and one's feet do in another way. All Jurgen's adventures, whether he is traveling backward in time to the Garden between Dawn and Sunrise, or forward to postmortem conditions, are just so many windows through which he may behold himself. . . . So, none of our experiences is a direct expression of ourselves; but their sum, interpreted in the light of our knowledge of the hieroglyphic language of which they are letters, is an intelligible artistic symbol thereof.

Thus we find Cabell constantly breaking up the conventions of human experience in order to demonstrate the ultimate independence of true Self-Consciousness. He enables us to become free from our natural tendency to mistake the alphabet of the intellect for the Word of the Soul. He makes Life intelligible by releasing it from the obsession that any of its phenomena are in themselves finally significant. Yet he avoids the pitfall of the ordinary mystic; he does not tell us that any experience, even the slightest, is "illusion." Every impression that we receive is . . . a necessary term in our Personal Equation, although its function only applies indirectly and symbolically, having no true meaning in itself.

This intrinsic depth of Cabell's thought is to be found, in one way or another, in all his writing. Here it is only possible to explore tentatively the main branch of the Mammoth Cave of his mind; his philosophy leads into many obscure and tortuous side-issues. Equally there is apparently no limit to the range of his raids upon humanity; time, race and caste oppose no barriers to his forays.

It is for these reasons that this brief introduction may be summed in the statement that he is at once the most ambitious, the best worth study, of living authors. To attempt to do more would be presumptuous and futile: each man for himself must bring his own bucket to these springs of deep yet sparkling water. It is no unworthy service to mankind to urge it to look for light to the nebula James Branch Cabell. (pp. 912-14)

> *Aleister Crowley, "Another Note on Cabell," in* The Reviewer, *Vol. III, Nos. 11 & 12, July, 1923, pp. 907-14.*

H. L. MENCKEN (essay date 1927)

What gave ["**Jurgen**"] its evil name is not anything that Cabell himself put into it, but simply the dreadful things that the pornographic Comstocks read between the lines. Who remembers that a New York court decided that the Comstocks were fools? Not many. So "**Jurgen**" lives in the finishing-schools as a wicked book, and the fact that it is a noble work of art is half forgotten. Worse, it is often forgotten that Cabell has also written many other books, and that some of them are even better. Such are the penalties that a moral Republic lays upon an artist, bogged in its swamps. If he is not hot for virtue, it is assumed at once that he is in the service of sin. (p. 7)

What is it, in brief, that the artist tries to do? The orthodox American answer is that his purpose is, first, to depict the life that he observes about him, and, second, to criticise it—in other words, to show how it could be improved, and to argue for his private scheme of improvement with all the voluptuous eloquence that he can muster—in yet other words, to make ideas appetizing by wrapping them in beauty. From this Cabell dissents sharply. The true artist, he says, has no such pupose, save in the sense, perhaps, that "prison-breaking is a criticism of the penitentiary." His real aim is not to suggest improvements in the life about him; it is to escape that life altogether. What he tries to do is to construct a world that shall be better than the world of everyday. He does not denounce his fellow-men for being satisfied with that everyday world, and he does not urge them to improve it; he simply invites them to take a ride with him and enjoy the lovelier scenery that he has discovered. The butt of his dream, if a dream may be said to have a butt, is not man, but God. It is his business to show that the stupendous achievements described in Genesis I, praiseworthy though they were, were yet not the last word in cosmic engineering—that immense progress has been made since then, theoretically if not actually, and that man, as artist, can now imagine a world as much superior to the one we all know as the one we know is superior to the city dump of Harrison, N.J.

Such notions, of course, have a contumacious and even ribald smack, and so the artist is doubly suspect—first, because he is devoid of moral purpose and seems to be anaesthetic to the

Larger Good, and, secondly, because he approaches Genesis I in a bilious and insolent spirit. This is sufficient to explain, says Cabell, the artist's general disrepute in society. When he is admired at all by respectable folk it is somewhat sneakingly, as a bootlegger is admired. Mainly, he is not admired at all, but distrusted and disliked, and whenever moral passions begin to run high he gets a kick or two, and maybe a coat of tar and feathers. . . . His offending, in the last analysis, lies in the simple fact that he doesn't take life seriously enough. He is too willing and eager to turn his back upon it, and seek release and happiness on the high peaks where goats run wild, and the cities appear as mere smudges of smoke upon the horizon, and there are no policemen. He is a traitor to responsibility, to high purpose, to duty. While the jails and lunatic asylums bulge, and the hangman misses meal after meal, and thousands come down with high blood pressure and diabetes, he departs for the hills with a banjo and a ham sandwich, and entertains himself matching his fancy with God's. (pp. 8-9)

How long will "**Jurgen**" last? How long will Cabell last? I venture the prophecy that he and all his books will last a long while. There is in him, indeed, more assurance of permanence than in any other contemporary American of his trade. The rest bind themselves too tightly to the current scene. Their books will go out when the United States becomes civilized, just as the novel of seduction has gone out, now that women are no longer seduced. Cabell, wandering through his charming Poictesme, the seat and stamping-ground of Everyman, will suffer less than his competitors from such changes. His tales are all generalizations—and generalizations always outlast the observations upon which they are based. He has sought to get at the primary elements of man's vain and endless combat with his fate. The struggles on the surface do not interest him; he has no eye for transient agonies, aspirations, modes, manners. What engages him is the primary quest of all of us, at all times and everywhere—for ease and delight of the body, for tranquillity of the mind, for comfort of the soul. He reduces that quest to a simple formula—and its cruel and inevitable failure to another. One could put the argument of all his books into a few sentences. He is right, fundamentally, in trying to make them appear as no more than volumes of the same work, variations upon the same unchanging theme. They have infinite variety, but they all go back to one tune. It is a simple tune and a plaintive one, but it has outlasted many grandiose military marches and sonorous hymns to God. (pp. 21-2)

> *H. L. Mencken, "James Branch Cabell" (1927), in* James Branch Cabell: Three Essays *by Carl Van Doren, H. L. Mencken, and Hugh Walpole (reprinted by permission of Kennikat Press Corp.), Kennikat, 1967, pp. 7-22.*

PAUL ELMER MORE (essay date 1928)

[**Jurgen**] is an allegory of life expressed in weird adventures and weirder symbols, wherein fragments of all the mythologies of mankind are woven; it is meant to be sly and ironical and disillusioned and disturbingly profound, and it certainly is always erotic. The method might be described as a compound of Maurice Hewlett and Anatole France, an attempt to reach the last refinement of conscious art by an assumption of innocent simplicity. For my own part, I confess that I was caught by passages here and there, even by whole chapters, which through the affectations of jollity gave hints of a sad and chastened wisdom born from too much brooding on the transience of all earthly things; and then a false note, a lapse into provincial English, a flash of cheap smartness, would break the charm, and make me feel that the erudition so lavishly displayed was more superficial than solid, the art more sophisticated than fine, and the superiorities of manner rather snobbish. A vein of unfulfilled genius *Jurgen* undoubtedly has, sufficient to explain its attraction for a certain class of critics; but I cannot help asking myself whether its wider reputation does not depend chiefly on its elusive and cunningly suggestive lubricity.

Besides *Jurgen* Mr. Cabell has written a group of novels conceived on a scale which, if you will take the word of his admirers, overtops the combined ambitions of Balzac and Zola. (p. 59)

The novels are fairly clever, fairly entertaining, and in their more fantastic parts have sometimes a vein of wistfully ironic wisdom; but they are trivial things in the end, with no mark of greatness. To compare them with the *Comédie Humaine* is to display an ignorance of art and life. . . . (p. 60)

To my taste the most interesting of Mr. Cabell's books is his *Beyond Life,* wherein he sets forth his personal theory of art in direct opposition to the creed and practice of the realists. . . . Its latent treachery is brought out by Mr. Cabell's attitude towards the relation of romance to the ethical basis of life. Literature, he insists, quoting the Sophoclean maxim from Aristotle, aims to portray men not as they are but as they ought to be. Very well; any good classicist will stand with Mr. Cabell on the side of Sophocles against Euripides. But what does Mr. Cabell mean by "ought to be"? "It can hardly be questioned," he says, "that 'good' and 'evil' are aesthetic conventions, of romantic origin," and "what men 'foolishly do call virtue' is thus relegated to a subsidiary position, in comparison with beauty, not as being in itself unimportant, but as being of no very potent value aesthetically." In Mr. Cabell's vocabulary "ought to be" proves to mean simply that the characters of a book should be allowed to follow the pretty vagaries of vice without any of the ugly consequences that overtake a sinner in the actual flesh. This is not quite to despise morality as "moralism" and "religionism"; but it does make a divorce between the true in life and the beautiful in art which must spell death to any serious emotion in literature. (pp. 60-2)

> Paul Elmer More, "Modern Currents in American Literature," in his The Demon of the Absolute (copyright 1928 by Princeton University Press; copyright © renewed 1956 and assigned to Princeton University Press for the Estate of Paul Elmer More; reprinted by permission of Princeton University Press), Princeton University Press, 1928, pp. 53-76.*

ARTHUR HOBSON QUINN (essay date 1936)

[Cabell has,] through revision and rearrangement of his books in his latest editions, sought to connect his modern American characters like John Charteris and Felix Kennaston with his medieval creations, Jurgen and Manuel, into one cycle of romance. This effort makes a purely chronological discussion of his books less important than a classification based upon the romantic impulse they represent.

Yet chronology in Cabell's case is not without value in any appraisement of his significance. His first book, *The Eagle's Shadow,* . . . is hardly more than an example of the lighter forms of romance then popular. As Cabell solemnly tells us, so that we shall not miss the moral, it is a study of various people as they are affected by the worship of money. At times

he is undoubtedly satirizing the current style of romance. But he is never quite sincere in his satire, for he treats seriously the curious jumble of signed and unsigned wills, with a hero incredibly stupid and a heroine, supposedly of breeding, who talks at times like a fishwife. . . . [The stories which make up *The Line of Love*] represent the sophisticated romance of history, the other field in which Cabell has labored. Here he did his most artistic work. . . . [In the short fictions of *Gallantry*] he caught fairly accurately the cold-blooded atmosphere of the eighteenth century. But no character remains like [Booth] Tarkington's Monsieur Beaucaire, and the situations grow tiresome in repetition. Much better were the stories gathered together . . . as *Chivalry,* where the scenes are laid in England and the Continent during the fourteenth and fifteenth centuries. It is not necessary to discuss the various imaginary historical references with which Cabell apparently seeks to give an air of authority to his romances. He would be the last person, I imagine, to wish them taken seriously. But he has read widely in medieval history and in "**The Story of the Tenson**" he gave Edward I of England the personal courage, the military skill and the steadfastness which seated him firmly upon the English throne. The varying moods of Richard II and the audacity of Henry V are also correctly portrayed in *Chivalry,* but it is to be noticed that when Cabell deals with a character of his own devising as in "**The Story of the Satraps,**" when he imagines an older brother for Richard II, he fails. When the characters are provided him from history, he can dress them up with a dramatic surrounding. But his own inventive powers are not strong, as his constant repetition of situations sufficiently indicates.

To the same group of his writings belongs *The Soul of Melicent* [revised as *Domnei*]. . . . It is a romance in which three persons, Perion of the Forest, Demetrios and Melicent, betrothed to King Theodoret, vie with each other to prove their standards of pride and honor. Especially in the final recognition by Perion of the spiritual quality of Melicent, transcending the physical beauty that lured him and other men, Cabell rises to at least a partial understanding of the medieval worship of "the lady" associated with the adoration of the Virgin. His remark in the "Afterword" that "it was also a malady and a religion" shows that he did not comprehend it completely. But *Domnei* is one of the best of his books, and the sly suggestiveness of his later work is happily minimized. *The Certain Hour* . . . has less vitality and less unity, for the episodes run from the thirteenth to the twentieth centuries. There are some good ironical situations, especially in the stories which deal with Wycherley and Pope, but Cabell should have let Shakespeare alone.

The stories laid in America have not the interest of the medieval romances. The heartlessness of Robert Townsend in *The Cords of Vanity* . . . is not as interesting as the ruthlessness of Perion. There is a fair picture of the emotional development of a writer who "has not been intimate with anybody" but the incidents and characters are forgotten as soon as the book is finished. *The Rivet in Grandfather's Neck* . . . is characteristic of Cabell's uncertainty of method. Viewed as romance, it might be a celebration, through Colonel Rudolph Musgrave, of the gallant sacrifice of his reputation when he takes the blame for an illicit affair which really belongs to the writer, John Charteris, or of his attempted sacrifice when he is willing to give up Patricia Stapylton to a younger man. We are even invited to believe that he prevents Charteris from running away with Patricia for the sake of Anne, and the old romantic clichés are trotted out in the extraordinary monologue he delivers to the eloping pair when they are sneaking away in the early morning and the Colonel's "eyes were like chill stars." But all the time Cabell is inserting sly digs at the permanence of marital love and the worth of the ideals Musgrave represents. His satire upon the feminine psychology which forgets and ignores what it wishes to disregard and yet lashes the object of its regard with bitter upbraiding, belongs to an ironic manner which sits uneasily upon the foundations of romance. Cabell's attitude toward the South is equally inconsistent. He cannot make up his mind whether the loyalties which tradition and breeding have cherished and preserved are important, or whether Charteris, who is a coward and a liar but who has accomplished something, is the only important product of the town. . . . [In *The Cream of the Jest*] Cabell attempted to join the modern and the medieval interests through Felix Kennaston, the writer who passes into dreamland in search of Ettare, the ideal of beauty. But as soon as he touches her, the dream vanishes. The last sentence of the book, "I reflected that it is only by preserving faith in human dreams that we may, after all, perhaps some day make them some true," represents Cabell in his most attractive mood. But it is not the mood of the book, which is sardonic. Its satire of pretense we can enjoy thoroughly, but the mummery about the mirror is boring because it leads nowhere.

With the publication of *Jurgen* . . . Cabell entered into a new phase, both in his work and in his popularity. . . . [While] the attempt to suppress *Jurgen* was silly, there is an odor of decay about it which is repulsive to any healthy minded reader. Cabell protests in the "Foreword" to the revised versions, that such choice passages as those describing Jurgen's stay with Anaïtis have no double meaning. If this be true and they are not implicit dabblings in perversion, they are nonsense. But in any event they are dull.

In *Figures of Earth, A Comedy of Appearances* . . . , the character of Manuel of Poictesme, of whom much had been hinted in the earlier books, especially in the revised versions, emerged. Elaborate maps have been drawn of this mythical country, but its location does not really matter, nor does the plot. At first glance Manuel seems to be the symbol of individualism in its protest against all restriction. "I am Manuel: I follow after my own thinking and my own desire, and if to do that begets loneliness I must endure it." Even his ruthlessness in his various amours are not incompatible with his return to Niafer, the woman whom he idealizes, or his excursion through the magic third window into the sorcerer's land to win back the lock of hair of Melicent, his child, and his final sacrifice to Death, to save Melicent. His quest for the unattainable which drives him on, while not a new note in fiction, is also in keeping with the character of Manuel. And there are some fine passages in *Figures of Earth*. . . . (pp. 609-12)

Manuel is a symbol of the complete pessimism of the bankrupt spirit, more insidious than the objective criticism of the realistic school, for it strikes at the roots of faith and of hope. He is the Byronic hero who is weary because his inmost thoughts cannot be expressed even to the woman he loves. It is perhaps this quality which caught the fancy of the young generation who rebel against this inevitable law and have not grown to an understanding that the very possession of these desires and longings should be a resource that reconciles human creatures to their loneliness.

The parallelism of Manuel's career to that of Christ, beginning with his virgin birth and leading to his "Eucharist," including the spending of three days in a tomb before his resurrection, is offensive, of course, and in bad taste, but it is all the more

inexcusable because it is dragged in. Cabell of course does not mention Christ, and he attempts to forestall criticism by a marshalling of characters to whom tradition has attached somewhat similar events. But the implication is clear enough. It is even clearer in *The Silver Stallion, A Comedy of Redemption* . . . , for the legend of Manuel the Redeemer is carried on by his wife and his apostles, and by Jurgen, in whose mouth are placed the actual words of Christ. If there is a central idea which ties together the adventures of the companions of Manuel, it is the depiction of the gradual growth of a legend concerning a lofty character whose memory the people worship and who, in reality, was a murderer and an adulterer. Moreover, his resurrection rests upon the empty tomb and the unsupported word of the child, Jurgen, who, it is implied, has made up most of the story. Between *Figures of Earth* and *The Silver Stallion* had appeared *The High Place* . . . another tale of Poictesme, but this rather stupid dream story of Florian de Puysange, descended from Manuel, hardly needs discussion.

After *The Silver Stallion*, Cabell seems to have lost completely the sense of standards once his. *The White Robe* . . . is a fantastic account of a werewolf whose sexual adventures give the author an opportunity to pass the limits which divide beasts from men. So does *Something About Eve, A Comedy of Fig Leaves* . . . , a transmigration of one of the Musgrave family into peculiar regions where the curious in abnormality may find pleasure. *The Way of Ecben* . . . repeats the earlier theme of the seeking after the unattainable, but the look adds nothing of importance except some quite pertinent observations upon Cabell's own generation of novel writers in America. Cabell is indeed quite penetrating in his criticism, which is distributed through his "Forewords" and has its most organic body in *Beyond Life* . . . a series of essays. His creed is definitely that of a romanticist, and his scorn of realism, which he seems to think is the antithesis of the romantic, is complete. It is not necessary here to discuss his theories except to remark in passing that a critic who believes Wycherley to have been the first example in English drama of "stooping to real life" is hardly a perfect guide.

Cabell's latest flair seems to be for autobiography, which it is to be hoped, is partly fiction. *These Restless Heads* . . . is ostensibly a series of personal reminiscences written with ease and studded with epigrams. But the book is spoiled by the pitiful spectacle of an elderly gentleman gloating over his amorous successes of bygone days. Beneath these depths it is difficult to go. On the border land of fiction and personal history, *Special Delivery* . . . , a series of letters to various correspondents, first the one Cabell sent and then the one he might have written, and *Ladies and Gentlemen* . . . , letters to historic characters, have a certain cleverness, but that is all. (pp. 612-14)

If it were not for one quality in the fiction of James Branch Cabell it would be sufficient simply to note the passing of his vogue, established by the incorruptible testimony of the recession in the library demand for his books. That lack of popularity is no evidence of lack of merit hardly needs emphasis, but what is most striking is the quick decline of his vogue. It came, I believe, from an inherent flaw, a lack of sincerity, both moral and artistic. According to his own theories of art in *The Certain Hour*, "a book's subject is of extremely minor importance" and the only important quality is beauty. But beauty of form is not the only beauty in literature. There must also be beauty of conception, and one great element of that beauty is sincerity. A novelist must respect his own creations, and though he may make them capable of crime, even murder like Donatello, or adultery like Hester Prynne, he must never make them embodiments of a vice that leads a reader to despise them. Many great novels have been based upon the passionate relations of men and women, outside the conventions of society or the laws of marriage, but no great novel has been based upon those abnormal practices which take from man his manhood or woman her womanhood. And above all else, no novelist of sincerity will titillate his readers by such tricks as the carefully placed series of dots and dashes, or the eternally recurring phrase "then he did what was necessary," which are frequent mannerisms of Cabell. They are unworthy of any artist.

Cabell's fall from grace is to be regretted, because he had one quality of the artist, that of style. He had not much of a story to tell, but he had the gift, especially in his early work, of the well-chosen word, the charming phrase, and the sentence whose proportions are a delight. There were few writers of his generation who had such control over the resources of the English tongue. Had he chosen to clothe great historic figures with some salient quality as he did in *Chivalry,* or to personify an idea of beauty as he did in *The Soul of Melicent,* he might not indeed have become a great writer, but he would at least have retained the respect of the discriminating. But instead, he chose to pass into the cave of moral twilight with *Jurgen,* and he has never come out again into that clear light of artistic truth by which alone literature of importance can be written. (pp. 614-15)

> *Arthur Hobson Quinn, "Booth Tarkington and the Later Romance," in his* American Fiction: An Historical and Critical Survey *(© 1936, renewed 1963; adapted by permission of Prentice-Hall, Inc., Englewood Cliffs, N.J.), Appleton-Century-Crofts, 1936, pp. 596-622.*

OSCAR CARGILL   (essay date 1941)

[To] undertake the re-reading of James Branch Cabell is to suffer monstrously on the rack of one's innocence. We were bored with him at the outset, yet read from a sense of duty; our minds atrophy, our organs decay, our flesh shreds from our bones as we whip ourselves through him again. He is, beyond all shadow of a doubt, the most tedious person who has achieved high repute as a *literatus* in America, and only Wells surpasses him among the English. Beside the eighteen volumes pompously called **"The Biography of Manuel"** the Congressional Record is sprightly entertainment and the *Novum Organon* a bacchanalian revelry. Yet this is the man whom H. L. Mencken in 1927, declared came nearer to being a first-rate artist than any other American of his time [see excerpt above]. . . . (p. 495)

Now, it seems to us that Cabell's reputation as a stylist is overblown. Once a man has been described as a stylist primarily, critics seem much more willing to accept and to repeat the tribute than to challenge the judgment. If one cites examples of downright bad writing, they are likely to be treated with indulgence: they are exceptions in the work of the artist, "Homer nods," etc. Yet open any Cabellian masterpiece and the chances are, if you are not sleepy, you will find something that irritates you *as writing.* Here are some specimens of his "excellence":

1. "For all this seemed remarkably remote from my introductory remark about Marco Polo."

Has he no ear?

2. ". . . and that after his departure northward, when his lieutenants had failed to take Bellegarde after a six weeks' siege, Poictesme was not molested further."

Would not a stylist boggle over the repetition of "after"?

3. ". . . and there in a snug room, with supper laid, sat Dame Lisa about some sewing, and evidently in a quite amiable frame of mind."

Or would he have adorned the last page of *Jurgen* with this ill-begotten sentence?

Truth is, whoever first acclaimed Cabell as a stylist mistook as a mastery of prose writing his ability to turn an occasional sentence happily. (pp. 495-96)

[In Cabell] one will detect prose which sounds like Stevenson, Harland, Hope, James, Pollard, Thompson, Barrès, France, Mencken, and Edgar Saltus! In fact, so many and varied influences intrude and there is so little synthesis of them that Mr. Cabell can hardly be said to have a style at all—not one of his many ways of writing may be said to be characteristic of him or his own. Cabell the stylist is more of a phantom than any of the mirages he has raised in his fiction. (p. 497)

> *Oscar Cargill, "The Intelligentsia," in his* Intellectual America: Ideas on the March *(reprinted with permission of Macmillan Publishing Co., Inc.; copyright 1941 by Macmillan Publishing Co., Inc.; renewed 1969 by Oscar Cargill), Macmillan, 1941, pp. 399-536.*

ALFRED KAZIN   (essay date 1942)

With his flair for literary jokes, his elaborate parody of the apparatus of scholarship, his pleasing grace, his effortless cynicism, his palpable contempt for the mob, Cabell did present the twenties with the homemade portrait of a Major Writer and nothing more. (p. 232)

Under his tutelage literature became a game that rivaled mahjong in popularity. Sitting in the Harding-Coolidge era, with its ridiculous standards and general dullness, one traveled in armchairs two spaces west to Poictesme, and two south to the Forest of Acaire. One played with tokens marked life, fate, love, which one could arrange in many pleasing and even hilarious combinations, since they were all equally illusory and always a little sad. One dealt with imaginary scholia, giggled over Cabell's cosmogony of a legendary world, and with Jurgen won the ultimate victory over the feigned protests of many a faire ladye. It was a pleasing game: so suggestive of life, and yet so superior to reality; so erudite, albeit so careless.

Unlike that other artificer of the medieval, Thomas Chatterton, Cabell never persuaded himself; and he had no need to persuade his readers. They wanted just what he gave them: the touch of life bereft of life's prosaic sordidness; an easy road to wisdom; a masquerade of the soul in which, by mocking the daydreams of the great herd, one could liberate and enjoy one's own. Cabell did not pretend to be an "escapist"; he was a realist whose cynical appreciation of reality encouraged him to make it ridiculous. By dismissing the superficial world of the present, he illuminated its pathos, lightly and fleetingly. The eagle in *Figures of Earth* was so indisputably a caricature of Woodrow Wilson, Cabell's lyrics to the good red wine of Provence so clever a thrust at Prohibition, that even the absurdities of one's own day gained a final grace.

What Cabell was writing, though no one would have admitted it at the moment, was not allegory but innuendo; the innuendo became tiresome when it became clear that his delight in his own cleverness would inevitably become the final content of his books. Behind their imposing façade, their glossy finish (*gonfalon* was the word then), lay something so stringy in its poverty, so opposed to all that is high, noble, and intense in art, that nothing could long conceal it. The trouble, at bottom, was complacency. Cabell was a keen and amusing ironist, but even his most ambitious satires suggested a perpetual smirk. He did satirize the leavings of traditional romance, but it was not enough to carry him through; after thirty years he was still parodying the Genteel Tradition under the delusion that he was a master of philosophy. A later generation would wonder why, in summing up his critical position in *Beyond Life,* Cabell found only one redoubtable antagonist, Booth Tarkington; but it was clear that Tarkington, not to say Marie Corelli and Robert W. Chambers and Winston Churchill, still represented everything Cabell had ever fought against. His own romanticism was thus only one step from the girlish innocence of the traditional Virginia romance to the charming and elusive demimonde of Poictesme, in which girls were never innocent and men were rarely dull. The critical Babbitts might think Cabell a satanic figure, but he was not even attempting to *épater le bourgeois;* he sought only to amuse him. Reading his books, good middle-class fathers and citizens, like good middle-class undergraduates, enjoyed the luxury of a depravity that was as synthetic as breakfast cereal, and as harmless.

Cabell's great secret, indeed, was that he made almost no demands upon his readers; and since he took such pains to be cute, it was impossible to resist him. He was not a decadent at all, but a mischievous and tryingly whimsical old uncle. The books were all comedies, and they were to be enjoyed for their pleasingly mundane tricks, like that top of a cold-cream jar which Felix Kennaston mistook for a prefatory sigil, or the archness that made the vulgarity of *Jurgen* so picturesque but homely. Yet he had one fatal weakness. He sought so energetically to keep his readers from being bored that he became a bore himself, and when he lost his charm even the famous style seemed ridiculous. "Henceforward you must fret away much sunlight by interminably shunning discomfort and by indulging tepid preferences. For I, and none but I, can waken that desire that uses all of a man, and so wastes nothing, even though it leave that favored man forever after like wan ashes in the sunlight." Could it be that, hiding archly behind his lovely fake ruins, there was nothing but such fantastic rhetoric and the disclosure, so long delayed, that Jurgen was quite a feller? It was a terrible and dismaying thought, a thought that swept away all those lovely ladies, all that mock learning, all the glories of a fabulous satire, and left nothing, nothing at all. (pp. 233-35)

Alfred Kazin, "The Exquisites," in his On Native Grounds: An Interpretation of Modern American Prose Literature *(copyright 1942, 1970 by Alfred Kazin; reprinted by permission of Harcourt Brace Jovanovich, Inc.), Reynal & Hitchcock, 1942, pp. 227-46.**

EDMUND WILSON   (essay date 1956)

[Cabell's] first ambition, he says, was to emulate the popular fiction of Anthony Hope, Henry Harland and Justus Miles Forman, and write novels "about beautiful fine girls and really splendid young men, and everything would come out all right in the end"; and for a time he is quite successful. His stories appear in *Harper's,* with pictures by Howard Pyle, and they are brought out as Christmas books, handsomely boxed, with the illustrations in color. But something is off-center in these stories. The editors of magazines are obliged to expunge certain kisses between persons not properly married, certain coarse references to Falstaff's "belly." When the heroine of a light little novel laid in contemporary Virginia makes use of the current American slang and, in a moment of crisis, says, "Damn you!," a controversy is stirred that goes on for months in the New York *Times Book Review,* as to how a young "gentlewoman" in fiction should be allowed to express herself. Cabell's illustrator, Howard Pyle, begins to complain that his stories "are neither exactly true to history nor exactly fanciful . . . that they are not true to medieval life, and that they lack a really permanent value such as I should now endeavor to present to the world." One of Cabell's medieval romances, the amusing and quite brilliant *Domnei* (then called *The Soul of Melicent*), a story of impossible prodigies of prowess and long-term fidelity, performed by a knight for his lady, seems almost—with its fairytale extravagances and its unexpected peripeties—to be getting out of hand. Cabell says that he had not known how to bring the book to a close, and we feel that he has stopped just in time to avoid an effect of comedy, since Melicent, finally deserved and won, could hardly have been worth all that trouble, and we are given the impression that her worshipper has become a good deal more interested in his semi-fraternal contests with his rival than in the object of these contests herself. Cabell points out, in this connection and in the case of others of his books, that he was always, in his earlier period, allowing his original hero, a conventional model of chivalry, to be played off the stage by a character—in *Domnei,* the ruthless rival—who makes hay of the chivalric code and eventually reduces it to absurdity. (pp. 298-99)

The Rivet in Grandfather's Neck appears to start out in a conventional way, but then performs surprising pirouettes and turns into—for Southern fiction—a new kind of rather Shavian comedy, in which the author pulls out rugs and chairs from under the Southern conventions. Yet Colonel Musgrave, the principal character—a professional genealogist and old-school Virginian snob—is made, in his outmoded way, to stand for something honorable and rather fine. The *Rivet* is a subtler and more serious, as well as more complicated, *Colonel Carter of Cartersville,* that once popular half-sentimental novel by F. Hopkinson Smith. . . . But [Cabell's] powers are not to find their fullest scope in presenting the contemporary South. He tells us that he was stopped, in this earlier phase, from dealing with some local subject by considering the fates of George W. Cable and other Southern writers when they tackled uncomfortable themes. The particular theme that made Cable an object of detestation on the part of his fellow-Louisianians—the difficult situation of persons of mixed black and white blood—is touched on by Cabell, though tellingly, only in *The Rivet in Grandfather's Neck.* One could not open up with impunity these old and sore scandals of the South, and it is quite impossible for Cabell to interest himself in the "New South." He cannot pretend to live in the accepted world of Southern legend; he is sure to give away the imposture. On the other hand, the Richmond of the Chamber of Commerce, the flourishing of which can bring nothing but a further *embourgeoisement,* is even more alien to him; it arouses distaste, and it bores him. The novelist hero of his next Southern book—*The Cream of the Jest* . . . gets away from this bourgeois Virginia by reverting in a series of daydreams to the fairy-tale world of *Domnei.*

The author of *The Cream of the Jest* will himself now remain in this fairy-tale world, but he will draw into it all his others. The Middle Ages, the seventeenth and eighteenth centuries, the inescapable mediocrity of modern life will now all be mixed up together and merged with the goblins and marvels of innumerable scrambled folklores. His mythological books of this period are undoubtedly Cabell's best, and they are also to become his most famous. (pp. 301-03)

[The] critical success of *The Cream of the Jest* and Cabell's other books, the attempted suppression of *Jurgen,* the failure of this attempt, and the excitement that accompanied the episode must have had the effect of arousing him to transcend his previous efforts. In the four major fantasies that follow—all written in the decade of the twenties and all part of the same cycle as *Jurgen*—Cabell called into play his full powers, put on his most dazzling performances, and established his most serious claims to be rated as a first-class poet. For it is perhaps less misleading to speak of these fantasies as "poems" rather than "novels." In creating a poetic convention, Cabell thus stands a bit aloof from the other Americans of his period, who for the most part—and even in the case of a writer so poetic as Hemingway—have always remained more or less loyal to the established conventions of realism.

Cabell himself, in his critical writings, has somewhat confused this question by rejecting what he refers to as "realism" with a certain superciliousness, apparently unaware that to glorify the "dream" as against the "real" is merely to express a preference for one kind of fictional convention rather than another. The convention, for example, of a Hemingway insists that an illusion be given of a consistency different from Cabell's, but his stories are waking dreams as much as Cabell's are. The work of Cabell differs also from that of most of the writers who were fashionable in the twenties in that he does not regard human destiny as tragic. Cabell is a *comic* poet, though one of—for modern times—almost unexampled splendor. Life, to be sure, he shows us, is full of discomfiting ironies, but they are rarely a reason for weeping. And life, in the long run, is scarcely susceptible of improvement. It is true that, at the end of *The Cream of the Jest,* he does go so far as to say that "it is only by preserving faith in human dreams that we may, after all, perhaps someday make them come true." (Cabell seems to confuse the "dream" as "ideal" with his other sense of "dream" as a non-realistic poetic convention.) But this has quite a different ring from the assurance, for example, of Anatole France—to whom Cabell is sometimes compared—that "Slowly but inevitably humanity realizes the dreams of the sages." Anatole France is a child of the Renaissance, of the Enlightenment, of the French Revolution, and this aphorism stands at the head of his collected political papers; we know the direction of those dreams of his that he believes will inevitably be realized. But in Cabell's case the Renaissance is a period of gorgeous costumes, lovely women and outrageous crimes, the age of Voltaire and Rousseau a carnival of wicked gallantries; and in his own country, itself revolutionary, he has been alienated from its progress in innovation. What *are* the "human dreams," for Cabell, that our faith in them may "make come true"? In these books, so crowded with heroes and gods, with adventurers, kings and enchanters, we may look for an answer in vain.

The key figure here ought to be Manuel, the protagonist of *Figures of Earth.* Manuel, Cabell tells us, is intended as a type of the man of action, in contrast to Jurgen, the man of intelligence, and, in taking account of what is likely to seem the relative unsatisfactoriness of Manuel, we come to realize the special conditions that limit his creator's dream. Manuel is meant to be sensual, unscrupulous, treacherous, brutal. He begins as a swineherd and ends as an emperor. We are shown first, in *Figures of Earth,* Manuel as he lived; then, in *The Silver Stallion,* the legend that is created about him after his death. He has come to represent an ideal, and the people of Poictesme are made more virtuous as well as more civilized through believing in his prowess and wisdom. They expect him to return again and to lead them to further triumphs. Now, this in itself is a good idea. The author is aiming to dramatize the process by which the beast who has made himself what we call human may also—through following his instincts, improvising his policies, taking advantage of his happy chances—arrive at a position of power over other men less pushing and lucky; to demonstrate how these, in their need for self-confidence, their thirst to exalt themselves, may imagine him, once he is gone, a faithful and fearless spirit, a past-master of statecraft and strategy. But the trouble is that Cabell's Manual seems to offer too little basis for such a myth. In reading *Figures of Earth,* we are likely to feel that we are following the adventures of a less sympathetic Jurgen. Yet the author has tried to bring out from the first his hero's strong will to power. "Will you remodel the world?" he is asked. "Who knows? . . . At all events, I do not mean to leave it unaltered." And he is made to repeat again and again his undiscouraged intention of following after his "own thinking and desires." . . . But in following the career of Manuel one finds no indications of greatness. It is true that he is made creative to the extent of animating some figures of clay, which come out, however, more or less botched. But he is otherwise such a coward, such a double-crosser, has so little continuity of purpose that he seems to give little real ground for his eventual apotheosis. In order to grow a great reputation, do you not need the seeds of qualities that suggest nobility or mastery, and qualities at least in the direction of those with which reputation credits you? This man of action of Cabell's is given, to be sure, bursts of eloquence which sometimes turn into verse and the effect of which is half-ironic, yet which represent dreams of glory that are evidently meant to raise him above the common run. But if Manuel's deeds seem too rascally for a hero, these soliloquies seem too literary for a rascal. (pp. 305-08)

If Cabell's Poictesme is lacking in the elements that provide stability, it is marvellously happy in rendering the unstable aspects of life—the fluidities, hoaxes, surprises; illusions that conceal their opposites. . . . All this quicksilver phantasmagoria—I take the phrase from Fernanda Pivano who refers to Cabell's work as "a great globe of scattering quicksilver"—is the author's "criticism of life." It is a unique artistic achievement, and one which it was possible to arrive at only by breaking through into a non-realistically conditioned world. (pp. 310-11)

One should warn the prospective reader of a generation which does not know Cabell that his art is a little encumbered by ornamentations in an antique mode, which do not always make for lightness. (p. 312)

But do not, in any case, let it put you off; you will soon forget about it. Hardly hedged by these arid frills lives the quicksilver world I have spoken of—a world of swift and witty colloquies, of vivid and enchanting colors, of continual metamorphoses. These fantasies are not logical allegories; it is one of their great virtues that they are not. They are closer to the psychology of dreams, and this gives them their uncanny effectiveness. The popularity of *Jurgen,* I believe, beyond the other books of its series, was due not to its superiority or to its publicized erotic interest—from this latter point of view, all these books of Cabell's are about the same—but to its being somewhat less elusive. If it is not a clear allegory, it has an element of the Odyssean and an element of the picaresque. And it is easier for the ordinary reader to understand and sympathize with the hero, to identify himself with Jurgen, than with Manuel or the heroes of the later books. These, however —[*The High Place* and *Something About Eve*] . . .—seem to me more interesting creations. I agree with Mencken that *The High Place* is one of the best of Cabell's books. Here the dream evanescences and the images cast from mirrors reach a point of expert juggling that half conveys disquieting meanings. The element of the macabre increases. Is the author still pursuing his original aim—repeated so many times—"to write perfectly of beautiful happenings"? Most of the happenings in these books are not beautiful. It would surely be more accurate to say that he is here writing brilliantly of happenings that are awkward, embarrassing or bitter, and I suggest that there is a strong strain in Cabell's work of something I have not found suspected. . . . [There is] a sense of morality, though this usually becomes explicit only when Cabell is talking about his art. You find it when he says that he fears he may not have earned the reputation that came to him on account of *Jurgen;* you have it when he says that the possession of talent imposes the obligation to make of it the fullest use—a principle that he is put to some trouble to reconcile with his other statement that "the literary artist . . . labors primarily to divert himself." There is even, on the next page to the passage just noted—in the book of essays, *Straws and Prayer Books*—a kind of non-literary self-castigation: "No man," he goes on to say, "cares quite to face the truth about himself." Looking back upon the past, he continues, he finds "much of what to the first glance seems shirking and equivocation, so much of petty treacheries, of small lies, and of responsibilities evaded, that I am wholeheartedly glad to reflect my private observatory is not, and never will be, open to the public." And though it is true, as Alfred Kazin says, that there is something in Cabell of complacency [see excerpt above], it seems to me also true that the supports upon which this complacency rests are always made to seem rather dubious, and that what, in the long run, he arrives at is a mastery in rendering the dubious. (pp. 312-14)

Edmund Wilson, "The James Branch Cabell Case Reopened" (originally published in The New Yorker, Vol. XXXII, No. 9, April 21, 1956), in his The Bit between My Teeth: A Literary Chronicle of 1950-1965 (reprinted by permission of Farrar, Straus & Giroux, Inc.; copyright © 1956, 1965 by Edmund Wilson), The Noonday Press, 1965, pp. 291-321.

DOROTHY B. SCHLEGEL   (essay date 1958)

The chivalric aspect of Southern Romanticism provided the richest nourishment to the genius of the *younger* James Branch Cabell. The tendency of the Southerner to see himself as a knight in shining armor riding forth to fight for a cause which he believed to be right provided Cabell's multi-volumed **"Biography of the Life of Manuel"** with many a crusader, who is set upon doing what he believes to be his duty, at no matter what expense to himself, or to anyone else either, as the *older* Cabell added ironically in a later volume. The chivalric thread in Southern Romanticism enabled Cabell to create, also, his never-never land of Poictesme, that region so much like Virginia and yet so different from it, wherein the artist might

move at will and breathe freely without fear of recrimination from his readers.

Later, instead of returning to the Age of Chivalry, the Southern mind preferred, after the events of the mid-nineteenth century, to go back only so far as its own Golden Age, the eighteenth century, the Age of Classicism, that age when men assumed the gallant attitude toward life which enabled them, as Cabell wrote, "to accept the pleasures of life leisurely and its inconveniences with a shrug." (p. 2)

This second reversion to the past, to the ideas of Neoclassicism, contributed likewise to the genius of Cabell. First, on the negative side, it furnished him with the impetus to rebel violently against the ways of the South which attempted to confine in a strait jacket the nonconforming artistic temperament. On the positive side, it provided him with the inspiration for his tales contained in the book specifically entitled *Gallantry,* which dealt with life in the seventeenth and eighteenth centuries. It also gave a *modus vivendi* to many of his middle-aged characters, in his books other than *Gallantry,* and to his younger protagonists when they had lost their chivalric illusions; for the chivalric attitude was, in the main, that of youth—of a young man or of a young nation—whereas the gallant attitude was that of the coming of age of an individual or of a people.

There was, in addition, a third attitude toward life, isolated and labeled by Cabell, an attitude which Cabell felt was peculiar to romantic artists, among whom he invariably classified himself. This attitude, termed by Cabell the *poetic* attitude, causes the artist, who rebels against the imperfections and the unnecessary strictures of the world about him, to create from the raw material of everyday life a far better world than that which he has ever known. If Cabell's criterion is applied to the South, the South, in its turn, shared with the romantic artist the poetic attitude, for the Southerner likewise attempted to create in his own mind a far more beautiful world than that which surrounded him. The South, then, by virtue of its very chivalry and its gallantry, was itself poetic. (pp. 3-4)

In contrast, Cabell's mind ranged through all of time and all of space—through all myths and all history. In this process he became a mental vagabond upon the surface of the earth, a François Villon, who was bound to differ violently from his more provincial neighbors. He came to look upon himself as a Wandering Jew among men, one who had lived through the ages. In fact, time and time again in his romances, taking a cue from this favorite myth of his, he referred to himself as a Peripatetic Episcopalian. He was a modern-day Faust, who was content with no pat explanation of the universe. To this wanderer through all of time and all of space, the temporal, the finite, the particular took on a cosmic insignificance in the total scheme of affairs. The insistence of his neighbors upon their fixed little notions of life seemed ludicrous to this rebellious cosmopolite in a world "where almost anything is rather more than likely to happen." (pp. 4-5)

As Cabell grew older and suffered the inevitable disillusionments of maturity, among which might be reckoned the shattering condemnation of *Jurgen* in the 1920's, he perfected a technique which had been practiced widely by such eighteenth-century critics of society as Montesquieu, the author of the *Lettres Persanes.* He developed more and more their habit of looking at himself and at his own people with the cold, impersonal eyes of a traveler from a far country. As a result of his observations, this stranger from Parnassus grew ever more rebellious against the fixed mores of his fellow Southerners, and he came to feel that the Southern chivalric attitude toward life, involving as it did a strictly fundamentalist religious position, created in the minds of the individuals who subscribed to it a deplorable priggishness and intolerance. He complained bitterly of these traits as he saw them manifested in his own people. In *Let Me Lie* . . . he wrote of the average Virginian: "No power can shake his belief in his own eternal rightness," and likewise "no power in nature can upset the faith of a Virginian of the old school as to the myths among which he was reared, and of which he needs to be worthy." (pp. 5-6)

If Cabell had limited himself only to a carping criticism of the ways of the South, he and his work would have amounted to nothing. But this was not the case. From Cabell's rebellion against the world about him were born his speculations as to the springs of all human behavior. The best and most complete expression of his conclusions is contained in his **"Biography of the Life of Manuel,"** that long allegory of the struggles of the human race from the thirteenth-century redeemer who had pulled himself up from the mire by his own bootstraps to the Virginians of Cabell's own lifetime.

Because of Cabell's dismay at the average Southerner's unwillingness to face what Cabell deemed to be the truth, and perhaps because of a similar inability which he must, at times, have detected in himself, he studied the phenomenon of human illusions in general. From this he came to the realization that mankind as a whole is loath to face reality. Man, it seems, must live by his dreams. He will not and cannot accept things as they are. Man dreams either of the past, when he believes that life has been better, or of the future, when he hopes that it will be better. (p. 7)

[Like] Heine, who bitterly burst romantic bubbles that he had created, so Cabell rebelled even against his own dreams. Suppose his dreams were to come true? Would he be content? Would man be satisfied with what he had, if he had what he wanted? The answer to that question Cabell provided in *Jurgen*.

In *Jurgen* the Romanticist is vouchsafed a prolonged residence in Poictesme. And what does he find there? His beautiful maidens are for the most part a dreadful disappointment to him. (p. 10)

Through all of Jurgen's journeyings through the various dream worlds, he can have and can be just what he wants. . . . But never is he completely satisfied, and even on the very throne of God he feels a gnawing discontent, for always a shadow had attended him, "a shadow that makes all things not quite satisfactory, not wholly to be trusted, not to be met with frankness." (pp. 10-11)

As even Heaven itself fails then to satisfy this fastidious visitor from Earth, Jurgen, the knight-errant, shrugs his shoulders, thereby indicating his transition from the chivalric to the gallant attitude towards life, and asks one of the four archangels who are in attendance upon him, "the quickest way out of Heaven," for he wishes to return to the more congenial illusions of Earth. Although he has admired and envied much that he has seen in Heaven, he feels that he cannot really believe in what he has seen. Certainly there is little satisfaction to be derived from the vague, empty beauty of Heaven. Instead, he is beset with a great longing for that comfortable, prosaic life of his on Earth, and so he returns of his own volition to the everyday world and to his own wife, Dame Lisa, who nags frightfully, but who, nevertheless, is a companion to whom he has become accustomed. His residence in the lands beyond common sense has stripped him of all his illusions. Heaven is no more sat-

isfactory than Earth. This ideal destination of man is scarcely worth the struggle of attaining it. (pp. 11-12)

> *Dorothy B. Schlegel, "James Branch Cabell and Southern Romanticism" (originally a lecture delivered at Longwood College in 1958), in her* James Branch Cabell: The Richmond Iconoclast *(copyright © 1975 by Dorothy B. Schlegel), The Revisionist Press, 1975, pp. 1-17.*

ARVIN R. WELLS (essay date 1962)

A world-view such as Cabell's may underlie a variety of possible attitudes toward existence. It may issue in the mournful "all is vanity" of Ecclesiastes, in the somewhat brittle stoicism of Russell's "A Free Man's Worship," or in the tragic vision of Miguel de Unamuno. Of all the possibilities, the comic vision seems on first consideration the least likely. (p. 24)

What Cabell came in time to write are fantasies or, more accurately, comic allegories compounded of myth and folklore refurbished for new allegorical and symbolic purposes. As Cabell himself explained it, he created Poictesme—the sometimes mythical, sometimes pseudohistorical realm in which his fantasies take place—because he needed in his art to be omnipotent; he needed a world unencumbered by any laws other than those of his own making. As the completed *Biography of Manuel* now stands, it is the story of man's relations, both personal and indirect, with that mythical realm.

What Cabell gained by means of his technique of comic allegory and fantasy is manifold. By carrying the reader to a land beyond common sense, Cabell achieves that atmosphere of holiday detachment which John Charteris in *Beyond Life* recommends, without having to resort to the rather stale and sterile setting of the drawing room or somebody's house party. By plunging the reader into a milieu which superficially has little or nothing to do with the familiar world, Cabell succeeds in putting to rest all the numerous predispositions and affections which ordinarily determine the way in which man views his own most serious doings as well as those of his fellows. More important than this, however, by borrowing widely from myth, legend, and folklore, Cabell is able to give concrete, dramatic expression to his otherwise abstract concepts. Out of the fragments of many mythologies and folklores, augmented by his own invention, Cabell created a pantheon of deities who, besides being susceptible to comic treatment, bring with them a nimbus of far-reaching associations. Their presence gives, without discourse, an immediate depth of meaning. Moreover, they combine in themselves two aspects which are fundamental to the expression of Cabell's world-view; they simultaneously represent the dead dreams by means of which man has in the past explained his world and himself, and the living forces that continue to shape man's life both from within and from without. Somewhat similarly the pseudolegendary figures whom Cabell uses as his comic protagonists extend the meaning without sacrificing either action or comedy. For without losing their own individuality they subsume the characters of other significant legendary figures. Thus, Jurgen is not Faust nor Odysseus nor the Wandering Jew but partakes of all of them and yet remains Jurgen. The consequence is that Jurgen's deeds and experiences are broadly representative, or at least suggestive, of general human experience in a way in which, say, Colonel Musgrave's or George Bulmer's can never be.

The service of these useful allegorical and symbolic figures is not the only advantage that Cabell drew from his interest in myth and folklore. Equally important is the fact that in the conventions of myths and folk tales he has found the basis for the laws of Poictesme. These conventions are particularly well suited to the expression of Cabell's vision of man as journeying through an irrational universe in which he blunders from mystery to mystery feeling himself assaulted and moved by strange forces but sustained by faith in his own sanity and cleverness; a universe in which nothing is what it appears and in which ends are predictable but seldom implicit in beginnings. Moreover, while the conventions of myths and folk tales do not conform to what science describes as the natural laws of the universe, they do express fundamental dreams and experiences of the human psyche, and these dreams and experiences are, of course, for Cabell the really important stuff of every human life and, thus, of the comedy of human existence. It may be, too, that the general association of fantasy and fairy tales with childhood helps to foster the playfulness which, initially at least, is essential to the experience of comedy.

All in all, the technique of fantasy and comic allegory which Cabell ultimately developed makes it possible for him to deal with the broad general patterns of human living without sacrificing either concreteness or the playfulness and the comic irony which are fundamental to his point of view. (pp. 65-7)

Cabell's first attempts at writing full-scale comedies were *The Eagle's Shadow* [and *Gallantry*]. . . . Both are in some sense comedies of manners, though the second is a historical set piece and the first is an attempt to render contemporary manners. Both are, in Cabell's term, mundicidious—light, worldly comedies which play superficially with human foibles. Both depend upon stock characters and stock situations, but *Gallantry,* because it is constrained and shaped by the spirit of the eighteenth century as that spirit had been defined in literary convention dating back at least to *Henry Esmond* and because it pretends to be nothing very serious, is the more successfully comic. Neither, however, has thematic complexity, and though many light ironies play over their surfaces, there is no fundamental underlying irony such as the later comedies are built upon.

The Eagle's Shadow is an old bag of tricks not very adroitly played. . . . [Cabell's] objective was obviously the playfulness of light comedy. Unfortunately, the house-party setting is not in itself sufficient to insure such playfulness, especially when—and this is true of Cabell's story—there is a trite but ostensibly serious theme, in this case the corrupting influence of money, which suggests that the characters and their experiences are after all to be taken with some seriousness. Such a suggestion is inevitably fatal when, as here, the characters are the almost wholly un-refurbished stock characters out of the frothiest sort of stage comedy—the gruff but tender-hearted father, the quarrelsome but meant-for-each-other young lovers, the foppish but gifted artist, the self-seeking philanthropists who, it turns out, have hearts of gold. (pp. 72-3)

Gallantry pretends to no serious theme and to no profound irony. The book explores an attitude as it was supposedly manifested in the eighteenth century, an attitude which by intention is resolutely superficial and of which the broad outlines at least are given by convention; consequently, the writing of it involved few problems of distance or of verisimilitude. Moreover, not only does the book seek merely to incarnate the conventionally defined spirit of an earlier period, it depends largely for its comic effect upon the borrowed literary devices of that period. All the tricks of eighteenth century melodrama and farce are exploited—the unpredictable shifts in plot and

character relationships arising out of concealed motivation, the farcical mix-ups (Captain Audain suddenly finds he has become his sweetheart's grandfather), and the high-flown language and sentiments that fall so readily into burlesque. Moreover, the characters themselves, though like the characters in *The Eagle's Shadow* they are all stereotypes, are drawn from a more vigorous variety of comedy, and they bring with them a certain talent for witticism and repartee. They make no demand to be taken seriously by the reader; they resolutely refuse to take themselves seriously. They ask only that the reader appreciate their wit, in which after all the comedy is largely invested. (pp. 74-5)

Gallantry, however, is a long way from *Jurgen.* In the former the gallant attitude and the gallant point of view are displayed only upon a narrow, conventionalized stage, and the gallant characters, clear sighted and worldly wise though they are intended to be, very rarely look beyond their immediate surroundings and their own localized doings. (p. 76)

[*The Cords of Vanity, The Soul of Melicent,* and *The Rivet in Grandfather's Neck*] were all written within a period of five years, 1907 to 1912. The first and last of these explore two of the basic human attitudes toward life—gallantry and chivalry, respectively—as these are manifested in a more or less contemporary (1900 to 1910) Southern milieu. They are comedies, or perhaps more accurately satires of contemporary manners. *Domnei,* on the other hand, is ostensibly a romance in the medieval manner, but conceived ironically and enlivened with the somewhat gaudy colors of Pierre Louÿs. (p. 77)

[These] comedies of what might be called the middle period lack "gusto," a quality which Cabell posits as a necessary ingredient of literature that endures. They lack also the thematic scope of the later comedies; they are in fact decidedly mundicidious—not precisely in the sense that *Gallantry* is so, but mundicidious in that they are bound to a particular earthly time and place which shapes theme and style as well as characters. This remains true despite the fact that all three make use of a variety of techniques designed to suggest the possibility of finding a broader and more general significance in the action.

All three comedies do, however, show marked gains in maturity of interest and technique: in each there is, besides the multiplicity of superficial ironies, a fundamental underlying irony which, so to speak, emerges to envelope the whole action; and in each Cabell is less concerned with gesture and attitude in themselves and is more deeply concerned with the psychology that lies behind the gesture. And when the three are considered together, they reveal a significant though as yet slight drift toward the use of folklore materials and motifs. (pp. 77-8)

[*The Cream of the Jest*] is in many ways a transitional comedy. It is a bridge between this world of ordinary experience and that other world which is ambiguously of the mind and imagination and yet a place in itself, a world in which everything is pregnant with meaning and through which man either picks his way gingerly or, with sublime unconcern, stumbles on from unguessed mystery to unguessed mystery. Here Cabell seems to have seen his kingdom clearly but has not yet entered in and taken possession of it. (p. 95)

The reader of this Comedy of Evasion finds himself suspended between two worlds, neither of which can in any ultimate sense be called *the* real world except by courtesy of convention. One of these is the world of ordinary experience. The other is an idealized dream world penetrated by Felix Kennaston with the aid of the spurious Sigil of Scoteia. Both worlds as Kennaston early comes to realize are worlds of impenetrable illusion, differing only in that the world of ordinary experience is defined by habit and convention while the other world is fashioned by the inborn yearning of man for a place "wherein human nature has kept its first dignity and strength; and wherein human passions are never in a poor way to find expression with adequate speech and action."

The immediate source of humor and irony in *The Cream of the Jest* is the contrasting interplay of these two worlds. The commonplace world in which Kennaston lives with his friends and neighbors is presented in a series of small domestic comedies, and naturally and appropriately enough the comedy of this world is the comedy of inadequacy; greatness is made to go in the tattered rags of worn-out clichés, talent rises on the wings provided by prurience and fad, and all conversation, however intimate the situation, runs in the barren gulches of the conventional and expected. The general inadequacy which is exposed by these comic techniques is boldly underscored by constant juxtaposition with that other world in which speech and action are always commensurate with the occasion, whether of good or evil, joy or sorrow. The actual embodiment which Cabell gives that other world in this comedy consists of many brightly colored fragments of historical romance.

Clearly this is not yet Cabell's mature manner, the manner of *Jurgen, Figures of Earth,* and *Something About Eve,* which forces the reader to enter a world that is frankly fantastic and alien yet symbolically the real home of the human psyche. The method of *The Cream of the Jest* is only in part dramatic and only in small part symbolic. By and large, it is discursive. The reader shares Kennaston's experiences, but the meaning of those experiences is to a large extent given in Kennaston's discursively elaborated meditations and in the digressive commentaries of the narrator, Richard Harrowby.

Nonetheless, this transitional comedy does decidedly point the way to the allegorical and symbolic comedies that are to follow. (pp. 96-7)

The comic pattern which emerges clearly for the first time in *The Cream of the Jest* was to remain the essential comic pattern of the later comedies. This pattern as the comic protagonist experiences it consists basically of three steps or movements: first, the felt awareness in various terms of the finite predicament, that is, of the humanly irremediable condition of incompleteness and imperfection; second, the struggle against the limitations implied in the finite predicament; and third, the acceptance of the human condition as, for all its limitations, upon the whole satisfactory. The third step is fairly complicated, involving acquiescence in the mystery of being as well as the reasonably complacent perception that however radically defective in some respects, the conditions of human living do nonetheless provide for both practical security and poetic beauty. From the reader's point of view the pattern is one of almost instinctive evasions by means of which the comic protagonist protects his ego against the corrosive, disillusioning truths which his struggle forces upon him and by means of which, also, he provides for his own more or less happy ending. (p. 103)

[*Jurgen*] was the first of Cabell's comedies written in what we may call his mature style and from his mature point of view; after *Jurgen* no further significant development takes place. (p. 105)

[The major comedies—*Jurgen, Figures of Earth, The High Place, The Silver Stallion,* and *Something About Eve*]—are all of a type. This is not to say, as numerous reviewers and critics have said, that these comedies are repetitious. The charge of repetitiousness betrays either a superficial reading which is impressed only with such common techniques as displacement and double-entendre or a reading which grasps only the broad pattern and none of the nuances or variations. The fact that all of the major comedies are written from the same point of view should forestall any surprise over the fact that the essential pattern remains the same. Moreover, it should be remembered that for the comic writer in general and for Cabell in particular all human experience is at bottom probable and therefore undifferentiated. The unity of human experience, however, does not preclude the possibility of variety, for though human experience is broadly uniform and normative, it has many facets. Each of Cabell's major comedies takes up a different facet, elaborates a closely related but different theme; each refers to and contributes to the same core meaning but it does not exhaust that core meaning. In other words, while Jurgen and Gerald Musgrave confront a similar world and endure a similar fate, their comedies do not repeat one another; their comedies taken together make a larger and more complex statement than does either taken separately.

What first and most forcefully impresses itself upon the reader who comes to the major comedies after having read the earlier comedies is the marked gain in gusto, due primarily to the broad comic treatment of sexuality and to the ever increasing dependence upon often recondite folklore materials. As outstanding as these things are, however, they are only secondary characteristics; the primary characteristics, those which are essential to the definition of Cabellian comedy as something distinct, are the peculiar qualities of the fantasy world in which the comedies take place . . . and the unorthodox character— or perhaps more accurately, situation—of the comic protagonist. (pp. 105-06)

Jurgen, Manuel, and Gerald Musgrave are, initially, all committed to the hopeless pursuit of impossible perfection. They are animated by a dissatisfaction which leads them to reject the probable norms of human experience and sends them journeying into the wonderful in search of ideal fulfillment and satisfaction. Thus, Jurgen sets out in search of justice, that is, in search of that which will satisfy his deep yearnings for love, beauty, and holiness. Justice in this sense refers simply to the seemingly rational demand that there should be no desire without a corresponding object or that the universe should provide that which is commensurate with man's dreams and in which, consequently, he may find total satisfaction. In Jurgen's case the complex objects of yearning are gathered up and projected in the symbolic figure of Helen of Troy, a variation upon the traditional unattainable princess of folklore. Similarly Manuel, too, is aroused by Horvendile, the spirit of romance, and sent forth in search of another version of the unattainable princess. And Gerald Musgrave sets forth to redeem the mythical kingdom of Antan and, more significantly, to reinstate himself as a god in his appropriate mythology. (pp. 107-08)

As rebels against imperfect, probable human experience, then, and as searchers into the wonderful, Jurgen, Manuel, and Gerald Musgrave would seem at the outset to be cast in the traditional role of the tragic hero. There is, of course, no confusion of tone. The appropriate comic tone—the tone of playful detachment—is established at the very beginning of each of the comedies and predominates throughout. *Jurgen* opens with the logical but comic because morally inappropriate defense of the devil; *Figures of Earth* opens with the ironic but humorous miscomprehension of the expression "to make a figure in the world"; *Something About Eve* opens with a mildly satirical treatment of the Southern code of chivalry. This is only to say, however, that the comic intention is declared at the outset. The fact remains that in subject matter, in the situation of the comic protagonist, these comedies trespass upon the domain of tragedy and raise the theoretical problem of how this domain is to be subjugated to the comic spirit. (pp. 108-09)

When one reads through the **Biography** as Cabell finally arranged it, he finds the comic vision re-enforced in several ways. The underlying irony of the **Biography** is that each individual life, for all its felt uniqueness, is merely one more essentially undifferentiated beat in the monotonous rhythm of life flowing down from Manuel. Negatively considered, this is a satire upon all concepts of progress and amelioration, but positively it means that the human spirit endures and with it the dreams and illusions and the comic pattern of life. To be sure, as one follows the life of Manuel from Poictesme to Lichfield the action seems to fall away into the inconsequential; there seems to be a considerable loss of scope and meaning. If, however, the modern Lichfieldians play out their comedies on a much smaller stage, it is not because anything essential has been subtracted from them, but because the free play of the imagination, which is needed to project their comedies upon the plane of symbol and myth, has been circumscribed by realism and scientism. And just as the second book in the **Biography,** *The Silver Stallion,* gives assurance that human dreams are indomitable and that in their imperiousness and ruthlessness they can thrive upon the most unlikely materials, so the last book, *The Cream of the Jest,* gives assurance that the power of the imagination does not diminish; for those who can avail themselves of it, it can still transfigure human living. (pp. 125-26)

> *Arvin R. Wells, in his* Jesting Moses: A Study in Cabellian Comedy *(copyright, 1962, by The Board of Commissioners of State Institutions of Florida), University of Florida Press, 1962, 146 p.*

DESMOND TARRANT   (essay date 1967)

Cabell's later writings consist essentially of five trilogies. The first trilogy is entitled *Their Lives and Letters,* and it stands as a prologue to the later novels while a second nonfiction trilogy is called *Virginians Are Various* and acts as the epilogue. The first of the trilogies of novels is *The Nightmare Has Triplets;* this comprises [*Smirt, Smith,* and *Smire*]. . . . The second is *Heirs and Assigns,* consisting of [*The King Was in His Counting House, Hamlet Had an Uncle,* and *The First Gentleman of America*]. . . . The third and last trilogy of fiction is called *It Happened in Florida,* and is composed of a history, [*The St. Johns,* and two short novels, *There Were Two Pirates* and *The Devil's Own Dear Son*]. . . . (p. 209)

The development and literary status of these later works are significant. After completing the **Biography,** Cabell omitted his first name; in a special sense, he is a different person and his art reflects this fact. . . . This is not to say that Cabell's art goes to pieces on completion of the **Biography**—far from it. Nevertheless he does seem to be like Napoleon returning from Moscow, although he fights every inch of the way, frequently halts for stubborn rear-guard actions, and even at times—as in *Heirs and Assigns*—makes recognizable if temporary advances. The nonfiction remains consistently superb. This last fact may be the clue to the total development. Cabell's earliest

writings dealt with contemporary life and more satirically with people and personal relations as in the first novels and short stories. Then he plunged into an ironical treatment of the relations between men and the gods as he produced his best works culminating in Gerald Musgrave's "camping" on the very borders of Antan. Now, Cabell deals increasingly again with the satiric; he gradually abandons the depths of irony even as he begins to move again toward the present in time. (pp. 209-10)

The matured and skilled intellect that produced the author's notes to the Storisende Edition carries over directly into the prose works and is apparent in *Their Lives and Letters.* (p. 212)

In his introduction to *These Restless Heads* [the first book of this trilogy] Cabell observes that it is "a cohering trilogy which concerns itself . . . with one main theme and with one protagonist." In the second part of the book Cabell takes up the account in his own person, day and place. This second part occupies most of the book and shows Cabell as an essayist in the very finest manner of the classical tradition. (p. 213)

It may be said that where the first book of the trilogy deals with Cabell's art and attitude in general, *Special Delivery* [the second book of this trilogy] deals with himself and his ideas most personally, while the third book, *Ladies and Gentlemen,* deals more specifically with the sources, the archetypes, of his own mythology. Thus each volume of this trilogy fills in details of related personal aspects of Cabell's attitude and art, as the earlier prose essays of *Beyond Life* and *Straws and Prayer Books* do for his thought and philosophy.

These prose writings also provide, although not to such profound depths, germinal analysis from which came later syntheses. For example, many of these ten replies touch satirically upon the nature of Virginia, the U.S.A., and modern life everywhere in the west. . . . There is a very sharp edge to these letters even as there is in most of the later writing, as the urbane impersonal irony yields to observations closer to the present in time and in person. After all, Cabell's position was so clearly unique: here is a civilized writer with mind and heart fully attuned to skills and concepts immortal who was free to express himself to the fullest of his range. Where so many were producing more marketable goods, here was the genuine artist cast in the mold of the ancients but with full command of the present. Not often has this century produced such a coincidence of circumstance and ability in letters. Cabell looks from Olympus upon the antics of his own era and a fine spectacle is finely portrayed—not by the usual topical means but through the gaze of eternity. (pp. 218-19)

Smirt, Smith, and *Smire* comprise Cabell's first substantial fiction after the completion of the **Biography of Manuel.** In *Their Lives and Letters,* Cabell had clarified many ideas about the causes and effects of modern life in general; many of these ideas were now to be presented in *The Nightmare Has Triplets.* He is still rather uneasy at finding himself outside Poictesme even though he symbolizes it by Branlon and occasionally re-enters it.

In *Smirt,* Cabell undertakes to depict a "real" dream in the mode of Lewis Carroll. Whereas all his previous books dealt with men's dreams, those dreams had been, in effect, artistic representations of instinctive racial desires. But what of the equally illogical nightly dreams also made by Miramon Lluagor? Cabell uses the technical method or machinery of a real dream and embarks upon a survey of modern life and letters. The schematic devices are devilishly ingenious. Using flippancy, irreverance, and the profoundest clichés of a reading public, Cabell expresses not only the essentials of modern living but also a conception which hints at age-old hypotheses amounting to a form of deism. Here Cabell's intellect is clearly paramount. There emerges both a satiric portrait of a life dominated by dullness and mediocrity and an astute rerendering of Cabell's long-held view of domesticity; both aspects are united by a treatment which hints at deeper hypotheses from reincarnation to a planned and ordered universe. In addition, balance is maintained by the acknowledgment, implicit in the name *Smirt,* of the artist who is not only subject to the dangers of hubris but frequently, in his innermost thinking, an "embarrassed booby." Smirt is rather like a more topical Jurgen. He meets the public at large and notes the workings of the gods as expressed in the daily headlines; he visits the gods themselves and the creator of the universe, who is the author of that best seller the Bible; he considers the magnificent lineage of the bluebottle fly and meets lost Arachne as well as other notable females who all have technical and spiritual as well as physical parts to play; in the end, even as a bluebottle fly, but with one important proviso, Smirt happily enters the web of Arachne, heroine of the lost legend which Smirt was to rediscover for her. (pp. 237-38)

Smith is subtitled "A Sylvan Interlude," and it recaptures much of the sunny tone and atmosphere of *The High Place*. It is one of the later novels that most nearly returns to Poictesme in treatment and significance. If, on the whole, it is not so profound, it by no means lacks substance—everything is relative. (p. 244)

Smire may be the best of this trilogy. Cabell completes his disengagement from Poictesme and deals, in a detached manner, with his own transition. While still meeting with the public at large, while still upon his eternal quest, he reflects a spirit of reconciliation and acceptance; this pervades the well-chosen material to produce a smoothly-flowing music that frequently echoes the orchestration of *Jurgen* in its sombre and majestic overtones. Where dialogue was later to diminish to ineffectuality, in *Smire* the loquacity is apt, very funny, and yet fraught with substantial meaning as Cabell in effect winds up his long personal, if fictional, versions and estimates. Yet the spirit of acceptance does not betoken compromise, and *Smire* offers precise confirmation of the essential ideas in *Beyond Life*. The reconciliation is with the gods rather than with the public at large.

Smire, reduced yet a step farther in his status, returns to various key episodes in literature and history: to Dido prior to the arrival of Aeneas; to Gabriel, who, in some slight embarrassment it seems, is about to arrange an immaculate conception; to the Almighty again; and to Moera, who, like Egeria, rules over all. Smire gives generously of his advice and guidance; he knows everything from how to tell a painter what is wrong with his picture to explaining the meaning of honesty to a statesman. Yet he remains modest in his persistent avoidance of *hubris*. Always the intellectual subtlety of dialogue and ingenuity of situation are underscored by the slow rhythmic sense of tragedy.

Here is abundant confirmation of the myth-making chemistry of Cabell's art. For example, in Chapter XXIV, "To the Public at Large," Cabell supplies a convincing distinction between realism and romance. In doing this he distinguishes between the copyist and the creator. We see how the poet, as the mythmaker, creates that which man desires and pursues while the copyist attempts to photograph and annotate that which actually

is. Only the poets—Cabell includes Homer, Shakespeare, Shelley, and Milton, as well as Walter Scott and Conan Doyle—create. (pp. 247-48)

Heirs and Assigns appears to contain, not Cabell's last fiction, but his last substantial fiction. On the other hand, these three novels [*The King Was in His Counting House, Hamlet Had an Uncle,* and *The First Gentleman of America*] . . . may well be the best of the later fiction, the backbone of the writings after the **Biography**. In *The Nightmare Has Triplets,* Cabell was disengaging himself from Poictesme; he dealt with the familiar themes even as he gave them more topical treatment and made greater use of the dramatic devices of his earlier short stories. Still making magnificent use of myth (as in Elaire's farewell to Astrild, Chapter XXI in *Smirt*) to probe the profoundest possibilities of human feeling and meaning, precisely in accordance with the primordial mechanics of human motivation as illustrated by Jung, Cabell also gave increasing play to his intellectual gifts for satire, to embody pungently standard elements of modern American, indeed all Western life. (p. 251)

In different ways, all three of the novels in *Heirs and Assigns* are excellent. After forty years of creative activity with words, Cabell here still displays versatility and variation in ever fresh forms, without appearing repetitious. The preface . . . to *The King Was in His Counting House* states the theme explicitly. Where Cabell's previous poet-heroes, such as Jurgen and Gerald Musgrave, eventually relinquished their spiritual guests to relapse into domestication, in this work Cabell deals at length with what happens to the poet as he turns to his practical vocation rather as he might deal with the reign of Shakespeare's Hamlet had Hamlet conquered Claudius. . . . All are poets in their youth, with the flourishing self-conceit and rebelliousness and self-sufficiency of the poet. But after boyhood comes "the marked respect for altruism" or, at least, the need to acknowledge the needs of others. Cabell describes this realization as "the supreme shape-giver of human character . . . the most dynamic of all strong forces in human life and in human civilization." It is most relevant to note in this work what is possibly the clearest statement of Cabell's implicit, if not belief, then certainly idea, of a force which uses humans in proportion to their usefulness for its own ultimately constructive ends. All whose characters do not develop to recognition of an acquiescence in the need to harmonize with these social forces are destroyed. Each character who dies ("excepting only chance-murdered Gratiano") does so "through a pursuit of some private interest which is at odds with implacable altruism." (pp. 252-53)

As Shakespeare brought into *Hamlet* his theories on the nature and performance of drama, Cabell introduces—and much more relevantly—ideas on the nature and performance of poetry.

Many are the subtle meanings thus interwoven (including Hamlet's Promethean use of a bundle of kindling twigs) in *Hamlet Had an Uncle,*—perhaps Cabell's subtlest work. It is a superb imaginative representation of the death of Hamlet and the life of his Uncle, which gives lastingly to eternal mysteries the emphasis and imprint of our times. . . .

[*The First Gentleman of America*] concludes this trilogy of inheritance. It also begins the last phase of Cabell's fiction, a phase in which he deals with semihistorical, legendary, and national material to present lasting traits of human nature in their more satirical perspective. Of this last phase, including this work and the trilogy following under the collective title *It Happened in Florida, The First Gentleman of America* seems the most substantial. So with this third work of *Heirs and Assigns* we see Cabell's last major novel. (p. 263)

The basis of *The First Gentleman of America* is the activities of the Spanish, French, and English as they endeavored to extend their possessions in America. Already in America were the Indians. Taking these two sides—the invaders and the invaded—Cabell presents his sardonic portrayal of the real and ostensible motives of human conduct as they went into the making of this new world in his comedy of conquest. (p. 264)

Whereas in *The First Gentleman of America* Cabell was freely making use of facts, in *The St. Johns* he makes use of his facts very freely with the result that the book becomes a satirical pageant of human faults and foibles. Brilliantly the saga of history up, down, and around this river is used to illustrate again, but much more intellectually, the discrepancy between ethics and morals, the ostensible intention and the actual outcomes, of human behavior. Thus the book becomes a shrewd combination of wit, fiction, and historical fact illustrating, in a manner midway between Gibbon and Thackeray, vice and folly and misfortune. Yet, while the fun remains fast and furious, while the craftsmanship, the style, the execution, are excellent, profundity is now replaced by shallows, however sparkling. Yet the intention was probably not otherwise, and the aim probably fully achieved.

As a work of art, *The St. Johns* fulfills its purpose. That this purpose is a pageant of the grotesque seems to speak for itself. Certainly over such a full range of material the purpose could hardly have been other. Yet themes which Cabell had previously dealt with very differently are now represented more for their ridiculousness than for their deeper, if ironic, significance. (p. 268)

Cabell's last two novels are slighter. Structurally they are clever and skilled, but the ingenuity does not include much of the substance or content. *There Were Two Pirates* . . . tells, in the first person, the exploits of a Spanish pirate José Gasparilla off the shores of Florida as he attempted to accumulate enough savings to return to his beloved in Spain. Cabell uses "flashbacks" and a magic green stone which can release one from one's shadow, but the substance is slight for all the technical skill and the novel becomes no more than a pleasant pastime, although that, in itself, may be achievement enough. With *The Devil's Own Dear Son* . . . , the background is more topical in that it consists of a tourist home in Florida. St. Augustine again features prominently, but dialogue tends to extend and extend without real justification as we experience the life of an embryo Rotarian who journeys to the castle of his youth's dreams through a universe akin to Florida itself. The scheme gives opportunity for satire but—except in scenes among the devils who serve in a democracy under a chief executive called Satan—it is now a little too contrived, while power and spontaneity are slowly diminishing. (pp. 270-71)

The three [volumes] which make up [*Virginians Are Various*] complete Cabell's writings by illustrating his place in the evolution of American and Western culture. European culture, with its classical foundations, must now interact with forces from Russia on the one hand and America on the other. Is it a question of Europe, as an extension of the classical, having to withstand the onslaughts of the barbarians? Will the barbarians dominate and destroy the cultural endeavors (various as these are) of thousands of years to the complete elimination of things spiritual? Or will the dynamic energies of the New World revitalize the old even as they become civilized, to the ultimate benefit of both? Cabell's art lies at the heart of this dilemma and shows how it can be satisfactorily resolved. In *Let Me Lie* he considers American Life in Virginia; in *Quiet Please* he deals with his own personal development within this framework; and in *As I Remember It* he illustrates more intimately the individuals who have influenced his art and himself. (p. 271)

The mind at work in *As I Remember It* bestrides the scene like enough to a colossus. The urbanity and humor are as good here as ever and the touch is surer than it sometimes is in the later works. (p. 276)

> *Desmond Tarrant, in his* James Branch Cabell: The Dream and the Reality *(copyright 1967 by the University of Oklahoma Press), University of Oklahoma Press, 1967, 292 p.*

MAURICE DUKE (essay date 1975)

[Cabell] is not as he appears at first sight. Although in subject matter he remained apart from the literary mainstream of the 1920s, his world view belies, as do the world views of many of the decade's major writers, his concept that life is an emotional, cultural, and intellectual vacuum. For Cabell the dream may be the ultimate reality, but it offers no more than a diversion from those parts of existence which man, because of various self-constructed codes by which he lives, will not allow himself to face. Thus, from the point of view which forms the philosophical basis of the Cabellian world, existence offers only appearances, never realities. And, if the appearance is the reality, then there is no still point, no central solid core in human life. (p. 76)

What is the statement made by Cabell's ambitious **Biography of the Life of Dom Manuel** . . .?

If we use Eliot's *The Waste Land*, probably the central poem of the first half of the twentieth century, as a touchstone or organizing metaphor, we see that in subject matter and social comment, the two writers are poles apart. *The Waste Land* paints for us a world in which we hear the pub keeper calling time, in which the sex act is as mechanical as putting a record on the gramophome, in which the meaning of our myths and the richness of our culture have somehow been inverted, a world in which "in this decayed hole among the mountains" we stand waiting for cleansing and renewing rain but hearing only thunder. On the surface, Cabell's world is obviously not like this. Cabell chides us with his urbanity, dazzles us with his ironical wit and captivates us with the beauties of Poictesme, a realm which is more perfect than any which we will ever be privileged to see. Beneath the surface, however, lies a kind of spiritual wasteland, not unlike Eliot's, in that in Poictesme nothing is really worth the effort because nothing can really ever be accomplished. Cabell's chivalric heroes, those who view life as a testing, find that there is really nothing to rest oneself against because the myths which form the core of existence have been fabricated both by chance and by opportunism. The gallant figures, those to whom life is a toy, a diversion, find a similar world facing and opposing them. These characters—Jurgen, for example—are the defeatists who live their lives by compromise. Knowing full well that their codes of behavior and the operation of the real world are alien to each other, they nevertheless, like J. Alfred Prufrock, "prepare a face to meet the faces" that they meet, perennially venturing forth to attend their ritualistic, and metaphorically insignificant, tea parties. The way of poetry offers little more, because in the Cabellian world it is impossible to be both poet and person. One must choose, and in the choosing one will invariably feel unfulfilled because he can have only half of what he feels the life of art should afford him.

Eliot's wasteland and Cabell's Poictesme are not too far apart then. In the former, man is out of touch with his mythology; in the latter his mythology is seen as being his hostage against mediocrity, but it is false. Again, in the former the mainstream of western culture—its art in the largest sense—is seen as being degraded while in the latter we see a world in which art counts less than the inventions of a Thomas Edison and a Henry Ford. Finally, in the former there is a cancerous malady at the core of society. In the latter the same malady is obviously there, but Cabell attempts to conceal it in artifice. These two writers never met. The one was a central figure in both the European and American literary scene while the other worked quietly in his private study in Richmond, Virginia. There can be little doubt, however, that both saw the world from a quite similar point of view. (pp. 85-6)

> Maurice Duke, *"The Baroque Waste Land of James Branch Cabell," in* The Twenties: Fiction, Poetry, Drama, *edited by Warren French (© copyright 1975 by Warren French), Everett/Edwards, Inc., 1975, pp. 75-86.*

ADDITIONAL BIBLIOGRAPHY

Canary, Robert H. "Cabell's Dark Comedies." *Mississippi Quarterly* XXI, No. 2 (Spring 1968): 83-92.
    Discussion of Cabell's attitude toward male and female sexuality.

Canby, Henry Seidel. "Persons and Personalities: James Branch Cabell." In his *American Estimates*, pp. 70-9. 1929. Reprint. Port Washington, N.Y.: Kennikat Press, 1968.
    Considers Cabell's themes trite and repetitive while admiring his style and use of myth.

Davis, Joe Lee. *James Branch Cabell.* New York: Twayne Publishers, 1962, 174 p.
    Comprehensive study designed to establish Cabell's importance as an American author.

Flora, Joseph M. "From Virginia to Poictesme: The Early Novels of James Branch Cabell." *Mississippi Quarterly* XXXII, No. 2 (Spring 1979): 219-39.
    Study of Cabell's apprentice novels and how they fit into *The Biography of Manuel.*

Godshalk, William Leigh. *In Quest of Cabell: Five Exploratory Essays.* New York: Revisionist Press, 1975, 97 p.
    Biographical, critical, and scholarly essays.

Himelick, Raymond. "Figures of Cabell." *Modern Fiction Studies* 2, No. 4 (Winter 1956-57): 214-20.

Examines the nature of the fantasy world in Cabell's fiction.

Hinz, Evelyn J. and Teunissen, John J. "Life beyond Life: Cabell's Theory and Practice of Romance." *Genre* X, No. 3 (Fall 1977): 299-328.
    Insightful examination of *Beyond Life* as "an indispensable point of reference for an introduction to Cabell's art as a romancer as well as to the theory and practice of the romance in general."

Howard, Leon. "Figures of Allegory." *The Sewanee Review* XLII, No. 1 (January-March 1934): 54-66.
    Analyzes *Figures of the Earth, Something About Eve,* and *Jurgen* as allegories of illusion and disillusionment.

Jack, Peter Monro. "The James Branch Cabell Period." In *After the Genteel Tradition,* edited by Malcolm Cowley, pp. 141-53. New York: W. W. Norton & Co., 1937.
    Attack on Cabell and his proponents.

Macy, John. Introduction to *Between Dawn and Sunrise: Selections from the Writings of James Branch Cabell,* by James Branch Cabell, edited by John Macy, pp. ix-xxvii. New York: Robert M. McBride & Co., 1930.
    Introduction to Cabell's dominant themes and a descriptive study of selections from *The Biography of Manuel.*

Millett, Fred B. "James Branch Cabell." In *Minor American Novelists,* edited by Charles Alva Hoyt, pp. 41-66. Carbondale, Edwardsville: Southern Illinois University Press, 1970.
    Descriptive survey of Cabell's major works and their critical reception.

Parks, Edd Winfield. "Cabell's *Cream of the Jest.*" *Modern Fiction Studies* 2, No. 2, (May 1956): 68-70.
    A gloss on Cabell's various uses of the phrase "cream of the jest."

Rubin, Louis D., Jr. "A Southerner in Poictesme." In his *No Place on Earth: Ellen Glasgow, James Branch Cabell and Richmond-in-Virginia,* pp. 50-81. Austin: University of Texas Press, 1959.
    Cabell as a Southern writer, with a consideration of him as a "realistic" author for the imaginative truth of his themes and characters.

Van Doren, Carl. *James Branch Cabell.* New York: Robert M. McBride & Co., 1925, 87 p.
    Critical study.

Wagenknecht, Edward. "James Branch Cabell: The Anatomy of Romanticism." In his *Cavalcade of the American Novel: From the Birth of the Nation to the Middle of the Twentieth Century,* pp. 330-53. New York: Holt, Rinehart and Winston, 1952.
    Descriptive overview of Cabell's works and their critical reception.

Wilson, Edmund. "James Branch Cabell: 1879-1958." In his *The Bit between My Teeth: A Literary Chronicle of 1950-1965,* pp. 322-25. New York: Farrar, Straus and Giroux, 1965.
    Observes a deepening of Cabell's pessimism in his later fiction.

Wright, Cuthbert. "The Best Butter?" *The Dial* LXXVI, No. 4 (April 1924): 361-63.
    Critique of Cabell's more enthusiastic critical admirers.

Karel Čapek

1890-1938

Czechoslovakian novelist, dramatist, short story writer, journalist, and essayist.

Čapek is best known for his antiutopian works, such as *R.U.R. (Rossum's Universal Robots)*, *Ze života hmyzu (The Insect Play)*, and *Válka s mloky (War with the Newts)*, in which he warns against the dehumanizing aspects of modern civilization and satirizes a plethora of social, economic, and political systems. These innovative and well-crafted fantasies are credited with changing the direction of science fiction and with bringing the genre of science-fiction drama into its own. Čapek's masterpiece, however, is the trilogy of novels *Hordubal*, *Provětroň (Meteor)*, and *Obyčejný zivot (An Ordinary Life)*. In these works he explores his most important theme, the plurality and relativity of truth.

Čapek was born in northeastern Bohemia. A frail and sickly child, he was favored by his older brother, Josef. As adults the brothers enjoyed a close relationship, frequently collaborating on short stories and plays. Josef, an artist, also illustrated several of his brother's books. In 1917 Čapek embarked on a career in journalism that lasted the rest of his life. In essays and articles he championed the causes of Czech nationalism and liberalism. Thus, the post-World War I independence of Czechoslovakia largely influenced the author's life. He was intensely involved in his country's politics; his enthusiasm for the new democratic government effected a personal friendship with Tomáš Masaryk, Czechoslovakia's first president, resulting in a biography and several chronicles. As World War II approached, the Čapek brothers, who had bitterly denounced fascism in their articles, cartoons, and plays, were advised to leave Prague. They chose to stay and continue their fight. Čapek died three months before the Nazi's invaded Prague; the secret police, unaware of his death, arrived at his home, seeking his arrest.

Čapek was a prolific writer who attempted many genres, but it was through the plays *R.U.R.* and *The Insect Play* that he achieved international acclaim. *R.U.R.*, which introduced the word robot to the world, was an immediate success. Though Čapek liked *R.U.R.* least of all his dramas, audiences were both fascinated and terrified by its vision of a technically advanced society unable to control its ultimate labor-saving creation, the robot. Playgoers ignored the obvious gaps in structure and argument, focusing instead on the drama's theatrical effectiveness and originality. *The Insect Play* and, to a lesser extent, *Věc Makropoulos (The Makropoulos Secret)* were also well received. The former, a parable on human vices and weaknesses, was deemed ingenious, if somewhat shallow and repetitious. And *The Makropoulos Secret*, with its strangely pessimistic view of eternal youth, aroused debate when critics suggested that it was written in answer to Bernard Shaw's *Back to Methuselah*.

Although *R.U.R* and *The Insect Play* brought Čapek worldwide attention, critics maintain that his science-fiction novels are of greater literary significance. *Krakatit* and *War with the Newts* are Čapek's most fully realized and eloquent antiutopian works. The potential misuse of technology is the focal

point in all of Čapek's science fiction. He was not against progress or scientific inventiveness; rather, he feared how these inventions and discoveries would be employed. In *Krakatit* he foresees the destructive potential of atomic energy. *War with the Newts* is a biting, multileveled satire aimed at the exploitive elements of capitalism, communism, and fascism. Readers find it still timely and prophetic. In both novels, as well as in the trilogy, Čapek departs from his usual flat, allegorical method of characterization and fashions complex characters. In the trilogy, which some critics consider his best work, Čapek probes the relativity of truth and reality by examining various external and internal points of view. The three novels also provide psychologically subtle studies of the human personality.

Much of Čapek's work, particularly his novels and short stories, manifests the influence of G. K. Chesterton's and H. G. Wells's antiutopian and utopian works. While critics have compared him favorably to both authors, they note that the overall quality of Čapek's work is uneven. In his plays, themes and ideas often impede the development of plot and characterization. His novels, albeit more successful, tend to be thematically ambiguous and episodic in style and technique. Nevertheless, Čapek is considered one of Czechoslovakia's

foremost writers and the father of Czech drama. His novels and dramas, which reflect a vivid interest in humanity and its future, have been widely praised.

PRINCIPAL WORKS

Zářivé hlubiny [with Josef Čapek] (short stories) 1916
R.U.R. (Rossum's Universal Robots) (drama) 1921
    [*R.U.R. (Rossum's Universal Robots)*, 1923]
Trapné provídky (short stories) 1921
    [*Money and Other Stories*, 1929]
Lásky hra osudna [with Josef Čapek] (drama) 1922
Továrna na absolutno (novel) 1922
    [*The Absolute at Large*, 1927]
Věc Makropoulos (drama) 1922
    [*The Makropoulos Secret*, 1925]
Ze života hmyzu [with Josef Čapek] (drama) 1922
    [Published in England as *And So Ad Infinitum (The Life of
        the Insects)*, 1923; published in the United States as *The
        World We Live In (The Insect Comedy)*, 1933, and as
        The Insect Play in *R.U.R. and The Insect Play*, 1961]
Krakatit (novel) 1924
    [*Krakatit*, 1925]
Adam stvořitel [with Josef Čapek] (drama) 1927
    [*Adam the Creator*, 1930]
Povídky z druhé kapsy (short stories) 1929
    [Published in *Tales from Two Pockets*, 1932]
Povídky z jedné kapsy (short stories) 1929
    [Published in *Tales from Two Pockets*, 1932]
Hordubal (novel) 1933
    *[*Hordubal*, 1934]
Obyčejný zivot (novel) 1934
    *[*An Ordinary Life*, 1936]
Provětroň (novel) 1934
    *[*Meteor*, 1935]
Válka s mloky (novel) 1936
    [*War with the Newts*, 1937]
Bílánemoc (drama) 1937
    [*Power and Glory*, 1938]
Matka (drama) 1938
    [*The Mother*, 1939]
Život a dílo skladatele Foltýna (unfinished novel) 1939
    [*The Cheat*, 1941]

*These novels were published as *Three Novels* in 1948.

ASHLEY DUKES (essay date 1923)

The strength of Karel Capek's *R.U.R.* lies even more in its hour than in its subject. The mechanical figures made by men in their own image are bound sooner or later to usurp world-dominion and exterminate their masters. We foresee the development of the "Robots" from industrous automata into creatures with whims and passions, moods and frenzies, a heart and a soul. We even foresee dimly the day when the last surviving man, a white-bearded scientist, will seek in his laboratory the lost formula for manufacturing inhabitants of this earth. If there be no more men, let there at least be Robots.

A dead planet cries for life. One step farther and we foresee the Adam and Eve of the Robot family in the earliest stage of courtship, ready to repeople the earth with a race that shall be no longer mechanical, but human and humane. In their garden lurks as yet no serpent. There is little originality in the idea. You may piece it together, bit by bit, from all the classical and modern tales of men who made beings like themselves. . . . The motive is always recurring in literature, like the motive of the heavenly visitor who is taken for a man. . . . The last man in a plague-stricken world, driven to the woods by hordes of wild creatures that invade his empty cities, lies on a bough and watches eagerly the anthropoid apes who fumble with bits of wood and stone. This year perhaps they will carve a weapon; next year maybe a tool; next decade a dwelling; and in centuries or ages a cathedral. The watcher will die, but the race will go on. It is a subject for "fantastic melodrama," as this play is well called.

Fortunately, there is something more in it than the sensational power of the old tale. That something is Capek's instinct for feeling the response of his audience at every given moment—an instinct sincere but unerring. The play is not a piece of dramatic literature; it is scarcely even a deep or thoughtful work. It is a piece of brilliant journalism of the stage, a work of temperamental power that "carries," as actors say, because the author believes in it, and believes in his audience, and is interested in their reaction to what he has to say. . . . But Capek goes farther than belief. He has a natural understanding of crowds and crowd psychology. Europe of to-day is his stage and the world his audience, not because we feel his plays to be immortal, but because we feel them to be inevitable. They are as inevitable as the leading article on the morrow of the Budget—good journalism, well phrased, well presented, and, above all, well timed. They have more to do with passing events than with enduring symbols.

Day-to-day work is stamped with a certain fleeting character that cannot be disguised. So it is with the work of Karel Capek, and with *R.U.R.* in particular. (pp. 114-16)

The sensations of his play are epic, magnificent. What headlines they would make! What headlines, in fact, they do make! "Rossum's Universal Robots—Men Manufactured—Too Old at Twenty—Seekers after Souls—the Fight for the Formula—Revolt of the Robots—Nature set at Naught." And how absorbing, too, are the questions that the author raises! Are Robots right or wrong? Is Progress right or wrong? Should Robots fight for men, or only work for them? Should Robots vote? Should Robots have a soul? In every question there is matter for an autumn newspaper correspondence, if not for an election address. . . . The question of the desirability of progress is an interesting one, if only Mr. Capek would not obscure the issue with his confounded dramatic sense. But of course we ought to be grateful for the quality. His dramatic sense is the life-blood of *R.U.R.* For my part the author may keep his questions and the answers to them, if he only shows us towering factories built by Robots, swung on cranes, and Robots looming up gigantic at the window against a flaming sky, and Robots chanting their cry for a posterity as they advance in regular formation and rhythmic gestures. These dramatic pictures have a certain style and importance.

For the rest of his dramatic effect, Capek borrows freely from his audience. His Robots not only work in factories and add up figures in counting-houses, but they are hired by governments for armies, and they kill each other and mankind with a cool precision quite devoid of ill-feeling. (For Robots read chemists, and we have the probable forecast of the next war.) They likewise have a tendency to band themselves together. "It was a mistake to make them international," says one of their inventors. "We must have national Robots; then they will speak a different language and really hate each other." A bitter saying. It is certain that our sympathy for the Robots increases as the play proceeds, if only because they are more interesting than the human beings who claim to have made them. Eventually we begin to wonder whether we ourselves may not be Robots—a theatre full of Robots waiting for an awakening. Yes, the author throws out his hints very skilfully. . . . When you have thought them over, you find there is no more in them than in yesterday's or to-morrow's newspaper head-line; but they have interested you all the same. In that sense *R.U.R.* is an intensely interesting play. (pp. 117-19)

Ashley Dukes, "Expressionists," in his The Youngest Drama: Studies of Fifty Dramatists, *Ernest Benn, Limited, 1923, pp. 107-40.**

H.T. PARKER   (essay date 1924)

"The Makropoulos Secret" was first played in the National Theater of Prague in November of 1922, and it was then that Karel Capek wrote to his audience:

"The idea of this new comedy first occurred to me about three or four years ago, before writing 'R. U. R.' It seemed then to be an ideal subject for a novel, but that is a form of writing I do not care for. The idea itself came from the theory of Professor Mecnik, that age is caused by an auto-intoxicating organism.

"I make these statements because Bernard Shaw's new play, 'Back to Methuselah,' which I have seen in synopsis only, appeared this winter. In actual measure, it is very impressive. It, too, has the motif of longevity. This likeness in theme is entirely accidental, and, it seems to me from the synopsis, that while Bernard Shaw comes to the same conclusion as I do, it is in quite the opposite manner. Mr. Shaw believes that it is possible for an ideal community of people to live several hundred years in a sort of paradise. As the play-goer perceives, long life in my play is treated quite differently; I think that such a condition is neither ideal nor desirable. Both ideas are purely hypothetical since neither has the proof of experience. Yet perhaps I may say this much: Mr. Shaw's play is a classic example of optimism, and my own—a hopeless instance of pessimism.

"Whether I am called an optimist or a pessimist, will make me neither happier nor sadder; yet, 'to be a pessimist' implies, it would seem, a silent rebuke from the world for bad behavior. In this comedy I have striven to present something delightful and optimistic. Does the optimist believe that it is bad to live sixty years but good to live three hundred? I merely think that when I proclaim a life of the ordinary span of sixty years as good enough in this world, I am not guilty of criminal pessimism. If we say that, at some future time, there will be no disease, misery, or poverty—that certainly is optimism. If we say that this daily life of ours, full of deprivation and sorrow, is not really so irreconcilable, but has in it something of immense value—is that pessimism? I think not. One turns from bad to higher things: the other searches for something better and higher in ordinary existence. The one looks for paradise— there is not a loftier vision for the human soul—the other strives for recompense in life itself. Is this pessimism?" (pp. 5-6)

The technician and the layman sit alike in admiration before a playwright who can arrest attention and kindle interest in the very first speeches of his play; who can coördinate the intro-

duction of the personages into the progress of the narrative; who from the interaction of both can quicken premises into curiosity aroused and suspense set a-vibrating. Of such a Capek is the first act of "The Makropoulos Secret." Before it is done we are engrossed in the suit of Gregor against Prus—a hundred years old; in Emilia Marty, singing-woman, mysterious intervener and informer; in the spell she lays with nearly every contact; in the fulfilment forthwith of her sayings. Prus, Gregor, Vitek, Kolonaty have all come, as well, into individual human and theatric being.

A second act that apparently begins in decoration, only deepens the mystery and intensifies the fascination hanging about Elina-Emilia. Incidents that pass as the embroidery, almost the digression of the moment—say the interchanges between the young lovers—speedily contribute to the main course of the dramatic narrative, the rising current of dramatic suspense. For the while, Capek seems to be taking the permissible privilege of the playwright to amusing conversation—and lo! almost every sentence is contributing to the riddle of Emilia. (pp. vii-viii)

A third act ensues—of the steeled Emilia caught in a press that may crush even steel; of Emilia spent, desperate, menaced, disclosing at last the mystery that has haunted the play. Again there are interludes—Prus's discovery of the suicide of his son because the father had won the woman that the youth also craved; the foolish interventions of old Hauk-Sendorf. Yet the one is as the red bolt to pierce these darkening clouds; the other as the irony attending nearly every human crisis. "The melodrama, the staginess, the superfluity of the mock mediaeval inquisition!" the reader is quick to say, as he cons the manuscript. Capek, however, writes for the stage, not for the easy-chair. In the theater these trappings retort with spell against spell upon the wavering Emilia. (p. ix)

The woman reveals [her secret] and the suspense of the play seems ended—only to renew itself. For what shall be done with life everlasting? And in the next room Elena-Emilia waits. There is debate, in which the debaters speak also in character and with emotion. There is human decision. For Elena-Emilia there is also human release. So does the masterful Capek, abounding round a play that emotionally and suspensively seemed already full-circled.

Such work of the theater stirs the pride, quickens the zest of those who still love it. . . . Yet Capek and "The Makropoulos Secret" would not so prevail unless they carried freight of matter to engage the mind, quicken the imagination, stir the spirit—matter, moreover, intrinsically human in content and implication, by the playwright and the stage vitalized. "The Makropoulos Secret" is the secret of life unending. The mystery of Emilia Marty, born Elena Makropoulos, is the mystery of endless existence dovetailing into the daily lives of men and women that are mortal. Her spell is the spell of a woman persisting and all-knowing, case-hardened in the virtue and vice, the experience and the sensation, of a life that has ceased to begin and wax, to waver and decline—a life that is perpetual. (pp. ix-x)

Matter of fantasy, it is true, but matter that weaves these imaginings into the actualities of human experience. Matter of the theater, it is also true, but matter impregnated with human content and choice, speculation and even philosophy. Matter indeed of substance and vitality for the mind, the imagination and the spirit. (p. xi)

H. T. Parker, "Introduction" (1924), in The Makropoulos Secret *by Karel Capek, edited by Randal*

C. Burrell, John W. Luce & Company, 1925, pp. v-xii.

WILLIAM A. DRAKE (essay date 1928)

The extraordinarily rapid rise of Karel Capek from comparative obscurity to world-wide acclaim, the exceptional vitality and fecundity of his talent, and the exigent social and moralistic preoccupations which control his work, are all, in a fundamental and impressive sense, suggestive of the psychological situation of the newly triumphant Czechoslovak Republic. (p. 310)

The whole nature of Capek's genius is Czech. The leader of the young generation which, since the war, has superseded that of Vrchlický, Březina, Machar, and Sova, he perfectly exemplifies the type of his special group. In his novels and plays, the classic Europen forms, introduced into Bohemian literature chiefly through the translation of Vrchlický, are cunningly adapted to the impulsive, informal utterance of the new age, and salted with occasional, tactfully blended admixtures of German Expressionism, Russian Rayonnism, and the Cubism which Josef Capek has borrowed from the French. Technically, Capek's work is anomalous, for it is as distinctly in the classical tradition as it is in the modernist. The singular effectiveness of his novels arises from this duality, as well as from the author's trick of lending his narrative a structure and climactic arrangement similar to that which he employs in his plays.

But Karel Capek's really important point of departure is not one of technique, but one of character. The first notable poet of Czech nationalism, the nature of Capek's inspiration is conspicuously Slavic. . . . [In] Capek's audacity of invention, in his Olympian disdain of the strait prescriptions of form, and above all, in his intense social consciousness, his sense of responsibility, his fundamental uprightness, his apprehension of God in the spirit of life, and his tenderness for every living creature, we perceive the original Slav.

The problems of humanity are never absent from Capek's work. If his novels and plays are in themselves thrilling, adroit, and occasionally beautiful, they are so merely because Capek is one of the most accomplished living publicists. The Czechs, of necessity, became masters of subtle evangelism under the Habsburg censorship. The only instrument of expression which was left to them was the theater, so they made the theater a national forum, with a completeness hardly equaled since the time of the Greeks; by recalling the heroic deeds of their past, by impassioned lyricism or purposeful innuendos, by scrupulous symbolism, even in their marionette shows, they constantly reminded one another that the ancient spirit of their nation still lived. Capek employs the technique which was then developed as an approach to what he conceives to be the fundamental problems of life. (pp. 310-12)

In his more mature work, Capek's curiosity is toward life itself. In his first play, *The Robber*, . . . the central character is symbolical of the energetic and willful spirit of youth. *R.U.R.* is a symbolical melodrama of the mechanization of the proletariat. *The Insect Comedy* . . . is an ironical fantasy of human egoism and weakness. *The Makropoulos Secret* is a satirical demonstration of the worthlessness of human life. Each of these plays is theatrically perfect, tense in action to the point of melodrama, ingenious in execution, and conspicuously original in conception. . . . But as symbolical drama, it must be confessed that none of these plays will bear scrutiny. Their failure in this respect is too obvious to need a bill of particulars: in

R.U.R., for example, one notes the needless sexual differentiation of the Robots, Helena's unreasonable decision to remain on the island, the feebleness of her humanitarianism. . . . One admits the principles of the plays intellectually, but one never feels them. One sees through the whole fabric, as clearly as one follows a proposition in logic. It is Capek's creative instinct that is here at fault. . . . These deficiencies do not prevent the plays from reaching an astonishing degree of theatrical effectiveness, but they emphasize Karel Capek's creative limitations. The intrusion of the thesis impedes and sometimes, despite the author's ingenuity, arbitrarily determines the development of the drama. The instinct of the dramatist, on the contrary, confounds the exposition of his symbolism. The result is that, fine as Capek's plays undoubtedly are, they have in no case fully accomplished the possibilities of their original design.

Capek has lately found a more gracious vehicle for his symbolical evangelism in the novel; and it is in the novel (paradoxically, since the nature of his talent is essentially dramatic) that he has, for the first time, succeeded in expounding his theses comprehensively and without violence to the artistic development of his incidental plots. The faults which we have remarked in the plays are still present in the novels, but they are fewer and less conspicuous. . . . Capek, the novelist, has been profoundly influenced by the work and thought of H. G. Wells. *Krakatit,* that cyclonically dynamic romance of the Engineer Prokop, who has discovered an incredibly destructive explosive, which he guards for the service of mankind, immediately recalls *The World Set Free.* . . . [The] whole of Capek's art is an abstraction. He is too clever a dramatist—a publicist, if you will—to ignore life, so in *Krakatit* he gives us the delectable picture of Annie's *Frühlingserwachen,* and shows us Prokop ready to deliver his discovery into the hands of the philistines and the haughty Princess ready to betray her rank and friends, for love of one another. But one sees a new symbol even in these rare human episodes.

In *The Absolute* Capek has achieved a still greater abstraction—a Wellsian novel which the best of Wells's does not surpass, developed to the perfection of its genre, and charged with the most brilliant, acrid, and withal despairing irony. As in *Krakatit*—and again, *The World Set Free*—the situation in *The Absolute* hinges upon a pseudo-scientific hypothesis: the discovery of a means to utilize the internal energy of the atom as a motive power. . . . The cataclysm comes about in a strange and surprising way. Instead of making men less rapacious and liberating them, this closeness to the mysterious center of all energy makes them religious. Therein they approach the Absolute, and the Absolute, as medieval experimental science knew it, is God. So a reign of pugnacious godliness ensues, which eventually reduces the earth to chaos. . . . Rival religious sects, bitterly embattled against one another, arise everywhere, and a great religious war rages thorughout the world, until depletion brings the struggle to an end and the old order is restored.

One must watch Karel Capek. He had done much, but he has still more to do. The signs promise richly for him. . . . [He] is already famous; he possesses a rich and audacious talent; he is in the intellectual mid-current of a new national spirit which has but lately become conscious of itself, and which is determined to be great. (pp. 315-16)

William A. Drake, "Karel Capek," in his Contemporary European Writers, *John Day, 1928, G. G. Harrap, 1929, pp. 310-16.*

RENÉ WELLEK (essay date 1936)

[Most] English readers do not know that Karel Čapek is an extremely ambitious and subtle practitioner of the craft of fiction, a philosopher-poet passionately interested in the problems of truth and justice, in short, a great artist who has to be reckoned with as one of the major figures of contemporary literature. (p. 46)

Čapek's earliest writings reach back to pre-war times. . . and inevitably bear the traces of the time and the youth of their author. Čapek then wrote in conjunction with his elder brother Joseph, who has since become a distinguished modernist painter. . . . *Krakonoš's Garden* [a collection of their stories] is a curious mixture of little burlesque tales, anecdotes and epigrams, prose-poems and phantasies. Parodies of the style of symbolism clash piquantly with quotations from telegrams and newspapers. Much in the book is crude and naïve: but some numbers present a certain interest as they anticipate later developments, for instance **"System"**, which, in a grotesque fashion, treats the problem of the robots before the name was adopted. (pp. 46-7)

The very early comedy *The Fateful Game of Love* . . . succeeds very much better. There is no denying the artificiality of the trifle, a sort of *commedia dell'arte* with a tragic leading motive in an ironic setting. Gilles, the romantic weakling, is killed in a duel by the bullying ruffian Trivalin, but the lady is carried off by the plotting Brighello. This traditional theme, which is treated in very musical blank verse, is lightened by a series of devices that purposely bridge the gulf between the public and the actors. For instance, the doctor asks the audience why they came at all, Trivalin suddenly refuses to go on acting or challenges anybody in the audience. . . . All this deliberate spoiling of the theatrical illusion is very amusing, though the device is, of course, known since the times of Ludwig Tieck at least. The very same ironic and melancholy setting of the dying "rococo" recurs in the best story of the next collection of tales. *Luminous Depths* . . . contains a story, **"L'Eventail"**, which also could be called the fateful game of love. The garden-party of Principe Bodoni in 18th century Naples catches the right flavour of the time: the automatic dolls of M.J.L. Droz are worthy of E.T.A. Hoffmann though the Čapeks aim at something more restrained and objective. The preceding **"Red Story"** does not come off so well, possibly because of the inherent improbabilities of the very sanguinary action, or because Čapek does not quite succeed in catching the right matter-of-fact tone which we find in Stendhal's *Chroniques italiennes*. . . . The range of the whole collection is remarkable, the advance compared to *Krakonoš's Garden* quite undeniable. The Čapeks have discovered the charm of sheer story-telling, and they move easily from one style to the other among the most various settings. There was, however, no further development towards the style of the Italian "novelle", though **"L'Eventail"** was a promising piece of work. But the rather awkward and wasteful *Luminous Depths* point to the future: to a new and original mystery-story. (pp. 47-8)

[*Wayside Crosses* is] a collection of "detective stories". But they are very unusual detective or rather mystery stories, without any solution for the mysteries. The very disappointment of our expectation is their main point: just the most important part of the event told remains behind the scene. The justification of this interesting technical device is, of course, in the view of life the stories are meant to convey. *Krakonoš's Garden* was full of a naïve scepticism and an irreverence which rather enjoyed demonstrating that there are no absolute values. But

in the *Wayside Crosses* the joy has turned into bitterness. The world appears as a whirlwind of chance and contingencies without deeper coherence. . . . *Luminous Depths* covers huge stretches of time in a few sentences; *Wayside Crosses* concentrates on single mysterious moments. The following *Painful Stories* [translated into English under the title of *Money and Other Stories*] . . . return to the normal epical form, though they do not imply a substantial change of outlook. Life is again arbitrary and disconnected, brutal and disconcertingly illogical, The stories are "painful", because they are so inconclusive, because they frequently end with a submission after a very unheroic revolt. A husband takes money from his wife which he must know she gets from her lover (**"Three"**); an intelligent girl throws herself suddenly at the mercy of a man who does not care for her and rejects her (**"Helena"**). . . . [These] are some of the themes which contrast a very trivial outward occurrence with an inner drama of painful resignation. The supreme instance is possibly the first story, **"Two Fathers"**. A child dies, and the supposed father breaks down in grief on her grave, while the real father—as everybody knows in the village—is singing lustily in the choir. There is an atmosphere of heavy, melancholy fatality in these stories, which can be very well compared with some of the "painful" stories in Maupassant or Chekhov. (pp. 48-50)

Painful Stories very worthily concludes the extremely interesting period of Čapek's early writings. Then came immediately the success of *R.U.R.* . . . , which shows a complete change of style and outlook. . . . *R.U.R.* took the world by storm, and there were some good reasons for this success. The main idea of the robots (the word, derived from robota, drudgery, was suggested by Joseph Čapek) was timely: the discussion of the whole problem of progress and of man's relation to machines was, so to say, in the air just after the War. The whole tendency of the play, its warning of mankind against the dangers of a machine-civilisation, seemed very healthy, and the final optimism, declaiming belief in the power of love and the survival of life, sounded very reassuring. The play has also considerable theatrical qualities: the men-automatons moving stiffly like dolls, the tension of the great revolt, the striking types of men—all this testifies to Čapek's lively sense for the stage. If we, however, examine the play in cold blood, the fissures in the structure and the gaps in the argument become obvious: the robots which are conceived as men-machines without soul or feeling, are changed during the play by a sleight of hand into real men. There is no revolt of robots, but a revolt of oppressed men: one race of men is simply dethroned by another and the whole story loses its point. It all comes to an attack on human ambition, and a recommendation of simple humanity: of love, laughter and tears. The science displayed with much ingenuity is, after all, pseudo-science: a sort of magic by which men are made artificially with bones, veins, muscles, etc., just as any man, though on some mythical chemical basis other than man's.

The second play in this vein, *The Life of the Insects* . . . , seems to me very much better. Of course, its texture is looser: it is almost a ballet, or review. The breathless speed of the dialogue avoids the mistakes of the rather bookish theorising which vitiates the later plays. (pp. 50-1)

[*The Macropoulos Secret*] is again a play about a scientific invention, the magical character of which is here frankly admitted. . . . This looks like a counterpart to Shaw's *Back to Methuselah*, but Čapek's play was written before he had heard of Shaw's, and his tendency is exactly the opposite one. The heroine has lost all joy in life and all desire for further life, all those around her finally reject the use of the recipe and a sensible young girl burns it. So youth has destroyed the fear of death. A life lived decently for sixty years is more valuable than three hundred. The setting of this moral in a legal comedy is not always convincing, however, and the figures remain puppets. The last of Čapek's dramas, *Adam the Creator, . . .* is rather disappointing. The idea seems a good one: Adam has destroyed the world, and God is asking him to recreate it. But he has no ideas of his own: everything he creates makes an even bigger mess of life, and when there is a chance to destroy the second world, he very properly refuses. It seems to be a little unfair to deprive mankind of any right of criticising because it would not be able to create, and the moral to be drawn seems a little too self-righteous about the present state of affairs: but obviously this quietism suited Čapek at a certain point of his development, and one must understand his impatience with all salvationists and world-reformers. But the execution of the idea is not very successful. (pp. 50-2)

Contemporaneously with the plays Čapek started to write utopian romances. The first is *The Absolute at Large* . . . which again starts with a brilliant idea: an engineer is able to burn matter so completely that only the Absolute remains and is liberated. Though the invention is excellent from the economic point of view as one pound of coal is burning weeks and weeks, the general consequences are disastrous: people become affected with religious mania, start to distribute their belongings, preach sectarian fanaticism, etc. This is very amusing satire on the gulf between theory and practice in religion, but after a few chapters Čapek gives the topic up in despair: the Absolute suddenly begins to work all the machines, and overproduction suffocates all economic life, the religious mania leads to endless wars of sects, ending in complete exhaustion. . . . But though the book contains some brilliant humorous scenes, especially on a barge and on a merry-go-round, its main conception is uncertain and the design becomes very loose towards the end. The "utopian" or rather anti-utopian phase of Čapek's writings finds its fullest expression in *Krakatit* . . . , Čapek's longest book. Again the satire is directed against any titanism, and the moral drawn is the moral of resignation. Prokop, the great specialist in high explosives, invents the deadly Krakatit, capable of blowing up anything. Throughout the whole of the novel he fights for withholding his secret, which, if betrayed, might become the end of civilisation. . . . There are many beautiful and striking scenes in *Krakatit;* especially the idyll in the country, which has obvious autobiographical touches, is in Čapek's best vein. But this solid piece of writing clashes curiously with the latter scenes in Balttin, where Prokop is confined. The love-scenes between him and the Princess Wille suddenly take on a phantastic colour of brutal violence which reminds us of some of the most painful scenes in D. H. Lawrence. The whole setting in a fanciful and grotesque aristocratic society, ingredients of melodrama, sex psychology, technological speculation, feverish dreams are mixed up disconcertingly with curious allegorising. The Princess Wille has an allegorical name, and D'Hémon or Daimon is a figure out of fairyland with burning hands. Many of the fever-hallucinations of Prokop are managed very interestingly, and there is a certain largeness in the whole conception, and a fierce intensity in some of the scenes—however absurd their rational connection: but the book drags on many points and the violent changes of style and technique make it incoherent.

Side by side with the plays and romances the essayist Čapek developed his powers. He settles down, so to say, and writes

a number of very pleasant, very sensible and humorous books of sketches, essays, travels which in one way or the other express his deep humanity, his belief in ordinary man, his sense of the bewildering variety and beauty of the world. His optimism is sometimes a shade too cheerful, and does not altogether avoid a certain contempt for all that is greatest is man. (pp. 52-3)

Čapek's deep humanity, his astonishing power of observation, come out best in his travel-sketches. The first were the *Letters from Italy* . . . , full of lively reflections on art and architecture, aggreeably set off by genre-pictures of the life of Italian towns, villages and ports. The book shows Čapek's love for the primitive painters, his real appreciation of early mediaeval Italy, while he is obviously uneasy before Renaissance and Baroque developments. The book is frankly the diary of a holiday tour, very short and very fully enjoyed, and does not pretend to any full comprehension for Italy's past or present. The *Letters from England* . . . show a very much deeper understanding for the character of the people. They are, it is true, light travelling sketches and the surprised attitude of the provincial and continental, battered by first impressions of London traffic, are sometimes a little too self-conscious. Čapek is rather interested in the daily life around him, the English landscape and the English character, than in history or art or anything out of the way. But inside these limits he manages to convey a great deal of subtle observation, quiet fun and real understanding. (p. 54)

The vivid interest in men, their habits of life and their institutions, is the starting-point of Čapek's political interests. A collection of papers, *On Political Things, or Zoon Politicon* . . . , says many sensible things on Czechoslovak and general problems. Čapek is a genuine democrat and has always advocated a humane, tolerant, and liberal government against extremists both on the right and on the left. (p. 55)

[Čapek] is interested very much in a vital question of modern literature: how can literature again appeal to the masses, while keeping a high artistic standard? The way to this ideal seems to lie in a development of the popular *genres* of literature, which should be exalted by the writer while remaining comprehensible to the common mind. This explains his special interest in the despised forms of "low" literature to which he has devoted a brilliant collection of sociological studies: *Marsyas, or on the Margin of Literature.* . . . There he tells us about journalism, the psychology and typology of anecdotes, writes about popular humour and proverbs, collects a series of extremely funny poems from the suburbs of Prague, has his say on pornography, on stories in calendars, novels read by maid-servants, etc. He is sceptical about consciously "proletarian" art, praises very properly the resources of the Czech language, and devotes much space to an illuminating discussion of two genres: the fairy-tale and the detective-story.

Fairy-tales are Čapek's speciality. . . . [His own *Fairy-Tales*] are a veritable treasure-house of pure aimless story-telling. His fairy-world is a happy one: full of sensible little dogs and cats, forward witches, genial, slangy water-sprites, pigmy postmen, ridiculous detectives, polite brigands. These things may look slight to grave pundits, but they are really very difficult to do without becoming sentimental or crude, and Karel Čapek succeeds because he never loses a sincere understanding of childhood, a sense of humour and the light touch. (p. 56)

The mystery-story has interested Čapek since the *Wayside Crosses.* Two new brilliant volumes of tales, [*Tales from One Pocket* and *Tales from the Other Pocket*] . . . develop this popular form along new lines. The stories have become very much more concise, brighter, their point very much more epigrammatic compared to the older volume. If we except a few trivial pièces, they are all genuinely concerned with problems of truth and justice, though they seem to be written only for excitement and amusement. Some of the stories, especially in the first volume, praise the intuition and the instinct of ordinary man in preference to the ways of calculating reason, the sagacity of common sense defeating far-fetched speculation. A police agent finds the man who stole an important military document from the larder where it was hidden, because he is not looking for sinister spies but for simple larder-burglars. . . . The second series, though the stories are hardly different in type, is composed differently: while the first is told in the usual objective manner, the second is composed of tales told to other people. They are associated loosely by verbal links which enhance the illusion of spontaneous reminiscence. But there is never any description of the story-tellers or their setting. The style is more colloquial in accordance with this fiction, and the structure looser. (pp. 56-7)

The poet, the writer of tragedy who seems to have slumbered through the period of very pleasant tales and plays and essays celebrating life's fullness and ordinary humanity, awakes again in [*Hordubal, Meteor,* and *An Ordinary Life*]. . . . Though every one of these novels is completely distinct in theme and method, there is a common conception underlying them all. All of them retell the very same story from different points of view and thereby enhance its variety of meaning, the mysteriousness of ultimate reality. Possibly Karel Čapek has learned directly or indirectly something from the masters of perspective in modern fiction—from Henry James or Joseph Conrad, or even more likely he has himself developed a method in his search for truth which remains always in perspective only. (p. 58)

The very last book by Karel Čapek, *War with the Newts* . . . is a return to the utopian romances of former years. Some of the parallels with the *Absolute at Large,* such as the figure of the Jewish captain of industry, are even deliberate. But in distinction to the earlier book, *War with the Newts* has a much better design, and the main idea is carried out with consistency. . . . The book contains very good genre-pictures in Čapek's best vein and delineates very nice human types, such as Captain Van Toch. . . . There is plenty of good, topical satire on modern science and pseudoscience, on recent politics and a lavish display of Čapek's quite extraordinary power of mimicry of styles: scientific, journalistic, colloquial, dialectical, etc. But one feels that much of this power is wasted on a topic rather too well worn since [William] Morris and Samuel Butler, Wells and Chesterton and Huxley and scores of others.

We must not forget that Karel Čapek is still a comparatively young man at the height of his powers. But his work as it stands now commands admiration by the very variety of his achievement, by the range of his powers, by its earnest striving after the highest goal. . . . In a few books, Karel Čapek has achieved real greatness, even measured by the highest standards. And obviously he should be judged by his best. (p. 61)

René Wellek, "Karel Čapek" (originally published in The Slavonic Review, *Vol. XV, No. 43, July, 1936), in his* Essays on Czech Literature *(© copyright 1963 by Mouton & Co., Publishers), Mouton Publishers, The Hague, 1963, pp. 46-61.*

V.S. PRITCHETT   (essay date 1941)

I have always had two sensations after reading a book of Capek's or seeing one of his plays: first, that something was missing; they had not quite come off and had faded like ghosts. Secondly, that this impression was false; what they really left one with was not a sense of failure but of loss. *Our* loss, not his. Borne on by the main stream, Western European culture was making heavy weather and we looked back upon little islands still in view, but hopelessly out of our reach—the small nationalist movements of the last generation which preserved a pure, naive and local poetry gone from us for good. Partly it was that we were seeing the last of the peasant, the last of a provinciality, circumscribed but strangely vital. (p. 141)

And to their native quality, those literatures occasionally rose to a tentative but often devastating comment on the greater cultures. It is a great advantage to a writer to work within strict limits providing the quality of life is intense within them; so much that is irrelevant never comes near enough to distract. It must have been for this reason that Capek was able, almost spritishly, to impose the word "robot" on Europe and to carry over the world so slight a thing as *The Insect Play.* Those two works, and his later novel *The First Rescue Party,* have a European standing. I do not think that English literature of the mines, which has lately been considerable, approaches the quality of that particular novel.

Of course, one may be deceived here by Capek's pure originality. He does manage to bounce you into the belief that he is writing about something which has never been seen or written about before. One may be mistaking freshness of eye for strength of mind. If so, the answer must be that, whether as travelling journalist, novelist or playwright, Capek could tread the most well-trodden ground, without drawing on the huge tradition of the banal. *The Cheat* is an unfinished and posthumous novel and illustrates the feckless variety of Capek's interests. . . . This time the subject is the always engaging one of the fake artist. Beda Foltyn is an amateur of music with romantic notions about the life and prestige of artists, and we see his life story from the point of view of a number of people who know him from his schooldays to his death. . . . He gives Capek an opportunity of defining the artist's business in life, in a very remarkable passage at the end of the story in which he compares the artist to the God of *Genesis,* who found the earth without form and void and gave it its form and outline. The Devil in art is the personal, the idle pourer-out of the self. Capek's own achievement springs from such a detachment from himself— though he is a writer with an unmistakable personal accent. *The Cheat* is not a work of much range and Foltyn is too feeble to hold up a very serious structure; but the second chapter in which a young girl describes her halting, silly, capricious love affair with Foltyn, is a masterpiece of character-drawing. Capek always astonishes us by his intuitions of reality, which go so lightly into the heart that one is inclined to pass them by as merely charming. They are a good deal more than that. . . . (pp. 141-42)

[The girl's description of her affair with Foltyn] has that restless evasive humour which plays with the reader and which is not a little fey; but Capek was an expert in the flat innocence of human egoism; whether it is in the grotesque form of the awful bourgeois beetles of *The Insect Play* rolling along "our little property" of dung; or in such a portrait as this one from *The Cheat.* Such as idiosyncrasy as his is inconceivable in our society, and one looks mournfully at the crushing of European variousness which has taken place since his death. (p. 142)

V.S. Pritchett, "The Last Capek," in The New Statesman & Nation *(© 1941 The Statesman & Nation Publishing Co. Ltd.), Vol. XXII, No. 546, August 9, 1941, pp. 141-42.*

GEORGE JEAN NATHAN   (essay date 1949)

I have seldom found profitable plays that deal with the imaginary relationship of animal life to human life. And that holds also for those about insect and fowl life. Once in a blue moon a Rostand's lyrical line may make something like *Chantecler* tolerable in spite of the spectacle of a lot of actors foolishly covered with feathers and pretending to be barnyard poultry identified with *Homo sapiens*. (p. 48)

The use of animals, fowl or insects for dramatic purposes, except in the higher reaches of classical drama, seems to be simply the strategem of inferior playwrights in substituting a superficial originality for their inability to achieve a profounder. (p. 49)

This revival of the Čapeks' play [*The Insect Comedy*] is responsible for these reprehensions. As those oldsters who saw it when it was performed here twenty-seven years ago under the title, *The World We Live In,* may recall, it again pursues the analogy business, this time between insects and human society which, as things stand today, seems pretty hard on the insects. There is some ingenuity in the treatment but once more the venerable stunt becomes recognizable before long and for the rest of the evening the effect is largely of a man peforming over and over the same card trick and merely varying the accompanying patter. (pp. 49-50)

George Jean Nathan, in his review of "The Insect Comedy" by Karl Čapek, in his The Theatre Book of the Year, 1948-1949: A Record and an Interpretation *(copyright 1949 by George Jean Nathan; reprinted by permission of Associated University Presses, Inc., for the Estate of George Jean Nathan), Alfred A. Knopf, Inc., 1949, pp. 47-50.*

WILLIAM E. HARKINS   (essay date 1957)

There is little doubt that Karel Čapek's trilogy of novels, [*Hordubal, Meteor (Povětron)*, and *An Ordinary Life (Obyčejný život)*], represents his crowning achievement, perhaps that of modern Czech literature. . . . [The] three novels of the trilogy represent serious attempts to develop new forms for the modern novel. In them Čapek comes to grips with the philosophical problem of truth and reality, as well as the esthetic problem of the representation of reality in the novel.

One's first impression is that the theme of the three novels, as for so much of Čapek's work, is merely that of the relativity and plurality of truth. For Čapek there is no single truth; there are a multiplicity of truths depending on the personality of the observer and the viewpoint from which he observes. This is Čapek's relativism, which brings him close to Pirandello among modern writers. But in fact relativism is only the starting-point of the three novels, and in the end they surmount the anarchy of a purely relativistic point of view. (p. 92)

The conflict in *Hordubal* is that of internal and external points of view; in *Meteor* it is between different external views. In *An Ordinary Life* the final possibility is exploited: a conflict of different internal points of view, of a relativistic pluralism in the individual's conception of himself. (p. 94)

On the philosophical plane, Čapek's trilogy is an attempt to deal with the problem of truth; on the artistic plane, it represents an effort to break through the form of the conventional novel and its representation of reality. The conventional, "realistic" novel assumes that reality is single and objective, while the novel of introspective experience suggests, at least in its method, that reality is merely relative and subjective. Čapek avoids both these extremes, for he is seeking to reconcile subjectivity and objectivity, relativism and absolutism, pluralism and monism. Thus he creates a new form of novel, neither objective nor introspective, which can reconcile these dialectical antitheses in man's perception of reality.

The three novels of the trilogy represent three separate attempts to create such a novel. In *Hordubal* this is achieved by destroying unity of point of view, in the conventional novel customarily one and the same. The first part of Čapek's story is told, for the most part, as Hordubal's own inner monologue, while the last two parts (which are in effect but one), describing the police investigation and the trial, are conventional, externalized narratives which depict Hordubal's death as seen by the village in which he lives, by the police and the court. . . . Philosophically, of course, this transition from inner monologue to external narrative reflects the opposition of subjective and objective points of view which is the novel's theme.

In *Meteor* Čapek departs even further from the technique of the conventional realistic novel. There is only a dying man, a wrecked plane, and a mystery: why and where did this stranger rush in such a storm? Behind these slight indications lies a reality of unknown aspect and dimensions. Čapek has almost entirely destroyed the "realistic" side of the novel: the objective world is reduced to an absolute minimum: all is fantasy and imagination. But the author destroys to create anew: reality returns as something deeper, not as a chain of trivial details in the life of a stranger, but as the essence of human life as such, which the stranger possesses in common with the three narrators. They can tell his story because they share his nature as a human being. . . . We can know the mysterious stranger's fate . . . for we know man. But we know man, in turn, because we know ourselves. We share the human essence; we ourselves have the potentiality of all human action. (pp. 94-6)

[Hence *An Ordinary Life*] must be written to complete the trilogy. To know others—to know man in the abstract—we must know ourselves. And in this final part of the work conventional narrative form is again shattered. To be sure, novels have often been cast in the form of diaries or confessions. But in Čapek's novel this choice of form is not external or incidental. . . . Here the form is directly linked to the philosophical theme. A man records his own life, not from vanity, but out of a desire to record an "ordinary" life, which appears to him, paradoxically, as insignificant and yet, somehow, as singularly important. In a sense it is not his own life even, which he is recording, but "ordinary life" as a universal.

And, in turn, the form of the personal confession is violated by Čapek for the sake of philosophical insight into man's reality. The confession ends abruptly, as the hero discovers that he is not merely an "ordinary man," but a host of personages. . . . The smooth narrative form breaks down, and a hectic dialogue begins, as each of the personalities in turn interrogates the others, each asserting his right, too, to be counted and to exist. This dialogue of interrogation and counter-interrogation is clothed in a rough, clipped style which is the very antithesis of the peaceful narrative of the "ordinary man." Thus rational reminiscence is destroyed, giving way to a breathless, irrational dialogue of almost primitive artistic immediacy. And finally the multiplicity of personalities within one man is identified with the plurality of society: the world of personages within us is the same as the world without. (pp. 96-7)

The three-part division of a trilogy suggests a dialectic path to truth, and in a philosophical novel we might justly expect it. But the three novels do not represent the simple working out of the formula of thesis, antithesis and synthesis. Rather it is within each novel that we find the dialectical triad exemplified.

In *Hordubal* the three parts of the novel are in fact two, as has already been suggested. . . . And this novel in fact gives us only the two-part formula of thesis—antithesis. The thesis is Hordubal's love; the antithesis, the failure of the world to understand his love. The novel ends without reconciliation. . . . The synthesis can come only with the meaning of the trilogy as a whole: each love is essentially unknowable, but all human love is of the same essence.

In *Meteor* the three narratives . . . apparently do not yield to the dialectical formula. In fact, as Čapek himself has pointed out in the Epilogue, there are not three narratives, but four. Besides these three reconstructions, there are the deductions of the two physicians made from the medical evidence. This, rather, constitutes our thesis: the ''objective truth'' about the unknown man. The three narratives, in turn, constitute an antithesis: they present an ''intuitive'' comprehension of the man's life. Their essential likeness to one another is suggested by the fact that Čapek is able to differentiate them only with difficulty. . . . The narrative of the poet is distinct, it is true, and is itself a kind of synthesis of objective and intuitive approaches, for the writer relies on deduction (though he is far less cautious in his deductions than the physicians) as well as on personal intuition and pure fantasy. But his tale resembles that of the clairvoyant in its essential subjectivity; it is as much a reflection of himself as of external reality. Subjective intention thus plays the role of antithesis in the novel. The synthesis of objective and subjective roads to truth is found in the fact that both of them agree at the end (the news despatch that the stranger in fact came from Cuba). Such a synthesis, however, may seem forced. A better one, perhaps, can be found within the writer's tale itself. Here the stranger has no identity; in this state he lacks definite personality: he can be anything, assume any character or profession, however ridiculous or vile. But in the end he discovers his identity and returns to claim it, to become himself; in other words, he does have an essential self, and his life is no mere illusion. Man is infinite potential, Čapek seems to be saying, but a potential which is at the same time constantly becoming actualized and defined.

In *An Ordinary Life* we find a multiplicity of personalities, and the triad formula is again not obvious. But we can construct an ethical triad (or a psychological one) with little violence to the novel: the ''ordinary man'' is good as he appears to himself; his life is contented and productive. But underneath lurks a self which is slothful, discontented, brutal, and perversely evil. . . . The synthesis then appears in the discovery that personality is manifold. Good and evil, conscious and unconscious become mere aspects of reality, ways of viewing the complex which is a living being. (pp. 97-8)

Only time can tell whether Čapek's experiments with the form of the novel have been successful. Perhaps he was more a destroyer of old forms than a true innovator. But whatever their esthetic suitability, the appropriateness of the forms which he created for his philosophical ideas can hardly be denied. On the philosophic plane there is little doubt that he is successful; in spite of the diversity of the three novels which constitute the trilogy, there is a remarkable unity in their view of reality. Here the author has finally rescued himself from the anarchy of philosophical relativism without losing the sense of freedom and the richness of experience which the relativist, pluralist viewpoint can give.

Perhaps Čapek's greatest achievement, however, in the trilogy is that of the humanist and democrat: his three heroes, moving and sincere portrayals, exemplify the measure of his faith in the nobility of the common man. The blind, inarticulate peasant with his pathetic love; the unknown man who finds his true self only to perish; the ''ordinary man,'' great in nothing but his humanity—they are among the author's finest creations. (pp. 99-100)

William E. Harkins, ''Form and Thematic Unity in Karel Čapek's Trilogy,'' in Slavic and East European Journal *(© 1957 by AATSEEL of the U.S., Inc.), Vol. XV, No. 2, Summer, 1957, pp. 92-100.*

WILLIAM E. HARKINS   (essay date 1962)

The title of the play, *R.U.R.* or ''Rossum's Universal Robots,'' is the name of a fictitious corporation, and is in English in the original. This would suggest a British or American setting for the play. But the names of the characters are multi-national; here as often later, Čapek tried to create a deliberately international background for his theme. A number of references are made in the play to the commercial interests of Europe, and there is no suggestion that American or Britain alone is guilty of a technological revolution which might submerge the human race.

The idea of a robot, an artificial man, is of course very old. One source is the Jewish legend of the Golem of Prague, which turned against those who misused its sacred power. Mary Shelley's novel *Frankenstein* is another manifest source. . . . (p. 84)

What is new in Čapek's play is the complex meaning of the symbol of the robot, which represents not only the machine and its power to free man from toil but, at the same time, symbolizes man himself, dehumanized by his own technology. From the technical point of view, man is an inefficient instrument, whose emotional and spiritual life only impedes the drive of modern technology. Either he must give way to the machine, or he himself must become a machine. . . . Last, the robot symoblizes man dehumanized by the very freedom from toil which the machine assures him; gone are the struggle of life and the challenge to man's spirit. In *R.U.R.* man loses even his ability to reproduce, the last thing which distinguishes him from the robot. The complexity of the robot symbol must be realized for a proper understanding of Čapek's play. He was too honest a writer to create a superficial melodrama about man-like machines which revolt against man—though this is obviously the aspect of the play which made it so popular. (p. 85)

In *R.U.R.* man's soul is described as standing in the way of mechanical perfection: man plays the violin, goes for walks, and has children—all impediments to his role as an integer in the modern world of industry and commerce. . . . [Technology] reaches a limit of the irrational which it cannot control: . . . the formula creates mere robots, but in the end robots become men. Man's spirit cannot be regimented, Čapek is saying, even by misapplication of his own reason and science. (pp. 85-6)

Čapek has blended expressionism with realism. In fact, only the figure of the robot itself (and the final transformation of robots into men) is expressionistic; otherwise Čapek's treatment is conventional and realistic. This mixture of styles was hardly a concession to popular appeal, for it was just the expressionistic symbol of the robot which made the play so popular. What Čapek was seeking, rather, was a humanization of the play, and in this he at least partly succeeded. . . . *R.U.R.*, for all its sins against the stage, remains moving and human. (p. 86)

The expository section of the Prologue introduces us to two contrasting aspects of the robot symbol. Their inventor, Old Rossum (the name is derived from Czech *rozum*, "reason") was a rationalist who sought to create life as a proof of the nonexistence of God. He had no interest in the economic exploitation of his discovery. For this type of scientist Čapek always had the warmest praise, though he was fully aware of the limitations of such a point of view. . . . In his zeal for pure science Old Rossum had striven to create man with everything Nature had given him—even an appendix. It was his nephew, rather, who simplified his discovery, created the robot, and set up manufacture on a mass-production basis.

The "comedy" element of the Prologue arises from Helena's inability to distinguish robots from humans. In one scene she refuses to believe that a robot is not a woman; later she mistakes the directors of the factory for robots, and tries to incite them to revolt. The humor here is not gratuitous; it introduces us directly to the theme of the play. The point is that man is already dehumanized, and so Helena cannot tell the difference. . . .

The Prologue is set apart from the body of the play because it is comedy, while the play proper is drama. Act I is the kernel of *R.U.R.*; in fact, the dramatic conflict is essentially resolved by its finish, and what follows is largely anticlimax. In this act we learn that robots all over the world have risen against their masters, and that man is doomed. We also learn that man has lost his power to reproduce his kind. (p. 87)

Once we know that man has lost his ability to reproduce, and that the robots have risen against him, the outcome is obvious. Yet Čapek delays the inevitable ending by introducing an electrified barrier which the robots cannot cross until they have taken the factory power plant. This delay is dramatically necessary; otherwise the play would be over by the end of the first act. . . . The author needed time to comment on what was happening if the play were to be a drama of ideas, and not a mere melodrama. In the Prologue and Act I the whole burden of argument is against technology. Such an opposition of black and white was foreign to Čapek's purpose. There is no reason to suppose, as some critics have, that he was opposed to human inventiveness as such; in fact, several of his essays welcome new inventions. Moreover, Čapek was a relativist. Domin too has a share of the truth in his dream of a world in which man is freed of toil and his energies are released to pursue the things of the spirit. This dream is depicted in the second act.

Of course, Domin could have described his dream in Act I, and the robots could have launched their attack during Act II. This would have been the more conventional dramatic procedure. But it would have deprived the author of a solemn moment in the symbolic plane of the drama: the awful realization that mankind is passing from the earth.

Čapek later wrote that he conceived *R.U.R.* as a eulogy to man. . . . (p. 88)

Of course Čapek exaggerates here; the note of eulogy is not the final one. The end of the play is the miracle of life, the transformation of robots into men. But even if his dramatic means are questionable, Čapek was right to introduce this philosophical note into his play. For the threat to man's existence can be meaningful only if the spectator really grasps that man is about to pass from the earth, if he comprehends what a "great thing" it was "to be a man."

Both capitalism and communism must share the responsibility for the robot uprising. It is not technology which destroys man, the directors conclude at one point, but greed for profits and the inevitable law of supply and demand. And when Domin reads a manifesto addressed to "robots of the world," he asks who taught them such phrases. Here the robot uprising appears as a symbol of socialist revolution; may not man forfeit even his own humanity to gain a materialist utopia, whether achieved through capitalism or socialism? (p. 89)

Act III is . . . a dramatic anticlimax, but it likewise is necessary for the philosophical point of the play. Alquist is alone, the only human spared by the robots. In despair at man's passing, he tries to discover the secret of manufacturing life. The robot leaders order him to dissect live robots. He attempts this, but his nervous hands cannot hold the scalpel. As he mourns his lack of resoluteness, he observes that his two robot servants, Primus and Helena, have fallen in love. . . . Alquist tells them to go and be man and wife to one another. . . . "Life will not perish," he concludes.

Ideologically the play thus turns in a circle, denying the very thesis it had asserted for dramatic purposes. This thesis, that modern civilization threatens to destroy man by removing the element of struggle from life, is contradicted: life and love will not perish. This contradiction is no inconsistency, but a deliberate use of a false dramatic resolution followed by the true one. This is why the construction of *R.U.R.*, with its two acts of apparent anticlimax, is so unorthodox. (pp. 89-90)

As Čapek states, the second idea of the play is that of the "comedy of truth," the conflict of pieces of relativist truth, each of them in itself quite valid. There are four such points of view expressed in the play. Domin stands for man as master of the universe . . . ; his is the dream of freedom for man from toil. Opposed to him is Nána, . . . a peasant woman of strict religious persuasion. For her "all inventions are against the Lord God." A more sophisticated variant of her belief is presented by Alquist, the construction engineer. Though he is not certain whether God exists, he recognizes the importance of spirit and moral law, and he prays. He has an almost Tolstoyan faith in work. His profession symbolizes his creativity, which for him is the inner goal of the human need to work. But Alquist forgets that work and creativity are not the same. . . . (p. 92)

Finally, there is Helena's viewpoint. Her name, which is also that of the beautiful robot girl, symbolizes her nature as eternal woman. She acts instinctively, out of feeling, not reason. But she too is doomed, for she does no work, and, though she desires children, she does not have them.

The chief fault in the interplay of these four points of view is that there is no acceptable ideology to counter that of Domin, only the logic of events themselves. Nána's viewpoint . . . would return man to an animal existence. Alquist's philosophy of creative work is a personal faith, for not every man is born to create. Helena's intuitive approach to right and wrong has no objective foundation. Though she is in touch with life, she is cut off, paradoxically, from reality. . . . (p. 93)

Čapek was aware of the defects of *R.U.R.*, and liked it least of all his plays. In an interview with Dorothy Thompson he confessed that he was unable to comprehend what people saw in *R.U.R.* But he declined to say what was wrong with it, observing only that the spectator can see for himself. "It is a play that anyone might have written," he added. For years he refused to go to see *R.U.R.*, and gave in only when trapped in a small Czech town by the director of the local theater. (p. 94)

In spite of the faults of *R.U.R.*, it is safe to say that no other play on modern technology has so captured the public's imagination. Perhaps, in view of the great urgency of its theme, it has a just claim to be Čapek's most popular work. (p. 95)

Adam the Creator is [a] comedy on a utopian theme, and continues the tradition of *R.U.R.* and *The Makropulos Secret*. It shows more influence, however, of an earlier play by Josef Čapek, *The Land of Many Names* (1924), than of Karel's utopian comedies. In *The Land of Many Names* a new continent rises above the surface of the ocean, offering men hope of a new life. But instead of prosperity and freedom, it brings new war, exploitation, and struggle. Finally it disappears in a second earthquake. The similarity of the two plays suggests that Josef Čapek was actually a full-fledged partner in the collaboration, and not a subordinate, as some critics have maintained. Only the optimistic note of the ending—the acceptance of the world as the best of all possible worlds—is more typical of Karel than Josef.

Like *The Land of Many Names*, *Adam the Creator* is expressionistic in technique. Its characters are little more than symbols or abstractions. The events of the play—the destruction of the world by Adam, its recreation according to his personal ideas of reform, his final acceptance of life as it is—all these are subjective attitudes objectivized as reality. Only the ending departs from expressionism, though in its philosophical implications rather than its technique: Adam accepts the world with all its limitations.

Besides the earlier plays of the two brothers, Shaw's *Back to Methuselah* seems to have had marked influence on *Adam the Creator*. Indeed, *Adam the Creator* (and not *The Makropulos Secret*) may be regarded as a specific answer to Shaw's play. Man cannot will to be something better; he only remains what he already is. Adam's repeated comment on how difficult the task of creation is seems a parody of the Shavian concept of creative evolution through the application of will and intelligence. (pp. 115-16)

The conception of the play is brilliant, and, it seems, completely original. . . . Adam is characterized as a disgruntled anarchist who hates his fellow men because no one will heed his manifestoes. He fires the Cannon of Negation, an expressionistic symbol of his nihilistic will, and all is destroyed. . . . The Voice of God then bids him create the world anew. A heap of earth is to serve as the Clay of Creation.

Adam's first efforts at creation turn out disastrously. Finally he hits on the idea of creating his own double, so that he can discuss with him his plans for creation. He gives life to Alter Ego, who is to think exactly as he does. But he forgets that Alter Ego will treat him as he, Adam, deals with others. Alter

Ego turns out quarrelsome, suspicious, and opinionated. He insists on dividing the world into equal shares, and on receiving half the Clay of Creation for himself.

Adam and Alter Ego now undertake to compete in creation. Adam is an individualist, who makes each person different. . . . Alter Ego follows modern, "scientific" methods, and realizes the concept of the "mass." He makes a mold and shapes his people exactly alike. This dichotomy parodies the ambivalence of the modern radical intellectual, who inclines to individualism, at least for himself, but fancies that totalitarian methods are an easier and quicker way of perfecting the social order.

The first four scenes of the play are imaginative and quite funny. What follows, however, is a rather tedious allegory of world history. The new personages introduced are hardly characterized, and the sense of recognition granted the spectator, that the "new" world is actually his own, is hardly a sufficient reward. (pp. 116-17)

The play suffers from a number of inconsistencies. For example, the characters of Adam and Alter Ego change without motivation from scene to scene and even from moment to moment. Nor do the created beings always live up to the specifications for their creation. But these are hardly serious defects in a frankly expressionist work. What is more significant is the play's ideological weakness.

The thesis of the play is vitalistic: life itself is superior to all man's schemes for improving it. But this is demonstrated negatively. The beings Adam creates have faults, but so do those which life creates. Moreover, the play brings no argument on the side of life itself, no example of life worth living. Instead we have only strife, hatred, greed, and stupidity. . . . To be sure, Zmetek is presented as an example of life creating independently of Adam, and he is intended as the positive figure of the play. Zmetek is a beggar who lives as best he can. He is generous; he has hope for a better future; he believes in life. . . .

Thus we are left with a double resolution. On one hand life is evil, and cannot be improved. On the other, life with all its ills is good, and Zmetek even has the temerity to hope in a better future.

These conflicting views are unresolved, and no doubt rightly so from the standpoint of the authors. Life is a paradox. But the point of the play remains cloudy at best. To what extent, precisely, ought man to be content with life as is and not strive to improve it? . . . The question can never, of course, receive a complete answer. But just because of this, it would seem that the brothers might have had more modesty, and refrained from implying even a tentative solution. (p. 118)

William E. Harkins, in his Karel Čapek *(reprinted by permission of the publisher), Columbia University Press, 1962, 193 p.*

ALEŠ HAMAN and PAUL I. TRENSKY   (essay date 1967)

Satire is one of the most common features of [Čapek's] writing, in his fiction and dramas as well as in his newspaper work. . . . To see in this aspect of his work its greatest value (as is sometimes done) would be, of course, to vulgarize it. The very use of satire, however, is distinctive for Čapek's art. It reflects better than anything else Čapek's constant preoccupation with general problems, his weighing and judging of the world and society. There is a pronounced moral standpoint behind this aspect of his art. It is not accidental that we constantly encounter motifs of judiciary proceedings in his work, for they reflect the author's moral attitude toward life; he presents to his audience the conflicts of this world while passing judgment on them. It is the paradox of Čapek's work that despite its pragmatic relativism, it is built upon a practical, personal morality. (p. 175)

Čapek's relation to Romanticism and Realism is also derived from his moral attitude and its poetic implications. The understanding of this relation is an important clue to the basic axioms of his art. Čapek's attitude toward Romanticism is ambivalent. On the one hand, he often regarded it as something tasteless, perverted, and false. . . . [On the other hand,] he was frequently attracted to the Romantic mode of artistic expression, as in the exotic and fantastic *Meteor, Krakatit,* and *The Blue Chrysanthemums*. . . . It appears that here one finds the permanent dramatic focal point of Čapek's art—the tension which was transforming every tendency toward epic fiction into a dramatic illusion. . . . Between the two poles, then—Realism, whose most natural milieu is the epic, and Romanticism, the most natural milieu of which is the lyric—fluctuates Čapek's own art. The result of this polarity is the dramatic dual appearance of his world. . . . Čapek's world breaks up into dream and reality, shadow and light. Nothing can escape the dialectical relativism of positive and negative, creation and destruction, joy and suffering. (pp. 176-77)

Ordinary, trivial reality is present in his feuilletons and editorials, as well as in his fictional prose. This "reality," however, undergoes a strange transformation in his stories, novels, and dramas. On the one hand, it develops into an endless chain of disillusionments and embarrassments, while on the other hand, it coexists with dreams in an extraordinary symbiosis of an "everyday" miracle. Visionary dreams play a major role in Čapek's fiction in general. . . . Everyday reality was apparently not sufficient grounds for Čapek's art. It had to be extended and deepened with fantasies, desires, and dreams.

Čapek's creative design transforms everyday reality into a miracle—the motif of dream being closely related in his work to the motif of miracle. . . . In *The Stories from One Pocket,* miracle is conceived of as something completely beyond human principle and understanding. Miracle is here juxtaposed to the notion of order, the maintenance and comprehension of which, according to the author, is the essential sign of true humanity. (It has to be emphasized, however, that in Čapek's work, order has meaning only in practical life and is never worshipped as an independent value.) Čapek was well aware of the chaotic state of the soul of modern man. . . . (pp. 177-78)

[His] pessimistic analysis of the modern world brings us to some of the most important features of Čapek's art, one of which is the conflict between spirit and matter. Čapek was a master in the description of the animalistic side of human nature. Impulsive sexuality destroying all beauty and dignity can be found in many scenes of his work . . . ; we often witness the tragic power of passion driving man to the brink of lunacy. The one thing that can save man from destruction is his reliance upon reason, so often celebrated by Čapek. . . . It would not be Čapek, however, if he did not have ambivalent feelings about the power of the spirit. Grave skepticism about the reasoning ability of man can be found in many pages of his works, where he shows how reason can work against human interest, creating a mechanized, technocratic society. Too much reason can be as destructive as a lack of it—a discovery which further

complicates the conflict. From this deeply tragic, insoluble situation, Čapek sometimes tries to find an escape into an idyllic world. Thus, *Krakatit* ends with a pastoral scene. . . . (pp. 178-79)

If we penetrate still deeper into Čapek's world, we find still another conflict and another cause for the dramatic character of his art. It is the feeling of uncertainty and confusion concerning the nature of life, and the search for support against it, especially in tradition. . . . In many places in Čapek's work we can find descriptions of senseless flight, of falling through empty space, etc., symbolizing the anxiety of man deprived of his certainties. Escape into tradition [is] the remedy against this destructive feeling. . . . (p. 179)

There is a still deeper, metaphysical conflict in Čapek's art. At the very bottom is a feeling of existential loneliness and the horror of a man who finds himself thrown into this world and yearns for a lost unity with the universe. We can find these feelings in almost all of Čapek's work. . . . Čapek is horrified by man's abandonment in the universe, and as a reaction against this feeling, he develops his myth of "home." In almost one half of the author's feuilletons we can find variations of this theme—the building of one's house, its furnishing, etc., home being the symbol of man's accommodation to the world and of his security. . . . The essential theme of Čapek's work is the dramatic search for home and the escape from solitude.

From this search derives also Čapek's ideal of a universal brotherhood, and the vision of the human race unified by a common fate. . . . This near-mystical idea . . . contained a potential danger. It threatened to create an idealized abstraction out of man, thereby reducing his opportunity to live a full life. . . . [Čapek] was not unaware of the pitfalls of an *a priori* philanthropy and idealism. His weapon against dogmatic abstraction and schematization is humor.

Stemming from the discovery of an ambivalent character of the world, his humor helps him to create his image of man, criticizing the follies of romantic titanism and of pettiness. It enables him to descend to the banalities of life in order to rise from there to the idea of real humanity. Čapek's humor, like all humor, embodies in itself the tension between the comic and the tragic. (pp. 180-81)

An essential feature of Čapek's art is the humorous miniaturizing of human hopes, sufferings, and frailties; it brings the big problems of the world within the reach of one's everyday experience, making them simpler and more understandable. All this is part of Čapek's ultimate axiom: the vision of man involved in an endless, incessant struggle with the absolute. (p. 181)

The absolute, however, is also hidden in man himself. A moment of weakness, and it emerges on the surface in the form of rationalistic megalomania, pathetic heroism, messianic titanism, blind bigotry, and other fanaticisms. Čapek was the advocate of a healthy skepticism, which he defined as a "dislike of verbal solutions, distrust of big nebulous words, and a minimal abuse of the intellectual ability to make generalizations." Some saw in this a lack of confidence in the strength of the human mind, but it was in reality rather the awareness of the dialectical ambivalence of man's thinking and acting and of his relativistic nature. Čapek was always searching for a middle road; the newt-like anonymity of the crowd was for him as terrifying as the demonic solitude of a genius.

Čapek belongs to the twentieth-century authors who understand the modern predicament. . . . God has ceased to be the creator of order for Čapek; He has become a gigantic maniac generating and destroying without plan—a blind, irrational force. The consequence of this discovery was the belief that man had become the measure of all things and that he had to create his own world, relying on his own potential as well as limitations. The renunciation of the absolute is supposed to lead man to a greater responsibility in life, and ultimately perhaps to greater happiness. (p. 182)

> Aleš Haman and Paul I. Trensky, "Man against the Absolute: The Art of Karel Čapek," in Slavic and East European Journal (© 1967 by AATSEEL of the U.S., Inc.), Vol. XI, No. 2, 1967, pp. 168-84.

GEORGE A. TEST   (essay date 1974)

War With the Newts presents a more terrifying fantasy world than either [Aldous Huxley's] *Brave New World* or [George Orwell's] *1984,* and in any case complements these works by encompassing the economic sphere of life, an area of little concern for either Huxley or Orwell.

The reasons for the present neglect of Capek's satire are not difficult to establish. Although Capek is one of the three Czech writers of the twentieth century with international reputations (Kafka and Hasek are the others) it is [for] the play *R.U.R.* that Capek is best known . . . *War With the Newts* suffered mixed or indifferent reviews and inevitable comparison with *Brave New World* when translations appeared in England and America. . . . None of the major studies of satire in the last ten years has acknowledged its existence. . . . (pp. 1-2)

Even as satire, *War With the Newts* is unconventional. Episodic in extreme, without a central hero, a grab bag of satiric techniques, Capek's work will not satisfy readers and critics who come to the book with conventional novelistic expectations. To call it episodic is in fact generous. A major portion of the novel is really a mock-historical narrative interspersed with various kinds of documents exhibited in mock-scholarly style. Although *War With the Newts* has several richly realized characters, the scope of Capek's satire would have been undesirably restricted by the convention of a novelistic hero. The action of Capek's satire is concern with the Newts, their discovery, their development, and their conflict with man. Since the Newts are a multi-faceted metaphor, the action is in effect the creation of that metaphor. . . . Whether a device such as Gulliver or Candide would have served Capek's purpose is impossible to say. On the other hand, the vastness of Capek's concept comments implicitly on the parochial nature of Huxley's and Orwell's satire.

If Capek fails (or chooses not) to provide his readers with a conventional novel-like book, he amply compensates for these features, especially for the reader attuned to the techniques and devices of satire. Moreover Capek's satiric commentary, while grounded in conditions and events of the thirties, has the merit of still seeming prophetic while describing reality more accurately with each passing day. (p. 2)

The Newts are, at the simplest level, Capek's convenient animal metaphor for man and his culture, for from the first time that Van Toch comes upon these writhing, grotesque beasts in their protected backwater habitat, they dominate this Menippean satire despite their being submerged throughout.

Actually the Newts' metaphorical function is far richer than this account suggests. Van Toch, their "liberator," exemplifies a paternalistic racism, despite his generally humane attitude.

In developing the concept of the Newts as a new labor force to be exploited, Capek builds in significant parallels with the slave trade of the eighteenth and nineteenth centuries. Later Capek mocks do-gooders who seek to make over educationally and culturally in their own image the emerging Newt population. As a symbol for the non-white races, Capek uses the Newts to comment on racism as it manifests itself in exploitation and in attempts to integrate non-white races into Western society. . . .

But the Newts also symbolize what sociologists have come to call "the mass man." The Newts have a deleterious influence on language. Art and music hold no interests for them. The worship of Moloch is the only religion that takes any extensive hold on the Newts. But above all the Newts are consumers and producers without parallel. (p. 3)

The Newts come ultimately to stand for society itself. Economic development, technological changes, and universal armament are forces set in motion by man's greed and thirst for power. Capek pictures these forces as irreversible and self-destructive. Like all the great satirists, Capek is attacking man's pride, man's failure to impose reasonable limitations on what is and is not proper, man's refusal to come to terms with the limitations imposed by his nature and his environment. . . . He seems to suggest that man can find happiness within these limitations, unhappiness and frustration outside them. To try to be more than a man is to transgress an unchangeable rule of nature at one's own peril.

Capek's arsenal of other satiric techniques is as rich as his major metaphor. Unfettered by the demands made by a conventional plot and hero, Capek tells his story and develops his metaphor in a virtuoso performance of parody, travesty, and burlesque. (p. 4)

One especially delightful travesty exploits the famous controversy over the fossil remains discovered near Oeningen, Switzerland by Johannes Scheuchzer in 1726 which he argued were human remains, "relics of the accursed race that perished with the Flood.". . . The paleontologist Cuvier later identified the remains as those of giant salamanders of the genus *Andrias* and named the species *Scheuchzeri!* Capek reprints a picture of Scheuchzer's fossil as part of a mock-scientific report on the geneology of the Newts and quotes from Scheuchzer's *Homo Diluvi Testis.* Capek's device not only satirizes senseless religious controversy and scientific attempts to establish human geneology, but also establishes the metaphorical connection of the Newts with the "that accursed race" before the Flood. Later Capek uses the Scheuchzer fossil to satirize the German pure Nordic race myth. (p. 5)

Ultimately Capek pictures a society so locked into production and consumption that its fate is irreversible. Business responds to warnings that the Newts threatened human civilization with counterwarnings that an attempt to restrict supplies to the Newts would precipitate a slump in production and a "serious crisis in many branches of human industry." (p. 8)

It may be that Capek's success as a satirist in *War With the Newts* is the most damaging statement one can make about him. Unlike Huxley and Orwell whose fantasies are projected into the future where man and his institutions have changed, Capek takes the world before World War II and injects a device of fantasy, the Newts. Neither time, place nor characters have to be changed. In fact Capek uses real places and the names of actual people. The introduction of the Newts is a simple device, but one that makes Capek's book even more terrifying, ultimately, than Orwell's. For in both *1984* and *Brave New World* the future is given, the reader must willingly suspend his disbelief. Capek's device forces the reader to participate in the coming of the future.

Both *1984* and *Brave New World* deal with dictatorships, . . . one concerned with the price of happiness, the other with the threat of naked power. Capek's concerns are much more mundane, fictionally speaking. His Newts fit into the scheme of things as they are. Life goes on as it always has, only more so. Business prospers, governments govern, education, religion and science flourish. But one day life ends terrifyingly in a watery grave. No one seizes power, no one applies behaviouristic psychology. The forces and institutions of society merely destroy themselves. No hedonistic new society, no pathological coercion of man's mind. Only God's voice over the silent deep. Who is responsible? No one. Everyone. We have met the enemy and he is us.

Capek's global view and his social and economic emphasis are unmatched in either Huxley's or Orwell's books. . . . [Capek] manages to yoke events of a global nature with commonplace simplicity of detail which are perhaps more invidious in their impact than the remote melodrama of either Huxley's or Orwell's works. Brainwashing and test tube babies still make Sunday supplement reading, but the threat of a black man or a foreigner taking one's job, the pollution of streams and oceans, and the artificiality of an economy based largely on military consumption are everyday realities. (p. 9)

As a satiric writer Capek combines the rich comic inventiveness of Huxley with the unnerving desire to see the thing as it really is of Orwell. This is only to say that Capek is an effective satirist. But unlike either of them, Capek does not fraction his view of man so completely as they seem to. . . .

Literary history is filled with examples of neglected works that posterity has raised to the status of classics, and conversely with overvalued works that have sunk into oblivion with the years. Capek's *The War With the Newts* was not overvalued when it was first published; it would be foolhardy to proclaim it as a future classic. It is safe to claim however that it is an undeservedly neglected modern satire and compares more favorably with Orwell's and Huxley's classics than its present reputation would indicate. (p. 10)

> *George A. Test, "Karel Capek's 'War with the Newts':*
> *A Neglected Modern Satire," in* Studies in Contem-
> *porary Satire, Vol. 1, No. 1, Spring, 1974, pp. 1-*
> *10.*

DARKO SUVIN (essay date 1979)

There is both irony and poetic justice in the fact that Karel Čapek is today, at least outside the Slavic countries, remembered mainly as the creator of the word *robot*. . . . A second irony is that Karel Čapek's eight plays are, despite the world popularity of some among them . . . , the weakest part of his opus. . . . The poetic justice, however, stems from the fact that a quite central preoccupation of his was with the potentials and actualizations of inhumanity in twentieth-century people, and that this preoccupation was throughout his whole opus translated into the image of the Natural Man versus the Unnatural Pseudo-Man. (p. 270)

Čapek's grandparents were peasants, and some of his most stubborn values and prejudices can be traced back to the traditional peasant confidence in the immediately available, se-

cure, everyday things and relationships of the little people, as opposed to the *hubris* of the hustling and bustling modern industry and the swift changes it brings about. In the plays, this attitude is openly expressed by his small people who act as ideological arbiters . . . ; in the novels, it is implied by strategic collocations of key actions, such as the return to normality at the endings of *Krakatit* and *The Factory for the Absolute;* but as a rule, it pervades all of Čapek's works. On the other hand, he was "enchanted and terrified" by the world of factories and technology—the workers' districts of Prague and the miners of his childhood days—as well as the "pride, power, wealth" of the capitalists. . . . Čapek's SF was written to deal with "great social interests and collective spiritual problems" arising out of "the leading ideas of science, guesses about the future, feats of technology"—that is, to deal with the destructive menaces which the irruption of modern mass production brings to the little man.

Therefore, in Čapek's first SF phase, which extends through the decade following World War I, there is a basic tension between the "natural," average little people, representative of the audience he was writing for, and the catastrophic forces of inhuman violence amid which they have to live, suffer, and die. For Čapek, inhuman, large-scale technology and industry lead in politics logically to international and civil warfare. A fatal ambiguity between the menace to Man as such and the menace to the middle-class man vitiates this whole phase of his work, its qualities lying in what he managed to do in spite of and on the margins of such an ideological muddle. For the menace to Man's existence arises from aliens created and abetted by large industry and its capitalist masters and engineering managers; but the menace to middle-class life arises from the workers, who had in Russia just seized power in the Bolshevik revolution. . . . [In] Čapek robots are not only stand-ins for workers but also—in an ideological mystification which brought him instant fame because it corresponded to deep needs for self-delusion in his audience—inhuman aliens "without history." . . . But at the end of the play, the robots . . . grow more like a new human order than like inhuman aliens. . . . For all the interest inherent in the basic concept and the theater tricks of Čapek's, this fundamental oscillation between mutually incompatible ways of envisaging the robots—which also means an oscillation between old-fashioned psychological and modern "collective" drama—has by now dated this play. (pp. 271-72)

Čapek's real strength as an SF writer lies in his novels. . . . The concept [in *The Absolute at Large*] is a fortunate one, combining wildly hilarious with weighty philosophical possibilities. And the novel is chock-full of irony and satire on the uses and abuses of the Absolute by church and state, corporations and individuals, academics and journalists. (p. 273)

However, it is not clear why the "mystical Communism" of the Absolute must bend itself to the capitalist forms of economic organization and to individualist competitive psychology, which are illogically assumed to be stronger than even an absolute power. Further, the disparate workings of the Absolute in things (overproduction of industrial goods only, not of farm produce or communications) and in people (destructiveness to match the overproduction) do not follow any consistent pattern either. Thus, instead of being a true Absolute, the power which is unleashed by the atomotors is for Čapek simply a chaotic magnification of the antagonisms inherent in acquisitive economics and psychology. This makes for brilliant if spotty social satire, but hardly for consistent SF conceptualization. . . . The only people who retain a tightfisted "normality" are the farmers, and the final chapter culminates in a typically Czech beer-and-sausage feast of the little people, which is consecrated as the highest achievable form of tolerance and everyday happiness. As already seen in *R.U.R.*, any high-minded idea leads necessarily to huge disasters, and one should stick to the pragmatic immediacy of people believing in other people. Not even the Absolute can improve men, religions, or the bourgeois institutions: the paradoxes of this creed explain but do not cancel out the inconsistencies of the novel.

The parallel of men and matter is carried forward in Čapek's most unjustly neglected work of SF, the novel *Krakatit*. . . . [This] bulky novel is as full of Dostoevskian fevered dreams and nightmares, dissociations of memory, and explosive human encounters as of physical explosions, fights, and escapes. . . . Čapek has in *Krakatit* made a conscious and significant attempt to integrate popular paraliterature—in particular the detective story and the epic adventure from Homer through the folktale to pulp thrillers—into sophisticated, poetic SF dealing with central questions of modern life. He wanted to fuse the "love and heroism" of a sensational newspaper story . . . with a psychological narrative, and the overtones of countercreation inherent in a mad scientist story with a sympathetic, suffering and relatively complex hero whose education advances through a series of erotic-cum-political temptations. For once, Čapek's hero rejects not only the militarist temptation of established power and the nihilist temptation of new, personal power . . . , but also the small-town idyll or island of repose. . . . From the fog of suffering and yearning, the hero has finally emerged into the clarity of moderation: his earth-shaking invention will be refunctioned. Though the novel has not quite succeeded in fusing realism and allegory, because it has not quite solved how to fuse ethical moderation with the certainties of the folktale, it is a largely successful first try at transcending the sterile opposition between scientific progress and human happiness which has haunted science fiction from Swift and Voltaire (Čapek's teachers) to the present day. For the first and last time in Čapek's SF, a believable hero fights successfully back at the destructive forces within himself and society.

The second phase of Čapek's SF was the result of the rise of Nazism, which threatened directly both his native land and his basic values. It comprises a few minor stories on the margins of SF, satire, and fantasy, as well as the novel *War With the Newts* . . . and *The White Sickness*. . . . By this time Čapek had shed many of his illusions, in particular his prejudice in favor of the little man's instinctual rightness and of everybody having his own truth. . . . [After] the rise of Hitler, Čapek reconsidered the role of the intellect which he satirized earlier. . . . Now he wrote sharply against an intellect that is giving up its rights "in favor of irrationalism and daimonism, be it the cult of will, of the land, of the subconscious, of the mass instincts, or of the violence of the powerful—that is a decadent intellect because it tends toward its own downfall." A limit was found beyond which the pseudo-human became clearly evil; that limit is reached when the new creatures in *War With the Newts* grow into an analogy to the Nazi aggressors. That is why in his final SF novel Čapek's satire is most clearly focused, the development of the novum most consistent, and there is no conciliatory happy ending. (pp. 274-76)

The satire is aimed at the fictions of mankind which prevent it from seeing the rise of a catastrophic menace. . . . Professional scientists and academics are shown to be as myopic, timid, and ideologically limited—especially in their national-

istic subservience to the powers that be—as the public at large; in the Hitler decade Čapek noted with a sinking heart but firm glance that the treason of the intellectuals to their humanist calling was proceeding apace. But the real political villains were the capitalists who financed the menace to humanity (Nazis as well as Newts). . . . (pp. 276-77)

[In] a brilliant use of satire, it is mankind that not only abets [the Newts] but also teaches them the inhuman combination of slavery and stock-market, warlike aggression and ideological propaganda—in brief, the corruption of reason for violent purposes. (pp. 278-79)

[Čapek's satire is] most bitter and topical, though no less precise [in the third part of the book]. Briefly but impressively, the nodal points of defeatism in face of rising Salamandrism (read fascism) are passed in review, from the Spenglerian philosopher Meynert, through "Salamandrist" fashions in art and entertainment, to the secret deals of the bourgeois states with it and the public hypocrisy of international conferences. The military successes of the Salamanders run parallel to the failures of reason and humanism among men. In a startling maturation for Čapek, even his beloved small Czech people are found guilty of neutralist complacency in the person of Povondra, the only character to be found in all parts of the novel.

In a way, the satire of literary, journalistic, and essayistic forms in *War With the Newts* is also a critique of past and (unintentionally) of subsequent SF. The history of the Salamanders starts with an echo of H. G. Wells' *Island of Dr. Moreau*, as well as of Arthur Conan Doyle's *Lost World*. . . . It proceeds with a global overview which latches onto Wells's later SF, from *The World Set Free* to *The Shape of Things To Come*, as well as onto Anatole France's ironic *Penguin Island*. It ends with havoc-wreaking aliens out of *The War of the Worlds* or "In the Abyss." But instead of Wells's alternatively pessimistic and optimistic outcomes, Čapek's end is, much more realistically, an open question. . . . Čapek [is] the pioneer of all anti-fascist and anti-militarist SF in the world, from the later Wells and Sinclair Lewis to the postwar American and Slavic writers. And he is still one of the best among them.

The enduring power of *War With the Newts* . . . is due to Čapek's mastery of stylistic strategies for building up his vision. In the first part of this mosaic the events are introduced and refracted in comically conflicting, individual though typical, points of view. As the focus of the action widens, impersonal points of view from articles and documents become more and more important, and the third part is mainly a kind of historicophilosophical essay emotionally strengthened by what one could call a tragic lampoon. The traditional individualist psychology is used in a masterly—though mainly comical and abbreviated—fashion where necessary, but it has been found insufficient for events of a global character. (pp. 279-80)

[In] a few works, such as *War With the Newts* he has left us a precious legacy. It may not be as significant as that of his countrymen Franz Kafka or Jaroslav Hašek; but these are the highest standards applicable. And for SF at least, he—rather than Edgar Rice Burroughs or Hugo Gernsback—is the missing link between H. G. Wells and a literature which will be both entertaining (which means popular) and cognitively (which means also formally) avantgardist. He took the adventure novel and the melodramatic thriller, the legacy of French and British SF as well as of German fantasy from the Romantics to the Expressionists (Hoffman, Meyrink, Kaiser), and infused all this with the prospects of modern poetry, painting, and movies, with an eager and constant interest in societal relationships, in natural and physical sciences, and above all in the richly humorous and idiomatic language of the street and the little people. In that way, he is the most "American" of the often elitist European SF writers; and yet he is also not only intensely Czech, but a "European local patriot" for whom Europe meant culture and humanism. (p. 282)

> *Darko Suvin, "Karel Čapek, or the Aliens amongst Us," in his* Metamorphoses of Science Fiction: On the Poetics and History of a Literary Genre *(copyright © 1979 by Yale University), Yale University Press, 1979, pp. 270-83.*

ADDITIONAL BIBLIOGRAPHY

Bradbrook, B. R. "Karel Čapek's Contribution to Czech National Literature." In *Czechoslovakia Past and Present,* edited by Miloslav Rechcigl, Jr., pp. 1002-11. The Hague: Mouton, 1968.
    Examines Čapek's cultural impact on Czechoslovakia and concludes that the author's versatility and originality place him among the leading Czech writers.

Chandler, Frank W. "Hungarian and Czech Innovators: Molnár and the Čapeks." In his *Modern Continental Playwrights,* pp. 438-64. New York: Harper & Brothers, 1931.*

Descriptive overview, with some critical commentary, of the Čapek brothers' plays.

Harkins, William E. "Karel Čapek and the 'Ordinary Life'." *Books Abroad* 36, No. 3 (Summer 1962): 273-76.
    Study of Čapek's epistemological approach to "familiar reality." Harkins focuses on *An Ordinary Life,* finding that its series of paradoxes best exemplify the author's basic philosophy.

Mann, Erika. "A Last Conversation with Karel Capek." *The Nation* 148, No. 3 (14 January 1939): 68-9.
    A moving interview, held just after the 1938 Munich pact. Mann suggests that Čapek's death was brought on by the "white sickness," a sickness of the spirit described in one of his last dramas.

Matuška, Alexander. In his *Karel Čapek: An Essay,* translated by Cathryn Alan. London. George Allen & Unwin Ltd., 1964, 425 p.
    An important study of Čapek's themes, method, vision, and characters.

Moskowitz, Sam. "Karel Čapek: The Man Who Invented Robots." In his *Explorers of the Infinite: Shapers of Science Fiction,* pp. 208-24. Cleveland: The World Publishing Co., 1963.
    Assesses Čapek's role in the development of science fiction. Moskowitz contends that with the popular and critical success of *R.U.R.* "science fiction as meaningful drama came into its own."

Němeček, Zdeněk. "Karel Čapek." In *World Literatures: Arabic, Chinese, Czechoslovak, French, German, Greek, Hungarian, Italian, Lithuanian, Norwegian, Polish, Romanian, Russian, Scottish, Swedish, Yugoslav,* pp. 53-65. Pittsburgh: University of Pittsburgh Press, 1956.
    Reminiscence of Čapek, incorporating brief summaries of the author's major works.

G(ilbert) K(eith) Chesterton

1874-1936

English novelist, short story writer, poet, critic, essayist, journalist, biographer, historian, and dramatist.

Regarded as one of England's premier men-of-letters during the first half of the twentieth century, Chesterton is best known today as a colorful *bon vivant,* creator of the Father Brown mysteries and the fantasy *The Man Who Was Thursday.* He is also acknowledged as a witty essayist and formidable Christian polemicist.

Chesterton showed a talent for journalism as a young man, working for the leftist newspapers *Speaker* and *Daily News.* He first gained public attention as a social and literary critic. *Heretics* and *Charles Dickens* are among the outstanding works of Chesterton's canon before 1910, the latter book establishing him as an insightful Dickens scholar. With *What's Wrong with the World* he achieved recognition, along with Hilaire Belloc, as a leading exponent of Distributism, an economic system similar in vision to feudal Europe's society of small proprietors. Chesterton and Belloc were close friends and literary associates, sharing similar beliefs on history, Christianity, and politics. Bernard Shaw described them jointly as "the Chesterbelloc," an absurd, elephantine creature with medieval beliefs. Chesterton's half of the beast often debated Shaw on social, political, and economic issues; and through his platform appearances, essays, and rollicking verse, the persona of G.K.C. developed, opposing G.B.S. in thought and manner.

Chesterton's fiction and poetry written after 1910 reveal a puckish, childlike *joie de vivre,* a reflection of his pronounced Roman Catholic beliefs. He particularly elaborated on these in *Orthodoxy* and *The Everlasting Man,* although most of his work—widely varied as it is in subject matter and genre—is colored by his faith. *The Man Who Was Thursday,* a parable in the form of a detective story which ascends into fantastic epiphany, is perhaps his foremost work of prose fiction in this regard. Among Chesterton's poems, the epics *Lepanto* and *The Ballad of the White Horse* are considered his best efforts, although his strength lay mainly in light verse, such as the drinking songs collected in *The Flying Inn.* In 1916 he began editing the magazine *New Witness,* which later, as *G. K.'s Weekly,* served as an organ of Distributism. The periodical failed to sell, and to support its publication Chesterton wrote the Father Brown stories, which proved his most popular works.

Chesterton is recognized as a master of the irreverent paradox; a recognition of this expert control is crucial to understanding him. Through paradox the seemingly self-evident is turned upside-down, causing readers to view their initial beliefs in a different light. This was part of Chesterton's purpose, as well as his "chief idea of life": the awakening of a child's sense of wonder as if experiencing things for the first time. His essay "A Defense of Nonsense" perhaps best summarizes his views on this method: "Nonsense and faith (strange as the conjunction may seem) are the two supreme symbolic assertions of the truth that to draw out the soul of things with a syllogism is as impossible as to draw out Leviathan with a hook."

Despite Chesterton's popularity, critics generally agree that with his wide spectrum of subjects, his self-proclaimed role as

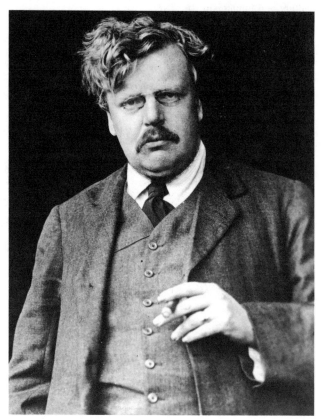

a "mere journalist," and his tendency to clown for the sake of clowning, Chesterton is indeed a "master who left no masterpiece."

(See also *TCLC,* Vol. 1.)

PRINCIPAL WORKS

The Wild Knight and Other Poems   (poetry)   1900
The Defendant   (essays)   1901
Twelve Types   (essays)   1902
Robert Browning   (criticism)   1903
The Napoleon of Notting Hill   (novel)   1904
Heretics   (essays)   1905
Charles Dickens   (criticism)   1906
The Man Who Was Thursday   (novel)   1908
Orthodoxy   (essays)   1908
George Bernard Shaw   (criticism)   1909
The Ball and the Cross   (novel)   1910
What's Wrong with the World   (essays)   1910
The Ballad of the White Horse   (poetry)   1911
The Innocence of Father Brown   (short stories)   1911
Manalive   (novel)   1912

BERNARD SHAW (essay date 1922)

[Mr Chesterton] has many magical arts and gifts at his command. He can make anything that can be made with a pen, from a conspectus of human history to a lethal jibe at the Lord Chancellor; and to utilize this practically boundless technical equipment he has enormous humor, imagination, intellect, and common sense.

Now in respect of the humor and imagination, his integrity can be depended on; but when you come to the intellect and common sense, you have to be careful, because his intellect is fantastic and his common sense impatient. That is because his humor and imagination will creep in. . . . [Mr Chesterton] may stray up an intellectual blind alley to amuse himself. . . . (pp. 94-5)

Thus Mr Chesterton, who once lived near the Home For Lost Dogs in Battersea, has a whimsical tendency to set up a Home For Lost Causes, in competition with Oxford University, in his half explored blind alleys. Like the Home in Battersea, they are not popular with the lost ones; for the final hospitality offered is that of the lethal chamber. The Lost Causes like their last ditches well camouflaged. Mr Chesterton scorns concealment: he stands on the parapet, effulgent by his own light, roaring defiance at a foe who would only too willingly look the other way and pretend not to notice. Even the Lost Causes which are still mighty prefer their own methods of fighting. The Vatican never seems so shaky as when G.K.C. hoists it on his shoulders like Atlas, and proceeds to play football with the skulls of the sceptics. Pussyfoot's chances of drying the British Isles seldom seem so rosy as they do the morning after Mr Chesterton has cracked the brainpans of a thousand teetotallers with raps from Gargantuan flagons waved by him in an ecstasy in which he seems to have ten pairs of hands, like an Indian god.

Nature compensates the danger of his defence by the benefit of his assault. He went to Jerusalem to destroy Zionism; and immediately the spirit of Nehemiah entered into him, and there arose from his pages such a wonderful vision of Jerusalem that our hearts bled for the captivity, and all the rival claimants, past and present, silly Crusader and squalid Bedouin in one red burial blent, perished from our imaginations, and left the chosen people of God to inherit the holy city. He attacks divorce

with an idealization of marriage so superhuman (without extraordinary luck) that all his readers who have not yet committed themselves swear that nothing will induce them to put their heads into the noose of that golden cord. He stated the case for giving votes to women so simply and splendidly that when he proceeded to give his verdict against the evidence it passed as a misprint. Really a wonderful man, this Chesterton; but with something of Balaam in him, and something of that other who went whither he would not.

His latest book is called **Eugenics and Other Evils**. It is a graver, harder book than its forerunners. Something—perhaps the youthful sense of immortality, commonly called exuberance—has lifted a little and left him scanning the grey horizon with more sense that the wind is biting and the event doubtful; but there is plenty of compensating gain; for this book is practically all to the good. The title suggests the old intellectual carelessness: it seems mere nonsense: he might as well write Obstetrics and Other Evils, or Dietetics or Esthetics or Peripatetics or Optics or Mathematics and Other Evils. But when you read you find that he knows what he is about. The use of the word Eugenics implies that the breeding of the human race is an art founded on an ascertained science. Now when men claim scientific authority for their ignorance, and police support for their aggressive presumption, it is time for Mr Chesterton and all other men of sense to withstand them sturdily. Mr Chesterton takes the word as a convenient symbol for current attempts at legislative bodysnatching—live-bodysnatching—to provide subjects for professors and faddists to experiment on when pursuing all sorts of questionable, ridiculous, and even vicious theories of how to produce perfect babies and rear them into perfect adults. At the very first blow he enlists me on his side by coming to my own position and reaffirming it trenchantly. "Sexual selection, or what Christians call falling in love," he says, "is a part of man which in the large and in the long run can be trusted." Why after reproducing my conclusion so exactly he should almost immediately allege that "Plato was only a Bernard Shaw who unfortunately made his jokes in Greek," I cannot guess; for it is impossible to understand what the word "only" means in this sentence. But the conclusion is none the less sound. He does not follow it up as I do by shewing that its political corollary is the ruthless equalization of all incomes in order that this supremely important part of man shall no longer be baffled by the pecuniary discrepancies which forbid the duchess to marry the coalheaver, and divorce King Cophetua from the beggar maid even before they are married. But that will come in a later book. (pp. 95-7)

Bernard Shaw, "Chesterton on Eugenics and Shaw on Chesterton" (originally published in The Nation, *London, Vol. XXX, No. 24, March 11, 1922), in his* Pen Portraits and Reviews, *revised edition, Constable and Company, Ltd, 1932 (and reprinted by Scholarly Press, Inc., 1971), pp. 94-104.*

J. C. SQUIRE (essay date 1927)

A great deal of Mr. Chesterton's verse has serious, though usually not ruinous, faults. He is a very exuberant man. The coupling of complete, and full-blooded, self-expression with fastidious care is unusual. Carefulness normally leads to cramping and timidity, and gusto to carelessness. Mr. Chesterton has always scorned to conceal even his most "vulgar" tastes, and he has let his genius take him wheresoever it would. If the pomposity of an under-secretary moves him to compose a metrical squib, he composes, rather rapidly, the metrical squib. Having composed it he publishes it; having published it, he reprints it. It may amuse others, as it has amused him; it would be hypocritical to pretend that he had not written such things; anyhow, how can they make any difference, one way or the other, to the merits of his love sonnets or his religious odes? The mixture does no harm; it is all to the credit of his honesty in a frightened neighbour-watching age; it is a great thing that on one page there is to be found a poem beginning, "A word came forth in Galilee, a word like to a star," and on the next one which opens with "Jones had a dog: it had a chain." But the fine spontaneity, the devouring zest, the unaffected willingness to engage (for he constantly sees the eternal behind the temporal) in any ephemeral controversy with any obscure combatant, do carry with them a tendency to be content with improvisation, where second thoughts might mean improvement, and to present the public indifferently with fine and momentous poems side by side with trifles that are anything but "tremendous trifles."

Mr. Chesterton is very careless and rather undiscriminating; he also has a propensity to rhetoric. Years ago he wrote an essay in which he described his notion of bliss. It was to lie on his back in bed and paint large sweeping fantasies on the ceiling with a brush ten feet long in the handle. For all I know he may now actually do this, at Beaconsfield, every morning. But he has always done the equivalent thing in print. He "chucks it about" in chunks. The unit is not the word, but the phrase, which is marked by all the stigmata which sometimes captivate, and sometimes irritate, in his prose. The less excellent of his poems are bewildering webs of rhetorical phrases, which roar like cataracts, but convey the vaguest impression of their meaning, sometimes because their sweep carries one away before one can look at them, sometimes because it has carried the author away before *he* could look at them. He is intoxicated with words, words that blare like trumpets, or reverberate like thunder; the more of them there are together the merrier he will be; his fine economical felicities come in pauses of the tumult; for the rest it is hit or miss. Metaphors and similes tumble over each other in the eloquent flood; alliterations charm the ear and distract the attention; antithetical constructions superficially titillate the reader so that too often the profound meaning which lies beneath them escapes him. . . . (pp. 47-8)

His defects are the defects of his qualities; his ear for splendid sound, his intellectual agility, his natural un-self-conscious copiousness. Lesser men often have fewer obvious faults; and, were he scrupulously to use the file, something would go besides the clogging epithets, the inaccuracies and superfluities, the pot-shots, the rhetorical counters, the automatic Swinburnian alliterations and the lazy obscurities. Such characteristic weaknesses as he has are chiefly evident in those poems (such as "St. Barbara," of which I can scarcely understand a line), in which he limits himself to the extent of being wholly serious; he is most frequently flawless when the whole man speaks in verses wherein irony covers passion, and religion is wedded to buffoonery, and romance is wedded to puns: the challenges of a Falstaffian Quixote and the quips of a Puck in Paradise. The greatest of all his poems, "Lepanto" and "The Ballad of the White Horse," hardly come into this category; they are the work of an artist more impersonal than usual, and engrossed in his theme. Sometimes, when Mr. Chesterton is chivalrously declamatory, one has a feeling that he has braced himself to it. Not so in "Lepanto" where his gorgeous vision has entire hold of him; not so either in the quieter, graver tributes and lamentations of "The White Horse," in which an old story has served him as a vehicle for all that he most deeply feels about the life of man, and only occasional side-glances are thrown at his modern bugbears. But beyond these and a few shorter poems, though many are starred with glorious lines, the most memorable of his poems are of the kind described. (pp. 49-50)

[It] was long ago said that Mr. Chesterton's value as a moralist was largely based on the fact that he made virtue amusing. Yet even when he is most vigorously jousting against slimy monsters or caitiff knights his spear usually has a few balloons tied on to it, and can be used, when he tires of the more formal tourney, as a quarterstaff or even a slapstick. His jests are mingled with his protestations of anger and love, as his newspaper magnates are mingled with his medieval knights. Tom Hood and Hans Andersen meet in him; he has one foot in fairyland and another in Fleetstreet—a logical development of which image might lead to the conclusion that this most persuasive of men was a centipede. Consider the series of Ballades and the "Songs of Education," Consider the mingling of sheer poetry and foolery, sentiment and irony, golden oratory and extravagant colloquialism in the songs from *The Flying Inn*, where the moods flit over the surface of the stanzas like cloud-shadows over the downs: "The Song against Songs," "The Good Rich Man," "The Saracen's Head," "The Song of Quoodle," "The Rolling English Road," and that intoxicating song about the elusive town of Roundabout. . . . (p. 51)

In many of the political poems, notably the superb Ode to Lord Birkenhead, there is the same unique mixture, chemical compound rather: elements which no deliberate artifice could blend, being perfectly united by sheer force of spontaneity. Tom Hood was mentioned just now. Our fathers were familiar with two volumes, one entitled *Hood's Serious Poems*, and the other, *Hood's Humorous Poems*. A publisher who should endeavour thus to divide the Chestertonian sheep and goats would soon discover most of them to be hybrids. Comic poetry is as rare as comic verse is common; Mr. Chesterton has written more comic poetry than any Englishman on record. And, to complicate the achievement, he has contrived to make a great deal of it didactic, without falling into the perils that beset didacticism.

His work, in verse as in prose, will have a definite influence. He expresses many opinions with vigour and an instinctive forensic genius. Many of them, notably those which bear particularly upon industrial civilisation, have been expressed by others, and are widely shared, though his remedies are perhaps not as generally approved as his diagnoses. But it is not as a critic of current politics, or of political history, that he is most especially remarkable, great though may be his gifts in these regards. His greatest distinction lies in the hold he has upon the fundamentals of human life, considered both in its social and its metaphysical aspects. In an age of new questions he has reiterated old answers; in an age of scepticism he has laughed at the laughers with a hilarity less hollow than theirs; in an age which tends to excuse baseness, even when it does not explain it away, he has flown the banners of honour, fidelity, and generosity; in an age of mass-regimentation he has stood for the sanctities of the individual soul. And above all— a fact in whose presence all his levities, quibbles, occasional injustices, easy assumptions, and prejudices pale into insignificance—living in a period when the value of life itself has been widely questioned (and, by that very fact, impoverished) he has maintained that "it is something to have been," showing the world the spectacle of one man enjoying the thousand miracles of the day, though the sword of Damocles hang over his head as it hangs over the heads of us all. There lies his ''optimism''; not in any shallow Panglossian delusions, either about the present or about the future. (pp. 52-3)

> *J. C. Squire, ''Mr. Chesterton's Verse'' (originally published in* The Observer, *July 3, 1927), in his* Sunday Mornings *(reprinted by permission of the Estate of the author), William Heinemann Ltd, 1930, pp. 45-54.*

C. S. LEWIS (essay date 1946)

Opening *The Listener* a few days ago I came upon an article on Chesterton by Mr James Stephens—an article which seemed to me ungenerous and even unjust. There were two main charges made against Chesterton; the one, that he was too public (for on Mr Stephens's view poetry is a very private affair) and the other, that he was ''dated''. The first need not, perhaps, be discussed here at very great length. Mr Stephens and I find ourselves on opposite sides of a very well-known fence, and Mr Stephens's side is, I must confess, the popular one at present. It still seems to me that the burden of proof rests on those who describe as ''private'' compositions which their authors take pains to have multiplied by print and which are advertised and exposed for sale in shops. It is an odd method of securing privacy. But this question can wait. It certainly would not have worried Chesterton. Nor would the maxim that any poetry which is immediately and widely acceptable (like that of Euripides, Virgil, Horace, Dante, Chaucer, Shakespeare, Dryden, Pope, and Tennyson) must be merely ''peasant'' poetry have offended a man who desired nothing so much as the restoration of the peasantry. But the question of ''dating'' remains. . . .

The truth is that the whole criticism which turns on dates and periods, as if age-groups were the proper classification of readers, is confused and even vulgar. . . . It is vulgar because it appeals to the desire to be up to date: a desire only fit for dressmakers. It is confused because it lumps together the different ways in which a man can be ''of his period''.

A man may be of his period in the negative sense. That is to say he may deal with things which are of no permanent interest but only seemed to be of interest because of some temporary fashion. Thus Herbert's poems in the shape of altars and crosses are ''dated''; thus, perhaps, the occultist elements in the Celtic school are ''dated''. A man is likely to become ''dated'' in this way precisely because he is anxious not to be dated, to be ''contemporary'': for to move with the times is, of course, to go where all times go. On the other hand a man may be ''dated'' in the sense that the forms, the set-up, the paraphernalia, whereby he expresses matter of permanent interest, are those of a particular age. In that sense the greatest writers are often the most dated. No one is more unmistakably ancient Achaean than Homer, more scholastic than Dante, more feudal than Froissart, more ''Elizabethan'' than Shakespeare. (p. 1070)

The real question is in which sense Chesterton was of his period. Much of his work, admittedly, was ephemeral journalism: it is dated in the first sense. The little books of essays are now mainly of historical interest. Their parallel in Mr Stephens's work is not his romances but his articles in *The Listener*. But Chesterton's imaginative works seem to me to be in quite a different position. They are, of course, richly redolent of the age in which they were composed. The anti-Germanicism in the **Ballad of the White Horse** belongs to a silly and transitory historical heresy of Mr Belloc's—always, on the intellectual side, a disastrous influence on Chesterton. And in the romances, the sword-sticks, the hansom cabs, the anarchists, all go back both to a real London and to an imagined London (that of *The New Arabian Nights*) which have receded from us. But how is it possible not to see that what comes through all this is permanent and dateless? Does not the central theme of the **Ballad**—the highly paradoxical message which Alfred receives from the Virgin—embody the feeling, and the only possible feeling, with which in any age almost defeated men take up such arms as are left them and win? (pp. 1070-71)

Read again **The Flying Inn**. Is Lord Ivywood obsolete? The doctrinaire politician, aristocratic yet revolutionary, inhuman, courageous, eloquent, turning the vilest treacheries and most abominable oppressions into periods that echo with lofty magnanimity—is this out of date? Are the withers of any modern journalist quite unwrung when he reads of Hibbs However? Or read again **The Man who was Thursday**. Compare it with another good writer, Kafka. Is the difference simply that the one is ''dated'' and the other contemporary? Or is it rather that while both give a powerful picture of the loneliness and bewilderment which each one of us encounters in his (apparently) single-handed struggle with the universe, Chesterton, attributing to the universe a more complicated disguise, and admitting the exhilaration as well as the terror of the struggle, has got in rather more; is more balanced: in that sense, more classical, more permanent?

I will tell Mr Stephens what that man is like who can see nothing in these stories but an Edwardian ''period'' piece. He is like a man who should look into Mr Stephens's *Deirdre* . . . and having seen the names (Connohar, Deirdre, Fergus, Naoise) should mutter ''All the old Abbey Theatre stuff'' and read no more. (p. 1071)

> *C. S. Lewis, ''Notes on the Way'' (reproduced by permission of Curtis Brown Ltd., London, on behalf of the Trustees of the Estate of C. S. Lewis), in* Time and Tide, *Vol. 27, No. 45, November 9, 1946, pp. 1070-1071.*

RONALD KNOX (essay date 1954)

When you take to writing detective stories, the measure of your success depends on the amount of personality you can build up round your favorite detective. . . . [Whether] because Sherlock Holmes has set the standard for all time, or because the public does not like to see plots unravelled by a mere thinking-machine, it is personality that counts. . . . It is because he drops his parcels and cannot roll his umbrella, because he blinks at us and has fits of absent-mindedness, that Father Brown is such a good publisher's detective. He is a Daniel come to judgement. (p. viii)

The real secret of Father Brown is that there is nothing of the mystic about him. When he falls into a reverie . . . the other people in the story think that he must be having an ecstasy, because he is a Catholic priest, and will proceed to solve the mystery by some kind of heaven-sent intuition. And the reader, if he is not careful, will get carried away by the same miscalculation; here, surely, is Chesterton preparing to show the Protestants where they get off. Unconsciously, this adds to the feeling of suspense; you never imagine that Poirot will have an ecstasy, or that Albert Campion will receive enlightenment from the supernatural world. And all the time, Father Brown is doing just what Poirot does; he is using his little grey cells. He is noticing something which the reader hasn't noticed, and will kick himself later for not having noticed. (p. x)

Father Brown began life as short stories in the *Saturday Evening Post,* and short stories he remained; for an author so fertile in ideas, perhaps it was the simplest arrangement. But it must be confessed that this enforced brevity produces a rather breathless atmosphere; the more so, because Chesterton was an artist before he became an author, and occupies a good deal of his space with scene-painting. And the scene-painting takes up room—valuable room, the pedantic reader would tell us.

What scene-painting it is! The Norfolk Broads, and the house full of mirrors standing on its lonely island; or that other island on the Cornish estuary, with its wooden tower—you would expect the second of these passages to be little more than a repetition of the first, but in fact it is nothing of the kind; in the one case you have the feeling of being in Norfolk, in the other you have the feeling of being in Cornwall. The atmosphere of that dreadful hotel in *The Queer Feet;* the atmosphere of a winter-bound summer resort in *The God of the Gongs;* the (quite irrelevant) effect of bitter cold in *The Sign of the Broken Sword*—what a setting they give to the story! (pp. xi-xii)

But it does take up room. And, if only because the canvas is so overcrowded, you must not expect in these stories the mass of details which you would expect of Freeman Wills Crofts; the extracts from Bradshaw, the plan of the study with a cross to show where the body was found. Hence the severely orthodox readers of detective stories, who love to check and to challenge every detail, must be prepared for a disappointment; Chesterton will not be at pains to tell us whether the windows were fastened; how many housemaids were kept (in defiance of modern probabilities), and which of them dusted the room last . . . , and so on. Even the unities of time and place are neglected; you can never be quite sure whether it is next morning, or a week later, or what. Consequently, you never quite feel 'Here am I, with all the same data at my disposal as Father Brown had; why is it that his little grey cells work, and mine don't?' Not that there is any deliberate concealment of clues, but the whole picture is blurred; the very wealth of detail confuses you. All you can do is to set about eliminating the impossible characters in the hope of finding, by a process of exhaustion, the villain. Women can be ruled out; there is only one female villain in the whole series—it is part of Chesterton's obstinate chivalry that he hardly ever introduces you to a woman you are meant to dislike. People with Irish names (how unlike Sherlock Holmes!) are fairly certain to be innocent. But, even so, the characters of the story elude you; you do not feel certain that you have been told quite enough about them.

For Chesterton (as for Father Brown) the characters were the really important thing. The little priest could see, not as a psychologist, but as a moralist, into the dark places of the human heart; could guess, therefore, at what point envy, or fear, or resentment would pass the bounds of the normal, and the cords of convention would snap, so that a man was hurried into crime. Into crime, not necessarily into murder; the Father Brown stories are not bloodthirsty, as detective stories go; a full third of them deal neither with murder nor with attempted murder, which is an unusual average nowadays; most readers demand a corpse. The motives which made it necessary for Hypatia Hard to elope with her husband, the motives which induced the Master of the Mountain to pretend that he had stolen the ruby when he hadn't—the reader may find them unimpressive, because there is no black cap and no drop at the

end of them. But, unless he is a man of unusual perspicacity, he will have to admit that he also found them unexpected.

The truth is that what we demand of a detective story is neither sensations, nor horrors, but ingenuity. And Chesterton was a man of limitless ingenuity. . . . All those brilliant twists which a Mason and an Agatha Christie give to their stories, Chesterton, when he was in the mood for it, could give to his. . . . A ship could be lured to its doom by lighting a bonfire which would confuse the appearance of the lights in the tideway; you could gag a ruler so securely that he would be unable to answer the challenge of his own sentries, and would be shot. They are all ideas we might have thought of, and didn't.

Whether such expedients would be likely to be adopted in real life is perhaps more questionable. But then, how far is the writer of mystery stories bound by the laws of probability? Nothing could be more improbable than Father Brown's habit of always being on the spot when a crime is committed; but he shares this curious trick of ubiquity with Hercule Poirot. The thing is a literary convention; it may not be a good one, but it is well worn. No, when we open a detective story we leave the world of strict probability behind us; we must be prepared for three or four quite independent pieces of shady business happening to happen in the same country house on the same evening. And Chesterton's imagination was flamboyant; he was like a schoolboy on holiday, and could sit as light to realism as P. G. Wodehouse. If you meet him on his own ground—that is, halfway to fairyland—you will have to admit that for sheer ingenuity he can rival Miss [Dorothy] Sayers herself. Cast your mind back to your first reading of the Father Brown stories, and ask yourself whether you saw what was the missing factor which linked all the various exhibits in Glengyle Castle, or why *The Insoluble Problem* was insoluble.

No, if we are to judge the Father Brown cycle by the canons of its own art, we shall not be disposed to complain that these are something less than detective stories; rather, that they are something more. Like everything else Chesterton wrote, they are a Chestertonian manifesto. And it may be reasonably maintained that a detective story is meant to be read in bed, by way of courting sleep; it ought not to make us think—or rather, it ought to be a kind of *catharsis,* taking our minds off the ethical, political, theological problems which exercise our waking hours by giving us artificial problems to solve instead. If this is so, have we not good reason to complain of an author who smuggles into our minds, under the disguise of a police mystery, the very solicitudes he was under contract to banish?

I am inclined to think that the complaint, for what it is worth, lies against a good many of the Father Brown stories, but not all, and perhaps not the best. Where the moral which Chesterton introduces is vital to the narrative, belongs to the very stuff of the problem, the author has a right, if he will, to mystify us on this higher level. In the over-civilized world we live in, there are certain anomalies which we take for granted; and he may be excused if he gently mocks at us for being unable, because we took them for granted, to read his riddle. There is something artificial in a convention which allows us to say that nobody has entered a house when in fact a postman has entered it, as if the postman, being a State official, were not a man. . . . But it must be confessed that in some of the stories, especially the later ones, the didactic purpose tends to overshadow, and even to crowd out, the detective interest; such stories as *The Arrow of Heaven,* and *The Chief Mourner of Marne.* If we read these with interest, it is not because they are good detective stories, but because they are good Chesterton. (pp. xii-xvi)

Ronald Knox, "Introduction" (1954), in Father Brown: Selected Stories *by G. K. Chesterton, edited by Ronald Knox (reprinted by permission of Oxford University Press), Oxford University Press, London, 1955, pp. vii-xvii.*

DUDLEY BARKER (essay date 1974)

The most obvious feature of Chesterton's work is its quantity. (p. 3)

It is astonishing that a man who wrote so much, so quickly, should also often have written so well. Two of his novels seem secure of their place in the literature of twentieth-century England. Half a dozen of his poems are still familiar, as is his fine English epic. At least one of his religious books is still widely read; so are many of his light essays and some of his literary criticism. He is accepted as the best English aphorist of our century. His little priest, Father Brown, ranks among the dozen best-known detectives of fiction. In addition to all that, of course, he wrote a huge amount of ephemeral, tired, worthless prose, and a very great deal of nonsense.

He first emerged as an essayist who had published in periodicals a few short poems which people remembered; notably '**The Donkey**' and '**By The Babe Unborn**'. He had in fact, in 1900, published two volumes of verse, one of nonsense verses and the other, which his father paid a publisher to put out, a pompous, boring verse play together with the reprinted short lyrics. Few noticed the volumes. (pp. 3-4)

However, the money that verse would not provide began to flow from essays. . . . His first essays appeared in the *Speaker* [a radical weekly] and were soon widely noticed.

From them he formed his third volume, *The Defendant;* each essay a defence of something, such as of Penny Dreadfuls, of Nonsense, of Heraldry, of Ugly Things. . . .

But most of the *Defendant* essays are light-hearted, chuckling, showing already Chesterton's superb knack of the neat phrase, and his love of paradox and logic of the absurd. (p. 4)

His second volume of essays, published in 1902 . . . , was collected chiefly from the *Daily News.* He had been invited at first to write on literary subjects, and these essays, collected as *Twelve Types*, established him as a literary critic and decided the direction of his writing life. His criticism, rarely profound, was remarkably perceptive. . . . Chesterton could plunge his pen into any hackneyed subject—Charlotte Brontë, say, or Pope, or Scott or Stevenson—and pluck out its core in a few fresh phrases. (p. 5)

The freshness of it introduced Chesterton to the literary gaffers of his day . . . [among them,] John Morley, then editing the 'English Men of Letters' series. Morley invited him to write the volume on Robert Browning. . . . Max Beerbohm advised him to accept, since he was still young enough to say something original. Chesterton's *Robert Browning* amplified the remark. As he admitted, with a chuckle, there was not much about Browning in his book; and what there was, was mostly inaccurate. It was chiefly a book about Chesterton's thoughts on poetry, life and religion. . . . Most of Browning's lines were misquoted, and there was one which Browning might well have written in 'Mr Sludge the Medium', but, as it happened, had not. (pp. 5-6)

Nevertheless, Chesterton's *Browning* was an immediate and lasting success. It enlarged him from journalist to author, though the journalism flowed merrily alongside. Indeed, the two streams often merged. Essays in the *Daily News* were the nucleus of his book *Heretics*, a couple of years later, attacking the philosophies of contemporary writers, with incidentally a good deal of straightforward literary criticism. The freshness of view persisted. . . .

But the true successors to *Robert Browning* were two more literary biographies. First came a short, vivid account of a great Victorian artist, *G. F. Watts;* then, in 1906, *Charles Dickens,* Chesterton's happiest book. (p. 6)

Part of the value of his *Charles Dickens* . . . is that it was written with devotion. But there is much more. Chesterton's ability to probe straight into essentials and illuminate them with a few phrases was never stronger. Of a subject which had been so worked upon he had fresh things to say, and they have formed more of the public image of Dickens, and the public appreciation of his novels than the writings of many another critic or biographer. He was the first to assert clearly that 'Dickens's work is to be reckoned always by characters, sometimes by groups, oftener by episodes, but never by novels.' . . . Chesterton's second basic clarification was that 'Dickens did not strictly make a literature; he made a mythology. . . . He did not always manage to make his characters men, but he always managed, at least, to make them gods.' (pp. 6-7)

Unfortunately, *Charles Dickens* proved the summit of Chesterton's literary criticism. He wrote several more books which could thus be catalogued, and hundreds of essays, articles and prefaces, but nothing ever again so good. Of the books, the one that has lasted best is the extended essay *The Victorian Age in Literature* . . . It starts brilliantly with an essay on the spirit of England in the nineteenth century, and flows well to the great Victorian novelists and philosophers. Scattered across it like sun-sparkles on a stream are vivid phrases and sentences setting down the essence of a writer: 'There was about John Stuart Mill even a sort of embarrassment; he exhibited all the wheels of his iron universe rather reluctantly, like a gentleman in trade showing ladies over his factory.' . . . Then the book goes on to the great Victorian poets, and the sparkle inexplicably vanishes, as though Chesterton, of all men, felt that he had nothing he particularly wanted to say about poets. (pp. 7-8)

He wrote only two more books, years later, in which literary criticism was the major factor. His *Robert Louis Stevenson,* containing more an account of Chesterton's youth than Stevenson's, is only, as criticism, a development of an early essay in the *Daily News.* His *Chaucer,* written a few years before his death, is one of the few Chesterton books in which dullness predominates. That he wrote badly about a subject so dear to him was perhaps because the pressures of journalism and an absurd back-to-mediaevalism politics, undertaken as a duty towards his dead brother Cecil, had by then sapped too much of his health and vigour. Or perhaps he was by then too old. For he aged as a writer far more quickly than as a man.

Most of his best work, indeed, was done in little more than the first decade of his writing life. . . . [Half] of his books were yet to come, as well as the great bulk of his journalism; but of the books, only five are of much consequence, and little of the journalism can compare with that of his Fleet Street decade. And he wrote no more poetry, only occasionally verse.

In that first decade of writing, however, he was brilliantly spontaneous. He started as novelist as suddenly and effectively as he had become essayist. *The Napoleon of Notting Hill* is one of the most unusual first-novels of modern times. Chesterton's tale of war of the future, between the London boroughs which had become separate little states in mediaeval trappings, is amusing enough in itself (and an odd prophecy of urban guerrillas). But it is subsidiary to the theme of conflict between Auberon Quin, the satirical King of England (elected from the Civil Service—and thought to have been modelled on Max Beerbohm) and Adam Wayne, the stern, fanatical Lord High Provost of Notting Hill. It is these two who, when the fighting at last is over and mankind laid low in grief and suffering, come together as two lobes of the same brain, the humorous and the fanatic, finding a philosophical justification for existence clearly derived from the Book of Job. . . . The novel does not deal with human relationships; it contains, for instance, no women. It is rather a statement of political beliefs, and a philosophical allegory. (pp. 8-9)

This first novel was followed by two others, *The Ball and the Cross* and *The Man Who Was Thursday*. . . . (p. 9)

The Ball and the Cross has now largely been forgotten, although it should rank not far below the others. Like them it is an allegory, told in jesting narrative until the closing scenes. An atheist and a devout Catholic swear to fight a duel because the Catholic considers the atheist has insulted the Mother of God. But they are continually thwarted. . . . At last they are trapped in the garden of a lunatic asylum, the madness of the world, in which two themes are worked out; on the spiritual plane, the struggle between good and evil; on the political, a prophecy of the authoritarian State which Chesterton clearly saw approaching. A comparison with Kafka is unavoidable, and curious; at that time, of course, Chesterton knew nothing of Kafka. There are the similarities of naturalistic dialogue in a mad setting, of incessant awareness of actual and positive evil and persecution, both spiritual and human. The chief dissimilarities are that Chesterton's surface narrative is light-hearted, often comic; and that he had, by then, emerged from an adolescence of despair and doubt into an unshakeable acceptance of orthodox Christianity.

His adolescent despair, which had been unusually severe and brought him near to mental breakdown, was the origin of his third novel, *The Man Who Was Thursday,* unquestionably his best. The surface narrative of this allegory is melodrama. The man who was Thursday—a detective smuggled on to the inner council of seven anarchists who aim to destroy the world, each bearing as code-name a day of the week (and of the Creation)— is engaged in successive wild combats with the others, only to find, in turn, that each is also a detective in disguise. Only Sunday remains, to be chased madly through London and at last to emerge as the Sabbath, the peace of God. Chesterton said that he did not intend Sunday to represent the Deity, 'but rather Nature as it appears to the pantheist, whose pantheism is struggling out of pessimism.' But this is not the impression that the reader receives by the final chapter, which is, once again, a direct reference to the Book of Job. The Kafkalike method of realistic dialogue and action in irrational circumstances is even more pronounced that in the earlier novels. But the theme is ever more strongly that of faith and optimism.

In the same year, 1908, Chesterton published *Orthodoxy,* in which he stated this faith without a veil of fiction. (pp. 9-10)

In the decade of his best novels, literary biographies, essays, and definitions of his religious and philosophical position, Chesterton also set out his somewhat odd political theories (in a book called *What's Wrong With The World*) unduly influenced by Hilaire Belloc and by his own brother Cecil, and composed nearly all his poetry. (p. 11)

Nobody, I imagine, would call Chesterton a great poet. Yet there are not a few of his lyrics that somehow stick in the general memory, poetry that most people have actually heard or read. . . . But the [lyric] songs were by no means all. There was the occasional thrust, such as the famous exhortation to Birkenhead ('Chuck it, Smith!'). There was the epic, especially *The Ballad of the White Horse.*

This was the only work in his life which he pondered and drafted over several years. The idea was that King Alfred's long defeat by the Danes, then his victory at Ethandune—but victory never complete, always having to be guarded and fought over again—is a microcosm of the English throughout their history. (pp. 11-12)

In the circumstances of defeat and victory, it *fits* the English as perhaps no other poem does. (p. 12)

A familiar comment on Chesterton is that he was a master who left no masterpiece. It may be that, of all he wrote, *The Ballad of the White Horse* is the only possible refutation.

Certainly the work by which he is now best known to a wide readership cannot make claim. Father Brown is a familiar fictional detective. But the Father Brown stories are not a masterpiece in the way that those of Sherlock Holmes are, or those of Maigret, or even of Poirot or Perry Mason. Many have ingenious ideas, particularly those written during Chesterton's prolific decade and published in the first collection as *The Innocence of Father Brown*. . . . Chesterton's original idea of a priest knowing more about evil than most criminals (because of the confessions of others) scarcely lasted intact through the first two volumes, *The Innocence* and *The Wisdom.* By the third volume, *The Incredulity of Father Brown,* twelve years later, Chesterton was deeply engaged as editor of his *G.K.'s Weekly.* . . . [He] kept the magazine in existence only by subsidizing it with money he earned by writing. Father Brown became then the chief provider, and the rest of the Father Brown stories were potboilers.

Not much needs to be said, indeed, about most of what Chesterton wrote after 1914. During the first world war his books were only war-propaganda pamphlets, and a *Short History of England* which is chiefly about the delights of mediaevalism. The fiction he wrote in the Twenties and Thirties falls well below his former standards. He collected into volumes some lively newspaper and magazine articles on his travels to Ireland, to Palestine, to the United States of America and to Rome, but these books are essentially sheaves of travel articles, little more.

His move from the Anglo-Catholic into the Roman Catholic Church in 1922, however, revived in him some of his earlier powers. The next book he wrote, a short biography of *St Francis of Assisi,* is as clear, simple and charming as anything he produced. His picture of St Francis, who had been one of his heroes since boyhood, is drawn with such affection that it was at once a success.

His second book of this period was provoked by Wells's *Outline of History.* Chesterton attacked Wells's theme of the steady betterment of mankind in *The Everlasting Man,* essentially a Christian view of history, centred around the brief life on earth of Jesus. In a sense it is the sequel to his earlier *Orthodoxy,* the completion of his journey from non-belief to complete and immovable religious conviction.

In spite of the vast writing output which Chesterton maintained until the very week of his death in 1936, there is not much more of his work that needs noting. . . . But there was one more biography to come towards the close of his life; a brief account of *St Thomas Aquinas,* companion to his *St Francis of Assisi* which it matches in length and simplicity, but well exceeds in profundity. To attempt to depict, in so brief a space, the greatest of Christian philosophers, as Chesterton insists that St Thomas is, and to show how he reconciled the Christian with the great pagan philosophies, was daunting indeed. Chesterton achieved it with, as he puts it, only 'a popular sketch of a great historical character who ought to be more popular . . . a rough sketch of a figure in a landscape, not of a landscape with figures.' The sketch is not only a convincing portrait of the saint, but makes clear to an ordinary reader how St Thomas 'did not reconcile Christ to Aristotle; he reconciled Aristotle to Christ.' It was the last book that Chesterton wrote (apart from a few more collections of newspaper essays and magazine stories); it is satisfying and right that it should be so good.

Although Chesterton's *Autobiography* was published shortly after his death, he had written most of it some ten years earlier, and laid it by. Its publication, however, beautifully rounded off his life. For all its inaccuracies (his memory failing him quite often, usually to soften things), and its omissions (such as practically any mention of his marriage and his private life thereafter), it is a book of delights. This kindly, generous, immensely courteous, often stubborn and pig-headed, portly man, so immensely filled with the sense of comedy, and with the certainties of faith, never drew a more agreeable portrait than this of himself. (pp. 13-15)

> *Dudley Barker, ''A Brief Survey of Chesterton's Work''*
> *(copyright © 1974 by Dudley Barker; by permission of Barnes & Noble Books, a Division of Littlefield, Adams & Co., Inc.), in* G. K. Chesterton: A Centenary Appraisal, *edited by John Sullivan, Barnes & Noble, 1974, pp. 3-15.*

IAN BOYD (essay date 1975)

There are two general conclusions which may be drawn from a study of Chesterton's novels. The first concerns the somewhat unexpected political view which an analysis of them reveals, and the second the correlation between their political meaning and their literary value.

It is of course true that the fiction does reflect fairly accurately the political thought which one finds in the other writing. Early novels such as *The Napoleon of Notting Hill* and *The Ball and the Cross* and pre-World War One novels such as *Manalive* and *The Flying Inn* again and again echo essays written at the same time. The preoccupation with Distributism which characterizes the post-War essays is also characteristic of the post-War novels and short stories. (p. 191)

But the most interesting and important feature which a study of the fiction reveals is the treatment of medievalism in the novels. The common view of Chesterton's social philosophy is that it expresses a longing for a literal return to medieval times. A careful study of the novels indicates the falsity of such a view. The shortest summary of what they have to say about the restoration of a medieval social order is that it is a dangerous political dream. In *The Napoleon of Notting Hill,* Adam Wayne's neo-medievalism brings back poetry and pageantry to modern life, but it also creates a neo-Imperialism which is as oppressive as the Imperialism it was supposed to

replace. In *The Ball and the Cross,* MacIan's dream of a medieval theocracy turns out to be a nightmare of authoritarian terror and oppression. Even in a later novel such as *Tales of the Long Bow,* which corresponds most closely to the popular view of his medievalism, surprisingly little is said about a return to a medieval past: what is achieved by the successful Distributist revolution is the protection of a newly created and broadly based agrarian society.

But the most subtle and ironic treatment of medievalism is found in . . . [*The Return of Don Quixote.* It is] perhaps the best example of the way in which the best fiction is at once sophisticated and well-balanced propaganda for a political philosophy and extraordinarily effective literature. The medieval experiment which the hero introduces does little to alter the political realities of modern life, except to the extent that it distracts the people from the existence of the real social problems which it leaves unaltered. The restoration of pageantry and colour to political life which delights Herne and his followers is also a means of deceiving them. It might be argued that the Distributist criticism of State Socialism and Capitalism is now turned against Distributism itself. Certainly nothing that Chesterton's critics have written about the folly of romantic medievalism in politics hits as shrewdly as his own criticism of it in what is ostensibly his most flamboyantly medieval novel.

The novels also associate the illusion which medievalism represents with the unreality of the medieval world which is actually restored. The medievalism of Notting Hill depends ultimately on the frivolous improvisations of Auberon, who not only claims no special knowledge of history but in fact regards the entire project as a joke. The medievalism of *The Ball and the Cross* and that of *The Return of Don Quixote* are equally bogus and egotistical and invite the same kind of doubts. There is, for example, no reason to believe that Herne's few days of antiquarian research have really qualified him as the medieval specialist he is supposed to be, and the result of this hastily conducted research shares something of the theatrical quality of the amateur play-acting with which it begins.

At the same time the ironical treatment of medievalism does not imply the rejection of 'medieval' values. The dream of restoring a medieval social order may be a dangerous illusion, but there is a sense in which the illusion is necessary. It has in fact the qualities of a myth. Those who mistake it for a reality destroy the society they are trying to reform, but those who recognize it as an ideal possess a valuable means of understanding and judging the modern world. Perhaps the best example of the way in which medievalism becomes a way of understanding modern political life is found in *The Man Who Knew Too Much.* The medieval pageant in which Horne Fisher takes part provides him with the historical perspective he needs in order to understand the squalid charade of modern politics in which he is also involved. Sometimes those who misunderstand the function of the medieval myth and those who understand it are the same people. Adam Wayne and Evan MacIan learn eventually from the romanticism which at first deludes them. And in *The Return of Don Quixote,* Herne's superficial studies finally provide him with the principles which enable him to condemn his own medieval political experiment.

Another way in which the novels reveal an unexpected side of Chesterton's political and social philosophy is more directly related to their allegorical quality. This has to do with the use of opposed but complementary characters who help to define a complete and balanced political point of view. The success with which this method is used varies greatly from novel to novel, and indeed it is fully used only in the early novels and in a certain number of the novels which were published in the early and mid twenties. The elements involved in the balance remain remarkably constant. The main conflict is always between a kind of idealism on the one hand and a kind of irony on the other, and the resolution of the conflict always involves a reconciliation of the political forces which have been previously opposed. In *The Napoleon of Notting Hill,* Auberon's irony and Adam's fanaticism are finally revealed as the two essentials of political sanity which achieve their equilibrium in the Chestertonian common man. In *The Ball and the Cross,* the quarrel between MacIan and Turnbull dramatizes the conflict between romantic Christianity and revolutionary Socialism, and is finally resolved by an affirmation of the values which each of them represents. In the other pre-War novels little attempt is made to create a political synthesis in this way. Nonetheless in *Manalive,* Innocent Smith derives a kind of cumulative wisdom from the various political types whom he meets on his journey around the world, and in *The Flying Inn,* Humphrey Pump represents a complete expression of what Chesterton meant by the common man.

It is in the early post-War Distributist novels that the use of political and social typology achieves its most interesting form. In *The Man Who Knew Too Much,* Horne Fisher makes a far more detailed case against the corruptions of parliamentary government than one finds in *The Flying Inn.* Admittedly the emphasis is generally negative, but in a story of almost unrelieved political disaster, some attempt is made to understand the motives of those who bring the disaster about. In *Tales of the Long Bow,* a series of marriages between different political and social types illustrates the pastoral side of Distributism. But the most successful use of typology is found in *The Return of Don Quixote.* Themes that were treated individually in the earlier novels are now brought together as the first complete expression of the Distributist political and social viewpoint. The political forces which are reconciled in the final synthesis are various and unexpected. Instead of the familiar opposition between characters representing idealism and irony, the novel introduces three central characters, each of whom possesses valuable political insights and dangerous political limitations. Herne, a romantic idealist in the tradition and Wayne and MacIan, is ostensibly the directing force of the novel's action. Braintree, who has affinities with Turnbull and Lord Ivywood, is at once the embodiment of the revolutionary spirit which demands social justice and the doctrinaire spirit which ignores the variety and complexity of real life. Murrell, who recalls the ironic detachment of Auberon, also represents a kind of Tory scepticism about the possibility of political improvement, which was characteristic of Horne Fisher.

The kinds of women these men fall in love with and the part played by women add a further complexity to the novel. Herne's impersonal idealism turns into a kind of neo-Fascism under the influence of the strong-minded Rosamund Severne; whereas Braintree's Syndicalism is eventually humanized under the influence of Olive Ashley's romantic idealism. Murrell undergoes a rather different transformation. His attempt to find the lost illumination colour becomes a romantic quest during which he falls in love and discovers an instance of the social injustice which is the real subject of the book. There is little in Chesterton's other writing which prepares one for the surprising resolution of this many-sided conflict. The resolution involves first of all a sharp distinction between religion and politics. The idealism which leads to political disaster also leads to religious conversion. But the movement of disillusioned romantics towards medieval religion involves a corresponding affirmation of the Syndicalist solution of worker-control for the social problem which romantic medievalism was unable to solve.

It is also important to note that this grouping and re-grouping of political types is achieved not by the mechanical manipulation of characters, but by purely literary means. The action is controlled by a developing pattern of imagery which changes as the story proceeds. The pageant which becomes a real-life drama and the quest for colour which brings the pageant to an end are symbolic as well as literal events. The broken monument in the park represents the vague romanticism which inspires much of the action of the novel, but it also represents the tragic separation of religion and idealism, which is one of the novel's central themes. In a novel which Chesterton called a parable for social reformers, the monument of the dragon standing alone without the angel that destroys it is an emblem of the need for a balance between the ideal and the practical sides of life. And the crimson illumination-paint which Olive Ashley seeks is at once the colour of the stained-glass window, which represents the religious values that are absent from modern life, and the colour of Braintree's revolutionary red tie, which represents the political solution to modern problems.

The way in which the novels sometimes fail to use imaginative means successfully is best illustrated perhaps by the final group of novels. The chapters which make up *The Poet and the Lunatics* are never more than random illustrations of a central theme, and they are illustrations that do remarkably little to advance the main action, which remains curiously static. The order of events is entirely haphazard, and the chapters seem merely to mark time until the somewhat predictable conclusion is reached. Even the elaborate and ingenious attempt to unify *Four Faultless Felons* does not quite disguise the essential dissimilarity of the stories that are supposed to be unified. And in *The Paradoxes of Mr Pond* the breakdown in unity is so complete that instead of a novel one is left with a series of loosely related short stories. The defects of the earlier novels are also present and present in an exaggerated form. The intrusive symbolism which occasionally mars some of the earlier novels is also found in the later fiction where the heavy-handed symbolic details have little relevance to the action they are supposed to clarify: every garden is an ironic Eden and every sunrise and sunset the symbolic background for a trivial event or a minor climax.

More significantly the literary decline is a political decline as well. The definition of social sanity in *The Poet and the Lunatics* is as vague and confused as the manner in which the story is narrated. It is also difficult to say what coherent political meaning emerges from the bewildering mixture of political and social themes which one finds in *Four Faultless Felons.* It is perhaps significant that most of the themes which are treated in the later novels have received their successful and definitive treatment in the early fiction. Indeed much of the repetitiousness and sense of fatigue which characterize the literary decline in the late novels can be explained in terms of their almost parasitic dependence on the political concerns of the earlier fiction. This apparent need to rely on reworking old material may explain why so much of the action of the later novels is set in an indeterminate period of the past and why so much of the political background is concerned with the politics of Edwardian rather than contemporary times.

It would not be difficult to multiply examples of the new vagueness of outlook and the new lack of imaginative grip.

The effect is not always an unhappy one. The rather confused tolerance which is now expressed for Imperialism is balanced by the new tolerance which is extended towards the Jews, who for the first time are represented in something like a favourable light. The old hostility towards Germany is also modified, and in *The Paradoxes of Mr Pond,* the very effective Polish propaganda of 'The Three Horsemen of Apocalypse' includes a defence of German romanticism; and 'A Tall Story', the final chapter of the book, may be read as a kind of apology for Chesterton's contribution to anti-German hysteria during World War One. But the most important example of what the new blandness and loss of imaginative power involve is provided by the treatment of the theme of kingship in the final novels.

It is of course true that the exploration of this theme provides a partial exception to the general absence of contemporary politics in the late novels. To some extent at least the treatment of this theme represents Chesterton's last attempt to come to terms with a political force which he recognized as genuinely modern. But the treatment of the theme owes as much to the earlier fiction as it does to any new awareness of what was happening in contemporary politics. The king, who makes his appearance in *Four Faultless Felons* as Clovis the Third of Pavonia, and in Mr Pond's imaginary republic as the Unmentionable Man, derives his real interest from being a member of the group of monarchs which begins with Auberon Quin in *The Napoleon of Notting Hill* and ends with Michael Herne in *The Return of Don Quixote.* In relation to these figures from the earlier fiction, the king of the later fiction is a new and somewhat disquieting version of a very familiar Chestertonian type. At first the change in his role seems to be entirely an improvement. Instead of the ineffectual romantic who releases political forces he can neither understand nor control, he is now the practical statesman standing above party politics, but ready to intervene in them when the interests of the nation require. Saving the people from a corrupt parliament seems to be his favourite occupation. In Pavonia, he prevents a revolution by championing the policy of reform that the politicians have neglected, and in Mr Pond's anonymous republic he succeeds in reconciling the conflicting values of revolutionary Socialism and Liberal idealism. In a word, he represents an easy solution to the difficult problems of modern politics. (pp. 192-98)

[What] at first seems to be the one important imaginative development in the late novels is in fact a final indication of the way in which they represent a failure in political imagination. The greatness of the failure can be measured only by a comparison between what the king had been with what he has now become. The comic subtlety that gave an unexpected meaning to medievalism, and the delicate balance between a multitude of political types that gave an extraordinary power to the best of his fiction have disappeared, and one is left instead with the grim and humourless figure of a king whose negative qualities make him an Auberon who has lost his wit and a Herne who has learned nothing from experience. (p. 198)

> *Ian Boyd, in his conclusion to his* The Novels of G. K. Chesterton: A Study in Art and Propaganda *(copyright © 1975 by Ian Boyd; by permission of Barnes & Noble Books, a Division of Littlefield, Adams & Co., Inc.), Barnes & Noble, 1975, pp. 191-98.*

KARIN YOUNGBERG   (essay date 1976)

[*The Man Who Was Thursday*] is the best-known and most successful of Chesterton's bizarre fantasies. The book is an imaginative exploration of the perilous land of unreason, of the intellectual and artistic world of London in the first decade of the twentieth century. . . . (pp. 240-41)

But, in some respects, *The Man Who Was Thursday* is also a detective story, traditionally the most intellectually demanding and carefully structured of fictional genres. Although Chesterton's book is often more melodramatic and swashbuckling than most detective stories, its police-detective heroes are faced with a series of puzzling and painful riddles which they attempt to solve. In their pursuit of the Ultimate Criminal, the Moriarty of the Cosmos, the detectives face many of the questions which the modern world has found most troublesome: the nature of God; the relationship of faith and science, of intuition and reason; and, most importantly, what C. S. Lewis has called "the problem of pain."

The hero of the tale is Gabriel Syme, poet and employee of Scotland Yard. . . . His seemingly impossible mission, given to him by a man in a dark room whom he has seen only from behind, is to discover and to expose the New Anarchists whose motto is, "We dig you deeper and blow you higher." As the story unfolds, Syme the philosopher-policeman undertakes a dangerous battle of wits with the Central Anarchist Council, called the Council of Days because its members have assumed the pseudonyms of days of the week. The members of the Council present some of the many faces of modern pessimism, which for Chesterton was the New Anarchy. At the head of them all is the enigmatic and elusive Master Criminal, the ultimate representative of intellectual anarchy, known only as President Sunday.

By a brilliant and brazen strategem Syme assumes the identity of Thursday, one of the Central Anarchist Council, to infiltrate the conspiracy. (pp. 241-42)

The first line of action consists of a series of surprising revelations in which each of the Anarchists on the Council (with the notable exception of Sunday) is exposed to the others as a fraud; each is in reality a card-carrying member of Scotland Yard, commissioned by the same Man in the Dark Room who first sent Syme out on his mission. But what does Chesterton intend by such an outrageous reversal? Is everyone and everything simply a disguise for something else?

In order to suggest an answer to these questions I have chosen to concentrate on the second lines of action in *Thursday,* that involving the Council's relationship to Sunday. (p. 242)

[In the] frantic pursuit of the President, there is no occasion for the application of deductive logic, the stock-and-trade of detectives. Chesterton's philosopher-policemen have little to do with deduction from evidence or with what Hercule Poirot would call "the little grey cells."

Instead Chesterton seems to have imagined the adventure, danger, and mystery of detective investigation as something akin to the perilous realms of knight-errantry. . . . [The] detective Chesterton has in mind is a romantic figure engaged in a quest that is somehow bigger than life, a kind of intellectual St. George going forth on a journey into the heart of a modern city to confront the Dragon of Mystery. . . . In *The Man Who Was Thursday* Syme and other detectives make the journey and achieve the confrontation, but a satisfying answer to the meaning of mystery alludes them. (p. 243)

The detectives seek from Sunday answers to questions about his nature and intentions and about their own being and purpose, questions not unlike those of Shakespeare's King Lear as he challenges the pain of life and the apparent injustice of the gods. And they learn through the exhausting chase what it means to take up the burden of mystery.

Perhaps this experience of Syme and his companions can be clarified by a somewhat analogous situation in another detective story of sorts where the "meaning of mystery" is explored, *The Book of Job.* (p. 244)

The Man Who Was Thursday as a detective story seeks to deal with the riddle of life, to bring man to the limits of his logic, face to face with the "huge and undecipherable unreason of it all." Job questions Yahweh asking, "Hast Thou sent the rain upon the desert where no man is?" Gabriel Syme puzzles over one of nature's oddities, a hornbill, "a huge yellow beak with a small bird tied on behind it." The bird seems to him a living question mark, an emblem of that "undecipherable reason" which man tries vainly to fathom.

So insistent are the echoes of *Job* in *The Man Who Was Thursday* that Sunday's dramatic confrontation with the detectives on the hotel balcony recalls unmistakably the Voice which speaks to Job out of a whirlwind. . . . Sunday, the Master Conspirator apparently intent upon man's ruin, is identical to the dimly perceived Chief of Philosophical Policemen who is man's last hope. Thus the answer to the riddle of Sunday is a paradox which defies logical explanation.

Left without satisfying answers to their questions, the detectives experience a growing bewilderment which finally becomes a sense of awe or wonder, a response of great spiritual importance to Chesterton. Although the mystery remains, the six detectives "hear their questionings echo into nothingness in the face of infinite mystery and the glory." All questions "seem to lose their urgency in the greater experience of an encounter with God." (pp. 244-46)

The tone of *The Man Who Was Thursday* (like that of *Job*) modulates in the last chapters from complaint to contemplation and comfort. The pursuit of Sunday ends in a beautiful twilight garden at Sunday's house to which the six exhausted, defeated detectives are conveyed. In the purple shadows and drifting darkness of the trees, they are transformed into six philosophers wearing garments suggestive of the six days of Creation.

Although some of the events in Sunday's garden have the quality of a restful dream, paradoxically some features of the nightmare and nonsense of the chase remain and even become the source of what Chesterton calls "the last adventure of comfort." The six philosophers experience a wild, phantasmagoric vision of "topsy-turvydom," of the world turned upside-down. Unreason and nonsense, paradox and mystery have now become the basis for a new spirituality. But in order to understand this scene, it is necessary to consider more precisely the role of nonsense in *Thursday.* (p. 246)

While it can reveal to man something of what he cannot know, [nonsense] can also give him a fresh view of what he already knows; that is, it can give him a new perspective on the familiar and the commonplace. (pp. 247-48)

The fascination which paradoxical statement held for Chesterton is well-known and may in part account for his interest in the renewal of perspective through nonsense. Paradox, two assertions which seem to contradict each other yet which are nevertheless both true, he describes as "truth standing on her head to attract attention." In somewhat similar terms, he pictures nonsense as "an exuberant capering around discovered truth." Both the incongruities of nonsense and the contradictions

of paradox cause a kind of mental shock which may "wake men up to a neglected truth." For Chesterton, even detective fiction can have this power of evoking a sense of the mysterious possibilities of life. . . . So even though most of the detective's questions have been left unanswered, there remains the hope that "man can understand everything by the help of what he does not understand." (p. 248)

A sense of wonder is the subject of "The Ethics of Elfland," a chapter in *Orthodoxy* which Chesterton published in 1908, the same year that he published *The Man Who Was Thursday*. The ordinary man, wrote Chesterton, has the capacity to find life precious because he can find it surprising, and meaningful because it confounds meaning. (p. 249)

In *Thursday*, this sense of wonder, man's "ancient instinct of astonishment," is aroused by the strange experience of the six philosophers in Sunday's garden. The six find themselves guests at a gala masquerade. . . . The scene creates a mood of celebration and anticipation, and perhaps is a fictional realisation of Chesterton's own instincts about the nature of the universe which he had described in *Heretics* a few years earlier:

> About the whole cosmos there is a tense and secret festivity—like preparations for Guy Fawkes's day. Eternity is the eve of something.

The "eternal jig" is a bizarre version of the celestial music of the Cosmic Dance, ancient symbol of harmony. As the fires fade in the garden and the last stray merrymakers disappear, only the hum of insects and the distant song of a single bird remain. And the six philosophers grow drowsy and serene, finding their comfort in the presence of the Seventh—of Sunday, of *Shabbaoth,* the Peace of God.

But one final revelation is reserved for Gabriel Syme. Gazing at Sunday's face, he sees a strange smile reminiscent of the maddening grin which so often during the chase had been a source of exasperation and pain to the detectives. "Have you ever suffered?" he cries defiantly to the President. Then as he watches horrified, Sunday's face grows larger and larger until it fills the whole sky. "In the blackness before it entirely destroyed his brain he seemed to hear a distant voice saying a commonplace text he had heard somewhere, 'Can ye drink of the cup that I drink of?'"

This enigmatic climax can best be understood in light of Chesterton's perception of the paradoxical quality of *The Book of Job*. Ultimately he came to see the meaning of Job's sufferings in the strange contradiction that Job is tormented not because he is the worst of men but because he is the best of men. . . . [Chesterton] regards Job as a prototype of Christ, the Suffering Servant. And the suffering of Syme and the other philosopher-policemen is resolved in the paradoxical figure of the Man of Sorrows who wears the fool's cap—of Christ, the Harlequin, who celebrates in his pain the secret festivity of an eternity "that is the eve of something."

Thus both detective tale and nonsense literature under the magic of Chesterton's imagination become means to spiritual revelation. The Metaphysical Detective and the Metaphysical Jester combine in the figure of Gabriel Syme, God-Seeker and holy fool—a policeman who bears the name of an angel.

The Man Who Was Thursday is a fantasy-search for meaning in the modern world. Its detectives discover Sunday, seek from him rational answers to rational questions, and are painfully frustrated by the maniacal and nightmarish world in which they find themselves. Yet it is the mad nightmare which arouses in the detective a "transcendental instinct," an instinct satisfied in a most singular way—through the paradoxical, the nonsensical, and the grotesque. In one of his essays Chesterton wrote of his art, "I have to carve the gargoyles because I can carve nothing else; I leave to others the angels and the arches and the spires." *The Man Who Was Thursday* is surely one of his most successful gargoyles. (pp. 249-51)

> *Karin Youngberg, "Job and the Gargoyles: A Study of 'The Man Who Was Thursday'," in* The Chesterton Review *(© 1976 The Chesterton Review), Vol. II, No. 2, Spring-Summer, 1976, pp. 240-52.*

MARSHALL McLUHAN (essay date 1976)

One reason why Chesterton exasperated many fastidious souls relates to what I am going to illustrate as his concern with formal causality. He was vividly aware of his public and of its needs both to be cheered and to be straightened out. So pervasive is this feature in Chesterton that it scarcely matters at what page one opens in order to illustrate it. (p. 253)

[The] formal cause, or the public itself, is in perpetual flux and always in need of clarification and re-focusing of its problems. Style itself, whether in poetry or painting or music, is a way of seeing and knowing, which is otherwise unattainable. . . . The style is the response of the artist to his audience and its needs. Chesterton's style was playful in an age that was very earnest, and his perceptions and thoughts were paradoxical or multi-faceted in a time that was full of intense specialism in politics and economics and religion. (p. 254)

Perhaps, before moving on, I should pause to indicate why Western philosophers and scholars may have shirked consideration of formal causality in the study of the arts and science. Since scarcely anybody has studied the audience of any writer from Plato to the present, there must surely be both a profound and a simple reason for so vast and consistent an omission. I suggest that this reason is to be found in the visual bias of Western man. Visual man is typically concerned with the lineal and the connected and the logical. Visual order has regard to *figure* and not to *ground*. The audience is always the hidden *ground* rather than the *figure* of any discourse. The *ground* is discontinuous, murky and dynamic, whereas the *figure* tends to be clear and distinct and static. However, without the interplay of *figure* and *ground*, no art or knowledge is possible. It might even be argued that the abrupt and bumpy and grotesquely sprockety contours of Chesterton's prose are very much a response of his sensitivity to a perverse and misbegotten public that he earnestly but good-naturedly was determined to redeem from its banalities. (p. 255)

In the everyday order, formal causality reveals itself by its *effects*. There is a strange paradox in this, because since the effects come from the hidden *ground* of situations, the effects usually appear before their causes. When a Darwin or an Einstein appears, we say "the time was ripe" and that the *figure* appeared in its natural *ground*. Chesterton was almost Oriental in his sensitivity to effects, his capacity for noting the consequences embedded in innovations and special attitudes or situations. In fact, Chesterton was always aware of "the law of the situation." This phrase was much used by Mary Parker Follett, the inventor of modern management studies. She was always concerned with discovering the question rather than the answer. It was she who began to ask managers: "what business do you think you are in?" They would point to the *figure* in their enterprise, and she would give the *ground*, or the *effects*

of the *figure*. She would point out to a windowblind manufacturer that he was really in the business of environmental light control. . . . Chesterton's awareness of the *figure/ground* consequences pervades his studies of history and human thought in general. It made it easy for him to enter the field of detective fiction, since the detective story is written backwards, starting with the effects, and discovering the cause later, and, as it were, incidentally. The history of detective fiction, at least since Edgar Poe, relates to the law of the situation very intimately.

Poe is perhaps best known for his account of the composition of "The Raven." He explained that, seeking in the first place to achieve an effect of maximal melancholy and gloom, he set about discovering the means to *get* this effect, noting that art must always start with the *effect*. This is another way of saying that art must start with formal cause, and with concern with the audience. Sherlock Holmes frequently explained to Watson (who was typical of the unenlightened public) that the detective must put himself in the place of the criminal. The criminal is the person who is entirely concerned with *effects*. He considers the entire situation as one to be manipulated, both *figure* and *ground*, in order to achieve a very special effect. The criminal, like the artist, takes into account both the *figure* and the *ground*, that is, the work to be done in order that the effect may be achieved. It is this interplay between *figure* and *ground*, and the confronting of the latter in the situation, which gives to the detective story so much of the poetic character. Chesterton's *Father Brown* is always sensitive to the hidden laws of the situation that are so easily obscured by the ordinary concern with *figure* and points of view: for it is of the essence of formal causality that it is not a point of view, but, rather, a statement of a situation. (pp. 256-57)

It was the "rhetorical" interplay between philosophy and its public which was eliminated by Descartes in the seventeenth century with the result that formal cause was transferred from the public to the subjective life of the individual philosopher or student of philosophy. The further consequence was that the "content" of philosophy and the arts became relegated to efficient causality. Formal causality simply ceased to have any *conscious* role in the arts and sciences from then until our own day. Chesterton was part of the *avant garde* in re-discovering formal causality in his multi-levelled grasp of his public and his themes. (p. 259)

> *Marshall McLuhan, "Formal Causality in Chesterton," in* The Chesterton Review *(reprinted by permission of McLuhan Associates, Ltd.), Vol. II, No. 2, Spring-Summer, 1976, pp. 253-59.*

PETER R. HUNT (essay date 1981)

If there is no doubt of the quite strong influence of the Pre-Raphaelites on Chesterton's imaginative writing, it seems equally clear that the influence of Dickens is at least as significant, but has, surprisingly, received very little attention. Yet it is the all-pervasive Dickensian elements in his writing, especially in his fiction, which allows us to realise the relationship between his Dickens criticism and his other writing, and between his rejection of Pre-Raphaelite mediaevalism and his love of Dickens. . . .

The Dickens influence is everywhere. (p. 37)

To see the Dickens's influence on Chesterton as an early one, it is necessary to look at some of the early stories he wrote.

Exemplary of the influence of Dickens and of Chesterton's affinity with 'his thought and style are two stories written at the age of sixteen, later reprinted in *The Coloured Lands:* "**The Wild Goose Chase**" and "**The Taming of the Nightmare.**" In the first of these two stories, the humour which mingles with the haunting, Hans-Andersen-like fairy-tale narrative, is Dickensian in its lightness and festive laughter, though here and there it has, too, a not unrelated touch of Lewis Carroll especially in its nonsensical images of the various creatures the Little Boy meets in his search for the elusive wild goose. The whole tale has an allegorical or parabolic character typical of Chesterton's fiction, but certainly not far removed from the fables of Dickens. The successful blend of fable, pathos and a sense of comic irony which makes stories such as *A Christmas Carol, The Chimes,* and *The Cricket on the Hearth* so successful and so essentially the work of Dickens is unmistakeable in Chesterton's early stories. . . . [The overall development of "**The Wild Goose Chase**"] is reminiscent of Andersen's "The Snow Queen" but, throughout, it resembles Dickens most. Despite the levity of its opening and of much of its incident, it manages to express a real pathos, especially in the passages which describe the boy, grown to manhood, climbing rocky slopes, a staff in his hand, trying to capture the one goose which was wild enough to fly away when he frightened it. Towards the end of the tale, the boy, now a man, is presented as follows:

> But over the darkening sea there came a sudden, strange, wordless song as of a flight of wild birds, and a glimmer of white wings seemed floating towards him. He gave a great cry and leapt forward; and no man ever saw him again on earth.

This leads into a hint of the theme as suggested in the sentence: "And must not all stories of brave lives and long endeavours and weary watching for the ideal so end, until all be ended?" This, of course, as well as occasional ironic references to "survival of the fittest," reveals Chesterton's quite early emphasis on adventure and striving, pursuit and brave reaching for the ideal. (pp. 38-9)

It should also be noted that the theme of a constant journey, a wandering search, with its inevitable picaresque structure, is a foreshadowing of the typical Chestertonian plot which is invariably like that of *Pickwick,* as we shall see presently. But the important thing to note at this juncture is the tone of its opening which is so close to the Dickensian comic rhetoric and humorous understatement. However, this story is merely a foretaste of the much more striking resemblance of Chesterton's style to that of Dickens in the other story, "**The Taming of the Nightmare.**" (p. 39)

Chesterton's novels and short-stories are filled with a spirit of adventure, but they are also often boisterously humorous, as though sheer foolery and a fantastic sense of the absurd were constantly taking over in Chesterton's mind. But the humour, the nonsense, the mood of the jester is not merely an addition or intrusion. Nor is it a caving in to a sense of mirth, as it may seem to be when we detach ourselves from the narratives and their relationship to all the rest of Chesterton's work. It is integral to his vision, which, as Michael Mason says, in another context, is "the centre of hilarity" for Chesterton. This centre of hilarious vision is seen especially in the early novels, and it is woven into plots which are invariably picaresque, either in terms of the actual series of events or in the narratives retold within the overall framework. Thus, for instance, *Manalive,*

whose main surface action takes place in a room, recounts the wandering of Innocent Smith around the world, and his various encounters with different people and situations, in a fashion clearly related to the whole tradition of the picaresque novel, and is especially Pickwickian in its blend of adventure and humour, though definitely Chestertonian in its peculiar metaphysical jesting. Similarly, *The Man Who Was Thursday* and *The Ball and The Cross,* have rambling "plots" in which the characters are moving from one place to another, and, like Pickwick, from one adventure to another. Chesterton ever loved the wandering story, the journey and the scrapes and encounters which go with it. Novels which are made up of many related tales in which main characters participate, such as *The Man Who Knew Too Much, Tales of the Long Bow, The Poet and the Lunatics, The Paradoxes of Mr. Pond, The Club of Queer Trades,* and *Four Faultless Felons,* all have this picaresque shape, this sense of strange happenings in the next village, town or house, this constant journeying and returning, in sum, this eighteenth-century tradition of the novel, surely related to Chesterton's love of Dickens's early books, though naturally innate in Chesterton's own personal enthusiasm for apparently aimless wandering. We recall as well, that the very first Father Brown story, probably the best, "**The Blue Cross,**" consists mainly of a narrative about the detective Valentin pursuing Father Brown and the disguised thief across London, and that this journey is highlighted by strange signs or clues, such as the soup being thrown across the wall, or the barrow being upset, all ridiculously strange events, ending with the strangest event of all, the conversation on Hampstead Heath. But the mention of Father Brown reminds us, as in a flash, of what it really is that makes these fictions so Dickensian while still being inimitably Chestertonian. Father Brown has a round, spectacled face, and, at least in all the earlier stories, is genuinely naïve as a child is naïve, though wise and preternaturally observant. His moon face, his cherubic innocence, is Pickwickian. There is no doubt that the character owes much to Pickwick. This, in turn, brings images of Sunday and Innocent Smith and Mr. Pond before us. Sunday, the mysterious leader of the "Anarchists" who turns out to be an allegorical giant of cosmic wisdom, is also child-like in his boisterous fun, his ardent enjoyment of letting the members of the whole group pursue him across London, even to the point of a trying to catch him as he rides an elephant from the zoo and takes a balloon up into the sky. There has been much good, but perhaps over-solemn, discussion of the meaning of Sunday, but at least one meaning is that he is wise because he is innocent, humorous because he is humble, though at first he seems almost sinister, later baffling, and finally reassuring to the men who, fearful of his mystery, are shown his benevolence. And part of this widsom and innocence is his sense of the absurd and his rollicking capacity for fun. His throwing of buns from a speeding coach, the gloriously-irrevelant scribbled messages he flings from the vehicles he flees in, or on, are all made for laughter, the element of farce being Chesterton's sense of the elfish queerness of life, and of the conviction that being serious and jesting are not only not opposites, but are inextricably related, a fusion of humility and humour. The tale is Chestertonian, but it is also shot through with a Dickens spirit; and the related feeling that the streets of London have all kinds of wild possibilities and a poetry to be discovered is not just a Stevensonian sense of romance but a Dickensian one. There is more of Dickens's novels in it than there is of Stevenson's harder fictions. Innocent Smith of *Manalive* is also like Sunday in his baffling behaviour which seems mad to those who do not see his sanity. Both figures are also rather like Chesterton himself.

The Napoleon of Notting Hill is less obviously like Dickens's work, though even here, despite the apparent concern with mediævalism, the real point is one which accents the need for more than a dedication to the restoration of mediæval chivalry and local autonomy and heraldry, represented by Adam Wayne the idealist. The novel is, in part, almost a satire or at least ironic allegory on the kind of retrospective mediævalism Chesterton experienced in his youthful reading of the Pre-Raphaelites, for it also has Auberon Quin, the incurably ironic humorist, who sets Wayne's movement going by a practical joke. Chesterton brings out the need for both "serious" dedication and humour. The first without the second can be proud, absurdly ruinous and even ultimately tyrannical. Thus, humour, associated in all his work with an English tradition, is Chesterton's greatest difference from those so often thought to be his chief mentors; and it is his closest point of resemblance to Dickens. And even in a figure like Gabriel Gale whom we think of as partly a Pre-Raphaelite-type poet, the impress of a character like Dick Swiveller is clearly visible. Lastly, in the brief sketch of some Dickens influences and affinities in Chesterton's fiction, we may cite the case of *The Return of Don Quixote* which, in its very title, illustrates the picaresque tradition. This novel's parallels with the Cervantes masterpiece, introduced for purposes of satirical allegory, show in fictional form, once and for all, Chesterton's deliberate contrast between the mediævalism he is rejecting and the spirit he regards as more truly mediæval, and which, in all his Dickens criticism, he associated with Dickens. Here, the librarian, Herne, moves from an absent-minded and enthusiastic absorption in the ancient civilisation of the Hittites to a discovery of mediæval ways, but in so doing, falls into the trap of trying to impose a pseudo-mediæval pattern on everybody. But Braintree, the Syndicalist radical, with his desire to bring about revolutionary change towards worker-ownership, is, as it turns out, and as Herne belatedly recognises, more in harmony with the fighting mediæval spirit which does not linger in the past, but applies perennial principles and vision to the social order. In *Charles Dickens,* and elsewhere, Chesterton makes a precisely similar point about Dickens's "democracy" as compared with the Toryism of the late-Victorian disciples of Carlyle and Ruskin.

Chesterton's essays, too, show again and again affinities with Dickens, in both their wandering or discursive structure, and in their humour, and some anecdotes and scenes are reflections of Dickens's scenes. . . . [Indeed, in his introduction to *Fancies Versus Fads,* he] brings together the Chestertonian idea of life and fiction as elvish, wondrous, and fantastic, and, moreover, wandering or freshly adventurous. From Chesterton's thousands of essays we can think of many which have the wandering quality and few of them without a Puckish, jesting humour which is tinged with the kind of farce and vision of eccentricity which we see in Dickens. It is a humour related to the way that Dick Swiveller sees streets as "closed" to him because of his debts, . . . or Mr. Pickwick chasing his hat. We cannot help being reminded of Pickwick in the essay **"On Running After One's Hat,"** or of a Dickens's street scene of coaches and traffic in **"An Accident,"** or of Mugby Junction in Chesterton's relation of an adventure in **"The Secret of a Train."** And in the essay, **"The Modern Scrooge,"** we have an allegorical essay which is inspired by a satiric image of a "modern" educator who wants to introduce charwomen to good literature by reading them *A Christmas Carol* after a lecture which tried to explain that Dickens was prone to present terribly exaggerated characters. This essay is simply a narrative, like a short story, and its outcome is one in which Vernon-Smith, the emblematic figure, is shocked into humanity by the snowballing assaults of the street boys. It is not the only essay which uses a fable-like structure and direct reference to Dickens. **"The Dickensian,"** for instance, tells of Chesterton's actually meeting an old man who, nostalgic for Dickens, scorns the modern amusements at Yarmouth, until Chesterton the narrator, resisting the allurement of romantic nostalgia, says, "Let us have no antiquarianism about Dickens." He says that Dickens looks forward as though with "Great Expectations" rather than back to books in "An Old Curiosity Shop." Here we see, of course, a bridge between his own essay-fictional method and his Dickens criticism. His love of Dickens resisted Dickensianism. There are many Chesterton essays which refer to Dickens. There are also countless essays which have a semi-picaresque narrative method again combined with poetical humour, as in **"A Piece of Chalk,"** about going out to draw with chalk and, finding no chalk with him, discovering that he is on a whole chalk landscape. . . . It is symptomatic that the volume which is perhaps richest in the picaresque and lightly humorous or jesting strain is *Tremendous Trifles,* published in 1909, in the midst of Chesterton's great period of Dickens writing. A wonderful power of *reductio ad absurdum* humour, similar to that of *Oliver Twist* or of Dickens's great satires of Chancery and Circumlocution, runs through many of Chesterton's essays of this period: typically priceless is the exquisitely funny essay **"The Little Birds Who Won't Sing"** which may be taken as reaching the best of Chesterton's lighter pieces in its suggestion of songs for modern work.

These are only indications; enough examples have been given to remind the reader of innumerable other ones. And none of this tracing of Dickens's influence on Chesterton's essays is meant to suggest that Chesterton's style is anything but his own. His particular humour, though definitely somewhat Dickensian, is a peculiar blend of a capacity for surprise, fantasy, and metaphysical enchantment with being, an awareness of that oddness of people and things which is reached in the manner exemplified by Chesterton's description of the horse as a fantastic creature in his "Introduction" to *The Everlasting Man.* Moreover, the "wandering," ruminative quality runs through his most serious works, and through his criticism. It may, in fact, reflect his whole speculative temperament, his awareness of multitudinous angles of vision and perspectives intrinsic to man's finite condition and the nature of his existence. Still, whether mainly nurtured in him by early Dickens influence, or innate, these qualities, though more intellectually shaped than in Dickens, share some of Dickens's most charactteristic ways of seeing. Perhaps the most revealing example of the intimate relationship between Dickens and Chesterton is to be found in **"The Ethics of Elfland"** in *Orthodoxy* (and probably, indeed, in the whole book) with its amazing blend of a critique of Victorian and Edwardian rationalism and a celebration of fairyland and miracle; especially with the suggestion that, though the world seems ruled by inevitable physical laws, perhaps God says to the sun each morning, "Do it Again," a poetical way of saying that all being is contingent on Being. Dickens did not engage in such metaphysical exploration, but his vision did embrace that sort of wonder.

The Dickens influence is less evident in Chesterton's poetry, though even there many of his satirical verses share a radical ridicule of pompous wealth and bureaucracy with Dickens, as in poems such as **"The Song Against Grocers,"** or **"Songs of Education,"** or **"Mr. Mandragon, the Millionaire."** **"Lepanto"** and **"The Ballad of the White Horse,"** are strongly related to the traditions and manner of Chesterton's early contemporaries, most notably Morris and Swinburne, and the colours of many poems are aglow with Pre-Raphaelite fire. . . . Philosophy, foolery, fantasy and fairy tale abound in his work. Chesterton's fecundity is similar in kind to that of Dickens. Both shared the oldest and richest English traditions.

All of this indicates, though it does not explore at all fully, the Dickens influence on Chesterton's literary tone and style. How much of the comic vision and poetic humour was native to Chesterton and how much was nurtured by his response to Dickens is impossible to say. It seems probable that, temperamentally, Chesterton was attuned deeply to Dickens's humour, but that also means that he was heir to a long English heritage. As for Dickens's influence on Chesterton's social compassion and desire to free the poor from officialdom and bureaucratic philanthropy, that is more evident in books such as **What's Wrong With the World, Utopia of Usurers, An Outline of Sanity,** and **Eugenics and Other Evils.** The strange truth about his Dickens criticism is that, although it does show his perpetual concern with the need for "looking up to the people," and his sympathy with the Dickens vision of festive joy among the poor, it shows relative (and I stress "relative") neglect of the more poignant and miserable scenes and the more bitter revelations of extreme poverty and degradation in Dickens's novels. This is partly bound up with Chesterton's view of Dickensian pathos, but largely with the nature of Chesterton's comic vision. (pp. 41-8)

Peter R. Hunt, "Dickens's Influence on Chesterton's Imaginative Writing," in The Chesterton Review (© *1981* The Chesterton Review), *Vol. VII, No. 1, Winter, 1981, pp. 36-49.*

ADDITIONAL BIBLIOGRAPHY

Barker, Dudley. *G.K. Chesterton: A Biography*. New York: Stein and Day, 1973, 304 p.
    An excellent and complete biography.

Canovan, Margaret. *G.K. Chesterton: Radical Populist*. New York: Harcourt Brace Jovanovich, 1977, 175 p.
    A study of Chesterton's concern for common people and of his rejection of all social schemes calling for the subjugation of the people by a self-styled elite.

Clemens, Cyril. *Chesterton as Seen by His Contemporaries*. 1939. Reprint. New York: Haskell House Publishers, 1969, 180 p.
    A biography of Chesterton, composed largely of the anecdotes of his contemporaries.

Evans, Maurice. *G.K. Chesterton*. Cambridge: Cambridge University Press, 1939, 157 p.
    Cogent criticism of Chesterton's essays, poetry, and fiction. The critic dubs G.K.C. "the last of the Crusaders."

Lewis, D.B. Wyndham. Introduction to *G.K. Chesterton: An Anthology*, by G. K. Chesterton, edited by D.B. Wyndham Lewis, pp. ix-xxi. London: Oxford University Press, 1957.
    A brief biographical and critical introduction to Chesterton and his work.

Joseph Conrad

1857-1924

(Born Teodor Józef Konrad Nalecz Korzeniowski) Polish-born English novelist.

Conrad is considered an innovator of novel structure as well as one of the finest stylists of modern English literature. His novels are complex moral and psychological examinations of the ambiguity of good and evil. His characters are repeatedly forced to acknowledge their own failings and the weakness of their ideals against all forms of corruption; the most honorable characters are those who realize their fallibility but still struggle to uphold the dictates of conscience. To examine these dilemmas Conrad devised narrative techniques that more completely involve the reader in the conflicts of his characters than did traditional novels.

Born in Poland, which was then under Russian rule, Conrad accompanied his parents to northern Russia when they were exiled for participating in the Polish independence movement. After the deaths of his parents Conrad wandered to France, where he began his career as a seaman. Though he knew very little English at the time, he joined the British merchant service in 1878, and in less than ten years rose to the rank of captain and mastered the English language. Although he wrote his first novel, *Almayer's Folly*, while still in the service, it was poor health, not a new career, which forced him to resign his commission, and it was several years before he gave up the idea of returning to the sea. Conrad struggled for the rest of his life to earn his living as a writer. In addition to his financial difficulties, Conrad found writing itself to be a slow and agonizing ordeal, and many critics have noted the effects his neurasthenia and lifelong fear of inadequacy had upon his work. In spite of such influential friends as Henry James, H. G. Wells, and Stephen Crane, it was not until the publication of *Chance* in 1913 that he was truly successful.

Throughout his career Conrad examined the impossibility of living by a traditional code of conduct: his novels demonstrate that the complexity of the human spirit does not allow absolute fidelity to any ideal, or even to one's conscience. In Conrad's work failure is a fact of human existence and every ideal contains the possibilities for its own corruption. This is portrayed most effectively in *Nostromo*, which deals with revolution, politics, and financial manipulation in a South American republic. All the characters in this novel are corrupted by their ambitions, which range from greed to idealistic desires for reform, and all ambitions lead to disaster—the nobler the ideal the greater the self-disgust the character experiences at the outcome.

Most of Conrad's greatest works take place on board ship or in the backwaters of civilization; a ship or a small outpost offered an isolated environment where Conrad could develop his already complex moral problems without unnecessary entanglements that might obscure the situations. Isolation allowed a concentration of tragedy. The two greatest examples of moral tragedy in his work are *Lord Jim*, which examines the failures of a man before society and his own conscience, and *Heart of Darkness*, in which Kurtz, a man who seeks to improve the condition of African natives, succumbs to the evils of life unregulated by the laws of civilization.

In both of these novels an understanding of the role of the narrator, Marlow, is crucial to an understanding of Conrad's intentions. Marlow offers a tentative view of a complex and ambiguous world. The reader should not accept all of Marlow's judgements as the only interpretations of events. Marlow is the most refined example of Conrad's use of an unreliable narrator, but in all of his works he relies upon time shifts, flashbacks, and multiple perspectives of several characters to portray the unreliability of human perception. Albert Guerard called Conrad's best works new forms of the novel, works that involve a reader completely in psychological and moral dilemmas by offering no consistent viewpoint. The reader is constantly forced to interpret the information given in the novel. In his preface to *The Nigger of the "Narcissus,"* an essay that has been called his artistic credo, Conrad expressed his intention of forcing the reader's involvement in his work: "My task which I am trying to achieve is, by the power of the written word, to make you feel—it is, before all, to make you *see*. That—and no more, and it is everything."

Conrad's style contributes immensely to his themes. Critics have called it a lush and dense style, one in which image is piled upon image, yet the characteristic rhythm of Conrad's prose keeps it from becoming ponderous. Unfortunately, many critics have concluded that Conrad's novels after *Chance* have little more than style to recommend them. In his later works his presentation of the ambiguity of good and evil breaks down into a stylized presentation of absolute good versus absolute evil. His best novels, however, are acknowledged masterpieces of English literature.

(See also *TCLC*, Vol. 1.)

PRINCIPAL WORKS

Almayer's Folly (novel) 1895
An Outcast of the Islands (novel) 1896
The Nigger of the "Narcissus" (novel) 1897
Tales of Unrest (short stories) 1898
Lord Jim (novel) 1900
The Inheritors [with Ford Madox Ford] (novel) 1901
Typhoon (short story) 1902
Youth (short stories) 1902
Romance [with Ford Madox Ford] (novel) 1903
Nostromo (novel) 1904
The Mirror of the Sea (autobiography) 1906
The Secret Agent (novel) 1907
A Set of Six (short stories) 1908
Some Reminiscences (autobiography) 1908; also published
    as *A Personal Record*, 1912
Under Western Eyes (novel) 1911
'Twixt Land and Sea (short stories) 1912
Chance (novel) 1913
Victory (novel) 1915
Within the Tides (short stories) 1915
The Shadow Line (novel) 1917
The Arrow of Gold (novel) 1919
The Rescue (novel) 1920
Notes on Life and Letters (essays) 1921
Notes on My Books (essays) 1921
The Rover (novel) 1923
The Nature of a Crime [with Ford Madox Ford] (novel)
    1924
Suspense (novel) 1925
Tales of Hearsay (short stories) 1925
The Sisters (short stories) 1928

JOSEPH CONRAD (essay date 1897)

A work that aspires, however humbly, to the condition of art should carry its justification in every line. And art itself may be defined as a single-minded attempt to render the highest kind of justice to the visible universe, by bringing to light the truth, manifold and one, underlying its every aspect. It is an attempt to find in its forms, in its colours, in its light, in its shadows, in the aspects of matter, and in the facts of life what of each is fundamental, what is enduring and essential—their one illuminating and convincing quality—the very truth of their existence. The artist, then, like the thinker or the scientist, seeks the truth and makes his appeal. Impressed by the aspect of the world the thinker plunges into ideas, the scientist into facts. . . . (p. 49)

It is otherwise with the artist.

Confronted by the same enigmatical spectacle the artist descends within himself, and in that lonely region of stress and strife, if he be deserving and fortunate, he finds the terms of his appeal. His appeal is made to our less obvious capacities: to that part of our nature which, because of the warlike conditions of existence, is necessarily kept out of sight within the more resisting and hard qualities—like the vulnerable body within a steel armour. His appeal is less loud, more profound, less distinct, more stirring—and sooner forgotten. Yet its effect endures for ever. The changing wisdom of successive generations discards ideas, questions facts, demolishes theories. But the artist appeals to that part of our being which is not dependent on wisdom; to that in us which is a gift and not an acquisition—and, therefore, more permanently enduring. He speaks to our capacity for delight and wonder, to the sense of mystery surrounding our lives; to our sense of pity, and beauty, and pain; to the latent feeling of fellowship with all creation—and to the subtle but invincible conviction of solidarity that knits together the loneliness of innumerable hearts, to the solidarity in dreams, in joy, in sorrow, in aspirations, in illusions, in hope, in fear, which binds men to each other, which binds together all humanity—the dead to the living and the living to the unborn.

It is only some such train of thought, or rather of feeling, that can in a measure explain the aim of the attempt, made in [*The Nigger of the 'Narcissus'*], to present an unrestful episode in the obscure lives of a few individuals out of all the disregarded multitude of the bewildered, the simple, and the voiceless. For, if any part of truth dwells in the belief confessed above, it becomes evident that there is not a place of splendour or a dark corner of the earth that does not deserve, if only a passing glance of wonder and pity. The motive, then, may be held to justify the matter of the work. . . . (pp. 49-51)

Fiction—if it at all aspires to be art—appeals to temperament. And in truth it must be, like painting, like music, like all art, the appeal of one temperament to all the other innumerable temperaments whose subtle and resistless power endows passing events with their true meaning, and creates the moral, the emotional atmosphere of the place and time. Such an appeal to be effective must be an impression conveyed through the senses; and, in fact, it cannot be made in any other way, because temperament, whether individual or collective, is not amenable to persuasion. All art, therefore, appeals primarily to the senses, and the artistic aim when expressing itself in written words must also make its appeal through the senses, if its high desire is to reach the secret spring of responsive emotions. . . . And it is only through complete, unswerving devotion to the perfect blending of form and substance; it is only through an unremitting never-discouraged care for the shape and ring of sentences that an approach can be made to plasticity, to colour, and that the light of magic suggestiveness may be brought to play for an evanescent instant over the commonplace surface of words: of the old, old words, worn thin, defaced by ages of careless usage. (p. 51)

To snatch in a moment of courage, from the remorseless rush of time, a passing phase of life, is only the beginning of the task. The task approached in tenderness and faith is to hold up unquestioningly, without choice and without fear, the rescued fragment before all eyes in the light of a sincere mood. It is to show its vibration, its colour, its form; and through its movement, its form, and its colour, reveal the substance of its truth—disclose its inspiring secret: the stress and passion within the core of each convincing moment. In a single-minded attempt of that kind, if one be deserving and fortunate, one may perchance attain to such clearness of sincerity that at last the presented vision of regret or pity, of terror or mirth, shall awaken in the hearts of the beholders that feeling of unavoidable solidarity; of the solidarity in mysterious origin, in toil, in joy, in hope, in uncertain fate, which binds men to each other and all mankind to the visible world. (p. 52)

> *Joseph Conrad, in his preface to his* The Children of the Sea: A Tale of the Forecastle, *Dodd, Mead and Company, 1897 (and reprinted as "'The Nigger of the "Narcissus"'," in his* Conrad's Prefaces to His Works, *edited by Edward Garnett, J. M. Dent & Sons Ltd, 1937, pp. 49-54).*

HENRY JAMES   (essay date 1914)

[Mr. Joseph Conrad's "Chance" is] an extraordinary exhibition of method by the fact that the method is, we venture to say, without a precedent in any like work. It places Mr. Conrad absolutely alone as a votary of the way to do a thing that shall make it undergo most doing. The way to do it that shall make it undergo least is the line on which we are mostly now used to see prizes carried off; so that the author of **"Chance"** gathers up on this showing all sorts of comparative distinction. He gathers up at least two sorts—that of bravery in absolutely reversing the process most accredited, and that, quite separate, we make out, of performing the manoeuvre under salvos of recognition. It is not in these days often given to a refinement of design to be recognised, but Mr. Conrad has made his achieve that miracle—save in so far indeed as the miracle has been one thing and the success another. . . . What concerns us is that the general effect of **"Chance"** is arrived at by a pursuance of means to the end in view contrasted with which every other current form of the chase can only affect us as cheap and futile; the carriage of the burden or amount of service required on these lines exceeding surely all other such displayed degrees of energy put together. Nothing could well interest us more than to see the exemplary value of attention, attention given by the author and asked of the reader, attested in a case in which it has had almost unspeakable difficulties to struggle with—since so we are moved to qualify the particular difficulty Mr. Conrad has "elected" to face: the claim for method in itself, method in this very sense of attention applied, would be somehow less lighted if the difficulties struck us as less consciously, or call it even less wantonly, invoked. . . . We take for granted by the general law of fiction a primary author, take him so much for granted that we forget him in proportion as he works upon us, and that he works upon us most in fact by making us forget him.

Mr. Conrad's first care on the other hand is expressly to posit or set up a reciter, a definite responsible intervening first person singular, possessed of infinite sources of reference, who immediately proceeds to set up another, to the end that this other may conform again to the practice, and that even at that point the bridge over to the creature, or in other words to the situation or the subject, the thing "produced," shall, if the fancy takes it, once more and yet once more glory in a gap. . . . We usually escape the worst of this difficulty of a tone *about* the tone of our characters, our projected performers, by keeping it single, keeping it "down" and thereby comparatively impersonal or, as we may say, inscrutable; which is what a creative force, in its blest fatuity, likes to be. But the omniscience, remaining indeed nameless, though constantly active, which sets Marlow's omniscience in motion from the very first page, insisting on a reciprocity with it throughout, this original omniscience invites consideration of itself only in a degree less than that in which Marlow's own invites it; and Marlow's own is a pro-

longed hovering flight of the subjective over the outstretched ground of the case exposed. We make out this ground but through the shadow cast by the flight, clarify it though the real author visibly reminds himself again and again that he must—all the more that, as if by some tremendous forecast of future applied science, the upper aeroplane causes another, as we have said, to depend from it and that one still another; these dropping shadow after shadow, to the no small menace of intrinsic colour and form and whatever, upon the passive expanse. What shall we most call Mr. Conrad's method accordingly but his attempt to clarify *quand même*—ridden as he has been, we perceive at the end of fifty pages of **"Chance,"** by such a danger of steeping his matter in perfect eventual obscuration as we recall no other artist's consenting to with an equal grace. This grace, which presently comes over us as the sign of the whole business, is Mr. Conrad's gallantry itself, and the shortest account of the rest of the connection for our present purpose is that his gallantry is thus his success. It literally strikes us that his volume sets in motion more than anything else a drama in which his own system and his combined eccentricities of recital represent the protagonist in face of powers leagued against it, and of which the dénouement gives us the system fighting in triumph, though with its back desperately to the wall, and laying the powers piled up at its feet. This frankly has been *our* spectacle, our suspense and our thrill; with the one flaw on the roundness of it all the fact that the predicament was not imposed rather than invoked, was not the effect of a challenge from without, but that of a mystic impulse from within. (pp. 345-49)

> *Henry James, "The New Novel" (1914), in his* Notes on Novelists, with Some Other Notes *(copyright 1914 by Charles Scribner's Sons; copyright renewed 1942 by Henry James; reprinted with the permission of Charles Scribner's Sons), Charles Scribner's Sons, 1914, pp. 314-61.**

ERNEST HEMINGWAY   (essay date 1924)

It is fashionable among my friends to disparage [Conrad]. It is even necessary. Living in a world of literary politics where one wrong opinion often proves fatal, one writes carefully. (p. 132)

It is agreed by most of the people I know that Conrad is a bad writer, just as it is agreed that T. S. Eliot is a good writer. If I knew that by grinding Mr. Eliot into a fine dry powder and sprinkling that powder over Mr. Conrad's grave Mr. Conrad would shortly appear, looking very annoyed at the forced return, and commence writing I would leave for London early tomorrow morning with a sausage grinder. (pp. 132-33)

The second book of Conrad's that I read was **Lord Jim.** I was unable to finish it. It is, therefore, all I have left of him. For I cannot re-read them. That may be what my friends mean by saying he is a bad writer. But from nothing else that I have ever read have I gotten what every book of Conrad has given me.

Knowing I could not re-read them I saved up four that I would not read until I needed them badly, when the disgust with writing, writers and everything written of and to write would be too much. Two months in Toronto used up the four books. . . .

In Sudbury, Ontario, I bought three back numbers of the Pictorial Review and read **The Rover,** sitting up in bed in the Nickle Range Hotel. When morning came I had used up all my Conrad like a drunkard, I had hoped it would last me the trip, and felt like a young man who has blown his patrimony. But, I thought, he will write more stories. He has lots of time.

When I read the reviews they all agreed *The Rover* was a bad story.

And now he is dead and I wish to God they would have taken some great, acknowledged technician of a literary figure and left him to write his bad stories. (p. 133)

> *Ernest Hemingway, "Conrad, Optimist and Moralist" (originally published in* Transatlantic Review, *October, 1924), in* By-Line, Ernest Hemingway: Selected Articles and Dispatches of Four Decades, *edited by William White (copyright ©1967 by By-Line Ernest Hemingway, Inc.; reprinted with the permission of Charles Scribner's Sons) Charles Scribner's Sons, 1967, pp. 132-36.*

DONALD DAVIDSON   (essay date 1925)

The reader who approaches Conrad for the first time is inevitably struck by his daring disregard of chronological order in narrative. The resulting complexity is naturally baffling to one accustomed to the orthodox methods of fiction. . . . It is Conrad's habit to twist events out of their regular order, to turn them completely around, so that there is, in effect, an inversion. To this characteristic of technique, which appears consistently in most of his work, the term 'inversive method' seems applicable. (p. 163)

[Conrad] discounts the purely animal curiosity which we may all have as to the outcome of his drama by telling us at the beginning (of course with great reserve and subtlety) just what the end of a given episode will be. He secures a satisfying relevance . . . by rearranging events with regard to import rather than chronology, slicing into his main narrative, whenever he pleases, any needful portions of history or incident. The effect at its best, when the involution is not too complex, is to throw the emphasis on the underlying significance of the human situation, thus rendering possible a discreet and serious treatment of melodramatic material. The reader, possessed in advance of knowledge which the participating characters do not have, looks down on the scene with Olympian foresight and with pity for brave mortal strife. Like the audiences in the golden age of the Attic theatre, he witnesses a drama the outcome of which he knows in advance. His emotions are thereby released and tempered for the suspense of an evolving character rather than for mere incidental outcome. He is prepared to receive the calm and studied impression of that art which Conrad himself defined as "a single-minded attempt to render the highest kind of justice to the visible universe by bringing to light the truth, manifold and one, underlying its every aspect" [see excerpt above]. It is this feature of Conrad's technique, more than any other, which throws into sharp relief the sought-for truth of art and life; and it is the search for this truth, through all complexities, which gives unity where at first there may seem to be chaos.

A precise definition of Conrad's method is difficult to give. Any term used to characterize it must possess the character of invention, since Conrad's method, in its scope and boldness, is unique in English fiction. The inversive method, described briefly, consists in transposing the natural order of incidents, so that they are presented to a large extent in non-chronological order. It is often a veritable turning upside-down of chronology, so that the story moves backward rather than forward. More frequently it consists in the interruption of a narrative to treat of prior events, and, even then, not in a summary form, but in direct, dramatic narrative. (pp. 165-66)

An analysis of Conrad's total production shows that inversion occurs in nearly all his works. . . . But it is in *Lord Jim* that we first find inversions used with much complexity,—so much in fact, that the book has an experimental air. In the massive *Nostromo,* published five years later, the inversive technique achieves its first unqualified success, in binding together, motivating, and electrifying the sprawling bundles of material. (pp. 169-70)

Major instances of inversion from the novels will reveal ready evidence of the varieties of use which the inversive method may serve. It is interesting to speculate what sort of novels they would have been if the inversive technique had not been applied. But to see just what Conrad has done, let us rearrange in a chronological order the major incidents in the first part of *Lord Jim.* In strict order of time, the events run about as follows: (1) the voyage of the *Patna;* (2) the passage over the derelict; (3) Jim's act of cowardice in deserting the ship; (4) the court of inquiry; (5) Jim's isolation and sense of defeat; (6) Marlow's interference in Jim's destiny; (7) Jim's wanderings and experiences as water-clerk. This is the order of events which we should expect any novelist but Conrad to follow. Conrad, however, pays no attention to chronology. He begins at Episode 7, with a brief sketch of Jim as water-clerk. He next presents Episode 1 and part of Episode 2, omitting a full account of what happened when the *Patna* struck the derelict. Then comes Episode 4, the court of inquiry scene, with Jim in disgrace, and much later the detailed account from Jim's own mouth of his fatal and almost inexplicable desertion of the ship. In other words, Conrad breaks off his narrative at a crisis, and delays an important and exceedingly interesting episode until we have already gained a general idea of its outcome and tragic effect.

The results of this tangled inversive proceeding are various. In the first place, instead of getting the suspense of mere melodrama, of rapid, thrilling narrative (which Conrad, when he likes, can execute perfectly), the reader is inveigled into a different sort of suspense, akin to the curiosity of the scientist examining under his microscope a portion of diseased tissue. It is a suspense as to character. Something is fatally wrong with this man. What is it? we ask ourselves, just as Marlow asked himself. And we follow the story's windings and delvings with an interest wholly concentrated on the personality of Jim. The incidents of the tragic act are in themselves irrelevant—only so much machinery. The point is, what is this man's relation to the events? Conrad answers the question by having Jim, the victim, burdened by a weight of scorn and defeat, pour his story into the sympathetic ears of Marlow, at a time when the reader is best attuned to receive this delicate communication. So that, besides changing the quality of suspense, and diverting the attention from the action *per se,* the inversion throws Jim's character and acts into a correct light and puts the emphasis on the question: When is a man a coward? It is true that in this book the inversive method is sometimes tedious or bewildering. Conrad risks clarity of narrative; he makes the book difficult, perhaps unnecessarily so. But at the close, the man Jim stands complete in the reader's mind. From the various weavings and cross-weavings of the narrative one constructs a character sympathetically amplified by a thousand connotations and associations, just as in real life one gradually builds up the character of a friend from numerous loosely associated and noncoherent incidents that merge into a harmonious conception. (pp. 170-71)

[The inversive method] eliminates the meaner elements which in the history of fiction have so often operated to hold the novel down to cheap and mechanical formulas; it brings into emphasis the inner forces which should dignify great narrative art; it puts a thoughtful cast on the face of melodrama itself. And as a final word, it is possible to assert that in Conrad's work it is in line with a predominant tendency in every field of modern art—the tendency to overthrow the old fallacy that art should represent life in a photographically methodical way. In the new scheme of art, distortion becomes an inevitable feature. The artist conceives life, not in terms of the flat realities of nature, but in terms of his own spirit, through which his expression must find its own unique form. (p. 177)

> *Donald Davidson, "Joseph Conrad's Directed In-*
> *directions," in* The Sewanee Review, *Vol. XXXIII,*
> *No. 1, January, 1925, pp. 163-77.*

ALBERT J. GUERARD (essay date 1958)

The universality of *Lord Jim* is . . . obvious, since nearly everyone has jumped off some *Patna* and most of us have been compelled to live on, desperately or quietly engaged in reconciling what we are with what we would like to be. (p. 127)

The impulse to discriminate between what we are and what we do, or to dissociate our*selves* from what exists in our unconscious, is a form ancient enough of making excuses. And the experience in Patusan, which to some critics seems irrelevant, corresponds to the fairly common dream of a second chance and total break with the guilty past. "A clean slate, did he say? As if the initial word of each our destiny were not graven in imperishable characters upon the face of a rock." Jim can only go to meet that destiny or await it, since it exists in his temperament; his failure is tragically certain. But he is one of those great fictional characters whose crime, like Michael Henchard's [in Hardy's *The Mayor of Casterbridge*] makes as well as breaks him. A Henchard who did not sell his wife would have been a haytrusser to the end of his days. . . . So too Jim, had the *Patna* not struck a derelict, would presumably have drifted through life seeking ever softer and more suspect berths. The first four chapters show him clearly headed down that path, and content to substitute revery for action. It is discomforting but true to say that involuntary crime brings him into the moral universe. (pp. 127-28)

[*Lord Jim* rests] on the bedrock of a great story and an important human situation; it has some appeal even for the casual reader who moves through a novel as clumsily as he moves through life. And yet it is, of course, an art novel, a novelist's novel, a critic's novel—perhaps the first important one in England after *Tristram Shandy*. This means that it becomes a different novel if read very attentively; or, becomes a different novel when read a second or third time. (pp. 129-30)

[The] casual reader usually ignores or minimizes the important evidence *against* Lord Jim, is insensitive to ironic overtone and illustrative digression, assumes that Conrad wholly approved of his hero, and is quite certain that Jim "redeemed himself" in Patusan. Thus this casual reader, identifying with Jim so completely, is incapable of responding to the novel's suspended judgments and withheld sympathies; he has committed himself, simply and unequivocally, to a highly equivocal personage. . . . So too, since his whole concern is with Jim, the casual reader regards Marlow as no more than an irritating technical device. And he responds not at all to structure and

style, to the beauty and meaning inherent in the elaborate ironic play of recurrence and reflexive reference. (pp. 131-32)

The differences between first and second readings are more striking as we look at whole chapters. For with *Lord Jim,* and specifically with the beginning of Marlow's narrative in Chapter 5, Conrad gives truly free play to his temperamental evasiveness, and to his delight in digression and distorted perspective. And now we are exposed to Marlow at his most exasperatingly roundabout: refusing to tell us the few facts we need to know, refusing to stay put in place or time, and offering a complex flow of thought and feeling over a situation of which we know next to nothing. (pp. 134-35)

[Such] is the perverse and wandering movement of [Chapter 5] that, at a generous estimate, [it] advances our knowledge in less than one line out of ten and . . . actively deceives us in far more than one out of ten. We can experience its full drama and irony only if we are aware of the difference between reality and the illusion under which the *Patna* officers still live; however, we are bound, through a first reading, to share that illusion almost completely. The experience, through that first reading, must rather be one of exploring and groping in a dense mist, with only the gravity of a guiding voice to sustain us. Through the strange chapter Marlow is creating an impression—and first of all an impression of himself as a man of intense curiosity and intensely conservative ethic, who is in some respect insecure and who likes to speak of "secret motives." At the expense of dramatic obfuscation he is establishing a serious atmosphere. He is also, through the vividness and ease of his digressions, thoroughly establishing his authority as someone who knows very well this Eastern world.

Yet the critic hostile to Marlow might point to this chapter as a useful exhibit of an alleged pervasive fault: that Marlow and hence Conrad make a great deal out of nothing. For the Jim who immediately provoked such a strong emotional and moral response in Marlow has done nothing, through Chapter 5, except stand in the street looking unconcerned. For the moment he is nothing, or nothing but his plight. The common impression received on a first reading of the whole novel (that Jim is an exceedingly complicated person) has in fact much excuse but little solid foundation. Conrad is closer to the truth in his Author's Note when he refers to Jim as "a simple and sensitive character." So too is Marlow when he says that Jim "complicated matters by being so simple." Simple he is, in the strength and pertinacity of his several urgent longings. . . . In fact not very much may seem left of Jim, after we have discounted Marlow's partialities and distortions. He is a rather adolescent dreamer and "romantic" with a strong ego-ideal, who prefers solitary reveries of heroism to the shock and bustle of active life. Hence he is lazy and a poor seaman. (The sea's only reward, perfect love of the work, "eluded him"; he chose the easier way of service with Eastern owners and native crews.) He has a strong visual imagination and vividly foresees the worst; this faculty, combined with other temperamental traits, tends to immobilize him in crisis. He seems radically incapable of acting properly at the important junctures of his life. Sometimes he cannot act at all. He differs from other introverted dreamers chiefly in the degree of his Bovaryism; he can literally confuse reality and dream at times, and so can hardly believe his own disreputable acts. But, precisely because the jump from the *Patna* so offends his dream of self, he enters into active if self-destructive life. He tries to live his dream. So too, though living in the dreamer's natural isolation, he wants the confirmation of other men's admiration and love and at the least needs one man (Marlow) who will believe in him. Shock, shame, or guilt, the loyalty of Marlow, the challenging opportunity of Patusan—these very nearly carry him out of his dreaming solitude and mist of self-deception. Yet in Patusan, as the dream gets some encouragement from life, revery and reality interfuse more than ever. Thus Jim can come to half-believe in the supernatural power with which local legend has endowed him.

There is a little more to Jim than this unsympathetic outline suggests. But there is nothing radically abnormal or obscure in his "acute consciousness" of lost honor, nor even in the durability of his romantic egoism and the magnitude of his self-deceptions. Our sense of depth comes rather from the complexity of Marlow's spiraling response to this not abnormal man, who is "one of us." It comes partly too from Marlow's long deceptive insistence on Jim's "truth" and "constancy": deceptive, since they turn out to be a truth and constancy to the exalted egoism rather than to Marlow's own strong sense of community obligation. And our sense of depth comes also from the paradoxical nature of Marlow's psychologizing. For Marlow insists on the "mysterious" or "inscrutable" side of Jim only when speaking of matters that are familiar enough to all of us (though they may indeed be "mysteries"): the selfish potentialities of idealism or the saving potentialities of egoism, the human capacity for evasion and self-deception, and so forth. (Unquestionably too he interjects these comments on the mysterious and the inscrutable for the dramatic purpose of disengaging the reader from present action or scene, of controlling distance and perspective.) But Marlow does not comment, or comments very little, on the occasions when Jim's actions are truly complex or truly enigmatic. Here the healthy novelistic impulse—to dramatize rather than explain important psychological insights—nearly always prevails. (pp. 139-42)

Lord Jim is a novel of intellectual and moral suspense, and the mystery to be solved, or conclusion to be reached, lies not in Jim but in ourselves. Can we, faced by the ambiguities and deceptions of life itself (and more!), apprehend the whole experience humanly? Can we come to recognize the full complexity of any simple case, and respond both sympathetically and morally to Jim and his version of "how to be"? The reader, in a sense . . . turns out to be the hero of the novel, either succeeding or failing in his human task of achieving a balanced view.

The "simple" Jim provokes then, within the largest question of whether he is "in the clear," certain basic questions of moral response:

1. *Guilt and disgrace: the moral character of the psychomachia.* "I don't mean to say that I regret my action," Marlow remarks, "nor will I pretend that I can't sleep o'nights in consequence; still the idea obtrudes itself that he made so much of his disgrace while it is the guilt alone that matters." To what extent does Jim see his jump from the *Patna* as a crime to be atoned for, to what extent as an "opportunity missed"? To what extent is "facing the music" (and the inquiry) a moral act, and to what extent an act of pride? And how pejorative or favorable a construction are we to give to the word *romantic* in "the reproach of his romantic conscience"?

2. *Is self-destructive behavior moral, and courageous?* Marlow raises these questions in connection with Jim's sudden departures from his jobs when reminded of the *Patna*. "Obviously Jim was not of the winking sort; but what I could never make up my mind about was whether his line of conduct amounted

to shirking his ghost or to facing him out . . . It might have been flight and it might have been a mode of combat." (pp. 142-43)

3. *Does Jim redeem himself in Patusan?* He wins the confidence and love of the natives, and (temporarily) brings them order and justice. But Marlow realizes he has not escaped the egoism and pride which menaced him from the start. . . . (p. 144)

4. *How to be?* We are thus asked to evaluate a romantic pride, a romantic conscience, an exalted egoism as solutions to the essential problem of "how to be." We must locate on a moral spectrum "a sort of sublimated, idealised selfishness." What we as readers are likely to think of such attitudes, or of Jim as a person, will depend partly on the persons we are, and not merely on the novel's success or failure. But *Lord Jim*'s impressionistic structure prevents us from bringing to bear too easily our preconceptions. Its shattering complexity compels us to set out anew. (pp. 144-45)

Lord Jim, then, is an intricate novel about possible emotional and moral responses to a relatively simple man, even to a "type" of man. However, it would be a mistake to dwell too much on Jim's simplicity, or to say that there's "nothing there." For this man repeatedly taken "unawares," and who is possessed by what he thinks he possesses, offers a major dramatic image of the will and the personality in conflict, of the conscious mind betrayed by the unconscious, of the intent rendered absurd by the deed. The conscious mind discovers, belatedly, what the betraying dark powers have accomplished: "I had jumped, it seems. . . ." (p. 145)

Simple Jim may be. But there is nothing simple about Conrad's own understanding of him. We must, as always, except Dostoevsky: the first Freudian novelist and still the greatest dramatist of half-conscious and unconscious processes. . . . Otherwise, *Lord Jim* is perhaps the first major novel solidly built on a true intuitive understanding of sympathetic identification as a psychic process, and as a process which may operate both consciously and less than consciously. (pp. 146-47)

Dramatically as well as theoretically, *Lord Jim* is a story of sympathies, projections, empathies . . . and loyalties. The central relationship is that of Marlow and Jim. We can see why Jim needs Marlow, as an "ally, a helper, an accomplice." He cannot believe in himself unless he has found another to do so. And he needs a judge, witness, and advocate in the solitude of his battle with himself. All this is evident. But why does Marlow go so far out of his way, very far really, to help Jim? Why does Marlow need Jim? He speaks of the fellowship of the craft, of being his very young brother's keeper, of loyalty to "one of us," of mere curiosity, of a moral need to explore and test a standard of conduct. And we may say with much truth that this is a novel of a moving and enduring friendship between an older and a younger man. But Marlow . . . acknowledges a more intimate or more selfish alliance. He is loyal to Jim as one must be to another or potential self, to the criminally weak self that may still exist. . . . (p. 147)

[The] central preoccupation of Conrad's technique, the heart of the impressionist aim, is to invite and control the reader's identifications and so subject him to an intense rather than passive experience. Marlow's human task is also the reader's: to achieve a right human relationship with this questionable younger brother. Marlow must resist an excessive identification (which would mean abandoning his traditional ethic); he must maintain a satisfactory balance of sympathy and judgment. No easy task, since Jim demands total sympathy. . . . And this is, far more than in most novels, the reader's moral drama and situation: to be subjected to all the phantoms in possession, to be exposed to a continuous subtle and flowing interplay of intellectual appeals to his judgment and poignant appeals to his sympathy.

The reader must survive this experience and go through this labyrinth of evidence without the usual guide of an omniscient author or trustworthy author-surrogate. The reader (looking incorrigibly for the author's convictions and final decision) is likely to put his trust in Marlow, including the Marlow who speaks of Jim's "greatness," "truth," and "constancy." But he does so at his peril. (p. 152)

Doubtless the common impression left by a first reading is that the formal rational evidence is preponderantly favorable to Jim, and that the novel finally reaches a lenient verdict, even a judgment of "approval." Jim emerges as, simply, a hero and a redeemed man. But the evidence (as we discover on rereading) is by no means preponderantly favorable; and *Lord Jim* is as much a novel about a man who makes excuses as a novel that makes excuses. Our first impression that the novel "approves" Jim turns out to derive not from the area of rational evidence and judgment but from the area of novelistic sympathy; we discover, as we look a little more closely, that Marlow has repeatedly taken us in. He is a considerably more lenient witness than his austere moralizing tone suggests. On various occasions he brings in the damaging evidence (he is, after all, obliged to bring it in) very casually and digressively, as though inviting us to overlook it. So too, when we are inclined to judge harshly, Marlow diverts our attention from the suffering, "burning" Jim to those who merely rot in the background, or who live safely in a world of untested rectitude. "You've been tried." Jim has, at least, been tested and tried. Therefore he exists. (pp. 153-54)

[The use of] sudden corrective juxtaposition is at once the novel's characteristic way of redressing a balance of meaning and its chief way of moving us emotionally. It may operate in both directions, of course: correcting an excessive austerity of judgment or correcting an excessive sympathy. The matter is not easy to sum up, and my conclusion is perhaps debatable. But here is it: that on a first reading we are inclined to think Marlow's own judgment of Jim too harsh (since we have missed some of the evidence that led him to that judgment); that on a second reading (because we are discovering that evidence with a force of delayed impact) we may think Marlow's judgment too lenient. In other words, the unfavorable evidence that Marlow had half-concealed through deceptive casualness of manner grows upon us at a second or third reading, and becomes more difficult to discount. But meanwhile our natural sympathy for Jim—the center of attention, the man on the rack, the conscientious sinner, the man who has been "tried"—has correspondingly diminished. (p. 154)

This then is *Lord Jim*'s chief way of provoking in its readers a strong human response and meaningful conflict: to interweave or suddenly juxtapose (rather than group logically and chronologically) the appeals to judgment and sympathy, to criticism and compassion. A man is what he does, which in Jim's case is very little that is not equivocal. But also he "exists" for us by the quality of his feeling and the poignant intensity of his dream. He is not "good enough" (as Marlow tells Jewel, as the Malay helmsman and other witnesses verify) yet his childish romanticism may be preferable to a cynical realism. In any event, as Marlow goes on to say, "nobody is good enough." This is not a relativistic conclusion. It reminds us rather how

strong Marlow's moral and community engagement was, against which his brotherly and outlaw sympathy contended.

These peculiar groupings—of incident and witness and evidence, of intellectual and emotional appeal—distinguish *Lord Jim* from most earlier fiction. But imagery also leaves us in provisional and perhaps lasting uncertainty. Is Jim "in the clear"? The novel's chief recurrent image is of substance and reality obscured, often attractively so, by mist or by deceptive light. *Fog, mist, cloud,* and *veil* form a cluster with *moonlight,* and with *dream,* to dramatize certain essential distinctions: between the conscious mind and the unconscious, illusion and reality, the "ego-ideal" and the self's destiny as revealed by its acts. Imagery is supposed to reveal an author's ultimate and perhaps unconscious bias. But much of the imagery here is grouped fairly consciously as part of a multiple appeal to the reader. These images—if they do form a cluster, if we do properly take them together—should help determine the delicate relationship of idealism and self-deception. (pp. 161-62)

At a first reading all this imagery of nebulosity may magnify and glamorize Jim . . . , and also may be partly responsible for our first impression that Jim is an exceedingly mysterious person. (p. 162)

The meaning of *mist,* as we look at its various appearances, is clearer than we might have expected. It can refer generally to ambiguity but more centrally refers to the aura of deception and self-deception that surrounds Jim's reality. Now and then Marlow has a "glimpse through a rent in the mist in which he moved and had his being," as Jim says something truly revealing: as he tells of his impulse to go back to the spot of the *Patna*'s abandonment, or as he recognizes the good Marlow does him by listening. But the mists close again at once when Jim refers to his plight as "unfair." Thus we may call the mist his illusion of self or ego-ideal, which is in turn responsible for the deceptions; it may impose the "mask" of a "usual expression." Reality can then appear in an "unconscious grimace," or through rifts caused by the inward struggles. He stumblingly reveals the truth; or, we stumble upon it. (pp. 162-63)

Discussions of *Lord Jim,* concerned as they are with interpretive and structural problems, regularly neglect the purely novelistic side of vivid particular creation. Mine has been no exception. Yet without the particulars of place and person, without the finely evoked atmospheres and brilliant minor vignettes, the novel's amount of brooding debate might have become intolerable. Its pleasures in any event would have been different ones. Page by page, *Lord Jim*'s consistent great appeal largely depends on its changing of the lens, on its sudden shifts from a distant and often nebulous moral perspective to a grossly and superbly material foreground. Marlow's tendency to make such shifts is his most personal and most useful mannerism. It lends reality to the unsubstantial reveries, as gross substance is bound to do, yet invites us to look at them more critically. But most of all it offers the pleasure of a creative surprise. (p. 171)

Albert J. Guerard, in his Conrad: The Novelist *(copyright © 1958 by the President and Fellows of Harvard College; excerpted by permission), Cambridge, Mass.: Harvard University Press, 1958 (and reprinted by Harvard University Press, 1965), 322 p.*

FREDERICK R. KARL (essay date 1969)

As a first novel, *Almayer's Folly* paradoxically displays the exhaustion and "sucked-out" quality of a very old and disillusioned novelist. Published in 1895, it manifests the language, the tones, the characteristic rhythms, and most of the mannerisms of *fin de siècle* literature. *Almayer's Folly* is a prose counterpart of 1890's poetry. . . . Conrad's novel, as befitting its background, is one of decadence and breakdown, a pageant of retreat, of dreams, of filmy torpor and fatigue. His method of developing this theme of exhaustion is through emphasis on a certain type of language and through his choice of characteristic images.

Conrad's settings in *Almayer* and his second novel, *An Outcast of the Islands,* are exotic, full of jungle scenes, semi-civilized natives, and violent emotions. These images—the basic stuff of his early work—are found later in new settings but with the same purport, transformed into the storm images of *The Nigger of the "Narcissus,"* the natural descriptions of *Nostromo,* the city backgrounds of *The Secret Agent* and *Under Western Eyes,* the island backdrop of *Victory*. No matter what the setting—in city or jungle or sea—Conrad used imagistic devices as objective correlatives to create the narrative.

The chief images in *Almayer* are those of languor—a languor of character, of language, and of setting. (pp. 91-2)

So overwhelming is the presence of the jungle and so overpowering the slow rhythm of this vast primeval slime that the people in contrast seem mere pawns in the grasp of uncontrollable forces. Conrad's description of background drives home their severe isolation; the vast swamp of trees and roots and mud seems to suck up every semblance of life and to reduce man to insignificance. Supplementing the jungle, Conrad uses the symbol of storm, an oft-repeated phenomenon in his later work, as an epitome of nature's power and man's insignificance. (pp. 93-4)

In his conception of character as well, we find that same sense of desolation, frustration, and exhaustion. The comedy of Almayer—a man of great hopes and only moderate abilities, an expedient man who found out that circumstances were set to destroy him—is played out against a vast panorama of natural forces which he is unable to control or even understand. It is an old Almayer we see falling further and further into personal and social isolation. . . . (pp. 97-8)

As a sequel in reverse to *Almayer's Folly,* Conrad's second novel, *An Outcast of the Islands,* goes back to an earlier period in the lives of the characters of the first book. The structure and language also return to those of *Almayer* rather than suggesting any new developments. That same sense of debility and exhaustion prevalent in the earlier book is present in *An Outcast,* but here attached to a dominant death theme; for the jungle has gained in malevolence, and the sea is an ambivalent force of life and death.

Conrad began *An Outcast* not as a novel, but as a short story, and perhaps its thinness and deficiency of substance can be traced to its original conception. The vast panorama of jungle creates a scenic background far in excess of what the characterization can sustain. (p. 100)

In *Almayer's Folly* and *An Outcast of the Islands*, Conrad worked through imagery and description to create an obvious world of man and nature, of greed and passion—obvious because discursive and labored: in short, too talky and too stagey. But in *The Nigger of the "Narcissus"*—still about man and nature, greed and passion—we have Conrad's first significant attempt to understate, to create a world through less obvious verbalizations, and to comment through a construct and not through

a patchwork of discourse. *The Nigger* is Conrad's first nondiscursive work, full of suggestive overtones that are neither pushed nor forced. (p. 108)

This book, Conrad implied, is a microcosm of a universal situation; that is, the inarticulate confusion of men of vague convictions when confronted by fear and superstition. . . . (p. 109)

Conrad's concern at this time was with the ever-shifting relation between the individual and society, and the role that each must play in conflict with the other. One can remark that James Wait stands as a symbol of the ethical demand that human beings in distress exert upon others, for Wait's predicament upsets the solidarity of the crew and creates a disturbance that can be reconciled only in moral terms. . . . Wait, in his role of seagoing confidence man, finds his counterpart in the fraudulent Donkin and in the vague fears and susceptibilities of an ignorant and superstitious crew. How Conrad develops this relationship, how the nature of Wait's illusory attraction conflicts with a crew rooted in reality and survival, becomes the stuff of the book.

Within this dialectic of illusion and reality, Conrad has placed a representative group of characters who become symbols of their type. In Singleton, whose name suggests his character, we see a mythological figure, a man of duty of whose fiber gods are made. . . . The chief mate Baker is dutiful like Melville's Starbuck, and though lacking in imagination, stolid, fair, just, withal a good seaman, a "model chief mate." Captain Allistoun . . . has an implied complexity which results in a keen sense of moral values; as Captain, he of course makes his decisions in the "loneliness of command," a godly function of whose powers he is aware and of whose rights he partakes judiciously. The crew as a whole, then, with its sense of duty, provides a stable background of moral conduct. (pp. 111-12)

Beneath every settled and ordered mind lies a stubborn anarchy which pokes through the surface under provocation. Donkin, together with Wait, is the first of a long line of Conradian anarchists; not men who throw bombs, but those who refuse their duties and know nothing of courage and endurance and loyalty; men who know only of their rights. . . . Conrad's anarchists, so often misunderstood, are objects of ridicule not so much for active behavior against society as for their refusal to accept their duties in a common fate. . . . To refuse duty, Conrad implies, is to be criminal, and in this sense the criminal equals the anarchist. . . . In conjunction with Wait, Donkin is able to demoralize the men by breaking through their surface serenity to their inner fears. While Donkin strikes into their minds, Wait, as a complement, throws terror into their hearts. (pp. 112-13)

With the unfathomable sea outside and Wait working on the unfathomable within, the crew breaks into disorganized pieces on which the storm itself is more than sufficient comment.

The storm—excepting that of *"Typhoon,"* perhaps the greatest description in sea literature in any language—baptizes the crew, in time unifies it, and further isolates Wait and Donkin, who lose identification through their refusal to coöperate. Although Wait retains his hold on the men by means of his very helplessness (virtually a Mother-Father and Child relationship), their sense of plight gives them a solidarity hitherto either missing or dormant. (p. 114)

In that central scene in which the crew attempts to save Wait entombed in his cabin, we have a symbolic presentation of

Wait's relationship to himself, to the crew, and, finally, to the reader. This scene . . . is an epitome of the entire book, summing up all the themes and gathering all the threads. Pounded by the sea at the height of the storm, the crew tries to get to Wait's coffined prison, only to find a wall of nails from the carpenter's stores covering the bulkhead beneath which the prisoner screams out his dread. Wait is, as ever, unable to act, able only to cry out in mortal fear, lacking will, entirely passive and acted upon. . . . He becomes flabby, boneless, a helpless child unable to stand or even to clutch at his rescuers. They handle him like the prodigal son, hating him and mothering him: "The secret and ardent desires of our hearts was the desire to beat him viciously with our fists about the head: and we handled him as tenderly as though he had been made of glass. . . ." (pp. 115-16)

In these central pages, Conrad, through a single dramatized scene, presents the major tensions and suggests the various aspects of the conflict. Like Jonah, Wait creates dissension among the men; in his own person, he symbolizes the anxieties that lie between life and death, between psychical fear and reality. If I were to cite one advance Conrad had made between *An Outcast* and *The Nigger,* I should point to his use of scene as symbol. (p. 116)

[Conrad's next novel, *Lord Jim,* is] a rich and varied experience. Jim in his semi-articulate and stumbling way, in his sense of almost complete failure, in his inability to act powerfully and wisely, is a compelling guide to the modern temper; and his frustrated quest for personal salvation in an indifferent or hostile world is Conrad's distressing prophecy for the twentieth century. (p. 131)

The psychological possibilities of Conrad's handling of Jim are immense. *Lord Jim* is often called existential or at least discussed in existential terms. However, if we read Conrad correctly in this novel, unconscious impulses, such as Jim's self-destructive promptings, make hash of any existential interpretation dependent on man's conscious choices. Questions of identity, good faith, attitude, even of life style, have no significance if the impulses directing one's conduct derive from unconscious sources. Under such conditions, one can only, like Jim, seek external explanation and yet continue to pursue a self-destructive course of action. (pp. 131-32)

Although *Lord Jim* is often more imposing in its parts than as a whole, it nevertheless retains a power and a force rarely duplicated by Conrad's contemporaries or by Conrad himself in his later work; obviously, Conrad's way of conceiving this novel makes *Lord Jim* his as yet most comprehensive statement on man. His ability to suggest and evoke is evident, and from here to "Heart of Darkness" is not a great step.

Contemporaneously with *Lord Jim,* Conrad wrote "Youth" and "Heart of Darkness." . . . (p. 132)

In reading "Youth," one is aware of how high its critics have placed it in the Conrad canon; yet it can rightfully be praised only in terms of a small job neatly performed within severe limitations. (p. 133)

From "Youth" to "Heart of Darkness" is indeed a step from youth to maturity as Conrad was aware. (p. 134)

"Heart of Darkness" is possibly the greatest short novel in English, one of the greatest in any language, and now a twentieth-century cultural fact. Like all great fiction, it involves the reader in dramatic, crucially difficult moral decisions which

parallel those of the central characters, here Marlow and Kurtz. (pp. 135-36)

"Heart of Darkness" is one of our archetypal existential literary documents in which all is contingency. It fits the categories; it has the right psychology. The reader can, if he wishes, see the novella as a delineation of absurdity—that term applied to man's skew relationship with objects, with his milieu, inevitably with the universe. The images of the narrative, like images of a poem, intensify man's sense of alienation—right into the appearance of the pale, white-skulled, ailing, then dying Kurtz, an elongated image of wasted power and fruitless endeavor, the humanitarian now inhuman.

Possibly it is this sense of absurdity and discontinuity which so impresses Marlow that he returns a changed man. All his inner computers have broken down. (p. 140)

Since he is a man of order and moral courage, Marlow expects similar restraints to prevail elsewhere. As a captain he of course knows that such qualities are essential to preserve life at sea. Carrying them over into civilian life, they become for him psychological expectations. Marlow acquiesces to the world's work as basically just and fundamentally good, even necessary, provided it is done by enlightened men. (p. 141)

Marlow's great revelation comes when he sees that the world is not arranged this way—and here the Congo is a microcosm of the great world in which those who can, plunder those who cannot. Marlow's awareness of evil comes when he notes that many men, and those the most willful, do not share his belief in an orderly, enlightened society. Theirs is one of chaos, anarchy, "unspeakable rites." They approve human sacrifice, and they eat their victims. This is Conrad's existential wedge, so to speak. A law-abiding, morally sensitive man enters an avaricious, predatory, almost psychopathic world. For the moment he sees that civilization brings dubious rewards. He learns the harsh vocabulary of reality. He matures. The nineteenth century becomes the twentieth. (p. 142)

Nostromo displays a large number of significant qualities, for with this novel, Conrad became a major author. . . . In Nostromo, as in his other novels, it was not Conrad's ability to achieve new and original techniques that makes his work distinctive, but rather his resourcefulness in organizing and revamping the conventional matter of the novel. . . . *Nostromo* is one of the first of the "difficult" modern novels, requiring . . . a close attention to word and scene. (pp. 153-54)

Conrad gains cumulative rhythms through special awareness of both the sounds and silences inherent in language, rhythms which grow in significance and intensity as the novel progresses. The *progression d'effet* which Conrad and Ford strove to reach through careful selection of word and phrase is conveyed in *Nostromo* through ever-increasing sub-surface rhythms. It is Conrad's delving into these subconscious rhythms, as much as his "underground" scenes and characters, which makes *Nostromo* intrinsically significant as well as important in the history of the novel. (p. 155)

The Secret Agent is at once one of Conrad's simplest and most elusive works. With a surface that betrays little complexity, the unpretentious story encompasses the ideas of a major novel. The exotic settings of *Almayer's Folly, An Outcast, Lord Jim,* and *Nostromo* have been subtly transformed into the city settings of London, and in their ramifications these city images are even more mysteriously suggestive than the jungle backgrounds of the Malayan novels. (p. 191)

The city and their ironic position in it are the twin aspects of the ungracious existence of Adolf and Winnie Verloc. Every element of Verloc's existence partakes of the desolation of a modern city. He is an organic part of its grubbiness, and through him the city lives. A seller of shady wares, he is of fatty build and unprepossessing in appearance; married by Winnie not for love but for security, he is an ineffectual Prufrock, who in anarchistic circles possesses not even a name but a designated mark. Nameless, loveless, and unable to function effectually as a counter agent, Verloc is as impotent as the gloomy city which enfolds his activities. (p. 193)

As part of city life, the central scene of the book—the lugubrious cab ride of Winnie, Stevie, and their mother to the charity home—is first and foremost a symbol of complete desolation. . . . The ride conveys the hopelessness of spirit in a modern city and creates a sense of "impending chaos," although the chaos is not that of political anarchism or anarchists. *The Secret Agent* possesses only superficial resemblance to a police story. Its chronology defeats the main elements of the detective novel, for the very arrangement of the book destroys suspense. We can reason that if the police are aware of who planted the bomb almost as soon as the reader, then the chase or the activity of anarchists is evidently not of primary importance. The theme, like that of *Nostromo* and "Heart of Darkness," is surely a presentation of moral corruption as it spreads back and forth from city to character. Conrad's aim is the ironic castigation of modern life, particularly the middle-class worship of science and materialism and the drab world it has built for itself. If *Victory* presents a dialectic of the forces that created the First World War, then no less does *The Secret Agent* convey a view of spiritual despair haunting a world which looks only toward its own materialism. (pp. 194-95)

Razumov in *Under Western Eyes* tries to pry himself from human solidarity in order to go his own way, a decision that inevitably proves self-destructive. Conrad, we remember, rarely equated self-imposed isolation with independence or individualism. Freedom from others is burdensome, an incubus and not a release, which in most cases leads to personal catastrophe. Conrad's conception of the individual is, ironically, a person who, once thrown out of society, must recognize the terms of his existence and then try to re-enter or else be overcome by a hostile world. His way of re-entry, in so far as he has a choice, can be through conquest or renunciation. Razumov makes the latter choice, and paradoxically his renunciation leads to both his destruction and acceptance, in each case by the same people.

But this overt theme is surely not the sole importance of *Under Western Eyes,* for Conrad not only pioneered the political detective novel in English, but he also knew how to provide effective psychological drama. *Under Western Eyes* is full of subtle devices which by appearing at nearly every turn in the novel replace a direct narrative line and provide psychological depth for otherwise superficial political and social activity. As in "Heart of Darkness," *Nostromo,* and *The Secret Agent,* Conrad in *Under Western Eyes* attained psychological depth through certain professional touches: the placement of a crucial image, the sudden shift of narrative, the use of a large symbolic scene which draws together various elements of the plot, or simply an ironic comment which cogently suggests another dimension. (pp. 210-12)

Despite a narrative that is only occasionally intricate and a group of characters that lacks the variety and range of his other major novels, Conrad was able to give *Under Western Eyes* the

elements of literary greatness. There are a thickness and density of tragic event and an awareness of the complex things of this world which we usually find only in great literature. The conclusive element in *Under Western Eyes* is perhaps its irony—not the pervading ironic comment of *The Secret Agent*—but an irony, rather, that is evoked through the juxtaposition of people and objects, an irony less of word than of scene. (p. 213)

Of the three stories in the volume ['*Twixt Land and Sea*] only "The Secret Sharer" need command our attention. . . . "The Secret Sharer," though surely not so profound and far-reaching as "Heart of Darkness," is for several reasons one of Conrad's major stories. (pp. 230-31)

"The Secret Sharer" has been the target of more many-sided interpretations than any other Conrad work with the possible exception of "Heart of Darkness." Rather than repeat the literal, ethical, psychological, and aesthetic meanings of the story, I should prefer to examine "The Secret Sharer" in a context that partakes of all the other possibilities and still remains true to Conrad's work as a whole. "The Secret Sharer" deals principally and simply with the theme of apprenticeship-to-life, which is the same theme of growing up and maturing that Conrad treated in many other stories and novels. Placed in this large category, the story can then be seen, as necessary, in its various subdivisions of ethical, psychological, and aesthetic development. (p. 231)

"The Secret Sharer" is the other side of *Under Western Eyes*. . . . The two works taken together pose a double question and show the consequences leading from both answers: what happens when you betray a trust? and what happens when under duress you remain true to your secret? It is the Captain's recognition of these points that sustains the dramatic interest of the story.

Professor [Morton Douwen] Zabel, in his well-known essay "Joseph Conrad: Chance and Recognition," remarked that the crisis in every one of Conrad's novels and stories arrives when by accident, decision, or error a man finds himself abruptly committed to his destiny. This recognition, Zabel says, occurs through a series of steps: isolation of the character from society; his recognition of his situation in a hostile world; and then, once self-knowledge is attained, his way . . . of either solving or succumbing to his problem. This is also the problem of the artist; and Conrad through his particular way of developing "The Secret Sharer" was able to relate the psychological and moral contradictions in human nature to the ambivalence of reality as art embodies it, and finally to a searching analysis of value itself. (p. 232)

[The] Captain in "The Secret Sharer" is faced by the stern materials of his salvation and is courageous enough to act on his problem once he has intuitively formulated its substance. This story, then, becomes a microcosm of Conrad's major themes; but for all its suggestiveness, it is, paradoxically, one of his most straightforward and obvious works. Its narrative is a model of clarity. . . . (p. 233)

The scenes and images of "Heart of Darkness," for example, are of a variety which permits extension, and an almost limitless number of references are possible. But "The Secret Sharer" is notable for its lack of variety, for the sameness of its images, for its failure to conceptualize the material in less direct form. This is surely not to denigrate the story, but only to show where analysis is possible and where excessive probing may go wrong. I want to emphasize that even though "The Secret Sharer" does not contain cosmic significance, it is, concerning matters of doctrine as well as intrinsically, among Conrad's more important works. The surface in this case *is* the story, and the surface is the arrival of the Captain at a degree of maturity in which he gains self-respect and confidence. This is the obvious fact of **"The Secret Sharer,"** and it must remain of the greatest import. (p. 234)

[*Chance* is] Conrad's only novel of the maturing of a girl to a young lady; all his other novels of growing-up are concerned with the apprenticeship of men. Flora de Barral has to overcome all the frustrations and barriers facing . . . [Conrad's male characters], but because of her sex, she lacks their mobility. Her role is necessarily more passive, and her first important decision is the only one she really ever must make, the choice of Anthony rather than her father. . . .

Typical of the problem of growing-up is the relation between parents and children: between the isolated Flora and her swindler father, between Captain Anthony and his poet father. Despite riches, position, a name, and a personal governess, Flora was, says Conrad, "the captive of the meanest conceivable fate." . . . Thrown out by society because of the nature of her father's past, Flora is as cursed as Jim. . . . Yet original sin is not hers; she is faultless, and perhaps for this reason her sanity prevails, and instead of being forced into self-destruction she endures her tormentors. (p. 237)

If human relationships are the center of the novel, then they are relationships responsible only to the consciences of individuals, never to the dictates of God. Conrad's atomic view of sin and salvation, the necessity for the individual to be aware of his rights and wrongs, makes each person accountable only to himself. There is no squaring of accounts with heaven. Rewards are on this earth, and hell exists solely as a conscience in each man's heart. (p. 239)

Despite his Catholic rearing, Conrad presents a view of man that is entirely secular; for him, the universe was man-directed. Earlier in his work, nature had been paramount and its mysterious workings conveyed some of the qualities of an inscrutable God; but in this, his middle period, Conrad's emphasis was clearly on man as center, directing his own affairs and assuming final responsibility for his decisions. (p. 240)

Despite the conscious formalism of *Chance,* with its involved construction that seems strikingly contemporary, it is, rather, Conrad's humanization of his subject matter that marks a precedent for the secularity of several major contemporary novelists. By de-emphasizing the relation between man and some murky God or between men and an organized Christian morality, Conrad subscribed to an atomistic view of morality in which self-responsibility determines individual action. Not only does this view of personal morality cut deeply into twentieth-century literary ideas, but it is also close in its general notions to the philosophic existentialism theorized by Sartre and Camus. (pp. 241-42)

Together with Mann's *The Magic Mountain*—a more fully wrought work which Conrad's novel resembles in many significant ways—*Victory* interprets several of the events that foreshadowed the First World War. But lest *Victory* become too closely identified with matters of war and peace, we should point to its aesthetic significance and its poetic nature, to its quality as "pure art," which harks back to Shakespeare's *The Tempest.* (pp. 246-47)

To bring together all the diverse elements of *Victory* Conrad used, in the figure of Axel Heyst, a human symbol of large

dimensions; analogously, in the novel's setting, in its shifting chronology of narrative, and in its various subsidiary symbols of sight and sound, Conrad has made the book a model of arrangement and suggested meanings. (p. 247)

For the first sixty-two pages—Part One of the novel—we see Heyst only indirectly. Built up and filled in by seemingly scattered details, Heyst comes to the reader just as Nostromo earlier, but with this difference: Heyst's activities *are* the center of a book which directly or indirectly he dominates in a way that Nostromo does not dominate *Nostromo*. What Heyst does and thinks determines *Victory* on all its levels at once. He is the central figure as well as the central symbol. *Victory,* therefore, seems a more unified book. (p. 248)

The sympathetic relationship between Heyst and his father is especially important for the novel's social and political theme. The elder Heyst had tried to sustain a form of idealism that constantly ran counter to reality. . . . [The] elder Heyst could not live by means of illusions while tacitly doubting their existence. Axel is a true offspring of that silent advocate of "Look on—make no sound"; long buried with the father is a substantial part of the son. Retreating into himself, Axel tried, like Villiers' Axel, to avoid the compromising contamination of human matter. But unlike Villiers' Axel, he even disbelieves in the efficacy of spiritual perfection; his despair is secular, heaven holds no reward and hell no punishment for his disenchantment. What is not dust is ashes; love is vanity, and attachment is momentary weakness. The pure life, the perfect life, is not for him a positive ordering of virtuous acts, but a complete negation of action.

This spirit of withdrawal should be stressed, particularly that influenced by the elder Heyst, for it extends from the individual to society at large. . . . Heyst realizes, though too late to save himself, that immersion in the realities of life may indeed be melancholy advice, but it is, nevertheless, the only way to survival. (pp. 251-52)

In Heyst, Conrad delineated possibly his most poignant character and his most significant human symbol. When we talk of Conrad's experiments with the novel, we must always take into account his characters, who suggest much in twentieth-century life and literature. Heyst is still attractive, perhaps because of his very ineffectuality and not despite it. As a symbol of anti-power and anti-action, he becomes in his world-weariness a strong reminder of everyman's desire to escape social pressures and to be himself, despite the nagging knowledge that this is impossible of attainment. (pp. 255-56)

[Granting] that the later fiction is indeed a letdown after the profundity of *Victory*, it is still of great importance as a mirror of the established, but exhausted, novelist, who, no longer able to experiment, had to draw upon all his practical skill to produce five more novels.

Many reasons, all speculative, could be advanced for the directness of Conrad's later style: advancing age that possibly brought with it a clearer vision and an accompanying simplicity of technique; or, a steady loss of conceptual power; or, the desire to appeal to larger audiences on their terms; or, a growing inability to turn waning personal experiences into imaginative fiction. . . . Many of the later novels and long stories—*The Arrow of Gold, The Shadow Line,* and *The Rescue* among others—are either almost direct reproductions of personal experiences or thinly veiled restatements of earlier material and methods. How different this work is from *Nostromo, Victory, Under Western Eyes,* and *The Secret Agent,* all of which were imaginatively created from the merest of suggestions or from the slightest of personal adventures! . . . The point is that the later work shows a smothering of method owing either to Conrad's refusal or inability to turn personal material into conscious art forms. (pp. 268-69)

Frederick R. Karl, in his A Reader's Guide to Joseph Conrad *(reprinted by permission of Farrar, Straus & Giroux, Inc.; copyright © 1960, 1969 by Frederick Karl), revised edition, Farrar, Straus & Giroux, 1969, 310 p.*

DOUGLAS HEWITT   (essay date 1975)

We cannot fail to observe, if we approach Conrad's work without preconceptions, that in almost all his earlier books a penetrating scrutiny is directed against the simple virtues of honesty, courage, pity and fidelity to an unquestioned ideal of conduct. (p. 16)

In particular we notice the recurrence of one situation which, though it occupies a subordinate place in two or three of the works, dominates many—the situation in which a man who relies on these simple virtues is confronted by a partially apprehended sense of evil against which they seem powerless. The mere realization of the existence of this evil overwhelms him with a sense of insecurity and casts doubt on the supposedly secure foundations of the ideals themselves; the virtues at last become suspect. Moreover, because of the peculiar structure of Conrad's works, the sharp immediacy of the problems which the confrontation raises and the clear knowledge of the significance to others of the main character's actions combine to prevent these realizations from being disregarded as vague self-questionings or moods which can be ignored. This awareness is often brought about through the recognition by the central character of an obscure link between himself and a manifestation of the evil which he cannot fail to know for what it is. (p. 17)

The choice of the word 'evil' to describe this seems inevitable. I have used the word . . . without apology and without explanation. This is not merely because it is the word which Conrad himself so often uses, but because it corresponds to his entire outlook on moral issues. We can discuss many novelists without using this term, speaking of aberrations of conduct, regrettable failings, weaknesses of character and the like, but the most cursory glance at Conrad's work is enough to convince us that he has a conception of a transcendental evil, embodying itself in individuals—a sense of evil just as great as that of any avowedly Catholic or Calvinist writer. (pp. 22-3)

In a chronological study of a writer who, like Conrad, did his best work comparatively early, we may be left with a sense of disappointment. Such a feeling should be dissipated when we reflect that, though his reputation rests upon part only of his output, it is not a particularly small part—certainly not less than four novels and rather more tales of varying length. Not many English novelists can claim more. The only point of noting a decline is to emphasise what he declined from.

His work is remarkably varied; the books between **'Youth'** and *The Secret Agent* manifest a restless exploratory energy. But they share . . . an individual vision, a cast of mind, which confronts us, upsettingly, with certain repeated situations. Conrad's concern is with a powerful sense of potential weakness and betrayal lurking under an apparent confidence in an established code of behaviour and waiting for the right circumstances of stress to emerge, often with devastating power. His technical

method of isolating his characters enables him to project these states of mind very forcefully through objects and circumstances which are both physical, natural, inevitably imposed by the real world, and at the same time symbolic of the plight of the characters.

To put matters thus may suggest that Conrad is essentially a systematic metaphysical thinker. This seems to me to be inaccurate. Certainly he employed large quasi-metaphysical terms, especially in his least successfully rhetorical moments, and he speaks of human behaviour roundly in terms of good and evil. Certainly, too, he encountered at second and third and fourth (and occasionally perhaps even at first) hand metaphysical doctrines which were being discussed at the time, and we can sometimes trace echoes of them in his work. But this is a very different matter from being a systematic metaphysical thinker. . . . There are, of course, occasions when, rather unconvincingly, he offers general statements as if he believes that they encapsulate meanings. The Marlow of *Chance* is given to this indulgence, but so, more damagingly because the novel has more in it to be damaged, does the Marlow of *Lord Jim*. But when he is writing at the height of his powers Conrad's individual vision is presented in a remarkably complex and often indirect manner, involving not only such basic fictional methods as engaging our sympathies, often surprisingly, with his characters and generating suspense and resolving it, but also shifts of tone and disconcerting juxtapositions of happenings. When we harden this dense and complex effect into doctrines it is often because of a tendency to support our view by what seem appropriate quotations. (pp. 129-30)

What lies at the heart of Conrad's work is surely not metaphysics but politics—politics understood in the widest sense. Much of private life—sexual relationships, family, neighbourly friendships, domestic rhythms—is of little interest to him, and when he writes about such matters, as in *Chance* and *Victory,* he displays his weaknesses rather than his strengths. His interest lies in the interplay of groups, the conflict between personal feelings and professional duties; he sees men as fulfilling public roles as well as leading private lives and he focuses attention upon their shared efforts and their conflicts of interest. Few novelists have written so much about work as Conrad, though the fact that the work is so often that of ship-handling— an exotic task for most readers—has tended to make us overlook the fact. But his tales of the sea are essentially about what we might call the politics of shipboard life. Even so apparently private a study of self-doubt as **'The Secret Sharer'** gains its force from the narrator's awareness of professional responsibilities and his relationship with the crew over whom he has power but whose judgements he cannot ignore. (pp. 130-31)

There is, however, one characteristic of [Conrad's sea] stories which distinguishes them from the strictly political novels, *Nostromo, The Secret Agent* and *Under Western Eyes;* in them at least one limited aim is clear and unquestionable—to navigate the ship and to preserve life at sea. The isolation of the situation concentrates the problems and convincingly limits them; Conrad does not have to consider such matters as the economic issues of the trade in which they are engaged nor the morality of sending men to sea in leaky ships. . . . Nothing is allowed to question the simplicity of the immediate task— as, indeed, nothing would in real life. It is interesting to observe in **'Heart of Darkness'**, where the morality of the trading is an issue and therefore the purpose of the voyage, that even though Marlow speaks of the therapeutic value of getting his ungainly steamboat to work he comes back down the river ill, a passenger and not a commander.

The pessimism of the sea stories is thus modified because Conrad's positive values, a belief in doing one's job properly, in fairness, in courage, in the stoic acceptance of blows, have a real, if limited, value. His protagonists may find themselves thrust into situations where the code by which they regulate their conduct seems precarious, unlikely to defend them against all the forces which may be arrayed against them, but at least in the situations which immediately confront them their duty is clear and they can win a limited victory.

In the overtly political novels there is no such unquestioned aim. There may be actions in which the practical virtues remain unquestionable but they are subsumed under larger themes where the end cannot claim legitimacy. Conrad's political view is one of gloomy scepticism, spiced with the sardonic humour of one who watches the futility of all political effort. (pp. 131-32)

But in truth his scepticism is more corrosive than we may think; attempts to change society may be futile but authority has no moral force. Nowhere is this more clearly shown than in Winnie Verloc's attempt to explain to Stevie the function of the police. He, in his pity for the cabman and his horse, has formulated his judgement as 'Bad world for poor people' and invokes the police as agents for righting wrongs—'He had formed for himself an ideal conception of the metropolitan police as a sort of benevolent institution for the suppression of evil'. Winnie feels the need to put him right and she also knows that the word 'steal' upsets him; she chooses, therefore, a formula upon which the Professor could hardly improve: 'They are there so that them as have nothing shouldn't take anything away from them who have.'

This view of politics—one which has no faith in the legitimacy of established order but also no faith in progress through political development and which sees men as almost inevitably corrupted by the public roles which they have to play—finds expression most fully in Conrad's masterpiece, *Nostromo*. (pp. 133-34)

But if *Nostromo* is, as many believe, the best political novel in the language this is not just because of the shrewdness of its analysis of the exploitation of an underdeveloped country by the invested capital of the 'Anglo-Saxon' powers, but rather because the complex form of the book does justice to the double vision of men and women as both individuals and as socially determined beings. The very frustrations which this arouses in the reader serve the meaning of the book.

In all substantial novels there is an inherent tension between our perception of form, of controlling structure, and our interest in the characters as individuals. In *Nostromo* this tension is very powerful; there are many elements in the book which are potentially or actually frustrating or irksome but to which, in the long run, we give our assent. The tension thus set up is in effect a political statement. (p. 134)

It is, of course, by the omnipresent symbolism of the silver of the mine, with which is linked the legend of the treasure seekers of Azuera, that the political judgement of the book is most enforced. There are times when this, too, may seem overdone, when its predetermining power constrains the characters' freedom so that they are perilously close to seeming puppets. As one gets to know the book better one realises that they are, indeed, puppets, but not those of a puppet-master novelist so much as of a political situation whose central controlling symbol seems not imposed by the writer but elucidated by him from the facts of the situation.

The structure, with its great use of time-shifts and changes of viewpoint, also functions to show the futility of the struggles of individuals within a political and economic situation which dwarfs them. The book's method is to plunge us into situations where we feel for characters faced by danger or the need to make decisions and then, without comment, to see these personal predicaments as part of a process which diminishes them. (pp. 135-36)

Nostromo does not merely express a political attitude; it embodies it, in the sense that the process by which the reader comes to understand it, changing his viewpoint and coming to terms with certain muddles and disappointments, is the political statement itself. It is this, above all, which gives the novel its extraordinary impression of density, solidity, which can only come from a large theme which finds its appropriate form. Maturity of outlook and originality of technique are perfectly matched. Had Conrad written nothing else his place would be assured. When we add to it **'Heart of Darkness'**, *The Secret Agent*, *Lord Jim* and half a dozen other works we recognize a body of work which makes all but a handful of other English novelists look superficial. (p. 136)

> *Douglas Hewitt, in his* Conrad: A Reassessment *(© 1975 Douglas Hewitt), third edition, Rowman and Littlefield, 1975, 142 p.*

ROBERT SCHULTZ (essay date 1981)

In *The Secret Agent*, Conrad penetrates London's gloom to give us a view of it from the inside. On a bright morning, the smog—which we have seen from the outside as a dark, brooding cloud—simply diffuses the sunlight so that nothing has a shadow and everything is tinged with a rich, gold, rusty color. In the book's first scene, this is the light by which Mr. Verloc considers the city's "opulence and luxury" which his efforts as a secret agent are supposed to protect. (pp. 218-19)

[We] will soon find out that, morally speaking, London has many shadows, and that many of its evils arise from the fact that the city's golden lustre of wealth and ease does not shine upon all its inhabitants.

Veroc watches the rich in the park and considers with satisfaction that the need to protect their ease insures his own. . . . Conrad's contempt for the "hygienic idleness" of the upper classes is matched by his disgust for the parasitic sloth of the revolutionists that he introduces a few pages later. . . . In Conrad's vision of society, the laziness of the revolutionists and the idleness of the upper classes mirror each other.

The mirroring of society's opposing factions is carried on throughout the book, and it has the effect of denying Conrad's readers the comfort of sitting back in complacent scorn for the revolutionary underworld. Some of that scorn inevitably reflects back upon the "respectable" social establishment. Conrad's description of the reciprocal relationship between society and its discontents extends whatever blame we may lay upon one group throughout the entire social organism. Clashing groups are in secret cooperation: the terms of their conflict are defined by shared conventions perhaps neither is fully conscious of. To Inspector Heat, though he is "not insensible to the gravity of moral differences," the idea of thieving seems as normal as the idea of property. "It was a form of human industry, perverse indeed, but still an industry exercised in an industrious world." . . . Policemen and burglars are "products of the same machine." The effect of this perception is to broaden whatever moral judgment we may pass on theft to include the "machine" which produces thieves, necessitating police. Any moral indictment must now include the entire social system which encourages the private accumulation of wealth and, therefore, encourages theft. Or it must be an indictment of human nature, in general: where there is property, there will be theft. (pp. 219-21)

A reader presented with Conrad's notion of the intimacy between society's conflicting factions will find it difficult to judge one good and the other evil. Private wealth and theft are two sides of a coin, and the conventions and restrictions required for social stability breed anarchists and revolutionaries. The former call the latter into being with a dialectic certainty. Law and lawlessness are the two heads of man's innate and monstrous depravity. This similarity between conventional society and its enemies is made explicit by the book's crowning irony: it is a highly conservative European government that actually perpetrates the bombing of the Greenwich observatory, in order to provoke a backlash of repression.

Only the Professor completely shares Conrad's perception of the interdependence of opposing forces. And so he has chosen to disengage himself completely from the entanglements of life, and even from the hidden alliances of opposition, by siding completely with death. In wiring himself with explosives and resolving to blow himself up along with his assailants at the first serious challenge, he achieves a form of independence. He can be eliminated, but it would be his own choice, and his final act would be in perfect accord with his insane ideology. His "program" is absolute negativity; he is the perfect anarchist. (pp. 221-22)

Though the Professor is perhaps the most purely repellent character in *The Secret Agent,* his knowledge brings him into a surprisingly close relationship with the story's narrator. He is the only character who shares Conrad's understanding that legal society and its challengers are interdependent institutions within a single corrupt social body, and his decision to stand alone as a purely destructive force gives him an independence analogous to that of the narrator. Turning this analogy around and reflecting it back upon the narrator, himself, we can ask whether Conrad's picture of society and his prevailing tone of contempt make his voice in this book a purely destructive force, as well. (pp. 222-23)

Is there anything in [the book] for a reader to affiliate himself with aside from the narrator's scorn, or are all possible positions exploded? Conrad's preface to *The Secret Agent*—written thirteen years after the book itself—displays his continued worry over the problem of how a reader is to respond to this story. Its final sentence is something like a promise, asking for the reader's trust.

> I will submit that telling Winnie Verloc's story to its anarchistic end of utter desolation, madness and despair, and telling it as I have told it here, I have not intended to commit a gratuitous outrage on the feelings of mankind. . . .

However, Conrad is defending himself against a charge few of his present readers take seriously: that the book was written merely to shock and surprise us with its ugliness. More troubling now, perhaps, is the comprehensive sweep of Conrad's scorn communicated by his ironic narration and the absolute separation that it enforces between the narrator and his fictional world. A moral condemnation of this extent, which can envision no defensible alternatives to the characters, the actions,

and the society it judges, and only lead to moral paralysis— or, in Conrad's more striking terms, to "utter desolation, madness and despair." (pp. 223-24)

In the case of *The Secret Agent,* Conrad tells us that he was inspired to write by "indignation and underlying pity and contempt." . . . He wants us to *see* the "criminal fatality" of the revolutionary and anarchistic activities that he despises as a "brazen cheat exploiting the poignant miseries and passionate credulities of a mankind always so tragically eager for self-destruction." . . . It is a noble motivation. Conrad exposed, however, much more than the revolutionaries and the anarchists—the guilt his book points out bleeds throughout the entire social fabric. And we, as readers attempting to respond to his vision, find all available ground blown out from under our feet. The experience is much like Marlow's in *Heart of Darkness* as he peers over the brink of the abyss that Kurtz has opened before him. Marlow judged Kurtz a moral hero for his direct stare into the "heart of darkness" and for his candid judgment of its horror. . . . Marlow, if he were to read *The Secret Agent,* would probably find a similar moral victory in the narrator's ruthless exposition of the depravity at the heart of man and of the institutions man constructs. (pp. 224-25)

[The reader] is drawn into a relation with Conrad like the one that develops between Marlow and Kurtz in *Heart of Darkness.* As Marlow found himself looking into the dark abyss that Kurtz had opened before him, the reader of *The Secret Agent* witnesses Conrad's plunge into civilization's "heart of darkness." As Marlow judged Kurtz's proclamation of "the horror" to be a kind of "affirmation," a "sort of belief" expressed with a terrible candor and "vibrating" with a "note of revolt," so we might judge Conrad's expression of his indignation and contempt to be a kind of moral heroism. But unless the involved reader can call upon something outside the world presented in *The Secret Agent,* his response cannot be much different from that of Marlow to Kurtz's horror.

Marlow survived—by not looking clear to the bottom of Kurtz's vision—but he is a maimed man as he narrates his experience. Marlow is haunted by his memory of Kurtz "opening his mouth voraciously, as if to devour all the earth with all its mankind." . . . Likewise, we watch, fascinated into helplessness, as Conrad, in *The Secret Agent,* swallows up everything in his vision of evil. The book is his "perfect detonator," by which he explodes an entire fictional world. And we are left in our own world, sifting rubble, searching for something that has survived the blast. (pp. 228-29)

> *Robert Schultz, "'The Secret Agent': Conrad's Perfect Detonator," in* The Midwest Quarterly *(copyright, 1981, by* The Midwest Quarterly, *Pittsburg State University), Vol. XXII, No. 3, Spring, 1981, pp. 218-29.*

ADDITIONAL BIBLIOGRAPHY

Baines, Jocelyn. *Joseph Conrad: A Critical Biography.* New York: McGraw-Hill, 1960, 523 p.
    Called an indispensable work by many critics. Baines includes detailed biographical material in her study of Conrad.

Conrad, John. *Joseph Conrad: Times Remembered.* New York: Cambridge University Press, 1981, 218 p.
    Reminiscences by Conrad's youngest son.

Crankshaw, Edward. *Joseph Conrad: Some Aspects of the Art of the Novel*. London: John Lane, 1936, 248 p.

Important early study of Conrad's literary artistry which treats his novels as wholly unified artistic achievements.

Geddes, Gary. *Conrad's Later Novels*. Montreal: McGill-Queen's University Press, 1980, 223 p.

Reasses Conrad's last six novels, which have been almost universally condemned. Geddes believes that critics misread these works by examining them with the same criteria used to judge Conrad's earlier psychological novels; instead, these novels should be read as a unique form of ironic romance which Conrad exploited to examine many of the concerns of his previous novels.

Karl, Frederick R. *Joseph Conrad: The Three Lives*. New York: Farrar, Straus and Giroux, 1979, 1008 p.

Most thorough biography of Conrad.

Krzyzanowski, Ludwik. *Joseph Conrad: Centennial Essays*. New York: The Polish Institute of Arts and Sciences in America, 1960, 174 p.

A collection of essays, the most interesting of which is a discussion by several prominent American writers of Conrad's influence upon American literature.

Schwarz, Daniel R. *Conrad: "Almayer's Folly" to "Under Western Eyes."* Ithaca, N.Y.: Cornell University Press, 1980, 230 p.

Treats the first fifteen years of Conrad's career as a movement from "a quest for identity" to an interest in politics. Schwarz finds Conrad to be a humanist who considered himself a perpetual outsider, yet sought to affirm "the primacy of family, the sanctity of the individual, and the importance of sympathy and understanding in human relations." Nevertheless, his novels vividly dramatize his internal conflicts between humanism and skepticism, between subjective experience and objective reality, between the desire for facts and the necessity of illusions, and between public goals and individual needs.

Stallman, R. W. *The Art of Joseph Conrad: A Critical Symposium*. East Lansing: Michigan State University Press, 1960, 354 p.

Excellent collection of essays including works by Andre Gide, Vernon Young, and Albert Guerard.

Watt, Ian. *Conrad in the Nineteenth Century*. Berkeley: University of California Press, 1979, 375 p.

Important study of the first half of Conrad's career. Watt provides excellent in-depth readings of the early novels and relates Conrad's artistic accomplishments to contemporary developments in literature and the arts.

Wiley, Paul L. *Conrad's Measure of Man*. Madison: University of Wisconsin Press, 1954, 227 p.

Discussion of Conrad's protagonists as men divided between mind and will, virtue and vice, morality and instinct.

Gabriele D'Annunzio

1863-1938

(Also spelled Gabriel or Gabbriele; also d'Annunzio) Italian novelist, playwright, poet, short story writer, and journalist.

D'Annunzio is one of modern literature's most flamboyant personalities. While the sensationalist press reported the romantic scandals of his life (including a prison sentence for adultery), literary journals criticized the moral outrages of his works (the Catholic Church placing them on its Index of Forbidden Books in 1911). Nevertheless, he was renowned in his lifetime as Italy's leading artist, a consummate stylist who combined the poetic grandeur of Dante and the classical writers with contemporary trends of naturalism, symbolism, and decadence.

Born in the small town of Pescara, Abruzzi, D'Annunzio had little opportunity for artistic development until he attended Cicognini College at Prato. While in college, he composed the poems of his first collection, *Primo vere,* and had them published at his father's expense. These lyrics displayed the linguistic virtuosity that remained D'Annunzio's most conspicuous skill. In *Intermezzo di rime* he focused on themes of decadence which glorify morbid and perverse experience in art and in life, particularly romantic life. His poetry finally evolved into a celebration of existence in the series *Laudi del cielo, del mare, della terra e degli eroi,* his highest poetic achievement. Glauco Cambon's analysis of "Assisi," a poem found in the second of the four volumes in this series, points out its representative traits of turmoil, sensual exuberance, and a glorification of nature.

D'Annunzio's early fictions in *Terra vergine* are regional tales in the naturalist tradition of Giovanni Verga, the chief author of the Italian *verismo* movement. Joseph Hergesheimer calls the short stories of peasant strife in *Le novelle della Pescara (Tales of My Native Town)* "the heroic spectacle of humanity pinned by fatality to earth but forever struggling for release." In his novels D'Annunzio was also influenced by literary movements of the late nineteenth century, from mystical symbolism to opulent decadence. His willingness to take up artistic fashions, and the ease with which he did so, is frequently criticized. *Il piacere (The Child of Pleasure)* is the ornate biography of a voluptuary in the style of such French novelists as Joris-Karl Huysmans, and *Le vergini delle rocce (The Maidens of the Rocks)* echoes French symbolists while displaying a unique D'Annunzian combination of imaginative vigor and verbal invention. *Il fuoco (The Flame of Life)* exemplifies its author's practice of using his love affairs as the basis for his fiction, in this case the account of his relationship with the celebrated actress Eleonora Duse, for whom D'Annunzio wrote a number of plays. *Il trionfo della morte (The Triumph of Death),* considered D'Annunzio's prose masterpiece, reflects the influence of Nietzsche for its grandiose tragedy and the amoralism of its superman hero.

While D'Annunzio's poetry and fiction have been criticized for their sensationalist morbidity, it is in his dramas that critics observe the highest concentration of horror. *La città morta (The Dead City),* one of the earliest plays, is derogated by Frank Moore for offending "not our morals but our taste" with its

Culver Pictures

display of eye-gouging, decapitation, and incest. R. Hastings explains that the physical and moral atrocities of the plays, the "orgiastic" experiences, are designed as a catharsis for the audience in the manner of Greek theater. D'Annunzio's dramas are nonetheless esteemed for their tragic beauty, with *La figlia de Iorio (The Daughter of Jorio)* usually called his best work in this genre. In his essay on *La gioconda,* Francis Thompson neatly illustrates the critical ambivalence toward D'Annunzio's work, objecting to the morality of "this excessively self-conscious Latin decadent" while praising the "imagination and form" of his art.

Besides enjoying an extremely successful literary career, D'Annunzio was an important figure in public life. He served in the army and air force and as a deputy in the Italian Parliament. During the First World War he distinguished himself with notable feats of heroism, and his speeches were instrumental in persuading Italy to join the war on the side of the Allies. He is occasionally referred to as a proponent of Italian Fascist ideology, though his biographers point out that in practice Mussolini and D'Annunzio had little use for each other's politics. By the end of his life D'Annunzio had amassed an estate of considerable wealth. He had also created a body of

writings that is valued for its linguistic beauty and imaginative extravagance.

PRINCIPAL WORKS

Primo vere (poetry) 1879
Terra vergine (short stories) 1882
Intermezzo di rime (poetry) 1883
Il libro delle vergini (short stories) 1884
Il piacere (novel) 1889
  [*The Child of Pleasure*, 1898]
La chimera (poetry) 1890
Giovanni Episcopo (novel) 1892
  [*Episcopo and Company*, 1896]
L'innocente (novel) 1892
  [*The Intruder*, 1898]
Il trionfo della morte (novel) 1894
  [*The Triumph of Death*, 1896]
Le vergini delle rocce (novel) 1896
  [*The Maidens of the Rocks*, 1898]
La città morta (drama) 1898
  [*The Dead City*, 1902]
La gioconda (drama) 1899
  [*La Gioconda*, 1901]
Il fuoco (novel) 1900
  [*The Flame of Life*, 1900]
Francesca da Rimini (drama) 1901
  [*Francesca da Rimini*, 1902]
Le novelle della Pescara (short stories) 1902
  [*Tales of My Native Town*, 1902]
*Maia (poetry) 1903
*Alcione (poetry) 1904
  [*Alcyone*, 1978]
*Elletra (poetry) 1904
La figlia de Iorio (drama) 1904
  [*The Daughter of Jorio*, 1907]
Forse che sì forse che no (novel) 1910
Le martyre de Saint-Sébastien (drama) 1911
Contemplazione della morte (meditations) 1912
*Merope (poetry) 1912
Notturno (meditations) 1921

*These four collections comprise the series *Laudi del cielo, del mare, della terra e degli eroi.*

EUGENE BENSON (essay date 1896)

[With] our modern literature there comes in a new element, pagan, chivalric, refined; the worship of woman, the cult of beauty. The most brilliant examples of it are still Italian. And it is not only the woman, but the lady, who is enthroned in the new art.

The new prose and the new romance are the work of Italy's new poet, Gabriele d'Annunzio, who, in *le Vergine delle Rocce,* seeks to make prose do all that poetry has done, that is, yield itself to every breath of emotion, pliant to every sensation. He would make it like Shelley's verse. And it is claimed that he has enlarged the domain of language. The uses to which he has put his prose imply a less trammelled life than that which our moralists accept. His style is the result of an unfailing sense of beauty, of a passion for, and power to express life,

without which it would be but a wordy and incontinent thing, flaccid, nerveless, swollen, ineffective and fatiguing. (p. 286)

Vividly as [d'Annunzio's characters] are presented [in *le Vergine delle Rocce*] there is little of the shock of action; the dramatic movement is so suave, it is as though they came and went according to some rhythmic law, to the sound of music, graceful, harmonious, beautiful. There is an air of high breeding, of melancholy, of reserve, as in Poe's *Ligeia*, as in his *Fall of the House of Usher;* there is the sense of latent passion, of malady, of mysterious destiny; but the reader is kept this side of the dangerous edge of circumstance; reflection takes the place of action. One follows their personal life at intervals not only to be led by curiosity to know their fortunes but to get the most brilliant expression of a beautiful mind. For the obvious sense of the hero's situation, involving his choice of a wife, has yet a richer interest. The writer touches the profoundest elements of life with such high Italian dignity and grace that he is never betrayed into anything unworthy his fine art, and he shows complete deliverance from the rank company of realism; he is poetic; his work is a work of art, as art has been understood in Italy before it was infected with the baser things of its decadence. (p. 288)

We wonder that a writer of the highest artistic gifts deals with diseased and degenerate types, showing the same fevour and interest that he does when he deals with health and beauty. Under the pretext of science or truth, he serves a bad turn to art; he confounds beauty and the normal life with all life; affects to be god-like, superior to matter, and handles the unclean and the clean, forgetting that the first business of the man and the artist is to discriminate between good and bad. The error of not choosing the better part will correct, or rather it has corrected itself, since the writer has turned from the romance of the street to the romance of the garden.

It is in d'Annunzio's new romance that we see his choice is determined by a higher ideal of life than in his former prose, that the things not nice of realism are abandoned, left buried with the *débris* of their day; their corruption dooms them to be forgotten. Pestiferous literature has short lease of life. If one goes to *L'Innocente* and *Giovanni Episcopo* to learn more about d'Annunzio, one is in danger of taking his exuberant fiction for fact. They but show the rank "dressing" of his former days. Most readers stop at that, unmindful of, or without seeing, the perfect flowers of beauty grown out of it. It is true that the heroes of his earlier romances are not only slaves to animal functions, but they are more dangerous than animals: they are fatal to the very women they love; they have the taint and the action of madness. They are not so aspiring as Milton's lion "pawing to get free his hinder parts"; at the best they are but like dolphins showing their backs above the element they delight in; they have no more moral sense than a water snake; they have something of Borgia, of Cellini, of Aretino, of Casanova; they are stiffening and repugnant to our sense of rectitude, for they illustrate not rectitude but excess. The experiences d'Annunzio has written of, with consummate gifts of expression, in *L'Innocente* and in *Giovanni Episcopo,* are usually confined to clandestine books, and are seldom presented in literature, seldom invested with art, at least outside France and Italy. To match it you must go to that native of Roman Gaul, the satirist of Nero, who alone is rivalled by the later Pagan, feeling responsible not for the story he tells, but for how he tells it, and determined to tell it in all its details with unmitigated truth. He shows the utmost unconcern as to what you may think of it. You have the right to say you do not like his choice of subject. (pp. 291-93)

D'Annunzio's phrase as a prose writer is supple and opulent: his word is vivid; his feeling intense; he is alway serious. He lacks playfulness. Without a sense of humour, seldom or never with the purpose of a humourist, without the sport of wit, he yet holds one fascinated by his word as he tells his tale; while he tells it he charms one with the music, the splendour, the colour and the grace of his language, and one wonders at the sustained flow and harmony of his periods. The secret of his style is that it is ever informed by an imaginative mind, shaped by a never failing sense of art. He seems denied lordship over laughter and tears. *That* belongs to the poet, and the dramatist, and the story-teller of simpler aims and humbler sympathies than the aristocratic and fastidious artist. He is like a musician who writes—the melodious element prevails; he is like a painter who paints—colour prevails; he is like a worker in marble or metal—form prevails. He is a writer who, like George Sand, like [Theophile] Gautier, like [Charles Algernon] Swinburne, has measureless power and a supreme sense of beauty to express his sense of life and art. Individual and intense, he looked isolated, like [Charles] Baudelaire, with questionable tendencies and preferences. He seems to have escaped the abasement of the unclean, stained, but not transformed by the thing he worked in when dealing with the baser experiences of life. (pp. 293-94)

> Eugene Benson, "*Gabriele d'Annunzio: The New Poet and His Work,*" *in* The Yellow Book, *Vol. XI, October, 1896, pp. 284-99.*

ARTHUR SYMONS (essay date 1898)

D'Annunzio comes to remind us, very definitely, as only an Italian can, of the reality and the beauty of sensation, of the primary sensations; the sensations of pain and pleasure as these come to us from our actual physical conditions; the sensation of beauty as it comes to us from the sight of our eyes and the tasting of our several senses; the sensation of love, coming up from a root in Boccaccio, through the stem of Petrarch, to the very flower of Dante. And so he becomes the idealist of material things, while seeming to materialise spiritual things. He accepts, as no one else of our time does, the whole physical basis of life, the spirit which can be known only through the body, the body which is but clay in the shaping or destroying hands of the spirit. And, in spite of a certain affectation of ideas, not always quite happily selected from Nietzsche and others, he takes nature very simply, getting sheer away from civilisation in his bodily consciousness of things, which he apprehends as directly, with however much added subtlety, as a peasant of his own Abruzzi. (p. vi)

[D'Annunzio] has shown us the working of the one universal, overwhelming, and transfiguring passion, with a vehement patience, and with a complete disregard of consequences, of the moral prejudice. To him, as to the men of the Renaissance, moral qualities are variable things, to be judged only by aesthetic rules. Is an action beautiful, has it that intensity which, in the stricter sense, is virtue? Other considerations may, if you please, come afterwards, but these are the essential. For to d'Annunzio life is but a segment of art, and aesthetic living the most important thing for the artist who is not merely an artist in words, or canvas, or marble, but an artist in life itself. These passionate and feeble and wilful people of his are at least trying to come near such an ideal. Not every one can become the artist of his own life, or can have either the courage or the consistency to go on his own way, to his own end. It

is needless to moralise against such an intention. Few will attain it.

It is but in the natural process of a deduction from these principles that d'Annunzio chooses to concern himself, in his novels, with temperament, not with either character or society. His novels are states of mind, sometimes, as in *Le Vergini delle Rocce,* not leading to any conclusion; and these states of mind interest him supremely, for their own sake, and not for the sake of any conclusion to which they may lead. We should not recognise one of his persons if we met him in the street; but his jealousy, or his corrupt love of art, or his self-pity, will seem to us part of ourselves, seen in a singular kind of mirror, if we have ever been sincere enough with ourselves to recognise an obscure likeness when we see it. The great exterior novels, we may well believe, have been written; the inter-action of man upon man has been at least sufficiently described; what remains, eternally interesting, eternally new, is man, the hidden, inner self which sits silent through all our conversation, and may sit blind to its own presence there, not daring to find itself interesting. (pp. viii-ix)

[With] d'Annunzio it is important to remember, that he was a poet long before he ever wrote novels, and that his novels, as he gets more and more mastery over his own form, become more and more of the nature of poetry. His early stories were crude, violent, done after the French models of that day; the man himself coming out in them only in the direct touch, there already, on physical pain, more than on physical pleasure. But with *Il Piacere* he has begun, a little uncertainly, to mould a form of his own, taking the hint, not only from some better French models, but also from an Englishman, [Walter] Pater. There is still much that is conventional and unskilful in a book which, it must be remembered, was written at the age of twenty-five; but how it suggests, already, the free form of the *Trionfo della Morte* and *Le Vergini delle Rocce*! how the imaginative feeling of the descriptions of Rome struggles with the scraps of tedious conversation between 'golden' young men at the club or on the course! It is the book of youth, and has the over-plenitude of that prosperous age. *L'Innocente,* which shows a new influence, the Russian intimacy of Tolstoi and Dostoievsky, deviates in form, but narrows the interest of the action still tighter about two lonely figures, seeming to be cut off from the world by some invisible, impassable line. In the *Trionfo della Morte* form, subject, are both found. This study in the psychology of passion is a book scarcely to be read without terror, so insinuatingly does it show the growth, change, and slowly absorbing dominion of the flesh over the flesh, of the flesh over the soul. (pp. x-xi)

Le Vergini delle Rocce begins with a discourse, and ends as a poem. Here there is not even so much of plot as the mere progression of states of mind to an arresting conclusion. The action, when it can once be said to begin, remains at the same point to the end. A marvellous sensation is given, but it is as if a picture found words. . . . (p. xii)

> Arthur Symons, *in his introduction to* The Child of Pleasure *by Gabriele D'Annunzio, translated by Georgina Harding, William Heinemann Ltd., 1898, pp. v-xii.*

FRANCIS THOMPSON (essay date 1901)

To the plain man, the man who hates all affectations, poses, and exotics, the man who remembers the perfect sincerity and straight-forwardness of the classic masterpieces, there is something disconcerting, if not actually repellent, in the first glimpses of [*Gioconda*]. It seems to be deliberately unusual, it seems wantonly to annoy that precious instinct of common sense and social decency which always prevents the man of right reason from appearing too conspicuously different from his fellows. The dedication runs: "For Eleanora Duse of the beautiful hands." Why for, instead of to? Why of the beautiful hands? Is it entirely correct thus publicly to particularise the charms of a woman whom one admires? Why Eleanora Duse at all—after the singular, the unspeakable portrait of La Foscarina in the author's novel *Il Fuoco*? The stage directions begin: "A quiet foursquare room, in which the arrangement of everything indicates a search after a singular harmony, revealing the secret of a profound correspondence between the visible lines and the quality of the inhabiting mind that has chosen and loved them. . . . Two large windows are open on the garden beneath; through one of them can be seen, rising against the placid fields of the sky, the little hill of San Miniato. . . and the church of the Cronaca, 'la Bella Villanella,' the purest vessel of Franciscan simplicity." The plain man naturally exclaims: "Secret of a profound fiddlestick!" He thinks of Bedford Park, minor magazines of high culture, and all Artiness and Craftiness. He stolidly objects to the commingling of architectural criticism with instructions to a stage-carpenter; there is a time for all things, and he is well assured that D'Annunzio has chosen the wrong moment to inform him that a certain church is the purest vessel of Franciscan simplicity. In one word, one word at once vulgar and unavoidable—Rubbish! (pp. 268-69)

We do not wish to lay too much stress on the lesser phenomena of D'Annunzio's productions. But these dedications, these solemn asides, and a thousand other trifles in his plays and his novels, do really point to the gravest defect of his individuality—namely, the tendency to magnify Art—with the majuscule—at the expense of all else, to pretend that nothing is worth aught save artistic beauty and the ability to perceive the same, and finally to go about beneath a banner with the legend: "Watch me, I am an artist, not a man." The fact is, D'Annunzio is as foolishly sentimental about Art as your English novelist is about Love. He can't talk about anything else. He has got it on the brain. He is a creature of one idea.

And having so vented our English spleen against the antics of this excessively self-conscious Latin decadent, we are at liberty to say with all heartiness that, in the essential qualities of imagination and of form, *Gioconda* is an extremely fine play—nearly fine enough to crush the prejudice which it arouses. Of course it is preoccupied with Art, and of course the hero is an artist. These things must be, with D'Annunzio. Lucio Settala is a sculptor, and at the beginning of the piece we find him recovering from an attempt to commit suicide. Lucio was hopelessly divided in his allegiance between two women, his wife, Silvia, and Gioconda, the woman whom the artist in him loved. He sought death as an escape, but failed. (p. 270)

The moral which D'Annunzio would have us draw is, no doubt, that Silvia's sacrifice and ruin were part of the tribute which omnipotent art may rightfully demand from life. . . . But we are well aware, and every plain person is well aware, that such a moral is absolutely wrong. No beauty and no force can give authority to the antique pretence that the artist, alone of all men, may obey "his own law" in "exceeding the laws of right." D'Annunzio's play is of "the present time." It is meant for spiritual realism of to-day. But strip off the embroidery of beauty, the verbal charm; forget the dramatic appeal; remove the scene from "Florence and the coast of Pisa" to London.

Put the house in Redcliff-square and the studio in the Boltons. Conceive the actual trio of people; conjure up the very circumstances; and then dare to say that Lucio was not either a scoundrel or a coward, or perhaps both. The moral position is untenable, and if D'Annunzio were fifty times D'Annunzio, he could not hold it against the attack of the simplest soul that lives. D'Annunzio is an extraordinary artist; he can do everything except the impossible; but that he cannot do. And so *Giocanda* remains a fairytale, unconvincing as a fairytale, vicious and handsome. (p. 273)

Francis Thompson, "The Claim of the Artist" (originally published in The Academy, *Vol. 61, No. 1536, October 12, 1901), in his* The Real Robert Louis Stevenson and Other Critical Essays, *edited by Rev. Terence L. Connolly, S.J. (copyright © 1959 by University Publishers Incorporated), University Publishers, 1959, pp. 268-73.*

H. D. SEDGWICK, JR. (essay date 1903)

It is not easy for an American, bred in the habits, notions, and prejudices which we call Anglo-Saxon education, to be just to d'Annunzio, even as a poet; for we are almost sure to approach his poetry through his novels, and these revolt all our natural sentiments. We are separated from him by the gulf of race. Even his virtues, in great part, are beyond our sympathies; for we, on our side, do not belong to the *gentil sangue Latin*, nor do we understand d'Annunzio's most sincere, most praiseworthy trait,—the conscience of the artist, a conscience as imperious, as self-sufficient, as disdainful as that of the Puritans.

To d'Annunzio himself, his aim is spiritual; yet to say in English that d'Annuzio labors for the spiritual life is to impose a strange burden upon those already heavily laden words. His understanding of the spirit is different from ours; Americans are prone to separate the spiritual from the intellectual, d'Annunzio is inclined to confound the two. He aims to enfranchise the intellect, to rescue it from the bonds of an ignorant social order, to enlarge the horizon of men by poetry. For him, intellectual exploitation of the senses is spiritual, it is man's highest life; and the expression of that intellectual enjoyment is poetry. He is a great artist; he has propriety, order, gradation, harmony, in word and thought; instinctively he shudders at formlessness. He is not inspired; he is the product of modern culture, not a natural force expressing itself under the ordinary impulses of life. He has lived more on other men's thoughts than on his own; a careful perusal of his books shows the periods in which different masters were in the ascendant. He has not the power of assimilation, that predatory habit of happy genius bestowed upon a Raphael or a Keats; on the contrary, his very lack of capacity to force the ideas and methods of other men to deny their creators, as it were, and serve him, marks the limit of his genius. Nevertheless he has a clever knack of cribbing. (pp. 7-8)

A lyric poet is, and must be, exaggeratedly personal in his relations to us. . . . With d'Annunzio, it is not so. From the first, we feel in our bones that he cannot be *our* poet. . . .

Whether he is our poet or not, his is a very interesting personality. Behind his sensuous descriptions is not feeling, but intellect; behind his intellect is not genius, but a Roman will, which joins with his ambition in high resolve to achieve a new life for Italy, and wills to use poetry as its instrument. Nevertheless, will and intellect, applied to lyrical talents, will not, without the addition of experience, turn a poet into a play-wright; and in d'Annunzio's plays we miss experience of the stage. He should have been apprenticed to a scene-shifter, cursed by the stage-manager, bullied by the second lady, and thus have acquired the lore of stage-craft. No genius can supply the lack of long familiarity with the stage. Of such knowledge the novelist, who desires to become a playwright, and more than all others the psychological novelist, stands in especial need: in the drama, living actors are the medium of expression; in story-telling, printer's ink,—and the difference is immense.

Among the defects of d'Annunzio's novels are intense subjectiveness, narrowness of human interest, and an indefatigable prolixity. The same defects hurt his plays; but the exigencies of the stage have helped him; they limit, if they cannot abolish, the author's soliloquies, and they discourage prolixity. His earlier plays, *La Gioconda* and *Città Morta,* mark the period of his apprenticeship. (p. 8)

In [*La Gioconda*] d'Annunzio has chosen the tragic and ethical theme that a man cannot serve two masters; but in his endeavor to portray an ethical situation he has only succeeded at the expense of human interest. The two women who struggle for the artist's soul are but two conflicting moral principles, and nobody cares what becomes of the soul.

La Città Morta ("The Dead City") is a play of greater ambition. D'Annunzio has attempted what he perhaps would call a younger sister to the Attic dramas; he has taken what he believes to be a Greek theme, and in order to strengthen his situation he has laid the scene near Mycenae. The characters are a poet, his blind wife and a brother and sister engaged in excavating the tombs of Agamemnon and Cassandra. Both husband and brother fall in love with the sister; there is no action; the brother, overcome by horror at his own love, and not untouched with jealousy, drowns his sister. The horror of the plot is dulled by prolixity, and by the lack of human interest in the characters (dreams of a morbid scholar), who spend their immense leisure in talking of the Antigone, of Cassandra, of the plains of Argos and the gulf of Corinth, not for the menial purpose of carrying forward the plot, but to awake a chill sense of the past, and to recall the cold presence of the long dead.

Tragedy requires some unreality; it requires isolation from daily life, whose unheroic little needs comfort humanity and spoil tragedy; but the strained quality of d'Annunzio does not transport us into the heroic unreality of Attic tragedy, it only carries us into a breezeless atmosphere of morbid psychology. The play is a mere study of abnormal psychic conditions, too abnormal for general interest, too subjective for the stage. . . . (pp. 8-9)

> *H. D. Sedgwick, Jr., "D'Annunzio, Poet and Play-wright," in* The Dial, *Vol. XXXIV, No. 397, January 1, 1903, pp. 7-10.*

FRANK MOORE COLBY   (essay date 1904)

[D'Annunzio] seems a monotonous and unsmiling young man of restricted interests, who, failing in the effects of art, falls back upon the merely horrible. With murder or mutilation or incest in the wind, you will stay on to the end, and there is never a moment when it is not in the wind. Portents and premonitions, fever fits and chills keep the doom incessantly impending, and the unfortunate characters are not human beings at all, but merely foregone conclusions. It fixes the attention as surely as the gong of an ambulance. It is the interest of

deferred brutality, the common device of those who seek a short cut to strong writing, for people will often confound the sources of their emotion and define a primitive animal zest in complicated art terms. . . . In the *Dead City* the fictitious element of mere ghastliness is so nearly the whole thing that there is nothing left for art to do. In this uninspired following of the *Oedipus,* ancient Greek seemliness gives way to modern Latin unreserve, and Nemesis becomes a buzzard, and a little man bustles officiously among horrors which only a genius could discreetly deal with.

The offence of the plays is not in their subjects but in their methods, and the offended part of us is not our morals but our taste. The irksome continuity of the passions, the fewness and fixity of the ideas, the unauthenticated emotions, the fatal absence of humor leave us with the sense of humanity unrealized and a world shut out. While there are afflicted people like those in the *Dead City,* it is cheerful to think that there are at least sanitariums with kind attendants and capable house physicians, and that one encounters them singly in the outside world, never a whole troop of them at once. D'Annunzio measures tragedy by the mere bulk of suffering. If murder is to be done in the end, he sprinkles blood in the first act, gouges out an eye in the second, cuts off a head in the third. He supplements adultery by the amputation of a woman's hands, and enhances incest by a most pathetic case of total blindness and a final drowning scene. Not that this is the whole story. There is symbolism, and there are the Herculean efforts of a minor poet to rise to the height of his great argument. And it is well known that minor poetry is of all things the most perishable. Truth may traverse many languages and laughter may drift around the world, but minor poetry dies on the frontier of its own barnyard. It is a field of endeavor wherein the taste of the words makes all the difference. But Ibsen can hold up his head in English, and so can Sudermann, and it is hard to believe that d'Annunzio, as a playwright, would so ignominiously disappear if there had been more of him to start with. (pp. 134-37)

> *Frank Moore Colby, "On Certain 'Problem' Plays," in his* Imaginary Obligations *(copyright, 1904 by Dodd, Mead and Company), Dodd, Mead & Company, 1904 (and reprinted by Dodd, Mead, 1913), pp. 134-44.**

PIETRO ISOLA   (essay date 1907)

D'Annunzio has surely given [Italians] a new language and a new impetus. He has reaffirmed our national conscience. He has revealed all the potency, the glow, the color, the life, and the heretofore almost unknown beauties of our tongue. For years we have been servile imitators of our neighbors; we have gorged ourselves with Gallicisms, not deeming our language capable of expressing all that others could express. D'Annunzio has changed all that. He has given us immeasurable power. He stands to-day as our great Stylist. He has felt and feels the civic dignity of the writer—'no longer to be considered as the subtile ornament of an industrious, laborious civilization, but as the first among its citizens; as the highest example of the product of a people; as the interpreter, the witness, and the messenger of his time.' . . .

Notwithstanding his defects, and they are many and grave, let us give him due credit; let us be unstinted in the praise he deserves; if we cannot offer him all the love and admiration we should like to bestow upon a noble man and leader, we must hail him as a great factor in our contemporary literature. He has given us a greater prose, he has, as he promised, rehabilitated and dignified our narrative and descriptive prose; he has given us unsurpassable poetic gems; he has commanded attention and admiration by a branch of art of which we knew little,—dramatic art. . . . (p. 488)

In his art D'Annunzio has been very versatile; delightfully eclectic, he has been realist, psychologist, symbolist, mystic. He has learned much of all writers; Doumic, Mendes, Rabusson, Maupassant, Baudelaire, Rossetti, Tolstoy, and others among the Russians. In style and defects he seems to have a strong affinity with Théophile Gautier. He has, in fact, been called a Frenchman writing in Italian, but what Italian! By some he has been called an imitator, by others a plagiarist. These of course are the accusations *'a la mode du jour.'* He has too much individuality to be an imitator. . . . He lacks originality, and in **'Piacere'** Andre Sperelli shows this point very clearly, when D'Annunzio makes him say: 'Almost always before beginning to write he needed a certain musical intonation coming to him from some other poet, and he usually sought it among the old Tuscans; an hemistich by Lapo Gianni or Cavalcanti or Cino Petrarch or Lorenzo; a note; a *La* as a foundation for his first harmony.' That is also what D'Annunzio needs, which, let us admit, is very far from imitation. No one accuses Raphael of imitation or plagiarism, yet even in his greatness he needed similar intonation. It is what takes place within; the transformation wrought by genius that renders the work original. D'Annunzio is Italian, his land is of the Abruzzi, and he is himself: therefore, the pollen gathered among the flowers of Italian or European literature could only bring forth blossom with special characteristics and coloring. (p. 489)

I have already remarked that D'Annunzio lacks originality or inventiveness. And we find no plot in any of his stories.

In **'Piacere'** we have simply a large canvas upon which the artist has drawn one salient figure and two accessory ones. Andrea Sperelli, a most sensuous, abject being; Donna Elena Muti, a perverse, sensuous, handsome creature; Donna Maria Fleres, a woman of high ideals and culture, soon to fall in the mire at the feet of Andrea. (p. 491)

In his preface [to **'Piacere'**] D'Annunzio told us that there was only one study for him, only one object, Life! Is it Life he gives us? When bitterly attacked by his critics, he asserted, and most impudently, that in Andrea he had portrayed the ideal type of a Roman nobleman of the nineteenth century. That is false, of course. Art does not recognize classes in Italy. There may have been one such man in Rome as there is but one D'Annunzio, but no more. I say one D'Annunzio, because, notwithstanding all his platitudes about depravity and duplicity, he portrays with so much spirit, with so much minuteness, he lingers on the character with so much gusto that we are compelled to realize that in the mind of the writer Andrea is not half bad. All the moral baseness, all the moral stench and soul putrefaction of the profligate Andrea is put into language that is as beautiful and limpid as the mountain springs and as sweet and fragrant as the violets and roses of our hills. That is not Art, because it is not art to give us what is abnormal and solitary, as representative, beautiful life. Therein is contained the immorality of the book; it is not the erotic element it contains that renders it immoral, but what is false, the creation of a neurotic mind. (p. 493)

[In the preface to the **'Trionfo della Morte'**] we find explained what use he will make of observation, life, and method. It is his aim, he says, to enrich the vocabulary of our language, to fit the word to the meaning, and to re-establish the narrative

and descriptive prose of Italy. Here he has triumphed. Universal verdict accords him that honor. Brunetière pronounced **'Trionfo'** a work unsurpassed by any of the naturalistic school. With no plot whatever, but on the usual broad canvas, the figure of Giorgio Aurispa is put before us. There is nothing to be learned from the book except how to speak and write Italian with the utmost virtuosity. The character of Giorgio is weak, unsound. It is plain that unqualifiedly inert love, impure love is the theme. That is all this author ever sees. Only once has he given us Love, and that is in **'The Daughter of Jorio.'** (p. 496)

This book abounds in beautiful descriptions, and the language is ever adequate and harmonious. All the sapiency of D'Annunzio as a psychologist does not satisfy us. Although we discover a great power of observation, the poet and literatteur ever predominate over the scientist. I should like to say that **'Trionfo'** is a great book for the sum of relevant and useful truth it reveals to us. But I cannot. I can say, however, that it reveals the great artist, and as such, no student of literature should let this book pass unread. (p. 500)

Pietro Isola, "Gabiele D'Annunzio," in Poet Lore, Vol. XVIII, No. IV, Winter, 1907, pp. 487-500.

JOSEPH HERGESHEIMER (essay date 1920)

The attitude of mind necessary to a complete enjoyment of the tales in [**"Tales of My Native Town"**] must first spring from the realisation that, as stories, they are as different from our own short imaginative fiction as the town of Pescara, on the Adriatic Sea, is different from Marblehead in Massachusetts. It is true that fundamentally the motives of creative writing, at least in the Western Hemisphere, are practically everywhere alike; they are what might be called the primary emotions, hatred and envy, love and cruelty, lust, purity and courage. There are others, but these are sufficient: and an analysis of **The Downfall of Candia** together with any considerable story native to the United States would disclose a similar genesis.

But men are not so much united by the deeper bonds of a common humanity as they are separated by the superficial aspects and prejudices of society. The New England town and Pescara, at heart very much the same, are far apart in the overwhelming trivialities of civilisation, and Signor D'Annunzio's tales, read in a local state of being, might as well have remained untranslated. But this difference, of course, lies in the writer, not in his material; and Gabriele D'Annunzio is the special and peculiar product of modern Italy.

No other country, no other history, would have given birth to a genius made up of such contending and utterly opposed qualities: it is exactly as if all the small principalities that were Italy before the Risorgemento, all the amazing contradictions of stark heroics and depraved nepotism, the fanaticism and black blood and superstition, with the introspective and febrile weariness of a very old land, were bound into D'Annunzio's being.

Not only is this true of the country and of the man, the difference noted, it particularly includes the writing itself. And exactly here is the difficulty which, above all others, must be overcome if pleasure is to result from **"Tales of My Native Town."** These are not stories at all, in the sense of an individual coherent action with the stirring properties of a plot. The interest is not cunningly seized upon and stimulated and baffled up to a satisfactory finale. The formula that constitutes the base of practically every applauded story here—a determination opposed to hopeless odds but invariably triumphant—is not only missing from **"Tales of My Native Town,"** in the majority of cases it is controverted. For the greater part man is the victim of inimical powers, both within him and about; and fate, or rather circumstance, is too heavy for the defiance of any individual.

What, actually, has happened is that D'Annunzio has not disentangled these coherent fragments from the mass of life. He has not lifted his tales into the crystallised isolation of a short story: they merge from the beginning and beyond the end into the general confusion of existence, they are moments, significantly tragic or humorous, selected from the whole incomprehensible sweep of a vastly larger work, and presented as naturally as possible. However, they are not without form, in reality these tales are woven with an infinite delicacy, an art, like all art, essentially artificial. But a definite interest in them, the sense of their beauty, must rise from an intrinsic interest in the greater affair of being. It is useless for anyone not impressed with the beauty of sheer living as a spectacle to read **"Tales of My Native Town."** (pp. vii-ix)

[In] **"Tales of My Native Town"** erotic gestures and thoughts, libidinous whispers, play their inevitable devastating part.

Yet this is not a book devoted to such impulses; one tale only, although in many ways that is the best, has as its motive lust. It is rather in the amazingly direct treatment of disease, of physical abnormality, that it will be disturbing to the unprepared reader from an entirely different and less admirable, or, at any rate, less honest, convention. Undoubtedly D'Annunzio's unsparing revelation of human deformity and ills will seem morbid to the unaccustomed mind; but, conversely, it can be urged that the dread of these details is in itself morbid. (pp. x-xi)

Such horror as exists here is the result of D'Annunzio's sensitive recognition of the weight of poverty and superstition crushing men into unspeakable fatalities of the flesh. A caustic humour, as well, illuminates the darker pits of existence, ironic rather than satirical, bitter rather than fatalistic; and then admirably exposing the rough play of countrymen like the rough wine of their Province. In addition there is always, for reassurance, the inclusion of the simple bravery that in itself leavens both life and books with hope.

Yet, with the attention directed so exclusively upon national differences, equally it must be said that no individual has ever written into literature a more minute examination of actuality than that in **"Tales of My Native Town."** Indeed, to find its counterpart it would be necessary to turn to the relentlessly veracious paintings of the early Dutchmen, or the anatomical canvasses of El Greco. D'Annunzio's descriptions of countenances are dermatological, the smallest pores are carefully traced, the shape and hue and colour of every feature. (p. xii)

Tales and stories exist as a source of pleasure, but men take their pleasures with a difference; and for any who are moved by the heroic spectacle of humanity pinned by fatality to earth but forever struggling for release **"Tales of My Native Town"** must have a deep significance. (p. xv)

> *Joseph Hergesheimer, in his introduction to* Tales of My Native Town *by Gabriele D'Annunzio, translated by Rafael Mantellini, Doubleday, Page & Company, 1920 (and reprinted by Greenwood Press, Publishers, 1968), pp. vii-xvii.*

MICHAEL MONAHAN (essay date 1926)

No small brother of Dante is Gabriele D'Annunzio. The milk of the She Wolf is in his veins. The old terrible Latin fire glows in his heart and brain. He is the greatest living poet of his country—it may be of the whole world.

I have lately read his **"Francesca da Rimini"**. . . . Is there any English play—I do not except even the best tragedies of Shakespeare—that surpasses this in depth and intensity of passion? If there is I have no knowledge of it. The love of Romeo and Juliet seems a mere boy-and-girl flirtation compared with the fateful, flame-like, irresistible passion which leads D'Annunzio's Paolo and Francesca to their tragic end. No doubt the old play is much staled by age-long familiarity—we have seen it too often and we know the lines by heart—and Shakespeare always makes his people talk too much. The Balcony Scene is, it may be granted, the finest piece of sentimentalism ever written. On the other hand, the Tower Scene in D'Annunzio's play has, it seems to me, a more grandly conceived and intensely realized tragic value than any single episode in "Romeo and Juliet."

But making full allowance for the depreciation which time and use have visited upon Shakespeare's play, the superiority of the Italian's work, in certain respects, is still manifest. The conception of love has changed since the Elizabethans, and the modern world apprehends it as a cleaner and finer and grander thing, involving "ultimate issues" undreamed of by Shakespeare, great as was his vision. In proof of this assertion,—which I am well aware will startle many—the entire lovemaking of Paolo and Francesca may be cited. Who will deny that it is on a plane of passion far higher than Shakespeare gives us or seems to have understood—passion which, though glowing with the white fires of the Italianate imagination, still renders such an account of the soul's participation in the tragedy as you will vainly seek in Shakespeare? Read, in particular, the last scene of the play, with the speeches of the lovers before they are surprised and slain by the Lamester. (pp. 221-23)

Again I dare avow that if there be anything in English dramatic literature that will sustain an adequate comparison with D'Annunzio's tragedy of Francesca da Rimini, in the respects above noted, I am not acquainted with the work. (p. 226)

> *Michael Monahan, "The She Wolf's Milk," in his* Nemesis, *Frank-Maurice Inc., 1926, pp. 221-26.*

DOMENICO VITTORINI (essay date 1930)

Gabriele D'Annunzio marks the decadence of Naturalism. Not, indeed, a melancholy and sad decline, but one which reminds the reader of a tropical sunset: a gorgeous blood-red sky, while the earth exhales its most penetrating perfumes and passions burst forth with the violence of a volcano.

D'Annunzio derives his art from Naturalism, as evidenced by his descriptions of the minutest details, by his study of country life, and by the analysis of sensations.

In him, however, Naturalism is accompanied by an extreme aestheticism, for D'Annunzio is a highly sophisticated writer who constantly seeks the beauty of expression and of words, and sets the analysis of passion as the chief goal for his art. If we compare him with Verga, Fogazzaro, and other great contemporaries who did not take lust as an end in itself but as a means of creating spiritual contrasts and drama, D'Annunzio is a decadent.

In D'Annunzio, morality, conscience, and thought are absent, and they are replaced by the author's belief that life is wholly in the senses. This belief makes him a perfect artist in the field of sensations, but causes him also to disregard the study of regions in the human heart which lie deeper than our senses. (pp. 36-7)

D'Annunzio's first book, *Primo vere* ("Spring") . . . was written in the primitive province of Abruzzi, where he spent his youth. After wavering between themes derived from Giosuè Carducci (Neoclassicism) and from Giovanni Verga (Naturalism), D'Annunzio found his own way and resolutely followed it. Rejecting Carducci's ethical content and Verga's mystic grief, he unfalteringly proclaimed his faith in a joyous Materialism. Life became for him the exalted expression of all the senses of a youth eager to grasp it like a mellow fruit and suck with greedy lips all its richness. (p. 37)

Primo vere, an essentially lyric period, was followed by [*Terra vergine* ("Virgin Soil"), by the *Libro delle Vergini* ("Book of the Virgins"), and by *San Pantaleone* ("St. Pantaleone")], . . . three collections of short stories in which the author reveals his dionysiac sense of life by portraying peasant men and women as he saw them in the quiet country of Abruzzi. The world appears to him as pure sensuality, and he succeeds in etching out strong figures and in analyzing the primitiveness of his characters with the exactness required by Naturalism. (p. 38)

In *Le Vergini* ("The Virgins"), he analyzes the physiological life of Giuliana, a girl who is convalescing from typhus and feels life ebbing back into her veins, until she is contaminated by a repulsive cripple.

This period is to us the best of D'Annunzio's career. His characters are still human enough to be conscious of the morality or immorality of their acts. In *Nell' assenza di Lanciotto* ("During the Absence of Lanciotto"), the author says of Francesca and Gustavo, who betray the absent Lanciotto, "They avoided everything that might lead them to an introspective analysis of their conscience." This factor, conscience, disappears later on, and its elimination brings about an art which lies outside of life and humanity. There is in these short stories a freshness and spontaneity in the very description of nature which is lost altogether in the rococo pictures that weigh down his later fiction. . . .

[In *San Pantaleone*] the joyous sense of life that we have noticed gives place to an exaggerated description of the Abruzzi and to a pathological delight in bloody scenes. Men are here transformed into heroic and barbaric beings of gigantic proportions, herculean strength, and savage looks. Their deeds are naturally heroic. One of them in *L'Eroe* ("The Hero"), having had his hand crushed by the weight of a saint's statue, goes to the church and cuts off this crushed member as an offering to the patron saint. (p. 39)

[D'Annunzio's] fiction from [*Il Piacere* ("Pleasure") to *Forse che si, forse che no* ("Perhaps Yes, Perhaps No")], . . . represents a brilliant treatment of the queries: What is pleasure? What is passion? Can we find in them happiness and the goal of our existence? (p. 41)

Il Piacere remains the best of D'Annunzio's novels, for the query "What is pleasure?" instills life in the tiresome account of Sperelli's amour. There are in the book two contradictory answers. In the dedication, addressed to his dear friend, the great painter, Francesco Michetti, he proposes as an answer "the misery of pleasure." The novel itself contains, on the contrary, the glorification of it. Never had the apotheosis of pleasure been made in more glowing and glorious terms. (p. 42)

At best, D'Annunzio shows the perversity of pleasure. Misery of pleasure implies detachment from it, nausea of it, yet in the novel, Andrea Sperelli sets pleasure as the only goal of his life. . . . Thus, the theme that D'Annunzio had proposed to develop is overwhelmed by his own sensual temperament. (pp. 42-3)

As a whole, however, the novel is weak. The author has exercised his sensitiveness only on the subject of lust, which creeps into everything and dwarfs his sense of life, rendering sterile the aspirations towards a superior life, to which his characters constantly refer. (pp. 43-4)

The years 1892-1894 were very active ones in D'Annunzio's literary life, since he completed then three complex novels: [*Giovanni Piscopo, L'Innocente* ("The Innocent"), and *Il trionfo della morte* ("The Triumph of Death")]. . . . (p. 44)

In the above-mentioned novels the theme remains the same as in *Il Piacere*. D'Annunzio is still asking himself whether or not passion is the great dream and goal of life. Apparently the novelist wants to show that lust creates in us an unspeakable void. Giorgio Aurispa, in *Il trionfo della morte,* proclaims that "the true, deep, sensual communion is a sheer chimera." Yet the very insistence on this theme and the adjectives *true* and *deep* show that the author was more steeped in his subject-matter than he was in the days of *Il Piacere*. (p. 45)

Are these great novels? The inner and ideal texture of the novel is entirely lacking. Their interest rests on the pictorial skill of the writer, whether he describes the flowers of Villa Lilla and the hieratic grandeur of the sower in *L'Innocente* or the pilgrimage of Casalbordino and Wagner's symphony in *Il trionfo della morte*.

Love now appears accompanied by death, and the heroes, not finding in passion what they expect, kill their lovers while they still thirst for a deeper and more perfect passion. At this point, we notice the appearance of the thesis: Have these individuals the right to kill? (pp. 45-6)

It is at this point that there appears in his works the superman that Nietzsche had fashioned. D'Annunzio uses him as a means of giving free play to his theme of lust which can be restated thus: "Everything is permissible, provided we realize the dream of a perfect passion."

To us, by adopting the morality of the superman, D'Annunzio placed his fiction outside the realm of true and human art. We do not deny to him the right of fashioning a superman. We contend that his superman bears only the name, and that his deeds are only the complication of sexual activity, and as such we cannot accept them as exploits of a superior life.

D'Annunzio envelops the queer mixture of sensuality and grandeur in the veils of symbolism, but the only factor that stands out is the theme of his first book: sensuality.

To this stage belong the most decadent of D'Annunzio's novels: [*Le Vergini delle Rocce* ("The Maidens of the Rocks"), *Il Fuoco* ("The Flame of Life"), and *Forse che si, forse che no* ("Perhaps Yes, Perhaps No")]. . . . The author has now reached the firm belief that lust is the supreme goal of man and that we must disobey human laws and morality that try to restrain it. We cannot conceive that D'Annunzio believed such a thesis. To us, this absurd axiom is a rhetorical means of continuing the theme of the sanctity of the flesh. (pp. 46-7)

As in all of D'Annunzio's novels, the value of *Il Fuoco* rests in the finished workmanship of certain parts and not in its totality. D'Annunzio is like a skillful architect who is capable of drawing a magnificent door, a perfect window, graceful arches, and stately columns, but who cannot put them together and create a harmonious whole. The importance of *Il Fuoco* centers around the author's analysis of his artistic experience, his theories of art, his description of the beauty of Venice and of Murano. (pp. 47-8)

The truth is that D'Annunzio has excluded the human soul from the domain of his art and for this reason he can render (and he does this admirably) only the inanimate world. For this very reason, however, his characters have no psychological depth and their life is narrowed down to pure sensuality. This fact engenders tediousness and weariness in the reader, who receives great promises of Life and ultimately discovers that Life is entirely reduced to a love affair. No novel glorifies the expectation of life more than *Il Fuoco,* yet no novel exudes more slime than this, in the description of the relation between Stelio and Foscarina. (p. 48)

D'Annunzio reached the lowest point of decadence in *Forse che si, forse che no*. . . . Here incestuous love takes the place of passion, a change determined by the fact that the author has to continue to complicate his original theme if he wants to write another novel. Although full of aeroplanes and automobiles, the novel is the most rhetorical of all his works. (p. 49)

The war brought out [D'Annunzio's] love for chivalrous adventures, but did not change the man as he lives in his art. His *Notturno* ("Nocturne") . . . , not only continues, but accentuates, the aestheticism of his previous works. The author presents himself as he lies on a bed, temporarily blind and in great suffering. Memories come to him and he describes them with all the pomp and burdensome grandeur that is characteristic of him. He sees the war, air raids, a daring sea raid. From the war he wanders back to his childhood, to his mother. His inability to see whets in him the desire to contemplate all that life has to offer to our eyes. Heavy perfumes of flowers, glittering beauty of plumage, the carnage of the war, all this passes before us enveloped in the courtly prose of *Notturno* without awakening any other feeling except one of wonder at the perfect technique of the author. The fact is that the human note is completely absent from it.

If we compare this war book with the books that younger men have written inspired by the war, we shall be able to account for the adverse criticism that *Notturno* has received and shall also be able to notice the change that has taken place in the generation of today.

Critics have exaggerated the complexity of D'Annunzio's art and temperament. Both his temperament and his art become easily understood if we consider his fiction as a document showing the author's inability to break away from the formula of the days of his youth. The falseness of his life generated falsity in his art and it prevented his great talent from creating a genuine, lasting, and great work. (p. 50)

Domenico Vittorini, "Gabriele D'Annunzio," in his
The Modern Italian Novel, *University of Pennsylvania Press, 1930, pp. 36-52.*

E. M. FORSTER (essay date 1938)

Poet, hero, and cad, D'Annunzio presents a test problem to the Englishman. Byron, to whom he has been compared, was difficult enough, and was sent by us on a continental pilgrimage from which he has never returned. D'Annunzio is even more troublesome, since his poetry is more poetical than Byron's, his heroism more histrionic and his caddishness not an aristocratic freak but innate in his bones and bowels. And he has no sense of humour—the "saving grace" as we are pleased to call it. Faced by such a problem, the Englishman becomes uncritical and unjust, thinks himself profound when he castigates and acute when he is merely being nasty, refuses to admit that an ill-bred egoist can be a genius and a leader of men, and suspects shoddiness because there is no underlying moral worth. D'Annunzio, a very great southerner, is not thus to be judged. His standards are not ours, and if we ask him to sign a suburban gentlemen's agreement he will impale us contemptuously upon the point of his pen as he did President Wilson. How are we to approach him? (pp. 238-39)

His leading passion was the Renaissance passion for earthly immortality. And he knew that immortality cannot be won by talking. Effort must accompany advertisement, and as a writer, a patriot, and a lover, he worked very hard. By the time he died he had a number of books to his credit, a still larger number of mistresses, and the city of Fiume. It is no small haul. It is a substantial hostage against oblivion. So long as Italy is Italy, he will not be forgotten. He, Paderewski, and T. E. Lawrence stand out as the three artists who achieved fame as men of action during the last war period, and of the three he is the most spectacular. He will win the prize which he wanted and which he certainly deserves. (p. 239)

D'Annunzio was full of spiritual ideas, but he could not use them until he had had the good fortune to see Ida Rubinstein dancing in a ballet. Then he exclaimed, "Here are the legs of St. Sebastian for which I have been searching in vain all these years," and poetry poured from his pen. No doubt the anecdote exaggerates, still it emphasises the point that his contacts with life were sensuous and local in their character; certain gestures, certain limbs, certain spots of soil in the Abruzzi and elsewhere, served as jumping-off grounds for his art, and impelled him into orations about human destiny. Nothing he writes is profound. Yet he is never superficial, because he is excited by what he touches and sees, or hopes to touch. "We ate oranges as if they were bread." Why has this phrase, in its half-remembered Italian, lingered in my mind for nearly thirty years? It is a phrase from his drama *The Dead City,* and, placed where he placed it, it brought out the taste of the newly picked fruit and the feeling of it between the lips and the teeth; not pulp, not juice, but a unity, bread-like, divine. The characters—poor mortals, they had fallen in love as they should not—discussed such an orange amidst the aridities of Greece, and it passed as a tangible presence behind the veil of their prose, it lent importance to their fate, like the peaches and pears surrounding a Crivelli Madonna. (pp. 239-40)

[D'Annunzio] could write like music, like scents, like religion, like blood, like anything, he could sweep into the folds of his magnificent prose whatever took his fancy, and then assert it was sacred. There has been nobody like him. Fascism wisely accepted him after a little demur, and we had better do the same. We can anyhow hail him by two of the titles which he claims: poet and hero. (p. 241)

E. M. Forster, "A Whiff of D'Annunzio" (copyright 1938 by E. M. Forster; copyright 1966 by E. M. Forster; reprinted by permission of Harcourt Brace Jovanovich, Inc.; in Canada by Edward Arnold Ltd.), in his Two Cheers for Democracy *Harcourt, 1951, pp. 238-41.*

RUDOLPH ALTROCCHI (essay date 1944)

The Crusade of the Innocent (*La crociata degli Innocenti*) [is] a mystery in four acts. The very title, then, indicates religious drama, therefore to be perused in genuflectent piety. But the piety it exhales has, this time, certain libidinous admixtures. (pp. 23-4)

In all justice to the author I should say that this *immorality* play was originally composed for the movies, or rather, it was first intended to be a libretto, to be set to music by Puccini (in whom, apparently, it failed to arouse lyric inspiration), and then was arranged for the movies. (p. 30)

Now, if it were a normal piece of literature, we should first examine the form and the spirit of the finished product. Odious as the terms romanticism, realism, and other -isms are, we might feel prompted to see into which category this composition might fit. Probably it would not fit into any, for it is in a class by itself, for which we should have to invent a new -ism, possibly deliriumism or celestial leprosism. But this sort of stuff got its original nourishment from the crumbs that fell from the mad Nietzsche's table. For it was Nietzsche who nobly said : "every wicked thing, terrible, tyrannical, resembling a savage animal and a serpent, contributes to the elevation of the species man as much as its opposite." And D'Annunzio was a disciple of Nietzsche.

After having so pigeonholed this play, we should proceed to discover the source material, to appraise the poetic transformation of mere history or legend, which is the skeleton of fiction, into poetry and drama, which is the flesh added on by the artist. But since this is only a scenario, it has . . . hardly a form. The poet divides it into acts and scenes, to be sure, and here and there, intoxicated with his own scaffoldings, bursts into half a dozen lines of verse, but never does this rise above versified sketchiness or lyricized melodrama. We may let this pass, however, assuming that in movie scenario technique the poet need only suggest the effects which the producer will pictorialize. But, as I said before, we must also examine this composition as literature, for D'Annunzio's every word, he knows, *is* literature! (p. 31)

[This] is perhaps D'Annunzio's most pitiless book—and that is saying a great deal. . . . In this play, more than elsewhere in D'Annunzio's works, I feel that he lays on his brutality thickly and does it with sadistic enjoyment. It is the primitive in him and the decadent. Let us go so far as to admit that, to some extent, we are all primitive and decadent. But though few of us may have placed upon our instinctive primitiveness so rich a layer of cultural polish as has this poet, few of us also so love to uncover it, and still fewer of us are so fashioned as to find any artistic satisfaction in the interplay of such foul motifs as lechery, leprosy, and fratricide; few of us can visualize without gastric repulsion an ocean bestrewn with innumerable baby corpses. In D'Annunzio's imagination, instead, corpses are among his favorite bric-a-brac, especially bloody ones, and still more so if, before death, they are presented as richly sprinkled with diseases, and accompanied by degenerates, courtesans, homicidal maniacs and other brutally pathological cases. With most of us, thank God, a little of this goes a long way. We prefer to consider sadism as an attribute which, if present (and it does not have to be), should be squelched, instead of being flaunted. And this not for reasons of prudery alone. A morality play need no more be moral, let us grant, than a comedy comical, but for reasons of art. It does not make for artistic enjoyment; it leaves us cold, and we therefore not only cease sharing with the dramatist but are also repelled. In

this *Crusade* more than elsewhere in D'Annunzio's erratic writings, horrors are accumulated; he spares nobody, neither his characters nor his audience, not even the most defenceless of his victims, the property man. We, at least, can laugh or "take a walk"; he cannot.

In connection with humor and pity, neither of these qualities is consistent with sadistic pleasure. Sensuality and cruelty, however, are good bed comrades. Furthermore, we cannot even say that this poet is interested in the tragedy of the flesh rather than of the spirit, for even the catastrophes of the body must have, in the drama, some sort of motivation, a motivation plausible to the audience, even if mysterious to the personages involved. The audience or reader also fails to be inspired with pity for the sufferings portrayed, when these are not so plausibly motivated as to force him to share them. He sees with amazement or horror occurrences due to abnormal folly and his only reaction, to the plight of the personages, besides disgust, is: It served them right.

For all too often passion is, in D'Annunzio, more intentional, if I may say so, than consequent. It is not the inevitable result of circumstances beyond the control of the humans involved, nor the result of their normally unwise actions; rather, it is the result of the mania in pathological personages to attain abnormal pleasure, a quest which, pressed to extremes, becomes exhaustion, which in turn translates itself into bestial folly and communal disaster. Surely, in the psychological jargon of today D'Annunzio's heroes would be called, at the very least, antisocial; we used to call them, more simply, swine.

Passion impels the hero to commit a foul act; recurring waves of more passion reimpel him to recommit it or another crime, *ad nauseam,* until he is satiated; then he kills, but not himself, alas, which would be a laudable and highly deserved dénouement. No, it never occurs to D'Annunzio's profligate hero to demolish himself and thus put his dear readers out of their misery; invariably he prefers to slay an entirely innocent person, a young woman, who happened to be born lovable, or still better, a child. This repeated twist in this poet's plots is monotonously annoying. In *The Dead City* (*La città morta*), for example, the hero who remains for hours in the throes of incestuous temptations (incest is another of D'Annunzio's favorite themes), prefers to slay his pure sister; in *The Innocent* (*L'Innocente*), a man slays the son, by another man, of his concubine, by exposing it cruelly to freezing weather, thus destroying the only guiltless party in the dirty story. Incidentally, why did this poet try so many times to portray the innocent? Is it because "like cures like"? ("Like," as Wordsworth said, "but oh how different.")

These general defects of D'Annunzio's imagination and of his interpretations of life are found in doses altogether too profuse in *The Crusade of the Innocent,* which, in a jumble of mediaevalism, religiosity, and impossible nature, presents a plot devoid of real emotions universally felt, driving inevitably to catastrophe. It merely sketches nasty crimes, puffed up to look like the results of passion overwhelming. Instead of leaving us terror-stricken, they leave us cold. Indeed, overstressed as they are, they make us laugh, when we are not too nauseated—a reaction most disastrous to tragedy.

Terror, of course, *is* a quality expected in tragedy. Does this *Crusade* inspire terror? My answer would be: horror, yes, but not terror. And the horror is of a physical kind; disgust, not emotional horror, since we are not stirred. That terror which leaves us appalled at the blind persecutions of the gods or of life, is not evoked by this play in which, I repeat, the catastrophe is gratuitous and absurd. In short, instead of drama, we have melodrama, or rather, sheer folly, and instead of poetry, rhetoric, or rather, hallucination. (pp. 32-5)

> *Rudolph Altrocchi, "Lust and Leprosy," in his* Sleuthing in the Stacks *(copyright © 1944, copyright renewed © 1972, by the President and Fellows of Harvard College; excerpted by permission), Cambridge, Mass.: Harvard University Press, 1944, pp. 23-50.*

ERNEST HATCH WILKINS   (essay date 1954)

[Gabriele d'Annunzio's] first collection of poems was published, under the Latin title *Primo vere,* **"In Early Spring,"** while he was still in school. These earliest poems are largely imitative, the dominant influence being that of Carducci: some of them are *odi barbare*. With all their immaturities they show certain characteristics that were to mark most of D'Annunzio's poetry: great linguistic and metrical facility (later to develop into an opulent virtuosity); an overloading with classic allusions; a remarkable gift for vivid description; and, most of all, an unlimited *joie de vivre*. (p. 464)

In the *Intermezzo di rime* . . . D'Annunzio plunges with a hectic abandon into the excesses of decadentism. . . . By the time of the publication of this volume D'Annunzio, through his luxurious extravagances, his ultrasophisticated aestheticism, his overt shamelessness, and his unquestionable brilliance, had attained a histrionic prominence that he continually cultivated, and never lost.

Decadentism and a somewhat recondite aestheticism prevail in *Isaotta Guttadauro* . . . , which contains, however, some pleasantly pictorial poems. The collection called *Elegie romane* . . . gathers D'Annunzio's impressions of contemporary Rome. In the *Odi navali* . . . he begins to blow the imperial trumpet: he loved the sea and ships; he was convinced of the importance of the sea in international conflict; and he had become a propagandist for Italian naval armament. The *Poema paradisiaco,* **"A Poem of Gardens"** . . . , breathes in a few of its poems a momentarily redemptive longing for the home and the surrounding family love of his boyhood. (pp. 464-65)

Between 1893 and 1900 he had written rather less verse than formerly: his only wholly new volume of verse was published in 1899 with the resounding title *Laudi del cielo del mare della terra e degli eroi,* **"Praises of the Sky, of the Sea, of the Earth, and of Heroes."** This collection proved to be the first form of D'Annunzio's most ambitious undertaking: the *Laudi* were to be expanded—retaining their original title—into a series of seven Books, each bearing the name of one of the Pleiades. Of the seven proposed Books, however, only four were completed: [*Maia,* subtitled *Laus vitae; Electra* and *Alcyone,* and *Merope*]. . . . They constitute an exuberant celebration of the joys of life as D'Annunzio felt them—joy in the perception of beauty in the actual world and in the worlds of art and poetry and legend, joy in vivid experiences of sense, joy in exciting and, at the best, heroic action. But D'Annunzio's joy is utterly self-centered, even dictatorial; and he appears to be insensitive to the joys of thought and of spirit.

In *Alcyone,* highly perfected in its artistry, all that is best in D'Annunzio comes to fulfillment. With four dithyrambs serving as its main structural elements, it gathers poems, many of them of great beauty, that renew the myriad sensations of a Tuscan summer—colors, melodies, silences, fragrances, tastes, dawns, burning noontides, starlit evenings, harvests, voices of crickets, of nightingales, of the rain, of brooks, and of the sea. (p. 465)

[D'Annunzio] tried to do for the peasant life of his native Abruzzi what Verga had done for the peasant life of Sicily. In sheer descriptive skill he excels Verga, and his most vivid stories, once read, are hardly to be forgotten; but his persons have no richness of individual life, and his realism, often barbaric, is unrelieved by any breath of compassion or any touch of humor. (pp. 465-66)

> *Ernest Hatch Wilkins, "Pascoli and Other Poets," in his* A History of Italian Literature *(copyright © 1954 by the President and Fellows of Harvard College; excerpted by permission), Cambridge, Mass.: Harvard University Press, 1954, pp. 460-69.**

GIOVANNI GULLACE   (essay date 1960)

The French writings of Gabriele d'Annunzio are of peripheral importance in his literary career. They reveal no new aspect of his artistic talent and add nothing to his reputation. Critics, in fact, have seldom given much heed to the poet's French literary production. His three French plays—*Le Martyre de Saint Sébastien, La Pisanelle, Le Chèvrefeuille*—were widely discussed at the time of their first theatrical presentations and either highly praised or mercilessly condemned; then, except for occasional references in general studies of the author, they were completely forgotten.

From the artistic point of view they perhaps deserved no more. But, if they do not offer much in artistic interest per se, they are important in the study of D'Annunzio's relations with French culture. The poet considered France his "seconda patria," and his French works, inspired by a strong affection for his adopted land, show the extent to which he assimilated its language and culture. (p. 207)

In 1896 D'Annunzio began to aspire to poetic laurels in his second language. Convinced that translations would never show Frenchmen the real dimensions of his poetic talent, he composed directly in French a series of twelve *Sonnets cisalpins* in a classical tone after the manner of Ronsard. . . . (p. 208)

D'Annunzio was not yet completely at ease with French. The *Sonnets cisalpins* lack the suppleness and rhythm of his Italian poems. One feels here and there a certain strain and affectation in the expression, due to insufficient mastery of the language. Some of them, however, are remarkably suggestive. . . . [The poems] often echo motifs dear to the poet, now spurred by a new daemon—the idea of the superman. The desire to rise above himself, to conquer himself and others, to ascend to the heights of pure art, is a theme recurring in nearly all these poems. Their form is characterized by that labored stylistic refinement characteristic of D'Annunzio—the choice of rare and musical words, the preference for archaisms, the use of sensual expressions. At times his French phrases seem to be a translation from his native tongue. . . . (pp. 210-11)

If the *Sonnets cisalpins* was a timid effort in the poetic use of French, *Le Martyre de Saint Sébastien* stands out as an ambitious and almost rash enterprise. A mediaeval mystery play in 1910 was, indeed, an unusual literary event, and only D'Annunzio's temerity could have conceived such a project. (p. 212)

The *Martyre* is divided into a prologue and five "mansions" which appear as loosely connected episodes. As a result, the play lacks real dramatic crescendo and unity, and has the fragmentary character of the mediaeval compositions of the sort. Moreover, D'Annunzio crystallized the various elements in the immobility of lyric presentation, failing to give the story even the little action it had in the *Golden Legend*. (p. 213)

The equivocal religious nature of the play is unquestionable. In *Saint Sébastien* there is such a strange mixture of pagan fervor and Christian tenderness that the martyr is often confounded with Adonis. . . . The dramatic tone of certain passages recalls vaguely Wilde's *Salomé*. The figure of the saint seemed to be profaned not only by the poetry but also by the music [by Claude Debussy], which became more suggestive at the very moment when the poet's inspiration, freeing itself from empty rhetorical forms, assumed an ambiguous mystical tone which was nothing but the exaltation of the senses. The Christian spirit which the work was to express is thus paganized and sacrificed to the idea of physical beauty, which dominates the play. . . [Rather] than a contrast between the Christian and the pagan worlds, D'Annunzio's play was meant to be a synthesis. (p. 216)

[The *Martyre de Saint Sébastien* was followed by] another French play, *La Pisanelle ou la mort parfumée*, a three-act drama in verse. . . . Although D'Annunzio called it a comedy, *La Pisanelle* is more of a romantic drama, in which shrieks, blood, and dances create an atmosphere both horrifying and voluptuous. The story is presented as a series of picturesque scenes in which the caustic and coarse spirit of the *fabliaux* is blended with the pathos of mediaeval romance. The protagonist is a harlot, native of Pisa, who bewitches the young and romantic king of Cyprus. The queen mother, in order to get rid of the adventuress, secretly lures her to court, and, after offering her drink, invites her to dance. While the girl dances before the admiring court, a shower of blossoms falls upon her until she succumbs under the weight of the petals.

The diffuseness noticed in *Saint Sébastien* is even more pronounced in *La Pisanelle,* where cumbersome details, especially seafaring terms and images, unduly burden the development of the drama. The play also contains the same pompous glorification of lust and blood which is found in *La nave* and *Il sogno d'un tramonto d'autunno*, and all the usual lust-laden clichés, calculated to raise every motif to ecstatic heights. What is significant is not the death of the protagonist but the manner in which she dies—under a shower of flowers. D'Annunzio's aestheticism is now aggravated by cold and verbose erudition and by an immorality to which he vainly tries to give a tragic sense. An effeminate St. Sebastian who perishes at the hands of his archers (the attempt to kill him under the flowers failed) and enjoys the sight of his own blood, and a Pisanelle voluptuously smothered under a shower of blossoms, express a sensualism too decadent to be dramatic.

The French of the play is even more artificial than that of *Saint Sébastien;* and at times it is more obscure. D'Annunzio had already acquired a close familiarity with mediaeval and Renaissance writers, and from their works he had derived a strange language compounded of Latinisms, Italianisms, lofty expressions and idiotisms, archaic and modern forms, the whole resulting in a sort of bizarre linguistic potpourri conspicuous for its inconsistency. (pp. 219-20)

The theatrical failure of *Saint Sébastien* and *La Pisanelle* did not disturb D'Annunzio in the least. . . . [A] new French drama of his entitled *Le Chèvrefeuille* (a three-act tragedy in prose) was produced on the Parisian stage. (p. 222)

Le Chèvrefeuille is a gloomy drama of passion. Although its title reminds one of Marie de France's lay, the theme echoes,

Aeschylus, Shakespeare, and Bourget. The protagonist is an enigmatic girl who finds herself in a situation similar to that of Electra, Hamlet, or André Cornélis. She senses that her father was murdered, suspects the complicity of her mother, and seeks vengeance. The plot unfolds in an atmosphere of mystery and terror, strange visions, hatred, and jealousy. Artistically it offers nothing new. It repeats psychological attitudes and motifs of earlier works by D'Annunzio, such as *La fiaccola sotto it moggio, La gloria, Più che l'amore,* etc. The tendency to evoke the invisible behind the visible, and to suggest mysterious secrets behind the uttered words is reminiscent especially of *Fedra* and *Forse che si forse che no.* Although carefully planned in its structure and close to traditional tragedy in its mood, there are puzzling obscurities in *Le Chèvrefeuille* which seem intentional. (pp. 222-23)

Giovanni Gullace, "The French Writings of Gabriele d'Annunzio," in Comparative Literature *(copyright © 1960 by University of Oregon), Vol. XII, No. 3, Summer, 1960, pp. 207-28.*

ANTHONY RHODES (essay date 1960)

[D'Annunzio's sensual nature is to be found] in his first set of short stories, *Tales of the Pescara,* where it seems that there is no joy other than physical joy, just as there is no pain other than physical suffering. They contain an astonishing mixture of cruelty and sex. . . . In *La Veglia Funebre,* the widow and the brother of a dead man, in the presence of his decomposing body, give themselves to one another feverishly, as they roll on the ground before him. . . . In *La Madia* we see a deformed man who is hungry and who, while he is stealing a loaf of bread, has his hand crushed by his own brother who shuts the heavy iron bin on it.

Impassively, without indignation, without tears or laughter, the young D'Annunzio examines, notes and describes these cruel things precisely. The volume of some of his collected stories is called *Il Libro delle Vergini,* its jacket depicting three naked women dancing in a Bacchanalian orgy. D'Annunzio described it himself to his publisher. "I think it should please the public for its air of sanctity combined with audaciousness. Its scenes alternate between the church and the brothel, between the odor of incense and the stink of decay."

I Romanzi della Rosa, his first full length novels, carry this process a stage further. They are, as their title suggests, placed under the sign of the Queen of flowers—mistakenly, one might say, for the rose is the symbol of burning but at least of pure love, whereas these novels are concerned exclusively with cerebral love and lust. D'Annunzio seems to have set out to be the Italian representative of the *fin de siècle* writers already well known in France and England. In *I Romanzi della Rosa,* he develops his special Cult of the Beautiful in a manner reminiscent of Baudelaire or Pater, adding to it his own special Italian element, a kind of Machiavellianism of Beauty. Every act committed for the sake of Beauty, even a sin or a crime, is justifiable and excusable. Just as Machiavelli exalted Cesare Borgia into a superman in spite of his crimes, so D'Annunzio exalts his heroes who, in order to live their life of Beauty, do not hesitate to commit sins, including the special D'Annunzian one of incest.

For such men a special set of rules exist. He describes Andrea Sperelli, the hero of *Il Piacere,* in these terms, "He was completely saturated with Art, to the extent of being corrupted by it, demanding only experience and more experience of the sharpest kind to feed it. He was always prodigal of his own energy, for the powerful force within him was ever expressing itself—but only at the expense of another force, the moral force. Gradually, he found that he lied to himself as much as to other people; it became absolutely natural, and necessary.'' Andrea Sperelli is a kind of autobiographical hero, a man of great culture, taste and verve, who moves through innumerable intrigues and amorous adventures, duels and balls, from fox hunts and horses to the composition of elegant works of art printed on special paper for a restricted number of friends.

A passage like the following from his next novel, *L'Innocente,* seems today like a parody of Oscar Wilde: ''. . . perverse and curious, I thought how she would seem if I made love to her when she was ill. Would not the voluptuousness have something incestuous about it? If she were to die? I thought . . . . Why must there be a germ of sadist perversion in everyone who loves and desires . . .?''

Here, the hero is a man who desires certain sensual spasms which he cannot find in his lover. Realizing that he can never obtain the unnatural delights he craves, he takes his pleasure in nostalgically imagining them.

In *Il Trionfo della Morte,* D'Annunzio goes further. Aurispa, the hero, loves a woman so intensely that he feels he must destroy her. He is a self-indulgent young man who passes from mad adoration of a woman to nausea for her. D'Annunzio emphasizes this by recounting her physical and mental defects, the manner in which his hero views the deformity of her feet as they walk on the warm sand of the beach, the physical disgust his mistress is beginning to awaken in him. He feels he can neither live with her, nor without her, that she will somehow destroy him. The book reaches its climax with a long and gloomy meditation on sin as the supreme joy, the hero obsessed by the thought of death, wishing to die and cause to die. These two acts can best be combined in a sexual embrace, so, after a fearful hand-to-hand struggle with the unfortunate heroine, he assaults her and pulls her to death over a precipice. (pp. 31-4)

Il Trionfo della Morte is perhaps D'Annunzio's best novel because it possesses unity. The problem of this kind of dissatisfied lover is stated in the opening pages, and is carefully worked out to its conclusion. This can hardly be said for the other novels, in which the actions and the emotions which inspire them are often unconnected. As for the writing and the technique, they are always undisciplined. Even in *Il Trionfo della Morte,* D'Annunzio introduces a long exposition of one of Tennysons' poems, as well as a disquisition on Wagner. (p. 34)

The worst quality is the verbiage. The ability to convey meaning and atmosphere by a word or short phrase is entirely absent. In this, D'Annunzio was probably not very different from other writers of his time, French and English. The huge crowded canvases of contemporary writers and painters are all much the same, with their varied groups and contorted attitudes. D'Annunzio's descriptions are often mere inventories, painfully minute, like a mosaic with millions of little word cubes—a multiplicity of words which frequently conceals a poverty of ideas.

Against this, the incessant search for what is loathsome and cruel, the physical and moral leprosies, the verbiage, must be set D'Annunzio's very great powers of observation and description. Seldom can a writer have been so influenced by the early surroundings of his native land as D'Annunzio. The whole Adriatic coast, from the mouth of the Tronto to the banks of the Trigno, its innumerable gulfs and bays and the barren Maiella

behind, together with the primitve traditions and barbarous customs of the race, appear in his early work. There is something pantheistic in his identification of the characters with the natural world around them, a kind of intoxication in his love of sounds and colors. (p. 35)

Among D'Annunzio's novels of the first period was *Le Vergini delle Rocce* which, if not the best, is certainly the most important, because it announces the Superman, the theme which he introduced into Italy from his reading of Nietzsche. If *I Romanzi della Rosa* all show the same kind of aesthete-hero, subject to a special set of laws, they also foreshadow the Superman. Most of the heroes live in a rarefied, sub-lunar atmosphere, and rarely come down to earth, to act. But Claudio Cantelmo of *Le Vergini delle Rocce* is an Italian Zarathustra. He speaks like a Teutonic man of action: ''I am grateful to my ancestors, an ancient and noble race of warriors, for having given me their rich and fiery blood, for the beautiful wounds and beautiful burnings they inflicted in the past, for the beautiful women they raped, for all their victories, their drunkennesses, their magnificence . . .''. (p. 39)

Zarathustra says that there is one law of nature for all animals, including the human animal—that the strong shall have everything because he is strong, and the weak have nothing, because he is weak. (p. 40)

Such ideas appealed to D'Annunzio, and he started reading Nietzsche. . . . D'Annunzio no longer wanted to write poems and novels about decadents, but to create an epic in which he could express Italian ideals, like Virgil's and Dante's, only brought up to date, in a vast vision of the opening century, and Italy's imperial role in it. (p. 42)

The poem *Maia* which he wrote about his trip to Greece, inspired by the idea of Ulysses in these waters, is often considered his finest, and it is certainly his most patriotic, work. ''From the furnace of my mind,'' he wrote, ''has appeared the only poem dealing with life completely which has been written since *The Divine Comedy.*'' Like *The Divine Comedy,* it is also a comment on the Italy of the day, for the later added sections about Rome and Italy—in a vast vision of the opening twentieth century, when a new sort of satanism was brewing and the world was changing with such rapidity. The poem expresses the anomalies of the time; a thirst for world domination in every European country—and yet visions of Arcadian peace; a mad armaments race—and yet congresses and prizes for that peace. It was the age of the Futurists, who sang only of the punch and the slap; of the Pope excommunicating the Modernists, and the Modernists excommunicating the Pope; of aristocrats becoming democrats—and democrats badly concealing their desire to become aristocrats. D'Annunzio's *Laus Vitae* is a poem about this modern Chaos, in an age of chaotic men, without religion or belief. This is the twentieth century.

True to the Neitzschean ideal, the poem shows no respect for Christianity. The quiet doctrines of Jesus seem futile; the only Gospel is that of Pan, or, as D'Annunzio calls it, ''Desire, Voluptuousness, Pride and Instinct, the Imperial Quadriga.'' ''With what ardor,'' he cried, ''we passed the limits of all the wisdoms and ran along the edges of the precipices of the world!''

The first part, *Maia,* is an idealized version of Greece as D'Annunzio saw it, written in 8,400 lines of blank verse, in the form of an itinerary, form the moment when he and his friends set out from Calabria in a yacht, until he left them in Athens two months later. It is a comprehensive portrait of Greece, its men, heroes, mountains, museums, statues, air, sea and sky; and Ulysses is its hero. (pp. 43-4)

Ulysses had long been important to Latin literature, from Dante, and back again to the Latins before him, through Plutarch, Ovid and Virgil into the mists of Homeric legend, where he possesses wisdom, cunning, and, above all, curiosity, or the desire to learn. D'Annunzio's vision of Ulysses is this classical one, but overlaid with Nietzsche's Superman. More than the desire for Knowledge, it is the desire for Power which drives him on; *virtute* has submerged *conoscenza*, and D'Annunzio's Ulysses tends towards the Superman. There is something of this in all D'Annunzio's heroes, from Claudio Cantelmo in *Le Vergini delle Rocce* to Corrado Brando in *Più che l'amore.* Anyone who has lived a life more violent and powerful than that of others is to D'Annunzio a potential Ulysses, the Mediterranean Superman. (pp. 44-5)

> *Anthony Rhodes, in his* D'Annunzio: The Poet As Superman *(© 1960; reprinted by permission of ASTOR-HONOR, INC., New York, NY 10017), 1960, 299p.*

GLAUCO CAMBON (essay date 1960)

An exuberant writer, Gabriele d'Annunzio . . . deserves to be known for some of his remarkable lyrical verse rather than for the sumptuous rhetoric of his plays or the overblown sensuality of his novels. His flamboyant personality dominated the nineties and the early decades of this century in Italy, carrying literary paganism far beyond the limits touched by his admired model, Carducci. In view of this, it is exciting to see what he does with St. Francis of Assisi in ["**Assisi**," his] smooth sonnet from the *Città del silenzio* series, made up of several poems on the silent charm of Italian towns that have outlived their medieval and Renaissance glories. Although d'Annunzio had much more of Nietzsche than of the seraphic saint in his make-up, he referred to the latter at several points in his work. His major collections of verse, published around the turn of the century, take their general title *Laudi (Songs of Praise)* from the Franciscan *laudes,* and the third volume *(Alcyone)* contains pantheistic addresses to the olive-tree or to the ear of wheat, intentionally worded after the refrain of St. Francis' *Cantico delle creature.* He did something of the sort even with the austere Dante, so totally unlike him, when he inserted in his poems quotations from well-known episodes of the *Commedia.* The result varies—but at times is convincing.

"**Assisi**," which belongs to the second volume of *Laudi,* is particularly successful because instead of trying to recapture the chaste folk-poetry of St. Francis, it evokes the suffering saint from the landscape itself. It does this in a highly personal way, which we must call baroque or expressionist. The unfailing association of Assisi in the general mind is with serenity, but the eager d'Annunzio breaks into this peace with the turmoil of his own sensual yearning, and at once everything is distorted into an erotic fury; we get an imagined flood, a madly thirsting riverbed, flamelike olive trees à la Van Gogh, spirals of desire, and Francis himself tortured by the carnal demon: a Bernini statue, a Jesuit counter-reformation painting, or perhaps a Munch. The poem, therefore, is not an act of surrender to Assisi and its great poet-saint, but a violent appropriation; and the clash is frankly stated at the outset by the forcefully egocentric poet. This frankness, averting pretense and insincerity, saves the day for d'Annunzio. By focusing on the ascetic ordeal of the renowned convert as sublimated sensuality, the modern Pan stays

within the range of his competence and makes his *self*-portrait acceptable. (pp. 290-91)

With his soft southern ear for music, d'Annunzio exploited the name of Assisi for all it was worth, placing it in relative isolation at the very beginning. We get an impression of the hill-town rising before us amid hushing whispers, as if we were taking the famous approach from Perugia. Peace, deepened by the pause after "Assisi," suffuses the restful solemnity of this first line—but the expectation thus aroused is immediately thwarted by the sharp change of tone. The lines that follow gather momentum, and their dizzy career shatters the initial promise and the tranquil vision. . . .

After that climax of fury and rapidity, the torrid final tercet on St. Francis himself is almost a relief, although it naturally springs from the accumulated tension of the preceding lines as an epitome of the landscape seen as quivering libido. . . . We see and feel the pain of a self-torturing Eros, rather than an achieved peace. Francis is still this side of Paradise. At the same time his offered blood can appease the thirst of the stony landscape, as a ritual of fertility. In his assimilation of the saint, d'Annunzio retained an unusual (for him) amount of taste; and it is to his credit that he addressed only the town in the second person, using the more distant third person for Francis himself. (p. 291)

> *Glauco Cambon, "Gabriele d'Annunzio," in* The Poem Itself, *edited by Stanley Burnshaw & others (copyright © 1960 by Stanley Burnshaw; reprinted by permission of Holt, Rinehart and Winston, Publishers), Holt, 1960, pp. 290-91.*

THE TIMES LITERARY SUPPLEMENT (essay date 1966)

Few Englishmen have been able to see why Italians should make such a fuss over D'Annunzio.

The aesthetic he had taken up was soon out of date and now seems to have no content beyond a self-absorbed sensationalism.

It might have worn better had it not been expressed so copiously and enthusiastically in the mannerisms of the decadence, though these bought D'Annunzio rapid fame. . . . Signor Praz has aptly called him the most monumental figure of the decadence; his works are encrusted with the commonplaces and populated with the lay-figures of decadence, from the *femme fatale* of Byzantium to the golden-hearted prostitute. His plots creak with the machinery which contrives the situations and set pieces of sadistic luxury. At times they are mere horror-comic stuff; he could today have written excellent examples of the James Bond genre of thriller, so susceptible was he to the verbal lure of brutality and voluptuousness. For a different era, his writings are a literary museum of a dead culture . . . . (p. 1197)

He was also dated in another way. The foundation of his power as a writer was an immense (and spontaneously growing) vocabulary both of words and images drawn from classical tradition. Much of his verse is so knowingly and elaborately written that even the classicist finds it hard; the imagery and machinery are sometimes so artificial and complex that they defeat the most determined rummager in the reference books. He was a very literary man of letters, finding his stimulus in literature as much as in life. When he wants to write about Garibaldi he deliberately takes up the form of the *chanson de geste.* Besides making some of his verse unapproachable simply because of its incredibility, this academicism is also deterring because it contains a large element of pure vanity. D'Annunzio is like the rich young men at lunch with their *poules de luxe* whom he brilliantly described in *Il Piacere*: they toss Latin quips about and tease the girls by talking over their heads about artists of whom they have never heard. Clearly D'Annunzio saw himself among the young men (malicious jibing was the only evidence he ever gave of a sense of humor) and showed off his reading and sensibility in much the same way. Unfortunately, it often led to stylistic failure: if ever a man sought *l'épithète rare* it was D'Annunzio, but the result was often only grotesque. (pp. 1197-98)

It is also irritating to discover what a hotch-potch of borrowings from other authors there is in D'Annunzio's work. It is stuffed like a department-store with fashionable furniture. (Sometimes this seems precisely as well as figuratively true; it abounds with voluptuous sofas, marble garden seats borrowed from Leighton and Alma-Tadema, heavy tapestries and so on.) But the borrowings go further than decor; the fashionable general ideas of the epoch flow through his writings (the Superman of the novels is a notorious example), and there are more specific verbal repetitions, too. . . . D'Annunzio quarried his predecessor and sometimes, to their annoyance, his contemporaries, but he did not fail to make them his own. Unfortunately, ideas once fresh and novel now seem stale and obtrusive and D'Annunzio is so obsessed with some of them that he is boring. He is the unsilenceable autodidact, regurgitating Nietzsche, Huysmans or whoever is the latest author to attract him . . . to anyone listening, whether they want the programme or not.

There is, therefore, a great effort to be made and much to be penetrated before we arrive at the D'Annunzio who lies behind fashion and manner. He can be seen at his best when he is most detached from the subject matter. This is what gives vitality and evocative power to many passages of narrative and descriptive prose—the form in which, he said, he above all wanted to excel. Often these are about natural objects or human beings observed with such objectivity that they have become facts of natural history to the observer; here he can surpass even a Maupassant just because of the linguistic resourcefulness at the service of his observation. All his works, and not only his prose, have passages of this kind and provide good anthology material. But often his art is sporadic; his great creative power sustains only a brief burst of flight and this is reflected in his own accounts of his method of work; he liked the sense of possession by his daemon. The act of expression satisfied him: what resulted was secondary. (p. 1198)

> *"Allalà!" in* The Times Literary Supplement *(© Times Newspapers Ltd. (London) 1966; reproduced from* The Times Literary Supplement *by permission), No. 3383, December 29, 1966, pp. 1197-98.*

ROBERT M. ADAMS (essay date 1968)

[When he sat down] to establish himself as his nation's foremost novelist, Gabriele D'Annunzio had in mind a characteristically magnificent scheme. He would write, not one novel, but nine, in three groups of three, to be called romances of the rose, the lily, and the pomegranate. His numerical scheme, so reminiscent of Dante's triplicity, was supplemented by a fruit-and-flower symbolism; the rose, it is fair to guess, represented novels of passion, the lily novels of asceticism and denial, while the pomegranate suggested novels of triumphant ego-affirmation, novels of rebirth invoking the promises of eternity. No doubt fortunately, the grandiose plan remained largely in-

complete, the last two categories being represented by but a single novel apiece. *Le vergini delle rocce* stands alone to represent the "lily" program; *Il fuoco* is all that was ever written of the pomegranate. But the romances of the rose, perhaps because they appealed more richly to his imagination, flowered into three books [*Il piacere, L'innocente,* and *Trionfo della morte*]. . . . (p. 260)

Trionfo della morte had aroused D'Annunzio's special devotion; though he was a fatally fluent composer, he worked five years over this novel, deepening and intensifying it as, unfortunately, he did with too few of his other productions. His theme was the slow, almost eventless disintegration of a personality; his protagonist was young, sufficiently gifted, sufficiently attractive, and quite sufficiently wealthy; he was in full possession of an adored and endlessly seductive mistress. Yet an unbroken chain of "states of consciousness" was to lead Giorgio Aurispa fatally, and in the end avidly, to a blind wrestle of love and hate atop a precipice from which he and his entangled mistress Ippolita must ineluctably, despairingly, triumphantly fall. *Trionfo della morte* was as free as any of D'Annunzio's other stories from the laborious logic of a developing plot. But it had, unlike most of the others, a sustained inner tension, an undercurrent of destructive violence tugging at the fragile structure of reason—which still lend it immense dramatic power. *Il fuoco* preaches, and at artless length; *Trionfo della morte* dramatizes. (p. 261)

At first glance, the most striking aspect of D'Annunzio's program is the abandonment of plot, in the sense of a particular sequence of exterior happenings developed more or less logically from a beginning through a middle to an end. And it is true that what we casually call "nothing" keeps happening throughout *Trionfo della morte*. D'Annunzio has made the aimless nothings of exterior inaction precisely the strongest and most dramatic counterpoint of his inexorable inner story. He has not merely abandoned plot, he has made positive, active use of the reader's expectation of plot, as a desire to be disappointed. . . . External circumstance thus becomes the material, not for an action, but for an anti-action; the over-powering mastery of psychological obsession is rendered precisely by the tug of unrepresented immobility against the obvious needs, of the reader outside the story, of the characters within it, for Something To Happen.

When the story is not stretched out like a string, it may be arranged in numerous interesting patterns—for example, in the form of a circle. *Trionfo della morte* opens with Giorgio Aurispa and Ippolita seated on a bench in the Pincio looking out over Rome; they are disturbed by a shout, investigate, and discover to their horror a crowd gathered about the stained street where a man has flung himself off the cliff. Periodically, through the novel, the image of Uncle Demetrio Aurispa appears before Giorgio, as he was in the last days before his suicide; and the two streams of imagery flow together in Giorgio's final, fatal leap from another cliff, with Ippolita in his arms. The devices of thematic repetition, of recollection and recapitulation, thus tend to replace those of progressive narration. Thematic repetition implies a pre-existing pattern for the novel's action; the motion of the fiction does not so much exploit a freedom or develop an assumption as discover a presupposition—the pattern proposed by D'Annunzio is akin to that known to students of Ibsen as "retrospective exposition," in which a minor step forward in time and action leads to a major reassessment of the action's predicates. In traditional romance, the adventurous hero makes, undoes, and remakes his destiny afresh on every page; the supreme question is, What will he do next? Not only does the D'Annunzio hero look inward and back; he is fulfilling a destiny which has already been spelled out, if only he can read the writing. He is a reader who deciphers the signatures of things, even as the reader deciphers him. Reality is diaphanous; the adventure of the hero is to look through it, and to allow himself to be looked through; both processes are aided by the example of other works of art. What the explication of *Hamlet* is to *Ulysses,* the account of *Tristan und Isolde* is to *Trionfo della morte;* through a Wagnerian glass darkly the hero looks to intuit the laws of existence which are exemplifying themselves silently, ineluctably, in his own being. Life is a forest of symbols, which Art does not imitate so much as continue; it must be explored not just unidirectionally, but through a complex crisscross of simultaneous interrelationships and juxtapositions—through the ineluctable modality of the visible rather than of the audible. The novel must take on, in the full sense, spatial dimensions, and hence be seen, like an artifact, outside time, in the simultaneous tension of its particulars. (pp. 267-69)

The failure of Gabriele D'Annunzio as a novelist by altogether in the unforeseeable collapse of his middle and later career. Looking upon *Trionfo della morte* as the work of a young man barely entering his thirties, one can scarcely imagine a more impressive exordium in the art of fiction. . . . D'Annunzio turned back after his one unalloyed triumph, and the marks of regression are on *Il fuoco.* . . . The prose is no longer ingeniously imitative, or not to such a degree; its aim is to be plastic, "fine," Chateaubriandesque. It is as if Joyce, after the radical experimentation of the later *Portrait,* had turned toward a fictional style founded more frankly on Newman. (p. 278)

Robert M. Adams, "The Operatic Novel: Joyce and D'Annunzio," in New Looks at Italian Opera: Essays in Honor of Donald J. Grout, *edited by William W. Austin (copyright © 1968 by Cornell University; used by permission of the publisher, Cornell University Press), Cornell University Press, 1968, pp. 260-81.**

R. HASTINGS (essay date 1971)

Standard critical judgement of D'Annunzio's theatre, while fundamentally sound, is not comprehensive. . . .

D'Annunzio has been misunderstood because he was trying to do something completely new with the medium of the theatre—or rather something so very ancient that it had become quite foreign to the prevailing conception of the nature and function of dramatic convention.

D'Annunzio was fascinated throughout his life by all manifestations of the phenomenon of orgiastic experience. By an 'orgiastic' experience I mean one in which the subject is aroused by sensual stimuli to a pitch of nervous excitement where a cerebral fit occurs, producing a trance state in which he experiences hallucinations of divine possession, and transcendental revelation, and terminating in a phase of physical and mental collapse. It is a safety valve for the release of pent-up emotions and accumulated nervous tension, making possible a return to stable controlled behaviour once the excess has been worked off in this intense emotional catharsis. The subject enjoys a profound sense of relief, satisfaction, and well-being, and emerges calm and serene in a mood of radiant euphoria. (p. 85)

[Such] experiences were at the centre of [D'Annunzio's] art, and the communication of these experiences (and of the philosophy he associated with them) the principal preoccupation of his writings. This preoccupation is discernible in his novels and his poetry. But it is nowhere more nakedly manifest than in his theatre.

He was familiar with Nietzsche's theories on the origins of tragedy, and subscribed to them in their entirety. Nietzsche held that Greek theatre, and particularly the tragic spectacle, originated in Dionysian rites, and evolved from the musical ritual and representational dances that accompanied them. It thus inherited certain essential characteristics from the religious ceremony: the choral musical element, the supernatural element, and so on. Most important, it remained an orgiastic experience with a therapeutic cathartic function.

This explains why he took so enthusiastically to the theatre: because he saw it was the medium par excellence for communicating the orgiastic experience which so absorbed and fascinated him. It lent itself naturally to ritualistic inducement of orgiastic crisis through group excitement and mass hysteria, because it was a communal medium (unlike novels or poetry) born originally of an identical need. With this in mind, D'Annunzio set out to recapture the 'authentic' flavour of Greek tragedy on the modern stage of twentieth-century Italy. His main aim was to communicate an experience which he found intensely meaningful and satisfying.

But there is also a polemical element in D'Annunzio's drama. The plays are propaganda for the superman philosophy as interpreted by D'Annunzio. He saw himself as a prophet with a mission, a message to preach. And here we can appreciate the potential efficacy of the design despite the ham-fistedness of the execution. D'Annunzio had hit on the perfect method of popularizing his Nietzschean doctrine. For when the subject reaches a state of extreme sensitivity verging on trance, any concept or dogma assimilated at this stage assumes, by association with the intensity of the experience, the same peculiarly meaningful quality. The subject emerges convinced of its validity, not by any rational argument but because he has 'seen the light'. Because the execution is crude, the techniques of stimulation laboured and obvious, the method fails. But had he been more subtle and insidious, the workings of the human brain are such that in all probability we would emerge from the theatre convinced and fanatical D'Annunzio disciples. (p. 86)

D'Annunzio's cult of the primitive, so marked in the poetry and novels, reaches grotesque and gargantuan proportions in the theatre. He is trying to show how man has remained as he was in the prehistoric state, governed by the same basic drives of hunger, fear, aggression, and sex. He was convinced that the superstitions, desires and aversions of our remote ancestors were still dominant and controlling forces in the subconscious of modern man, that civilization was just a veneer superimposed on an immutably primitive personality . . . D'Annunzio accordingly recreates in his plays an uncivilized world of naked elemental passions, the original world of primitive man as depicted in the tragedies of ancient Greece.

This primitive tone is conspicuous in the setting and action of all the plays. *Figlia di Iorio* presents a savage Abruzzi peasant community. *La Nave* relives the barbaric days of the emergence of the Venetian republic from the bloodbath of the Middle Ages. But the unremitting savagery of this world is nowhere more dramatically highlighted than in *Città Morta,* where modern man has the primitive core of his nature exposed when he is 'possessed' by the ancient passions of the tenants of the tombs he is excavating. . . .

The introduction of succubus figures constitutes another attempt to recreate primitive mentality. The aim is to resuscitate. the primitive psychological attitude to woman. (p. 87)

Succubus figures abound in D'Annunzio's theatre. Almost all his women are vamped up as primeval goddesses, omnipotent female deities, cold impersonal beings to be worshipped and feared, not individuals or real people. The symbolism of sacrifice to the deity is particularly clear with Basiliola, who as the goddess 'Diona' is to drink the blood of her sacrificial victims. But the underlying symbolic value is the same in Pantèa, Angizia, Comnena, Gioconda, and Fedra: always it is 'Woman' in the abstract, an incarnation of the eternal mystery of life and sex. The reason for this constant highlighting of atavistic traits is simply that it is on the primitive, instinctive, irrational, emotional elements in our make-up that D'Annunzio must play to arouse his audience to the point of orgiastic crisis.

To what stimuli does D'Annunzio resort to arouse and excite his audience and how are they effective? The first essential is to provoke a violent reaction. So D'Annunzio employs deliberate shock tactics. He sets out to startle and astound. His stimuli are all extreme, excessive, overwhelming. They are also stimuli to which we are particularly vulnerable: D'Annunzio exercises a careful choice of phenomena to which we possess a conditioned sensitivity, and which get us 'on the raw', arousing basic drives, primitive instincts. atavistic fears and desires. All adverse reaction is as effective as a favourable one . . . . So D'Annunzio's stimuli can be attractive, appealing, fascinating, but can also be repulsive and revolting (horrific and terrifying; outrageous and scandalous; or disgusting and nauseating).

The first technique is a wholesale assault on the senses by extravagant stage spectacle; scenery, lighting, sound and special effects. Ideally, he wanted his plays to be performed in the open countryside, beneath starry skies, to recapture the atmosphere of the wild nocturnal revels of the Dionysiacs on the hillsides of ancient Greece. (p. 88)

Dramatic use of lighting is also intended to disturb and arouse the spectator by its disquieting surreal effects. Lurid skies and the peculiar unreal luminosity of the bright slanting rays of the setting sun are exploited to suggest the hypersensitivity of sensory perception of the orgiastic. Everything is made more intense, more immediate than normal. (pp. 88-9)

Emotive sound effects are employed: faint, confused, far-off sounds of cockcrow, sheep bleating, music, plainsong, oars on water; insistent oppressive noises—the clamour of the mob, the wild clanging of bells, the braying of trumpets; intense silences, broken only by minute sounds that emphasize the prevailing hush. Finally, there are special effects: the lighting of burning pitch and firing of flaming arrows in *Francesca* (the introduction of the naked flame on stage is again calculated to excite and disturb). All these effects and many more are expressly prescribed in the stage directions.

D'Annunzio develops the ritual elements of Greek tragedy, capitalizes on the stimulating upliñing effects of ceremony, liturgy, chorus, music, drums, and dancing. Many plays were set to eerie suggestive music by Debussy, Malipiero, Mascagni, and Pizzetti. Of the dance sequences the most striking are the erotic dances of Basiliola in *La Nave* and the harlot in *Pisanelle*.

The ballerina Ida Rubinstein played the lead in *Pisanelle* and *Martyre de Saint Sebastien.*

Another notable stimulus is the exasperation of sexual and aggressive instincts. Provocative dances, seduction scenes, even striptease is brought into play. In *La Nave* Basiliola prances across the stage, her naked bosoms heaving in the spotlight. . . . (p. 89)

The most characteristic technique is the use of abnormal, extraordinary, exceptional phenomena, the exploitation of that peculiar intensity of stimulus, extreme provocation, and unique power to thrill and exhilarate of strange, bizarre, sensations. Firstly, the stimulus of the terrifying and horrific. This takes two forms: the disturbing fascination of all things mysterious, uncanny, and weird—myth and legend, folklore, superstition, above all magic (the spells and incantations of *Tramonto* and *Fiaccola sotto il moggio,* the sorcery of Mila and Angizia, the Theban herbalist in *Fedra,* the slavegirl Smaragdi in *Francesca*); and the sight of mutilation and deformity—the maimed, the crippled, the blind, and the mad parade before us to unsettle us with their grotesque, macabre appearance (the hideous cripple Malatesta, the gruesome spectacle of the gaunt and charred sockets of the shambling Orso Faledro, the wild staring eyes and demented anguish of Teodata, the crushed and bleeding hands of Silvia, her wrists reduced to blunted bloodstained stumps). Magic arouses fear and desire, is simultaneously attractive and repulsive. Deformity also arouses atavistic fears and provokes a violent shudder of horror, but again the revulsion is coupled with an awful fascination.

Second comes the excitement of scandal and outrage. Here we encounter deliberate violation of taboo, harnessing the peculiar stimulus of guilt and contamination, sinful pleasure and the exquisite taste of forbidden fruit. D'Annunzio represents violation of religious taboos by littering his plays with desecration, sacrilege, anathema, black magic, sorcery, and witchcraft: the demonic rites of Diona in *La Nave* when black mass is said in the basilica; the satanic curse of Gradeniga and the wax image stuck with pins in *Tramonto;* in *Martyre de Saint Sebastien* the worship of pagan idols, the diabolic arts of necromancy, and the profanation of martyrdom in the erotic ecstasy of the saint.

Moral taboos are violated by perverted forms of violence: matricide, patricide, fratricide, and uxoricide. And especially by perverted forms of sex. The plays are bathed in a turgid, pathological eroticism. There is a deliberate cult of corruption and depravity, which is nauseating, 'stomachevole', but hypnotic and compulsive. He exploits the sexual deviations of incest (*Città Morta, Fedra, Francesca,*) and narcissism and transvestism (Ida Rubinstein as the saint in *Martyre de Saint Sebastein*). But his favourite abberration is sadomasochism. In *Martyre de Saint Sebastien* the forehead of an oracle is branded with a flaming torch (male sadism), and the torture and execution of Sebastien, who walks on burning coals and is shot to death with arrows, exhibits both male sadism and female masochism (the actress revels voluptuously in her torments). (pp. 89-90)

[D'Annunzio] had no real sense of the dramatic. For all his efforts he was usually unable to inspire his audiences as he intended. His genius was principally lyrical. His preposterously impractical stage instructions . . . amply illustrate that he was in the theatre a fish out of water. Only a poet would have failed to see it. And D'Annunzio was a poet. (p. 93)

R. Hastings, "D'Annunzio's Theatrical Experiment," in The Modern Language Review (© Modern

Humanities Research Association 1971), Vol. 66, No. 1, January, 1971, pp. 85-93.

PHILIPPE JULLIAN (essay date 1971)

[In] studying a literary achievement that has suffered much at the hands of time and the greatest beauties of which can be appreciated only by Italians, it would be futile to emphasize the borrowings and the failures. Rather that a series of pastiches, as his enemies have described it, the work of d'Annunzio was the emanation of his time, above all of the Decadent movement which occupied the latter years of the nineteenth century, and which he prolonged until the eve of the last war. (p. xvi)

[*Intermezzo di rime*] confirmed what was already a bad reputation. In these poems d'Annunzio appeared as the flaunter of vice and, what is even worse in Italy, of sacrilege—a formidable example of the Decadence that was already raging in Paris. The motto taken from the Apocalypse gave the collection a vaguely Satanistic invocation: *In fronte ejus nomen scriptum: Mysterium.* ('On her forehead a name was written: a Mystery'.) The poems were as deplorable from the literary as from the moral point of view. A few titles will give an idea of their tone: *The Blood of the Virgins, The Thirteenth Labour;* twelve sonnets each devoted to a famous adulterer, including one called *Godoleva* which is almost obscene. The following lines from *Four Nude Studies* are enough to explain the scandal which the volume provoked:

> Beautiful breasts with your flowery points, you
> on which my weary head falls at dawn when,
> in the supreme prostration of pleasure, I stiffen
> and lose my strength . . .
>
> (p. 53)

[The poet] recognized his weakness in verse: 'My barbarous and vigorous youth is slain in the arms of women'; and also in prose, in a letter to [his publisher Angelo] Sommaruga (24 June 1884): 'The *Intermezzo* is the product of an illness, of a feebleness of mind, of a momentary decadence. The reasons for *Intermezzo* are to be found in my way of life at that false period. The *Intermezzo* is not a pornographic book; it is a human document; it is a manifestation of an unhealthy art . . . Now I am renewed and fortified . . .' (probably by marriage).

The words 'barbarous' and 'decadence', inseparable from this period, reveal the poet's inward contradictions and the absurdities which have too often prevented his work being taken seriously. They also indicate a certain lucidity, which in this 'barbarian' sometimes compensated for his complete lack of a sense of humour. . . .

[D'Annunzio] also wrote some very pretty love-poems for his wife and some realist stories for his publisher.

Here is yet another contradiction: if *Le Novelle della Pescara* outdo even the French Naturalist school in their treatment of the sordid, the poems in the collection *Isaotta Guttadauro ed altre poesie* are permeated with a Pre-Raphaelite sweetness. (p. 54)

The novel [*Il Piacere* ('**The Child of Pleasure**')] is a work of art composed with the utmost care, engraved with marvellous detail, encrusted with unforgettable phrases and some purple passages. (p. 61)

Il Piacere is an excellent novel which can be read at a single sitting, though some minutely detailed descriptions can be skipped. Like Huysmans, Wilde and, a little later, Elémir Bourges, d'Annunzio was a born interior decorator: how he indulges his love of Genoa velvet and Casteldurante majolica! The auction . . . is one of the best chapters of the book. The writing is most dated when the language of the soul is employed. Maria Feres abuses such language in the same way as the Présidente de Tourvel abuses religious expressions in *Les Liaisons dangereuses.* (pp. 63-4)

The whole novel does seem to bear out d'Annunzio's own words: 'I am the mythical composite of all fruits, of all secret gardens—a bee that plundered freely from French flower-beds.' In more than one passage of the novel d'Annunzio plagiarized *L'Education sentimentale;* he also borrowed from a story by Jean Lorrain in which the heroine, like Elena Muti, describes too explicitly the pleasure that she experiences in dancing. The description of the dinner and the meeting with Elena, in the very first pages of the book, might almost come from a novel by Alphonse Daudet—*L'Immortel,* for example; the description of the cutlery is pure Goncourt; the teas under lamp-shades and the frequent use of English expressions recall the novels of Paul Bourget. The scene at the races calls to mind a similar episode in *Nana.* These Parisian frills were skilfully superimposed on a solid Roman architecture. By a highly effective contrast, the open-air cure in the Baroque villa where Scarlatti is played charmed those ladies who were rather disconcerted by the raciness of certain pages. . . . The crude pleasantries of Sperelli [the protagonist] might appear shocking if one did not remember that this hero is above all laws, even those of decorum. His laugh is the laugh of Boccaccio. In this contempt for the proprieties, coupled with a contempt for women, *Il Piacere* is a work in the main stream of the Aesthetic Movement; it has its Nietzschean aspects, but it is almost certain that d'Annunzio did not read Nietzsche until two or three years after writing this novel (and then in a French translation). (p. 64)

[The] poems of *La Chimera* hark back to the voluptuous themes of the *Intermezzo di rime;* they parade all the monsters from the menagerie of the Decadence—Gorgons, Mandragoras, Medusas, succubae, and hermaphrodites. Yet these fashionable myths do not prevent the reader from believing in the agony of their insatiable hero. The poem *A Andrea Sperelli* contains the most beautiful flashes of late Romanticism . . . (pp. 68-9)

Never did d'Annunzio so thoroughly indulge his taste for the morbid [as in *Trionfo della Morte*]. This novel is a *danse macabre* of the kind painted in charnel-houses: intestines protrude from under dresses and bones clatter. At the beginning of the novel, Giorgio and Ippolita witness a suicide; from that moment onwards, death stands between them, even during the frantic week of love at Albano. The hero has to go away to arrange the affairs of his family, whose situation has been jeopardized by a ghastly father. In the house at Pescara, haunted by childhood memories in the form of senile aunts, he finds the weapons of an uncle who killed himself. To escape the phantom of suicide, he sends for Ippolita and installs her in a hermitage amid glorious countryside. But his idyllic existence is disturbed by the repulsive squalor and disease rife among the local population. In his long description of the pilgrimage—reminiscent of both Huysmans and Zola, the fair on the church terrace and the beggars' camp—d'Annunzio invites the reader to a festival of human depravity. (p. 75)

This novel, the action of which takes place in the middle of the summer, reeks of sweat and filth. Yet it would be unfair to d'Annunzio not to recognize the insights which it contains, with its long meditations on death. Illusory or not, this communication with the world beyond transformed the writer's view of everyday life, leading him to despise the uninitiated and to indulge in every sort of extravagance in order to explore all the possibilities of an existence which it seemed futile to confine within the limits of the rational. (p. 76)

Around 1960 an Italian film [*Mondo Cane*] lyrically described scenes of cruelty taken from everyday life (though largely from exotic environments), both in the animal world and among human groups on the fringe of our society. The world of d'Annunzio the realist was a *mondo cane* both comic and primitive. . . . The first short stories, *Terra vergine* ['Virgin Land'] . . . , which he described as 'physiological studies', are permeated with the provincial atmosphere of the *veristi*. *The Bellringer*, with its lyrical realism, is reminiscent of Zola's *La Faute de l'abbé Mouret*, but *The Sister-in-law*, which is set in a Chekhovian world, is much more disturbing and heralds the great novels: an aristocratic atmosphere, temptations of incest, guilty hands meeting in the hair of a small girl. . . . The influence which the *veristi* novelists could claim to have exerted on these stories came not so much from Zola as from Maupassant and Flaubert; thus, the story *Vergine Anna* is a pastiche of *Un cœur simple* both in subject and in style. Generations of critics—d'Annunzio has always exasperated academic critics—have emphasized the links between the Abruzzi of d'Annunzio and the Normandy of Maupassant. The narrative methods of the two writers are the same; their characters, equally lacking in intellectual and spiritual depth, are exactly the opposite of the characters Chekhov was beginning to create. (pp. 80-1)

If the stories are read one after the other, they become rather monotonous. The protagonists, described from the same viewpoint of burlesque, eventually come to resemble one another: they are all scrofulous invalids and alcoholics. The women are mostly idiots or whores. The comedy is a humourless buffoonery. Humour requires self-analysis on the part of the writer, and the faculty for looking at oneself with detachment is very rare in Mediterranean countries. Basically, the comedy in these tales is like that provided by monkeys: a guffaw followed by disgust. In the *Trionfo della Morte*, the descriptions of the peasants exhausted with fever and squalor and the pilgrimage of cripples provoke revulsion without inspiring the slightest pity. This is a subhuman world, like that of Swift's *Yahoos*. . . . (pp. 81-2)

Giovanni Episcopo, a shorter tale of more concentrated depravity, [was influenced by Dostoevsky's story *The Eternal Husband*]. . . . But d'Annunzio's story is devoid of the slightest hint of charity and shows utter contempt for heroes who are from the very lowest orders, procurers and drunkards, a riff-raff with pretensions. . . . This tale of masochism is thus comic rather than sad, written as it is without a trace of compassion. In the *mondo cane* of the Roman petty bourgeoisie, the portraits of the procuress and the jovial commerical traveller are admirable. (p. 84)

[*Le Vergini delle Rocce* ('The Virgins of the Rocks'),] represents the best of d'Annunzio, free as it is of the excessive preciousness of *Il Piacere* and the vulgarity of *verismo*. It is essentially d'Annunzian because, despite pages that bear the imprint of the period, written in a mood of grey and morbid languor, the irrepressible vitality of the author bursts forth in dazzling passages, exciting even when his exuberance becomes entangled

in fantasies and is expended in the pursuit of creatures belonging to another world. (pp. 97-8)

The Venetian novel *Il Fuoco* ('The Flame of Life') . . . was a splendid but morbid tribute to this capital where the Byzantine mingles with the Rococo. (p. 109)

The difference between *Il Piacere* and *Il Fuoco* is like that between a richly stocked antique-shop and a famous museum; but, as in the first novel, *Il Fuoco* is a book dedicated to a city and one which for a long time was read as a supplement to Baedeker by visitors strolling through Venice. With the ease of a Veronese or a Tiepolo, d'Annunzio gave an allegorical quality to characters set against a background of architecture and gardens; perhaps these characters, like the figures in the frescoes, possess more movement and colour than personality. There is a greater vigour in the Roman novel, a greater languor in the Venetian one; if d'Annunzio had imagined himself as Andrea Sperelli, it could be said that, ten years later, he was almost Stelio Èffrena. (p. 110)

Today, d'Annunzio's first drama [*La Città morta* ('The Dead City')] which is still the most admired, seems weighed down by interminable monologues and by a rhetoric that does not bear translation (these rhetorical passages must be seen as an imitation of the Wagnerian recitative). The influence of Maeterlinck is as evident as in *Le Vergini delle Rocce;* the play owes to Maeterlinck its blind character (nearly every Symbolist drama had one), the monologues interspersed with repetitions and silences, and the stage-directions which could almost have been taken straight from *Pelléas et Mélisande:* 'The loose hair spreads over the shoulders of the virgin and falls onto the blind woman's dress, flowing like water, Anne's hands follow its streams . . .'. The last act, with the brother and the lover beside the girl who has drowned in the pool, is pure Maeterlinck, but in the character of the blind woman there is also an echo of Sophocles; the idea of the right of the creator to cultivate his ego belong to Nietzsche, and the style of the play is strongly influenced by Leconte de Lisle's archaic translation of Homer. Yet the vigour of d'Annunzio, the incredible richness of the images, the underlying harshness and the suggestion of incest, give the play its originality. In a theatrical world whose masterpiece was [Giovanni Verga's] *Cavalleria rusticana*, it represented an extraordinary step forward; the whole text of the play seems to have been written with the purpose of grouping the protagonists sculpturally against an immortal backdrop, which should have been that of the Roman theatre at Orange; alas, the effect was more like a museum of plaster-casts. (pp. 116-17)

[In 1908 d'Annunzio] started work on a story which he intended at first to call *Il Delirio* and which, after two years of writing, was to become the best of his novels, the most 'd'Annunzian': *Forse che sì forse che no* ('Perhaps so, perhaps not'), a title taken from a motto painted on the ceiling of the ducal palace in Mantua. Beside this work the other novels are rather like museums, antique-shops of the aesthetes or the ready-made products of realism. In *Forse che sì forse che no* d'Annunzio recorded the memories of his great love-affairs, but without retracing them in the same precise detail that had characterized *Il Fuoco* and *Il Trionfo della Morte*. He succeeded in embellishing the descriptions with the poetic *élan* of the *Laudi;* at the same time, the great scenes in the novel have a dramatic power unequalled in the tragedies. The hero of the novel was, of course, d'Annunzio himself, in a new incarnation both mythical and very modern: Icarus the aviator. (p. 177)

D'Annunzio was the first writer of his time to understand that speed would become the great need and pleasure of the modern world. The aesthete, abandoning his trinkets, became a mechanic and valued the beauty of an engine almost as much as that of a work of art. At first, he was fascinated by the automobile less as a means of transport than as a machine in which to play with death. The beginning of the novel is a glorification of danger such as was to be seen fifty years later in the film *Rebel without a Cause*, in which James Dean foreshadowed his own death. The now familiar images of a life cut short by speed are to be found for the first time in *Forse che sì forse che no* . . . , the only one of d'Annunzio's novels that nowhere invites comparison with any foreign work. (p. 179)

With the coming of war our syphilitic, debt-ridden Don Juan, whose now mediocre works brought compliments only from broken-down women and bored snobs, was transformed into a d'Annunzian hero, discovering a second youth much more exciting than the first had been. This rather fishy individual, now the comrade-in-arms of soldiers much younger than himself, outshone them in bravery and gave magnificent expression both to the intoxication of this new life and to its inevitable horror. D'Annunzio's energy was from now on directed too much towards action to give him time to write a single work; later, haphazardly gathered together under various titles—*Envoi à la France, Notturno, Per la più grande Italia, Il Libro ascetico*—he published the proclamations and the dreams, the memories and the polemics, the meditations and the projects of this period; through these pages, as beautiful as the broken sculptures and overturned columns of an overgrown ruin, we can follow five of the most exhilarating years in the poet's life. These fragmentary texts, like the pieces of a broken bas-relief which enable us to appreciate its quality, possess a truth not to be found in the sumptuous façades of the d'Annunzian basilicas. Once again, however, one must refrain from moral judgements; for d'Annunzio the heroic life became a work of art, and what matter if it struck reasonable people as absurd, if to the erudite it sometimes seemed difficult to reconcile with the dull reality of the facts? (pp. 248-49)

[*Notturno*] is a series of meditations on death, on memories of flowers and music, written with the detachment of one who is no longer of this world. There is no apparent order: after the evocations of violets gathered with La Duse [actress Eleonora Duse] during a shower in Pisa, and of the paths of Sorrento strewn with orange-blossom, the images of death loom up like the skulls in paintings of the *vanitas* genre. . . . [The] most beautiful pages are devoted to the poet's comrade, Giuseppe Miraglia: the death of the pilot, in the sea, the return of his body to the chapel of the military hospital between candles and bayonets, the four days of vigil amid the stifling odour of the flowers, during which time the handsome face changed so horribly that d'Annunzio eventually fainted; and, finally, the procession across the lagoon to the Island of the Dead. This book is permeated with the awesome simplicity of those Baroque canvases in which ecstasy verges on the charnel-house, in which roses lie scattered over livid flesh. (p. 273)

[A bizarre book made up bits and pieces and entitled *Cento e Cento e Cento e Cento Pagine del Libro segreto di Gabriele d'Annunzio tentato di morire* ('Hundreds . . . of Pages of the Secret Book of Gabriele d'Annunzio Tempted by Death') may not be on the level of Montaigne's *Essais*, which d'Annunzio knew well, but a similarly desultory manner is to be found in the meditations and the quotations. It is not directly comparable with the *Memoirs* of Casanova, but the memory of a night with

La Casati, a kiss stolen in a museum in Florence at the age of sixteen, or the skin of Elena Sangro, could still set the old man dreaming. Nor is it comparable with the *Mémorial de sainte-Hélène*, but how beautiful are the insights into past greatness and power. The *Libro segreto* . . . is superior both to *La Contemplazione della Morte* and to the *Notturno,* to which it forms a sequel. As in the other two books, the best passages are meditations on death and the vanity of glory, by a man who has had everything: 'I no longer accept anything that comes from outside. I can no longer tolerate anything foreign. I do not believe that anybody or anything is capable of enriching my life.' . . . The book ends with four lines of verse written in 1902: 'The whole of life is unchanging. Melancholy has but one face. The summit of all thought is folly. And love is inseparable from treachery.' This is the disenchantment of an ascetic raised in the mould of Christianity, but who, despite little comedies with neighbouring monks, was to remain faithful to his pagan ideal: 'It is better to believe in the body than in the soul, in the limits of the body than in the excesses of the soul. Too often the soul is merely a lie of the flesh.' (pp. 346-47)

> *Philippe Jullian, in his* D'Annunzio, *translated by Stephen Hardman (copyright © 1971 by Librairie Artheme Fayard, Paris; translation copyright © 1972 by Pall Mall Press; reprinted by permission of Viking Penguin Inc.; originally published as* D'Annunzio, *Librairie Artheme Fayard, 1971,) Viking Penguin, 1973, 366 p.*

ADDITIONAL BIBLIOGRAPHY

"The Theater of Gabriel D'Annunzio." *The American Monthly Review of Reviews* XXIX, No. 172 (May 1904): 622.
> Quotes French critic Jean Dornis's important review of D'Annunzio's plays in which he compares them to Shakespeare's.

Antongini, Tom. *D'Annunzio.* Boston: Little, Brown and Co., 1938, 583 p.
> Biography written by a long-time friend of D'Annunzio's; includes much quoted material from the author's letter, literary works, and conversation. Much of this work is a defense of D'Annunzio's unconventional character traits and countless scandals.

Boyd, Ernest. "Gabriele D'Annunzio." In his *Studies from Ten Literatures,* pp. 147-54. New York: Charles Scribner's Sons, 1925.
> D'Annunzio's popular reception abroad.

Collins, Joseph. "Gabriele D'Annunzio—Poet, Pilot, and Pirate." In his *Idling in Italy,* pp. 44-69. New York: Charles Scribner's Sons, 1920.
> Bio-critical survey.

Griffin, Gerald. *Gabriele D'Annunzio, The Warrior Bard.* 1935. Reprint. Port Washington, N.Y., London: Kennikat Press, 1970, 288 p.
> Critical biography focusing on D'Annunzio's military career, stating that he will "go down to posterity as the Saint John the Baptist of Fascism."

Gullace, Giovanni. *Gabriele d'Annunzio in France: A Study in Cultural Relations.* Syracuse: Syracuse University Press, 1966, 243 p.
> Book-length treatment of the subject of his 1960 essay (see excerpt in entry above).

Harding, Bertita. *Age Cannot Wither: The Story of Duse and d'Annunzio.* Philadelphia, New York: J. B. Lippincott Co., 1947, 281 p.
> Popular biography of his famous romance.

Isola, Pietro. "Gabriele D'Annunzio's Dramas." *Poet Lore* XIX, Nos. I, II (Spring 1908; Summer 1908): 111-19, 215-24.
    Critical survey "frank in condemnation and admiration."

Kennard, Joseph Spencer. "Gabbriele D'Annunzio." In his *Italian Romance Writers*, pp. 389-449. 1906. Reprint. Port Washington, N.Y.: Kennikat Press, 1966.
    Survey of the major works.

MacBeth, George. "The John the Baptist of Mick Jagger: On D'Annunzio." *Encounter* XL, No. 5 (May 1973): 76-80.
    Sees D'Annunzio's personal and literary scandals, sensational behavior, and flamboyant lifestyle as prophetic of the conduct of modern media idols such as Mick Jagger. The title of this article is an adaptation of Gerald Griffin's characterization of D'Annunzio as "the Saint John the Baptist of Fascism."

"Some Translated Novels: *Episcopo & Co.* and *The Triumph of Death*." *The Nation* LXIII, No. 1644 (31 December 1896): 500.
    Review characterizing D'Annunzio as a "dismal naturalist."

Symons, Arthur. "Francesca da Rimini." *The Fortnightly Review* n.s. LXXI, No. CCCCXXII (February 1902): 236-46.
    Primarily a discussion of the poetic techniques and devices used in this drama.

Walkley, A. B. "Francesca da Rimini." In his *Drama and Life*, pp. 255-59. London: Methuen & Co., 1907.
    Comments that this is not a "first rate drama" but one that has "filled out the story with the *maximum* number of dramatic episodes."

Rebecca (Blaine) Harding Davis

1831-1910

American short story writer, novelist, and essayist.

A pioneering realist, Davis was the first American author to write about the lives of factory workers. Her first published story, "Life in the Iron Mills," was in its time both hailed as a dramatic exposé of the conditions endured by iron workers, and reviled as a piece of sensationalistic "muckraking." Critic and author Tillie Olsen has referred to the story as "the *Uncle Tom's Cabin* of Capitalism," citing it as another instance of an author daring to portray the negative aspects of a profitable and accepted system.

Davis, born in Washington, Pennsylvania, moved with her family to what was then Wheeling, Virginia, where she grew up in a unique environment midway between the traditional south and progressive north. Virginia, for example, was a border slave state, but Wheeling was a heavily industrialized city, active with the iron works that inspired her most critically acclaimed story. During a trip to New England following the publication of her first book, *Margret Howth: A Story of To-day*, Davis became acquainted with the literary greats of the day: Nathaniel Hawthorne, one of her primary literary influences; Ralph Waldo Emerson; A. Bronson Alcott and his daughter, Louisa May; Oliver Wendell Holmes; as well as her future husband, L. Clarke Davis, then a journalist and law student. With her marriage in 1863, Davis moved to Philadelphia, and most of her works are set in Pennsylvania or in Virginia.

Critics agree that Davis's first two works, "Life in the Iron Mills" and *Margret Howth*, were her best. Her artistic talent was thwarted, thereafter, by literary and personal pressures. After an editorial "suggestion" led her to bring *Margret Howth* to a more cheerful (and saleable) conclusion than she had intended, Davis began to employ a formula of closing her stories and novels with often inappropriately happy endings. Following her marriage, her time was consumed by the demands of her growing family and she wrote mostly trite love stories and Gothic mysteries which she sold, unsigned, to various magazines to supplement the family income. Her originality and skillful characterizations were hampered by a melodramatic, didactic style and by her reluctant attempts to infuse her gloomy tales with the optimism needed to make them marketable. Most of her short stories saw print only in popular monthly journals such as *Harper's*, *Scribner's*, *Lippincott's*, and have never been gathered together and reprinted.

Davis did, however, continue to attempt serious themes, and her subsequent work, though not of the same quality as "Iron Mills" and *Margret Howth*, included several more pioneering firsts: among them, the use of blacks as major characters, a call for reform of Pennsylvania's insanity laws, and stories of talented women frustrated by the choice between career and family. Feminists today interpret these last stories as Davis's way of expressing dissatisfaction with the status of women in nineteenth-century America. Even in an antisuffrage tract in *Pro Aris et Focis*, Davis called for more acceptable occupations to be opened to single women.

Davis's starkly realistic portrayals of the commonplace have caused critics to compare her with French author Émile Zola—forgetting that she preceded him by half a dozen years. Since Davis never lived up to the promise of her first efforts in fiction, she is virtually unknown as a writer today. Though she was the first American realist to write extensively about everyday affairs, she was eulogized, and is chiefly remembered, as the mother of "roving correspondent" Richard Harding Davis.

PRINCIPAL WORKS

Margret Howth: A Story of To-day (novel) 1862
Dallas Galbraith (novel) 1868
Waiting for the Verdict (novel) 1868
Pro Aris et Focis (essays) 1870
John Andross (novel) 1874
Silhouettes of American Life (short stories) 1892
Doctor Warrick's Daughters (novel) 1896
Frances Waldeaux (novel) 1897
Bits of Gossip (reminiscences) 1904
*Life in the Iron Mills; or, The Korl Woman 1972

*This work was originally published as "Life in the Iron Mills" in *The Atlantic Monthly*, April, 1861.

LOUISA MAY ALCOTT (essay date 1862)

Saw Miss Rebecca Harding, author of "**Margret Howth**," which has made a stir, and is very good. A handsome, fresh, quiet woman, who says she never had any troubles, though she writes about woes. I told her I had had lots of troubles, so I write jolly tales; and we wondered why we each did so.

> *Louisa May Alcott, in her diary entry of May, 1862, in her* Louis May Alcott: Her Life, Letters, and Journals, *edited by Ednah D. Cheney, Roberts Brothers, 1890, p. 130.*

THE NATION (essay date 1867)

Mrs. Davis intimates in her dedication that her book ["**Waiting for the Verdict**"] treats of "the weak and wronged among God's creatures," and that it is written in their behalf. It can hardly be said, however, that the persons she has brought upon the scene have, with perhaps one or two exceptions, any great wrongs to complain of or any extraordinary weakness to contend with—unless it be that their grievances may be resolved into the fact that Mrs. Davis has undertaken to write about them. The exceptions, of course, are in the case of certain individuals of negro blood. The story moves on two distinct lines, each with its separate hero and heroine. . . .

The subject—the leading idea—strikes us as a very good one. It was a happy thought to attempt to contrast certain phases of the distinctively Northern and Southern modes of life and of feeling, and to bring two intelligent Southerners, such as Miss Conrad and Garrick Randolph, into contact with Northern manners in such a way as to try their patience and their courage. The chief fault, artistically, in working out this idea is that she has made two complete plots with no mutual connection. The story balances in an arbitrary manner from Ross Burley to Margaret Conrad and from Randolph to Dr. Broderip. The authoress might have strengthened the links between the two parties by making more than she has done of the relations between Randolph and Miss Conrad. . . . [Nevertheless,] the idea is good, and if the execution had been on a level with it, "**Waiting for the Verdict**" might have claimed, without reproach, that much-abused title, "A story of American life." As it stands, it preserves a certain American flavor. The author has evidently seen something corresponding to a portion of what she describes, and she has disengaged herself to a much greater degree than many of the female story-tellers of our native country from heterogeneous reminiscences of English novels. She has evidently read Dickens with great assiduity, to say nothing of "Jane Eyre" and "Wuthering Heights." But these are great authorities, and on this ground we suppress our complaints, the more readily as we find ourselves in conscience unable to give the book in any degree our positive commendation.

Mrs. Davis has written a number of short stories, chiefly of country life in Virginia and Pennsylvania, all distinguished by a certain severe and uncultured strength, but all disfigured by an injudicious straining after realistic effects which leave nature and reality at an infinite distance behind and beside them. The author has made herself the poet of poor people—laborers, farmers, mechanics, and factory hands. She has attempted to reproduce in dramatic form their manners and habits and woes and wants. The intention has always been good, but the execution has, to our mind, always been monstrous. The unfortunate people whom she transfers into her stories are as good material for the story-teller's art as any other class of beings,

but not a bit better. . . . They are worth reading about only so long as they are studied with a keen eye versed in the romance of human life, and described in the same rational English which we exact from writers on other subjects. Mrs. Davis's manner is in direct oppugnancy to this truth. She drenches the whole field beforehand with a flood of lachrymose sentimentalism, and riots in the murky vapors which rise in consequence of the act. . . . In her desire to impart such reality to her characters as shall make them appeal successfully to our feelings, she emphasizes their movements and gestures to that degree that all vocal sounds, all human accents, are lost to the ear, and nothing is left but a crowd of ghastly, frowning, grinning automatons. The reader, exhausted by the constant strain upon his moral sensibilities, cries aloud for the good, graceful old nullities of the "fashionable novel." (pp. 410-11)

> *"'Waiting for the Verdict','' in* The Nation, *Vol. V, No. 125, November 21, 1867, pp. 410-11.*

THE NATION (essay date 1868)

This new novel of Mrs. Harding Davis ["**Dallas Galbraith**"] is better than her last, which we had occasion to notice a year ago [see excerpt above]. Certain offensive peculiarities of style which we then attempted to indicate have not, indeed, disappeared, but they are less prominent and various than in "**Waiting for the Verdict**." The story, the fable, to begin with, is very much more simple and interesting, and is, in fact, very well conducted. A really simple and healthy writer the author of "**Dallas Galbraith**" never will be; but on careful consideration we think it would be unjust not to admit that in the present work she has turned herself about a little more towards nature and truth and that she sometimes honors them with a side glance. In the conception and arrangement of her story, moreover, she displays no inconsiderable energy and skill. She has evidently done her best to make it interesting, and to give her reader, in vulgar parlance, his money's worth. She may probably be congratulated on a success. For ourselves, we shall never consider this lady's novels easy reading; but many persons will doubtless find themselves carried through the book without any great effort of their own. (p. 330)

Mrs. Davis, in her way, is an artist. And yet . . . "**Dallas Galbraith**" is a book about which it is very easy to make talk which is not too valuable. . . . Mrs. Davis's stories are habitually spoken of as "earnest" works, and it is not hard to detect in reading them a constant effort to deserve the epithet. Their pretensions are something very different from those of the simple novel of entertainment, of character, and of incident. The writer takes life desperately hard and looks upon the world with a sentimental—we may even say, a tearful—eye. The other novel—the objective novel, as we may call it, for convenience—appeals to the reader's sense of beauty, his idea of form and proportion, his humanity in the broadest sense. Mrs. Davis's tales and those of her school appeal, we may say, to the conscience, to the sense of right and wrong, to the instincts of charity and patronage. She aims at instructing us, purifying us, stirring up our pity. Writers of the other school content themselves with exciting our curiosity. A good distinction to make, we should say, is that with the latter the emotion of sympathy is the chief agent, and with the former the feeling of pity. . . . [The] great "objective" novelists, from Scott to Trollope, are almost innumerable. It is our impression that Mrs. Davis might, by taking herself in hand, make a very much better figure in this company than she has heretofore done in the other. (pp. 330-31)

[The characters in **"Dallas Galbraith"**] seem to us, one and all, essentially false. The hero himself is a perfectly illogical conception. He is too unreal to take hold of; but if he were more palpable, and, as it were, responsible, we should call him a vapid sentimentalist. He is worse than a woman's man—a woman's boy. Active and passive, he is equally unnatural, irrational, and factitious. . . . George Laddoun, the villain of the tale, is scarcely a more successful portrait. The author has confused two distinct types of character, and she seems never quite to have made up her mind whether this person is a native gentleman, demoralized by vice and whiskey, or a blackguard, polished and elevated by prosperity. Laddoun, however, is better than Madam Galbraith. Where the author looked for the original of this sketch we know not; she has only succeeded in producing a coarse caricature. . . . The author has, of course, had in her mind an ideal model for this remarkable figure; but she has executed her copy with a singular indelicacy of taste and of touch. A self-willed, coarse-grained, rugged, and yet generous old woman was what she wanted for her story, but her manner of writing is so extravagant, so immoderate, so unappreciative of the sober truth, that she succeeds only in producing a vulgar effigy. In Mrs. Duffield, Galbraith's mother, she has adhered more closely to the truth. Nature here is represented and not travestied. In spite of the faults of conception and of style exhibited in these characters, we think that Mrs. Harding Davis might yet, with proper reflection, write a much better novel than the one before us. She has a natural perception, evidently, of the dramatic and picturesque elements of human life, and, in spite of all her weakness, there is no denying her strength. **"Dallas Galbraith,"** as we have intimated, is *almost* interesting. What does it need to be truly so? The materials, the subject are there. It needs that the author should abjure her ultra-sentimentalism, her moralism on a narrow basis, her hankering after the discovery of a ghastly moral contortion in every natural impulse. (p. 331)

> *"'Dallas Galbraith',"* in The Nation, *Vol. VII, No. 173, October 22, 1868, pp. 330-31.*

THE ATLANTIC MONTHLY   (essay date 1874)

John Andross is certainly a very readable novel. Mrs. Davis writes well; with all her grimness she has a very agreeable humor and if about all the men there is a certain exaggeration of their prominent qualities, the women—both the serious and sensible one whom the men of the story consider dull, and the frivolous and pretty one whom they will equal unanimity take for charming and loving—are very well described. The scene of the story is laid in western Pennsylvania, in the coal and oil region, and in Philadelphia and Harrisburg, and the local color is very well given. . . . [There] is a chance that the power of a "whisky ring" is somewhat exaggerated, for the plot of the novel turns on the sufferings of an amiable but weak man, who, partly by his own fault and partly by force of circumstances, has got into the power of a "ring." . . . The hero, John Andross, is the victim and tool of the ring, and the position in which he is placed is certainly a very dramatic one; he is struggling to free himself from its clutches; he has fled to this unknown region, where he has found a benefactor in Dr. Braddock, who in his ungainliness and shyness is a trifle overdrawn, although his principal qualities are well set before us. . . . The acquiescence of a weak man [Andross] is admirably given, better than the idealized patience of Dr. Braddock. It is alone quite good enough to make the novel a success.

The weak woman, Anna Maddox, is, as we have said, well drawn. . . . All the love-making is well told, and full weight is given to the momentary influence which such women get over men. Very different is Isabella. The interest rather flags, it must be said, in the last half of the novel; but on the whole the book is very entertaining. It is an American novel in which the American part does not outweigh everything else; it has those other qualities more important than geographical accuracy; it is clever and interesting.

> *"Recent Literature: 'John Andross',"* in The Atlantic Monthly, *Vol. XXXIV, No. 201, July, 1874, p. 115.*

THE BOOKMAN New York   (essay date 1896)

[**Dr. Warrick's Daughters**] may have been better reading as a serial than it is as a book. A few pages of microscopic study of the least interesting aspects of provincial life might make an acceptable weekly article, but three hundred consecutive pages of the same cannot make a good novel. Only a firm central motive could give form to such a shapeless mass; and the cathode rays would hardly discover anything of the kind in **Dr. Warrick's Daughters.** Touching many things, the work seems without definite meaning. . . . [The] doctor himself appears to be characterised in so many different ways that he seems to be several men—a fussy tyrant capable of sacrificing the family's necessities to his selfish whims; a crushed creature who dreads to ask for a few cents of his own money; and two or three other opposite characters. Nor are the daughters much more convincing when they finally appear. It is true that one is represented as being always tall, and the other as always short; but beyond this their characterisation is almost if not quite as various as that of the father. And it really looks as if they changed places sometimes in the author's imagination. (p. 166)

[The] whole portion of the book dealing with Southern types and social conditions is flat, stale, and unprofitable, and the dreariest thrashing of old straw. All these absurdities have been perpetrated again and again. Surely the Northern reader must be tired and sick of them; Southern readers are tired—and sore. Let us hope, then, that this may be the last of its moss-grown kind; that no more attempts may be made to cover a great country with a tape measure's length. (p. 167)

> *"Novel Notes: 'Dr. Warrick's Daughters',"* in The Bookman, *New York, Vol. III, No. 2, April, 1896, pp. 166-67.*

THE CRITIC   (essay date 1897)

The tragedy of the strenuous mother and the inadequate son makes a theme for literature whose interest cannot be exhausted until the novelist has used as material the thousand forms of masculine inadequacy possible from the maternal standpoint. In [**"Frances Waldeaux"**] Mrs. Davis presents the case of an intense and passionately self-sacrificing gentlewoman who thinks that she sees in her self-complacent heir the fulfilment of all her own thwarted hopes. . . . The after-effects of the son's marriage upon the mother's character open up for the latter depths of emotion and actualities of evil in her own soul which she had never faintly suspected. . . . In the very end, everyone is made happy, even the son, who does not deserve it, unless weakness and amiability constitute a claim upon fate for happiness. The concession of a good ending, however, is not made by the author to the reader, but by Providence to Frances Waldeaux's intensity, which is so great that it imposes the fulfilment of her desires even upon the universal order of things. The story of her later life is conceived with power and told with directness.

The characters of the book are seen with a single eye and drawn with a steady hand, and the minor personages are as carefully characterised as the more important ones. If one were to complain of anything in the book, it would be of its excess of lucidity. The style is concise to the point of dryness. We are told only the things which are directly pertinent to the tale, and the result is a certain lack of atmosphere. The characters stand out with the crystalline brilliancy of figures seen through an expanse of plate-glass, and in admiring their clearness we forget now and then that the reader's task is that of sympathy.

"Literature: 'Frances Waldeaux'," in The Critic, *Vol. XXVII, No. 790, April 10, 1897, p. 251.*

FRED LEWIS PATTEE   (essay date 1923)

[In] April, 1861, came a bit of realism as depressed as anything ever produced by the Russian school—Rebecca Harding's short story, **"Life in the Iron Mills,"** a glimpse into the hell of the Pittsburgh roller mills in the unrecorded days. Influenced though it may have been by Kingsley's *Alton Locke* (1850), by Mrs. Gaskell's *Mary Barton* (1848); and by Reade's *It is Never Too Late to Mend* (1856), the tale has a convincingness and a sharpness of outline that were its author's own and that place her among the pioneers of American fiction. The setting of her picture is Doré-like in its remorseless black and white. . . . The hero and heroine, or rather the central characters, are of a piece with this background—victims struggling in the grip of hell and powerless. (pp. 171-72)

At the end a crime forced upon [the hero] by the woman who thought she was helping him to escape from the grip of the Mills, desperation, horror, suicide in a prison cell with a bit of sharpened tin can, and then:

> Silence deeper than the Night! Nothing that
> moved, save the black, nauseous stream of blood
> dripping slowly from the pallet to the floor.

A tale by Gogol could not be more hauntingly depressing. Shuddering realism at every point, and yet nothing too much: the reader cannot shake the effect of the thing from him for hours. (p. 172)

Fred Lewis Pattee, "Lowell and 'The Atlantic Monthly'," in his The Development of the American Short Story: An Historical Survey *(copyright 1923 by Harper & Row, Publishers, Inc.; renewed 1950 by Fred Lewis Pattee; reprinted by permission of Harper & Row, Publishers, Inc.), Harper, 1923 (and reprinted by Biblo and Tannen, 1966), pp. 166-90.*

FAIRFAX DOWNEY   (essay date 1932)

It was the lot of Rebecca Harding Davis, paladin for mill workers and slum dwellers, to see decades pass before her onslaught gained ground. Then, ironically, the memory of her own early challenge had faded.

The Civil War in prospect or in progress failed to divert the attention of the country from the short story and the serial in which Rebecca Harding first espoused her cause. They won her a triumphal trip to Boston there to be welcomed into the exclusive fold of literature by Emerson, Holmes, and Hawthorne. . . . The blows she struck for labor resounded but they were premature for the assurance of her own fame; they sank unseen foundations on which later reformers built. . . .

The spark for her tinder glowed in her home town of Wheeling. Pity had enlisted her in what would later be called settlement work among the Welshmen and other immigrants. They toiled harshly and squalidly, the men in the iron mills, the women as cotton spinners. She grasped her pen and unsparingly pictured the sullen smoke settling everywhere, the foul smells, the stagnant and slimy life of the workers in the mills and their miserable hovels, the furnaces glowing by night like a street in Hell, the nightmare fog of an existence from which drunkenness was the only escape. . . . Through her inferno scenes she wove the tale of a young Welsh puddler with a genius for sculpture and of the deformed girl who adored and stole for him; a stark, powerful story ending with suicide in a jail cell. She did not sign it. People were sure a man must have written it, probably some Russian revolutionary. It was incredible as the work of a young American woman in the year 1860. . . .

[In **Margret Howth,** Rebecca Harding] had broken away from the ultra-romantic, sickly-sentimental trend of the period to do pioneer work, and she realized it. "A Story of Today," she called it, but not the today of 1862. "I write from the border and the battlefield," she began it, "and I find in it no theme for shallow arguments and flimsy rhymes. The shadow of death has fallen on us; it chills the very heaven. No child laughs in my face as I pass down the street. Men have forgotten to hope, forgotten to pray." Her book, she promised, would not echo the hackneyed cant of men and bloodthirstiness of women in the fervors of war feeling; it would tell a plebeian story of everyday drudgery, a great warfare as old as the world, and readers might like it or not.

Amazingly, they liked it, this novel whose heroine was a homely woman bookkeeper and whose men included the hero who abandoned his career as a merchant prince for her and a reformer who strove in the foul stratum of the under-life of the American slums. Her thesis was that the great idea of American sociology is *to grow.* . . .

Critics agree that the later writings of Rebecca Harding Davis failed to fulfill her early promise. Her novels fell into the conventional grooves of the period. Love vs. money is often their conflict. Their homely scenes wear the color of authenticity, they reveal the beauty and sincerity of her own life and through them runs an under-current of deep religious faith. Her theme in **Dallas Galbraith** declared that "in the story of the humblest man there is no such thing as luck or chance—that God is under the hardest circumstances, and that God is good." These books are outmoded for the taste of the cynic who believes in the "breaks," for the modern reader impatient of moralizing and insistent on pace.

Yet the arresting quality of her articles on social subjects survives, as does the charm of her reminiscences, especially in **Bits of Gossip.** . . .

Fairfax Downey, "Portrait of a Pioneer," in The Colophon, *Vol. 3, Part 12, 1932.*

ARTHUR HOBSON QUINN   (essay date 1936)

Rebecca Harding Davis is significant in her revelation of woman's nature, in her long period of production, and in the variety of her scenes. . . . [She] has suffered from a lack of appreciation of her great significance in the development of realism. . . .

Her first significant contribution to realism was a short story, **"Life in the Iron Mills."** . . . It is uncompromising in its grim picture of the iron worker, Hugh Wolfe, and of "Deb" who loves him. (p. 181)

Next came a novel, *Margret Howth* . . . , which is laid in and near a milling town, settled by New England and Pennsylvania people. It comes near to being a great novel—marred by too much preaching at the end; but the characters are vividly etched against a background of real life that could have been depicted only by an artist who saw clearly and was filled with human sympathy. (p. 182)

Rebecca Harding had an ability to bring a spiritual value out of realism which is very rare. . . .

[The main portion of *Margret Howth*] is one of the best that the period produced. It actually throbs with the sense of pity for the oppressed, for those whose lot is hard, and with a faith that is triumphant over all the apparent brutality of life. (p. 183)

[Mrs. Davis's short stories] are of uneven merit, but in **"John Lamar,"** and **"David Gaunt"** she drew realistic pictures of the Civil War in the mountain region of what is now West Virginia. There is no glory of war, but rather its cruelty manifested by the poisoning of wells and the burning of the houses of the noncombatants by both sides. . . . [**"David Gaunt"**] is a fine study of the way the Civil War remained a personal matter in a disputed border country. The attitude of the regular army soldier, Douglas Palmer, who has already become a professional, is well established. So is the character of "Dode" Schofield, "the only creature in the United States who thought she came into the world to learn and not to teach." In Mrs. Davis's next story, **"Paul Blecker,"** the analysis of the women's characters is made more prominent than the picture of war, for she represents them as restless, a bit morbid, but determined to control their own lives. (p. 184)

One of the best of the short fiction is **"The Wife's Story,"** a powerful narrative revealing the processes of a woman's mind. . . .

[Mrs. Davis] returned to the novel with *Waiting for the Verdict* which, if it had not been overloaded with propaganda, would have been a great one, and which, even as it is, ranks with the best of this period. The characters are finely drawn. (p. 185)

It is a pity Mrs. Davis turned the novel into an appeal so definitely to the nation—for the Negro—waiting for its verdict, but she knew both sides and saw the problem clearly, even in 1867 . . . and realized the handicaps of the Negro and the Northern attitude of hostility to him. . . .

[*Dallas Galbraith*] is a good study of an inarticulate boy who suffers for another's crime. The plot is at times melodramatic, especially in the scenes which prove his innocence, but the characters of Dallas and of his grandmother, dominating her property in West Virginia, and all her family, are excellent. (p. 186)

The best of her fiction of the 'seventies, however, was *John Andross* . . . , a story of character as affected by political corruption, the Whiskey Ring, and corporation lobbying in Pennsylvania. It begins in the coal and iron region near Lock Haven, and moves into Philadelphia and Harrisburg. John Andross, a charming but easily swayed young man, is the center of the book. He is ruined by his passion for Anna Maddox, a

remarkable picture of the vampire. . . . As a contrast to Anna, Isabel Latimer, the slower but more substantial woman . . . , is also well done. The background of corruption is not over stressed, and the description of the iron furnace is realistic. . . . A bit too much Evangelicalism and a looseness of structure, but also passionate devotion to the right, animate the book. (p. 187)

[*Silhouettes of American Life* is a collection of short stories originally] published in magazines during the 'seventies and 'eighties. She treated a variety of places and themes in these two decades, always with a decided realism. (p. 188)

The faults of Rebecca Harding Davis are clear to anyone who reads her critically. She repeats her plots, which are her weakest elements; there are improbabilities in her best stories, but she was a master in character drawing. No one in American fiction before her had painted with such skill two individuals: first, the woman of moderate means, working and directing her household and shaping the lives of those around her without demand or display; and second, the apparently light and dependent woman, who grips the lives of the men who love her relentlessly and brings them to ruin. She must have known one or both of these women; perhaps she was the first. It is our misfortune that some of her best work lies unreprinted in the pages of the magazines, and that she told the truth too uncompromisingly before it had become the fashion to do so. (p. 190)

Arthur Hobson Quinn, "The Transition to Realism," in his American Fiction: An Historical and Critical Survey *(© 1936, renewed 1963; adapted by permission of Prentice-Hall, Inc., Englewood Cliffs, N.J.), Appleton-Century-Crofts, 1936, pp. 159-204.**

JAMES C. AUSTIN (essay date 1962)

Pioneer realist and sociological fiction writer Rebecca Hardin Davis . . . was born too early. In her struggle with the nineteenth century, the century won too many of the victories. . . .

Her merits as a writer were her accurate observation of local color, her social consciousness, and her awareness of suffering. Her native defects were a ponderous and overinsistent style, a certain lack of form, and a proneness toward the hackneyed kind of philosophizing popular in her time. (p. 44)

[Her first published work, **"Life in the Iron Mills,"**] suggests the gloomy tone of much of the author's best work, a gloominess that was strongly objected to. The story depicts in realistic detail the lot of the mill workers, whose only hope is in a pitying God. . . .

Besides writing about the exploited laborer, the author was also among the first of American fiction writers to deal realistically with war and with race prejudice. In **"David Gaunt"** . . . , she described the splitting apart of families and friends that the Civil War brought to the region that was yet to become West Virginia. In *Waiting for the Verdict* . . . , she attacked prejudice against Negroes without indulging in the violent biases of either the North or South.

The underlying theme in Miss Harding's early writing was the romantic demonstration that love is important regardless of defeat. This was the conclusion in **"Life in the Iron Mills,"** the ending of which was otherwise utterly black. In *A Story of To-Day* . . . , (later entitled *Margret Howth*) and in **"David Gaunt,"** the author dramatized the conflict between human love and loyalty to particular creeds or dogmas. In *Paul Blecker*

..., the vague ideal of Duty was shown to be less commendable than a trust in benign instincts. ... (p. 45)

The author's distrust of abstract creeds and principles is something we could wish she had been more consistent in. ... Mrs. Davis excelled at portraying the backbone of fact. But the eternal verities were in demand and it is perhaps the author's major fault that she willingly complied with the demand. Her philosophizing was nearly always aesthetically impertinent. In the novelette *Natasqua,* for example, she tells us gratuitously that ''love and patience and common-sense can conquer anything in time,'' though the story itself contradicts this dictum: love conquers, indeed, but only through a tragic accident brought about by impatience and lack of common sense.

Mrs. Davis is also faulty in style and form. She probably would have preferred to let her story grow organically out of the characters. ... In 1861 she complained to the editor of *The Atlantic Monthly* that she needed ''room'' to develop a story and did not like to be restricted in length. But she was restricted ... and she learned to adapt. Her plots became more slick and melodramatic and her style more sprightly as her matter became less consequential.

But it was Mrs. Davis' ''gloominess'' that caused her the most trouble, and it is here that we can trace the pressures of the age most clearly. Again it was the editor of the *Atlantic,* James T. Fields, who first brought it up. ... The editor originally rejected Miss Harding's *A Story of To-Day,* but later printed it in the magazine after the ending had been brightened. (pp. 45-6)

The author's solution to the problem of satisfying her editor [by appending inappropriate happy endings to her stories] turned out to be a formula which she used repeatedly thereafter. ... The solution is not satisfactory to the twentieth-century reader, and it probably constitutes the chief reason her stories are not read today. ...

[There] is no doubt that readers of the 1860's wanted ''sunshine.'' (p. 46)

The somberness of Mrs. Davis' writing was also noted in the reviews of her books. ... It is significant that Mrs. Davis' work was never puffed or over-rated, though excessive praise was common in the reviews of other writers.

By the 1890's tastes had changed, but Mrs. Davis' approach remained as it was. ... The revolutionary character of Mrs. Davis' writing was no longer noticeable or objectionable. She had anticipated the tastes of the nineties and subsequent decades, but she had made her compromise with the sixties, and although she continued to write about as well as she began, she did not progress.

The pressures on Rebecca Harding Davis as an author were neither logical nor aesthetic. But they were certainly part of the cultural climate of the nineteenth century. (pp. 47-8)

> *James C. Austin, ''Success and Failure of Rebecca Harding Davis,'' in* Midcontinent American Studies Journal *(copyright, Midcontinent American Studies Association, 1962), Vol. 3, No. 1, Spring, 1962, pp. 44-9.*

WILLIAM FRAZER GRAYBURN (essay date 1965)

[Rebecca Blaine Harding Davis] began her literary career with **''Life in the Iron Mills''** ..., the story that secured her place in the history of American literary realism. Her other works are not well known, nor is the truth that she matured along with the realistic movement that she helped to launch. She contributed not only an eloquent outcry against social injustices, but also excellent realistic characterizations, memorable satire, and great common sense.

Some defects in her fiction detract from even her best work, however: she largely outgrew her early straining for realism, her sermonizing, and her sentimentality; but she did not discard trite and melodramatic plots. Neither are her philosophic positions uniformly attractive. Sometimes they create unresolved contradictions; and too often Mrs. Davis equates the real and the good with mediocrity, with consequent downgrading of the excellent.

Closer analyses than have heretofore been made of some of her major fiction will reaffirm several earlier estimates of her work. Such analyses may also identify qualities in her fiction not yet adequately discussed.

''Life in the Iron Mills'' did much to define Rebecca Davis's realism; it is still impressive in its eloquent complaint against social injustice and in its realistic descriptions. Although the characters are flat types, the author's purpose is well conveyed, partly by excellent symbolism. The realistic creed suggested in this story was further clarified and defined in her first novel, *Margret Howth* ..., one of her best pieces of fiction. It was here that she invited readers to look into ''this commonplace, this vulgar American life'' for a significance not yet understood. ...

[**''John Lamar''** and **''David Gaunt''**] were among the first Civil War stories ever published; but in spite of the author's commonsense tolerance toward both sides, the stories disappoint. Even more disappointing is her most pretentious novel, *Waiting for the Verdict* ..., an ambitious but overly complicated and propagandistic attempt to show the white man what he owed to the black man.

Social protest was absent in [*Dallas Galbraith, Natasqua, Kitty's Choice; or Berrytown,* and *Earthen Pitchers*]. ... These are marked by pleasantness of conception and outcome. Although none of them is perfect in execution, with melodrama and trite plots the principal defects, all show improvement in Mrs. Davis's ability to characterize and to satirize with sharp effectiveness. ...

[In *John Andross,*] an underrated work, she wrote perhaps her best novel, through combining social protest with mature characterizations. This exposé of the whiskey ring is most distinguished in its characterizations of Houston Laird and Anna Maddox.

Although Rebecca Davis did not return to social protest after *John Andross,* her last major fiction shows continued growth of her powers. The novel *A Law unto Herself* ... marks a transition from her older approaches to character and satire to those of her most mature works, which often contain mellower, more tolerant satire. *Silhouettes of American Life* ..., a collection of late short stories, illustrates her versatility and excellence in characterizing women; but conventional plots continue. **''Mademoiselle Joan,''** a good story of the supernatural, probably influenced Henry James's *The Turn of the Screw.* ... [*Dr. Warrick's Daughters*] comes close to being a completely unified novel—something Mrs. Davis never achieved; it is distinguished not for its artistic unity, however, but for its character studies and its satire of a provincial Pennsylvania town. *Frances Waldeaux* ..., her last novel, breaks down badly in its conventional plot; but it, too, is memorable for its potentially great characterization of Mrs. Waldeaux, a mature woman of great complexity.

> William Frazer Grayburn, "The Major Fiction of Rebecca Harding Davis" (originally a dissertation presented at the Pennsylvania State University in 1965), in Dissertation Abstracts (copyright © 1965 by University Micro-films International; reprinted with permission), Vol. 26, October, 1965, p. 2211.

TILLIE OLSEN (essay date 1972)

It was in front of the Harding house that the long trains of mules dragged their masses of pig iron and the slow stream of human life crept past, night and morning, year after year, to work their fourteen-hour days six days a week. The little girl who observed it grew into womanhood, into spinsterhood, still at the window in that house, and the black industrial smoke was her daily breath. (p. 69)

The slow-moving thoughtful Rebecca absorbed them into herself with the quiet intensity that marked all her confrontation with life, and with an unshared sense of wonder, of mystery. (p. 70)

In Rebecca's first published fiction, there is a gallery of girls before marriage, devoted to their families, especially their usually difficult fathers. (p. 77)

Throughout her work, there is another recurrent figure: proud, vulnerable young women, subjected to indignities and rejection because their appearance and being do not fit the prevailing standards of female beauty or behavior. (pp. 77-8)

There are older women, realizing that theirs is to be the social obloquy of the unchosen, the unmarried. . . . Like the younger women, they school themselves to maintain dignity, integrity; they armor, imprison themselves in "the great power of reticence." (pp. 78-9)

With Rebecca's younger women, they comprise the most openly physical women in the fiction of the time. (p. 79)

To the readers of that April 1861 *Atlantic, Life in the Iron Mills* came as absolute News, with the shock of unprepared-for revelation.

In the consciousness of literary America, there had been no dark satanic mills; outside of slavery, no myriads of human beings whose lives were "terrible tragedy . . . a reality of soul starvation, of living death." When industry was considered at all, it was as an invasion of pastoral harmony [to the spirit]. . . . (p. 88)

[*Life in the Iron Mills*] was an instant sensation; it was recognized as a literary landmark. A wide and distinguished audience, shaken by its power and original vision, spoke of it as a work of genius. (pp. 88-9)

[In *Margret Howth: A Story of Today,* the] tacked-on happy ending is grotesquely evident, a contrived reformation. . . . (p. 95)

It is an awkward book, sometimes embarrassingly bad. Nevertheless, it is also a rewarding, fascinatingly native book of substance and power. . . . Essential reading for any literary or social historian concerned with the period, *Margret Howth: A Story of Today* justifies re-evaluation, perhaps resurrection. (pp. 95-6)

[The] most chilling and perfectly executed of her stories [is] "**John Lamar.**"

Set in the West Virginia hills in icy November, where Secesh Bushwhacker atrocities have been followed by Union Snake-hunter reprisals, John Lamar, a Georgian slaveowner, is being held captive by Union forces under the command of his closest friend since childhood, Captain Dorr. Lamar is planning escape, an escape completely dependent on his barefoot body slave, Ben, to whom the North secretly means freedom. (pp. 97-8)

[Rebecca wrote] another Civil War story, *David Gaunt.* [But] a love theme (she Confederate, he Northern, of course) twines mawkishly through it all, and there is a distraught, watery, hasty quality to the writing. (p. 102)

[The] July 1864 *Atlantic* featured ["**The Wife's Story**"] as its lead piece. It deserved that honor, and perhaps a more permanent one. . . .

["**The Wife's Story**" is about a woman who] had married fifteen months before into a ready-made family. . . .

She yields [to the temptation of an artistic career]—to discover that the talent itself is mediocre, a delusion; the world in which it has to function, commercial and degrading; and the end result is shame, death to her loved husband, the fate of a social outcast for herself.

But wait: it is all in the fantasies of a brain-fever dream; it never happened. The wife wakes from the nightmare illness. . . . (p. 120)

Happy conclusion, and satisfyingly reassuring to the prevalent attitudes of her readers. But there is anguish in the story. . . .

"**The Wife's Story**" is important (and fascinating) for the detailing of this anguish, the working of woman's conflict between commitment to other human beings and the need to carry on serious work. The literature of this anguish is sparse. "**The Wife's Story**" is the first, and still among the most revealing. . . . (p. 121)

Waiting for the Verdict, finished in 1868, was intended to pose what Rebecca considered the basic question of the time: how was the nation going to redress the wrong of slavery? Were the freed slaves to have work, education, respect, freedom? The blacks, the nation, the future, were waiting for the verdict. (p. 129)

[There are numerous characters and situations, and] surprising depths in the development of the main characters, most in Nat, Rosslyn, and the unprecedented, complex Dr. Broderip, torn between his whiteness and blackness. There is stereotype, slush, excess, caricature, melodrama, and occasional racism on Rebecca's part.

Waiting for the Verdict never became a great book. More than anyone else, Rebecca knew that she had failed. She had conceived, intended to write, a great novel. She had failed to write it; had not given (had) the self and time (or always the knowledge) to write it. . . . She never attempted an ambitious book again. (pp. 131-32)

Waiting for the Verdict was a book of far more substance and compass than anything else being written—and praised—at the time; and . . . it alone recorded, tried to make sense of, the seething currents of the Civil War period. Partly because of the unselected unwieldness, the first-draft character of some of the pages, partly because of disturbing truths and portents in the book, understandings far ahead of the time, almost no one recognized this. (p. 132)

[In 1870 Rebecca] published *Pro Aris et Focis* (For Altar and Hearth), a small book all for domesticity, motherhood—and against women's rights. (p. 137)

For all the insights throughout her writings on the narrowness, triviality, drudgery, hurts, restrictions in women's lives, she could not envision women "as they might be." Of their domestic fourteen-hour-a-day, seven-day work week, she did not ask Hetty's question, so terribly punished in **"The Wife's Story"**: "Was [it] for this reality that God made me?" (p. 139)

Rebecca wrote another revealing **"Wife's Story"** but this time there is neither terror nor temptation in it: the gift is used—without punishment—for family needs; the anguish is explicit only on the last page.

She called it *Earthen Pitchers,* . . . about the fate of two young women earning their living professionally at a time when professional women were an extreme rarity.

Jenny, "built for use but not for show," is a no-nonsense journalist, with no pretensions to art. (pp. 139-40)

Audrey is a musician—violinist, singer, composer. She has been rigorously training herself since early childhood, eight to ten hours a day, for a life in music. Music "is all there is of me," she says. (p. 140)

Both women are disillusioned in marriage but manage what happiness they can. (p. 142)

[Audrey] had forsaken her heavenly call, taken up what was "no better work in life for a woman." She had literally made herself a visible Providence for her husband and child. The punishment came anyway. It was her birthright world of art out of which she was cast, whose faces were averted. The death was to the self that had had the power to achieve, the murder had been to her calling, the practice of art which was her life. (pp. 144-45)

[In 1874 Rebecca] published *John Andross,* calling attention to the control of government by special interests, through bribery of legislators, gangsterism if necessary; and the corruption of character through subservience to wealth. It was the first novel of this kind. . . .

[Earlier] she had written another first book of its kind—a defense of the rights of supposedly insane persons. . . . Now her *Put Out of the Way,* . . . along with editorials and articles by [her husband, journalist L. Clarke Davis], resulted in getting the Pennsylvania lunacy laws changed. (p. 146)

Her first critical and popular success in years came . . . with *Silhouettes of American Life,* her first collection of stories. A strain from *Earthen Pitchers* and from **"The Wife's Story"** sounds within it: the power for art wasted and gone. . . . (p. 150)

In her seventies, she still kept grinding [books and stories] out. This is but a sampling: **"Temple of Fame," "Curse of Education," "Ignoble Martyr," "Country Girls in Town," "The Disease of Money-Getting," "Is It All for Nothing?" "In the Gray Cabins of New England"** (about the "starved, coffined" lives of spinsters), **"New Traits of the New American," "Under the Old Code," "The Black North"** (about the furor aroused by President Roosevelt's inviting Booker T. Washington to dine at the White House—nothing so delighted Rebecca as exposing racist hypocrisy), **"Recovery of Family Life," "Story**

of a Few Plain Women," "Undistinguished Americans," "Unwritten History." (pp. 151-52)

Rebecca Harding Davis is a name known today only to a handful of American Studies people and literary historians. Few have read any of her work; fewer still teach any of it. . . .

To those of us, descendants of [industrial workers of the last century], hungry for any rendering of what they were like, of how they lived, Rebecca Harding Davis's *Life in the Iron Mills* is immeasurably precious. Details, questions, Vision, found nowhere else—dignified into living art.

She never wrote anything of its classic quality after. (p. 154)

A scanty best of her work is close to the first rank; justifies resurrection, currency, fame. Even that best is botched.

Here or there in even her most slipshod novels, stage-set plots, moldering stories: a grandeur of conception ("touches, grand sweeps of outline"), a breathing character, a stunning insight, a scene as transcendent as any written in her century, also confirm for us what a great writer was lost in her.

Even in the tons of her ephemera, of the topical nonfiction, there is vitality, instructive range—and a fascinating native quality in its combination of radicalism, reaction, prophecy, piecemeal insights, skepticism, idealism, all done up in a kind of exasperated plain-spokenness.

The strong pulse of her work . . . evidences that—botched art or not—a significant portion of her work remains important and vitally alive for our time.

She is more than landmark, of contemporary interest only to literary historians—though she is that too. There is an untraced indebtedness to her in the rise of realism. She maintained that fiction which incorporates social and economic problems directly, *and in terms of their effects on human beings*.

She was more than realist. (pp. 155-56)

She was not derivative. Her pioneering firsts in subject matter are unequaled. She extended the realm of fiction.

Without intention, she was a social historian invaluable for an understanding access to her time. On her pages are people and situations that are discovery, not only of the past, but of ourselves. (p. 156)

Tillie Olsen, "A Biographical Interpretation" (copyright © 1972 by Tillie Olsen), in Life in the Iron Mills; or, The Korl Woman *by Rebecca Harding Davis, The Feminist Press, 1972, pp. 69-174.*

NORMA ROSEN (essay date 1973)

"Life in the Iron Mills" was written 112 years ago by Rebecca Harding Davis, the mother of Richard Harding Davis, whose name everyone knows, if not whose work. Rebecca's name and work were both forgotten, until this new publication. . . .

The book is set in an ugly iron works town in Virginia. The hero is the 19-year-old, self-taught genius sculptor, Hugh, in the mill since the age of 7, who snatches time from his slave-life of 14-hour shifts to carve a life-size figure from the refuse product, korl. . . .

Tillie Olsen [see excerpt above] claims for this story "the weight of a novel." It has that weight—in the scenes of brutalizing work, the shriek of the engines, the glare and smoke of the fires in the mill; in the evoking to one's own touch the feel of lives in the damp hovels. . . .

But of course it isn't quite a novel. It is too hasty, too intensely brief. Nor is the writer, for all the unforgettable scenes of the millworks, completely a novelist. . . . This talented woman . . . never developed as an artist. . . .

"**Life in the Iron Mills**" was a success, both as a work in itself and as a means of drawing attention to the abuses it depicts. Hawthorne and Emerson praised it. . . .

[After her marriage] Rebecca discovered that she had a talent for writing romantic, serialized stories that paid. So for the rest of her life, Rebecca wrote those to support her large household. Her husband and son went on to careers in letters that took them to the centers of intellectual life. Rebecca stayed home, looked after the children and the house and spun her romances that sold. . . .

[Again] and again her stories evoke the anguish of the woman who renounces personal goals. In one astonishing story . . . ["**Earthen Pitchers**"], a woman gives up the career in music for which she has great gifts, and then finds that she has lost her voice. In a hasty resolution, Rebecca Harding Davis has her heroine shake off her pain and say that it is enough for her that she leaves a child to the world. . . .

You must read this book and let your heart be broken by it. You will never again want to glue it up with the sticky and lying sentiments that flow all around us (still!). The ordeal of Rebecca Harding, the carver and abandoner of her own korl-woman, reminds us that for women the task still remains what another writer, Anton Chekhov, said it was for him: To squeeze the slave out of the soul.

> *Norma Rosen, "The Ordeal of Rebecca Harding,"* in The New York Times Book Review *(© 1973 by The New York Times Company; reprinted by permission), April 15, 1973, p. 39.*

COPPÉLIA KAHN (essay date 1974)

[Rebecca Harding Davis] wrote in passionate sympathy for the obscure, the ignorant, the oppressed. . . . [She] enjoyed an initial critical success, but dropped into oblivion thereafter, the startling promise of her first work blighted by maladies now easily recognizable as characteristic of women writers. . . .

Rebecca Harding was a 30-year-old spinster, the "house-bound, class-bound, sex-bound" daughter of a successful businessman in Wheeling, (then) Virginia, when she wrote this novella or parable ["**Life in the Iron Mills**"]. Its subject and treatment were wholly new to American literature. In it she tells the story of Hugh Wolfe, furnace tender in an iron mill, who has the "fierce thirst for beauty" and genuine artistic talent of a genius. But he is so debased by the bestial conditions and grinding toil of his life that he has lost the capacity for anything save despair and anger. (p. 36)

The moral passion, or rather agony, which propels this narrative is intense; at times, nearly unendurable. It is not the physical degradation and violence of the workers' lives which is so painful to read about, though that is rendered deftly; it is the spiritual torture suffered by a man of superior talent and sensibility [Hugh Wolfe] for whom there is no possibility of fulfillment, for whom the daily starvation of mind and spirit is worse than the physical starvation which accompanies it. Wolfe himself is depicted as barely articulate, and utterly un-

comprehending of the social and economic forces which have enslaved him. (pp. 36, 117)

It is the narrator's voice, accusatory, prodding, impassioned, which reveals Wolfe's inner dimensions and makes him representative of all oppressed people. Though short scenes and bits of dialogue are finely realized, they function almost as *exempla* in a medieval sermon, and the fiction as a whole works like a sermon, a direct bombardment of the reader from different angles with the terrible question: what is the meaning of this suffering? The sole weakness of the book, I think, is that Davis hints vaguely at some doctrinal, probably Christian answer to the question, when she has embodied the only convincing response to it in the hero himself—in his ability to assert his vision of his situation when life only mocks the attempt. His death is tragic, in that it is finally the only means of such an assertion. (p. 117)

> *Coppélia Kahn, "Lost and Found," in* Ms. *(© 1974 Ms. Magazine Corp.), Vol. II, No. 10, April, 1974, pp. 36, 117-18.**

LOUISE DUUS (essay date 1974)

While it is true that the realists [in American fiction] held to the notion that marriage is sacred and that the possibility of independence for female characters remained limited, they at least allowed for a greater variety of individuality in the women so entrapped. . . .

As early as 1862, Rebecca Harding Davis in *Margret Howth: A Story of To-day,* takes a step toward providing an accurate picture of the commonplace life of the American woman. The novel is understandably much neglected in favor of Mrs. Davis' "**Life in the Iron Mills.**" . . . The plot is negligible, the characters sketchy, and the prose awesomely bad. (p. 276)

[*Margret Howth: A Story of To-day*] is standard sentimental fare, and yet, having acknowledged this, one is obliged to recognize the degree to which Mrs. Davis anticipates both the theory and the practice of later realists. In an apology for the crudeness and homeliness of the tale, Mrs. Davis attacks her readers' preference for "idylls delicately tinted; passion-veined hearts, cut bare for curious eyes": "You want something, in fact, to lift you out of this crowded, tobacco-stained commonplace, to kindle and chafe and glow in you. I want you to dig into this commonplace, this vulgar American life, and see what is in it. Sometimes I think it has a new and awful significance that we do not see." She objects to the notion that all heroines "glide into life full-charged with rank, virtues, a name three-syllabled, and a white dress that never needs washing." . . .

Her heroine, Margret, is the essential domestic "blonde" heroine, but in fact she is a quiet, dark girl with a dull skin and dead-dull eyes. . . . Further, she has a complicated inner life. She has moments of real truculence about the sacrifices she has been forced to make and grows pettish on busy days. She feels balked and thwarted by the bleakness of her working world and the "white leprosy of poverty" that characterizes her desolate and shabby home. . . . She is neither saint nor sinner, nor does she provide an improving model for her female readers. She is simply a girl who has been disappointed in love and tries as best she can to cope with this fact.

Mrs. Davis can not, unfortunately, release her character from the old formula that the only true source of happiness is marriage; and, for all we know, in Margret's case this formula will work. . . . Later realists would explore more fully the cruelty of the idea that marriage brings happiness. . . .

But Margret is most interesting as a character when she finds herself without a goal, for it is in this condition that the plight of women is most keenly felt. (p. 277)

In their quest for verisimilitude, objectively rendered, it was inevitable that the realists call attention to the social and economic limitations imposed on women. (p. 278)

> *Louise Duus, "Neither Saint Nor Sinner: Women in Late Nineteenth-Century Fiction," in* American Literary Realism 1870-1910 *(copyright © 1974 by the Department of English, The University of Texas at Arlington), Vol. 7, No. 3, Summer, 1974, pp. 276-78.**

WALTER HESFORD (essay date 1977)

[Rebecca Harding Davis's **"Life in the Iron-Mills"**] is the first notable work of fiction to concern itself with the life of the factory worker in an industrial American town. In literary histories, the story is usually treated, if treated at all, as a forefunner or early example of American literary realism. That it should receive such treatment is natural. Davis takes pains to initiate us into the knowledge of hitherto little acknowledged social realities; she seems a pioneer exploring a territory which, by the end of the nineteenth century, would be recognized as the new American wilderness. Yet the significance of **"Life in the Iron-Mills"** can better be appreciated, I think, by setting it in several other literary contexts: the achievement of Nathaniel Hawthorne, the writer to whom Davis owed most; the tradition of the social novel; the religious, apocalyptic bias of mid-nineteenth-century American literature. Set in these contexts, Davis's story comes to life not as a work which is admirable because it is almost realistic, but as a work which astonishes and informs its past and present readers because it shares in and extends the accomplishments of the romance. (p. 70)

What concerns us here is the life-long attraction Hawthorne's efforts held for Davis.

The three tales [of Hawthorne] Davis read as a child—"A Rill from the Town Pump," "Little Annie's Ramble," and "Sunday at Home"—are hardly of major stature. Their very slightness helps teach the lesson valued by the young girl: the world around us is as enchanting as the world served up by Bunyan and Scott. . . . (p. 71)

Taken together, the three tales suggest that the phenomena which fall within our daily observation and experience have moral, historic, and imaginative significance, and participate in an on-going mystery and revelation. They suggest the manner in which the great subject of the Hawthornian romance, "the truth of the human heart," establishes its presence within the context of this mystery and revelation. (pp. 71-2)

Davis presents herself as writing **"Life in the Iron-Mills"** in an upper-story room of the house in the cellar of which dwelt, thirty years previously, her working-class protagonists. What we read is "a story of this old house" . . . ; though not so old as the House of the Seven Gables, nor so rich in recorded history as the Salem Custom House, it contains fit material for the writer of romance—a richly symbolic work of art. Her situation, moreover, offers a strategic perspective. The thirty year old author is separated by the span of her life and a storey or two from the situation of her protagonists, which continues

to be the situation of the mass of workers she sees in the street beneath her window. Her imaginative position affords her at once an immediacy of apprehension and an effective working distance from which she can see her story whole. (pp. 72-3)

From her strategic vantage point, Davis imaginatively descends into the mire of her story, and insists that the reader accompany her. . . . The "real thing" at the core of nightmare experience is not the socio-economic "reality" of the "realist"; it is, rather, a secret, a mystery, an unanswered question raised by the "dumb" masses. The secret is not easily revealed, the question not easily answered. The reader may finish **"Life in the Iron-Mills"** without knowing exactly the revelation, the answer Davis intends to offer. This much, however, is clear: the common laborer, though he works in a type of Hell, though his existence is seemingly meaningless, has a soul, and is as worthy of redemption as "you," the middle-class reader. He is capable of love and sacrifice, of aspirations and the appreciation of beauty. He has his role in the moral drama which, for the romantic historian, constitutes history.

A work of art by Hugh Wolfe, Davis's working-class hero, raises the question at the heart of the story most explicitly. The meaning of Wolfe's life, of **"Life in the Iron-Mills,"** comes into focus around the statue of a strong, naked woman he carves from korl, an industrial waste product, as is, in a sense, Wolfe himself. (pp. 73-4)

We first come upon the statue as a group of local "representative men" come upon it in the course of a midnight tour of the iron mill. Initially, they are frightened; they begin to dispute its meaning. . . . Only a cynical aesthete sees in the figure Wolfe's hunger for life. . . . He no more than the others, however, is ready to answer the "awful question" the "dumb face" of the korl woman asks: "What shall we do to be saved?" (p. 74)

Like so many of Hawthorne's romances, . . . **"Life in the Iron-Mills"** evolves its significance, its evaluations and revelations, through a work of art. One is reminded especially of *The Marble Faun,* published the year before Davis' story. . . . Of course it is a long way from Rome to Wheeling, from marble to korl. Hawthorne and Davis do not cover the same ground or sculpt the same material. (p. 75)

Hawthorne and Davis both feel that we are involved in a common mystery, a common romance, though we may not care to acknowledge our commonality. He is chiefly disturbed by the "great gulf" that exists between one man and the next, she by the "great gulf" that exists between classes. . . . Yet Davis too knew the importance of contact between individual souls. The saddest moment in **"Life in the Iron-Mills"** comes when Wolfe, in jail, about to commit suicide, longing to be "spoken to" one last time, calls out "Goodbye, Joe" to a lamplighter. Joe, uncertain of what he hears, passes on without responding. Only a jailer responds, telling Wolfe to "Be quiet," striking the cell door with his club. . . . Yet Wolfe's isolation and doom seem less final than that suffered by a fair number of Hawthorne's characters because of the revelation wrought in and by his korl woman. One might contend that Davis has more faith in romantic resolutions than Hawthorne, her literary mentor.

In placing **"Life in the Iron-Mills"** in the tradition of the social novel, I do not mean to suggest immediate influences so much as common intentions, interests, perspectives, and patterns. Fiction "with a purpose" and fictions which address the "problem" or "condition" of the working class are bound to introduce the reader to a certain quantity of socio-economic reality, which is the province of literary realism. Such literature, however, in probing the *meaning* of apprehended reality, in rendering resolutions, often reveals its affinity to the ideology and form of the romance. (p. 76)

In the middle of **"Life in the Iron-Mills,"** the debate over the meaning of the korl woman leads to a debate over what can be done for such men as Wolfe. . . . It is argued that money is the one thing needful. Wolfe's hunchback cousin, Deb, who unrequitedly loves him and wants the best for him, is led by this argument to pick the pocket of one of the gentlemen engaged in the debate. Wolfe is brought into the crime, and suffers temporary delusions about the power of money, which lock his fate. . . . The korl woman's hunger can be honestly and permanently satisfied only with spiritual food. (pp. 76-7)

In the second quarter of the nineteenth century in England, the romance of the working man captured wide interest. In this period in America, racial divisions loom larger than class divisions; for the whites, the Indian and the black slave are the great subjects of romance. . . . [Davis] might well be pronounced a pioneer romancer for extending the territory of the form to include the American worker at, for America, so early a date.

Davis begins her work, as we have noted before, with a description of the environment which defines the life of the working class. After breathing in the air and the smoke of the laborer, she takes in the town. . . . (p. 78)

"Life in the Iron-Mills" succeeds in giving poverty a local American industrial habitation. It is noteworthy, however, that the resolution of the action of the story involves an escape from the confines of the city landscape, as does the resolution, indeed, of a number of social novels. (p. 79)

In **"Life in the Iron-Mills"** there are no outbreaks of working-class violence, aside from the petty theft of Deb and Wolfe. The potential, however, for an outbreak, for danger, even for revolution, is evident. It is embodied in the korl woman. . . . Davis leads the reader to speculate on the possibility of revolution. . . . (pp. 80-1)

The revolution which Davis seems to consider is chiefly spiritual rather than economic. Through his social crime and death, Wolfe can serve as a Christ-like martyr to the cause. . . . Wolfe does not develop into [a working-class Messiah], but he does begin to see what he might do for his class, and his death prepares the way for the regeneration and redemption of Deb.

The romance form is open to mythic dimensions, prone to rely on mythic patterns for its resolutions. Motifs of death and rebirth are common to the social novel. . . . **"Life in the Iron-Mills"** bears witness to the promise of a revolutionary dawn. There is also a reliance on cyclical patterns to achieve unity of presentation and to confirm or reveal the author's hope: . . . the action of Davis' story chiefly falls between one night and the next, while she presents herself as writing from one dawn to the next; here, the pattern of telling, the rhetorical pattern, rescues, properly interprets, the dramatic pattern. (p. 81)

"Life in the Iron-Mills" could, and can, arouse a "revolutionary attitude towards reality" because it offers both an incarnation of "real existence" as Davis witnessed it and a sense of "the potential" hidden within the life of the iron-mill worker, a potential to be in time revealed. (p. 82)

In her own right, Davis carried on the work of liberation. Her "business" as a romancer engaged her in rescuing the worker from neglect; in subsequent fiction, she carries on her mission to blacks and prostitutes. Not that she preaches, not that she indulges in loose sentimentality. In her early stories, at least, she maintains a kind of Hawthornian economy, together with a commitment to "real existence." Under her auspices, the romance does not preclude an apprehension of reality, but includes it, and involves it in a drama of historic, mythic significance. The romance gives dynamic, accessible import to Davis' social concerns. (pp. 84-5)

> *Walter Hesford, "Literary Contexts of 'Life in the Iron Mills'," in* American Literature *(reprinted by permission of the Publisher; copyright 1977 by Duke Univeristy Press, Durham, North Carolina), Vol. XLIX, No. 1, March, 1977, pp. 70-85.*

ADDITIONAL BIBLIOGRAPHY

Langford, Gerald. *The Richard Harding Davis Years: A Biography of a Mother and Son.* New York: Holt, Rinehart & Winston, 1961. 336 p.
> Thorough account of Rebecca Harding Davis's life and her beginnings as a writer. The critic treats extensively the close lifelong relationship between Rebecca and Richard Harding Davis.

Spiller, Robert E.; Thorp, Willard; Jonson, Thomas H.; and Canby, Henry Seidel; eds. "Realism Defined: William Dean Howells." In *Literary History of the United States,* pp. 878-98. New York: The Macmillan Co., 1948.*
> Places Davis in relation to other early American realists.

F(rancis) Scott (Key) Fitzgerald
1896-1940

American novelist, short story writer, essayist, screenwriter, and dramatist.

Fitzgerald was the spokesman for the Jazz Age, America's decade of prosperity, excess, and abandon, which began soon after the end of World War I and ended with the 1929 stock market crash. The novels and stories for which he is best known examine an entire generation's search for the elusive American dream of wealth and happiness.

The glamour and insouciance portrayed in *This Side of Paradise, The Beautiful and Damned,* and *The Great Gatsby* were derived from Fitzgerald's own life and that of his wife and friends. But the early gaiety shows only one side of a writer whose second and final decade of work portrayed a life marred by alcoholism and financial difficulties, troubled by lost love, and frustrated by lack of inspiration.

The son of well-to-do midwestern parents, Fitzgerald was a precocious child with an early interest in writing plays and poetry. As a young man he emulated the rich, youthful, and beautiful, a social group with whom he maintained a lifelong love-hate relationship. His first stories appeared in Princeton University's literary magazine, which was edited by his friend and fellow student Edmund Wilson. Leaving Princeton for the army during World War I, Fitzgerald spent his weekends in camp writing the earliest draft of his first novel. The eventual acceptance of *This Side of Paradise* by Charles Scribner's Sons in 1919 enabled Fitzgerald to marry Zelda Sayre, whom he had met and courted during his army days.

The jaded, rebellious "flaming youth" of the new era, brought to life in the popular *This Side of Paradise,* were soon imitated nationwide, with Scott and Zelda Fitzgerald serving as models. Zelda significantly affected her husband's life and career. During the 1920s she was Fitzgerald's private literary consultant and editor, while publicly she matched Fitzgerald's extravagant tastes and passion in living for the moment. Her gradual deterioration from schizophrenia and eventual breakdown scarred Fitzgerald, contributing to the deep, self-reproaching despair that brought his career to a near standstill in the mid-1930s.

While continuing to illuminate the manners of the Roaring Twenties, Fitzgerald's second and third novels, as well as the story collections published between novels, evidenced a growing awareness of the shallowness and brutal insensitivity that are sometimes accoutrements of American society. These weaknesses and America's lost ideals are movingly described in Fitzgerald's strongest and most famous work, *The Great Gatsby.* Although it gained the respect of many prominent American writers and is now considered a classic, *Gatsby* was not a popular success and marked the beginning of the author's decline in popularity. Another commercial disappointment, *Tender is the Night,* reflected the disillusionment and strain caused by the Great Depression and Zelda's breakdown. Fitzgerald's downwardly spiralling career is described in detail in the three confessional "Crack-Up" essays of 1936, which bril-

liantly evoked his pain and suffering. Trying to start anew, he became a motion picture scriptwriter and began *The Last Tycoon,* a novel based on his Hollywood experiences, which remained unfinished when Fitzgerald died in late 1940.

In a 1920 interview Fitzgerald called himself "a professed literary thief, hot after the best methods of every writer in my generation." He considered Edmund Wilson his "intellectual conscience," and through his first three novels and ill-fated drama Fitzgerald looked to his former editor for advice and discipline. Ernest Hemingway was Fitzgerald's "artistic conscience," a friend and competitor who often rebuked Fitzgerald for writing slick, but well-paid, magazine stories.

At the time of his death, Fitzgerald's work was forgotten or unread. But a growing Fitzgerald revival, begun in the 1950s, has led to the publication of numerous volumes of stories, letters, and notebooks that indicate the author's importance as a profound and sensitive artist, as well as the unmatched voice of the Jazz Age.

(See also *TCLC*, Vol. 1, and *Dictionary of Literary Biography,* Vol. 4: *American Writers in Paris, 1920-1939;* Vol. 9: *American Novelists, 1910-1945.*)

PRINCIPAL WORKS

Flappers and Philosophers (short stories) 1920
This Side of Paradise (novel) 1920
The Beautiful and Damned (novel) 1922
Tales of the Jazz Age (short stories) 1922
The Vegetable; or, From President to Postman (drama)
  1923
The Great Gatsby (novel) 1925
All the Sad Young Men (short stories) 1926
Tender Is the Night (novel) 1934
Taps at Reveille (short stories) 1935
The Last Tycoon (unfinished novel) 1941
The Crack-Up (essays, notebooks, and letters) 1945
Afternoon of an Author (short stories and essays) 1957
The Pat Hobby Stories (short stories) 1962
Letters (letters) 1963
*Dear Scott/Dear Max: The Fitzgerald-Perkins
  Correspondence* (letters) 1971
*As Ever, Scott Fitz: Letters Between F. Scott Fitzgerald and
  His Literary Agent Harold Ober, 1919-1940* (letters)
  1972
The Basil and Josephine Stories (short stories) 1973
*Bits of Paradise (short stories) 1973
The Notebooks of F. Scott Fitzgerald (notebooks) 1978
The Price Was High (short stories) 1979

*This collection also includes stories by Zelda Fitzgerald.

H. L. MENCKEN (essay date 1920)

The best American novel that I have seen of late is also the
product of a neophyte, to wit, F. Scott Fitzgerald. . . . In **"This
Side of Paradise"** he offers a truly amazing first novel—original in structure, extremely sophisticated in manner, and adorned
with a brilliancy that is as rare in American writing as honesty
is in American statecraft. The young American novelist usually
reveals himself as a naïve, sentimental and somewhat disgusting ignoramus—a believer in Great Causes, a snuffler and
eye-roller, a spouter of stale philosophies out of Kensington
drawing-rooms, the doggeries of French hack-drivers, and the
lower floor of the Munich Hofbräuhaus. . . . In brief, a fellow
viewing human existence through a knot-hole in the floor of a
Socialist local. Fitzgerald is nothing of the sort. On the contrary, he is a highly civilized and rather waggish fellow—a
youngster not without sentiment, and one even cursed with a
touch or two of pretty sentimentality, but still one who is many
cuts above the general of the land. More, an artist—an apt and
delicate weaver of words, a clever hand, a sound workman.
The first half of the story is far better than the second half. It
is not that Fitzgerald's manner runs thin, but that his hero begins
to elude him. What, after such a youth, is to be done with the
fellow? The author's solution is anything but felicitous. He
simply drops his Amory Blaine as Mark Twain dropped Huckleberry Finn, but for a less cogent reason. But down to and
including the episode of the love affair with Rosalind the thing
is capital, especially the first chapters.

> *H. L. Mencken, in his essay in* The Smart Set, *Vol.
> 62, No. 4, August, 1920 (and reprinted as part of
> "'This Side of Paradise'," in* F. Scott Fitzgerald:
> The Critical Reception, *edited by Jackson R. Bryer,
> Burt Franklin & Co., Inc., 1978, p. 28).*

EDMUND WILSON, JR. (essay date 1923)

F. Scott Fitzgerald's play **The Vegetable** . . . is, in some ways,
one of the best things he has done. In it he has a better idea
than he usually has of what theme he wants to develop, and
it does not, as his novels sometimes have, carry him into
regions beyond his powers of flight. It is a fantastic and satiric
comedy carried off with exhilarating humor. One has always
felt that Mr. Fitzgerald ought to write dialogue for the stage
and this comedy would seem to prove it. I do not know of any
dialogue by an American which is lighter, more graceful or
more witty. His spontaneity makes his many bad jokes go and
adds a glamor to his really good ones.

> *Edmund Wilson, Jr., "A Selection of Bric-à-Brac:
> Two Comedies," in* Vanity Fair *(courtesy The Condé
> Nast Publications, Inc.; copyright © 1923, renewed
> 1950, by The Condé Nast Publications, Inc.), Vol.
> 20, No. 4, June, 1923, p. 23.**

MAXWELL E. PERKINS (essay date 1924)

I think you have every kind of right to be proud of [**The Great
Gatsby**]. It is an extraordinary book, suggestive of all sorts of
thoughts and moods. You adopted exactly the right method of
telling it, that of employing a narrator who is more of a spectator than an actor: this puts the reader upon a point of observation on a higher level than that on which the characters stand
and at a distance that gives perspective. In no other way could
your irony have been so immensely effective, nor the reader
have been enabled so strongly to feel at times the strangeness
of human circumstance in a vast heedless universe. In the eyes
of Dr. Eckleberg various readers will see different significances; but their presence gives a superb touch to the whole
thing: great unblinking eyes, expressionless, looking down upon
the human scene. It's magnificent! (pp. 82-3)

The amount of meaning you get into a sentence, the dimensions
and intensity of the impression you make a paragraph carry,
are most extraordinary. The manuscript is full of phrases which
make a scene blaze with life. If one enjoyed a rapid railroad
journey I would compare the number and vividness of pictures
your living words suggest, to the living scenes disclosed in
that way. It seems in reading a much shorter book than it is,
but it carries the mind through a series of experiences that one
would think would require a book of three times its length.

The presentation of Tom, his place, Daisy and Jordan, and the
unfolding of their characters is unequalled so far as I know.
The description of the valley of ashes adjacent to the lovely
country, the conversation and the action in Myrtle's apartment,
the marvelous catalogue of those who came to Gatsby's house,—
these are such things as make a man famous. And all these
things, the whole pathetic episode, you have given a place in
time and space, for with the help of T. J. Eckleberg and by
an occasional glance at the sky, or the sea, or the city, you
have imparted a sort of sense of eternity. You once told me
you were not a *natural* writer—my God! You have plainly
mastered the craft, of course; but you needed far more than
craftsmanship for this. (p. 84)

> *Maxwell E. Perkins, in his letter to F. Scott Fitz-
> gerald on November 20, 1924, in* Dear Scott/Dear
> Max: The Fitzgerald-Perkins Correspondence, *edited
> by John Kuehl and Jackson R. Bryer (copyright ©
> 1971 by Charles Scribner's Sons; reprinted with the
> permission of Charles Scribner's Sons),* Charles
> Scribner's Sons, 1971, pp. 82-4.*

EDITH WHARTON (essay date 1925)

[Let] me say at once how much I like Gatsby, or rather His Book, & how great a leap I think you have taken this time—in advance upon your previous work. My present quarrel with you is only this: that to make Gatsby really Great, you ought to have given us his early career (not from the cradle—but from his visit to the yacht, if not before) instead of a short résumé of it. That would have situated him, & made his final tragedy a tragedy instead of a "fait divers" for the morning papers.

But you'll tell me that's the old way, & consequently not *your* way; & meanwhile, it's enough to make this reader happy to have met your *perfect* Jew, & the limp Wilson, & assisted at that seedy orgy in the Buchanan flat, with the dazed puppy looking on. Every bit of that is masterly—but the lunch with [Wolfsheim], and his every appearance afterward, make me augur still greater things! . . .

> *Edith Wharton, in her letter to F. Scott Fitzgerald on June 8, 1925, in* The Crack-Up, *edited by Edmund Wilson, New Directions, 1945, p. 309.*

JOHN PEALE BISHOP (essay date 1937)

In Fitzgerald the romantic will is strong, all its pursuits subject to disillusionment. In his novels, these pursuits are many, and love is among them, particularly the first loves of endowed youth, prolonging anticipation, delaying those satisfactions which are of the feelings rather than the senses. For his young men are assuaged by what stirs them, the scents, dresses, the slippers of silver and gold. He lingers with knowledge over these adolescent sentiments, confined, like those nostalgic dance tunes which recur through his pages, to the shortest of seasons. Obviously he prefers these young attachments, in which the emotion, part vanity, part desire, has been just felt and is not yet proved by performance. He has not, however, evaded his responsibilities as a novelist; he has seen his lovers through, to tell what becomes of them later. Afterwards come the broker's office, the bank, the racket; the sad young men take to drink; successful or failures, they know the discouragement of a predatory civilization. For let no one be mistaken: though love is always in the foreground in the sentimental world of Fitzgerald, no allure is so potent as money.

"The rich are not as we are." So he began one of his early stories. "No," Hemingway once said to him, "they have more money."

This belief, continually destroyed, constantly reasserted, underlies all that Fitzgerald has written. It made him peculiarly apt to be the historian of the period. Those who have wealth have an assurance that those without cannot hope to have; they dance, they play, they marry none but the loveliest girls; they beget their own kind. They dare where others falter. Pretty much anything goes, so long as there is money. At their worst, the successful will still have the air "of having known the best of this world." They must have spiritual possessions to match their material accumulations.

That the rich are a race apart is a current and not always complimentary assumption. In the Midwest where Fitzgerald grew up, it was the common dream that riches made the superior person. To the acquisitive powers all others would be added. His America, at least in recollection, was that country which, with a sort of ignorant corruption, could profess its love for Lincoln while completely satisfying the appetites of

James K. Hill. And worse than Hill. The Great Gatsby is the Emersonian man brought to completion and eventually to failure; he has returned to the East; the conditions which could tolerate his self-reliant romanticism no longer exist. (pp. 72-3)

> *John Peale Bishop, "The Missing All" (copyright, 1936, by* The Virginia Quarterly Review, *The University of Virginia; copyright renewed © 1964 by Margaret G. H. Bronson as widow of the author), in* The Virginia Quarterly Review, *Vol. 13, No. 1, Winter, 1937, (and reprinted in his* The Collected Essays of John Peale Bishop, *edited by Edmund Wilson, Charles Scribner's Sons, 1948, pp. 66-77).*

GLENWAY WESCOTT (essay date 1941)

I remember thinking, when the early best sellers were published, that [Fitzgerald's] style was a little too free and easy; but I was a fussy stylist in those days. His phrasing was almost always animated and charming; his diction excellent. He wrote very little in slang or what I call babytalk: the pitfall of many who specialized in American contemporaneity after him. But for other reasons—obscurity of sentiment, facetiousness—a large part of his work may not endure, as readable reading matter for art's sake. It will be precious as documentary evidence, instructive example. That is not, in the way of immortality, what the writer hopes; but it is much more than most writers of fiction achieve.

This Side of Paradise haunted the decade like a song, popular but perfect. It hung over an entire youth-movement like a banner, somewhat discolored and wind-worn now; the wind has lapsed out of it. But a book which college boys really read is a rare thing, not to be dismissed idly or in a moment of severe sophistication. Then there were dozens of stories, some delicate and some slap-dash; one very odd, entitled *Head and Shoulders.* I love *The Great Gatsby.* Its very timeliness, as of 1925, gave it a touch of the old-fashioned a few years later; but I have reread it this week and found it all right; pleasure and compassion on every page. A masterpiece often seems a period-piece for a while; then comes down out of the attic, to function anew and to last. There is a great deal to be said for and against his final novel, *Tender Is the Night.* On the whole I am warmly for it. To be sane or insane is a noble issue, and very few novels take what might be called an intelligent interest in it; this does, and gives a fair picture of the entertaining expatriate habit of life besides.

In 1936, in three issues of *Esquire,* he published the autobiographical essay, *The Crack-up,* as it were swan-song. . . . There is very little in world literature like this piece: Max Jacob's *Defense de Tartuffe;* the confidential chapter of *The Seven Pillars of Wisdom,* perhaps; Sir Walter Raleigh's verse-epistle before his beheading, in a way. Fitzgerald's theme seems more dreadful, plain petty stroke by stroke; and of course his treatment lacks the good grace and firmness of the old and old-style authors. Indeed it is cheap here and there, but in embarrassment rather than in crudity or lack of courage. Or perhaps Fitzgerald as he wrote was too sensitive to what was to appear along with it in the magazine: the jokes, the Petty girls, the haberdashery. He always suffered from an extreme environmental sense. Still it is fine prose. . . . It also, with an innocent air, gravely indicts our native idealism in some respects, our common code, our college education. (pp. 119-20)

He had made a great recovery from a seemingly mortal physical illness; then found everything dead or deadish in his psyche, his thought all broken, and no appetite for anything on earth. . . . His trouble just then and his subject was only his lassitude of imagination; his nauseated spirit; that self-hypnotic state of not having any willpower; and nothing left of the intellect but inward observation and dislike. (pp. 120-21)

Especially the first half [of *The Crack-up*] is written without a fault: brief easy fiery phrases—the thinking that he compared to a "moving about of great secret trunks," and "the heady villainous feeling"—one quick and thorough paragraph after another, with so little shame and so little emphasis that I have wondered if he himself knew how much he was confessing. (p. 121)

> Glenway Wescott, "In Memory of Scott Fitzgerald" (copyright by Glenway Wescott), in The New Republic, Vol. 104, No. 7, February 17, 1941 (and reprinted as "The Moral of Scott Fitzgerald," in F. Scott Fitzgerald: The Man and His Work, edited by Alfred Kazin, The World Publishing Company, 1951, pp. 116-29).

CHARLES E. SHAIN (essay date 1961)

This Side of Paradise is usually praised for qualities that pin it closely to an exact moment in American life. Later readers are apt to come to it with the anticipation of an archeologist approaching an interesting ruin. Its publication is always considered to be the event that ushered in the Jazz Age. (p. 20)

Today, the novel's young libertines, both male and female, would not shock a schoolgirl. Amory Blaine turns out to be a conspicuous moralist who takes the responsibility of kissing very seriously and disapproves of affairs with chorus girls. (He has no scruples, it must be said, against going on a three-week drunk when his girl breaks off their engagement.) At the end of the story he is ennobled by an act of self-sacrifice in an Atlantic City hotel bedroom that no one would admire more than a Victorian mother. For modern readers it is probably better to take for granted the usefulness of *This Side of Paradise* for social historians and to admire from the distance of another age the obviously wholesome morality of the hero. Neither of these is the quality that saves the novel for a later time. What Fitzgerald is really showing is how a young American of his generation discovers what sort of figure he wants to cut, what modes of conduct, gotten out of books as well as out of a keen sense of his contemporaries, he wants to imitate. (p. 21)

The novel is very uneven, and full of solemn attempts at abstract thought on literature, war, and socialism. It has vitality and freshness only in moments, and these are always moments of feeling. Fitzgerald said of this first novel many years later, "A lot of people thought it was a fake, and perhaps it was, and a lot of others thought it was a lie, which it was not." It offers the first evidence of Fitzgerald's possession of the gift necessary for a novelist who, like him, writes from so near his own bones, the talent that John Peale Bishop has described as "the rare faculty of being able to experience romantic and ingenuous emotions and a half hour later regard them with satiric detachment." (p. 22)

His success arrived almost overnight: 1920 was the *annus mirabilis*. In that year, the *Saturday Evening Post* published six of his stories, *Smart Set* five, and *Scribner's* two. (p. 23)

The first collection of Fitzgerald's stories in 1921 was timed by Scribner's to profit from the vogue of *This Side of Paradise*. It was called *Flappers and Philosophers.* A second collection, *Tales of the Jazz Age,* was published a year later in the wake of his second novel, *The Beautiful and Damned.* The nineteen stories in the two collections represent with more variety and perhaps more immediacy than the two first novels the manners and morals that have come to compose, at least in the minds of later historians, the Jazz Age. (p. 25)

The Beautiful and Damned was an attempt to write a dramatic novel about a promising American life that never got anywhere. . . . It was the first and least convincing of what were going to be three studies of American failures. As he started the novel in August 1920, Fitzgerald wrote to his publisher that his subject was ". . . the life of Anthony Patch between his 25th and 33rd years (1913-1921). He is one of those many with the tastes and weaknesses of an artist but with no actual creative inspiration. How he and his beautiful young wife are wrecked on the shoals of dissipation is told in the story." (p. 28)

The Beautiful and Damned is a novel of mood rather than a novel of character. The misfortunes of Anthony and Gloria are forced in the plot, but the mood in places is desperate. Fitzgerald does not know what to do with his hero and heroine in the end but make them suffer. The novel will place no blame, either on the nature of things or on the injustices of society. Anthony and Gloria are finally willing to accept all the unhappy consequences as if they had earned them, but the reader has stopped believing in the logic of consequences in this novel long before. The failure of *The Beautiful and Damned* suggests where the soft spots are going to occur in Fitzgerald's art of the novel, in the presentation of character and motivation. With Anthony Patch Fitzgerald assumes that if he has displayed a man's sensibility in some detail he has achieved the study of a tragic character. The "tragedies" suffered by Anthony and Gloria, Fitzgerald's members of the lost generation, lack a moral context as the characters in *The Sun Also Rises* do not. Fitzgerald's fears of his own weaknesses and the excesses that, according to his troubled conscience, he and Zelda were learning to like too easily, endowed the parable of the Patches with moral weight and urgency for its author; but the reader had to invent the worth of the moral struggle for himself. (p. 30)

The Great Gatsby has been discussed and admired as much as any twentieth-century American novel, probably to the disadvantage of Fitzgerald's other fiction. None of its admirers finds it easy to explain why Fitzgerald at this point in his career should have written a novel of such perfect art—though it is usually conceded that he never reached such heights again. (p. 32)

Gatsby's mingled dream of love and money, and the iron strength of his romantic will, make up the essence of the fable, but the art of its telling is full of astonishing tricks. To make the rise and fall of a gentleman gangster an image for the modern history of the Emersonian spirit of America was an audacious thing to attempt, but Fitzgerald got away with it. His own romantic spirit felt deeply what an Englishman has called the "myth-hunger" of Americans, our modern need to "create a manageable past out of an immense present." The poignant effect of the final, highly complex image of the novel, when Gatsby's dream and the American dream are identified, shows how deeply saturated with feeling Fitzgerald's historical imagination was. From his own American life he knew that with his generation the midwesterner had become the typical American and had returned from the old frontier to the East with a new set of dreams—about money. (p. 34)

The whole novel is an imaginative feat that managed to get down the sensational display of postwar America's big money, and to include moral instructions on how to count the cost of it all. *The Great Gatsby* has by this time entered into the national literary mind as only some seemingly effortless works of the imagination can. We can see better now than even some of Fitzgerald's appreciative first reviewers that he had seized upon an important set of symbols for showing that time had run out for one image of the American ego. Poor Gatsby had been, in the novel's terms, deceived into an ignorance of his real greatness by the American world that had for its great men Tom Buchanan and Meyer Wolfsheim, the Wall Street millionaire and his colleague the racketeer. The story does not pretend to know more than this, that Americans will all be the poorer for the profanation and the loss of Gatsby's deluded imagination.

The principal fact in Fitzgerald's life between his twenty-eighth and thirty-fourth year was his inability to write a new novel. (p. 35)

Between 1925 and 1932 he published fifty-six stories, most of them in the *Saturday Evening Post*. (pp. 36-7)

The best stories of those years he selected for two collections [*All the Sad Young Men* and *Taps at Reveille*]. . . . Two recently published collections, *The Stories of F. Scott Fitzgerald*, edited by Malcolm Cowley, and *Afternoon of an Author*, edited by Arthur Mizener, have assured the modern availability of all the good magazine fiction of Fitzgerald's last fifteen years. (p. 37)

During three years beginning in 1928 he sent the *Saturday Evening Post* a series of fourteen stories out of his boyhood and young manhood. The first eight were based on a portrait of himself as Basil Duke Lee. The last six were built around Josephine, the portrait of the magnetic seventeen-year-old girl of his first love affair. It was characteristic of Fitzgerald to relive his youth during the frustrated and unhappy days of his early thirties. His characters always know how much of their most private emotional life depends upon what Anson Hunter calls the "brightest, freshest rarest hours" which protect "that superiority he cherished in his heart." (p. 38)

Fitzgerald's big novel *Tender Is the Night* was written in its final form while Fitzgerald was living very close to his wife's illness. . . . Their life together was over. It is astonishing that, written under such emotional pressures, *Tender Is the Night* is such a wise and objective novel as it is. (p. 39)

Tender Is the Night is Fitzgerald's weightiest novel. It is full of scenes that stay alive with each rereading, the cast of characters is the largest he ever collected, and the awareness of human variety in the novel's middle distance gives it a place among those American novels which attempt the full narrative mode. Arnold's assumption that how to live is itself a moral idea provides the central substance of the novel. The society Dick has chosen is a lost one, but Dick must function as if he is not lost. To bring happiness to people, including his wife, is to help them fight back selfishness and egotism, to allow their human imaginations to function. To fill in the background of a leisured class with human dignity does not seem a futile mission to Dr. Diver until he fails. For Fitzgerald's hero "charm always had an independent existence"; he calls it "courageous grace." A life of vital response is the only version of the moral life Fitzgerald could imagine, and when Dr. Diver hears the

"interior laughter" begin at the expense of his human decency he walks away. He returns to America and his life fades away in small towns in upstate New York as he tries unsuccessfully to practice medicine again. (p. 41)

Nearly all the influential critics discovered the same fault in the novel, that Fitzgerald was uncertain, and in the end unconvincing, about why Dick Diver fell to pieces. . . . [Fitzgerald's] short stories in *Taps at Reveille*, the next year, were greeted by even more hostile reviews and the volume sold only a few thousand. . . . And between 1934 and 1937 his daily life declined into the crippled state that is now known after his own description of it as "the crack-up." (pp. 41-2)

Fitzgerald's public analysis of his desperate condition, published in three essays in *Esquire* in the spring of 1936, will be read differently by different people. (p. 42)

The crack-up essays have become classics, as well known as the best of Fitzgerald's short fiction. . . . The grace of the prose has made some readers suspect that Fitzgerald is withholding the real ugliness of the experience, that he is simply imitating the gracefully guilty man in order to avoid the deeper confrontation of horror. But his language often rises above sentiment and pathos to the pure candor of a generous man who decided "There was to be no more giving of myself" and then, in writing it down, tried to give once more. (pp. 42-3)

For several months in 1939 he was in a New York hospital but by July he was writing short stories again for *Esquire*. He wrote in all twenty-two stories in the eighteen months remaining to him, seventeen of them neat and comic little stories about a corrupt movie writer named Pat Hobby, and one little masterpiece, **"The Lost Decade,"** a sardonic picture of a talented man who had been drunk for ten years.

During the last year of his life Fitzgerald wrote as hard as his depleted capacities allowed him on the novel he left half-finished at his death, *The Last Tycoon*. It is an impressive fragment. (p. 44)

The Last Tycoon had the mark of the thirties on it as surely as his early novels had the American boom as their principal theme. The subject was Hollywood as an industry and a society, but also as an American microcosm. Instead of drawing a deft impression of American society as he had in his earlier fiction, Fitzgerald now wanted to record it. The first hundred pages of the novel take us behind the doors of studios and executive offices in Hollywood with the authority of first-rate history. The history fastens on the last of the American barons, Hollywood's top producer, Monroe Stahr, and we watch him rule a complex industry and produce a powerful popular art form with such a dedication of intelligence and will that he becomes a symbol for a vanishing American grandeur of character and role. "Unlike *Tender Is the Night*," Fitzgerald explained, "it is not the story of deterioration—it is not depressing and not morbid in spite of the tragic ending. If one book could ever be 'like' another, I should say it is more 'like' *The Great Gatsby*. . . ." The plot was to show Stahr's fight for the cause of the powerful and responsible individual against Hollywood's labor gangsters and Communist writers. Violent action and melodrama were to carry the story, like a Dickens novel, to seats of power in Washington and New York. . . . The action is brilliantly conceived and economically executed. Fitzgerald's style is lean and clear. His power of letting his meanings emerge from incident was never more sharply displayed. At the center of his hero's last two years of life is an ill-starred love affair, like Fitzgerald's own, that comes too late and only reminds him of his lost first wife. But Fitzgerald kept his romantic ego in check in imagining Stahr. What obviously fascinated him was the creation of an American type upon whom responsibility and power had descended and who was committed to building something with his power, something that would last, even though it was only a brief scene in a movie. (pp. 44-5)

> *Charles E. Shain, in his* F. Scott Fitzgerald *(American Writers Pamphlet No. 15; © 1961, University of Minnesota), University of Minnesota Press, Minneapolis, 1961, 45 p.*

CLEANTH BROOKS (essay date 1971)

Whether we Americans are really innocent or whether we are not, we have had with us for a long time the notion that Americans *are* innocent and that their innocence is of a peculiar and special sort. In recent years, this notion has come in for increased attention. Americans, in their growing self-consciousness, try to analyze the ways in which their experience differs from that of Europe and the possibly different perspectives in which they are forced to see the claims of the past and the promise of the future. (p. 181)

What I propose to talk about is the way in which three great American novelists have treated the "innocent" American. My texts will be [Henry James's *The American*, F. Scott Fitzgerald's *The Great Gatsby,* and William Faulkner's *Absalom, Absalom!*]. . . . (p. 182)

[Fitzgerald's hero, Jay Gatsby, is] a self-made man. His fortune was built up rapidly during the Prohibition era, and though we are not told in detail just how it was accumulated, his financial manipulations clearly will not bear inspection. But Gatsby, though his great wealth is tainted, is in his own way an idealist—he lives for an idea—and manages to preserve a kind of innocence which, in the total context, is not simply amusing and odd, but magnificent.

Before making his fortune, Gatsby has fallen in love with a young woman named Daisy, but as a soldier preparing to be sent overseas in the First World War, a man moreover without money, he is not able to marry the girl, and Daisy lands in the arms of Tom Buchanan, an eligible suitor who has money and some kind of social position.

The chalice of love that poor deluded Gatsby—born Gatz—bears for four years, safely through the jostling throng, is his idealistic love for Daisy. It is for her that he has accumulated a fortune, and now in the monstrously big house that he has bought across the harbour from the Buchanans, he looks wistfully every night at the little green light on the Buchanan dock. Finally, Gatsby meets Daisy again and tries to reclaim her for true love. The effort fails, of course, as it must; but in contrast to the shoddy, plutocratic society which has swallowed up Daisy, Gatsby's innocence—even though we must put it very carefully within quotation marks, shines with a hard and gem-like flame—or if you prefer Shakespeare to Pater—shines like a good deed in a naughty world. Fitzgerald makes it quite plain that the world inhabited by the Buchanans is a naughty world. (p. 183)

[A] close look at [James's] Newman, Gatsby, and [Faulkner's Thomas] Sutpen ought to tell us a great deal about the nature of innocence, for in spite of the differences among these three characters, each is obviously to be regarded as in some sense innocent. But since the nature of innocence is the problem at issue—the matter to be defined—let us begin with more objective matters. What is common to the backgrounds of these men?

In the first place, all three, in effect, come out of nowhere: their families can give them nothing and do not share their ambitions. There is no process of nurturing, no family tradition that is handed on. Each of our heroes leaves his family early and strikes out on his own. (p. 184)

What is true of all of these men is not that they are all "self-made" merely in the fact that they did not inherit their wealth. In a far more important way, they are self-made—in the sense that they have created their own personalities and disciplined their minds in the service of a dream. Fitzgerald tells us that "the truth was that Jay Gatsby . . . sprang from his Platonic conception of himself." So it is with Thomas Sutpen. Sutpen once told his sole friend in the community that he knew that he possessed courage and as for the cleverness, "if it were to be learned by energy and will in the school of endeavor and experience" he would learn. Sutpen's deepest belief is that a courageous man, if he plans carefully enough, can accomplish anything.

Though Gatsby will seem, when measured against Sutpen's intensity, somewhat relaxed and offhand, his creed is much like Sutpen's. He is possessed by the same kind of devouring idealism. When Gatsby's friend tries to suggest to him that what has happened has happened, and that one simply "can't repeat the past," Gatsby cries out incredulously: "Can't repeat the past? Why, of course you can!" (p. 185)

Sutpen has not only a "design," as he calls it in his conversation with General Compson, but he has also what he calls his schedule—that is, his time table—in accordance with which the design is to be realized.

Jay Gatsby, of South Dakota, lived by a schedule too. One of the most poignant things about this young gangster-idealist is a scrap of paper that turns up late in the story. After Gatsby's death, Nick Carraway comes upon a bit of paper dated September 12, 1906, bearing the word "schedule." . . . It is touching to see how this seventeen-year-old boy sought with a fierce austerity to pull himself up by his own bootstraps. But the discovery has its ominous side, for men who rule their lives in this way are likely to suffer from an elephantiasis of the will. In both Thomas Sutpen and Jay Gatsby that faculty is developed to the point of deformity. (pp. 186-87)

[James's] Newman sees himself as a kind of St. George sallying out of the new world to save a beautiful maiden from the clutches of an old-world dragon, but he fails in his mission. Had Jay Gatsby had better luck and rescued his maiden from her dragon, would he have been happy? Perhaps, but there is nothing in the novel to make one think so, and there are some things in it that seriously call in question any supposal that he and his dream girl—for that is literally what she is—could have lived happily ever after. It is not merely a question of Daisy's superficiality—of her initial weakness or of the corrupting influence of her life with Tom Buchanan. The most ominous portent lies in the character of Gatsby himself—in his "innocence." For Gatsby is a man in the grip of a powerful illusion and his image of Daisy surely could not have survived the flesh-and-blood experience of the actual Daisy. Fitzgerald has hinted that Gatsby himself may have sensed this possibility. Early in his courtship of Daisy, Fitzgerald tells us, Gatsby had a sort of vision: in the evening light the blocks of the sidewalk seemed to form a ladder that "mounted to a secret place above the trees—he could climb it, if he climbed alone, and once there he could suck on the pap of life, gulp down the incomparable milk of wonder.'' Nevertheless, he seeks Daisy's lips and ''forever wed his unutterable visions to her perishable breath.''

Here it is appropriate to observe that both Newman and Gatsby dismiss the claims of family, of the past, and of society in general in favor of the intimate communion of two people who feel they need nothing for their happiness but each other. This notion, whether or not it is to be called innocent, is good American doctrine. . . . Fitzgerald, who is not innocent in this sense, gives more than a hint that he knows how things would have gone with Daisy and Gatsby. . . . (p. 190)

But what of innocence? (p. 192)

[In his *The American Adam*, R.W.B. Lewis] tells us that James's treatment of the theme of innocence involved a ''very long series of innocent and metaphorically new-born heroes and heroines,'' and he points out further that these qualities of innocence are treated by James ''with every conceivable variety of ethical weight.'' Even in *The American* it is plain that James regards the innocence of a man like Newman as not merely, and not wholly, admirable. Lewis remarks that in his fiction James made it quite clear that ''innocence could be cruel as well as vulnerable.'' (p. 194)

Even Fitzgerald seems to imply such a conception of innocence, for his Jay Gatsby is not the only innocent in his novel. Consider Daisy and Tom Buchanan. The term that Fitzgerald applies to them is, to be sure, not innocent but ''careless.'' He has Nick Carraway observe that ''They were careless people, Tom and Daisy—they smashed up things and creatures and then retreated back into their money or their vast carelessness. . . .'' This is Nick's bitter final characterization of the pair. Nick had meant to reproach Tom Buchanan for having in effect connived at Gatsby's murder. But in his final interview with Tom, Nick tells us: ''I felt suddenly as though I were talking to a child.'' In saying this, Nick is indeed very close to calling Tom ''innocent''—that is, a man who has not yet found out what reality is like and who has not yet transcended the child's self-centered world.

This discussion has seemed to imply that innocence is not a quality wholly good or desirable; that, on the contrary, it is something to be sloughed off in process of time—a state to be grown out of—a negative thing that ought to disappear with the acquisition of knowledge and moral discipline. I plead guilty to this emphasis, but it does seem to be the emphasis of two, and perhaps of all three, of the novelists we have been considering. . . .

In order to make a case for innocence as a positive virtue, I shall appeal to one of the great poems of our century, a poem about innocence written not by an American but by the Irishman, William Butler Yeats. . . .

Yeats's ''A Prayer for My Daughter'' was written in 1919. The occasion is a storm howling in off the Atlantic, sweeping past the tower home near the west coast of Ireland in which Yeats was then living. The poet's infant daughter lies asleep in her cradle, and the father, dreading what the future may have in store for his child, makes his prayer for gifts and qualities that shall stay her against the destructive forces that threaten her future. (p. 195)

The murderous innocence that is amoral and that is associated with the storm winds off the Atlantic is set over against a radical innocence—that is, an innocence *rooted* like the laurel tree. And nature as capricious and cruel, mere brute force, is contrasted with a human nature which is very much like the Platonic view of the soul. One may hope to find in its depths norms and archetypes of order, indeed a reflection of the divine order. (p. 196)

[We] are in the habit of thinking of innocence and beauty as the gift of nature; and we commonly oppose them to custom and ceremony, for we think of custom and ceremony as tending to sophisticate, and even to corrupt. Yeats inverts these relations. Innocence and beauty, he maintains, are not the products of nature but the fruit of a disciplined life. They spring from order. They are not capriciously given. They come from nurture and tradition.

The innocence with which we are born—if we *are* born innocent—does not suffice.

Seen in this perspective, the term ''self-made'' itself takes on new meanings. The self-made man has, to be sure, made his fortune and may have made his ''world,'' but can he be called truly self-made? Or at least *well made* if he is merely *self-made*? Isn't man too much a social and political animal for such self-creation to be other than fantastic? I think that our three American novelists are in agreement on this point. Fitzgerald's remark that Gatsby ''sprang from his Platonic conception of himself'' hangs somewhere between amused admiration and sardonic awe. . . . (p. 197)

> *Cleanth Brooks, ''The American 'Innocence' in James, Fitzgerald, and Faulkner'' (copyright © 1964 by Cleanth Brooks; reprinted by permission of Harcourt Brace Jovanovich, Inc; in Canada by Methuen & Co. Ltd; originally published in a slightly different form in* Shenandoah, *Vol. XVI, No. 1, Autumn, 1964), in his* A Shaping Joy: Studies in the Writer's Craft, *Methuen, 1971 (and reprinted by Harcourt, 1972), pp. 181-97.**

LELAND S. PERSON, JR. (essay date 1978)

Few critics write about *The Great Gatsby* without discussing Daisy Fay Buchanan; and few, it seems, write about Daisy without entering the unofficial competition of maligning her character. . . . A striking similarity in these negative views of Daisy is their attribution to her of tremendous power over Gatsby and his fate. Equating Daisy with the kind of Circean figures popular in the nineteenth century, the critics tend to accept Gatsby as an essential innocent who ''turn[s] out all right at the end.'' Daisy, on the other hand, becomes the essence of ''what preyed on'' Gatsby, a part of that ''foul dust [that] floated in the wake of his dreams.'' . . . (p. 250)

Such an easy polarization of characters into Good Boy/Bad Girl, however, arises from a kind of critical double standard and simply belittles the complexity of the novel. Daisy, in fact, is more victim than victimizer: she is victim first of Tom Buchanan's ''cruel'' power, but then of Gatsby's increasingly depersonalized vision of her. She becomes the unwitting ''grail'' . . . in Gatsby's adolescent quest to remain ever-faithful to his seventeen-year-old conception of self . . . , and even Nick admits that Daisy ''tumbled short of his dreams—not through her own fault, but because of the colossal vitality of his illusion. It had gone beyond her, beyond everything.'' . . . Thus, Daisy's reputed failure of Gatsby is inevitable; no woman, no human being, could ever approximate the platonic ideal he has invented. If she is corrupt by the end of the novel and part of a "conspiratorial" . . . coterie with Tom, that corruption is not so much inherent in her character as it is the progressive result of her treatment by the other characters.

In addition to being a symbol of Gatsby's illusions, Daisy has her own story, her own spokesman in Jordan Baker, even her own dream. Nick, for example, senses a similar "romantic readiness" in Daisy as in Gatsby, and during the famous scene in Gatsby's mansion, Daisy herself expresses the same desire to escape the temporal world. "'I'd like to just get one of those pink clouds,'" she tells Gatsby, "'and put you in it and push you around'." . . . If Daisy fails to measure up to Gatsby's fantasy, therefore, he for his part clearly fails to measure up to hers. At the same time that she exists as the ideal object of Gatsby's quest, in other words, Daisy becomes his female double. She is both anima and Doppelgänger, and *The Great Gatsby* is finally the story of the failure of a mutual dream. The novel describes the death of a romantic vision of America and embodies that theme in the accelerated dissociation—the mutual alienation—of men and women before the materialistic values of modern society. Rather than rewriting the novel according to contemporary desires, such a reading of Daisy's role merely adds a complementary dimension to our understanding and appreciation of a classic American novel.

A persistent problem for the contemporary critic of *The Great Gatsby* is the reliability of Nick Carraway as narrator, and certainly any effort to revise current opinion of Daisy's role must begin with Nick. Without rehearsing that familiar argument in detail, we can safely suggest that Nick's judgment of Daisy (like his judgment of Gatsby) proceeds from the same desire to have his broken world "in uniform and at a sort of moral attention forever." . . . Returning to a Middle West which has remained as pure as the driven snow he remembers from his college days, Nick flees an Eastern landscape and a cast of characters which have become irrevocably "distorted beyond [his] eyes' power of correction." . . . Life, he concludes, is "more successfully looked at from a single window, after all" . . . , and the same tendency to avoid the complexity of experience becomes evident in Nick's relationship to women.

While he is far more circumspect and pragmatic than Gatsby, in his own way Nick maintains a similarly fabulous (and safely distanced) relation to women. In effect, he represents another version of that persistent impulse among Fitzgerald's early protagonists (e.g., Amory Blaine, Anthony Patch, Dexter Green, Merlin Grainger of **"O Russet Witch!"**) to abstract women into objects of selfish wish-fulfillment. Nick, after all, has moved East at least in part to escape a "tangle back home" involving a girl from Minnesota to whom he is supposedly engaged. . . . And in New York he has had a "short affair" with a girl in the bond office but has "let it blow quietly away" because her brother threw him "mean looks." . . . In both cases Nick seems desperate to escape the consequences of his actions; he prefers unentangled relationships. Indeed, he seems to prefer a fantasy life with Jordan and even with nameless girls he sees on the streets of New York. . . . Even with Jordan, Nick manifests the sort of attraction to uncomplicated little girls that will seem almost pathological in Dick Diver of **Tender Is the Night.** Jordan, he enjoys thinking, rests childlike "just within the circle of [his] arm" . . . , and because he has no "girl whose disembodied face floated along the dark cornices and blinding signs" . . . , Nick tightens his grip on Jordan, trying to make her what Gatsby has made of Daisy.

Despite the tendency of critics to view her as a "monster of bitchery," Daisy has her own complex story, her own desires

and needs. "'I'm p-paralyzed with happiness'" . . . , she says to Nick when he meets her for the first time, and even though there is a certain insincerity in her manner, Daisy's words do perfectly express the quality of her present life. In choosing Tom Buchanan over the absent Gatsby, Daisy has allowed her life to be shaped forever by the crude force of Tom's money. According to Nick's hypothesis, "all the time [Gatsby was overseas] something within her was crying for a decision. She wanted her life shaped now, immediately—and the decision must be made by some force—of love, of money, of unquestionable practicality—that was close at hand." . . . Yet Daisy discovers as early as her honeymoon that Tom's world is hopelessly corrupt; in fact, Daisy's lyric energy (which so attracts Gatsby) must be frozen before she will marry Buchanan.

In a scene which has attracted remarkably little critical attention, Jordan tells Nick of Daisy's relationship with Gatsby in Louisville and of her marriage to Tom. Despite the $350,000-dollar string of pearls around her neck, when Daisy receives a letter from Gatsby the night before the wedding, she is ready to call the whole thing off. Gatsby's appeal far surpasses Tom's, and the pearls quickly end up in the wastebasket. The important point to recognize is that Gatsby is as much an ideal to Daisy as she is to him. Only Gatsby looks at her—creates her, makes her come to herself—"in a way that every young girl wants to be looked at some time." . . . Thus, it is only after she is forced into an ice-cold bath and the letter which she clutches has crumbled "like snow" that Daisy can marry Tom "without so much as a shiver." . . . She has been baptized in ice, and with her romantic impulses effectively frozen, Daisy Fay becomes "paralyzed" with conventional happiness as Mrs. Tom Buchanan. Her present ideal, transmitted to her daughter, is to be a "beautiful little fool" because that is the "best thing a girl can be in this world." . . . (pp. 250-53)

Although Fitzgerald certainly depicts Daisy as a traditionally mysterious source of inspiration, even here he dramatizes the limitations of the male imagination at least as much as Daisy's failure to live up to Gatsby's ideal. Gatsby's world is founded on a fairy's wing . . . , and as the discrepancy between the real Daisy and Gatsby's dream image becomes apparent, Nick observes, Gatsby's count of "enchanted objects" is diminished by one. . . . In effect, Gatsby scarcely apprehended or loved the real Daisy; she was always an "enchanted object": initially as the "first 'nice' girl he had ever known" . . . , and then as the Golden Girl, "gleaming like silver, safe and proud above the hot struggles of the poor." . . . The essence of Daisy's promise, of course, is best represented by the magical properties of her voice; yet the process by which Nick and Gatsby research the meaning of that essentially nonverbal sound progressively demystifies the archetype. When Gatsby weds his unutterable vision to Daisy's mortal breath, he immediately restricts the scope of her potential meaning. Much like Hawthorne in *The Scarlet Letter,* Fitzgerald demonstrates the recovery and loss of symbolic vision in *The Great Gatsby.*

Early in the novel, for example, Nick only faintly apprehends the uniqueness of Daisy's voice. Like a fine musical instrument, Daisy's voice produces a sound so impalpable and suggestive that it seems purely formal. (p. 254)

A vivid expression of an archetype which is fluid in form yet suggests nearly infinite designs, her voice inspires both Nick and Gatsby to wild imaginings. Nick, in fact, hears a quality in Daisy's voice which seems at first to transcend the meaning of words. "I had to follow the sound of it for a moment, up and down, with my ear alone," he says, "before any words came through." . . . Daisy's effect is thus linked explicitly to the kind of auroral effect that a truly symbolic object produces on an artist's mind, "bringing out a meaning in each word that it had never had before and would never have again." . . . She seems able to transform the material world into some ephemeral dreamland in which objects suddenly glow with symbolic meaning. Thus, Gatsby "literally glowed" in Daisy's presence "like an ecstatic patron of recurrent light" . . . , and the objects he immediately revalues "according to the measure of response [they] drew from her well-loved eyes" suddenly seem no longer real. . . . Existing within a realm of as yet uncreated possibility, Daisy's essential meaning, in short, suggests a psychic impulse too fleeting to be articulated or brought across the threshold of conscious thought. Frantically trying to comprehend the impulse within himself which Daisy's voice evokes, Nick concludes: "I was reminded of something—an elusive rhythm, a fragment of lost words, that I had heard somewhere a long time ago. For a moment a phrase tried to take shape in my mouth and my lips parted like a dumb man's, as though there was more struggling upon them than a wisp of startled air. But they made no sound, and what I had almost remembered was uncommunicable forever." . . . (pp. 254-55)

Like Gatsby with his "unutterable vision," then, Nick admits his failure to realize (and communicate) the essence of Daisy's meaning. Together, both men effectively conspire to reduce that meaning to a "single window" perspective. As successfully as the townspeople of *The Scarlet Letter* in their efforts to confine the punitive meaning of Hester's "A," Nick and Gatsby progressively devitalize Daisy's symbolic meaning until she exists as a vulgar emblem of the money values which dominate their world. Her voice was "full of money," Nick agrees; "that was the inexhaustible charm that rose and fell in it, the jingle of it, the cymbals' song of it. . . . High in a white palace the king's daughter, the golden girl. . . ." . . . Paralleling Fitzgerald's sense of America's diminishing possibilities, Gatsby's action has the added effect of forfeiting forever his capacity to reclaim Daisy from Tom's influence. When he tries to become a *nouveau riche* version of Tom, Gatsby ceases to have the power to take Daisy back to her beautiful white girlhood. No longer does he look at her with the creative look the "way every young girl wants to be looked at"; instead, Daisy becomes the victim of what has become Gatsby's irrevocably meretricious look.

Because she, too, seeks a lost moment from the past, Gatsby succeeds momentarily in liberating Daisy from Tom's world. However, just as the shirts in his closet "piled like bricks in stacks a dozen high" . . . signal the disintegration of Gatsby's obsessively constructed kingdom of illusion, Daisy's uncontrollable sobbing with her magical voice "muffled in the thick folds" . . . represents the end of her dream as well. Even as Nick apologizes for its simplicity, Daisy is simply "offended" by the vulgarity of Gatsby's world. . . . Thus, although both characters do enjoy the moment "in between time" possessed of "intense life" . . . which they have sought, Gatsby and Daisy inevitably split apart. When Tom reveals the real Gatsby as a "common swindler" . . . , Daisy's own count of "enchanted objects" also diminishes by one. She cries out at first that she "won't stand this" . . . , but as the truth of Tom's accusation sinks in, she withdraws herself from Gatsby forever. For the second time, Tom's crude, yet palpable force disillusions Daisy about Gatsby, and in spite of the latter's desperate attempts to defend himself, "with every word she was drawing further and further into herself, so he gave that up, and only the dead dream fought on as the afternoon slipped away, trying

to touch what was no longer tangible, struggling unhappily, undespairingly, toward that lost voice across the room." . . . Because she cannot exist in the nether world of a "dead dream" which has eclipsed everything about her except the money in her voice, Daisy moves back toward Tom and his world of "unquestionable practicality." Reduced to a golden statue, a collector's item which crowns Gatsby's material success, Daisy destroys even the possibility of illusion when she runs down Myrtle Wilson in Gatsby's car.

Not only does she kill her husband's mistress, thus easing her reentry into his life, but she climaxes the symbolic process by which she herself has been reduced from archetype to stereotype. At the moment of impact—the final crash of the dead dream into the disillusioning body of reality—it is surely no accident in a novel of mutual alienation that Daisy and Gatsby are both gripping the steering wheel. Daisy loses her nerve to hit the other car and commit a double suicide (thus preserving their dream in the changelessness of death); instead she chooses life and the seemingly inevitable workings of history. She forces the story to be played out to its logical conclusion: Gatsby's purgative death and her own estrangement from love. Despite Nick's judgment of her carelessness and "basic insincerity," her conspiratorial relationship with Tom, Daisy is victimized by a male tendency to project a self-satisfying, yet ultimately dehumanizing, image on woman. If Gatsby had "wanted to recover something, some idea of himself perhaps, that had gone into loving Daisy" . . . , if Nick had nearly recovered a "fragment of lost words" through the inspiring magic of her voice, then Daisy's potential selfhood is finally betrayed by the world of the novel. Hers remains a "lost voice," and its words and meaning seem "uncommunicable forever." (pp. 255-57)

Leland S. Person, Jr., "'Herstory' and Daisy Buchanan," in American Literature *(reprinted by permission of the Publisher; copyright 1978 by Duke University Press, Durham, North Carolina), Vol. L, No. 2, May, 1978, pp. 250-57.*

MALCOLM COWLEY (essay date 1979)

[Fifty stories], or nearly one-third of Fitzgerald's magazine work—are collected for the first time in **"The Price Was High."** "There isn't any more now," the editor says a little wistfully. The barrel has been turned upside down, but I was happy to find that there are things other than dregs at the bottom of it.

There are, for example, several remembered stories that I read again with pleasure and with greater admiration than I had expected to feel. Among them, **"Dice, Brassknuckles & Guitar"** . . . is almost pure froth and lightheartedness. The Southern hero, with his touring car that keeps coming apart and his brassknuckled finishing school for the subdebs of Southampton, evokes a mixture of hilarity and affection. Plot? There's too much plot, as often with Fitzgerald, but one can forget about it.

"The Love Boat" . . . marks a new stage in Fitzgerald's career as a magazine writer; it is the first of his mature stories about the search for irrecoverable illusions. . . . As always, they center on a girl. "Her smile came first slowly, then with a rush, pouring out of her heart, shy and bold, as if all the life of that little body had gathered for a moment around her mouth and the rest of her was a wisp that the least wind would blow away." Here the romantic music resembles the grand opening scenes of Alain-Fournier's "The Wanderer."

"The Bowl" . . . is Fitzgerald's only college-football story, much as he loved the sport. It also expresses his lasting admiration for what he called the "final people" in any profession. "All these," I once wrote of the story, "had an authority and, he believed, a sense of kinship that was based on their common respect for disciplined effort. 'Why, I'm Dolly Harlan,' the football hero says, in the same spirit that the author would like to have said, 'Why, I'm Scott Fitzgerald.'"

"The Rubber Check" . . . is about the usual Fitzgerald young man, this time depicted frankly as a fortune hunter. He falls in love with Ellen Mortmain, whose "childish beauty was wistful and sad about being so rich and sixteen." But later, "all around her he could feel the vast Mortmain fortune melting down, seeping back into the matrix whence it had come." Reduced to working as a gardener, Val Schuyler reflects: "Society. He had leaned upon its glacial bosom like a trusting child, feeling a queer sort of delight in the diamonds that cut hard into his cheek."

"More Than Just a House" . . . is about the same Fitzgerald hero, though it casts him in the role of a rising businessman. . . .

Those five are my favorites among the stories overlooked by previous editors (including myself), but there are others I was glad to see collected in this book of last things. One of them is **"Image on the Heart"** . . . , a story based on Zelda Fitzgerald's passion for a French aviator and the ambiguous feelings it left behind. Another is **"Discard"** . . . , for which Fitzgerald's title was "Director's Special"; it is the double portrait of a Hollywood star and of the younger woman who tries to devour her, lock, stock and top billing, husband and house. **"A Freeze-Out"** . . . , **"Three Acts of Music"** . . . and I could name a few others that present new facets of Fitzgerald's talent.

The sad fact remains that three-fourths of the stories in **"The Price Was High"** are below his usual level of achievement. In general they depend too much on coincidence, melodramatic turns of plot and information withheld from the reader until the last moment so as to end the story with an O. Henry twist. More fatally, they reveal an innocent snobbery, a resentful tribute paid to inherited wealth and position—a habit of mind that went out of fashion in the Depression years and that now seems archaic.

Yet I was glad to reread all 50 stories, including the weakest of those rescued from the bottom of the barrel. Almost all of them contain something to surprise us, if only a sentence or a passing observation of the sort that Fitzgerald squirreled away in his notebook for possible use in a novel after the story itself had been (as he used to say) "junked and dismantled." "Abruptly it became full summer," we read in **"A Freeze-Out,"** one of the dismantled stories. "After the last April storm someone came along the street one night, blew up the trees like balloons, scattered bulbs and shrubs like confetti, opened a cage full of robins and, after a quick look around, signaled up the curtain upon a new backdrop of summer sky." Those lines are romantic poetry, a mixture of Keats and Cummings with a dash of Jerome Kern, but they bear the distinctive Fitzgerald stamp.

"The day of his elopement with Lucy," we read in another dismantled story, **"The Adolescent Marriage"** . . . , "had been like an ecstatic dream; he the young knight, scorned by her father, the baron, as a mere youth, bearing her away, and all willing, on his charger, in the dead of the night." That too

bears the Fitzgerald stamp; in a few phrases it gives us the Lochinvar legend that was his favorite theme. Obsessed with time, he was a master at rendering ecstatic dreams or moments of felt beauty. . . . Such moments are still there for Fitzgerald's readers, and they are a sound reason for preserving even the weaker stories in this final collection.

Malcolm Cowley, "A Book of Last Things," in The New York Times Book Review *(© 1979 by The New York Times Company; reprinted by permission), March 4, 1979, p. 7.*

ROBERT MURRAY DAVIS   (essay date 1979)

The forty percent of Fitzgerald's notebooks not included in **The Crack-Up,** together with the corrected version of that material and "a selection from the miscellaneous notes" written for the Hollywood novel "which do not seem to bear directly on **The Last Tycoon,**" are [presented in **The Notebooks of F. Scott Fitzgerald,** edited by Matthew J. Bruccoli] . . . with what seems to be careful editing and intelligent but sometimes too unobtrusive annotation. Aside from noting the irony of publishing these fragments when better than competent writers—like Fitzgerald himself in the late 1930s—cannot remain in print, one can speculate on the use to which the notebooks can be put. Perhaps least important, except for specialists who will pursue the topic further and who will be indebted to Bruccoli for the annotations, are the relationships between the notebooks and Fitzgerald's fiction. More important to the general reader is the way in which notebooks of any writer reveal the essence of the talent prior to the obscuring excitements of plot or illusions of form.

Thus, to use Fitzgerald's own categories, he was not really very good at Jingles and Songs or Ideas; rather poor at Rough Stuff, Slang, Nonsense and Stray Phrases, Anecdotes or Bright Clippings; and no good at all at Epigrams, Wise Cracks and Jokes. He was not at all bad at Observations and first-rate at Descriptions of Things and Atmosphere. He could see the motives which actuate many of us much of the time, especially the vanities and insecurities which stem from too much or too little looks, money, position. And he had an obsession with and something like a genius for the rhythm—a key term—of a situation or a personality.

In fact, the notebooks underscore the fact that Fitzgerald was essentially a lyric writer who tried, by cultivating a sense of history, to become epic or dramatic and sometimes succeeded in being elegiac. He seemed to believe that the right verbal formula could transmute anything. This is not a belief which makes a major writer, but it is far from the worst illusion a writer can have.

Robert Murray Davis, "Miscellaneous: 'The Notebooks of F. Scott Fitzgerald'," in World Literature Today *(copyright 1979 by the University of Oklahoma Press), Vol. 53, No. 4, Autumn, 1979, p. 689.*

GORE VIDAL   (essay date 1980)

Although very little of what Fitzgerald wrote has any great value as literature, his sad life continues to provide not only English Departments but the movies with a Cautionary Tale of the first magnitude. Needless to say, Scott Fitzgerald is now a major academic industry. . . .

For Americans, a writer's work is almost always secondary to his life—or life-style, as they say nowadays. This means that the novelist's biographer is very apt to make more, in every sense, out of the life than the writer who lived it. Certainly, Fitzgerald's personal story is a perennially fascinating Cautionary Tale. As for his novels, the two that were popular in his lifetime were minor books whose themes—not to mention titles—appealed enormously to the superstitions and the prejudices of the middle class: *This Side of Paradise* and *The Beautiful and Damned*—if that last title isn't still a lu-lu out on the Twice-born circuit . . . , I will reread the book. But when Fitzgerald finally wrote a distinguished novel, the audience was not interested. What, after all, is the *moral* to Gatsby? Since there seemed to be none, *The Great Gatsby* failed and that was the end of F. Scott Fitzgerald, glamorous bestseller of yesteryear, bold chronicler of girls who kissed. It was also to be the beginning of what is now a formidable legend: the "archetypal" writer of whom Cyril Connolly keened . . . "the young man slain in his glory." Actually, the forty-four-year-old wreck at the bottom of Laurel Canyon was neither young nor in his glory when he dropped dead. But five years later, when Wilson itemized the wreckage [in *The Crack-Up*], he recreated for a new generation the bright, blond youth, forever glorious, doomed.

Professor Bruccoli's edition of [*The Notebooks of F. Scott Fitzgerald*] comes highly recommended. Mr. James Dickey, the poet and novelist, thinks that "they should be a bible for all writers. But one does not have to be a writer to respond to them—these *Notebooks* make writers of us all." If true, this is indeed a breakthrough. (p. 12)

Professor Bruccoli is understandably thrilled by *The Notebooks* which "were [Fitzgerald's] workshop and chronicle. They were his literary bankroll. They were also his confessional." Edmund Wilson disagrees. In the introduction to *The Crack-Up*, Wilson notes that, even at Princeton, Fitzgerald had been so much an admirer of Butler's *Notebooks* that when he came to fill up his own notebooks it was "as if he were preparing a book to be read as well as a storehouse for his own convenience. . . . Actually, he seems rarely to have used them."

The entries range from idle jottings, proper names, and jokes to extended descriptions and complaints. I fear that I must part company with Wilson who finds these snippets "extremely good reading." For one thing, many entries are simply cryptic. "Hobey Baker." That's all. Yes, one knows—or some of us know—that Baker was a golden football player at Princeton in Fitzgerald's day. So what? The name itself is just a name and nothing more. As for the longer bits and pieces, they serve only to remind us that even in his best work, Fitzgerald had little wit and less humor. Although in youth he had high spirits (often mistaken in freedom's home for humor) these entries tend toward sadness; certainly, he is filled with self-pity, self-justification, self . . . not love so much as a deep and abiding regard.

In general, Fitzgerald's notes are just notes or reminders. (pp. 12-13)

There is a section devoted to descriptions of places, something Fitzgerald was very good at in his novels. Number 142 is a nice description of Los Angeles, "a city that had tripled its population in fifteen years," where children play "on the green flanks of the modern boulevard . . . with their knees marked by the red stains of the mercurochrome era, played with toys with a purpose—beams that taught engineering, soldiers that taught manliness, and dolls that taught motherhood. When the dolls were so banged up that they stopped looking like real babies and began to look like dolls, the children developed affection for them." That is sweetly observed. But too many of these descriptions are simply half-baked or strained. The description of a place or mood that is not in some way connected to action is to no point at all.

Those journals and notebooks that are intended to be read must, somehow, deal with real things that are complete in themselves. Montaigne does not write: "Cardinal's house at Lucca," and leave it at that. But then Montaigne was a man constantly thinking about what he had read and observed in the course of a life in the world. Fitzgerald seems not to have read very much outside the Romantic tradition, and though his powers of observation were often keen and precise when it came to the sort of detail that interested him (class differences, remembered light), he had no real life in the world. Early on, he chose to live out a romantic legend that had no reference to anything but himself and Zelda and the child.

As I read *The Notebooks,* I was struck by the lack of literary references (other than a number of quite shrewd comments about Fitzgerald's contemporaries). Although most writers who keep notebooks make random jottings, they also tend to comment on their reading. Fitzgerald keeps an eye out for the competition and that's about it. . . .

There are lines from *The Notebooks* which have been much used in biographies of Fitzgerald; even so, they still retain their pathos: "1362 I left my capacity for hoping on the little roads that led to Zelda's sanitarium." But most of the personal entries are simply sad and not very interesting. To hear him tell it, again and again: once upon a time, he was a success and now he's a failure; he was young and now he's middle-aged. (p. 13)

Gore Vidal, "Scott's Case," in The New York Review *of Books (reprinted with permission from* The New York Review of Books; *copyright © 1980 Nyrev, Inc.), Vol. XXVII, No. 7, May 1, 1980, pp. 12-20.*

BRIAN WAY (essay date 1980)

Scott Fitzgerald has never received his due as a writer of short stories. His tales have been relegated to a minor position: they are too often discussed as if they mattered only as aids to the understanding of his major novels. It is symptomatic of this situation that some fifty of them remained uncollected for four decades after the author's death. And yet Fitzgerald deserves the same respect as the undisputed masters of the genre among his American contemporaries—Sherwood Anderson, Hemingway and Faulkner. (p. 72)

I shall not spend any time cataloguing the weaknesses of his poorer stories, but concentrate all my attention upon those tales which ought to have a secure place alongside the best short fiction of the twentieth century. Given this framework of analysis, his dislike of short-story writing instead of being an obstruction to the understanding of his work becomes potentially illuminating: it provides a deeper insight than any other aspect of his career into the difficulties he experienced because of his complex attitude to his role as an author; and it helps to draw attention to the exacting nature of his conception of short-story form.

Fitzgerald's ideas about the function of the artist . . . are divided by a central conflict: on the one hand he believes that the artist is a heroic figure, and the values of art supreme; and, on the other, that writing is a middle-class vocation which involves the author in a network of responsibilities and obligations to other people. (p. 73)

[In one sense], Fitzgerald's best tales have no plots at all; and it is here that we see the full significance of his claim that 'all my stories are conceived like novels, require a special emotion, a special experience.' The structure of any one of these is a matter of subtle connections and transitions, something too complex to be discussed adequately through any notion of plot. They differ from *The Great Gatsby* and *Tender is the Night* only in scale, not in kind. . . . Of all Fitzgerald's tales, it is **'The Rich Boy'** which most completely realizes his exacting sense of the possibilities of the genre, but even in a good commercial story like **'The Bowl'**, we find the same density of texture, a similar multiplicity of characters and episodes, and an extended time scale. It is surely no accident that three of his finest short stories, **'May Day'**, **'Absolution'** and **'One Trip Abroad'**, were fashioned out of material originally intended for inclusion in novels. (pp. 76-7)

In **'Echoes of the Jazz Age'** . . . , Fitzgerald names May Day, 1919, as the day on which the Jazz Age actually began, and in his story **'May Day'** . . . , he attempts, with an extraordinarily sure instinct for the shape of things to come, to evoke the atmosphere of the postwar era. The story is made up of the interwoven actions and feelings of several groups of characters, in New York, between early morning on 1 May 1919, and early the following morning. (pp. 77-8)

'May Day' not only conveys the atmosphere of a historical moment with incomparable vividness: it is also a triumph of artistic form. In order to write it, Fitzgerald had to find a way of representing social chaos which would, nevertheless, avoid condemning his story to a similar formlessness. He began with a device common to much naturalistic fiction—that of taking a single day in the life of a city—but went on to discover a far more subtle and creative structural principle: that the rhythms of city life could be made to function as the rhythms of his story. The various groups of characters are drawn together and flung apart again as these rhythms exert their influence. During the daylight hours, they are mostly apart, occupying themselves with their own private concerns: Philip Dean shopping and gossiping; Gordon worrying about money; Edith at the hairdresser's; the soldiers searching hopefully for liquor and entertainment. Then, during the climactic pleasure-seeking hours between ten and one, they are all brought together in the dance at Delmonico's, which is for that night the city's great revel, and therefore a centre of magnetic attraction. In the secret time between one and four, they disperse again, and then reassemble at Child's, Fifty-ninth Street, to refresh their tired bodies and jaded nerves with coffee and scrambled eggs. . . .

One of Fitzgerald's greatest gifts as a social novelist is this sensitivity to the rise and fall of nervous energy by day and night, which produces the rhythms of social life. His success in **'May Day'** depends not merely on moving his characters through the right places and activities at the right times, but on a deep understanding of moods and atmospheres. A long night's revel, in particular, develops a subtly shifting pattern of sensations—anticipation, excitement, fatigue and depression. In order to give this pattern its full value, he had to master many contrasting modes of social comedy: the frothy absurdity of Edith's conversation with her dancing partners; the slapstick adventures of the two soldiers; and the bacchanalian fantasy of Mr In and Mr Out. This comedy has, in turn, to be balanced against other elements—unhappiness, strain, hysteria and de-

spair—before the full complexity of the story can emerge. This is the artistry which enabled Fitzgerald much later in his career, to evoke the atmosphere of Gatsby's parties and Dick Diver's Riviera days. (p. 79)

In Fitzgerald's view, Americans, characteristically, attach more importance to dreams than to grasped experiences: their inner lives may be rich and colourful, even when their outer circumstances are conventional, drab or sordid. Their youth is filled with dreams of an 'orgastic' future (the word he uses on the closing page of *Gatsby*). Later, they become victims of nostalgia, and their lost youth, which slipped by in mere anticipation, now seems to them the period when they truly lived. Finally, with middle age, comes disillusionment: the inner life of dreams loses its power, and they find themselves alone in the emptiness of a purely material universe. The whole pattern, foreshortened in time though not in emotional fullness, is explored in *Gatsby*, but aspects of it form the basis for many of Fitzgerald's stories, particularly in the 1920s. . . .

[**'Absolution'**] is a story about the origin of dreams. It has a Middle Western setting, though of a very different kind from those in **'Bernice Bobs her Hair'** and **'The Ice Palace'**. Its two principal characters, Rudolph Miller and Father Schwartz, are remote from the wealthy and comparatively sophisticated life of the country clubs and the big cities—they live in a lost Dakota prairie town. The habit of dreaming is born out of the circumstances of their lives. After the brief exciting drama of frontier life, the town stagnates in an atmosphere of perpetual anticlimax. Theoretically, this is still a land of opportunity, but in fact the inhabitants are condemned to lives of isolation, monotony and inaction. Only dreams can fill the vast vacant spaces of their boredom. The brutal violence of the Middle Western climate, and the meagre but garish sensations of prairie life, ensure that their dreams take on a sensuous if not a directly sexual character. (p. 80)

By giving Father Schwartz's dreams a social, indeed a historical origin, Fitzgerald overcomes one of the main difficulties inherent in his theme. A story which deals with a man's hidden imaginative life is capable almost of vanishing through the sheer tenuousness and vagueness of its material. This had already happened in the case of a slightly earlier piece, **'Winter Dreams'** . . . , where the hero has no tangible human existence at all. Such a story needs ballast in the form of precise social observation and intense poetic images. These elements, which are clear enough in Fitzgerald's portrayal of Father Schwartz, are still more apparent in his treatment of Rudolph Miller.

Rudolph's dreams are given an added dimension by the fact that he is eleven years old and on the brink of adolescence. He has been avoiding confession for a month because he is ashamed to tell Father Schwartz about his 'impure thoughts'; and yet these thoughts have become the most exciting part of his imaginative life. He manages to convey the external facts to the priest—how he lingered to eavesdrop on a pair of lovers in a barn—but he cannot tell him 'how his pulse had bumped in his wrist, how a strange, romantic excitement had possessed him when those curious things had been said.' Adolescence, as Fitzgerald sees it, intensifies and complicates a child's imaginative life, driving his thoughts inwards as he attempts to make sense of the turmoil of his feelings. Rudolph is torn between new, half-understood, romantic emotions and old idealisms. (pp. 80-1)

But when he goes to Father Schwartz the same afternoon, to ask for absolution from his mortal sin, his feelings are unexpectedly placed in a new light; and, by the end of the interview, he is led to believe that 'there was something ineffably gorgeous somewhere that had nothing to do with God.' Father Schwartz's behaviour is disconcerting to say the least. Having dismissed Rudolph's spiritual problems with a comically brusque scrap of pastoral theology, he begins to talk about that other forbidden world which so fascinates them both. The lonely, half-crazy, old man struggles incoherently to put into words thoughts he has never dared to acknowledge before. He speaks of people for whom things 'go glimmering', and of a great light in Paris bigger than a star; but it is in [the bright amusement parks of] the Middle West itself that he eventually finds the image he is groping for. . . . In 'Absolution', this image is the poetic and dramatic climax of the story: it draws Rudolph and Father Schwartz together in a new secret community of feeling; and it turns their dreams into something more than mere personal fantasies—into expressions of the American consciousness. For Rudolph in particular, it becomes a symbol of the future, hovering before him, leading him away from old allegiances towards the lure of a more expansive life.

'Absolution', a fairly early story, deals, appropriately, with the origin of dreams, but, by the late 1920s, Fitzgerald was becoming more interested in nostalgia as a fictional subject. Of the group of stories which reflect this concern, '**The Last of the Belles**' . . . is very much the best. Superficially, it seems a mere reworking of some of his most familiar romantic properties—the War, the wayward aristocratic Southern girl, and the Northern suitor whom she rejects. In fact, however, he brings a more complex attitude, and a greater subtlety of narrative method to these materials than anywhere else except in *Gatsby*.

The design of '**The Last of the Belles**' is like a woven fabric, with threads which go this way and that. The long threads of the warp are provided by its extended development in time. It tells the story of a beautiful Southern girl, Ailie Calhoun—how she is gradually transformed from a Southern belle of the old-fashioned type into a flapper of the later Jazz Age. At the same time, it conveys a sense of the more general changes in American manners which have formed the background to her career. More important still, it is the history of one man's dreams, of the narrator's growing nostalgia for the lost romance of his youth. The cross threads of the woof are woven into the story by the action of the narrator's own voice—his ironic and yet absorbed commentary upon all the changing elements of the situation. (pp. 81-2)

The narrator is saved from sentimental fatuity by his ironic self-awareness: he sees clearly that, in his infatuation with Ailie, genuine romance and tawdry illusion are inextricably mingled. Nevertheless, he achieves a fine balance in his feelings towards her: he is prepared to love her in spite of her defects—indeed, he realizes that he finds her defects an integral part of her charm. He regards with amused regret the very quirk of character which leads her to reject him. Throughout their acquaintance, he is puzzled by her insistence that her admirers should be 'sincere': it intrigues him that she should value a quality which she herself so evidently lacks, but at last he grasps what she means. In spite of her air of being an 'instinctive thoroughbred', she too has an accurate sense of her own deficiencies, and cannot believe that any man who sees them can really love her. . . . The complexity of attitude which makes the narrator interesting to us, is the very trait which renders him forever untrustworthy to her. (pp. 83-4)

Between 1920 and 1924, Fitzgerald lived almost continuously in New York or within commuting distance of it, and during this period the nature of his understanding of city life changed profoundly: in 'May Day' he had shown the insight of the brilliant outsider, but by the time he wrote '**The Rich Boy**' in 1926, he possessed the deepened awareness of the settled resident. None of the characters in the earlier story actually belong to New York, and they experience only those sensations which are accessible to the casual visitor or the tourist. But Anson Hunter, the hero of '**The Rich Boy**', is an entrenched member of the city's upper class, and his life is an expression of its underlying structure, not its glittering surface. (p. 84)

This is still substantially the world of *The House of Mirth* and *The Custom of the Country*: Anson Hunter, just like the Trenors, Dorsets and Van Degens of Edith Wharton's novels, owes his wealth, position and manners to the Gilded Age. Fitzgerald's narrative style, too, is remarkably close to Mrs Wharton's—indeed this seems to me a case where one can reasonably speak of a direct influence upon his work. As a rule, the most distinctive quality in his writing is the constant delicate play of atmospheric and poetic suggestion, but what impresses one particularly in '**The Rich Boy**' is the sustained pressure of a fine moral intelligence. The tone is dispassionate, sober, analytical; it does not rise to high points of climactic intensity or wit, and so, unlike most of Fitzgerald's writing, it is not especially quotable. . . . Fitzgerald maintains this tone, with its carefully judged inflections of irony and sympathetic insight, throughout the story—a degree of artistic control which is unique in his short fiction.

The character of Anson Hunter is Fitzgerald's one unquestioned success in portraying the sophisticated Eastern rich. As a possible American aristocrat, Anson is a failure, but his inadequacies lurk beneath the surface of an apparently flawless good form. In this respect, it is interesting to contrast him with rich Middle Westerners like Tom Buchanan and Baby Warren: he could never be guilty of their crude and frequent lapses—Tom's outbreaks of uncouth violence, Baby's rudeness and her tantrums. Even his coarseness is of a subtler kind than Tom's. Tom's affair with Myrtle Wilson is merely sordid—it represents the breakdown of a style. Anson's gentlemanly dissipations, on the other hand—the ritualized college drunkenness he keeps up with his Yale Club friends, and his adventures with 'the gallant chorus girls'—are the expression of a style; he knows how to choose women of a certain class for a party, how much to spend on them, and how to get rid of them.

The essence of his failure lies still deeper, however, in that complex area where the psychology of an individual and the manners of a class become alternative expressions of the same situation. Fitzgerald believed that people who possess enormous wealth, particularly wealth acquired in an earlier generation, constitute a distinct psychological and moral type. . . . This inbred sense of superiority does not make Anson in any simple sense arrogant or snobbish: it is, rather, the basis of his cynicism and his indifference. Life has given him so much already, that he cannot believe that any of the remaining prizes are worth a serious effort. (pp. 84-6)

Anson finds himself increasingly alone with his own sense of superiority, and his story broadens into a further chapter in Fitzgerald's history of the Jazz Age. His class, the pseudo-aristocracy of the Gilded Age, are being rapidly engulfed in the [postwar decade's] onward rush of new conditions. When his father dies, Anson is disconcerted to find that the family isn't even particularly rich by current standards; and he is dismayed when his younger sisters insist on selling up the baronial country estate in Connecticut, which they regard as an irrelevance and a bore. His Yale Club cronies get married and disappear one by one, either to live abroad, or to settle into the new and unassuming style of domesticity which, even for the rich, has replaced the portentous splendours to which Anson is accustomed. One hot Saturday afternoon in New York, he finds himself a stranger and alone, in the city which once belonged, by dynastic right, to the Hunters and a handful of other leading families. As he gazes up at the windows of one of his clubs, he catches sight of a solitary old man, staring vacantly into the street. It is a portent of the future, an image of the isolation and neglect which await a man whose habits of thought and feeling no longer have any relation to the society he lives in.

But, although Anson's feelings of superiority are not supported by any external social reality, they are still psychologically necessary to him. At the end of the story, he leaves New York, the city which has forgotten him and his family, for a vacation in Europe. As soon as he boards the liner, he begins a flirtation with the most attractive girl on the ship, and it becomes clear that the admiration of women is his one remaining resource; only by making them respond to him and love him can he sustain a little of his accustomed sense of himself.

Anson Hunter's life in New York ends with his departure for Europe. Countless well-to-do Americans were to make the same journey by the end of the 1920s, as Paris and the Riviera, rather than New York, became the setting for the most extravagant manifestations of the Jazz Age. In Fitzgerald's fiction, this shift is reflected not only in *Tender is the Night,* but in an important group of short stories. (pp. 86-7)

[Impaired] or broken marriages are an important element in all of Fitzgerald's best international stories. **'One Trip Abroad'** . . . traces the gradual deterioration of Nelson and Nicole Kelly's relationship during a period of four years' travel overseas. Fitzgerald put the story together from a discarded early version of *Tender is the Night,* and in both works, his sense of place is always made to serve a dramatic purpose or to strengthen his moral and social analysis—he is never merely picturesque or anecdotal. (pp. 89-90)

As in all Fitzgerald's best short stories, the form of **'One Trip Abroad'** is a particularly felicitous expression of the underlying structural necessities of its subject. Its episodes succeed each other like a series of moral tableaux—a kind of Jazz Age *Rake's Progress*—and within the broad canvas of each picture, there are striking vignettes, the excellent satirical sketches of minor expatriate types. Count Chiki Sarolai, the exiled Austrian nobleman who sponges on rich Americans in Paris, is a well observed case of the aristocratic confidence man. Better still are Mr and Mrs Liddell Miles, a pair of professional cosmopolitans, who turn even their ignorance and boredom into a pretext for feeling superior to their fellow travellers.

The expatriate life portrayed in . . . **'One Trip Abroad'** came to an end with singular abruptness: within a year of the Wall Street Crash of 1929, the swarms of Americans with their millions of dollars had vanished from the European scene. The opening pages of **'Babylon Revisited'** . . . are an evocation of the silence and emptiness in the Ritz bar, which had been filled only a year or so earlier with a shouting drunken crowd. When Charlie Wales asks the barman for news of old friends, the latter responds with a litany of ghosts—the names of men who have lost their health, their reason or their money. Later that same evening, he wanders through the city like a man in a state of shock, recognizing everything he sees and yet not

feeling a part of it. He looks in at a Montmartre night club which had been one of his favourite haunts back in the 1920s. It is as quiet as the grave, but at his appearance, it explodes into a grotesque semblance of gaiety: the band starts to play; a couple of employees masquerading as patrons leap to their feet and begin to dance; and the manager rushes up to assure him that the evening crowd is about to arrive. In this macabre image of the unfamiliarity of the familiar, Fitzgerald conveys the first shock of the Depression more effectively than any other American writer. (pp. 90-1)

In many ways, as this account indicates, **'Babylon Revisited'** is a simple story, and its strength lies in its simplicity. Like a lyric poem or a folksong, it deals directly with deep and powerful emotions: a father's love for his daughter, the ugliness of family quarrels, the disturbing way in which ghosts may return from a seemingly buried past. In one important respect, however, the story is extremely subtle—in its treatment of the psychology of disaster and the nature of recovery. For Charlie, the suddenness of the Depression has produced a sense of dislocation, a feeling that he is living in two worlds at once: he is committed to the idea of recovery and to the new way of life he has painstakingly created, but he still clings half-consciously to many of the mental habits which he formed during the Boom. . . . Charlie's personal experience is a distillation of the social history of the age: during the period of economic chaos which followed the stock market collapse, President Hoover became notorious for his facile promise that recovery was 'just around the corner'; but Fitzgerald understood, with his usual fine instinct for the spirit of the age, that the Depression was going to last a long time. (pp. 91-2)

Most of the stories I have discussed so far deal with members of the leisure class, but during the 1930s Fitzgerald became increasingly concerned with people whose lives must be measured in terms of professional dedication or creative achievement. This is apparent in his novels—Dick Diver is a doctor and Monroe Stahr a film producer—and is also reflected in some of his stories. In these, the main characters are usually artists or entertainers, and the principal theme often arises from Fitzgerald's sense of the dual nature of the artist. . . . (p. 92)

Fitzgerald's best stories between 1920 and 1932 convey an overall impression of consistency rather than change. There are shifts of emphasis in his choice of subject matter, but few fundamental departures from the concerns already apparent in **'May Day'** and **'Absolution'**. From this point of view, his international stories are not so much an innovation as a variation within the pattern of his understanding of the Jazz Age. Similarly, his attitude to the form of the short story remains substantially the same, even though he made enormous advances (particularly in the earliest years of his professional career) in his mastery of fictional technique. But after 1932 the nature of his short fiction changed radically. (p. 95)

The most strikingly novel characteristic of these tales is how short they are—often no more than five or six pages. In the main, this was undoubtedly a response to . . . new commercial pressures . . . , and in particular to the fact that, after 1936, the main outlet for Fitzgerald's work was *Esquire,* whose editor preferred short pieces, and in any case paid such small fees that there was no incentive to write at length. These *Esquire* stories, however, are far from being mere truncated versions of Fitzgerald's earlier tales. They represent a fundamentally new approach on his part to the problem of short-story form, in which he was led to adopt a position very close to that of the modernist writers and critics. Like them, he now appeared to prefer the form of the sketch or episode, as practised by Chekhov and Joyce, Sherwood Anderson and Hemingway. This type of story is compressed and oblique; it relies on poetic evocation or outright symbolism, it eliminates authorial intervention and dispenses with fictional narrators; its rhetorical mode implies an attitude of complete objectivity. Joyce's 'Clay', Anderson's 'Hands', and Hemingway's 'Hills Like White Elephants' are particularly clear examples. A number of Fitzgerald's most successful late stories conform to this pattern.

In subject matter, the contrast with his earlier fiction is less clear-cut . . . , stories like **'Three Hours Between Planes'** and **'News of Paris—Fifteen Years Ago'** carry forward old preoccupations into the new form. Nevertheless, there is one important development which it is impossible not to associate with his crack-up—a group of tales which deal with personal disaster and unhappiness, alcoholism, mental illness, psychological trauma, broken marriages, the sense of failure, and the increasing loneliness and declining vitality of middle age.

'Afternoon of an Author' . . . the best of all these stories, gives an almost unbearably painful sense of the author's exhaustion, discouragement and loneliness after some unspecified illness or breakdown. . . . Because of the dry, ironic impersonality and wit of its narrative style, this sketch does not have a trace of the self-pity and exhibitionism which frequently disfigure the crack-up essays.

In **'Afternoon of an Author'** (and other similar late stories), the extent to which Fitzgerald's attention is directed towards the inner, psychological condition of his characters has an interesting effect upon his treatment of the outer social reality which surrounds them. Here it is convenient to make use of an image from the story itself: as the author rides downtown, the overhanging branches of trees brush against the windows of the bus, and, in the same way, random impressions of the city flicker across his mind in vivid but unstable succession. In his shaky mental state, the disintegration within seems matched by fragmentation without. The real significance and value of this new way of looking at social life, however, is that it represents much more than simply the reflection of a sick mind. It corresponds very closely with Fitzgerald's conviction that the solid fabric of American wealth and American manners which he had made imaginatively his own, had collapsed in the Crash of 1929 leaving only shattered memories behind. He makes this view explicit in **'My Lost City'** and **'Babylon Revisited'**, and his late stories—**'The Lost Decade'**, **'Financing Finnegan'**, **'Afternoon of an Author'** itself—are filled with the reverberations of a vanished era. The new impressionistic technique which he began to develop in the last named of these, was admirably suited to the exploration of the unstable consciousness and shifting reality of recent American conditions. . . . (pp. 95-7)

There are several other excellent late stories—for example, [**'I Didn't Get Over,'** **'An Alcoholic Case,'** and **'The Lost Decade'**] . . .—but there is one, **'Financing Finnegan'** . . . , which has a special interest. It reflects obliquely on those personal problems in the life of an author which became pressing for Fitzgerald after his crack-up, but its main concern brings us back full circle to the point where we began—to a renewed awareness of Fitzgerald's conflicting ideas about the artist's role. Finnegan himself, the hero of the story, is pre-eminently the artist as conqueror: half wayward genius and half confidence-man, he rises superior to the conventions of professional reliability, financial probity and sexual morality, but does undeniably produce on occasion work which is incomparably fine.

He never appears in person, but his mysterious doings, magnified by hearsay, are relayed to us through the conversations of his agent and publisher, who have invested so much in him in the form of loans and advances, that they have come to regard him with a mixture of infatuation and dread. The whole situation is described, with ironic disapproval, by a narrator who is in every way Finnegan's antithesis, a sober hard-working professional writer who possesses all the good qualities that Finnegan lacks, and is at the same time without a trace of the latter's genuine distinction. By pushing these alternative possibilities to the extreme, Fitzgerald is able to create a story which is at once a brilliant farce in the manner of **'News of Paris—Fifteen Years Ago'**, and something more—a uniquely clearsighted view of the disturbing cross currents always present in his conception of art.

Indeed from several points of view, **'Financing Finnegan'** is a good story with which to conclude a discussion of Fitzgerald's short fiction. Like so many of the other tales we have considered, it shows his consummate skill at blending the social with the individual: Finnegan's obscure difficulties are set against the wider context of the Depression, and the problematic nature of recovery acquires a double sense. Above all, this story gives evidence of the strong element of continuity in Fitzgerald's development, his ability to keep returning to certain themes with a fresh awareness of their potentialities; and at the same time his adaptability, the way in which he could always respond creatively to new conditions both in his professional work and in the social life around him. (p. 97)

> *Brian Way, in his* F. Scott Fitzgerald and the Art of Social Fiction *(© 1980 Brian Way; reprinted by permission of St. Martin's Press, Inc.; in Canada by Edward Arnold Ltd.), St. Martin's, 1980, 171 p.*

LEO MARX (essay date 1981)

I want to suggest that Hawthorne's theory and practice will serve as an almost paradigmatic example of the way the classic American writers treat the environment. (pp. 73-4)

A distinguishing feature of this body of writing is its domination by protagonists, like Hester, whose deepest yearnings are expressed in numinous visions of the natural landscape. She might be speaking for any one of them when she urges Dimmesdale, in the forest, to '''Begin all anew! Hast thou exhausted possibility in the failure of this one trial?''' I am thinking of that familiar roster of pastoral figures: Natty Bumppo, the ''I'' of Emerson's *Nature* and Thoreau's *Walden,* Ishmael, Christopher Newman, Huckleberry Finn, Jay Gatsby, Nick Adams and Ike McCaslin. All of these characters enact the ideal life of the American self journeying away from the established order of things into an unexplored territory we tend to think of as Nature. The object of the journey, implied or avowed, is the nearest possible approximation to the situation of the autonomous, unencumbered self. (p. 74)

The truth is that not one of the works in question finally can be described as an unqualified ''pastoral of success.'' *Walden* comes as close as any to being that, but the more carefully one reads the book the more narrowly personal and limited Thoreau's triumph seems. Since Thoreau's time, in any event, our best writers working in this mode increasingly have tended to compose pastoral romances of manifest failure. They continue to enact the retreat/quest, but it would seem that they do so chiefly in order to deny it, and the resulting state of mind is one of structured ambivalence.

Perhaps the most revealing twentieth-century instance of this mode of rendering the modern industrial city is *The Great Gatsby*. Fitzgerald's fable is particularly useful for our purposes because he has Gatsby (and, to a lesser extent, Nick Carraway) assimilate their conceptions of New York to an illusionary pastoral viewpoint. That that is Gatsby's mode of perception becomes evident to Nick, in his role as narrator, in the famous ending when he finally discovers the clue to Gatsby's character. Lying on the beach, looking across the Sound at dusk, Nick suddenly recognizes that all of the incongruities of Gatsby's behavior can be explained by his characteristically American propensity to credit the pastoral hope. It is a view of life which initially had been fostered in Europeans by the image of the beautiful, rich, vast, seemingly unclaimed continent. The physical reality of the place, all that it promised in the way of material satisfaction, also was assumed to have made available an inner freedom and fulfillment such as Gatsby seeks. In the beginning of the European settlement of America, at least, there had been reason to believe that the actualizing of the ancient pastoral dream really might be feasible in such a "new" world. A palpable sense of that possibility is another distinctive quality of American pastoralism. As Nick puts it, Gatsby's dream of Daisy, represented by the green light, "must have seemed so close that he could hardly fail to grasp it"—another way of saying what Hester had tried to convey to her self-hating lover by pointing to the unbounded forest: "'There thou art free! So brief a journey would bring thee from a world where thou has been most wretched, to one where thou mayest still be happy!'" But if that possibility had existed a long while ago, Nick realizes, and what Gatsby did not know is that it "was already behind him, somewhere back in that vast obscurity beyond the city [before America had become an urban industrial society], where the dark fields of the republic rolled on under the night."

Gatsby's failure to grasp this historical truth is of a piece with his distorted view of certain realities before his eyes, and Nick's view of the world is only somewhat less skewed by a similar susceptibility to illusion. Nowhere is this more obvious than in Nick's account of New York itself. He sees the city from the vantage of an ambitious young man, like Gatsby, just in from the western provinces. To him it is a ceaselessly beckoning fairyland. . . . Nick pastoralizes the streets of Manhattan as naturally as Thoreau does the landscape at Walden Pond. "We drove over to Fifth Avenue," he says, "so warm and soft, almost pastoral, on the summer Sunday afternoon that I wouldn't have been surprised to see a great flock of white sheep turn the corner." This image occurs to Nick shortly after he has described an appalling urban wasteland—a passage which in fact gives us our first sight of the city proper in *The Great Gatsby*. (pp. 75-6)

This is the modern city at its worst, and it has no place in a green vision of America like Gatsby's. His inability to recognize the discrepancy between the underside of urban industrial society, as embodied in this valley of ashes, and the idealized world of his aspirations is the direct cause of his death and his failure. Every significant element of the tale, indeed—the characters and landscape and action—has discrepant meanings in accord with this duality. As Nick describes it, this other workaday city is utterly remote and unreal. Its ashen inhabitants, who dimly go about their obscure operations, already are crumbling in that polluted air. These are people, like the auto mechanic, Wilson, whose lives are largely circumscribed by material conditions, and who share none of Gatsby's gratifying sense of a dream about to be consummated. Glimpses of this

other New York, composed of the material and human detritus of industrial society, are fleeting but crucial in *The Great Gatsby*. They provide the measure by which we know that the main characters inhabit a realm shaped by myth as well as wealth. Near the end, when Nick tries to imagine how the world might have looked to Gatsby when divested of its mythic veil, he describes it hauntingly as "A new world, material without being real, where poor ghosts, breathing dreams like air, drifted fortuitously about . . . like that ashen, fantastic figure gliding toward him through the amorphous trees." The ashen figure is Wilson on his way to kill Gatsby. He kills him because of Gatsby's unwillingness—or inability—to let go of his patently false conception of Daisy and, by extension, of the world.

In *The Great Gatsby* and *The Scarlet Letter* human habitations derive their meanings from essentially the same conflict of views. At one extreme we are shown a town or city as it exemplifies the writer's highly critical conception of the dominant culture. This is a real place represented at its worst by emblems of oppression and suffering like the valley of ashes or the scaffold. At the other ideological extreme, we are given the perception of that place by a pastoral figure like Hester or Gatsby. It is true, of course, that Hester is alienated from Puritan Boston—is eager to get away—whereas Gatsby and Nick are more or less enthralled by the glamour and excitement of New York. But this difference is not as significant, finally, as the similarity in their viewpoints and its ultimate implications. Gatsby and Nick (until the very end) see New York from an idealized perspective very much like the one to which Hester lends expression in the forest. ("'I'm going to fix everything just the way it was before,'" Gatsby says of his relations with Daisy.) But Fitzgerald points to Europe as the truly significant place from which the symbolic disengagement has been made, and for Gatsby all America—urban, rural, wild—retains the attributes of that fresh green breast of the New World envisaged by arriving Europeans. This is the illusion that ashen-faced Wilson finally destroys. Thus the outcome of the action in both works may be understood as exposing the glorious impracticality of the alternative each has posed to urban reality. (pp. 77-8)

> *Leo Marx, "The Puzzle of Anti-Urbanism in Classic American Literature" (© 1981 by Leo Marx; from a paper originally presented at the Conference on Literature and the Urban Experience held at Rutgers University in April, 1981), in* Literature and the Urban Experience: Essays on the City and Literature, *Rutgers University Press, 1981, pp. 63-80.*

ADDITIONAL BIBLIOGRAPHY

Bruccoli, Matthew J. *Some Sort of Epic Grandeur: The Life of F. Scott Fitzgerald*. New York, London: Harcourt Brace Jovanovich, Publishers, 1981, 624 p.

    The latest biography; complete and highly informative.

Bruccoli, Matthew J., and Bryer, Jackson R., eds. *F. Scott Fitzgerald in His Own Time: A Miscellany*. Kent, Ohio: The Kent State University Press, 1971, 481 p.

    Important collection of works by and about Fitzgerald. The volume's first section contains early, unreprinted material by Fitzgerald. The second part contains valuable critical essays on his work.

Bryer, Jackson R., ed. *F. Scott Fitzgerald: The Critical Reception*. New York: Burt Franklin & Co., 1978, 386 p.

Collection of reviews, valuable for the insight provided into Fitzgerald's reception by his contemporaries.

Eble, Kenneth. *F. Scott Fitzgerald.* Rev. ed. Boston: Twayne Publishers, 1977, 187 p.
    Biographical and critical study.

Fitzgerald, F. Scott. "An Interview with F. Scott Fitzgerald." *Saturday Review* XLIII, No. 45 (5 November 1960): 26, 56.
    An interview written entirely by Fitzgerald a few weeks after the publication of *This Side of Paradise.* The interview is interesting for the author's perceptions of himself and his craft at the outset of his career.

Goldhurst, William. *F. Scott Fitzgerald and His Contemporaries.* Cleveland, New York: The World Publishing Co., 1963, 247 p.
    Traces Fitzgerald's friendships with Ring Lardner, Edmund Wilson, H. L. Mencken, and Ernest Hemingway, and the influence these writers had upon his work.

Kuehl, John. Introduction to *The Apprentice Fiction of F. Scott Fitzgerald: 1909-1917,* by F. Scott Fitzgerald, pp. 3-16. New Brunswick, N.J.: Rutgers University Press, 1965.
    Surveys Fitzgerald's earliest short stories and dramas, emphasizing in the essay's second half the prefigurations of the *femme fatale,* a character type that dominated the author's professional work.

Lehan, Richard D. *F. Scott Fitzgerald and the Craft of Fiction.* Carbondale, Edwardsville: Southern Illinois University Press, 1966, 206 p.
    Study of Fitzgerald and the Romantic tradition, with critical treatment of *This Side of Paradise, The Great Gatsby, Tender Is the Night,* and other works.

Long, Robert Emmet. *The Achieving of "The Great Gatsby": F. Scott Fitzgerald, 1920-1925.* Lewisburg, Pa.: Bucknell University Press, 1979, 226 p.
    Detailed study of patterns and characters in *The Great Gatsby.*

Scribner, Charles, III. Introduction to *The Vegetable; Or, From President to Postman,* pp. v-xx. New York: Charles Scribner's Sons, 1976.
    Follows Fitzgerald's writing and revisions of his dramatic flop, *The Vegetable.*

Sklar, Robert. *F. Scott Fitzgerald: The Last Laocoön.* New York: Oxford University Press, 1967, 376 p.
    Biographical and critical study, and discussion of Fitzgerald's importance.

Turnbull, Andrew. *Scott Fitzgerald.* New York: Charles Scribner's Sons, 1962, 364 p.
    The definitive Fitzgerald biography.

Tuttleton, James W. "F. Scott Fitzgerald: The Romantic Tragedian as Moral Fabulist." In his *The Novel of Manners in America,* pp. 162-83. Chapel Hill: The University of North Carolina Press, 1972.
    Examines Fitzgerald as a social historian.

Twentieth Century Literature, F. Scott Fitzgerald Issue 26, No. 2 (Summer 1980): 130 p.
    Contains essays by Richard Lehan, Jeffrey Steinbrink, Scott Donaldson, and Ruth Prigozy. The issue concludes with two helpful bibliographical chapters.

Wilson, Edmund. *Letters on Literature and Politics: 1912-1972.* Edited by Elena Wilson. New York: Farrar, Straus and Giroux, 1977, 767 p.*
    Contains letters to Fitzgerald offering opinions on the author's works and works-in-progress.

(Pearl) Zane Grey

1872?-1939

(Born Pearl Zane Gray) American novelist and essayist.

Grey, who has been called the "father of the western," holds an important place in American popular culture. A pioneer of the western novel, Grey played a major role in creating the myth of the American cowboy. This myth extolls the independent, virile male in a rugged, demanding environment, praising the virtues of the primitive West over the cultivated, but enervated, East. Though he has been called a hack writer by some, Grey's sixty-odd formula pieces won him immense popularity, especially in the decade following World War I when his novels continuously reached the best-seller list. His themes of simple morality and self-reliance echoed the sentiments of a war-weary, nostalgic, and isolationist public looking for escape from a troublesome world.

Following in the footsteps of his father, Grey began his career as a dentist in New York. From 1898 to 1904 he struggled to establish his practice, and it was during this period that he began writing articles on outdoor life for popular magazines such as *Field and Stream*. Out of either acute boredom or a desire to lead a more fulfilling life, Grey closed his practice in 1904 to devote his time to writing. His first fiction, *Betty Zane*, a historical romance based on a maternal ancestor, found no publisher, and Grey published it at his own expense. It was not until he made a fruitful trip to the Southwest that he acquired the personal experience and understanding which formed the basis for the success of his later works. Many critics believe that the novels immediately following Grey's encounter with the West are among his best: *The Last of the Plainsmen*, *The Heritage of the Desert*, and *Riders of the Purple Sage*, the last of which won its author instant reknown.

Grey's first western romance, *The Heritage of the Desert*, introduced the thematic pattern that he used repeatedly throughout his career—the "rite-of-passage." This pattern consisted of the innocent initiated into a new world, the outsider who must face conflict and emerge as a hero or heroine with a new understanding of life. For Grey the West, with its distinctive moral and symbolic landscape, offered a unique setting for the development of this theme. The harsh realities of the country and the violence of a lawless society provided a field of action wherein his protagonists, usually high-bred Easterners, would learn to confront their environment and discover their basic human values. This pattern was used more effectively, and with some variations, in *Riders of the Purple Sage*. Many critics believe *Riders of the Purple Sage* is Grey's best novel, mainly because he loosened the restraints of his formula and allowed the story to grow at its own pace.

Grey never received the critical acclaim his popular audience felt he deserved. Many critics attacked the lack of realism in his novels, pointing out that his stories were melodramatic and nostalgic, that he fumbled love scenes to an embarrassing degree, that his plots were often unbelievable, and that his characters were never complete. Other critics, apologizing for his faults, attempted to illustrate his literary attributes. Grey was the first writer, for example, to create the mysterious and alienated figure of the heroic gunfighter or outlaw; he was the

Culver Pictures

first novelist to write a western story from a woman's point of view in *The Light of Western Stars;* and he was the only western writer of his time to elevate the natural environment into a transcendent religious and moral force. Recently, critics have become receptive to the works of Zane Grey, suggesting that Grey be approached as a writer of romance, a peculiar literary genre outside the rules and criteria of realism.

Despite the critical debate as to his place in the literary world, there is no doubt that Zane Grey was a first-rate storyteller. His novels have reached an estimated fifty-one million readers, and more than fifty movies have been adapted from his works. Through his colorful descriptions and romantic images, Grey brought the Old West to life for millions of readers.

(See also *Dictionary of Literary Biography*, Vol. 9: *American Novelists, 1910-1945*.)

PRINCIPAL WORKS

Betty Zane (novel) 1904
The Spirit of the Border (novel) 1905
The Last of the Plainsmen (novel) 1908
The Heritage of the Desert (novel) 1910

Riders of the Purple Sage   (novel)   1912
Desert Gold   (novel)   1913
The Light of Western Stars   (novel)   1914
The Lone Star Ranger   (novel)   1915
The Rainbow Trail   (novel)   1915
The U.P. Trail   (novel)   1918
To the Last Man   (novel)   1922
The Call of the Canyon   (novel)   1923
The Thundering Herd   (novel)   1925
The Vanishing American   (novel)   1925
Nevada   (novel)   1928
Arizona Ames   (novel)   1931
The Hash Knife Outfit   (novel)   1933
Code of the West   (novel)   1934
Western Union   (novel)   1939
30,000 on the Hoof   (novel)   1940
Boulder Dam   (novel)   1963

THE NEW YORK TIMES   (essay date 1908)

Lovers of adventure in the wild and woolly West will find in Zane Grey's **"The Last of the Plainsmen,"** . . . a book of heart's delight. Buffalo Jones, picturesque and practical "Preserver of the American Bison," is its central figure, and the volume is an exposition, in the form of stirring narrative, of the man's character and of some of his boldest deeds. The author took an extended trip through the Northern Arizona desert last year with the old hunter, and in this book he tells the story of how they traveled and of what they did, how they roped cougars and chased wild mustangs and rounded up the buffalo herd, interspersed with tales of some of Jones's adventures in former years. Dr. Grey has a vivid style and a keen sense of dramatic situation, as well as poetic appreciation of the weird beauty and sublimity of the country through which he journeyed. With many little touches of characterization he makes an intimate picture of Buffalo Jones, "a simple, quiet man, who fits the mountains and the silences and the long reaches of distance."

> *"With Buffalo Jones," in The New York Times (© 1908 by The New York Times Company; reprinted by permission), September 12, 1908, p. 502.*

THE NEW YORK TIMES   (essay date 1910)

[In **"The Heritage of the Desert"** Zane Grey] has staked out a region hitherto unknown in American fiction. It lies in that almost inaccessible country of Southern Utah and Northern Arizona bordering on the rim of the upper reaches of the Grand Canyon of the Colorado, and the story deals mainly with the life, family and fortunes of a Mormon patriarch on a desert oasis made by his own hands.

The story is one of unusual power and picturesqueness. Its hero, a young New Englander, is found on the desert, almost dying of illness, exposure and thirst, by a Mormon elder, carried to the oasis home, made virtually one of the patriarch's family and brought back to health and vigor. . . . For the most part it is a man's story, concerned with the clashing of wills, the crossing of purposes, with dare-devil courage and grim determination. Except for the heroine, Mescal, the women in it are not much more than names. But some of the men loom

big in the reader's interest, and wonderfully alive and real. Especially is this true of August Naab, the Mormon. The time of the story goes back a quarter century or more, before plural wives were under the ban of the law, and the picture of this old patriarch at the head of his swarming family, surrounded by the prosperity and comforts which his years of toil as farmer, engineer, mason, carpenter, road builder, experimenter, have wrested from the desert, is intensely interesting as a part of the social history of the West. For it is true to life and its living counterpart might have been found in hundreds of fertile spots scattered over the southwestern desert.

For his method the author has gone to the great realists, and he paints the surroundings and conditions of this desert life with an attention to detail that makes it all stand out before the reader's eyes exceedingly vivid and convincing. Mr. Zane Grey . . . has some half-dozen books to his credit. But in **"The Heritage of the Desert"** he has set a new standard for himself and established his right to be classed among the best of those American novelists who have chosen the frontier as their field.

> *"A Tale of the Desert: Mr. Zane Grey Finds a Novel Setting for a Stirring Romance," in The New York Times (© 1910 by The New York Times Company; reprinted by permission), October 8, 1910, p. 558.*

FREDERIC TABER COOPER   (essay date 1910)

The Heritage of the Desert, by Zane Grey, is a book full of crudities which we nevertheless forgive because of that saving grace, the quality of sincerity. It is a story laid in the early days of the settlement of the Southwest; and the chief factors are a colony of Mormons who have been crowded out of Utah to take refuge in the inaccessible vastnesses amid the Arizona deserts; secondly, the Navajo Indians; and, thirdly, organised bands of cattle-thieves. The specific romance which binds the various ingredients of this story together is the attachment between a half-breed Indian girl, adopted daughter of a Mormon prophet, and an invalid from the East whose one hope of life lies in the curative properties of the Arizona air. We have had more novels built from this material than could easily be counted. This particular one, however, is its own best excuse for existence. It presents certain types of Mormons in a rather new light that somehow carries conviction with it; it gives us some rather graphic pictures—perhaps all the more graphic because a little crude and sketchy—of the rugged scenery, the intolerable heat, the agony of thirst, the brutality of man when the veneer of civilisation drops away. In the absence of any specific information regarding the author, one ventures the opinion that if this is a first effort he is likely to go a long way forward in the near future, and therefore is distinctly one of the writers who are worth watching. (p. 295)

> *Frederic Taber Cooper, "The Value of Sincerity," in The Bookman, New York, Vol. 32, No. 3, November, 1910, pp. 290-96.**

OUTLOOK   (essay date 1912)

The purple of the sage and of this title [**"Riders of the Purple Sage"**] seems to have found its way into the author's style. Zane Grey is a capital writer of plot stories of the kind which rough-and-ready critics say are "full of good, red blood." This book has incident, plot, imagination, and romance; it would have been a quite unusual book in its class if it were not here and there over-written and over-sensational.

"The New Books: 'Riders of the Purple Sage'," in Outlook, *Vol. 100, February 3, 1912, p. 289.*

THE NEW YORK TIMES　(essay date 1912)

[In **"Riders of the Purple Sage"**] Zane Grey returns to the scenes which he portrayed so powerfully and entertainingly in **"The Heritage of the Desert."** The mountains and sage-grown plains of Southern Utah furnish the setting of his tale, and the conflicts between the Mormons and Gentiles and the depredations of cattle rustlers in the early 70's, the motives from which he derives a thrilling, well-constructed, and well-told story. It is a better novel than was **"The Heritage of the Desert"**—striking and clever as was that book—more closely knit in its construction, better balanced in its component elements, deeper and more poignant in its emotional qualities.

Its heroine, Jane Withersteen, is a Mormon heiress, whose father, a power in the church, had left her mistress of wide stretches of upland and valley, and of herds of cattle. She is young and beautiful, strong-charactered, and capable, and her many-sided nature is portrayed with a good deal of skill, though she lacks a certain flame of reality and alertness with which the author has endowed his hero, Lassiter, the avenging Gentile who marks his trail about and across Utah with death and destruction. . . . [Jane] is wilful, passionate, stiff-necked, and the more ruin thunders about her, the more she invites. Her religion is deeply rooted in her heart, and she has many fierce struggles with herself in her endeavor to reconcile it with other demands that seem to her quite as vital and as holy. She is a strong and appealing figure, though not so striking as the taciturn Lassiter, bent with his avenging revolvers upon his mysterious quest, a quest which finds its goal in a secret grave upon Jane's estate.

The book is one of the best of recent western novels, stirring in its rush of action and incident, vivid with local color, strong and human in its emotional interest.

"A God Western Novel," in The New York Times *(©1912 by The New York Times Company; reprinted by permission), February 18, 1912, p. 82.*

THE AMERICAN REVIEW OF REVIEWS　(essay date 1912)

To go back to the Utah of the year 1871, we have a strange, wild romance of the strife between the Mormon and the Gentile over the cattle ranges of the Mormon country,—Zane Grey's **"Riders of the Purple Sage."** It is exaggerated fiction, but it is not servile to any European model; it brings us to the top of a desert hill whence we can see the long, level stretches of mesa stained with the "purple sage." The ruthlessness of Mormonism in that period of western development is laid bare with great accuracy and the literary artistry of the book is superior to that of many that have been praised above it.

"Popular Novels and Short Stories: 'Riders of the Purple Sage'," in The American Review of Reviews, *Vol. 45, No. 6, June, 1912, p. 762.*

THE NATION　(essay date 1914)

In **"Desert Gold"** Mr. Grey gave us a stirring melodrama, written against a background of the plains and desert mountains of the Southwest. **"The Light of Western Stars"** has a similar setting, described with the same imaginative sweep and vigor. But the story itself is far inferior to **"Desert Gold."** The author

has fallen back upon conventional material—the rich and beautiful Eastern girl transplanted to the West, and the English lord among cowboys. He has taken over his opening situation from Charles Alden Seltzer's "The Trail to Yesterday." In both books the Eastern heroine, arriving alone at night, comes into the power of a more or less drunken cowboy, who forces her to go through the form of a marriage with him by threatening to shoot the priest or minister. In both cases the cowboy turns out to be an admirable man whom the heroine is ultimately glad to claim as a husband. The original suggestion for this situation may perhaps have come from Moody's "The Great Divide." If we add to the conventional elements, borrowings, and repetitions certain up-to-date properties, such as a high-powered automobile and a number of Mexican rebels of the most villanous type, we have summed up the book pretty well.

"Current Fiction: 'The Light of Western Stars'," in The Nation *(copyright 1914 The Nation magazine, The Nation Associates, Inc.), Vol. 98, No. 2540, March 5, 1914, p. 239.*

WILLIAM MORTON PAYNE　(essay date 1914)

"The Light of Western Stars," by Mr. Zane Grey, is a stirring romance of the southwestern desert, the scene being laid in Mexico, close to the Mexican border. . . . A young woman of wealth and social distinction is the heroine. Becoming weary of the round of gaiety which has been her normal existence, and fairly loathing its emptiness, she cuts loose from it all, and sets out to visit her brother, who is a rancher in New Mexico. Her adventures begin the moment she steps off the train at the frontier station. . . . It is all stagy and conventional stuff, but good of its kind, skilfully managed, and effective. Now and then, the writer seems to be planning effects for us which do not quite come off and leave us rather disappointed. . . . But there is no lack of excitement in the narrative, which has also a considerable admixture of romantic glamour and poetic charm. It "reads" from beginning to end and mingles a good deal of humor with its melodramatic plot. (pp. 424-25)

William Morton Payne, "Recent Fiction: 'The Light of Western Stars'," in The Dial, *Vol. LVI, No. 670, May 16, 1914, pp. 424-25.*

ZANE GREY　(essay date 1921)

[Today] it is not possible to travel into the remote corners of the West without seeing the lives of people still affected by a fighting past. How can the truth be told about the pioneering of the West if the struggle, the fight, the blood be left out? It cannot be done. How can a novel be stirring and thrilling, as were those times, unless it be full of sensation? My long labors have been devoted to making stories resemble the times they depict. I have loved the West for its vastness, its contrast, its beauty and color and life, for its wildness and violence, and for the fact that I have seen how it developed great men and women who died unknown and unsung.

In this materialistic age, this hard, practical, swift, greedy age of realism, it seems there is no place for writers of romance, no place for romance itself. For many years all the events leading up to the great war were realistic, and the war itself was horribly realistic, and the aftermath is likewise. Romance is only another name for idealism; and I contend that life without ideals is not worth living. Never in the history of the world were ideals needed so terribly as now. Walter Scott wrote romance; so did Victor Hugo; and likewise Kipling, Hawthorne, Stevenson. It was Stevenson, particularly, who wielded a bludgeon against the realists. People live for the dream in their hearts. And I have yet to know anyone who has not some secret dream, some hope, however dim, some storied wall to look at in the dusk, some painted window leading to the soul. How strange indeed to find that the realists have ideals and dreams! To read them one would think their lives held nothing significant. But they love, they hope, they dream, they sacrifice, they struggle on with that dream in their hearts just the same as others. We all are dreamers, if not in the heavy-lidded wasting of time, then in the meaning of life that makes us work on.

It was Wordsworth who wrote, "The world is too much with us"; and if I could give the secret of my ambition as a novelist in a few words it would be contained in that quotation. My inspiration to write has always come from nature. Character and action are subordinated to setting. In all that I have done I have tried to make people see how the world is too much with them. Getting and spending they lay waste their powers, with never a breath of the free and wonderful life of the open! (pp. v-vi)

> *Zane Grey, in his foreword to his* To the Last Man: A Novel *(copyright © 1921 by Harper & Brothers; copyright renewed © 1949 by Lina Elise Grey; reprinted by permission of Zane Grey, Inc.), Harper, 1921, pp. v-viii.*

T. K. WHIPPLE   (essay date 1925)

Mr. Grey has received justice only from his millions of devoted readers—and some of them, I fear, have been shamefaced in their enthusiasm. The critics and reviewers have been persistently upstage in their treatment of Mr. Grey; they have lectured him for lacking qualities which there was no reason for him to possess, and have ignored most of the qualities in which he is conspicuous. (pp. 19-20)

Mr. Grey himself emphatically believes in the truthfulness of his record [see excerpt above]. Above all else he prides himself upon his accuracy as a historian. . . . One must admire and be thankful for Mr. Grey's faith in his own veracity; but to share it is impossible. Zane Grey should never be considered as a realist. . . . I grant that Mr. Grey does not portray the world as I know it, that he is not an expert psychologist, that his is no refined art in the subtle use of words—that in competition with Henry James, Jane Austen, George Eliot, and Laurence Sterne he is nowhere.

But what of it? There is no reason for comparing him with anyone, unless perhaps with competitors in his own genre. If he must be classified, however, let it be with the authors of *Beowulf* and of the Icelandic sagas. Mr. Grey's work is a primitive epic, and has the characteristics of other primitive epics. His art is archaic, with the traits of all archaic art. His style, for example, has the stiffness which comes from an imperfect mastery of the medium. It lacks fluency and facility; behind it always we feel a pressure toward expression, a striving for a freer and easier utterance. Herein lies much of the charm of all early art—in that the technique lags somewhat behind the impulse. . . . Mr. Grey's style has also the stiffness of traditional and conventional forms; his writing is encrusted with set phrases which may be called epic formulae, or, if you insist, clichés. These familiar locutions he uses as if they were

new, to him at least—as if they were happy discoveries of his own. So behind all his impeded utterance there makes itself felt an effort toward truth of expression—truth, that is, to his own vision, for we must never ask of him truth to the actual world as we know it.

That Zane Grey has narrative power no one has denied, but not everyone is pleased with his type of story. . . . They are, of course, sensational melodrama, as "improbable" as plays by Elizabethan dramatists. They roar along over the mightiest stage that the author has been able to contrive for them. They tell of battle and bloodshed, of desperate pursuits and hairbreadth escapes, of mortal feuds and murder and sudden death, of adventures in which life is constantly the stake. These stories move on the grand scale; they are lavish in primitive, epic events. Mr. Grey does not dodge big scenes and crises, in which plot and passion come to a head; he has a distinct liking for intense situations. . . . Though melodrama is not in style at the moment, the human taste for tremendous happenings is not likely to die for some centuries yet. Mr. Grey has the courage of his innocence in tackling difficulties which cautious realists know enough to avoid.

And no more than in his stories does he dodge the heroic in his characters. His people are all larger than life size. They may be called cowpunchers, prospectors, ranchers, rangers, rustlers, highwaymen, but they are akin to Sigurd, Beowulf, and Robin Hood. Just at present, heroism, of all literary motifs, happens to be the most unfashionable, and disillusionment is all the cry. But it is tenable surely that the heroic is not incompatible with literary merit. . . . (pp. 20-3)

Of these heroic figures Mr. Grey's portrayal is crude and roughhewn. Their speech is often far from the talk of actual men and women; we are as much—and as little—conscious of the writer's working in a literary convention as when we read a play in blank verse. His characterization has no subtlety or finesse; but, like his style, it is true—again, of course, I mean true to the author's own conception. That conception of human nature is a simple one; he sees it as a battle of passions with one another and with the will, a struggle of love and hate, of remorse and revenge, of blood lust, honor, friendship, anger, grief—all on a grand scale and all incalculable and mysterious. The people themselves are amazed and incredulous at what they find in their own souls. (pp. 23-4)

In Zane Grey's conception of human nature nothing is more curious than his view of sex. In *Riders of the Purple Sage* a young man and a girl live alone together for weeks in a secret canyon; in *The Lone Star Ranger* the hero rescues an innocent girl from a gang of bandits and roams about Texas with her for a long time—and all [in a harmless fashion]. . . . Nothing shows more clearly how far away Mr. Grey's world is from actuality; his Texas is not in the Union, but in fairyland. His heroes, to be sure, have occasional fierce struggles with their "baser natures"—a difficulty, by the way, from which his heroines are exempt. Not all his women, however, are altogether pure; from time to time a seductress crosses the path of the hero, who usually regards her with indifference. These women, incidentally, are often among the best-drawn of Mr. Grey's characters. In his treatment of sex as in other respects Mr. Grey is simple and naïve; his conventions are as remote as those of the medieval Courts of Love, and must be taken for granted along with the other assumptions of his imaginary world.

Mr. Grey's heroic ideal looks a little strange in the twentieth century. It is; it belongs more naturally to the sixth century; it is the brutal ideal of the barbarian, of the Anglo-Saxons before they left their continental homes. . . . [Mr. Grey] democratically insists on loyalty and generosity between friends, and on independence and self-reliance. And to this code he adds an element which is no doubt a kind of residuum from Christianity: he likes to see hatred and desire for vengeance supplanted by forgiveness and love. The process of purification or redemption is a favorite theme of his; sometimes it is brought about by the influence of a noble and unselfish man or by the love of a pure and innocent girl, but more often by the cleansing effect of nature in the rough. If one is to take Mr. Grey's ethics at all seriously, one must of course find fault with them. . . . [However] we may insist that a storyteller's merit is not dependent on the validity of the lessons which he teaches. There is something of the savage in most of us, so that we can respond imaginatively to Mr. Grey without our all rushing off to the wilds to be made men of.

Not that Mr. Grey regards nature as always a beneficent force. Rather, he portrays it as an acid test of those elemental traits of character which he admires. It kills off the weaklings, and among the strong it makes the bad worse and the good better. Nature to him is somewhat as God is to a Calvinist—ruthlessly favoring the elect and damning the damned. Mr. Grey sees in nature the great primal force which molds human lives. . . . This setting of desert, forest, mountain, and canyon, great cliffs and endless plains, has been made familiar to us all by the movies if not by travel; but as seen through Mr. Grey's marveling and enhancing eyes it all takes on a fresh and unreal greatness and wonder. For his descriptive power is as generally recognized as his narrative skill; indeed, it would be hard for anyone so overflowing with zest and with almost religious adoration to fail in description. Mr. Grey's faculty of wonder, his sense of mystery, is strong; it shows itself in his feeling for the strangeness of human personality and also more outwardly in the air of strangeness with which he invests his lonely wanderers or outlaws who from time to time appear out of the unknown—but most of all it shows itself in his feeling for the marvelous in nature. So far as he indicates a religion, it is a form of nature worship; when he is face to face with the more grandiose aspects of the earth's surface, he feels himself in the presence of God.

Mr. Grey differs from many nature lovers, that is to say, in that his fervor is altogether genuine. His enthusiasm is not assumed because it is the proper thing; on the contrary, he feels much more than he can manage to express. And here, I think, we come to the secret of his superiority to most of his contemporaries and competitors: he is sincere and thoroughly in earnest. He really cares, he gets excited about what he is writing. His books have not the look of hackwork. It is true that they are uneven, that he has not been immune to the influences of his own popularity and of the movies, that he must often have worked hastily and carelessly—but he has never written falsely. He is genuine and true to himself, an artist after his fashion. Furthermore, he possesses a powerful imagination, of the mythmaking type which glorifies and enlarges all that it touches, and in his best work, such as *Riders of the Purple Sage*, he uses his imagination to the utmost. The whole story, the situations and people and settings, are fully living in his mind, and he gets them into words as best he can. Of course he has an amazing, an incredible simplicity and unsophistication of mind, a childlike naïveté—but that is what makes him what he is, a fashioner of heroic myths. . . . [In] Zane Grey we have a real, not a would-be, primitive mirac-

ulously dropped among us; yet we accord him no recognition at all—except an astounding popularity. (pp. 24-8)

The glorification of the redblooded he-man, the pioneer ideal, is a national trait, and even those who have learned better cannot rid themselves of a sneaking respect for the brute in their hearts. . . . No, the American forte is not sophisticated disillusion—it is much more likely to be something on the order of Zane Grey's work. Of course everyone is at liberty not to like such literature, which belongs by right to the infancy of the race, and to disagree with Mr. Grey's view of the world. Indeed, if one asks of books a valid criticism of life as we experience it, Mr. Grey has little to offer. But let us look at him for what he is, rather than what he is not. Then, whether or not we happen to care for his work, I think we must grant him a certain merit in his own way. We turn to him not for insight into human nature and human problems nor for refinements of art, but simply for crude epic stories, as we might to an old Norse skald, maker of the sagas of the folk. (pp. 28-9)

T. K. Whipple, "American Sagas" (1925), in his Study Out the Land: Essays *(copyright © 1943 by The Regents of the University of California; copyright renewed © 1970 by Mary Ann Whipple; reprinted by permission of the University of California Press)*, University of California Press, 1943, pp. 19-29.

DOUGLAS BRANCH (essay date 1926)

[About] the literary abilities of Zane Grey there is a discreet silence, except for innumerable semi-apologetic tributes to his "well-known descriptive powers." For the critics, it seems, Grey is:

> A man whom few there are to love,
> And none who dare to shoot.
>
> (pp. 249-50)

The broad appeal of Zane Grey is the romantic West. (p. 250)

But his romances, as he calls them, are the grim, gory conflicts of Sadists who are also supermen, women who are hypersexual yet strangely virginal. Stewart, his typical hero, is "a combination of fire, strength, and action. There was something vital and compelling in his presence." The superman again! (pp. 250-51)

I believe [there] is legitimate explanation for his success; for interwoven with the appeal of a romance-laden West is practically every popular "appeal" that has enlivened the whole body of domestic fiction, from the glory of the Flag to the glory of woman's virginity, from a fiery democratic Americanism to the mystery of God-ordained love between man and woman, from the avenging strength of fighting men to the caveman tactics of lovers. (p. 251)

[In *The Light of Western Stars*] Grey describes the hero's love-tactics thus: "He had said straight out that he loved the girl— he had asked her to marry him—he kissed her—he hugged her—he lifted her upon his horse—he rode away with her through the night—and he married her." (p. 252)

The niceties of structure in these tales are suspiciously like the niceties of structure in a five-reel photoplay; the novels are dreams made to order, and if the cowboy is only a lover he has played his part. These romances, though they may preserve a journalistic attention to broad detail, are not based in their characterizations and in their motives on the truth of human experience; and they are not true romances. (p. 253)

Douglas Branch, "The Aristocracy of Novelists," in his The Cowboy and His Interpreters *(reprinted by permission of Hawthorne Properties (Elsevier-Dutton Publishing Co., Inc.), copyright © 1926 D. Appleton and Co.; 1954 Douglas Branch),* Appleton, *1926, pp. 236-53.**

HAMLIN GARLAND   (essay date 1932)

Grey was walking on deck as I came up at seven this morning. I introduced myself and for an hour we walked and talked about whales, sharks, swordfish, and finally of Arizona and New Mexico. The deeper I got into his thinking, the more I liked him. He is like his books, manly, adventurous, clean-minded and wholly American in his excellencies as well as in his faults. He lacks in literary subtlety and grace of speech just as in his writing. He was not in the least boastful as he might very well have been over men who like myself are failures from the commercial point of view.

It is plain that he feels his isolation from his fellow writers and is a bit bewildered by the failure of the critics to value his work for the excellence which he believes it to possess. He seemed to regard me as an elder and wiser brother and treated me with candid respect.

As for me, I regarded him as an amazingly significant literary phenomenon. He confirmed all his publisher's reports of his royalties and they were enormous, more than any other fictionist in our time or in any other time. (pp. 139-40)

He told me of his mother's asking him when a lad to sign the Francis Murphy pledge. "I did so and I have never tasted whiskey or any other intoxicant. I don't smoke and I don't tell smutty stories." These peculiarities increased my respect for him. They explained his stories, which are without offense in this way. He admitted that he found little companionship among the Hollywood men. "I hate all this pornography of Hollywood, as you do."

The longer we talked the more we had in common. We are both what would be called "puritans." He knows much of the Hollywood corruption and keeps clear of it. That he is a man of power of resolution, no one can deny. He has made his great sales as Edgar Wallace did, without resort to pornography, and what he lacks in literary taste and charm, he makes up in sincerity and vigor. (p. 140)

Hamlin Garland, in his journal entry of November 20, 1932, in his Hamlin Garland's Diaries, *edited by Donald Pizer (copyright © 1968), The Huntington Library, 1968, pp. 139-41.*

BURTON RASCOE   (essay date 1939)

[Zane Grey] represented a story-telling tradition that is peculiarly American. . . . [He] had his literary ancestry in the dime novels about Kit Carson, Buffalo Bill, and the Wild West. . . . Grey brought about the vicarious wish-fulfillment of millions of sedentary workers in the office warrens of cities and industrial towns—of imprisoned men to whom a new Zane Grey novel was a splendid escape into a wild, free dreamland of limitless horizons, where the problems of life are reduced to the simplest elements and where justice triumphs over evil, the

wages of courage and uprightness are true love and genuine happiness, and where man may breathe in freedom. . . .

[Zane Grey] was a star. It is difficult to imagine any writer having less merit in either style or substance than Grey and still maintaining an audience at all; but his yarns had the requisite setting and they did possess the quality of speed and action which is suited to the accelerated speed of modern travel. . . . There is [little] likelihood that Grey's novels will find new readers years hence, for each generation produces its own Zane Greys. But Grey's was a success story that was peculiarly American. . . .

Burton Rascoe, "Opie Read and Zane Grey," in The Saturday Review of Literature *(copyright © 1939, copyright renewed © 1966, by Saturday Review; all rights reserved; reprinted by permission), Vol. XXI, No. 3, November 11, 1939, p. 8.**

FRANK LUTHER MOTT   (essay date 1947)

[Only] two of Zane Grey's stories qualify for top-bracket position as best sellers—*The Spirit of the Border* and *Riders of the Purple Sage*. . . . [*The Spirit of the Border*] is a violent, bloody, and crudely written story of fighting against the Indians and their renegade allies. "The author does not intend to apologize for what many readers may call the 'brutality' of the story," begins the Introduction. Apology was not what was required. The story of the death of Girty is revolting in the extreme, though one might accept it if it were supported by historical authority. *Riders of the Purple Sage* was also an early number. It has a sensational Mormon theme in connection with the love story, and more than the usual amount of hard riding and miraculous shooting. (pp. 237-38)

Grey's stories were stimulating to boys who wanted imaginative excitement and to men without developed literary taste who wanted only escape. Their plots displayed an unusual talent for invention, and the narration was swift. . . . [Grey] was also a product of his times. Though unliterary, he belonged definitely to the rough-and-tough school of letters of the Roosevelt-Kipling era, whose typical hero was . . . a superman whose will was iron, whose nerves were steel, and whose manners were brass. And if . . . Grey mixed blood plentifully with his ink, that too was part of the technique of his school. His love passages are far too often downright funny, not in intention, but in their naïve attempts to depict passion. (p. 238)

Frank Luther Mott, "The Great Open Spaces," in his Golden Multitudes: The Story of Best Sellers in the United States *(reprinted with permission of the Estate of the author; © 1947 by Frank Luther Mott; copyright renewed © 1974 by Mildred Mott Wedel), The Macmillan Company, 1947, pp. 233-40.**

JAMES K. FOLSOM   (essay date 1966)

[How] to rehabilitate the Indian is the basic concern of *The Vanishing American*. . . . Grey sees the most serious particular evil in white programs to modernize Indian life as the presence of missionaries. *The Vanishing American* is filled with dastardly men of God. . . . In Grey's pages the ministers are not only misguided and bigoted but lecherous, greedy, and even traitorous. In contrast to these melodramatic stereotypes stand the good white traders and the better Indians. The best Indian of all is the chief Nophaie, *alias* Lo Blandy, who had been carried off as a youth and given the advantages of a white education. . . . When the United States becomes involved in the first World War the Indians, for some obscure motivation Grey never bothers to clarify, rush to the colors, and honorably acquit themselves in various ways overseas. (p. 156)

Grey's real concern is not with Indians in particular or even society in general. . . . Grey ignores both Indians and history. Garland's bitter, uncompromising, often misguided, and sometimes evil characters become in Grey's hands nothing more than stereotypes. Nowhere is this more evident than in Grey's discussion of attempts to Christianize the Indians, an aspect of white policy which both men understand is at the heart of the Indians' cultural future. Unlike Garland, Grey never faces the problem squarely. We discover early in the book that Nophaie has lost both his white and Indian religions, and in the face of this catastrophe minor problems such as white maltreatment of Indians, poor sanitary conditions on the reservations, inadequate medical care, and indeed the threatened extinction of the entire Indian race dwindle to matters of almost no importance. At the end of *The Vanishing American* Nophaie comes to the comforting realization that the God of the Indian and the God of the white man is the same. The rush of insight which opens his mind to this complacent universal truth also elevates him to a pinnacle of philosophical understanding where he can realize that ''the tragic fate of the vanishing American . . . ceased to exist.'' . . . Secure in this profound knowledge he can—and does—die happily, untortured by the doubts which have pursued him throughout the book.

The Vanishing American, then, becomes escape literature of the most insidious kind. Grey is interested in nothing other than the most complacent romanticizing. The fate of the Indian is exploited to lend to the book a dim melancholy quality and, hopefully, the illusion of profundity to a story which celebrates nothing more profound than a total retreat from life. The stereotyped characters—evil missionaries and nefarious agents on the one side and noble Indians and sympathetic traders on the other—serve only to reveal the utter conventionality of Grey's mind. In his hands a great and tragic theme is reduced to the most insipid bathos. (pp. 156-57)

> *James K. Folsom, ''Good Men and True,'' in his*
> The American Western Novel *(copyright © 1966 by*
> *College and University Press Services, Inc.), College*
> *& University Press, 1966, pp. 99-140.**

KENNETH W. SCOTT (essay date 1970)

[In] the spring of 1907, at thirty-five years of age and with two unread novels to his credit, Easterner Grey made his first trip to the Far West. . . . The purpose of Zane Grey's journey to the Southwest was to write a book on Buffalo Jones. . . . Grey wrote the Jones book—*The Last of the Plainsmen* . . .— but it was not until a few years later, with the publication of *The Heritage of the Desert,* that he began to use his western experience in fiction. ''Just what happened to my soul on this trip I am now trying to discover,'' Grey wrote in a letter in 1908. When the revelation of the West came to Grey—as it comes to Majesty Hammond, to John Hare, and to many other Easterners in his novels—it enabled him to write the Western romances that were to make him for many years one of the most popular authors of his time. (p. 10)

[*The Heritage of the Desert*] was Grey's first successful novel, and it marked the beginning of his lifelong association with Harpers. . . . [As] Grey worked on it in the comparative tranquility of his Lackawaxen cottage and recollected his trips to

Jones's ranch, and his emotional response to the West and its ways, the novel took on a strong primitivistic flavor.

The Heritage of the Desert opens with Connecticut-raised John Hare found ''almost dead'' in the desert of southern Utah by a party of Mormons. Ill with tuberculosis, Hare has traveled to the West ''because the doctors said [he] couldn't live in the East.'' . . . When the Mormons come upon him, he is in danger of death not only from his illness but also from exposure in the desert, to which he has fled following an encounter with an outlaw named Dene. But Hare's malaise is of the spirit, as well as of the body, for in this novel, as in many that Grey wrote after it, the East symbolizes an effete and bloodless way of life, in contrast to the hardy, vigorous West. . . .

The young man is taken by [August] Naab to his homestead in the desert where the Easterner finds a ''land overflowing with milk and honey.'' . . . (p. 11)

August Naab, the man who has created this Eden out of the wilderness, is Grey's idealized portrayal of the Westerner. Naab is the symbol of creativity, a man in harmony with the productive and positive forces of the natural world, a man of peace; he is also strong, virile, and capable. . . . In the act of creation, in making the desert bloom, Naab literally has become a man made in the image of God; the many descriptive terms applied to Naab—physician, carpenter, preacher, shepherd, pacifist—are those traditionally associated with the Deity and with Christ. . . .

Grey's desert Eden, along with the God-like father-figure of Naab, includes an Eve. She is Mescal, half-Spanish, half-Indian, the adopted daughter of August, and the eventual helpmeet of John Hare after he has become healthy, sturdy, and self-reliant. Like Naab, she assists in the young man's rebirth and growth. Her name—that of the familiar desert plant—links her to the Western wilderness and suggests her role in the novel. (p. 12)

As has been suggested, Grey's use of image and symbol to support his theme reveals considerable skill; less successful are his characterizations. The villains—the outlaw Dene, Holderness the land agent, who shuts off Naab's water supply to force him to sell his homestead, and the drunken Snap Naab, lustfully eyeing Mescal—are a colorless trio. Even Hare is too often a cipher. And Mescal . . . is too beautiful, too ingenuous, too passionate—too good, finally, to be believed. . . . Only August Naab, the sturdy old Mormon who embodies Grey's primitivism more successfully than either Hare or Mescal does, is genuinely convincing.

The traditional elements of the Western story are given little play in *The Heritage of the Desert.* The long chases, the shoot-'em-ups, the last minute rescues are there, but not much space is devoted to them. The emphasis instead is on Hare's discovery that a life lived simply and naturally in the wilds is the most meaningful one. And Grey's technique, though limited at times, is more than adequate in many places. Much of the novel is descriptive, and here Grey rarely falters; every chapter reveals his ability to render the colors, shapes, and astonishingly varied beauty of the desert. Furthermore, he skillfully exploits the limited third person point of view, forcing us to experience the power and majesty of the West as they are revealed to Hare. . . .

Zane Grey used the thesis of *The Heritage of the Desert* many times in the more than fifty novels that he wrote after it. The Easterner who can discover a meaning to existence only amid the rugged grandeur of the American West is a recurring character who appears, with only slight modifications, in [many of his novels]. . . . Each novel is, in its way, a recreation of the author's first experience with the West, the 1907 visit to Buffalo Jones's desert ranch. After *The Heritage of the Desert,* Grey's most successful fictional reworking of this revelatory period in his life is *The Light of Western Stars*. . . . In this novel, Majesty Hammond, an overrefined, overeducated young New York girl, is the female counterpart of John Hare. At first hostile to the West and its ways, the young woman comes to find it the only satisfying life. On a simple level, the novel seems to suggest that operas, trips to Europe, and visits to Old World shrines are as nothing when compared with the glory of a desert sunset; on a more complex level, the novel demonstrates the relationship of environment to character development. It is the West, with its greater demands, rather than the listless East, that brings out Majesty's best qualities: her generosity, her courage, her ability to love. Here again, Grey limits his point of view to that of the central character, and *The Light of Western Stars* is something of a novelty in western romances in that it is told entirely through the consciousness of a woman. . . .

Grey's mellifluous style, sustained use of symbolism in the stars to suggest aspiration and spiritual illumination, and carefully controlled point of view make *The Light of Western Stars,* after *The Heritage of the Desert,* perhaps Grey's most satisfying novel. But it lacks the strength, the sense of revelation, that the earlier work has. The moment of discovery is missing from this work, as it is from all of the later novels that employ the same theme. As Grey moved further away in time from his 1907 western trip, the freshness and vitality of the experience diminished in his many retellings of it. *The Heritage of the Desert,* Zane Grey's first fictional attempt to impart the meaning of this experience, still stands alone as the most successful account of his discovery of the West. (p. 13)

> *Kenneth W. Scott, "'The Heritage of the Desert': Zane Grey Discovers the West," in* The Markham Review *(© Wagner College 1970), Vol. 2, No. 2, February, 1970, pp. 10-14.*

RICHARD W. ETULAIN   (essay date 1970)

There is little neutral ground in reactions to the writings of Zane Grey. On one side, numerous academic critics contemptuously dismiss his work as damnable sub-literature and not worth reading; on the other, thousands of steak and potato readers devour his Westerns and enjoy them, because they are lean on hidden meanings and spare on symbolism. Unfortunately, there has been little analysis of Grey as a writer; no one has spent sufficient time and energy to understand the man and his books. (p. 217)

Grey chose to be a formula writer and to repeat a successful pattern in his works. In *Riders of the Purple Sage,* his most popular book, the typical qualities of his Westerns are clearly delineated. Set in Mormon country in Southern Utah in the 1870s, the story centers on two hero-heroine relationships: Bern Venters and the Masked Rider (Bess Oldring); and Jane Withersteen and Lassiter. Venters is a physical weakling until he encounters the catalytic purple sage, a moral weakling until he meets Bess. The metamorphosis of Lassiter is in the other direction. Known beforehand as a hotshot gunslinger, his character changes under the influence of his devotion for Jane Withersteen. . . . [He] is refined and gentled because of the love of a woman. (p. 218)

Riders of the Purple Sage contains the essential ingredients of the Zane Grey Western: romance, action, and good versus evil. The author, however, creates a closed fictional society; and the characters are maneuvered to fit preconceived notions. His men and women are "flat" characters: those who represent an idea are in conflict with persons who epitomize opposite concepts. Another weakness prominent in this Western is Grey's inability to handle human emotion. His heroines overact emotionally; they are too often crying or fainting. Such weaknesses are not allowed in the heroes, but they are repeatedly "shocked," "stunned," or "astounded." Grey is not able to hint at feeling; he is too explicit and oversimplifies the feelings and actions of his characters.

At the same time, it is evident that the author knows how to tell a story. The suspense and drama are there. The narrative flows along without getting caught in whirlpools of flashbacks and subplots. Also appealing is Grey's descriptive ability. . . . He did not entirely succeed in juxtaposing action and description smoothly, but few will fault his descriptive passages as much as his treatment of character. (p. 219)

However one reacts to the opinions of . . . other interpreters, what is evident is the need for less castigation and more consideration of Grey and his writings. As the father of the Western, he occupies an important position in American popular culture, and one would hope that future interpreters would spend more time in scrutinizing the techniques and ideas of Zane Grey, than in condemning him to the nether region set aside for writers of Westerns. (pp. 219-20)

> *Richard W. Etulain, "A Dedication to the Memory of Zane Grey: 1872-1939," in* Arizona and the West *(copyright 1970 by the Arizona Board of Regents), Vol. 12, No. 3, Autumn, 1970, pp. 217-20.*

RUSSEL NYE   (essay date 1970)

[Zane Grey's] popularity was neither accidental nor undeserved. Few popular novelists have possessed such a grasp of what the public wanted and few have developed Grey's skill at supplying it. . . . He combined adventure, action, violence, crisis, conflict, sentimentalism, and sex in an extremely shrewd mixture, adding just enough history, scenery, and seriousness to give it the unmistakable stamp of a Zane Grey story.

Action came first. A master of the chase, the Indian ambush, the gunfight, the stampede, the fistfight, and the walkdown, Grey weaved them together with consummate skill and sufficient restraint to keep them believable. All the classic conflicts appeared in his novels: rancher and settler, sheriff and outlaw, gunman and gunman, cowboy and Indian, Indian and white, Eastern "culture" and Western society. His most notable contribution to the roster of characters was the gunfighter, the good-bad man who might be on either side of the law—rootless, lonely, a doomed wanderer through a society which had no place for him. . . . Though the term existed in the seventies, Grey was the first writer of popular Westerns to seize and to capitalize on the "gunfighter" image. After he created the original model a hundred novelists and scriptwriters began producing it in quantity.

In an unobtrusive way the action in Zane Grey's work was surprisingly violent. . . . But Grey's real skill lay in his ability to ring changes on standard plots, combining them with sufficient historical data to make them plausible. *Riders of the Purple Sage* placed a pretty, headstrong girl together with an outlaw gunman in the Mormon-Gentile wars of the seventies. *The U.P. Trail* set a handsome, young construction engineer and an orphaned girl against the background of the building of the transcontinental railroad. *Western Union* used the building of the first transcontinental telegraph, Indians, a prairie fire, a buffalo stampede, a flood, and a bandit gang to provide interest. In *The Vanishing American* and *Heritage of the Desert* Grey introduced and then edged away from a problem he apparently preferred to evade: the first suggests "passionate and unconventional love" between a young Indian chief and golden-haired Marian Warner from the East, the second something of the same sort between a rich Eastern boy and a half-Indian girl. (pp. 294-95)

Grey introduced sex, good and bad [to the Western]. Good women, he emphasized, were the best of all creatures this side of heaven, and their pure love the world's greatest ennobling force. (p. 296)

Grey drew women better than he did men, though he leaned heavily for both on stereotypes taken out of the popular novel. Except for his gunmen, his heroes tended to be bland, a trifle too noble, a bit too upper class. . . . More interesting were his semioutlaws—Lassiter, the doomed gunman in *Riders of the Purple Sage;* Nophaie, the bitter young Nopah warrior in *The Vanishing American;* Buck Duane, the agonized killer of *Lone Star Ranger* and the cold, tawny gunfighter Poggin, in the same novel. Some of Grey's women, excluding the prevalence of schoolma'm types and Eastern heiresses, could be interesting—Beauty Stanton, the regally-beautiful madam in *The U.P. Trail;* Fay Larkin, "fair as a Sago lily," the captive girl of *Rainbow Trail;* Mescal, the half-Navajo girl of *Heritage of the Desert,* purchased as a toy; Jane Withersteen, the proud Mormon girl of *Riders of the Purple Sage.* (p. 297)

> Russel Nye, *"Sixshooter Country,"* in his The Unembarrassed Muse: The Popular Arts in America (© 1970 by Russel Nye; reprinted by permission of The Dial Press), Dial, 1970, pp. 280-304.*

GARY TOPPING (essay date 1973)

The all-important idea in Zane Grey's conception of the uniqueness of the West was that nature is a purifying force, purging man of the superficiality and corruption of Eastern over-civilization. This idea was far from original with him; in fact, when he began writing in 1903 it had become a standard ingredient in the Western myth. (p. 681)

Grey's interest in this idea received much encouragement from the sense of loss Americans began to feel as a result of the end of the frontier. The rapid increase in the urbanization of American life with its attendant corruption reinforced in Grey's mind the idea that the open West had indeed served as the source for much that was virtuous and creative in American history. With the end of that source, it seemed to many that America was truly becoming indistinguishable from the Old World in its increasing weakness of moral fiber. This explains much of the longing for a lost world that characterizes Grey's fiction. (p. 682)

[How] did Grey's background influence his particular view of the West? First, it is significant to note the simple fact that Grey was sincere: he thought his view of the West was essentially true. . . .

The critics have not recognized this fact, and prefer to dwell upon the romanticized aspects of Grey's novels. His treatment of sex is a good case in point. . . . [While] acknowledging the validity of [this argument], one must note a more realistic side to Grey's novels as well. For one thing, they abound in rapes, both attempted and successful (although the successful ones occur off stage). His *The U.P. Trail* features a whorehouse madam as a major character and describes her establishment in great detail. Also, in both that novel and *Riders of the Purple Sage,* female breasts are bared (although only for medical reasons in both cases). All this is remarkably daring and realistic for pre-1920 fiction.

Moreover, compared to many of his successors, Grey seemed to relish violence very little. . . . Much of the carnage in his novels takes place off stage, as does the massacre of the wagon train early in *The U.P. Trail.* Most of the violence is simply necessary, and well integrated with the plot. Also, Grey's most violent heroes, Buck Duane of *Lone Star Ranger* and Jim Lassiter of *Riders of the Purple Sage,* take little pleasure in the violent acts they must commit. (p. 683)

Finally, although he was admittedly biased in his observations, Grey knew the West . . . from personal experience. . . . As a result, his novels often contain graphic descriptions of Western life, such as his description of boom town life and railroad construction in *The U.P. Trail,* or his explanation of the practical effects of a drift fence in the novel of that name. (pp. 683-84)

But perhaps Grey's most original contribution to the view of the West found in his novels was his Darwinism. Other Western novelists could wax eloquent over the nobility of the mountain man and cowboy, but Grey attempted to explain in detail just how it was that the Western environment operated to create such people. . . .

Contact with raw nature was the vital factor in Grey's West, not the strife of man versus man. . . .

[Further,] one can see the extent to which nature was, to Grey, not only the philosophical explanation for his Western characters but also a great cause. . . . Nature in his novels is the one great fact of Western life that cannot be ignored or cheated. (p. 684)

A standard Zane Grey plot for expounding his Darwinian West is the story of an Easterner who comes to live in the West and is gradually educated to Western ways. Comparing the two ways of life, the Easterner realizes the essential artificiality of his former life and is converted to the primal wholesomeness of Western life. (p. 685)

How then can we characterize in general terms Zane Grey's West? First, it is a romanticized creation directly in line with the mythical tradition dating back to the eighteenth century. Although to say, with Whipple [see excerpt above], that Grey's Texas is in fairyland rather than the Union is a bit extreme, it is true that Grey never really appreciated the West on its own terms. He saw the West the way he did, one might say, because he saw the East the way he did.

Secondly, however, Grey has never received due credit for the comparatively high degree of realism in his books. His cowboys, for example, actually raise cattle, get tired, dirty and drunk, and curse, albeit mildly, when angry.

Finally, Grey was philosophically a child of his times. In an age that extolled moral incorruptibility, the manly virtues and "the strenuous life," Grey's novels revealed a world in which those values reigned supreme. (p. 687)

Gary Topping, "Zane Grey's West," in Journal of Popular Culture (copyright © 1973 by Ray B. Browne), Vol. VII, No. 3, Winter, 1973, pp. 681-89.

DANNEY GOBLE (essay date 1973)

[Zane Grey's] *Riders of the Purple Sage* established a new style of adventure story. Quick in pace, the book matched a super-human hero with a virginal heroine and placed them against a backdrop of ruggedness and violence in a struggle against un-mitigated evil. Within a few years the plots and characters would become standard. But Grey's combination of brutal vi-olence and saccharine romance—a heady mixture all but un-known to his predecessors in the writing of frontier fiction—established his claim to a gold mine which he exploited time and again. (p. 64)

[If] only in terms of the audience that Zane Grey has reached, the message of his novels is a deserving subject for serious study. Undeniably, his Western novels have played a major role in setting the American cowboy upon a magnificent myth-ological steed and sending him galloping across the plains of our imagination. But to dismiss his works as having importance only as a rather ridiculous prod to fancy would be gross over-simplification. The man was more than a hack writer who discovered a popular theme and rode it to riches. There is more to his novels than the invincible and virtuous cowboy-hero triumphing through swiftness of mind and six-shooter over black-hearted villains. . . . Using the format that he inadvert-ently hit upon in *Riders of the Purple Sage,* the novelist came to articulate a coherent approach to what he perceived to be the problems of his own time. To a generation embittered by war, disillusioned by peace, and searching desperately to regain a sense of normalcy in a world frighteningly abnormal, Zane Grey purposely and consciously offered a view of society which, beneath the blood and smoke, reaffirmed the traditional values seemingly jeopardized by European war and the swirling social currents of the 1920s. (pp. 64-5)

At the height of his popularity, [Grey] offered his audience a rare glimpse into what he took to be the message of his frontier novels [see excerpt above]. . . . Zane Grey labored to present to Americans a romantic world of "idealism": innocence and rugged virtue untainted by European war and the complexities of modern life. . . .

The precise nature of the "ideals" that Grey felt his nation so terribly needed becomes clear in examining the qualities that the novelist bestowed upon his heroic characters. His leading men were uniformly handsome beyond compare and possessed unmatched skill with firearms. They were most striking, how-ever, in their all-but-absolute virtue, and at the bottom of this steadily flowing well of virtue is the simplicity and naturalness of spirit that the novelist feared was disappearing in his own times. (p. 66)

[In a sense] Grey portrayed his characters as an undisciplined breed of men—undisciplined by the compulsions of a complex, urbanized society. . . . And yet their simple, natural, elemental existence generated qualities which a complex, artificial, and sophisticated environment could not. . . .

To Zane Grey it was clear that the era of the cowboy had produced men of moral qualities sadly lacking in his own time. The coursing floods of social change had eroded the environ-ment that had produced such hardy and admirable specimens, and yet he felt that the still "lonely and hidden wilderness of the West" in his own day might continue to produce those "hard men of the open . . . who climb to the heights of nobility and sacrifice." This hope was the theme of several novels that he set in the contemporary period. In each book he demon-strated that the West continued to stand in striking contrast to the effete and decaying life of the rest of America. (p. 67)

Grey's cowboy-hero may be viewed as personifying traditional American values at a time when, in Grey's mind, the nation was in terrible need of them. By avoiding the false sophisti-cation of the East and living a simple, natural, and self-dis-ciplined life close to the soil, the cowboy-hero becomes nothing less than the central character in a modern morality play. With justice at his hip, unsoiled love in his heart, and honor in his every deed, he is doubly a man on horseback.

But if the nature of Grey's heroes suggests the contrast between his fictionalized West and post-war America, a look at his heroines makes the antithesis more explicit. In writing of the frontier era, Grey carefully delineated the earlier qualities of greatness that he understood to be disappearing in the hollow-ness of the modern woman. Like other authors of frontier fiction, Grey enveloped his heroine with "a gossamer web of refinement and gentility." . . .

She and her sisters are agents of morality and civility in a raw and rugged land. (p. 69)

In spite of her civilizing role, however, the heroine's nature is one of near-total dependence and innocence. (p. 70)

Perhaps because of this indelible strain of innocence, Grey consistently pictured his heroines as dependent on the very men they hoped to "civilize." . . . On the frontier, woman might represent all that was gentle and pure, but in the harshness of the primal environment, her ambitions were doomed to come short of success. The cowboy's rugged virility—to use one of Grey's favorite terms—was destined to triumph over the softer graces of the woman.

Collectively, then, Grey's heroines were created of almost equal parts of morality, innocence, and dependence. Their col-lective nature was thus quite different from the worldly indi-vidualism that he thought typical of women in his own era. The contrast, always implicit in the frontier novels, became explicit when he set a story in the contemporary period. A central figure in many of these books is the woman who comes from the modern life of the East to encounter the rugged sim-plicity of the changeless West. (pp. 70-1)

[For Grey real] progress depended upon recapturing simpler virtues, elemental life-styles, and time-honored morality. Prog-ress meant male virility and female dependence. Progress de-manded a return to Zane Grey's West.

This message rang through Grey's fiction, and it provoked in 1939, the year of his death, *30,000 on the Hoof,* the most absorbingly written of his many novels. It was his third story centered upon World War I. (pp. 72-3)

[With] the guns of Europe firing again and America's role in the growing world conflict under fervent debate, Grey for the last time set a novel against the backdrop of the First World War. Passionately and eloquently, Grey's last and best novel captured the fears and hopes that lay behind his popular suc-cess. (p. 73)

30,000 on the Hoof is a bitter and powerful novel that provided popular literary ammunition for those who dreaded American participation in a second great European war. Neither glory nor adventure waited outside the isolated Arizona canyon [where the novel takes place], only shame and misery. But it was not just war that Grey feared lurking beyond the canyons of the West; it was even more the modern world of moral erosion and swiftly paced change that he had come to perceive as the inevitable product of foreign involvement. It was not, in Grey's final view, enough for Americans to avoid another war; rather, they must seek with him . . . the simplicity and virility of the unchanged and rugged West. (p. 74)

> Danney Goble, "The Days That Were No More: A Look at Zane Grey's West," in The Journal of Arizona History (copyright © 1973 by the Arizona Historical Society), Vol. 14, No. 1, Spring, 1973, pp. 63-75.

ANN RONALD (essay date 1975)

[Zane Grey's] novels transport the reader to a simpler life where the scenery is beautiful and the people are predictable, where choices are clear-cut and obstacles surmountable. But most important, Grey's books renew the spirit of the frontier that has almost vanished from the life of the typical American. By providing a new frontier, albeit an idealized version of the West, he offered a distinctly American Shangri-La to readers caught in everyday lives in everyday places. Using a formula that became increasingly familiar, he aimed his novels directly at middle America and gave that audience comfortable conservative answers to questions of law and order, justice, morality, religion. His ideas provided an ethical oasis in what must have seemed to them a desert of changing mores. Because the scope of his writing is tied inseparably to the needs of his readers, then, the various aspects of his work must be seen primarily in terms of their popular appeal. (p. 6)

Most of his novels used the basic formula which he had established at the beginning in *The Heritage of the Desert,* although he offered enough variations to keep the public interested. That formula is both a key to his popular success and a reason for his literary failure. Psychologically, it is immensely satisfying, but he repeats it too often, and after the first fifteen novels or so his books take on a sameness that seems almost mechanical. The formula is not uniquely Grey's. It is a cross between James Fenimore Cooper and Owen Wister, an echo of Grey's admiration for the Leatherstocking series and his recognition of *The Virginian*'s (1902) popularity. It is also a restructuring of the Horatio Alger success story, which at that time had a huge following that copied it exactly, and a smaller group that used its pattern for inspiration. Most important, the Zane Grey formula is an outgrowth of the author's personal experiences, a reiteration of his own journey to the frontier.

An Easterner—that is, an innocent—arrives in the West. He, or she, has been a failure in the past and seems unprepared to meet the challenges ahead. The land at first seems harsh and unforgiving—the sun is too hot, the canyons too deep, the peaks too rugged, the rivers too swift. Problems are compounded by the appearance of evil, of men who live by their guns and who care nothing for the rights of others. Gradually, however, the neophyte becomes a man. Rather than be beaten by the environment, he learns to conquer the elements, and in doing so he acquires a deep appreciation for the land. Rather than see innocent people tormented by evil, he learns to fight and to protect those he has come to love. The West, seeming

almost a Garden of Eden, becomes a proving ground for man. Here he loses his innocence and gains knowledge. In Grey's words, the hero learns "the heritage of the desert" exactly as the author did on his first trip with Buffalo Jones, and exactly as he hopes the reader will do while reading each of his novels. (pp. 12-13)

[In] *The Heritage of the Desert* and in most other Grey books, we have a novel of education, one that initiates a character into manhood through a series of masculine rites and challenges.

For the process to work, that character must begin as an innocent. . . . Actually [the person] is an author-reader surrogate, the kind of character we can easily identify with, one with whom we can experience many things vicariously. And this quality is the first key to Grey's popularity. His heroes, or heroines, generally start out as people like us.

The next step in the formula is essential: Grey places his main character in a special setting, the American West. He includes numerous, extensive, effusive descriptions of this physical environment until he has created almost a visual onslaught of shapes and colors. Indeed this visual richness is what readers remember most clearly about his books, even years after they read them. Grey himself felt that this was the most important element of his novels, but his actual use of setting is even more meaningful than he might have suspected. In the "Preface" of *To the Last Man* . . . he said, "My inspiration to write has always come from nature. Character and action are subordinated to setting" [see excerpt above].

The first half of his statement is accurate. We know that a close correlation exists between the places he visited and subsequent settings of his novels. . . . The second half of his statement does not give him enough credit. Character and action are not subordinated to setting, but rather are developed by it. The three work together, with setting providing the impetus for change. (pp. 14-15)

[The] particular setting implies all the things that a Grey Western environment accomplishes during the course of a novel. First, it is a pictorial rendition of a specific place previously unfamiliar to both the main character and the reader. The shift of scene takes the reader away from his own everyday surroundings and gives the character an environment where he can have a fresh start. The fictional setting, in effect, provides a frontier. Second, the setting is initially seen as hostile. . . . Increasing familiarity will make the land seem less harsh, and each succeeding step in the action will lead toward a fuller sense of its benevolence. Last—and this is how setting determines character—we learn "the heritage of the desert." . . . Innocence is replaced by experience . . . through [the character's] confrontations with nature. . . .

So setting has led character through the initiation process, and this process is synonymous with the action of the novel. . . . Each action leads to another action that leads to another that leads to manhood, and each action is first precipitated by setting. (p. 16)

Just as the author himself went to the West as a failure and turned the experience into success, most of his protagonists do the same. And the reader, looking from his vantage point in middle America, can vicariously enjoy similar sensations while reading the books. This formula of turning failure into success gives a psychological lift that can be immensely satisfying.

But eventually the formula itself becomes the failure. The chief reason why Zane Grey has never been recognized as a significant American novelist is that his formula always remains a formula. Several key phrases that are appropriate to Grey's work—Garden of Eden, innocence and experience, survival of the fittest—might suggest a mythic pattern. But the novels never rise to the level of myth because the formula, rather than setting the characters free, only binds their actions by restricting their choices. Life in a Zane Grey novel is too simple to create mythic patterns. His men and women are too rigidly characterized, their problems too clear-cut, the solutions too easy. Ultimately we read his books not because he tells us about life, but because he does not. For this failure the critic can find fault and the scholar can condemn. But one must credit him for giving his readers exactly what they want—escape fiction, novels that let those readers forget their own comparatively colorless existence while they live alongside the characters. (p. 17)

[Grey's] books have sold millions of copies because he told people like him stories about people almost like themselves. He understood their dreams, their hopes, their needs; and he fed them vicarious success to satisfy their appetites. They let themselves be initiated into his Western world, with its strong masculinity and its staunch morality. They relished his hints of lawlessness, sexuality, and violence. They believed his historical re-creations. They heard his concerns about contemporary issues. They appreciated his religious views. They did not resent the paradoxes or the open contradictions which appeared throughout. They enjoyed their escapes from their everyday surroundings into the romantic West of the author's imagination. They wanted that last glimpse of the frontier, with its simple ethical system. They adored the comfortingly repetitious formula that carried them along.

Zane Grey was a literary phenomenon unequaled in this century because he knew his audience perfectly and because he answered their needs. (p. 41)

> *Ann Ronald, in her* Zane Grey, *edited by Wayne Chatterton and James H. Maguire (copyright 1975 by the Boise State University Western Writers Series), Boise State University, 1975, 46 p.*

DANIEL J. WILSON (essay date 1976)

At the turn of the century there was a revival of an interest in nature, a period that Roderick Nash characterized as the era of the "wilderness cult." Americans, removed from the land by the growing industrial civilization, experienced a strong urge to reassert the traditional ties to the wilderness. . . . These changes in the American relationship to nature and the particular responses of men at the turn of the century and after found expression in . . . this popular literature, especially in the Westerns of Owen Wister and Zane Grey. (pp. 42-3)

With the writings of Owen Wister and Zane Grey after 1900 there was a return to the more wide-ranging philosophical concerns evident in the dime novels. The major difference is that these men developed this philosophy at greater length, considered it more carefully, and integrated it more fully into the structure of their stories. In general, their philosophy encompassed the belief in beautiful, benign, and bountiful nature but they expressed their beliefs in several specific ways. They believed that some sort of superior being was present in American nature and that sensitive people could make contact with it. Wister and Grey also thought that man needed and could

have a special relationship to the land. Unlike the overwhelmingly favorable relationship of the dime novelists, their beliefs were marked by an ambivalence: a need for escape and a need for restraint. Finally, in the novels of Zane Grey, there are occasional suggestions that he realized that the relationship of man and nature may not be mutually beneficial, that in fact, man may be destroying the very nature he needs.

A recurrent idea for these two novelists was the notion of some primal creative force present in the wilds of nature. This primal natural spirit was, at its heart, the creative urge of the world, which, in all probability, was identical with the Christian God. The most sustained dialogue about these spiritual forces occurs in Zane Grey's *Wanderer of the Wasteland.* The hero, Adam, flees to the desert thinking he has killed his brother. . . . After several years of wandering and helping people in distress, Adam reaches a new understanding about the primal spirit and God. He realizes that man is moved by an urge toward unattainable perfection and of mastery over base instincts. Adam finally realizes that this creative evolutionary spirit embraces both the natural spirit he has come to understand and the Christian God he can not give up. The tension obvious in this novel between a wholly naturalistic religion and the Christian God is characteristic of Grey's treatment of the subject, though this novel is unusual in its extended treatment.

Like the local color authors, Owen Wister and Zane Grey presented nature as a necessary escape from the hectic civilized life of modern man. Like them also, they felt that man could not simply return to nature. For Zane Grey, especially, there was a strong belief in the necessity for restraint in man's relationship with nature; if man gives in to his primal urges completely then he violates the higher necessity for progress and the upward evolution of man. (pp. 47-8)

Zane Grey was the only author who manifested any awareness of the detrimental actions of man on nature. In many of the works written after the 1870's there is a nostalgic, elegaic tone which mourns the passing of a way of life. However, it was only Grey who directly confronted the destruction of nature by man. (p. 49)

> *Daniel J. Wilson, "Nature in Western Popular Literature from the Dime Novel to Zane Grey," in* North Dakota Quarterly *(copyright 1976 by The University of North Dakota), Vol. 44, No. 2, Spring, 1976, pp. 41-50.*

GARY TOPPING (essay date 1978)

In attempting an objective evaluation of Grey's literary worth, one might as well begin with the frank admission that he did indeed possess some grave deficiencies. One of the most fundamental indictments the literary critic must bring against Grey is the stifling predictability of his plots. Most of his plots are only slightly varying fictionalizations of Grey's own experience of the West: an Eastern dude comes West and sheds the superficialities of his Eastern cultural background, finding physical health, moral strength, philosophical enlightenment, or true love. Once the names of the characters, the specific geographical setting, and the exact nature of the Easterner's problems are established, often the only interest remaining is to find out which of the stock catalysts Grey will use to effect the cure: stampede, Indian attack, kidnapping, exposure to the elements, and so on.

Complementing Grey's rigidly formulaic plots are his morally naive, simplistic, and stereotyped characters. There are important exceptions, especially his morally ambiguous gun-fighter heroes of whom Lassiter of *Riders of the Purple Sage* and Buck Duane of *Lone Star Ranger* are perhaps the best examples. (pp. 52-3)

Given Grey's fundamental belief in the West's restorative, indeed redemptive, mission in American history, it is perhaps to be expected that his characters would have a high moral tone, to the point of becoming unpalatable to more cynical modern readers. . . . [Grey's characters] lack even a temporary moral indecisiveness, to say nothing of a fully developed tragic flaw, that would interest us and involve us in their fate. Undoubtedly, in an age that had not yet learned to give cynical acceptance to moral cowardice and compromise, [Grey's] characters . . . would be appealing to a sizeable audience, but they lack the complexity necessary for generating deep and sustained literary appeal.

Furthermore, Grey lacked a fundamental control over his prose, especially when describing the physical setting and developing the psychology of his characters. In great literature such things usually build gradually and in subtle ways so that the reader has time to assimilate their effect. Grey, however, too often preferred simply to open the floodgates and let the verbal deluge overwhelm the reader suddenly. Such moments of descriptive eloquence can, of course, have great effect, as they sometimes do in Grey's books, but more often they impress the reader with a sense of poor taste and unwarranted verbal extravagance. (p. 53)

Grey could not hint at emotion. Granted, the limitations of the frontier environment that Grey's books attempt to approximate obviously render improbable a character with the emotional subtlety of a Lambert Strether. But there remains a lot of literary potential in the area between Strether and Grey's emotionally juvenile characters. Grey's Eastern dudes generally convert to Western ways not by gradual rational persuasion or through the slow blossoming of a new insight but . . . in a catastrophic emotional upheaval that leaves them grovelling on an Arizona desert. His Westerners are no better; they resort to fists or guns in response to the slightest frustration, or if female, to those universally appropriate responses so typical of sentimental literature—tears or the swoon.

The speech Grey puts in the mouths of his characters is another major liability. . . . [Making] fictional people talk like real people is not the simple task it seems. The difficulties multiply under Grey's goal of making cowboys sound natural while expounding some fairly sophisticated ethical concepts and historical theories.

All such difficulties aside, however, the fact remains that Grey was a miserable failure at creating realistic speech. (p. 54)

Grey appreciated to a high degree the literary value of a setting and incidental details rooted deeply in the real world, and his best novels show a skillful use of factual material. Unfortunately, he did fall at times into using a compilation of facts as a substitute for literary imagination rather than as a support to that imagination. (p. 55)

The social philosophy and historical theory that Grey crowded into many of his novels are often equally gratuitous. Grey saw the American West as a primitive, Darwinian social environment that nourished fundamental virtues and physical capabilities that were basic ingredients in all vital civilizations and that were especially needed in twentieth century America, which he regarded as increasingly and dangerously effeminate, su-

perficial, and over-civilized. Unfortunately, Grey lacked the literary skill to integrate those ideas into the various novelistic elements of plot, character, setting, and tone. Consequently, his stories, novelistically considered, never add up to the lofty meanings he wanted them to convey, and as a means of filling that gap, he pads them with page upon page of tiresome soliloquies and orations designed to supply as an essayist a substance he could not impart as a creative artist.

Of the several avenues by which one might explore Grey's literary strengths, one that immediately suggests itself is to carry the battle back into the realists' camp. A broader acquaintance with Grey's work . . . provides evidence of numerous realistic elements. Grey's historical novels often show careful research, some of which, admittedly, is dropped into the text in undigested chunks, but at other times helps lend credence to the fictional element. (pp. 55-6)

[Also] Grey's treatment of sex is considerably more realistic than even some sympathetic critics like T. K. Whipple have thought [see excerpt above]. Viewed in the context of his time and especially in the context of Western fiction at that time, Grey was not so prudish as is commonly believed. (p. 57)

T. K. Whipple attempts another avenue of investigation by considering Grey as a writer of primitive epics. . . .

The flaw in Whipple's thesis is that he did not take into consideration Grey's own conception of what he was doing. Grey was, in fact, not a writer of primitive epics, but a writer of romances. Whipple was mistaken in identifying Grey's literary mode, and the only thing that kept him from going as far astray as those who castigated Grey from a realist or naturalist perspective is the fact that the romance and the primitive epic have a considerable number of features in common. (p. 58)

Grey repeatedly refers to his books, especially in his autobiography and in an unpublished essay, "My Answer to the Critics," as "romances," rather than "novels" or "epics." Furthermore, he acknowledged as his mentors and models not Homer and *Beowulf*, but Hugo, Stevenson, Kipling, Tennyson, and Poe.

My thesis is that while the realist and naturalist critics such as Burton Rascoe [see excerpt above], demanded too much of Grey's novels, Whipple demanded too little; if Grey's healthy chunks of romance clogged the fine mesh of the realists' nets, they slipped too easily through the coarse mesh of Whipple's. Considered as more or less a peer of Scott, Cooper, or Stevenson, then, how does Grey measure up?

The romance critic can begin by expropriating most of the positive qualities noted by Whipple, since they are not unique characteristics of the primitive epic, but appear as well in the romance. The first of these is the grand scale of scenery and action in Grey's stories. These appear to best advantage, as Whipple saw, in Grey's masterpiece, *Riders of the Purple Sage*. The balanced rock, the hidden canyons, the waterfall, and the vast prairies of purple sage provide fully as appropriate and memorable a background for the intense passions of *Riders of the Purple Sage* as the murky bogs do for *Beowulf* or the woods and castles and pageantry do for *Ivanhoe*. The action, too, is appropriately intense yet extravagant, and vividly portrayed. (pp. 59-60)

A great deal of the charm of many of Grey's books is to be found in his descriptions of the minutiae of common Western life: his railroad boom towns in *The U.P. Trail*, the cowboy's daily routine in *The Drift Fence* and *The Trail Driver*, and the historical vignettes in *Western Union* and *To the Last Man.* Grey may have fallen short of what Emerson had in mind in "The American Scholar" in calling for a literature on indigenous American themes, but for millions of readers he did provide an introduction, at least, to the literary potential of many common aspects of Western life. Grey's pages swarm with character types and themes that writers had previously ignored and in some cases have yet to receive adequate literary attention: Mormons, Mexicans, buffalo hunters, forest rangers, fishermen, the railroad, the telegraph, labor radicalism—and the list could be extended even further.

Grey's exoticism is also characteristic of the romance. In one sense, Grey merely emphasized the exotic implications and aspects of characters and themes he inherited from other writers and acquired in his own experience of the West. In spite of his attention to detail and reality, many of his cowboys are much more than mere herders of cattle and menders of fence, for Grey raised them to the same colorful never-never-land of Ivanhoe and Long John Silver. (pp. 60-1)

Another typically romantic characteristic of Grey's books is his nostalgia for an earlier, simpler, and morally more vital time, which grows out of a disenchantment with modern bourgeois culture. . . . Grey's heroes are more than merely larger-than-life doers of mighty deeds that rebuke the weaklings of the present (although they are that); there is a more highly developed philosophical discontent behind their exploits. . . . Grey's "flappers" and effeminate Eastern dudes represent the decadence and failure of bourgeois cultural aspirations that can only be cured by a return to a more natural moral system. In fact, while Grey indulges in a nostalgic romantic escapism, he makes his reasons for the escape even more explicit than most of his predecessors in the Romantic movement, thus showing his debt to the Victorian writers as well. Briefly, although Grey is nostalgic, his nostalgia is much more deeply rooted in explicit social criticism than the primitive epics, and sometimes even exceeds that of his Romantic mentors. . . .

There is, admittedly, far too much gratuitous and simplistic moralizing in Grey's books, but at times he shows glimpses of more mature moral conceptions. An example would be the tragic element in the moral constitution of some of his gunfighter heroes, especially Jim Lassiter of *Riders of the Purple Sage* and Buck Duane of *Lone Star Ranger*. (p. 62)

The tragic element in Lassiter and Duane is that they are the harbingers of higher civilization coming to a raw frontier society, yet the violent deeds they must perform to pave the way for the arrival of that civilization must inevitably be condemned when it does arrive. Grey thus perceived, however dimly, an ironic component at the center of the process of refining a frontier society: civilization, once established, can operate by means of rationally-derived laws and social mores, but it can only be established by means of vigilantism and other extralegal and antisocial behavior.

Grey's best characters are those who are caught in the moral borderland between the two worlds of the raw frontier and the ordered civilization that slowly pushes west. Desiring the advent of the new civilization, they realize, nevertheless, that they are too rooted in primitive frontier ways to survive its coming. They are the willing tools of those who seek their ultimate destruction, martyrs at the altar of social and moral progress. It would be absurd to claim that Grey brings the ironic potential of these characters to full literary realization—indeed, the infrequency of his attempts to exploit the theme

seriously rather than simply suggest it indicates that he largely failed to appreciate its profound possibilities—but he does succeed in exploring it enough to impart a special interest to those characters. (p. 63)

There is no doubt that the experienced literary critic, approaching Grey's novels for the first time, will be much more impressed by the fumbled opportunities, the unrealized literary potential in many of the themes Grey pursues, than in the positive literary value of his books. But upon further reflection, the critic who would be really fair to Grey must acknowledge that there is some real merit in certain aspects of his work. Romance, after all, is one of the perennially valid literary modes. As a writer of romances, Grey had some strong qualities, and, however disappointing his failures in other areas may have been, he deserves credit for that. (p. 64)

> *Gary Topping, "Zane Grey: A Literary Reassessment," in* Western American Literature *(copyright, 1978, by the Western Literature Association), Vol. XIII, No. 1, Spring, 1978, pp. 51-64.*

ADDITIONAL BIBLIOGRAPHY

Arrington, Leonard, and Haupt, Jon. "Community and Isolation: Some Aspects of 'Mormon Westerns'." *Western American Literature* VIII, Nos. 1-2 (Spring-Summer 1973): 15-31.
    Examines the portrayal of the Mormon community in western American fiction, using *Riders of the Purple Sage* as a framework.

Gruber, Frank. *Zane Grey: A Biography.* Cleveland: The World Publishing Co., 1970, 284 p.
    Detailed account of Zane Grey's life and the events surrounding his career as a writer. In a biography commissioned by the author's estate, Gruber traces the development of Zane Grey from childhood to his death, painting a portrait of the man and writer through interesting and numerous anecdotes and events.

Jackson, Carlton. *Zane Grey.* New York: Twayne Publishers, 1973, 175 p.
    Study of Zane Grey's life with respect to the themes and concerns the author developed in his numerous writings. Jackson categorizes Grey's novels into five major types—desert, mountain, horse, historical, and cowboy—and discusses each in turn to demonstrate the attitudes held by Grey.

Karr, Jean. *Zane Grey: Man of the West.* New York: Greenberg, Publisher, 1949, 229 p.
    Detailed study of Zane Grey's life with some critical analysis of his works. Karr discusses the major events surrounding Grey's literary career and adds a descriptive bibliography of his novels through 1948.

Powell, Lawrence Clark. "*Riders of the Purple Sage:* Zane Grey." In his *Southwest Classics: The Creative Literature of the Arid Lands; Essays on the Books and Their Writers,* pp. 203-15. Los Angeles: The Ward Ritchie Press, 1974.
    Discussion of Zane Grey's life and the influence of the western environment on his writing. Powell argues that Grey wrote his best novels immediately following his experience with the West, and that his later works suffered as he moved away from the impact of that experience.

Stott, Graham St. John. "Zane Grey and James Simpson Emmett." *Brigham Young University Studies* 18, No. 4 (Summer 1978): 491-503.*
    Discussion of Zane Grey's friendship with James Emmett, a Utah Mormon, and the latter's influence on Grey's writing. Stott notes a number of Grey's Mormon characters modeled after James Emmett.

(Cyprien) Max Jacob

1876-1944

(Also wrote under pseudonyms of Leon David and Morven le Gaelique) French poet, novelist, short story writer, critic, biographer, translator, and librettist.

Jacob's literary contribution is most significant in the genre of the prose poem, a form largely advanced by the French symbolists of the nineteenth century. Producing much of his work during an era of flourishing new movements in the arts, Jacob sought poetic beauty in forms that were self-consciously modern. Along with his contemporary Guillaume Apollinaire, he celebrated the "new spirit" of the Paris avant-garde. The movement of cubism in the visual arts, into which Jacob's background as a painter gave him particular insight, influenced his conception of multiperspective writing, though this was only one technique among an array of verbal devices that some critics have found serious and others trivial.

Jacob was born to Jewish parents at Quimper, Brittany. He studied law at the Ecole Coloniale, leaving the school in 1894 to pursue painting and literature. In Paris he entered into the society of artists gathered around Montmartre, and numbered Picasso and Apollinaire among his intimate friends. During this time Jacob lived in severe poverty, working at several jobs in order to support a life of indulgence in a thriving bohemian scene. In 1909 he experienced a vision of Christ and became a convert to Christianity. A second vision occurred in 1914 at a cinema, this episode forming the inspiration for "Le Christ au cinéma" in *La défense de Tartufe*. Initially refused baptism (because of his reputation his sincerity was doubted), Jacob was received into the Catholic Church in 1915. For a time afterward he carried on a schizophrenic life of revelling followed by penitent prayer, finally retiring to a semimonastic existence in 1921 at Saint-Benoit-sur-Loire. Here the Nazis seized the converted Jew during the Second World War and placed him in a concentration camp at Drancy, where he died.

Jacob wrote a great deal, much of his work in what might be considered marginal genres such as religious meditations, children's literature, "unactable" plays, imaginary conversations, and epistolary novels. The early novel *Saint Matorel* contrasts imaginative fantasy with realistic observation, burlesque humor with deep religious feeling. These polarities came to be associated with Jacob the clowning saint. With the prose poems of *Le cornet à dés (The Dice Cup)*, written over the course of a decade, Jacob gained critical recognition that endures to this day.

In his "Preface of 1916" Jacob explained some of his aesthetic principles: the preference for will and emotion over intellectual analysis, an emphasis on poetic form rather than prosaic statement, and the concept of the prose poem as a genre "situated" between the initial feeling of the artist and that stimulated in the reader. He also distinguished his prose poems from those of his symbolist predecessors Baudelaire and Mallarmé, to whose formal precision Jacob added chance images and associations from the unconscious. The poet remarked that he "set about by attempting to seize, from within myself, in any way I could, the imperatives of the unconscious: words given liberty, risky associations of ideas, dreams both day and night,

hallucinations, etc." Along with this "liberty," Jacob combined his skill as a highly conscious manipulator of words, earning notoriety for his puns, neologisms, and general wordplay. However, he considered this skill as merely a prerequisite, and not a substitute, for realizing one's artistic worth and expressing a personal vision.

Jacob's major collections of poetry, including *La défense de Tartufe, Le laboratoire central*, and *Le sacrifice impérial*, display the same bizarre originality as his prose poems. Because of his absence from the Paris literary scene in the 1920s, Jacob did not receive the recognition he might have from the members of the new surrealist movement, whose technique of automatic writing duplicated Jacob's unconscious outpourings earlier in the century. André Breton, leader of the notoriously antireligious surrealists, disdained Jacob's achievement as that of a promising experimentalist who sold out. Later commentators have established the surrealists' profound debt to Jacob. This debt is shared by several modern French poets, such as Jean Cocteau and Jacques Evrard, to whom Jacob offered his literary insights and guidance through his voluminous correspondence. Jacob is now acknowledged as one of the most significant poets and aestheticians to come after the symbolists,

**and an artistic force important to the inauguration of the
modernist period in literature.**

PRINCIPAL WORKS

L'histoire du roi Kaboul ler et du marmiton Gauwain
    (juvenile fiction) 1904
Saint Matorel (novel) 1909
*Les oeuvres burlesques et mystiques de frère Matorel mort
    au couvent* (novel) 1912
Le cornet à dés (prose poems) 1917
    [*The Dice Cup,* 1979]
La défense de Tartufe (poetry and prose poems) 1919
Le laboratoire central (poetry) 1921
Le roi de Béotie (short stories and dramas) 1921
Art poétique (criticism) 1922
Filibuth (novel) 1923
L'homme de chair et l'homme reflet (novel) 1924
Visions infernales (poetry) 1924
Les pénitents en maillots Roses (poetry) 1925
Le sacrifice impérial (poetry) 1928
Rivage (poetry) 1931
Ballades (poetry) 1938
Conseils à un jeune poète (criticism) 1945
    [*Advice to a Young Poet,* 1976]
Derniers poèmes en vers & en prose (poetry and prose
    poems) 1945
Drawings and Poems (poetry) 1951
Lettres, 1920-1941 (letters) 1966

MAX JACOB (essay date 1916)

Everything that exists is situated. Everything that's above matter is situated; matter itself is situated. Two works are unequally situated either by the authors' minds or by their artifices. Raphael is above Ingres, De Vigny above Musset. Madame X is above her cousin; the diamond is above quartz. Maybe this is the result of the relation between morale and morality? In the past they believed that artists were inspired by angels and that there were different categories of angels.

Buffon said: "The style is the man." Which means that a writer must write with his blood. This definition is beneficial, it doesn't seem exact to me. What is the man is his way of using words, his sensibility; it's right to say: express yourself in your own words. It's wrong to believe that that's style. Why should we want to give style in literature a different meaning from the one it has in the other arts? Style is the will to exteriorize oneself by one's chosen means. Generally, as in Buffon, language is mistaken for style, because few men need an art of the will, that is, art itself; and because everyone needs a human quality in their way of expressing themselves. During great artistic epochs, the rules of art that are taught from childhood on constitute canons which furnish a style: the artists are then those who, despite the rules they followed since childhood, find a living way of expressing themselves. This living way of expressing oneself is the charm of the aristocracies, it's that of the 17th Century. The 19th Century is full of writers who understood the necessity of style but who didn't dare come down from the throne which their desire for purity constructed. They created shackles at the expense of life. [In a footnote Jacob states: The prose poem must have, despite the rules which

style it, a free and vital way of expressing itself.] The author, having situated his work, can use all his charms: language, rhyme, musicality, and feeling. *When a singer has found his voice, he can have fun with the vocal flourishes.* To really understand me, compare Montaigne's familiarities with those of Aristide Bruant or the elbowings in a hack's diary to the brutalities of Bossuet knocking the Protestants around.

This theory isn't ambitious; it's not new, either: it's the classical theory that I'm modestly resummoning. The names I mention aren't there to hit the "moderns" with the club of the "ancients;" these are incontestable names; if I'd mentioned others that I know, perhaps you might have thrown away this book, which I don't want; I'd like you to read it not for a long time, but often: to make something understood is to make something loved. Only long works are held in esteem; it's hard now to be beautiful for a long time. One can prefer a three-line Japanese poem to Péguy's *Eve,* which is three hundred pages, and one of Madame de Sévigné's letters full of joy, daring, and ease to-one of those old-fashioned novels made of patchwork pieces which claim to have done enough for good behavior, if they'd met the requirements of their thesis.

Many prose poems have been written in the last thirty or forty years; I hardly know of any poet who's understood what it's all about and who's known how to sacrifice his ambitions as an author to the prose poem's formal constitution. Dimension counts for nothing in the beauty of a work, its situation and its style are everything. And, I maintain that *The Dice Cup* can satisfy the reader from this double point of view.

Artistic feeling is neither a sensory act nor an emotional act; otherwise nature alone would suffice to give it to us. Art exists, the point being that it corresponds to a need: art is actually a *distraction.* I'm not mistaken: it's theory which has given us a marvelous population of heroes, powerful evocations of environments where the legitimate curiosities and the aspirations of bourgeois who are prisoners of themselves are satisfied. But the word distraction must be taken in an even broader sense. A work of art is a force which attracts, which absorbs the forces at the disposal of the one who approaches it. There's something like a marriage here and in it the amateur plays the wife's role. He needs to be seized by a will and held. Will, therefore, plays the leading role in creation, the rest is only the bait in front of the trap. Will can only be exercised on the choice of means, because the work of art is only a collection of means and we arrive at the same definition for art as the one I gave for style: art is the will to exteriorize oneself by one's chosen means: the two definitions coincide and art is only style. Style is considered here as the use of materials and as the composition of the whole, not as the writer's language. And I conclude that artistic feeling is the effect of a thinking activity on an activity that has been thought. I use the word "thinking" with regret, because I'm convinced that artistic feeling ends where analysis and thought intervene: making someone reflect on something is not the same as creating the feeling of beauty. I put thought with the trap's bait.

The more active the subject, the more intense will be the emotion given by the object; therefore the work of art must be distant from the subject. That's why it must be *situated.* Here we can refute Baudelaire's theory about surprise: that theory is a bit crude. Baudelaire understood the word "distraction" in its most ordinary sense. To surprise is nothing much, one must *transplant.* Surprise charms and prevents true creation: like all charms it's harmful. A creator only has a right to be charming after the fact, when the work is situated and styled.

Let's distinguish a work's style from its situation. The style or will creates, that's to say separates. The situation distances, that is, it excites the artistic feeling; one recognizes that a work has style if it gives the sensation of being self-enclosed; one recognizes that it's situated by the little shock that one gets from it or again from the margin which surrounds it, from the special atmosphere where it moves. Certain of Flaubert's works have style; none of them is situated. Musset's plays are situated but don't have much style. Mallarmé's work is the paradigm of the situated work: if Mallarmé weren't affected and obscure, he'd be a great classic, Rimbaud has neither style nor situation: he has Baudelairean surprise; he's the triumph of romantic disorder.

Rimbaud expanded the field of sensibility and all men of letters owe him a debt of gratitude, but the authors of prose poems can't use him for their model because the prose poem, to exist, must submit to the laws of all art which are style or will and situation or emotion, and Rimbaud only leads to disorder and exasperation. The prose poem must also avoid Baudelairean and Mallarméan parables if it wants to distinguish itself from the fable. It's understood that I don't consider as prose poems the notebooks of more or less curious impressions which my excessive colleagues publish from time to time. A page of prose isn't a prose poem, even when it frames two or three lucky finds. I would consider as the said "lucky finds" those presented with the necessary spiritual margin. While we're on the subject, I'm putting the authors of prose poems on guard against too-bright precious stones which catch the eye at the expense of the whole. The poem is a constructed object and not a jewelry store window. Rimbaud is a jewelry store window, he's not the jewel: the prose poem is a jewel. (pp. 5-7)

> *Max Jacob, "Preface of 1916," translated by Zack Rogow (1916), in his* The Dice Cup: Selected Prose Poems, *edited by Michael Brownstein (© Editions Gallimard 1945; translation copyright © 1979 by Sun; originally published as* Le cornet à dés, *Gallimard, 1945), Sun, 1979, pp. 5-7.*

RÉGIS MICHAUD (essay date 1934)

Max Jacob's poems are one-third lyricism and two-thirds humor. We cannot help wondering when we read him whether words, rimes and sounds are as safe vehicles to travel in as we thought. Who knows but that poetry so called is only a deceit and a play on words in the long run? Jacob had doubts in this respect, and he retired to his "central laboratory" (*Le Laboratoire Central*) to solve the problem. After mixing in his retorts parody, fun and emotions, it looked as if the poetic game was nothing but another kind of jugglery, and that anybody could, with some imagination, associate, dissociate and upset words as he wanted. A word caught a word, a rime caught a rime, and there was no limit to the absurdities which words could lead to. Yet one could make poetry out of nonsense by playing with words. Words had a meaning in spite of themselves, and by juggling them one could challenge logic and turn it upside down. One threw the dice and collected what they brought in the way of good luck and surprises.

This game of dice was played most skilfully by Jacob in *Le Cornet à dés,* a collection of midget poems in prose where words are used as cubes and writing is only a pretext to make quaint mosaics out of them. . . . When he throws his dice Max Jacob must know that divine providence is on his side and that even an acrobat cannot scare the Muse away. His most absurd poems are full of precious findings of images and emotions.

Humor once more stands at the gate to turn off all those intruders who would take inspiration too much in earnest, but inspiration is there in the disguise of a lightmindedness which is only a form of humility. His poems require special optics and the gift, on the part of the reader, to seize their plastic objectivity. They must be focused with particular attention on the retina in order to come out not as mere words but as pure bits of poetic creation.

Max Jacob's novels, *Cinématoma, Le Roi de Béotie, Filibuth ou la montre en or, Le Terrain Bouchaballe, L'Homme de chair et l'Homme reflet,* have the same purpose as his experimental poems. They puncture people's foibles and absurdities through verbal cartoons, fun and parody. Characters, like feelings, are verbal illusions, and personalities are mostly made out of words. The lives we live as well as the novels we read are nothing when all is told but burlesque talkies, which Max Jacob unreels with perfect gusto. Parrot talk, as it is used in that burlesque epic *Le Phanérogame,* may well make at least two-thirds of our sentimental life, and we are not surprised that he fled to a monastery to avoid so much inanity. Better flee to a monastery than to an insane asylum.

To say that Max Jacob was the greatest contemporary poet and creative artist, as have some critics, is to pronounce a verdict that should be taken not with one but with several grains of salt—as Jacob himself would probably do. But it is undoubtedly true that this mystic epicure and "pince-sans-rire" can be safely credited with having made a great contribution to the rejuvenation of French verse and prose. (pp. 163-65)

> *Régis Michaud, "The Medley of Arts: Cubism and Modernism in Poetry," in his* Modern Thought and Literature in France *(reprinted by permission of Harper & Row, Publisher, Inc.), Funk & Wagnalls, 1934, pp. 149-65.**

S. J. COLLIER (essay date 1957)

Jacob obviously conceived the prose-poem as a carefully-fashioned, autonomous unit, delicately composed, hermetic, possessed of an inner dynamism, transposed from normal reality by methods known to himself, of limited length but infinite suggestion, and requiring a specific type of vision and an unorthodox use of language. The first and most striking impression one receives from the poems of the *Cornet* is that of their finished quality, their compact unity, and their internal tension.

The collection is divided into two parts—one might infer from the number of scriptural or semi-religious subjects in the second part that the reason for the division is chronological—and contains two separate sections, *Le Coq et la Perle* and *Exposition Coloniale,* where many of the so-called 'poems' are no more than single-line notations. The first hundred poems date from the period preceding 1914, while those in the second part, as well as the *Cornet à Dés: Adde* were composed in the three final years before publication.

There are at least a dozen poems bearing simply the title '**Poème**', some are called '**Anecdote**', but the majority have titles which might well be those of magazine-articles: '**Mémoires de l'espion**','**Moeurs Littéraires**', '**La Situation des bonnes au Mexique**', '**Autour de la Bible**', '**1889-1916**', '**Littérature et Poésie**', and so on. Generally speaking, the title bears some relation to the subject-matter, though very often it is highly allusive and tangential to the main theme. . . . (p. 151)

Jacob can be the most laconic and elliptical of poets, the most deceptively simple and unassuming commentator, the most disturbing of guides. He is never diffuse or flamboyant, he never shows his cards twice; a fleeting glimpse is all we are permitted as the elusive vision slips by and on into the white blank of the page. (p. 154)

It would be a mistake to suppose that Jacob understood, or even cared about the theoretical bases of the [Cubist] movement, but its strict formal economy, its power of evocation, its incongruous juxtaposition, and the poetry it could conjure up from the unusual grouping of common objects and the angle from which they were seen, attracted him. (p. 155)

The poems, or dice, of the *Cornet à Dés* appear, on examination, as symmetrical cubes, on each of whose six faces an image may be projected. These images are correlated, but confusion and incoherence may arise because any one face of the dice may be contiguous with four others at any one time, and as the dice lies upon the table, one face remains permanently hidden—except, that is, from the eye of the poet. (p. 156)

Examination shows that the longer poems are mainly of the 'récit' type, whereas the shorter ones crystallize an image, a tableau, a momentary vision, or simply a *boutade*. Whatever the dimension of the poem, once the original impulse has failed, Jacob does not . . . continue to spin a thread of images. . . . The *poèmes-récits,* which take the form of the anecdote, or short story with a moral, usually ironic are generally comprehensible; obscurity usually arises from the isolation of a single, unexplained scene or episode. . . . (pp. 157-58)

In the incoherence of certain poems, the actual thread of the récit is relatively unimportant; what matters is the reproduction of a disturbing *angoisse solitaire,* the distress of the poet lost in a nightmare world where common objects, losing their normal identity, close in upon him. . . . These dream-transformations are not explained, they are merely enumerated, though an impalpable thread reminds us the transcription is conscious. . . . (p. 158)

Throughout *Le Cornet,* Jacob uses deceptively simple, colloquial language, never striving after nobility of expression or the balanced line, yet avoiding the cliché—or rather, should one say, *creating new clichés*. The verbs *être* and *faire* are adequate for most purposes; *c'est, il y a* and their Imperfect forms, almost always followed by a Relative . . . and occasionally by defective syntax . . . are common throughout. There is no attempt at syntactical variety, only exclamation-marks, interrogation-marks, and *points de suspension* serving to diversify the simple scheme: subject-verb-complement. (pp. 158-59)

It is not with the words themselves, but rather with their mutual and reciprocal influences that Jacob is preoccupied. This playing with verbal reactions is obvious at first glance, and probably explains the dismissal of *Le Cornet* as a compendious funbook. . . . This 'juggling' with words was, for Jacob, a method, a means of filtering their hidden substance, of seeing beyond their literal meaning, of distilling their poetic essence. (p. 159)

The poetry of the *Cornet* is largely an experiment in new vision, an attempt to *see,* and to see clearly, a casting of the net on the opaque waters of the subconscious, a throwing of the dice and the subsequent surrender to the muscular rhythm of their syllabic dance. It is from this close perception and verbal experiment that the images arise, images born from the illumination, sudden and brilliant, of the apparently insignificant detail, and crystallized in concrete language. (p. 160)

Here we can formulate the only just criticism which can be levelled at *Le Cornet à Dés,* and it is a damning one. Despite its freshness, its richness, its brilliant imagery, despite the new lease it gave to poetic style, content and vocabulary, the signposts it erected for the guidance of poets to come, one has only to read Apollinaire, Valéry, Aragon, or Eluard to see clearly its one crowning defect—its almost total lack of musical harmony. It is strange that Jacob, the musician, the close friend of Erik Satie, should have been so incapable of verbal melody. Yet these poems of *Le Cornet,* so pleasing, so charming to the eye and the imagination, how flat, jerky and inharmonious do they become when read aloud! The aural effect, where it is not frankly cacophonic, is almost entirely absent. Max Jacob worked with words, not with sounds, and the words betrayed him. There is little doubt that he knew this and, *faute de mieux,* found a malicious delight in the sudden and unaccountable fracture of the lilting rhythm. . . . It is not the least part of Jacob's disparate and fragmentary genius that he possessed the private vision, the painter's sense of colour, grouping and perspective, the gift of immediate image-transformation, and the verbal power to produce a type of poetry which, if it is perpetuated, will probably never be surpassed or equalled. By the experiment of *Le Cornet,* he attempted to rid poetry of the extravagance of the Romantics and the vaporous imprecision of the Symbolists, pleading the cause of what Jean Cocteau later called *la poésie pourrie,* the poetry which lies hidden in the banal objects which clutter our lives until the poet's eye and sensitivity come to give it release.

Le Cornet constitutes an *art poétique* which cannot be ignored when the poetic trends and achievements of this most complex of centuries come to be assessed. Nor, on reading it, can one fail to see how faithfully it reflects the tone and atmosphere of an epoch. Here is the Paris of gas lamps and kinematographs, tramways and cabs, *corsets et corsages, redingotes et chapeaux-melons;* the President of the Republic visits the horticultural show, Sarah Bernhardt, Monsieur de Max, Mademoiselle Ratkine and Mounet-Sully appear nightly, soldiers with epaulettes walk the streets, *La Gioconda* has just been stolen from the Louvre. Jacob is here the poet of society, painting, without malice, the *petit bourgeois,* the provincial family, the *concierge,* the *patron d'hôtel,* the journalists, the sailor, the broken-down actor, the priest, the librarian, the *petit employé*. They are portrayed, not satirized; their assimilation is an element of his aesthetic; they are amusing, but sympathetically so. When Jacob wrote *Le Cornet,* he was as far removed from the pastoral idyll of his youth at Quimper as he was from the sackcloth and ashes of the retreat at Saint-Benoît. Hence the mature humour of many of its poems, not the bitter, disillusioned, twisted, corrosive humour of later years, but the genial transparent laughter of the timid parodist, the compassionate smile of the transient man, painfully conscious of his impermanence.

Yet, despite the great pride Jacob took in this, his first successful collection, it has not the passionate sincerity of the 'stoppered vials' of *Le Laboratoire Central* or the simple dedication of the later Catholic verse. The deliberate *fantaisie* of *Le Cornet* has somehow lost its appeal in a world in which our ear is attuned to the desperate song of the *poète engagé,* where the poet seeks more and more the complex form, the elaborate construction. Yet Jacob's place among the poets of this century is high, his influence fertile. He brought to French poetry not only the discordant music of the Jazz age, and the independent intelligence of the free artist; he also offered it new possibilities, cutting across the current of traditional verse, attacking *le grand style* with the weapon of his own *baroquisme*. (pp. 163-65)

S. J. Collier, "Max Jacob's 'Le cornet a dés': A Critical Analysis," in French Studies, Vol. XI, No. 2, April, 1957, pp. 149-66.

THE TIMES LITERARY SUPPLEMENT (essay date 1959)

The rewards offered by Max Jacob's letters are many, but it must be said that they are of no great value for the literary history of the period. He gives no information about the beginnings of Cubism. There is no exchange of letters with Picasso and in fact after 1917 they rarely met. There is little of the gossip such as Salmon and Léautaud retailed. The bulk of the letters were written when he had left Paris and there are no signs that he wanted his friends to report the talk of the cafés. What he missed in his exile was the audience which had adored his *numéro*. . . .

The main interest of the letters and their importance is their reflection of a poet's mind. Max Jacob, with Apollinaire, Cendrars and Salmon had rescued poetry from the impasse of post-Symbolism in the years before the First World War. By 1921, when Max left Paris, the Surrealists had begun to take possession, and if they remembered Apollinaire they forgot Jacob who had committed the *bêtise* of becoming a Christian as well as taking out a patent for certain poetical procedures they were anxious to claim as their own. . . . It was not until the younger poets began to rebel against surrealist tyranny that he found himself once again accepted. By then (1936) he had returned to St.-Benoît where he was to remain until his death at Drancy in 1944. These years, which might have been unendurable (he had to wear the badge of the Jews during the Occupation), were lightened by the affection of Rousselot, Cadou and Béalu, the young poets who had turned to him for guidance. For them, in letter after letter, he poured out the long meditated wisdom of what he called his aesthetic.

This aesthetic was in no sense a system. Max began early to establish his verities and in the letters to Jacques Doucet he was already taking up positions from which he never departed. The soundness of these principles was that they allowed him to develop. There were but two: first, a poem must be given *la marge* if it is to be a true poem; secondly, the poet, if men are to hear him at all, must make his poems with *la pleine poitrine*.

By *la marge* he meant that the poem must be given objective existence. . . .

The experience of the poet, accepted and deepened in the processes of suffering until it has become (in a title he gave to one of his books) *le laboratoire central*, is what he understood by the *pleine poitrine*. . . . Rimbaud, as it seemed to him, was the evil genius who had tempted poets to deny their human nobility and grandeur. He had made them ashamed of expressing feelings in the language of feeling. "Rimbaud is the disorder I execrate." "It is only since Rimbaud," he wrote, "that the poet-as-monster has been set up in opposition to the citizen-poet." The modern poet is the perfect bourgeois in the stupid orthodoxy of revolt, his conformity in non-conformity, his terror of speaking from the heart. "I believe poetry to be *la pleine poitrine* and that the great poets Pushkin, Byron, Dante have been *pleines poitrines*."

It was not surprising that Paris ceased to speak of the poet who uttered these uncomfortable platitudes. But was Max Jacob's

poetry in accord with his preaching? . . . [In] *Fond de l'eau,* in *Sacrifice Impérial* and *Rivage*—all published *hors commerce* and never reprinted—there were poems which had begun to synthesize the two principles of Jacob's "aesthetic": *la marge* was being "aerated" by *la pleine poitrine.* An extraordinary *souffle* became apparent, as if Harlequin at last had dared to speak without his mask. . . . But with *La Maison Mystérieuse* (in the *Ballades* of 1938) the liberty-in-constraint was fully achieved. . . .

The Abbé Garnier speaks of "the extraordinary and unfortunately impossible dialogue between Max Jacob and his epoch" and indeed this dialogue can be traced in all the correspondence. But this dialogue concealed another dialogue which was fully explicit only in the meditations he scattered through the post. Max Jacob's conversion has been both underplayed and overplayed. For those who were unable to take it seriously and saw it as yet another facet of the clown, it was proof of his fundamental insincerity. For those who saw it as something which might be used to sectarian advantage it had a disconcerting inability to conform to type. Max was both too complicated and too simple; he was a Jew and he was Breton. . . . The importance of Jacob is that he called in question the modern concept of poetry as an instrument of *connaissance*.

"Le pauvre Max," in The Times Literary Supplement (© Times Newspapers Ltd. (London) 1959; reproduced from The Times Literary Supplement by permission), No. 3006, October 9, 1959, p. 576.

WALLACE FOWLIE (essay date 1967)

[Jacob's] religious spirit penetrated everything, even his most burlesque writings. His nature was one of great expansiveness. He needed to confess his acts and thoughts, the best and the worst. André Blanchet, in his admirable critical edition of *La Défense de Tartuffe,* justifies his belief that Jacob remained always very close to Jewish tradition in his life of a Christian. The apparition of 1909 which changed his life, was Judaic in its form and intimacy. He studied Judaic theosophy, both orthodox and non-orthodox. The apparition of Christ on the wall of his room on that day in 1909 when he returned from the Bibliothèque Nationale, never ceased to count in his life, and never lost its mysteriousness of an enigmatical sign. Both as a poet and as a believer, Max Jacob waited for signs, expected signs, remained in a state of availability. (p. 191)

From *Saint Matorel* to *La Défense de Tartuffe,* the five poems on Jacob's conversion underwent several changes. . . . In *La Révélation,* the mysteriousness of the apparition is restored by a suppression of passages of explanation. The action moves swiftly, from the moment of the poet's return from the Bibliothèque Nationale to the apparition on the red tapestry of the wall. . . .

The text of the second piece, *Visitation,* was especially abridged and tightened. Here the casualness and familiarity of Christ's apparition to Max Jacob is stressed. . . .

The other three poems are less narrative in form. They combine the elements in the life of *Saint Matorel,* burlesque and mystical elements. They are far more typical *poèmes en prose* of Max Jacob than the first two poems.

Entrevue describes a vision: a golden ray forming a crown over the poet's bed. The elements of the vision are apocalyptic (the horse dominating the sea) and familiar (a poet at the piano). It is a picture that is drawn, a Marc Chagall assemblage of objects that do not usually go together and that appear in unusual places. There is a reminiscence of Rimbaud in the phrase: *Des incendies s'allument au loin.* And at the bottom of the picture, in miniature, the poet: a slave on his knees, whose expression is so changed that he does not recognize his own face.

In *Significations,* the poet is a terrified monk praying before a stained-glass window of St. Eustache. The poet explains his belief in symbolism. (p. 193)

The problem of understanding the incomprehensible is the theme of the fifth poem: *Exhortations.* . . .

The unusual religious experience of the poet is thus related in five poems where he plays five slightly different roles. (p. 194)

These poems transcribe a very personal experience, and announce a poetic method. Max Jacob felt in his room the supernatural presence of God. As a poet, he will have to project this experience by means of color and form and reminiscences. After being invaded by a Presence, he will become the prey of images. He will never dissociate poetic creation from divine revelation. The passivity he knew at the moment of revelation, he will continue to know at the moment of poetic creation. In the choice he has between the head and the heart, he chooses the heart. The apparitions of God to Abraham, to Moses, and to other Old Testament figures, often took place in familiar casual settings. The apparitions of Max Jacob in a Montmartre cinéma and in his room on the rue Ravignan could be interpreted as belonging to a Judaic tradition. (p. 195)

In the diversity of Max Jacob's writings, which reflect the burlesque and the mystical, the parody and the very serious, he created a form, a genre, which he called *le poème en prose.* Baudelaire composed his *poèmes en prose* with a very specific subject matter, but avoided all poetic effects, all picturesqueness. Mallarmé reduced in his *poèmes en prose* the subject matter and emphasized picturesqueness. Jacob, in his *poèmes en prose,* reduced both subject matter and picturesqueness. His use of parody was almost a discipline for him. . . . (p. 196)

The serious study of Max Jacob's art has barely begun. It will include, as time goes on, a study of the way he presents a word in different meanings, from different angles, a method very close to cubism. It will also study the ways by which he destroys emotion by means of irony and parody, his art of transposing traditional themes. When he decomposes the elements of a city scene or a landscape, in order to recombine the elements in a new way and reach a new total effect, he was practicing the aesthetics of cubism, and he was combining in the same poem ideas that do not ordinarily cohabit one with the other. The universe is one, for Jacob, and therefore everything can cohabit with everything else: judgments, emotions, memories, sensations, philosophical concepts, literary allusions. The subconscious dictates to the poet. Long before the surrealists defined this practice as orthodox, Max Jacob practiced it. His poems often appear to be fortuitous inventions, devoid of any visible relationship with the real world. The final poem could therefore be a total surprise to the poet. Something monstrous or diabolical would be perpetrated without the creator being fully aware of how it had appeared and from what sources.

The art of Max Jacob was a series of efforts to write a poem that had no subject, or one that would have only the slightest trace of a subject. (p. 197)

The source of the poem for Jacob was an experience, and more often than not, a spiritual experience, but the poem itself was an experiment. And since the daily life of a Christian is a constant struggle, Jacob's laboratory of experiments on poetry was always open. His faith added a great richness of details to the experiments, but all forms of experimentation are disguises, and ways of approaching a problem from a great variety of possibilities.

About 1910 a major battle for modern art was being waged by Apollinaire and Picasso. Certain texts of Max Jacob define the theories and aims of this new art, as lucidly as some of his prose poems illustrate it. By far, the principal text is the six-page preface to *Le Cornet à dés.* . . . But important concepts are discussed in [*Lettres à Jacques Doucet,* in the short *Art Poétique,* in *Conseils à un jeune poète*] . . . , and in the general correspondence which Max carried on with countless young poets during the last fifteen years of his life. He was, in his own way, a theorist, a teacher. (p. 198)

In the earliest texts he speaks of the "situation" of a work of art, of the atmosphere in which it is placed, and of the necessary distance from the reader it must occupy. In later texts he seems to emphasize the importance of emotion and of the perfecting of an artist's inner life. He repeats many times that emotion is the true sentiment of the heart and that the first gift of the poet is the power of articulation, the actual volume of his voice, the will to exteriorize his feelings by specfic means. . . . The public is attracted if the writer's heart reveals its violence, because the public is anthropophagic. It devours the writer's ego. Art must therefore effect a union between words (*mots*), if the artist is poet, and the disastrous experiences of the heart, evils (maux), which Jacob calls them in a letter to Emié, in order to repeat the same sound: *mots—maux.*

Jacob claims that the writer has the choice of two possibilities: that of writing (*écrire*) and that of moving his reader (*émouvoir*). If he chooses the second, there is a chance that he will become an artist, a man able to describe and measure his sentiments, to make their mobility felt by means of syntax, to demonstrate their power by means of a well-composed sentence.

Max Jacob believed that he was the inventor of the true *poème en prose,* that before him the genre had been impure. The poems included in *Le Cornet à dés* were written during the years when he lived on the rue Ravingnan, and his friends— Picasso, André Salmon, MacOrlan—often called on him in the morning to ask to read the poem they were sure he had written the night before. In a lecture given at *Le Salon des Indépendants* in 1907, Apollinaire called attention to his friend Max Jacob. This was the first public acknowledgment of Jacob's work, but he had already for some time been composing poetry in accordance with principles that would eventually be taken over by the surrealists. These principles centered on the subconscious, on the poet's effort to apprehend in every way possible the acitivity of the subconscious . . . , to grant freedom to words as they enter the poet's consciousness, to welcome free associations of ideas, to draw upon the stories and situations of dreams, to transcribe hallucinations and obsessions. These principles, referred to by Jacob himself in a brief historical notice written in 1943 for an edition of *Le Cornet à dés,* are identical to many of the precepts of surrealism. He believed that most surrealist poetry illustrated simply a freedom of words and did not reflect the power of the emotions. On this point he believed his art was different from theirs. (pp. 198-99)

A poem, as well as a human being, has a situation in the world, and this situation is determined both by the mind of the poet and by the way in which he writes, by all the artifices of his craft. In other words, the poet's sensibility is exteriorized by language. He restates a famous belief of Poe and Baudelaire that beauty is so intense that it cannot last long, that there is no such thing as a long poem. . . . Art, in terms of the artist, answers for Jacob a need of his nature. For the reader, art is a magnetic force attracting him, absorbing his vitality. A marriage takes place between the poet and the reader, in which the poet is the male and the reader is the female, who has to be subjugated, whose will has to be forced. A work of art is "situated" far from its subject matter, far from the initial emotion which brought it into existence. But this very distance, this "situation" stimulates another kind of emotion in the reader, an artistic emotion. (pp. 199-200)

Poetry would seem to be for Max Jacob the control of violence, the control of remorse. In reading the finished poem which is "situated," the reader finds himself situated in another universe from which he can see many things: reflections, irruptions, dreams, enthusiasms undermined by irony, incoherences of man that are parodied, examples of the universal stupidity of man (as in the portraits of *Cinematoma*).

The prose poems of *Le Cornet à dés* cannot be summarized or paraphrased because they are themselves the paraphrase of some dream, of some intuition, of some memory, which is copied down in its initial incoherences, with its unusual juxtapositions. (p. 200)

All worlds are juxtaposed in these poems of *Le Cornet à dés*. The title is appropriate, because from a dice box fall the dice, and each time with a different result, with a different sum. A surreal picture, such as that of seven galley ships can be traced back to its origin in the mind's memory, to the seven murdered wives of Bluebeard; a Marathon soldier, back to a man who has lost his reason; Dostoievsky, back to a ragpicker; a convert, back to the poet Max Jacob living on the rue Ravignan, in Montmartre, in the first decade of the twentieth century. (p. 201)

> *Wallace Fowlie, "Max Jacob: Violence of the Supernatural," in his* Climate of Violence: The French Literary Tradition from Baudelaire to the Present *(reprinted with permission of Macmillan Publishing Co., Inc.; copyright © 1967 by Wallace Fowlie), Macmillan, 1967, pp. 188-202.*

ANNETTE THAU (essay date 1972)

Jacob's published writings include not only a staggering variety of works of fiction and non fiction, but a corpus of writings which may be grouped under the heading of esthetic reflections. These are scattered in a variety of works, divergent in form, written between 1907 and 1944, which may be classified as belonging to four main groups. First, entire books concerned with esthetics. These include [*L'Art poétique* and *Conseils à un jeune poète*], . . . both primarily collections of aphorisms. Secondly, brief articles, mainly written for small literary reviews or provincial newspapers. . . . Thirdly, prefaces written by Jacob to some of his other books. The most important of these is the 1916 preface to *Le Cornet à dés,* which purported to set forth the laws of the prose poem in particular, and art in general. The bulk of Jacob's esthetic writings are contained in a fourth group, i.e., the many volumes and articles of his published correspondence, in which Jacob endlessly poured out advice and opinions concerning literature.

These texts, which constitute the least well known part of Jacob's work, thus comprise a heterogeneous collection, varying in form and intent. It must also be remembered that they were composed (improvised might be a more accurate term) during a span of more than 37 years, during which French poetry, including that of Jacob, exhibited extraordinary change and variety.

Nonetheless, these texts are inchoate only at a superficial level. Their coherence derives from the fact that Jacob's ideas concerning poetry crystallised around several broad problems, to which he returned continually throughout his life, and which he redefined over and over again. This process of redefinition resulted in a deepened understanding of his basic esthetic ideas. Jacob's disclaimers notwithstanding . . . these ideas, once established, changed very little. Surprisingly, Jacob's view of the poet is far closer to that of his contemporary, Valéry, than it is to those who are usually thought to be his spiritual brothers, namely, the dadaists and surrealists, in that Jacob ascribed no mission to the poet other than that of engaging in an autonomous activity of the mind while emphasizing the need for self-development and technique. (pp. 800-01)

Jacob's thought is shaped both by the tenets of symbolism and the revolution which occurred in art (particularly painting) at the beginning of the twentieth century. The cornerstone of his esthetic thought is basically that of Baudelaire: namely, that the artist does not imitate or study reality, but rather, that he creates works independent of reality, through the imagination. This idea was expressed by Jacob through his various definitions of the concept of *création*, a term which occurs often in his criticism where it is frequently coupled or used interchangeably with the terms *invention* and *idée poétique*. . . . The implication is clearly that Jacob considers creation in art or literature to be a function of form, i.e., in literature, of the way in which the writer uses words. His point of departure is that of the symbolists, namely, that the function or role of words in poetry differs from its function or role in non-poetic usage, i.e., that poetic language ought to convey feelings ordinarily expressed in some other way, or which ordinarily cannot be expressed at all. His definitions of this function are reminiscent of those of Mallarmé and Valéry. (pp. 801-02)

On a number of occasions, Jacob attempted to define more precisely the key formal characteristics of poetry. Again, such definitions are heavily reminiscent of those of the symbolists. Thus, Jacob defined as non-poetic or as tending towards prose any usage relying primarily on the denotative function of words. . . . Jacob stressed the importance of the most intangible, most imprecisely definable aspects of poetry, such as music or euphony. This he sometimes described as a function of the quality or distribution of sounds, a position analogous to that of the proponents of *poésie pure*. . . . At other times, he made it clear that he considered that music is not an independent quality, which can be divorced from meaning, but that the two are indissolubly linked, especially in lyric poetry, where music is the result of the tension or depth of feeling expressed. . . . (p. 802)

By and large, however, Jacob's comments rarely remain at this level of generality. Much of his esthetic writing takes the form of advice to would-be poets, and definitions cannot help anyone to write a better poem. . . . While these comments follow logically from Jacob's definition of poetry, they are far more precise, deriving from his personal experience as a writer. Two types of considerations are relevant: the conditions which make it possible for an artist to create, which I shall call considerations on the artist, and more technical advice, relating to style. (pp. 802-03)

Jacob occasionally affirmed that poetry is a special aptitude or gift. . . . Such a statement serves to correct Jacob's usual emphasis on technique, his insistence that poetry is first of all a language, and the poet, a technician. Jacob's thought is entirely free of any romantic view of the artist as a being different from ordinary mortals. . . . The serious artist, however, according to Jacob, must possess a number of characteristic personality traits and attitudes.

An artist is first and foremost a person with a very deep need to create. Something in the true artist demands expression. For Jacob, the metaphor of a subject seeking its writer out is more than a metaphor. A subject which does not possess the writer, clamoring for expression, will not result in anything of importance. . . . Jacob often expressed his dislike of what he called contemptuously ''les beaux arts,'' excellence of the ''prix d'excellence'' type, or even ''french literature'' (sic), by which he meant a kind of superficial polish and style. . . . More precisely, he sought to distinguish between a truly creative artist, who feels compelled to create, and the esthete, whose sensations and art exist only at a superficial level. . . . (pp. 803-04)

As Jacob explained . . . it does not suffice to study literature or art: The artist must acquaint himself with the entire universe, he must cultivate all aspects of the human condition, including the ordinary life of the ordinary people. . . . (p. 804)

The connection between *vie intérieure* and poetry is a complex one, not fully explained by Jacob. It represents for him an intuitive truth, demonstrable and fundamental. . . . We must bear in mind, however, Jacob's insistence that art is an activity of the imagination, and description, antipoetic, the function of poetry being to express *l'inexprimable*. Thus, the purpose of the poet who develops his inner life cannot be that of a realist, taking notes to document his work. Jacob made it abundantly clear that he was not advocating a return to a literature (or a poetry) of ideas. . . . He did, however, leave some hints as to how he conceived the relationship between *vie intérieure* and poetry in such statements as the following: ''la philosophie incluse et invisible, c'est l'idéal'' . . . , the idea being that the artist is reflected in the poem, but indirectly.

A rich inner life contributes to the work in a number of ways. It would, Jacob felt, lend depth and weight to the texts, and prevent the writer from dealing with trivial subjects or themes. . . . The reason for this, according to Jacob, is that indirectly, one's entire experience of life is reflected in the literary works one produces. The quality of one's inner life thus determines the quality of the literature. . . . (pp. 804-05)

Implicit in this last statement, there is another, more subtle, yet more basic connection between *vie intérieure* and the literary work, which is related to Jacob's concept of poetic creation. This he conceived primarily as a process whereby the writer plunges deep within the self, to the very sources of the imagination, in order to express a personal vision. This has nothing to do with realism, or even lyricism. Rather, art is conceived as a means of creating unique and therefore, new, personal statements. Self-development, as well as the practice of double vision, of watching one's self, which are basic to the development of *vie intérieure,* thus become a necessary prelude to the act of writing, and the development of one's inner life, inseparable from one's artistic development. All of

this is made very clear through Jacob's various definitions of style. . . . (pp. 805-06)

The term style is given a number of meanings by Jacob. Prominent among them is the normative definition of style as a specific set of techniques which any writer must acquire. . . . His correspondence is filled with very precise technical advice, usually relating to specific poems submitted to him. . . . Thus it is clear that Jacob considered writing a craft, and the ability to manipulate words as essential for any poet. But the technique of a poet must progress beyond the initial acquisition of tools, since for Jacob, poetry is born during the tension of an encounter between something which demands to be expressed, and a technique adequate to express it. . . . (p. 806)

It is at this point that the relevance to the poet of developing his inner life in depth becomes clear. Jacob posited that there is a region of the self, a level of consciousness (the same level of consciousness at which a mystic finds union with his God) which the poet must strive to reach, and it is at this level, the deepest region of the self, that he must write. . . . Technique, thus conceived, consists of far more than the mechanical application of specific rules. Style is redefined as the vehicle for the expression of the poet's deepest artistic ideas, through poetic phrases which arise from the depths of the consciousness . . . . (p. 807)

Jacob's criticism is remarkable for the precision with which he defined the qualities of the poetic phrases he had in mind. He called them variously *mot, mot-plaie,* or *la sensibilité approfondie,* and through specific examples, described their formulation. . . . The general emphasis is on the representation of an inner reality through concrete images. . . . Such poetic phrases are thus the result of a complex interplay of acquired technique, *travail sur soi* demanded for a developed *vie intérieure,* and descent into the self. This process is at the antipodes of any realism since, as Jacob makes clear, the poet uses elements of external reality in order to intuit and define his poetic ideas.

The main characteristic of any poetic idea (called by Jacob *idée poétique* or *création poétique*) is an intangible one, the characteristic of invention in depth. Jacob defined that concept in [a] definition of imagery, in which truly new, truly invented poetic images are contrasted with those which are new only at a superficial level. . . . Very much like Breton and Reverdy, Jacob considered the element of surprise to be paramount. He defined novelty, however, in absolute terms: it was his belief, made explicit through the phrase in italics, and through the fanciful etymological breakdown of *images,* that artistic creativity is analogous to any creative process in that it results in totally new artifacts, in the case of the poet, poetic images or phrases. It may be pointed out, in this connection, that Jacob rarely singled out the conventional figures of rhetoric, such as simile, or metaphor, for special analysis. . . . The distinguishing characteristics of images, their concrete character, and the element of surprise, can be and are characteristic of any ''*mot*'' as well. Jacob considered any of these equally effective in poetry, as long as they met the criteria of vividness and invention in depth.

Jacob's concept of style helps to explain how he understood the phenomenon of inspiration. He defined it as the sudden emergence to the surface of the consciousness of a poetic idea which demands to be expressed. . . . Jacob's insistence, however, on the necessity of control, of technique, would lead us to predict that he would not advise the writer to submit blindly to its dictates. . . . In this, he differs most notably from the surrealists who wished the writer to abdicate insofar as possible all rational control, in order to abandon himself to the message of the collective unconscious, to turn himself into a kind of receiving apparatus for a message originating elsewhere than the conscious mind.

Jacob's belief that the artist should work only at the deepest levels of the consciousness has as its logical correlative a parallel belief that poetry should not be too easily accessible to the reader. . . . While this is a direct and inevitable consequence of the emphasis on the uniqueness of the personal vision of the artist, it is also supported by a theory of the nature of esthetic pleasure, which is defined by Jacob as doubt, deriving from the surprise value of the work.

Again, this theory owes a great deal to Baudelaire. In the 1916 preface to *Le Cornet à dés* . . . , Jacob sought to set up precise distinctions between his own thought and that of Baudelaire. He did so, no doubt, partly in order to shock, by alluding to Baudelaire's theory as "un peu grosse," but also, in an attempt to characterize with some precision what he meant by surprise. He characterized the esthetic pleasure afforded by art as "une distraction," by which he meant gratuitous pleasure. He further specified that the reader has a need to have certain "forces disponibles" captured and held by a work of art. The relationship between the work of art and the reader is explored through an analogy whose import is that reader, artist, and work of art each have a specific role to play if the reader is to experience "artistic emotion." The artist's will must shape the work, calculate its effects. The work of art exerts a kind of force which holds and attracts the attention of the reader. The reader's activity is determined both by the will of the artist and by the force exerted by the work of art. . . . Artistic emotion is thus proportional to the efforts the reader must expend in order to come to grips with the work of art. . . . What Jacob was demanding of the reader is thus a process of "creation" (see below) analogous to the one which the artist undergoes in creating the work of art; the work must be sufficiently difficult to enable the reader to feel totally involved, and his mind and spirit on a real journey. . . . (pp. 807-10)

The difference between Jacob's thought and that of Baudelaire is thus subtle, yet nonetheless real. Baudelaire, in his article on *Madame Bovary,* had sought to recreate within himself the mental processes which had led Flaubert the author, to compose *Madame Bovary.* Jacob is asking the reader to go a step further, to become while reading so immersed in the work that he will totally lose consciousness of his own identity, becoming Emma Bovary, or acting out the poem in his soul. In essence, Jacob is saying that the poem must be sufficiently difficult to totally absorb all of the reader's mental energies, rather than merely allowing him to stand outside of it, as an amused observer, charmed by his own cleverness and perception. Jacob occasionally added that the poet should not cultivate obscurity for its own sake, but should be obscure only when the subject demands it. Such disclaimers notwithstanding, however, it is clear, given the emphasis, on the one hand, on totally new poetic phrases, and on the other hand on difficulty in the text, that for Jacob, as for the symbolists, good poetry must necessarily be obscure.

Jacob's emphasis on the creation or recreation of reality in and through the work of art, on obscurity, on descent into the depths of the self, on poetry as a language, all of these place him very much in the mainstream of twentieth century esthetic thought.

Jacob, however, differed with many twentieth century theoreticians of poetry, chiefly those who considered poetry to have a goal other than itself. Unlike the surrealists, for example, he clearly restricted the domain of poetry. . . . Jacob made it clear that he did not believe that poetry may be a source of quasi-mystical experiences for the poet, or that the poet is a kind of super-human, whether rebel or *suprême savant.*

While Jacob did not believe that art is entirely gratuitous, the utility he posited for it is a very limited one: that poetry is an activity of and for the imagination and that it affords "joy" for both the reader and the author. . . . The true creator provides his reader with a feast for the imagination and the mind. The poet writes to give pleasure and because he must. Ultimately, nothing justifies the writer other than his own need to create. No other justification or utility is necessary. (pp. 810-12)

Annette Thau, "The Esthetic Reflections of Max Jacob," in The French Review (copyright 1972 by the American Association of Teachers of French), Vol. XLV, No. 4, March, 1972, pp. 800-12.

S. I. LOCKERBIE (essay date 1973)

The two strongly marked poles of the work of Max Jacob are represented, on the one hand, by the bizarre and enigmatic prose poems of *Le Cornet à dés,* and, on the other, by the fervent mysticism of the main parts of *La Défense de Tartufe, Le Laboratoire central* and many other works. At neither pole is the concept of 'realism' a very relevant critical or exegetical tool. In his poems of spiritual aspiration Jacob turns away from reality and the social situation, sometimes, although not always, with a Christian horror of the world as a place of sin and evil. In his prose poems he departs from it no less radically, although this time to create a strange and bewildering universe which disturbs by its apparently gratuitous nature. Nightmarish visions, dream sequences, satirical sketches, parodies, jokes and puns all follow each other rapidly throughout the book and leave the reader amazed and disorientated.

A desire to transfigure the real, to place the poem at a considerable remove from everyday experience, occupies, indeed, a central position in Jacob's aesthetic. He develops this belief in the preface to *Le Cornet à dés* itself, and in many other writings, using terms like *situation* or *marge* to define the quality of a poem which successfully divorces it from the real. (p. 149)

[Yet] there is a great deal in Jacob's work that testifies to his strong interest in social life and manners, and his considerable powers as an observer of society. A satirical depiction of human behaviour is a predominant feature of his prose fiction, and *Le Cornet à dés* itself contains many sketches and pen-portraits of the life and people of his times. (p. 150)

It might be helpful, therefore, to see Jacob's poetic work as describing an arc between the two poles we have identified. At the two extremes, the subject matter, tone and atmosphere of the poems place them at some distance from reality. At various intermediary points, however, there is a greater approximation to the real, so much so that the poems stimulate a type of interest in social life and everyday experience that is rather rare in modern poetry.

Probably at the centre point of the pendulum swing stands a small group of verse poems, written at various times during Jacob's career, but mainly concentrated in the 1910-20 period.

Those that will be considered appear in [*La Défense de Tartufe,* in *Le Laboratoire central,* and *Les Pénitents en maillots roses*]. . . . The characteristic of these poems is that while they may be 'situated' in Jacob's sense, the transposition is achieved through a fantasy that is much milder in tone than the vigorous burlesque of many of his prose poems. It is a playful fantasy that fuses with observations of life to produce a relationship to reality for which a term like realism does not, on occasion, seem too inappropriate. It is not, of course, a realism like that of the nineteenth-century novel, with its case histories of typical figures, its searching analysis of character and situation, and its deterministic assumptions. It will be a much more intimate and evocative form of realism, concerned with conjuring up the 'ordinary texture of reality', with making us feel the atmosphere of everyday living in a given place at a given time. The expression *réalisme du quotidien* has sometimes been used to describe it, and the term conveys well enough the limited goals that such an aesthetic sets itself, at the same time as it hints at its importance. However vast their general ambitions, all the great realist writers were aware of the peculiar fascination that the *quotidien*—the ordinary unstressed moment of ordinary life—has for all of us and in moments of stasis and insight tried to record it in their works. This is what Jacob also tries to do, although by different means.

The social life and environment that Jacob knew best were those of Paris. This was particularly true between 1904 and 1920 when he was immersed in the avant-garde of painters and writers headed by Apollinaire and Picasso, which, although it was cosmopolitan, was nonetheless the very incarnation of the Parisian spirit. Paris therefore looms large in all his early work, but it is especially in the opening section of *La Défense de Tartufe* that he tries to catch the mood and tempo of Parisian life.

The perspective is not limited to the present, for three poems are entitled **'1867', '1889'** and **'1900'**. Jacob seems to have had in mind almost a social history of Paris, past, present and future. . . . (pp. 150-51)

In this formulation, however, the theme is wrongly conceived, as Jacob quickly realized. The so-called prophetic poems (in prose) and the *tableaux du passé* (in verse) are works very different in tone, and represent two themes in his literary output rather than one. The first are hullucinatory in style, and belong perfectly to the more hermetic atmosphere of *Le Cornet à dés* where they were finally published. In the second the emphasis falls clearly on an attempt to evoke the social climate and manners of Paris at various points in the recent past. It is understandable, therefore, that they should have been separated off and grouped with other poems in *Tartufe* which have a similar range and ambition, but with reference to the present.

The prevailing mood in the whole group of poems, whether they be contemporary or *tableaux du passé,* is undoubtedly one of gaiety. (p. 151)

In the *tableaux du passé* [an] attitude of humorous indulgence is adopted towards the periods being evoked. What is especially picked out for comment are the fashions in dress, leisure and entertainment peculiar to each age and such an emphasis produces in poet and reader alike a reaction of amused interest. . . . Many of the graver issues of each period are in fact alluded to: political repression and social injustice under the Second Empire; Boulanger and anarchism; the Dreyfus case. But in this context these issues lose the impact they have in political history. They are lightly passed over and become only part of the general texture of the age, without disturbing the overall tone of the poem. In their place other aspects of human affairs are highlighted, which are much more important in determining the mood and atmosphere: simple *faits divers,* typical utterances of the *vox populi,* the vogue names of the period. It is through his use of these vivid little particulars that Jacob can create a generalised impression of each age that is essentially light and carefree.

Humour is, therefore, an important characteristic of Jacob's approach to reality. His particular version of realism is one in which life is observed and recorded in a spirit of relaxed enjoyment. That this mood has not featured greatly in the main areas of the realist tradition is not a fact that should blind us to its relevance and value in another context. A *réalisme du quotidien* will often be lighter in tone than more serious forms of the aesthetic, and there is no reason why it should not be compatible with an attitude of warm amusement at human behaviour. (pp. 151-53)

No doubt, in such a context, humour must be kept within certain bounds, and it is arguable that in the poems mentioned so far, whether contemporary pieces or *tableaux du passé,* it is allowed too much play. Satirical exuberance is sometimes unrestrained, as at the end of **'1867'** or the brilliant beginning of **'1889'** which vividly captures the giddiness of *La Belle Époque.* . . . [But despite] touches of the burlesque, these poems reveal a genuine interest in the world of human affairs and real powers of outward-going observation. If they do not represent quite the ideal balance between observation and humour, they suggest that, with only a slight adjustment in tone, this balance could be achieved—and this is indeed what happens in the major poem in the section, **'Printemps et cinématographe mêlés'.**

Two interrelated themes dictate the whole tone and tempo of this poem and make it the essential statement of Jacob's delighted contemplation of Parisian life *circa* 1914: joy in spring, and pleasure in the urban surroundings and way of life of Paris. If the first theme spreads a note of gaiety through the poem, emanating from all the traditional ingredients of spring poetry, the second theme is no less vital, in that it diverts all these associations towards an urban scene and anchors the poem firmly in a precise milieu. For we do not see spring or nature as they would have been sung by a Romantic poet. It is nature as it is seen in the park of a big city, and spring as it is experienced by a city dweller. . . . (p. 153)

It is precisely to the urban preoccupations that the title of the poem relates. Although reference is made to the cinema in only one stanza, it is rightly promoted to a position of prominence because the implication is that it is one of the central features of the new life style of urban man. The exhilaration that spring arouses in the poet naturally prompts a desire to walk in the park. But no less naturally and spontaneously—indeed within the same stanza—it prompts a desire to go to the cinema. For modern man, so the title suggests, one impulse is really inseparable from the other. The joys of spring immediately evoke the joys of new collective forms of pleasure, typical of the urban twentieth century, and both are needed to bring fulfilment to a contemporary poet. . . .

[On this occasion] a balance is kept between the free play of fantasy and faithfulness to external experience. The poet's enjoyment of spring and the Parisian scene, his sharp eye for sensuous details in the real world—which are caught in vivid little cameos throughout the poem—act as restraining factors on his imagination. His fantasy blends with perceptions of the real world, but does not obliterate them.

Where this balance can best be felt is in the language and rhythm of the poem, where Jacob achieves with great success the kind of effect for which he was obviously striving in the other poems as well. The effect could best be described as that of a feigned casualness. The aim is to defeat expectations of a well-made poem by the use of a colloquial, off-hand style, marked by a certain flatness in both diction and rhythm. (p. 154)

It is a style which perfectly captures Jacob's approach to reality as he tried to crystallise it in all these Parisian poems. It is an approach that can both be compared and contrasted with a similar attitude to be found in other sectors of the avant-garde of his day. A desire to catch the essence of the twentieth century scene and an urban way of life was common to such poets and groups as Guillaume Apollinaire, the Futurists and the Un-animists. All wanted to break out of the enclosed atmosphere of late Symbolism and create a new poetry for a new age. But whereas others were concerned to reflect the dynamism of the new century, with its rapid means of transport, its instant communications and its energy, the carefree mood and casual spontaneity of Jacob's poem proclaim that he is interested in the more intimate, small-scale texture of modern life. The Paris that emerges from his work is quite different from either the corrupt capital of so much nineteenth-century literature, or the pulsating metropolis of the modernists. The city has become simply the natural habitat of man, providing an environment and a life style in which the poet takes an equable and absorbing pleasure.

By its totally good-humoured acceptance of an environment and way of life, in the way that the tempo and atmosphere of Parisian life in Jacob's day are warmly brought alive, while at the same time being subjected to a degree of ironic distanciation through humour and fantasy, **'Printemps et cinématographe mêlés'** is thus one of the best examples of Jacob's type of realism.

The mood it represents, however, soon disappears in *La Défense de Tartufe*. The rest of the volume becomes the poignant, and often anguished record of Jacob's conversion to Catholicism and his meditations on his new faith. The experience of the revelation led him naturally to quite different themes, a wider range of moods, and writing that is generally more highly charged. In the new spiritual atmosphere of the later sections, even his view of Paris begins to change, with the city tending to take on new associations as a place of darkness and sin.

The contrast, indeed, between the very secular nature of the Parisian poems and the rest of the volume is so marked that Jacob tried to rationalise it in a preliminary note to the opening section. . . . To find a more convincing reason for the juxtaposition within the volume of two apparently very different kinds of inspiration—apart from the drastically simple one of the conveniences of publication—one has to look for another form of continuity.

It can be found in the fact that, although the *mood* of the poems in which Jacob recounts his discovery of Christ is naturally very different from that of the secular pieces, the variation in the *tone* of his writing is not always so marked. His conversion was distinguished by the unpropitious circumstances in which it took place. (pp. 155-56)

It is in such an infiltration of banality even into a dramatic event that one discerns a deeper continuity between the secular

and some of the Christian poems. An instinctive feeling for place, and a spontaneous preference for low-toned aspects of reality still seem to be guiding Jacob. (p. 157)

Three poems from *Les Pénitents en maillots roses*, **'Voyages'**, **'Nice'** and **'Dimanche à Marseille'** show the mood beginning to change. All have passages in the deliberately free and easy-going style with which we are now familiar. In **'Nice'** there is particularly deft use of casual observations and reflections which are blended together by discreet repetition to form a smooth impressionistic flow. . . . (p. 159)

But **'Voyages'** alone maintains to the end this equable note, heightening it in the last lines with a touch of burlesque humour. In the other two the mood threatens to turn sour. A disgust with the selfish opulence he saw around him on the Côte d'Azur, and with the whole materialistic bias of contemporary civilisation, emerges in both poems, springing clearly from the poet's Christian convictions. The vision in **'Dimanche à Marseille'** has particularly sombre moments, yielding a black and striking picture of the dockland area. . . . Here, obviously we are nearer to the Baudelairean image of the poet as an exile in the modern city than to Jacob's earlier picture of urban man happily adjusted to his milieu.

However, the revulsion is not total. In both poems, despite the sombre moments, Jacob continues to note small details of the scene with the light quiet touch of the amused observer. (pp. 159-60)

As with **'Le Christ au cinématographe'**, therefore, these poems generate a tension, both thematically and stylistically, between two contrasting attitudes. Against the more powerful images and rhythms expressing horror at the godlessness of the contemporary world, we find a less powerful but pervasive impressionism working to capture the atmosphere of a given place and inviting poet and reader to immerse themselves in it. Although from 1921 onwards, with Jacob's retreat from the world to a life of meditation, the pendulum will swing markedly toward the more forceful spiritual vision, it is possible to say, here again, that in the equilibrium it establishes with a conflicting principle, the impulse towards the real in Jacob's imagination proves itself to be tenacious and genuine.

In conclusion, one cannot claim that the kind of atmospheric realism we have been discussing is a major aspect of Jacob's work in either a temporal or a quantitative sense. It produced relatively few poems in a prolific writing career, and, while these may be found episodically in later periods, the best examples seem concentrated in the 1910-20 decade. But some of these poems are among the most attractive that Jacob ever wrote, and for this reason alone deserve to survive. They throw light on an unexpected and under-appreciated aspect of a poet whose whole work has, anyway, not yet been properly assessed, and they provide a basic point of reference from which to investigate the many other ways in which Jacob comments on his society and his age. (pp. 160-61)

S. I. Lockerbie, "Realism and Fantasy in the Work of Max Jacob: Some Verse Poems," in Order and Adventure in Post-Romantic French Poetry: Essays Presented to C. A. Hackett, *edited by E. M. Beaumont, J. M. Cocking, and J. Cruickshank (© 1973 by Basil Blackwell), Basil Blackwell, 1973, pp. 149-61.*

ANNETTE THAU   (essay date 1976)

Although Max Jacob is now regarded as one of the major French poets of the twentieth century, only limited aspects of his poetry have received critical attention. Much of the considerable critical literature concerning Jacob dwells on his extraordinary personality. Published studies of his poetry are fragmentary or concentrate on aspects of his early volumes characterized variously as cubist or hermetic or the like. These studies fail to convey the complexity and variety of Jacob's poetry, or its range. In an unpublished letter to Mlle. Marguerite Mespoulet, Jacob identified three tendencies in his work: *"humour"* (wit), *"amour"* (love, lyrical elements), and *"inconscience"* (chance, the subconscious). He added that these three had always coexisted, but that, early in his career, in the *rue Ravignan* days (when Jacob's painter friends and close associates were creating cubism), he had been drawn by his entourage in the direction of *"inconscience"* whereas later *"humour amour"* dominated. This statement accurately describes Jacob's evolution as a poet. More importantly it identifies tendencies which were present at every stage of his long and prolific poetic career. In most volumes of his poetry, and indeed in many poems, these three tendencies coexist. To explore Jacob's art as a poet fully, one must study the stylistic features of his poetry—not merely those used in the early works that made his reputation but those that characterize his entire poetic output. (p. 15)

The critical literature on Jacob condemns a number of aspects of his poetry, chiefly those associated with elements of play and humor. Those elements analysed . . . as "association of words on the basis of sounds" have particularly aroused the ire of critics. Yet, a number of them have been so struck by Jacob's verbal play that they have ignored almost everything else in his poetry and remember him only as the poet who wrote poems based on association of sounds. . . . These critics have not articulated the reasons for their objection to this type of verbal play in poetry. But it is clear that Jacob's poems violate their expectations of what a poem is or should be. The concept underlying this attitude is a variation of the classic injunction against mixtures of style, based on the assumption that there are, or ought to be, distinctions between the noble or elevated style of poetry or tragedy and a low style in which humor may be used. Jacob's use of playful structures as elements of his poetic style is thus considered by critics as too vulgar, or too frivolous, and hence destructive: in a word, "anti-poetic."

These objections are related to another aspect of Jacob's style, . . . namely, the dissociation between poetry and beauty, and the fact that Jacob's poetic language or level of style is devoid of poetic diction—indeed, at times, close to the vernacular. Clichés, snatches of conversation, ordinary, even pedestrian objects, and the like dominate many poems. This gives his poetry a surface appearance of banality, possibly of triviality. Again, this may appear "anti-poetic."

Yet it ought to be evident that one cannot isolate those aspects considered "anti-poetic" from the rest of Jacob's work, or from the rest of a poem. The very fact that these aspects have been singled out for criticism or are considered by some as the central element of Jacob's poetry underlines their importance. (pp. 16-17)

One can meet these critical objections only by analysing impartially and objectively the function of Jacob's structures, and by regarding poetry as, among other things, a special use of words that seeks to extend them beyond their ordinary dimensions, so as to reveal unsuspected meaning. The element of obscurity, or mystery, which is an integral aspect of Jacob's poetry, is hence viewed as a necessary concomitant to the

particular use of language in a given text. From this view, any structure that renews the reader's perception of language and reality, whether it involves the use of nonsense, fantasy, antirational and prosaic elements, chance, etc, or the use of more traditional figures such as imagery, is intrinsically poetic, and therefore, legitimate. The poetic value of a structure is judged by criteria related to such questions as: How is this structure used in this text? In what way is the meaning of a word enriched or a new meaning created? What precisely adds the element of surprise or mystery? What gives new or unexpected dimension to a text? Can it be read on a number of levels? and the like.

It has been said that Jacob deliberately mystified his readers, that nothing in the poems is what it seems to be. This is not always a pejorative judgment, but rather . . . a characterization of Jacob's poetic universe, a recognition of the importance of the element of ambiguity in his poetry. . . . Ordinary objects or scenes—such as a wheelbarrow, a hole in the wall, a corn on one's foot—appear in the poems only to mislead the reader into thinking he is reading about a familiar, mundane world. Invariably, however, another dimension intrudes, or is revealed. The structures which contribute the most to this effect of ambiguity or mystification are a function of Jacob's use of imagery. They are also intimately linked to his "anti-poetic" structures, especially play with words or sounds, and parodies. These do not, however, result uniquely in effects of humor or ambiguity, as has been assumed implicitly or explicitly by Jacob's critics. (pp. 18-19)

Jacob's poetic output is divided into prose and verse. This raises some delicate questions, mainly because a precise definition of the prose poem has yet to be established. A number of general tendencies are more readily identified with Jacob's prose poetry than with his verse poetry: in prose poems, the "I" tends to be absent from lyrical contexts, resulting in more "objective" poems; humorous contexts are frequently associated with effects of nonsense, fantasy, or ambiguity in that the reader often has to invent varying interpretations. These distinctions are far from absolute, however. Nor do they necessarily hold for anyone other than Jacob. As used herein, prose poetry and verse poetry indicate only typographical disposition, "verse poetry" designating poetry presenting itself in separate lines *(vers)*, whether free or based on conventional syllable counts; and "prose poetry" designating poetry presenting itself in paragraphs, or in the case of very brief poems, in run-on phrases or sentences. (p. 19)

I have repeatedly stressed two themes: that Jacob's poetry makes use of many devices or aspects of language which had been considered either apoetic or antipoetic because associated with "low" or "humorous" contexts; that it uses them to force a re-examination of the meaning of these words, to show them in a new light. (p. 110)

The difference between puns and metaphors lies not in the supposed frivolity of one as opposed to the power of revelation of the other; rather, each affects meaning in different ways. Puns focus on the multiple existing meaning of words. This device achieves great density by making it possible to compress within one utterance a number of seemingly unrelated meanings; or to contrast these meanings (in the case of paronomasia) in a particularly striking context. The result is an exploration of language in depth. Metaphors, on the other hand, create new meanings for words by encapsulating many meanings that cannot be expressed in other ways: it is impossible to paraphrase the full meaning of a metaphor. The result is an outward expansion of language. Midway between these two is the device I have called "substantives expressive in a number of ways at once." Characteristic of this device is the fact that the existing meanings of words, often drawn from the vernacular, are not altered. Commonplace objects are evoked concretely, yet they acquire additional overtones which may be affective, psychological, metaphysical, etc. Complexity of meaning can be signaled by rhetorical or syntactical devices; or, in the case of metaphors or puns, can result from the devices themselves. In Jacob's poetry, it also relates to a conception of the universe that is anachronistic to the twentieth century because it is based on occult beliefs that situate objects in the material world in a system of correspondences with a spiritual reality and attributing quasi-magical powers to them and perhaps to language as well. This conception of the universe becomes a source of imagery, as well as a means of transforming objects. (pp. 110-11)

Jacob found his poetic material everywhere: whatever suits the logic of a poem is by definition poetic. Jacob, moreover, composed individual poems in the same way he composed his entire work: longer poems, are composites in which all or many of the devices studied are blended together.

This does not mean, however, that Jacob's poetry is indiscriminate, or that it lacks individuality and character. Jacob's imprint is unmistakable. His originality derives from the unique way in which the various devices are combined in his poetry to become one voice, one presence. At the level of language and structure, this voice is especially marked by the use of prosaic elements, nonsense, sound and word play, parodies; at the thematic level, by the extensive use of dream images, and the intrusion into the everyday of the supernatural. The exclusion from my analysis of any biographical considerations does not mean that the world of Jacob is absent. On the contrary, Jacob's particular vision of reality must be referred to constantly: it is, however, contained in the poems themselves. It is, after all, his poetic universe which interests us. The world that emerges is one in which the familiar reveals itself as multi-layered, multi-dimensional; a world where there is no visible separation between myth, reality, and dream, where the commonplace is the supernatural, a little girl, the devil, and a cloud, an angel. The familiar, be it a familiar meaning, a familiar object, is transformed. Meaning, rationality, logic, nonsense are reinterpreted. Poetry dwells in the ordinary—and everywhere else.

Jacob's reputation as a poet, up to now, has primarily been that of an innovator, not a poet so much as, in the formula coined by Gabriel Bounoure, "un inventeur de poésie." Nevertheless, the variety of devices, as well as Jacob's mastery in utilising fully the resources of language, testify that his accomplishments are those of a poet of considerable stature. (pp. 112-13)

> *Annette Thau, in her* Poetry and Antipoetry: A Study of Selected Aspects of Max Jacob's Poetic Style *(© North Carolina Studies in Romance Languages and Literatures), U.N.C. Department of Romance Languages, 1976, 128 p.*

JUDITH MORGANROTH SCHNEIDER (essay date 1978)

Jacob's religious beliefs were characterized by consistency amidst contradiction. While his opinions on dogma wavered, his faith had its foundation in a constant anti-rationalism. He was a mystic whose religion came to life from his visions. He be-

lieved in the invisible presence of the divine in the material world. (p. 23)

Jacob's mystical way was of his own invention. If his convictions exhibited an affinity with several acknowledged forms of mysticism, they were positively identified with none. There were two principal correlatives to his belief in the hidden presence of divinity in the terrestrial sphere. First of all, manifestations of the spirit belonged to one of two categories—the good or the evil. Behind the phenomena of everyday reality antagonistic moral forces perpetuated a struggle, which might be represented in Christian, kabbalistic, or astrological terms. The second corollary of Jacob's vision was the notion of communicating with invisible spiritual entities. Whether they took the form of devils, angels, genies, saints, Satan, or Christ, Jacob attempted to reach these beings through direct address.

Such was the spiritual atmosphere pervading Jacob's religious poetry. As he stated in his *Art poétique,* he sought to transform the commonplace into the miraculous. . . . (p. 24)

The title of the present study, *Clown at the Altar,* comes from a list of alternative titles proposed by Max Jacob for *Les Pénitents en maillots roses.* Each of the paradigmatic substitutes suggests the antithesis of the mystical and the burlesque. . . . At the time Jacob wrote these poems, the clown was an established archetype in literature and painting. Yet, although the theme had become a cliché, the contexts created by Jacob invested the figure with renewed poetic force. In his life and in his texts, the clown embodied the principle of contradiction. . . . The condensation of contraries, the alternation of opposite states, the asymmetrical couple or double man, these movements of division associated with the clown motif, in Jacob's writings, reached the painful intensity of a quest for identity, as well as a salvational Passion. . . . (pp. 25-6)

If the clown signified antithesis, the clown at the altar was a hyperbole of contradiction, emphasizing an ironic view of the penitent as a caricature of the true convert. Just as the clown's flights of fancy are inevitably undermined by humiliating reminders of his gross physicality, Jacob's *vieux personnage* parodied the roles assumed by the new man. And in depicting the penitent as a clown, his poetry dramatized the poet's relation to the public, a society of disbelievers to whom his mysticism appeared, at the least, anachronistic and ridiculous, or, at the worst, hypocritical and ridiculous. It is as if, through his own skeptical attitude, Jacob attempted to forestall the skepticism of others. The figure of the clown, moreover, was not the only sign of contradiction in his writing, where the interpenetrating levels of form and theme manifested a determinant pattern of antithesis. . . . The religious poetry of Max Jacob consisted not of harmonious verses, reflecting the faith of a tranquil *dévot,* but of dynamic texts, transcribing the agitation of a Christian poet, who doubted the authenticity of his religious beliefs, his aesthetics, and his art. (p. 26)

[Consistency] is not a prerequisite for poetry, nor is contradiction a sign of artistic failure. In the poetics practiced by Jacob, he effectively balanced the antitheses which undermined his theoretical affirmations. The immeasurable affect of mystical inspiration was complemented by technical skill. The contrariety of conscious and unconscious modes of writing, unresolved in theory, created expressive stylistic contrasts in his poems. And, through a counterpoint of oneirism and lyrical confession, Jacob dramatically transposed the conflict of the occult and the orthodox. Opposition, contradiction, discordancy were the characteristic elements of his poetry. (p. 63)

[The] *Défense de Tartufe,* as its dedicatory remarks claimed, manifested an evolution of his poetic method. The subtitles of its four parts—"L'Antithèse," "La révélation," "La décadence ou mystique et pécheur," "La vie dévote"—suggest a dialectic in which the antithesis of scepticism and faith produces a spiritual conflict resulting in the new life of the penitent Christian. And, to a certain extent, this process was stylistically actualized: the first group of poems relied on burlesque techniques; the second section created primarily visionary effects; the third contrasted the three major tendencies of Jacob's style; and the last group depended on the confessional mode. Yet the significant factor in terms of Jacob's stylistic evolution was not the simulated progress towards devotional lyricism, but the juxtaposition (in the *Défense* as a whole and in its individual texts) of incongruous effects. For the early poetic devices by no means dwindled away in the later poems. On the contrary, a consistent pattern of stylistic contrasts . . . determined the structure of his religious poetry.

A brief analysis of several prose poems of the *Défense* will demonstrate the contrast of confessional and enigmatic effects. Jacob's multifold devices for expanding the connotations of ordinary language, which produced an atmosphere of mystery in the *Oeuvres burlesques et mystiques* and the *Cornet,* continued to function in the *Défense.* But, while his earlier texts heightened ambiguity by avoiding explanations of personal symbolism, his later prose poems provided clues to interpretation. Titles, parenthetical expressions, appositives, interjections, exclamations, interrogations typically served as indicators of the emotive meaning of the text. . . . In respect to aesthetics, such rhetorical devices suggest the deliberate activity of the poet, while . . . contrasting oneiric techniques give the impression of verbal association without reflective ordering. The poem . . . transposes the antithesis noted earlier in Jacob's poetic theories: the opposition of automatic or unconscious writing to conscious composition. (pp. 73-5)

It was not a question in the *Défense*'s contrasts of the negation of one tendency by another, nor of synthesis, for Jacob's poetic method relied upon the maintenance of tension. Just as, in his religious experience, sin generated remorse and remorse entailed self-deprecation, so in his poetry the visionary and the burlesque induced confession and confession, in turn, became the parody of confession. (pp. 76-7)

Similarly, a thematic antithesis of faith and skepticism emanates from the stylistic structure of "**Le Christ au cinématographe,**" where parodic effects counterpoint a predominantly confessional orientation. The verse poem evokes a dramatic situation autobiographically inspired by Jacob's second revelation: the poet in a movie house, a cloak-and-dagger film, the arrival of a mysterious heavenly spirit, the apparition of a Christ-like figure on the screen. . . . In "*Le Christ au cinématographe*" the immediate juxtaposition of emotive and burlesque contexts produces comic surprise, but in the wider context of the poem the antithesis concretizes the disquietude of a contradictory spiritual experience. (pp. 77-8)

The project of uniting disparate poetic tendencies through contrast was the common design of the poetry written by Jacob after the *Défense de Tartufe.* Although not yet developed in the *Laboratoire central* . . . , where verbal experimentation predominated, the contrastive method prevailed in the [*Visions infernales,* in *Pénitents en maillots roses,* in *Fond de l'eau, Sacrifice impérial, Rivages,* and in the posthumous collections, *Derniers poèmes* and *L'Homme de cristal*]. . . . Yet the pattern of stylistic oppositions did not serve a monolithic function in

these poems. Contrasts between burlesque, enigmatic, and confessional contexts intensified expressiveness by creating a variety of effects. As we observed in several pieces of the *Défense,* a frequent result was the reinforcement of thematic contradictions, such as the antitheses of temptation and penitence, of doubt and faith, of occultism and orthodoxy. Or, stylistic polarization might emphasize semantic complementarity, as in the instance of interpretative emotive statements and of oneiric signifiers serving as an objective correlative to lyrical motifs. The general function, however, of the formal antithetical structure of Jacob's religious poetry was to recreate the dramatic atmosphere of his spiritual life. (p. 80)

Parody of religious themes, through the contrast of burlesque and confessional effects, typifies the self-consciousness of Jacob's poetry. If the *Cornet à dés* parodied the style of other writers, the later poems constantly referred to his own *écriture* with a parodic intention. (p. 88)

As a result of these parodic contrasts of confession and burlesque, of the penitent and the impostor, of devotional poetry and the parody of devotional poetry, the reader is left in a state of doubt. Not as to the religious orientation of the texts, but regarding the resolution of their dramatic tension. . . .

By retaining his early tendencies toward the burlesque and the enigmatic, Jacob succeeded in avoiding the "Lamartinian" sentimentality, which he feared at the outset of his conversion. The spiritual experience he transposed into poetry was one of conflict, of movement, of process, reflected aesthetically in a structure of stylistic contrasts: The opposition of enigmatic imagery and confessional interpretation, as well as the emotive refutation of oneirism and word-play, corresponded to the occult and orthodox poles of his metaphysics. Juxtaposition of confession and burlesque reflected the struggles of conversion, the self-doubts of the penitent, the contradictions of the devotional poet. While the persistence of irony in Jacob's religious poetry has been taken as a sign of insincerity, if his poetic method is to be interpreted as an indication of his faith, it might just as reasonably be considered a figure of his aversion to complacency and facile acceptance of dogma. In fact, it would have been inauthentic for his poems not to embody a dialectic. (p. 90)

Jacob's writing on poetry reflected the contradictions of his metaphysics. Poetic theories defining the poem as an aesthetic object contradicted statements allowing poetry the function of mystical cognition. In descriptions of poetic execution, Jacob emphasized, alternatively, antithetical notions: style (technique) and situation (affectivity), interiorization (inspiration) and exteriorization (fabrication), maturation in the unconscious (automatism) and surveillance (conscious control). These contradictory theories matched his ambivalent attitude toward the relation of poetry and faith. At times, he stressed the compatibility and complementarity of the two domains; on occasion, he declared them irrevocably opposed. (p. 118)

[For Jacob] contradiction was not limited to a single conceptual antithesis; it was a psychological and ontological reality at the center of the human condition.

This incessant mechanism of duplicity might be looked at in two ways, either positively or negatively. . . . The sense of inconsistency suggested by Jacob's figures of the double man, the actor, or the clown, frequently evoked anxiety. It was a mode of consciousness equivalent to Sartre's explication of the awareness of human freedom, which he exemplified by the dizziness of a man on the edge of a precipice. This dizziness is caused not by fear of accidentally slipping, but by the anguish inherent in the possibility of choosing to throw oneself into the abyss. Jacob, similarly, was afraid of sinful temptations, but felt anguish at the knowledge of his freedom to sin, at the distance between intention and act. (pp. 118-19)

Confession was the mode chosen by Max Jacob to transcend duality, and the mirrors in which he sought his undivided image were prayer and poetry. . . . Like devotional confessions, Jacob's religious poetry dramatized a quest for salvation, or wholeness, through the avowal of duplicity. And these poems, paradoxically, derived unity from their multiform exhibition of the double man. (pp. 120-21)

> *Judith Morganroth Schneider, in her* Clown at the Altar: The Religious Poetry of Max Jacob *(© North Carolina Studies in Romance Languages and Literatures), U.N.C. Department of Romance Languages, 1978, 136 p.*

MICHAEL BROWNSTEIN (essay date 1979)

The young Surrealist poets who succeeded Max and ignored him for "political" reasons ironically have left us with no long poems that equal what was achieved with *The Dice Cup*. In terms of a reorientation of reality through art they talked a spectacular game, they did and made much, but I suggest that the single most extensive poetic source for experiencing what happened to the white psyche between, say, Baudelaire and the present moment, lies within the modest cylindrical space of a leather dice cup. The title itself suggests inventiveness as a state of being—the perpetual remaking of the grounds of art that characterizes the modern artist. It is also a sexual or at least procreative image, with the throw of the dice creating in each poem a detailed and unique whole, replicating the genetic process of chromosomes mixing and matching their strands of DNA into you and me and Mom.

Max's achievement was the creation of a work owing its captivating and surprising existence to a total assimilation of modern day life. He created a world that can be savored in all its complexity and variety to an extent shared by few other long poetic works in this century. Though the machinery behind the spectacle can be felt to an exquisite degree, its nature remains just beyond our reach. Max's work is never didactic, it never argues for artistic method or philosophy. His revolutionary contributions to poetic method, however, should be mentioned.

Cubism in art is as inevitable in the twentieth century as romanticism was in the nineteenth. Max's aesthetic concerns paralleled those of the early cubist painters with whom he lived, who, according to Juan Gris, were reacting against elements employed by impressionist painters. Max followed his painter friends when they gave up attempting to make a two-dimensional canvas represent a three-dimensional scene. Duality, plurality and simultaneity of vision were introduced to demolish the everyday world and build up a new one. In painting, movement around objects captured fragments of appearances which fused into a single new image. In poetry, Max was involved in destroying and recreating the conventional subject, anchored as it was in realistic imagery. As he wrote in **"The Cock and the Pearl,"**

> When one paints a picture, it changes completely with each touch, it turns like a cylinder and is almost endless. When it stops turning, that's because it's finished. . . .

Like still lifes of Braque or Gris, the poems in *The Dice Cup* are possessed of an interior equilibrium. Not an outmoded equilibrium imposed from without in the form of a ruling taste, but a new one created by the poet. As cubist painting contradicts temporal logic and spatial logic, *The Dice Cup* contradicts temporal logic and accepted semantics. Max achieved this through incessant puns, clashing imageries, reorientation of perspective, cutting across literary styles and social distinctions, montage of dictions, slang, disregard for conventions of logic, tonal disturbance, lack of transitions, arbitrary fragmentation, shifting focus, personal associations and private vocabulary. These elements resolve themselves in each poem into an immobile constellation, as when the dice finally come to rest on the table. The poems are kaleidoscopic, images growing out of puns transformed into new images. Max also was the first to write one page novels; that is, he was the first writer to realize the sheer speed with which people see each other today. And yet for all that his prose is clean, alive, exact.

The plurality of consciousness in *The Dice Cup* implies a simultaneous universe (the age of electricity, the telephone, flying machines) while it embodies rebellion against artistic and behavioral norms of his time, a rebellion also evident in the works of contemporaries like Apollinaire, Pierre Reverdy and the Futurists. The way in which things change in *The Dice Cup* is mysterious—what makes things happen remains inexplicable and therefore unsettling. Contradictions are felt as related to each other *simply because of context*—"Everything that exists is situated," as Max wrote in the *Cornet à dés* "Preface of 1916." For example, the solipsistic nature of our culture makes an argument or opinion seem perfectly obvious only to the person putting it forth. By adapting such facts of life to his art, Max Jacob revealed a fine awareness of the relativity of all perceived existence.

Thus *The Dice Cup* provides a more accurate and intense experience, for my money, than similar extended creations by Max's French contemporaries, or even than the one concocted in Ezra Pound's symphonic typewriter. This is because the poems in *The Dice Cup* disrupt and realign the mental status of the reader, taking him to a very modern place—where the farthest is also the nearest, where elements of memory, perception and identity are constantly changing. *The Dice Cup* also is alive and familiar in its language and emotive impact in ways that works by Roussel, *et al.*, though fascinating, are not. (pp. iii-v)

> *Michael Brownstein, "Introduction" (copyright © 1979 by Michael Brownstein), in* The Dice Cup: Selected Prose Poems *by Max Jacob, edited by Michael Brownstein, Sun, 1979, pp. i-v.*

ADDITIONAL BIBLIOGRAPHY

Adlard, John. Introduction to *Advice to a Young Poet*, by Max Jacob, translated by John Adlard, pp. 7-9. London: The Menard Press, 1976.
    Presents brief excerpts from Jacob's letters, organizing them into a general exposition of his poetic thought.

Collier, S.J. "The Correspondence of Max Jacob." *French Studies* VII, No. 3 (July 1953): 235-56.
    Reprints and analyzes nine unpublished letters "in an attempt to clarify Jacob's position at the time of his first retirement" at Saint-Benoit "and to give some account of his state of mind then."

Collier, S.J. "Max Jacob and the 'poème en prose'." *Modern Language Review* LI, No. 4 (October 1956): 522-35.

Jacob's position in the development of the prose poem in French literature. The critic argues that "the prose-poems of *Le Cornet* are not Jacob's best work" because they are spoiled by his oneiric technique and verbal acrobatics.

Fowlie, Wallace. "Homage to Max Jacob." *Poetry LXXV*, No. 6 (March 1950): 352-56.

Sympathetic bio-critical essay which states that Jacob's art "resembles the buffoon's, without being it too literally, in which disorder is a saving grace."

Hubert, Renée Rièse. "Max Jacob: The Poetics of *Le Cornet à dés*." In *About French Poetry from DADA to "TEL QUEL": Text and Theory*, edited by Mary Ann Caws, pp. 99-111. Detroit: Wayne State University Press, 1974.

General analysis of themes and techniques in the prose poems.

Kamber, Gerald. *Max Jacob and the Poetics of Cubism*. Baltimore: Johns Hopkins Press, 1971, 182 p.

Close analysis of Jacob's prose poems, with a comprehensive examination of the theoretical background of cubist aesthetics.

Schneider, Judith Morganroth. "Max Jacob on Poetry." *Modern Language Review* 69, No. 2 (April 1974): 290-96.

Contends that "an 'esthétique de Max Jacob' is questionable," in contrast to Annette Thau's ideas in "The Esthetique Reflections of Max Jacob." [See excerpt in entry above].

Thau, Annette. "Max Jacob and Cubism." *La revue des lettres modernes*, Nos. 474-78 (1976): 145-72.

Concludes that "Jacob's poetry owes very little to theories, cubist or otherwise."

M(ontague) R(hodes) James

1862-1936

English short story writer.

James is considered the creator and foremost craftsman of the modern ghost story. Writing in the tradition of Joseph Sheridan Le Fanu, whom he thought stood "in the first rank as a writer of ghost stories," James avoided the atmospheric Gothicism in his predecessor's work and instead employed a simple narrative style designed to heighten the terrifying effect of his tales. In Le Fanu and other Gothic writers, terror arises from both psychological and supernatural sources; but in James the agency of fear is entirely an objective phenomenon outside character psychology. As critics have pointed out, his characters are pursued to their unpleasant doom for no apparent reason aside from their being in the wrong place at the wrong time.

James was raised an Evangelical Christian. His father was rector of the Suffolk village of Livermere, and James maintained his childhood faith with complete orthodoxy throughout his life. An intensely studious child, he grew up to devote himself to studying apocryphal documents connected with the Old and New Testaments and cataloguing medieval manuscripts, on which he was a world renowned authority. His academic offices included fellow, provost, and vice-chancellor at King's College, Cambridge, and provost of Eton. He wrote his first ghost stories to be read at meetings of the Chitchat Society, a Cambridge literary club organized "for the promotion of rational conversation." James was urged to produce more stories, which were collected as *Ghost Stories of an Antiquary*, with illustrations by James McBryde. It was for McBryde's daughter that James wrote a children's book, *The Five Jars*, which never gained the renown of his supernatural fiction. Collections of James's ghost stories were immensely popular, and his Christmas Eve readings at Cambridge, by candlelight, became a tradition.

Though not a professional or even frequent writer of fiction—he wrote his stories strictly to amuse himself and friends—James was a self-conscious artist who followed specific literary guidelines in his tales of terror. Realistic setting and characters, use of often scholarly detail, and finally the intrusion of malevolent supernatural forces are all integrated to form the model ghost story. But while lesser artists also adhered to this formula, James added to it a genius for generating highly original specters in a genre of well-worn possibilities. Rather than mobilizing the familiar wispy apparition, James's tales commonly feature horrors of chilling substance: the tentacled companion in "Count Magnus," the hairy-handed thing in "Canon Alberic's Scrapbook," or simply the ever-present creeping shape spied out of the corner of its victim's eye.

Criticism of James's work primarily indicates the success of his ambitions as a virtuoso of the spectral chiller. Maurice Richardson's psychoanalytic interpretation, which finds symbols of repressed and perverse sexuality in the ghost stories, is an interesting exception to the rule. Deliberate symbolism is more characteristic of contemporary supernatural authors such as Ramsey Campbell and Robert Aickman, who nonetheless acknowledge James's stylistic influence on their work.

Courtesy of Mansell Collection

For James himself it was only important that his tales infect the reader with a pleasurable uneasiness and possibly with the thought that "If I'm not very careful, something of this kind may happen to me!"

PRINCIPAL WORKS

Ghost Stories of an Antiquary   (short stories)   1904
More Ghost Stories of an Antiquary   (short stories)   1911
A Thin Ghost and Others   (short stories)   1919
The Five Jars   (juvenile fiction)   1922
A Warning to the Curious and Other Ghost Stories   (short stories)   1925
The Collected Ghost Stories of M. R. James   (short stories) 1931

THE ATHENAEUM   (essay date 1904)

Read in suitable circumstances, *Ghost Stories of an Antiquary* . . . cannot fail to produce a series of thrills. Dr. James uses his multifarious erudition with effect to produce a background of vraisemblance. We see no particular reason to lament the fact that the stories are scholarly in their setting rather than journalistic. It is possible to be vivid without being vulgar. As a matter of fact each of the eight stories is simply told, and the Latin used is explained, while the humour is lightly touched in, and the offensive stupidities of the common funny man are wholly avoided. In most of the cases here the ghost has definite reasons to worry the person who sees it, the said percipient being, consciously or unconsciously, the aggressor. Thus some of the effective vagueness of real ghost stories is lost. On the other hand, there are no feeble explanations of the whole thing being a dream or the result of disordered brain or body. In fact, the thing is done in the best way—the way to carry conviction. The best story, to our thinking, is **"O whistle and I'll come to you, my lad,"** but all the eight maintain a very level quality of excellence, and do credit to Dr. James's imagination.

> *"Our Library Table: 'Ghost Stories of an Antiquary',"* in The Athenaeum, *No. 4025, December 17, 1904, p. 842.*

H. P. LOVECRAFT   (essay date 1927)

[Gifted] with an almost diabolic power of calling horror by gentle steps from the midst of prosaic daily life, is the scholarly Montague Rhodes James, Provost of Eton College, antiquary of note, and recognized authority on mediaeval manuscripts and cathedral history. Dr. James, long fond of telling spectral tales at Christmastide, has become by slow degrees a literary weird fictionist of the very first rank; and has developed a distinctive style and method likely to serve as models for an enduring line of disciples. (pp. 408-09)

In inventing a new type of ghost, he has departed considerably from the conventional Gothic tradition; for where the older stock ghosts were pale and stately, and apprehended chiefly through the sense of sight, the average James ghost is lean, dwarfish, and hairy—a sluggish, hellish night-abomination midway betwixt beast and man—and usually *touched* before it is *seen*. Sometimes the spectre is of still more eccentric composition; a roll of flannel with spidery eyes, or an invisible entity which moulds itself in bedding and shows *a face of crumpled linen.* Dr. James has, it is clear, an intelligent and scientific knowledge of human nerves and feelings; and knows just how to apportion statement, imagery, and subtle suggestions in order to secure the best results with his readers. He is an artist in incident and arrangement rather than in atmosphere, and reaches the emotions more often through the intellect than directly. This method, of course, with its occasional absenses of sharp climax, has its drawbacks as well as its advantages; and many will miss the thorough atmospheric tension which writers like [Arthur] Machen are careful to build up with words and scenes. But only a few of the tales are open to the charge of tameness. Generally the laconic unfolding of abnormal events in adroit order is amply sufficient to produce the desired effect of cumulative horror. (pp. 409-10)

Dr. James, for all his light touch, evokes fright and hideousness in their most shocking form, and will certainly stand as one of the few really creative masters in his darksome province. (p. 412)

> *H. P. Lovecraft, "Supernatural Horror in Literature" (1927), in his* Dagon and Other Macabre Tales, *edited by August Derleth (copyright 1965, by August Derleth; reprinted by permission of Arkham House*

Publishers, Inc.), Arkham House, 1965, pp. 347-413.*

M. R. JAMES   (essay date 1931)

I am told [my ghost stories] have given pleasure of a certain sort to my readers: if so, my whole object in writing them has been attained, and there does not seem to be much reason for prefacing them by a disquisition upon how I came to write them. Still, a preface is demanded by my publishers, and it may as well be devoted to answering questions which I have been asked.

First, whether the stories are based on my own experience? To this the answer is No: except in one case, specified in the text, where a dream furnished a suggestion. Or again, whether they are versions of other people's experiences? No. Or suggested by books? This is more difficult to answer concisely. Other people have written of dreadful spiders—for instance, Erckmann-Chatrian in an admirable story called *L'Araignée Crabe*—and of pictures which came alive . . . and so on. Places have been more prolific in suggestion: if anyone is curious about my local settings, let it be recorded that S. Bertrand de Comminges and Viborg are real places: that in *Oh, Whistle, and I'll come to you,* I had Felixstowe in mind; in *A School Story,* Temple Grove, East Sheen; in *The Tractate Middoth,* Cambridge University Library; in *Martin's Close,* Sampford Courtenay in Devon: that the cathedrals of Barchester and Southminster were blends of Canterbury, Salisbury, and Hereford: that Herefordshire was the imagined scene of *A View from a Hill,* and Seaburgh in *A Warning to the Curious* is Aldeburgh in Suffolk.

I am not conscious of other obligations to literature or local legend, written or oral, except in so far as I have tried to make my ghosts act in ways not inconsistent with the rules of folklore. As for the fragments of ostensible erudition which are scattered about my pages, hardly anything in them is not pure invention; there never was, naturally, any such book as that which I quote in the *Treasure of Abbot Thomas.*

Other questioners ask if I have any theories as to the writing of ghost stories. None that are worthy of the name or need to be repeated here: some thoughts on the subject are in a preface to *Ghosts and Marvels* [an anthology edited by V. H. Collins]. . . . There is no receipt for success in this form of fiction more than in any other. The public, as Dr. Johnson said, are the ultimate judges: if they are pleased, it is well; if not, it is no use to tell them why they ought to have been pleased.

Supplementary questions are: Do I believe in ghosts? To which I answer that I am prepared to consider evidence and accept it if it satisfies me. (pp. iii-v)

> *M. R. James, "Preface" (1931), in his* The Ghost Stories of M. R. James *(copyright © 1931 by M. R. James; reprinted by permission of St. Martin's Press, Inc.; in Canada by Edward Arnold Ltd.), second edition, St. Martin's, 1974, pp. iii-vi.*

MARY BUTTS   (essay date 1934)

It is the writer's belief that if Doctor James had chosen to write stories about any other subject under the sun, he would be considered the greatest classic short story writer of our time. Yet, in his case, it is more than usually silly—so completely fused with one another are his style and his subject—to suggest such a thing. It is impossible to think of him as writing about anything else than what is rather foolishly called "The Unseen." Idiotically, in his case. "Unseen," indeed! When the essence of his art is a sudden, appalling shock of visibility. The intangible become more than tangible, unspeakably real, solid, *present*. He is not a writer—say like Mr. Algernon Blackwood—who relies on suggestion, a strengthening atmosphere in which very little ever happens; or rather one is not sure whether it has happened or not. It is what his people *see* that Doctor James is busy with; not how it affects them. After it has happened they either die, or leave home or go to bed; or, years after, tell it to him, with permission to make a story out of it. It sounds simple. It is not. It is matter-of-fact. A very different thing. Yet in its unpretentiousness, in its absence of worked-up atmosphere, its lack of hints, it carries the driest, clearest kind of conviction. If his stories were about anything else (which heaven forbid) Doctor James would be praised for something of the same qualities for which we praise Horace and Catullus and Villon, for something terse and poignant and durable, and looked at with both eyes wide open. (p. 307)

It is strange: to try and separate Doctor James' precise, elegant, detached style, where never a word is wasted, from his matter; to wish, even to imagine, it employed in any other direction, is to dislocate one's imagination, one's sense of what is conceivably possible, so perfectly is the instrument adapted to its end.

His matter. It is taken from his own surroundings and experience, in the University town, the library, the cathedral, the country inn and the country house. His people are the people who live and work in such places; the country gentleman, the student, the don. They are going about their business. Then, as a man might turn a corner or the page of a book, they meet the Unspeakable. Are brought up sharp against the dead who are not dead; who are out and about on hellish business; who, if they have long remained quiescent, are stirred by some trivial accident into hideous activity.

Or these tranquil ordinary men of learning come suddenly upon creatures, tangible as men, but of a different order; intelligences 'less than that of a man, more than that of a beast'; and of the malignancy of hell. Sometimes they escape. Not always. While neither Doctor James' Dead nor his Demons appear in any of the categories or conventions which other writers, using tradition, or maybe their own experience, have accustomed us. His ghosts, demons, 'elementals' are utterly original. New minted. And owing nothing (while at the same time everything) to the vast corpus of tradition—and whatever truth lies behind it—on the existence of such things. (pp. 307-08)

Passing tactfully by the real effect on their nerves and on their sense of truth by the matter of Doctor James, the critics often reserve their praise for his incomparable evocation of the past. "Here," they say, "is imaginative scholarship. How he uses his research to take us back three centuries, or two, or one." . . .

[James' settings] are more than a historic reconstruction, however skilfully done. There is something distilled about them. It is not as if one were in a picture gallery, a spectator, but inside. How does he do it? Doctor James has waved his hand, but what is the spell? Again, it is by a kind of simplicity, a directness of attack. People are confused about this. If the attack comes from an unexpected quarter, they will call the work obscure; not told in the right way. This is not what they mean. The point is that the essential meaning of a tale—from

whatever quarter—must "come at" the reader, undeflected, at its proper pace; which, in works of Doctor James' kind, is usually swift; so that *everything*, however brilliant or diverting, must be omitted that interferes with "telling the tale." (p. 309)

The economy is the same in his display of character. His presentation owes something to Dickens, but all are observed, not without sympathy, but with complete ironic detachment. The marvel is that, when he tells us so little, without, for instance, a hint of physical description, that we know so much. It is true he has no time to make us acquainted at length. He has to get on at once to his point, to the appalling experience that is in store. Many writers would have been content with lay figures; yet, on learning what sort of an inheritance was Mr. Humphreys', one finds out what sort of a man he was. As unlike Dennistoun or Mr. Poynter, Dr. Haynes, or Squire Richards in nature, as he resembles them in representing a class of our society. While in dealing with their servants, Doctor James may be said to let himself go. They are as full of 'humours' as an Eighteenth Century play; more tenderly handled, but as little sentimentalised. He has no objection to driving in the obvious nail, that the better educated you are, the more you are likely—if not to experience—to observe, to be affected, to understand, to be curious about what is happening to you. (p. 310)

[Pages] of analysis would not tell essentially more about them than we gather from a few swift pages, whose motive is not primarily to shew character at all. It is one of the mysteries of classic art, that so little should be enough. As it is one of its supreme beauties that, out of what is said, there is not a word wasted.

In the same way, with the same excellence of proportion, Doctor James attends to the other part of his setting, the place and the weather. A great many pages have been written of good, bad and indifferent prose, on the south-west wind. In *Lost Hearts*, he opens with it. It is his wind. (p. 311)

He has an affection also for some very plain, very subtle, very unambitious English landscapes it takes a long time to appreciate and understand. Scenes that have an affinity with Constable; and which are not there, like mountains and savage valleys and rainbow-filled cataracts and eternal snows to awe and stun us and take away our breath. That ask instead years of patient contemplation and silent love—and even a silent tongue.

Here one might speak of his one book for children [*The Five Jars*]. . . .

It is not a perfect book. The idea is 'genial' and cries aloud for a sequel; but the rather Elizabethan 'Little People,' who appear in flights, with a too rational—a wish-fulfilment—life of their own, have a slight school-mastering touch. They are too much well-bred boys, dressed-up. Created as it were out of the wrong stuff, they jar on the rest of the book, which, with its ordinariness, is steeped in the magic which belongs to Doctor James and to no one else on earth. How plain it is, how mysterious, how lovely. Even those Little People would be another writer's excellence. (p. 312)

What is Doctor James writing about? What is a ghost-story? . . . And why is it, as he has said himself, that no other subject has ever attracted him? While how is it that the ghost stories he has written are incomparable and unique; that he has found a formula for their telling more effective and like that of no other writer? In English we have a considerable literature of the occult. One wishes one knew enough to compare it with that of other countries. One imagines French to be deficient, and German to be very good. Is it partly a question of language? Yet an audience has shivered at Doctor James, put into clumsy French. (He would translate, where a more 'atmospheric' writer would not.) Anyhow, with us, it is almost a special branch of letters, and includes some masterpieces. Some more ambitious writers are concerned with the theory of such things; with reasons, scientific or mystical, how and why they happen. In Doctor James there is not a hint of this, not the faintest breath of explanation. It is all statement; all the directest narrative.

These questions are unanswerable directly. Only one thing can be said. Years ago, he found a magical receipt, and has spent his life in perfecting the use of it. With it he can raise the evil dead; summon the abominable familiars, whose place is just across the threshold of human life. As in his longest story, *Casting the Runes*. One which happens over a longer period of time than is usual with him, and so allows for an ever-so-slightly-evoked, yet sufficient, atmosphere of suspense. A critic once said that it was work that left one saying: "If I am not very careful, this sort of thing will happen to me." That is certainly true here, as the events move, delicately, inevitably, from slight point to slight point. (pp. 312-13)

If Doctor James were to get up and say that he believes every word he has written, that he has evidence for the essential truth of each one of his stories, he would be believed, in the same way that a scientist is believed. He is the sort of man whose word is taken. While he is a great scholar, and the scholar is elder brother to the scientist.

In one form or another, his subject has haunted man's imagination since the beginning. The Un-Dead Dead, and the potencies, good and evil, but more noticeably evil, which have been thought to crowd about between the threshold of his life and any other forms of life that there may be. (p. 315)

For Doctor James is pitiless. People do not easily escape from his creatures. They fall a victim to them. More often the bad or the disagreeable person, but the amiable and charming Mr. Humphries did not escape "concussion of the brain, shock to the system, and a long confinement in bed." (He later married Lady Wardrop's niece, so that was all right.) But Mr. Poschwitz, the Jew dealer, who stole the prayer books from Brockstone chapel, died by the most hideous death it is possible for the mind to conceive. (pp. 315-16)

Perhaps the doubt felt about Doctor James' subject is not only shallow scepticism, but sound, self-protective sense. Better not—certainly for the majority—better not enquire too closely; ask too many question as to the existence of such things. Everyone who has lived much out of doors *feels* something of what he tells. Not by association with tradition, but by a direct kind of awareness, an impact on the senses—and something more than the senses. It can be a recurrent, almost an overwhelming, experience. Much ancient bogey-lore was a rationalisation of it. To-day we talk of suggestion, exorcise with the magic word "unscientific." But I doubt if our ignorant scepticism is any nearer truth than our ancestors ignorant credulity.

It is certainly safer as it is, safer to have Dr. James give us the experience at second hand. Work his magic; imprison such things safely for us inside the covers of a book, an enduring book. And remember that, thanks to him, we have undergone an adventure which might have been deadly, with more than safety, with delight. (p. 317)

Mary Butts, "The Art of Montague James," in The London Mercury, *Vol. XXIX, No. 172, February, 1934, pp. 306-17.*

PETER PENZOLDT (essay date 1952)

There are many reasons for James' extraordinary success. One is certainly that he is the most orthodox ghost-story writer among his contemporaries. His stories are straightforward tales of terror and the supernatural, utterly devoid of any deeper meaning. They are what the orally-told ghost stories originally were: tales that are meant to frighten and nothing more. They contain no study of human nature as do those by W. F. Harvey, Walter de la Mare, Robert Hichens, Conrad Aiken and others of his contemporaries, and no moral lesson as do Dickens' and Stevenson's tales. They have none of Kipling's poetry. In this respect James can only be compared with F. M. Crawford, though the two authors differ fundamentally in taste, style, technique and the atmosphere of their stories. It can therefore be said with truth that James is at once an orthodox and original writer. Orthodox, because he chose for his tales a form that is older than fiction itself; original, because he alone in the 20th century still believed that the simple ghost story could be thrilling if only it were well enough told. (p. 191)

Naturally, such tales as James chose to write demand a far more elaborate form than most types of ghost story. A horror with a natural explanation, e.g. an illusion caused by mental disease, appears to the reader as being at least possible. Such a story can be presented in a very direct fashion. But when a manifestation of the supernatural forms the climax of the story, and no natural explanation is vouchsafed, the tale becomes far less acceptable to the reader, who because he does not, as he once did, believe in the supernatural, has to be approached with care and brought gradually into a state in which his disbelief is suspended. James's success proves both that he has perfected the technique of 'make believe' and that a large public prefers his kind of story to those with a natural explanation. (pp. 191-92)

In all James' story the reader guesses the supernatural quality of the climax long before any one of the actors does. James probably tried to increase the horror of his tales by making the actors be taken unawares: he counted on the reader identifying himself with the principal actor, and so, seldom described the emotions of his characters. The reader is expected to guess their reactions or rather feel them. As do most ghost-story writers, James tried to create the impression that it was not a third person, but the reader himself, who was undergoing these horrifying experiences. The actors are merely a vehicle for identification. The ghost story should 'happen' between the reader and the ghost. (p. 196)

He opens his stories with a leisurely description of some place or character. This beginning is usually written very much like the opening of a novel. The author seems to have all the time he needs and refuses to hurry towards the action as do most short-story writers. Then suddenly the rhythm changes. As soon as James thinks that the reader has been sufficiently introduced to the scenery and the actors, he deliberately cuts short his description in a single sentence. This sentence clearly proclaims its function; the author makes no mystery of his intention. For instance: . . . 'It is no part of my plan to repeat the whole conversation that ensued between the two'. . . . ; or 'Lake expressed his concurrence with Worby's views of restoration, but owns to a fear about this point lest the story proper should never be reached. . . .', or something of that kind. From this point on everything that does not directly concern the action is, as a rule, merely sketched. Conversations, for example, give the impression of being overheard telephone calls: The answers of one partner are simply omitted. James is not even afraid to use an 'etc., etc.', to get on faster, for example: '. . . You'll excuse me mentioning it, only I thought it a very nice evening for a ride. Yes, sir, very seasonable weather for haymakers: let me see, I have your bike ticket. Thank you, sir; much obliged: you can't miss your road, etc., etc.' New actors that appear on the stage are no longer introduced with a description but simply reveal their characters in speech and action. In this respect, of course, James does not differ greatly from most modern short-story writers. Sometimes he goes a little too far in stressing the picturesque. There are too many frightened maids and butlers, who deliver speeches in cockney or dialect, and too many characters who always repeat the same proverb. Such devices are amusing once, but when they appear again and again they become rather tiresome. They are, however, excusable, if we remember that the author is chiefly interested in the supernatural part of his story, and if he describes reality it is chiefly for the contrast with the apparition. James' masterly imitation of the legal and ecclesiastical cant of past centuries adds much more to the atmosphere of his stories than do his modern cockney speeches. Being a student of ancient and medieval lore, he also had a general interest in history and was extremely well read. The exact language of the century in which he places his stories, or from which he 'quotes documents', gives his stories an air of authenticity which is missing from the work of most ghost-story writers who take their themes from the past.

It is in the direct presentation of the supernatural, that is to say in the climax, that James' style is most remarkable. He uses short, impressive sentences and simple words. All that is glimpsed of the apparition is described with great directness and precision. Of course, James is careful to ensure that not too much is seen, and what he reveals of the ghost always leaves plenty of room for the reader to imagine additional horrors. (pp. 197-98)

> *Peter Penzoldt, "Dr. M. R. James (1862-1936)," in his* The Supernatural in Fiction *(copyright 1952 by Peter Penzoldt; reproduced in Canada by permission of The Hamlyn Publishing Group Limited), P. Nevill, 1952 (and reprinted by Humanities Press, 1965), pp. 191-202.*

MAURICE RICHARDSON (essay date 1959)

[Freud] deals with the subject of ghost stories in *The Uncanny*. . . . He begins by defining the uncanny as 'that class of the terrifying which leads back to something long known to us, once very familiar'. He then examines the etymology of the German word *unheimlich* (uncanny) and concludes that its 'meaning develops towards an ambivalence until it finally coincides with its opposite'. (pp. 419-20)

Freud also points out the difference between fairy stories, 'where the world of reality is left behind from the very start and the animistic system of beliefs is frankly adopted', and ghost stories in which the writer often pretends to move in the world of common reality; he not only accepts all the conditions operating to produce uncanny feelings in real life, but he can increase his effects by so doing. 'He takes advantage, as it were, of our supposedly surmounted superstitiousness'. (p. 420)

Let me now see how I can apply these ideas to one or two old favourites. . . . I will begin, then, with perhaps the best known English ghost story, M. R. James's *Oh, Whistle And I'll Come To You, My Lad*. . . . (pp. 420-21)

Most readers of M. R. James are agreed that this is his best story. It is one of what Edmund Wilson, who is otherwise apt to be too severe on him, calls his flashes of really fiendish fancy. It seems to have something personal in it. (James admits that the bedclothes taking shape was partly suggested by one of his own nightmares.) It is also more plausible than most of his stories, in too many of which, as Wilson says, the hobgoblins are almost parodies of themselves. The device by which the evil spirit is made to animate the bedclothes is very effective, the kind of thing that might almost happen to anybody. In its construction, with the *heimlich* and the *unheimlich* elements succeeding one another like an alternating current, it conforms very closely to the pattern which Freud outlines in his paper.

(The uncertainty about whether an object is alive or not is another factor which Freud points to as helping to awaken uncanny sensations.)

And when you start examining it with a view to spotting repressed infantile complexes, it turns out to be almost embarrassingly rich.

In the first place there is the symbolism of the whistle which is both phallic and anal. (p. 423)

A further indication in the story of the omnipresent castration complex to which a psychoanalyst would point is the blindness of the ghost, which has come to recover its purloined phallus. The evidence for the equation of blindness with castration is, as Freud remarks, 'plentiful in dreams, myths and fantasies, as well as in the analyses of neurotic patients'. It is not easy to demonstrate it to the satisfaction of the layman, who is inclined to reject it out of hand on rationalistic grounds, maintaining that the eyes are equally precious organs and it is only natural that they should be guarded by proportionate dread.

Significant, too, are the circumstances of the finding of the whistle. These are described in a wealth of detail. 'And when he introduced his hand it met with a cylindrical object lying on the floor of the hold.' It is almost as if [the protagonist] Parkins is removing it from a living body. He himself continues to display an odd doubt about what it is that he has found. 'I suppose,' he says, 'I am a little rusty in my Latin. When I come to think of it I don't believe I even know the word for whistle.'

Then there is the ingenious dramatic device of the Latin inscription. Here for a moment, James, as narrator, is slyly gloating over the unfortunate Parkins's predicament, even though he must to some extent be identified with him. Parkins has enough Latin to translate *Quis est iste qui venit?* as 'Who is this who is coming?' But the little cryptogram defeats him. Add *bis* to *fur*, *fle*, and *fla*, and you have the second person singular of the future tense of the verbs *Furo*, I rage or go mad; *Flo*, I blow; *Fleo*, I weep or grieve. The arrangement in diamond formation allows one to translate it in any order. It can be rendered with a little licence as: *You will blow. You will be sorry. You will go mad.* You might expect a cryptogram to contain the key to the story. Does this one contain it? It is impossible to prove it, but the idea at once occurs to anyone with a little experience of psychoanalysis that blowing the whistle is an act in some way associated with masturbation, to be visited by the fearful penalties attaching to masturbation in the child mind. This squares with the attitude of the colonel, the heavy father figure. He knows perfectly well what Perkins has been up to. He as good as says to him: 'You've brought this on yourself, my boy, and you'll have to take the consequences.' The duplication of the father figures, with the reappearance of Rogers, [a bluff father-figure], at the end, which is unnecessary to the story, is an example of the tendency to reiteration or repetition compulsion and duplication as in dreams to which Freud draws attention.

The final haunting of Parkins in the bedroom by the animated spare set of bedclothes has all the ambivalence which we have been led to expect in a ghost story. The attack which the ghost figure makes upon him is peculiarly intimate and takes on something of the nature of a sexual assault. It reminds one of Dr Ernest Jones's dictum, 'All the beliefs about the nightmare in whatever guise proceed from the idea of the sexual assault that is both wished for and dreaded.'

There is one more significant feature in the story which should not be overlooked and that is the Templar's Preceptory. The inference at the conscious level is that the evil spirit which is attached to the whistle is that of a Templar; what were the Templars notorious for, whether deservedly or not? their homosexuality. That there should be a homosexual element in the story is not surprising, especially if you take into account the fussy henlike personality of Parkins, which has a distinct hint of epicenity about it.

Few, if indeed, any short ghost stories are quite so rich as this one in evidence of repressed infantile complexes. . . . (pp. 423-25)

> *Maurice Richardson, "The Psychoanalysis of Ghost Stories," in* The Twentieth Century *(© The Twentieth Century, 1959), Vol. 160, No. 958, December, 1959, pp. 419-31.*

COLIN WILSON (essay date 1962)

One of [Joseph Sheridan] Le Fanu's most fervent admirers was M. R. James, a Cambridge don who gained a limited fame with his *Ghost Stories of an Antiquary*. James is by no means as good as Le Fanu, but the reader of the *Ghost Stories of an Antiquary* will be . . . struck by the physical violence in them. James's ghosts are very likely to strangle their victims or to inflict some horrible disfigurement on them. What is most significant, however, is that they completely lack a centre of gravity. Poe's tales are all expressions of Poe's temperament; Lovecraft's all center upon the same mythology. James's stories seem to be all over the place. They might almost have been written by several different men. (p. 143)

There would be no point in detailing . . . James's plots; he wrote only thirty stories, and most of these have physical ghosts or "creatures". Again, one observes that the quiet, retired writer, living in relative comfort—even luxury—feels the compulsion to create physical horrors, ghosts that, after all, could frighten no one but a nervous schoolboy. (Towards the end of his life, James wrote a few ghost stories for schoolboys; they are incredibly bad.) Adults continue to read James's stories, not because their horrors are convincing, but because James had a certain pedantic, scholarly cast of mind that somehow makes a delightful contrast with his ghosts and bogies. At his best, in **"Casting the Runes"** or **"The Stalls of Barchester Cathedral"**, there is a gentle, ironic delicacy of touch that

brings to mind—strangely enough—Max Beerbohm. (pp. 144-45)

> *Colin Wilson, "The Powers of Darkness," in his* The Strength to Dream: Literature and the Imagination *(copyright © 1962 by Colin Wilson; reprinted by permission of Houghton Mifflin Company; in Canada by Bolt & Watson, as agents for the author), Houghton, 1962, pp. 128-56.**

AUSTIN WARREN (essay date 1969)

Montague James's ghosts are those of people who in their lives were set apart—witches, wizards, unjust judges, specialists, and traffickers in the occult. But those to whom they, or their effects, appear are themselves ordinary sensible people—"patients," to use his own word—with whom the reader can identify: indeed, only for a here and now normal reader can there be a real supernatural. (p. 96)

[James's] stories are all meticulously and lovingly framed in time as well as localized in setting. For time in his tales, James has at sensitive command the centuries from the Middle Ages (and their medieval Latin) on; he empathizes their concerns, their view of the world. Our antiquary can veraciously imitate their literary styles, whether of letter writing or journals, or, in more and dignified urbanity, of sermons and contributions to the *Gentleman's Magazine*.

The antiquary and the mimic combine in the delight, and the skill, with which James varies the time of his stories. The time is often double: the traditional device of the discovery and reading *now* of some document written in the remote or more recent past. (p. 99)

There is another and differently constituted framing of the [*Ghost Stories of an Antiquary*], one which no single story completely exemplifies but which is the pervasive pattern. This framing is partly a matter of social classes. The outermost framework is that of the educated and socially well-placed—which is either the world in which James lived, the world of scholars, of professors and fellows and the cathedral clergy, or the world he well knew—that of the landed gentry—good, cultivated, sensible gentlefolk. These, persons not easily hauntable, are the "patients" of his tales. They are such persons as Dr. and Mrs. Ashton of Whitminster or the Anstruthers of Westfield Hall, Essex, in **"The Rose Garden,"** with their golf, their gardenings, and their sketching, or antiquarians like Dennistoun of Cambridge. (p. 101)

[By] the pleasurably winding road which leads into the stories—the time, the place, the normal and living, we reach their eruptive center—the horror, about the nature of which something explicit must be said.

There are verses in the thirty-fourth chapter of Isaiah (one of them James cites in a tale) which picture the horror of desolation—the wasted land inhabited by cormorants and bitterns and owls and dragons. "The wild beasts of the desert shall also meet with the wild beasts of the field, and the satyr shall cry to his fellow: the screech owl also shall rest there . . . then shall the vultures also be gathered, every one with her mate."

Except for the *satyr*, a mysterious word which means either a compound of man and ape, or the *lamia,* that famous monster in half human shape which sucks the blood of children, these are all traditional *natural* objects of human aversion, beasts and birds of ill omen associated with death and the devouring of dead bodies. In James's stories, owls, bats, and rats and spiders, the traditionally ominous creatures of the night are frequent. But more terrifying than the literal creatures are their properties, operating of themselves: multiple tentacles, for example, which reach out and entwine themselves stranglingly about the human intruder.

Hair is invoked in double signification: often the creatures are described as having their arms or what pass for their bodies covered with gray or grisly hair; a hairy man is a primitive like the Ainus of Japan; he recalls our anthropoid ancestry. But then there is another, opposite but equally repellent, signification of hair: the effeminate long hair of Sir Everard Charlett, the long hair of Absalom, the King's son, who was caught by his hair as he rode horseback through the forest, who was hanged by his own hair. The wallpaper made from a stuff pattern of Sir Everard's hair, the rippling lines, the almost curling waves of tresses, have their serpentine terror, their menace of entanglement. These are the rival fears of the primitive and the decadent.

More characteristic of James's terrors is the terror of the amorphous. In **"Whistle and I'll Come to You, My Lad,"** the only tale which incorporates one of James's own dreams, the presumed figure of a Knight Templar, perhaps of the fourteenth century, materializes itself out of "the bed-clothes of which it had made itself a body": the living spectator's face; and, as he looks, he sees the face of the other, "an intensely horrible face of *crumpled linen.*" (pp. 102-03)

Ghosts, as commonly conceived of—white, visual images—rarely appear, and then at some distance. More frequently they are heard in cries, moans, or (more disturbing yet) whispers and murmurs; or their presence in a room, or a landscape, is felt. When, however, the evil dead are menaced, they come close and grow heavy. James rarely uses the word 'nightmare,' and then not with technical accuracy, yet his chiefest horror is some version of the incubus—something partly human, partly animal, partly *thing* which presses down, grasps and grips, threatens to strangle or suffocate, a heavy weight of palpable materiality—not 'psychic' but sensually gross—a recall not of shroud but of corpse, of a living dead or death. (p. 104)

The tales of Dr. James are a continuing delight. Indeed, they are so rich in detail, and told with such seemingly artless art, that it is only upon repeated readings that they are properly cherished—so far are they from being mere shockers the pleasure of which is exhausted after the first blunt impact is spent. They have, indeed, to be read closely, for they are to be read for their surface as well as their structure—so far as these two can be disengaged.

James is the author of much more than a few anthology pieces. The two commonly included, **"Casting the Runes"** and **"Whistle and I'll Come to You, My Lad,"** are both excellent stories and excellent James stories; but the level is extraordinarily high. Of the thirty included in *Collected Ghost Stories,* there are, say, eighteen others as good, some of them better. . . . Even this narrowing down has required sacrifices; for it must be said that in every story of James there are touches, 'passage-work,' phrasings not to be missed. And, for his reader who has the tastes of a scholar, there is the recreative research of tracking down his allusions, which, according to his scholarly fancy, are sometimes genuine and sometimes feigned—to discover whether there was a minor Greek author called Polyaenus or a seventeenth-century English organ builder named Dallas, or even to learn what Dr. Blimber really said in Chapter XII of *Dombey and Son.*

This last item . . . is one of Dr. James's own extranarratorial touches, discoverable upon close examination of the stories. He does not hesitate to appear in his own person, either in stories told in the third person or by a feigned narrator. Strictness of 'point of view' is no fetish of his. Yet such are his lowness of pitch and ease of manner (both despite the *horrendum* which awaits us) that no desirable illusion is shattered. He is a born storyteller with no sense of shame at being one—no sense of 'stories' as undignified or even untrue because they are not 'history.' Born storytellers are oral storytellers, and the sound of the storyteller's voice as well as of the many mimicked voices is heard in all James's writing; it not only abounds in dialogue but is itself speech pleased with the resources of speech. (pp. 104-05)

The ghost stories of Montague James have their rightful place in the final chapter of recent books on the tradition of the Gothic Romance. Even such parts of its 'machinery' as the gloomy old press with its secrets, James can use, with the affectionate, half-parodic bow of an antiquarian. But he is the master of a new and probably inimitable mode in his special combination of erudition, dry, precise, rather donnish style, realistic dialogue, humor, and treatment of the supernatural—a supernatural never explained away but variously interpreted by characters dramatically differentiated. He has common sense, and uncommon, too. (p. 107)

Austin Warren, "The Marvels of M. R. James, Antiquary" (1969), in his Connections *(copyright © by The University of Michigan 1970), University of Michigan Press, 1970, pp. 86-107.*

E. F. BLEILER (essay date 1971)

James considered himself a follower of J. S. LeFanu, whom he thought the greatest writer of supernatural fiction. . . . To a modern reader, however, the linkage between LeFanu and James is somewhat tenuous, and James seems much more original than he realized himself.

The "evil that dieth not but lieth in wait" is usually the theme of James's stories, presented in many rich situations built from James's scholarly resources. No one (with the lesser exceptions of Vernon Lee and R. S. Garnett) has ever made use of the exotica of antiquarianism so well and with so much originality. While his stories may seem unconventional in form, sometimes even a little awkward in structure, this difficulty vanishes when one remembers that these originally were stories to be read aloud, not stories to be looked at. His achievement can be measured more accurately if his stories are compared with the material-horror stories of his contemporaries, or with the work of his countless imitators. Within the parameters that James himself set, no one has ever told a better ghost story. (p. 6)

E. F. Bleiler, in his introduction to Ghost Stories of an Antiquary *by M. R. James (copyright ©1971 by Dover Publications, Inc.), Dover, 1971, pp. 3-6.*

JULIA BRIGGS (essay date 1977)

As an author, James maintained an attitude of critical detachment which seems to have been the exception rather than the rule. He did not share the concern shown by other writers ([Algernon] Blackwood or [Joseph Sheridan] Le Fanu, for instance) with the significance of spirits, the state of mind in which ghosts are seen, or the condition of a universe that permits the maleficent returning dead. His stories assert a total acceptance of the supernatural that his scepticism apparently denies. It is as if the implications of what he wrote never disturbed him, and he enjoyed writing them primarily as a literary exercise, governed only by certain rules he had evolved. A classicist both by temperament and profession, James had read a great many ghost stories and worked out from them his own methods, employing traditional themes in highly original settings.

His scepticism about ghosts did not derive from a general agnosticism. The son of a clergyman, M. R. James was a committed Christian and theologian who spent many years collating the Apocryphal Gospels, perhaps in the hope that they might provide some independent evidence of Jesus's supernatural powers with which to refute the 'Higher Criticism'. His ghost stories seem almost to parody his scholarly investigations into Holy Writ, for they frequently adduce biblical or literary references to prove the existence of spiritual forces, yet these appear to be introduced in the spirit of an academic joke, to show that anything can be proved by the citation of learned texts. Such allusions also function as an effective device for convincing the reader, by giving a spurious air of academic authenticity. (pp. 124-25)

Like Henry James and Vernon Lee, M. R. James admitted to finding places 'prolific in suggestion'. . . . (p. 125)

James describes scenery and domestic architecture with knowledge and affection, but when he comes to ecclesiastical architecture, he is in his element. (p. 126)

Accurate and vivid description becomes of primary importance when particular objects play key rôles in the story, as they so often do: 'Canon Alberic's Scrap-Book', 'The Mezzotint', the Anglo-Saxon whistle in '"Oh, Whistle"', the stained glass window with its odd juxtaposition of Job, John and Zechariah in 'The Treasure of Abbot Thomas', 'The Tractate Middoth', 'The Stalls of Barchester Cathedral', and 'The Uncommon Prayer-Book'. In each case, the style and period of the object is carefully established. . . . In describing objects such as the scrapbook, James not only conveys their physical appearance, he also provides them with inscriptions, often in Latin, in the correct style for the period. In fact there is a great deal of literary pastiche throughout his work. Nineteenth-century diaries and letters are imitated in 'The Stalls of Barchester Cathedral', 'The Residence at Whitminster' and 'The Story of a Disappearance and an Appearance'. 'Mr. Humphreys and his Inheritance' includes an ornate passage from an imaginary seventeenth-century sermon, and 'The Diary of Mr Poynter' itself also dates, supposedly, from the same period. 'Martin's Close' is the most sustained of his inventions for it takes the form of a verbatim account of a trial before Judge Jeffreys. His peculiar ability to imitate the different styles and tricks of different periods, in both English and Latin, was probably linked with his powers of mimicry, which he first demonstrated at prep. school. (pp. 126-27)

Yet despite his ability to re-create the past in lucid pictorial detail, James gives several of his most fearful spirits, quite ordinary, even prosaic locations. He understood the importance of a 'fairly familiar' setting, and some of his worst moments take place in modern hotel bedrooms, or even in one case, on an electric tram. . . . [In 'Casting the Runes' the] fatal runes are planted on the victim in the British Museum Reading Room, and returned in a railway carriage. An advertisement in a tram window becomes a portent of death, and the victim, putting his hand under his pillow to find a match, discovers—well,

something very unpleasant. The idea of an invasion of one's bed, of a horror lurking beneath the pillow (the very place where one expects to feel secure) is deeply disturbing. If we are not safe in our beds, then the last sanctuary has gone. The peculiar sense of violation that arises at the thought of one's bedroom being invaded is effectively exploited in '"Oh, Whistle"', where the bedclothes on an empty bed are possessed by an evil spirit. Many sensitive readers have subsequently experienced a certain reluctance to sleep in a room containing an unoccupied bed. And if hiding under the bedclothes is one traditional resort better avoided, so is pulling the curtains to shut out the dark, for the curtains themselves may be harbouring a restless ghost, as they do in 'The Diary of Mr Poynter'. James has shown us fear in a handful of dust, in a Punch and Judy show, and a fragment of wet cloth sticking out of a cupboard.

Fear of the supernatural is essentially circular, for what we fear most is the sensation of being afraid, which endows the most familiar objects with frightful possibilities. The source of terror in a ghost story may be totally irrational, and even incapable of inflicting anything but the experience of fear itself, as in '"Oh, Whistle"', perhaps the most terrifying of all. Here the 'intensely horrible face *of crumpled linen*' seems to possess this power alone: 'The Colonel . . . was of the opinion that if Parkins had closed with it, it could really have done very little, and that its one power was that of frightening.' Yet this is a far more effective piece than the otherwise similar story, 'A Warning to the Curious,' where the phantom actually murders the victim. By placing too great a strain on the reader's credulity, the effect of terror is here diminished, rather than increased. (pp. 127-28)

Sometimes there are allusions to incidents that are never actually related, for example, at the end of 'Casting the Runes', 'Harrington repeated to Dunning something of what he had heard his brother say in his sleep: but it was not long before Dunning stopped him.' Such vague allusions help to prod the imagination into action. They are also part of a more general use of understatement that characterizes James's style. Implicit in the restrained, gentlemanly, even scholarly tone is the suggestion that it would be distasteful to dwell on unpleasant details, and this consistent 'meiosis' serves to increase our apprehension. Recognition that the story teller is deliberately understating his case serves to increase its effectiveness. James may have learnt the use of a deadpan narrative technique from such French exponents of *Grand Guignol* as Mérimée, Maupassant and the Erckmann-Chatrian collaborators, but it was quite evidently a tone that came perfectly naturally to him, perhaps because it is also a characteristically English one. (p. 129)

M. R. James adapted a variety of time-hallowed themes from folklore and legend, myth and ballad, and his stories are largely constructed from such traditional elements. Recognizing this process, he wrote: 'I have tried to make my ghosts act in a way not inconsistent with the rules of folklore.' . . . He found in the ballad a useful source of supernatural episodes, and was particularly interested in the Danish and Breton versions. It is worthwhile, in the light of his interest in the ballad, to consider how far his own narrative technique was influenced by it. The prosaic, matter-of-fact tone with which natural and supernatural events alike are presented, the build-up of suspense by steps, the overall importance of the action and the subordination of characterization to it, the stiff and conventional nature of the character-drawing, and perhaps above all, the sense of a background of shared traditional beliefs conveying further implications to the audience—all these qualities are present in James's work. We need to know something of the hats o' the birk and the red cock to understand the events of **'The Wife of Usher's Well'**, just as we need to know something of the associations of witches and ash-trees for **'The Ash-Tree'** to work on us as its author intends. It may be that the self-effacing story-teller, the impersonal narrative technique and the extensive use of understatement were characteristics that James took over from the ballad, the supreme form for a tale of terror, as the Romantic poets had realized.

Much of the effect of his stories depends on our recognizing certain archetypal patterns of temptation and vengeance as typifying the workings of the supernatural world. The different allusions in a single story do not derive from any one origin, however, but from a compound of sources both in literature and folklore. It is often difficult to distinguish these elements completely, since ancient beliefs survive in a variety of contexts. In **'"Oh, Whistle, and I'll come to you, My lad"'** the malevolent spirit that appears in response to Parkins' blowing the whistle may be connected with the sailors' superstition about whistling on deck, the prototype of which is at least as old as Homer, and Odysseus' *contretemps* with the bag of winds. Witches, too, traditionally had power over the winds, as Shakespeare showed in *Macbeth*. . . . Thus the very antiquity of a superstition is put forward as some sort of evidence of its validity. The horrible thing that responds to the summons is bodiless, as traditionally spirits often were, so it has to assume the body of bedlinen. (pp. 132-33)

For James, the plot was of paramount importance, and characterization is accordingly reduced to a minimum. In this respect his practice contrasts strikingly with that of Henry James, who felt 'the thickness in the human consciousness' to be essential to the ghost story since it is 'the only thickness we do get'. M. R. James keeps his characters thin to the point of transparency. They are quite deliberately washed free of all subtlety or complexity which might cloud or impede the all-important progress of the plot. In the delineation of character James employed no tricks; there were no new developments, no sudden revelations to catch the audience unprepared, for all the devices of surprise are limited to that element of the story which concerned him most, the plot. Psychology is totally and defiantly excluded from his writings. (pp. 134-35)

[James's central characters are] transparent, anonymous heroes, often distinctively twentieth-century in their practical, sceptical approach to life, are frequently academics of some kind, if their professions are referred to at all. They have a selfless enthusiasm for knowledge (or perhaps a fatal curiosity) which ironically leads them on 'where angels fear to tread', as old Cooper warns Mr Humphreys. From one angle the hero is thus a reflection of his sceptical and detached creator; from another he is the clear window through which the reader perceives the plot unfolding, unfolding far faster than the hero himself realizes. For this hero unknowingly inhabits an animistic world where anything might happen, a world into which only the minor characters are given intuitive glimpses so that they may warn the protagonist of what impends. But the hero's materialism, his doubt, prevents him from giving due weight to the warnings he receives.

Such a warning is usually provided in the early stages of the tale, partly in order to increase the sense of suspense and imminent danger, but also to provide an element of dramatic justice. In everyday terms, the hero is mildly culpable in that he wilfully rejects, because of his scepticism perhaps, the ad-

vice of wiser or older men. In metaphysical terms, his refusal to be warned is symptomatic of a wider rejection of unproven forces and inexplicable powers, and hence is duly revenged by these powers, whether they are conceived as emerging from an outer darkness or an inner id. Nearly all of the stories provide this warning element in some form or another: in **'Canon Alberic's Scrapbook'**, there is not only the excessive anxiety of the sacristan and his daughter, but even the sight of the fearful drawing itself; in **'The Ash-Tree'**, the Bishop of Kilmore warns Sir Richard with his allusion to Irish peasant beliefs. . . . Thus the hero has to some extent wilfully placed himself 'on the edge'. In the rare cases where visitations fall on the totally innocent, as in **'Casting the Runes'**, the victim is provided with helpful friends, as Dunning is with Henry Harrington, whose advice he is only too eager to adopt.

The warnings constitute dramatic justice only, however, and there is inevitably a degree of disproportion in their working. Yet there is nearly always a distinct moment when the hero commits some error, perhaps a form of hubris, by taking a wrong decision, or by choosing against advice to prosecute some scheme or investigation on hand. What impels him to press on at this juncture in the plot may be one of a variety of emotions; it may involve avarice or covetousness, but equally it may be simply a desire to carry through a projected plan perfectly innocent in itself, such as having curtains made up in an eighteenth-century design, opening up an old maze, or building a rose garden. There is no apparent folly in such undertakings and the act of hubris then lies in not heeding warnings or signs. But perhaps the emotion that most frequently lures the unwitting hero on is curiosity, sometimes quite justifiable, and at other times, strange, even perverse. (pp. 136-37)

A more sinister and reprehensible curiosity is the subject of James's stories of black magic, and its disastrous consequences for those who practise it. . . . In the tales based on this theme, a necromancer ventures too far in his dark enquiries, loses control of the spirits he has summoned up, or perhaps tries to evade the final reckoning, and is destroyed by the spirits he has attempted to exploit, or otherwise carried off. James first used this motif in an early tale, **'Lost Hearts'**, but it occurs more frequently in his later work, for example in **'The Residence at Whitminster'**, **'An Evening's Entertainment'** and **'A View from a Hill'**. These three pieces are elaborately and amusingly presented, but their denouements are marred by the excessive violence which often weakens his handling of this theme. (p. 138)

The last group of James's stories, considered thematically, is perhaps the most classical and traditional: these are stories of revenge spirits, familiar from Shakespeare and his contemporaries, as well as from the great Victorians such as Dickens, Wilkie Collins and Le Fanu. As in *Richard III* or *Macbeth* the ghosts of the murdered appear to haunt the murderer and hasten his final downfall. These spirits seem to derive their power from the guilt caused by a forbidden action, such as murder, particularly of the helpless or weak. This classic pattern is used in **'Martin's Close'**, **'The Stalls of Barchester'** (where further spirits come to effect the punishment of the guilty) and **'A Disappearance and an Appearance'**, each time with ingenious elaborations on the basic pattern of murder revenged. (pp. 138-39)

[James's] avowed motive in writing was to tell a good story, and having discovered from his wide reading certain well-established structural patterns, he adopted them and made them the bases on to which he grafted a variety of settings, incidents and characters. Throughout his work, he was strictly regulated by his particular notions as to how the suspense and climax should be achieved, and his practice reveals a close adherence to a limited number of techniques that he had evolved for himself, through his acquaintance with so many examples of the genre. He was perhaps the only writer who deliberately studied the ghost story in order to write it himself, and the resulting pieces exhibit a unique degree of critical control and an exceptional grasp of the force of traditional elements. Without being in any sense experimental or exploratory, his stories demonstrate the power that the classically well-made tale may still exert over a modern reader. (p. 139)

> *Julia Briggs, "No Mere Antiquary: M. R. James,"*
> *in her* Night Visitors: The Rise and Fall of the English
> Ghost Story *(© 1977 by Julia Briggs; reprinted by*
> *permission of Faber and Faber Ltd.), Faber and*
> *Faber, 1977, pp. 124-41.*

JACK SULLIVAN (essay date 1978)

"Count Magnus," from M. R. James's *Ghost Stories of an Antiquary,* is haunted not only by its own ghosts, but by the ghost of Sheridan Le Fanu. Mr. Wraxall, the hero of the tale, dooms himself by peering at a terrifying sarcophagus engraving which should have remained unseen and opening an obscure alchemy volume which should have remained closed. By doing these things, he inadvertently summons the author of the alchemy treatise, the dreaded Count Magnus, from the sarcophagus. To make matter worse, he also summons the count's hooded, tentacled companion. Anyone who has read Le Fanu's "Green Tea" knows that such creatures are easier summoned than eluded. Mr. Wraxall flees across the Continent, but his pursuers are always close behind. They arrive at his remote country house in England before he does and wait for him there. Not surprisingly, he is found dead. At the inquest, seven jurors faint at the sight of the body. The verdict is "visitation of God," but the reader knows that he has been visited by something else.

In both incident and vision, "Count Magnus" is darkened by the shadow of Le Fanu. The basic dynamic of the story, the hunt, is symbolized by the sarcophagus engraving:

> Among trees, was a man running at full speed, with flying hair and outstretched hands. After him followed a strange form; it would be hard to say whether the artist had intended it for a man, and was unable to give the requisite similitude, or whether it was intentionally made as monstrous as it looked. In view of the skill with which the rest of the drawing was done, Mr. Wraxall felt inclined to adopt the latter idea.

Upon reading this insidiously understated passage, the reader who is familiar with Le Fanu immediately knows two things: that the fleeing figure will soon be Mr. Wraxall himself and that the outcome of the pursuit will be fatal for him. Such a reader will not be surprised by the mysterious illogic of the plot, the absence of any moral connection between the hunter and the hunted. Mr. Wraxall is no Gothic villain or Fatal Man; he is a singularly unremarkable, almost anonymous character. He resembles several Le Fanu characters (especially in "Green Tea" and "Schalken the Painter") in that he is a pure victim, having done nothing amiss other than reading the wrong book and looking at the wrong picture. We are told in an ironic

passage that "his besetting fault was clearly that of over-in-quisitiveness, possibly a good fault in a traveler, certainly a fault for which this traveler paid dearly in the end." . . . We are not told why he is any more overly inquisitive than James's other antiquaries, many of whom are never pursued. The narrator sums up the problem near the end of the story: "He is expecting a visit from his pursuers—how or when he knows not—and his constant cry is 'What has he done?' and 'Is there no hope?' Doctors, he knows, would call him mad, policemen would laugh at him. The parson is away. What can he do but lock his door and cry to God?" . . . This fragmented summary of Mr. Wraxall's final entries in his journal suggests that the horror of the situation is in the chasm between action and consequence. In the fictional world of Le Fanu and James, one does not have to be a Faust, a Melmoth, or even a Huckleberry Finn to be damned. The strategy of both writers is the same: to make the reader glance nervously around the room and say, "If this could happen to him, it could happen to me."

The style also owes much to Le Fanu. In an odd sense, "Count Magnus" is more in the Le Fanu manner than Le Fanu. James's use of innuendo and indirection is so rigorous that it hides more than it reveals. Le Fanu creates a balance between uneasy vagueness and grisly clarity. But James tilts the balance in favor of the unseen. Tiny, unsettling flashes of clarity emerge from the obscurity, but usually in an indirect context. We are allowed to see the protruding tentacle of one of the robed pursuers, for example—but only in the engraving, not in the actual pursuit. In the most literal sense, these are nameless horrors.

James also follows Le Fanu's example in his use of narrative distance, again transcending his model. Le Fanu separates himself from his material through the use of elaborate, sometimes awkward prologues and epilogues which filter the stories through a series of editors and narrators. Sometimes, as in "Mr. Justice Harbottle," the network of tales within tales results in a narrative fabric of considerable complexity. In "Count Magnus," the narrator is an anonymous editor who has access to the papers Mr. Wraxall was compiling for a travelogue. The story consists of paraphrases and direct quotations from these papers, a device which gives the narrative a strong aura of authenticity. The transitions from one document to the other, occurring organically within the text, are smooth and unobtrusive. They are also strangely impersonal, as if the teller in no way wishes to commit himself to his tale.

James's reticence probably relates as much to personal temperament as to the aesthetic problem of how to write a proper ghost story. It is commonly accepted, largely because of the work of James and Le Fanu, that indirection, ambiguity, and narrative distance are appropriate techniques for ghostly fiction. (Material horror tales, such as [H. G.] Wells's "The Cone" and Alexander Woollcott's "Moonlight Sonata," are another matter.) Supernatural horror is usually more convincing when suggested or evoked than when explicitly documented. But James's understated subtlety is so obsessive, so paradoxically unrestrained that it feels like an inversion of the hyperbole of Poe or Maturin. I find his late work increasingly ambiguous and puzzling, sometimes to the point of almost total mystification. It is as if James is increasingly unwilling to deal with the implications of his stories. What begins as a way of making supernatural horror more potent becomes a way of repressing or avoiding it. Often he appears to be doing both at once, creating a unique chill and tension. (pp. 69-71)

James's aggressively deflationary attitude toward himself and his material is part of the mystique of his fiction. The stories use every available verbal resource to avoid calling attention to themselves, as if the otherworldly phenomena are creepy enough on their own not to require a loud voice for their exposition.

Moreover, the stories fit thematically into this context, for they often imply a kind of emptiness and restlessness on the part of the characters. It is not "overinquisitiveness" that gets Mr. Wraxall into trouble so much as ennui. James's stories assume a radical breakdown of the work ethic in which the forces of evil take advantage of idleness. Mr. Wraxall is like most of James's heroes in that he is a roving antiquary, a bachelor who is wealthy and cultivated but seems to have no fixed place in society. . . . Though James does not make much out of the idea, the supernatural in his stories has a way of materializing out of a void in people's lives. In **"The Uncommon Prayer Book"** (one of his happiest titles), Mr. Davidson spends a week researching the tombs of Leventhorp House because "his nearest relations were enjoying winter sports abroad and the friends who had been kindly anxious to replace them had an infectious complaint in the house." . . . Even those who have a "settled abode" are curiously unsettled.

There is thus an implicit "Waste Land" ambiance to these stories. The characters are antiquaries, not merely because the past enthralls them, but because the present is a near vacuum. They surround themselves with rarefied paraphernalia from the past—engravings, rare books, altars, tombs, coins, and even such things as doll's houses and ancient whistles—seemingly because they cannot connect with anything in the present. The endless process of collecting and arranging gives the characters an illusory sense of order and stability, illusory because it is precisely this process which evokes the demon or the vampire. With the single exception of Mr. Abney in **"Lost Hearts,"** James's men of leisure are not villainous, merely bored. Their adventures represent a sophisticated version of the old warning that idleness is the devil's workshop.

This is a crucial difference between James and Le Fanu. In Le Fanu, supernatural horror is peculiarly militant—it can emerge anytime it pleases. In James's antiquarian tales, horror is ever-present, but it is not actually threatening or lethal until inadvertently invoked. For Le Fanu's characters, reality is inherently dark and deadly; for James's antiquaries, darkness must be sought out through research and discovery.

It is true that the final discovery is always accidental: James's stories are distinctly different from the more visionary stories of [Algernon] Blackwood and [Arthur] Machen, stories with characters who are not bored, but stifled, and who consciously seek out weirdness and horror. Nevertheless, there is a half-conscious sense in which the antiquary knows he may be heading for trouble but persists in what he is doing. An example is Mr. Parkins in the (again) wonderfully titled **"Oh, Whistle and I'll Come to You, My Lad,"** a man whose bed clothes become possessed. Parkins brings this singularly unpleasant fate on himself by digging up a dreadful whistle and having the poor sense to blow it. He doesn't *have* to blow it. He is given ample warning—certainly more than any of Le Fanu's victims ever get—from a Latin inscription on the whistle: "Quis est iste qui venit?" ("Who is this who is coming?") "Well," says Parkins with a nice simplicity, "The best way to find out is evidently to whistle for him." . . . (pp. 74-6)

[James's] contribution is to demonstrate that the old forms of supernatural evil are still respectable, still viable, if seen through different glasses. It is as if the reader were looking through

the haunted binoculars in **"A View from a Hill,"** watching a familiar landscape transform itself in sinister, ever-changing ways. Vampires, for example, are familiar enough by the twentieth century, but in **"An Episode of Cathedral History"** James creates a vampire posing as a saintly relic in a fifteenth-century cathedral altar-tomb. The church renovators, surprised at finding a full-length coffin in the altar, are more than surprised when the red-eyed inhabitant of the coffin, annoyed at being disturbed, leaps out in their faces. Witches are also commonplace in fiction, but James's witch (who inhabits **"The Ash Tree"**) has some uniquely unsavory traits, among them the ability to breed gigantic spiders. In all cases, James moves from the traditional concept to his own variation with such swiftness and conciseness that the reader almost forgets he is reading a reworked version of old, sometimes trite material.

On rare occasions, James makes manifesto-like statements about the need for linguistic economy. The Ezra Pound of ghost story writers, James once criticized Poe for his "vagueness"; for his lack of toughness and specific detail; for the "unreal" quality of his prose. The charge is similar to Pound's denigration of Yeats's early poems. Actually, Poe and James were attempting very different things. Poe's tales are not ghostly but surreal. They immerse themselves in the irrational, whereas James's tales only flirt with it. The power of James lies in his ability to set up a barrier between the empirical and the supernatural and then gradually knock it down—to move subtly from the real to the unreal and sometimes back again. The distinction between the two is much more solid than in Poe, where nightmare and reality constantly melt into one another. James's stories assume a strong grounding in empirical reality. In this context, his refusal to accept the existence of ghosts until he encounters "conclusive evidence" is consistent with the attitude of his stories. The stories are consciously addressed to skeptical readers, readers with a twentieth (or eighteenth) century frame of reference. In making us momentarily accept what we instinctively disbelieve, the burden falls heavily on the language. The way to reach such a reader, James implies, is through clarity and restraint: the hyperbole and verbal effusiveness of the Gothic writers are to be strictly avoided, as are the "trivial and melodramatic" natural explanations of Lord Lytton and the neo-Gothic Victorians. To James, both overwriting and natural explanations in ghost stories are related forms of cheating. Although James usually avoids issuing these anti-Gothic manifestoes, he indirectly pans the Gothic tradition in the introduction to the *Collected Ghost Stories* by refusing to acknowledge any literary debt to it [see excerpt above]. (pp. 78-9)

In James, even the visionary scenes seem almost prosaic—yet strangely effective for being so. (p. 79)

One exception to James's habitual terseness can be found in the descriptions of some of his settings. If the present is lacking, the past is always alive. Whenever James describes the antiquarian lore which provides the settings for all of his stories, his prose instantly becomes crowded with historical or scholarly detail. (p. 80)

The paradox in James is that this very oldness is invariably a deadly trap. If antiquarian pursuits provide the only contact with life, they also provide an immediate contact with death. Even in tales where there is no dramatic coffin-opening scene, there is always an implicit analogy between digging up an art object and digging up a corpse. In the antiquarian tale, evil is something old, something which should have died. Old books are especially dangerous as talismanic summoners of this evil.

The danger is trickier in James than in similar evil-book tales by James's contemporaries in that neither the nature nor titles of the books necessarily betrays their lethal potential. [Robert W.] Chambers's *The King in Yellow*, Yeats's *Alchemical Rose*, and Lovecraft's *Necronomicon* (all imaginary books) are works with spectacularly demonic histories which the collector in a given story opens at his own risk. But James's collectors are liable to get in trouble by opening almost anything. In **"The Uncommon Prayer Book,"** a remarkable rag-like monstrosity is summoned by a psalm (admittedly a "very savage psalm") in an eighteenth-century prayerbook. For James's antiquaries, even the Holy Scriptures can become a demonic text. Undermining the very thing they celebrate, the plots seem to symbolize, perhaps unconsciously, the futility of the entire antiquarian enterprise.

In a curious way, the style reinforces this contradiction. The most striking aspect of this style, even more striking than its ascetic brevity and clarity, is the gap between tone and story. This gap is especially telling in the more gruesome tales. In **"Wailing Well,"** a small boy is tackled and brought down, much as in a football game, by an entire field of vampires. He is found hanging from a tree with the blood drained from his body, but he later becomes a vampire himself, hiding out with his new friends in a haunted well. (James wrote this cheerful tale for the Eton College troop of Boy Scouts.) More gruesome yet is **"Lost Hearts,"** which tells of an antiquary who, in following an ancient prescription, seeks an "enlightenment of the spiritual faculties" through eating the hearts of young children while they are kept alive. (James is as unsparing of children as Le Fanu.) In the end, the children rise from the grave to wreak a bloody, predictably poetic justice. In both stories, the style is distinguished by a detachment, an urbanity, and a certain amount of Edwardian stuffiness which are entirely at odds with the nastiness of the plots. The narrators seem determined to maintain good manners, even when presenting material they know to be in irredeemably bad taste. Alternating between casualness and stiffness, chattiness and pedantry, James's narrators maintain an almost pathological distance from the horrors they recount. This contradiction between scholarly reticence and fiendish perversity becomes the authenticating mark of the antiquarian ghost story. For James's narrators, sophisticated literary techniques are a form of exorcism in a world filled with hidden menace. To stare the menace in the face is unthinkable; to convert it into a pleasant ghost story is to momentarily banish it. The reader, however, experiences an inversion of this process: the very unwillingness of the narrators to face up to implied horrors makes the stories all the more chilling and convincing. (pp. 80-2)

Another device James uses to disguise or distance his horrors is humor. Humor and horror . . . are often two sides of the same coin. Eliot's famous reference to "the alliance of levity and seriousness (by which the seriousness is intensified)" is useful, for James's humor does not defuse horror so much as intensify it by making it manageable and accessible. Without James's deadpan wit, these stories might seem unreal and "Gothic" to a sophisticated reader. (p. 85)

A more underhanded means that James uses to create distance is deliberate obscurity. Occasionally he moves so far in the direction of mystification that he runs the risk of leaving us completely behind. This device, James's ultimate disguise, occurs with increasing frequency in the later stories. **"The Story of a Disappearance and an Appearance," "Two Doctors," "Mr. Humphreys and His Inheritance"** and **"Rats"**

read more like dark enigmas than finished works of fiction. The narrators often seem aware of the problematic nature of this material, even to the point of sometimes warning the reader in the opening paragraph. The narrator of **"Two Doctors,"** for example, describes his tale as an incomplete *dossier*, "a riddle in which the supernatural appears to play a part. You must see what you can make of it." . . . James ungraciously provides only the outline of a gruesome tale in which one doctor uses an unexplained supernatural device to do in another. The tale is densely packed with fascinating hints: a rifled mausoleum; a reference to Milton ("Millions of spiritual creatures walk the earth/Unseen both when we wake and when we sleep."); a haunted pillow which enfolds the head of the sleeping victim like a strange cloud; a recurring dream of a gigantic moth chrysalis disclosing "a head covered with a smooth pink skin, which breaking as the creature stirred, showed him his own face in a state of death." . . . Since there are so many ways to piece together the information, the tale becomes more ominous with each reading. The initial reading is curiously empty and frustrating, almost as if James demands that we try again.

Furthermore, he takes it for granted that we know his earlier stories which, for all their nonrational connections, are easier to fathom. The structure of **"Two Doctors"**—a sketchy presentation of lawyers' documents—is so fragmented that whatever piecing together we do must be based, at least in part, on patterns from *Ghost Stories of an Antiquary*. "Death By the Visitation of God," the surgeon's verdict, makes little sense unless we see it as a reference to the same verdict in the earlier **"Count Magnus,"** a story which has its own stubborn mysteries, but which is clearly a tale of demonic pursuit. (pp. 87-8)

These sly cross references are another indication of the self-referential character of James's fictional world. His narrative posture, at least in the late tales, assumes an audience of connoisseurs, an elect readership which can extrapolate a plot from a sentence. The demands James makes on his readers are somewhat at odds with his determination to present himself as an aggressively "popular" writer whose sole function is to entertain and amuse in as undemanding a way as possible. This is minor fiction to be sure, but fiction which nevertheless succeeds in creating a universe of its own which can be apprehended only through careful, thoughtful reading. Like so much quality ghostly fiction from this period, James's stories fall into the uniquely alienated category of being too controlled and sophisticated for "horror" fans, yet too lightweight for academics. In his relation to twentieth-century culture, James is very much a ghost himself, or very much like his own Mr. Humphreys in **"Mr. Humphreys and His Inheritance,"** a man lost in a haunted maze.

If James is not a major writer, he nevertheless deserves a larger audience than he currently enjoys. His fictional palate is admittedly restricted, even in comparison with other writers of ghostly tales. His stories have considerable power, but only muffled reverberation. He exhibits little of Henry James's psychological probity, none of Poe's Gothic extravagance, none of Yeats's passion—but he delivers a higher percentage of mystery and terror than any of these. If he is merely a sophisticated "popular" writer, content with manipulating surfaces, those very surfaces are potent and suggestive. (p. 89)

This is the delightful paradox of James's ghost stories: the more of his stories we read and reread, the more we know what to expect, but that very reservoir of expectations infuses each reading with added menace. The sheer pleasure of these gentlemanly horror tales continually rejuvenates itself. (p. 90)

> *Jack Sullivan, "The Antiquarian Ghost Story: Mongatue Rhodes James," in his* Elegant Nightmares: The English Ghost Story from Le Fanu to Blackwood *(copyright © 1978 by Jack Sullivan; reprinted by permission of Ohio University Press, Athens), Ohio University Press, 1978, pp. 69-90.*

ADDITIONAL BIBLIOGRAPHY

Aickman, Robert. Introduction to *The Fourth Fontana Book of Great Ghost Stories,* edited by Robert Aickman, pp. 7-10. New York: Beagle Books, 1967.*

> Critic remarks that "certain of M. R. James's stories contain an element of patronage: one becomes aware as one reads of the *really* great man, the Provost of Eton . . . all too consciously descending a little to divert, but also still further to edify, the company."

Campbell, Ramsey. "Interview: Ramsey Campbell." *Fantasy Newsletter* 3, No. 4 (April 1980): 15-20.

> Cites James as a major influence on Campbell's supernatural fiction.

Cox, J. Randolph. "Ghostly Antiquary: The Stories of Montague Rhodes James." *English Literature in Transition, 1880-1920* 12, No. 4 (1969): 197-211.

> Includes bibliography of critical writings on James.

Lubbock, S. G. *A Memoir of Montague Rhodes James.* Cambridge: Cambridge University Press, 1939, 86 p.

> Casual reminiscence, mentioning the ghost stories only in passing.

"The Ghost Collector." *The New York Times Book Review* (22 July 1905): 483.

> Plot outlines of *Ghost Stories of an Antiquary,* concluding that James's stories "are not quite the real thing in spite of the pains he takes to pile up detail in the setting and leave the horror itself as undefined, shapeless and elusive as may be."

Pfaff, Richard William. *Montague Rhodes James.* London: Scholar Press, 1980, 461 p.

> Definitive biography with a brief survey of the ghost stories and their critical reception.

Stevenson, Lionel. "Purveyors of Myth and Magic." In his *The History of the English Novel,* pp. 111-54. New York: Barnes & Noble, 1967.*

> Judges James to be "probably the greatest master of sheer spine-tingling dread."

Wilson, Edmund. "A Treatise on Tales of Horror." In his *Classics and Commercials,* pp. 172-81. New York: Farrar, Straus and Co., 1950.*

> Makes the passing comment that James "never took any trouble to make his stories seem even halfway plausible, so his hobgoblins are always verging on parody."

Franz Kafka

1883-1924

Austro-Czech novelist, short story writer, and diarist.

Kafka's works form a major literary expression of modern humanity's loss of personal and collective order. Alvin J. Seltzer calls *Der Prozess (The Trial)* "one of the most unrelenting works of chaos created in the first half of this century." The term Kafkaesque has come to be applied to situations of psychological, social, political, and metaphysical instability and confusion, defining a state of nightmare without the assurance of relief. Kafka's characters suffer a process of dehumanization which critics have seen as definitively modern, and his plots are rituals of persecution often considered prophetic of later European dictatorships. In terms of everyday life Kafka's stories portray commonplace frustrations of the western individual faced with the bureaucratic complexities of society. Critics have characterized the world of these stories as hostile and profoundly enigmatic.

Born in Prague into a financially secure Jewish family, Kafka apparently had a difficult childhood and youth. His relationship with his strong-willed father was always an uncomfortable one, as is evidenced by his *Brief an den Vater (Letter to His Father)*, and he found life as a German-Jew among Christian Czechs to be lonely. In addition, his simultaneous aversion and attraction to bourgeois family life posed a lifelong personal conflict which he never satisfactorily resolved. He was employed by a government insurance bureau until 1917, when he discovered he was tubercular. The remaining years of his life were for the most part spent in sanatoriums, where he devoted himself to writing.

Plagued by doubts about his work, Kafka published only a few short stories during his lifetime. Among them were *Die Verwandlung (The Metamorphosis)* and *In Der Strafkolonie (In the Penal Colony)*. These are characteristic Kafkaesque fantasies of psychological and physical brutality which suggest a variety of alternative readings; even contradictory readings are made possible by the obscure nature of the events in these stories. The issue of obscurity is central to criticism of Kafka's fiction. While he is noted for his precise and lucid style, critical difficulties arise when attempting to apply a simple interpretation to narratives founded on philosophical, psychological, and religious mysteries. In particular, the transformation of Gregor Samsa in *The Metamorphosis* from a man into an insect remains for critics one of the prototypical enigmas in modern literature.

Kafka's literary reputation rests largely upon the posthumous publication of his novels *Amerika (America)*, *The Trial*, and *Das Schloss (The Castle)*. All remained unfinished at the author's death. He left instructions to destroy them, but each was later edited and published by his friend Max Brod. Like Kafka's other works, these novels relate surreal, nightmarish stories of alienation; they are located for the most part in a dreamworld which operates according to cryptic and undiscoverable laws. The protagonists of all three novels find themselves on a quest consisting of a series of frustrations without ultimate resolution. The resulting ambiguity leaves these novels open to diverse critical analyses. Few writers have had

their works subjected to as many kinds of interpretation as Kafka: his fiction has been variously described as allegorical, autobiographical, psychoanalytic, Marxist, religious, existentialist, expressionist, and naturalist. Most critics are in agreement, however, concerning the importance of Kafka as a genius who gave literary form to the disorder of the modern world, turning his private nightmares into universal myths.

(See also *TCLC*, Vol. 2.)

PRINCIPAL WORKS

Betrachtung   (short stories)   1913
  [*Contemplation*, 1940]
Das Urteil   (short story)   1913
  [*The Judgment*, 1948]
Die Verwandlung   (short story)   1915
  [*The Metamorphosis*, 1937]
In der Strafkolonie   (short story)   1919
  [*In the Penal Colony*, 1941]
Ein Landarzt   (short stories)   1919
  [*The Country Doctor*, 1940]

Ein Hungerkünstler (short stories) 1924
    [*Hunger-Artist,* 1938]
Der Prozess (novel) 1925
    [*The Trial,* 1935]
Das Schloss (novel) 1926
    [*The Castle,* 1930]
Amerika (novel) 1927
    [*America,* 1938]
Beim Bau der Chinesischen Mauer (short stories) 1931
    [*The Great Wall of China and Other Pieces,* 1933]
Tagebücher, 1910-1923 (diaries) 1951
    [*The Diaries of Franz Kafka,* 1948-49]
Briefe an Milena (letters) 1952
    [*Letters to Milena,* 1953]
Brief an den Vater (letter) 1953
    [*Letter to His Father* published in *Dearest Father: Stories and Other Writings,* 1954]
Brief an Felice und andere Korrespondenz aus der Verlobungszeit (letters) 1967
    [*Letters to Felice,* 1973]
Letters to Friends, Family, and Editors (letters) 1977

FRANZ KAFKA   (essay date 1913)

While I read the proofs of *The Judgment,* I'll write down all the relationships which have become clear to me in the story as far as I now remember them. This is necessary because the story came out of me like a real birth, covered with filth and slime, and only I have the hand that can reach to the body itself and the strength of desire to do so:

The friend is the link between father and son, he is their strongest common bond. Sitting alone at his window, Georg rummages voluptuously in this consciousness of what they have in common, believes he has his father within him, and would be at peace with everything if it were not for a fleeting, sad thoughtfulness. In the course of the story the father, with the strengthened position that the other, lesser things they share in common give him—love, devotion to the mother, loyalty to her memory, the clientele that he (the father) had been the first to acquire for the business—uses the common bond of the friend to set himself up as Georg's antagonist. Georg is left with nothing; the bride, who lives in the story only in relation to the friend, that is, to what father and son have in common, is easily driven away by the father since no marriage has yet taken place, and so she cannot penetrate the circle of blood relationship that is drawn around father and son. What they have in common is built up entirely around the father, Georg can feel it only as something foreign, something that has become independent, that he has never given enough protection, that is exposed to Russian revolutions, and only because he himself has lost everything except his awareness of the father does the judgment, which closes off his father from him completely, have so strong an effect on him.

Georg has the same number of letters as Franz. In Bendemann, "mann" is a strengthening of "Bende" to provide for all the as yet unforeseen possibilities in the story. But Bende has exactly the same number of letters as Kafka, and the vowel *e* occurs in the same places as does the vowel *a* in Kafka. (pp. 278-79)

Franz Kafka, in an entry in his diary on February 11, 1913, in The Diaries of Franz Kafka: 1910-1913, *edited by Max Brod, translated by Joseph Kresh (reprinted by permission of Schocken Books Inc., copyright © 1948, copyright renewed © 1975, by Schocken Books Inc.), Schocken Books, 1948, pp. 278-79.*

EDWIN MUIR   (essay date 1930)

[Kafka's three long stories form] a trilogy corresponding with grotesque differences to the *Divine Comedy.* **The Trial,** which is his "Inferno", deals with a victim of divine justice who does not know even the offence for which he is summoned, and whose judge remains to the end concealed behind an army of subordinate prosecutors and advocates with very questionable credentials. **America,** his "Purgatorio", deals less directly with supernatural powers, and relates the adventures of a German boy who goes to the United States, is exploited by rogues, and falls from one misfortune into another. He is Kafka's most charming character, and somewhat resembles Prince Myshkin in *The Idiot.* He is more credible, however, and there is in his presentation, as Herr Brod has pointed out, a touch of Chaplinesque humor. If it were possible to conceive of a perfectly natural boy performing the office of a Myshkin with something of the air of one of Charlie Chaplin's heroes, one would have some idea of this delicious figure. The third story, **The Castle,** is Kafka's curious version of the "Paradiso", a Paradiso which is never reached. (p. 236)

For this elaborate allegory there are symbols enough to be found. To Herr Brod, for instance, the castle represents divine grace, so mysteriously granted to some, so mysteriously withheld in spite of their intensest efforts from others; while the village is the community, in which one can find one's true place only by deciphering and following the guidance of God. This, indeed, seems to be the meaning of the fable; yet an allegory has not justified itself if it contains nothing more than its interpretation; and the logic of Kafka's narrative is so close that it builds up a whole particularized system of spiritual relations with such an autonomous life of its own that it illumines the symbol rather than is illumined by it. It is almost certain, moreover, that Kafka put together this world without having his eye very much on the symbol; his allegory is not a mere re-creation of conceptions already settled; and the entities he describes seem therefore newly discovered, and as if they had never existed before. They are like additions to the intellectual world.

America stands somewhat apart from the other two books. The action takes place in time, and the characters have, like Dostoievski's, a mixture of the natural and the preternatural which makes their outlines periodically dissolve and combine again in a continuously more mythical pattern. There are scenes in *America* as good, I think, as some of Dostoievski's, and in this respect better: that they are corrected, even at their wildest, by a fantastic sense of comedy. The fault of the book is that its setting shifts uneasily between the metaphysical and the actual, and that while its scene is a fantastic version of the United States, it occasionally crosses to a province which is not of the actual world at all. It is the most uneven of his works.

In the other two stories, however, the action takes place entirely in this other province, and everything, the characters, the setting, the development, is part of a metaphysical or theological construction. These intellectually fashioned worlds have their own laws and their own geography. Time, space, custom, right and|wrong, have undergone a subtle but decisive change; trifles are crucial; subtle questions are more important than general ones; and every motion is judged by a different standard from that of the world. Yet it is difficult to define what principle it is which causes all those modifications, or to establish the laws or the geography of those two worlds; for their validity resides purely in their imaginative justice, and measure in their symmetry. Except for this we have only one clue to lead us through them: Kierkegaard's theory, which influenced Kafka very deeply, of the incommensurability of the divine and the human moral law. With this clue we are led through maze after maze in which everything is changed and yet real; in which every thought is judged by an intuition of the divine law and in which we recognize objects without being able to give them a name; and simply by doing this find that we have acquired a new understanding of the most ordinary and even the most trivial diurnal things. The architecture of those worlds is consummate, and every feature is interesting; for Kafka was a master of construction and of fascinating detail. In realistic novels excessive detail is a defect, for it catalogues things which we could better have imagined; but the author of a purely imaginative world is in the same position as a traveller who has returned from an unknown country, and who interests us more by the faithfulness with which he can describe a native broomstick than by anything else. So Kafka's detail is always fascinating, but it is full of meaning as well; for it is the last working-out of a conception which to be perfect had to inform all its parts. (p. 237)

The main ideas which run through Kafka's work may be condensed into four axioms. The first two are, that compared with the divine law, no matter how unjust it may sometimes appear to us, all human effort, even the highest, is in the wrong; and that always, whatever our minds or our feelings may tell us, the claim of the divine law to unconditional reverence and obedience is absolute. The other two are complementary: that there is a right way of life, and that its discovery depends on one's attitude to powers which are almost unknown. In his two allegories [*The Trial* and *The Castle*], Kafka sets out to discover something about those powers, to prove where he can that they are necessarily right, and to read from his intuition of their nature and aims the only true way of life for his hero. To most modern eyes this must seem from the start a hopeless, indeed a foolish, attempt. The interesting point is that when one surveys it it strikes one as neither Quixotic, nor as lacking in valuable results. It is not only a possible attempt; in Kafka's case it has obviously been a richly fruitful one.

By many of his German admirers Kafka has been called a mystical writer. The adjective seems singularly ill-chosen, however, for the one thing which his heroes never succeed in achieving is a moment of mystical illumination in which their problems might find alleviation. Like Pascal, whom he resembled in many ways—in the daring and solidity of his thought, and in his purgatorial temper—he was a religious genius who, though his faith was unshakable, found little rest in faith; and whose deepest intellectual agonies were caused by the problem of religion itself. He had a singular knowledge of the intricacies of spiritual experience; yet he seems to know them only as possibilities; he remains outside them, as if cut off by an invisible barrier; and his heroes stand in much the same relation to the worlds they traverse as Dante to the worlds in his poem. Sometimes, indeed, his voice has the note of a Calvinist who sees and acknowledges his own reprobation, who accepts the scheme, but is not himself accepted. At those moments his hero seems to be wandering in a vast logical nightmare; the

realization comes to him that he has lost his way, the story becomes like a protracted anxiety-neurosis, and one feels the tension has to snap. Then he always starts anew from something ordinary and concrete, from a sober formulation of the hero's ostensible position, for instance: "It may not be much, but I have a home, a position and real work to do, I have a promised wife who takes her share of my professional duties when I have other business. I'm going to marry her and become a member of the community". Coming where they do in the story, those summaries have always an overwhelming pathos; and in general, indeed, Kafka's pathetic effects are secured simply by defining the hero's situation, or by noting that there is a moderate hope for him. The pathos of moderate hopes, which in spite of their moderation are yet worthy of being clung to, even with desperation; this is a province which Kafka has made his own. Those hopes—and this adds to their pathos—are invariably founded on experience. "Once answer a false ring at your night-bell," the country doctor says in one of the short stories, "and you can never repair the damage." Or again—a passage which Kafka afterwards deleted: "If you have the strength to look at things steadily, without, as it were, blinking your eyes, you can see much; but if you relax only once and shut your eyes, everything fades immediately into obscurity". Or, from *America:* "It is impossible to justify yourself if there is no good-will". These axioms do not sound, it is true, like the utterances of hope; yet in their context they do, for there every practical rule, however limited in application, is a help. Their pathos consists in their inadequacy to the vast journey which still lies before the hero, and in the fact that they are founded on experience which must needs be invalid for the problems which will confront him there. Yet they have some kind of use; their existence helps him, even if when he comes to apply them at some future time they will be found mysteriously lacking.

It is a practical temper, a temper which scrutinizes every hope, and yields to no access of despair, which informs all Kafka's work, informs every manifestation of it. It determined the form into which he threw his two great religious narratives: the form of the allegory. For this was the only one which by its very structure was bound to carry him forward to the end he set in front of him. . . . [Kafka postulated] a hero whose only passion was to discover religious truth; and once that was done the hero's passion was no longer relative, like that for example of the characters in Dostoievski's novels, but absolute, and capable of being logically worked out. The action in his allegorical narratives is a sort of dialectic; one position has to be established before we advance to the next, and every advance takes us in the direction we wish to go. So, I think, for anyone who wants to have a serious imaginative treatment of religion, Kafka is infinitely more satisfying than Dostoievski.

There remains his superb literary art. In the difficult *genre* which he essayed he left nothing partly fashioned, no obstacle which he did not merely overcome, but overcome with apparent ease. Temper, method, style: all are consummate. His diction is of the utmost flexibility and exactitude, and of an inevitable propriety. His conduct of the sentence is masterly. Flowing without being monotonous, his long sentences achieve an endless variety of inflection by two things alone: an exact skill in the disposition of the clauses, and of the words making them up. I can think of hardly any other writer who can secure so much force as Kafka by the placing of a word. Yet in all his works he probably never placed a word unnaturally or even conspicuously. He had, it seems to me, all the intellectual and imaginative as well as the technical endowment of a great writer. (pp. 239-41)

Edwin Muir, "A Note on Franz Kafka," in The Bookman, *New York, Vol. LXXII, No. 3, November, 1930, pp. 235-41.*

RUDOLPH BINION (essay date 1961)

The first generation of Franz Kafka's critics has construed *The Metamorphosis,* like his other enigmatical tales, diversely as a fusion of naturalism and supernaturalism, or of realism and surrealism; or as an allegory, or as a mere psychotic projection. Gregor Samsa's metamorphosis into a bug serves, if supernatural, to magnify his natural anguish or despair; if surrealistic, to illumine the categories of the self, of the absurd, or of nonentity; if allegorical, to figure the reincarnation of Christ, the isolation of the artist, neurotic illness, or alienation at large. If, finally, it expresses literally Kafka's own view of the world, then its significance is autobiographical rather than artistic. (p. 214)

[The] tale does afford full *internal* evidence that Kafka meant Gregor's illness as mental and not physical.

For *The Metamorphosis* is simply a conventional account of a natural occurrence. It is the story of a man who thinks he has become a bug, told as if the content of his delusion were physical reality. The narrator's perspective is equivalent to that of the hero himself, who, like a typical victim of hallucinosis, sees the world accurately in all of its particulars save one. Thus what crawls out of Gregor Samsa's bedroom one morning, naked and drooling, to astound his parents and the chief clerk is not a man-sized bug but Gregor physically intact. Indeed, what other explanation is there for their instantly recognizing him?—or for the charwoman's mere playfulness with him later, or the lodgers' mere amusement?

The best way to grasp what Kafka has done is to imagine him having first invented his hero, then decided to tell his hero's story in accordance with his hero's own outlook. To devise a narrative idiom in accordance with the hero's perspective on reality is common literary practice in our century: Thomas Mann's narrators are as reflective as his heroes, Hemingway's as primitivistic, Camus' as absurd. And neurotic heroes too are common in our time. What is singular about *The Metamorphosis* is only Kafka's use of this narrative technique in the case of a *hallucinated* hero—though here of course the oddity of the effect far exceeds the singularity of the means employed. (p. 215)

[The] narrative respects the manner as well as the content of Gregor's delusion. Following his peculiarly psychotic pattern of awareness it tends to fix unnaturally on single elements of a whole physical complex, ones having special meaning for Gregor, which then become self-sustaining and quasi-absolute: the father's uniform of office, which dominates the father and through him the whole household, or the sound of the lodgers' teeth, which drowns out the other sounds of their eating "as if thereby to apprise Gregor that one needs teeth in order to eat." Also like Gregor's own mind the narrative notes sights and sounds by preference, it notes them in simple perceptive sequence, and it notes them indifferently as it were, in their bare externality, such that when quoted in bits and snatches it even appears naturalistic—especially the dialogue, which it records as if in stenographic transcript. Again like Gregor's own consciousness it prohibits direct evidence against his de-

lusion, such as his being called a lunatic, and registers no contradiction when he sees only kindness in his mother's and sister's removing his furniture, or "foresight and thrift" in his father's having kept a nest egg on the sly.

His delusion is once extended, to include the lodging of an apple in his back—the hallucinatory conversion into a somatic trauma of a psychic one: his shock at his father's bombarding him with apples. The presentation of the scene according to Gregor's mode of perception brings out the affective basis for his shock. The rhythmic pursuit of Gregor by the father, agitated and erect in his uniform, followed by Gregor's slow passage through a double door back into his dark chamber, the father loading his pockets with apples and then discharging them while the mother, giddy, disrobed, "embracing him, in complete union with him—but here Gregor's vision was already failing—her hands behind the father's head, pleaded for Gregor's life"—the scene requires only an instant's elaboration by Gregor to become a fantasy of his own procreation, hostile and violent. Presumably it revives in him a like pseudomemory at the root of his illness. Schizophrenics have fantasies of the sort often enough without the benefit of provocation, so strong in them is the urge to undo their birth and conception. Obedient to this urge Gregor reverts to primary narcissism, simulates embryonic life in the sickroom, and finally curls up and dies. (pp. 217-18)

Kafka may well have been a prepsychotic who elaborated his fantasies into works of art as a defense against converting them into symptoms; but elaborate them he did, and into works of art as close to reality as any literary convention will permit.

Gregor's predicament is, like neurosis, common in our time. It deserves to be shocking; Gregor himself makes it so through his choice of illness, and the narrative follows suit. By dint of entering into his symptomatic perspective the narrative renders his choice of illness plausible at least, if not appealing. Then, by showing how weirdly well the family's treatment of him— not an unconventional treatment at the time—accords with such a perspective, it is able to make certain facts about families evident. This is doubly ironical: because the perspective is a false one, and because Gregor, whose perspective it is, does not himself see the evidence. The narrative technique is ironical also in a philosophical sense. In the end Gregor is, existentially, nothing if not a bug, since others deny him his old identity— "Indeed, how can it be Gregor?" asks the sister—and refuse to accept him under any other.

In sum, Kafka exposes an everyday social and domestic situation as psychologically destructive. Gregor's protest against his job is profoundly human. . . . So too is his revolt against not being loved save as son-provider—"the disgusting circumstances reigning in this house and family," as the chief lodger puts it—profoundly human. He is, however, no extraordinary young man. He lacks the intellectual and moral resources for his revolt to be anything but neurotic. As such it is as fatal to his personality as resignation would have been. It is, however, beneficent to his family—his decline revitalizes them—and so by way of his morbid choice, a free and deliberate one in the end, he acquires tragic dignity. His dilemma from start to finish is a specifically modern one, arising as it does out of conditions of financial insecurity and dehumanized social labor. Through it Kafka points to a vast historical problem, that of mankind's having generated social and domestic institutions destructive of its own humanity. (pp. 219-20)

Rudolph Binion, "What 'The Metamorphosis' Means," in Symposium *(copyright © 1961 by Syr-*

acuse University Press), Vol. XV, No. 3, Fall, 1961, pp. 214-20.

RONALD GRAY (essay date 1962)

[Kafka is not] a writer of horror stories pure and simple. Only a small proportion of his writings portray hideous scenes after the fashion of Edgar Allan Poe, with whom he has some affinity. (A comparison of **The Penal Colony** with *The Pit and the Pendulum* would show Kafka's sober confrontation with the meaning of suffering in stark contrast to the hysterical horror-mongering of Poe's tale.) More often, he conveys a sense of insidious, indefatigable evil sapping silently all the time at the roots of human existence. . . . The oppressive sense that comes from both of them is more a matter of the mind. . . . He does not really belong with Poe at all, but with a poet like Rimbaud who lived his Season in Hell and named it for what it was. (pp. 61-2)

To write, in Kafka's sense, was to be open completely to every impression, not rejecting the worst that might be suggested to him, or the best, but setting it all down faithfully. (p. 63)

There was nothing Kafka admired so much as ordinary everyday happiness. . . . Thus, far from seeing human life as a temporal evil, Kafka envisaged it, under certain circumstances, as a means of realizing holiness here and now. This was consistent with his basic belief in the absolute supremacy of good. (p. 68)

Ronald Gray, "Kafka the Writer," in Kafka: A Collection of Critical Essays, *edited by Ronald Gray (copyright © 1962 by Prentice-Hall, Inc., Englewood Cliffs, New Jersey), Prentice-Hall, 1962, pp. 61-74.*

ELIAS CANETTI (essay date 1969)

I found [**The Letters to Felice**] more gripping and absorbing than any literary work I have read for years past. They belong among those singular memoirs, autobiographies, collections of letters from which Kafka himself drew sustenance. He himself, with reverence his loftiest feature, had no qualms about reading, over and over again, the letters of Kleist, of Flaubert, and of Hebbel. . . . In the face of life's horror—luckily most people notice it only on occasion, but a few whom inner forces appoint to bear witness are always conscious of it—there is only one comfort: its alignment with the horror experienced by previous witnesses. . . .

To call these letters a document would be saying too little, unless one were to apply the same title to the life-testimonies of Pascal, Kierkegaard, and Dostoevski. For my part, I can only say that these letters have penetrated me like an actual life, and that they are now so enigmatic and familiar to me that it seems they have been mental possessions of mine from the moment when I first began to accommodate human beings entirely in my mind, in order to arrive, time and again, at a fresh understanding of them. (p. 4)

The richness of [Kafka's] memory for concrete detail is shown in the amazing sixth letter to Felice, dated October 27, in which he describes their meeting in the most precise terms. Seventy-five days have elapsed since [their first meeting on] the evening of August 13. Of the details of that evening, recorded in his memory, some have more importance than others. Some he notes almost, one might say, with truculence, to show her that

he had missed no detail of her person, that nothing had escaped him. He shows how much he is a Flaubertian writer, from whom nothing is trivial as long as it is right. With a touch of pride he presents the whole picture, doing a twofold honor— to her, because she was worthy to be comprehended, at once, in every detail; but some honor he does also to himself, to his own all-seeing eye.

On the other hand he observes one or another detail because it has significance for him, because it conforms to important traits in his own nature, because it balances out some deficiency of his, or because it astonishes him and brings him, through wonderment, physically closer to her. These are the details to be discussed here, because it is these that shape his image of her during the next seven months. That image persists until he sees her again, and about half of their very ample correspondence consists of letters written during these seven months. (p. 8)

The correspondence developed rapidly, with daily letters coming from Kafka and Felice soon replying at the same rate (only his letters are preserved). It has certain quite astonishing features: for an open-minded reader, the most noticeable is the amount of complaining, on Kafka's part, about his physical states. These complaints begin as early as the second letter, still somewhat veiled: "Oh, the moods I get into, Fräulein Bauer! A hail of nervousness pours down upon me continuously. What I want one minute I don't want the next. When I have reached the top of the stairs, I still don't know the state I shall be in when I enter the apartment. I have to pile up uncertainties within myself before they turn into a little certainty or a letter. . . . My memory is very bad . . . my halfheartedness . . . I remember that I once actually got out of bed to write down what I had thought out for you; but I promptly returned to bed, because—and this is my second failing—I reproached myself for the foolishness of my anxiety." . . .

One can see that what he is describing here is his indecisiveness, and with this his wooing begins. But soon everything is brought into relation to his physical states.

He begins the fifth letter with a reference to his inability to sleep, and he ends it with an account of interruptions in the office where he is writing. From now on, there is hardly a single letter without complaints. At first they are outweighed by interest in Felice. He asks a hundred questions, wants to know everything about her, wishes to be in a position to imagine exactly what goes on in the office where she works and in her home. But that sounds far too general—actually his questions are more concrete. He asks her to tell him when she arrives at her office, what she has had for breakfast, what sort of view she has from her office window, what sort of work she is doing. . . . He will not let any contradiction pass, and he asks for immediate explanations. Of Felice he demands a precision equal to that with which he describes his own states of mind. (pp. 11-12)

[Let] us keep in mind Kafka's deeper intent during the first period of this correspondence: he was establishing a connection, a channel of communication, between her efficiency and health and his own indecisiveness and weakness. Across the distance between Prague and Berlin he wishes to hold fast to her robustness. The weak words that he is permitted to address to her come back from her ten times stronger. He writes to her two or three times a day. He fights—contrary to his assertions about his weakness—tenaciously, even unyieldingly, for her answers. She is—in this one respect—more capricious than he; she does not have the same obsession. But he succeeds in imposing upon her his own obsession: soon enough, she too is writing him a letter a day, sometimes two.

The struggle to obtain this strength which her regular letters bring him does have meaning. It is no empty exchange of letters, no end in itself, no mere self-gratification: it helps his *writing*. Two nights after his first letter to her he writes **"The Judgment,"** at one sitting, during a single night, in ten hours. One might say that with this story his self-assurance as a writer was established. He reads it to his friends, the story's authenticity is beyond doubt, and thereafter he never repudiated it as he did so many other writings. During the following week he writes **"The Stoker,"** and then inside the next two months five more chapters of *Amerika,* making six chapters altogether. During a two-week pause in the writing of the novel, he writes *The Metamorphosis.*

So it is a magnificent period, and not only from our later standpoint; few other periods in Kafka's life can be compared with it. To judge by the results—and how else should one judge a writer's life—Kafka's attitude during the first three months of correspondence with Felice was entirely the right one for him. He was feeling what he needed to feel: security somewhere far off, a source of strength sufficiently distant to leave his sensitivity lucid, not perturbed by too close a contact—a woman who was there for him, who did not expect more from him than his words, a sort of transformer, whose every technical fault he knew and mastered well enough to be able to rectify it at once by letter. (pp. 12-13)

What he writes to her are not unique things which are set down once and for all; he can correct himself in later letters, he can confirm or retract. And even volatility, which with his controlled intelligence he begrudges himself in the single diary entries, because he regards it as being disorderly, is quite possible in the sequence of the letters. But doubtless the chief advantage, as already indicated, is that repetitions, veritable litanies, are possible. If anyone was ever cognizant of the need and function of "litanies," it was Kafka. Among his very pronounced characteristics as a writer, it is this that has most often led to the "religious" misinterpretations of his work. (p. 14)

[Once] the reader has learned to read the litany of complaint as a sort of language into which everything else has been brought for shelter, he realizes that in this medium, a continuously expressive one, highly remarkable statements are being made about Kafka, with a precision and truth granted to few other writers.

The degree of intimacy in these letters baffles imagination: they are more intimate than any complete description of happiness might be. There is no other account of hesitancy to compare with this one; no other self-revelation has such fidelity. For a primitive person this correspondence would be almost unreadable; he would think it a shameless display of psychic impotence: for it is all here—the indecisiveness, the fearfulness, coldness of feeling, detailed description of lovelessness, a helplessness so vast that only excessively exact description makes it believable. Yet it is all so composed as to become, instantaneously, law and knowledge. Somewhat incredulous at first, but with rapidly increasing assurance, one finds that none of it can ever again be forgotten, as if it were written, as in **"In the Penal Colony,"** on one's own skin. There are writers, admittedly only a few, who are so entirely them-selves that any utterance one might presume to make about them must seem barbarous. Franz Kafka was such a writer; accordingly one must adhere as closely as possible to his own utterances, with the risk that one might seem slavish. Certainly one feels diffident as one begins to penetrate the intimacy of these letters. But the letters themselves take one's diffidence away. For, while reading them, one realizes that a story like *The Metamorphosis* is even more intimate than they are; and one comes at last to know what makes it different from all other stories. (pp. 29-30)

Of all writers, Kafka is the greatest expert on power. He experienced it in all its aspects, and he gave shape to this experience. (p. 80)

Here some apology might be due for the naïve use of the word "power." Yet Kafka himself uses it unhesitatingly, in spite of all its ambiguities. The word appears throughout his writings in the most varied contexts. Due to his shunning "big" words, overcharged words, there is not a single "rhetorical" work by him. Accordingly, he will never become less readable; the continuous emptying and refilling of words, a process that induces aging in practically all literature, can never affect him. But he never shuns the words *"Macht"* ("power") and *"mächtig"* ("powerful"); both are among his unavoided, unavoidable words. It would certainly be worth the trouble to trace all the passages where they appear in his writings, diaries, and letters.

It is not, however, only the word, it is also the thing, in all its infinite complexity, that he articulates with unrivaled courage and clarity. For, since he fears power in any form, since the real aim of his life is to withdraw from it, in whatever form it may appear, he detects it, identifies it, names it, and creates figures of it in every instance where others would accept it as being nothing out of the ordinary.

In a note to be found in the volume *Dearest Father,* he renders the animal nature of power, a stupendous cosmic image in eight lines: "I was defenseless confronted with the figure, calmly it sat there at the table, gazing at the table-top. I walked round it in circles, feeling myself throttled by it. And around me there walked a third, feeling throttled by me. Around that third there walked a fourth, feeling throttled by him. And so it went on, right out to the circling of the constellations, and further still. Everything felt the grip at the throat."

The threat, the throttling, spreads from the inmost center, where it originates, a gravitational force of strangulation, which sustains each concentric circle "right out to the circling of the constellations, and further still." The Pythagorean harmony of the spheres has become a sphere-system of violence, with human gravity predominating, each individual representing a separate sphere. (pp. 86-7)

In a letter to Felice he coins the appalling phrase "the terror of standing upright." He interprets a dream of hers that she has told him; the interpretation is such that one can gather the content without much difficulty: "Had you not been lying on the ground among the animals, you would have been unable to see the sky and the stars and wouldn't have been set free. Perhaps you wouldn't have survived the terror of standing upright. I feel much the same; it is a mutual dream that you have dreamed for us both." . . . One must lie down with the beasts in order to be set free, or redeemed *(erlöst).* Standing upright signifies the power of man over beast; but precisely in this most obvious attitude man is exposed, visible, vulnerable. For this power is also guilt, and only on the ground, lying among the animals, can one see the stars, which free one from this terrifying power of man. (p. 88)

Elias Canetti, in his Kafka's Other Trial: The Letters to Felice, *translated by Christopher Middleton (reprinted by permission of Schocken Books, Inc.; translation copyright © 1974 by Schocken Books, Inc; originally published as* Der andere Prozess *(copyright © 1969 by Carl Hanser Verlag), Carl Hanser Verlag, 1969), Schocken Books, 1974, 121 p.*

ALVIN J. SELTZER (essay date 1974)

The world of Franz Kafka is immediately familiar to anyone who has ever had a nightmare. Here are our everyday lives transformed into strange yet recognizable aspects whose reality is so overpowering that we never think to question the outrageous situations in which we suddenly find ourselves. A man turns into a bug and wonders not how such a thing could have happened, but only how he can best maneuver his new body. In a world where probabilities are replaced by possibilities, we are kept too busy adapting to new contexts and assumptions to waste time on useless speculation. If, in our dreams, we find ourselves in a river infested with alligators, we immediately become too preoccupied with getting out alive to consider how we got there in the first place, or just how unreasonable our predicament is. Reasonable or not, our lives are in terrible jeopardy, and we had better concentrate on getting back safely to land. (p. 141)

What seems to me most significant about Kafka is the utter integrity of his vision—his refusal to apologize for it or somehow make it more palatable for the conventional reader. He simply propels us into his world without explanation and shows us what goes on there without comment or interpretation. Whether it resembles our literal reality or not, it contains a psychological reality which enables us to accept it without question. In this completely chaotic atmosphere, our concern must be with survival, not edification. Kafka's novels do have a philosophical dimension, but their power lies elsewhere. It is the intensity of his vision which holds us, the unremitting emotional force with which he keeps us trapped in his reality.

The Trial is surely one of the most unrelenting works of chaos created in the first half of this century, and critics have done it the honor of interpreting it on many levels of significance, including the view that implies it is a rather tame novel dramatizing specific institutions and their effect on the individual. But while the book certainly invites interpretations of a social, political, and religious nature, Kafka seems to have wanted it to evade any facile explanation. It is important that we make no attempt to reduce the unknown in his world to manageable analogies of the known in *our* world. . . . It seems to have been his intention to create a world in which things happen arbitrarily to people whose only fault is in being there at the time. Joseph K. may or may not deserve his fate more than another man, but once we decide that he has been chosen by hostile forces for particular reasons, we have forced a meaning onto his experience that Kafka has taken great care to prevent. As soon as we find causes to justify effects, things start making sense in a reassuring way that dispels the chaotic potential in our lives and stills terror until it is made to submit to our intelligences. Like all our dreams, *The Trial* embodies enough elements from our everyday realities to tempt us to search for meanings as we would during a normal day when the intellect seems adequate to interpreting events. But it is obvious that Kafka has no intention of providing this kind of security for the reader: those passages which seem to explain why K. should

be an appropriate victim have been purposefully deleted to discourage us from viewing his plight as an expressionistic examination of his own repressed guilt. Certainly, the trial itself is a metaphor, but to what extent can we explicate it without falsifying Kafka's vision? (pp. 142-43)

Essentially, *The Trial* is really about one man who did not "make it" upon waking up one morning; in this riskiest moment of the day, he finds his life completely altered by the fact of his arrest. Physically, of course, his situation is little different from that of the day before, and it is this which misleads K. into thinking that he is still living in the same world, predicated on the same laws, values, and assumptions. Therefore, he continues to lead his previously normal life and to regard his strange arrest in the light of everyday reality. As such, it is probably a mistake, possibly a ruse; certainly a problem and inconvenience—but something, in any case, that can be dealt with in a sensible, rational way. From this point on, he continues to fight his case by appealing to authorities, arguing as his own counsel, finding connections in the court, gathering information, hiring and then firing a lawyer, etc.— all reasonable actions to take in such a dilemma. But why, then, are they all ineffective? Why does K. get nowhere in his struggle to defend his innocence? (pp. 143-44)

From the moment K. is placed under arrest, his previously secure world is replaced by one filled with unknowns. Even though his arrest leaves him free to continue his normal life, K.'s life is never the same again because he can never accept his new mysterious condition. Although he insists on his innocence throughout, he never even learns of the charges against him, and so he can never know what is helping him or hurting him in his mad effort to defend himself. In this new context, he never knows who his judges are, what their criteria may be, and what new rules he must follow to impress them favorably. Yet the silence of his opposition drives him into a frenzied activity that is totally gratuitous. . . . He eventually becomes so aggressive in his struggle to reach and identify the higher officials that he seems to be pulling destruction down upon himself; more and more his fight resembles shadowboxing, as his prosecutors retain their silence and anonymity. Their invisibility works increasingly on his imagination, forcing him to become more and more deeply involved as each day fails to bring any new progress. At first annoyed by the mystery of his trial, he is later haunted by it and finally plagued by it, until it becomes the sole concern of his life. He is trapped in a void by his own imagination, tormented by his own intelligence, and defeated by his human nature.

There seems to be no hint in the novel that, beyond the first mere statement of arrest, the court intends to take an active role in bringing K. to trial. Had he accepted the fact of his arrest without question, he might have continued his routine life until his natural death, for there is never any suggestion that the court imposes punishment after its judgments. One remains under the court's power for his whole life, but that need not restrict his movements, alter his life style, or cause him undue concern. But psychologically, of course, such a situation is intolerable, and it is also intellectually untenable. Our minds cannot rest in the face of mystery: they insist on finding the proper causes for effects, resolving contradictions into some form of useful knowledge, and providing faces and features for the unknown. The concept of nothingness is insupportable for an intelligence that needs to presume the validity of logic before it can go to work. (pp. 144-45)

The parable of the doorkeeper seems to reemphasize the ultimate isolation of the man who knocks at the door of the Law, since each door is intended for only one man. But the parable also sums up K.'s situation from the beginning of the novel, as the doorkeeper becomes the spiritual equivalent of the inspector, the lawyer, the painter, and various women such as Leni (who guarded the entrance to the lawyer's rooms). The parallels become more and more striking as the parable progresses, until the court seems to embrace all the institutions that evaluate man; whether personal, political, social, artistic, or theological, all become analogous with and implicit to the court where K. seeks admittance. Yet this story is subject to so many alternative interpretations that K. finally finds it as impossible to cope with as the lawyer's technical advice. It is not surprising when, upon turning to leave the cathedral, he reaches a nadir of confusion, helplessness, and despair as he pathetically discovers that he cannot find his way alone in this darkness. As in the last chapter of Melville's *Confidence-Man*, the darkness becomes an immediate metaphor for man's basic condition in this world. (p. 146)

As soon as he resolves to be cool and logical to the end, K. for the first time becomes his own judge, and from then on, *he* begins to lead his captors, who immediately fall into perfect rhythm with his own footsteps as the three move harmoniously as one "solid front." Yet how are we to interpret this new resignation on K.'s part? Does it make him more or less admirable than he had seemed before? In one sense, we respect his new position of leadership—at last he is no longer a victim, but the instigator of his own judgment. Or is he really more a victim now than he ever was? By accepting and justifying his guilt, he has merged into the very force he had been fighting and finally becomes indistinguishable from the Court itself. Furthermore, his intention to keep his intelligence calm and analytical to the end would suggest that he has still not recognized its uselessness in trying to clarify a situation it cannot comprehend. (pp. 147-48)

[The] ending seems hopelessly ambiguous, but K.'s sudden change of heart is quite clear. Suddenly all his old doubt returns to torment him—although this time he challenges the supremacy of logic, which cannot withstand a man who wants to go on living but must submit to a higher authority of human instinct and will that ultimately holds life above reason. Unreasonable living is preferable to reasonable dying—and what is reason anyway but an arbitrary way of looking at things which are, from all accounts, invisible to begin with? What proof had he, after all, of the Court, of the Judge, of all those presences and forces which preyed upon his mind, yet had, perhaps, no real existence outside of that mind? Since the priest has denied the Court's interest in K. ("The Court wants nothing from you. It receives you when you come and it dismisses you when you go"), he might really have doomed himself to this wretched death by failing to acknowledge the total absence of all authority higher than himself. Instead he had created laws to fill the vacuum and had become so entangled in them that they ended by controlling his life and death. (p. 149)

If we learn nothing else from K.'s struggle, we are at least forced to recognize the futility of trying to work with a world that simply will not relate to our rational faculties. Things *happen* regardless of whether we can account for them, and we cannot expect to bargain our way to a more comfortable position, a more tolerable destiny. Our freedom, if real, *is* limited. Life finally *is* a nightmare, because there are inscrutable forces beyond our control that no amount of psychological health can protect us from. Annihilation is not a choice but a fact; the only choice left to us is whether to accept it or continue

to struggle against it. We die either way, but the implication is that K. might have died with a little more dignity than a dog.

K.'s death ultimately is as inexplicable as his arrest, for the reader, like K., must finally accept what he cannot understand. It seems fitting, though, that the book ends as inconclusively as K.'s life, because our resultant discomfort is really the most suitable response to Kafka's vision of reality. (pp. 150-51)

Alvin J. Seltzer, "Waking into Nightmare: Dream as Reality in Kafka's 'The Trial'," in his Chaos in the Novel, the Novel in Chaos *(reprinted by permission of Schocken Books Inc.; copyright © 1974 by Schocken Books Inc.), Schocken Books, 1974, pp. 141-52.*

ERICH HELLER (essay date 1974)

[In **"The Judgement"**] Georg Bendemann, son of an aging and recently widowed businessman, is writing a letter to a bachelor friend who years before had left their common home town to settle in Russia. Considerations of exceptional delicacy have hitherto prevented Georg from telling his friend that a month earlier he had become engaged to a girl called Frieda Brandenfeld. Now, at last, urged by his fiancée who is disturbed by Georg's withholding the fact of their engagement from his friend, he does give him the news, inviting him at the same time to their wedding. Then he walks across the corridor to his father's room, apparently to seek his approval of the letter containing the important announcement. It is now that the transition takes place. What up to this point was an ordinary and perfectly comprehensible situation suddenly assumes the character of a *danse macabre*, a sinister *pas de deux* of father and son; this "going over" is accomplished so effortlessly that in retrospect the reader may believe he had detected evil specters lurking in the interstices between the words of the story's first sentence, short and serene: "It was a Sunday morning in the very height of spring"; or that the twice-mentioned river of the first paragraphs and the bridge had struck him right away as ominous signals of destiny. For the story ends with Georg's carrying out the death sentence passed upon him by his father: he swings himself over the railings of the bridge and lets himself drop into the water. (pp. 8-9)

[The] father is vigorously determined to punish his son. For what? Above all, it would seem, for his decision to get married from disreputable motives: "'Because she lifted up her skirts,' his father began to flute, 'because she lifted her skirts like this, the nasty creature,' and mimicking her he lifted his shirt . . . , 'and in order to make free with her undisturbed you have disgraced your mother's memory, betrayed your friend, and stuck your father into bed so that he can't move. But he can move, can't he?'" Never before or after, it seems, has Freud ruled so supremely over a piece of literature. (pp. 10-11)

With Kafka, the offense, far from being an adequate motivation of the punishment, is often not at all recognizable. What, in the first chapter of *Amerika*, is the guilt of the Stoker? And if he is not guilty, it is more likely, to judge by the surrounding circumstances and the removal from the scene of his enthusiastic advocate, young Karl Rossmann, that "justice" will not be done. Or later in the novel, how almost imperceptible is the offense for which Karl is sent into the American wilderness by his uncle! Or what is the crime of Joseph K. in *The Trial*? Or the wrongdoing, in *The Castle*, for which K. is tormented by an endless sequence of promises and rejections (not to mention the other victims of the Castle's capriciously cruel dispensations)? (p. 17)

["In the Penal Colony"] contains the starkest exposition, indeed the "guiding principle," of the terrible incongruity between any possible guilt and a horrible penalty, and this despite the rare fact that here the offense is clearly stated: the soldier who is to die under torture has, by falling asleep, involuntarily disobeyed an order. . . . (p. 18)

But what exactly *is* the Law upon which the judgment is founded? And who—in the name of whom?—is the law giver? Is it, in the penal colony, the commandant, who is already "soldier, judge, mechanic, chemist, and draftsman," a parody of God, a god, however, unable to prevent the final destruction of his machine? Or is He, in **"The Metamorphosis,"** represented by the simple vitality that "in spite of all the sorrow of recent times" and all the insect trouble suffered by the family, allows Gregor Samsa's sister in the end to blossom into an attractive young woman ready to find a husband and bring forth healthy children? Or, in **"The Judgment,"** is it the father, pronouncing the sentence of death upon his "devilish" son? Or, in *Amerika,* is it the incongruously offended uncle who punishes his nephew? Or, in *The Trial* and *The Castle,* is it the unapproachable and invisible authority that condemns, torments, or executes its appointed culprits? And why, if it is a matter of *universal* guilt, does it fall to the lot of an undistinguished son to play the role of the sacrificial lamb? Why is it an ordinary commercial traveler, or an all but anonymous land surveyor, who must carry upon his shoulders the sins of the world?

There is no answer to any of these questions; indeed, there is no *answerable* question to be found anywhere in the works of Kafka. For it is in the nature of his questions that they allow of no answers: in the unfinished story **"Investigations of a Dog,"** the "investigator" says of himself that, like every other dog, he has the impulse to question as well as the simultaneous impulse "not to answer." It is even true to say that Kafka's questions are not only unanswerable but also unquestionable. This is one of the secrets of his art: he wields the magic by which to remove the question mark from the questionable. Where he succeeds, the questions have been transformed into an indisputable givenness, something as affirmative as trees or mountains or oceans. . . . (pp. 19-20)

The Law without a lawgiver, original sin without a god to sin against: this is the essence of the negative theology that pervades Kafka's stories and novels. The protagonists are sinful almost *because* there is no God to disobey, guilty almost *because* there is no Sinai, for although there is no God and no lawgiver, their souls are cast in the mold in which the fear of God and obedience to His laws is inscribed. Sin and guilt more often than not appear to lie not in any *doing,* but in *being,* in being a separate individual, or, to use Schopenhauer's terms, in the *principium individuationis* itself—an unprincipled *principium individuationis,* as it were, for it is only individual sons and not the individual fathers and friends, only the Gregor Samsas and not the parents, sisters, or lodgers, only the K.'s and not the other citizens in their towns or villages who are fatally affected by the principle's machinations. (p. 22)

[The] first and fundamental design of **"The Judgment"** or **"The Metamorphosis"** or **"In the Penal Colony"** is unequivocally Schopenhauerian: to be an individual is a culpable encroachment upon the peace of nonbeing, or at least of not being an individual. (p. 24)

Where deliverance from the *principium individuationis* is near, and be it in the most cruel circumstances, there often appears in Kafka's works the reflection of a transcendent light on the faces of those about to be freed from their guilty individual state. While Schopenhauer is fond of thus interpreting the peace that shows in the features of the dead, with Kafka it sometimes seems that the lifting of the curse of individuation is welcomed ecstatically, that the victim himself rejoices in the fulfillment of the Law exacting the supreme penalty for the sin against the original all-oneness. It is as if many a terrible dying described by Kafka were perverse love-deaths, partaking of the raptures of a final reunion after the sorrows of a long deprivation. (p. 25)

[In] *The Trial,* where Joseph K. suffers a death of unrelieved shame, all those who stand accused and in all probability will be sentenced to death, are beautiful, as the Lawyer explains, meaning that they have *become* beautiful "in the process" of their having been drawn into the net of the Law (process = *Prozess* = trial); and the beauty they have thus acquired seems to mark a stage on the journey beyond the principle of individuation, inviting as it does the self-abandonment of the eruptive, impersonal "unindividualized" sexual relations between Joseph K. and Leni, the Lawyer's maid. And *Amerika*—Kafka's first attempted novel and one which, to judge by the fragment that exists, would certainly not have resisted a happy ending—was meant to issue in the great utopia of "The Nature Theatre of Oklahoma," where "everyone is welcome" to take part in the vast all-embracing play of the world. In the "almost limitless" spaces of this theater, the self, having suffered the pains of division and isolation, would be most joyously and "as if by some celestial witchery" received again into the unity from which it had been separated. (p. 26)

Although the guilt that lies in being an individual is, with Kafka, the *ultimate* justification of all punishments, it would be naïve to believe that this almost theological sin explains all his obscurities. At best it illumines the innermost chamber of the edifice, but the surrounding labyrinth remains. In its twisted architecture there still lurks, among others, the question: what is the specific guilt of the culprits, and what is the specific law in the name of which they are sentenced? Despite one's awareness of the ultimate sin, it is impossible to suppress such questions. They are inevitable; and if the inevitable is also the legitimate, they are legitimate questions, even if Kafka's art is such that it deprives them of their self-confidence; for the labyrinth not only houses the questions but is filled with those mysteriously transparent vapors of senselessness that all but choke them. Still, the questions survive simply because the stories are stories and are therefore about individuals who live among other individuals, differing from them by their particular destinies and guilts, and what is true of **"The Judgment,"** **"The Metamorphosis,"** *The Trial,* and *The Castle* is certainly true in a much more complicated way of **"In the Penal Colony."** The complication is not that the guilt, although clearly defined, is so horribly outdistanced by the punishment that it amounts to no definable guilt whatever; it lies rather in the insinuation that the law behind the lethal torture of the condemned is at least as justified as the leniency of the more "humane" new commandant; that the old order, confusingly allied to the newest technology and automation—"Up till now a few things [in the machine] still had to be set by hand, but from this moment it works all by itself"—evokes a faith that the faithful believe is worth dying for, while the convictions of the liberal visitor are not even strong enough for him to help soldier and condemned man to escape from the abominable penal colony. "It's always a ticklish matter to intervene decisively in other people's affairs,'' he says to himself. (pp. 37-8)

Kafka's imagination, indissolubly wedded to his intelligence, was helplessly attracted by the Law without being able to form a clear idea of it, such as would be the condition of uninhibited moral judgments, the condition too of any sensible adminstration of justice beyond—or before—the acknowledgment of that universal guilt which arises from individuation itself. As the nature of the light reveals itself to the moth that circles it with insatiable curiosity only by burning the moth in the end, so for Kafka the sole proof of the Law was in the indisputable punishment it exacted from him. Therefore he was unable to sustain any particular indictments against anyone except himself—and even not quite against himself. The **"Letter to His Father"** comes closest to being an accusation of another, but even this document is imbued with a sense of guilt that is in "being" rather than in "doing," in an unfathomable dispensation of nature rather than in misdeeds. At the end of the **"Letter,"** or almost at the end, as if he was writing a drama, he allows his father to speak in his own defense, indeed to counterattack, and this in so subtly intelligent a manner as would have exceeded the father's intellectual gifts: "At first," says the father, speaking a text invented by the son, "you repudiate . . . all guilt and responsibility; in this our methods are the same. But whereas I then attribute the sole guilt to you as frankly as I mean it"—for the father believes that he *does* know the Law, and with unbroken spontaneity distinguishes what he takes to be right from wrong—"you want to be 'overly clever' and 'overly affectionate' at the same time and acquit me of all guilt." Yet it only *seems* so: in truth, it is the son's most clever ruse. What can be read between the lines of his letter, despite all the niceties about "character and nature and helplessness," is that actually "I [the father] have been the aggressor while everything you were up to was self-defense." By this most sophisticated method—and this the playwright son writes into the part of his father—the son has shown not only that he is himself without guilt but that, on the contrary, all the guilt is with the father. Nonetheless the son, the innocent, is willing to forgive and most magnanimously suggests that in the final resolve the father, too, is without guilt. (pp. 38-9)

The part of the father is endowed with at least as much inner conviction as is the part that the son delivers in his own person. It is the art of a truly dramatic writer that has gone into this letter: whoever it is that holds the stage at any particular moment is in the right. And the final truth—if this situation permits of such—is contained in the words with which the son begins his last reply to the father: "My answer to this is that, after all, this whole rejoinder . . . does not come from you, but from me"; the son, that is, being in control of the whole epistolary scene, might have suppressed this ultimate touch of moral inconclusiveness. But it only seems that he had this choice. The truth is that he couldn't help writing as he did. For this fanatically honest writer—always ready to suspect himself of dishonesty (and only very rarely right in doing so, unless we conclude that his kind of self-consciousness renders "honesty" impossible)—was quite unable to reverse **"The Judgment"** and wholly to condemn his father, as unable as he was unequivocally to define guilt in **"The Judgment"** and **"The Metamorphosis"**; or to take sides in the struggle between cruel orthodoxy and vague liberality in the **"Penal Colony"**; or even to hint at an unrestrained disapproval of the dissolute guardians of the Law in *The Trial;* or to arbitrate between the claims of the Hunger Artist and those of the young panther;

or even, in his own case, to make up his mind whether he should marry or else remain an ascetically dedicated bachelor writer. . . . (pp. 40-1)

In the case of Kafka, and *The Trial* in particular, the compulsion to interpret is at its most compelling, and is as great as the compulsion to continue reading once one has begun: the urgencies are identical. For Kafka's style—simple, lucid, and "real" in the sense of never leaving any doubt concerning the reality of that which is narrated, described, or meditated—does yet narrate, describe, or meditate the shockingly unbelievable. While it is in the nature of Biblical parables to *show* meaning, through concrete images, to those who might be unable to comprehend meaning presented in the abstract, Kafka's parables seem to insinuate the meaninglessness through nonetheless irrefutably real and therefore suggestively meaningful configurations. (p. 72)

It has been said that *The Castle* is a religious allegory, a kind of modern *Pilgrim's Progress;* that the unattainable building is the abode of divine law and divine grace. This would seem to be a misapprehension reflecting a profound religious confusion, a loss of all sureness of religious discrimination. Where there is a spiritual famine, *anything* that is of the spirit may taste like bread from Heaven, and minds imbued with psychology and "comparative religion" may find the difference negligible between Prometheus, clamped to the rock, and the martyrdom of a Christian saint; between an ancient curse and the grace that makes a new man.

The Castle is as much a religious allegory as a photographic likeness of the devil in person could be said to be an allegory of Evil. Every allegory has an opening into the rarefied air of abstractions and is furnished with signposts pointing to an ideal concept beyond. But *The Castle* is a terminus of soul and mind, a *non plus ultra* of existence. In an allegory the author plays a kind of guessing game with his reader, if he does not actually provide the answers himself; but there is no key to *The Castle.* It is true that its reality does not precisely correspond to what is commonly understood in the "positive" world as real, namely, neutral sense perceptions of objects and, neatly separated from them, feelings. . . . In Kafka's novels there is no such division between the external sphere and the domain of inwardness, and therefore no such reality. There is only the tragic mythology of the absolutely incongruous relationship between the two worlds. (pp. 102-03)

Erich Heller, in his Franz Kafka, *edited by Frank Kermode (copyright © 1974 by Erich Heller; reprinted by permission of Viking Penguin Inc.), Viking Penguin, 1974, 140 p.*

CHRISTINE W. SIZEMORE (essay date 1977)

One of the most fascinating and yet discomforting aspects of Franz Kafka's fiction lies in its attack on the reader's sense of reality. Kafka's work reflects simultaneously a realistic and yet a dreamlike situation. At first the reader thinks he recognizes Kafka's world as that of his own. The realistic detail, the straightforward logic, the muted tone, the ordinary characters convince the reader that the fictive world is close to his own experience. No sooner does the reader acknowledge the reality of Kafka's world, however, than the events change. The new events contradict the reader's understanding of reality, and yet, since they are presented with the same precise detail, the same matter-of-fact tone, and the same unexcited characters as before, the reader cannot quite dismiss these new events as mere dreams or symbols. An uncomfortable dichotomy arises, producing a growing uneasiness in the reader. . . . The uneasiness created by these two conflicting viewpoints increases as Kafka's works progress. That which cannot happen does happen. The reader hopes to resolve the dichotomy by finding some clue that the seemingly unreal events are purely imaginative, but that clue never comes. The two irreconcilable interpretations of reality remain. (pp. 380-81)

The reader first notices that most of the details of Kafka's world are too close to his own to be able to call Kafka's world a mere fantasy. Kafka's style and tone are clearly that of realism, but nonetheless, some of the events seem impossible. The reader next tries to integrate these seemingly impossible incidents with his own concept of reality by attempting an explanation: those incidents are part of a dream or the narrator is hallucinating. Kafka often seems to invite this hypothesis because sometimes his works begin with a protagonist just awakening from sleep [for instance, in *The Trial* and "Metamorphosis"], but the disturbing events are soon proved to be no dream. They seem dreamlike, to be sure, but there is no doubt that they happen. The reader who nonetheless tries to rationalize away these disturbing events will find no criteria in Kafka's text to separate them from the familiar events and details. Kafka's reality cannot be assimilated into the reader's. (p. 382)

[Anxiety] is produced by almost all of Kafka's fiction, but it is perhaps most easily demonstrated by one of Kafka's simpler works, a narrative excerpt from his diary dated January 19, 1915. This period is that of Kafka's mature work since by this time he had completed several of his short stories and was writing *The Trial*. Thus this excerpt provides a typical, although short, illustration of Kafka's method and the anxiety it generates in the reader. Kafka begins his entry dated January 19, 1915, with a comment that his factory job interferes with his writing. He continues with some speculations about Sweden's relationship with the Triple Entente. The reader is initially grounded in the reality of autobiographical and historical events. The next paragraph begins the narrative. The even tone and the first person point of view do not change. The only differences are a shift into the past tense and an increase in detail:

> I had agreed to go picnicking Sunday with two friends, but quite unexpectedly slept past the hour when we were to meet. My friends, who knew how punctual I ordinarily am, were surprised, came to the house where I lived, waited outside awhile, then came upstairs and knocked on my door. I was very startled, jumped out of bed and thought only of getting ready as soon as I could.

The reader is curious as to why the speaker has overslept and is prepared by the detail and suspense for an anecdote or story, but the account is so realistic that the reader still does not know whether this event is autobiographical or fictional. In either case the events and details conform to the reader's sense of reality and there is no dissonance.

The suspense builds as the friends greet the narrator and discover a new aspect of the narrator's experience:

> When I emerged fully dressed from my room, my friends fell back in manifest alarm. "What's that behind your head?" they cried. Since my awakening I had felt something preventing me from bending back my head, and I now groped

for it with my hand. My friends, who had grown somewhat calmer, had just shouted "Be careful, don't hurt yourself!" when my hand closed behind my head on the hilt of a sword. My friends came closer, examined me, led me back to the mirror in my room and stripped me to the waist. A large, ancient knight's sword with a cross-shaped handle was buried to the hilt in my back, but the blade had been driven with such incredible precision between my skin and flesh that it had caused no injury.

Suddenly a new and conflicting cognitive element is introduced into the narrative. (pp. 382-83)

The reader next tries to assimilate the new cognitive element by presuming that the narrator is hallucinating. This solution is the familiar one of Poe's "Tell-Tale Heart" in which the reader integrates his knowledge that a dead man's heart cannot beat with the sounds heard by the "I" narrator by assuming that the narrator hears the sounds only in his mind. In the Kafka story, however, two narrative elements undermine this possibility. First of all, there is no indication by either style or tone that the narrator is hallucinating. . . .

Another element in the story that tends to negate the possibility of the narrator's hallucinating is the other characters' recognition of the sword. They point it out to the narrator. Not until he reaches around his back and feels the sword and then is shown it in the mirror is the narrator even aware of its existence. Furthermore, although the friends are initially alarmed, they soon calm down and do not treat the situation as extraordinary. When the narrator first grasps the sword, they merely warn him, "Be careful, don't hurt yourself." This admonition particularly disturbs the reader because it establishes the reality of the sword, but it contradicts the reader's experience by refusing to recognize the event as unusual. (p. 384)

The reader's uneasiness grows because the logical methods by which he might integrate Kafka's world and his own experience have been undermined. When he finds himself unable to integrate the two worlds, the reader tries to reject Kafka's world entirely, but the reader is usually already too involved in the story and too convinced by its details to dismiss it as mere fantasy. The reader's anxiety is increasing by this point, and although it would be comforting to be able to resolve the dissonance of the two realities by denying Kafka's, it is impossible for the careful reader.

In his narrative of the sword, Kafka intensifies the reality of his world just as the reader seeks to deny it. By his concrete description and precise detail, Kafka gives the sword an unchallengeable visual reality: "a large ancient knight's sword with a cross-shaped handle." If the description of the sword had been hazy, the reader perhaps could have forgotten the character's acceptance of it as real, but now not only do the characters acknowledge the sword's reality, but the reader is also given a vivid mental picture of the sword. Moreover, not only is the sword minutely described, but it is also given an exact location, buried up to the hilt just between the skin and the flesh. This second statement increases the reader's uneasiness still more. The specificity of detail reinforces the reality of the sword and at the same time forces the reader to focus his attention so carefully that he is given no chance to question further the detail's reality. (p. 385)

Kafka does not yet effect a confrontation of the two realities. . . . He rather smothers the reader's incipient questions with a continuing accumulation of detail. From a precise description of the sword, the narrative moves to a detailed account of the sword's removal. . . . No questions are left unanswered in the passage except the one large question that the events contradict the reader's experience.

All the literary techniques of the passage, however, work to suppress that question. The narrator's credibility is reinforced as he briefly echoes the reader's doubt as to the existence of the sword without a wound, but the doubt is removed as the friends calmly "assure" the narrator of the sword's existence and proceed to remove it. The specific details of the action, the friends' need to stand on chairs, the slowness of the sword's extrication, and the logical progression of these details emphasize the reality of the experience. (p. 386)

In this Kafka narrative all the fictional elements work together to establish a believable world; the reader is left alone with his protest that it is not believable because it does not conform to the reader's experience.

The story ends with a metaphysical question, and there is no further entry for January 19. The narrator asks:

> Who tolerates this gadding about of ancient knights in dreams, irresponsibly brandishing their swords, stabbing innocent sleepers who are saved from injury only because the weapons in all likelihood glance off living bodies, and also because there are faithful friends knocking at the door prepared to come to their assistance?

Since this question provides some distance from the immediate events of the sword's discovery and its removal, the reader looks anxiously for a clue which will allow him to resolve the two conflicting realities.

The narrator's comment answers two of the reader's questions, but hardly in a satisfying way. The narrator first suggests that the answer to the question of how he was stabbed is that a knight from a dream thrust the sword into his back. The reader is astonished by the word "dream." He hopes briefly that he can resolve his anxiety by returning to his original assumption that the narrator is dreaming, but this hope is soon destroyed. The reader approaches a point of horror as he realizes that the narrator is calmly implying that the events of dreams continue into the waking state. (pp. 386-87)

The narrator's second suggestion answers the question of why the sword causes no wound, but the narrator does not seem to recall the events accurately. He says that he was "only saved from injury because the weapons in all likelihood glance off living bodies." . . . The sword penetrated the narrator's body, but it did not wound him, make him bleed, or even cause pain. There are no satisfying explanations. The narrator's implications only serve to bring the two conflicting realities to a confrontation.

The reader is left in a state of anxiety. . . . The reader has tried to integrate Kafka's world with his own, but that is not possible. Kafka's fiction is too close to the reader's world to be dismissed as fantasy, but there is no way to assimilate the disturbing events. Kafka's techniques of realism and vivid details create a compelling world, but once the reader is within it, he finds that it is the world of horror. Alternatively, to resolve the dissonance by embracing Kafka's world and denying one's own previous experience with reality is to admit madness and descend into a world of horror. In spite of the pressures to resolve dissonance and the intense anxiety accom-

panying dissonance, the reader is unable to escape it. The two realities cannot be merged. To renounce one's own is madness, but it is impossible to give up Kafka's. The literary experience of reading Kafka is thus the experience of anxiety, or for those who choose to resolve the dissonance in favor of Kafka, the experience of horror. (pp. 387-88)

> *Christine W. Sizemore, "Anxiety in Kafka: A Function of Cognitive Dissonance," in* Journal of Modern Literature *(© Temple University 1978), Vol. 6, No. 3, September, 1977, pp. 380-88.*

ROBERT T. LEVINE (essay date 1977)

Kafka, in one diary entry, refers to "my talent for portraying my dreamlike inner life." Indeed, he had the energy and the courage to hold on to thoughts from the unconscious so that he might memorably depict what we others allow to recede into the comfortable darkness of oblivion. His comments about writing **"The Judgment"** [**"Das Urteil"**] imply that it contains much dreamlike inner life: he records that the story emerged from him "like a real birth, covered with filth and slime," and that as he composed it he had "thoughts about Freud." But most significant, of course, is the texture of the story itself. Upon close reading, we find the sort of irrationality customarily found in dreams, an irrationality that is imposed on verboten unconscious thoughts by the censorship of the preconscious to make them less threatening to the ego. (p. 164)

From the story's first paragraph, we learn that Georg and his father reside in a "ramshackle" house. . . . But as the story unfolds, we learn that the family business is unbelievably successful. Georg thinks to himself that his father "is still a giant of a man." . . . But he treats his father like an infant, undressing the father and carrying the father to bed in his arms. . . . And then there is the matter of the friend in St. Petersburg. At first, the father denies that such a friend exists: "You have no friend in St. Petersburg." . . . But later on, the father claims that not only does he know the friend well . . . but he has maintained a steady correspondence with the friend. . . . (pp. 164-65)

As startling as the story's contradictions are its non sequiturs. For example, in the exchange between Georg and his fiancée concerning Georg's friend, Georg explains to her that he has not told the friend of their engagement. She asks: "But may he not hear about our wedding in some other fashion!" Georg answers: "I can't prevent that, of course, but it's unlikely considering the way he lives." And then comes Frieda's illogical retort: "Since your friends are like that, Georg, you shouldn't ever have got engaged at all." . . . (p. 165)

I wish to focus on other absurdities in **"The Judgment."** We are told that, because he doesn't want to make his friend feel like a failure, Georg "could not send him any real news." . . . Now this extreme statement—"*any* real news"—is typical of the hyperbolic, hysterical, paranoic aspect of the story. Another ridiculously extreme statement is that Georg "had not entered for months" . . . his father's room. The explanation for Georg's absence is pathetic in its attempted reasonableness: "There was in fact no need for him to enter it, since he saw his father daily at business and they took their midday meal together at an eating house." . . . We must be alert to *superficial* rationality. Freud has discussed the process in which unconscious material, having been distorted by the censoring preconscious, undergoes a second censorship because the material is still too threatening to the ego. In this second censoring process, which Freud terms "secondary revision," the unconscious material acquires a superficial logic that tames heretofore threatening elements: the secondary revision makes these elements less conspicuous by minimizing their absurdity. Thus the secondary revision, in Freud's words, "fills up the gaps in the dream-structure with shreds and patches." . . . [When] we carefully examine **"The Judgment,"** when we apprehend its dreamlike structure, then the feeble logic of secondary revision quickly breaks down. (p. 166)

Undeniably, **"The Judgment"** is riddled with illogic. Whatever veneer of logic may be present in the opening scene as Georg contemplates his situation, dissipates once Georg enters his father's room. We might even contend that the story shows an awareness of its irrationality. In the first paragraph, we are told that Georg is behaving "in a slow and *dreamy* [or languorous] fashion" . . . ; while near the end of the story, the father says to Georg, "I suppose you wanted to say that sooner. *Now it does not fit* any more." . . . And, in fact, the whole story proceeds like a dream, where thoughts, speeches, and actions do not quite fit. Let us then apply to **"The Judgment"** a critical method that can deal with the story's irrational, dreamlike structure. Such a method is Freud's dream-analysis.

Freud has emphasized that dreams contain the disguised thoughts of the unconscious mind. The concept of disguise is crucial to understanding dreams. The unconscious cannot express itself undisguised because its thoughts, unacceptable to the ego, will be rejected unless they can pass into the dream-world unnoticed. In **"The Judgment,"** the principal disguise involves the friend, who really represents Georg. Whereas numerous critics have argued that the friend represents some part of Georg's personality, I suggest a complete identification of the friend with Georg. Here, I am following Freud's belief in the egoistic nature of dreams: "All of them [dreams] are completely egotistic: the beloved ego appears in all of them, even though it may be disguised." (pp. 166-67)

By being able to represent Georg in the guise of his friend, the dream/story can express certain ideas that otherwise might be rejected by the censoring ego. Georg appears to be succeeding *in propria persona*. He is doing well in business. He is doing well in relationships with women. But actually, I would suggest, he is not doing well in either endeavor. His failures, unacceptable to the ego, are assigned to the friend. In contrast to the successful Georg, the friend has a business that is "going downhill," . . . and "he was resigning himself to becoming a permanent bachelor." . . . That the friend represents Georg explains the intensity of Georg's remark to Frieda about the friend: "He'd have to go away again alone. Alone—do you know what that means?" . . .

But despite these failures economically and socially, the friend has achieved something that Georg hasn't: he has escaped from the home environment that a dominant father makes stifling. The dream/story disguises the wish to escape from home by giving the impression that to leave home is undesirable. In truth, however, Georg longs to escape to "a foreign country" from the overshadowing father who "had hindered him from developing any real activity of his own." . . . (p. 168)

As critics have perceived, a major part of the story deals with the Oedipal competition between father and son. Sometimes, the father is ascendant, demonstrating that he remains "a giant of a man." At other times, Georg asserts his power by treating his father as a child: undressing the father, carrying him to bed, and tucking him under the sheets. The story ends with a disguised parricide. The father crashes, but Georg—thanks to the distorting process imposed by the ego censor on unacceptable material—is not to blame. As Georg is mysteriously "urged from the room," . . . he seems dissociated from his father's fall. Yet, truly, it is the act of parricide rather than the preoccupation with himself that makes Georg "a devilish human being" . . . and merits the judgment of death by drowning.

Having sketched the conflict between Georg and his father, we must now complete our account of the Oedipal situation by focusing on the mother, for whose love the father and son are rivals. One recent critic has suggested that the "rivalry for the mother" is *not* an important element in **"The Judgment"** and has characterized the rivalry as "a Freudian idea which seems to have made little impression on Kafka." But I would maintain that, consciously or unconsciously, Kafka has expressed this rivalry in his writing. Consider **"The Metamorphosis"** [**"Die Verwandlung"**] which, like **"The Judgment"** and so much of his work, has a distinct Oedipal content. (p. 169)

If we are to understand the mother's role in **"The Judgment,"** we must again be alert to disguise. In the dream/story, as we have earlier observed, both Georg and his friend have not shown a proper attachment for the mother, have indeed exhibited toward her a certain coldness: the friend has "expressed his sympathy . . . dryly" over her death . . . ; the father reminds Georg, "The death of our dear mother hit me harder than it did you"; . . . and the father avers to Georg, "You have disgraced your mother's memory." . . . But the actual situation is just the reverse. Georg, as part of his sexual predicament, is *too much* attached to his mother. One hint of this attachment is the father's reference to the mother as "*our* dear mother." . . . As she is *our* dear mother, so by displacement is she *our* dear wife—wife to both husband and son who compete for her love. A second hint is Georg's offer to the father, "You can lie down in my bed for the present." . . . If the father sleeps in Georg's bed, Georg can be free to sleep with the mother in the father's bed.

The "latent disease" . . . afflicting the friend may be interpreted as Georg's Oedipal fixation. Georg needs to be cleansed of his Oedipal love for his mother and hate for his father. . . .

In my opinion, the Freudian approach yields valuable insights about the story that are not otherwise to be obtained. But I do not want to deny the legitimacy of other approaches. For example, while in the cluster of meaning I have been exploring the friend represents Georg, the friend may well have other significations; and the friend's escape to Russia may signify many other things besides the breaking away from the father. A dreamlike structure such as **"The Judgment"** can bring together significations almost as unending as the stream of traffic just going over the bridge. (p. 170)

Robert T. Levine, "The Familiar Friend: A Freudian Approach to Kafka's 'The Judgement' ('Das Urteil')," in Literature and Psychology (© Morton Kaplan, 1978), Vol. XXVII, No. 4, 1977, pp. 164-73.

VLADIMIR NABOKOV (essay date 1980)

[Franz Kafka] is the greatest German writer of our time. Such poets as Rilke or such novelists as Thomas Mann are dwarfs or plaster saints in comparison to him. (p. 255)

Before starting to talk of "The Metamorphosis," I want to dismiss two points of view. I want to dismiss completely Max Brod's opinion that the category of sainthood, not that of literature, is the only one that can be applied to the understanding of Kafka's writings. Kafka was first of all an artist, and although it may be maintained that every artist is a manner of saint (I feel that very clearly myself), I do not think that any religious implications can be read into Kafka's genius. The other matter that I want to dismiss is the Freudian point of view. His Freudian biographers, like Neider in *The Frozen Sea* . . . , contend, for example, that "The Metamorphosis" has a basis in Kafka's complex relationship with his father and his lifelong sense of guilt; they contend further that in mythical symbolism children are represented by vermin—which I doubt—and then go on to say that Kafka uses the symbol of the bug to represent the son according to these Freudian postulates. The bug, they say, aptly characterizes his sense of worthlessness before his father. I am interested here in bugs, not in humbugs, and I reject this nonsense. Kafka himself was extremely critical of Freudian ideas. He considered psychoanalysis (I quote) "a helpless error," and he regarded Freud's theories as very approximate, very rough pictures, which did not do justice to details or, what is more, to the essence of the matter. This is another reason why I should like to dismiss the Freudian approach and concentrate, instead, upon the artistic moment.

The greatest literary influence upon Kafka was Flaubert's. Flaubert who loathed pretty-pretty prose would have applauded Kafka's attitude towards his tool. Kafka liked to draw his terms from the language of law and science, giving them a kind of ironic precision, with no intrusion of the author's private sentiments; this was exactly Flaubert's method through which he achieved a singular poetic effect.

The hero of "The Metamorphosis" is Gregor Samsa (pronounced *Zamza*), who is the son of middle-class parents in Prague, Flaubertian philistines, people interested only in the material side of life and vulgarians in their tastes. . . . Gregor is mostly away traveling, but when the story starts he is spending a night at home between two business trips, and it is then that the dreadful thing happened. "As Gregor Samsa awoke one morning from a troubled dream he found himself transformed in his bed into a monstrous insect." (pp. 255-56)

Now what exactly is the "vermin" into which poor Gregor, the seedy commercial traveler, is so suddenly transformed? It obviously belongs to the branch of "jointed leggers" (*Arthropoda*), to which insects, and spiders, and centipedes, and crustaceans belong. If the "numerous little legs" mentioned in the beginning mean more than six legs, then Gregor would not be an insect from a zoological point of view. But I suggest that a man awakening on his back and finding he has as many as six legs vibrating in the air might feel that six was sufficient to be called numerous. We shall therefore assume that Gregor has six legs, that he is an insect.

Next question: what insect? Commentators say *cockroach,* which of course does not make sense. A cockroach is an insect that is flat in shape with large legs, and Gregor is anything but flat: he is convex on both sides, belly and back, and his legs are small. He approaches a cockroach in only one respect: his coloration is brown. That is all. Apart from this he has a tremendous convex belly divided into segments and a hard rounded back suggestive of wing cases. In beetles these cases conceal flimsy little wings that can be expanded and then may carry the beetle for miles and miles in a blundering flight.

Curiously enough, Gregor the beetle never found out that he had wings under the hard covering of his back. (This is a very nice observation on my part to be treasured all your lives. Some Gregors, some Joes and Janes, do not know that they have wings.) Further, he has strong mandibles. He uses these organs to turn the key in a lock while standing erect on his hind legs, on his third pair of legs (a strong little pair), and this gives us the length of his body, which is about three feet long. In the course of the story he gets gradually accustomed to using his new appendages—his feet, his feelers. This brown, convex, dog-sized beetle is very broad. . . . In the original German text the old charwoman calls him *Mistkafer,* a "dung beetle." It is obvious that the good woman is adding the epithet only to be friendly. He is not, technically, a dung beetle. He is merely a big beetle. (I must add that neither Gregor nor Kafka saw that beetle any too clearly.)

Let us look closer at the transformation. The change, though shocking and striking, is not quite so odd as might be assumed at first glance. A commonsensical commentator (Paul L. Landsberg in *The Kafka Problem* . . .) notes that "When we go to bed in unfamiliar surroundings, we are apt to have a moment of bewilderment upon awakening, a sudden sense of unreality, and this experience must occur over and over again in the life of a commercial traveller, a manner of living that renders impossible any sense of continuity." The sense of reality depends upon continuity, upon duration. After all, awakening as an insect is not much different from awakening as Napoleon or George Washington. (I knew a man who awoke as the Emperor of Brazil.) On the other hand, the isolation, and the strangeness, of so-called reality—this is, after all, something which constantly characterizes the artist, the genius, the discoverer. The Samsa family around the fantastic insect is nothing else than mediocrity surrounding genius. (pp. 258-60)

Let me sum up various of the main themes of the story.

1. The number *three* plays a considerable role in the story. The story is divided into three parts. There are three doors to Gregor's room. His family consists of three people. Three servants appear in the course of the story. Three lodgers have three beards. Three Samsas write three letters. I am very careful not to overwork the significance of symbols, for once you detach a symbol from the artistic core of the book, you lose all sense of enjoyment. The reason is that there are artistic symbols and there are trite, artificial, or even imbecile symbols. You will find a number of such inept symbols in the psychoanalytic and mythological approach to Kafka's work, in the fashionable mixture of sex and myth that is so appealing to mediocre minds. In other words, symbols may be original, and symbols may be stupid and trite. And the abstract symbolic value of an artistic achievement should never prevail over its beautiful burning life.

So, the only emblematic or heraldic rather than symbolic meaning is the stress which is laid upon *three* in "The Metamorphosis." It has really a technical meaning. The trinity, the triplet, the triad, the triptych are obvious art forms such as, say, three pictures of youth, ripe years, and old age, or any other threefold triplex subject. Triptych means a picture or carving in three compartments side by side, and this is exactly the effect that Kafka achieves, for instance, with his three rooms in the beginning of the story—living room, Gregor's bedroom, and sister's room, with Gregor in the central one. Moreover, a threefold pattern suggests the three acts of a play. And finally it must be observed that Kafka's fantasy is emphatically logical; what can be more characteristic of logic than the triad of thesis, antithesis, and synthesis. We shall, thus, limit the Kafka symbol of three to its aesthetic and logical significance and completely disregard whatever myths the sexual mythologists read into it under the direction of the Viennese witch doctor.

2. Another thematic line is the theme of the doors, of the opening and closing of doors that runs through the whole story.

3. A third thematic line concerns the ups and downs in the well-being of the Samsa family, the subtle state of balance between their flourishing condition and Gregor's desperate and pathetic condition.

There are a few other subthemes but the above are the only ones essential for an understanding of the story.

You will mark Kafka's style. Its clarity, its precise and formal intonation in such striking contrast to the nightmare matter of his tale. No poetical metaphors ornament his stark black-and-white story. The limpidity of his style stresses the dark richness of his fantasy. Contrast and unity, style and matter, manner and plot are most perfectly integrated. (pp. 282-83)

> Vladimir Nabokov, "Franz Kafka: 'The Meta-
> morphosis'," in his Lectures on Literature, edited by
> Fredson Bowers (copyright © 1980 by the Estate of
> Vladimir Nabokov; reprinted by permission of Har-
> court Brace Jovanovich, Inc.), Harcourt, 1980, pp.
> 251-83.

PETER STINE (essay date 1981)

"I am separated from all things by a hollow space," Kafka wrote in his diary in 1911, "and I do not even reach to its boundaries." And in another entry of 1913: "Everything appears to me constructed. . . . I am chasing after constructions. I enter a room, and I find them in a corner, a white tangle." Such strange (yet vaguely familiar) moments are faithfully recorded in the *Diaries*, which Kafka clung to as a mode of self-rescue; for he experienced the present as a "phantom state" in which the self, flickering and unknowable, forever merged into its opposite under the exigencies of living. (p. 58)

Kafka investigated this condition by writings whose mark of integrity is their resistance to interpretation. "Our art," he wrote, "consists of being dazzled by the Truth. The light which rests on its distorted mask as it shrinks from it is true, nothing else is." This aesthetic was continuous with the unknowable self in all its enigmatic purity. . . . His art, far from neurotic, reflects a higher lucidity, offering us the wisdom of a clairvoyant stutterer, due, as he says, to his habit of "introspection, which will suffer no idea to sink tranquilly to rest but must pursue each one into consciousness, only itself to become an idea, in turn to be pursued by renewed introspection." For Kafka there was no escape from this. Man's "own frontal bone bars his way," for the present is perpetually invaded by a dizzy recapitulation of those discarded "selves" receding into oblivion. Kafka's challenge as an artist, then, was to discover a strategy that allowed "the exchange of truthful words from person to person." What his inner dreamlife struck upon was the process of metamorphosis—an image that was commensurate with the opposite yet integral modes of being that exist within a single searching mind. W. B. Yeats remarked at the dawn of a modern age that the truth can be embodied but not known, and Kafka's animal world became his prize embodi-

ment of human truths that evade the grasp of analysis. (pp. 59-60)

His animals emerge as indicators of the far pole of dispossession from ourselves and each other, and we stand in the same relation to them as God does to us. (p. 61)

In *The Metamorphosis,* then, Kafka grieves about living under the invisible constraints of a family, and the enabling condition is Gregor Samsa's metamorphosis into a gigantic insect: "It was no dream." Gregor's body is so alien to him that his transformation has no effect upon his mental life, which initially sets in motion droll and terrible ironies. Gregor imagines his family will take his change "calmly, he had no reason to be upset". . . . It is only when his Father drives this literalization of "troubled dreams" into his room with a newspaper—"Shoo!"—and locks him there as a prisoner, a more forcible and telescoped version of his life as son and servant of officialdom, that Gregor starts to touch reality. Indeed, his metamorphosis is less a tragedy than a naked clarification of all Gregor's relations to the world, a restoration of Truth—in particular, the hidden rage of the Father who has been battering on him like an insect.

And yet Gregor is as far removed from this "dazzling" recognition as the gap between his consciousness and his numerous waving legs. Having toiled for years to bail his parents out of debt, he now feels "guilt and shame" . . . that they must work and finds "cheerful" the news that his Father has been duplicitous about finances and has been hoarding his son's contributions. There might be hope that Gregor experienced anger, had he in fact been guilty of the venality the chief clerk accused him of earlier, but he has no individual thoughts apart from his filial loyalty. (p. 63)

Gregor's only real pleasures and resentments—what we might call his real or hidden self—arise out of that admittedly despicable, forgotten, yet indestructible side of being, his animality. This is reflected humorously in Gregor's first sight of garbage, whereupon "his legs all whizzed towards the food," and in his discovery of the autoerotic freedom of crawling the walls and hanging from the ceiling: "one could breathe more freely, one's body swung and rocked lightly; and in the blissful absorption induced by the suspension it could happen . . . that he let go and fell plump on the floor. . . . Such are the freakish and regressive antics of a sexuality too long deferred. When Grete comes to dispossess him of his room, Gregor, whose sex life as a man (when not studying timetables) consisted in gazing at an innocently lewd picture of a lady on his wall, with rare self-assertion "crawled on the lady muffled in so much fur . . . which was a good surface to hold on to and comforted his hot belly". . . . In this way Kafka . . . is able to draw the link between repression and pornography without propagating it in human terms. What we witness instead is a kind of trans-Freudian comedy as Gregor breaks free on three occasions into the domain of his Mother's livingroom, only to be repelled with increasing violence by the "giant soles" of his advancing Father. Such humor is not psychological, but rather (as the pun on "giant soles" implies) ontological: "The noise in his rear sounded no longer like the force of one single father". . . . Indeed, Gregor is dealing with all fathers through time—these primal scenes take us back to the dawn of creation. At one point Gregor is trapped between his Mother, who has fainted in his room in a swamp of petticoats, and the stalking wrath of his Father, and suffers bombardment with apples for bumbling into this tableau that parodies the Biblical Fall. Under this cosmic burden of the past, Gregor might very well choose to forget his "animality" and embrace his "human" consciousness.

But it isn't easy. Gregor touches on reality only when he acknowledges his pain and its causes through his body, a result of the social reorganization of the household. The ministrations of Grete, which start to lapse into neglect and indifference, soon oppress him. A bony charwoman becomes his keeper, and now just an "old dung beetle," he grows more rebellious as he moves toward starvation. Hunger is real. . . . At last Gregor accepts the family verdict upon him, cooperates with their desire he be gotten rid of, and expires "thinking of his family with tenderness and love". . . . There is no resistance to fate here, for what else could have happened given this family and this metamorphosis? Nothing is more surprising about Kafka than the serenity with which he views his own failure and explores that theme for all of us. Gregor, as he discovered with bleeding jaws that first morning, did not need a locksmith to get out of his room. As Nabokov was fond of reminding his pupils at Cornell [see excerpt above], he was a species of dung beetle that could fly and might have zoomed out the window at any time. (pp. 64-5)

Impelled as an artist with a Messianic urge to "raise the world into the pure, the true, the immutable," [Kafka] fell wondrously short of his goal and in the pursuit became a scapegoat for mankind instead. The modern age was his only sacred text, shifting under the gaze of a metamorphosing self, and animals offered him a means for endless reflection on that present without presuming to grasp it. "Everything appears to me to be an artificial construction of the mind," he concluded. "Every remark by someone else, every chance look throws everything in me over on the other side, even what has been forgotten, even what is entirely insignificant. I am more uncertain than I ever was, I feel only the power of life." This power is reflected in the enigmatic clarity of his prose, and yet where did that prose lead? . . . Language will never be more than a lurching probe of life, and Kafka's led into the far recesses of the negativity of our era, both private alienation and coercion by emerging social norms that are the beneficiaries of our guilt under the evacuated heavens. For this saintly genius, all was a temptation to despair that made his own works suspect. W. H. Auden shrewdly observed that "one should only read Kafka when one is in a eupeptic state of physical and mental health," and has a hunch that he wished his works destroyed because he "foresaw the nature of too many of his admirers." But another reason suggests itself. If writing was an "act of prayer," all of Kafka's work reduced to a serene and secular act of attention: he regarded himself as a failure, and everything else followed, including his sense that he was like a banished animal dreaming of home. (pp. 79-80)

Peter Stine, "Franz Kafka and Animals," in Contemporary Literature (© *1981 by the Board of Regents of the University of Wisconsin System), Vol. 22, No. 1, Winter, 1981, pp. 58-80.*

ADDITIONAL BIBLIOGRAPHY

Cox, Harvey. "Kafka East, Kafka West." *The Commonweal* LXXX, No. 20 (4 September 1964): 596-600.
    States that Kafka's work represents a serious challenge to the Christian doctrine of salvation and the social salvationism of Marxists.

Gray, Ronald. *Kafka's "Castle".* London: Cambridge University Press, 1956, 136 p.
    Eschews theological, philosophical, or psychoanalytic approaches to this novel in favor of a strictly literary interpretation.

Emrich, Wilhelm. *Franz Kafka: A Critical Study of His Writings.* New York: Frederick Ungar Publishing Co., 1968, 561 p.
    One of the most comprehensive studies of Kafka's works.

Flores, Angel, ed. *The Kafka Debate: New Perspectives for Our Time.* New York: Gordonian Press, 1977, 453 p.
    Collection of essays by various critics, including Christian Gooden, Malcolm Pasley, and Walter H. Sokel.

Flores, Angel, ed. *The Problem of "The Judgment."* New York: Gordonian Press, 1977, 265 p.
    A new translation of "The Judgment," along with essays examining its structure, symbols, biographical background, and critical reception.

Flores, Angel, and Swander, Homer, eds. *Franz Kafka Today.* Madison: The University of Wisconsin Press, 1958, 289 p.
    Critical essays divided into sections on the short stories, novels, diaries, and letters, including studies by R. W. Stallman, Carl R. Woodring, and Maurice Blanchot.

Janouch, Gustav. *Conversations with Kafka.* New York: New Directions, 1971, 219 p.
    Memoir of the author's friendship with Kafka.

Politzer, Heinz. *Franz Kafka: Parable and Paradox.* Ithaca, N.Y.: Cornell University Press, 1966, 398 p.
    Critical study focusing on structural and stylistic analysis of Kafka's fiction.

Ziolkowski, Theodore. "Franz Kafka: *The Trial.*" In his *Dimensions of the Novel: German Texts and European Contexts,* pp. 37-67. Princeton: Princeton University Press, 1969.
    On the use of time, the nature of guilt, and the motif of the circle in *The Trial.*

(Clarence) Malcolm Lowry

1909-57

English novelist, short story writer, poet, and screenwriter.

Lowry's *Under the Volcano* is a classic of modern literature. A richly allusive and complex work, it is, like Joyce's *Ulysses*, an exemplum of the novel as a meticulously structured work of art. An anatomy of a man's psychic and spiritual collapse, *Under the Volcano* has been interpreted in many ways, from a political allegory of contemporary society to a personal confession of its author's moral foundering. Lowry conceived *Under the Volcano* as the *Inferno* section of a modern *Divine Comedy*, the central work of a novel series to be called *The Voyage That Never Ends*. The project was never finished, however, because it was Lowry's practice to revise his works incessantly without completing them. None of his other works of fiction can match the intensity and brilliance of *Under the Volcano*, and his reputation rests on this achievement.

Although the son of a prosperous cotton broker, Lowry never followed a conventional vocation but spent his life wandering. In his teens Lowry joined the crew of a British freighter, an experience that provided the material for his first novel, *Ultramarine*, which explores the spiritual agonies of its protagonist, Hilliot. This examination of Hilliot's nightmarish interior world is also an analysis of Lowry's personal dilemmas. Like Hilliot, all of Lowry's protagonists are in some way a projection of himself.

After his service as a seaman, Lowry attended Cambridge. Upon graduation he traveled to Spain, where he met his first wife, and then later went on to the United States. In New York he committed himself to Bellevue Hospital for treatment of alcoholism, a lifelong malady. "Lunar Caustic" is a fictional account of this episode and an introduction to the alcoholic traumas more fully explored by the Consul in *Under the Volcano*. After leaving Bellevue, Lowry moved to Cuernavaca, Mexico, the Quauhnahuac of *Under the Volcano*.

Lowry's most successful description of his hectic life and his tenacious devotion to the novelist's art is found in *Under the Volcano*. Though Lowry was intimate with the cultural and geographical background of the novel, the story essentially takes place, as William Gass puts it, in a "Mexico of the mind." By the criteria of realistic fiction, critics have judged the novel a failure, for it lacks dramatic tension, and its characterizations are vague. Commentators have also noted, however, its considerable achievements as a symbolic work detailing the protagonist's fallen state and final loss of salvation. While much of the novel is autobiographical, *Under the Volcano* transcends confessional fiction by the artistic achievement of its design. Throughout the novel Lowry interweaves a vast number of motifs based on occult, religious, and philosophical systems. Critical explication of these systems is invaluable, and the most cogent explication came from Lowry himself in a long letter to his publisher, Jonathan Cape—essential reading for any student of Lowry's novel.

Lowry finished *Under the Volcano* in Dollarton, British Columbia, where he lived for several years with his second wife. Dollarton became fictionalized in Lowry's later works as Eridanus, an Edenic haven where his characters seek spiritual

redemption. *Dark as the Grave Wherein My Friend Is Laid* is the author's fictional account of a return to Cuernavaca which contrasts the Mexican inferno with a Canadian paradise. *October Ferry to Gabriola* also examines the opposition between an idyllic natural existence and the perils of Western civilization. Though Lowry never finished these novels, critics regard them as valuable to an understanding of his artistic vision. The author's struggle to realize this vision is a major theme in the short stories of *Hear Us O Lord from Heaven Thy Dwelling Place*, a collection that provides great insight into Lowry's literary aims and self-image.

Although Lowry never completed *The Voyage That Never Ends*, his extant works have attracted an impressive amount of critical attention. In particular, the complex artistic achievement of *Under the Volcano* assures him a place among the seminal authors of modern literature.

PRINCIPAL WORKS

Ultramarine (novel) 1933
Under the Volcano (novel) 1947

Hear Us O Lord from Heaven Thy Dwelling Place   (short stories) 1961
Selected Poems   (poetry) 1962
Lunar Caustic   (novella) 1968
Dark as the Grave Wherein My Friend Is Laid   (unfinished novel) 1968
October Ferry to Gabriola   (unfinished novel) 1970

———————

DEREK VERSCHOYLE   (essay date 1933)

[*Ultramarine*] is not specifically a book about the sea. It is an illustration in particular of circumstances which share their effects with many others. . . . Mr. Lowry's writing is disastrously mannered. He attempts to describe the mental conflicts of a sensitive young man who, on the rather speculative assumption that the experience will be of spiritual value, signs on as deck boy on a tramp sailing to the East. The book suffers from a mixing of conventions. It combines the psychology of the mere analytical type of school story with a manner largely derived from *Ulysses*. Some of Mr. Lowry's scenes are excellent (notably his description of the ship leaving an eastern port), and his account of any particular episode is generally in itself satisfactory. But the different styles which he employs produce effects which are neither cumulative nor adequately complementary. There is no unity of impression.

> Derek Verschoyle, "Fiction: 'Ultramarine'," *in* The Spectator (© *1933 by* The Spectator; *reprinted by permission of* The Spectator), *Vol. 150, No. 5478, June 23, 1933, p. 920.*

MALCOLM LOWRY   (essay date 1946)

I feel that the main defect of *Under the Volcano,* from which the others spring, comes from something irremediable. It is that the author's equipment, such as it is, is subjective rather than objective, a better equipment, in short, for a certain kind of poet than a novelist. On the other hand I claim that just as a tailor will try to conceal the deformities of his client so I have tried, aware of this defect, to conceal in the *Volcano* as well as possible the deformities of my own mind, taking heart from the fact that since the conception of the whole thing was essentially poetical, perhaps these deformities don't matter so very much after all, even when they show! But poems often have to be read several times before their full meaning will reveal itself, explode in the mind, and it is precisely this poetical conception of the *whole* that I suggest . . . [might be] missed. But to be more specific: your . . . main objections to the book are:

1. The long initial tedium. . . .

2. The weakness of the character drawing. This is a valid criticism. But I have not exactly attempted to draw characters in the normal sense—though s'welp me bob its only Aristotle who thought character counted least. But here, as I shall say somewhere else, there just isn't *room*: the characters will have to wait for another book, though I did go to incredible trouble to make my major characters seem adequate on the most *superficial* plane on which this book can be read, and I believe in some eyes the character drawing will appear the reverse of weak. (What about female readers?) The truth is that the character drawing is not only weak but virtually nonexistent, save

with certain minor characters, the four main characters being intended, in one of the book's meanings, to be aspects of the same man, or of the human spirit, and two of them, Hugh and the Consul, more obviously are. I suggest that here and there what may look like unsuccessful attempts at character drawing may only be the concrete bases to the creature's lives without which again the book could not be read at all. But weak or no there is nothing I can do to improve it without reconceiving or rewriting the book, unless it is to take something out—but then, as I say, one might be thereby only removing a prop which, while it perhaps looked vexing to you in passing, was actually holding something important up.

3. "The author has spread himself too much. The book is *much too long* and over elaborate for its content, and could have been much more effective if only half or two thirds its present length. The author has overreached himself and is given to eccentric word-spinning and too much stream-of-consciousness stuff." This may well be so, but I think the author may be forgiven if he asks for a fuller appraisal of that content—I say it all again—in terms of the author's intention as a whole and chapter by chapter before he can reach any agreement with anyone as to what precisely renders it over-elaborate and should therefore be cut to render that whole more effective. If the reader has not got hold of the content at first go, how can he decide then what makes it much too long, especially since his reactions may turn out to be quite different on a second reading? And not only authors perhaps but readers can overreach themselves, by reading too fast however carefully they think they are going—and what tedious book is this one has to read so fast? I believe there is such a thing as wandering attention that is the fault neither of reader nor writer: though more of this later. As for the eccentric word-spinning, I honestly don't think there is much that is not in some way thematic. As for the "stream-of-consciousness stuff," many techniques have been employed, and while I did try to cut mere "stuff" to a minimum, . . . a lot of the so-called "stuff" I feel to be justified simply on poetical or dramatic grounds: and I think [one] would be surprised to find how much of what at first sight seems unnecessary even in this "stuff" is simply disguised, honest-to-God exposition, the author trying to proceed on Henry James' dictum that what is not vivid is not represented, what is not represented is not art. (pp. 59-61)

[*Under the Volcano*] is written on numerous planes with provision made, it was my fond hope, for almost every kind of reader, my approach with all humility being opposite, I felt, to that of Mr. Joyce, *i.e.,* a simplyfying, as far as possible, of what originally suggested itself in far more baffling, complex and esoteric terms, rather than the other way round. The novel can be read simply as a story which you can skip if you want. It can be read as a story you will get more out of if you don't skip. It can be regarded as a kind of symphony, or in another way as a kind of opera—or even a horse opera. It is hot music, a poem, a song, a tragedy, a comedy, a farce, and so forth. It is superficial, profound, entertaining and boring, according to taste. It is a prophecy, a political warning, a cryptogram, a preposterous movie, and a writing on the wall. It can even be regarded as a sort of machine: it works too, believe me, as I have found out. In case you think I mean it to be everything but a novel I better say that after all it is intended to be and, though I say so myself, a deeply serious one too. But it is also I claim a work of art. . . .

This novel then is concerned principally, in Edmund Wilson's words (speaking of Gogol), with the forces in man which cause him to be terrified of himself. It is also concerned with the guilt of man, with his remorse, with his ceaseless struggling toward the light under the weight of the past, and with his doom. The allegory is that of the Garden of Eden, the Garden representing the world, from which we ourselves run perhaps slightly more danger of being ejected than when I wrote the book. The drunkenness of the Consul is used on one plane to symbolize the universal drunkenness of mankind during the war, or during the period immediately preceding it, which is almost the same thing, and what profundity and final meaning there is in his fate should be seen also in its universal relationship to the ultimate fate of mankind. (p. 66)

[*Under the Volcano*] was so designed, counterdesigned and interwelded that it could be read an indefinite number of times and still not have yielded all its meanings or its drama or its poetry. . . . (p. 88)

> *Malcolm Lowry, in his letter to Jonathan Cape on January 2, 1946, in* Selected Letters of Malcolm Lowry, *Harvey Breit, Margerie Bonner Lowry, eds. (copyright © 1965 by Margerie Bonner Lowry; reprinted by permission of Literistic, Ltd.), J. B. Lippincott Company, 1965, pp. 57-88.*

MARK SCHORER (essay date 1947)

"Under the Volcano" is, ostensibly, the story of a man's disintegration and death, but within this appearance is the deeper reality of man's fall from grace, the drama of how we are damned and who shall be saved, the basic contrast in human history of the mind confronted by destiny. One other novelist in this century, James Joyce, has brought into his fiction such primary experience, and devised a good method whereby the naturalistic surface opens into endlessly amplifying symbolic depths, a style capable of posing these final questions in an esthetic unity, of holding event and symbol, story and meaning absolutely together, of preventing, that is, allegory. It would be no service to Mr. Lowry to push the comparison further. . . . [He] has set for himself literary ambitions of the Joycean order if not of their full complexity, and within the smaller frame of his novel, he has achieved them. . . .

The "downward flight" of Geoffrey Firmin is executed with skill. . . .

We have had, in our time, many poems and plays and stories about alienated and disintegrating spirits, but I know of few which convey so powerfully the agony of alienation, the infernal suffering of disintegration. The characteristic treatment of these themes has been through arid characters, Hamletlike men sucked dry of all but nostalgia, shaken by violence, perhaps, but not violently shaken. Malcolm Lowry reverses this treatment. The consciousness of his central character is unraveled as he sinks deeper into his moral depths, as he comes face to face with the slimiest horrors of experience and is granted no relief whatever in any compromise with evil. Instead of narrowing down to a more and more precise pathos, like so much of our best literature, this novel simplifies into wider and wider meanings to the limits of experiences, not merely literary myth, and one is left at the end as after tragedy, at once exhausted and exhilarated. Following Geoffrey Firmin so utterly into the abyss, we are, through the paradox of all genuine esthetic experience, ourselves released from it.

Mr. Lowry writes with superb vigor and depth dash and he creates, through his style no less than through his acute capacity

for sensuous observation, a novel of opulent texture and consequently resonant meaning.

> *Mark Schorer, "The Downward Flight of a Soul," in* New York Herald Tribune Book Review *(© I.H.T. Corporation), February 23, 1947, p. 2.*

JACQUES BARZUN (essay date 1947)

[*Under the Volcano*] strikes me as fulsome and fictitious. Mr. Lowry is also on the side of good behavior, eager to disgust us with subtropical vice. He shows this by a long regurgitation of the materials found in *Ulysses* and *The Sun Also Rises*. But while imitating the tricks of Joyce, Dos Passos, and Sterne, he gives us the mind and heart of Sir Philip Gibbs. His three men and lone woman are desperately dull even when sober, and, despite the impressive authorities against me on this point, so is their creator's language. I mean the English language, since Spanish also flows freely through his pages. "The swimming pool ticked on. *Might a soul bathe there and be clean or slake its drought? . . .* The failure of a wire fence company, the failure, rather less emphatic and final, of one's father's mind, what were these things in the face of God or destiny?" What indeed when so reported? Mr. Lowry has other moments, borrowed from other styles in fashion—Henry James, Thomas Wolfe, the thought-streamers, the surrealists. His novel [is only] . . . an anthology held together by earnestness.

> *Jacques Barzun, "New Books: 'Under the Volcano'," in* Harper's *(copyright © 1947 by Harper's Magazine; copyright renewed © 1974 by Minneapolis Star and Tribune Company, Inc.; all rights reserved; reprinted from the May, 1947 issue by special permission), Vol. 194, No. 1164, May, 1947, p. 486.*

GEORGE WOODCOCK (essay date 1958)

[In] the bare outline of its actions, *Under the Volcano* might appear a rather sophisticated variant of those sensational novels expounding the evils of drunkenness which were published in our fathers' days by the Society for the Propagation of Christian Knowledge. In fact, however, the element of moralism (as distinct from morality) enters hardly at all; rather, the qualities that impress one in *Under the Volcano* are its compassion for the agonies of all its characters, and the sense of looming tragedy with which one beholds the nightmare world of the alcoholic. The death of the Consul is not seen in terms of the just punishment of the weak and wicked; it is rather the ineluctable culmination of a chain of tragic events which take place in the Consul's soul that day—the physical end that merely terminates the series of spiritual defeats he has suffered and accepted during his descent into degradation.

Yet, though *Under the Volcano* poses no moral judgment, it nevertheless proceeds on an allegorical level to a consideration of the destiny of man. This fact is important, for, if we were to consider the novel only according to the canons of naturalistic realism, it would clearly have to be accounted a failure. The action is too contrived with the intention of fitting an ordained pattern, the succession of coincidence is too obviously repetitive, and events are built up with an improbable intensity that is reminiscent of the Jacobean tragedies of Webster and Tourneur.

However, though there are many passages of vividly realistic description of certain aspects of Mexican life, it is evident that these are used by the author in the same way as surrealistic painters will render some parts of their pictures with meticulous realism in order to enhance the dreamlike and incongruous quality of the whole, and that his general intention is to depict in symbolical terms the terrors of the underworld of spiritual torment and death. In relation to its success or otherwise in this task we must judge *Under the Volcano.* (p. 153)

The kind of exuberant mass of fantasy and philosophy, of symbolism and sheer human agony, which Lowry has crammed into *Under the Volcano* might easily have disintegrated in the hands of a lesser craftsman into an amorphous chaos; at times, indeed, when the author's fancy has been ridden with too loose a rein, it does seem as though the whole novel is about to suffer just such a breakdown. But this is always averted by the carefully jointed structure which holds the plot together; only a writer with a really close prose discipline could steer so near to shapelessness and escape.

This disciplined structure, however, is closely connected with the faults as well as the virtues of *Under the Volcano.* It is achieved, not organically out of the growth of the characters, but through a fatality externally imposed, a kind of patterned Karma which, while it may have a certain poetic and symbolic validity, has a great deal less of fictional reality. For Lowry's treatment of character and of human destiny is basically mechanical. (p. 155)

Yet, while I believe this criticism to be fundamental, pointing to a serious lapse from that organic development which should be the aim of the novelist's art, I still think there are qualities—the exuberant yet sure handling of words, the sense for tragedy and the touch of compassion, the poetic eye for image and symbol, the complex and fascinating erudition—which make *Under the Volcano*, considered as a prose composition and apart from its psychological validity, one of the most interesting productions of the past decades. (p. 156)

> *George Woodcock, "Malcolm Lowry's 'Under the Volcano'," in* Modern Fiction Studies *(© copyright 1958 by Purdue Research Foundation, West Lafayette, Indiana), Vol. 4, No. 2, Summer, 1958, pp. 151-56.*

PHOEBE-LOU ADAMS (essay date 1961)

[The stories in *Hear Us O Lord from Heaven Thy Dwelling Place*] are so intensely introspective and so limited in theme that it is perhaps a mistake to consider them as stories at all. They are rather elaborations of mood and revelations of the workings of the author's disintegrating mind, with the intensity and egocentricity of lyric poetry; and, like poetry, they demand a degree of empathy that not all readers will be able, or willing, to supply.

Involving symbolic voyages, confused identities, and inexplicable Nirvanas, the stories are held together by the fisherman's hymn of the title and the sound of the ship's engines chanting *Frère Jacques.* Between the dream of paradise embodied in the former and the mundane racket of the latter, Mr. Lowry's character (there is only one, although he has several names) hovers, lost and uncomprehending, in a limbo of his own creation. . . . He is alienated, to use the fashionable term. The only consolations in his wilderness of difficulties are the beauties of the sea and the Canadian landscape—both of which Mr. Lowry describes with immense skill—and love, which he interprets as the possession of a mattress which can cook and make pretty remarks about the scenery.

The sense of suffering in these stories is acute and at times moving, but it is the suffering of a mind closed in on itself, of an extreme neuroticism for which no cause is ever given. Mr. Lowry implies that the world is mean and man uncouth, but why this well-known fact should have reduced his hero to such a state of cowering withdrawal is not explained. Indeed, there is no evidence that this introverted man has ever looked at the world long enough to see what it is, or become acquainted with any man but himself.

Mr. Lowry's prose has brilliance and vitality, but whole paragraphs can be lifted out as pure James, pure Melville, pure Conrad, and even, heaven help us, pure Kathleen Norris. As a record of private experience, the stories are interesting, if incomplete. As a comment on the experience of humanity in general, they are of debatable relevance.

> *Phoebe-Lou Adams, "Neurotic Limbo," in* The Atlantic Monthly *(copyright © 1961, by The Atlantic Monthly Company, Boston, Mass.; reprinted with permission), Vol. 208, No. 2, August, 1961, p. 96.*

J. R. COLOMBO (essay date 1963)

[In his poetry we see that] Lowry's view of life was as pessimistic as Housman's, but there is nothing sweet or serious to it. Lowry was inclined to sympathize with himself and then laugh it off, giving his poetry a half-hearted seriousness. He was usually too drawn to man as a silly spectacle to take the plight of man seriously, in the poetry in any case. Occasionally he would catch himself in a line: "And pray that his prove no titanic case," but he would either end the poem there or lose himself again. His lack of taste and tact is unfortunate, because Lowry was sensitive and intelligent:

> Tenderness
> Was here, in this very room, in this
> Place, its form seen, cries heard, by you.

He strikes this note in **"Delirium in Vera Cruz"** but not in many other poems.

The *Selected Poems* is a medley of moods, genuine poetry, ragged verse, doggerel, stances, statements—everything from the showy to the shoddy. Full of echoes, Lowry is made to resemble the Ahab he writes about "whose rhetoric's however not his own." But Lowry has his own individuality. He is one of the few modern poets who can write convincingly about animals, birds and fish, and he handles images of ships and sea with a freshness not with the savour of the usual salt.

His poetic measures are straight-forward and traditional, but his lines always sound as if they were in the middle of their second draft, which in fact they might have been. In fact, much of the pleasure in reading these poems comes from one's willingness to appreciate fragments: verse experiments and poetic exercises. His longer poems he seemed to rush through, and where his poems are of any length they are seldom integrated. In turn, Lowry can be seen joining wit with intelligence and wit with mood. . . . As with all "doomed" poets, we end up with a choice of half-a-dozen hastily scribbled epitaphs and self-parodies, like **"The Pilgrim."** . . . But there is seldom a complete poem which rings true. A number, however—poems like **"Without the Nighted Wyvern," "A Poem of God's Mercy"** and **"For** *Under the Volcano"*—are individual and satisfying, often for entirely different reasons. (p. 62)

[Lowry] had all the ingredients [of a popular poet]: the iambic line, unexpected rhyme, the obsession with self and personal death. He has a touch of the Villon to him (**"Men with Goats Thrashing"**), a quick bit of Zen (**"The Comedian"**) and an appreciation of nature (**"Nocturne"**). He could write a Tennyson-like musing (**"No Still Path"**) and a Whitman-esque fantasy (**"The Volcano"**). In addition, he possessed that single indispensible ingredient, the romantic outlook. This is shown in the Bliss Carman and school-book simplicity of **"The Flowering Past,"** as well as in the excruciatingly romantic ending of **"The Days Like Smitten Cymbals."** . . . (pp. 62-3)

[Earle Birney remarks] that Lowry's poetry is "without disguise" and "innocent of defenses." With a man of Lowry's unpredictable nature, this is a doubtful virtue at best. A bit more attention to statement and form might have sharpened the sentimentalizing and barbed the language. (p. 63)

> *J. R. Colombo, "Poetry and Legend," in* Canadian Literature, *No. 16, Spring, 1963, pp. 61-3.*

CONRAD KNICKERBOCKER   (essay date 1964)

"Under the Volcano" combines the terror and inevitability of **"Moby Dick"** with the virtuosity and density of **"Ulysses."** Although the book recasts total despair, it plays a counterpoint of ecstasy. Lowry understood the drinker's (and mystic's) dictum that it takes hell to know heaven. The frightfulness of Firmin's predicament becomes bearable from moment to moment because it is also ridiculous. . . .

Stumbling through the lowering Mexican landscape, pursued by his brother and wife, he reenacts the expulsion from Eden. . . . His experience reaffirms in modern terms the mythic truths of the Faust legend and the Divine Comedy. If life for Lowry was an approximation of art, art explained more about life than life ever could. The Consul carries on his shoulders the very stones of Western civilization, and like Faust, he knows too much. (p. 64)

[Lowry] wanted to penetrate the outer limits of literature, to untangle and follow out the experience of 20th-century derangement, but part of him held fast to the plain 19th-century virtues of his upbringing—courtesy, generosity, decency in extremis.

His poems reveal this aspect of his morality. They are the most private of his writings. . . . Formal and almost courtly, they have the faintly declamatory tone of a man who sees in poetry the final resort of order and simplicity. . . . [They] show that if he had focused his efforts, he would have found a public voice in poetry as strong as that of his fiction.

Of all his work, his verse . . . is the most English. If Lowry acknowledged in his style any debt to his homeland, it was to the poetry of England. As a shy and sardonic schoolboy, he had written, "When I am dead,/Bring me not roses white . . . but roses red." The rhetoric of Romanticism, the declaration of life as a mysterious voyage, sustained the schoolboy and the man. (p. 65)

> *Conrad Knickerbocker, "Paperbacks in Review: Malcolm Lowry," in* The New York Times Book Review *(© 1964 by The New York Times Company; reprinted by permission), November 8, 1964, pp. 64-5.*

STEPHEN SPENDER   (essay date 1965)

Under the Volcano is, it is true, perhaps the best account of a "drunk" in fiction. The Consul's addiction is treated as a kind of tragic game, in which there are as many moves as moods, played by the Consul to deceive the others, but still more to deceive himself. The root cause of his drinking is loneliness. The early pages of the book in which M. Laruelle meditates on his boyhood friendship with the Consul indicate this clearly enough. For those who seek it out, the clinical history of the Consul's longing for companionship, fear of sex, deeply idealistic puritanism, rejection of the world, and suppressed homosexual tendency, is embedded in the narrative. By the time we have finished this novel we know how a drunk thinks and feels, walks and lies down, and we experience not only the befuddledness of drinking but also its moments of translucent clairvoyance, perfected expression.

All the same, that Lowry elaborates the distinctions between beer and wine and Bols and the Black Mass experience of mescal is only incidental to the Consul's real tragedy, which concerns this world in these times. Fundamentally *Under the Volcano* is no more *about* drinking than *King Lear* is *about* senility. It is about the Consul, which is another matter, for what we feel about him is that he is great and shattered. We also feel that he could have written the novel which describes his downfall, and this means that, considered as an art of consciousness attained, this is no downfall, but his triumph.

Most of all, *Under the Volcano* is one of a number of works about the breakdown of values in the twentieth century. Just as the collapse of power in *King Lear* is envisioned through the shattered mind of the king, so in *Under the Volcano* is the tragic despair of Mexico, and, beyond Mexico, the hopelessness of Europe torn by the Spanish Civil War, seen magnified and distorted in the minds of the Consul and of Hugh.

The Consul, then, is a modern hero—or anti-hero—reflecting an extreme external situation within his own extremity. His neurosis becomes diagnosis, not just of himself but of a phase of history. It *is* artistically justified because neurosis, seen not just as one man's case history, but within the context of a wider light, is the dial of the instrument that records the effects of a particular stage of civilisation upon a civilised individual: for the Consul is essentially a man of cultivation. The most sensitive individual, although not the most normal, may provide the most representative expression of a breakdown which affects other people on levels of which they may be scarcely conscious. Yet seeing the needle on the disc of the recording instrument, they know that what it registers is also in some sense their own case. (pp. viii-x)

The hero of *Under the Volcano* is the autobiographic consciousness of the Consul, who is a mask for Malcolm Lowry. Lowry is concerned with the ability of the Consul conditioned by circumstances which are partly those of his own psychology, partly imposed by "the times," to wrest a triumph from himself, to create an order out of the material which is his own fragmented consciousness. *Under the Volcano* is not a statement about civilisation so much as an account of one man's soul within the circumstances of a historic phase. In this sense it belongs not to the literature of the "picture of the West" of the 1920s but to the more restricted literature related to that time and more especially to the 1930s. (pp. xii-xiii)

The more one reads his work and about Lowry, the more one has the impression that he did write about almost nothing which he had not himself seen or experienced. But that is not what is profoundly autobiographical in him. What I mean by calling him an autobiographer is that in his writing he constructs a picture of the world by piecing together situations which are self-identifications. *Under the Volcano* is his best book because it seems to contain the whole sum of these identifications. The agonies he endured in Mexico provided a catalyst which enabled him to express his deepest feelings about his life, his vision of ''the times.''

Lowry's work is not, as I have pointed out, ''an escape from personality.'' It is the putting together of a great many situations which he had himself experienced. By comparison with *Under the Volcano* most of his other work suffers from the limitation that the central character is Lowry himself and that the other characters are two-dimensional. In *Under the Volcano* this defect is avoided, or compensated for by the fact that he has distributed his own personality among several characters. It is clear that Hugh, the Consul's half-brother, is the Consul in his youth, and that both are aspects of Malcolm Lowry. Mr. Laruelle is a mirror of the Consul, as his meditations at the beginning of the novel, which are entirely about Geoffrey Firmin, show. (p. xviii)

The central paradox of *Under the Volcano* is that it is a novel about action, that is, about action negated. At the centre, there is an impassioned cry that men should attain simplicity of being, love and live and act in a world of simple choices. Conrad Knickerbocker quotes Lowry: ''The real cause of alcoholism is the complete baffling sterility of existence as *sold* to you.'' This implies a spiritual isolation. . . . Lowry had isolation which condemned him to perpetual self-searching, in which the mind creating is inextricably involved in the work created. Because there is no solution in the contemporary world of bogus solutions, art itself becomes a form of defiant action, and here Lowry anticipates later artists—Jackson Pollock, for example—self-involved yet selfless, intoxicated yet wholly lucid, drinking themselves into sobriety, who in their very excesses seem to acquire some quality of saintliness, as though undergoing what in others might appear to be vices, for the sake of the rest of us. (p. xxiii)

[The] theme of the Consul's fatality is to be found on almost every page of [*Under the Volcano*], however great the variations of his mood—themselves distorted and exaggerated by drink. The life of the Consul resembles variations on a theme of music by some composer such as Beethoven where the greatest possible variety of moods and rhythms are gone through without the elements of the theme being fundamentally altered. Yet perhaps this is to emphasize too much the side of the novel which embraces the Consul's will to self-destruction. One also remembers this book for marvellous scenes of affirmation. The alternate life, although rejected, does appear. There is the wonderful scene in which Hugh and Yvonne—physically healthy, beautifully attractive, conscious of the world and their responsibilities public and private—walk through the valley and then ride the horses which they hire, with the fools running beside them. This is the open air life of physical well-being and frank communication, yet it is subtly meretricious; they (Hugh, especially) too consciously act out their roles. Later in the novel, parallel with the scene between Hugh and Yvonne, there is the moment when drunk to the point of sobriety the Consul suddenly speaks to her openly, not concealing his true feelings. And contrasted with almost all the book there is the sun overhead, and across half the world there are people fighting for their freedom, first in Spain and later against Hitler. *Under the Volcano* is an authentic modern tragedy because somehow the

murder of the Consul by the fascist police transforms his life into a convincing affirmation of values which he deeply knew, and which in his own consciousness he did not destroy. The conclusion must be that it is religous: the contradictions of a hero who does not act and who fails to be a hero, the insistence implicit that the Consul is the writer, and living and dying for all of us, the concern for values which are outside the time in a world entirely contemporary, are resolved in the theme of the Divine Comedy, the progress of the soul. (pp. xxv-xxvi)

Stephen Spender, ''Introduction'' (copyright © 1965 by J. B. Lippincott Company; reprinted by permission of J. B. Lippincott, Publishers), in Under the Volcano *by Malcolm Lowry, J. B. Lippincott Company, 1965, pp. vii-xxvi.*

DENIS DONOGHUE (essay date 1966)

[If] Lowry is weak in the creation of character, if he is unable to conceive of people distinct from himself, he has many other resources. He is remarkable for the plenitude of his sensations; this is clear in *Under the Volcano* and some of the short stories. Many scenes in the novel, in **''Strange Comfort''** and **''The Forest Path to the Spring,''** are almost entirely static. They do not lose the name of action, for the sufficient reason that they have never had it. But they are extraordinary in the richness of their sensations. . . . [The] sensations released are remarkable. Lowry found it hard to discriminate between one sensation and another: he was not impeccable in judgment. *Under the Volcano* was re-written several times, but the final version contains pages of ''Pure Poetry'' which read like anyone's loose imaginings. The fact that most of them are assigned to the Consul is neither here nor there. And there is a certain amount of residual ''Lowromancing,'' as Lowry called it in a severe moment. (pp. 17-18)

[He] was tempted to load every vein with ore. If you have reduced the whole world to your own sensations, you can't afford to slight even one of them. This is why *Under the Volcano,* remarkable as it is, gives the impression of being overwritten. After a few chapters we long for something casual, even a mistake, anything to relieve the pressure of deliberate significance. In the event, the only relief from the demand of one sensation is the arrival of another. Everything is so knowingly placed, the ''depths'' so carefully enforced, the mysteries so Eleusinian, the names so cunningly chosen, that only the inescapable density of the writing keeps us going. And because Lowry acknowledged the stress of independent existence so rarely and ambiguously, he could not rely upon its power. This is why he seized upon Baudelaire's remark that life is a forest of symbols. It had to be; otherwise it was nothing. If a tree was just a tree, how dreadful; Lowry had to rescue it from its finitude. Charles Tomlinson has a poem about ''the proper plenitude of fact.'' This is not Lowry's idiom, ornithologist or not. To him, plenitude was the virtuosity of sensation, a conjuror's flair. If facts are not significant, you must ensure significance by surrounding them with a halo of your own desire. . . . So *Under the Volcano* is a forest of symbols. . . . Nothing is ever wasted. In these rituals Lowry endows the objects with the wealth of his own sensation. . . . (p. 18)

Denis Donoghue, ''Ultra Writer,'' in The New York Review of Books *(reprinted with permission from* The New York Review of Books; *copyright © 1966 Nyrev, Inc.), Vol. VI, No. 3, March 3, 1966, pp. 16-18.**

DALE EDMONDS   (essay date 1967)

Lowry was *not* a "born short story writer"; many of his works of short fiction do not succeed by themselves, nor do the later stories constitute the interrelated whole Lowry visualized. However, two of his short works, **"The Forest Path to the Spring"** and **"Through the Panama,"** may be considered minor triumphs, and several of the other stories are worthy of attention for the occasional flashes of the brilliance of *Under the Volcano.*

Lowry's short fiction may be grouped into three categories for convenience of discussion: uncollected short works, most of them early; **"Lunar Caustic"**. . . ; and *Hear Us O Lord from Heaven Thy Dwelling Place.* . . . The early and uncollected works are, on the whole, of little save historical and curiosity value; **"Lunar Caustic"** is of debatable overall merit, though it has certain undeniable strengths; *Hear Us O Lord* contains Lowry's most fully realized works of short fiction, two of which bear consideration as substantial contributions in English short fiction in the post-World War II period. (pp. 59-60)

"Lunar Caustic" is a disappointing work. . . . (p. 65)

[It has a not] unpromising plot, but it does not have sufficient interest and dynamic quality in itself to "carry" the story through its weak moments (as in **"Through the Panama"**), nor does Lowry create an effective story by means of his style (as he was able to do with **"The Bravest Boat,"** which actually has little plot).

"Lunar Caustic" is less a study of the horror of the alcoholic's withdrawal from, and subsequent return to, drink, than an occasionally effective protest against stultifying bureaucracy and disgraceful inefficiency on the part of the staff of a public hospital. In this respect the story contains the most explicit social criticism of Lowry's published writings.

Bill Plantagenet, if that is his name, is another of Lowry's sensitive drinkers, a musician this time, in the mold of the protagonists of the *Hear Us O Lord* stories. (pp. 65-6)

[In the long central section of the story the] customary Lowry themes appear: drunkenness, madness, exile, the failure of love, the sorrowful state of the world, the difficulty of communication between human beings. There are some fine descriptions in this section of the world inside the hospital and of the world outside as apprehended from within. Plantagenet's friends, Garry, Mr. Kalowsky, and Mr. Battle, are good studies in the results of neglect and misunderstanding. They are troubled and lost, but deserve more suitable treatment than they are receiving. (p. 66)

The last section of the story begins, "Once more a man paused outside the City Hospital. Once more, with a dithering crack, the hospital door had shut behind him." . . . Plantagenet has stayed sober while in the hospital, but to what end? This is the question Lowry leaves with Plantagenet—and with the reader. Assailed as we are in fiction by outcries at the futility and horror of existence, we require something more. (p. 67)

Lowry's description of Plantagenet's passage through increasingly shabby streets toward the waterfront brings to mind a similar passage in Stephen Crane's *Maggie, a Girl of the Streets.* Lowry, like Crane, attempts to present, in telescoped fashion, downward progression over a period of years. When Plantagenet smashes his bottle against the obscene sketch of a girl in the tavern washroom, one thinks of the scene in *The Catcher in the Rye* when Holden Caulfield rubs out an obscene phrase in the hallway of his sister's school. Although Lowry probably

did not intend to emulate these well-known passages, the result is that the reader is likely to think that he has read all this before.

Lowry's presentation of the inner workings of a public hospital is vivid and thought-provoking; his descriptions of the mentally ill characters are effective and moving; his treatment of the drunkard is believable. But **"Lunar Caustic"** fails as a work of fiction because of Lowry's uncertainty of intention and inconsistency of style. (pp. 67-8)

Most critics [of *Hear Us O Lord from Heaven Thy Dwelling Place*] commented upon the autobiographical nature of the stories. At times Lowry does include extraneous or cloying autobiographical material (as in **"Strange Comfort"**), and it is true that the most successful story in the collection, **"The Forest Path,"** is the one in which Lowry keeps the greatest distance from his protagonist's personality. However, in the second most successful story, **"Through the Panama,"** the protagonist, Sigbjorn Wilderness, bears strong resemblance to his creator, both in the external details of his life and in his emotional complex. Thus it is not the presence or absence of autobiographical elements that determines the success of the stories.

Perhaps the chief weakness in the stories is a lack of movement and development (**"Through the Panama"** and, perhaps, **"Gin and Goldenrod"** may be excepted here). Often there is no satisfactory progression toward a resolution of some kind. Obviously Lowry did not attempt to provide a plot, in the usual sense of the term, but several of the stories simply do not have sufficient vitality. The protagonists of these stories, particularly of **"Strange Comfort,"** **"Elephant and Colosseum,"** and **"Pompeii,"** are virtual slaves to their introspective tendencies, with the result that the stories seem static.

The recurring motifs, themes, and symbols occasionally have the effect of boring the reader with repetitiveness, rather than tying the stories together, as Lowry hoped. At times certain themes which are relevant in one story will seem artificially engrafted onto another. For instance, the sound of the freighters' engines—"Frère Jacques, Frère Jacques"—while believable when apprehended by Wilderness on his voyage through the Panama Canal, seems incongruous amid the reflections of Kennish Drumbold Cosnahan at the Rome zoo in **"Elephant and Colosseum."** (pp. 69-70)

The women in these stories are poorly drawn, although one need not go so far as one critic who described Lowry's ideal woman as "a mattress which can cook and make pretty remarks about the scenery" [see Adams excerpt above]. The Lowry woman must be pretty, gay, helpful, and understanding. The quality of understanding is most important: she must understand the almost inconceivable problems that beset a sensitive drinking writer (perhaps one should say "sensitive writing drinker"). She must remain faithfully at his side, always patient, ready to give succor, and eager to interpret natural phenomena in images of textiles and jewelry. These women may be called Primrose, Lovey, Tansy, or simply "my wife," but they are the same charming, articulate, unconvincing woman.

The character Sigbjørn Wilderness, central figure in three of the stories, is perplexing. It is difficult to reconcile the Wilderness of **"Through the Panama"** with the Wilderness of **"Gin and Goldenrod,"** and either or both of these with the Wilderness of **"Strange Comfort."** In **"Gin and Goldenrod"** Wilderness resembles the figure Lowry once described as "a sort of underground man . . . disinterested in literature, uncultured, incredibly unobservant, in many respects ignorant, without faith in himself, and lacking nearly all the qualities you normally associate with a novelist or writer. . . . he sees practically nothing at all, save through his wife's eyes. . . .'' In this story, while Wilderness feels remorse about his debauchery and loss of money to a bootlegger, he seems most interested in whether there will be a drink waiting for him at home. The Wilderness of **"Through the Panama"** has his troubles with drink, but far from being ''disinterested in literature,'' he is obsessed by it: literary references fill his journal. Neither of these figures seems compatible with the comparatively sane and self-possessed Wilderness of **"Strange Comfort,"** an American writer in Rome on a Guggenheim Fellowship, who scrupulously takes notes and quietly reads them over a few *grappas* (albeit a letter he discovers in an early notebook suggests the problems of the other Wildernesses). Thus there is not one Sigbjørn Wilderness, but three—Lowry failed to make him consistent among all three stories, an indefensible lapse, since he used a single name. (pp. 71-2)

Lowry's style in these stories at times becomes excessively mannered. He seems to have grown more digressive, reflective, introspective than when he wrote *Under the Volcano*. There is nothing here to restrain him as effectively as did the necessities of plot in the novel. . . . (p. 72)

In the foregoing discussion I have dealt mainly with the weak points of the stories in *Hear Us O Lord*. The strong points, if they do not entirely compensate for the weaknesses, at least give the collection a substantial claim on the reader's attention. The constantly reiterated themes do provide a certain continuity. For example, by the time he reaches the end of the book, the reader is not likely to forget the ''Frère Jacques'' sound of the freighters' engines. The constant repetition of this phrase, which suggests the sound of eternity, impresses upon the reader the endless cycle of existence. (p. 73)

Of the recurring themes in *Hear Us O Lord,* one of the most prevalent is that of the opposition of nature and civilization. Throughout his life Lowry felt his greatest happiness away from cities and in close touch with nature. This Rousseauistic attitude appears in nearly all his mature writings. As Lowry sees it, the world is in a state of chaos because man has ''civilized'' nature. This theme is expressed powerfully in **"The Bravest Boat."** (p. 74)

While Lowry's style in these stories at times lapses into obscurity, overrichness, or excessive mannerism, it rises at times to the level of excellence reached in *Under the Volcano*. These stories ''live'' in the sense that Lowry's perception enables him to convey, in a manner both exactly and poetically, the texture of life. (pp. 75-6)

In these stories one finds the same rich irony and humor, the same delight in puns and word play, that suffuse *Under the Volcano.* (p. 76)

If **"Through the Panama"** is Lowry's best short fiction piece dealing with the dark side of the human condition, then **"The Forest Path"** is his best short work dealing with the positive aspects of man's existence. . . . Throughout the story Lowry successfully sustains the tone of high seriousness, and by so doing makes the protagonist a consistent character and the story an aesthetic whole.

Lowry planned to use **"The Forest Path to the Spring"** as the coda to his projected cycle of works, **"The Voyage That Never Ends."** He wanted the beauty and happiness of this story to stand at the end of his work as an antithesis to the darkness and despair of some of the earlier works. He did not live to complete his **"Voyage,"** but **"The Forest Path"** exists to show the reader the ultimate goal he envisioned. (pp. 79-80)

> Dale Edmonds, ''The Short Fiction of Malcolm Lowry,'' in Tulane Studies in English *(copyright © 1967 by Tulane University), Vol. XV, 1967, pp. 59-80.*

DOUGLAS DAY (essay date 1967)

Malcolm Lowry was not really a novelist, except by accident. It is difficult to know what to call him: diarist, compulsive notetaker, poet *manqué*, alcoholic philosophizing rambler—any of these would do for a start, but only for a start. . . . [The] word one hears most often used to describe Lowry is *genius;* and the word, for once, is apt. Even his least successful works are clearly the products of a mind and a sensibility quite different from yours and mine. The second most frequently used epithet is *unique,* and it applies as well as *genius* does: there has never been, one is sure, anyone even remotely like Lowry. (p. ix)

[Readers] have sought to find in his works what is not there, except peripherally: external action—''plot,'' as we used to call it—and realized conflict between characters. Nobody moves anywhere; nothing *happens*. But if there is no external action, there is almost a surfeit of movement internally; and there is enough tension within the mind of the protagonist to render any other conflict superfluous. Lowry was really, for all his romanticism, for all the exoticism of his prose, the most cerebral of writers, a real intellectual's delight. What sustains all his works is not plot, nor dialogue, nor movement, but the spinning up and down of a mind which is genuinely amazing, in all the senses of the word. The pace of this mind is such that it generates great tension and excitement, so that the ''plot'' of a Lowry novel is the movement of the mind of the author—or, shall we say, the mind of the protagonist. Whenever he lets his protagonist think, Lowry becomes a great writer. Whenever he tries to invent action, or dialogue, or to create believable characters other than himself, he is on very thin ice indeed. Sometimes, as with Juan Fernando Martinez in [*Dark As the Grave Wherein My Friend Is Laid*], he succeeds in interesting us in another person—but Juan Fernando never appears in the novel, except as remembered by Sigbjørn Wilderness. And when, in this novel, we are moved by the awesome Mexican landscape, we must realize that it is not Mexican at all (except by accident of geography): it is an inner landscape. . . . (p. xii)

Lowry was nothing if not a symbolizer: whatever happened, whatever he heard or saw, had to *mean* something, however obliquely. Sometimes he could be embarrassingly amateurish in his symbolizing, as when in Chapter VI he evokes ''the bilingual moonlight, that spoke at once the language of love and madness.'' But at his best—which is occasionally in *Ultramarine, Lunar Caustic,* and *Dark As the Grave,* and almost always in *Under the Volcano*—his mind reaches deeply and broadly, drawing from the world, from his own considerable intellect, from his subconscious, new visions of the great old symbols. Not the authentic simple forms of vine, plate, wine, stone, woman, tree—Lowry was after bigger game: the archetypal daemonic forms of abyss, labyrinth, burnt forest, monster, blighted garden, ruined castle, dark and ominous forces at work in an ancient and dangerous world. Thus Sigbjørn

Wilderness is . . . a Dante or a Virgil on his way down into the Inferno. And more than they, because he is going back a second time. And the hell is no one else's but his own.

The first swooping, breathless paragraph of *Dark As the Grave* throws us and Sigbjørn in this downward direction. There he is, pretending he is on a vacation, this writer who cannot write, this would-be hero who has missed World War II (just as his alter ego, Geoffrey Firmin of *Under the Volcano,* had missed the Spanish Civil War), this reformed drunk who has begun to drink again. He has left the security of his Canadian home because a malignant fate has burned it down, and he and his wife have not had the will to finish rebuilding it. He is a middle-aged Lord Jim who no longer has illusions about his honor; he admits his fear of everything but death—which is actually what he is seeking in Mexico. . . . In Mexico he hopes to find Juan Fernando Martinez, whom he thinks of as his good angel—a fellow drunk, but one of nature's noblemen: horseman, swordsman, idealist, true friend. (This same man had also been a presence in *Under the Volcano,* both as the offstage hero Juan Cerillo, and the bibulously *simpático* Dr. Vigil.) Juan Fernando is really the key to Sigbjørn Wilderness, and to this book, in spite of the fact that he never appears: for Sigbjørn comes ultimately to realize (in Chapter IX) that, though he has all these years thought of Juan Fernando as a symbol for life and vitality, he actually is equally symbolic of *death,* in its most attractive forms. When Sigbjørn learns this, he knows then the real reason for the pilgrimage that he is making into his past, which he had hitherto thought of as sordid: he had somehow been *happy* in the bad old days; he had possessed something then that had slipped away from him in the intervening years. This "something" emerges as more than youth, or inspiration, or happy irresponsibility, though these were parts of it: really, what he had known then was the exhilaration that comes from proximity to danger—and the danger for him had not simply been physical, but spiritual as well. In the old days he had been, like Faust, flirting with damnation, and enjoying the flirtation. For Primrose, his pleasant yet not overly perceptive wife, the pilgrimage has the function of vacation-*cum*-exorcism: Sigbjørn is to visit the scenes of his earlier downfall, and lay the ghosts that have plagued him ever since. But Sigbjørn learns that he really does not *want* to lay the ghosts, but to rejoin them—and this is what makes his descent into the Mexican hell truly perilous. (pp. xvii-xix)

Now, this book is no *Under the Volcano.* It might have been but it isn't. There are too many loose ends, too many undeveloped ideas, too many images of intended great significance which never seem more than vaguely portentous. Sometimes Lowry's prose is hasty, even slovenly. The dialogue is often surprisingly wooden. The flight to Mexico with which the novel begins is probably the longest literary journey since that of the *Pequod;* and the evening that Sigbjørn spends talking about his fiction with Eddie and Hippolyte is nearly as lengthy. And improbable to boot: who could talk as long as Sigbjørn does? Who could listen as long as Eddie and Hippolyte do? And who, really, *are* Eddie and Hippolyte, other than receptacles for Sigbjørn's prolixity? Why is Primrose such a lightweight, alternately gushing and carping? How can one understand what is going on in *Dark As the Grave* unless he has a copy of *Under the Volcano* beside him as he reads, in order to keep track of the allusions, to recall characters and incidents? (p. xxi)

Yet in spite of all its flaws, *Dark As the Grave Wherein My Friend Is Laid* needs only so many apologies; for the book has genuine merit as it stands. There is real Lowryesque comedy

in it: the impossible bathroom in the Hotel Cornada; Sigbjørn's envious reflections about the robust virility of other novelists; . . . Sigbjørn's morning swim; Sigbjørn with a hangover—and so on. (p. xxii)

Dark As the Grave Wherein My Friend Is Laid is a work of embryonic greatness. We can lament its imperfect state, but we can also be glad to have it even as it is. Sigbjørn Wilderness, like his creator, was a man worth knowing. (p. xxiii)

> *Douglas Day, "Preface" (1967; reprinted by permission of Brandt & Brandt Literary Agents, Inc.; copyright © 1968 by Douglas Day), in* Dark as the Grave Wherein My Friend Is Laid *by Malcolm Lowry, edited by Douglas Day & Margerie Lowry, The New American Library, 1968, pp. ix-xxiii.*

PERLE S. EPSTEIN (essay date 1969)

Following in the tradition of the Christian Cabbala, Lowry freely incorporated myths and symbols from many other cultural sources. However, still intent on maintaining the Cabbalistic substructure, or what he referred to as the "poem" of [*Under the Volcano*], he utilized the stylistic method of the *Zohar* itself, a book that is entirely composed of allegorical correspondences. Take, for example, the external world of nature as a representation of inner states of consciousness; the Consul's alcoholic bliss is denoted by his idyllic descriptions of the cantinas; his anguish is symbolized by the vultures, dogs, and overgrown gardens. Then there are the seemingly casual references to themes like anti-Semitism that later emerge as motifs of great significance with regard to the plot structure itself. Each of the twelve chapters is really one degree in the twelve stages of initiation. . . . In addition, each tarot suit is embodied in its own particular symbol: wands—the Consul's ever-present walking stick; cups—the drinking theme; swords—a razor and later a machete; pentacles—the zodiac.

A magical aura is diffused by the heightened awareness, the sensitivity to an animistic nature featuring astrological coincidences and spirit messages that characterize the Consul's state. These supernatural components are bound together by the central image of initiatory wine, which bears the property of divine and demonic communication; in this case, mescal. . . . The "occult ordeal" is carefully framed not only in traditional numerological detail but is equally evident in the dominating symbolism of the volcano (or the pilgrimage of ascent) and the barranca (descent into the abyss). Archetypal in its significance, the volcanic peak usually symbolizes the home of the god or gods from which emanate thunder and lightning. Located at the base of the volcano is the cavernous abyss that represents hell.

In view of the ambiguous overlapping of above and below, the initiate cannot be sure of attaining his goal. He may be ritually tortured nevertheless, his only reward being a glimpse into a new dimension.

By way of Böhme and the Cabbala (especially in its Messianic emphasis), the Consul found that evil and self-sacrifice must be accepted before they can be rejected. Largely incorporated in the last three chapters of the novel, the culmination of the initiation in ritual sacrifice is presented in terms of the Mithraic bull sacrifice, the Eleusinian mystery feast, and the Kelipathic accusers.

Keeping in mind that the microcosmic initiation process is directly related to the external world, we learn that Geoffrey's destruction mirrors the coming destruction of nations by war, that Hugh's commitment to the democratic cause foreshadows American intervention in the war, and that Yvonne's barren-ness, her denial of femininity, corresponds to the destructive nature of modern woman. Encompassing these characters and events is the ominous Mexican setting chosen because ". . . It is the ideal setting for the struggle of a human being against the powers of darkness and light."

Mexican lore, with its death preoccupation, which goes to the point of devoting an entire day to the dead on November 2, contributed its share to the darker aspects of the novel. Certain Indian tribes in Mexico outline an elaborate seven-day journey to be taken by the souls of the newly dead, which involves a trial descent into the darkness of the abyss. In the novel, we accompany the Consul on this downward journey from 7 A.M. to 7 P.M. by means of M. Laruelle's opening reflections from the heights overlooking the barranca in Chapter One, all the way through to Geoffrey's final plunge in Chapter Twelve. The route the Consul follows is derived largely from Lévi and Dante, whose vision of hell is that of a narrow end of a conical pit at the center of the cosmos. Here lie Satan's quarters. For one to find one's way out it would be necessary to discover the secret path of the initiate, the path where hell meets heaven and where God and Satan are one—hence the double signifi-cance implied in the Consul's assertion as he heads down the path to Parián: "I like hell."

The astronomical setting of the initiation process is also of great importance. Inextricably combined with astrology and numerology, the novel is loaded with zodiacal significances. Included, for example, in the references to the action taking place "in Scorpio" (the death sign) are reminders of Agrippa's contention that Christ's statement "Are there not twelve hours in a day?" alluded to favorable or unfavorable astrological times for self-purification. (pp. 47-9)

As for the numerical reiterations, we find emphasis primarily on the numbers 666 (the beast in Revelation, but also, in occult circles, symbolic of completion of the "great work of initia-tion") and 999 (666 seen upside down by the Consul), a number of Zoharistic importance. The number 7 can stand for nearly anything, but in *Volcano,* it becomes the Pleiades, a traditional Old Testament number designating sacrifice, as well as the number of heavenly palaces and tower steps to heaven or to hell, and the ledges of purgatory. Moreover, 12 can be mag-ically transposed into a form of 7; both contain 3 and 4, and both control time and events in our universe by means of the seven days of the week and the seven planets, twelve hours of the day, and the signs of the zodiac.

The characters are interrelated, as are the cosmic correspon-dences. Geoffrey is surrounded by wife, half brother (Hugh), and childhood friend (Laruelle); all are connected further by Yvonne's adulterous liaisons with both Hugh and Laruelle. At some point in the novel the protagonists are or have been alter egos to Geoffrey or lovers to Yvonne. Magically speaking, therefore, people who have had contact in the past maintain an underlying magnetism that enables them to continue to in-fluence, and even to symbolize, each other. In this fashion, Geoffrey often seems to be willing the actions of the others, and Yvonne can "plead with" Geoffrey to extricate himself from danger when she is not physically present.

The Consul is, in effect, the central figure of two interlaced triangles. In alchemy, the interlaced triangles stand for the fundamental elements of transmutation: fire and water. The

magician's function is, of course, to maintain the equilibrium between the opposing elements. Geoffrey, victimized by "fire water," has lost his balance. (pp. 49-50)

The most compelling symbol by far is, of course, the Consul himself. Overtly compounded of parts of Faust, Dante, and Bunyan, the roots of his mysterious nature reach deeper into the legendary levels of the book. Morally, he is identified with the strange William Blackstone, a seventeenth-century believer in witchcraft who came from Cambridge to New England much as Lowry himself had done, a man whose writings, like Low-ry's, were destroyed by a fire similar to the one described in Yvonne's dying vision of Geoffrey's burning "great work." And it is as "William Blackstone" that the Consul meets his death. (p. 51)

Each of the twelve chapters [of *Under the Volcano*] follows the hermetic scheme in which human punishment is projected by the twelve zodiacal signs, with suffering decreasing as the initiate ascends by abandoning the seven vices, and increasing as he descends to lower stages of matter. The first ten chapters represent the Sephirotic stages [of the Cabbala], while the elev-enth and twelfth chapters symbolize the culmination of the undertaking in death. Because events actually occur on two levels—the earthly and the astral planes—the dialogue often appears to be ambiguous, the inner monologues confusing or seemingly irrelevant to the exterior action. On these occasions, particularly with regard to Geoffrey's "hallucinations," the reader is usually being presented with some form of Cabbalistic reference. One of the clearest examples of this technique occurs in the scene during which Geoffrey's rumination about his spiritual life is reflected by his lovemaking. (p. 52)

[The] fate suffered by his four characters indirectly corresponds to that of the four sages who, according to perhaps the most famous of the Cabbalistic legends, enter a garden. One looks upon it and dies, a second goes mad, a third turns away from it and becomes an atheist, while the last looks upon it and returns home. For to the Cabbalist, the Garden of Eden was actually no more than the human mind, in which God had planted the choice between good and evil. And as Geoffrey states himself at one point, "equilibrium is all" in this garden where the life is balanced between two scales of opposing forces. Destruction resides in such unbalanced forces as the fascist police who rule the Mexican gardens. Positive power resides in the hands of the world restorers (in this case, the socialists) who reconstruct the ruined world from the remnants of the primordial world of the seven kings of Edom whose possessions had been broken up and dispersed after their de-struction. Herein lie the Cabbalistic underpinnings of the nov-el's political theme.

The ruined, infertile state of Geoffrey's garden, with its thorns and weeds, indicates that there is a breach between upper and lower planes, that is, between God and man. Therefore, in the recurring allusion to the ruined palace of Maximilian is implied not only the death of earthly love but also the forfeiture of communion between the heavenly palace and the kingdom be-low.

Only man himself can seal this breach, and because the Cabalist regards all mankind as one great totality, "one great united stream of life," the suffering of one man atones for all. It becomes the responsibility of this man to penetrate the secrets of the terrestrial, the astronomical, and the undefined worlds by means of his own corresponding channels of communication in order eventually to reunite those worlds. The Consul has apparently accomplished the first two stages, but by misusing his power he has lost control of the undefined world, becoming victimized by it instead. From this world emerge all the haunting demons and hallucinations that overcome him. Here too lies the territory for the ecstatic experience that is likened by Cabbalists to a sense of drowning or sinking (the manner in which the Consul ultimately ends his life). (pp. 53-4)

> *Perle S. Epstein, in her* The Private Labyrinth of Malcolm Lowry: "Under the Volcano" and the Cabbala *(copyright © 1969 by Perle S. Epstein; reprinted by permission of Holt, Rinehart and Winston, Publishers), Holt, 1969, 241 p.*

WILLIAM H. GASS (essay date 1970)

[Is] *Under the Volcano* really a biography, a one-day history of a man, and is its advantage in being imaginary that it can with confidence report details biographers can rarely have? Novels are made of such details, no doubt of that. But what biographer would want them?. . . [Facts by the thousands here]— all trivialities, items which could never find their way into any serious history. (p. 56)

We shall never verify this history. It rests nowhere in our world. Our world, in the first place, lacks significance; it lacks connection. If I swallow now—what of it? if I pass a cola sign— no matter. . . . And the real mountains of Mexico, those two chains which traverse the republic, exist despite us and all our feelings. But the Popocatepetl of the novel is yet another mountain, and when, in the first chapter, we are taken on a tour of the town, the facts we are given have quite a different function. Lowry is constructing a place, not describing one; he is making a Mexico for the mind where, strictly speaking, there are no menacing volcanoes, only menacing phrases, where complex chains of concepts traverse our consciousness, and where, unlike history, events take place in the moment that we read them—over and over as it may be, irregularly even, at widely separated times—whenever we restore these notes to music. Each of us, too, must encounter and enter the book alone, bring our lifetime to it, since truly it is a dark wood, this Mexico, a southern hell we're being guided through, and although simply begun, it is difficult to remain, to continue so terrible a journey. In this conceptual country there are no mere details, nothing is a simple happenstance, everything has meaning, is part of a net of essential relations. Sheer coincidence is impossible, and those critics who have complained of this quality in Lowry have misunderstood the nature of the novel. They would not complain of the refrain of a song that its constant reappearance was coincidence. So the Ferris wheel of the festival—for this is the Day of the Dead, after all—will turn in our eyes as it turns in the Consul's, the burning wheel of Buddhist law, "its steel twigs caught in the emerald pathos of the trees," appearing just as often as design demands.

Nothing like history, then, *the Volcano* ties time in knots, is utterly subjective, completely contrived, as planned and patterned as a magical rug where the figure becomes the carpet. Nothing like a country or a town—no Oil City—*the Volcano* is made of a series of names which immediately become symbolic, and reverberate when struck like a hundred gongs. Even drunkenness has a different function, for the Consul does not drink so we may better understand drunkenness, and though he is ridden with guilt, his guilt is as fictional as he is. The Consul's drinking frees the language of the book, allows it to stagger and leap like verse, gives Lowry the freedom to construct freely. The Consul's stupors are the stupors of poetry,

as madness was for Lear and his fool, and chivalry for Cervantes.

The Volcano is a mountain. We must climb. And it is difficult to maintain a foothold at first. Yet soon we begin to feel the warmth at its core, and few books will finally flow over us so fully, embed us in them as the citizens of Pompeii were bedded by their mountain, the postures of their ordinary days at once their monuments, their coffins, and their graves. Of novels, few are so little like life, few are so formal and arranged; there are few whose significance is so total and internal. Nonetheless, there are scarcely any which reflect the personal concerns of their author more clearly, or incline us as steeply to a wonder and a terror of the world until we fear for our own life as the Consul feared for his, and under such pressures yield to the temptation to say what seems false and pedestrian: that this book is about each of us—in Saint Cloud, Oil City, or Bayonne, N.J.—that it is about drunkenness and Mexico, or even that it is about that poor wretch Malcolm Lowry. (pp. 57-9)

> *William H. Gass, "In Terms of the Toenail: Fiction and the Figures of Life," in his* Fiction and the Figures of Life *(copyright © 1970 by William H. Gass; reprinted by permission of International Creative Management), Alfred A. Knopf, Inc.; 1970, pp. 55-78.*

MATTHEW CORRIGAN (essay date 1971)

As a piece of writing [*October Ferry to Gabriola*] achieves moments of lyric and philosophic grace that equal anything written in the twentieth century; moments that spring from such a quietness of spirit (a *quietus,* even) that it is difficult to peruse them in the context of a work that describes itself on the surface as a novel.

The infernal and paradisiacal (Eridanus) poles that divided and ruled Lowry's thinking are felt once again, though the pull is positive throughout, inclining finally toward a synthesis of salvation, even of grace. The theme is dispossession, eviction. Ethan and Jacqueline Llewelyn are under edict of eviction from their squatter's shack at Eridanus, on the north shore of Burrard Inlet, opposite Vancouver. They have shared two years of extraordinary, primitive joy: a joy based on the near totality of their rebellion against a polluted, plastic age (the year is 1949); based on a simple return to nature and a learning to love the elements of that nature; but based also on an Ockham balance achieved between reality and fear. . . . (pp. 71-2)

Essentially the novel takes place in Llewelyn's consciousness, though of such a symbiotic and cosmic nature is that consciousness that it tends to become whatever it considers or momentarily takes cognizance of. The book is this consciousness in the state of becoming. Present action takes place on a bus from Victoria to Nanaimo, where the Llewelyns board a ferry for Gabriola Island. They have heard of a sea-captain's house for sale on the island and they are journeying to inspect it. . . . Present experiences tend to be few and far between— an incident in a Nanaimo tavern, something seen from the window of a bus—experiences which propel Llewelyn back into his past. The trip is laced with minute correspondences which secure the past in a state of webbed terror. Most of the time we are delving so deeply into the past that its own past becomes significant. The past within the past is explored in depth, so that everything gives way to and becomes part of everything else: a single continuum of consciousness in which time is technically suspended.

The ferry is actually taken but returns because of a sick passenger. The whole trip (Eridanus: Vancouver: Victoria: Nanaimo) seems to enact a geographic flirtation with Eridanus, as though something in the elements refused to let them travel far from home; at several junctures they find themselves pointed homeward, the significance of which does not escape Llewelyn. The book ends with the travellers once again ferrying across the strait to Gabriola. Instead of taking us to the island, however, Lowry lets Llewelyn envision their new life there, a vision very close structurally to the one at the end of *Volcano*, where Firmin imagines a similar Canadian paradise. This sudden projection forward optimistically at the end presages an escape for the Llewelyns from the past that has terrorized them. At least this seems to be Lowry's intention. When the ferry returns to discharge its sick passenger the evening newspapers are taken on board. As the ferry approaches Gabriola they read that city council has reprieved the squatters at Eridanus. They are free to return from exile. Since they are already on their way, the prospect of a more permanent home on the island takes on a new significance. It is as though they have eased clear of their own doom, have escaped the punishment that has been threatening throughout. Salvation is felt as a moment of release that comes when least expected in the throes of an ordeal; it is something to remain humble about, for it retains as its present heritage the remembrance of what it is like to suffer in exile. Such is the Lowry synthesis. We glimpse it partially in **"Forest Path to the Spring"** and in *Dark as the Grave;* in *Gabriola* it is given its longest moment. What is amazing is that it thrusts through the unfinished manuscript with the clarity and consonance of a single state of mind, suggesting that all of Lowry's later work was reaching toward this conclusion. (pp. 72-3)

That Ethan Llewelyn is a forty-year-old retired criminal lawyer is almost irrelevant to the book. Why he has given up his Toronto law practice to settle in a west coast shack is never explained. . . . What is most unfinished in this book concerns Llewelyn the lawyer and the reasons for his retreat. Lowry's working notes indicate some of the things he intended to add to facilitate our believing in his character on objective as well as personal grounds. Evidently, we were to be shown how Llewelyn had defended a man he believed innocent, only to learn he was a murderer. Thus his disillusionment and his retreat from civilization. That the book works as well as it does despite its factual imperfections and its structural imbalance indicates, I think, the degree to which Lowry was no mean characterizer, and no ordinary novelist. Finally, it doesn't matter who Llewelyn is trying to be; he is the Lowry persona— he could be no other. The book is the mind of the author at work phenomenologically on the raw substance of experience, narrowed as that experience was through his choice of lifestyle, through his consciously cultivating one species of suffering, through his latent Manicheism.

Llewelyn's external world makes a bizarre kind of sense. It is constantly telling him something about himself, pumping him with information to help overthrow the fear that the world has gone mad. There are few inert or isolated facts. Films that Llewelyn sees become more real than life itself. He becomes the "Wandering Jew" in a film of that title. He suffers that becoming. Nothing exists for him with prehension, without intentionality. (pp. 73-4)

Everything is connected with everything for those with pure vision. The men's section of a bar in Nanaimo (which has "an ugliness the world had not thought of before") seems to take on the "perfect outward expression of his own inner soul, of what it meant, of what it did, even of what awful things could happen in it." Words overheard are "addressed mysteriously to Ethan himself; and moreover . . . every phrase [has] another meaning, perhaps many meanings, intended for his ears alone." (p. 74)

When things are going well there is this pefect symbiosis between man and environment, between self and God. Their shack, unlike their other two houses (both of which burned to the ground mysteriously), means more than the usual abode: "they wear it like a shell," they "love it like a sentient being." Eridanus exemplifies a religious wholeness; and love is the cement that secures it fast. Eviction, or its threat, is thus taken as symptomatic of some overlooked and unconfessed evil. Llewelyn has no difficulty screening his past for the appropriate evidence. He sees himself responsible for his friend's suicide; he sees himself a failure as a lawyer who might plead eloquently for the abolition of capital punishment, and for the life of a boy murderer. There is even the fear that he has become too possessive for Eridanus. Guilt is never that simple or unilateral, however. Llewelyn has the added torment of terrible visions— visions of chaos and not of some principle of good controlling the reeling world. His greatest despair comes when under the influence of alcohol.

Significantly, Llewelyn cannot avoid peering into such depths. He needs a sense of hell in his life almost in order to keep his joy sensibly bound. Once he envisions this hell it is enough. An inverse spirit resembling hope begins to point him in the opposite direction and he sees with cleared vision. (p. 75)

The only drama is that between present and past consciousness; the only action the will of the moment grappling with a mute past, not so that it can strike out in pure action, but rather so that it can enlarge upon itself, so that it can know itself. The process is self-defeating because of its intoxication, its solipsism. Few prose writers of the modern period have tried (have tormented) the moment of consciousness as Lowry does in this work. What he seems to be emphasizing is the compulsion of modern man to rework past consciousness; suggesting that if man is to constitute himself as a free individual he must first make sense of the nightmare of his past. The posture of Lowry's later work is *retrospective* in this sense. Terror is something experienced when one realizes the significance of the past, when one sees the connection; it does not consist of any present threat. Since all of this ratiocination is intended as a kind of reparation for the future, the present moment tends to be overlooked, if not also to be underlived. There is almost no active present tense in this work. (pp. 75-6)

Lowry's is the problem of the poet turned mystic, a problem of learning to face the fact that everything that comes from his creative unconscious is part of everything else in the order of creation, and must be attended to, must be set down in chiselled stone prose, if the final balance is to be maintained. Editing, or what for the average novelist amounts to an ordinary task, is lost sight of in Lowry's later work. Certain parts of *Gabriola* give the feeling that at some later rereading the author would have trimmed or deleted them. Yet the same pieces show us something of the difficulty of doing this for Lowry, because in some way they control parts of the larger whole; they give the feeling of belonging. There is a strange logic behind the excess (the plethora) of this manuscript, a logic akin to that of dreams. It defies ordinary daylight understanding yet demands our attention. I am thinking of the way a person we know reveals himself or herself totally in a dream, becoming through word or deed a full being and doing so in terms that seem totally appropriate to that person; so that on awakening we think, "Yes, that is exactly what she would say, how she would act." Though nothing of the sort had taken place or would ever take place in real life the dream had effected the imaginative leap that life was too shy or slow to make. The ontological accuracy of the thing strikes us. It is the same with the manuscript of *Gabriola*. . . . Reading Lowry, if one does it properly, requires more than the usual suspension of disbelief. If the writing works for us, it does so not because it is fiction on its way to becoming a novel, but because it entails a vision of a higher order of creative existence altogether than we ordinarily get in modern literature. (pp. 76-7)

> Matthew Corrigan, "Lowry's Last Novel" (reprinted by permission of the author), in Canadian Literature, *No. 48, Spring, 1971 (and reprinted as "The Writer as Consciousness: A View of 'October Ferry to Gabriola'," in* Malcolm Lowry: The Man and His Work, *edited by George Woodcock, University of British Columbia Press, 1971, pp. 71-7).*

RICHARD HAUER COSTA   (essay date 1972)

Lowry's dilemma as a craftsman is not to be solved by a balancing of assets and liabilities. He possessed the virtues of his defects; without the flaws, the undeniable powers might have been diminished. (p. 157)

Lowry was a *conductor* of what one unsympathetic reviewer called "mescalusions" but which really come close to being in Carl G. Jung's terms "archetypal fragments" or "primordial images." These visions—I shall define their Jungian equivalents shortly—obsessed Lowry to the point that their incidence outpaced his ability to assimilate them into artistic fiction.

Except for *Under the Volcano,* a handful of short stories, and several fragments of *October Ferry to Gabriola,* all of Lowry's prose boils down to being a catalogue of one protagonist's inner visions and lacking "the final expurgatory look." If we did not have the evidence of *Volcano,* it would be easy to conclude that Lowry was incapable of transmuting vision into viable fiction.

One of the keys to understanding Malcolm Lowry as conductor of mystic impulses may come less from literature than from modern psychology—the writings and theories of Jung in particular. (pp. 157-58)

Lewis Mumford has written that for Carl G. Jung dreams were more gripping than wakeful life. He often felt himself living simultaneously in two different ages and being two different persons. This feeling of double life, which persisted to the very end of Jung's life, haunted Lowry daily. In his earliest fiction, dream was a favored narrative device. Lowry conceived of dream as bearing the same relationship to the dreamer as film to the viewer.

This idea can best be illustrated by reference to an early and little-known story, **"The Bulls of the Resurrection."** . . . Two Cambridge undergraduates, Rysdale and Sam, stand at a bar in Granada, Spain. Like all the names of places in Lowry's writings, the designation of the tavern is significant. It is Café Fray Diego de León. A girl named Terry, their companion on the trek to Spain, has deserted them for a third young man, Smith. The resentment of Rysdale, the girl's original lover, spills over as he recounts to Sam his dream of the death of Terry and of the execution by beheading of Smith. The scene

is characteristically Lowryan, Jungian: the hero's youth and early manhood are merged. The dream takes place in a prison where Rysdale and Smith are simultaneously inmates and pupils; the setting is concurrently Spain (the present) and Dartmoor (the past), where the two men had played as children. Sam asks if the dream might not have been evoked by a haunting El Greco original they had seen. Rysdale explains that

> it was like El Greco gone mad. No, I'll tell you what it was like. It was as though a moving picture had been projected onto a Greco instead of onto a screen. There was this fixed, timeless, haunted background, but this was not part of what was going on, this was only the relief against which it could be seen, the means by which it became visible.

Here, in an apprentice story, Lowry provides in capsule his concept, not then refined, of the interplay between linear time-space and flux; that is, between place frozen in time and movement and change that are continuous.

By the time of *October Ferry to Gabriola,* Lowry had refined the literary apparatus by which Ethan Llewelyn's visions could be made viable in fiction. At the end of the extraordinarily rich "fire" sequence at the heart of the book, Ethan sits alone in a hotel beer parlor. He has had a quarrel with Jacqueline over the series of fires which, coupled with reverberations and correspondences in his current reading, have placed him "in the current," at the threshold of consciousness transcended. He becomes aware of something which Freud described, writing of the epilepsy of Dostoevsky, as a "mind explosion."

> . . . something more frightening yet taking place in his mind. It was a feeling that permeated the high ill-lit yellow walls . . . , the long dim corridor between the two beer parlours, on which the door now seemed to be opened by an invisible hand. . . .

Ethan finds this collective mental image held unwaveringly if instantaneously "on the screen of his mind." The unconscious, hiding place of demons, has not only been opened (". . . the home also of more conscious mental abortions and aberrations; of disastrous yet unfinished thoughts, half hopes and half intentions . . . where precepts, long abandoned, stumbled on") but become the province where a peak at Creation is vouchsafed (". . . why, then, should he have rushed to the conclusion that . . . this collision of contingencies, was in its final essence diabolical, or fearful, or meaningless? . . . Mightn't he equally well consider that he'd been vouchsafed . . . a glimpse into the very workings of creation itself . . .")

Lowry wisely undercuts the messianic thrust of the vision by allowing it to happen while Ethan is downing one beer after another. Nevertheless, the juxtaposing of motifs from one of his earliest stories and his last book reveals that Lowry never ceased in the quest to pin down "the constant irrelevant relevancies of life—the 'thinginess' of life—impinging on us, expanding, diminishing, falling away . . . as mind moves through landscape, or landscape through mind (it is all one)." But if mind and landscape indeed are all one, it took Lowry a lifetime of trial-and-error, revision-on-revision, to dissolve the false boundaries erected by every novelist until Sterne and most of those following Sterne until the arrival of Joyce and Proust.

It is necessary here to try to summarize those aspects of Jungian psychology which have pertinence in being linked to Malcolm

Lowry's life and works. In general, Jung's stress on the manifestations in art of unconscious *expresson* over Freud's concern with the morbid effects of unconscious *re*pression make his findings of enormous relevance to so tireless a collector of the residue of the unconscious as Lowry. Jung's impulse was that he had located in the unconscious "the matrix of a mythopeic imagination that has vanished from our rational age." Lowry, through the Consul, felt himself a survivor of a sensibility that has disappeared in this century. The heroes of **"The Forest Path"** and *October Ferry* live visionary lives dreaming that they have found an earthly paradise out of time and place. (pp. 159-61)

Jung departs from Freud in his belief that it is not necessary to use a dream as *the* point of departure for the process of "free association." . . . When dreaming becomes obsessive and dreams highly charged, the personal associations produced by the dreamer do not usually suffice for a satisfactory interpretation. Elements often occur, according to Jung, that are *not* individual and that cannot be derived from the dreamer's experiences. Their presence cannot be explained by anything in the individual's own life: they seem to be aboriginal, innate, and inherited shapes of the human mind. Jung calls them "archetypes" or "primordial images." "The archetype," he writes, "is a tendency to form . . . representations of a motif—representations that can vary a great deal in detail without losing their basic pattern."

I do not believe it an oversimplification to say that Malcolm Lowry's life was itself an archetype. And, because all of his fiction except for *Volcano,* duplicated his life, the fiction, too, is archetypal in the Jungian sense: representational of a motif. What, then, is the motif, the archetype?

Throughout his life, Lowry retained as the title for the whole under which all the fictinal parts would eventually be grouped, **The Voyage That Never Ends.** He saw life in a series of compensatory metaphors that recur in his fiction: water and fire, the river and the ravine, the volcano as emblematic of life and death. The dramatic tension, symbolized by these metaphors, was always the possibility of salvation, the chance for rebirth. (pp. 161-62)

The Consul's visions run a vertically cyclical path—from the snowy peak of Himavat and the summits of the twin volcanoes to life under the volcano, the depths of the barranca "through the blazing of ten million burning bodies falling. . . .'' The volcano, at once infernal and redemptive, provides the book's title and its most insistent symbol. The path is both an ascent and a descent: an ascent from fire to light—Yvonne's death vision—and a descent from light to fire—the Consul's.

The Consul's obsessive thoughts of fire always produce the compensating image, the opposite symbol of water. One cannot help but note the water imagery of the Consul's vision in the Garden Chapter (V) just before he flees to his overrun flowers seeking the bottle he has hidden among them. He imagines himself on Mount Himavat, pausing in his ascent to slake his thirst. . . . (p. 163)

The profusion of language suggestive of regenerative water is unmistakable [in this section]. Finally, in his vision, the Consul realizes that he is drinking not water but "certainty of brightness." The scene represents the Consul's loftiest aspiration until the final pages: the closest he comes to salvation. At the last, seven chapters—perhaps seven hours, but, in terms of *rendered time,* a lifetime—later, the Consul's ears pick up "the distant clamour of a waterfall and what sounded like the cries

of love." . . . But the dream of Eridanus—the life-renewing river that legend says received the dead Phaethon—gives way as the Consul, dying, is borne to the edge of the barranca to the accompaniment of "the noise of foisting lava in his ears." . . . (p. 164)

[Lowry's] fondest hope was that he, like Orpheus, would soar from—transcend—the ashes of his fiery life. Life as a wheel continuously turning forward and backward on itself—life as a river (Eridanus and Styx alike) that contains at once the beauty of flow and the murk of stagnation: these are the major motifs in Lowry's working in life and art of an archetpe to which now can be applied this name: the Pilgrim's Everlasting Return. Or—better—the Everlasting Voyager. For, as Ethan Llewelyn muses near the end of *October Ferry,* everybody was on the homeward-outward-bound voyage. (p. 166)

"It is quite within the bounds of possibility for a man to recognize the relative evil of his nature," Jung declares, "but it is a rare and shattering experience for him to gaze into the face of absolute evil." The Consul looks on the dark side of his nature with an intensity that is rare in modern literature. *Under the Volcano* is the story of a possessed man that could only have been written by a possessed man. Yet the always lucid evocation of the Consul's madness is the product of an artist who was in control of his Jungian labyrinth. The contrapuntal resonances by which Lowry built his symphonic novel echo only occasionally in the inner monologues of Sigbjørn Wilderness, Ethan Llewelyn, and all the Lowryan personae of the subsequent fiction. After a novel in which nearly everything—at last—worked, nothing really worked again. . . . In life, Lowry enacted daily Jung's concepts of the Unconscious. In art, Lowry's attempts to metamorphose Jung-like impulses failed and eventually overwhelmed him. (pp. 166-67)

> *Richard Hauer Costa, "The Jungian Conductor,"*
> *in his* Malcolm Lowry *(copyright © 1972 by Twayne*
> *Publishers, Inc.; reprinted with the permission of*
> *Twayne Publishers, a Division of G. K. Hall & Co.,*
> *Boston), Twayne, 1972, pp. 155-67.*

DOUGLAS DAY (essay date 1973)

[*Under the Volcano* is] a deeply moral work. To say that it advances its cause on several levels at once is to state the obvious—but the obvious is necessary, here. I can, still foreseeing the eventual *Gestalt* approach to the novel, discern at the moment five such levels, all in motion, all interdependent, all pointing toward the inevitable conclusion.

The first of these is that which we might label *chthonic:* the earthbound level, composed of natural elements either on or beneath the earth and (for purposes of neatness in classification) man-made elements which are made to function in accord with Lowry's chthonic grand scheme. Here also belong all subhuman living creatures. Above all, of course, is the great volcano, Popocatepetl, the Smoking Warrior, standing guard over his sleeping mate, Ixtaccihuatl, and serving as representative of all the world's magic mountains: the real ones of Hawaii, Yvonne's birthplace, and of Karakoram and the Hindu Kush, looming in the far north of Geoffrey's native Kashmir; and the mythic or literary ones of the *Divine Comedy,* the *Mahabarata,* and the Hellenic Mount Erebus. In Lowry's novel the conventional salvific notions about ascent of the magic mountain are employed only ironically, negatively; what really concerns him is what, after all, is *under* the volcano: the frightening realm of Tartarus, the infernal abyss below Hades. His characters may walk on the surface of the earth, but they are constantly being reminded of what is below them: the treacherous and fetid *barranca* winds through Quauhnahuac, and yawns also behind the Farolito in Parían, waiting to receive the body of the Consul. (pp. 326-27)

The chthonic imagery is, clearly, archetypally demonic in nature: that is, it employs the traditional affirmative apocalyptic images of the Mount of Perfection, the fertile valley, the cleansing stream or fountain, and the blossoming garden, but employs them in an inverted, ironic form. What had indicated fruition, now indicates sterility; what had represented cleansing, now represents corruption, and what had symbolized the soul's striving upward toward salvation, now symbolizes the descent into damnation. It is of a world turned upside down that Lowry writes. (pp. 329-30)

The novel swarms with scorpions, spiders, vultures, armadillos, hideous and starving pariah dogs, and horses straight from the Apocalypse. . . . Other than the ever-present pariah dogs, the animal Geoffrey Firmin sees most often is probably the figure on the label of bottles of Anís del Mono: a red and grinning monkey, brandishing a pitchfork and wagging his barbed tail.

These are the paramount images on the chthonic level of the novel. There are others that the ultimate *Gestalt* interpretation must encompass: the signs, posters, and illustrations along the way, some highly portentous . . . , some as mere distractions, used to indicate that the senses of the central characters are constantly being assailed by one appeal after another; until, surrealistically, the gratuitous signs come to seem as momentous as the crucial ones. There are the twisted railway tracks and roads: a grand American-style highway, for instance, enters Quauhnahuac from the north, but becomes lost in the narrow streets of the town and emerges from the south end as a goat track. And, of no small importance, there are the two chief attractions of the carnival that is taking place in Quauhnahuac: the Máquina Infernal, by now surely familiar to us, and the Ferris wheel, looming above the town, and carrying all the symbolic weight Lowry can give it. . . . The main point to understand about all of this chthonic imagery is that it is the very opposite of static. Even the volcano seems to be in constant motion, brooding ominously one moment, smoking benignly in the distance the next. . . . It is this chthonic level that gives the work its extraordinary textural density, its oppressiveness which is sometimes almost insupportable. Everything in nature is rendered alive and febrile, as in a woodcut by Munch or an oil by Ryder. Such vitality is initially exhilarating, but—like a fever—ultimately exhausting.

Fortunately, there are other levels than the chthonic in *Under the Volcano*. Sometimes they intensify the fever, but occasionally they distract us from it. The second, or *human,* level does both. The background figures seem for the most part to have been suggested by Breughel, or perhaps drawn from Buñuel or Eisenstein films set in Mexico: there are noseless peons, legless beggars, exalted madmen, loathsome old crones, brutal, mustachioed policemen. . . . These extras are really part of the setting, and scarcely function as characters. But there are minor figures who do indeed come across as recognizably human. Dr. Vigil, for instance, is a small triumph: he is not only two kinds of physician, advertising himself publicly as a specialist in illnesses of childhood and nervous indispositions, and privately—in men's rooms—as a clinician for all manner of sexual disorders; he is also a sportsman, a gentleman, and almost as great a drunk as his friend the Consul. Through

precise and deft descriptions of a few of his mannerisms (the quick flick of his wrist, say, as he whips his cigarette lighter from his pocket), Lowry conveys to us exactly what sort of person the agreeable Dr. Vigil is: concerned, elegant, intelligent, but perhaps too much of a playboy to take himself or his profession very seriously—a well-meaning but finally rather inadequate Virgil to the Consul's Dante. (pp. 331-33)

The emphasis on the human level of *Under the Volcano* is of course on the four chief characters. . . . [It] is these four who bear the burden of realistic delineation in the novel. Geoffrey Firmin, then, may be any number of extraordinary things, but he is first of all a man, and a man of definable qualities. He has been a very vulnerable and touching kind of orphan, a champion boy golfer, an eccentric sort of scholar, a naval hero, a diplomat. He has for years been engaged in writing a book on "Secret Knowledge," which shows no signs of being completed. He has been, for probably not more than four or five years, a serious drinker. (p. 334)

Though his alcoholism is bad indeed, it is not the worst of the Consul's problems—is, in fact, only a symptom of something far more dangerous. (p. 335)

[He] drinks to shatter his consciousness; and to avoid responsibility, he tries to convince himself that his magical dabblings have doomed him, that he has turned his back on God, and come to long for hell. But he still hears that voice—even as he is only minutes away from his death: in the Farolito, after he has had intercourse with the whore, María he feels that now surely he is completely damned, and slides into what theologians would recognize as the gaiety of despair. But, even as he is aware of a desire for "complete glutted oblivion," a voice seems to be saying in his ear, "Alas, my poor child, you do not feel any of those things really, only lost, only homeless." He may think of himself as playing Hephaestus to Yvonne's promiscuous Aphrodite, or Prometheus, or Faust, or the failed Cabbalistic adept, or the guilty warrior; and he may posture about how much pleasure he derives from his torment; but actually—on the human level—he is only pathetic: a good man self-destroyed by his inability to overcome whatever it is that prohibits him from loving.

With the three other principal characters, there is not so much that needs to be said, especially if we take Lowry seriously when . . . he says that all four characters are meant not to be considered as individual entities, but as parts of one larger personality. Since all three men have in fact possessed Yvonne, the four have at least a certain sexual connection; and there are other interesting possibilities if we should choose to assign the four traditional familial roles, so that Geoffrey becomes Father (he calls himself "Papa," as do Yvonne and Hugh, who are both twelve years younger than the Consul), Hugh becomes Son (since Geoffrey has served in a more-or-less parental relationship to him), and Jacques, who is Geoffrey's age and who had been a close childhood friend, becomes Brother, or—let us say, since the song was to become a refrain in *Hear Us O Lord From Heaven Thy Dwelling Place*—Frère Jacques. This leaves Yvonne in the role of *das ewig Weibliche*: the eternal feminine, mother, mate, sister, and daughter, all things to all men. If they are not all the same man, as Lowry claims, they might at least constitute one standard Freudian family. (pp. 338-39)

On the third level of meaning, that which I shall call the *political,* we are still mimetically oriented. Now Mexico becomes the earthly paradise first as ruined by exploiting *conquista-*

dores, and then as jeopardized by left-versus-right revolutionary activity in the late Thirties of this century. (p. 341)

[There can] be little dispute about the political significance of the ruined-garden motif. . . . [The] cautionary sign that the Consul sees everywhere applies not just to him, as an Adam who has sullied his paradise, but to mankind at large. Now the earth is a garden, in imminent danger of destruction by the forces of oppression (whether Communist or Fascist); and the reason for worldwide peril is announced by the inscription on Jacques's wall: one can't live without loving. Thus it is not only the Consul who has failed to love, but all of the rest of us hypocrite readers as well. And when the Consul dies, civilization is also perishing. . . . (pp. 341-42)

The political level bears its relation to the fourth, or *magical* level of the novel. If we choose to take this level seriously (as Lowry pretended to do, but I suspect did not—quite), then we can say that, because every element, every symbol in *Under the Volcano* is an integral part of that infernal machine, then even the most insignificant details have their share in affecting the downfall of Geoffrey Firmin. Everything, moreover, is related to everything else: Geoffrey's world is a world of occult and total correspondence, one in which there is a vital connection not only between things material and things spiritual, but also in a very mysterious way between all things that have concrete existence. Geoffrey is—or had been, before the gods turned against him—an adept in a number of esoteric cults; he had been a magus, a dark magician who was privy to the innermost secrets of alchemy, Rosicrucianism, Swedenborgianism, and—most importantly—the Cabbala. . . . (pp. 343-44)

On the magical plane . . . it is not enough to say simply that Geoffrey Firmin is a drunk: he is—or had been—a mystic, an adept in the most esoteric varieties of occultism; and his drunkenness is for him no mere vice, but a depravity of awesome proportions, a sickness of the soul, perhaps even—because he comes to embrace his depravity, and consciously to seek his destruction—a perverse way to spiritual enlightenment. Thus his final, suicidal debauchery is more than just that: it is a frenzied and headlong leap into the abyss, a deliberate and successful attempt at self-damnation. This failed Consul, this erratic and faintly ludicrous drunk, is nothing less than a modern-day type of the Faustian-Promethean rebel, a man who turns his back on Grace, and who seeks by doing so to acquire diabolical wisdom and power. He knows, like Rimbaud, Baudelaire, and the rest of the *poètes maudits,* that the way down and the way up are one and the same; and he, like them, prefers the way down. (p. 345)

The crucial component in Geoffrey Firmin's character is that he lives in continual terror. Not Angst, nor *Weltschmerz,* nor even simple fright: *terror.* All his magical posturing is only a way of hiding first from the world in which he has so signally failed, but chiefly from God, who, Geoffrey Firmin is sure, must hate him.

Which brings us to our fifth, or *religious* level. In the never-posted letter to Yvonne which Jacques Laruelle reads on the anniversary of the Consul's death, the Consul had written: "Love is the only thing which gives meaning to our poor ways on earth: not precisely a discovery, I am afraid." (p. 348)

It is the Consul's failure to experience love in the sense of *logos* (roughly, devotion to the Divine Word, or to God's authority) that concerns us on the religious level. Like Marlowe's Faustus, Geoffrey Firmin knows that one has only to

love God and ask for salvation in order to be saved; and, like Faustus, he cannot love, cannot ask. (p. 349)

And the Consul *is* damned. One can't live without loving. On the religious level, Fray Luís de Leon's words take on their ultimate meaning: without loving God, one cannot live eternally. *Under the Volcano,* then, gives us an immensely detailed and precise portrait of the failure and self-destruction of a good man who finds truth too simple, and who must complicate his life in order to function at all. The too-simple truth that he cannot bring himself to face, is that in order to survive, he must love his wife, his fellow men, and his God. And if Kierkegaard is correct in saying that love is not an exclusively personal attribute, but an attribute by virtue of which or in which one exists for others, then we can say that Geoffrey Firmin aspires to love, prays for the ability to love, but never succeeds in escaping from what he calls "this dreadful tyranny of self" enough to exist in any real way for others. The Consul is right: he already is in hell, and the hell is himself. (pp. 349-50)

> *Douglas Day, in his* Malcolm Lowry: A Biography *(copyright © 1973 by Douglas Day; reprinted by permission of the author and Oxford University Press, Inc.),* Oxford University Press, New York, 1973, 483 p.

MALCOLM BRADBURY (essay date 1973)

When the postwar English novel comes under fire for failing to continue with the traditions, ambitions, and artistic pretensions of the modernist movement, and for lapsing into literary quietism, there are a few names we can produce to refute the charge. (p. 181)

[In the case of Malcolm Lowry it is possible] to suppose that the modernist air was not a fully assured possession, was a commitment that divided his power or else stood in excess of what those powers could achieve. An inspection of the *Selected Letters of Malcolm Lowry* . . . an anguished and engaging compilation of the greatest fascination for anyone interested in the contours of modern creativity, further exposes and extends this problem, which had been growing more and more apparent in Lowry's later work. That collection makes it that much clearer that his work was conceived of as a life-dedication, the dedication of a man of great intelligence and critical instinct attempting a full and responsible achievement. It also makes even clearer what one might also suspect from the work, which we still have only incompletely (plenty of manuscript remains to be released)—that that life-dedication proceeded according to the evolution of a nurtured creative instinct that was always working to place and shape an abundance of material which constantly challenged its producer. One of Lowry's favourite phrases in these letters is 'design-governing postures'—those techniques, often borrowed from others, which compose a wealth of matter already in a sense achieved, but which place and make resonant that matter. At the same time there are numerous uneasy signs of a creative direction never fully achieved, a bewilderment about the potential public meanings of his own type of creativity, a sense, not uncommon in modern writing, that what has been written is not of itself complete, or rightly acquired. Part of this may well be due to Lowry's unhappy dealings with publishers. But the problem strikes deep into his very creativity, and comes out (as it also does in Dylan Thomas) as a principle of vacillation between an extreme artistic ambition and the sense of never having achieved a proper subject-matter to serve it. Like Thomas, Lowry was a middle-class provincial boy for whom the dedication to art brought a species of suffering, and this suffering becomes a staple of the writing; if one presses personal passions and myths hard enough art will emerge, but as a kind of testimony to one's seriousness. So Lowry can say, in a letter to his Random House editor about *October Ferry to Gabriola,* a book still somewhat clumsily personal in its unfinished, posthumously published form: 'the bloody agony of the writer writing it is so patently extreme that it creates a kind of power in itself that, together with the humour and what lyricism it may possess, takes your mind off the faults of the story itself. . . .'

Of course this sort of appeal is not worthless; there are kinds of writing—for instance the poems of Hart Crane—where the sense of what literary effort can't achieve *is* so patently achieved that we recognize worth and distinction. But such writing is more obviously romantic than modernist; and that is also very true of Lowry. Though certain modernist features seem essential to his work, his posture in relation to them is oddly oblique, incomplete. One can follow this out, for instance, in the pattern of his expatriation, which for most modernists was a movement to culture capitals, the new urban contexts of art and the centre of new movements and fashions in literary thought. Beckett and Durrell, for example, expatriated themselves via well-forged cosmopolitan links—Beckett to *avant-garde* Paris, Durrell to that and also to Mediterranean life and writing. But Lowry made only the most tentative links with established literary scenes and contexts (in Cambridge, Paris, and New York) and rather expatriated himself away from artistic centres, and to the idea of exile and voyage itself. . . . He was equally uneasy about identifying his art or purposes with any particular literary centre or literary tendency. He was apt, in the later period, to regard himself as an American or a Canadian writer—but casually and very much, it would seem, in the mood of his hero in **'Elephant and Colosseum'**, in *Hear Us O Lord From Heaven Thy Dwelling Place* . . .—a Manx author living in America because 'the people who believed in him were all Americans, and even here in Europe—once more came that inexplicable childish pang, yet so deeply he couldn't believe its cause was mean or unworthy—he'd received no word from the heart.'

And typically Lowry liked to stress the lonely nature of his genius, his general separateness from influence, even his ignorance. In a letter to Jacques Barzun, who had written a review of *Under the Volcano* attacking it as 'an anthology held together by earnestness' [see excerpt above], he complained: 'Having lived in the wilderness for nearly a decade, unable to buy even any intelligent American magazines (they were all banned here [Canada], in case you didn't know, until quite recently) and completely out of touch, I have had no way of knowing what styles were in fashion and what out, and didn't much care.' Obviously, as the stories in *Hear Us O Lord* . . . make evident, he was widely read and had assimilated a good deal from many twentieth-century moderns; there is clear influence from Joyce (after a Joycean punning bout he speaks, in a story and also in his letters, of being 'Joyced with his own petard'), from Thomas Wolfe, from D. H. Lawrence, from Scott Fitzgerald (whose *Tender Is the Night* he adapted as a reputedly brilliant scenario, never made into a film). But a more obvious debt is to the Romantic poets, particularly those associated with voyage and/or suffering. And his two great modern literary heroes were characteristically oblique ones—Conrad Aiken and the Norwegian writer Nordahl Grieg, both novelists of voyage to whom *he* voyaged in youth, shipping on freighters to the States and Norway in order to meet them. All the voyage and journal

material of the (posthumously published) collection *Hear Us O Lord* . . . is bound together in a complex structure of literary allusion, founded on a wide range of reading from Prescott to Baudelaire, Marx to Wolfe, and some of it is clearly excessively literary; even so, there is a secure truth in Lowry's claim that (so he paraphrased his admired Melville) a cargo ship was his real Yale and Harvard. To a considerable extent, then, he was the romantic autodidact, and this element is sharply there in the work.

So it is that there lies, behind the experimental and modernist spirit, a deep vein of romanticism. The signals of modernism are evident enough; the texture of deep literary allusiveness, the commitment to formal experiment, the quality of strain and anguish which itself, as Stephen Spender stresses in a useful introduction to . . . *Under the Volcano* [see excerpt above], links Lowry with the other central modernists in his concern with the 'modern breakdown of values'. Yet, as Spender says, Lowry's view of life is individualistic in a way in which those of the leading moderns are not, since through them a consciousness that is ultimately historic and even collective speaks. But Lowry's work is primarily *self*-projection, and the surrounding world tends to be solipsistically merged into that of the hero. Lowry's essential assumptions about art thus tend to be purist romantic ones, art seen as imaginative voyage and representative suffering, all this in the cause of a final transcendence, the fulfilment of a paradisial opportunity. It is against this that he introduces, modernly, a sense of tragedy; his primary themes are then the despoliation of the world by man, and the tragic condition of the serious spirit in the modern world. His heroes move through landscapes of destruction and waste, landscapes of hell in which symbolic ruination abounds, seeking the restitution of the paradisial garden. To some extent, as in Fitzgerald's work, the tragic derives from a sense of necessary identification with that world, a need to know its nature; and in Fitzgerald this view is supported by a superb cultural and historical awareness. But in Lowry the tendency is rather towards an auto-destruction in excess of what conditions it; at the same time, the imagined world of his books approves the nobility of that destruction. He tended to associate this scaled-up romantic dream of the self with creativity, which he saw as the principle by which we compose our lives. In the later work, I think, he sees the difficulty, and the stories in *Hear Us O Lord* . . . are marked by situations in which fiction, or the created romantic view of the self, is violated by reality; or else romanticism is dissipated by a critique of it, as in **'Through the Panama'**, where the need for talent to be uncritical of itself is played off against the need for criticism, and a notion of equilibrium emerges: 'And yet there has never been a time in history when there was a greater necessity for the preservation of that seemingly most cold-blooded of all states, equilibrium, a greater necessity indeed for sobriety (how I hate it!).' The confession is surely crucial, and at the heart of Lowry's artistic difficulties throughout his whole *oeuvre*. In consequence, Lowry's 'large' romantic heroes, both in battle with the universe and striving to attune themselves to what is transcendental in it, are at once somewhat overly regarded *personae* for Lowry himself, and the subjects of the author's own criticism and even his uncertainty. The result is an achievement that has a fascinating development, an achievement at once magnificent and incomplete. (pp. 182-85)

Malcolm Bradbury, "Malcolm Lowry As Modernist," in his Possibilities: Essays on the State of the Novel (copyright © 1973 by Malcolm Bradbury; reprinted by permission of Oxford University Press), Oxford University Press, London, 1973, pp. 181-91.

TERENCE BAREHAM   (essay date 1974)

Lowry's last novels are too often seen as a sadly incomplete coda to *Under the Volcano,* or as existing in a parasitic limbo. Perhaps the sheer flamboyance of *Under the Volcano* inevitably led to this, for neither *Dark as the Grave Wherein My Friend Is Laid* nor, particularly, *October Ferry to Gabriola* seeks to impress with quite the same theatrical bravura. (p. 349)

In all his books, men in action scarcely exist. He seems to feel that in the world man has involuntarily created for himself action is superannuated or superrogatory. Men thinking rather than men acting are Lowry's speciality, and while thought *is* action of a kind, it is (Hamlet-like) precisely the converse inwardly. Neither Sigbjørn Wilderness nor Ethan Llewelyn *act* themselves towards the edge of the maelstrom. It is by the quality and nature of what they experience and *think* that we discern their problem and their potential salvation. To both the very act of cognition begins as physical torture. In this they are clearly blood brothers of Geoffrey Firmin in *Under the Volcano.* But in both the later heroes, the will to fight back against the possessing demons, ultimately to accept the guilt and despair which thinking too precisely brings with it, wins the struggle. Sigbjørn, at the nadir of his experience in Cuernavaca, finds himself physically unable even to lift himself from his bed . . . and Ethan arrives at the point where the simple action of asking the time of departure of a ferry has become impossible for him. But both men have been led to this point by an acutely honest capacity for self-assessment and, more important, both progress from it by an act of will which lifts them from the Valley of the Shadow. They convert accidia into a potential to redirect or subdue their fears. . . .

Beyond walking, drinking, or taking a journey, nothing seems to happen on the plot-surface of a Lowry novel. Both *October Ferry* and *Under the Volcano* occupy only one day in their ostensible time span, but both plunge us long years backward into the hero's "interior" life. (p. 351)

In *October Ferry,* which is the last of Lowry's novels, the journey is to new environments, to places never previously visited, which offer at least the potential of a better future. *Dark as the Grave* is halfway between this new standpoint and the destructive retrogression, both mental and physical, of *Under the Volcano.* The conscious retesting of the self against previously "infernal" places and associations is the emotional center of interest in *Dark as the Grave.*

Characteristically Lowry created layers of narrative fact on top of each other. Ostensibly Sigbjørn Wilderness revisits Mexico, where years earlier he had written a novel called *The Valley of the Shadow,* and had experienced harrowing agony during separation from his first wife. On one level, of course, what we are dealing with is Lowry's trip in 1945-46 to Cuernavaca, the town where in the late thirties he had written *Under the Volcano* while becoming estranged from Jan, his first wife. The boundaries between fact and fiction are wider than this suggests, however, for Sigbjørn's rediscovery of himself is part of the cumulative experience shaping *The Voyage that Never Ends,* and hence in the novel it has meanings and alternatives which were not Lowry's own. So this book, like all the others, is striving to turn inchoate experience into a pattern, where the ultimate goal is salvation and liberation. "We progress towards equilibrium this time instead of in the opposite direction," as one of his letters declares.

It is towards this equilibrium that the reader of Lowry's later novels feels himself drawn, and towards which the individuality

of each one contributes, rendering them free of the taint of parasitic dependence on *Under the Volcano,* even while they are inevitably linked to that work by grand thematic purpose and sometimes by specific verbal and situational cross-reference. In both the later novels the journey begins downward, towards the barranca of self-destruction which Geoffrey Firmin sought. . . . But if all three heroes share this sense of descent . . . , Ethan and Sigbjørn achieve the journey back. They do not "love hell" as Geoffrey has come to. (pp. 352-53)

Though the final marshalling of detail may be incomplete in *October Ferry,* the book as it stands is a remarkable achievement. Its central integrity is intact, and its "message" clearly worked through. . . . But no Lowry novel would ever be completely finished, and whatever the posthumous books lack in final touches, they contain essential and valuable statements on issues which preoccupied Lowry's haunted and searching mind, and both put the man, as a major novelist, within a broader and more complete frame of reference. (p. 361)

> Terence Bareham, "After the Volcano: An Assessment of Malcolm Lowry's Posthumous Fiction," in Studies in the Novel (copyright 1974 by North Texas State University), Vol. VI, No. 3, Fall, 1974, pp. 349-62.

KRISTOFER DOROSZ   (essay date 1976)

[Judged] by the standards of realistic fiction, *Under the Volcano* must appear a failure. Deficient in adequate character drawing, it does not depict "man in society". There is almost no "story", no external action that would lend coherence to the "eccentric word-spinning" saturated with exuberant imagery. The book seems misshapen and overwritten. But the essential features of Lowry's writing are never embedded in the traditional art of the novel. . . . Hence the absence of full-blooded characters. However desirable in most novels, they seem inconsistent with Lowry's fundamentally poetic conception of *Under the Volcano.* . . . (p. 10)

Considered by poetic standards, *Under the Volcano* must indeed appear a considerable achievement. Its "significant expression" evidently relies on the word rather than event. The reader is invited not so much to follow the story as to contemplate the extraordinary verbal display composed of layers upon layers of meaning. Lowry, however, never went as far as Joyce, who in *Finnegans Wake* made individual words carry whole constellations of semantic charges. Instead, he counterpointed themes, images, and metaphors turning them into the fundamental units of his art. Yet his brilliant polyphony, unsupported by the solid framework of a plot, seems to lose itself in stream of consciousness and drunken phantasmagorias. To recover it, it is necessary to approach *Under the Volcano* the way most poetry is approached. (p. 11)

We cannot grasp *Under the Volcano* all at once, and our understanding of it grows with each successive reading. Time and again the reader must probe the apparently amorphous mass of details until it reveals an immensely intricate network of relationships: a scaffolding, or a multitude of scaffoldings, on which larger thematic patterns may be fashioned. Nor is this all. The labour of poetic reconstruction is further stimulated by the novel's wheel-like structure which leads the reader on an endless circular course through the protagonist's life. "The book was so designed", Lowry informs Cape [see excerpt above], "counterdesigned and interwelded that it could be read an indefinite number of times and still not have yielded all its meanings or its drama or its poetry''. . . . Obviously no or-dered 'reading', no linear argument can do justice to all this profusion of meanings. (p. 12)

To complicate matters further, *Under the Volcano* is *par ex-cellence* a symbolic novel. Like the French symbolists, Lowry used the poetic resources of language not only to evoke and suggest rather than state, but also to present ''a reality on one level of reference by a corresponding reality on another''. Thus the ruined garden, for example, one of the recurrent motifs in the novel, does not merely signify a plot of land in a state of confusion, abandoned and covered with weeds. Symbolically, it reflects the protagonist's ruined life, neglected love and de-stroyed marriage, or the earth in danger of destruction by the forces of political oppression. As a mythical symbol, both Christian and Cabbalistic, it refers to the lost paradise and the abuse of mystical powers and occult knowledge. The garden is one of the more comprehensive symbolic images in the novel, comprising all the five levels of meaning distinguished by Douglas Day in his analysis of *Under the Volcano:* the chthonic, the human, the political, the magical, and the religious [see excerpt above]. But ''life is a forest of symbols'', as Lowry liked to repeat after Baudelaire, and any detail, however in-significant, may reveal unsuspected depths of meaning. The hero's dark glasses, which on reflection turn out to symbolize his fear of light, truth and salvation, are a case in point. Like-wise, the apparently casual references to Atlantis implicate us in the theme of destruction by fire and water, a symbolic re-flection . . . of the tragedy depicted by the whole novel.

But how to find one's way in this forest of symbols where the often unmarked paths and misleading signposts seem to mock our sense of orientation? How to approach the variety of myth-ical and literary allusions which, in order to evoke and sym-bolize, are severed from the cohesion of our non-poetic ev-eryday experience? How to come to terms with motifs from Christianity, Greek, Aztec, Buddhist, and Hindu mythology; from the occult sciences such as the Cabbala, alchemy, as-trology, the Tarot; from the sacred literature of the Old and New Testaments, The Cabbalistic *Zohar,* the Hindu *Mahab-harata,* or the *Rig Veda;* and, finally, from the works of Mar-lowe, Dante, Shakespeare, Goethe, Blake, Boehme, Pascal, and many others?

Certainly we cannot afford an immediate response to all these messages assembled from systems of ideas accessible to us mostly through scholarship. Together they have never formed any living, cultural or religious, tradition; nor have they been ordered within an organic whole until the creation of *Under the Volcano*. Their guiding principle therefore lies in the novel itself and has to be discovered there. Otherwise Lowry's sym-bols might appear simply as ''a heap of broken images'', to borrow T. S. Eliot's phrase. Uninformed by a common faith and cultural tradition, dependent for their elucidation on learn-ing and research, they might often be found to mean practically everything and nothing. Indeed, the science of comparative religion has often demonstrated that, above the common ar-chetypal substratum, mythical symbols display a variety of meanings determined by particular mythologial and religious contexts. Therefore most images, whose context in *Under the Volcano* suggests a nonliteral symbolic and mythical signifi-cance, are exposed to what Karl Jaspers calls ''the random interpretability of symbols''. (pp. 12-13)

[In] *Under the Volcano,* we have to assume that all the arcane sciences, all the myths and literary allusions of which it is composed, are analogous to foreign languages inaccessible to most speakers of English. We may regret the situation on cul-tural, but not necessarily on aesthetic, grounds. If so, we shall ascribe the obscurity, the lack of cohesion, or the fragmentar-iness not so much to the shortcomings of the writer but to the breakdown of a culture. Because European civilization—less and less permeated by a universal faith and by the canons of a common literary tradition—is increasingly incapable of rean-imating whatever ''broken images'' it still cherishes, the twen-tieth-century writer has often had to rely on the power of his own personal vision and the resources of other cultures. (p. 14)

An essentially romantic piece of fiction, remote from the at-mosphere of a well-tempered classicism, [*Under the Volcano*] tends, as I have been trying to point out, to escape our grasp and understanding. Through all-embracing poetic evocation it can work at all sorts of levels, its wheel-like structure creates perpetually open meanings, and its manifold symbolism, rooted in a variety of cultural and religious traditions, can make it both inaccessible and unduly ambiguous. Not surprisingly Lowry critics have on the whole concerned themselves with various aspects of the novel, without attempting what Douglas Day terms a ''*Gestalt* approach''. (pp. 14-15)

[In *Under the Volcano*] the fundamental moral issue is embed-ded in Lowry's complex mythical polyphony, unsupported, as I have already pointed out, by the solid framework of a plot. To come to terms with the moral problem of the book, there-fore, we shall have to search for some order in the confusion of mythical and literary evocations. This will expose us to the dangers of a reductive interpretation, but to leave *Under the Volcano* working at ''all sorts of levels'' is to miss its specific essence or *Gestalt*. . . . [The guiding] principle, in as much as it creates a pattern underlying the protagonist's moral prob-lem and radiating throughout the whole of *Under the Volcano,* will reveal the peculiar essence of the novel. . . . [This] fun-damental pattern springs from the motif of black magic and permeates the book as the *Gestalt* quality of ''infernal para-dise''.

Nevertheless, our search for the *Gestalt* quality of ''infernal paradise'' will not enable us to disentangle all the complexities of Lowry's work or fill out all the obscure areas. The discovery of the underlying pattern of *Under the Volcano* may reveal its essential quality but it cannot remove its essential flaw: the overabundance of suggestive detail which, while creating many potential rather than actual meanings, sometimes tends to dis-solve the imaginative experience of the novel. (pp. 15-16)

Now in order to indicate in a preliminary way the meaning of the quality of ''infernal paradise'' we shall have to anticipate our discussion of the novel's esoteric layer and take a short look at the theme of black magic. *Under the Volcano* is, as most critics agree, based, at least to a certain extent, on the Jewish esoteric wisdom, the Cabbala. At the same time it contains, if only by poetic implication, a host of other esoteric and mythical ideas and images. Of these the most important—and in my view more important than the Cabbala—is the theme of black magic and the black magician. Black magic is evoked by allusions to Faustus, Prometheus, the destruction of Atlan-tis, which in esoteric tradition is said to have perished through necromantic practices, and to the Tower of Babel, built, ac-cording to a Cabbalistic legend, by means of magical sciences and for the purpose of man's self-deification. But the magical substance, so to speak, conjured up by many mythical allusions of which I have given just a few examples, is constantly reflected by the more tangible reality of the novel, that is, by the protagonist's drunkenness.

Although drunkenness is the main theme of Lowry's book, "the drunkenness of Geoffrey Firmin", as a critic puts it, "is the correlative of the drunkenness of the world as seen by both Dostoevsky and Hesse, a world reeling down the corridors of disaster filled with the sins of both commission and, particularly, omission, a world which had apparently condemned itself to impotence in the dark night presided over by palpable evil". More specifically, the alcoholic addiction depicted in *Under the Volcano,* because it creates a confusion of heaven and hell, is the correlative of the quality of "infernal paradise".

Consul Geoffrey Firmin is no ordinary drunkard who in alcohol seeks merriment or forgetfulness. On the contrary, in drinking the Consul finds mystical enlightenment and fulfilment of his spiritual aspirations. He appears as a mystic in search of the lost paradise and eternity. He drinks as if he "were taking an eternal sacrament" . . . , often regarding mescal, his favourite drink, as the nectar of immortality. At the same time, he is suffering the "tortures of the damned" . . . , on the magico-mystical plane manifested by sheer demonic horrors, and on the human, by profound estrangement and an almost total inability to love. Obviously there is something amiss with his mysticism. It seems that he is trying to reach divinity by way of hell, without being fully aware of it. Overwhelmed by despair and surrounded by darkness, he fondly imagines that he has reached a state of bliss. Darkness appears to him as light, and the true light, of which he is mortally afraid, as darkness. One of the cantinas for which his whole being yearns is significantly called "El Infierno". Just as significantly perhaps a "lamp of hope" is hanging over its door; a lamp of hope, of course, since alcohol provided by the cantinas appears as the way to God and eternity. (pp. 16-17)

[The] Consul's search for celestial joys in the inferno and his constant confusion of good and evil bespeak a diabolic mysticism as practised by a would-be saint or contemplative.

Perhaps Geoffrey's demonic magic, buried in countless evocations, symbolized by his drunkenness and never stated as fact, would be better left alone, were it not for its overall effect upon the whole novel. Since it truly radiates throughout *Under the Volcano,* it gives the novel a characteristic stamp and becomes a central metaphor, capable of ordering the significance of the book. As a demonic inversion it has permeated each of the five levels distinguished by Day. . . .

[The] magical inversion has spread itself onto the eight fundamental themes of Lowry's novel. Like the Cabbalistic Tree turned upside down, the eight themes represent man's spiritual aspirations brought down by the powers of evil. We see ascent turned into downfall, light into darkness, immortality into perdition, a search for eternity and paradise terminated in hell, love and charity giving way to lovelessness and indifference, life transformed into death, salvation appearing as damnation, and freedom as captivity.

But the demonic inversion in *Under the Volcano* involves much more than a transformation of one thing into its opposite. It is an attitude, a state of mind, or an atmosphere which envelops events, motifs, fragments of dialogue, sometimes even single phrases and words. Not confined to images, symbols, ideas, themes, or metaphors, it is something which permeates *Under the Volcano* through and through. It cannot be enclosed by any of the objects in the world depicted by the novel nor by any of the common categories of literary criticism. It appears there-fore that demonic inversion has in *Under the Volcano* assumed the role of a quality, a *Gestalt* or essential quality, peculiar to the novel as a work of art. Hence the proper subject . . . is not the protagonist's black magic but its thematic and aesthetic consequence, the quality of "infernal paradise". (p. 18)

"The gods exist, they are the devil" . . . , the Consul is told by a randomly singled-out quotation, which succinctly characterizes the mental and physical world he inhabits. We shall now examine this world by selecting out of its complexity different themes, strands, and motifs, and organizing them within some more inclusive and basic patterns. In this way I hope to bring out the quality of "infernal paradise" and show how it permeates the eight fundamental themes of *Under the Volcano.* The first of these, "Ascent", prepares the ground for the moral issue of the novel. Through the mountain-volcano symbolism and its negative counterpart of the fall, it shows man in the context of his highest aspirations and their failure. "Light", the second of the themes, reveals the demonic inversion in the dialectics of light and darkness. "Draught of Immortality" brings us close to the central issues in the protagonist's predicament. We see how Geoffrey's spiritual and physical thirst cannot be quenched by alcohol, notwithstanding its mystical faculties. These indeed turn out to be deceptive and, instead of mystical illumination and eternity the Consul finds destruction and death. The fourth theme, "Eternity" contains the essence of his mystical-metaphysical strivings. Through a variety of mostly mythical evocations it shows him as a former mystic and an earnest seeker for God and eternity, now turned into black magician and bound for hell. "Love" brings into view a world contaminated by estrangement and indifference, devoid of charity and genuine personal relations, while "Life" presents the exuberance of vital forces turned into disintegration and death. "Salvation" discloses the spuriousness of human efforts towards rebirth and redemption. So great is the spuriousness that genuine salvation appears as damnation and vice versa. "Freedom", finally, gives us a picture of the Consul's abuse of freedom and its transformation into spiritual imprisonment. And since the abuse of freedom implies its initial existence, the theme reveals the protagonist as essentially and fundamentally free, responsible for his actions and the tragedy depicted by the whole novel. (pp. 20-1)

[These eight fundamental themes in Lowry's *Under the Volcano*] reveal the metaphysical quality of "infernal paradise". (p. 22)

> *Kristofer Dorosz, in his* Malcolm Lowry's Infernal Paradise *(originally a dissertation given at the University of Uppsala in 1976; © Kristofer Dorosz; reprinted by permission of the University of Uppsala and the author), Almqvist & Wiksell International, 1976, 166 p.*

RICHARD K. CROSS (essay date 1980)

Ultramarine allows us to chart the development of a writer whose apprenticeship was coming to a close and who showed considerable promise as a stylist. . . . [The] central flaws of the novel are embedded in its very design and reflect the author's immaturity at the time of its conception. These problems cannot be remedied simply by cutting or by rewriting passages here and there. Probably the most satisfactory disposition of the material in *Ultramarine* was the use to which Lowry put it in the *Volcano;* that is, investing Hugh Firmin with a seafaring past similar to Dana Hilliot's. (p. 12)

[Two] short stories from this period, **"Hotel Room in Char-tres"** and **"In Le Havre,"** . . . prefigure in a number of significant details the theme of marital discord in *Under the Volcano.* In **"Hotel Room in Chartres,"** as in all Lowry's works, "the world is a forest of symbols." (p. 13)

"In Le Havre," the other story that reflects Lowry's unresolved ambivalence toward . . . marriage, is thematically less rich than and technically inferior to **"Hotel Room in Chartres."** The latter represents a modest advance on the method of *Ultramarine* in that the protagonist's monologues have a more intimate connection psychologically with the passages of dialogue from which they flow and to which they return than do Dana Hilliot's. **"In Le Havre,"** consisting entirely of a conversation between a self-involved young Englishman and a case-hardened American newspaperman, reads like a poor pastiche of "Hills like White Elephants." (p. 16)

Lowry's experience of New York crystalized in a work whose original title, *The Last Address,* refers to the site, near Bellevue, where *Moby-Dick* was completed, and the story is in fact "about a man's hysterical identification with Melville." In *The Last Address*—or *Lunar Caustic,* as the novella came to be called—the protagonist [Bill Plantagenet] walks the city streets as though he were Ahab "stumbling from side to side on the careening bridge, 'feeling that he encompassed in his stare oceans from which might be revealed that phantom destroyer of himself'." . . . Lowry shared Melville's belief that "some certain significance lurks in all things" as well as his radical skepticism about the possibility of defining precisely what that significance is. The two novelists' concern with epistemological problems is of course the seal of their modernity. They challenged the opacity of the world with the only weapon their vocation afforded, the imagination, at the same time questioning its efficacy, for they had no assurance that meaning inhered in the objects they contemplated. "Isolatos" cut off from any firm sanction, metaphysical or moral, for their art, both feared that they were falling victim to their own projections. Given this set of mind, even the minutiae of daily life become appallingly ambiguous. (p. 19)

A thwarted religious sensibility characterizes the protagonists of both *Lunar Caustic* and *Under the Volcano;* each yearns for a grace that will deliver him from the hell of self-involvement. Unable to find rest in the bosom of mother church, they fall back on alcohol to console themselves. Juxtaposed with the longing for maternal solace is the hostility of Bill and Geoffrey toward most other female forms. (p. 23)

Lowry cast much of *Under the Volcano* in an apocalyptic-symbolist mode that springs from a correspondence between the "subnormal world" without and the "abnormally suspicious delirious one within him." (p. 26)

[On the axis of] contending forces—hope and despair, salvation and doom, Eros and Thanatos—the action of the *Volcano* turns. Unfortunately the protagonist's dialectical balancing, his "teetering over the awful unbridgeable void" . . . , ends in paralysis rather than the equilibrium he seeks to maintain. The knowledge of a path through the Inferno Geoffrey attributes to Blake, reconciler of antinomies, whose imaginative reach he at moments rivals but whose grasp—the will to act on his perception—he lacks. (p. 33)

One can unravel [the] paradoxical commingling of Eros and Thanatos most effectively by examining the reasons for Geoffrey's drinking. As we have observed in *Ultramarine* and *Lunar Caustic,* alcohol serves Lowry's protagonists as an ersatz for the maternal breast if not the womb. But with the Consul the longing goes even further back: he craves ultimately a reversion to the tranquility of the inorganic, the stony peace of the grave, which represents for him both a symbolic reunion with his lost parents and an actual one with the "elements" from which he has become estranged. . . . His drinking is a form of chronic suicide, a means of shortening the detour to death. (p. 46)

At the end of chapter 10, the Consul gives voice to the resolve that has long been shaping itself in his heart: "I love hell. I can't wait to get back there. In fact I'm running." . . . Implicit in his choice is the doleful assumption that one can spite death by refusing to live. (p. 58)

[Of] the six volumes of [Lowry's] fiction to reach print, four have appeared since his death in 1957. Among novelists the case of Franz Kafka comes to mind. Unfortunately the parallel between the two writers' posthumously published books turns on their number and the agonizing circumstances of their composition rather than on their merits, for none of Lowry's later writings, in the form he left them, begins to rival *Under the Volcano.* (p. 65)

Whatever faults the *oeuvres posthumes* may have, they do illumine the cast of Lowry's mind, the circumstances in which he wrote, and the new terrain he was staking out for his art in the final years of his life. Furthermore, several of the shorter narratives—**"Ghostkeeper"** in *Psalms and Songs* . . . and **"The Bravest Boat," "Strange Comfort Afforded by the Profession"** and **"The Forest Path to the Spring"** in *Hear Us O Lord*—have substantial intrinsic worth. Indeed **"The Forest Path"** ranks as an impressive contribution to a genre in which distinction has been rare, the mode of pastoral confession whose prototype is *Walden.* (p. 67)

In *Dark as the Grave* one finds little of the opulent style and none of the labyrinthine structure that characterize the *Volcano.* Occasionally there is a Melvillean period reminiscent of that earlier glory. . . . These summits are encompassed, however, by vast stretches of prose so flat and arid one hesitates to quote from it. At other moments the writing descends into excruciating self-parody, for instance, when the protagonist likens a hotel elevator to "a station of the cross, in the unfinished Oberammergau of his life". . . . (p. 69)

Under the Volcano is no less autobiographical in origin than *Dark as the Grave,* yet one feels that at every crucial turn the former follows the *cammin di nostra vita,* the route of broadest significance, whereas the latter remains, as Lowry acknowledged, "a sidestreet to [his] own consciousness." (p. 74)

October Ferry represents an attempt to work through neurotic problems the author could resolve neither in art nor apart from it. . . . Perhaps the most fruitful way to respond to this book, whose biographical overtones are more compelling than its vision or artistry, is to refine and coordinate the insights it offers into the malaise that Lowry shared with his persona.

Unlike most of the protagonists in the later fiction, Ethan Llewelyn is not portrayed as an expatriate English writer but rather as a native-born Canadian attorney. . . . (p. 76)

By attributing a calling remote from his own to Ethan, the artist apparently meant to endow him with a measure of autonomy. In actuality the protagonist of *October Ferry* is as little distinguished from his creator as Sigbjørn Wilderness has been. Each is in essence a poet-mystic, a Kierkegaardian figure whose soul has become "sick almost to death." . . . (p. 77)

[In *Hear Us O Lord from Heaven Thy Dwelling Place* the] protagonists, artists and seafarers who can be distinguished from one another only by their names and superficial differences in their personal histories, are all transparent masks for the author. . . . [The] pieces are more nearly akin to meditative-descriptive lyrics than they are to traditional narrative modes. . . . Read in sequence, even though the order in which they appear does not correspond precisely to his design, they do form what might fairly be described as a symphonic prose poem. (p. 88)

Lowry meant *Hear Us O Lord* to be a kind of "*Volcano* in reverse," and indeed the tragic vision of his masterwork and the comic spirit of **"The Forest Path"** do ultimately come together, with the hero of the latter enjoying the rebirth that eludes Geoffrey Firmin. . . . The journey on which Lowry was embarked, a passage undertaken by many poets and seers before him, involves a dying away of the old self into a more authentic mode of being where one discovers the myth he must render into life. (pp. 105-06)

> *Richard K. Cross, in his* Malcolm Lowry: A Preface to His Fiction *(reprinted by permission of The University of Chicago Press; © 1980 by The University of Chicago), The University of Chicago Press, 1980, 146 p.*

ADDITIONAL BIBLIOGRAPHY

Bradbrook, M. C. *Malcolm Lowry: His Art & Early Life; A Study in Transformation.* London: Cambridge University Press, 1974, 170 p.

> Introductory study interweaving biography and criticism. An appendix reprints two early stories: "A Rainy Night" and "Satan in a Barrel."

Costa, Richard Hauer. *Malcolm Lowry.* New York: Twayne Publishers, 1972, 208 p.

> Study of Lowry's major fictional themes and the significance of autobiography in his work. This book features a detailed examination of the influence of Conrad Aiken and James Joyce on *Under the Volcano,* with a coordinating analysis of the successive revisions of this novel.

Creswell, Rosemary. "Malcolm Lowry's Other Fiction." In *Cunning Exiles: Studies of Modern Prose Writers,* edited by Don Anderson and Stephen Knight, pp. 62-80. Sydney: Angus and Robertson Publishers, 1974.

> Sees Lowry's fiction before and after *Under the Volcano* as concerned with the artist's relationship to his work.

Dodson, Daniel B. *Malcolm Lowry.* New York, London: Columbia University Press, 1970, 48 p.

> Introductory examination of Lowry's novels, short stories, and poetry, offering biographical background and plot outlines of the major works.

Durrant, Geoffrey. "Aiken and Lowry." *Canadian Literature,* No. 64 (Spring 1975): 24-40.*

> Correlates the use of Psyche and Ulysses myths in Aiken's *Blue Voyage* and Lowry's *Ultramarine.*

Flint, R. W. "Weltschmerz Refurbished." *Kenyon Review* 9 (Summer 1947): 474-77.

> Considers *Under the Volcano* largely a failure, denying that it ranks with the innovative works of Joyce, Lawrence, Fitzgerald, and Djuna Barnes.

Knickerbocker, Conrad. "Malcolm Lowry and the Outer Circle of Hell." In *Lunar Caustic,* by Malcolm Lowry, edited by Earle Birney and Margerie Lowry, pp. 5-7. London: Jonathan Cape, 1968.

> Biographical background to the novella.

Lowry, Margerie, ed. *Malcolm Lowry: Psalms and Songs.* New York: New American Library, 1975, 308 p.

> Reminiscences of Lowry by Conrad Aiken, David Markson, William McConnell, and others, with a critical study of the author's literary development from his school days at Cambridge to the final novels and short stories.

Markson, David. *Malcolm Lowry's "Volcano": Myth, Symbol, Meaning.* New York: Times Books, 1978, 241 p.

> Chapter by chapter explication of themes, symbols, allusions, and organizing structures of *Under the Volcano,* paraphrasing the novel "in terms of those Joycean utilizations of myth and symbol that comprise its texture, dictate much of its interior form, and evince most of its meaning."

Perlmutter, Ruth. "Malcolm Lowry's Unpublished Filmscript of *Tender Is the Night.*" *American Quarterly* XXVIII (Winter 1976): 561-74.

> Examines Lowry's use of cinematic effects in his filmscript, concluding that although it is "an anachronism today, it is a triumph of the classical narrative film."

Pritchett, V. S. "New Novels: *Ultramarine.*" *The New Statesman and Nation* V, No. 122 (24 June 1933): 850-51.*

> Brief review calling *Ultramarine* "self-conscious, monotonous, and unrevealing."

Snow, C. P. "Wolfe's Clothing." *Financial Times,* No. 25,546 (2 September 1971): 10.

> Review describing *October Ferry to Gabriola* as a dithyramb and praising its visual sense.

Steiner, George. "Cold Ash." *The Nation* 192, No. 21 (27 May 1961): 465-66.

> Comments that the short stories in *Hear Us O Lord from Heaven Thy Resting Place* are mostly mediocre, but that "Through the Panama" was Lowry's highest achievement after *Under the Volcano.*

Tiessen, Paul G. "Malcolm Lowry and the Cinema." *Canadian Literature,* No. 44 (Spring 1970): 38-49.

> Examines cinematic techniques and allusions in *Under the Volcano.*

Wood, Barry, ed. *Malcolm Lowry: The Writer and His Critics.* Ottawa, Canada: The Tecumseh Press, 1980, 278 p.

> Reprints important reviews and critical essays on the novels, short stories, and poetry, including Lowry's letter to Jonathan Cape.

Woodcock, George, ed. *Malcolm Lowry: The Man and His Work.* Vancouver: University of British Columbia Press, 1971, 174 p.

> Critical and biographical essays, including studies by Woodcock, Anthony R. Kilgallin, Geoffrey Durrant, W. H. New, and Perle Epstein.

Wright, Terence. "*Under the Volcano:* The Static Art of Malcolm Lowry." *Ariel* 1, No. 4 (October 1970): 67-76.

> Sees *Under the Volcano* as concerned with presenting a static "contemplation" of the Consul's fallen state rather than the changing "process" of his fall into death and disintegration.

Osip (Emilievich) Mandelstam

1891?-1938?

(Also transliterated as Ossip; also Emil'evich or Emilevich; also Mandel'shtam, Mandelshtam, or Mandelstamm) Russian poet, novelist, essayist, critic, and translator.

The evolution of Mandelstam's poetry represented a trend in early twentieth-century Russian literature away from symbolism and toward what came to be called acmeism. Along with Nikolay Gumilyov and Anna Akhmatova, Mandelstam epitomized the ideals of the new movement. While symbolism looked outside the world to a transcendent realm apprehended through poetic form, the poetics of acmeism demanded attention to immediate, physical reality: the rose as sensuous object rather than symbol. Stylistically Mandelstam's most characteristic poems display the acmeist emphasis on a neoclassic formalism combined with contemplation of the nature of art itself. As one critic expresses it, Mandelstam's is a "poetry of poetry."

Born to middle-class Jewish parents in Warsaw, Mandelstam soon afterward moved with his family to St. Petersburg. He described his ethnic background as the "Judaic chaos," and he always experienced a tension between his Jewish homelife and western European culture. He was especially attracted to the Gothic spirit of the Middle Ages, Notre Dame cathedral representing for him the ideal creative act which gives human life meaning. Through his travels in Europe and the Mediterranean, he developed an admiration for the historic lands of Christianity, and he eventually embraced a Christian theology. Mandelstam also derived much of his inspiration from sources foreign to his cultural background, including Dickens, Poe, the French symbolists, the medieval Italian poetry of Dante and Petrarch, and the classical mythology of the Hellenic world. For Mandelstam Hellenism, like the Gothic, meant the ambition to humanize an indifferent environment. Though a man of wide cultural sympathies, Mandelstam was somewhat estranged from the politics of the Russian revolution. Like many Russian artists he welcomed the utopian ideals of the revolution but later shrank from the reality. At one point he was exiled for three years to the city of Voronezh for criticizing Stalin in a line of verse. Later, Mandelstam was arrested and sent to a camp for political prisoners, where he died under brutal conditions.

Mandelstam began his literary career with a series of poems published in the journal *Apollon*. His first collection of poetry, *Kamen'* (*Stone*), exhibits the transition from an early symbolist aesthetic to the new tenets of acmeism. The poems of this and the second collection, *Trista* (*Tristia*), are architectural in style and sometimes in subject. Some of the most famous lyrics celebrate the buildings of Paris, Moscow, and Constantinople, the poet striving in these works for a carefully constructed elegance. Metaphors drawn from music also characterize Mandelstam's technique of orchestrated grace and formal sophistication. A major criticism of these poems is the poet's impersonality and detachment from the concerns of the world outside of art. As critic Steven Broyde has demonstrated, however, Mandelstam often reacted to the events of the rapidly changing world around him, the poem "Vek" ("The Age"), for example, expressing his hopes and apprehensions for the

future of postrevolutionary Russia. Generally the poems in *Stone* and *Tristia* are judged superior to those Mandelstam produced in the 1930s, though Jennifer Baines's book-length study of the later poetry takes issue with this view.

Of comparable importance to his poetry are Mandelstam's prose works, comprising primarily the autobiographical essays of *Shum vremeni* (*The Noise of Time*) and *Theodosia*, and what is often described as a surrealistic novella, *Egipetskaya marka* (*The Egyptian Stamp*). Critics describe Mandelstam's prose as characteristic of a poet: rhythmic, image-laden, and somewhat baroque. These works are additionally valued as a source of biographical information on the author, particularly his impressions of childhood.

Since his death Mandelstam has been recognized as one of the most important Russian writers of the twentieth century, most significantly in his homeland, where he was once reduced to the status of a literary "nonperson." A Soviet encyclopedia succinctly summarizes Mandelstam's predicament during the Stalin era and the subsequent revival of the poet's reputation: "Illegally repressed during the period of the cult of the individual. Rehabilitated posthumously."

(See also *TCLC*, Vol. 2.)

PRINCIPAL WORKS

Kamen' (poetry) 1913
  [*Stone* published in *Complete Poetry of Osip Emilevich Mandelstam*, 1973]
Trista (poetry) 1922; published in Russia as *Vtoraya kniga*, 1923
  [*Tristia* published in *Complete Poetry of Osip Emilevich Mandelstam*, 1973]
Shum vremeni (autobiographical essays) 1925
  [*The Noise of Time* published in *The Prose of Osip Mandelstam*, 1965]
Egipetskaya marka (novella) 1928
  [*The Egyptian Stamp* published in *The Prose of Osip Mandelstam*, 1965]
O poezii (criticism) 1928
Stikhotvoreniya (poetry) 1928
  [*Poems* published in *Complete Poetry of Osip Emilevich Mandelstam*, 1973]
The Prose of Osip Mandelstam: The Noise of Time, Theodosia, The Egyptian Stamp (autobiograpical essays, novella) 1965
Razgovor o Dante (essay) 1967
  [''Conversation on Dante'' published in *Mandelstam: The Complete Critical Prose and Letters*, 1979]
Sobranie sochinenni. 3 vols. (poetry, autobiographical essays, novella, and letters) 1967, 1971
Complete Poetry of Osip Emilevich Mandelstam (poetry) 1973
Osip Mandelstam: Selected Poems [translated by Clarence Brown and W. S. Merwin] (poetry) 1973
Osip Mandelstam: Selected Poems [translated by David McDuff] (poetry) 1973
Osip Mandelstam: Selected Essays (essays) 1977
Mandelstam: The Complete Critical Prose and Letters (criticism and letters) 1979

LEONID I. STRAKHOVSKY (essay date 1949)

The poetry of Mandelstam is characterized ''by an attraction for classical examples, by a grandiloquent severity, by the cult of historical themes,'' but primarily by a balancing fusion of the outer and inner worlds expressed in swaying rhythms. There is a feeling of permanency in his lines even beyond living existence and a contempt for the momentary, the transitional, that which is today and gone tomorrow. And he paid particular attention to craftsmanship. (p. 87)

Although at first Mandelstam seems to be introspective, in reality he is impersonal. The ''I'' in his poetry may not be Mandelstam at all, but merely a reflection of himself as provided by his imagination. Even his emotionalism seems detached. . . . (p. 88)

Mandelstam loved ''heavy,'' ponderous words. There is an architectural quality in his poetry. He said himself: ''We do not fly, we merely ascend those towers which we can build ourselves.'' And he builds his poems, as once were built the Gothic towers of his beloved Notre Dame of Paris, of permanent material to last for ages. That is why the title of his first book, *Kamen'* (**Stone**), is so significant. But the choice of his material imposed upon the poet, the creator, the architect,

its own limitations; hence there is ''an imprint upon his poetry of artistic laconicism,'' which gives it a classical form. This tendency toward classicism also forced Mandelstam to remain within the framework of the established rules of Russian prosody. Therefore, the often startling effects of his poetry are achieved solely by his style and the inner content of his poems, and not by any innovations of poetical form.

Like [Anna] Akhmatova, he is epigrammatic in the recording of his impressions. But he does not prompt the reader by word-suggestions to perceive the mood of the picture he presents; on the contrary, he gives a precise and peculiar word formula of it.

It is interesting to examine closely how Mandelstam selects those particularities and details with which he re-creates the impression of this or that artistic presentation. Least of all can one call him an impressionist who reproduces directly and without selectivity, without any rational associations, those visual spots which are the first and as yet unrealized impressions of outer objects. At first glance the details consciously selected according to his artistic taste may seem accidental and unnoticeable; their meaning in the creative imagination of the poet is immeasurably exaggerated; a small item grows to fantastic proportions as if in a purposely distorted grotesqueness; at the same time the relation in perspective between insignificant and large objects disappears; the distant and the near-by in the projection on the surface appear of equal dimensions. But in this deliberate distortion and fantastic exaggeration a previously unnoticed particularly becomes expressive and characteristic of the subject under presentation. (pp. 89-90)

On the whole, as a poet, Mandelstam is not a realist as some of the other Acmeists were . . . , nor even a romantic realist as [Nicholas] Gumilyov was. He is more of a fanciful realist in the fashion of E. T. Hoffmann. According to his poetical technique he could be called a fantastic creator of words in the same manner in which the German poet could be called a fantastic creator of images and plots. Nevertheless, Mandelstam has a kinship with his generation of Russian poets ''in the absence of the personal, emotional, and mystical elements in their poetical presentation as well as in their conscious word technique, their love for graphic detail, and their consummate epigrammatic treatment of expression.'' (p. 92)

Together with Gumilyov and Akhmatova, he forms the immortal trinity on the poetical Olympus of Russia's literary renaissance of the twentieth century. (p. 97)

Leonid I. Strakhovsky, ''Osip Mandelstam: Architect of the Word,'' in his Craftsmen of the Word: Three Poets of Modern Russia, Gumilyov, Akhmatova, Mandelstam (copyright © 1949 by the President and Fellows of Harvard College; copyright renewed © 1977 by the President and Fellows of Harvard College; excerpted by permission), Cambridge, Mass.: Harvard University Press, 1949 (and reprinted by Greenwood Press, a Division of Congressional Information Services, Inc., Westport, CT., 1969, pp. 83-97).

NILS ÅKE NILSSON (essay date 1963)

The title [of Osip Mandel'stam's first collection of poems, **Stone** (**Kamen**),] seems to indicate a uniformity in motives and mood. Matters, however, are not as simple as they might seem at the first glance. On the contrary, Mandel'stam's first book is rather heterogeneous and ambiguous. The first thing to strike us is the fact that each poem is dated and included in the collection chronologically. This arrangement is not made unintentionally. What the poet wishes to say by this is obviously that the collection is intended to show some kind of development, the development of a poet or, possibly, of a form of poetics. This gives us, I think, a starting-point to an understanding of it.

There is, to be sure, a cycle of poems about stone buildings which forms, in a way, the centre of the collection—they all seem to fit the theme of the title. There are poems about Notre Dame, Sophia Cathedral in Constantinople, the Admiralty Building in Petersburg and of Roman architecture in Italy. Even landscapes are often considered architectonically; fields are compared to Roman forums and trees to colonnades.

The vocabulary too, contains many words which emphasize the concept of hardness suggested by the title. Most frequent, as might be expected, are the words "stone" and "stony" (*kamen, kamennyj*). Next follow "crystal" and "crystallic" (*xrustal', xrustal'ynj*), "heavy" (*tiazelyj*), "coarse" (*grubyj*). There are also isolated examples of more precious stones, especially in earlier poems, revealing a certain influence of Symbolist poetry: "diamond" (*almaz*), "gold" (*zoloto*), "mother-of-pearl" (*perlamutr*), "enamel" (*emal'*), "porcelain" (*farfor*).

Coupled with this vocabulary indicated heavy, solid objects, there is, however, a quite different one in exact opposition to it: a vocabulary of airy, weightless objects and concepts. There are adjectives like "tender" (*nežnyj*), "fragile" (*xrupkij*), "delicate" (*tonkij, tonenkij*), nouns like "foam" (*pena*), "reed" (*trostinka*), "straw" (*solominka*), "mist" (*tuman*), "cobweb" (*pautina*), "lace" (*kruževo*) and so on.

These contrasting elements of the vocabulary are most interesting. They seem to reveal a certain dualism in the poet's outlook on life. This world is not, as the title of the collection would seem to indicate, a solid world where all objects stand firmly in place. It is rather a dualistic world, a world in which a fatal and uncertain balance reigns.

This impression is stressed by a motif which is also built up on contrasts and introduced at the very beginning of the collection. It is a contrast between the fragility and shortness of human existence on the one hand, and the eternity of time and life in general on the other. This motif is a crucial one in Mandel'štam's poetry. (pp. 164-65)

The first part of the collection has, without a doubt, much in common with the poetry of the Symbolists. The dominant mood is one of nostalgia, sadness, depression; *pechal'* (sadness) is, in fact, a dominant word in the collection. The setting often emphasizes the impression of something unreal. It is, to be sure, our earth which is discussed but we can hardly discern any palpable details. People and objects are wrapped in a dreamlike, misty or bizarre fairytale atmosphere, creating thereby an impression of fear and emptiness. The world is empty, but the poet must nevertheless accept and love it, for this is the only world given to him. . . .

What Mandel'štam is concerned with in the first part of his collection may be described as the poet's return to earth after dwelling in the Symbolist realm of abstract, metaphysical speculation. Although the return is necessary it is by no means easy to make. It is a return to a bare world and the poet is at first frightened by its nakedness and meaninglessness. What is worldly reality without the promise of a greater reality? Life without

God seems to him as impalpable as mist, and he feels himself to be an empty cage from which God has flown like a bird. . . . (pp. 165-66)

But Man cannot live without reflecting on the mystery of life and death. He cannot live without the perspective of eternity. Eternity (*vechnost*) is, in fact, another frequent and important word in the collection. (pp. 166-67)

Without this hope of eternity man is frightened and this fear "is the awareness of emptiness" (*samy strax est' čuvstvo pustoty*). Therefore there is no choice, he must try to live for eternity. . . . (pp. 167)

In his search for a symbol of eternity within the realm of reality the poet introduces the symbol of stone, i.e. the building, the tower, primarily as contrast to the old image of the stars. . . . (p. 168)

In the earlier poems the contrasts of reality created a feeling of fear in the poet, an impression of something unreal. Now he knows: through art a certain balance can be attained, a new feeling of freedom. It is a fragile, an uncertain balance but it is the only one Man can attain. Facing a world in flux, a dynamic reality of contradictions and tensions, the artist is able in his art, by stones or words, to create an illusion of harmony and eternity.

The important thing is not the stability or the indestructibility but the transformation of the material. The "heaviness," reality as it is, is "no good" (*nedobraja*). It must be transformed into the artist's personal vision of the world. This, however, has a double danger. Reality is often transformed into something about weightless, clear and transparent, a structure of glass (. . . frequently "crystal" and "crystalline" are [found] beside "stone" and "stony"; a frequent word is also "transparent" [*prozračnyj*], getting still more frequent in the next collection) which can easily break down if the balance is upset, if the pressure of reality on art becomes too hard—and this . . . is exactly what happens with Mandel'štam's balance. The other point is that there is no real place for the poet himself in the harmony created by him. Art is a means by which the poet tries to bind chaos. It stands between him and reality. To attain the illusion of order and harmony he must remain something of an outsider, he must, as Mandel'štam says, "keep his distance."

If we now try to approach Mandel'štam's poetic style for some few general observations . . . we cannot expect to find a complete uniformity. In my opinion the first collection above all bears witness of a development towards a poetics and a view of the world. There is, without a doubt, a certain difference between the first poems and the last. Many of the earlier poems are, for instance, written in stanzas of two lines; they often seem to be something like miniatures, sketches, exercises. One is often given the impression of something unexpressed, something unaccomplished. This is stressed by the fact that he concludes by no means few poems with three dots (. . .). It is easy for us to notice a difference in the later poems. Not only are they built up more carefully, but also contain an often repeated device of more self-confident expression; in fact, many poems end with an exclamation mark, stressing the impression of something finished, definitive—or, at least, the impression that the poet tries to make himself believe in the definitiveness of his interpretation of reality.

But still the collection as a whole has many important points in common. The architecture of cathedrals being

Mandel'štam's model, we are able to understand his interest in the structure of the poems. He starts with the smallest units; more than any one of the other Acmeists his main concern is the word, the word *per se,* as it was at the same time for the Futurists. Perhaps the title of his collection has still another significance, suggesting the word as the basic element of poetry as the stone is that of architecture.

It is here not only a question of the careful choice of "the right word," the right syntagmas and their arrangement in the sentence. The important thing is the tension between the words, just as the secret of a building of stone lies in the tension between contrasting structural elements. There are many different devices of tension to be found in Mandel'štam's poetry; still they are not permitted to be an end in themselves. Reigning in the cathedral with its many contrasting elements is the plumb (see *Notre Dame*); reigning in poetry is the balance—this is the main feature of Mandel'stam's neo-classicism. (pp. 170-71)

We find these principles wholly at work in the central poems of the collection *Stone.* In his next collection they are developed into mature craftsmanship but also, as we shall see, in yet another direction. This collection he called *Tristia.* . . . The title seems to indicate that he is here continuing the mood of melancholy and sadness of the first collection. But there is more to the title: apparently Mandel'štam has taken it from Ovid. He evokes a parallel to the banished Roman poet's lamentations from the coast of the Black Sea (*Flebilis ut noster status est, ita flebile carmen . . .).*

The background to this new tone of sadness is the appearance of a new element of reality contrasting with the order and harmony finally created in the first book: this is the revolution and the civil war which the poet was forced to witness at first hand. He tries to keep these experiences at a poetic distance by clothing what happens in a garb of classical history and mythology. He sees them as a classical tragedy, as a part of world history's perpetual circulation: his Petersburg is consequently transformed to Petropolis.

It is clear from the poems of *Tristia* that in this period of apocalyptic upheaval his main concern is with art, poetry, the word. The question he puts himself is: will poetry survive? In the night, black as velvet, he goes out into the streets praying for the word. To be sure, this is a time full of words, of proclamations and speeches. But the word he is praying for is the word without meaning, the word of poetry. . . . (p. 173)

Generally speaking, Mandel'štam in *Tristia* develops and continues the principles of style of his first collection. The new painful themes do not shatter the verse form. His impressions of a time of chaos, his songs of sadness and loneliness are moulded into a verse with the same firmness as in *Stone.* He tries to keep a poetic distance to these new intrusive elements of reality. Even if his view of a world conquered with such difficulty in *Stone* is toppled he nevertheless endeavours to maintain the balance in his poetic form.

It is, however, easy to notice that the contrasts he is trying to balance have now grown in intensity and strength. The tension is much stronger, in fact approaching the limits of the possible: tension between words and groups of words, between sentences, between images (we notice, for instance, how he now quite commonly makes use of oxymorons and synasthesias: ("black ice"; "burning snows"). The imagery plays a more important part than before: daring images cross the poems like sudden flashes of lightning, many of them returning in other poems, reappearing in different contexts. His choice of ele-

ments of reality is more fastidious and elliptic, often leaving us with enigmatic gaps. (p. 175)

Mandel'štam became, as we know, a victim of the literary politics of the thirties. His poems preserved from this period are to be looked upon more as personal documents than as a real continuation of his earlier poetry. If many poems in *Tristia* deal with the vital problem at that time of whether poetry would survive the turmoil and the new demands put to it, the poems of the thirties reflect the more personal question of the poet's own survival. (p. 177)

Nils Åke Nilsson, "Osip Mandel'štam and His Poetry" (reprinted by permission of Scando-Slavica *and the author), in* Scando-Slavica, *Vol. IX, 1963 (and reprinted in* Major Soviet Writers: Essays in Criticism, *edited by Edward J. Brown, Oxford University Press, New York, 1973, p. 164-77).*

ISAIAH BERLIN   (essay date 1965)

[Mandelstamm's] poetry, although its scope was deliberately confined, possessed a purity and perfection of form never again attained in Russia.

There are poets who are poets only when they write poetry, whose prose could have been written by someone who had never written a line of verse, and there are poets (both good and bad) whose every expression is that of a poet, sometimes to the detriment of their work as a whole. . . . All that Mandelstamm wrote is written by a poet. His prose is a poet's prose—this he has in common with Pasternak. This, but little else. . . . He resembles his exact Western contemporaries, the imagists and the neo-classical poets; his self-imposed discipline derives ultimately from Greek and Roman, French and Italian models. If this conveys the notion of something cold and marmoreal, the impression is misleading. Concentration and intensity of experience, the combination of an exceptionally rich inner life, nourished by a vast literary culture with a clear vision of reality, as agonized and undeluded as Leopardi's, divided him from his more subjective and self-expressive Russian contemporaries. He began of course, as they did, in the shadow of French symbolism, but emancipated himself exceedingly early. Perhaps it was a conscious opposition to everything vague and indeterminate that caused him to cut his cameos so fiercely, to lock his images so firmly, sometimes a shade too firmly, in an exact, unyielding verbal frame. This tendency toward objectivity and his intimate relation to the great classical poets of Europe made him an original and somewhat Western figure in a country educated to confessional literature, and insistence and over-insistence on the social and moral responsibility of the artist. It was this that was described as lack of contact with reality,—self-estrangement from the national life and the people, for which he and his fellow Acmeists have been condemned since the early years of the revolution. (p. 3)

No doubt it would be better to read these haunted stories [in *The Prose of Osip Mandelstam*] without bearing in mind the fate of the author (as the poet himself would surely have wished one to do) but it is not easy to achieve detachment. Yet no matter how macabre the fantasies which Mandelstamm wrote in his peculiar prose, they achieve the tranquility of harmonious art—the Hellenic ideal which he inherited from [Innokenti] Annensky and, ultimately, the early German romantics. . . .

Mandelstamm's prose is scarcely translatable. The verse with all its fearful complexity and the tiers of meaning packed into the miraculously chosen words is, despite everything, more capable of being reproduced in an alien medium than his wildly eccentric, although rigorously disciplined, "prose." He intended to write in what he himself called "wild parabolas." He succeeded more often than not and to an astonishing extent. "A manuscript is always a storm," he wrote. But the writer keeps his head and dominates the storm. Sometimes he fails: then we have passages of brilliant virtuosity, the galloping wild horses of an exultant and disordered poetic imagination. But because Mandelstamm is a marvelous rider the wild leaps, even when they seem to vanish in mid-air, are exhilarating and never degenerate into a mere exhibition of skill or vitality. More often these pages obey a rigorous pattern. . . . For the cascades of Mandelstamm's glittering or tranquil images leaping out of one another, the historical, psychological, syntactical, verbal allusions, contrasts, collisions, whirling at lightning speed, dazzle the imagination and the intellect, not as an impressionist or surrealist cavalcade of haphazard violently contrasted elements, a brilliant chaos, but as a composition, as a harmonious and noble whole. . . . [Mandelstamm's images] are bold, violent, but fused into a disturbing, often agonized but demonstrably coherent, unity—a complex, twisted, over-civilized world (needing a sophisticated and widely read observer) in which there are no loose ends. All the strands are interwoven, often in grotesque patterns but everything echoes everything else, colors, sounds, tastes, shapes, tactile properties are related not by symbolical but literal—sensory and psychological—correspondences. It is all the product of a remorselessly ordering mind. The description of him by Russian critics as "architectural" is perfectly just.

In the center there is always a suffering hero—the martyr pursued by the mob, a descendant not only of Gogol's and Dostoyevsky's humble victims but (whether consciously or not) also of [Georg] Büchner's *Woyzeck*. . . . The suffering hero of **"The Egyptian Stamp"** is a Russian Jew. His prose is populated with figures and images of his Jewish environment, treated neither with condescension nor irony nor aggressive self-identification, indeed no self-consciousness of any kind. . . .

Two motifs run persistently through these strange pieces: one, that of a wistful, timorous, Jewish victim of men and circumstances. Literary historians will surely one day devote chapters and perhaps volumes to this stock figure of our time and trace his evolution from his gentile ancestors, from Peter Schlemihl to [E.T.A.] Hoffmann's terrorized creatures, from Dostoyevsky to [Leonid] Andreyev, until we reach Mandelstamm's Parnok, an obscure ancestor of Mr. Bellow's Herzog. Mandelstamm identifies himself with poor Parnok and at the same time prays passionately to be delivered from his characteristics and his fate. Pasternak took a different and much solider path to salvation in *Dr. Zhivago*.

The other motif is that of music and composers, Bach, Mozart, Beethoven, Schubert, and, at a different level, Tchaikovsky and Scriabin, the characteristics of whose art haunted Mandelstamm much as they did Pasternak; and are constantly used by him to describe other things. They are similes for nature, ideas, human beings: the comparison between Alexander Herzen's stormy political rhetoric and a Beethoven sonata in **"The Noise of Time"** is one of the most typical and brilliant of these. The two themes come together in the marvelous description of the contrast between two Baltic seaside resorts—the German resort where Richard Strauss is played before an audience from which Jews have been excluded, and the Jewish resort full of Tchaikovsky and violins: still more, in what is, if not the best,

the most directly emotional of all his lyrics, the poem about the gloomy Jewish musician Herzevich. . . . It is a poignant and profoundly upsetting piece, like the single Schubert sonata which the musician practices over and over again. . . .

In **"The Egyptian Stamp"** the hero's enemy—his *alter ego* descended from Hoffmann and [Adalbert von] Chamisso—is the stupid, brutal, handsome, insolent soldier, the *miles gloriosus*, who steals the hero's shirts, persecutes him, is admired while the hero is despised, and robs the hero of what he most ardently longs for. He is the terrible Double—the *Doppelgänger*—of the paranoiac imagination of the early German Romantics, the Drum Major in Wozzeck, the symbol of detestable strength and success, the mocking dismissal of all forms of inner life. . . .

As for **"The Egyptian Stamp,"** although the fantasy derives from nineteenth-century romanticism, it has points of similarity both with the phantasmagoria of Bely's *Petersburg* and the logic of Kafka's *Castle*. (p. 4)

Isaiah Berlin, "A Great Russian Writer," in The New York Review of Books *(reprinted with permission from* The New York Review of Books; *copyrights © 1965 Nyrev, Inc.), Vol. V, No. 10, December 23, 1965, pp. 3-4.*

CLARENCE BROWN   (essay date 1965)

[*The Egyptian Stamp* is] the single example of Mandelstam's narrative prose and one of the few examples of surrealist fiction to be found in all of Russian literature. We might take these words as a clue to the pattern of the tale itself, which is composed in a kind of delirious key and consists of just such a feverish babble of constant digressions. In Mandelstam's serious writing it is the nearest approach to dealing directly with the bleak reality of his time and place, though it can seem, in the flaunting of its various opacities, to be as remote from that reality as poems like **"Nashedshij podkovu"** (**The Finder of a Horseshoe**) or the terrible **"'Grifel' naja oda"** (**The Slate Ode**). It represents that reality in a fragmented, multifaceted manner which strives for an artistic equivalency to the fractured life of the period.

Perhaps there were other reasons, too, for the elliptical manner. The central character strikes one almost at once as a familiar figure: here is one of the legion of "little men," the spineless or hapless but in any case heroically weak victims of Russian literature, We know him. But as we read, our familiarity with him seems to grow and to become more specific, our sense of his significance deepens, and we are at the end finally aware that this late descendant of Akakij Akakievich [the protagonist of Gogol's *The Overcoat*] represents in the context of his time a statement which in a more naked form, shorn of the ambiguity of its many levels, might have been not only less poetic but certainly less prudent. (pp. 32-3)

For all the prismatic surrealism through which we see the background of the novella, it is still vividly the actual stone and glass of Petersburg. The same may be said of certain of the characters: they derive with hardly a change of name from actual acquaintances of Mandelstam. And it seems to me that the central event itself recapitulates, this time with considerably more disguise, an episode from Mandelstam's personal history.

His beloved Petersburg—the classical and eighteenth-century nature of which he caressed in his poetry with the Derzhavinian name "Petropol'"—has become animal: "loathsome as if it were eating a soup of crushed flies." Everything has gone to pieces, like the style of narration. Violence and lawlessness are unrestrained, since the government, "sleeping like a carp," has vanished. It is a background against which the impotence and futility of the dreamy little hero with the queer name of Parnok impress us all the more. But Parnok has the artist's antidote against horror—a retreat into his abstracted interior musing, the description of which vies with the external narration as the focus of the novella. There is in general an uneasy balance between the real and the imagined: Parnok's strabismal vision is forever half on one, half on the other. His inner thoughts are nostalgic, poetic, culture-laden; they sometimes descend into a fatigue-induced playing with words that have snagged his attention.

Pornok loves music, and his presence alone in the foreground of the narration is sufficient to scatter musical images throughout the description of his surroundings. [One] example of [Mandelstam's] saturation technique . . . is Parnok's entry into the Polish laundry, transforming it into a kind of Renaissance concert. (pp. 33-4)

[The events of Parnok's day] succeed each other in a curious mosaic pattern, the intrinsic charm of which seduces the attention from any direct concern with the events of the original narrative, which one feels to be taking its ordinary course just beyond or behind the language before us. This language has the qualities of Mandelstam's best poetry: condensation, form, grace, observation, wit. Were that its only reason for being, it would be sufficient, and the style in large measure *becomes* the plot of this *commedia erudita*. (p. 35)

The surface events of Parnok's day are indeed the surface, and below them one can discern at least two more levels: that of the literary tradition and that of autobiography. The former is the more important, and I deal with it first. (p. 37)

For all its vastly more complex and sometimes baffling structure and symbolism, *The Egyptian Stamp* presents the identical basic situation that we find in the works of Gogol and Dostoevsky: the hero, a helpless little man, finds his own identity split in two, the second half being endowed with all those attributes of power and invulnerable knowledge of the world lacking in the first. And the double uses his superiority to antagonize and persecute the hero. To put it briefly, Parnok is to Captain Krzyzanowski as Kovalëv is to the Nose and as Mr. Goljadkin the Elder is to Mr. Goljadkin the Younger. Mandelstam, like Dostoevsky in *Poor Folk,* makes his intention unmistakably clear to the reader by actually mentioning the hero of his model, and, moreover, by including that hero precisely in the list of Parnok's *ancestors*. . . . (pp. 38-9)

The parallel with [Gogol's] *The Overcoat* is striking indeed. It is enough to point out that Gogol's story is about Akakij Akakievich Bashmachkin, a kind of archetype of the civil servant—desperately poor, terrified of his superiors, the butt of his fellows—whose entire being is concentrated toward one end, the possession of an overcoat; that he is at the mercy of a malign tailor named Petrovich; and that he is finally robbed of his precious coat to realize how important are the links between it and *The Egyptian Stamp*. (pp. 42-3)

If Mandelstam's story is an ingenious combination of numerous elements from earlier works, the question why he did it may prove interesting. Are we to suppose him so poor in invention that he was compelled, in his only attempt at contriving an objective narrative, to borrow characters and situations from his predecessors? I do not think anyone even slightly acquainted

with Mandelstam's work could accept that explanation. . . . Audacity of purpose, not paucity of invention, led him to utilize for his own special aims Gogol's and Dostoevsky's themes and characters. In order fully to grasp this complexity and audacity, it will be necessary to turn to the third of the principal levels of *The Egyptian Stamp:* the elliptical and elusive references to Mandelstam's own life.

One must deal here with allusion, often cryptic enough, with "tone," and with scattered, fractional details which, taken separately, could scarcely be regarded as conclusive, but together impress one with the extent to which Mandelstam was writing of himself. We know little of his life, as I have said, but it is clear that we know quite enough to see that a good deal of it has found its way into the ostensible fiction which we are considering.

There are two sorts of autobiographical reference in *The Egyptian Stamp*. The first is thoroughly private and consists of occasional references to and verbal echoes from his own work, especially from *The Noise of Time,* and also of some of the personal characteristics of Mandelstam which we find abundantly in the memoir literature devoted to him. (pp. 44-5)

But I have called such references to his life "private," for they are revealed only by a special knowledge of Mandelstam's personal life and by the most sedulous collation of his published works. He could hardly have expected his audience to remark the significance of such things as the mention of Ejlers' flower shop on Ofitserskaja. But that he did intend his readers to be aware of the autobiographical elements in *The Egyptian Stamp* is evidenced by a second, more explicit type of reference to himself. The narrator of the story is ubiquitously present, like the ironic and whimsical narrator of Gogol's tales. He refers to his pen (the symbol of the very process that is creating the story before our eyes), which he has some trouble in subordinating to his will, and to the manuscript itself: "Destroy your manuscript, but save whatever you have inscribed in the margin out of boredom, out of helplessness and, as it were, in a dream." The most explicit implication of himself in the whole story is the already noted *cri de coeur*: "Lord! Do not make me like Parnok! Give me the strength to distinguish myself from him." This altogether ironic entreaty is echoed in the still more ironic exclamation: "What a pleasure for a narrator to switch from the third person to the first!" The irony is that he has inserted first-person narration throughout. Such inserted anecdotal reminiscences as those about Shapiro, the sooty lamp, Geshka Rabinovich, Aunt Vera, the little domestic dictionary are all, in the strictest sense, continuations of the autobiography in *The Noise of Time.*

The Egyptian Stamp would thus appear to be, to adopt one of E. M. Forster's phrases for the novel as a genre, "a queer blend of Poetry and History"—not, though, just any poetry and history. Let us ask why this particular poetry—the narrow, though dual, theme from Russian literature to which Mandelstam added his surrealistic extension—and why this particular history, his own and that of his times. (pp. 52-3)

Clarence Brown, "The Prose of Mandelstam," in The Prose of Osip Mandelstam: "The Noise of Time," "Theodosia," "The Egyptian Stamp" *by Osip Mandelstam, translated by Clarence Brown (copyright © 1965 by Princeton University Press; reprinted by permission of Princeton University Press), Princeton University Press, 1965, pp. 3-66.*

VICTOR TERRAS   (essay date 1966)

I believe that Mandel'štam's ideas in the fields of philosophy of language, aesthetics, and poetic theory, which he considers "hellenistic," have only a vague and an indirect connection with the world of the classics. . . .

The main object of Mandel'štam's "hellenistic" vision is the word (*slovo*). To use the poet's own definition, "the word, in a hellenistic conception, is active flesh, ready to give birth to the event." "It may be viewed not only as what is objectively given in consciousness, but also as a human organ, exactly as the liver, or the heart," a conception which leads to a poetics of "biological character." It may also be viewed as "a word-soul which hovers about things . . . like a soul about a deserted, but not forgotten body." The word realized in these terms is a frequently recurring motif of Mandel'štam's poetry. It is in this connection that [Gleb] Struve and [B.A.] Filippov rightly speak of Mandel'štam's "verbal magic." Such "magic" conception of the word is of course not specifically, much less exclusively, Greek, although it has found its most elegant and sophisticated formulation in Greek philosophy.

A "hellenistic" view of language is equated by Mandel'štam with "philologism," i.e., love and respect for the word as such. The word, "hellenistically" conceived, is in his opinion the greatest, perhaps the only asset of Russian culture. The most terrible thing that could happen to Russia is a victory of the enemies of the word, who would destroy its living spirit by making it, thoughtlessly, a mere signal of communication or, selfishly, a tool of mere self-expression. That his own age is guilty of a criminal destruction of the word, Mandel'štam sees clearly. (p. 252)

The "hellenistic" and "classicistic" nature of Mandel'štam's poetry has long been taken for granted. I find little substance in this notion—if it is to mean that Mandel'štam's poetic style resembles that of Greek and Latin poetry in general, or of any individual poets of classical antiquity in particular. Only of some late and very sophisticated ancient poets (such as Ovid) can it be said that their verses are "a quintessence of literature," which is true of the Parnassians, and of Mandel'štam. Yet Mandel'štam goes even further than the Parnassians in eliminating from his poetry all that is "non-poetry" (to use Croce's term). There is little rhetoric to be found in Mandel'štam, but plenty of it in Horace, Ovid, and even Catullus. True, the early Mandel'štam is the typical *doctus poeta,* who likes to shine with his erudition, but this is a trait he shares with many modern but not with all ancient poets. Mandel'štam's tendency to reduce poetry to "pure language" by eliminating the paralinguistic elements of abstract thought and logic, of subjective emotion, of personal involvement, and of actuality, this tendency reminds one of Mallarmé or of Valéry, and not of any ancient poet. Mandel'štam's poems may be called polyphonic verbal compositions with a multidimensional (rhythmic, architectonic, euphonic, synaesthetic, emotional, and intellectual) expressive effect. Such an effect may be found, occasionally and I believe accidentally, in Pindar and the Aeolian poets, but is of course a consciously pursued goal in Mallarmé, Stefan George, or Mandel'štam. It is quite untypical of the bulk of Greek and Latin poetry. (p. 253)

Still, Mandel'štam the modernist poet deserves to be called a hellenist. He deserves it for having stepped into the stream of time and retrieved from it (I am using a metaphor of Stefan George's) genuine fragments of the ancient world, visions of Hellas and Rome which are marvels of historical intuition in the Bergsonian sense. He does this on the strength of his own imagination (and erudition, too), although not without help from a very strong classical tradition in Russian poetry. (pp. 253-54)

[We] may say that a profound awareness of the continuity and unity of Occidental culture is the most characteristic trait of Mandel'štam's poetry. . . . He has been eminently successfull in realizing it. I believe that Mandel'stam's poetic conquests of "times lost" are due not only to his brilliant intuition but to solid philological erudition as well. . . . As to intuition, I think that he alone has actually succeeded in leaving the shores of his own age, entering the stream of time, and meeting there the spirits of forgotten ages. (p. 264)

Victor Terras, "Classical Motives in the Poetry of Osip Mandel'štam," in Slavic and East European Journal *(© 1966 by AATSEEL of the U.S., Inc.), Vol. X, No. 3, September, 1966, pp. 251-67.*

CLARENCE BROWN   (essay date 1967)

Mandelstam's earliest poetry is marked by an extraordinarily low temperature and a lack of movement that sometimes amounts to virtual stasis. It is characterized by quietude of manner, whiteness of color, elegance of form. The emotions are chaste, and there is a solemn ceremoniousness in the tones and attitudes of the speaker of the poems, whose presence is seldom felt. It is remarkable how often Mandel'stam's diction is colored by negative words. Here are a few examples: nežiloj ("uninhabited") . . . nezvučnyj ("soundless") . . . neživoj ("lifeless") . . . nepodvižnyj ("motionless") . . . . And so on. The list of such words could be a very long one, but these can serve to illustrate a frequent tendency of Mandelstam's: to summon up a quality or attribute only to deny it.

He was a master at describing emptiness, absence, vacancy, silence. I know of no equal to him in this regard, at least not in literature. In painting Andrew Wyeth often achieves a Mandelstamian feeling of emptiness, and I think the comparison is doubly apt since both Wyeth and Mandelstam lend poignancy to their "desert places" by including some reminder of human life. Both artists show us not the vacancies of the sea or the ininhabited steppe but the emptiness of rooms. I like to imagine to myself an illustration by Wyeth of a line that would seem peculiarly suited to his mood and talent:

> Silence, like a spinning-wheel, stood there in the
>   white room.

This blankness is not altogether dead, as it never is in Mandelstam. It has a human nerve in it. The more we perceive that remarkable figure of the spinning wheel to betoken a now ended human activity, the more we sense the peculiar stillness of a thing whose function is to move, the more densely does that image gather the silence around it.

Here is a poem which has been published in different variants. I take the version that appeared in Mandelstam's first book of poetry *Kamen* (**Stone**). . . .

> Hearing stretches its sensitive sail,
> The widened gaze grows empty
> And through the silence floats
> A soundless chorus of midnight birds.

(pp. 148-49)

How extraordinary and how daring these images are! And not merely daring, but permanently daring. Time has not effaced their originality, and one recalls Ezra Pound's having defined literature as "news that *stays* news."

Nor have they anything to fear from analysis, which is durability of a sort that again argues the genius of their author. What is their effect? In the first line

> Hearing stretches its sensitive sail

one is provided with a visual image which jolts the imagination through its equation of an abstraction (the sense of hearing) with a piece of maritime equipment. But the image is far more than visual. There is something tactile in our perception of the tautness of a sail stretched tight against the wind, and this sense is enhanced by the addition of the epithet *čutkij,* which means "delicately sensitive" in both the basic physical sense and in the transferred sense for which "tactful" is a common though not very satisfactory equivalent. And there is yet a third way in which this image strikes us, though I am not sure that I can find the words to express it (and I take such disability as the final proof that one is in the presence of poetic art of the highest calibre). "Auditory" is hardly the adequate description for a quality of sense perception which is not that of sound but of *silence* (it is later in the poem that one learns this particular aspect of the first image: the poem is about emptiness and silence). And the function of the sail metaphor is to make that silence almost palpable. This third way of perceiving the image is perhaps best expressed by calling it an intense, almost painful, *awareness* of the sense of hearing, but not of anything conveyed to the consciousness by that sense.

In the next image the sense of sight is treated in much the same way, and it has much the same sort of effect:

> The widened gaze grows empty.

Here one finds not the word for sight itself (zrenie) but the word *vzor* "gaze," which is a sort of buried hypostatic image: a piece of sight, an instance of sight. This hypostasized sight is made more material by the epithet that is applied to it: . . . "broadened, widened." And by the verb: it "becomes empty," which implies the condition of having been full, of having contained something.

This is a poem about emptiness so complete that it is hardly expressible, but obviously images and sounds must be found to convey the emptiness. That the dilemma can decidedly *not* be resolved by simple, declarative statement can be learned by looking at Milton's attempt to do something similar. In *Paradise Lost* (I/62-64) his purpose is to convey the absence of light, as Mandelstam's was to convey the absence of sound and vision:

> . . . . yet from those flames
> No light, but rather darkness visible
> Served only to discover sights of woe.

The phrase "darkness visible" appeals uniquely to the intelligence, to purely rational perception and to no other.

And so it is an inevitable contradiction that after the two images which transmit the emptiness of hearing and sight, one is presented with an image that is visual and auditory:

> And through the silence sails
> A soundless chorus of midnight birds.

Silence itself is materialized as a medium through which these midnight birds fly, and the fundamental contradiction is emphasized by a device which is frequent in Mandelstam: the *contradictio in adjecto—nezvučnyj xor:* soundless chorus.

The tenaciousness of early reputations is well known. The poems that I have been talking about—the cool, quiet, laconic poetry bathed in the pale radiance of other worlds—is the poetry of Mandelstam's earliest youth. It is regarded by many as his best work . . . but it would be a great mistake to regard it as his only work.

In a poem of 1912 Mandelstam had exclaimed of some ball "thrown from a dim planet"

> So there it is, a geniune
> link with a mysterious world!

But one year later this Symbolist link with other worlds had been abruptly transformed into a tennis ball, batted about in a real tennis game between a "sportive girl" and an ever-young Englishman." The pervading gloom of the Symbolist manner was replaced for a while by the Acmeist gaiety and delight in the things of this world. Mandelstam had written many poems filled with a longing for muteness—perhaps a remnant of the decadent *amor fati*—and this scheme was to return later in such superlatively moving poems as *To the German Language* but for the time being there was some delightfully witty poems to be written—poems about the cinema, about Carskoe Selo— perfectly empty little poems that reveal the poet disporting himself in his language and taking nonchalant delight in its consonants and vowels.

And the themes range over the whole world of art and all of Western culture. There are the famous poems in which the poet's vision caresses the immense perspectives and the classical architecture of his beloved Petersburg (to which he gave the Deržavinian and Hellenic name of Petropol), and the architecture of Paris (Notre Dame), of Moscow, where all the gentle churches lend their voices to a maidenly choir, and where Mandelstam was attracted as always by whatever seemed to him classical and Mediterranean in Russian culture. . . . His poem about the Hagia Sophia in Istanbul is one of his most beautiful and beloved.

Other themes come from literature—all the way from the epic poems of Homer through the classical tragedies of Racine to the Victorian novels of Dickens and the weird tales of Edgar Allan Poe. Whatever one may think of the Soviet critic Selivanovskij's other opinions about Mandelstam, there is much truth in his remark that Mandelstam's poetry is not a reflection of life, but a reflection of its reflection in art. And a critic who is far more well disposed toward Mandelstam, Viktor Žirmunskij, has applied to his work Schlegel's tag "die Poesie der Poesie."

This brings us to two remarks that are perhaps repeated more often than others about the poetry of Osip Mandelstam: that it is impersonal and that it is impenetrable.

Certainly there is enough on the surface of his poetry, and especially of the early and better known poetry, that would seem to many people impersonal. Those who call it so generally have in mind the little *thing* poems with their nearly Japanese laconism (The nameless fruit falling from the tree in four brief lines) or the architectural poems, or the meditative poems. In other poems, though a *persona* may be present, it seems to matter so little, it seems to be so much a part of the patterned movement that it becomes lost, as in a trick picture, in the general composition. In the body of his work—by which I mean those of his poems that have been heretofore published and are known to the general reader—there are so few poems that concern themselves with anything outside of poetry and the other arts, there are so few that seem, for example, to point a moral, or advance a cause, or tell an entertaining story, or in fact to solicit our attention on any ground at all that is not in the strictest sense poetic ground, that there seems to be a certain lack of warmth, of humanness, about them. Hence the recurrent phrases: pure poetry, a poet's poet, rarefied atmosphere, museum-like, etc.

As for the charge of impenetrability, this is made by people who fail to understand Mandelstam because they are looking for the meaning in a place where he did not put it. This is the more to be regretted since Mandelstam himself, who had one of the clearest and most elevated conceptions of poetry of any Russian writer of his time, left in his critical writings explicit directions for reading his poetry. Those who use the word *meaningless* against him generally have in mind the notion that few of his poems can be paraphrased. The poet himself, meanwhile, regarded whatever is susceptible of paraphrase as belonging outside of poetry proper. It was not his concern to couch a prose meaning in the outward form of metered language. (pp. 149-53)

As a prosaist, Mandelstam did not emulate the example of Puskin, who strove to exclude from his prose whatever seemed ornamental and "poetic." Mandelstam's prose is distinctly and avowedly that of a poet. It is in fact so closely linked to his poetry in technique—and often by specific figures—that what we say of one can largely serve for the other. It reminds me rather of the prose of Wallace Stevens, if only in this: that it often seems on the very verge of becoming poetry. The essay **"Language and Culture"** for instance, is actually a sort of contrapuntal arrangement of prose and poetry. Abundant quotation is of course no novelty. In Mandelstam, however, the essential difference is that the verse—much of it, by the way, his own—is not so much illustration or interlude as it is a sequential development of the argument. It does not accompany the prose: it momentarily replaces it. (p. 157)

[Mandelstam's] prose is probably the most consistently joyous creation to come from his pen. His work as a whole is marked at all periods by a strong undercurrent of Pushkinian gaiety, but nowhere does this find such free and masterful expression as in his prose. . . . Surely he was among the wittiest writers of his generation, if by wit one understands the inevitable companion and lightener of high seriousness. His prose exhibits the best qualities of his poetry—concision, observation, surprise—but for those interested in the man behind the poems it brings another advantage: it reveals Mandelstam himself, or it is, at least, as far as he ever went in self-revelation. Most of it is plain autobiography, some of it is elaborately camouflaged autobiography, but all of it is to a remarkable degree personal and immediate. (p. 158)

In two senses [*The Noise of Time*] is rather like the autobiography of Maksim Gorkij. It is, in the first place, a book of characters, sharply observed and reproduced with a kindly objectivity. And in the second place, the figure of the author himself is curiously marginal. He is a kind of ambulatory recording instrument moving unobtrusively among the scenes of his childhood and youth, picking up the flavor of a conversation here, the sounds of a concert, audience and all, there. But we must bring this comparison to a halt, for nothing else in Mandelstam is like Gorkij. . . . In whatever Mandelstam chooses to show us there is a compelling sense of relevance, of relatedness. Between the archeology of the family bookshelves, the sounds and odors of the railroad station in Pavlovsk, the chthonian delirium of a violin concert, the opening day exercises at

the Tensev School, and the geography of a Jewish spa we make our way with pleasantly mingled feelings of astonishment and familiarity, for however sui generis these people and scenes may be, they are bound together by the silver thread of that historical intuition. It, more than mere chronology, is the principle of order and arrangement.

The Noise of Time deals with Mandelstam's childhood and adolescence. Except for a brief but precious memoir by the late Mixail Karpovič, the years just following in Germany and Paris are surrounded by silence. Glimpses of Mandelstam the university student are also provided by others. In the autobiographical vein, we have only two more writings of any extent from his own hand. The first, *Theodosia,* comes nearer to being a continuation the *The Noise of Time.* . . . It is a record of certain people and impressions which Mandelstam encountered in the Crimea during the latter days of the Civil War when it was occupied by the dispirited Volunteer Army of Denikin and Wrangel. Everything about the situation—the desperate political collapse, the hopeless apprehension of disaster, the very topography of the little peninsula itself, protruding into the Black Sea like a springboard into exile—imparts to *Theodosia* a kind of ultimate refinement of that fin de siècle atmosphere which Mandelstam had portrayed in his earlier work. (pp. 158-59)

[The other] is the fascinating surrealistic novella entitled *The Egyptian Stamp.* It reminds one strongly of a much more extensive—but equally neglected—body of imaginative prose, that of the Futurist poet Velimir Xlebnikov, by which it was clearly influenced. But Mandelstam's novella had an added dimension, or dimensions, and if we call it fiction it is only to avoid some more cumbersome designation of its true nature, for it is about equally fiction, autobiography, and criticism. The plot is the merest nothing. A little man named Parnok runs about Petersburg during the Kerenskij summer between the two revolutions of 1917 trying to accomplish two things, to retrieve certain items of his clothing and to prevent a lynch murder, and he fails in both. On this frail narrative Mandelstam hangs a dream-like swarm of portraiture, city-scape, reminiscence, word-play, and cultured jottings of extraordinary variety. It is in part a strange little inventory of the interior museum in which his life was largely passed. There is a kind of contrapuntal rhythm among passages of hallucinatory nonchalance and passages thick with the smell of actuality. (p. 160)

Like all genuine originals, Mandelstam was always himself. His criticism is conveyed to us by the same instrument that produced the memoirs and the fiction. That is to say, he does not assume a manner of talking depending on the subject-matter. He talks about everything in his own manner. . . . It might as well be said at the outset that his being utterly true to his own nature is not always a good thing for his criticism. Some of it is too private for me, at least, to understand. Some of it, to use a distinction which he himself makes in **"The Morning of Acmeism,"** seems to be written not with the consciousness but with the word. I have said that his prose closely resembles his poetry. In the essay on Dante he presents us with a figure for the movement of a poem, and this figure is an example of how vividly and memorably Mandelstam can convey to his reader a critical notion and also an example of the procedures which render some parts of his criticism *not* vivid or even comprehensible. The figure is of a swarm of Chinese junks moving about in various directions on a river. The sense of a poem leaps from junk to junk in making its way across the river. As the junks continue to move this way and that, it is pointless even to try to reestablish the thought's hectic itinerary from one to the other. Poetry written in the spirit of this image is alive with a sense of daring enterprise and constant, unfailing amazement, but if critical prose makes its way thus eccentrically through a restless flotilla of assocations, the result will sometimes be vague.

Having broached Mandelstam's criticism with these negative reservations I now feel free to state that in spite of occasional baffling passages I find his little book *On poetry* and his other scattered essays on literary art to be laden with some of the most startling, impressive, and brilliant observations that I have ever read. (pp. 160-61)

I have just been turning through the pages of Mandelstam's critical essays, confident in the expectation of finding many brief passages that would lend themselves to quotation, but I must confess to a certain disappointment. I do not think that he is really very quotable, and the reason for this disability is a measure of one of his strongest qualities as a critic. There must be few who rely so heavily on context. Mandelstam's sharpest perceptions are so thickly interwoven with the fabric of his argument (and of his Argument) that they are extricated only at their, and the reader's, peril. His criticism is impressionistic (I do not think he would approve my saying this) and like all impressionism it demands to be taken whole. This is true even of the longest and most ambitious work, such as the "Razgovor o Dante," ("Conversation about Dante") and essay of rare intellectual passion and beauty. Here he moves over the vast range of his subject, from canto to canto of the great poem, attracted now by this, now by that quality, quoting, translating, bodying forth his thought with metaphor and imaginatively recreating the physical and mental world of the great Italian. The result is continous excitement that arises from one's almost palpable sense of the *Divina Commedia* not as a finished monument but as a poem in the process of becoming. (p. 162)

> *Clarence Brown, "On Reading Mandelstam" (reprinted by permission of Inter-Language Literary Associates), in* Osip Mandelshtam: Sobranie sochenenii, *Inter-Language Literary Associates, 1967 (and reprinted in* Major Soviet Writers: Essays in Criticism, *edited by Edward J. Brown, Oxford University Press, New York 1973, pp. 146-63).*

NADEZHDA MANDELSTAM (essay date 1972)

[Mandelstam] used to say people had destroyed Yesenin by telling him to write a long poem, a "major" work, thereby causing him to feel strain and frustration: as a lyric poet, he was incapable of turning out a full-length epic. M. was himself totally immune to the modern cult of bigness in all its forms. I put this down to the fact that he had arrived at his own conception of a "major" work in lyric poetry, namely a book of verse all composed during the same period and having a certain unity. Verse arranged in a volume like this—as an interlocking whole, covering a broad range, yet bound together by a single lyric concept and way of looking at the world—constitutes a special kind of literary form with its own type of subject matter and governed by its own rules. The arrangement of the material is sometimes worked out in accordance with a conscious plan. . . . (p. 388)

In *Stone* M. published by no means all of the poems from his first flow of inspiration. . . . *Stone* is a book of his youthful days, a time of wonderment at the world, of first endeavors to make sense of it ("Can I be real, and will death truly come?") and discover a firm core of life and culture. It used to be commonly said—this was the judgment of people debauched by the self-indulgence and wanton outpourings of the first decade and a half of the century—that M. was lacking in emotion, cold and "classical" (whatever this absurd word may mean). I believe they simply failed to read him properly—whom *did* they read properly?—and never noticed the youthful anguish of the early verse and the particular tone of the last third of the *Stone* poems, beginning with the one that mentions "Joseph sold into Egypt." In *Stone* life is still an accident, a mesh of pain in which M., a stranger among strangers, is searching for meaning, first discovering it in death. His interest in historiosophy already makes its appearance in *Stone* as a quest for the mainspring of life in society. At that period he saw its basis in the church—the Catholic one, moreover. This explains why he constantly harks back to Rome, right to the end of his life (one of his very last poems is about it). In his mature years he saw the central core of our society in Christianity and the European culture based on it—the culture whose desperate crisis we have witnessed in our lifetime. The architectural theme running through all his books is linked with his belief that man's task on earth is to build, to leave tangible traces of his existence—that is, to defeat time and death. (p. 390)

Each work—*Stone, Tristia, Poems* (1921-25), "New Verse," "Voronezh Notebooks"—has its leading idea, its poetic beam of light. In the early verse of *Stone* it is youthful anguish and his search for a place in life; in *Tristia*, coming to maturity, forebodings of catastrophe, the doom of a culture (Petersburg), and the search for salvation (St. Isaac's); the truncated, strangled book of verse **1921-25** shows the poet as a "drying crust" in an alien world; "**New Verse**" is an assertion of the value of life for its own sake, and also the sense of being an outsider among people who had turned their backs on values accumulated over the ages, a new awareness that his isolation was a form of opposition to the forces of evil; in the "**Voronezh Notebooks**" there is resigned acceptance of life for what it is, in all its vanity and with all its horrors, an awareness that this was the brink, the end, the era of wholesale slaughter, the "beginning of grim deeds." Here he names the "Judas of peoples to come." In the last year of his life there were two further bursts of poetry, but this has all been lost. These final poems expressed a new view of Russia as a country which, despite everything, still lived on, though dormant and oblivious of itself. In this lost verse the country stands up to the forces of destruction by its hushed silence, its passive resistance, its traditions, its self-sacrificing readiness for any ordeals. M. was impressed by the "fan-shaped lathwork of invincible sloping roofs." This was only the beginning of a new book, and there is no point in guessing what it would have grown into if it had not been abruptly cut short. (p. 398)

His notion of a "book," or a cycle, as a complete whole relating to a given period preserved M. from the sickness of the age—to which people succumbed as children do to measles or dogs to distemper; it took the form of a craving to write "major" works—novels, or if one was a poet, then at least a long narrative in verse, ideally an epic. "Major" works were demanded by the State, but the State was only responding to what was being urged in literary circles. (p. 399)

In the twenties everybody tried to reason with M., but in the thirties they were already pointing their fingers at him; not concealing his distaste, he went on living among the barbarians and did what he had to do. He was not tempted by the idea of a "major" work and never even gave it a moment's consideration, since he thought in terms of "books" and "cycles" of verse. There were sometimes also interconnected series larger than "cycles" and on a common theme; of these, using a precise musical term in preference to a vague literary one, he said that they were "like oratorios." It was thus that he referred to his "Verse on the Unknown Soldier" and the group of poems on the death of Andrei Bely. If he did not put the group of poems about Armenia into this category, it was, I believe, because he thought of an oratorio as having for its subject matter the crowning moment in the life of man and humankind as a whole: death. Dying, death, mass slaughter, and the general doom—such is the theme of M.'s two oratorios. (p. 400)

> *Nadezhda Mandelstam, "The Unbroken Flow," in her* Hope Abandoned, *translated by Max Hayward (reprinted by permission of Atheneum Publishers; translation copyright © 1973, 1974 by Atheneum Publishers; originally published as* Vtoraya Kniga, *Editions YMCA Press, 1972), Atheneum, 1974, pp. 388-400.*

DONALD RAYFIELD   (essay date 1973)

[I want] to write about some of the images and themes of the poems [in *The Gold-Finch and Other Poems*], to show how they grow out of Mandel'shtam's earlier more orthodox poetry and why he chooses such apparently esoteric devices. (p. 4)

The style of his poetry of the 1930s, particularly from 1935, is far more immediate, abrupt and intimate than the classical lyricism which, rightly or wrongly, one associates with the Mandel'shtam of the 1910s or early 1920s. His imagery incorporates a new terminology, sometimes banal, sometimes disconcertingly odd. Allusions extend in all directions to Dante, to modern cosmology, to biology.

There are moral reasons and environmental reasons for a sudden renewal and compression of Mandel'shtam's poetic thought from summer 1935 to spring 1937. In May 1934 Mandel'shtam had been arrested and exiled to the Urals. A nervous breakdown, successful intercessions and luck led to his being allowed to choose Voronezh, on the edge of the steppes, some 300 miles south of Moscow for the remainder of his four-year sentence. . . . There is fear in Mandel'shtam's poetry, but it takes the form of nervous haste, rather than a paralytic tremor, of strange rhythms, rather than inarticulateness.

Voronezh gave new landscapes to Mandel'shtam's work. His poetry up to 1915 (*Kamen', **Stone***) and from 1916 to 1921 (*Tristia*) is set in a highly stylised landscape, abstracted from a classical Black Sea dreamworld, a mediaeval Moscow or a neo-classical Petersburg. Russian forests and Russian steppes, however, played no part in his poetry until he was exiled to Cherdyn' among the great rivers and forests of the Urals and, soon after, to Voronezh, where the undulating country of European Russia meets the traditionally Scythian expanses of steppe. The impact of the new scenery was overwhelming.

Mandel'shtam was never an "open-air" poet. . . . [He] never let his mind fuse with nature. Trees and forests always threatened him with a sense of evil forces, of dark, folklore forebodings. (pp. 4-5)

All Mandel'shtam's work indicates both claustrophobia and agorophobia. His early poetry took him away from Jewish closeness into European landscapes; his Voronezh poetry shows

horror at an Asiatic immensity. What he constantly demanded was form, a sense of strata, direction, evolution. (p. 6)

The dominant theme of all the Voronezh poetry is the resemblance of the sky's starry firmament to the human head, its skull, sockets, the starry seams of its bones. Mandel'shtam thinks of the human head and its mind as a parallel creation, the death of a man being a microcosmic apocalypse. It was an anatomical analogy that first began in a poem of 1923, *The Age,* in which the image of a crushed backbone links the individual animal and the spirit of his times. In Voronezh it becomes a conceit which helps to express a feeling that Mandel'shtam was living through the last fears not only of his own life, but of human culture. The conceit gives several images that relate the dome of the thinking skull to the dome of the Voronezh skies. Hence . . . the barren skies and desolate human face are one in "temporo-facial ice" and "swollen azures of the eyes". Observer and object merge. Rivers flowing under the ice incorporate the poet's insomniac mutterings. Weather and poet confront each other, equally alienated and tense.

Yet in the Voronezh notebooks, as the scenery becomes less strange, we recognise the main features of Mandel'shtam's poetry in its search for poetic continuity, for revelations of poetic experience that date back to ancient Greek poetry, for form in matter. Mandel'shtam said in a vehement tirade of 1931, *Fourth Prose:* "What I like in a doughnut is the hole in the middle." The symbolic value of all his imagery is in "the hole in the middle". (p. 7)

Those who know Mandel'shtam's poetry will not have forgotten a long, rhetorical poem of 1923 called *The man who found a horseshoe*. It is a poem which attempts to set out a theory of poetry. The horseshoe is an image releasing all the energy of the galloping horse, all the hardness of the road and the sharpness of the sparks: it is an archetypal poetic symbol. In the Voronezh . . . poems about the "precious leavening of the world"—i.e. the airiness in texture and matter—and about the imp getting into "the traces of the hurrying hooves", the central idea is of the poetic sensibility as a road, on which the horseshoe of the outside world leaves imprints. These indentations fill with water—Mandel'shtam says "cupreous water", copper always being in his work an image of metallic struggle, of fatal confrontation. The poet's job is to record these imprints on his mind, before they cloud over with some "micaceous layer" that distorts the truth. The image of the mind as a road is effectively dynamic; basically, the idea of the imprint, "the hole", as more important than the concrete force that made it, stems from his poetic thought some fifteen years earlier.

But now, in Voronezh, demonic forces are at work. . . . Stalin furtively enters into his poetry. It was a lampoon on Stalin and a decree by Stalin that led to Mandel'shtam's exile. Stalin, his killer, lurks in many of the Voronezh poems. Mandel'shtam was struck by a number of resemblances between himself and Stalin. He was Osip, Stalin was Iosif, for one thing. Prey and predator share other likenesses. On the greatest of the Voronezh poems, "Inside a mountain an idol sits", gives a picture of decaying splendour and dehumanization which can be interpreted both as that of the poet's imagination and as that of Stalin's corrupt tyranny. (pp. 7-8)

From the beginning of the nineteen-thirties Mandel'shtam, and a few other poets, were fascinated by Italian poetry, particularly Dante, Petrarch and Aristo. The "Florentine anguish" that Mandel'shtam feels while the left and the right deviations are wiped out by Stalin, together with Russian civilisation, is almost pleasurable: it links the poet with Dante, writing poetry under not dissimilar tribulations, while Guelphs and Ghibellines murder each other. The mortal, vulnerable human skull recreates in his poem the firmament; the corollary for Mandel'shtam is that mortal anguish should call forth an eternal echo. . . .

If Dante had to endure the death of the old earth-centred cosmology of Ptolemy, Mandel'shtam has to put up with the extinction of the universe, centred on solar light and warmth, as he knows it. Stalin is reshaping the universe as fundamentally and irreversibly as Galileo or Copernicus. (p. 9)

> *Donald Rayfield, ''Introduction'' (copyright © 1973 by Donald Rayfield and The Menard Press), in* ''Chapter 42'' *by Nadezhda Mandel'shtam and ''The Goldfinch and Other Poems'' by Osip Mandel'shtam, The Menard Press, 1973, pp. 3-11.**

STEVEN BROYDE (essay date 1975)

[A] variety of critics have claimed that Mandel'štam was indifferent to his age: ''Characteristic of Mandel'štam's view of the world is a coldness of inner indifference to everything that occurs. The immense force of inertia which kept Mandel'štam's consciousness intentionally walled off from processes occurring in reality gave the poet the opportunity of preserving right up until 1925 a position of absolute social indifference.'' ''He has no social interests.'' Yet even [a] preliminary study of a single decade in Mandel'štam's career conclusively demonstrates that the poet's consciousness, far from shutting out contemporary reality, continuously confronted it in an effort to explore the possibilities of art. (pp. 1-2)

Mandel'štam was immensely involved in his age. His poetry represents a continuing commentary on it, an attempt to comprehend and record his reactions to an era which was changing if not disintegrating, before his eyes. Living at a time of profound social upheaval, Mandel'štam tried in his poetry and prose to understand the changes which were occurring with bewildering rapidity.

One recent scholar has written that ''Mandel'štam's purely political poems are, perhaps, his easiest ones, [but] some of his most difficult poems are those which deal with the nature of poetic vision, the social function of poetry, and the relationship between the poet and time.'' While the meaning of a political poem may be more obvious by providing a particular event on which to focus, the distinction between the two types of poems is not as clear-cut as this statement implies. Mandel'štam's poetry is never easy. Moreover, the political poems to a large extent explore precisely the relationship between the poet and time. . . . Mandel'štam reacts to events in a varied, complex, and constantly developing way. His responses are never doctrinaire; he does not view things from the vantage point of an already determined framework. Hence, at any point in time a new event can evoke a previously unfelt response. Moreover, it is important to see how Mandel'štam rethought previous solutions in the light of changes in the historical moment. (pp. 3-4)

[Many of his poems] are ultimately concerned with Mandel'štam's views on the fate of Russian culture, however one chooses to define this elusive word, at a time when the social order was in a state of near chaos; when some people feared for its survival, while others called for its destruction. Mandel'štam's most consistent belief during this period of tur-

moil was that Russia's cultural heritage must be preserved. However, his belief in the ability of the culture to survive in the midst of an inimical environment fluctuated. If in one poem he views the heritage as threatened and dying. . ., in yet another he can express muted confidence in the likelihood that it will survive, outlasting both those who would destroy it, and those who are attempting to protect it. . . . (p. 4)

Mandel'štam at various times professed an almost naive belief in, or perhaps hope for, the existence of a past and future golden age for humanity. This hope emerges at moments when one might expect the greatest despair: at the height of World War One (''Zverinec''), during the Civil War (''Na kamennyx otrogax Pierii'' [On the rocky spurs of Pireus]), at the time of a threatened Allied intervention (''Vojna. Opjat'raznogolosica''). Yet on the other hand, Mandel'štam sometimes was prey to a fear of an impending, never clearly delineated, cataclysm (''Koncert na vokzale'' [Concert at the Railway station], ''Veter nam utešen'e prines'' [The wind brought us consolation]). In fact. . ., both the fear of cataclysm and the belief in a golden future were expressed within one and the same poem (''Vojna. Opjat'raznogolosica''). The most optimistic interpretation of such a juxtaposition is that the cataclysm is the apocalyptic force which might initiate the new golden age; but Mandel'štam never made such a connection clear. (pp. 201-02)

Precisely because Mandel'štam's vision is so complex, it is often ambiguous. Ambiguity derives, not from any failure to focus his response exactly, but rather from being aware of the variety of possible responses. Refusing to accept the easy faith of the moment, Mandel'štam insists on measuring his experience against classical values or historical antecedents. Because he can comprehend intellectually both sides of an issue (or especially because in a period of cultural change he is excruciatingly aware both of what has been gained and what has been lost), complete emotional commitment to one side or another would be difficult if not impossible. Mandel'štam's choice instead is for complexity—to be inclusive rather than exclusive; to articulate all that he knows and feels, even if that knowledge is more painful to express than to ignore. Rather than sacrifice his awareness of or allegiance to one set of values for the sake of another, Mandel'štam remains detached and may seem aloof. (pp. 204-05)

Mandel'štam, in an attempt to be scrupulously exact, to preserve the situation in all its aspects, and to allow a variety of interpretations, may appear to be irresolute, undecided—either unclear in his own mind which interpretation he favored, or else certain himself, but maddeningly obscure to us. But the careful artist, the complex man who sees his own age intensively and can appreciate the past and future imaginatively and intellectually may be ambiguous because it is the only way to be perfectly true to his experience. To recognize the variety of responses may finally be much more demanding than deciding in favor of one set of values or one interpretation of events over another. Thus Mandel'štam's poems are ambiguous not out of perversity but out of accuracy. (p. 206)

> *Steven Broyde, in his introduction and conclusion to his* Osip Mandel'štam and His Age *(copyright © 1975 by the President and Fellows of Harvard College; excerpted by permission), Cambridge, Mass.: Harvard University Press, 1975, pp. 1-6, 200-06.*

SIDNEY MONAS (essay date 1977)

Mandelstam's criticism has to this day been seriously underestimated. He does not provide us with a new methodology, and in general tends to take a deflating view of the importance of methodologies. Nor is he quick to put on the Judge's robes and consign his fellow-poets to this or that circle of critical hell. There are poets he speaks of frowningly and with displeasure in one context, who often appear with vibrantly positive force elsewhere in his work. . . . He offers us neither the luxury of an imitable method nor that of an authoritative juridical decision, and so interest in him as critic in our age of luxurious criticism has been limited to the illumination his criticism provides his poetry.

This is of course no mean interest. He was a poet first, and no doubt his criticism must be approached from the perspective of his poetry and in relation to his poetic practice. At the same time, it becomes immediately apparent that the quality and gift of his criticism partakes of the quality and gift of his poetry while remaining, properly, prose.

Just as T. S. Eliot's interest in Dante and the English metaphysical poets, [Ezra] Pound's in the troubadours and Confucius, [Wallace] Stevens' Symbolist essays in esthetics, cannot be seen apart from their own poetry, so Mandelstam's **"Conversation about Dante"** has to be read, I think, as an incipient project for a new *Divine Comedy,* or at the least as the ringing affirmation of a sense of poetic identity so closely and passionately held as to make mere mistakes of historical detail or social interpretation seem relatively insignificant.

It is interesting to compare it with Eliot's essays on Dante. The poets attempt to rescue Dante from the Dante scholars. Each, while respectful of the need for knowledge about Dante's time and its cultural assumptions so very different from our own, makes a powerful effort to remain true to his own "amateur" reading of the poem. Each rejects the "antiquarian" Dante, and seeks in his work what is potentially alive as poetry.

Yet Eliot's Dante is more like that of the scholars—a formidable and remote figure. Eliot's immediate involvement is with the *visual,* not far away from the conceptual. "Dante's," he writes, "is a visual imagination," adding that "it is visual in the sense that he lived in an age in which men still saw visions." . . . The essays on Dante by Eliot are permeated by a nostalgia for a remote, more integral, more spiritually grounded age.

Mandelstam's involvement is immediate and personal. For him, the essential question is "how many sandals Alighieri wore out in the course of his poetic work, wandering about on the goatpaths of Italy?" For him, poetry is *movement,* the embodying, the incarnation of movement. Elsewhere, Mandelstam repeatedly refers to [Paul] Verlaine's *"L'Art poétique,"* and often he substitutes the word *"mouvement"* for Verlaine's *"musique."* His own synonym for poetry was "moving lips" and composition was inseparable from physical movement, from pacing and gesturing. Mandelstam *wrote* his poems—i.e., "fixed" them on paper; abstracted them—only after they had already been composed. The composition of a poem was a physical process and "another poet" a physical presence.

Mandelstam tries to erase the impression left by Dante's face in the well-known portraits; the aquiline profile, the haughty and superior gaze. Dante was an exile and a *raznochinets* (like Mandelstam!), a man of uncertain social background, nervous about his deportment in the presence of the mighty, all too capable of swinging to extremes of self-abasement and self-assertion. (pp. xii-xv)

The visual is by no means absent from the **"Conversation about Dante,"** and even the musical "instruments" with which the essay begins, soon turn out to be "images." It is not the visual stasis of a tableau. One senses the physical; incipient movement. In his obsession with architecture, Mandelstam sees the Goethean *erstarrte Musik,* "frozen music"; and in weaving, the flow of rivers. Music is motion; words are motion. When he writes about Italian vowels, he talks of their place in the mouth, the mode of their issuance, the movement of the muscles. In his discussion of the "mineralogical" nature of Dante's work—an image of stone borrowed from Novalis—he sees the most solid thing in the world, a rock, as a product of the motion of time and the weather.

It is not that Mandelstam has less than Eliot the sense of a "different" age. What he has is a physical confidence in the rightness of his own presence there, and it is a confidence that survives anachronism and incongruity. To catch the motion—*there* he concentrated. . . . This gift of physical sympathy, of susceptibility to motion, is apparent also in his almost physical sense for the presence and movement of cultural epochs. *Where does it come from? Where does it go?* These are questions he is always asking. For Mandelstam, an epoch is also a presence in motion. And he has the sense that Dante's epoch, like his own, is transitional. (pp. xv-xvi)

Like Jesus, the artist redeems the world; but in his art. (p. xvii)

The poet and the architect imitate Christ by endowing the world with meaning, by giving it a form and pattern in their works that is analogous to the form and pattern God made out of the world. The poet is a colonizer, a settler, a kind of St. George. . . . Anticipating Heidegger, Mandelstam wrote: "To build means to fight against emptiness, to hypnotize space. The fine arrow of the Gothic bell tower is angry, for the whole idea of it is to stab the sky, to reproach it for being empty." Poets were the shepherds of being.

This freedom of the artist and the builder is therefore not the empty liberty of the unimportant. His mission is to hypnotize space and, like Joshua in the Old Testament or the priest in performance of the Eucharist, to make time stand still. (p. xvii-xviii)

For all his juxtaposing of Chinese junks and racers at Verona, Jesus and Joshua, Beethoven and Dante, Verlaine and Villon, incarnation and Ovidian metamorphosis, Mandelstam knows very well what time it is. He never asks, as does the lyrical voice in a Pasternak poem, "What millennium is it out there?" His feeling for "the age" is one of the qualities of his gift. Not clock time . . . , time spatially conceived, but rather Bergsonian time, time as *durée,* a system of intuited inner connection. (p. xviii)

It is dangerous, the time he lives in. He feels the ominous shift of direction. The nineteenth century, weighed down by "the enormous wings" of its cognitive powers, cannot lift itself from the exhausted shore. One feels the shadow of an oncoming night. Those essays of the Civil War period, **"The Word and Culture"** and **"Humanism and the Present"** still vibrate with a certain optimism, still hold the early conjunction of his religious sensibility and his unorthodox interpretation of Marxism. He *hopes* for a new "social gothic," that universalized domesticity, an all-human family. But he *sees* the other alternative: a new Assyrian age in which "captives swarm like chicks under the feet of the immense king.

It is a time of crisis and there is magic in it; the tree is about to become a girl again. It is a time when

Social distinctions and class antagonisms pale before the division of people into friends and enemies of the word. Authentically, sheep and goats. I sense, almost physically, the unclean goat smell issuing from the enemies of the word. . . .

Who are these goat-smelling enemies of the word?

Those for whom the word had merely a denotative, a *utilitarian* meaning. Those for whom its living nature is a secondary or subordinate quality. Propagandists of political parties, philosophers, anthroposophists like Andrei Biely, who, in Mandelstam's view, yoked his great poetic gift to a "Buddhist" world view. Those who used the word as slave labor to support some other external structure—a church, a state, a party, a program.

"Friends" were those who believed in the sacred and redemptive power and the psychic nature of the word. (p. xix)

"Culture has become a church," Mandelstam wrote in 1921, and he hailed the separation of this "church" from the state. It is in this time of transformation and transfiguration that culture assumes a sacred quality, a sacred mission. Within the state, those are friends of the word who acknowledge the statutory independence of culture, who "consult" it, as the princes of old Moscow used to consult the monasteries. But within these monasteries, there were monks and laymen; and Mandelstam identified himself as a layman. Monkish structure—whether Byzantine, or whether the new monasticism of the secularized Russian intelligentsia—was hostile to the word.

Even Literature, with a capital *L,* was hostile. Mandelstam was an Acmeist, but he did not like schools. Still less did he like the way these schools were organizing themselves in the 1920's—preparation for their own slaughter, in which the Stalinist organization of Socialist Realism would later use the rivalries and the acrimonies as well as the phrases and slogans of contending schools in order finally to decimate them all. As the 1920's came to an end and Literature tightened the clamp on Mandelstam, invoking even anti-Semitism against him, Mandelstam increased the angle of the defiant tilt to his head. More and more he came to distinguish "poetry" from "Literature." (p. xx)

Mandelstam's Hellenism should not be confused with that program of classical studies that for so long dominated the higher education of Europe and Great Britain. It is not that aristocratic/priestly key to possession of a mystery that wielded power in a secularizing world still stunned by the sacred. For Mandelstam, "Hellenic" means "human." Perhaps it would be better to call it a kind of creative, procreative projection of the human onto the emptiness of the world. Crucial here is the conception of the *utvar'*, which one may translate as "utensil," except that it has at its root a sense that is not that of "use" but rather closer to the notions of "creation" and "creature," something "creaturized." It is, he tells us, the insistence on a relatedness between the warmth in the stove and the warmth in the human body. "Christianity," in Mandelstam's definition, "is the Hellenization of death."

Both Victor Terras and Clarence Brown have written eloquently of Mandelstam's "classicism," [see excerpts above]. It should not be confused with a preference for "high style" (p. xxi)

Nor is "the Classical" simply a matter of Greeks and Romans. "Classical poetry," Mandelstam tells us, "is the poetry of revolution." He is not referring to David's historical tableaux or to eighteenth-century pseudo-classical "tragedy." The clas-

sical is that which is remembered when the mere piety of remembrance fails. It is remembrance energized by a powerful sense of the new, by a sense of what the new requires from the past. The trouble arises, Mandelstam write "when, instead of the real past with its deep roots, we get 'former times.'" This is a poetry that has not had to wrestle with its conventions: "Easily assimilated poetry, a henhouse with a fence around it, a cosy little corner where the domestic fowl cluck and scratch about. This is not work done upon the word but rather a rest from the word." The Classical is what is required to complete a mode of experience: its *necessity*. In that sense, Mandelstam refers to the "genuinely Classic" style of Racine, and the Classical furies of André Chénier. (pp. xxi-xxii)

The Classic has nothing to do with lofty attitudinizing, but rather with the idea of a human potential fulfilled. In this sense Mandelstam speaks in his poems of the classic *lands* of the Mediterranean, of Italy and Greece, "those all-human hills" near Florence, and in the same sense, of the lands of the Caucasus and the Crimea which he associates with the Mediterranean, which for him are part of that "all-human" Mediterranean world. (p. xxiii)

> *Sidney Monas, "Introduction: Friends and Enemies of the Word" (originally published in a slightly different form in* Texas Studies in Literature and Language: Special Russian Issue, *Vol. XVII, 1975), in* Osip Mandelstam: Selected Essays *by Osip Mandelstam, translated by Sidney Monas (copyright © 1977 by University of Texas Press), University of Texas Press, 1977, pp. xi-xxvi.*

HENRY GIFFORD (essay date 1980)

It is fortunate that Mandelstam's criticism [in *Mandelstam: The Complete Critical Prose and Letters*] should be so markedly continuous with his poetry, serving both to facilitate its writing and to place it in an ample perspective.

The range of his literary knowledge and historical speculation is remarkable even for a Russian poet brought up in the shadow of Bryusov and Vyacheslav Ivanov. Many of his preoccupations were those of Eliot, with whom he must be compared both for his intelligence about poetry and his concern with "the mind of Europe". Neither of them could take for granted the tradition they cherished: it was necessary for them to overcome an initial displacement. Mandelstam contended that in criticism only one question "brings us at once to solid ground"—namely, "where did the poet come from?" He and Eliot had to ask it about themselves, and the answer gave each the capacity to "fare forward". . . .

[Philology] (love of the word) is what frames Mandelstam's conception of a living culture. There are two unusual aspects to his classicism—an insistence on the spoken word, and a passion for the domestic. . . .

The spoken word brings a human warmth to intellectual life, and poetry, as Wordsworth said before him, can make abstruse thought "a dear and genuine inmate of the household of man", The domestic and the physical help to determine Mandelstam's thinking about poetry, and each, when fully realized, leads inescapably to tradition. The household depends on an inherited way of life, a community within the nation, the nation within a wider community. Physical being includes more than the alert use of all the senses: it means also the language of the body—the actor Mikhoels's "thinking fingers" when he dances, gesture and facial expression, the familiar tones of speech and customary register of the voice as these are learnt in a given place by each generation.

A classicism that takes account of these principles will be at a far remove from what Mandelstam deplored in the age of the Encyclopaedists, which had "lost its direct link with the moral consciousness of antiquity". . . . For Mandelstam Dante was, in his wife's words, "the source form which came all European poetry, and the measure of poetic rightness". His concern was with future performance. Latin poetry he liked because

> the imperative rings more vividly in it. Such an imperative characterizes all poetry that is classical. Classical poetry is perceived as that which must be, not as that which has already been.

Mandelstam sends modern poets to school with Dante, the master of metamorphosis.

He was attracted, like many others by the philosophy of Bergson, which showed a way of apprehending "the internal connection among phenomena". Bergson's was "a profoundly Judaic mind" searching for unity—a search that dominates Mandelstam's own thought. . . .

Some of his earlier positions were extreme, and not without arrogance. He was driving an idea to its conclusion, with the impetuous absolutism that often characterizes Russian thought (not for nothing did he admire Chaadaev, the architect of a single masterly negation). But his criticism, again like Eliot's, always served the needs of his poetry. Hence the fine consistency of its development: one essay grows out of another, previous notions are stated with a subtler awareness, unity becomes ever more distinct. The triumph of Mandelstam's critical prose is enviable: his last enterprise, the *Conversation about Dante,* crowns the work. It was also a treatise on the dynamics of poetry, the future that lies in the ferment of old wine, and the meeting in poetry of the poet's mind and the reader's. (p. 827)

In his earlier years Mandelstram was bold in asserting the autonomy of his art. This position follows from the idea of rightness. He distinguishes in 1913 the poet from the prose writer or essayist, maintaining the opposition Verlaine had made between poetry and "literature". "Instruction is the central nerve of prose", and so puts a major constraint on the man of letters who must always consider a specific audience. Knowing whom he addresses, he will never be astonished either at his own words or at the astonishment of his auditors. But the poet who addresses an unknown reader in posterity gains the freedom through that ideal conversation—"without dialogue, lyric poetry cannot exist"—to discover what is new and really important.

In the fragmentary **"Pushkin and Scriabin"** (begun in 1915) he affirms the benefits of Christianity to the artist:

> No necessity of any kind . . . darkens its bright inner freedom, for its prototype, that which it imitates, is the very redemption of the world by Christ.

So Christian art can be joyful, whereas Hellenism, according to Gippius, was halted at "tragic pathos". . . . The appeal of Christianity for [Mandelstam] as for other poets of the time— Pasternak and Akhmatoya come particularly to mind—derives from an awareness of its central position in the culture which Bolshevism disowned in essence, while adapting it to other

ends. . . . Mandelstam was perfectly right when [he stated]. . . : "Social differences and class antagonisms pale before the new division of people into friends and enemies of the word. . . ." Friends of the word will find it at least possible to appreciate what the Word is to believers.

In the following year, 1922, Mandelstam published a major essay, **"On the Nature of the Word"**, which shows his continuing loyalty to Acmeism. In it he performs a double task, defining the responsible use of language in poetry after its maltreatment by the Symbolists. and considering the peculiar characteristics of Russian literature and society which make "philology" so important. . . .

Mandelstam is at one with Eliot in recognizing the importance of the historical sense "which we may call nearly indispensable to anyone who would continue to be a poet beyond his twenty-fifth year." . . . Eliot further observes that "the historical sense", taking in both the timeless and the temporal, is "what makes a writer most acutely consious of his place in time, of his own contemporaneity". The task before Mandelstam had always been to discover "that truth which helps us form some sense of our own selves in tradition". His efforts were rewarded by a supreme clarity about himself, the inheritor of diverse traditions—Russian literature with its moral and civic responsibilities, his racial consciousness as a Jew descended from "sheepbreeders, patriarchs and kings", and that Mediterranean culture in which Hellas and Rome, Judaism and Christianity were mingled to form (if it is possible to conceive such a thing) "the mind of Europe". Mandelstam is as deeply a historical poet as ever existed. (p. 828)

> *Henry Gifford, "Origins and Recognitions," in* The Times Literary Supplement *(© Times Newspapers Ltd. (London) 1980; reproduced from* The Times Literary Supplement *by permission), No. 4035, July 25, 1980, pp. 827-28.*

ADDITIONAL BIBLIOGRAPHY

Akhmatova, Anna. "A Portrait of Mandelstamm." *The New York Review of Books* V, No. 10 (23 December 1965): 8.
    Reminiscences of Mandelstam by a leading fellow acmeist.

Alter, Robert. "Mandelstam's Witness." *Commentary* 57, No. 6 (June 1974): 69-77.
    Examines Mandelstam's identity as a Jewish writer in relation to his later Christianity.

Baines, Jennifer. *Mandelstam: The Later Poetry*. Cambridge: Cambridge University Press, 1976, 253 p.
    Argues against the prevalent critical position that Mandelstam's poems of the 1930-37 period are "obscure and significantly weaker than his early poetry."

Brown, Clarence. *Mandelstam*. Cambridge: Cambridge University Press, 1973, 320 p.
    Definitive biography in English.

Bukhshtab, Boris. "The Poetry of Mandelstam." *Russian Literature Triquarterly,* No. 1 (Fall 1974): 262-82.
    Examines Mandelstam's method of revising his poems, which consisted primarily of adding or subtracting stanzas, observing that the connections between his stanzas are not of the "material-logical type" and that to an extent the stanzas are autonomous.

Ivask, George. "Osip Mandelstam's 'We Shall Gather Again in Petersburg'." *Slavic and East European Journal* 20, No. 3 (Fall 1976): 253-60.

Stanza by stanza close reading of this poem, viewing it as "the dramatic culmination of numerous poems of love and death written earlier."

Leiter, Sharon. "Mandelstam's Petersburg: Early Poems of the City Dweller." *Slavic and East European Journal* 22, No. 4 (Winter 1978): 473-83.
    Characterizes these poems written between 1912 and 1915 as "united by their image of the solitude and despair of the city dweller."

Mandelstam, Nadezhda. *Hope against Hope: A Memoir*. New York: Atheneum, 1978, 431 p.
    An account of life with Mandelstam by his wife, with portraits of many Russian literary figures of the time.

Mihailovich, Vasa D. "Osip Mandelshtam and His Critics." *Papers on Language and Literature* VI, No. 3 (Summer 1970): 323-35.
    Survey of critical reaction to Mandelstam, both in western countries and the Soviet Union.

Turner, C.J.G. "On Osip Mandelstam's Poem 'Vek'," nature of Dante's *Slavic and East European Journal* 20, No. 2 (Summer 1976): 148-54.
    Demonstrates how Mandelstam uses Greek myth as an analogy to modern Russian history.

Gregorio Martínez Sierra

1881-1947

María (de la O'LeJárraga) Martínez Sierra

1880?-1974

Spanish dramatists, novelists, essayists, poets, short story writers, and translators.

The dramas of the Martínez Sierras subtly examine the complexity of a woman's role in Spanish society while quietly arguing for a more vital social role for women. The Sierras' conception of change, however, was quite conservative and they usually reflected the Catholic heritage of Spain by promoting such traditional Christian values as restraint, fidelity, and self-sacrifice. Although the principal characters in most of their plays are strong and resourceful women, these characters triumph over adverse conditions only with the aid of a profound faith.

Gregorio Martínez Sierra and María de la O'LeJárraga began writing together in 1897 and were married in 1900. Their early publications include several volumes of poetry and short stories. Only the first of these, a book of poems entitled *El poema del trabajo*, is believed to have been written solely by Gregorio. It has long been known that all of the other works

signed by Gregorio were collaborative efforts with his wife María—what was not known was the extent of the individual contributions. For years critics believed that María's role was greater than she admitted; as evidence they pointed to the distinctly feminine sensibility that lay behind most of the couple's plays. Patricia Walker O'Connor's 1977 study of the Sierras supports the assertions of earlier critics. O'Connor's research indicates that María did most of the actual writing of the couple's vast output while Gregorio served as an editor, offering comments and suggestions for polishing the works. It was at María's insistence that the joint efforts be published under Gregorio's name, and she never admitted the large role she played in her husband's career. After Gregorio's death, however, she published many essays and stories and has come to be recognized as an important minor voice in twentieth century Spanish literature.

Gregorio and María's best writing was done during the years they collaborated. After the modest success of their early stories and poems the Sierras turned to drama and, over the next thirty years, wrote many popular plays. Their best work was done in episodic one or two act plays that examined the lives of strong women characters. The most famous drama of this type is *Canción de Cuna (The Cradle Song)*, a warm, almost poetic study of the lives of women in a Spanish convent.

The Sierras intended their work to be inspirational. Because they believed that human nature is basically good, virtue always triumphed over human failings in their plays. They did not address complex philosophical problems, and their social commentary is invariably tied to conservative Christian values. An example of such traditional messages is found in *Mama*, a loose adaptation of Ibsen's *The Doll's House*, in which the Spanish heroine, instead of abandoning home and family as Ibsen's Nora does, rejects her frivolous life and fights to keep her family together. The women of the Sierras' plays are quiet feminists who elect to reconcile differences and seek an equality of responsibility with men. Though carefully drawn, these characters are sometimes criticized for being idealized madonna figures. Similarly, the Sierras' emphasis upon characterization over plot often results in formless and unoriginal work. Nevertheless, the plays are consistently praised for subtly ironic dialogue and excellent dramatic techniques.

The Sierras' plays, progressive for their own time, no longer receive much critical attention. Gregorio, who formed his own publishing house and dramatic troupe, is now considered most important to Spanish literary history as a translator and promoter who introduced Spanish audiences to contemporary foreign dramatists such as Maurice Maeterlinck and Bernard Shaw. The work of Patricia Walker O'Connor, however, may lead to renewed interest in María Martínez Sierra as an early, somewhat hesitant feminist who examined the problems of women in an old and tradition-bound European culture.

PRINCIPAL WORKS

El poema del trabajo (prose poems) 1898
Diálogos fantásticos (prose poems) 1899
Sol de la tarde (short stories) 1904
Teatro de ensueño (dialogues) 1905
 [*Theatre of Dreams*, 1918]
Tú eres la paz (novel) 1906
 [*Ana María*, 1921]
Vida y dulzura [with Santiago Rusiñol y Prats] (drama)
 1907
La sombra del padre (drama) 1909
El ama de la casa (drama) 1910
Canción de cuna (drama) 1911
 [*The Cradle Song*, 1917]
Lirio entre espinas (drama) 1911
 [*A Lily among Thorns*, 1930]
Primavera en otoño (drama) 1911
 [*Spring in Autumn*, 1933]
Madrigal (drama) 1913
Mamá (drama) 1913
Los pastores (drama) 1913
 [*The Two Shepherds*, published in *The Kingdom of God
 and Other Plays*, 1923]
La mujer del héroe (drama) 1914
 [*Wife to a Famous Man*, published in *The Kingdom of
 God and Other Plays*, 1923]
El reino de Dios (drama) 1915
 [*The Kingdom of God*, published in *The Kingdom of God
 and Other Plays*, 1923]

Esperanza nuestra (drama) 1917
Sueño de una noche de agosto (drama) 1918
 [*The Romantic Young Lady*, published in *The Kingdom of
 God and Other plays*, 1923]
Feminismo, feminidad, españolismo (essays) 1920
Don Juan de España (drama) 1921
Cartas a las mujeres de América (essays) 1941

CHARLES ALFRED TURRELL (essay date 1919)

[Gregorio Martínez Sierra] is a journalist, novelist, poet and dramatist, the youngest of the popular playwrights of Spain today. A collection of dialogued poems in prose called, "Theater of Fantasies" (*Teatro de ensueño* . . .), was his first dramatic work. These are not real plays and were not intended for stage performance. In his fantasy and in his symbolism he has imitated [Maurice] Maeterlinck and [Gabriele] D'Annunzio; everywhere he is lyric and feminine. He is ultra-national in the idea pervading all his works that Spain is the most righteous, most noble land in all the world, and nowhere are women so virtuous and the family so sacred. This national spirit, coupled with a florid style, almost gongoristic, a beautiful blending of words, so pleasing to the Spanish ear, has won for him great popularity. Since 1905 Martínez Sierra has contributed many plays to the Spanish stage the best of which is "The Cradle Song" (*Canción de cuna* . . .). It is semi-romantic, but with many realistic touches, and the appeal is a universal one. The thesis of mother-love versus the convent life is real to the Spaniard, and Martínez Sierra shows the unrest that must arise from the crushing of the greatest longing of the woman-heart—motherhood. Of his other plays, some eight or ten are real dramas of domestic and social life; the rest are *zarzuelas* (musical comedies) and *sainetes* (skits) amazingly clever in plot and charming in composition. (pp. 19-20)

> *Charles Alfred Turrell, in his introduction to* Contemporary Spanish Dramatists, *translated by Charles Alfred Turrell, The Gorham Press, 1919, pp. 7-22.*

JOHN GARRETT UNDERHILL (essay date 1922)

In the beginning an intellectual by temperament and a word-painter by inclination, Martínez Sierra may be characterized as an impressionist, well-versed in the procedure of the modern French schools. (p. viii)

The first decade of the productivity of Martínez Sierra suggests little of the theatre. It was quietistic in feeling, essentially contemplative, a communion with idyllic and elegiac poets. Yet through these days another influence had been active, although less conspicuously, which in the end was to prove decisive. In the year immediately following the publication of "The Song of Labor," the Art Theatre was founded at Madrid by [Jacinto] Benavente. The coöperation of the more promising of the younger generation was enlisted, among whom was Martínez Sierra, who played the rôle of Manuel in support of Benavente in the latter's comedy "A Long Farewell" at the opening performance. The ensuing months were months of intimate association with a remarkable mind. "As I listened to him talk, the fundamental laws of the modern theatre were revealed to me and I have profited by his instruction unceasingly." So, properly, Martínez Sierra had already served an

apprenticeship in the theatre before he began to write plays. . . .
As Martínez Sierra's non-dramatic prose becomes most nicely
expressive, most pictorial and most imaginative in *Sol de la
tarde,* his comedy attains perfection in [*Canción de cuna* and
Los pastores, his] beautiful idyls of the religious life. Radiant
with the bland charm and luminosity of the Andalusian sketches
of the Quinteros, these comedies possess, nevertheless, a quality which is distinctive and personal, at once richer and humanly more significant than the work of any competitors in
the *genre*. No other plays convey so convincingly, or with
equal grace, the implications of environment as it interprets
itself in terms of character, not symbolically nor in any didactic
way, but directly and visually so that the ambient becomes the
protagonist rather than the individual, and the spirit of the
milieu is felt to express more clearly than words the fundamentals which condition its life. (pp. ix-x)

[Martínez Sierra's lesser plays] become an epitome of the
activities of the contemporary Madrid stage, broadened, however, by a thorough cosmopolitanism. They are eclectic, light-
hearted, persistently gay, and, upon the more serious side,
progressive documents considered from the sociological point
of view. As he has grown older, Martínez Sierra has come to
be interested not so much in the picturesque, in the life which
is about to pass, as it lies inert in the present with all the
remoteness of objective art, as he is in the future with its
promise of the amelioration of the life which he formerly portrayed. He is an apostle of the new order, which is to be assured in his conception through the dissemination of a wider and
more complete knowledge, a more truly international culture
and sympathy, a keener social consciousness, and, more precisely and immediately, through the promotion of certain reforms. The more significant of the recent comedies, **"The
Kingdom of God"** and *Esperanza nuestra* (**"The Hope That is
Ours"**) are indicative of this development. Although by no
means didactic, they are purely social in genesis and in trend.
Even his ***Don Juan de España,*** a re-embodiment of the traditional libertine celebrated by Tirso de Molina and by [José]
Zorrilla, is a Don Juan redeemed. Yet Sierra remains essentially
a man of the theatre. As a social thinker, his ideas are general,
by no chance controversial, rising little beyond a broad humanitarianism, temperately and engagingly expressed. **"Letters to the Women of Spain,"** **"Feminism, Feminity and the
Spanish Spirit,"** and **"The Modern Woman,"** all volumes of
frankly confessed propaganda, are more effective because they
persuade rather than provoke, avoiding partisan commitments
or advocacies of any sort. They are quite as dispassionately
impersonal as the plays. (pp. xii-xiii)

Martínez Sierra is no longer a young man of promise. Soon
he will be counted among the elders whose art has matured
and attained its full extension, consolidated and ripened by
experience. It is now possible to appraise his accomplishment
and to determine with relative certainty his contribution to the
contemporary theatre. (p. xiii)

Like the Quinteros, Sierra is primarily an optimist, a child of
the sun. . . . He is not, however, an optimist by virtue of high
spirits or uncommon enthusiasms, or because he has found life
pleasant and easy, but through his sensitiveness. It is an optimism that is partly aesthetic, partly emotional. His sympathies
have led him to hope. He has faith in the human equation,
trust in men rather than in measures. The law he esteems very
little in face of the gentle wisdom whose increment is sure
with the years. Social progress is individual progress and individual progress is spiritual progress whose conquests are re-

corded first in the heart. This, of course, is no new doctrine,
but it is the core of Martínez Sierra's philosophy and the mainspring of his art. In so far as the Church is a liberating and
humanizing force he is a Christian, but he is a dissenter from
all creeds and doctrines which restrict and inhibit the upward
march of man.

Curiously enough, as a playwright, Sierra, for all his tenderness, has little concern with the individual. This is the source
of his calm. One of the most sensitive of men, he is also one
of the most detached. His drama is expository, chiefly for the
reason that the inception of his plays is invariably generic and
abstract. They are illustrative each of some general axiom or
principle, whether human or social. He is no apostle of personal
causes. . . . The course of the story is the setting forth of the
idea, the impelling emotion in all its significant phases, now
by direct statement, now through contrast, but, in whatever
way it may be effected, the content is plainly implicit in the
theme from the beginning to become evident in detail as the
action proceeds. For this reason the volitional element, in so
far as it passes beyond mere childish caprice, is almost wholly
lacking. Sierra draws no villains, creates no supermen, heroically imposing their wills, inherits no complexes, and cherishes small love for the tricks of display. His taste is unfailingly
nice. Mystery, however veiled, he abhors, complication of
plot, all thrill of situation. He even flees those internal crises
of character which are so absorbing to the great dramatists,
through whose struggles personality is built up and self-mastery
won. These savor always of violence and conflict, no matter
how subjective or subtle they may be. They are drama of action,
and Sierra's drama is static drama. He is content to sacrifice
movement to visual quality, excitement to charm.

Although indubitably theatre of ideas, characteristically and
fundamentally this is emotional theatre. It is live and warm.
Naturally the spectacular ardors which have been associated
time out of mind with the so-called emotional play have been
discarded. Yet there is no more skilful purveyor of tears. The
feeling is always direct, the presentation transparently clear.
The playwright displays the intuitive grace of simple truth. The
spectator sees and is persuaded without argument at sight. Life
is depicted as a process of adjustment, a pervading harmony
which influences the characters and tempers them to its key,
so that they are never suffered to become intellectualized. This
is the most extraordinary of Sierra's gifts. His men and women
remain spontaneously human, unchilled by the ideas in which
they have previously been conceived. Standing by themselves,
it is true, they betray a tendency to pale and grow thin, because,
like the action, they have been born of the theme, and acquire
substance and vitality only as they fit into the general plan and
merge themselves with the incidents and scenes which reflect
their life history. It is an art compact of simplicities, so delicate
and frail that it can exist authentically only at propitious moments. Every element must concur in the perfection of the
whole. Absolute unity is indispensable. Character must syn-
chronize with theme, dialogue with action, situation with background, until each at last becomes articulate in the other, through
every shade of feeling and the concord of smiles and tears.
Otherwise the spell is shattered and ceases to be. Comedy and
pathos join as one. Sierra's art is a blending of the more tract-
able emotions, of technical elements and all the ingredients
which go to make up a play, that is so complete as not to stop
short of interpenetration. To achieve less for him means failure.
In the rehearsal of memory, the people of the plays do not
recur to the mind, nor the stories, nor any fragments nor striking

features, but the atmosphere, the feeling, the impression of the ensembles. The plays live as emotion, pictures.

When posterity comes to assess the fame of Martínez Sierra, the non-dramatic works, despite their undoubted merits, beyond peradventure will be set to one side. Time will ignore, also, as it has already done in large measure, the purely theatrical, occasional pieces contrived to meet the needs of aspiring actors or to tide over the exigencies of importunate companies, including specifically his own. There will remain a body of plays, considerable in bulk, and notable, at least superficially, in variety. A surprising amount of the best work must be assigned to the plays in one-act. Few have wrought more happily in miniature, or have qualified more instinctively in the lesser *genre*. The briefer pieces are without exception deft and tenuous, by their very nature peculiarly congenial to a temperament that is shy and retiring and a method that is tactful and restrained. Sierra's success has been unquestioned in this field. In two acts, he has shown equal facility, profiting in addition by the superior dignity and weight which are corollaries of the larger scale. "**The Cradle Song**" is Martínez Sierra, the epitome of his virtues and the confutation of his detractors, while into this group fall also the major number of his more serious efforts often, perhaps, only by limitation of subject inferior to those better known. In drama of greater extension and presumably more profound import, prolonged through three or more acts, he has been less impressive. The expository method here becomes treacherous, for either the play or the audience in the end is obliged to move. Confronted by this dilemma, Sierra falls back upon episode, and takes refuge in devices which temporize to sustain the interest, and at best are purely conventional. The most noteworthy of the longer plays such as "**The Kingdom of God**", are in consequence properly sequences of one-act units, carefully assembled and held together by a common subject or related, it may be, by a single character which runs its course through them all. Still they preserve unity of atmosphere, still they plead unobtrusively their causes and retain the freshness of their visual appeal, but the problem at full length is more complex, position and juxtaposition of incident are not so potent nor so suggestive, while even the most skilfully graduated emotion proves unable except in the rarest instances to dispense with progressive action and a continuous story artfully unrolled. These are multiple dramas, spoken pageants. They are chronicles of the modern stage. (pp. xiv-xviii)

[Sierra] has produced the popular masterpiece of the two-act style, already secure as an international classic. He has written also more perfectly than his contemporaries the Spanish realistic comedy of atmosphere, that gently sentimental, placid communion with patience and peace whose quiet falls like a benediction upon a restless world. (p. xviii)

> *John Garrett Underhill, in his introduction to* The Cradle Song and Other Plays *by G. Martínez Sierra, translated by John Garrett Underhill, E. P. Dutton & Co., Inc., 1922, pp. vii-xviii.*

HELEN GRANVILLE-BARKER and HARLEY GRANVILLE-BARKER (essay date 1922)

While there may be much to say, there is really very little to explain about the plays of Martínez Sierra, for they have in the first place the supreme dramatic virtue of explaining themselves. They are not (those at least now under review) strikingly novel in technique. They certainly carry no abstruse philosophical message. But they are notable, the present writer holds, for simple excellence as plays, for the directness with which they set out to—and the fine economy with which they do—achieve their purpose. And what better in this sort, can be said? Take for instance "**The Cradle Song**." Sierra has the idea—the charming, unrecondite idea—of a foundling baby thrust upon the mercies of a convent of nuns, who bring her up, spend upon her all they can recover of their suppressed motherly instincts, give her to a young man in marriage, and so back to the world. Mark his means to this effect. The foundling, a varied chorus of nuns—among them one who is emotionally the play's protagonist, an old doctor (the child must acquire a legal parent) and the young bridegroom. No intrigue, no thesis, no rhetorical enlargement; two acts because his theme needs two, and no convention-satisfying third, which it does not need. The whole result is a story perfectly told for the sake of its innate humour and feeling, a picture filled and rounded. (p. vii)

"**The Two Shepherds**" may be coupled with "**The Cradle Song**." It has the same simplicity of scheme, the same directness of approach. It is perhaps the more remarkable in that its action swings upon a stark fidelity of vision. And here is the chief of Sierra's dramatic (distinct for the moment from "theatrical,") virtues; he paints faithfully the thing he *sees*. Once he has his outline clear and true he may sentimentalise a little in filling in the detail; it is a venial fault. We could forgive, if need were, even more affectionate weakness on his creator's part for snuffy, frowsy, garlic-smelling old Don Antonio. . . . Again Sierra needs his two acts and no more, seventy minutes, perhaps, of playing time, but in that space he shows us a dozen characters, individual and alive, and a picture of a Spanish village so consistent that, experience apart, we know it to be true. . . . Sierra translates for us his Spanish village in terms, no doubt, of his own happy, humorous, ironic temperament. But he has seen it first without illusion, seen it naked, seen it true and, thanks to him, so can we—and have our fun into the bargain. (pp. viii-ix)

[In *Lirio entre espinas*,] Sierra has seen each single figure and has informed it with a life of its own before he started the mere making use of it for his group. . . . [One] is struck with the fine humanity of Sierra's treatment of his theme. No condescension either! He writes about the nun and the fallen women and the gay young blackguards, their visitors, alike without vulgar astonishment, unselfconsciously, with a perfect courtesy of mind. He writes as a gentleman should. (pp. ix-x)

El Reino de Dios ("**The Kingdom of God**") is in some ways the most considerable of Sierra's work. He devises for himself a larger canvas than usual and, if for nothing else, the play would be remarkable for the number, variety, fidelity, vitality of the sketched characters with which it is so economically filled. He demands great assistance from his actors, no doubt, but he sets them no problems of psychology, no modelling, so to speak, is asked of them, they have but to colour in "on the flat" the firm outlines of his drawing. And, for more immediate effect he places them against a background which is in itself dramatic, which in itself and in its changes, develops the action and purpose of the play. The action itself is unconventional more or less—though there is little in the shape of transgression against the unities which has not been tried in the post-Ibsen period of European drama by one dramatic experimentor or another. We mark Sierra yet once more as the accomplished man of the theatre by the ease and certainty with which he transgresses. He sacrifices everything to his purpose and contrives to sacrifice nothing. . . . [It] is instructive to the student of drama to note the use made of the material, the means by which Sierra appeals—and most legitimately—to our emotions. He is not concerned (as an English dramatist choosing such a theme to-day would almost certainly be) with the growth or wane of the woman's religious belief, nor yet . . . with her mental reaction to the social conditions she faces, not even with developing her ''character''; in fact, it is part of his theme that she does not bother, as certain of our self-conscious philanthropists do, with any such self-righteous thing—so why should he? He relies upon making as clear in his picture to us, as in the reality it was clear to her, the human needs and their claim upon us of disreputable age, sordid sins of the flesh, and of childhood, that will bate no claim, and should not, since upon it all the claims of the world must fall. And that he does so in terms which not the simplest soul in his audience can mistake, nor the most sophisticated deny, is, it may be claimed, an achievement—complete of its kind—in the reality of art. (pp. xi-xiii)

He seems incapable of writing anything ineffective, though now and then he may yield to the too obvious effect. That is a venial fault—in the actor's eyes at least. And Sierra, one may judge from this, does genuinely like, admire and understand the art of acting. (p. xiv)

> *Helen Granville-Barker and Harley Granville-Barker, in their introduction to* The Kingdom of God *and Other Plays by G. Martínez Sierra, translated by Helen Granville-Barker and Harley Granville-Barker (reprinted by permission of The Society of Authors as the literary representatives of the Estates of Helen and Harley Granville-Barker), E. P. Dutton & Co., Inc., 1922, pp. vii-xv.*

FRANCES DOUGLAS (essay dates 1922 and 1923)

Martínez Sierra lays special stress upon the sincerity of his productions. His writings are true to nature and true to art. They deal only with the simple, everyday events of life. . . . With light, seeming trivial matters . . . , he has said, his works are concerned, and yet, although so simple, the events represent life's complex. They bring both smiles and tears. His books should not be read hastily while making a dashing round of a city in the street car; they may better be appreciated in a softly lighted library during a long, rainy evening. They must be read in the original in order that the beauty and lyric charm of the diction may not be lost. (pp. 257-58)

The author has himself pointed out that in his works the events to which he gives expression are not unusual and remarkable. Indeed, many of them might have happened in America, or Russia, or China, as easily as in Spain. It is his peculiar delineation that makes them stand out as the product of genius. In Spain he has many imitators, and perhaps in future years he will rank as the founder of a school. None of his followers, however, achieve the effect produced by the master. (p. 264)

Canción de Cuna is generally conceded to be Martínez Sierra's magnum opus. While all of his works are intensely Spanish, *Canción de Cuna* could have been written nowhere except in Spain, and by no other author. Here his tender, sympathetic understanding of women, children, and all helpless creatures is revealed. . . . [The] subject matter is somewhat difficult and it is rather far removed from the comprehension of the protestant American; yet, with his charm of expression, and his grace of diction, the author arouses a sentiment of extreme cordiality between the reader (differences of religion and nationality notwithstanding) and the gentle nuns who exist behind

convent walls, whose faces are revealed to no man except the aged physician, and who hold a solemn discussion concerning the propriety of giving shelter to an abandoned child. (p. 266)

[Love,] humanity, piety, resignation, and above all, duty, are personified by the different characters. The work, while pervaded by the ascetic and mystic atmosphere of the morality plays of the Middle Ages, is at the same time not devoid of the humor, optimism, and brilliancy so characteristic of Martínez Sierra. (p. 267)

Martínez Sierra has no quarrel with the Church, nor with royalty. His characters, in faithful accord with Spanish life, to whatever social stratum they may belong, bear evidence of deep piety and thorough religious training. . . . Whenever religious characters figure in his novels or plays they are true to the benign and noble part they are most likely to assume in real life. (p. 268)

•　•　•　•　•

In the fall of 1919 a new play by Martínez Sierra, called *El Corazón Ciego*, was presented at the Teatro Eslava, by the company which he directs. This recent play proved to be quite in conformity with the philosophy set forth in his earlier works: true and lasting happiness is not to be found in the hectic flurry of perpetual entertainment and excitement; wealth does not bring happiness; felicity is to be found in service; between man and wife happiness results from mutual respect and coöperation in all matters pertaining to the home and to the business life. This constant reiteration of his general beliefs, sane and wholesome as they are, can but have a beneficial effect upon Spanish home life, proving a corrective for the restlessness prevalent throughout the world at the present time. A sermon may be delivered from the stage as well as from the pulpit. These sermons, however, are endowed with esthetic form, in a manner so attractive that a price is willingly paid to hear them. (p. 3)

Again and again Martínez Sierra in his writings strikes the same note, but always the message is delivered in so new and original a form that it is convincing: The world is big; work is good! A healthful message this, particularly for Spain, where work, except that of holding government office, used to be considered beneath the dignity of a gentleman. (p. 10)

Dr. Aurelio M. Espinosa has pointed out that in many of the works of Martínez Sierra it is a woman that saves the situation. This is true of Ana María in the novel *Tú Eres la Paz*. She is a realistic creation, an exquisite little woman, possessed of perfect refinement, who dresses in subdued tones and laughs softly, and yet she has a will power so virile as to resemble those Spanish women described by Havelock Ellis as masculine in their strength of character. . . . She is not lacking in sweetness and femininity, and in her passionate love, as in that of many of the feminine characters depicted by Martínez Sierra, there is a mingling of the maternal instinct. When his women love they seem to extend an encircling, protecting arm around the object of their devotion, as the mother does about her babe. . . . The charm of the book consists partly in the faithful portrayal of a group of characters thoroughly human and essentially Spanish, and partly in the beauty of the style. It presents an intimate view of life in a delightful corner of Spain where the sordid struggle of money-getting is forgotten. (pp. 12-13)

The large assemblage of characters created by Gregorio Martínez Sierra in his dramas and novels depict practically every phase of Spanish life. (p. 13)

Frances Douglas, "Gregorio Martínez Sierra: I. Stylist and Romantic Interpreter" and "Gregorio Martínez Sierra: II. Stylist and Romantic Interpreter," in Hispania, *Vol. V, No. 5 and Vol. VI, No. 1, November, 1922 and February, 1923, pp. 257-68 and pp. 1-13.*

WALTER STARKIE (essay date 1924)

Gregorio Martínez Sierra in his short dramatic career has achieved remarkable successes. His work has not been confined to drama: in his early years between 1900 and 1904 he wrote novels in a beautiful lyrical prose worthy to be compared with that of [Ruben] Dario. . . . [His] first attempt at drama was *Teatro de Ensueño,* a collection of fantastic plays which were intended for reading rather than acting. These symbolic plays by their sensitive imagery, their lyrical charm, resemble the fairy plays of [Maurice] Maeterlinck. Like Maeterlinck, Martínez Sierra followed Novalis, who proclaimed the absolute reality of poetry; his sensitive personality projected itself on every *nuance* in Nature. . . . Martínez Sierra adopts an impressionistic method in his early works; he develops his plays by prophetic intimations and subtle suggestion.

The short symbolic play, *El Palacío Triste* (**The Palace of Sadness**), . . . by its subtle descriptions recalls the Belgian master. An atmosphere of dejection and boredom surrounds Princess Teodora living in her palace with her three sons. She is a frail little thing . . . : she seems more of a child than her sons and, bereft of her husband who had been drowned, she lives on dreaming in that dreary palace surrounded on all sides by courtiers and conventions. Her daughter Marta has disappeared suddenly, and all believe her dead, but the mother feels in her heart that she will return, and has opened up a white path through the wood in order that she may find her way home. But Marta has not been killed: she had wandered away from the sad palace in order to reach the life of freedom, and now she returns to free her mother and brothers. . . . This play is a glorification of human will, and in the character Marta we can see the basis of all Martínez Sierra's later work. As a Spanish critic has said of him, hard winter pines should be placed in his hand to symbolise Will and Perseverance in an allegory of the moderns. By this optimistic glorification of human will Martínez Sierra is a contrast to Maeterlinck, who has generally depicted passive conditions of being rather than active conditions of doing. Maeterlinck was as pessimistic as Thomas Hardy, and believed that the power of human will is an illusion: Martínez Sierra, on the other hand, shows the moral triumph of human will. (pp. 199-200)

The twentieth century with its steel and stress is not propitious to the poet living in his enchanted castle; Martínez Sierra . . . left the realms of fantasy and turned towards the heated problems of modern life. . . . [In *Primavera en Otoño*] he studies married life. This play bears resemblance to Benavente's famous work, *Rosas de Otoño* (Autumn Roses). . . . In both plays the theme is the reconciliation between husband and wife after many sad years of misunderstanding. But there is great difference between the personalities of the two writers; Benavente is mainly an intellectual writer who lets his cold irony play with the follies of the world, and his satire does not kill at one blow, but little by little by dint of pinpricks; Martínez Sierra is more warm-hearted and full-blooded; his irony in its soft good humour never suggests the bitter grimace of Voltaire, but rather [a] cheerful laugh. . . . Owing to his optimism and his equable temper Martínez Sierra does not always awaken

deep emotion. He is too much occupied with his thesis that women are ever so much better than men, and consequently there is a tendency to over-elaborate feminine psychology and to leave masculine character to take care of itself. (pp. 200-01)

[In *Mamá*] the author develops his play round the same moral, but there is more truth to life. (p. 201)

It is in *Mamá* that we get the first complete exposition of Martínez Sierra's ideals with regard to women. The play seems to be a reaction against Ibsen's where the woman insists on living her own life. Martínez Sierra approves of Nora when she claims equality with her husband, but he holds that nowhere can woman be happy except in following her traditional duties as wife and mother. He also tries to prove in this play as in many others that man cannot understand the true meaning of love, and that it is woman only who can fathom its true significance. . . .

Martínez Sierra, in making woman represent the ideal in his art, has followed the general trend of Western civilisation. Like the ancient troubadours of Galicia his songs have ever been inspired by an ideal, sylph-like spirit, clad in woman's robe. He is untouched by Oriental civilisation with its hero Don Juan, that sinister but brilliant ruler of Spanish drama to whom women are immolated. In vain we look through his plays for one strong personality of the male sex. In *Madrigal* and *Pobrecito Juan* . . . , the two protagonists are entirely dependent on the courage and will power of the heroines. (p. 202)

Amanecer (**Dawn**) . . . introduces many socialistic ideas, but that does not prevent it from being one of Martínez Sierra's best plays. It is splendidly constructed, and is true to the traditions of the Spanish *comedia,* where tragedy is mingled with comedy right up to the end. The subject of the play proves how defenceless a household is when the head, the breadwinner, fails. It is a common subject, and has been treated with remorseless pessimism by Henri Becque in *Les Corbeaux* and with sadness by [Giuseppe] Giacosa in *Come la Foglie.* Martínez Sierra looks at the subject in a way that sums up the ideas of Becque and Giacosa. He shows with merciless satire the drab poverty and disillusionment following the father's disappearance, but he follows Giacosa in making the heroine a strong girl, who is determined to save the crushed fortunes of the house. (p. 204)

[*Amanecer*] is another very strong appeal for new feminist notions in Spain, and the author has not limited himself to preaching his new ideas from the stage. Many of the opinions put forward in his plays are to be found in his book on *Feminism in Spain* and also in his *Letters to the Women of Spain.*

The chief fault that is to be found with Martínez Sierra's dramas is that he has only thought of the heroine and has forgotten the hero. We always remember charming heroines . . . who by their courage are able to fight against any odds, but we do not remember any really strong man out of the big gallery of types. He has not described any character whose tragic power reaches the level of Santiago Rusiñol's Mystic. It seems as if Martinez Sierra started off with Ibsen's deterministic ideas and worked straight ahead. Like Ibsen, he makes all his heroines carry on a dialogue between their two egos— the momentary ego that they are and the ideal one towards which they strive. But Ibsen did not err in making the man characters merely a foil to the brilliant women, for Brand and Stockmann are as strong as Nora or Rebecca West. Perhaps one of the greatest virtues of Martínez Sierra is that he abolished that ideal of renunciation in drama which had lasted into the twentieth century, and had cast its pall over literature. His heroines do not, as many of the Benaventian heroines do, sacrifice themselves in order that others may be happy. . . . [There] has been too much renunciation in [Spanish] literature. The heroines of Martínez Sierra follow the precepts of Maeterlinck's *Sagesse et Destinée,* and devote themselves to sane, healthy life, not to death. And it is perhaps this splendid optimism and belief in life that makes the theatre of Martínez Sierra one of the durable edifices in this storm-tossed twentieth century. (p. 205)

> Walter Starkie, ''Gregorio Martínez Sierra and the Modern Spanish Drama,'' in Contemporary Review, Vol. CXXV, February, 1924, pp. 198-205.

AUBREY F. G. BELL   (essay date 1925)

[With Don Gregorio Martínez Sierra,] one feels that style and persons are the first consideration. One may take his play, *Primavera en Otoño* . . . , in which he perhaps purposely challenged comparison with his master [Jacinto Benavente]. *Rosas de Otoño* . . . is more closely reasoned; it is philosophical where *Primavera en Otoño* is lyrical. The atmosphere of the one play is prose, of the other poetry, yet both are realistic. . . . In *Rosas de Otoño* we are interested in the relations of Gonzalo to Isabel, as in the relations of any wife to any husband; in *Primavera de Otoño* we are interested in Elena and Don Enrique . . . and do not care about all the other wives and husbands in the world. The unity of place is perfect in Señor Benavente's play; in that of Señor Martínez Sierra the scene passes from Madrid to a Cantabrian village, but the unity is not lost, owing to our interest in the characters for their own sake. The *dramatis personae* are more numerous in *Rosas de Otoño,* more varied in *Primavera en Otoño;* those of the former are all of one class although of different countries (for the servant is merely a kind of telephone, a walking machine), those in the latter include a lady's tailor who has a good deal to say for himself and the very much alive servants Justa and Pura. In this the play is more indigenous, and it is perhaps also more universal, although less cosmopolitan; there is also more spirit and lyrical fire; on the other hand, in general psychology and subtlety and perfect control of his characters, Señor Benavente shows his masterly skill. Both plays are concerned with the gradual reconciliation between husband and wife; both are intense. In *Rosas de Otoño* the intensity is more intellectual; in *Primavera en Otoño* the intensity is of that more genuinely Spanish kind which permeates external objects as well as the mind, is compounded of heart and head (the whole man, a bundle of nerves perhaps, but never a cold abstraction) and succeeds in spiritualizing the material elements.

It is worth while to consider the unity in Señor Martínez Sierra's plays. It is a unity, not in any Aristotelian sense, but achieved through intensity, sobriety, economy in the means employed and consistent development of the characters. In the external building of his plays, he is unconventional. *Canción de Cuna* has two acts; *Don Juan de España* has seven. *Canción de Cuna* is a short comedy, or rather *comedia,* for with all its brightness and humour it ends fittingly with the tragic figure of Sor Juana de la Cruz alone, ''weeping bitterly.'' The characterization of this little masterpiece is skilful throughout; its poetry is never introduced at the expense of reality, which nevertheless is constantly bathed in charm and emotion. There is a gap of eighteen years between the first and second acts, while unity of place is strictly maintained. That of time is not really broken, for the character of the nuns develops quietly in their convent, the doctor is an old man in both acts, while Teresa figures in the first act only as a baby in a basket.

In *El Reino de Dios* the unity of the play is Sister Gracia. She is the centre of the three acts, which are set in three different places and at intervals of ten and forty years. And it is when one might expect to find her old and broken in the third act that she appears in all her strength, an unconquerable force before which the clamour of revolutionaries and the glamour of the young bullfighter's fame break as waves on a wall of granite. The triumph of character over circumstance is equally clear in *Los Pastores,* where the victory is with the aged priest going out abandoned and alone and not with the crowd feasting at the *alcalde's* house. So in *Lirio entre Espinas* Sor Teresa dominates a situation for which her training as a nun could scarcely have prepared her, and in *La Mujer del Heroe* Mariana's strength of will succeeds in a situation almost as difficult as that which faced Sor Teresa. (pp. 171-74)

[His characters] are presented so sharply and sympathetically that we are always glad to meet them and are left with a desire to hear more of them. As a correction of a tendency to sentimentalism, Señor Martínez Sierra can depend upon his humour and on the spirited animation of his plays. (p. 174)

The collaboration of Don Gregorio Martínez Sierra and of his wife Doña María Lejárraga is as closely interwoven as that of the brothers Alvarez Quintero in their *sainetes.* The sympathetic interest in the development of the female characters need by no means be the mark of a woman's hand, and a certain feminine strain might be characteristic of a modernist writer; but the feminist outlook in the *Sueño de una noche de Agosto, La Mujer del Héroe, Pobrecito Juan* and other plays no doubt represents the well-known feminist views of Doña María Lejárraga, to whom likewise may be ascribed something of the delicacy of the craftsmanship. (pp. 176-77)

> Aubrey F. G. Bell, ''The Drama,'' in his Contemporary Spanish Literature, Alfred A. Knopf, 1925, pp. 151-92.*

ERNEST BOYD   (essay date 1925)

While the qualities which Spanish criticism attributes to the dual personality implied by the signature of Martínez Sierra are evident in the author's verse and in the essays on feminism, they cannot fail to strike the readers of these plays. Sentimentality is their common feature and their outstanding virtue, or defect, as one prefers. He began by writing symbolical and mystical playlets in the manner of [Maurice] Maeterlinck, as the title of an early volume, *Theatre of Dream,* sufficiently indicates. He soon, however, found the vein of sentimental comedy which has produced the greater number of his characteristic works. (p. 116)

[*The Cradle Song*] is a typical Martínez Sierra play, with its slender story of a foundling child, who arouses the maternal instincts of the nuns in the convent where she has been left, is brought up by them, provided with a husband, and sent out happy into the world from which her mother intended to save her. Granville Barker, viewing it with the eye of an actor-manager, even rejoices in the fact that there are only two acts, ''because his theme needs two, and no convention-satisfying third'' [see excerpt above], so that we are asked to assume that the supreme excellence of the play is compensation for this violation of one of the practical rules of our own theatre. Equally slender is *The Lover*. . . . (p. 117)

[*Madame Pepita*] is also built up of the flimsiest materials. A fashionable dressmaker who is no better than she should be, an excessively innocent daughter, with a streak of real originality and character, and a world of crooked swindlers and decayed aristocrats. . . . In brief, a thoroughly conventional piece of stage mechanism which, in its innumerable indigenous forms, is sure to run for at least a year, and has then long life before it "on the road." (pp. 117-18)

In *The Kingdom of God,* which is probably Martínez Sierra's best play, we are again in a convent, but the heroine is a woman who has not taken vows. She is seeking the kingdom of God, first in an asylum for old men, then in a lying-in hospital for fallen women, and in her old age as the head of an orphan asylum. Here there is good character-drawing, if no great depth or novelty of treatment. . . .

Most English-speaking readers of these plays will be reminded of J. M. Barrie, and the comparison very fairly represents the status of G. Martínez Sierra in contemporary Spanish. (p. 119)

> Ernest Boyd, "Gregorio Martínez Sierra," in his Studies from Ten Literatures, *Scribner's 1925 (and reprinted by Kennikat Press, 1968), pp. 114-19.*

MAY GARDNER (essay date 1926)

In 1900 [Martínez Sierra] published his first story, *Almas ausentes.* This was followed during the next few years by *Horas de sol, Pascua florida, Sol de la tarde* and *La humilde verdad.* With the publication . . . of *Le humilde verdad* Martínez Sierra's reputation as a novelist was on firm ground. Later novels, *Tú eres la paz* and *El amor cardrático* and many shorter stories would have assured him a position as a novelist had his dramatic work not overshadowed them.

All the poetic nature of Martinez Sierra is in the lyrical prose of these novels. Vivid phrases give color and life to the simplest picture. He delights in the use of choice words. Noble words are to him as seed to germinate noble ideas. "I enjoy" he says, "repeating beautiful words as I enjoy looking at the flowers." There are lovely descriptions filled with the emotion of the landscape and the reaction of his soul to its beauties. He finds a kinship with all things in nature, the trees, the flowers, the sky and the sea. Beauty is essential to him and he finds it more real than the sordid things of life. Vice is ugly and he will not let it dominate a picture. Life for him has a smiling aspect and never does he forsake his optimistic belief and faith in human nature. He sees the noble passions which exalt the human soul rather than the vices which degrade it. (pp. x-xi)

Encouraged by his poet friends, Martínez Sierra wrote one volume of real verse, *La casa de la primavera.* It is a song of the joys and happiness of life—the optimistic outburst of a sensitive personality. (p. xi)

Much of the novelistic work of Martínez Sierra contains dramatic dialogue, so it is not surprising that the first dramatic work to appear should be half story, half play, and should appear in book form rather than on the stage. Grouped together under the title of *Teatro de ensueño* were . . . four fantastic little tales in dramatic form. They contain some of the author's most poetic descriptions, much of his romantic idealism and not a little symbolism. (pp. xi-xii)

The plays which have brought distinction to Martínez Sierra are the comedies of manners. These plays are essentially realistic, modern in subject and about people we seem to know, but at the same time they have an idealistic character which places them a little apart from the other realistic productions of the period. Real life is reflected in their scenes, life which is sincere, full of tender feelings and simple emotions. They picture a world in which reign not great passions but nobility, generosity and the finer qualities of human beings, a world in which simple virtues triumph over human weaknesses and happiness comes from well-doing. It is a world in which work is the joy of life and where there is still faith in dreams. Love, human and ideal, pervades the atmosphere and we are taught to believe that life is sweet and worth living. The plays are rarely concerned with a thesis and our souls are never left with the torment of unsolved problems. They always end happily because human nature can be counted upon to choose the right way in the end. An abundance of sentiment fills the plays but surprisingly enough, without undue sentimentality. In spite of a somewhat ideal atmosphere we move in a world intensely real. The scenes are as events passing before our eyes, with nothing foreign to the event finding a place in the picture. They are simple, natural and easy to understand. Plots are of small importance and factitious device entirely absent. The dialogue is sparkling and lively, but written with fine taste and free from vulgarity. . . . The action is simple and rapid. There is never anything superfluous in it. Scenes are not complicated by the crowding in of unnecessary figures. Each figure stands out in relief against a simple background. One has only to read the multiplicity of stage directions to realize how well the art of acting is understood by the author, how carefully all effects have been thought out and how carefully every sensation of the characters has been analysed and given the proper expression.

The theme of the comedies is usually some phase of married life and the power of women to control the destinies of the home. The same ideas are frequently repeated but there is no monotonous similarity among the plays. While the background is often the family living-room the characters are always new and the scene varied. A glance at the subject matter of a few of the plays will show that the action rarely fails to revolve about some woman character who by her innately feminine qualities brings happiness to those around her. (pp. xiii-xv)

There are really no great characters in the plays but all are very human and frequently lovable. To whatever class of Spanish life they may belong, they are in faithful harmony with their surroundings. We know that Martínez Sierra likes his characters because he makes us understand them and like them. He has the gift of letting us see their innermost soul, making them so real to us that we forget we are in the theatre. If he ever treats them ironically he does it so gently and with such subtlety that he seems to add rather than detract from our affection for them. Whatever he sees in them he paints with an unfailing sureness of touch. So accurate is he in characterization that the most insignificant character who walks across the stage leaves the impression of a distinct personality.

Women, as has been said, are objects of special interest in all the plays. They are women who are essentially Spanish in all their characteristics, but modern in their point of view. They are women who find their greatest happiness in being good wives and mothers but who demand and achieve a position of equality with their husbands. They are women with joyful natures, with a love of life and humanity, women to whom one can go for consolation. They are better than men and they inspire men to better things. They have developed their talents through education and are the intellectual companions of their husbands. They are women who have learned that a man respects them more if they are capable of earning their own living. . . . They are not afraid to look at the world face to face, and to make the best of life. If, as Mercedes [in *Mamá*], they are heedless women running up bills without knowing where the money comes from to pay them, they are only proof that women must know about their husbands' business if they are to take money matters seriously. And if they are forever seeking pleasures away from home they will only find disappointment. Only as wives and mothers will they be happy.

If they are young, and the Martínez Sierra theatre is filled with charming girls of eighteen or twenty, they are independent, self-sacrificing, self-respecting, serene in their ability to take care of themselves. If they are a bit frivolous in the beginning, as is natural, they become serious in the moment of necessity. Here is the new young woman of Spain, who is no longer waiting at the balcony window for a lover, but is studying, working, realizing that she is far happier alone than married to one she knows nothing of. Not that in her newly acquired independence she is expecting to find greater happiness outside of married life, but she will hesitate to marry until she is sure of being happy. (pp. xviii-xix)

Men in the Martínez Sierra theatre are frequently weak, especially the younger ones. So interested is the author in feminine psychology that he has given too little attention to the men. They suffer in contrast with the ideal character of the women. They are rarely of strong personality, but are as foils in the hands of the feminine characters. They are easily swayed for good or evil and are in constant conflict between love of home and the lure of the outside world. They are frequently selfish, looking only for their own pleasure or advantage. It is not given to them as to women to understand the true meaning of love, but they have a purity in their natural feelings to which women can appeal. Hence the great responsibility of women and the opportunity given her to develop into an ideal character. (p. xx)

> *May Gardner, "Introduction" (copyright © 1926 by Henry Holt and Company; copyright © 1953 by May Gardner; reprinted by permission of Holt, Rinehart and Winston, Publishers), in* Sueño de una noche de agosto *by G. Martinez Sierra, edited by May Gardner and Arthur L. Owen, translated by H. Granville-Barker, Holt, 1926 (and reprinted by Holt, 1953), pp. vii-xxv.*

L. A. WARREN (essay date 1929)

The works written under the name of Martinez Sierra are the joint production of husband and wife. This is an unusual combination, for no married pair, writing together, has ever before arrived at such literary distinction. These plays, therefore, have the promise of giving the merits of each sex, and of avoiding their respective defects. It is in the novel that the limitations of sex are most important, for there character is vital; few male novelists achieve great success over their heroines, and the portrayal of men is not as a rule the conspicuous merit of women authors. It cannot altogether be said that Martinez Sierra has the merits of both sexes and the defects of neither. This is partly because their best work has been in the theatre; in the theatre characterization is not everything, is not so all-important as in the novel, and the individualization is in large manner

achieved by the actors and actresses who impersonate the different rôles and not by the authors. Chiefly it is because the feminine is dominant in Martinez Sierra. The feminine shows itself more prominent in the early writings—poetry and novels. Here we have the minds, thoughts, emotions, inner life and being of women elaborately presented with feeling and truth; while there is no such detail and truthful psychology for the men. There is grace, delicacy and refined sensibility over all this early writing, and a total lack of force and vigour. In the plays, which are later, the delicate grace, the subtle female characterization continue; but the feminine is not so preponderant, increasing years and ripening experience give a seriousness which imparts a suggestion of the masculine. (pp. 577-78)

The early period from about 1900 to 1908 was given chiefly to poetry and novels, and with them verse and fiction are very similar; marked with a delicate feeling for scenery; a vagueness, an absence of the clear-cut and the concrete; a lack of strife and emotion, of humanity and action. Gradually in their development as experience ripens the human element begins to become prominent. . . . Sierra's verse, like most modern poetry, consists of a series of short detached pieces. In their case the verse is somewhat negative; it has not much form, has no subject, and is without great beauty. It is rather empty, the beauty of the words is not remarkable, nor is the depth of thought or power of feeling; they want power, force and energy; they have a certain sensibility, but have nothing to say either of dreams, emotions or concrete reality, a trait which is noticeable later on in their plays and which also is connected with the quality they show in drama of keeping to the middle path and avoiding extremes. They are the friends of modernistic poets and modernism shows, though not pronouncedly, in their verse; their fresh feeling for nature and scenery, a wholesome woman's mind and feminine taste, keep them from the decadents. It is not a great poetic talent, but a sweet, delicate, pensive charm is characteristic of their verse. They lack, at this stage, knowledge of character and experience of humanity; have not yet made the almost inevitable plunge into the middle of material life. . . . Their verse is of a customary kind which mingles a dreamy feeling for landscape with sentiments and echoes of sadness at the passing nature of mankind and the fleetingness of life. There is tranquillity, quiet happiness, lackadaisical melancholy. There is no substance, and this lack of solidity remains over into the period of their early plays. Many of their comedies are slight. But with the passing of time they have become ripe with knowledge. *Esperanza nuestra,* a later play, has as much solid matter in it as any drama of our time. (pp. 578-79)

[In *Tú eres la paz,* the] slight sentimentality is subdued by refinement and good taste; the work is attractive and delicate, full of sensibility; but there is a lack of gusto, it has the grace of woman, not the strength of man. It is full of description, of reflection, and of the garden; is of quiet beauty with minute character study. The women are better than the men; the heroine is a finished study, treated with sympathy, of a woman of good style, and quiet meditative temperament, but not intellectual. She is studied, felt and lived from within. She is introspective and lives in the garden in an atmosphere of delicate pensiveness. . . . (p. 580)

The descriptions are realistic; but when dealing with people the realism is refined into accounts of subtle shades of thought and feeling; while the environment is a secluded world of luxury and comfort away from a life of stress and struggle.

There is a tendency to modernism in that the delicate miniature realism is confined to an artificial paradise; slightly modernistic in that there is a current, an air of mistiness, of the unknown, the vague, elusive, enchanted. Just a trifle of the northern mists are caught, but they mostly escape, and we remain in a southern garden of clearness and sunshine.

It requires two to make a love-story. The heroine lives and feels with charm and subtlety. Not so the hero; he is viewed from the outside, and so seen is not satisfactory. As, however, during the last hundred years a vast majority of Spanish authors—novelists, dramatists and essayists—have agreed in showing up their men as wretched creatures, he must be accepted and we be thankful that he is not worse. For in spite of this the authors have dealt of love with feeling, grace, and reflective subtlety, for they are highly civilized. Passionate love and frantic jealousies are the tradition of Spain and the tone of its classical literature. . . . During the twentieth century love has been treated with a delicacy, a subtlety and an inner understanding which had been absent from the literature. This delicate understanding of love is a feature of Martinez Sierra, manifested again in their drama.

Their plays, perhaps the best now being produced in Madrid, possess no one particular outstanding quality, but the authors maintain an even balance of qualities required to make a successful play. Their pieces, unlike those of [Jacinto] Benavente and the Quinteros, are drama in the ordinary sense of the word; a situation is developed, wrought to a climax and brought to a definite conclusion; there is conflict of emotions and interests; there are situations; the dialogue is natural and realistic; the scene and settings are of to-day; while lastly the characters, especially the women, move, talk, act and feel each like a separate, definite human being.

Therefore, though they are in no one quality supereminent, yet from their being good in all, their drama is meritorious. It is often slight, as for example in *Sueño de una noche de agosto,* known in London under the title of the *Romantic Young Lady;* it has delicate charm and pleasant temperate realism, but is rather ordinary and thoroughly conventional. *La sombra del padre,* though with rather more in it, is also a somewhat slight comedy of manners. The play deals with a contrast and contest between a rich Indiano, who returns from America to join his family on the north coast, and that ultra-fashionable family, horrified at the father's uncouth manners. The contrast between the artificial family, fashionable in their manners and also fashionable in their habits, and the natural ungainly father is effective. The son has an affair on with a married woman, the married daughter's husband and the second daughter's fiancé are infatuated with some dancer. The father arrives expecting a joyful welcome, but the family, out of countenance because of his want of elegant manner and clothes, chill him with coldness and he is temporarily suppressed. Gradually the prestige of fashion loses its influence upon the father, he finds out about his children's ways of life—and asserts his authority. (pp. 580-82)

In *Nuestra Esperanza* the authors have written what I consider the best play of the modern Spanish stage; a piece full of substance, which is kept by graceful delicacy from being heavy. It is remarkable that so much can be condensed into so small a space: there are many characters, and several simultaneous problems all stated, developed, brought to a dramatic crisis and solved; looming large are the contrasts between town and country, old and new, one generation and another; and most notable of all is the problem of the land and the people on it,

and of their improvement—'nuestra esperanza.' . . . The play is more than an exposition of character and of problems, it is a drama. Things happen, a crisis develops. The young people manage to pull themselves together, exert some will-power, carry the father along with them, and seriously undertake to improve the people on their property. (pp. 583-84)

Martinez Sierra in the later plays excels for poetic sensibility, for gravity of subject combined with grace of manner, for knowledge of men and women, and for sympathy with humanity; these great qualities being served up in a form which is good drama. (p. 584)

> *L. A. Warren, "Martinez Sierra," in his* Modern Spanish Literature: A Comprehensive Survey of the Novelists, Poets, Dramatists and Essayists from the Eighteenth Century to the Present Day, Vol. II, *Brentano's, Ltd, 1929, pp. 577-84.*

DESMOND MacCARTHY (essay date 1932)

Facility in the blessed sense is . . . one of the marks of those plays of [Sierra's] which have reached us in translation. An immediate directness, an instinctive balance between subtlety and reticence are among their great merits. They run with a beautiful ease from beginning to end, and even when the theme is gravest there is a lightness and spontaneity in the treatment of it which suggests that the dramatist instantly knew what he wanted to do and how to do it. His plays possess the graces of superficiality as well as depth of insight. (p. 129)

What is it that makes [*The Kingdom of God*] remarkable? An unerring dramatic sense and a natural comprehension of goodness. A commonplace dramatist would have made Sister Gracia die in an atmosphere of impressive sanctity, instead of exhibiting her at her humdrum practical work. There is not a touch of sentimentality and, more remarkable this to an English audience, no dread of it in the play. The author takes for granted that there is such a character in the miscellany of human nature as the saint.

The same qualities, a direct dramatic instinct, and an understanding of goodness, underlie also *The Cradle Song.* . . . It is a plain story perfectly told and with much humour. There are two protagonists, the religious life and the worldly life, and justice is done to both. (p. 130)

> *Desmond MacCarthy, "Three Modern Spanish Dramatists," in* The New Statesman & Nation *(© 1932 The Statesman & Nation Publishing Co. Ltd.), Vol. IV, No. 75, July 30, 1932, pp. 129-30.**

STARK YOUNG (essay date 1948)

In the kind of modern plays we know best, plays Northern or Nordic in their quality and mind, such a story of a woman as this in *The Kingdom of God* would turn more on her inward state, her changes of mind, her development and growth through her experience. But in this Latin piece it is the background itself that carries the drama along. We see first the young girl working among the shreds of life in these old men; then as a woman confronted with the needs of her own body and soul, and with the problem of how life comes into the world, how it comes through the pain of others, how urgent it is and innocent and unceasing, how it cannot be denied; and finally as an old woman surrounded by the life that lies between birth and age, the promise of life opening in these boys and girls, to whom she gives her wisdom, strong rule, humor and love.

The theme of her is not inward, introspective, psychological in our familiar sense, but is set against the whole idea of woman the mother, the bosom of life, the love that mediates between harsh law and human needs, which the world of the Mediterranean understands so easily and has turned into the Madonna, the divine mother. Sister Gracia rests for her significance not on her individuality but on her eternity; and she derives her permanence from the need life has of her, moment by moment.

The play is foreign, too, is Latin, in the way the characters are put in, their strong outlining, the typicality of their self-revelation, and their habit of generalizing and running off into philosophic statement anywhere and everywhere. And most of all it is Latin in a particular respect that is difficult for us to understand and that misleads us constantly with regard to the depth of Latin art. I mean the manner in which the subtlety is achieved by a certain *combination* of single simple things instead of by some single complexity. When this method comes off supremely, as in the scene of the young bullfighter and the old Sister Gracia, we cannot see just what has been done but we feel that the sum of these simple motives that make up the scene is one of the most beautiful and moving moments in all the modern theatre. (pp. 103-04)

> Stark Young, "'The Kingdom of God'," in his Immortal Shadows: A Book of Dramatic Criticism *(copyright 1948 by Charles Scribner's Sons; copyright renewed; reprinted with the permission of Charles Scribner's Sons), Charles Scribner's Sons, 1948, pp. 101-05.*

PATRICIA WALKER O'CONNOR   (essay date 1966)

The heroine in the plays of Gregorio Martínez Sierra is essentially Spanish, but she is an independent young woman who desires and actively seeks full equality of opportunity and responsibility in a world that traditionally has favored men. She is attractive without being glamorous, and is poised and aggressive without being masculine. She is sympathetic, feminine, and strong, all at the same time, and is consistently able to solve the domestic problems which confront her and around which most of the plays revolve. Though it is true that the man playing opposite the heroine is often weak in comparison to her, she never intentionally makes him aware of this. She solves whatever situation arises discreetly and takes as little credit for the accomplishments as possible.

The heroine . . . is the subtle blend of the ideal and the real that has had such a long and successful tradition in Spanish literature. She has high ideals and ambitions, but never loses sight of the smallest problem of those around her. In the case of the heroine who is not a nun, religious fervor is not a factor, but she holds dear the sanctity of marriage and the home. Divorce never enters her mind as a solution to her marital problems. Rather, she seeks to solve them, when they arise, through planned action. She diagnoses the ills of her marriage, then sets about to correct them. She is not one either to bemoan her lot or to resign herself to a life of misery. She is essentially a woman of action. (p. 30)

While all of Martínez Sierra's plays seem to advocate marriage for women, it seems that he would not have them devote all of their time and talents to the home. The typical Martínez Sierra heroine successfully combines a career with marriage. No doubt the feminist María was responsible, to a great extent, for this factor in the plays. The right of the woman to work outside the home was defended in such a way as to indicate the writer's belief that the best wife and mother was the one who did not stagnate in the home, but who got out and developed her talents and intellect. He felt that she would thereby be better able to understand her husband and her children and would be contributing to the progress and economy of a country that stood sorely in need of both. We are shown the potential power of woman in various heroines who cherish their liberty and their right to take their place independently in a society that begins to cede them at least some professional equality. These are the capable, ambitious young women so admired by María Martínez Sierra.

The woman in these plays is never the feminist in the sense that she is part of an organization to fight for women's rights. Perhaps the Spanish personality is too independent to conform in such a way, or perhaps it would have been considered unfeminine. At any rate, the heroine who represents the modern woman in Martínez Sierra's plays exerts herself and is active because she herself *wants* to be, not because she is blazing a path for the future of womankind. Her brand of feminism is typically Spanish in that it is an individual effort and is only subtly related to feminism in the sociological sense of the word. (pp. 33-4)

That the woman is happier and the marriage more stable when husband and wife share responsibilities and work side by side is an idea portrayed repeatedly not only in the theater of Martínez Sierra, but in his novels and poetry as well. The importance of partnership in marriage was not just something that Gregorio and María Martínez Sierra wrote about; it was something they lived. Perhaps this explains the frequency with which the theme appears. (pp. 44-5)

[The heroine in Martínez Sierra's plays] is a lively Spanish girl who is not content to accept the traditions and conventions that have ruled her mother's life. She is strongly individual and feels the need for expressing herself, her talent, or her intellect outside of her home. While a career can never replace marriage and motherhood for her, she often feels that the best way to occupy her time until the right man comes along is to work. After marriage she often collaborates with her husband in his business or profession, or she may choose some career that will not take her too far from home. The heroine, unlike the ingénue, knows what she wants and how to get it. Unlike the conservative mother, she is free of religious dogmatism and would like to break with the traditions of the past, especially with regard to her right to a career, and to marry for love. She is a self-assured young woman who very much knows where she wants to go and is in command of herself at all times. The heroine, as seen in these plays, was more of a symbol of woman's aspirations than a reality in the author's lifetime. (pp. 50-1)

The pervading theme of almost all of Gregorio Martínez Sierra's plays is the idealization of womanhood; to him, the maternal instinct is the essence of feminity and is its loftiest expression. In many works, such as *El reino de Dios, Navidad*, and especially *Canción de cuna*, feminity and the maternal instinct are equated and almost inseparable. (p. 52)

In Martínez Sierra's plays, woman's love for her husband or her sweetheart often becomes mingled or confused with the maternal instinct. She wants to protect the man she loves, and the author portrays this idea without detracting from the feminity of the character. Indeed, in many instances this shielding of the man makes the woman appear softer and closer to her basic role in society as the comforter, the soother—in a word, the mother. The woman treats her man much as a mother treats her child. She understands his weaknesses and shortcomings, and overlooks them or forgives him for them even when they hurt her. (p. 63)

By the overwhelmingly large number of [Martínez Sierra's] heroines who successfully combine careers and motherhood, he suggests that career women are better mothers than their more conservative counterparts, who, in his plays at least, seem to stagnate at home. There is the suggestion, too, that women, aided by their maternal instinct, are better prepared to be doctors than men, who lack this special sensitivity. In *Cada uno y su vida,* for example, Irene and her sweetheart, Carlos, are fellow medical students. Carlos feels only repugnance in contact with illness or imperfection, while Irene feels compassion and the drive to alleviate suffering.

In his idealization of motherhood, . . . Martínez Sierra felt that the maternal instinct was only vaguely associated with the physical reality of motherhood. This instinct, when allowed to develop normally and freely, brings great happiness to both mother and child, as expressed by Sor Juana and Teresa in *Canción de cuna.* When unexpressed, it produces frustration and anxiety, as seen in some of the other nuns in the same play. The maternal instinct, Martínez Sierra seems to say, is what makes women better doctors and nurses than men; it is also intimately associated with the attraction which men and women feel toward one another. Some men seek out this appealingly feminine and soft quality in women, and some women are forever searching for someone to protect and love, whether this person be friend, husband, or child. The author seems to say that woman's ultimate aim, and the only one that will bring her true happiness and completion, is to marry and have children. While it is true that most of the women in Martínez Sierra's theater work, they do not aspire to be career women exclusively. The solution to the heroine's problem is almost always in marriage or in the resolution of a marital problem. All of the heroines are prospective mothers, whether they have their own children, act as mothers to their husband's children or, as in the case of some nuns, become mothers to mankind's forgotten children. (pp. 66-7)

[Often in Martínez Sierra's plays the mother who lacks the maternal instinct is a symbol of conservatism. This woman is usually the] mother of adult or nearly adult children whose ambitions differ markedly from the ambitions she has for them. She is an emotionally unbending woman, lacking in tenderness and understanding, and having none of the desirable characteristics that have been associated with the maternal instinct. This type of mother is conservative in her attitudes and has no patience with the liberal aspirations and ideals of the younger generation. Since the maternal instinct is so apparent in the plays of Gregorio Martínez Sierra, and since he treated the theme in such a delicate and almost sacred manner, the role of the mother would seem to be an enigma.

The mother, as she is portrayed here, is reminiscent of the many traditional mothers to be found in the Spanish literature of the nineteenth century. She is the product of a Victorian age and of a country that has always instilled prudishness in its middle- and upper-class women. She has been educated in a convent and has been well instructed in religious dogma. Her education has consisted largely of religion and the domestic arts, so it is not surprising that the mother should be convinced that her destiny was to be in the home. (p. 68)

Often her marriage was arranged by the family, so there was not necessarily a basis for companionship between husband and wife. The husband, in addition, was frequently quite a bit older than she, and his education, both formal and practical, was vastly more varied and extensive than hers. He had been educated in the universities, where few women ventured, and in life, where he was encouraged to explore. Don Juanism, in fact, was often equated in his mind with masculinity. Between this ultra-religious and rather naïve woman and her husband, there was often understandable antagonism. (pp. 68-9)

It is possible that the mothers in these plays may not have been inspired entirely by a large percentage of the mothers of her time. Gregorio Martínez Sierra may have observed his model at first hand in his own mother.

Considering how Gregorio Martínez Sierra felt about motherhood, it seems strange that he should have presented the mother in such an unflattering light. In his plays the abstract quality of motherhood is romanticized, while the mother is portrayed realistically to the extent that she represents the conservative faction. She is unrealistic, of course, in that she represents only one point of view.

At the time of the writing of Martínez Sierra's plays, Spain was in the throes of a great struggle between the forces of conservatism and liberalism. The former group would have Spain cling to the institutions that were associated with the Golden Age, the period of the country's greatest glory. The most prominent of these institutions was the Church. . . . In the nineteenth century, with the rise of liberalism in Spain, Rome evolved a policy of keeping its grasp firm on Spain to save it from liberal atheism. The Church, having already lost power in France, Germany, and Italy, spared no effort to retain control on traditionally faithful Spain. While the liberals were successful in establishing public schools and keeping them officially separate from the Church schools, the lay teachers were often conservative Catholics who spent as much time on religion and dogma as was spent in the religious schools.

The mother, then, is a product of family tradition, institutions, and conventions. She has been so completely indoctrinated that she fails or refuses to see that times have changed and that people must change in accordance with them. She would like to instill in her children, for example, the accepted traditions of her time, no matter how poorly they might fit the altered circumstances. (pp. 69-70)

The mother spends extravagantly and is a social climber, especially where her children are concerned. She expects them to marry within their social class or, preferably, higher. She is very much against careers for women in general, and particularly opposes those careers that involve any professional activity or active participation in public life—such as medicine, for example, or the stage. In the scheme of characters this mother is generally placed in opposition to a heroine with liberal ideas so that the struggle between mother and daughter may become a symbolical one in which tradition and a changing society lock horns. There is never any doubt, however, as to which force will be victorious, for the guiding hand behind the fracas, the author, is on the side of progress. If he were not, the mother would be the heroine and would be an attractive, lovable character whose daughter was an ungrateful brat given to rebellious and unladylike tendencies. (pp. 70-1)

The enthusiasm of the heroine for independence and a career is contrasted with the prudishness and conservatism of the mother. The mother again fares rather badly in comparison with the kindly, wise, and witty grandmother, who is no longer actively engaged in making her mark in society and has long ago stopped dreaming of the ideal marriage for her children. The appearance of things has ceased to be of consuming importance to her, and minutiae have lost their charm. Time and experience have changed her attitudes about many things, for she is free from the subjective pettiness that characterized the mother. Since she is free of many of the mother's responsibilities, there is less reason for her to be stubborn. The mother's frustration is augmented by her lack of culture and by her lack of any real authority. Her interest and abilities are quite limited. We see, however, that the extreme conservatism of the mother disappears with years and with the lessening of responsibilities and their inevitable frustrations. This does not mean that the domineering or reactionary grandmother did not exist; she did, of course, and she is portrayed in Doña Isabelita of *Esperanza nuestra,* but she is not the grandmother type that Martínez Sierra chose to immortalize on his stage.

The grandmother is probably the most universal type that Martínez Sierra created. . . . Martínez Sierra depicts a series of grandmothers that demonstrate the special personality—cynical at times, but always humane—that he apparently associated with this member of the family. She is not a stereotype or a theatrical device . . . but rather is taken whole from the society of her time and is very likely to be recognized by the viewer. When she is compared with the possessive and dictatorial mother, she is especially pleasing and amusing. Of course she has not acquired academic culture with her years, but she has acquired a sort of wisdom and philosophical resignation born of her past struggles and disappointments. She smiles, and tolerates youth's desire for progress. At times she is helpful, and at others she merely suspends judgment, and never does she set herself up as a supreme judge of right and wrong, as the mother usually does in the plays of this author.

If we consider the mother as the symbol of conservatism, we may consider the grandmother as the symbol of patience and kindness in relationship with the heroine. She understands and sympathizes with the aspirations of youth, if she does not encourage them. . . . In addition, she functions dramatically as a source of comic relief in some instances. She keeps the struggle between the heroine and the forces that oppose her from becoming too serious. . . . The grandmother may say things that might be offensive in another character, because she speaks affectionately, not derisively.

Just as the conservative mother is generally placed in opposition to her freedom-seeking daughter, a grandmother type often appears in the same plays and is a source of consolation and cheer to the depressed or irritated heroine. She is consistently sweet, human and lovable. She has a sense of humor, and tends to look on the brighter side of the past as well as of the future. She injects a note of optimism, which must be considered a distinguishing feature of the works of Gregorio Martínez Sierra. (pp. 86-7)

The ingénue depicted by Martínez Sierra is disturbingly unreal and in some cases is obviously forced. . . .

We may define the ingénue as a young unmarried girl, about eighteen years old, who has been sheltered all of her life and who reacts rather uncertainly and fearfully in her first encounters with men. She flusters easily and has no will of her own and can be talked into almost anything. She is frequently awkward in her dress, but her outstanding hallmark is her almost incredible naïveté.

Considering all of the various personality types created by Martínez Sierra, certainly the ingénue is the weakest and the

one least worthy of his dramatic genius. She is more entertaining than profound. This author is at his best in the creation of the woman with a serious purpose, and apparently he has little patience or charity for the rudderless, frivolous ingénue, whom he portrays in a most unflattering light. She suffers unquestionably in comparison with the beautiful, posed, intelligent, ambitious and long-suffering heroine.

There are many reasons why Martínez Sierra presented the ingénue as he did. First of all, the type did exist in real life, though rarely so extreme as the author depicts it. (p. 96)

In the ingénue, the author may have consciously presented a ridiculous type to show her in unfavorable contrast to the heroine. No doubt he was in favor of education and social reforms that might virtually eliminate from the Spanish scene this dewy-eyed dreamer who was so ill-prepared for the realities of life. (p. 97)

> *Patricia Walker O'Connor, in her* Women in the Theater of Gregorio Martínez Sierra *(copyright 1966 by Patricia Walker O'Connor), The American Press, 1966, 150 p.*

ROBERT W. CORRIGAN   (essay date 1967)

[In *Cradle Song*,] as well as in such ingenuous little idylls as *The Kingdom of God* and *The Two Shepherds,* [Martínez Sierra] succeeds by the irresistable force of simple humanity. He delineates characters who are real people with individual eccentricities. They are humble, religious people in uncomplicated situations, contending only with the corrigible faults of their own souls and the inevitable passage of time. Out of this almost unconscious flow of time, Martínez Sierra creates that ancient pathos of things passing, of good people growing old. But Martínez Sierra's characters are not ravaged by time; instead, they mellow with age, their simple lives free of remorse, and even as they proceed toward death we feel their agelessness. There is no philosophic pandemonium here, but rather the transforming power of human love. It is a context which, if we give ourselves over to it, disarms us with its peace and gentleness.

Martínez Sierra avoids sentimentality in these plays through his unfailing feeling for dramatic proportion and a certain ironic sense of humor. The theme of *Cradle Song* is tempting material for a fully orchestrated "tear-jerker"; but he keeps things under control, with the result that we are more conscious of the humaneness of his treatment of the situation than we are of its essential implausibility. Using two acts, he shows Teresa's arrival at the convent as a foundling and her departure eighteen years later to marry. Within this space he reveals the peculiarities of each of the nuns, and also shows their varying relationships to the girl committed to their charge.

Martínez Sierra's later drama is peopled with characters other than nuns and priests, but these plays do not measure up to his earlier work. (pp. 276-77)

> *Robert W. Corrigan, "Gregorio Martínez Sierra," in his* Masterpieces of the Modern Spanish Theatre *(copyright © 1967 by Macmillan Publishing Co., Inc.), Macmillan/Collier Books, 1967, pp. 275-350.*

PATRICIA W. O'CONNOR   (essay date 1977)

In the final decade of the nineteenth century, Spanish readers showed a preference for sentimentality and the evocation of mood through delicate rhetoric. Precisely because the early works of Martínez Sierra so thoroughly represented the tastes of the period, they are little read today. In these times of anguish and catastrophe, readers tend to demand an earthier realism expressed in violence, explicit sex, and four-letter words. Martínez Sierra's works, Modernist in style, idealistic, languid, pantheistic, moralistic, and melancholy in tone, run directly counter to current trends. . . . (p. 68)

Martínez Sierra shows a general kinship to early twentieth-century writers who praised nature as an antidote to encroaching industrialization. Unlike the writers of this group who saw factories and machines as the enemies and dehumanizers of man, Martínez Sierra wrote in a characteristically positive and optimistic way, accentuating the advantages of the simple life led in harmony with nature. Using a verbal palette lacking in harsh colors, he painted comforting pastel landscapes devoid of violence. Perhaps because he had lost faith in traditional religion, Martínez Sierra sought a universal order—and hence solace—in the beauties of nature. Recalling John Ruskin, he shows that this beauty has morally beneficial effects on society as well as the individual. Unlike Ruskin, however, he does not specifically condemn material progress as the natural enemy of human happiness.

What Martínez Sierra does suggest, however, is that in cities or in large crowds, there is decreased opportunity for direct contact with nature; God's message is therefore muted. A humane mystic . . . , this writer flees from the "worldly noises" of the city to a natural refuge of beauty, order and balance. Work is recommended as a salutory and desirable form of human consolation, but unlike his plays, many of the novels and stories end on an unhappy note. While the praise of work continues throughout his works, the pessimism of the early period vanishes in the more optimistic dramas. (pp. 68-9)

Although [Jacinto] Benavente assisted with the publication of [*El Poema del Trabajo*] *Labor's Poem,* his public sponsorship by way of the prologue was reserved—if not imperious and disdainful. Suggesting that the youthful Martínez Sierra had attempted more than he accomplished in his first effort, Benavente writes: "He sings of human strength, life and work; he is eloquent more for feeling than for words." . . . (pp. 69-70)

These allegorical prose poems, written largely in dialogue, extol the work of men and nature. . . . (p. 70)

In its political and cultural overtones, *Labor's Poem* can be compared to the attempt of the Generation of '98 to confront the problems of an ailing nation. Unlike other works of similar inspiration produced by members of the Generation of '98, the ideological thrust of *Labor's Poem* is positive, enthusiastic, and determined, which is unusual for this period of crisis and tremendous questioning. Indeed, *Labor's Poem* overflows with the enthusiasm, optimism, and reverence for work that were to characterize Gregorio Martínez Sierra, the dramatist. In its poetic language, symbolism, imagery, and delicate tone, this work represents Modernism in form as it reflects the concerns (but not the attitudes) of the Generation of '98.

Nine years later, however, . . . Martínez Sierra made this observation about *Labor's Poem:* "Don't read it if you have the chance: it has 122 pages—sincere, of course, but with a rash of adjectives that would stand your hair on end. . . . *Labor's Poem* had some success with the Socialists; a certain critic even called me a thinker—he really believed it." . . . (pp. 71-2)

The *Diálogos Fantásticos (Fantastic Dialogues* . . .), written in prose, are nine lyric, symbolic exchanges dedicated to Benavente, the first literary benefactor. Reminiscent of the traditional *autos sacramentales* (allegorical plays that exemplified the Church dogma, principally the Eucharist), the "speakers" (i.e., "characters") are Life, Death, Heart, Head, Soul, Truth, Fairies, Muses, Work, Idea, etc. Of the *Dialogues,* María writes: "In them, without realizing it, we were imitating our immortal Calderón who, three centuries ago, brought to life with human feeling and passion, abstract figures and mere theological concepts." . . . (p. 72)

Martínez Sierra's third work, *Flores de escarcha (Frost Flowers)* . . . contains twenty-four short stories in free verse that continue in the symbolic, languid, moralistic vein of *Labor's Poem* and the *Fantastic Dialogues.* Nature continues to play an important role, but there is a more decadent, pessimistic quality to this work that separates it from the mainstream of Martínez Sierra's writings. While Goldsborough Serrat calls *Frost Flowers* superior to the first two works, I must agree with María who, late in her life, judged this work rather harshly: "Those flowers aren't worth anything." (p. 73)

[*Almas ausentes (Absent Souls)*] is Martínez Sierra's first attempt at the novel. The narrator, a writer desiring to learn more about the mentally ill, spends some time in an insane asylum. . . .

This work, reminiscent of a gothic novel with its ghostly, castle-like asylum, its glimpses of tortured souls, and the floating image of the sweet, innocent, oblivious heroine, Anita, abounds in metaphor and poetic prose. The action moves fairly swiftly, however, through Romantic description and Realistic dialogue. (p. 74)

Absent Souls shows a trend toward a simple rather than complex plot, with a preference for describing moods and personalities rather than actions. Because simplicity and mood are difficult to sustain or extend, Martínez Sierra has been more successful in the short, contained forms, like the sketch, the short story, the novelette and the drama, rather than the novel. In *Absent Souls* he also shows a preference for reality, rejecting the allegorical approach of the first works. Both content and language shift from the poetic and the symbolic toward the mundane, a direction that was to continue.

Pursuing the short novel, Martínez Sierra produced *Horas de sol (Sunny Hours).* . . .

[*Sunny Hours*] is the romantic story of a wealthy, aristocratic city girl sent to the country for a vacation. There, in the sensuous yet pure atmosphere of raw nature, Hortensia falls in love with Carlos, a simple village boy. As in other works of this period, there is a pantheistic note, and the sun works its special magic. Hortensia seems mesmerized, almost inebriated with the warmth and life-giving force of the sun. (p. 75)

Under the spell of the sun and the beauty of nature, Hortensia believes that Carlos is the man destined to share her life. When she returns to the cottage one afternoon, however, a letter from a friend in the city thwarts nature's course. Amelia writes of the many festive parties in Madrid and that all her friends miss her. She also makes fun of the friends who have laughingly suggested that Hortensia might be having a "country idyll." Hortensia, a victim of *el qué dirán* ("what people will say") thereupon rejects her natural inclinations and decides to return to the city immediately. The novel ends, thus, on a sad rather than a happy note. (pp. 75-6)

Teatro de ensueño (Dream Theater) . . . is the first published attempt of Gregorio and María at theater. Because the pieces in this collection are experimental and Modernist, they were not performed at the time. (p. 80)

The first short piece of *Dream Theater,* "Along the Flowery Path," deals with some of life's harsher realities on an idealized and lyrical plane. While Dinko is traveling through Spain with his little Hungarian circus, Mirka, his wife, dies of starvation and overwork. In this sketch, Martínez Sierra again asserts his often-reiterated belief that one of woman's duties is to console; she must smile even when sad, and her laughter must give comfort and joy. . . . Because Mirka represented life and happiness to Dinko, he rejects the idea of her death and, unable to bear this final separation, refuses to allow her burial. Dinko's father finally convinces him to proceed with life because Mirka would not have wanted him sad. . . . Again illustrating the pantheism so much a part of his early style, Martínez Sierra suggests that Mirka has not ceased to exist; she simply exists in another form. She has become a part of all nature. Mirka now will be associated with light, with beginnings, and with the smiling encouragement and warm energy radiating out from the sun. This happy resolution became typical of Martínez Sierra's optimistic philosophy of life. (p. 81)

[*Tú eres la paz (You Are Peace)* was the] most popular work except for *Cradle Song*. This novel would reach a wide reading public of sighing young girls in both Spain and South America during the first part of the present century. . . .

In *You Are Peace,* the central figure, Ana María, modest, intelligent, optimistic, gay, and self-controlled . . . , is in love with her artist cousin, Agustín who, while abroad, has fallen in love with a beautiful model. (p. 85)

Ana María and Agustín, partially reared by their grandmother, had declared their love for each other prior to Agustín's departure. As the novel opens, Ana María and the grandmother . . . await the return of Agustín. Because in his absence Agustín has stopped writing, Ana María faithfully composes long, newsy, affectionate letters and passes them off as Agustín's to keep the grandmother happy. When Agustín returns, Ana María and Agustín, in order to preserve their grandmother's happiness, pretend that their relationship has not changed and that they will eventually marry as planned.

An interesting novelistic technique utilized in this work is the telling of the story from various points of view. The third-person narrator describes the pleasant rural setting and much of the action. Direct contact with reactions of the characters is provided through letters that Ana María and Agustín write to friends. The reader thus sees not only an objective description of what has taken place but subsequently views the scene as other characters have perceived it.

The novel revolves principally around the interaction between Ana María—proud, unselfish, maternal—and Agustín, the rather weak-willed young man who ultimately recognizes his need for her. (p. 86)

You Are Peace has a much more modern air than previous works. In addition to being quite realistic in setting, there is less description; the dialogue is the normal language of young people, and there are fewer rhetorical sentences couched in poetic, symbolic prose. Here, too, flesh-and-blood characters rather than symbols emerge strongly. Ana María is the prototype of the woman the Martínez Sierras admired and would portray again and again in the theater. In addition to being

Spanish (a very important virtue), this character is intelligent, modest, quietly aggressive, long-suffering, self-controlled, smiling, and gay. Juxtaposed to her is the prototype of the undesirable woman: not only foreign, she is designing, frivolous, unmaternal, and amoral. Agustín is a pleasant young man, but extremely weak. He needs a mother, and Ana María is quite willing to oblige. (p. 87)

In the twelve years from 1898 to 1910, the Martínez Sierras evolve from poetic, languid, colorist, Modernist diction to a simple, direct, realistic approach. Throughout the period, however, they continue to encourage man to follow his natural instincts and to take pride in accomplishment. Indeed, the admiration shown for work in *Labor's Poem* will persist throughout all their writings. There is also a shift from lengthy descriptions of life and nature through allegorical dialogue to a concern for real people in more and more localized surroundings.

Reflecting a desire for the fusion of body and spirit embraced by a kindly cosmos to form a balanced and happy universe, Martínez Sierra casts nature, work, love, art, ideas, and people as a harmonious whole. Frequently symbolized in the sun, this balance is a positive beacon, a magnet that points toward a positive natural order. All things seem to demonstrate an innate harmony. One must only listen to the natural signals they emit. Man, then, will gravitate toward what is good if he simply allows nature to lead him. The noises, artificial light, and cement of the city tend, on the other hand, to obscure nature's message. (p. 96)

Just as the Martínez Sierras recall Rousseau in their insistence on the goodness of the natural man and the ultimate treachery of civilization and material progress, they also suggest [Gabriele] D'Annunzio in their quasi-pagan joy of life and strong nationalism. They lack, however, the Italian's more refined enjoyment of sensual pleasures, for they were strongly moralistic and almost totally obedient to the bourgeois ethic. Their melancholy young men recall Goethe's Werther, and in the delicate imagery and Romantic expression of the inner life through poetic exchange, they show the influence of [Maurice] Maeterlinck. In the early period Martínez Sierra was, in fact, a curious amalgam of the poet, the pagan, and the mystic. (pp. 96-7)

Although totally different from the sentimental, domestic comedy for which Martínez Sierra is remembered, . . . [early works such as *Dream Theater* and *Aldea Ilusoria (Illusive Village)*] are interesting for the steady progression they document from symbolic, allegorical figures to flesh-and-blood characters, and from high-flown rhetoric to colloquial speech. Not theatrical in the commercial sense, the plays cast in dialogue are essentially poetic essays, while *Dream Theater,* Maeterlinckian, impressionistic, highly visual in thrust—and more appropriate for the contemporary art film—would have been difficult if not impossible to perform effectively on stage.

About 1907, the Martínez Sierras rather abruptly turned from the composition of colorist, Modernist pieces to focus on plays designed to please audiences. (p. 98)

[In *El ama de la casa (Mistress of the House),*] the Martínez Sierras have found their style, their characters, and their message. . . . [A strong woman] is contrasted to a well-intentioned but essentially weak man. Moreover, the central character shines by comparison to several negative examples of the Martínez Sierra feminine ideal. . . . [Conflicts] revolve around domestic problems that ultimately find solutions. . . . (pp. 102-03)

Carlota—in her determination, activity, and optimism—becomes a composite Martínez Sierra heroine, combining maternal sentiments and authority with the active optimism of the heroines. (pp. 104-05)

One curious facet of this play is the rather practical, nonsentimental approach to marriage. While Carlota and Félix are fond of each other, both confess in word and action that love was not a primary motive in their marriage. Carlota had desperately wanted a home—especially because she had lacked one as a child—and Félix was able to provide it. For Carlota, work in an office was only a temporary measure until a man could provide a home for her. Although a strong, accomplishing woman, Carlota has no feminist inclinations. . . .

In *Mistress of the House,* Martínez Sierra also touches on a theme that figures rather prominently in the feminist essays written years later. Carlota voices basic advice for her stepchildren later given in the feminist essays: she insists on proper diet, rest, simple attire, and cleanliness. . . . Such were the Martínez Sierras simple solutions for bodily ills. Their similarly uncomplicated prescription for mental health was hard work. (p. 106)

Because of a generally optimistic and frequently sentimental portrayal of life, Martínez Sierra has not been considered a revolutionary dramatist—or even a social critic, for that matter. His plays featuring religious figures, however—[*Canción de cuna (Cradle Song), Lirio entre espinas (Lily Among Thorns), Los Pastores (The Shepherds), El reino de Dios (The Kingdom of God), and Navidad (Holy Night)*] . . .—exalt the virtues of Christian charity and self-sacrifice at the same time that they criticize the existing social, religious, and political order. The revolution gently recommended in these plays is essentially a spiritual one involving a return to the universal fundamental of fraternal love. The thrust is consistently humane and vital rather than narrowly religious.

The nuns chosen by Martínez Sierra to convey the message of human charity are, first and foremost, human beings. They suffer, fear, cry, dream and, on occasion, lick cookie pots and stick out their tongues in pique. Despite their human qualities and limitations, these nuns symbolize distilled and sometimes idealized maternity. The selfless dedication shown by these women also functions as a metaphor for the human ideal of Christian charity. Not happy as contemplatives, they seek activity and involvement with living things and need to nurture, be it abandoned child, ailing invalid, hardened sinner, or wounded animal. (p. 107)

Illustrative of Martínez Sierra's ideas as well as his theatrical technique is his masterpiece, *Cradle Song*. Rather than develop a conflict or move toward any climax, this play reveals two moments of convent life as it explores feminine personality. (p. 108)

While some may see *Cradle Song* as the sweet expression of idealized and pure maternal love, it is, in addition, a drama of feminine frustration and, in some cases, of forced rather than voluntary renunciation of self. Although the motivations of the women in coming to the convent are not explored, the implication is that they came out of financial need and family or social pressure rather than an authentic religious vocation. In this sense, these women are like Teresa and her mother, victims of a social system that tended to channel women to the home, the convent, or the brothel. Although the Martínez Sierras recommend no solution to the various problems alluded to in

this play, they certainly suggest that the convent is not a happy solution for economic or social ills. (p. 111)

In *Lily Among Thorns,* the scene is a house of prostitution into which a nun stumbles—again by chance or divine plan—at a time of need. This "lily" briefly provides the "thorns" with the maternal care and spiritual orientation needed in a moment of crisis.

Lily Among Thorns combines elements of fantasy and reality as it recalls a moment of recent Spanish history: Barcelona's "Tragic Week" of 1909. During these bloody days, opposition to military service in Morocco had sparked a general strike, the burning of convents and churches, riots in the streets and general chaos. (p. 112)

In *Lily Among Thorns,* actual revolution forms a background for the exaltation of women and their natural maternal virtues. This one play involves a real rather than a symbolic revolution, and Lulu expresses the militant desire for a more just world, and a willingness to die for her beliefs. Sister Teresa, on the other hand, has given up all rights to assert herself. She is, nevertheless, a model for the spiritual and social revolution favored by the Martínez Sierras. Were everyone like Sister Teresa, the revolt of the streets would be quite unnecessary.

Of the three plays featuring maternal nuns, [*The Kingdom of God*] . . . is the one that most accentuates the theme of personal renunciation for the social good. Its philosophy, if generally adopted, would bring the "kingdom of God" to earth. . . . Like *Cradle Song,* it reveals decisive moments of feminine life. (pp. 114-15)

Although none of the plays featuring nuns focuses on the religious life as such, there is in *Cradle Song* an implied criticism of the cloister, for Martínez Sierra firmly believed that women needed active involvement with people. In *The Kingdom of God,* Sister Gracia is neither a cloistered nun nor does she take perpetual vows. As a Sister of Charity she takes vows only yearly. Moreover, her vocation is authentic, for as a member of a wealthy family, she came to the order freely, not out of economic necessity. (p. 115)

Precisely because Sister Gracia chooses to become a nun as well as remain one, her personal sacrifice is all the more admirable. (p. 116)

The three plays involving maternal nuns evince a progression from involuntary to voluntary renunciation of the world; from dedication to one individual—Teresa, of *Cradle Song*—to a dedication to all society in *The Kingdom of God.* Although [*Holy Night*] . . . features no nun, the Virgin Mary performs a similar function in a play identical in ideological thrust. *Holy Night* carries the renunciation theme to its limit as it portrays the woman chosen by God to be His mother—and hence the symbolic mother of mankind—performing the ultimate renunciation: she delivers her divine Child to the needy. After this play, a return to the theme of maternal renunciation would have been anticlimactic. Perhaps for this reason *Holy Night* is the final play in the cycle. (pp. 116-17)

In several ways, *Holy Night* is a more symbolic, more theological version of *The Kingdom of God.* In the latter play, Sister Gracia, a humanized "Holy Mother," ministers to the world's most needy as she renounces the comfort of home and family. In *Holy Night,* the Virgin makes the ultimate gesture of maternal renunciation as she delivers her divine and only child to the poor. Martínez Sierra suggests that human selfishness has obscured the meaning of Christ's birth. Beneath the false trappings imposed by a materialistic power structure, however, Jesus and his mother continue to set examples of sacrifice, humility, and love. They, like the nuns of the other plays, not only befriend outcasts of society, but reject the values of—and association with—a selfish and insensitive Establishment. In this sense all of these figures, like Jesus himself, are revolutionaries. On a hopeful note *Holy Night* implies, in its contemporary setting, that the miracle of two thousand years ago remains within grasp through a return to the simple traditions of brotherhood and love. (pp. 118-19)

> *Patricia W. O'Connor, in her* Gregorio and María Martínez Sierra *(copyright © 1977 by Twayne Publishers, Inc.; reprinted with the permission of Twayne Publishers, a Division of G. K. Hall & Co., Boston), Twayne, 1977, 155 p.*

ADDITIONAL BIBLIOGRAPHY

Chandler, Frank W. "Spanish Sentimentalists." In his *Modern Continental Playwrights,* pp. 487-502. New York: Harper & Brothers, 1931.
    Asserts that "at his best, Martínez Sierra breaks with the older artificial drama, writing simply, and allowing his matter to dictate the form."

Hatcher, Harlan. "Gregorio Martínez Sierra." In *Modern Continental Dramas.* Edited by Harlan Hatcher, pp. 427-31. New York: Harcourt, Brace and Company, 1941.
    Provides "a brief view of some of Martínez Sierra's typical and most widely known plays."

Young, Raymond A. "A Comparison of Benavente's *Rosas de Otoño* and Martínez Sierra's *Primavera en Otoño.*" *C.L.A. Journal* XI, No. 3 (March 1968): 206-20.*
    Elaborates on essay by Aubrey F. G. Bell [see excerpt in entry above].

Alice (Christiana Gertrude Thompson) Meynell

1847-1922

(Also wrote under name of A. C. Thompson and pseudonyms of Alice Oldcastle and Francis Phillimore) English poet, essayist, critic, journalist, editor, and translator.

Meynell, one of the first successful female critics of literature, was also one of England's foremost Catholic poets. Dubbed by Max Beerbohm "the literary queen of the 1890s," Meynell was admired by the great and near great writers of her time. They extolled her writings as well as her composed, intellectual, and hospitable personality, a personality reflected in much of her work. These attributes, combined with an inherent gentility and reticence, struck a responsive chord in late- and post-Victorian readers.

Meynell was born to wealthy, aristocratic, and artistically-inclined parents who counted Dickens and Tennyson as family friends. Though born in England, she spent much of her childhood in Italy, a country to which she frequently returned. At the age of twenty Meynell converted to Catholicism; she remained devoutly religious throughout her life, as the reverent themes of her verse demonstrate. Meynell's first collection of poems, *Preludes,* generated a great deal of critical attention. Though the general public ignored this first effort, John Ruskin, Christina Rossetti, George Eliot, and other prominent literary figures considered *Preludes* the work of a promising new talent. The volume also impressed Wilfred Meynell, a young journalist and critic, who asked to meet the author. They were married two years later, beginning a personal and professional partnership that lasted some forty years. To support their family, the Meynells coedited two journals, *Merry England* and *The Weekly Register.* In addition, she contributed articles, essays, and criticism to *The National Observer, Spectator,* and *The Pall Mall Gazette.* The publication of *Poems* and *The Rhythm of Life* in 1893 attracted the attention of several notable authors, and Meynell's home became a favorite gathering place for celebrities such as George Meredith, Coventry Patmore, and Francis Thompson.

The essays in *The Rhythm of Life, and Other Essays,* as well as those in *The Colour of Life, and Other Essays on Things Seen and Heard, The Spirit of Place, and Other Essays,* and later collections, were selected from her magazine and newspaper articles. The subject matter ranges from children and Italian landscape architecture to the practice of moderation in art and life. Interspersed are critical essays, collected in *Hearts of Controversy,* discussing the literary merits of Dickens, Thackeray, and the Brontës. Meynell's concise, controlled style and her simplicity and discipline of thought attracted readers on both sides of the Atlantic. She was as acclaimed in the United States, which she toured at the height of her career, as she was in her own country. Critics praised her subtlety and reticence, her ability to "say just enough," which allowed readers to think for themselves.

Meynell's verse displays the same controlled craftsmanship and command of language. Her most frequent theme is that of renunciation, the act of sacrificing pleasure and comfort to attain a purer state of being. Yet her poems also reflect the social concerns of her day, such as the need for women's suffrage and the horrors of World War I.

Meynell has fallen out of favor with modern critics, who find her style aloof and austere. They note, particularly in her criticism, a lack of humor and a forced satiric style. Moreover, critics conclude that her essays are too short—her subject matter calls for depth and scope rather than brief and highly subjective impressions. The subtle and reserved style so admired by her contemporaries is today considered obscure and affected. G. K. Chesterton attributed these flaws to the period in which Meynell wrote. Her peers encouraged extreme delicacy and reticence, he explained, and frowned upon experiments in style or literary explorations into the baser aspects of human nature. Although her literary reputation has declined considerably, Meynell enjoyed a lifetime of popularity and critical acclaim.

PRINCIPAL WORKS

Preludes [as A. C. Thompson] (poetry) 1875
Poems (poetry) 1893
The Rhythm of Life, and Other Essays (essays) 1893
The Children (essays) 1896
The Colour of Life, and Other Essays on Things Seen and Heard (essays) 1896

COVENTRY PATMORE (essay date 1892)

At rare intervals the world is startled by the phenomenon of a woman whose qualities of mind and heart seem to demand a revision of its conception of womanhood and an enlargement of those limitations which it delights in regarding as essentials of her very nature, and as necessary to her beauty and attractiveness as woman. She belongs to a species quite distinct from that of the typical sweet companion of man's life. . . . (p. 761)

I am about to direct the reader's attention to one of the very rarest products of nature and grace—a woman of genius, one who, I am bound to confess, has falsified the assertion which I made some time ago . . . , that no female writer of our time had attained to true "distinction." In the year 1875, Miss Alice Thompson (now Mrs. Meynell) . . . published a volume of poems, which were as near to being poetry as any woman of our time, with the exception perhaps of Miss Christina Rossetti, has succeeded in writing. But though this volume . . . far surpassed the work of far more famous "poetesses," it was not poetry in the sense which causes all real poets, however subordinate in their kind, to rank as immortals. There is sufficient intellect and imagination in Mrs. Meynell's *Preludes* to have supplied a hundred of that splendid insect, [Robert] Herrick; enough passion and pure human affection for a dozen poets like [Richard] Crashaw or William Barnes; they breathe, in every line, the purest *spirit* of womanhood, yet they have not sufficient force of that *ultimate* womanhood, the expressional *body,* to give her the right to be counted among classical poets. No woman ever has been such a poet: probably no woman ever will be, for (strange paradox!) though, like my present subject, she may have enough and to spare of the virile intellect, and be also exquisitely womanly, she has not womanhood enough.

The feminine factor in the mind of the great poet is, indeed, a greater thing than woman—it is goddess. Keats and Shelley, in their best works, were wholly feminine; they were merely exponents of sensitive beauty; but into this they had such an insight, and with it such a power of self-identification, as no woman has ever approached. (p. 762)

Mrs. Meynell's verse is true, beautiful, tender, and, negatively, almost faultless; but it does not attain the classical and only sound standard. Compared with that which is classical in the writings of second or even of third-rate poets, like Herrick, Crashaw, and William Barnes, it is "as moonlight unto sunlight." Our admiration is, indeed, strongly awakened by it, but we think of and admire the poetess still more than her poetry. It does not strain to rival man's work, as Mrs. Browning's does, nor to put forth the great, impersonal claims of great poetry, nor claim to have mastered the arduous *technique* whereby every phrase becomes a manifold mystery of significance and music. Mrs. Meynell's thoughts and feelings seem

to be half-suffocated by their own sweetness and pathos, so that, though they can speak with admirable delicacy, tenderness, and—that rarest of graces—unsuperfluousness, they cannot sing. With extraordinary power of self-judgment, she discovered this fact while she was as yet a mere girl, and, disdaining to do anything which she could not do, not only well, but best, and notwithstanding the encouragement to persevere in poetry which she received from a large and high class of critics, she gave up the attempt, and has hardly since written a line.

But, in a very small volume of very short essays [*The Rhythm of Life and Other Essays*] . . . , this lady has shown an amount of perceptive reason and ability to discern self-evident things as yet undiscerned, a reticence, fulness, and effectiveness of expression, which place her in the very front rank of living writers in prose. At least half of this little volume is *classical* work, embodying, as it does, new thought of general and permanent significance in perfect language, and bearing, in every sentence, the hall-mark of genius, namely, the marriage of masculine force of insight with feminine grace and tact of expression. Of the "sweetness and wit," which are said, by Donne, I think, to be woman's highest attainment, there is in these little essays abundance, but they are only the living drapery of thought which has the virile qualities of simplicity, continuity, and positiveness. The essays of Emerson, of which those of Mrs. Meynell will sometimes remind the reader, are not to be compared with the best of hers in these greater merits; moreover, the "transcendentalism" of the American writer afforded a far easier field than that chosen by the English lady. It is very easy to speak splendidly and profusely about things which transcend speech; but to write beautifully, profitably, and originally about truths which come home to everybody, and which everybody can test by common sense; to avoid with sedulous reverence the things which are beyond the focus of the human eye, and to direct attention effectively to those which are well within it, though they have hitherto been undiscerned through lack of attention, . . . is a very different attainment. Gaiety of manner with gravity of matter, truth perceived clearly and expressed with ease and joy, constitute the very highest and rarest of prose writing. . . . In the writing of Mrs. Meynell we have brightness and epigram enough, but they are but the photosphere of weighty, intelligible and simple human interest; and they never tempt her, as the possession of such wit almost inevitably tempts the male writer, to any display of scorn and contempt. She has always pity and palliatory explanation for the folly or falsehood which she exposes so trenchantly. Perhaps the unkindest hit in her book is that in which she laughs at the New-Worldling. . . . (pp. 763-64)

[In] all Mrs. Meynell's wit, the razor-edge cuts so keenly because of the weight at its back. In one little sentence she shatters a world of pretension which, without deceiving anyone, has puzzled most of us in the attempt to define and dissipate it; and henceforward we shall never be without an answer to the worn-out and vulgarised civilizee when he at once boasts of and apologises for being a fine young savage.

The title of the essay ["**Decivilised**"] . . . is a word invented by Mrs. Meynell, and not before it was wanted. We had "uncivilised" and "over-civilised," but no word to express the condition in which "Progress" has at last landed the world, especially the English-speaking part of it. The epithet "decivilised" is in itself an achievement of insight, and a word to conjure by. (p. 764)

In the way of art criticism very few have equalled Mrs. Meynell's little essay on Velasquez, "**Point of Honour,**" whom she calls "the first Impressionist." In this essay she, for the first time, and with the extreme brevity and fulness of genius, explains and justifies Impressionism, and abolishes the pretensions of almost all modern "Impressionists" to their self-assumed title. The best of this lady's essays, which seldom run to greater length than about two pages of this Review, are so perfect that to give extracts as samples is like chipping off corners of "specimen" rubies or emeralds for the like purpose. Their value is not in arithmetical, but in geometrical, proportion to their bulk. (p. 765)

The range of subject in this score of miniature essays is very large, and an extraordinary degree of finished culture in various directions is displayed, with an entire absence of pretension or even consciousness. . . . [These essays] bear no resemblance one to the other, except in their equal charm of fulness, brevity, original insight, experience, graceful learning, and unique beauty of style. The authoress never falls below the high standard she has attained in the two essays I have [mentioned], except in cases in which she has chosen matter unworthy of her powers. The merits of Lowell and Oliver Wendell Holmes, and the vulgarity of Dickens and the caricaturists of fifty years ago, may afford very good subjects for ordinary critics, but diamond-dust and a razor-edge, though it may have the weight of a hatchet behind it, are quite unadapted for the working up of blocks of teak or sandstone. There is a sort of sanctity about such delicate genius as Mrs. Meynell's which makes one shrink to see the robe of her Muse brush against anything common. Let her respect her own graceful powers and personality, as every man of true delicacy and insight must respect them, and she will become one of the fairest and steadiest lights of English literature, though she may remain unconspicuous to "the crowd, incapable of perfectness." (p. 766)

Coventry Patmore, "Mrs. Meynell, Poet and Essayist," in The Fortnightly Review, *Vol. LVIII, December 1, 1892, pp. 761-66.*

FRANCIS THOMPSON   (essay date 1893)

The poetry of Mrs. Meynell is of a peculiarly and indescribably evanescing quality: she deals with emotions which it might seem as impossible to communicate as to paint a wind. These, nevertheless, she conveys through a union of expression and suggestion that is absolutely adequate. It is diction rarefied to the vanishing point. She has a power quite extraordinary of uttering the many unspoken things through the one spoken thing, of stirring in the reader's mind many circles with the one pebble. The footfalls of her Muse waken not sounds, but silences. We lift a feather from the marsh and say: "This way went a heron." And so with her, the emotion sheds but a single phrase to betoken what manner of wings had lonely passage athwart her soul. In this respect she is a Coleridge of the feelings; she is volatilised feeling, as Coleridge is volatilised imagination. And, even as with Coleridge's imagination, her imagination is wholly of the etherealised quality; you must not look in it for ardour. (pp. 187-88)

It would be very false, nevertheless, to suppose her only an emotional poet. On the contrary, she is penetratingly thoughtful. But feeling is the essence of her verse; it is feeling oozed through the pores of thought. And profoundly imaginative her poetry always is, even when its emotion is too instant for thought. That thought itself, at its most characteristic, is typically imaginative thought. Much poetic thought can be divorced from its poetry, and rendered with completeness into

naked prose. But Mrs. Meynell's thought is as indissolubly wedded to imagination as light to colour. . . . [Divorce] her thought from its imaginative expression, and it might exist in her mind, but it would become invisible—that is, incommunicable. As a test, let anyone attempt to explain **"Builders of Ruins"** to a quite unimaginative person. He will soon conclude that, on the whole, it would be a more prosperous employment to translate Aquinas into Romany. And because this poem so centrally exhibits her characteristic of imaginative thought with feeling murmuring about its base, the poem is perhaps her greatest, or at least greatest of her longer poems. But it is not her most completely representative, because one quite personal note of hers is in it subduedly struck—her tenderness.

Entirely representative are **"The Poet to his Childhood"** and the **"Letter from a Girl to her Own Old Age."** The originality of their conception is quite singular. The spiritual perception of inclusions—of the blossom in the bud and the precedent bud in the blossom—which Mrs. Meynell, consciously or unconsciously, has developed from its germs in Shelley, is here carried to innovating lengths; lengths which, in fact, make the method so proper to herself, that it will be difficult henceforth for a poet to use it without arousing perilous comparisons. (pp. 188-89)

To choose among the briefer poems is a task at once bewildering and futile. The little book [*Poems*] was surely written to show that in short measures books, not less than life, may perfect be. It has no mere rhyme; it is all (in the Roman sense of the word) mere poetry—poetry with no allaying verse, *vinum merum* of song. **"Pygmalion,"** like much of her work, is a poet's poem, for probably only a poet can entirely know and feel its moving truth. (pp. 189-90)

Mrs. Meynell's metre echoes her diction—shunning elaborate form, but full of noiseless magic. Her hatred for the suspicion of insistence keeps the versification delicately numerous in an age whose metre tends to strong tuniness. Consequently the sweet and still modulation of its phrasing, the intelligent and vital niceties of its symmetry, will evade the untrained ear. **"The Poet to his Childhood,"** for example, is written in a metre which—in all other hands—is by nature lilting. Yet, without destroying its melodic form, she fingers it with a numerousness that gives it newly beautiful grace. So with the anapæstic **"Day to the Night"**—it is almost a new rhythm in anapæsts. Its lovely elegance of movement differs wholly from the rich luxury of movement in **"The Sensitive Plant"**; but for the quality of variousness, so rare and difficult in anapæsts, the two poems may rank together. Whatever her metre, her numbers are truly numbers.

Mrs. Meynell's is poetry the spiritual voice of which will become audible when "the high noises" of to-day have followed the feet that made them. . . . Foremost singer of a sex which is at last breaking the silence that followed on Mary's "Magnificat," she will leave to her successors a serener tradition than masculine poets bequeathed to men. She has reared for them an unpriced precedent, and she has given them the law of silence. That high speech must be shod with silence, that high work must be set forth with silence, that high destiny must be waited on with silence—was a lesson the age lacked much. Our own sex has heard the nobly tacit message of Mr. Coventry Patmore. But by an exception rare as beautiful, the woman's calm has been austerer-perfect than the man's. (pp. 190-91)

Francis Thompson, "Mrs. Meynell's 'Poems'," in Tablet, *January 21, 1893 (and reprinted as "Vic-*

torian Age: Alice Meynell,'' in his Literary Criticisms, edited by Rev. Terence Connolly, S.J., E. P.
Dutton and Company Inc., 1948, pp. 187-91).

THE BOOKMAN (London)   (essay date 1893)

['The Rhythm of Life' from the collection of the same name]
is the first of twenty short essays which are capable of causing
considerable irritation tempered by moments of pleasure. In
nearly every one of the twenty the writer convinces us that she
has something to say. This high praise is given ungrudgingly.
The book enshrines (no less solemn word would be adequate)
a few principles of life and art, and a few prejudices of a
superior order. It is free from conventionality of a commonplace kind. The point of view is for the most part negative.
The main object of attack—but attack is an inappropriate word,
and Mrs. Meynell makes us ponder our language—of reproach,
rather, is Vulgarity, or, as she prefers to call it, "insimplicity."
This is held to include, of course, everything Early Victorian,
the colonial muse and the colonial intellect generally, the "decivilised" provincials who go to ballad-concerts or daub door-
panels: in fact, all cheapness in literature and art and life.

Mrs. Meynell has pushed the artistic gift, or habit, of selection
to a point that must make the world a rather more difficult
place for her than even for other people. It is not only in country
lodgings she finds "the most ordinary things of design have
sifted down or gathered together, so that foolish ornament gains
a cumulative force and achieves a conspicuous commonness."
Even English landscape is under a ban. . . . On the other hand,
"Italy is slim and all articulate." Her love for simplicity finds,
however, it must be said, some better illustrations. Indeed, so
admirable is her understanding of the saving value of this essential of healthy life and art, that we are driven to wish with
real ardour that she would express it in a way that would not
urge unregenerate persons to cherish Early-Victorianism and
to commit with appetite all the other deadly Philistine sins.

"I could wish," she says, "abstention to exist, and even to
be evident in my words." No doubt it exists. . . . It is evident
probably, too, in the brevity, in the very thinness of the essays.
But abstention is apt to end in baldness and in very puzzling
ellipses. And then there is so much she does not abstain from.
Her love of "Latinity," a protest against the crudeness of
Teutonic expression, and a certain want of lucidity in her thinking, make up a difficulty which it is not always worth while
overcoming. Add to these the "preciousness," which is not
so much affectation as a symbol of over-conscious aloofness
from all the opinions of the many, and you get the components
of a style which at its worst can be described only by a word
forbidden by the code of the polite critic. Her admiration for
abstention, her fear of exaggeration and violence, find their
best expression in an essay in fine shades, called **"A Remembrance,"** the portrait of an "amateur at living." . . .

It is a pity that a book which has in it some very sane maxims
of life and art, some that need preaching lustily, should so
gratuitously prevent its own success. It is a voice crying, not
in the wilderness, but inside a high-walled garden, and faintly,
lest its timbre should suffer.

G. Y., "'The Rhythm of Life','' in The Bookman,
London, Vol. III, No. 17, February, 1893, p. 158.

THE SPECTATOR   (essay date 1893)

[There is not a poem in *Poems*] which does not display qualities
far above the level of the ordinary versifier. There is no indication of the commonplace, or of rhyming without a purpose,
to be found in these pages. The workmanship is always careful,
the thoughts often noble and beautiful. There is tenderness
without false sentiment, and high culture wholly free from
affectation; there is considerable command of language, and a
nobility of thought which turns instinctively to whatsoever things
are lovely and are of good report. So elevated is the feeling contained in some of the poems, that we do not wonder if readers
with large sympathies respond readily to the poet's words, and
find, perhaps, more in them than they can be justly said to
merit as poetry. In our judgment, the volume is the fruit of
culture, and of what may be termed spiritual instinct, rather
than of genius; and we are somewhat confirmed in this belief
by the fact that life, with all the treasures which it yields, has
not enlarged the faculty of song displayed by Mrs. Meynell in
her youthful days. . . . *Preludes,* the title of Mrs. Meynell's
youthful volume, appears to have suggested a hope on the part
of its author, that these early and tentative strains might be
followed by notes of more enduring charm.

This was not our expectation upon reading the volume with
care, and a considerable amount of pleasure; but Mrs. Meynell
has reversed our judgment, so far, indeed, as a single new
sonnet can reverse it,—a sonnet of so rare a charm, that it
merits a place among the most beautiful love-sonnets in the
language. If our readers know it already—for it has been printed
in a selection—they cannot fail to recall the lovely lines with
pleasure. It is entitled **"Renouncement."** . . .

A small volume [*The Rhythm of Life and other Essays*], corresponding in size and binding with the *Poems,* contains twenty
short essays, in which the author's good sense and good intentions are expressed in language which, if it have the merit
of subtlety, is assuredly far from lucid. The painful strain and
obscurity of Mrs. Meynell's style may possibly possess some
virtue hidden from the ordinary critic. He, at least, will be
inclined to complain that the author is unreasonably enigmatical, and to suspect that, if less effort had been used, both the
writer and her readers would have been gainers. It may be
possible, although we much doubt it, for an essayist to think
clearly and to utter his thoughts ambiguously; but while Mrs.
Meynell has succeeded in making her essays hard reading, it
is possible that the effort they demand from the reader is not
due to profundity of thought. Sometimes we are tempted to
smile when Mrs. Meynell is most serious,—as, for instance,
when she asks whether Dr. Johnson's noble English did not
control and postpone his terror of death? Mrs. Meynell appears
to think the Latinity of Johnson's language conduced to his
tranquillity, and she compares that tranquillity "with the stimulated and close emotion, the interior trouble, of those writers
who have entered as disciples in the school of the more Teutonic
English." (p. 326)

There is a vein of affectation in the author's complaints of our
working-day world, and in the ideal she holds up for admiration, of which, doubtless, she is guilty unawares. There is
no novelty in her argument. That all excess is allied to vulgarity, that the highest delights are the simplest, that moderation is a virtue in life as well as in art, and that it is our truest
wisdom to desire "plain living and high thinking," are familiar
truths which have been urged again and again, although never
in the peculiar style adopted by Mrs. Meynell. The author is
often thoughtful and occasionally witty, but the note of her
little volume is eccentricity, a characteristic not readily to be
tolerated either in life or in literature. (p. 327)

"Mrs. Meynell's Poetry and Prose," in The Spectator *(© 1893 by* The Spectator*), Vol. 70, No. 3376, March 11, 1893, pp. 326-27.*

EDMUND K. CHAMBERS (essay date 1896)

In attempting to analyse the impression which Mrs. Meynell's writing makes upon at least one reader, I shall not dwell at length upon her sex, and upon the fact that she is perhaps the first woman to make her way to the higher levels of criticism. . . . [Though] Mrs. Meynell is clearly touched by the fine issues which the problem of the future of her sex at this moment presents—we are grateful to her for her woman's protest against the gross defacement of woman by the pen of Dickens and the pencil of Leech—yet I think that she has always held herself characteristically aloof from the more revolutionary phases of the movement. That brave desire to arraign the whole of society as man has made it . . . could not be expected to evoke much but pity and amusement in the mind of one whose consciousness of the past is so strong, and who knows that, for women as for Americans, there is no beginning, but only a continuity. This, indeed, is the first point in Mrs. Meynell's critical temperament to which I would call attention. She has that sense of inheritance, of oneness with the past, which only liberal scholarship can give. (pp. 517-18)

[The] insistence on the literary point of honour, and a certain delicate psychology, define Mrs. Meynell's critical attitude. Of what is hackneyed she will have nothing; "habitualness," she says, "compels our refusals." Patent things, even patent truths, fail to arrest her; she prefers a more intimate, even if it be a lesser, truth; a truth that she can feel, that has some freshness about it, not a truth that she must merely accept and share. She will not willingly walk in the ways of common tread. Therefore she pushes analysis as far as it can be pushed, in the discrimination of subtle shades of sentiment, the exploration of secret distinctions which the blunter sense would disregard. And analysis frequently issues in paradox; a paradox, however, which is not often merely verbal, belonging, as it does, to the order of her thought and the structure of her material. For it is invariably truth itself that she seeks, and not the affectations of truth. No one, indeed, will prick you with more mordant wit the bubble of an affectation; the affectation, for instance, that finds pathos in what is really humorous, or the affectation of an impressionism that has no impressions worth recording. In this close power of penetration lies her delicate critical instrument; for in criticism, as in portraiture, it is the little touches that count, the barely noticeable curves and crow's-feet, that hold the secrets of mental history, and build up the ultimate ineffaceable personality. . . . Subtle herself, Mrs. Meynell demands some response of subtlety from her readers; she is difficult, because she is not facial. She is indeed unpardonable, because she requires, compels thought; compels even an effort of thought, grinds the edge of thought. And to-day we do not wish that thought should give us pause; we ask for books to satisfy easy mental processes, and not to awake complicated ones. (p. 518)

The subtlety of Mrs. Meynell's thinking determines also her vocabulary. She will not use synonyms as if they were equivalents, for she knows that usage is the deposit of history, and that cognate words have cognate, and not identical meanings. . . . Her words are not inanimate counters, but have their characters and their colours. The *epitheton constans* is no temptation to her, nor will she reproduce the second-hand quaintnesses of Wardour Street. Her tendency, indeed, is all to the Latin derivatives, so cool and quiet. . . . She seeks in style qualities that control rather than stimulate, is careless to cry aloud in the market-place, will not be clamant, and would rather have you not suspect the measure of her resources for the discretion of the art that conceals them. So that it will surprise you on analysis to find that she, who is never rhetorical, possesses and has used every artifice of rhetoric. (pp. 518-19)

[She] has the choicer equipment of a critic, the comprehensive experience of life and letters, the acute vision, the easy control of an exquisite medium. But from the absolute critics, the two or three who interpret to an age, more than this is required. Of such we ask in addition an unity, an organic unity, of purpose and of aim. Some fecund principle of thought, far-reaching in its scope, and bearing upon what is vital rather than what is accidental, this alone can give birth to a criticism that shall be creative, dynamic. For in the positive, not the negative pole of criticism, in its power to modify the old mental attitude and to suggest the new, must always lie its highest achievement. Nor can the operations of this principle be limited to any one department of human activity; on all alike, on art, on letters, on conduct, it will have its shaping word. Such a principle underlies Mrs. Meynell's work. It is rooted in a certain austere philosophy. "The half is better than the whole," cried the Greek; and Mrs. Meynell, too, solves many problems by her willingness to accept, and even appropriate the limitations of life. (p. 519)

Edmund K. Chambers, "Mrs. Meynell," in The Bookman, *New York, Vol. III, No. 6, August, 1896, pp. 516-19.*

GEORGE MEREDITH (essay date 1896)

[*The Rhythm of Life* and *The Colour of Life*] have, in these days of the overflow, the merit of saying just enough on the subject, leaving the reader to think. They can be read repeatedly, because they are compact and suggestive, and at the same time run with clearness. The surprise coming on us from their combined grace of manner and sanity of thought, is like one's dream of what the recognition of a new truth would be. . . . [Mrs. Meynell] has no pretensions to super-excellence, however confirmed her distastes. (pp. 762-63)

Her scorn, when it is roused, is lightly phrased, her wit glances, her irony is invisible, though it slays; and if she admires she withholds exclamations. Intemperateness, redundancy, the *ampoulé* and pretentious, are discarded by her, nor may her heroes be guilty. She cuts her way for herself through that wood to a precision never emphatic unless it be intentionally, for the signification; and this precision she contrives to render flexible, conversational even; she achieves the literary miracle of subordinating compressed choice language to grace of movement, an easy and pleasant flow until her theme closes. Her theme, too, is held in hand to be rolled out like the development of a sonnet. . . . The papers outside the descriptive and the critical are little sermons, ideal sermons—let no one uninstructed by them take fright at the title, they are not preachments; they are of the sermon's right length . . . , and keeping throughout to the plain step of daily speech, they leave a sense of stilled singing on the mind they fill. In all her writing we read off a brain that has found its untrammelled medium for utterance, with stores to deliver. Necessarily, where an intellect is at work, ours should be active, and we should know the roots of the words. She does not harp on a point; she pays her readers the compliment of assuming that they have intelligence. But she does not offer them puzzles. The writing is limpid in its depths.

By what strict discipline her task of preparation was done may be gathered in part from her Essay on *Composure* and on *Rejection.* They are lessons in the composition of sound and vibrant English, a sensitive English retaining dignity. Simple Saxon is too much a brawler; and emotion, imagination, the eye on things, will be shrouded by obtrusive Latin. . . . Mrs. Meynell's plea is not for a return to the learnedness of the old coining Divines, *bien entendu;* she pleads for the eighteenth century's happy refuge in the language of greater tranquillity, "Johnson's tranquillity," as an ethical need of our day. . . . Passion knows no tongue but plain Saxon with us. Mrs. Meynell's allusion is to the times for transmitting ideas, or summarily narrating events. . . . We are not, however, counselled to return to the Johnsonian stalk, the marching of words like men-at-arms in plated steel, under which the Saxon was a trampled stubble. . . . [By combining Saxon and Latin] our scholarly literature may get to a rhythm of life having the colour of life. (pp. 763-64)

Her eloquence is shown by repression with the effect. Occasionally, as in *The Lesson of Landscape, Sun, Cloud, Winds of the World,*—notably the great South-west—her hand is loosened. Her disposition is to a firm grasp of the reins, and her characteristic is everywhere the undertone. We have had our eminent masters of style. . . . Mrs. Meynell has much of Pyrrha's charm, the style correcting wealth and attaining to simplicity by trained art, the method unobtruded. Her probed diction has the various music in the irregular footing of prose, and if the sentences remind us passingly of the Emersonian shortness, they are not abrupt, they are smoothly sequent. It may be seen that she would not push for rivalry; the attraction is in her reserve. . . .

Her use of the undertone in the painting of a portrait, the sketching of a scene, is an artistic revelation. The few affirmative strokes placed among the retiring features of the Gentleman in a *Remembrance* surpass vividness in the impression. They make a Rembrandt canvas. The scene *At Monastery Gates,* soberly coloured as it is, remains with us; we are drawn by an allurement, that is not the writer's invitation, to share her feeling. She feels deeply, saying little. A funny incident occurring in the Monastery is related with an unformed smile, and the laughters are in it. Like the hero of her Portrait, she has "compassion on the multitude." The tenderness inspiring the thoughtfulness of the *Domus Angusta* is not stressed for an effect of pathos, but the reader's mind and heart are touched, enlarged, one may say with truth. (p. 765)

There is not the word of affectionateness [in the essays on children]; her knowledge and her maternal love of them are shown in her ready entry into the childish state and transcript of its germinal ideas, the feelings of the young,—a common subject for the sentimentalizing hand, from which nothing is gathered. Only deep love could furnish the intimate knowledge to expound them so. Perhaps the most poetic, most suggestive also, of the Essays in these two books is the one on *The Illusion of Historic Time,* treating of the child's views of historical events, illuminatingly and delightfully describing what the child has for his great possession in the early days, and what the man has lost, though not absolutely lost if he imagined when he was a child. . . . The Essay is in its essence a concentrated treatise on the imagination of childhood and the uses in nourishing it; a piece of work of more than the literary value for

which it is remarkable. It is work that philosophers may read with enlivenment; instructed, perhaps. (p. 766)

Through all Mrs. Meynell's writings there is an avoidance of superlatives. Rarely does she indulge in an interjection. One may gather that she would disrelish the title bestowed by enraptured reviewers on exceptionally brilliant gifts. . . . The power she has, and the charm it is clothed in, shall, then, be classed as distinction—the quality Matthew Arnold anxiously scanned the flats of earth to discover. . . . She has this distinction: the seizure of her theme, a fine dialectic, a pliable step, the feminine of strong good sense—equal, only sweeter,—and reflectiveness, humaneness, fervency of spirit. . . . A woman who thinks and who can write, who does not disdain the school of journalism, and who brings novelty and poetic beauty, the devout but open mind, to her practice of it, bears promise that she will some day rank as one of the great Englishwomen of Letters. . . . (pp. 769-70)

> *George Meredith, "Mrs. Meynell's Two Books of Essays," in* The National Review, *London, Vol. XXVII, No. 162, August, 1896, pp. 762-70.*

WILLIAM ARCHER   (essay date 1902)

Stern veracity, I fear, enforces the admission that few poetesses of the past have shown a very highly developed faculty for strict poetical form. I am not aware that the works of any woman in any modern language are reckoned among the consummate models of metrical style. . . . [Ladies] as a rule seem to have aimed at a certain careless grace rather than a strenuous complexity or accuracy of metrical structure.

In respect of accuracy, though not of complexity, Mrs. Meynell is one of the rare exceptions to this rule. Within a carefully limited range, her form is unimpeachable. Her grace is often exquisite, but never careless. She never strays beyond two or three simple iambic or trochaic measures, and her most elaborate stanza (the sonnet excepted) is one of five lines, with rhyme-scheme either *a a b b a* or *a b a b a.* Dactylic and anapæstic rhythms and intricate rhyme-patterns she altogether eschews. The sonnet in its strictest form she writes with real accomplishment; but the sonnet is really a very easy mould to fill. . . . The strict form is far more of a support than a burden. It serves as stays to a flaccid thought. It provides, so to speak, a ready-made effect of climax and antithesis, while a very little care in ordering the rhymes and distributing the pauses of the sestett will give it a highly creditable air of technical mastery. It is this amiable duplicity, if one may call it so, on the part of the sonnet—this apparent difficulty and real ease of manipulation—that has secured its vogue. I do not mean that it is easy to write sonnets as good as some of Mrs. Meynell's, but merely that her success in the sonnet form does not invalidate the remark that her metrical ambitions are carefully and judiciously limited.

Within the limits she has assigned herself, her accomplishment is real and delightful. There is scarcely a jarring note in all her measures; her rhymes, without purism, are true rhymes to the cultivated ear; and she habitually attains distinction-in-simplicity of phrase. Her diction is absolutely unaffected. There is not, in her little book of *Poems,* a single word dragged in for its own sake. Far be it from me to sneer at the poets who ransack the treasure-house of the language for jewels wherewith to encrust the hieratic vesture of their thought; but an exquisite simplicity is, in its way, at least as beautiful, and (to use the word without the slightest shade of disparagement) far more characteristically feminine. (pp. 264-65)

There is not a poem of Mrs. Meynell's that is not marked by [an] unobtrusive grace—a quality which, if the word could be divested of its unfortunate eighteenth-century associations, one would like to call elegance. At the same time, one cannot but feel that Mrs. Meynell's verse does but scant justice to her intellectual gifts. It is deficient, not only in dramatic, but in pictorial quality; it interprets a very narrow range of experience; and the thoughts it expresses are pretty rather than luminous or searching, ingenious rather than relevant or real. The charm of the poems . . . lies in the discreetly sincere expression of personal feeling; but the very discretion of these utterances condemns them to a certain monotony; and beyond personal feeling, into the regions of observation and speculation, the poetess seldom strays. But her essays have proved her capable of very keen observation and of real substantive thought, as opposed to mere air-drawn fantasy. One finds in her prose a far wider range of vision and faculty, a larger and deeper knowledge both of nature and of life, than is anywhere evidenced in her verse. Turn, for instance, to *A Letter from a Girl to her own Old Age,* one of her longest poems. The idea is ingenious, but the verses say little or nothing. There is charming sentiment, but practically no thought in them. One feels that the authoress of *The Rhythm of Life* would find something far more interesting to say were she now to approach the theme afresh. (pp. 267-68)

The truth is, of course, that her prose represents Mrs. Meynell's maturer experience and thought, her verse the emotion and sentiment of her girlhood. . . . It is not at all wonderful that a girl should write like a girl; the wonder is that a very young woman should possess the technical skill which is apparent throughout these poems. My regret, then, is not that the verses of "early youth" should express "transitory and early thoughts," but that the "verses written in maturer years" should be so few. (pp. 269-70)

> *William Archer, "Mrs. Meynell," in his* Poets of the Younger Generation, *John Lane, 1902 (and reprinted by Scholarly Press, 1969), pp. 164-70.*

G. K. CHESTERTON   (essay date 1911?)

I was recently re-reading some of the very small but very great essays of that great lady, Alice Meynell. I was much struck by a certain truth, for which she stood against very formidable antagonists, and which she triumphantly demonstrated in these little papers, often hardly longer than paragraphs. It is rather difficult to express; like so many truths that she expressed easily. It might be called the sentimentalism of the cynic; or, more correctly, the melodrama of the man of the world. It is the fact that the mere man of the world, when he lumps things together, always really groups them together by a convention like that of melodrama. He speaks so hastily that he always uses stock terms and therefore stale terms. He is none the less the dupe of romances because he refuses to take a romantic view of romances. But an unworldly woman like the woman poet I have named is not in any sense a romanticist. The unworldly woman is a realist; because she is a psychologist. Most people who talk about psychology probably do not remember the name of Psyche or remember that her emblem was the butterfly and her name the soul.

In one essay, Mrs. Meynell remarks that it grieves her greatly to have to contradict Thackeray. As a matter of fact, she is

perpetually contradicting Thackeray. . . . [She] was contradicting the whole of that attitude of tolerant and masculine scepticism which marks the man who has, indeed, seen much, but who has learnt to generalise much too easily. The experienced traveller who will tell you offhand what Chinks or niggers are like; the experienced man of pleasure who will tell you offhand what women are like; the experienced politician who will tell you offhand what crowds are like, because he only meets crowds, and never meets people—these were the spirits against which Mrs. Meynell was really waging ceaseless war till the day of her death. She was always interested in the intimate and individual story. Thackeray was always content to say that it was the old story. He meant that it was the ordinary story; but Mrs. Meynell had no difficulty in showing that it was really the ordinary made-up story. (pp. 176-77)

[There] is a far more complex and unexpected sort of psychology in the scenes of real life.

It was exactly that sort of complex and unexpected psychology that was the speciality of Alice Meynell's works. (p. 180)

> *G. K. Chesterton, "Contradicting Thackeray" (1911?), in his* Lunacy and Letters *(© Dorothy Collins, 1958; reprinted by permission of Miss D. E. Collins), Sheed and Ward, 1958, pp. 176-81.**

AGNES REPPLIER   (essay date 1923)

It is hard to think of Mrs. Meynell as even a beatified newspaper writer. Her genius does not seem to have been of the order which rejoices an editor's heart, or wins the careless approval of a hurried and preoccupied public. But she brought to bear upon journalism the quality of conscientious care which distinguished all her work, the clean-cut thoughts in clean-cut, polished sentences. It seemed to her worth while to write with this precision, and she was eminently wise. When Mr. Cust organized in the *Pall Mall Gazette* the daily columns known as "The Wares of Autolycus," he intrusted each column to the care of a distinguished woman author, who once a week produced a set of "Wares," differing widely from the assortment of her contemporaries, but of an unvaried excellence. There was not a writer on the staff who did not take a keen personal pride in this work; and the result was that happy combination of journalism and literature which to the French seems a matter of course, but which English and Americans are apt to consider as a forced and unnatural alliance.

The Friday column of "Autolycus" was contributed by Mrs. Meynell, and many of the papers were reprinted in the volumes of selected essays which she deemed worthy of preservation. (p. 722)

Mrs. Meynell was . . . essentially modern. . . . She could reproduce with absolute fidelity the medieval note, as in **"San Lorenzo Giustiniani's Mother"**; but, left to her own imaginings, she brought every subject up to date. That strange pacifist poem, **"Parentage,"** is a case in point; and so are the lines on **"Saint Catherine of Siena."** In the first she exalts the childless man, the barren woman, over those stronger, simpler mortals whose sons go down into the sea in ships, or hold their country's gates against the oppressor. . . . In the second she uses the beautiful old story of St. Catherine's triumphant struggle for the soul of the young patrician condemned to death, as an argument for woman suffrage. (p. 723)

Mrs. Meynell's childhood and youth were singularly fitted to equip her for her life's work. From her father, a man of "reticent virtues'' and wide cultivation, she acquired her literary tastes, her intellectual serenity. Part of her early life was spent in Italy, which she knew, and loved, and understood. (p. 724)

A convert to the Catholic Church, married to another convert, living in London, writing for English newspapers, she preserved inviolate the raptures of her wandering childhood, the secluded and delicate pleasures of the intellect, the clear flame of the spiritual life. (p. 725)

Mrs. Meynell's essays suffer from undue brevity, a brevity doubtless entailed by journalism. They are no shorter than were the eighteenth-century essays; but they are more critical, and criticism calls for scope. Moreover, the eighteenth-century essayists, when they wanted to be exhaustive, carried a subject through a half-dozen or a dozen papers, until the picture was rounded and complete. Mrs. Meynell's papers are for the most part snatches of thought, expressed in carefully and admirably chosen words. She was, in the best sense of the term, a *précieuse,* valuing the manner of the saying as highly as she valued the thing said. (p. 727)

Mrs. Meynell's literary sympathies are many and finely chosen. They never fail, save when her profoundly unhumorous mind is forced to the contemplation of a profoundly humorous writer like Jane Austen. All the distances that can be imagined, distances of time and space, of centuries and continents, are too narrow to reflect the measureless gap between these two English ladies. A conscientious effort to do justice to Miss Austen is a waste of good intentions. She is the solace and delight of our lives, or she is nothing. Mrs. Meynell, in an essay upon Thomas Lovell Beddoes, says that he "lacked humor." He certainly did. . . . But it is possible to write flawless lyrics without a sense of humor, and it is not possible to criticize Jane Austen's novels. Mrs. Meynell finds the art of *Emma* and *Persuasion* to be of "an admirable secondary quality," and their derision to be "caricature of a rather gross sort." . . .

Yet Mrs. Meynell understood and relished the more robust humor of Dickens, the humor which creates a type and holds it. I know of no such perfect comment as her brief description of Pecksniff—"a bright image of heart-easing comedy." This is so exactly what he is, and what Dickens should have permitted him to remain. (p. 728)

When Mrs. Meynell visited the United States, she lectured on Dickens as a master of words. It was a novel point of view. A master of style he certainly was not. . . . But the lecturer made good her point, showing over and over again, with admirably selected illustrations, that Dickens invariably chose the one and only word which exactly expressed his meaning. (p. 729)

Scattered richly through Mrs. Meynell's prose and verse, are brief, exquisite passages, recording a single impression, like the strange "November blue" of the lamp-lit, mist-wreathed London streets; a single conception, like the playfulness of children and kittens at the hour of dusk; a single insight, like the comprehensive pity for the man whose mean estate has denied him his share of the solitude which should be the common possession of mankind. And back of her graceful, austere, and beautifully finished work, are the steadfast strength, the crystalline sweetness of religion. All her delicate processes of thought spring from that sure foundation, and reach upward into imperishable light. (p. 730)

> Agnes Repplier, "Alice Meynell," in Catholic World,
> Vol. CXVI, No. 696, March, 1923, pp. 721-30.

OLIVIA HOWARD DUNBAR   (essay date 1923)

"The Rhythm of Life," "The Colour of Life"—these are happy titles, not chosen vaguely for their sound, but because they are precisely descriptive of their author's preoccupations. Absence of any conventional approach seems a positive grace. She arrives at her delicate impressions and analyses with the directness of a mathematician. Another writer, offering a mere page or two on such themes as "The Sun," "The Rain," could hardly escape seeming artfully artless. But it is only necessary to read a sentence to perceive that there is no trace here of deliberate wise-eyed wistfulness. Alice Meynell does not write at all until she has an authentic original impression to convey. And she conveys it with an individual and severe simplicity that is beyond praise, a simplicity that one can't imagine being either imitated or parodied. These are, of course, the attributes of a classic. . . .

Though she could write unabashed and wisely on universal things, it would, of course, be absurd to claim that she was a universal artist. But there were two worlds wherein she seemed to function without handicap or limitation. One was the world of field and sky and one the world of children. . . .

To insist, as one must, that her touch is firm and sure and perfect with a Greek perfection when she is noting the movement of a cloud or the speech of a child is perhaps to suggest that there are occasions when her line is less confident and precise. I think this is true. Yet she has a score of triumphs outside the limits I have mentioned. [There] is an admirable disquisition on "The Audience." And she is uncontrovertible, if rather merciless, in pointing out "the obsession of man by the flower"—in its inordinate use, she means, as an element of design. "In the shape of the flower his own paltriness revisits him."

But she did at times, move in directions where one follows her with a cooled rapture. The truth may be that when she ceases to function strictly as an artist she becomes another and considerably less important figure. In her critical work one misses not, of course, her gift of words, but her charm and the extraordinary balance that she characteristically has. She leans too far. It is true that we owe much to her generous enthusiasm. . . . But her expressed ardors have the effect of prejudices. It is scarcely possible to follow all her adulation of Dickens or to find illumination in her singling out of Lowell as the only American man of letters. . . . Her depreciation of Swinburne seems no less excessive than her praise of Patmore, whose voice she found "the voice less of a poet than of the very muse."

This extravagance in regard to Patmore does constitute, it is true, a special case. Between these two there was, of course, an uncommon accord. It wasn't merely that they were both Catholic poets—or that Patmore had called her, as well he might, "a woman of genius." But they were both aristocrats by temperament, both capable of enormous disdains and arrogances and exclusions. Alice Meynell was far freer than her older friend from the vices of this temperament, although I don't doubt that she too, may be detected in little British snobberies. . . .

No doubt, it will make for the permanence of her work that it is so utterly unviolated by any reference to the currents of her own day, political or other. It is easy to infer that her own conceptions were completely unmodern. She could as well have happened in one century as another. And, advocate as she was of reticence and austerity, her own century, whenever it might be, would doubtless fail to respond to her temperate expression. She is the type of artist of whom it is always left for some later century to make a cult.

Olivia Howard Dunbar, "Alice Meynell's Prose," in The Literary Review, *June 16, 1923, p. 763.*

J. C. SQUIRE   (essay date 1923)

[Mrs. Meynell's style is] personal without parade of personality, beautiful without parade of ornament, a style at its best approaching perfection. . . . Mrs. Meynell's prose is always clear; where her verse is at first sight difficult it is only so from the rapid flight of her thought. She had few mannerisms; an excessive fondness for a certain company of euphonious words, such as "uncovenanted" and "alien," may be noted as the chief of them. Nor are echoes, traces of derivation, often encountered in her work. No essayist altogether avoids falling at times into the accents of a previous essayist. When, very rarely, another voice mingles with Mrs. Meynell's it is seldom the elsewhere ubiquitous accents of the Lambs and the Hazlitts that we hear, but the older tones of [Francis] Bacon. . . . The affinity was natural with Bacon, whose prose was so frugal and close, and yet so beautiful; but if sometimes she borrowed a shape the content was always hers still. Usually her prose, free though it was from tricks, was unmistakably hers, and incontrovertibly good. It was, as was inevitable when a passion for accuracy and compression was united with a fastidious ear, fertile in striking and charming phrases. Discussing the raving tragedies of the time, she says "The eighteenth century stuck straws in its periwig"; such felicities came to her easily. With her, however, they grew out of their contexts; she was no phrase-maker in the ordinary sense, though many of her best passages are webs of good phrases. (pp. 111-12)

Mrs. Meynell's work had its limitations. She was aware of them, and some of them were imposed by her own will. She was one kind of writer and not another kind: an admiration for her does not preclude a still greater admiration for more voluminous artists like Dickens and more careless artists like Shakespeare. None of her writings is long: her aim was to compress all she could into a lyric or a few pages of prose, inspired by a thing seen and deeply felt or by some flash of vision into the ways of life. She never made the slightest effort to adapt herself to an audience; she would not withhold her knowledge, or modify her vocabulary, or win attention by facile confidences. She had a great passion for Dr. Johnson, but she could not have borne to brandish a bludgeon herself. She loved Falstaff and the broadest pages of Dickens, but her own works might be searched in vain for a single sentence which might be termed rollicking. . . . That was her way— the way of quietness and moderation. She moved "in captive flight". . . . Inclination and theory reinforced each other: she was inclined that way, and a decivilised world needed examples of restraint and care. One says a "world"; but she had no illusions about the narrowness of her direct appeal. She was writing with all the veracity of which she was capable, and using, consequently, all the education she possessed and every response she felt: the result was naturally a product only to be completely understood and appreciated by a public which was accustomed to fine distinctions, which would not miss her frequent allusions, and which could relish the precision of her language. What influence she could exercise would be chiefly indirect; it could not be helped, and she had no hankering at all for a more public platform. For all her restraint and her pains of craftsmanship, however, expression always remained

a means to her. What she wished to say still remained the dominant thing: the instrument was an instrument to an end. Here she differed in a marked degree from some of those moderns who have set themselves to make "emaux et camées," and who have ended by worshipping the picture, the cadence, and the word. Her style never became a Narcissus admiring himself in a pool. Casual readers sometimes thought her "precious"; no careful reader possibly could. She loathed the slipshod, but she regarded meretricious ornament with equal disgust; she refused to use a loose word but she disdained to use an affected word; under her firm surface was the fire of humanity. (pp. 115-18)

J. C. Squire, "Alice Meynell," in his Essays on Poetry *(reprinted by permission of the Estate of the author),* Hodder and Stoughton, 1923, pp. 98-121.

ANNE KIMBALL TUELL   (essay date 1925)

Mrs. Meynell's whole study of childhood [contained in *The Children, Childhood, Ceres' Runaway,* and *Children of the Old Masters*] is a considerable proportion among her essays. The *Pall Mall Gazette,* proud of its sponsorship, made for her a considerable claim: "It may almost be said of Mrs. Meynell that she has newly created the child in literature. . . . Hers may almost be called the 'new child'." It is best not to accept the superlative assertion of the *Pall Mall.* But if there is in any sense a "new child" in the nineties, he is the child as Mrs. Meynell perceives him.

He is intended to be "the real child," not—so to say—touched up. And so far he is new indeed; for literature has usually known the child mind heightened or colored or feelingly considered in adult regard. . . . Most frequent, in fiction at least, is the child created to constrain our pity, foreordained to patience and slaughter that our tenderness may indulge itself without confine. Such were always favourites. . . . There has been besides the more lugubrious and subtle pathos recognised by Mrs. Meynell—pity for "the child predestined not to die but to live." . . . (pp. 139-40)

The "new child" of the nineties was coming to be a subject sufficient unto himself, with a psychology and dignity of his own. (p. 141)

To take [a child's mind] seriously was to take it simply, just to see it alone, "when it is in no way displayed." The quotation is from the criticism of Mrs. Meynell in *Merry England* upon [Robert Louis] Stevenson. And to Stevenson, if to anyone, she would have ascribed the new creature. . . . [In a *Child's Garden of Verses*], as well as in the adventuring stories of the . . . treasure-seekers, she found "the simplicity of character and enterprise in day-dreaming of the real boy." . . . Of the same blood come the innumerable company of "real" children who have filed by in procession ever since, led by their knowing friends who have known enough to be respectful. Most courteous in some ways, most void of offensive "condescension" have been the unpretentious essays of Mrs. Meynell. She has waited in patience upon the opening consciousness of these young spirits, without forcing, without impertinence.

She drew, of course, a little from her early memories. . . . Her own childhood gave the clue. But for the most part she speaks from the one remove or the less than one remove of motherhood. (pp. 141-43)

Mrs. Meynell went joyously about her observations, without "pathos," recording, as she said of E. N. Shaw, "the gayest little facts.'' An unreprinted sketch, **"The Nursery,"** is full of memories—of long minutes wasted in choice among ''confectionary plums,'' of special signs without words understood between mother and nursery. . . .

She has watched the slow beginnings of the personal life. (p. 143)

With closer inspiration Mrs. Meynell has recaptured for us the greater intensity of the child's experience within the narrow range, his acuteness of sense and freshness of perception quite beyond our adult powers of recovery. (p. 144)

With a delicacy which will not press or handle, Mrs. Meynell respects the strange and baffling separateness of the child mind from our own alien habits, revealed now and then in some startling childish answer. From their distance we catch hints of a separate and special code of signals imperceptible to experienced minds. . . . And nobody has done better than Mrs. Meynell for the inscrutable age of twelve as she shows it in **"The Boy."**

Deepest perhaps is her compassionate understanding for the young will untaught in the uses of necessity. . . . Wistful in a beautiful comprehension is her watch over ''the child of tumult,'' the gusty spirit not yet prepared for its own danger. . . . (pp. 145-46)

Mrs. Meynell has ample time besides for the unready wit in a world too quick for its laggard mental pace. For the child mind, she tells us, does not, like its flitting body, take trips for the third part of a minute. It moves halting, making what unwieldy way it can amid the intricacies of life and a still more intricate grammar. (p. 146)

Eagerly too she defends the child from the adult zeal to amuse him. . . . [He] is not, Mrs. Meynell insists, essentially humorous. Why must we then be always busy ''to offer humour to those by no means trivial eyes?'' (pp. 146-47)

Her witness is valuable to the homely common sense of children, ignored in the popular insistence upon their fancy. . . . Characteristic is her protest at the pretty game played by the audience at the end of *Peter Pan*, wherein the children are called upon to declare their faith in fairies—''a game of men and women at the expense of children.'' For children, Mrs. Meynell is bold to assert, do not spend their time . . . listening to elves. They are tirelessly fertile in pretence to be sure. But they know what they are doing. The children of her knowledge are not friends of fancy but friends of fact.

Childhood remains to her, none the less, a mystery visited by revelation. Here is another witness, valid because unsentimental, to the inner sight of privileged children. Mrs. Meynell's kinship is with [Thomas] Traherne, who celebrated in simplicity and in philosophy a childhood of spiritual powers. . . . She remembers too with Wordsworth the exultation of the child's soul over ''beauty at its daybreak in the dark,'' recalling the childish sense for hillsides in wild flower, calm summer seas, and ''fields unprofaned.'' She derives from the boy Dante poetry's highest reach of spiritual love. (pp. 147-48)

[The] children of Mrs. Meynell are not oppressed by the weight of their immortalities. Theirs is a reality of flesh. And she finds them the more exquisite as the more real. . . . [Against] the old tradition of the child as diminished man, she sets in modern wise the frolic beauty in the real childish proportions, as Reynolds saw them: ''the irregularity of profile which is in fact a

child's regularity, the homeliness of the large head which is the child's elegance. . . .'' Early and late, too, she throws her gauge against Raphael ''who imposed the formula of grace upon all Europe.'' The child of grace, at least, is nowhere found in the pages of Mrs. Meynell. Her child, the true child, is never posed at all. He stands upon both feet, in ''stable equilibrium,'' taking what grip he can of the earth. (pp. 148-49)

The descriptive writings of Mrs. Meynell form that part of her work best known to the running reader. One is surprised to discover that of her complete product they represent but a slight proportion—so special is their quality and so considerable their number in the reprinted essays. Here, we may be sure, is something for which she singularly cared. She loved these memories of the wayfaring vision, these gleams of lights and waters.

Perhaps they achieve no less than the vindication of that old-fashioned thing, word-painting as an art form. The theorizers like to remind us that the days of descriptive writing are over. . . . [We shall not] find it any more alive than in the pages of Mrs. Meynell.

It is the art of a fine strung impressionism, as Mrs. Meynell understood the meaning of that unhappy word. We get her theory in a chance comment upon her sister, Lady Butler, ''She has, though not the method, yet the spirit of impressionism, in her instant and insistent grasp of the passing fact.'' She gives us more, therefore, than is commonly achieved of real sensation, with a memory caring far more for sense than for sentiment. (pp. 150-51)

Mrs. Meynell is felt always a presence in control. Each sketch is the product of alertness. Here is no mere drift of unrelated details, but a sure intention, able to heighten without the intrusion of a too intimate emotion.

We are far indeed from what Mrs. Meynell calls ''the extreme explicatory labour'' of a Ruskin, his over-courteous attention to the limitations of his reader lest we miss the entirety of his vision. Hers is the selectiveness of the fine impressionism—for in speaking of Mrs. Meynell one cannot without pedantry avoid the habit which she always deplored and frequently followed, of speaking of one art in terms of another. The friend and critic of painters, she might have been, had she chosen, . . . herself a painter of distinction—so extraordinary was her gift to perceive what she saw, to catch as swiftly as sunshine its salient places, to detect only with the emphasis of the perceiving eye. . . . Her little sketches are all tipped with ''instancy,'' the higher detection. Sentences taken almost at random have the effect of light suddenly shaken upon shady places.

Here is the fine vitality of a most rich sensation. One gets from her words a poignancy as of an incorrupt noble savagery seldom indeed to be recaptured among our urban habits and satieties. Or rather perhaps we might say that she has managed to preserve the stringency of the child's experience which we faintly remember as now torment and now delight. . . . Whatever the impression, her words prick a dulled memory for the actual pulse of things. (pp. 151-52)

Anne Kimball Tuell, in her Mrs. Meynell and Her Literary Generation, *E. P. Dutton & Company, 1925, 286 p.*

JOHN DRINKWATER (essay date 1925)

[*Preludes*] contained thirty-seven poems, and it shows the poet already in the full maturity of her powers. It is, indeed, difficult to think of any English poet who in early youth has published a book in which the fulfilment of design is so complete. Other poets in their first efforts may have had a more universal, perhaps a more passionate aim, but none has subdued his intention, whatever it might be, to a more perfect mastery. The workmanship of the book is exact and unfailing from the first page to the last, and although in the poems that were to come later there was no falling away from the exquisite standard set in the beginning, there could be no development of an art that seemed to have had no probation days. . . . *Preludes* at once displays the characteristics that have become familiar to the poet's admirers. Its general mood is one of affectionate resignation, with neither bitterness nor even regret. Throughout there is a spiritual humility that reminds us how little of true pride there is in the common self-assertions. There is here a surrender of soul, but it is consciously a surrender of something so rare and lovely that it can be made only to a supremely imagined purity. The poet is humble only because of the divine company in which she moves. This accounts for the fact that one note for which we commonly look in the poetry of youth, that of revolt, is entirely absent from *Preludes*. Anger and protest and denunciation, those ardours of rebellion that stir most generous young minds as they first realize the tyrannies of a stupid world, were nothing to this poet, who, however she might look upon the vulgar errors of society, could not conceive of them as food for the imagination. Not that she was careless of these errors on the one hand, or that her poetry was mere placidity on the other—nothing could be wider off the mark than to suppose either of these things. She took always a very practical, and even argumentative, interest in the thousand ways in which man teases and confounds himself in the ordering of his communities, but these were matters for the tea-table, not for the seclusions of art. (pp. 156-58)

Looking within this general mood, we may detect certain qualities of mind that were peculiarly Alice Meynell's own. First, perhaps, of these is an amazing gift for capturing with a phrase the most elusive turns of thought, for arresting the cloud shadows of emotions as they pass over the mind and giving them solid intellectual form. This was a faculty that she shared with her beloved seventeenth-century lyrists, with Donne and Crashaw and Vaughan, but in actual deftness of its exercise I think she excelled them all. Such poets as those, perhaps, burnt more fiercely than she, and were even more curious in spiritual skill, but none of them gave difficult thought so lucid a simplicity of statement. (pp. 158-59)

Together with this power of saying exactly what we might have supposed could not have been said even nebulously, a power constant in Alice Meynell's poetry, is the less rare but not less admirable power of sending tides of imaginative suggestion through a plain statement. . . . (p. 160)

Alice Meynell, writing but little, never wrote insignificantly, and each of her few poems presents its own attractive problems; but already in her first book certain themes are recurrent, and certain distinctions of style assert themselves. The communion of a mind with its other self, sometimes moving in its own recesses, sometimes in the person of a friend or lover, is one of her favourite preoccupations. It is to be found in *The Young Neophyte*, *The Visiting Sea*, and the *Girl's Letter*. . . . (p. 163)

This sense of an intimacy, a mystical understanding, that makes many things—perhaps, in the philosophic conclusion of the matter, all things—one, is, together with the instinct for surrender in service to some divine wisdom that alone can command service from a spirit so rare, the prevailing mood com-

municated by *Preludes*, and indeed by the later poems as well. "A poet of one mood in all my lays," she says, of herself we must suppose, and shapes of the world are subjected, in all their variety, to the influence of this mood, which is rightly the way of poetry. (p. 164)

Already the manner had that curious fastidiousness that was to mark it always, and to mark it apart. It was a manner rarely compounded, reticent, and yet precise and uncompromising in statement, shunning every kind of emphasis, and yet of the most lucid and ringing accent, shy of rich colours in diction, and yet making hard and prosaic phrases flush and glow with unexpected light. (p. 165)

Lyric poetry could hardly be simpler . . . , and at the same time it could hardly be subtler, or even more complex. . . . For a young poet so proudly of tradition, and so spiritually akin to one age at least of English verse, there is a surprising absence of apparent influences upon the actual phrasing of the poems. (p. 166)

[In Meynell's *Collected Poems*] small in size as the product of a long life, made up almost entirely of short lyrics, and yet very close and exacting in substance, there is hardly a stanza or even a line that the severest critical judgment would wish away. And yet of the work after 1875 there is little that is essential to be said that might not as well have been suggested by the first volume. The delight never fails, but it is not the less eagerly welcomed because it is not a new delight. It is the measure of Alice Meynell's excellence as a poet that after we know a dozen of her poems we feel that there is no possible further chance of novelty from her, and yet that there will never be a failure of complete and arresting originality. The more familiar we become with her work the more do we want it to go on being just what it is without change. In the later books the poetic life of *Preludes* is modified here and emphasized there, but no more, and we would not have it otherwise. On the whole there is, perhaps, a little more to question—that is to say, we are pulled up once in fifty pages now instead of once in seventy as before. Every now and again, very rarely, we wonder whether the intellectual deftness and the balanced mastery of language are not playing half a trick with the poet. One of her most celebrated lyrics is the [*Cradle-Song at Twilight*]. . . . It is idle to praise a thing so exquisitely done; the mastery is plain at once. And yet is there in its nature something not false but capricious, capricious in the presence of truth? Has the delight in saying a thing so beautifully for once led the poet from imagination to make-believe? (pp. 167-69)

Among the later poems are a few pieces that are more definitely occasional in character than anything in the first book, *November Blue*, *A Dead Harvest*, and *The Watershed*, for example, but they are all beautifully done. . . . Here and there is a touch of more explicit humour than we had found before. . . . (pp. 171-72)

We find sometimes, too, a more objective mood asserting itself, directed now upon problems of literary criticism, producing the specialized kind of poetry that William Watson has done so well, and in which Alice Meynell is certainly his equal, and again upon problems and aspects of modern civilization, as in the lovely and rather unexpected *Threshing Machine*. But for the most part the poetry of the later years is with that of the earlier, both in its concerns and in its methods. We have the same slow gracious movement of the verse, the same limpidity of phrase, the same fixed and piercing vision. . . . The line "She is so circumspect and right" might almost stand in a phrase as the key to Alice Meynell's style. It is the style always of a poet who possessed her soul and her imagination, one who was in the great line of English lyrists, and yet stamping personality upon every word she wrote. (pp. 172-74)

> *John Drinkwater, "The Poetry of Alice Meynell,"*
> *in his* The Muse in Council, *Sidgwick and Jackson*
> *Limited, 1925, pp. 153-74.*

OSBERT BURDETT (essay date 1926)

[Mrs. Meynell's poem **"Renouncement"** is] the one poem which will always be quoted from her. . . . To be identified with one work, in this sense, is to have attained the certainty of reputation. It is the most simple test, and the best. To revive the freshness of this familiar piece, let us note first that it is a sonnet, and secondly how it grew under her hand. The sonnet is properly the favourite form of the smaller poets. It is the favourite form because it is the shortest metrical scheme yet acclimatized to English prosody. While the great poets, like Wordsworth, have been the greatest masters of the sonnet, the poets of the second rank, like Rossetti, have done well, even excellently, in this form. Its narrowness is a quality, not a defect. . . . [Alice Meynell's] quality is a perfection of integrity which needs a small compass to display itself. Thus **"Renouncement"** suggests her range and is an instance of its quality. (pp. 101-02)

A small compass implies intensity, and intensity, together with a small compass, implies an absence of vitality in the larger sense. If we turn to the drawing by Sargent which adorns the volume of **Collected Poems,** what do we see? We see a tall, slender figure, the stem, as it were, of a delicate, refined face, a face a little weary, as if it were masked with the ashes of a fire which had wasted the spirit within. The distinction, the beauty, is apparent, but there is the sense, often to be observed in an aristocratic face, of the end, of the weariness of a long road, most of which lies behind the traveller. The thread which binds the sheaf of Mrs. Meynell's verses is a thread of sadness. . . . [Her] mind is preoccupied with tragic moments, moments bravely borne no doubt, but requiring bravery to bear them. Life is a burden to this poetess, not a joy. It imposes too great a strain upon her nerves. She has to brace herself to live, and is less conscious of life than of the daily price to be paid for living. In a poem entitled **"The Modern Mother,"** the mother hopes not for the love of her son but for his "forgiveness." Had she not bestowed upon him the tragic present of life? Again, in **"Parentage,"** a poem written before the War, we are told that women who bear children are the real slayers, because war and disease prey upon living things and everything which is born is led to the slaughter. The experiences which move her most, and the poignancy of which she uses all the resources of her art to prevent us from losing, are tragic, cruel moments; and these she contemplates with the fascination of a magnet to its pole. (pp. 102-03)

[It] is hardly too much to say that her imagination was only awakened fully by the spectacle of suffering, and when she sings it is in elegy. **"The Letter of a Girl to her own Old Age,"** with its long line of lamentation and the skilful droop of the feminine endings, is characteristic; and yet, if the spectacle of suffering were offered to her in its nakedness, as Mestrovic offered it to us all in his "Crucifixion," I fancy that she would turn away her eyes and declare that it was not bearable. Such a turning away I should regard as evidence of the truth of this criticism. We do turn away when we see

ourselves face to face. Consequently Mrs. Meynell must place herself slightly at an oblique angle, and view the moments which possess her mind a little from one side. She shoots beside the mark rather than at it; and her arrows, like the bright glances of the robin, fly the straighter because they seem to spy their object from one side. This gave a bird-like quality to her writing, which is at once intense but detached.

We gain from her work, then, this: not, at first, an extension of our humanity but an added sharpness to our consciousness. But in so far as this consciousness is concerned with experiences not peculiar in themselves, but common to all men, it is enriching. The experience of Strephon in **"St. Catharine of Siena"** is an experience of mankind; Catharine herself is feminine humanity. Hackneyed or official themes are transformed by this insight. . . . [The] death of Edith Cavell is seen as perhaps Edith herself saw it: a nurse who watched at her own death-bed, a woman who quietly waited for the dawn. We penetrate beyond the heroine of the copy-book to the natural woman, and go with her to her execution. This is the quality which raises Mrs. Meynell's verse to the highest point possible to its own order. Each poem, too, is carefully reasoned, and the reader who does not follow the argument will miss the whole; for intellectually no less than emotionally the verse has point. This intellectual concentration is a dangerous quality. **"Via et Veritas et Vita"** is an epigram, but a good one. **"Veni Creator"** and **"Why wilt Thou Chide?"** seem, or seem near to, intellectual conceits. The latter poem apparently offers an impossibly subtle consolation. Renunciation, consolation—how the theme recurs!

The limits of this poetry are sharply defined, and the substance is the clearer for them. That substance is true and genuine, but it is not gay or great. Joy is a quality of strength, and only in the great poets is intensity wholly free from tensity. The edge of a refined intelligence which we carry away from our reading has been gained by a tension of the nerves, which are robbed of some of their tone by the strain imposed upon them. We cannot repose upon this poetry. It is a tonic rather than a wine. It is life at its most intense, rather than at its highest, which we find here. For life at its highest is pure joy; at the centre of joy there is peace; and genius is too simple to be unhappy. (pp. 106-07)

> *Osbert Burdett, "The Poems of Alice Meynell," in*
> *his* Critical Essays *(reprinted by permission of Faber*
> *and Faber Ltd.), Henry Holt and Company, 1926,*
> *pp. 98-108.*

JOSEPH J. REILLY (essay date 1932)

"I think," wrote William Ernest Henley to Alice Meynell, "that you would write well about a broomstick." From the outspoken and exacting Henley this was rare praise. . . . [Henley was] sensitive to what are taken to be the infallible marks of true poets in their prose: the presence of imagination, aptness of metaphor, economy of phrase, and unfailing sense of the right word. And by "right" is to be understood not only precise but (to borrow Walter Pater's fine phrase), rich in second intentions.

Mrs. Meynell never wrote about anything so prosaic as Henley's broomstick, but of her varied subjects, many are a part of everyday: children, clouds, horizons, wells, flower designs in domestic art, laughter, hours of sleep, the reflection of stars in streams, and grass, that universal vagrant, which grows up unwanted among the flagstones of cities and upon ruined cornices. These subjects seem commonplace enough but Mrs. Meynell looked upon them with a vision as unspoiled as Wordsworth's and endowed them with freshness, novelty, and a new and exquisite meaning. (pp. 195-96)

Mrs. Meynell learned, as only a poet can, the mystery and the music of words. With an almost infallible sense of primary meanings and rich implications she sought and found those that stirred with life and carried the pulses of thought to the remote parts of her sentences. Words in groups, ready-made phrases fit for the facile employ of modern journalism, found no place in her work. Her essays are brief, her thoughts exact, her conceptions poetic; inevitably she looked upon words as a lapidary upon jewels. Each must itself be perfect and yet so subdued to the preordained scheme of color and form as to make harmony minister to beauty. She never (to use a phrase of her own) "lets a word run errands and serve the first purpose at hand"; for a poet to do that, even in prose, would be to sin against the light. Here are a few sentences taken at random; the lapidarian-like skill is unmistakable. "Poplars and aspens let the sun through with the wind. You may have the sky sprinkled through them in high midsummer, when all the woods are close." Again, writing of cascades, she says: "As from a strong stem a sapling wavers upwards, entangled at last in all the breezes, so the dropping brood wavers downwards to its last and lighter motion." (pp. 198-99)

Mrs. Meynell's concern with words may seem too nice, a species of over-refinement. It is, but only to those who regard words merely as a means of communication recruited from the jargon of the motor, the links, and the engine-room, and reinforced with "You know what I mean," that ubiquitous slavery in the House of Bromides. To read Alice Meynell is to learn from her preoccupation with her own and other's diction that words have an individuality, almost a personality, of their own and that the general disregard of their claims is a Bœotian offense against the noblest of living tongues. To read such an essay as her "Superfluous Kings" (the Romance adjective so sweetly wed to the Saxon substantive) is to approach a sanctuary where only the initiate may enter, to penetrate for a golden moment the mystery of words and sense the opulence of their second intentions. (pp. 199-200)

> *Joseph J. Reilly, "Alice Meynell: A Poet in Prose," in his* Dear Prue's Husband and Other People, *The Macmillan Company, 1932, pp. 195-213.*

VIRGINIA MOORE   (essay date 1934)

Alice Meynell had exceptional endowments in a richly endowed generation, but not genius. That gap, that faint defect, . . . which it seems ungenerous to mention, what was it? We read her exquisitely reserved essays, her disciplined poetry, and the ardent praise of her contemporaries, yet return stubbornly to our disappointment. . . . The mind or the heart, which failed?

Her mind, though not bold in speculation, nor wide-ranging, was a fastidious, sane and vigilant labourer in small plots. (p. 163)

[The heart that loved England and Italy], and her scholarly father, and her gifted mother, and the Catholic Church . . . , and her husband, and her eight children, and a multitude of friends, and found time to love, unfeignedly, all the aspects of a changing world, was a large heart, and a good one, without blemish.

Then was she too civilized for breathless evocation? From her birth . . . to her death . . . , her life was correct, punctilious and well-bred. She was attached to pleasant things, and devoted to everlasting ones, and did not overdo anything. . . . She worked conscienciously at writing, without in any way neglecting her [children]. . . . This admirable and at times almost heroic discipline is reflected by her poetry and prose.

But of the wild breaking forth of genius her writing shows no trace. Nothing overwhelms her; she is never mysteriously greater than she guesses. Nor was urbane civilization a loss to her: she preferred it. It was only, judging her by the strictest criterion, a loss to literature. For, reading her work, . . . one pays well-meant honest compliments—many compliments—while longing for a morass where roots plunder down deep and reckless, and trees rear so high one cannot count the leaves. One longs . . . for the minor poet to metamorphose into a major poet. No great battle, it seems, was ever fought on the field of her soul. What was there to fight over?—the elements of her nature were thoroughly in accord and under control. . . . It might be argued that she distilled the essence from passion, and therefore knew what passion was. But the splendid flavour from the mighty grapes is not there. . . . Her writing is the zenith of journalism; it is a little better than that. But it is not . . . that she drops a vast net into the sea and is surprised at her own catch. She wants a fish and a fish she catches. . . . But some have dragged the sea and brought up a great whale, thrashing. (pp. 163-65)

> *Virginia Moore, "Alice Meynell," in her* Distinguished Women Writers *(copyright 1934 by E. P. Dutton & Co., Inc.;* ©*, 1962 by Virginia Moore; reprinted by permission of the publisher, E. P. Dutton), Dutton, 1934, pp. 161-74.*

THE TIMES LITERARY SUPPLEMENT   (essay date 1940)

It is interesting to recall [the early praise of Meynell] as we turn to [*The Poems of Alice Meynell*], produced with a quiet distinction so appropriate to them. And inevitably that praise of more than half a century ago and from men so eminent to judge provokes the question how the rareness of her verse survives amid the so much louder and cruder noises of to-day, and to what extent its refinement dates it. To combine refinement with spiritual strength and depth is always hard. The cultivated sensibility so often grows weark at its roots. And a poet who published her first volume in 1875 was living in an age more favourable to the decorative than the creative, and to the sentimental than the imaginative.

There are signs of this in some of Alice Meynell's early verses. But it was typical of her spiritual integrity to succumb neither to the melodious sentiment of Tennyson in her youth nor to the nostalgic artistry of the nineties in her middle years.

Alice Meynell's verse owed its quality to the unusual degree in which she combined spiritual and artistic integrity. . . .

[She expressed with a rare individual awareness] the meaning of suffering, its cost, its dignity and its privilege. Yet her spiritual austerity only heightened her human tenderness and brought her nearer to the truth of nature, the wonder of childhood, the gay gallantry of youth, the wisdom of age.

It was because she strove to attune her ear to this music that her artistry, finely conscious as it became, never degenerated, as occasionally it did in her prose, into artifice. Art for her was a spiritual activity, a perfecting of the natural. . . .

[Those of her poems which once brought her most renown,] **"The Shepherdess"** or the sonnet **"Renouncement,"** will touch this age less than some among her maturest verses which possess a less obvious appeal. But in the best of what she wrote the spiritual voice which Francis Thompson recognized [see excerpt above] is as audible to-day as it ever was.

"The Spiritual Voice: Mrs. Meynell's Triumph," in The Times Literary Supplement (© *Times Newspapers Ltd. (London) 1940; reproduced from* The Times Literary Supplement *by permission), No. 2025, November 23, 1940, p. 594.*

G. ROSTREVOR HAMILTON   (essay date 1947)

[Alice Meynell's] work to-day has a special remoteness, above that of other Victorians: it is as though her quality, marked by so fine a certainty, a finish so nearly perfect, had for us, in our unresting confusion, something hard to endure.

Her poetry and her prose must be viewed together. They are too much akin to be merely complementary, for each springs from the close harmony of her nature. In some of the early work we may admire most, perhaps, an exquisite perception of landscape and a feeling, which was always hers, for the infinite gradations and subtleties of light. But already she sees with a tender affection, a lucid discrimination, attesting the union of heart and brain. Her vision is fastidious, at times, I think, even to excess. There is something of the aesthete exploring the last refinement of sense, which links her to the 'nineties. But there is a world of difference, for her senses are subdued—yet that is the wrong word for so delighted a service—to the spirit which may rather be said to heighten and clarify them. In her later work the critical intelligence comes increasingly into action, and here again is the characteristic mark, a fine relish and discrimination which call out the strength of her emotions. . . .

Alice Meynell was capable of severity, for she felt strongly and was unwavering in her loyalty to the severe standards of her making. . . . Her writing is a true expression of herself: we are aware of a distance that somehow goes naturally with the tenderness of her feeling. (p. 325)

The inequalities of Time fascinated her, and her treatment of them, always delicate and frequently moving, suffers now and then from an over-ingeniousness, which sometimes appears as a definite weakness in her penetrating mind. In the lines **"Length of Days—To the Early Dead in Battle"**, the thought of the long experience of the young and the child's sense of antiquity, despite the sincerity with which it is felt, offers too ingenious a comfort. (p. 326)

Alice Meynell used the discipline of prose to train herself in the varied powers of language, from the sensuous value of the concourse of syllables to the precise shade of intellectual meaning and the elusive aura of suggestion. With these she sometimes deals directly: **"Composure"** is a tribute to the dual derivation of the English tongue, and itself provides, in the deliberate poise and rhythm of its sentences, a fine example. . . . She brought this preoccupation with the word to her more avowedly critical writing, where it both gave a strength and imposed a limit. Again and again in her examination of particular line or passage—the compelling magic or, at an opposite extreme, the ruinous bathos—she pierces with absolute precision to her mark. . . . This unerring rightness is found in the admirable essay on Tennyson, with its distinction between "the great welcome style and the little unwelcome

manner". But indeed we may find it everywhere, for it is sign and seal of her quality. With it goes, not seldom, a certain shortening of perspective: the details are drawn with firmness of contour and bathed in revealing light, but something in the mass effect, felt by a less refined intelligence, appears to escape. Sometimes the reader asks for a broader and less exquisite treatment. . . .

I get a fuller satisfaction from the poetry. I began this paper by referring to the remoteness of Alice Meynell's work from to-day, and there is difficulty in due appreciation even of her poems. The reason is, perhaps, that, although poetry is the natural air which she breathes, her art takes so dominating a control. Mingled with our admiration is a slight discomfort, as we feel the calculation of her firm and delicate style. . . . [Yet] her calculation is never cold: nearly always her verses are warm with tenderness or with tempered passion. (p. 327)

The later poems are those with the securest title to fame. And yet the earlier, which she herself came to view with scant favour, hold a special attraction. They are, as a rule, looser in form, and the emotion is sometimes allowed to lead the thought, though not to run away with it. **"A Letter from a Girl to her own Old Age"** must always remain a most moving piece, and its tones are so true a prelude to those of the mature poet as to make the letter, in a double sense, prophetic. (p. 328)

She had her favourite themes, among them the intimacies of family life, the niceties of criticism, and, with a fresh approach, the great truths of Christianity. To all she brought her own original manner, constant in its regard for the half-shades of thought and feeling, and for the exact flavour—the personality, almost—of words. She is not afraid of a vast subject, but even in her boldest speculation we find the same minute precision of style. (p. 329)

G. Rostrevor Hamilton, *"Alice Meynell,"* in Poetry Review *(copyright © The Poetry Society 1947), Vol. XXXVIII, No. 5, September-October, 1947, pp. 325-30.*

HOXIE NEALE FAIRCHILD   (essay date 1962)

The ladylike, reticent verse of Mrs. Meynell [is] deft but scrupulously traditional in form, mildly pleasing but unadventurous in style. . . . (p. 33)

She might be described as a rhetorical lyricist: her poems are short versified essays in which she uses agreeable but never surprising images as a medium for the expression of ideas. Her desire to communicate what *she* feels is subdued by her desire for emotional privacy. Someone has said that both her religious conversion and her way of writing resulted from a wish to chasten her too passionate heart. Possibly so. One sees the restraint plainly enough; the fires which seethe beneath are much less obvious.

With a reminder that she also writes many secular lyrics about such subjects as nature and love (here she is especially ladylike), and about the writing of poetry *about* these themes, we may confine ourselves to her religious poems. . . . [She] makes no attempt to fabricate a personal interpretation of the sacred mystery of the universe. That mystery, she thinks, has been explained to her by Holy Church. If you asked her for a statement of her fundamental beliefs, she would simply recite the Apostles' Creed. Her poems are seldom theological, or mystical, or even personally devotional. With some interesting exceptions to be noted later she writes her little essays on various aspects of Catholic faith and practice in a spirit like that of the lady in her anthology-piece who, ''so circumspect and right,'' tends her quiet thoughts like sheep. Usually those thoughts concern, for example, the purity of little nuns, the necessity and joy and extreme difficulty of complete self-surrender, the changeless God of a changing world, Mary as representative of the bliss and pain of motherhood. (pp. 33-4)

Occasionally, however, she exploits the subtler resources of the Faith in a way that a more timidly conventional Catholic might regard as slightly bold. She hears a Hyde Park soapbox speaker whose compassion for the suffering poor has led him to deny with angry tears the existence of a loving God. That night, in her dream, the Lord of *all* compassion gazed into the atheist's face,

> And saw Himself, as one looks in a glass,
> In those impassioned eyes.

To her, however, according to another poem, the sufferings of the innocent are less appalling than the just punishment of the wicked. (p. 35)

Two poems—*only* two, I believe—suggest that the mind of a Catholic is not always impregnable against romantic infiltration. In *''I Am the Way''* she confesses that as a ''child of process'' she is by no means sure of attaining Christ as ''the goal,'' a definite ''end for me / Full of repose, full of replies.'' It is enough for her to know that He is ''the Way''—

> Access, Approach
> Art Thou, Time, Way, and Wayfarer.

Via, et Veritas, et Vita similarly subordinates both ''Veritas'' and ''Vita'' to ''Via.''

These poems smack a little too strongly of Browning's ''The prize is in the process.'' One might object that although Christ is assuredly the Way, what He offers at the end is the joy of absolute finality, not the joy of infinite wayfaring. But this is no more than a momentary lapse of spiritual taste. Alice Meynell is far from being a great religious poet, but she is a faithful representative of Catholic Christianity. . . . [Literary] and religious orthodoxy by no means necessarily coincide. This poet serves to remind us that they *may* coincide. (p. 36)

> *Hoxie Neale Fairchild, ''Old Wine, Old Bottles,'' in his* Religious Trends in English Poetry: 1880-1920, Gods of a Changing Poetry, Vol. V *(copyright © 1962 Columbia University Press; reprinted by permission of the publisher), Columbia University Press, 1962, pp. 13-36.**

THE TIMES LITERARY SUPPLEMENT   (essay date 1966)

In the 1890s the evening newspaper, the *Pall Mall Gazette*, ran a column [''The Wares of Autolycus''] as we should now say ''devoted to women''. . . . [In] among articles on garments, gardening and gastronomy by various forgotten women will be found literary criticism contributed anonymously by Alice Meynell. . . .

Alice Meynell is remembered rather as a poet than a critic, and the poetry of her sex in her generation is perhaps somewhat out of favour at present, even among anthologists. She had, however, a keen analytical intelligence, and a mode of expression often oblique but none the less pungent. As Autolycus her subjects were for the most part feminine—women writers of her own century (Jean Ingelow and Mrs. Browning), or earlier male poets (Lovelace and Waller) extolling women's

virtues or charms. But she is not particularly tender to her own sex. Indeed she is no respecter of persons, or of reputations. She can praise Vaughan and Keats and Coleridge, but is aware, too, of the ''secondary Vaughan'' and ''the deadly sickliness of 'Endymion''', and finds the author of ''The Ancient Mariner'' ''a poet almost incapable of thought''.

Her greatest bugbear is ''mediocrity''. She tosses the epithet alike at Harriet Martineau, Ouida and Gray's ''Elegy'', and by implication at any novelist or poet in whom she detects a deficiency of sincerity or passion. Her scorn for the mediocre parallels Virginia Woolf's for the middlebrow. . . .

Mrs. Meynell was less of a perfectionist; her early criticism, thoughtful as it always was, and well-supported by quotation, gives sometimes an impression of having been written off the cuff. Revision came later, usually with an opportunity of adapting old material to a new purpose.

> *''Reconsidered Trifles,'' in* The Times Literary Supplement *(© Times Newspapers Ltd. (London) 1966; reproduced from* The Times Literary Supplement *by permission), No. 3333, January 13, 1966, p. 26.*

GEORGE WATSON   (essay date 1967)

[*The Wares of Autolycus*] evokes the personality of Mrs. Meynell rather than that of any of the poets and novelists which it affects to describe. It is an amiable personality, seldom an arresting one; and the essays themselves often verge upon the limping and the inconsequent. Her notion of poetry hardly extends beyond the lyrical, . . . so that her handling of certain seventeenth-century ad romantic poets has only that slight and remote interest that this limitation confers: for her there is 'not a single moment of poetry', for instance, in the works of Crabbe. The memoirs of her friend Francis Thompson are mildly informative. But try as one may, it is difficult to see her in any light but that of a good lady out of her depth.

> *George Watson, ''Reviews: 'The Wares of Autolycus','' in* The Review of English Studies, *Vol. XVIII, No. 69, February, 1967, p. 96.*

PATRICK McCARTHY   (essay date 1968)

[The deepest strain in Alice Meynell's] work is the sense of privacy and the need for renunciation. In her most joyful moments she is conscious that each individual is separate from all others, like the mountains covered with the first snows of Winter that 'keep their counsel sealed and fast'. In *A Poet's Wife* the poet remains detached even when locked in his wife's embrace, and in *The Unknown God* Christ descends at communion into the man seated next to the poet, but He remains enclosed with 'this lonely conscience'. There is not in Alice Meynell the agonizing sense of man shut off permanently from other men, much less from God, for this same poem ends with a confident appeal to Christ. But she does feel that man must work out his salvation alone, and that the innermost recesses of the human personality cannot be invaded from outside.

Linked with this is an ascetic strain: a liking for self-discipline and an aesthetic distrust of the ostentatious. . . . Renunciation is seen as a condition of striving, and Alice Meynell seeks out the limits that man imposes on himself. Particularly relevant here is the poem *Renouncement* . . . where the poetess withdraws from any guilty love with the simple watchword: 'I must not think of thee'. This [is a] desire for law—the willingness to accept limits as the price and condition of the spiritual. . . . (pp. 183-84)

[One finds in Alice Meynell's writings] the sense that the spiritual is indeed a development of the human, but that limits must be set. (p. 186)

> *Patrick McCarthy, "Claudel, Patmore and Alice Meynell: Some Contacts With English Catholicism," in* Claudel: A Reappraisal, *edited by Richard Griffiths (© 1968 Rapp and Whiting Limited; reprinted by permission of Andre Deutsch Limited), Dufour Editions, 1968, pp. 175-87.**

ADDITIONAL BIBLIOGRAPHY

Alexander, Calvert, S.J. "Alice Meynell." In his *The Catholic Literary Revival,* pp. 113-28. 1935. Reprint. Port Washington, N.Y.: Kennikat Press, 1968.

   A brief biography of Meynell, characterizing her as the moving force behind the Catholic Literary Revival in England.

Brégy, Katherine. "Alice Meynell." In her *The Poets Chantry,* pp. 159-72. 1912. Reprint. Port Washington, N.Y.: Kennikat Press, 1970.

   An overview of the styles and themes in Meynell's poetry and prose.

Connolly, Terence L., S.J., ed. *Alice Meynell: Centenary Tribute.* Boston: Bruce Humphries, 1948, 72 p.

   Personal reminiscences of Meynell by Anne Kimball Tuell and other scholars, with commentaries on her literary achievements.

Mais, S.P.B. "Alice Meynell As Critic." In his *Books and Their Writers,* pp. 231-41. New York: Dodd, Mead and Co., 1920.

   Examines Meynell's critical evaluations of Dickens, Swinburne, and the Brontës.

Meynell, Viola. *Alice Meynell: A Memoir.* New York: Charles Scribner's Sons, 1929, 354 p.

   A remembrance of Meynell by her daughter.

Noyes, Alfred. "Alice Meynell." In his *Some Aspects of Modern Poetry,* pp. 1-9. London: Hodder and Stoughton, 1924.

   A study of Meynell's poetry, comparing it in quality to the best of Wordsworth and Tennyson.

Tuell, Anne Kimball. "Mrs. Meynell: A Study." *The Atlantic Monthly* 131, No. 2 (February 1923): 229-38.

   Discusses Meynell's influence on and importance to the literature of the 1890s.

A(lan) A(lexander) Milne

1882-1956

English dramatist, poet, short story writer, essayist, and novelist.

Milne is world famous for his children's verse and stories about Christopher Robin and Winnie-the-Pooh. In addition to his four books for children, Milne wrote numerous plays and essays, and several novels. Although contemporary readers know Milne almost exclusively for his Christopher Robin books, many of his plays achieved considerable success on the London and New York stages in their day.

Milne was educated at Westminster School and Trinity College, Cambridge, where he edited the undergraduate paper, *The Granta*. Upon completion of his degree in mathematics in 1903, he moved to London and worked as a freelance journalist. In 1906 he accepted an assistant editorship with *Punch*, where he worked for eight years contributing humorous essays and verse. By the time he joined the Royal Warwickshire Regiment at the onset of World War I, he had already published three collections of essays from *Punch* and was becoming well-known as a humorist.

While serving in the army, Milne wrote *Wurzel-Flummery*, his first play. Milne's friend, the dramatist James Barrie, was instrumental in arranging for the play's production. When Milne became ill soon after completing *Wurzel-Flummery*, he returned to England to recuperate and continue writing. Several of the plays written during this period, including *Mr. Pim Passes By*, *The Dover Road*, and *The Truth about Blayds*, were popular with contemporary theater audiences. However, most critics feel that after his second collection, *Second Plays*, he ceased to develop as a dramatist. Most of his plays are short, whimsical drawing room comedies; although they are noted for their wit, amusing dialogue, and entertaining quality, they are often criticized as superficial and sentimental.

Inspired by his young son Christopher Robin and memories of his own childhood, Milne began writing children's verse. These occasional verses quickly grew into the collections *When We Were Very Young* and *Now We Are Six*, which are ranked among the best of children's light verse. Displaying a genuine understanding of childhood experience, Milne skillfully mirrors the child's thought processes and impressions of the adult world. Both collections were instantly popular and are still widely read today. They were soon surpassed in popularity, however, by the stories in *Winnie-the-Pooh* and *The House at Pooh Corner*. Based upon Christopher Robin and his stuffed animals, the characters are whimsical caricatures of human nature and habit. Enjoyed as much by adults as by children for their gentle humor and wit, these stories are among the most-quoted children's classics.

Milne continued to write plays following the publication of *When We Were Very Young* and *Winnie-the-Pooh;* however, publishers were more interested in collecting his children's verse and stories than his plays. Milne once wryly expressed his frustration at how the tremendous popularity of these children's books had eclipsed his more serious work as a dramatist and essayist: "When I wrote them, little thinking/All my years of pen-and-inking/Would be almost lost among/Those four tri-

fles for the young." Although he would have wished otherwise, Milne's essays, dramas, and novels are now largely forgotten, and his place in world literature depends entirely upon his four well-loved and widely translated children's classics.

PRINCIPAL WORKS

Lovers in London (sketches) 1905
The Day's Play (essays) 1910
Wurzel-Flummery (drama) 1917
First Plays (dramas) 1919
Mr. Pim Passes By (drama) 1920
Second Plays (dramas) 1921
The Truth about Blayds (drama) 1921
The Dover Road (drama) 1922
The Red House Mystery (novel) 1922
The Great Broxopp (drama) 1923
Success (drama) 1923
When We Were Very Young (juvenile verse) 1924
Ariadne; or, Business First (drama) 1925
Four Plays (dramas) 1926
Winnie-the-Pooh (juvenile fiction) 1926
Now We Are Six (juvenile verse) 1927

The House at Pooh Corner   (juvenile fiction) 1928
It's Too Late Now (autobiography) 1939; published in the
    United States as *Autobiography,* 1939
The Norman Church (poetry) 1948
A Table Near the Band (short stories) 1950
Year In, Year Out (essays) 1952

THE TIMES LITERARY SUPPLEMENT   (essay date 1919)

[A. A. Milne's *First Plays*] were written for fun. They are
delightful parlour-games, all five. They do not affect, like the
newest of Mr. Shaw's parlour-games, to be fantasies in the
Russian manner. They are modestly and tactfully and good-
humouredly in the English manner. It is something nowadays
to find a playwright who doesn't take himself pontifically. . . .

We like best the one play we happen to have seen, *Belinda*.
That is to say, we like it best to read. Recollection of the acting
helps your reading, while there are no actors there now to put
you out. It is the ideal mode of enjoying a play—"emotion
recollected in tranquility." . . . [The] half-ability of recollection is more appropriate than the whole reality of presence to
a fantasy like *Belinda,* an "April Folly," as its author calls it.
It is all agreeable chatter, and agreeable chatter becomes less
and less agreeable when prolonged through three acts and in-
terchanged between real flesh-and-blood actors, determined not
to let you off a single word. . . . On the stage the people are
too real to be true. Belinda is an impossibly heartless coquette,
Baxter an impossibly unconscious bore, Tremayne an impossibility *tout court*. In the book they become possible again,
reduced to their proper scale of suggestions, adumbrations,
pretexts for bright talk—talk not only bright but coloured for
you now with the real voices you heard on the stage. With
such a play as *Belinda* our advice would always be: face it
bravely, go and see it acted, and then, having got your data,
go home and really enjoy it in the book.

Should we give the same advice about *The Lucky One*? We
are not so sure. We are inclined to think—perhaps because our
opinion is apparently in no danger of being put to the test—
we are inclined to think the play would be best enjoyed in
actual presentation. . . . [The] people are real, the whole scheme
of the play is real, and it would be helped by the reality of the
actors instead of being, like *Belinda,* hindered by it. There is
character as well as chatter in this play. And so, after all, we
find ourselves becoming endeared to Mr. Milne by agreeing
with him that it is the best play of the five. We agree, that is
to say, it would be the best to see acted. As, according to Mr.
Milne, there is no hope of its being produced, there can be no
risk of our agreement being upset. We must, then, remain
endeared to him forever. What luck!

> *"The Comedy of Chatter," in* The Times Literary
> Supplement *(© Times Newspapers Ltd. (London)
> 1919; reproduced from* The Times Literary Supple-
> ment *by permission), No. 926, October 16, 1919, p.
> 564.*

JOHN POLLOCK   (essay date 1922)

Mr. Milne in many respects—and what greater compliment
could be paid him?—is the legitimate successor of [the English
novelist and playwright Mr. F.] Anstey; he shares with the
author of *The Man from Blankley's* and *Lyre and Lancet,* immortal works that they are, the gift of catching the most quizz-
ical thoughts of ordinary men and women and prisoning them
in the simplest and most natural words. Perhaps this does not
furnish the chief attraction of **The Dover Road,** but if Mr. Milne
cares to develop this rare gift, for indeed it is one of the rarest,
he may become as much the perfect chronicler of the manners,
customs, and mentality of the nineteen-twenties as Mr. Anstey
was for the eighteen-nineties. To be truly consistent in its
success the Anstey method, if one may so call it, must be
applied to situations that are improbable, but never impossible;
not farcical, but within the frame of comedy. Its quizzicality
will then obtain the utmost scope, and the spectator, or reader,
will yet never cease to have the impression that he is observing
men and women of his own stamp and composition. In **The
Dover Road** Mr. Milne, it may be, somewhat oversteps these
limits: not from the nature of his original theme, but because
in its working out one or two of the scenes do cease from the
improbable, and, crossing the line that divides this from the
impossible, become farcical. (pp. 339-40)

Mr. Milne's other danger is that his dialogue flows with an
ease so prodigious as at times almost to carry him beyond the
scope of his subject. There must be tremendous temptations to
one capable of spinning a glittering web of amusing nothings,
until it ends like one of Edouard Strauss's waltzes that takes
its title from this method—"Sans fin." . . . But in Mr. Milne
the sense of the play, as opposed to that of the theatre, is too
strong for us to be in serious fear of such a fate overtaking
him. Throughout his lightest badinage, and underlying his
pleasantest epigrams, may be detected a healthy grip of the
one thing that makes a play, and differentiates it from the
hotchpotch of chatter that often passes for one—namely, the
plot. It is precisely the fact that Mr. Milne, save for a few
moments of diffuseness and redundancy, does not deviate from
the necessarily narrow lines imposed by his subject, and strictly
subordinates both characters and episodes to it, which allows
the hope that he will give to England of our days a comedy as
perfectly typical of it, and as typically perfect, as were, in
their centuries [Oscar Wilde's] *The Importance of Being Earnest,* [Richard Brinsley Sheridan's] *The School for Scandal,*
and [William Congreve's] *Love for Love.* In embroidery of his
theme, in the construction of cunning little climaxes that advance its action, he is already an artist to whom few are superior. (p. 340)

> *John Pollock, "Four Plays of the Season: 'The Dover
> Road'," in* The Fortnightly Review *(reprinted by
> permission of Contemporary Review Company Lim-
> ited), n.s. Vol. CXII, August 1, 1922, pp. 339-42.*

GEORGE JEAN NATHAN   (essay date 1923)

One of the weaknesses of the lesser British playwrights of the
day lies in the omnipresent dodge of attempting to brew laughter from the ancient device of bringing into sharp juxtaposition
two subjects violently out of key with each other. An irrelative
allusion to pigs interjected suddenly into a conversation on
love, an alien reference to sausages inserted into an observation
on cynicism, an extraneous mention of a bowler hat during a
discussion of poetry—these are the species of comic gold-fish
that such playwrights as A. A. Milne, for example, continually
pull out of their silk hats. And when they do not rely upon
sudden contrast as a comic device, their reliance is largely
upon such equally fragile devices as causing a comic character
to repeat the remark of a serious character directly after him,

mispronouncing a person's name, and confusing Eugene Aram with Enoch Arden. These playwrights suffer further from their heavy effort to be insistently light. Their lightness has about it not infrequently a sense of tug and strain. Where British playwrights like the late Haddon Chambers or Hubert Henry Davies, appreciating their shortcomings, promptly abandoned froth qua froth the moment they detected a bead of perspiration upon its brow, the lesser writers of today blandly wipe off the bead and plough determinedly ahead. The net impression that one takes away from their exhibits is, consequently, of having been present at a dinner party whereat all the exceptionally dull guests have endeavoured to be assiduously amusing. (pp. 131-32)

George Jean Nathan, "Theatre and Drama: The Lesser British Playwrights," in his The World in Falseface *(copyright © by Alfred A. Knopf, Inc.; copyright renewed © 1950 by George Jean Nathan; reprinted by permission of Associated University Presses, Inc., for the Estate of George Jean Nathan), Knopf, 1923, pp. 131-32.**

ASHLEY DUKES   (essay date 1923)

The discerning listener to *The Dover Road* will feel that he has not only travelled the main highway, but sauntered in every lane that turns out of it. They are green and pleasant English lanes, and boyish and innocent adventures are to be found in them. . . . Mr. Milne knows all about those lanes and saunters with you, as it seems, arm-in-arm, making observations not exactly about human nature, but about human oddities. His excellent jokes are like school-magazine jokes raised to the *n*th magnitude. . . . He has a keen sense of the unexpected and a high appreciation of the preposterous; and while he is practising a genius for the presentation of these absurdities, you get farther and farther down the lane and away from the turnpike road. The side-issues are the things that amuse Mr. Milne and therefore amuse you. Sometimes you suspect that he feels safer in the lanes than on the high road, and that the pace of the stroll is not quite free from calculation. But how companionable is the humour, how spirited the invention, and how amiable the dialogue!

Among the obvious fruits of divagation are a husband visibly breakfasting and shaving for twenty minutes by the clock; a too-affectionate wife reading Gibbon aloud; and the entire character of the rich man who intercepts would-be runaway couples and gives them time, in his comfortable mansion, to think better of their immoral project. . . . He is cynical, certainly, but how sweetly, how innocently cynical! The mentality of a really nice Oxford tutor hangs about him in spite of the Bohemian velvet jacket, the flowing tie, and the dashing eyeglass. Let us not quarrel with him for that; it is good to be so innocent. But let us not pretend, except for fun, that the gentleman ever kept the reformatory for eloping couples. He is only a green lane in which the author saunters—with an air. Such plays are easily seen and easily forgotten.

The Truth about Blayds was made (in the beginning) of more memorable stuff. It was an essay in serious comedy as opposed to pipe-and-slipper humour or bobbed-hair-and-jumper senti-ment. It had foundations of character. Old Oliver Blayds, that venerable relic of the Victorian era, lived in every line of his portrait. We saw him from various angles and in various lights. We sympathised with his grandchildren who found so great a grandfather hard to live up to. We bent the knee of homage with the deputation of younger writers who saluted the poet's

ninetieth birthday. We felt, with his fussy and pompous little son-in-law, that nothing short of an Abbey funeral would ul-timately meet the case. We approved the sacrifice of the daugh-ter who had given up her prospects of love and marriage to devote herself to the old man's care. And then Blayds died. He whispered on his death-bed the staggering truth that he was a charlatan. He had built up his reputation on another poet's treasure of manuscript. The fortune he had made in royalties was stolen property. All this venerable legend that had clung about him was naught, from his high-minded refusal of a peer-age to his sturdy damning of his creaky boots during a royal interview at Osborne.

Then the play should have begun. There were but two possible solutions. One was to make the confession public and surrender Blayds's fortune; the other to hush the matter up and pretend that the old man was suffering from delusions. The first was of dubious dramatic effect; the second promised success to a remorseless satirist. Mr. Milne, painfully aware of the di-lemma, confided himself to the tender mercies of the daughter who had been old Blayds's ministering angel and was now his sole executrix. The drama became, most disastrously, hers. Alas, we were not interested in this lady and her unborn chil-dren, but in old Blayds. His ghostly and admirable figure re-turned again and again to remind us that the dramatist had taken himself too seriously and his art not seriously enough.

The comedy of *Success* was as ambitious in conception and as slight in achievement. Here Mr. Milne chose one of the clas-sical dramatic plots, that of a sleeping memory awakened. (pp. 99-102)

[It is a] comedy of fine moments. Mr. Milne's emotional scenes are sincere and vivid while they last. The trouble is that he neither prepares them nor faces their consequences. In his ca-reer as an author he has not yet wrecked a happy home, or, for that matter, an unhappy one. We are touched, but we vaguely resent being touched in vain. These questions of love and marriage and fidelity are more significant than they appear when they are viewed through the wrong end of the opera-glasses in a really nice Milne comedy. (pp. 102-03)

Ashley Dukes, "Comedians," in his The Youngest Drama: Studies of Fifty Dramatists, *Ernest Benn, Limited, 1923, pp. 85-106.**

HELEN CADY FORBES   (essay date 1924)

[A. A. Milne's **"When We Were Very Young"**] is that rare thing, a book about children which they may enjoy. The rhythm alone would hold them entranced, even without the absolute rightness of the sense and nonsense. The book has the vitality that children crave; there is nothing conventional between its covers, not an insipid line, either in the verses or in the draw-ings that so perfectly illustrate them. Nor is there a trace of condescension. While the poems frequently mention a certain Christopher Robin, that child will have no reason to reproach his father by and by when he looks at the book with older, colder eyes. (p. 82)

"When We Were Very Young" is essentially different from other volumes of poetry about children. There is more variety of form and thought. The flying kites, the flying clouds, the tiresome rice pudding are taken more gayly, more tenderly, than usual. There are poems of quiet loveliness balanced by the most delightfully nonsensical stories. (p. 83)

Animals figure largely in these verses, as they do in children's interest, but these are no ordinary beasts. They possess personalities far removed from the animals of bedtime lore. (pp. 84-5)

Their elders may wish to read these poems aloud, but children will want to take the book away to read to themselves and to each other, to chant each rhyme as many times as they like before going on to the next. The very music of childhood is here, sung with a varied cadence peculiar to these poems, essentially and uniquely the dramatic expression of tenderness. (p. 85)

> Helen Cady Forbes, " 'When We Were Very Young',"
> *in* New York Herald Tribune Books (© *I.H.T. Corporation; copyright renewed © 1952; reprinted by permission), December 14, 1924 (and reprinted in* The Three Owls: A Book about Children's Books, Their Authors, Artists and Critics, *Vol. 1, edited by Anne Carroll Moore, The Macmillan Company, 1925, pp. 82-5).*

GRAHAM SUTTON (essay date 1925)

[A. A. Milne's *Wurzel-Flummery* is pure "Punch":] an artistic entity of gossamer farce unspoiled by the least touch of gravity. Alike in conception and in execution, it is informed by the authentic spirit of "Punch" which that journal maintains with such admirable consistency: the spirit of amateurdom in the best sense, of things done enthusiastically for the sheer fun of doing them, and without any staider thought of super-efficiency or of ulterior motive. As such, it marked the close of a period. For henceforward A.A.M. [the initials Milne used to sign his "Punch" contributions] was to collaborate with one Milne, ex-soldier. . . . In the twelve or fourteen plays which followed *Wurzel-Flummery* we may trace the progress of that alliance.

There is little enough of "Punch" in two early one-act plays, *The Boy Comes Home* and *The Camberley Triangle*—both presented as light-comedy, it is true, though the one leans as definitely towards farce as the other does towards drama. Scratch these (not very deeply) and their true nature appears as something far removed from the all's-well-with-the-upper-classes beatitude of A.A.M. They voice the returning soldier—a little puzzled, a little cynically amused, more than a little indignant—as he stands in ironic contemplation of the man to whom war has meant nothing but an increase of peace and prosperity. It is the voice of much modern literature. . . . [In] these plays, light though their treatment is, the wit is steely-hard and the old silly-ass note tuned to a new and sharper pitch. . . . *The Camberley Triangle* is in one act only; but [it] . . . illustrates, as well as anything in even the full-length *The Lucky One*, the peculiar vein of caustic, rather bitter-sweet comedy which runs through all the plays of Mr Milne's "first period," as opposed to *Wurzel-Flummery*, which uniquely constituted the "last period" of A.A.M. . . . I attach these labels with diffidence, partly because Mr Milne is not the sort of man to be pedantic about, and partly because what I have called his first period, in strict point of time, includes only *The Lucky One* and *The Boy Comes Home: The Camberley Triangle* and *The Stepmother* appearing as casts-back to the earlier style, written after their author had won popularity on more genial lines. . . . *The Lucky One*, then, though it has nothing to do with the war, holds the same hint of bitterness as the two topical plays; and like theirs, its comedy is spiced with a dash of drama. . . . *The Lucky One* is almost the only work of Mr Milne which lacks a London production, and it is good enough to make one sympathise with

his avowed regard for it as the ewe lamb of his flock; it is as delicate and sensitive as all his work; it is more subtle than most; yet one can't altogether blame the London manager for neglecting it. For one thing, it is non-popular: as the author himself admits, "the girl marries the wrong man": and for another, managers are bound to judge a play by its net result rather than by its aim. *The Lucky One* may be—it *is*—much more worth while than *The Dover Road*; it may be—but surely isn't?—more worth while than *Wurzel-Flummery*; but it is not so good of its own kind as either of these; also the kind is commoner. Other playwrights would call round with other *Lucky One*'s: but not with a *Wurzel-Flummery*. Yet again, the public knew its A.A.M. but knew nothing of Milne the dramatist. "Punch" and that first Punch-farce hung round Mr Milne's young neck; their names were inscribed, as it were, upon the visiting-card which he passed in at the manager's door. (pp. 119-24)

So it fell out that Mr Milne, with his instinct for something just a little more serious than we were prepared to accept from him, became the Jack Point of modern dramatists; but his rich wit enabled him to make the best of both his worlds without artistic heartbreak. His plays resolved themselves into a series of scarce-hinted gravities decked out in holiday ribbons: of wisdom masquerading as folly: of real people shimmeringly disguised in the costumes of make-believe. Superficially as farcical as *Wurzel-Flummery,* they have foundations of good sense and philosophy buried no deeper than was necessary to elude the too-cautious managerial eye. They are the googlie-bowling of dramaturgy, flicking your intellectual bails before you know that there is anything in them. *The Romantic Age* and *Mr Pim* and *Broxopp* are all capital fun, none the worse because you are not aware till afterwards that they have preached you as shrewd sermons on domestic life as many drearier plays. *Blayds,* on the other hand, just insomuch as it is less light than the other comedies, is less successful. It starts out on a larger scale than they, and then loses itself; it is modern comedy's counterpart to *The Jew of Malta;* a dramatic mermaid, at first promising well but ending in a tail whose wag is of the feeblest. . . . It is not easy to see how Milne could have written this piece without killing Blayds pretty early—Blayds' greatness being merely "situation" or postulate, and the play's theme the difficulties raised by his exposure—yet there is little doubt that one's memory of the first-act Blayds quite dwarfs the rest of the play. Perhaps even genuine greatness (Mr Milne being the dramatist) is the better the more lightly it is portrayed. (pp. 124-26)

Mr Milne like a good practical workman turned that A.A.M., who might have proved his incubus, to useful account. He consults him in all his plays, to their exceeding profit. . . . And in some plays he gives A.A.M. a free hand with purely farcical characters: Mrs Knowle in *The Romantic Age* is a case in point. At the same time he keeps him in his place by many sly digs: not only flashing unexpected lights on some of A.A.M.'s pet heroes, but finding unsuspected heroism in types which A.A.M., in his green days on "Punch," might have completely ignored. He develops sympathy with parvenus and such-like pariahs; worse still, he begins to poke fun at the Country Gentleman (that almighty man, as Tennyson has it), and at the Country House, that other Eden, demiparadise, that blessèd plot, that earth, that realm, that England round which, as a moat defensive to a house, succeeding generations of "Punch" have ranged themselves. The fun he pokes is not bitter, like that of Galsworthy in *The Skin Game,* but delicate loving little blasphemies, too slight to pierce the hide—nearly always, at all events. . . . *Broxopp* is Mr Milne pointing out to A.A.M. that the "best" people are not the only people: implying even that there might have been no best people, if some good second-best people had not tried to better themselves: that this bettering process, practised by the pure in heart and not by mere snobs, has its own proper beauty and may indeed be the true vision of civilisation. . . . (pp. 126-28)

Milne and [James] Barrie have often been compared—not without good reason. But the comparison has been too zealously concentrated on the children's plays, Milne himself setting the fashion when he wrote about *Make-Believe* that "the difficulty in the way of writing a children's play is that Barrie was born too soon." *Make-Believe* . . . is wholly a children's play. . . . Milne writes always about childhood, Barrie never. Barrie writes always as the man of the world, with whatever sentiment he may cloud his worldly issues; *Peter Pan* is childhood seen from the angle of sophistication, *Mary Rose* (most cruel and logical of plays) at once the result and penalty of being Peter Pan. But Milne's *Make-Believe* is a story of real children, seen with a child's eyes, not through the spectacles of a grown-up and (dare one say it?) slightly cynical uncle. Here is no trace of that artificial childishness, that unnatural refusal to grow up, which attracts yearly crowds of sentimental elders to *Peter Pan*, and which is so utterly untrue to the child's philosophy. Milne's children are all agog to be grown up; they look forward eagerly, wistfully, pathetically to adult life, even though only to a fantastic adult life of their own imagining. And this eager striving, paradoxically enough, is what keeps them young: younger by far than Barrie's petticoated little worldlings, whatever their age may be. Youth is the keynote of Milne's plays, whose best fun lies always in the by-play of his young people. . . . [The] sunny temperament of Mr Milne shines through his work, out-bluffing melancholy. Ever loath "that Youth's sweetscented Manuscript should close," he prolongs make-believe to the full prime of adolescence and beyond it. He is the apologist of youth.

In all which, as it seems to me, there is little or no trace of the Barrie philosophy. Nor do I think that Mr Milne (however modest his preface to *Make-Believe*) is at all unconscious of this, nor of the danger of confusing Barrie-ideas with his own different scheme. *Make-Believe*, we are told, is what the children *thought*. . . . (pp. 128-31)

But if Milne's philosophy touches Barrie's at hardly any point, their stage-conventions, or moulds in which each has chosen to create his image of life, are remarkably similar; and it is here in this more superficial resemblance that the value of the comparison lies. Both deal in the spiritual rather than in the physical. And since one of drama's disadvantages (from which even the subtlest acting only partly delivers it) is its obsession with the physical side of life at the expense of the spiritual, it follows that both these writers shouldered a much bigger job, when they ordained to express themselves in drama, than the majority of their rivals. . . . [It] was *The Dover Road*, more perhaps than any other Milne play, which furnished chapter and verse for endless critical discourses on Milne's Barriesque style. (pp. 131-33)

[Much] as I admired *The Dover Road* as an actors' play, I liked *Broxopp* better. *Broxopp* is the ideal blend of Barrie and Milne; a shade less farcical than the average Milne, it yet stops well short of the sentimentality with which the elder dramatist might have invested it. (p. 133)

> *Graham Sutton, "A. A. Milne," in his* Some Contemporary Dramatists *(reprinted by permission of*

Mildred Sutton), Kennikat Press, Inc., 1925, pp. 118-34.

MARCIA DALPHIN   (essay date 1926)

Writers for children have done stories about bears often enough, but it has remained for Milne to discover to us in "**Winnie-the-Pooh**" the essential wistfulness of these great lumbering, blundering creatures. Others have shown their clumsiness, their heavy, halting intelligence, their occasional flashes of sly humor, their greediness. Pooh has all these; but he has something else as well—a disarming humility in the presence of his quicker-witted fellows, a longing for approval, a desire to be correct (did he not take Stoutness Exercises in front of the glass?), a—well, there's no word for it but wistfulness—that goes straight to your heart. (p. 76)

As you read the conviction grows on you that Mr. Milne has done it again. There are not so very many books that, sitting reading all alone, you find yourself laughing aloud over. This is one of them. Here is nonsense in the best tradition; entirely plausible on the surface, as true nonsense always is, with good sense at its core, and the high seriousness about it that children and other wise people love. The illusion is perfect. You never forget that these are nursery animals, and that you exist as a reader only because you are allowed to see them through the eyes of a child. (p. 77)

> *Marcia Dalphin, "Mr. Edward Bear: His Book," in* New York Herald Tribune Books *(© I.H.T. Corporation; copyright renewed © 1954; reprinted by permission), October 17, 1926 (and reprinted in* The Three Owls: Contemporary Criticism of Children's Books, Vol. 2, *edited by Anne Carroll Moore, Coward-McCann, 1928, pp. 75-7).*

HELEN CADY FORBES   (essay date 1927)

Milne's is the freest and freshest light verse. It is impossible for him to be dull, and it would seem for him that rhyming is as easy as breathing. "**Now We Are Six**," if we had never seen "**When We Were Very Young**," would be a landmark in books of verses about children that could be enjoyed by the children, too. But the book cannot stand alone. The first thought of most of the thousands and thousands who took delight in the earlier volume will be to compare this with that and ask—"Is it as good?" Physically it is much the same because of the Shepard drawings, but the slight difference in text begins with the lettering on the jacket, not quite as spontaneous as that other zigzagging, sprawling title. Within the covers there is nothing to touch "**The King's Breakfast**." . . .

But Milne's fundamental characteristics are here, his whimsical humor his intelligent sympathy and understanding of a small boy's problems, his honest affection for children; neither has he lost his powers of observation. And his rhymes are perfect still, the cadence falling on the ear with all the charm that variety and the hackneyed can give. . . .

To the average adult the book will be another amusing lot of verses to read aloud, but children will be able to find matter for thought as well as rhythm, notions worth turning over. . . . Milne's Christopher Robin and his Johns and Elizabeth Anns think for themselves with much simple and inquiring comment on the habits of their elders.

Now and then there is a tendency toward sentimentality in "**Now We Are Six**," a suspicion of the commonplace. It is not that Mr. Milne doesn't do the sentimental as well as any one could, but it interrupts.

Helen Cady Forbes, "The Milne School of Verse," in New York Herald Tribune Books (© I.H.T. Corporation; copyright renewed © 1955; reprinted by permission), October 16, 1927, p. 8.*

FRANK SWINNERTON (essay date 1934)

Milne's first books consisted of reprinted pieces from *Punch*. . . . They were delightful nonsense. His children's verses are familiar, innocent, arch, and charmingly turned. His one detective story is high among the lighter examples of a popular craft. All these books have a polish and bubble iridescence that make them excellent in their own department of letters, and all have large numbers of admirers. But it is by his plays that Milne has made his most ambitious claim to attention, and, finally, it is upon his plays that the critic must concentrate.

The first of them, apparently, was *Wurzel-Flummery,* the story of a trick played upon two proud men by a dying eccentric who left each a fortune on condition that each changed his name to Wurzel-Flummery. A name . . . is not a strong theme for a play, and *Wurzel-Flummery,* which began in three acts, is now printed in one. *Belinda,* another trifle, remains in three acts, and is about an inconsequent woman, her daughter (newly returned from a convent school), a long-missing husband, and two absurd suitors—one of them a juvenile poet, the other a middle-aged statistician. Here again the theme is slight to tenuity. Here again the amusingness of the play lies almost entirely in the persiflage which passes between shallow and very pleasing persons until the curtain falls. Both plays were very much like *Punch* sketches written in dialogue form at greater length; both were extremely nonsensical. . . . [Neither] play had what may be called an "idea." The story in each case was just sufficient to hold together the various nimble sayings of the actors, and no more. But *Belinda* held the first of those former or missing husbands who have figured so prominently in the Milne drama.

Mr. Pim Passes By was about another of them;—but this time the husband did not appear, and in fact he did not (at the moment of the play's action) exist. . . . From *Mr. Pim* onwards, a Milne play has been a recognized type of theatrical entertainment. (pp. 122-23)

Both *Success* and *The Truth About Blayds* failed in the theatre; the latter not unexpectedly, the former through an error in popular judgment. *Blayds* began with a serious and deeply interesting first act; but as soon as the situation had been grasped the play ceased to amuse, and was even a cause of some discomfort to those who saw it. *Success* . . . was badly received by the dramatic critics, who thought that Milne had dared to presume upon their favourable verdict. It has more feeling in it than any other play of Milne's, is extremely skilful, as to both plan and character, and is full of good, quick, effective dialogue. It deserved quite another fate than failure.

But both plays have the weakness which it seems to me is apparent in Milne's work whenever he is most serious; that is, they suffer from a kind of punitive zeal against wrongdoing. Milne has such a contempt for backsliders and materialists and sycophants that he cannot withhold a moral foreclosure which affects the structure of his play. . . . *Blayds,* which might have been a great comedy about an impostor, shifts its centre to the impostor's dependants, ignominious indeed, but of no signif-

icance. To castigate the meanness and hypocrisy of those who, after an earthquake, are clinging to a lie, is the work of a zealot.

Similarly, in *Success,* although the reawakening of Mannock is made credible with extraordinary skill (this is quite Milne's best play), and his downfall before temptation is exciting and convincing, a moral judgment—not a doom—hangs over the entire play. It is not tragedy, but an arraignment. I suggest that owing to his knowledge that Mannock was going to collapse, and his bitter dislike of venality, Milne has been unable to allow Mannock as much character as he should have done. So the fall is not great enough, because Mannock has throughout flown too low: the failure of a bigger man would have been a greater loss to his true love, and would have moved us more. (pp. 124-25)

[Milne] was deficient in certain qualities of the great romancers. At times his invention is meagre; it is always hampered by a lack of boldness, an inability to shake off the author's strict moral standards. Thus, while in every play the dialogue is fresh and full of life, the content of the play, where it is not a jest, is too often conventional.

I do not mean only conventional in the theatrical sense, and yet it is true that on the whole these plays of Milne's deal with a life peculiar to the theatre. I say no more as to the husbands who turn up or who refrain from turning up; but what of the wives to whom these husbands have in the past belonged? They at least are principals in the action. If their husbands come and go in this wanton manner, do not the wives also lose something of acceptable reality? A husband who is mislaid as if he were an article of jewellery may serve as a pretext for drama; but the wife, charming chatterbox though she be, who merely resumes her life as if she said, "Dear me, I don't seem to have a husband this morning; never mind, I expect he'll turn up again some time," does put a slight strain upon our credulity. Of course these ladies are before us: we see them, we hear them, we relish their wit. But when they leave the stage, or when we leave the theatre, we cannot help feeling that they have been only make-believe wives, make-believe women, like the dolls which little girls ask to tea parties and forget as soon as they have been put to bed.

That is the character of the Milne drama—make-believe. In a sense it is the character of the Barrie drama. Here are embodied whimsies, delicious fancies, nonsensical dreams, tender memories of play and young illusion, an enchanting aptness of phrase, sometimes a piercing revelation of unseen things, a charm that is not half-real, half-arbitrary, in the manner of a child's game. But neither Barrie nor Milne ever, it seems to me, goes quite the whole hog. Neither deals quite with the real world or quite with the world of faery. The real world is too harsh, or at least too stubborn, for fanciful treatment; the world of faery too incredible. Once we listen to the coaxing, winning "Let's pretend," we are at the mercy of both Milne and Barrie; but they know as well as we do that they are pretending; a time will come when they will leave off pretending, put away the toys, and return to reality as represented by the grown-up evening newspaper; they dare not absolutely let go at any time of the pleasant normal circumstances of well-bred and easy-mannered society. If they could do so, and if Milne, in particular, could see a cad without wishing to punish him, or a leprechaun without suspecting that he was in the presence of a joke, the liberation which would follow would perhaps astound the world. (pp. 125-26)

Frank Swinnerton, "Fancy Fair: Barrie, Milne, James Stephens," in his The Georgian Scene: A Literary Panorama (copyright 1934, © 1962 by Frank Swinnerton; reprinted by permission of Holt, Rinehart and Winston, Publishers), Farrar & Rinehart, 1934, pp. 105-30.*

A. A. MILNE (essay date 1939)

In real life very young children have an artless beauty, an innocent grace, an unstudied abandon of movement, which, taken together, make an appeal to our emotions similar in kind to that made by any other young and artless creatures: kittens, puppies, lambs: but greater in degree, for the reason that the beauty of childhood seems in some way to transcend the body. Heaven, that is, does really appear to lie about the child in its infancy, as it does not lie about even the most attractive kitten. But with this outstanding physical quality there is a natural lack of moral quality, which expresses itself, as Nature always insists on expressing herself, in an egotism entirely ruthless.

Now it seems to me that the writer who is trying to put a child upon paper must keep these two outstanding facts about children before him, and endeavour to preserve his sense of proportion. A sentimental painter might leave out the wart on Cromwell's face; but the biographer who, priding himself on his realism, calls attention to the wart every time he mentions the face, is just as falsely sentimental, since any small blemish on the face of one we know soon passes unnoticed. A pen-picture of a child which showed it as loving, grateful and full of thought for others would be false to the truth; but equally false would be a picture which insisted on the brutal egotism of the child, and ignored the physical beauty which softens it. Equally false and equally sentimental, for sentimentality is merely an appeal to emotions not warranted by the facts.

To avoid equally these two sentimentalities is the difficulty in front of the writer. It is easy (at least, I suppose it is easy, if one is a painter) to paint a beautiful child, but it is not easy to describe one. Any attempt to do so will become either conventional or indescriptive. But it is possible to give what one might call 'an air of charm,' particularly when writing in verse, to any account of a child's activities, and it seems to me that this 'charm,' if one can convey it, should have as much chance in the printed page as in real life of hiding from the sentimentalist the uncharming part of a child's nature: the egotism and the heartlessness.

I shall now expose my own egotism by giving one or two examples of how I have tried to do this.

The mother of a little boy of three has disappeared, and is never seen again. The child's reaction to the total loss of his mother is given in these lines:

> James James
> Morrison Morrison
> (Commonly known as Jim)
> Told his
> Other relations
> Not to go blaming him.

And that is all. It is the truth about a child: children are, indeed, as heartless as that: but only in one sense have I made a song about it.

In *Buckingham Palace* Christopher Robin is taken by his nurse to see the changing of the guard. She tells him about the soldiers and the Palace and the King, and at the end of it all he has

only one question to ask: 'Do you think the King knows all about Me?' Could egotism be more gross? If you were to take an author up to your most admired friend—as it might be Lindbergh—and on the way were to whisper to him of all the wonderful things your hero had done, would you not be disgusted if his only remark were, 'Do you think Lindbergh knows all about Me?' But since a child of three can say these things, and be innocent and charming enough to make them sound innocent and charming, so then, in the poem, if a true picture is to be given, the egotism must be there for the unsentimental to find, but there must also be charm enough to give it at least a surface covering.

Finally, let me refer to the poem which has been more sentimentalized over than any other in [*When We Were Very Young*]: *Vespers*. Well, if mothers and aunts and hard-headed reviewers have been sentimental over it, I am glad; for the spectacle in real life of a child of three at its prayers is one over which thousands have been sentimental. It is indeed calculated to bring a lump to the throat. But, even so, one must tell the truth about the matter. Not 'God bless mummy, because I love her so', but 'God bless Mummy, I know that's right'; not 'God bless Daddy, because he buys me food and clothes,' but 'God bless Daddy, I quite forgot'; not even the egotism of 'God bless Me, because I'm the most important person in the house,' but the super-egotism of feeling so impregnable that the blessing of this mysterious god for Oneself is the very last thing for which it would seem necessary to ask. And since this is the Truth about a Child, let us get all these things into the poem, and the further truth that prayer means nothing to a child of three, whose thoughts are engaged with other, more exciting matters; but since the Truth about a Child is also that, fresh from its bath, newly powdered and curled, it is a lovely thing, God wot, why then, let us try, however inadequately, to get at least a hint of this upon paper, so that, if possible, the reader, no less than the spectator, may feel that Beauty is hovering. . . . (pp. 283-85)

A. A. Milne, in his Autobiography (copyright 1939 by Alan Alexander Milne; copyright renewed © 1967 by Daphne Milne; reprinted by permission), E. P. Dutton & Co., Inc., 1939, 315 p.

RAYMOND CHANDLER (essay date 1950)

Every detective story writer makes mistakes, of course, and none will ever know as much as he should. Conan Doyle made mistakes which completely invalidated some of his stories, but he was a pioneer, and Sherlock Holmes after all is mostly an attitude and a few dozen lines of unforgettable dialogue. It is the ladies and gentlemen of what Mr. Howard Haycraft (in his book *Murder for Pleasure*) calls the Golden Age of detective fiction that really get me down. (pp. 5-6)

Let us glance at one of the glories of the literature, an acknowledged masterpiece of the art of fooling the reader without cheating him. It is called *The Red House Mystery*, was written by A. A. Milne, and has been named by Alexander Woollcott (rather a fast man with a superlative) "one of the three best mystery stories of all time." Words of that size are not spoken lightly. The book was published in 1922 but is timeless, and might as easily have been published in July, 1939, or, with a few slight changes, last week. . . . It is an agreeable book, light, amusing in the *Punch* style, written with a deceptive smoothness that is not so easy as it looks.

It concerns Mark Ablett's impersonation of his brother Robert, as a hoax on his friends. Mark is the owner of the Red House, a typical laburnum-and-lodge-gate English country house. He has a secretary who encourages him and abets him in this impersonation, and who is going to murder him if he pulls it off. Nobody around the Red House has ever seen Robert, fifteen years absent in Australia and known by repute as a no-good. A letter is talked about (but never shown) announcing Robert's arrival, and Mark hints it will not be a pleasant occasion. One afternoon, then, the supposed Robert arrives, identifies himself to a couple of servants, is shown into the study. Mark goes in after him (according to testimony at the inquest). Robert is then found dead on the floor with a bullet hole in his face, and of course Mark has vanished into thin air. Arrive the police, who suspect Mark must be the murderer, remove the débris, and proceed with the investigation—and in due course, with the inquest.

Milne is aware of one very difficult hurdle and tries as well as he can to get over it. Since the secretary is going to murder Mark, once Mark has established himself as Robert, the impersonation has to continue and fool the police. Since, also, everybody around the Red House knows Mark intimately, disguise is necessary. This is achieved by shaving off Mark's beard, roughening his hands (''not the hands of a manicured gentleman''—testimony), and the use of a gruff voice and rough manner.

But this is not enough. The cops are going to have the body and the clothes on it and whatever is in the pockets. Therefore none of this must suggest Mark. Milne therefore works like a switch engine to put over the motivation that Mark is such a thoroughly conceited performer that he dresses the part down to the socks and underwear (from all of which the secretary has removed the maker's labels), like a ham blacking himself all over to play Othello. If the reader will buy this (and the sales record shows he must have), Milne figures he is solid. Yet, however light in texture the story may be, it is offered as a problem of logic and deduction.

If it is not that, it is nothing at all. There is nothing else for it to be. If the situation is false, you cannot even accept it as a light novel, for there is no story for the light novel to be about. If the problem does not contain the elements of truth and plausibility, it is no problem; if the logic is an illusion, there is nothing to deduce. If the impersonation is impossible once the reader is told the conditions it must fulfill, then the whole thing is a fraud. Not a deliberate fraud, because Milne would not have written the story if he had known what he was up against. He is up against a number of deadly things, none of which he even considers. Nor, apparently, does the casual reader, who wants to like the story—hence takes it at its face value. But the reader is not called upon to know the facts of life when the author does not. The author is the expert in the case.

Here is what this author ignores:

1. The coroner holds formal jury inquest on a body for which no legal competent identification is offered. A coroner, usually in a big city, will sometimes hold inquest on a body that *cannot* be identified, if the record of such an inquest has or may have a value (fire, disaster, evidence of murder). No such reason exists here, and there is no one to identify the body. Witnesses said the man said he was Robert Ablett. This is mere presumption, and has weight only if nothing conflicts with it. Identification is a condition precedent to an inquest. It is a matter of law. (pp. 6-8)

2. Since Mark Ablett, missing and suspected of the murder, cannot defend himself, all evidence of his movements before and after the murder is vital (as also whether he has money to run away on); yet all such evidence is given by the man closest to the murder and is without corroboration. It is automatically suspect until proved true.

3. The police find by direct investigation that Robert Ablett was not well thought of in his native village. Somebody there must have known him. No such person was brought to the inquest. (The story couldn't stand it.)

4. The police know there is an element of threat in Robert's supposed visit, and that it is connected with the murder must be obvious to them. Yet they make no attempt to check Robert in Australia, or find out what character he had there, or what associates, or even if he actually came to England, and with whom. (If they had, they would have found out he had been dead three years.)

5. The police surgeon examines a body with a recently shaved beard (exposing unweathered skin) and artificially roughened hands, but it is the body of a wealthy, soft-living man, long resident in a cool climate. Robert was a rough individual and had lived fifteen years in Australia. That is the surgeon's information. It is impossible he would have noticed nothing to conflict with it.

6. The clothes are nameless, empty, and have had the labels removed. Yet the man wearing them asserted an identity. The presumption that he was not what he said he was is overpowering. Nothing whatever is done about his peculiar circumstance. It is never even mentioned as being peculiar.

7. A man is missing, a well-known local man, and a body in the morgue closely resembles him. It is impossible that the police should not at once eliminate the chance that the missing man *is* the dead man. Nothing would be easier than to prove it. Not even to think of it is incredible. It makes idiots of the police, so that a brash amateur may startle the world with a fake solution.

The detective in the case is an insouciant amateur named Anthony Gillingham, a nice lad with a cheery eye, a nice little flat in town, and that airy manner. He is not making any money on the assignment, but is always available when the local gendarmerie loses its notebook. The English police endure him with their customary stoicism, but I shudder to think what the boys down at the Homicide Bureau in my city would do to him. (pp. 8-10)

There is a very simple statement to be made about [such] stories: they do not really come off intellectually as problems, and they do not come off artistically as fiction. They are too contrived, and too little aware of what goes on in the world. They try to be honest, but honesty is an art. The poor writer is dishonest without knowing it, and the fairly good one can be dishonest because he doesn't know what to be honest about. He thinks a complicated murder scheme which baffled the lazy reader, who won't be bothered itemizing the details, will also baffle the police, whose business is with details.

The boys with their feet on the desks know that the easiest murder case in the world to break is the one somebody tried to get very cute with; the one that really bothers them is the murder somebody thought of . . . only two minutes before he pulled it off. But if the writers of this fiction wrote about the kind of murders that happen, they would also have to write about the authentic flavor of life as it is lived. And since they cannot do that, they pretend that what they do is what should be done. Which is begging the question—and the best of them know it. (pp. 12-13)

Raymond Chandler, "The Simple Art of Murder: An Essay" (originally published in a different form in The Atlantic Monthly, *Vol. 174, No. 6, December, 1944), in his* The Simple Art of Murder *(copyright 1950 by Raymond Chandler; reprinted by permission of Houghton Mifflin Company), Houghton, 1950 (and reprinted by Ballantine Books, 1972, pp. 1-21).*

ELEANOR GRAHAM (essay date 1956)

It is the Christopher Robin books which place [Milne] beside the immortals—four little books, amounting to no more than 70,000 words in all (his figures), but preserving (even to the dry and sere) something of the unconscious joy and loveliness of childhood.

Twenty years ago people wrangled about them and made rude noises over **Vespers,** sympathising with the boy whose secret life had been thus thrown open to public view. If the work had been less good, it might have died under the angry criticism launched at it, but succeeding generations of children still take the verses to their hearts and remember them for life. Sensible people, trying them again in maturity, have to admit the perfection of form, and their genuine simplicity. (p. 52)

These verses were almost as much inspired by Milne's own memories as by the daily contact with his son, though without Christopher Robin they would certainly never have been written. Somewhere he said that childhood's world is a very small place, intimately known, mapped out and labelled in every part, but soon forgotten until and unless some other child recalls it. It seems to have been so with himself, and the interaction of the two impressions, the one observed and the other experienced nearly forty years earlier, seems to have shown him the very essence of childhood when imagination and make-believe are only an extension of reality. Such material is delicate and spoiled as easily as one rubs the bloom off a hot-house grape; but Milne caught it dexterously, and transferred it to paper without damage or distortion. Had he been less detached, had he felt the situations more poignantly (as sentimental readers have often done), had he been less practised a maker of verses, the bloom would certainly have been lost.

Yet, to compare his work with that of Walter de la Mare, is to see at once that they lived in different worlds. De la Mare would never agree that childhood's world is small or easily explored to the limits. For him, it never faded, though young eyes have illuminated parts of it afresh for him too. In a sense, Milne was the journalist, seeing and getting what he had observed on to paper with all the skill at his command. He had not the magic in himself to transmute the things his eyes had seen into other shapes and forms by virtue of imagination. He had imagination, but was plainly not of those who can *live* in it.

He says he was never a child worshipper, and that he wrote his books "not as a poet becoming playful, nor a lover of children expressing his love, nor as a professional writer knocking together a few jingles for the little ones, but as a light verse writer taking his job seriously even in the nursery." No one will question his having taken the job seriously; the verse is so good. (pp. 52-3)

He chose rhythms as carefully as he devised forms, and in **Buckingham Palace,** he used one which expressed exactly the to and fro pacing and stamping of the sentries. **James, James,** conveys admirably the often laboured pedalling on a tricycle of just such a three year-old as J.J.M.M.W.G. du P. The former also illustrated his dexterity in capturing moods. There is the first awe of the small child facing the great height and tremendous dignity of the soldier in red coat and busby, but so quickly brought to earth by Alice's matter-of-fact interpolations about such things as his socks. Nevertheless, there are verses in which he failed to appreciate the whole feeling of a situation. **The Wrong House,** for instance, misses the child's real shock at finding himself suddenly in unrecognisable surroundings.

Sometimes Milne remained wholly observer, and though the child might have made him look, what he saw he registered with his adult mind, and the verse then missed its proper relation to the very young. He knew that, and pointed it out in connection with **The Mirror.** . . . (pp. 54-5)

Perhaps Milne's particular genius lay in recognising the little things which make up a child's daily round, lighting them up, not exploiting them for his own amusement. He brought his adult powers into a perspective in which they would function truly though in miniature. For him writing had to be fun, no one can read the **Pooh** tales without feeling that, without being aware of the lightness of his touch, the constant and spontaneous bubbling of fun and laughter, and most important of all in a child's book, of his unfailing benevolence. There is no jealousy, no unkindness, no trickery in his children's books—and it is interesting to find that he had thought a good deal about the subject. He knew that a child creates its own fairyland in its own terms, and that no matter how carefully the parents may try to keep away such dangerous communications, they cannot really deprive their children of the fruits of imagination. The milkman, for instance, in a conscientiously factual bedtime story, is immediately transformed into a legendary figure in the child's mind, and fairyland creeps in. Milne realised also the moral values which belong to the genuine fairy tales, truth, honesty, simplicity; and he saw that there was no place in them for sophistication or *worldly* wisdom. (pp. 57-8)

Milne never seems to have been at a loss for a suitable small situation. He never faltered for the right word. He never, indeed, put a foot wrong in these books, and his care for the choice of the right word makes hay of the theories of limited vocabularies for young age groups. Only bad and careless writers really need such a discipline. Milne hands his five-year-old readers such phrases as "hostile intent," "customary procedure," "expedition," "ambush." He extends their vocabulary and there is never any danger of dead spots arising from any failure in contact. He either uses his words so aptly that no further help is required, or drops in an explanation so cunningly that it seems neither intrusive nor educative. (pp. 58-9)

Eleanor Graham, "A. A. Milne," in The Junior Bookshelf, *Vol. 20, No. 2, March, 1956, pp. 51-9.*

BARBARA NOVAK (essay date 1957)

A. A. Milne's poems for children are at once lyrical, whimsical, and intimate. Lyrical, because in the truest sense of the word they are singable poems with a rhythmic structure which is delightful to the ear. . . . Whimsical, because they are filled with humor and fantasy, frequently using sound for the sake of sound in nonsense words, with a kind of freedom of thought which captures the gaiety of a child's mind and suggests a positive attitude to life and a fresh appreciation of the smallest things, which is too often lost in the experience of adult living.

They are intimate poems because in their phrasing and mode of expression they have a kind of inner whispering quality which imparts the feeling that the poem is a conspiracy between the child and the poet. If it is true that they were originally conceived in this way because of the personal relationship between the poet and his own child, they still transcend their specific purpose with universal qualities which make them meaningful to a much wider audience. Their intimacy derives from the poet's ability to establish a really strong relationship with the child's mind—to speak to him in his own language, and to anticipate and often mirror his thought processes, the way he would look at the world about him. Milne accomplishes this through the subjects or content he chooses to deal with, as well as through the actual formal structure of his poems.

The poetry of Milne delves into many sources for content, from profound themes such as **"Explained,"** in which the child asks to be told how God began, to humorous sound poems like **"Sneezles."** All have a magical blend of the proportion of the serious and the gay, the profound, and the humorous which is, for each, most appropriate to the relative situation in living experience.

It is a kind of content that is rooted in experience, and that displays incredible understanding of the child's own world of experience. It draws, therefore, on the things which to a child are real: the reality of the fantasy companion Winnie the Pooh is brought out in such poems as **"Us Two,"** as is the reality of the imaginary, only-to-be-seen-by-the-child Binker, in the poem of the same name. We are confronted here with a poetic vision which digs deep into the spiritual and imaginative resources of the child, and says for him what perhaps he would like to say himself. . . . Indeed, we might almost say that Milne's poetic content falls into two broad categories: one in which the poet expresses something *for* the child, and one in which he expresses *to* the child.

In the former category, we may group such poems as **"Solitude,"** where the child himself, speaking in the first person, describes the house where he goes when he is seeking his own inner privacy, or **"Busy,"** where with joyous freedom of spirit he fantasizes about the many things he thinks he might be. There are, also, first person poems written as though by the child, which explore the specific pastimes of the child. . . . And too, there are poems which express the child's relation to others especially older people. (pp. 355-56)

When dealing with the child's relation to older people, Milne manages beautifully to hit upon the very things that to a child being reared in a grown-up world are most universally meaningful in a psychological sense, or perhaps really, to state it more simply, most naturally and humanly true to his own feelings. In such poems as **"The Good Little Girl,"** in which the child is asked that ever constant grown-up question "Have you been a good girl?," or even in the tongue in cheek, written as though by a grown-up **"Rice Pudding,"** Milne manages with subtle humor to touch again upon the child's sense that grown-ups do not understand, even when in the simple matter of asserting his individual rights he prefers not to eat what he does not want to eat.

Here, I think, we may expect that the child will understand immediately what is the matter with Mary Jane, because he will probably recognize his own behavior on past occasions,

even while the author-poet is professing bewilderment as the bewildered grown-up. This is the theme too, of the poem **"Independence,"** where the child states simply at the end:

> It's no good saying it. They don't understand.
>
> (p. 356)

Always these poems for the child written as though by the child have an extraordinary inner-thought kind of quality, as in **"Down by the Pond,"** where the child, fishing, half aloud, half to himself, cautions people not to come near for the fish might hear. In **"Spring Morning,"** too, there is the blitheful sense of the unity of a child with nature; the child as a natural, free, unaffected being. . . . (p. 357)

[**"The Island"**] could spark in itself a long consideration of Milne as a poet. Putting aside the lilting structure for the time being, there is here an incredible metamorphosis of fantasy into reality. The physical realities of the child's journey are graphically described. . . . [There] is a kind of poetic elaboration of detail which adds atmospheric reality to the fantasy of the mythical voyage to the distant isle. The child can climb, he can stagger, and stumble on his hands and knees, and hear the stones pattering down, and then finally, with ultimate satisfaction and a royal sense of achievement:

> And there would I rest and lie
> My chin in my hands, and gaze

Almost all of Milne's "I" poems have this immediate, true-to-the-child's-experience tone. Often too, they have the kind of nonsense whimsy which is too often lost in expression by and for adults. Thus, in **"Halfway Down,"** the child sits on a stair which really isn't anywhere but somewhere else instead. We are reminded here of E. E. Cummings' use of this sort of expression, though Milne's poetry differs in that it is not a sophisticated adult use of a child's manner of expression, but rather, the expression of a poet who has never lost the ability to think, feel, and express as a child.

In the category of poems in which he is expressing *to* the child, Milne himself appears for the most part in the clearly stated position of narrator, and again, establishes frequently what would seem to be a conspiratorial intimacy with his child listener. Many of these poems are distinct tales, often folk-lorish and adventurous in tone, and often, too, they deal with authoritative figures who are humanly appealing and not nearly as forbidding as their "positions" would lead us to suppose.

Thus, in **"King John's Christmas"** poor King John who was not a good man, yet had his hopes and fears, signed his Christmas wish not Johannes R. "but very humbly, Jack." (pp. 357-58)

The same kind of lack of affectation in **"Important People"** occurs when Teddy Bear has an adventure in the poem of the same name. Here he meets **"His Majesty the King of France,"** who is not too important to bow stiffly, remove his hat, and even stop, handsome if a trifle fat, to talk carelessly of this and that.

To the child, all of these **"Important People"** must seem no more or less important than other grown-ups; and Milne, therefore, would seem to me to be using them very wonderfully, simply to demonstrate their humanity, and perhaps to enable the child to identify more easily with all grown-ups, who must seem important in their very role as grown-ups. (p. 358)

[In **"The Emperor's Rhyme"**] it is significant that the emperor had a rhyme which he used when he felt shy with strangers, or when someone asked him the time when his watch didn't go. These are the sorts of experiences a child would have, and yet, they deal also with human characteristics which extend from childhood to adulthood: shyness with strangers, embarrassment, self-consciousness, etc. . . . Such a poem draws not only on the areas of human behavior common to adult and child with which a child can identify (though on occasion one feels that only Milne's adults are so wonderfully fresh in spirit), but also on the child's innate love of nonsense sounds, rhymes that need actually make no real sense except, very properly, that "then it's time for tea."

Milne uses his content, too, in a half-nonsense way that is best characterized, perhaps, as meaningful understatement. In "**The Four Friends**," for example, nothing really happens, and yet everything does. James was only a snail, who sat down on a brick. But there is, in this poem, a tone, sound, or mood, call it what we will, which is perhaps Milne's most meaningful mode of expression, and is contained actually in his manner of phrasing, and his method of statement, an integral expressive factor in the form of his poetry. It lies largely in his end line:

> But James was only a snail,

and in his pertinent repetitions of just this kind of understatement at the end of each stanza.

The simplicity, always, of his statements about James, after the more complex descriptions of the tempestuous activities and grand habitats of the other animals is extremely telling, telling of the simplicity of the snail itself, small, low-toned, humbly carrying his own house on his back, and no doubt the hero of the poem for the child. (pp. 358-59)

But [Milne's] content becomes expressive, meaningful, magical, wonderful, because of the way he uses words, and the "how" of this seems certainly within the realm of our investigation.

The obvious love of word sounds and love of repetition of word sounds in his poetry would be, in itself, enough to endear his poems to the child, who shares very naturally this enchantment.

But Milne combines this with the above mentioned feeling for understatement and with a sensibility to phrased rhythms which derive impact and power through variation and a change of pace. . . . [After every stanza in "**Buckingham Palace**"] it is the "Says Alice" which sets the tone, and by the very way in which it is spaced, off to the right like a signature, we know that this is somebody's statement, and almost, we feel, an aside.

The use, indeed, of parenthetical asides, is one of Milne's most delightful ways of introducing variation into his themes, adding an intimate aspect of direct conversation which should be most appealing to the child. (p. 359)

[One] of Milne's favorite modes of composing [is] a sort of repetition which is achieved by retaining the constancy of as many elements as possible, for the sake of rhythm and emphasis, as well as meaningfulness for the narrative. . . . (pp. 359-60)

Milne's poetry depends largely on the singing sounds of his rhythms, which are rooted in repetition and rhyme and are usually a lyrical combination of both. With Milne's poetry, too, humor and whimsy seem to set the tone more frequently than highly pictorial images. However, in some of his more serious nature poems, such as "**Spring Morning**," he does capture through his choice of words, the atmospheric magic of the descriptive phrase which is capable of evoking strongly vivid images for his audience.

Perhaps because they are so musical, so singable, in their rhythms, and in the sounds created by their rhymes and repetitions, Milne's poems lend themselves extraordinarily well to reading aloud. . . . Milne himself was strongly aware of the need for expressive and imaginative spacing, for variation of type, and for creative structuring of his words on the page, to help carry the mood of his poems, and as a guide for reading aloud, as well as silently.

He is extremely inventive in his use of italics: to indicate a change of tone and emphasis, to distinguish between speech and thought, or often too, to introduce his frequent asides, or inject the narrator's comments into a running narrative. . . . (p. 360)

The richness of Milne's poetry lies in the extraordinary wealth of variety in both form and content. The content of his poems, the mood he wishes to express: the delight in nature, the tall tale that he spins of the Old Sailor, the child's fantasy that he will elaborate, the every-day world pointed up by poetic magic, . . . the humor, the fun, the joy in being, all create through their own meanings and substance, the formal structures in which he will present them.

The whimsical poems, filled with humor, will have light, bouncing rhythms as in "**Busy**": "round about and round about and round about I go." The adventurous and narrative tales, very often, a ponderous note of the grandiose, as in "**Bad Sir Brian Botany**," combined often, as here, with a hilarious sense of the ludicrous and a joyous love of descriptive sounds. . . .

There is, very appropriately in [the nature] poems, an air of quiet tranquillity, a kind of peace-with-the-world note which is conveyed by the soft even tempo of the words.

There are, too, occasional moments of sharp, poignant wistfulness, and echoes of human disillusionment, shared certainly by the child, that are strangely evoked by the singing rhymes. . . .

We cannot exhaust Milne: the variety of his images or the richness of his vision. Nor should we hope to try. It would seem as though every phase of a child's experience is expressed and understood by a poetic form which is eminently suited in tone to its content. That Milne works with ideas and artistic forms which are universally appealing is perhaps best evidenced by the continued meaningfulness of his expression for a different generation of adults and children alike. (p. 361)

> Barbara Novak, "Milne's Poems: Form and Content," in Elementary English (copyright © 1957 by the National Council of Teachers of English; reprinted by permission of the publisher), Vol. XXXIV, No. 6, October, 1957, pp. 355-61.

THOMAS BURNETT SWANN (essay date 1971)

When Milne is at his best—as a novelist sharing the vagaries of Mr. Pim or solving the mystery in the Red House, as a fantasist whose animals are more engaging than people and to whom fairy-tale princesses seem as modern as suffragettes, as a formal or familiar essayist after World War I—his world is infinitely visitable, a welcome escape from the brothels and bars of Naturalist fiction.

But Milne in his early essays [collected in *The Day's Play*], the pieces which launched his first career, gives the unfortunate impression that he spends his days at golf and croquet, his nights at house parties, and that he writes between strokes or cocktails. He is less a humorist than a farceur; he is not so much nimble as he is trivial; his style had been called "feathery," but he accumulates feathers until they become as ponderous as an overstuffed mattress. (p. 17)

Even in his callow days with *Punch,* his pieces had fitfully glowed with warmth and charm: when he wrote about gardening; when he wrote for the first and second times about golf and cricket. In his postwar essays, the glow steadies into an almost constant flame. He has learned the difference between the playful and the trivial; that he can write formal essays as well as familiar; that it is not always necessary to be amusing even when he is familiar. . . (pp. 18-19)

Best of all, Milne became a literary critic whose outspokenness is balanced by his love for tradition and whose opinions are so artfully expressed that he is stimulating even when he is wrong. No critic has surpassed his evaluations of Kenneth Grahame, James Barrie, and Saki. . . .

Bad, better, or best, Milne's essays and sketches served the commendable purpose of launching and helping to sustain him as a writer. In the early pieces, successful with his readers but shallow, contrived and dated, he at least became a stylist and developed the flexibility which was destined to characterize his plays, juveniles, and novels. In the later and stronger pieces, he displays the mind, the manners, the tastes of a cultivated and highly companionable author. . . . (p. 19)

[The collection of essays] *Those Were the Days* is a faltering apprenticeship and not an attainment. The superficial humor is neither savagely curative like that of Swift nor rooted in universal human foibles like that of Fielding, and it is too contrived and precious even to succeed as farce. . . . The young Milne was reasonably topical (though his topics were slight), tenaciously whimsical, but no more subtle than a bear riding a velocipede. . . .

[He] helped to popularize a daft, impertinent dialogue which passed for the voice of the young generation newly emancipated from the shackles of Victoria. To some of Milne's compatriots, it was both novel and delightful to hear young people talk slangily and impudently and without regard for the traditions and conventions of their elders. . . .

But the slang and impudence of the young Milne, directed against a queen and an era which have now been so thoroughly exorcised that it is no longer necessary to reject them—indeed, it is possible to view them with nostalgia instead of rancor— have lost their audacity. (p. 22)

In spite of numerous failures and occasional adequacies . . . the two collections [*Not That It Matters* and *If I May*] include Milne's first literary criticism and a strong presentiment of the critic to come. . . . The few pieces of literary criticism in *If I May* and *Not That It Matters* indicate that Milne has served his apprenticeship and developed a clean, spare style and a perspicacious eye. When the right subject presents itself, he can meet its demands. Happily, his next collection, *By Way of Introduction* sparkles with right subjects, most of them literary. (pp. 24-5)

By Way of Introduction introduces Milne, the man, in the new flattering light of maturity. Gone is the empty-brained, foppish young editor of *Punch* who seemed to spend more time at house parties than at the office. He still writes occasionally about parties, cricket, and golf, but the subject of recreation

is less important than that of creation: how books are created and why they are written; why they succeed or fail. (p. 25)

By Way of Introduction introduces a frank and articulate author who has read and written some excellent books, and who has written about them with the excellence which they deserve. He always felt that his essays were incidental to his plays, but the public considered them as incidental to his juveniles. But *By Way of Introduction,* still in print, has proved more durable than most of the plays, and it frames and vivifies the juveniles which it can not equal. (p. 27)

Year In, Year Out, Milne's last book, is a random collection published . . . when the author was seventy. . . . *Year In, Year Out* is a gracious and graceful farewell to the audience which had followed him faithfully through his long career, had sometimes maddened him by forgetting that he had created Mr. Pim as well as Pooh, but had never denied him a chance to speak. (pp. 29-30)

Year In, Year Out is the self-portrait of a writer successful but not boastful—wise but not sententious, aging but not old— who for half a century, from his first adolescent trillings in *Punch* to this, his farewell without tears, has spoken his mind through the medium of his essays. (p. 31)

Like Oscar Wilde, Milne satirized society and loved what he satirized. But, unlike Wilde, Milne as a dramatist has gathered dust along with his drawing rooms. Amid his dark, ornate, and overabundant furniture, his plethora of portraits and landscapes, chaise longues, and presentation clocks, move people whose manners seem as elaborate and artificial as a rococo chair. (p. 34)

[All] in all, when the good and enduring are weighed against the bad, dull, and derivative, the plays of Milne are a barren Sinai in which the manna of excellence is delectable but much too infrequent for a sustaining diet. (p. 36)

Whether playing in puddles or talking to horses, rabbits, and a puppy, whether walking on the beach with his father or lying in wait for Brownies, the child of [*When We Were Very Young*]— Christopher, John, Jack, Emmeline, or Mary Jane—is persuasive and real. He is not a sentimentalized child, impossibly good or oppressively cute. (pp. 75-6)

Avoiding sentimentality, Milne also avoids the opposite extreme of condescension. He never looks down from the Olympian eminence of maturity to treat a child's follies as the amusing antics of a puppy or a kitten. He never intrudes what he calls "that strange but uninteresting person," the author, except in a single poem, "**Sand-between-the-Toes**"; and here he neither sentimentalizes nor patronizes but simply recounts the time when he and Christopher Robin walked on the beach. (p. 76)

In brief, Milne has surpassed Mother Goose as a model, improving her versification, updating her characters, and producing shapely poems instead of infectious jingles.

He also appears to have used some later models. . . . [Milne and Christina Rossetti] resemble each other not only in individual poems but in their view of the countryside, its flowers, and its animals. Like many of the best nature poets, they were city dwellers who sometimes visited the country; and they wrote, therefore, not with the jaded familiarity of a farmer or a dairyman, but with a freshness and awe which led them to personify flowers as ladies and to look upon even the commonplace cow with affectionate wonder. (pp. 77-8)

But Milne is the better children's poet. As a craftsman, Christina is little superior to Mother Goose. Most of her songs, naïve, unstudied, charm us with their spontaneity; but a few of them read like rough drafts, hummed or jotted between her household duties and never polished. (p. 78)

Milne's flowers and cows recall Christina Rossetti; but his wild animals—bear, lion, elephant, fox, wallaby, mingo, bison—recall Hilaire Belloc and his *Bad Child's Book of Beasts.* But Milne has designed *When We Were Very Young* for children who, on the whole, are well behaved; and his beasts, though various and often carnivorous, are rarely inclined to a diet of human beings. . . .

The lilt of Mother Goose, the rustic wonders of Christina Rossetti, the varied bestiary of Belloc: Milne has read and borrowed but remained himself, an adaptor and not an imitator. Guiltless of imitating poets, he is guilty, however, of a sometimes obnoxious attempt to imitate babytalk. . . .

But Milne's occasional lapses hardly diminish the magic of Christopher Robin, the real little boy whose realistic portrait unifies and sweetens *When We Were Very Young* to the stature of a small classic. (p. 79)

[The] charm and freshness of *Now We Are Six,* the fact that it is both a distinguished sequel and a superior book in its own right, are more than a matter of assembling attractive new characters with old characters who have aged becomingly. The story poems of kings and knights and shipwrecked sailors, designed for children of six, and even ten, are considerably more than the slight anecdotes of *When We Were Very Young,* they are fully developed tales, almost ballads with well-defined unheroic heroes. (p. 81)

In addition, the story poems no longer necessarily contain children for their heroes. In other words, they reflect the fact that, as children mature and leave the nursery, they learn to project themselves into persons foreign to their actual experience. They can read about pirates and Indians, sailors and soldiers, without the intermediary of a Peter Pan. The story poems in *When We Were Very Young* generally included children. . . . The story poems of the second volume, however, abound with adults. (pp. 81-2)

Furthermore, in *Now We Are Six* Milne seems less indebted to Mother Goose than to the more complicated craft of Robert Louis Stevenson's *A Child's Garden of Verses.* Always a careful craftsman, Milne rivals Stevenson in the glossiness of his lines, the assurance and yet the surprise of his rhymes, the variety of his forms.

Equal to Stevenson in craftsmanship, Milne surpasses him in characterization; in the ease with which he enters his subjects, whether children or adults, laughs with their laughter, stomps his foot with their pique; and avoids the preaching which makes a poem seem a lesson. (p. 82)

To summarize Milne's achievement as a poet for children: *When We Were Very Young* and *Now We Are Six* have captured a bright, appealing child in his everyday moments as no other poet could have captured him. *In his everyday moments* is also a clue to Milne's limitations, for he has not attempted the heights and the depths of a child's experience, such as sadness. In the Christopher Robin poems, there is pique, disappointment, and occasional loneliness, but there is no real sadness. (p. 83)

If Milne has omitted the depths of a child's sadness, he has also omitted the heights of his wonder; he has missed his closeness to the mysteries of creation, to what Wordsworth called the "clouds of glory." (p. 84)

Milne's limitations, however, are those of genius. Within his chosen range he is unsurpassed. Christina Rossetti, Stevenson, De la Mare, Lear, and Carroll: masters all of them—but which one has created the equal of Christopher Robin, who belongs to the world's children as Pooh belongs to Christopher? (pp. 84-5)

Most admirers of Pooh are not aware that 1925 saw the publication of a volume called *A Gallery of Children,* a bloodless and Pooh-less book of stories which taught the author to write the better stories about his famous bear. . . . Except for Poor Anne, whose hair turns an unbecoming red, the little heroes and heroines are as charming but unlikely as Hummel figures, whose place is a china shelf and not in a book of stories. (p. 86)

But Milne at least learned from his first book of stories for children that his next must assemble characters who were lively instead of pretty, and that he must characterize them by incidents as well as descriptions and dialogue. (p. 87)

It was not hard for Milne, who had profited from his mistakes in *A Gallery of Children,* to tell a whole book of stories about Pooh. (p. 89)

It goes without saying that Pooh, in text as well as illustrations, remains triumphantly and uproariously the hero of [*Winnie-the-Pooh*], a Sancho Panza without a Don Quixote, but one who has found his own windmills to tilt. Hinting for honey, breasting a flood atop a jar, or searching for Eeyore's tail, he is all the funnier because he is not aware of his fun. . . . (pp. 90-1)

But a clown, even an accidental one like Pooh, requires an audience to evoke his buffooneries; to inspire, reflect, and amplify; to act as foils. Pooh has a host of friends who are jesters in their own right and foils to the jests of the master. . . .

Pooh and his friends constitute what Ben Jonson would have called "humour" characters. In each of them, one characteristic is exaggerated for humorous effect—Pooh's gluttony, Owl's pedantry, Piglet's timidity, Tigger's energy. . . . The wonder is that Milne, working within such rigid limitations and forced to characterize with broad, brief strokes, has managed to create individuals instead of types. His secret is that he constantly reveals character through action. The animals meet, talk, and characterize themselves with tricks of speech—Pooh is diffident and halting except on the subject of food; Owl, verbose and pedantic—but they plan or adventure even while they talk. As in most books loved by children, action is never made to wait on words. The action may not be large. Pooh and Piglet may spend a chapter walking in circles. But always something is in doubt, something threatens or promises. (p. 91)

In addition to the animal characters, there is Christopher Robin, who comes up a hill or down from a tree when his friends get in trouble and, like a deus ex machina, extricates and advises them. Human beings as a rule should not be mingled with talking animals. . . . Christopher Robin could not be denied admittance to a story about his own animals and told for his own benefit. He could, however, be denied importance. Milne, an author as well as a father, has strictly limited his son's appearances and made him unobtrusive and unpatronizing when he does appear. . . .

Such characters—indispensable animals and incidental boy—deserve a setting which befits their antics; and Milne provides for them a forest which is never named but tantalizingly drawn by Shepard. . . . (p. 92)

Sensible Christopher Robin knows that the Heffalump and the Woozle exist only in the imagination of Pooh and Piglet. There may be threatening floods, but there are always honey jars to serve as boats. Oak trees spread their branches not to conceal Wizzles but to provide houses for Owl and Piglet. Caves hold Poohs instead of grizzly bears. The forest of Milne is not the haunt of Pan, lying in wait to terrorize travelers, but of animals kinder than the kindest men and of a little boy whose whistle is an incantation. (p. 93)

The House at Pooh Corner revisits the familiar and beloved characters but engages them in agreeably new adventures. . . . Considered together, the Winnie-the-Pooh books, even more than the Christopher Robin poems, represent the summit of Milne's achievement in all fields, a mountain so easily climbed that it seems a hill until we get to the top and find ourselves almost in the clouds. Lewis Carroll had caught the sensible nonsense of childhood; Barrie, the wonder and the wounding sadness. Kenneth Grahame had detailed the forests and fields, the rivers and islands of the English countryside with the accuracy of a naturalist and the language of a poet. But Milne captured, incomparably and enduringly, the frolic and indolence, the sweetness and foolishness, of animals which are also people.

His animals are laughable and, at the same time, lovable. They are laughable because they miniaturize our human eccentricities. Who has not met an over-indulgent Pooh among his acquaintances? Or a fearful Piglet? Or a pessimistic nay-sayer like Eeyore? (p. 94)

Milne, who loves his animals, never makes them figures of ridicule: foolish at times, yes; ridiculous, no. They are jesters but not caricatures. They are not vehicles for mordant satire or farcical burlesque. Even less than in *Once on a Time* is he writing an *Animal Farm* or a *Gulliver's Travels*. His fatherly warmth permeates the book, and his fondness for animals which, furry, hoofed, pawed, or striped, demand to be hugged instead of scolded. His animals are lovable because they are loving. Their claws do not rend, their hooves do not bruise. (p. 95)

Even the most ardent fans of Pooh and Christopher Robin are often surprised to learn that the author enjoyed a briefly successful but protracted career as a novelist for adults. Milne's misfortune was that he wrote his two best novels, *Mr. Pim Passes By* (adapted from the play) and *The Red House Mystery*, in the early 1920's and then overshadowed them with his own juveniles. . . . When he returned to the writing of novels in the 1930's and the 1940's, most of his readers either ignored him or reminded him that what they preferred was another Pooh and not a Mr. Pim. If they did read *Two People, Four Days' Wonder*, and *Chloe Marr*, they justly concluded that he should have said good-by to his novels instead of his juveniles.

Milne succeeds best as a novelist when he limits his canvas to a few people, a short time and a small scene—in other words, when he practices the Aristotelian unities which he learned as a dramatist. . . . True, he can fail even when he limits his time and his scene as in *Four Days' Wonder*. More often, however, as in *Mr. Pim Passes By* and *The Red House Mystery*, he seems to draw power and confidence from his self-imposed restrictions. (pp. 98-9)

Yet his very craftsmanship has worked to discredit him. In the first decades of the twentieth century, the well-made novel and the well-made poem fell into disrepute. Plot, it was widely argued, was an artificial order imposed upon the disorders which constitute life; and the honest novelist, the realistic novelist, as opposed to the mere practitioner for the popular magazines, should allow the thoughts of his characters to assume a chaotic stream of consciousness analogous to a patient's ramblings on a psychoanalyst's couch. . . .

In such a climate, it is not likely that Milne's novels—even his good ones—will return to favor. . . . [However, both *Mr. Pim Passes By* and *The Red House Mystery*] deserve renewed attention. In both of them Milne has more than fulfilled his theory of drama and fiction: he has shaped his materials, arranged, compressed, and neatened, and made his "characters behave unnaturally, in order that to the audience, looking in the mirror, they shall seem natural." On the other hand, when he apes the modern convention of formlessness in *Two People* and *Chloe Marr*—meanders instead of pursuing a recognizable plot, and ends with a whimper and not a bang—he fails as a novelist. (p. 99)

Like most of the best comic novels, *Mr. Pim Passes By* has a theme, a point, a significance. It harnesses laughter to the cart of wisdom. (p. 101)

[The protagonist Olivia] is the New Woman, and her triumph over [her husband] George exemplifies Milne's view that modern marriage should be a partnership and not an enslavement of wife to husband. In all of Milne's novels except *The Red House Mystery*, women are stronger, wiser, and infinitely more engaging than men. . . . [Olivia] is the New Woman but she is neither a blaring suffragette nor a cigarette-puffing Flapper; she is not free with a bottle or with her favors. She is new but also old; womanhood, eternal and unchanging—she is strong but she veils her strength with tenderness; wise but she never flaunts her wisdom; beautiful but she does not exploit beauty to achieve her goals. Inevitably, she overshadows George, but the shadow she casts is a soft suffusion rather than a blackness, and George is illuminated rather than obliterated—inspired to his best, excused of his worst. . . . Olivia humbles her husband without wounding his pride and asserts her right to be a comrade as well as a wife. (pp. 101-02)

The novel is, however, more than praise for a woman's charm and a plea for woman's rights. It is also an oblique assault on the outworn attitudes on the rustic aristocracy. . . . (p. 102)

The same Milne who, when young, had avidly collected invitations to English country houses now punctures the traditions and pretensions of the very people who were once his hosts. . . . He knew that it was time to reexamine the old morality and see how much of it was founded on true moral principles, and how much on arbitrarily defined manners. He may not have welcomed the future without reservations; . . . but in *Mr. Pim Passes By* he smiles wryly at change and holds out his hand. (pp. 102-03)

Plot summaries, usually dull, are totally inadequate for *The Red House Mystery*, which, when summarized reads like a farce of mistaken identity—in fact, like one of Milne's lesser plays. But Milne generates considerable and not in the least farcical mystification as Antony and Bill chase clues and a possible corpse through a secret passageway or search a muddy lake for a bundle which may be a body. . . . His clean, swift prose—the perfect exemplification of his principle that mystery writers should write simply—hurries Antony to a solution of the crime in four concentrated days.

Suspense, however, is not the chief excellence of the book. By present-day standards, and to readers addicted to the plenitude of thrills in Ian Fleming or Daphne du Maurier, the story may seem to be uneventful and even bland. (p. 106)

Milne's success, on the contrary, lies less in surprise or shock than in characters meticulously individualized against a convincing background. (pp. 106-07)

Milne was too scrupulous a storyteller to blur Antony. We know his background as a well-to-do young gentleman who chose adventure as some men choose security. . . . We know his mind and his heart; he is not a shell to be possessed by the reader like an empty conch by a hermit crab. He is Antony Gillingham, soldier of fortune. Most of Milne's heroes are silken and effete, if not effeminate. . . . But Antony is a welcome exception: he is manly without being tough, an adventurer without being a ruffian. (p. 107)

Versatility was a mixed blessing to Milne. . . . No sooner did he establish himself as an essayist than he hurried to write a play. Established as a dramatist, he turned to novels and juveniles. His four major careers sometimes complemented each other, but they also at times conflicted, drawing him in several directions at once, sapping his creativity, producing repeated failures along with memorable successes. As an additional drain on his powers, he also wrote three volumes of poems and three volumes of short stories. In neither of these areas can he be said to have carved an additional career—his offerings are too infrequent and undistinguished; they are afterthoughts, bagatelles. (p. 117)

Milne's final volume of verse was not a collection but a long single poem, *The Norman Church* . . . , the kind of book which publishers accept only out of deference to a writer who has supplied them through many years with better, more marketable books in other fields. (p. 120)

[Milne] has not achieved a great or even a competent poem. The first of [its] four divisions, which concerns a likable vicar who is content to teach the old platitudes without questioning them, is the best . . . but the following three divisions are notably less successful. Milne's forte is for people and places: for the human, not the cosmic. As soon as he departs from the vicar and the church and proceeds to question the accumulating legends and lies which have come to distort God, he departs from competence. . . . He lacks the largeness of expression or concept which large poetic themes demand, as well as the surprise and passion, the sweep and profundity. He lacks the grandeur, the resonance, and the verbal symphonics of Lucretius, Pope, and Tennyson. His jingling verses, his nine-line stanzas of three couplets and a triplet, are suitable to the unpretentious portrait of the vicar and his ''accidental village,'' but they cannot sustain the burden of major themes. The latter tinkle when they ought to reverberate. (pp. 121-22)

Considered together, [Milne's collections of short stories] *The Secret and Other Stories, Birthday Party,* and *A Table Near the Band* may be categorized and mildly approved by the adjective ''incidental.'' In the 1920's Milne's stories were incidental to his plays, novels and juveniles. In the late 1940's, when he turned in earnest to the writing of stories, he had passed his prime. At his rare best, he remained a first-rate raconteur like the Milne of *The Ivory Door* a purveyor of curious plots and arresting people. At his frequent worst, he spoke with a firm

voice and assured gestures but without the power and inventiveness which belong to the masters; and his tales seemed decorated incidents rather than fully realized stories. (p. 125)

> *Thomas Burnett Swann, in his* A. A. Milne *(copyright © 1971 by Twayne Publishers, Inc.; reprinted with the permission of Twayne Publishers, a Division of G. K. Hall & Co., Boston), Twayne, 1971, 153 p.*

GEOFFREY GRIGSON (essay date 1974)

A. A. Milne was a poet—he wrote poems, shall I say, no less than John Betjeman, or Eliot; or William Empson. Undeniably *When We Were Very Young,* his most successful book, is filled with poems. (p. 12)

The nature of the best-seller has to do with the nature of a class, its prime interest is one of sociology, not literature; which is the fun of such books. The readers have mattered most of all, and it is not difficult to be sure of the readers who have found a voice in A. A. Milne, to be sure of the readership (and the sociological writership) to which he belonged. From the poems you need only to deduce the keepings of Christopher Robin, and Percy, and John, and Mary Jane, and Emmeline, and James James Morrison Morrison Weatherby George Dupree.

The poems intimate that these children are of good family—at least up to the Forsyte standard. They have nannies and nurseries (*passim*). Maids are also in attendance—though not butlers (see *The Wrong House*).

Their homes, in London, are in the right squares, are not too grand and not too mean. (p. 13)

Their world is Us, and the Other People. Those of the Other People who sell in shops or work with their hands (Jonathan Jo the gardener) are a little queer, and perhaps need washing (see *Bad Sir Brian Botany*), but they must be treated with consideration; which averts revolution. (p. 14)

Conclusions? We may now be sure that of these children the males are earmarked for the better schools, then the better colleges, high on the river (*mens mediocris in corpore sano*), at one of the 'two' universities; and that male and female they come of families comfortable, secure, self-certain, somewhat above the middle of the middle class.

Are the poems for other children of such homes? No, rather than yes. Children, in my experience, of every generation since and including the Twenties, have found the poems nauseating, and fascinating. In fact, they were poems by a parent for other parents, and for vice-parental nannies—for parents with a war to forget, a social (and literary) revolution to ignore, a childhood to recover. *When We—We—Were Very Young* the book is named, after all, indicating its aim; which, like the aim of all natural best-sellers, was not entirely explicit, one may assume, in the author's consciousness.

Here mamas of the middle way, and fathers, and nannies, those distorting reflectors of the parental ethos, could be sure of finding Innocence Up to Date. . . . No hint in these poems of children nasty, brutish and short, as *Struwelpeter* or Hilaire Belloc made them (or as they are being re-established in newspaper cartoons).

Are there ever tantrums, as these nice children say 'cos', and 'most', and 'nuffin', and 'purfickly', and 'woffelly', in their nice accent? . . . If there are tantrums, it is rice pudding again;

but not the child psyche, not infant sexuality, not Freud, who had now entered the pure English world. (pp. 14-15)

The innocence of *When We Were Very Young*—of course it chimes with the last tinkle of a romantic innocence which by the Twenties had developed to whimsy. Christopher Robin comes trailing the tattiest wisps of a glory soiled by expectation and acceptance. The clouds have gone grey. The Child, in spite of Westminster and Trinity, is all too much at last the Father of the Man. (p. 15)

For some Poets Who Don't Sell, these poems for people towards the top with children beneath the age of literary consent have the qualities of rhythm, shape, economy, and games with words—good qualities, after all. Would it be too ponderous to say as well that they were poems for a class of middle to top people who had lost their intellectual and cultural nerve, who expected of right things which they had not earned, and who had scarcely looked a fact in the eye for fifty years? It might be too ponderous. But it would be true.

And sometimes out it comes in the charming sick, in the actual stuff, with an ironic unconsciousness. As Christopher Robin says, imagining himself on a desert island instead of his holiday coast of Cornwall, in the land of Betjeman:

> And I'd say to myself as I looked so lazily
>   down at the sea:
> There's nobody else in the world, and the world
>   was made for me.
>
>   (pp. 15-16)

Geoffrey Grigson, "The Mildly Monstrous," in his The Contrary View: Glimpses of Fudge and Gold *(© Geoffrey Grigson 1974), Rowman and Littlefield, 1974, pp. 12-22.**

ALISON LURIE   (essay date 1976)

In spite of their apparent simplicity, **"Winnie-the-Pooh"** and its sequel, **"The House at Pooh Corner,"** tell a story with universal appeal to any child anywhere who finds himself, like most children, at a social disadvantage in the adult world. What Milne has done is to turn this world upside down, so that Christopher Robin becomes the responsible adult, while everyone around him has turned into toys or animals, inferior in both size and authority.

Though the characters in **"Winnie-the-Pooh"** may have been drawn from Milne's own childhood, or his son's, they are also brilliant portraits of figures that might appear in any childhood. Who has not had a cheerfully reckless friend like Tigger, or a wryly gloomy one like Eeyore? . . . Even more to the point, what child—or adult—has not had days when he felt like Tigger or like Eeyore, or like Pooh himself? It was Milne's genius to have created, working from such apparently simple materials, these universal types.

Milne's other great achievement is to have created, out of a few acres of Sussex countryside, a world that has the qualities both of the Golden Age of history and legend, and the lost paradise of childhood—two eras which, according to psychologists, are often one in the unconscious mind.

The world of Pooh is without economic necessity or competition. There are no cars, planes, radios or telephones; war, crime and serious violence are unknown. Aggression is limited to the mildest practical joke, and even that generally backfires.

It is a society of loyal and eccentric friends, in which the main occupations are eating, exploration, visiting and sports. The greatest excitement centers around the capture of strange animals or the rescue of comrades in danger; but this danger is always from natural causes. Apart from occasional bad weather, it is a perfectly safe world.

"Winnie-the-Pooh" is essentially a modern version of an archetypal legend. It is a very old one—almost the first, in Biblical terms—the story of a peaceful animal kingdom ruled by a single benevolent human being. Milne even tells us that Christopher Robin, like Adam, gave names to his subjects.

It seems no accident, therefore, that the threat of change and loss enters this Eden in the shape of a tree of knowledge. One day, Christopher Robin is discovered to be missing from the Forest. He has gone to school for the first time and is learning his alphabet, beginning with the letter A. Eeyore comes across this letter A, arranged on the ground out of three sticks, and walks slowly around it: "'Clever!' said Eeyore scornfully. . . . 'Education!' said Eeyore bitterly."

He is right to be bitter. It is Education that will, by the end of **"The House at Pooh Corner,"** have driven Christopher out of his self-created Eden. No wonder many readers weep when they read the last chapter of this book. They know that they too have lost their childhood paradise. That is why, I think, they are so grateful to A. A. Milne, who managed to preserve one such world for generations past and those to come.

Alison Lurie, "Now We Are Fifty," in The New York Times Book Review *(© 1976 by The New York Times Company; reprinted by permission), November 14, 1976, p. 27.*

ELLEN TREMPER   (essay date 1977)

Apologies are due at the start of a paper that presumes to analyze the humor of Alan Alexander Milne. For, despite the buoyancy and irrepressibility of *Winnie-the-Pooh* and *The House at Pooh Corner*, the coldness of the analytical eye temporarily deadens what seem to me, by turns, the most delightfully arch, witty, and humorous books ever written for children or, I should say, for adults.

I make the correction of "adults" for "children" because while children certainly appreciate the stories, their sometimes exquisitely side-splitting humor is available almost exclusively to the grownups reading to the children. . . . [Now] that I have read the stories to my own child, it is easy to see why children respond to them with great earnestness while adults are bowled over by their profound funniness. (p. 33)

The universal appeal of [the] animals has little to do with a young listener's finding adequate representations in them of real life friends. Making such connections between fiction and life, indeed, being conscious enough of personality to discriminate Poohs, Piglets, and Eeyores among one's friends, requires sophistication that few five or six year olds have. It is much more likely, as [Alison Lurie] . . . states [see exerpt above], that a child will subconsciously sense that at one time or another he has been all of these animals himself. He identifies with them and for this very reason does not regard them as particularly funny. Seeing one's own behavior as humorous requires objectivity beyond the reach of children, if not of most adults.

The second, perhaps more important reason for a child's earnest response to the books concerns the character of much of their humor. Milne seems to have had a wonderful time creating these stories, writing them more for himself, I suspect, than for his son Christopher. They are filled, that is, with witty word play and ironic repartee way over a child's head. So while the popularity of these stories may well rest on children's primitive identification with archetypal figures and situations, their high comedy is grownup business, of value to their writer and readers, not to their listening audience. (p. 34)

[Their] charm depends upon the fact that the stuffed animals have been transformed into seemingly breathing ones with complicated lives of their own while Christoher Robin, and all children to whom they are read, wait, round-eyed and passive, for the grown-up magician to perform this miraculous life-giving metamorphosis.

But even Milne in [the first chapter of *Winnie-the-Pooh*] seems a little uneasy about the roles that he, Christopher Robin, and the animals will play. The dialogue between him and the listening Christopher Robin is henceforth given in italics. . . . After this chapter, the narrator conceals himself, and Christopher Robin is only a character in the stories. And while Pooh, in this first story, has been given life and then demoted to the status of stuffed toy . . . , he is ever after as alive as Christopher Robin. . . .

And, to adults, ten times as funny. Broadly speaking, the comedy in *Winnie-the-Pooh* and *The House at Pooh Corner* falls into the classical categories of humor and wit. Milne, it would seem, was guided by the dictionary definition of humor in creating the character of Pooh: "the ability to perceive that which is comical or ludicrous or ridiculous but connotes kindliness, geniality, sometimes even pathos, in the expression and a reaction of sympathetic amusement from the audience." All of the characters are humorous with the exception of Eeyore (whose funniness is pure wit . . .). (pp. 35-6)

As adults, we see our own children in different moods in these animals. Their transparent guile and artless devices are what make them humorous. We laugh with the baby who totters so comically as he takes his first steps. Likewise, we laugh in sympathetic amusement with these animals whose stratagems mimic, in childish fashion, the efforts of grown-ups to solve problems in the adult world.

The first difficulty that Pooh encounters in **"We Are Introduced to Winnie-the-Pooh and Some Bees, and the Stories Begin"** is, not surprisingly, how to get the honey from the bees' hive. In this adventure Christopher Robin is the knowing adult while Pooh is his inexperienced "child" whose honey-getting scheme is so amusingly disingenuous. (pp. 36-7)

Milne delights in exploding the idiomatic language of adults, so opaque to children, by supplying very literal translations that answer a child's desire for pictorial representation. He wittily points to the absurdities in language that we ignore but which become very amusing when we pay them any attention. (p. 40)

The narrator also relies on typography for the creation of visual jokes that seem to be made more for the reading adult than for the listening child. . . . Milne's capitalizing of descriptive words is another visual device that turns them into names reminiscent of the titles of religious tracts. Pooh, trapped in Rabbit's front door, asks: "'Then would you read a Sustaining Book, such as would help and comfort a Wedged Bear in Great Tightness?'". . .

But the narrator's allusions to emblem poetry and religious literature, or his examinations of idiomatic language pale beside the brilliance of Eeyore's devastatingly sarcastic and deadpan wit. He has "the ability to perceive the incongruous and to express it in quick, sharp, spontaneous, often sarcastic remarks that delight or entertain." Part of the pleasure we get from Eeyore's retorts is that their sarcastic drollness always hits the mark at once. He says, at the first go, what we wish we could have said at the time, if we had been thinking on our feet (as a four-legged beast like Eeyore usually does).

He is at his best, with a little descriptive help from the narrator, in Chapter VI of *The House at Pooh Corner,* **"In Which Pooh Invents a New Game and Eeyore Joins In."** (pp. 41-2)

The adult reader recognizes a number of allusions to growing up and maturing in the second volume, *The House at Pooh Corner.* The current is inescapable; even nature participates. . . . It seems to me no accident that it should be Eeyore who opens the subject of education and knowledge, for witty Eeyore (who was *never* a child) is the most adultly humorous of the animals. We can extend the obvious theological metaphor of the loss of Eden by considering it from a more positive perspective; that is, viewing it as some theologians have, as "the fortunate fall." With our adult knowledge of what we missed in childhood through ignorance and inexperience, indeed, with our knowledge of what we would miss in our reading of the *Pooh* books if we were children again, we cannot regret our banishment from Paradise. Hindsight teaches us that our grown-up appreciation of Eeyore's wit and Pooh's artless artfulness—appreciation that comes only through knowledge—is the prize A. A. Milne awards us for having left, as our first Parents did, "[. . . our] happy seat," to find "The World was all before [. . . us]." (pp. 43-4)

Ellen Tremper, "Instigorating 'Winnie the Pooh'," in The Lion and the Unicorn *(copyright © 1977 The Lion and the Unicorn), Vol. 1, No. 1, Summer, 1977, pp. 33-46.*

ROGER SALE   (essay date 1978)

I really am not able to read [A. A. Milne] as I once could. I loved the Christopher Robin books, but find only intermittent pleasure in them now, and when they fail to cast their old magic spell, I am not just bored but offended. As a child listening to and staring at [Jean de Brunhoff's] Babar books, I trusted the relation I was enacting with the adult doing the reading, because the adult was not trying to ask me to respond any differently than I was. But the adult reader of Christopher Robin implicitly seeks more with the child being read to than that. The adult is explicitly put in the position of Milne himself, the child in the position of Christopher Robin: "you" and "I," the text says clearly. This might be all right, or even fun, except that Milne is always nudging Christopher Robin, instructing him, urging upon him good manners and good spelling and obedience, and this makes it hard on me as an adult reader. It may also explain why many children, after they become old enough to read to themselves, don't read these books, because so much in them depends on the relation of reader and read-to, adult and child. (p. 15)

[All] too often in Milne, the essential action is to construct a hierarchy, to calculate one's superiority to someone else and then worry about who is superior to oneself. (p. 16)

The books are essentially about the fact that Christopher Robin is now too old to play with toy bears. He is given a world over which he has complete power, and if he is not very attractive as a deus-ex-machina in story after story, if he is never as interesting as the Pooh and Piglet to whom he condescends, the pleasures of his power are clear enough. Christopher Robin is now going to school, doing sums, spelling, worrying about not getting things right; he takes his fear of ridicule and his need to fit into a hierarchy and his schoolboy facts and imposes them on the animals in the Forest. Pooh is not, of course, a bear of very little brain, but Christopher Robin keeps putting him in situations where he will think he is, which is just what, one imagines, others are doing to Christopher Robin in his hours away from the Forest. Thus the alliance Milne seeks to create with Christopher Robin, whatever we may say of its entanglements otherwise shrewdly seeks to console Christopher Robin for the pains of having had to leave the Forest. Children, certainly myself as a child, are much more interested than students of college age in learning about the ways it is sad, but all right, that we grow beyond early childhood, and even the snobbish Milne offers the assurance that we are growing toward something as well as growing away from something else. (p. 17)

Milne's most explicit statement of this theme, which comes in the closing sentences of **The House at Pooh Corner,** always moved me very much. It has come time for Christopher Robin to say good-bye to the Forest forever, and he takes Pooh up to the top of the Forest and dubs him Sir Pooh de Bear. Then:

> So they went off together. But wherever they
> go, and what ever happens to them on the way,
> in that enchanted place on the top of the Forest,
> a little boy and his Bear will always be playing.

I do not think it particularly sentimental of me that I still find it hard to say these words without beginning to cry, though I am aware that my tears are for the lost boy I was who also once wept over them. The lies they tell are known to be lies, and that saves everything. Pooh and Christopher Robin do not go away together, and we know it. The Forest is forever closed, except to the memory, and that is not a sentimental fact.

What I never saw as a child, but see in many places now, is that the Forest is becoming tainted long before it is closed by the alien values of Christopher Robin's and Milne's world. The animals are forever deferring and being asked to defer. . . . That much is perhaps inevitable in most societies, but what makes it all painful is that Milne's view of schoolboy and adult life is so limited and empty, and his view of women, as seen in his digs at Kanga, is at the very least designed to foster the notion in Christopher Robin that one grows up by

finding mothers silly and fussy. Even when Christopher Robin is at his best, as when he announces that the stick in Pooh's hand is the North Pole, he is still finding ways to control others by hiding his own ignorance. Candor is generally a fugitive and discardable virtue in the Forest, except, I must hasten to add, for Eeyore. He is, though not just for that reason, the one character I enjoy now even more than I did as a child, and his jibes at Rabbit at the end of the game of Poohsticks still make me want to clap, with surprise at Eeyore's sudden burst of healthy bad temper and with delight that the neofascist Rabbit is finally told off. But for the rest, the pleasures seem to me awfully thin, or else worse. (pp. 17-18)

> *Roger Sale, "Introduction: Child Reading and Man Reading," in his* Fairy Tales and After: From Snow White to E. B. White *(copyright © 1978 by the President and Fellows of Harvard College; excerpted by permission), Cambridge, Mass.: Harvard University Press, 1978, pp. 1-22.**

ADDITIONAL BIBLIOGRAPHY

Adcock, A. St. John. "Alan Alexander Milne." In his *Gods of Modern Grub Street: Impressions of Contemporary Authors,* pp. 243-49. New York: Frederick A. Stokes Co., 1923.
    A survey of Milne's early career.

Brown, John Mason. "Mr. Milne Passes By." In his *Broadway in Review,* pp. 218-21. New York: W. W. Norton & Co., 1940.
    A contemporary review of Milne's *Autobiography.*

Crews, Frederic C. *The Pooh Perplex: A Freshman Casebook.* New York: E. P. Dutton & Co., 1963, 150 p.
    A parody of modern criticism. Through twelve imaginary critics, Crews examines Winnie-the-Pooh from the viewpoint of a Marxist, a Freudian, an Esthete, an Angry Young Man, and others.

Cunliffe, John W. "After War Playwrights: A. A. Milne." In his *Modern English Playwrights: A Short History of the English Drama from 1825,* pp. 211-16. 1927. Reprint. Port Washington, N.Y.: Kennikat Press, 1969.
    Survey of Milne's dramatic career which finds him an occasionally amusing minor playwright.

Harvey, Patrick. "E. H. Shepard, Illustrator of *Winnie the Pooh,* Now in His Nineties, Talks to Patrick Harvey." *The Listener* 84, No. 2163 (10 September 1970): 340-41.
    Shepard discusses his association with Milne and his illustrations of Milne's children's books.

Milne, Christopher. *The Enchanted Places.* New York: E. P. Dutton & Co., 1975, 169 p.
    A discussion by Milne about life with his father and the background to the Pooh stories.

Eugene (Gladstone) O'Neill

1888-1953

American dramatist.

O'Neill is generally considered America's foremost dramatist. His plays consistently examine the implacability of an indifferent universe, the materialistic greed of humanity, and the problems of discovering one's true identity. Because O'Neill's plays are bleak portraits of a world without ultimate meaning, critics have come to regard him as the most pessimistic of American dramatists.

The son of a professional actor, O'Neill was brought up on the road and acquired a precocious knowledge of the theater. His early years were profoundly affected by the pressures of his mother's recurring mental illness and his father's coldness, which he later vividly portrayed in *A Long Day's Journey into Night*. Although he was a voracious reader, O'Neill was a poor student; he preferred to spend his adolescence in barrooms with his profligate brother James. After expulsion from Princeton and a brief, unsuccessful marriage, O'Neill attempted suicide, then left his family for a life at sea. For two years he lived alternately as a seaman and a panhandling derelict in several South American ports, a period that provided material for many of his early plays. The turning point in his life came in 1912, when he suffered a mild attack of tuberculosis. While convalescing in a sanatorium he resolved to become a dramatist and spent the next several years assiduously studying his craft.

O'Neill's career can be divided into five somewhat distinct periods. The first, the period of his dramatic apprenticeship, lends nothing of consequence to his reputation. Included in this period is his first collection, *Thirst, and Other One Act Plays,* and the so-called *Lost Plays,* works so poor that O'Neill made no attempt to publish them.

O'Neill first gained recognition during his second period, which was devoted primarily to one act plays about the sea. According to some critics O'Neill's initial production, *Bound East for Cardiff,* marks the first departure from nineteenth-century melodrama and the beginning of serious American theater. All of these plays are slice-of-life dramas dealing with the delusions and obsessions of common people. *Ile* is particularly representative of this period with its naturalistic style, its tragic irony, and its use of the sea as a symbol of malignant fate.

During his third period, from 1920-24, O'Neill turned to longer plays. Foremost among these is *Desire under the Elms,* one of O'Neill's few conventional tragedies, which examines the power of repressed sexuality in a staid New England town. Throughout this period O'Neill exploited many experimental dramatic techniques. His most successful experiments were with symbolism in *The Emperor Jones* and expressionism in *The Hairy Ape,* a grim play in which a brutish laborer is destroyed by industrial civilization.

O'Neill's fourth, sometimes called his "cosmic," period extends to 1935. Throughout this era he was preoccupied with the problems of identity and the nature of fate, and these vast, sprawling plays are often much longer than traditional productions. O'Neill was still experimenting heavily with theat-

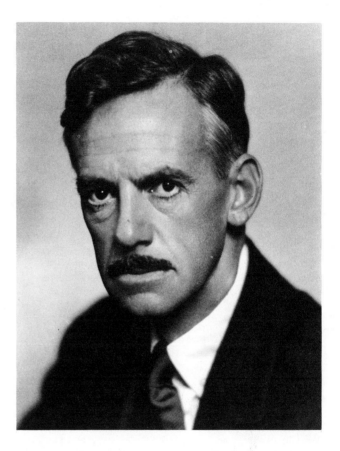

rical techniques and he successfully utilized such effects as masks, split personalities, and stream of consciousness monologues. The most important play of this era, *Mourning Becomes Electra,* is a powerful examination of the ways that guilt, jealousy, and sexual passion lead to the downfall of an old New England family. Uncharacteristic of this period, and of O'Neill's career as a whole, is *Ah, Wilderness!,* a nostalgic, idealistic comedy about adolescence that critics find one of his most unpretentious, and thus most successful, works.

Despite his award of the Nobel Prize in literature in 1936—he was the first American to receive that honor—O'Neill's reputation declined steadily after 1935. It was not until after his death that the plays of his last period gained recognition. Of these, *The Iceman Cometh,* a realistic study of the fragility of illusions, is generally considered his masterpiece, while *A Long Day's Journey into Night,* a portrait of a tormented, self-destructive family, is called one of the most powerful dramas in American theater.

It is generally agreed that O'Neill wrote some of the most important and some of the most lackluster of modern dramas. In his plays he experimented with almost every dramatic innovation of the early twentieth century. Unfortunately, experimentation with theatrical effects sometimes became an end in itself, and technique could not enhance such puerile, poorly conceived works as *The Great God Brown* and *Lazarus Laughed.* For this reason O'Neill's most realistic plays are considered his best. Similarly, while O'Neill was a master at sketching character, he also wrote melodramatic, needlessly verbose dialogue. It is such seeming contradictions that make O'Neill's work fascinating to contemporary critics; they often attack several elements of his plays while applauding the ultimate effects. O'Neill is universally acknowledged as an important tragedian who is credited with creating the traditions of twentieth-century American drama and is as integral to modern world literature as Bertolt Brecht and August Strindberg.

(See also *TCLC*, Vol. 1, and *Dictionary of Literary Biography*, Vol. 7: *Twentieth Century American Dramatists*.)

PRINCIPAL WORKS

Thirst, and Other One Act Plays   (dramas)   1914
Before Breakfast   (drama)   1916
Bound East for Cardiff   (drama)   1916
Ile   (drama)   1917
In the Zone   (drama)   1917
The Long Voyage Home   (drama)   1917
The Moon of the Caribbees   (drama)   1918
The Rope   (drama)   1918
Where the Cross Is Made   (drama)   1918
The Dreamy Kid   (drama)   1919
Beyond the Horizon   (drama)   1920
Diff'rent   (drama)   1920
The Emperor Jones   (drama)   1920
Anna Christie   (drama)   1921
Gold   (drama)   1921
The Straw   (drama)   1921
The First Man   (drama)   1922
The Hairy Ape   (drama)   1922
All God's Chillun Got Wings   (drama)   1924
Desire under the Elms   (drama)   1924
Welded   (drama)   1924
The Fountain   (drama)   1925
The Great God Brown   (drama)   1926
Lazarus Laughed   (drama)   1928
Marco Millions   (drama)   1928
Strange Interlude   (drama)   1928
Dynamo   (drama)   1929
Mourning Becomes Electra   (drama)   1931
Ah, Wilderness!   (drama)   1933
Days without End   (drama)   1934
The Iceman Cometh   (drama)   1946
*Lost Plays   (dramas)   1950
Long Day's Journey into Night   (drama)   1956
A Moon for the Misbegotten   (drama)   1957
A Touch of the Poet   (drama)   1958
*Hughie   (drama)   1959
Poems, 1912-1924   (poetry)   1980

*These are dates of first publication rather than first performance.

STARK YOUNG   (essay date 1922)

[The] most significant thing that can be said about Mr. O'Neill's plays at this stage of the game is that his qualities are funda-

mental theatre. He is like a sculptor who, good or bad, is a sculptor in that he models a form solidly; it is at least sculpture as far as it goes. The blackest artistic fault in the average painting is that it might have been said in sculpture, the average music in poetry, and drama in fiction. The primary and the rarest thing in any art is to attain to an expression that is in terms of the fundamentals of that art and that could be said in no other.

In *The Emperor Jones* and *The Hairy Ape* the pattern is a theatre pattern: their outline belongs to the stage. In *The Hairy Ape* Mr. O'Neill has done what happens only once in a dramatic generation and almost never then, he has invented a fable. He has created a story that begins and moves and ends in a line so right, so just, so simple and inevitable that it might easily be taken for granted by the imagination of the American theatre. The dialogue that Mr. O'Neill writes is in terms of his art; in his best scenes it has what you see only in one out of thousands of plays, a quality that might make it almost impossible as literature but yet moving and right as theatre. He has a current of thought and feeling that is essentially theatrical, taken off the stage it might often seem exaggerated, out of taste or monotonous. At his best he is in control of a flow of compelling emotion and a strange quivering intensity that is not equalled in recent English drama.

But in the very excellence of *The Hairy Ape* there is something implied that makes it necessary that Mr. O'Neill go on. The case of his dialogue parallels exactly the case of the plays in the large. The best examples of dialogue in his plays, like that in the first act of *Diff'rent,* or the first act of *Anna Christie* or *The Hairy Ape* are absolutely right as far as they go. The speeches carry us with them; they establish a stream of glowing and poignant and magnetic feeling. They bite; they have at times the precision and the thrill of poetry. But if you hear them often you begin to notice that they depend a good deal on single-track streams of emotion in the characters; they get results sometimes by repeating words over and over, sometimes merely by violent damns and oaths and unexpected frankness. You find them moving still but less engaging; you give to them more feeling than attention. These traits of dialogue need not in the least be faults in themselves. Yet the content of the dialogue would be deepened and widened if this secure and direct feeling were kept but at the same time there were more shading in the words themselves and more inclusion through these words of the whole content of the dramatic moment. Without lessening its strength or its force the dramatic texture of this dialogue might sometimes be enriched.

What holds for the dialogue fits the plays of Mr. O'Neill's future; they will bear enriching. In the greatest drama there is a distribution of elements. However, sweeping the emotion may be, the tragic beauty and the flight of the human spirit portrayed, there is in the whole sum of the work a balancing of things with a more complete view of the world and all that is in it. *The Hairy Ape* had only one thread. It was operatic, lyrical, in its interpretation of life. To think of it as a problem is absurd. It is what its author meant it to be, a powerful and picturesque statement of a thing that was insoluble. It was not even realism, but a sort of brutalism used lyrically. It was not revolutionary except in so far as it was a moving response to a certain human condition. *The Hairy Ape* was complete; what made it complete was not its comment on its material but its unity of emotion. In its high levels *The Hairy Ape* was perfect in its kind. But life nevertheless is more complex than all that. It was on the side of this larger complexity and grasp that

Diff'rent went to pieces at the end and *Anna Christie* failed, in so far as it did fail, to reach a bang-up and right conclusion. There are more and more elements to be considered as one's art develops. The intellectual weight and measure is one of the parts of us that drama involves as well as the more poignantly felt circumstance.

That this progression toward a wider complexity is dangerous, so sensitive a mind as that behind these plays knows, none better. One may be able to do a more or less single-minded thing well enough, but fail in others. A man like Mr. O'Neill may stumble and despair long before he finds—if he ever does—the same mastery in this more complex venture that he has achieved in his earlier work. (pp. 307-08)

I am not saying that Mr. O'Neill ought to do this, that or the other; such critical exhortation is a stupid intrusion—I am saying that from his best work I think that he will. (p. 308)

> Stark Young, "Eugene O'Neill," in The New Republic, *Vol. XXXII, No. 415, November 15, 1922, pp. 307-08.*

HUGO von HOFMANNSTHAL (essay date 1923)

Judging from those of [O'Neill's] plays with which I am familiar, his work is throughout essentially of the theatre. Each play is clearcut and sharp in outline, solidly constructed from beginning to end; *Anna Christie* and *The First Man* as well as the more original and striking *Emperor Jones* and *The Hairy Ape.*

The structural power and pre-eminent simplicity of these works are intensified by the use of certain technical expedients and processes which seem dear to the heart of this dramatist and, I may presume, to the heart of the American theatregoer as well; for instance, the oft-used device of the repetition of a word, a situation, or a motive. In *The Hairy Ape* the motive of repetition progresses uninterruptedly from scene to scene; the effect becomes more and more tense as the action hurries on to the end. Mr. O'Neill appears to have a decided predilection for striking contrasts, like that for instance, between the life of the sea and the life of the land, in *Anna Christie,* or between the dull narrowness of middle-class existence and unhampered morality, in *The First Man.* The essential dramatic plot—the "fable," that is—is invariably linked to and revealed by that visual element which the theatre, and above all, I believe, the modern theatre, demands. The dialogue is powerful, often direct, and frequently endowed with a brutal though picturesque lyricism.

In an American weekly publication I find the following judgment on Mr. O'Neill, written by an intelligent and very able native critic [Stark Young in excerpt above]: "He has a current of thought and feeling that is essentially theatrical. Taken off the stage it might often seem exaggerated, out of taste or monotonous." To this just praise—for it is intended as praise—I can heartily subscribe. But the same writer goes on to say, however, that in this dramatist's best scenes there is a power in the dialogue that is found in only one work among thousands. Granting that this is true, it seems to me that the manner in which Mr. O'Neill handles his dialogue offers an opportunity for some interesting speculations of a general character on the whole question of dramatic dialogue.

In my opinion, granting the primary importance of the dramatic fable, or plot, the creative dramatist is revealed through his handling of dialogue. By this, be it understood, I do not mean the lyrical quality or rhetorical power; these elements are in themselves of little importance in determining the value of dialogue. Let us assume a distinction between literature and drama, and say that the best dialogue is that which, including the purely stylistic or literary qualities, possesses at the same time what is perhaps the most important of all: the quality of movement, of suggestive mimetic action. The best dramatic dialogue reveals not only the motives that determine what a character is to do—as well as what he tries to conceal—but suggests his very appearance, his metaphysical being as well as the grosser material figure. How this is done remains one of the unanswerable riddles of artistic creation. This suggestion of the "metaphysical" enables us to determine in an instant, the moment a person enters the room whether he is sympathetic or abhorrent, whether he brings agitation or peace; he affects the atmosphere about us, making it solemn or trivial, as the case may be.

The best dialogue is that which charges the atmosphere with this sort of tension; the more powerful it is the less dependent does it become upon the mechanical details of stage-presentation. (pp. 249-51)

In the best works of Strindberg we find dialogue of this sort, occasionally in Ibsen, and always in Shakespeare; as fecund and strong in the low comedy give-and-take scenes with clowns and fools as in the horror-stricken words of Macbeth.

Measured by this high ideal, the characters in Mr. O'Neill's plays seem to me a little too direct: they utter the precise words demanded of them by the logic of the situation; they seem to stand rooted in the situation where for the time being they happen to be placed; they are not sufficiently drenched in the atmosphere of their own individual past. Paradoxically, Mr. O'Neill's characters are not sufficiently fixed in the past. Much of what they say seems too openly and frankly sincere, and consequently lacking in the element of wonder or surprise: for the ultimate sincerity that comes from the lips of man is always surprising. Their silence, too, does not always convince me; often it falls short of eloquence, and the way in which the characters go from one theme to another and return to the central theme is lacking in that seemingly inevitable abandon that creates vitality. Besides, they are too prodigal with their shouting and cursing, and the result is that they leave me a little cold towards the other things they have to say. The habit of repetition, which is given free rein in the plot itself as well as in the dialogue, becomes so insistent as to overstep the border of the dramatically effective and actually to become a dramatic weakness. (pp. 251-52)

[Mr. O'Neill's] first acts impress me as being the strongest; while the last, I shall not say go to pieces but, undoubtedly, are very much weaker than the others. The close of *The Hairy Ape,* as well as that of *The Emperor Jones,* seems to me to be too direct, too simple, too expected; it is a little disappointing to a European with his complex background, to see the arrow strike the target towards which he has watched it speeding all the while. The last acts of *Anna Christie* and *The First Man* seem somewhat evasive, undecided. The reason for this general weakness is, I think, that the dramatist, unable to make his dialogue a complete expression of human motives, is forced at the end simply to squeeze it out like a wet sponge.

I have no intention of giving advice to a man of Mr. O'Neill's achievements. . . . His qualities as a dramatist are already very great, and I have no doubt that he will make progress when, in the course of time, which is necessary to each man who creates, he shall have acquired better control over his materials, and above all over his own considerable talents. (p. 255)

Hugo von Hofmannsthal, "Reflections on Eugene O'Neill" (originally published as "Eugene O'Neill," translated by Barrett Clark, in The Freeman, *Vol. 7, No. 158, March 21, 1923), in* O'Neill and His Plays: Four Decades of Criticism, *edited by Oscar Cargill, N. Bryllion Fagin, and William J. Fisher, New York University Press, 1961, pp. 249-55.*

H. G. KEMELMAN (essay date 1932)

By the term melodrama as used in this essay will be understood the present meaning of exaggerated and unbalanced serious drama.

The popularity of the melodrama is due in great part to its romanticism. It presents in concrete form that vague, improbable, yet delightful daydream world which exists only in the unrestrained fancy of the individual. . . . The melodrama of the cinema is concerned with the romanticism of action, since physical prowess is for the movie fan the criterion of greatness. But there is another type of melodrama; a type which appeals to a more intellectual but no less romantic audience. This type, which we might call "highbrow melodrama", embodies intellectual and emotional romanticism. Highbrow melodrama is just as exaggerated and unreal as the melodrama of the movies, but the unreality is along different lines. And in this category of highbrow melodramas belong the plays of Eugene O'Neill.

In O'Neill we find no blond, curly-headed heroes foiling train robbers and no sleek, dark villains kidnapping heroines, but we do find two male types just as distinct and just as unreal as these. The male protagonist, or rather that male character who has the sympathy of the author, is the same in every play. He is always a sensitive soul with large, dark eyes and a face harrowed by lines of internal struggle. The other male type, the antagonist, although not always clearly defined since O'Neill's heroes do not always fight against individuals, is usually a thick-set, practical man with small, blue eyes. In the movie melodrama, virtue in the male was a matter of hirsutage on the upper lip; in the O'Neill highbrow melodramas, virtue depends on eye pigmentation. Let us examine the evidence.

In *The Great God Brown* the opposition between the two types is clearly stated. William Brown is first introduced to us as "a handsome, tall, and athletic boy of nearly eighteen. He is blond and blue-eyed, with a likeable smile and a frank good-humoured face, its expression already indicating a disciplined restraint. His manner has the easy self-assurance of a normal intelligence". The reader new to O'Neill is apt to jump to the conclusion that Brown is the hero of the piece, but the knowing will readily recognize the above description as typical of the O'Neill villain. "Frank good-humoured face", "disciplined restraint", "normal intelligence", and above all "blond and blue-eyed"—these are anathema to O'Neill. Consider now the hero of the play, Dion Anthony. "He is about the same height as young Brown but lean and wiry, without repose, continually in restless nervous movement. His face is masked. The mask is a fixed forcing of his own face—dark, spiritual, poetic, passionately supersensitive, helplessly unprotected in its child-like, religious faith in life—into the expression of a mocking, reckless, defiant, gayly scoffing and sensual young Pan." Here we have the opposition between two types that is to be found in most of O'Neill's plays: the lean, dark, sensitive, poetic hero and the thick-set, fair, normal villain. (pp. 482-83)

Suffice it to say that every male character who is described as dark-eyed and sensitive is a protagonist and every male character who has blue eyes is an antagonist. And it is obvious, I think, that all the O'Neill heroes are essentially one and the same person. They are as stereotyped and uniform as Ford cars; slight variations in body styles there may be, but the motors are of the same design. Nor need we speculate long as to who this person is who keeps popping up as the leading figure in most of the plays. It is Eugene O'Neill. (pp. 484-85)

It is important to note that these heroes of O'Neill's, although they are often described as poetic, are never poets. Their poetic natures do not help them to produce anything; they do not even bring them happiness, for in O'Neill plays the happiness of the hero is in inverse proportion to his sensibility. They are described as intelligent, but they manifest their intelligence only in their vague maunderings concerning their vaguer emotions. To exalt these pitiable figures, as O'Neill does, to establish them as Nature's noblemen merely because they have failed to find happiness is the height of romantic absurdity. And this high level of romantic absurdity O'Neill does not fail to maintain in the treatment of his female characters.

Although physically the female characters present no such uniformity as was found in the male characters, nevertheless they are emotionally all of a piece. Almost all are sexually abnormal; rare is the character who is not either a prostitute or a wanton or a nymphomaniac. . . .

There are a few normal female characters, but their very normality seems to gain for them the playwright's contempt. Almost invariably they are portrayed as narrow, petty, bigoted and lacking in understanding. They are in striking contrast to the sexually abnormal female characters, who are presented as noble, spiritual, sympathetic, and wise. (p. 485)

In *Anna Christie* the heroine, a former prostitute, shows the greatness of her character in refusing because of her past life to marry the man she loves. It is made plain that she is really "pure" in soul and that circumstance rather than desire led her to prostitution. Nevertheless she tells her lover what she has been, and he, as she expected he would, curses her and leaves her. This unselfish love, this quixotic disregard for their own happiness is common to almost all of the sexually abnormal female characters. Anna, Marthy, Cybel, Mrs. Fife, Pompeia . . . they are all so wise, so understanding, so generous, so noble—and so improbable. To sum up, when a woman walks on stage in an O'Neill highbrow melodrama, the chances are ten to one that she is in some way sexually abnormal and if she is, she is certain to be the finest character on the stage.

It is only to be expected that unreal and exaggerated characters will talk in an unreal and exaggerated fashion. The diction in O'Neill is just as grandiose and extravagant and unreal as the characters who use it. It is a rare O'Neill hero who does not stop the action of the play now and again to deliver a long metaphysical address on the meaning of his existence and it is a rare O'Neill prostitute who does not get off some good things on Life and Man and Love—in capitals. (pp. 485-86)

[In *Welded* the] sensitive O'Neill hero, engaged in the Higher Love, gives vent to his passion:—

> CAPE: Listen! Often I wake up in the night—
> in a black world, alone in a hundred million
> years of darkness. I feel like crying out to God
> for mercy because life lives! Then instinctively
> I seek you—my hand touches you! You are

there—beside me—alive—with you I become a whole, a truth! Life guides me back through the hundred million years to you. It reveals a beginning in unity that I may have faith in the unity of the end!

(p. 487)

Is there very much difference between the pomposity of the last passage, for example, and the line, "I scorn your filthy lucre, Jack Dalton!" Is not the one as unreal as the other? They are both examples of rant, of melodramatic diction and both are suited to melodramatic characters and melodramatic plots.

O'Neill's plot structure reveals a total lack of dramatic sense. The drama, because of its temporal and mechanical limitations, is a medium for the expression of swift, forceful, and animated action. In O'Neill the action consists almost entirely of a lumbering analysis of the obsessed and even insane minds of the characters in his plays. Insanity is to be found in most of his plays and in many cases the entire structure of the play is based on some mad obsession of one of the characters. In *Gold*, for example, the plot is woven around the obsession of Isaiah Bartlett that he has discovered a chest full of gold and jewels. . . . Later on he learns that the treasure is worthless, and, overcome by remorse, he drops dead. Isaiah Bartlett is presented to us from the very first scene as mad. The play is an analysis of a diseased mind, a case study for a psychiatrist; but it evokes no sympathy from the reader since the leading character is too far removed from the realm of common experience. The deaths of Isaiah and his wife are purely mechanical attempts to get at the emotions of the audience. I say mechanical, because the deaths are not justified either logically or emotionally.

This mechanical method of evoking an emotional response from the audience by depicting insanity, death, and suicide is characteristic of O'Neill plays just as it is characteristic of the melodrama in general. (pp. 487-88)

In the trilogy, *Mourning Becomes Electra*, O'Neill's latest contribution to the drama, the stage is converted into a veritable shambles. The toll of the Grim Reaper is two deaths by murder and two suicides out of a total of five principal characters. (p. 488)

Even in the less violent incidents of the plot O'Neill exaggerates his effects with all the melodramatic vigour at his command. In the handling of dramatic situations and of the reversals of fortune which befall the characters, he shows all the delicacy and subtlety of a circus advertisement. He uses dramatic irony, that delicate rapier, as a shillelah with which to cudgel his characters. He toys with them as a boy plays with a fly whose wings he has torn off. Indeed, an O'Neill character has only to express a desire for something in order to get just the opposite before the end of the act. (p. 489)

It must not be supposed that because so many O'Neill plays end in death or suicide that these endings are necessarily unhappy. On the contrary, almost all the plays end either happily or on an optimistic expression of hope. . . . The happy ending is a necessity in the melodrama and so it is not to be wondered at if O'Neill includes it in his box of tricks. He cudgels his heroes, who are projections of himself, with what can only be described as masochistic fury, but he makes it plain just before they die or commit suicide that they have in reality triumphed.

O'Neill has been called a great dramatic experimenter, but I think the value of his experimentation is greatly over-rated.

He experimented first with expressionism, chiefly in *The Hairy Ape* and in *Emperor Jones*. Both plays are psychological studies with almost no dramatic power. . . . [*Emperor Jones*] is a monologue which describes the successive mental states which fear and hunger induce in the central figure. In this play O'Neill introduces one of those novel tricks which have enhanced his reputation as an experimenter. From the beginning of the play to the end, the audience hears the sound of tom-toms. The tom-toms begin in a steady rhythm of seventy-two beats per minute, the rate of the normal pulse. Then as the play progresses the speed of the tom-tom is gradually and continuously accelerated until at the end of the play it is going at a feverish pace. The physiological effect on the audience is obvious. The psychological effect of the tom-tom is produced not through the speeches and actions of the characters, but directly by the sound itself. And the monotonous rhythm acts as powerfully on the audience as it does on Jones in the play. It is not my purpose here to discuss the propriety (in an artistic sense) of substituting for a more substantial plot structure a mechanical device in order to create the atmosphere for the play. I would merely point out that the tom-tom in *Emperor Jones*, although a new device, produced no change in the established technique of the drama. The use of the tom-tom is a trick whose only virtue is its novelty. (pp. 490-91)

In *The Great God Brown*, O'Neill tried another experiment. In this play the characters at times wear masks which are intended to symbolize the duality of their natures. When a speech is expressive of the outward character, the character which the world sees, the speaker wears a mask; when he speaks according to his true, inner nature, he takes off the mask. This "experiment", rightly considered, is merely a method of labelling the speeches of the characters. It cannot be considered an advance on modern dramatic technique. Indeed it is a step back, for only a poor artist needs labels to make his intentions clear.

In *Strange Interlude* O'Neill uses another type of label, the aside. Here the actors deliver the lines in the usual manner but follow each speech with an oral expression of their thoughts. In other words, the audience is treated to a series of explanatory notes on the true emotions of the characters in the play. It is a confession on the part of the playwright that he cannot express himself in the dramatist's medium.

This experimentation is intended only to hide defective craftsmanship and to tickle the fancy of the audience. It is mere pandering to the taste of the moment. The intelligentsia whose patronage has raised O'Neill to his present eminence, blinded by their intellectual and emotional romanticism, mistake these little tricks of the showman for bold originality. O'Neill shows them a succession of thin-skinned poeticules and they hail them as tragic heroes. He paints a picture of a chimerical, daydream world and they shout, "It is true reality". They mistake extravagant "purple passages" for poetry and a maudlin bathos for power. In short, they call that tragedy which is merely violent and unbalanced melodrama. (p. 491)

H. G. Kemelman, "Eugene O'Neill and the Highbrow Melodrama," in The Bookman, New York, Vol. LXXV, No. 5, September, 1932, pp. 482-91.

CAMILLO PELLIZZI   (essay date 1935)

[O'Neill's] **"Bound East for Cardiff"** shows a sailor, Yank, dying in his bunk as the result of a fall in the hold, while his rough companion, Driscoll, attends him and tries to comfort him as much as he can in his rude way. . . . The strange, broken, coarse dialogue of the two friends is among the noblest and most beautiful things in modern drama: their slang acquires a rhythm and a swing which make one think of Synge, by whom O'Neill was certainly influenced. The drama lies wholly in the contrast between these poor human creatures and the hostile elements which *live* all around them, between the spark of soul they reveal and their monotonous, brutal and obscure fate, between their timid, confused longing for affection and the death which takes place in the midst of the fog, without tears or lament. This is the drama, and yet, as also in [Giovanni] Verga, the ultimate artistic effect of the dialogue is *epical;* it is a confession, a pure poem, a song, which expresses the author's feeling in a fresh and ingenuous way. (pp. 353-54)

The hero [of *The Emperor Jones*] is a sort of negro tyrant who is seen, in the first act, enthroned ·in his palace; he is petulant and solemn, a mixture of the cruel and the grotesque. His enemies force him to leave the palace and flee into the jungle. In the six successive scenes we see him alone in the forest, a prey to ancient, atavistic fears. . . . All through these six scenes there is nothing but Jones's monologue, his rising madness, which, before these apparitions, these silent groups, pervades the scene. In the distance is heard the uninterrupted beat of the tom-tom of his enemies. (p. 354)

The tom-tom in *The Emperor Jones* can be compared to the repeated blast of the whistle in **"Bound East for Cardiff"**; some would call them stage devices to excite the nerves of the audience. In reality they are symbolical elements dramatized; they represent, in both cases, a brooding Fate, a predestination. . . . [Whether] O'Neill is dealing with ancestral terrors latent in the soul, as with Jones, or with a strange, cruel Nature, as in all his sea dramas, man's destiny, here, always depends on a terrible, unequal struggle between man and a *created* reality from which he is sharply distinguished. If Providence does not intervene and assist man with a power which is not wholly human, we know already that he will succumb. This attitude can be found even in the subsequent psychological and psychoanalytical plays. O'Neill, irreligious in his beliefs, does not perhaps perceive that, in his own particular form of anti-Puritanism there is implied a Catholic outlook in the strictest sense—the acceptance of the positive, powerful reality of evil, and the existence of grace and the miraculous. Fate, even when it interweaves itself with man, is always a *different thing* from man, who presses and struggles against it with all the violence of passion; with O'Neill, therefore, the tragical is hardly ever the contrast of distinct and opposed personalities, but the unequal and desperate struggle of each character against an *objective* reality which hangs over him. In this atmosphere the psychological elements also become the *object,* or tragic fate; and in this can perhaps be found the reason for O'Neill's *tragic* superiority over all other living Anglo-Saxon writers . . . , in the fact that he does not confuse man with his destiny, his internal passions or his follies; he sees man as a subject who is *struck,* even if it be in his most inward and secret fibers, by these passions, disasters and follies. (pp. 354-55)

Even when O'Neill, as in *Strange Interlude,* resolutely attacks a theme dear to psychoanalysts, that of "frustration," he extracts tragedy from it; for the heroine, Nina, who has lost her lover in the war and will remain all her life a woman unsatisfied in her profoundest needs and instincts, is still always a *subject,* a personality, a free human soul; and the frustration is like a disease, a profound impression which is made on her by outward circumstances, from which she will never be able to free

herself, and against which, eternally defeated, she will eternally rebel. (p. 355)

> *Camillo Pellizzi, in an essay in his* English Drama: The Last Great Phase, *translated by Rowan Williams (copyright 1935; reprinted by permission of Macmillan London and Basingstoke), Macmillan, 1935 (and reprinted as "Irish-Catholic Anti-Puritan," in* O'Neill and His Plays: Four Decades of Criticism, *edited by Oscar Cargill, N. Bryllion Fagin, and William J. Fisher, New York University Press, 1961, pp. 353-57).*

BERNARD DeVOTO (essay date 1936)

Unquestionably most of the critics and most of the public who think about literature at all will regard the award of a Nobel Prize to Eugene O'Neill as a gratifying recognition of a great dramatic talent. A minority will not, however, and because what may be a signal weakness rather than a great strength of our literature is involved, the *Saturday Review* cannot let the occasion pass without expressing that minority opinion. For the Nobel Prize, although it was once awarded to Rabindranath Tagore, is supposed to recognize only the highest distinction in literature, and Mr. O'Neill falls short of that. He falls short of it both absolutely and relatively. Whatever his international importance, he can hardly be called an artist of the first rank; he is hardly even one of the first-rate figures of his own generation in America. (p. 190)

He has had every kind of success that a playwright can have: money, fame, the best directors and designers and actors of his time, a sumptuous collected edition, a critical acclaim so reverent that the more recent treatises discuss him in language usually considered sacrilegious when applied to the merely mortal, and now the Nobel Prize. Here is a great triumph, but a very large part of it is due to prestige and publicity. At best he is only the author of some extremely effective pieces for the theater. At worst he has written some of the most pretentiously bad plays of our time. He has never been what the Guild and the Nobel jury unite in calling him, a great dramatist.

It is not a derogation but only a definition to say that workable theatricality is the measure of successful playwriting. In the theater the test is not: Is this true to the realities of human experience? Instead the test is: Is this fictitious representation satisfactory to the artificial conditions of the theater? With luck—or with genius—a play may pass both tests, but it must pass the second, and if they are in conflict, the first must yield. The theater is under many limitations: the exigencies of space and time; the dictation of the literal. . . . (pp. 191-92)

A great dramatist, I take it, is one who has somehow managed to transcend the limitations of the theater and, while preserving the theatrical values that pass the second test, to add to them some profundity of human experience, human understanding, or human enlightenment that brings the art of the theater into the same area as the highest art of fiction or poetry. Those who have transcended them—we need name no more than Shaw and Ibsen—have done so by reason of great intelligence, great imagination, and great understanding. The whole truth about Mr. O'Neill is that his gigantic effort to transcend them has been of an altogether different kind. He is a fine playwright who is not sufficiently endowed with those qualities to be a great dramatist and who has tried to substitute for them a set of merely mechanical devices.

Let us recall his works. The charmingly romantic one-act plays were young Greenwich Village. . . . They had novelties of decoration but their effectiveness, like the dialects spoken by the sailors, came from time-honored tricks by which generations of playwrights had lifted the audience out of their seats for the tense half-second that means effectiveness in the theater.

A group of miscellaneous plays followed, some expressionistic, some realistic, some successful in their own terms, some obviously tending toward the confusion that was soon to follow. Two of them, *The Emperor Jones* and *Anna Christie,* are among the best work that Mr. O'Neill has ever done; of his other plays, only *Ah, Wilderness!* is comparable to them. . . . *The Emperor Jones* was a trimphant experiment in the drama of phantasy, which may last longer than anything else he has written. It was a very effective assault on the emotions. . . . [*Anna Christie*] remains his most effective play. But note carefully that its effectiveness is theatrical—of the theater, not of life. The romantic conception of a prostitute, the Greenwich Village cliché of "dat ol dayvil sea," the flagrant falsification of life in the oath scene at the end were magnificent theater, magnificent craftsmanship, but surely they were an exact antithesis of great drama. It should be noted here, also, that with *All God's Chillun's Got Wings* he began the use of insanity as a solution of all dramatic problems, which makes for thrilling effects on the stage but falls short of explaining human life.

Mr. O'Neill then dived into the infinite. He undertook to transcend the theater, to break the shackles of mortality, to work with the immortal urges and the eternal truths. His characters would not be men and women merely, they would be Man and Woman, they would even be Earth Man and Earth Woman. And this mighty effort to be a great dramatist inexorably proved that he lacked intellectual, emotional, and imaginative greatness. In the theater he is a master of craftsman. But in the cosmos he is a badly rattled Villager straining titanically with platitudes, and laboring to bring forth ineffabilities whose spiritual and intellectual content has been a farcical anticlimax to the agonies of birth.

Lazarus Laughed, The Great God Brown, Marco Millions, Dynamo—one or another of them must be the silliest play of our time. (pp. 192-94)

Mr. O'Neill has called himself a poet and a mystic. In these plays he is trying to press beyond the theater into great drama by means of poetry and mysticism focused through symbolism. But it is the very essence of symbolism that the meaning symbolically conveyed must be a distinguished meaning—a meaning profound and exalted—or the result will be preposterous. And Mr. O'Neill has no such meaning to convey. He has only a number of platitudes which would be comfortably accommodated to the one-acters of Washington Square from which he graduated, or to Dads' Night at a prep-school drama festival, but which come out flat and unchanged through as elaborate a mechanism as was ever devised to amplify inanities.

The same lack of profundity, subtlety, and distinguished imagination is quite as clear in the next cycle where, turning from symbolism, Mr. O'Neill occupied himself with racial myths and the unconscious mind. Probably the Nobel award was based on *Strange Interlude* and *Mourning Becomes Electra,* and yet these plays only emphasize what the others had made clear. Here all the strains meet and blend—the novelties of the little theater substituting for knowledge of the human heart, dodges and devices, a fortissimo assertion of significance, and a frantic grappling with what seem to be immensities but turn out to be one-syllable ideas and mostly wrong at that. . . . [The] significances he announces to us are elementary and even rudi-

mentary. . . . What he tells us is simple, familiar, superficial, and even trite—where it is not, because of a shallow misunderstanding of Freud and a windy mysticism, sometimes flatly wrong. It is not great drama for it is not great knowledge. (pp. 195-96)

> *Bernard DeVoto, "Monte Cristo in Modern Dress,"* *in* The Saturday Review of Literature *(copyright © 1936, copyright renewed © 1963, by* Saturday Review; *all rights reserved; reprinted by permission), Vol. XV, No. 4, November 21, 1936 (and reprinted in his* Minority Report, *Little, Brown and Company, 1940, pp. 190-97).*

EDMOND M. GAGEY (essay date 1947)

In the many critical works about him Eugene O'Neill has been called variously realist, poet, mystic, seer, and plain writer of highbrow melodrama. These designations all fit to a certain degree, for, regardless of his eventual reputation, O'Neill remains a many-sided figure. . . . Furthermore, his plays were experimental—in style, in treatment, in the use of ingenious devices—and thus lent themselves readily to imaginative production.

O'Neill was twenty-six when his first work, *Thirst and Other One-Act Plays,* was published. . . . (p. 39)

The journeyman work of famous dramatists, while usually mediocre, is always revealing. O'Neill himself . . . selected *Bound East for Cardiff* . . . as most important in including the germ of his later work. Equally significant, however, are the five plays of the *Thirst* volume, despite their lack of merit. All are melodramatic and unhappy in ending. The title play, for instance, presents three persons—a girl in dancing costume, a gentleman, and a West Indian Negro—tortured by thirst on a raft in tropical seas until they become raving mad and die or kill off one another. Here we find already romantic setting and characters, exploitation of the sea, and a sense of malevolent destiny. (pp. 40-1)

[In] the collection as a whole, to summarize, are already discoverable many of the ingredients of his great successes: novelty of characters, realism of scene and language, romantic and unusual settings, interest in experimentation, use of melodramatic situations. Also we find O'Neill's identification of himself with the dreamer and the poet, tired of the world but looking with scorn upon the American business man, the pre-Sinclair-Lewis Babbitt. Finally, while fate appears as a tricky and ironic jade, O'Neill did not rule out in life the possibilities of mysticism and the religious spirit. (p. 42)

Taken as a whole, the one-act plays of [the] period from 1916 to 1920 are interesting and theatrically effective. They continue, with greater skill and power, the blend of romance and realism characteristic of his first published work. They are melodramatic, with violent and unhappy endings, dramatic irony, and occasional sentimentality. While most are about the sea, others deal with New England and several with Negro life. Four of the best-known sea plays are set on the same British tramp steamer and, as a matter of fact, were presented together . . . under the general title *S.S. Glencairn.* . . . [*Bound East for Cardiff*], which O'Neill found so significant in relation to his later work, deals with the affecting death at sea of Yank. . . . The play shows O'Neill's latent if unorthodox concern with life after death and with religion, his fine conception of friendship, and his common theme of "not belonging." . . . [*In the Zone*], the most popular of the one-acters both in America and abroad, dramatizes the sudden hysterical belief in the fo'c's'le that Smitty is a German spy. What the men later find in a black box which aroused their suspicion is merely a package of love letters revealing Smitty's unhappy love affair. The piece is sentimental but does not ring so false when we consider the time of its writing, when spy scares were commonplace and sentimentality more in vogue. *The Long Voyage Home* . . . tells the tragic and ironic story of a sailor who decides to give up the sea and return to his native Sweden, only to be drugged in a London dive and shanghaied on a windjammer going round the Horn. *The Moon of the Caribbees* . . . , probably the most interesting of the group, is a study in mood and setting. (pp. 42-3)

Of the other one-act plays special mention must be made of *Ile* . . . , a dramatic study of a whaling captain who chooses to let his wife go insane rather than bear the disgrace of returning to port without a full quota of oil. In melodramatic force this must be held one of O'Neill's best. (p. 44)

[O'Neill's first full-length play, *Beyond the Horizon*,] was a grim, modern tragedy of New England, intensely realistic yet not without poetic beauty, a play of frustration and irony that ended in wholesale disaster. Two brothers on a New England farm near the sea are of diametrically opposite character: Robert Mayo is poetic, restless, curious about what lies beyond the horizon; Andrew is matter-of-fact, practical, unimaginative, perfectly content with his lot as farmer. Fate intervenes with a typical O'Neill trick. As Robert is about to realize his lifelong ambition to travel the seven seas on a sailing vessel, he discovers and reveals his romantic love for Ruth, Andrew's sweetheart. She accepts him and he immediately forsakes his dream, with the result that it is Andrew who goes to sea and Robert who stays at home to tend the farm. The inevitable outcome is frustration and tragedy for the three principals, who discover that they have made an irrevocable mistake. The tragic impetus of the play proves truly affecting, though one must admit that the cards are stacked pretty heavily against the characters. . . . The play has faults of construction and characterization, but in opposition to the escapist pabulum of Broadway it won an enthusiastic hearing and a significant victory for the art theatre as well when it was awarded the Pulitzer Prize. (pp. 45-6)

O'Neill develops in [*The Emperor Jones*] the colorful and dramatic career of Jones, former Pullman porter, now self-styled emperor of an island, who claims he is invulnerable to any but a silver bullet. Fully prepared for an uprising of the people he has tyrannized, he escapes to the tropical forest as the sound of tom-toms in the distance indicates that the revolt is gathering strength. But night has come sooner than he expected and he loses his way in the forest, where in a series of terrifying visions he recapitulates not only the main events of his life but also the primitive history of his race. He ends by killing himself with his own last silver bullet after finding that he has traveled a wide circle during the night, while the beat of the drums becomes faster and more menacing. With his racy dialogue and superb strutting Jones possesses epic grandeur, so that we can only regret his downfall. . . . (pp. 46-7)

[The story of *Anna Christie*] is a realistic one about old Chris Christopherson, captain of a barge, who sentimentalizes over a daughter he has not seen for fifteen years; Anna, the daughter, who becomes regenerated from a career of prostitution as a result of her new life on the barge; and Mat, a loquacious Irishman, who falls in love with Anna and is tortured to drink and madness when he learns of her past life. From such a set of characters only tragic irony and suffering can result, and we find Anna voicing the theme of this as well as other early plays by O'Neill: "Don't bawl about it. There ain't nothing to forgive, anyway. It ain't your fault, and it ain't mine, and it ain't his neither. We're all poor nuts, and things happen, and we yust get mixed in wrong, that's all." (p. 48)

[*The Hairy Ape*] was immediately termed expressionistic, although O'Neill denied any direct influence from the expressionism of German writers. . . . Expressionism may be defined in simple terms as an attempt to portray inner reality in nonrealistic terms by the use of abstraction, symbolism, and distortion. . . . [*The Hairy Ape*] relates in a series of short scenes the story of a man who . . . loses his old harmony with nature. Yank, a stoker on a transatlantic liner, has always gloried in his work and in his brute strength until he is startled and infuriated when Mildred Douglas, spoiled daughter of a millionaire, visits the stokehold. Driven to thought and unable to rationalize his place in the scheme of things, Yank is obsessed by the idea that he "doesn't belong." He is clapped into jail for starting a riot on Fifth Avenue, and he is even thrown out of the I.W.W. as an unwelcome intruder. Finally he attempts to shake hands with a gorilla at the zoo but is crushed to death by the animal—O'Neill's symbolism for his inability to get back to a lower order of existence. The play, obviously, is concerned not so much with Yank as with Man and his struggle to find himself, and to bring out the symbolism O'Neill has departed from naturalism, as in the famous Fifth Avenue scene where the passers-by are represented as mere walking automatons. Reality is still present and recognizable, however, especially in the salty speech of the stokehold, and the play might very well be called another example of imaginative realism. (pp. 49-50)

[*All God's Chillun Got Wings*] represents the author's first extensive invasion of Freudian territory. *All God's Chillun* is a clinical study of miscegenation and racial hatred, handled with restraint and yet with dramatic power. (p. 51)

[*Desire under the Elms*] is a starkly realistic portrayal of a New England farm tragedy. Old Ephraim Cabot, seventy-five years old, stern and Bible quoting, has just taken to himself a third wife, Abbie. Partly because she wants an heir to insure her possession of the farm, she seduces Eben, Ephraim's son by an earlier marriage. From this illicit relationship a child is born which old Ephraim proudly believes to be his own. Eben and Abbie, however, have found themselves caught in a passion stronger than they. In a desperate attempt to prove her love Abbie smothers the infant and reveals its true paternity to old Cabot. Eben, who in his first horror has rushed to call the sheriff, realizes the depth of his love for Abbie, and the two lovers face the uncertain future with a sense of exaltation. It is this closing note that keeps *Desire under the Elms* from being merely sordid and endows it, according to various critics, with something akin to the catharsis of Greek tragedy. (p. 52)

[In *The Great God Brown* O'Neill] plunged boldly into symbolism, employing the ancient device of masks, which the players took off or put on or even exchanged to indicate changes in personality. The play, which almost defies analysis, deals with the fortunes of William Brown . . . and Dion Anthony . . . , both in love with the same girl at the time of their graduation from high school. It is the artistic and erratic Dion, however, and not Billy Brown, that Margaret prefers and later marries. After college Brown becomes successful as builder and architect but finds that he needs the aid of Dion's artistic genius. Dion, however is maladjusted and unhappy, in spite of his love for the faithful Margaret, who has borne him three sons. He is driven to drink and gambling, and finds his main solace with the town prostitute, Cybel. Eventually Dion dies in the house of Brown, who takes his mask (hence his personality) and poses sometimes as Dion, sometimes as himself, until his death in the arms of the sympathetic Cybel. This unusual plot becomes more intelligible when O'Neill explains that Dion Anthony represents a combination of Dionysus and St. Anthony, "the creative pagan acceptance of life, fighting eternal war with the masochistic, life-denying spirit of Christianity as represented by St. Anthony"; that Brown stands for the demigod of the materialistic American myth of success, "building his life of exterior things, inwardly empty and resourceless"; that Margaret is the eternal girl-woman, modern descendant of Marguerite in Goethe's *Faust;* and finally that Cybel personifies Cybele, the Earth Mother of Greek mythology. In his note to the Wilderness edition of his plays O'Neill states further that the play "attempts to foreshadow the mystical patterns created by the duality of human character and the search for what lies hidden behind and beyond words and actions of men and women. More by the use of overtones than by explicit speech, I sought to convey the dramatic conflicts in the lives and within the souls of the characters."

Confusing as are the theme and symbolism, as well as the use and exchange of masks, *The Great God Brown* remains an artistic success. Nowhere else is O'Neill's dialogue more charged with emotion and lyrical beauty. Even where we are uncertain about the meaning of the words, they offer at times sudden glimpses of the ineffable mystery of human life—something he never succeeds in doing in his more "philosophical" plays, such as *Lazarus Laughed.* Whereas most of O'Neill's prostitutes are unconvincing and juvenile, Cybel becomes much more than the personified abstraction she was meant to be. The other characters are equally well realized. It is only when Brown seizes the mask from the dead Anthony and starts putting it on and removing it at frequent intervals that the audience, not to mention Margaret, is lost in bewilderment. The play bogs down at this point, but perhaps a more conventional treatment would have meant a loss of vividness and dramatic power. (pp. 53-5)

[In *Marco Millions* O'Neill turned] to fantasy with a pseudo-historical background, adding only the new element of satire. In an ironical foreword he states his intention of whitewashing the soul of Marco Polo, which he proceeds to do by revealing him as a glorified traveling salesman, a true Babbitt—shrewd, aggressive, materialistic, uxorious, entirely devoid of sensibility. (p. 55)

[With *Strange Interlude* O'Neill revived] the ancient aside and soliloquy to express the inner thoughts of the characters. So completely were these last two devices used that one might almost say that O'Neill employed the regular dialogue to supplement the asides, rather than vice versa. This was an attempt, of course, to adapt in drama the stream of consciousness method of contemporary fiction, and except for slowing up the action it proved fairly successful. The nine acts of *Strange Interlude* represent the intimate relations of Nina Leeds, daughter of a college professor, to several men who affected her life, especially to three. Emotionally upset because of the death in France of her fiancé, Nina hates her father, whom she considers responsible for preventing their marriage. She leaves home to become a nurse and returns only at her father's death. She is then prevailed upon to marry Sam Evans, diffident and good-natured, and feels almost happy at the discovery of her

pregnancy until she learns of a strain of insanity in Sam's family. She resorts to abortion, but unhappy and maladjusted once more, she takes as her lover Dr. Darrell, who lives up to his bargain of supplying her with another child. As little Gordon grows up, he feels instinctive hatred for his real father but, ironically enough, loves Sam, his ostensible one. Later Nina goes through the maternal torture of losing Gordon, now grown up, to the girl he loves, and after the death of Sam Evans she decides to mary Charlie Marsden, a spinsterish childhood admirer, whom she has come to associate psychologically with her father. This fragmentary synopsis may suffice to indicate O'Neill's invasion of the novelistic medium and his dependence on Freudian psychology—the Oedipus complex and the father-daughter fixation, for example—in such manner that the soliloquies and asides become almost imperative to indicate inner motives, loves, hates, and by-plays. (pp. 56-7)

[What most critics consider O'Neill's masterpiece, *Mourning Becomes Electra,*] is described as a trilogy; the three parts, with a total of thirteen acts, were entitled respectively *Homecoming, The Hunted,* and *The Haunted.* . . . In the new play O'Neill attempts to reinterpret the old story of Agamemnon, Clytemnestra, Orestes, and Elektra in terms of modern psychology. The result is a New England tragedy, not particularly Greek, but remarkably effective and moving. The main incidents of the classic plot have been preserved. (p. 59)

Giving force and direction to this tragic plot, the Freudian concepts of the subconscious are employed freely to suggest a twentieth-century version of fate. Christine, having felt nothing but revulsion on her wedding night, hates both Mannon and her eldest child, Lavinia. The latter, on the other hand, starved for affection in childhood, is jealous of her mother and in love with her father. Her secret passion for Captain Brant, her mother's lover, who resembles her father, adds to this jealousy—her hatred being rationalized into a sense of duty to avenge her father's murder. After Christine's death Vinnie temporarily blossoms out and, interestingly enough, begins to affect her mother's dress and manner. But [her brother] Orin, victim of an Oedipus complex, transfers his incestuous love to Vinnie and becomes insanely jealous of her attentions to other men. "Can't you see," he exclaims, "I'm now in Father's place and you're Mother? That's the evil destiny out of the past I haven't dared predict! I'm the Mannon you're chained to!" Orin's rantings in the third part of the trilogy become a little tedious but nevertheless the underlying psychological motivation works out extremely well. (p. 60)

Up to this point a dominant note in O'Neill's plays . . . had been a sense of futility at the tragedy of human life, finding expression in dramatic irony or in the unhappy ending. At least, no one would have accused the playwright of philosophical optimism. Man might have an essential nobility of character, but Fate or God or his own self was always getting him "balled up." Lazarus expresses positive affirmation in the goodness of life, but in spite of his optimism his wife was poisoned and he himself burned at the stake. It came, therefore, as a distinct shock to find the author suddenly turned kindly, wistful, reflective, and reminiscent in his first comedy, *Ah, Wilderness!* . . . *Ah, Wilderness!* is a homely, bourgeois comedy of "the American large small-town at the turn of the century." . . . The protagonist here is really the entire family, typical American and upper middle-class, with the kindly father, the adolescent child, the maiden aunt, the family drunkard, and so on. All are depicted graphically with the faithfulness of portraits in a family album. (pp. 61-2)

[*The Iceman Cometh* shows O'Neill] concerned philosophically with the mystery of human illusion. Employing the bare yet leisurely simplicity of *Days without End*—in contrast to the more luxuriant and melodramatic style of his earlier work— he exhibits in *The Iceman Cometh* a group of down-and-outers that frequent Harry Hope's West Side saloon in 1912. The place is described sardonically by one of the characters as the No Chance Saloon, Bedrock Bar, the End of the Line Café, the Bottom of the Sea Rathskeller. And yet its habitués are far from unhappy; they manage somehow to remain drunk and they delude themselves "with a few harmless pipe dreams about their yesterdays and tomorrows." (p. 65)

As the play opens, the entire group of derelicts is waiting for the arrival of Hickey, a hardware salesman, who never fails to appear with plenty of money and jovial talk to celebrate Hope's birthday party. In the past Hickey has enlivened the occasion with comic gags, the favorite one being that he has just left his wife in the hay with the iceman. This time, how- ever, he is no longer the life of the party—he even refuses to drink with the gang. As he tells them, he no longer needs alcohol; he has faced the truth about himself and now, being at last without illusions, he is completely at peace. This peace he insists on bestowing on his comrades by the process of destroying their pipe dreams of yesterday and tomorrow. The task of thus saving them is both difficult and painful, resulting in quarrels and burning hatred. . . . By next day Hickey has driven most of his companions out of the saloon in an effort to bring their pipe dreams to the test of actual realization. They all rush back in panic, as he knew they would, but he believes that the shattering of their final illusions will bring them the peace that he has himself attained. But to Hickey's surprise they are completely licked; even when they drink they find the whiskey has lost its kick. In spirit and appearance they are dead. To convert them by his own example Hickey then tells them the sordid story of his marriage to Evelyn. In spite of his many moral lapses she always forgave him, deluding herself into thinking that this was the last time and that he would reform. The only way to free Evelyn from this pipe dream of reformation, to give her the peace she always wanted, Hickey tells the startled group, was for him to kill her. He insists he committed the murder with love, not hate, in his heart. But suddenly, in the course of his recital, Hickey comes to the unexpected realization that he too has been deluding himself, that he really killed Evelyn because he hated her. The revelation is too much for Hickey to face, and he says he must have been insane. Pouncing avidly upon this straw of Hickey's insanity, which would nullify the cogency of his persuasive arguments, Hope and most of his cronies regain their composure and their illusions, ending the play in a good old drunken brawl. (pp. 66-7)

It is evident that *The Iceman Cometh* presents an O'Neill so- bered by experience, a step further in philosophical disillu- sionment, concerned for the moment not with the inhumanity of God but with the mystery of man's own soul. Is it possible for mankind to live without pipe dreams, illusions? The answer seems to be no. In the course of the play Larry identifies the Iceman with Death, and Hickey's attempt to strip life of all rationalizations results in death—for his wife, for the young radical, for Larry perhaps, for the others temporarily; Hickey deceives himself that he has found peace, but it is the peace of insanity or maybe of the electric chair. . . . As in earlier plays, O'Neill writes much about tortured marital and filial relationships, but though Freud looms in the background, the language and the technique are no longer the professional psy-

chologist's. In fact, *The Iceman Cometh* gives rather the impression of being a modern morality play with its symbolism disguised in grimly realistic terms. As in the past the author makes no concessions to popular appeal, the play's theme, its characters, its length all militating against its acceptance. In deliberately avoiding the dramatic cohesion and sweep of his earlier work, O'Neill often makes his action seem slow and repetitious. Yet, if *The Iceman Cometh* falls short of his highest dramatic achievement, no one can deny on the other hand that it has a depth and power rarely found on the Broadway stage.

An accurate estimate of Eugene O'Neill's place in American drama cannot with justice be given until his work is com- plete. . . . His main contributions to American drama, very considerable ones as we have seen, belong mainly to his first ten years on Broadway. They may be summarized briefly as (1) revival of tragedy and the unhappy ending; (2) romantic novelty of scene; (3) realism of situation and character in the depiction of sailors, prostitutes, farmers, Negroes, and others of humble station; (4) use of profanity and realistic diction on the stage; (5) experimentation in form, including the use of multiple scenes and acts; (6) interest in symbolism, leading to unnaturalistic scenery, revival of masks, and other devices; (7) adoption of Freudian psychology with ingenious revival of the soliloquy and aside to represent the stream of consciousness; (8) development of historical fantasy, tending toward the mas- que form in such plays as *Marco Millions* . . . ; (9) passionate absorption in the problem of man's rapport with himself and with God, leading at various times to frustration, to dramatic irony, or to conversion. The enumeration may be incomplete but it will at least indicate the variety of O'Neill's interests and experiments. He was of particular significance as a pioneer, even when his innovations were considerably modified by sub- sequent writers. . . . He had, in short, the genius to select timely themes and techniques, and if some of his plays appear dated, the reason is partly that his innovations were so widely adopted that we no longer recall how revolutionary they once were. O'Neill's experimental boldness helped to establish his position as the first great dramatist of the art theatre and as a poet, but from the start he was also a realist and will probably best be remembered for those plays that show an ideal fusion of realism and imagination. (pp. 67-70)

> *Edmond M. Gagey, ''Eugene O'Neill,'' in his* Rev- olution in American Drama *(copyright 1947, Colum- bia University Press; copyright renewed © 1975 by Edmond M. Gagey; reprinted by permission of the publisher), Columbia University Press, 1947, pp. 39- 70.*

DORIS V. FALK (essay date 1958)

O'Neill thought of himself as a writer of "ironic tragedy," but irony requires a detachment which he found impossible. Pity, indignation, despair at the human position, robbed his tragedies of the irony he intended them to convey. The sneer became only the protective mask of a face distorted by suf- fering; the ironic words were drowned in cries of anguish. The plays are attempts to explain human suffering and, somehow, to justify it. The result is not irony, but the classic twofold justification of the ways of God—or fate—to man: first, that suffering and the very need to explain and symbolize it are the fountainhead of human action and creativity; and second, that fated though he may be, man is ultimately a free and responsible agent who brings most of his grief upon himself through pride. (pp. 3-4)

[Life] and action exist in a perpetual tension between opposites, each of which owes its existence to the presence of the other. This tension is the source of all change and growth, for as night exists only in contrast to day, so night flows eternally into day and day to night again. (p. 4)

The justification of the Fall through Pride also implies a pull between opposites, for here, too, man moves between relative values. The very pride which is the source of his aspiration, enabling him to transcend many of his limitations, can be his destruction when it ignores those limitations and covets godhead. Similarly, the humility which can lead to the *via media* and self-acceptance may take the sick, distorted form of paralysis and self-destruction. Man, according to O'Neill, must find his way somewhere between pride and humility. (pp. 4-5)

This view of life has, of course, a long, familiar history in philosophy and art. O'Neill's conception of process as the unity in which opposites are reconciled has numberless philosophical parallels and sources—in the works of Heraclitus, Plato, Aristotle, Lao-tse, Nietzsche, Emerson, to suggest only a few. The greatest heroes and heroines of O'Neill's plays belong to the literary tradition of the Fall through Pride—the tradition of Prometheus, Oedipus, Tamburlaine, Macbeth, Satan—and Adam, Faust, Ahab. (p. 5)

But O'Neill was after all not a Greek, nor an Elizabethan, nor a nineteenth-century Romantic. As a twentieth-century man, he had to interpret the ancient idea in twentieth-century terms and symbols. He found those in the conditions of modern living and in the language of psychoanalysis. O'Neill knew, of course, the general outlines of Freudian theory, but his imagination was stimulated most by the work of Jung, and especially by those Jungian concepts formulated by analogy to the universal human problems expressed in art, literature, and philosophy.

Jung sees man's primary need not in the desire to satisfy physical drives or to fulfill any single emotional necessity such as power, security, or love, but in a longing for a life of meaning and purpose—for a sense of order in the universe to which man can belong and in which he can trust. . . . O'Neill assumes, with Jung, that one's problems and actions spring not only from his personal unconscious mind, but from a "collective unconscious" shared by the race as a whole, manifesting itself in archetypal symbols and patterns latent in the minds of all men.

O'Neill uses many of the terms and ideas of the Jungian system, but most important is this conception of the unconscious as an autonomous force, existing independently of the individual man but expressed through him. All his life man is forced to wrestle with the unconscious in an attempt to reconcile its demands with those of his conscious ego. The Sin of Pride means to O'Neill what it does to Jung: Man is in fatal error when he assumes that his conscious ego can fulfill all his needs without acknowledgment of the power of the unconscious, the modern equivalent of the gods. Clinically speaking, the ignorance or suppression of unconscious needs results in neuroses and psychoses; poetically speaking, to consider oneself the sole arbiter of one's destiny is to court destruction. . . . O'Neill's answer, like Jung's, is the classic one. Men must find self-knowledge and a middle way which reconciles the unconscious needs with those of the conscious ego. This means that life inevitably involves conflict and tension, but that the significance of this pain is the growth which Jung calls "individuation"—the gradual realization of the inner, complete personality through constant change, struggle, and process. (pp. 5-6)

O'Neill was impelled by his own deep-seated needs to justify pain, and these needs were the greatest threat to the philosophy which grew out of them. Indeed, within O'Neill's very thesis lurked its antithesis. While he affirmed disintegration as the price of life and pain as the penalty for creativity, there was always the terrible possibility that life and art might not be worth the struggle. Perhaps the price was too high. Perhaps the constant need to establish reality in a world of relative values, to determine one's true identity amid opposite self-images, are sources of a torment as stultifying as it is creative. O'Neill's plays are a consistent chronological record of this torment, charting as clearly, perhaps, as historical biography the direction of his growth as man and artist. (pp. 9-10)

Long Day's Journey is excruciatingly powerful because it is so painfully and consistently realistic. That is not intended to imply that literal realism is generally a criterion of dramatic power, but only that it frequently is in O'Neill's work, where realism is so often lost among unintegrated symbols, O'Neill's attempt at poetry. (pp. 180-81)

For all its realism the play is full of symbols. The fog was O'Neill's first and last symbol of man's inability to know himself, or other men, or his destiny. In Act I of *Long Day's Journey* the sun is shining; in Act II the haze gathers; in Act III a wall of fog stands thick against the windowpanes. Through the fog at intervals a foghorn moans, followed by a warning chorus of ship's bells—the leitmotif of the family fate, sounding whenever that fate asserts itself.

The interior set has its symbolic value too. . . . All the visible action takes place . . . in a shabby, cheaply furnished living room lined with well-used books, the titles of which are largely those of O'Neill's acknowledged influences. The family "lives" in that mid-region between the bright formality of the exterior front parlor—the mask—and the little-known dark of the rear room.

In that living room the four Tyrones torment themselves and each other, gradually stripping away every protective illusion until at the end each character must face himself and the others without hope, but with a measure of tolerance and pity. The focal point of the play is the drug addiction of the mother and the family's early hope that she has been cured. As this "pipe dream" vanishes, the truths about the family emerge in anguished sequence. Each confession elicits another confession, but in spite of these often long and repetitious speeches the conflicts of hate and love, guilt and accusation, lead to tense, exhausting, and brilliant drama. The driving force of the family fate hurtles each of the characters into his own night and causes him to take the others with him. (pp. 181-82)

This is O'Neill's own family, and their story was torn from the depths of his consciousness. With an effort compounded of "tears and blood," O'Neill forced himself to examine them honestly and objectively, from their own points of view as well as his. The result was that the figures most deeply rooted in that consciousness have emerged from it not simply as symbols of their meaning to the author, but as memorable, fully created individual personalities. But in each of these full portraits lurks the outline of a psychological type who has appeared and reappeared in O'Neill's work. Each type with its problems dominated a period in O'Neill's development, but there are only four Tyrones, and there are more than four stages in O'Neill's own journey into night; the other stages are to be found in the themes of this play and in O'Neill's very compulsion to write it.

Just as O'Neill's life journey began with his mother his mature literary career began with "the searchers," those characters in his plays who were her direct descendants. Mary appears throughout the plays in two guises: what she was, and what her sons wanted her to be. She is the "eternal girl-woman," the wife and mother who longs to return (as in *Long Day's Journey* she does, in her drug fantasies) to the innocence of childhood and virginity. (pp. 182-83)

Mary is also the inverse image of the Earth Mother for whom her sons long. Her hair was once the same "rare shade of reddish-brown," which symbolized prenatal freedom, security, and warmth in *Mourning Becomes Electra;* but Mary cannot give her sons this peace, and her hair is white. (p. 183)

Mary describes the fate of all the searchers when she says "None of us can help the things life has done to us. They're done before you realize it, and once they're done they make you do other things until at last everything comes between you and what you'd like to be, and you've lost your true self forever." . . . Ultimately, of course, this describes the fate of most of O'Neill's characters, but it is most precisely and pointedly applicable to the protagonists of the plays from *Beyond the Horizon* to *Anna Christie.* (p. 184)

This bewildered, submissive mother was, of course, only one of the images by which O'Neill was haunted. The dominant image for the fanatics of the "extremist" plays (1919-21) is that of the ambitious, driving, and all but heartless father. The extremists find their way out of the fog by climbing to an aggressive, domineering image of the self. But this image turns out to be a false one, a mask which covers no face at all. The face, the real self, has been sold for the crazy power and illusive wealth represented by the mask. There can be no doubt, after reading *Long Day's Journey Into Night,* that regardless of what James O'Neill really was, to his son he represented this kind of pseudosolution to the search for self. (p. 185)

Tyrone, Sr., is the successful star actor of a romantic melodrama, as was the real James O'Neill. He has sacrificed wife and children to his need for secure wealth, denied him in his childhood. . . . Not only his desire for money, but his stubborn ignorance and defensive pride in his Irish-Catholic origin, reenforcing his drive to outdo the Yankees, have been at the root of the family ills. The tragedy of Tyrone is that, like the other extremists, he has sold his soul for the illusion of success. (p. 186)

Only the more sensitive of the extremists, like Tyrone, ever see the truth or realize that the real self has been lost. Indeed, among O'Neill's heroes, the sensitive ones alone are wholly alive, the sufferers and the creators. O'Neill took this positive view of sensitivity in the sequence of plays written between 1921 and 1927, when he believed most consciously and emphatically that the real order and justice of life lay in the tragic tension between opposites. His finders embrace this destiny and discover the answer to disunity in the unity of process, in the organic continuum in which opposition is the source of growth. In his own portrait of the artist as a young man in *Long Day's Journey,* O'Neill makes Edmund one of these tormented finders. . . . If he cannot find a home with his family or with society, he can at least be absorbed into the processes of nature, especially those of the sea, where nature and the unconscious become symbolically one. (p. 187)

[In "dream, drunkenness, death,"] Edmund has succeeded in losing the self which tortured him with its ambivalence—toward itself and toward the conflicting father and mother images

within it. In the "finders" period O'Neill saw, and demonstrated in his characters, the dualities which tore him apart. The only hope for integration lay, he knew, in his acceptance, if not reconciliation, of the dualities. But they could coexist only in the ecstatic visions of a transcendent oneness, visions which revealed themselves to be intellectualizations of real self-acceptance—theoretic, neurotic solutions to a neurotic struggle between the masks of the pride system. These may vanish for a while in the vision, but no real self is left to take their place—nothing but the mist, the fog, and through it the dismal horn of fate. (p. 189)

[In *Long Day's Journey,* O'Neill portrayed] his tragic conception of life as an endless struggle between opposite images of the self. Now, however, the conflict is not only hopeless . . . but worthless. Man is not even endowed with dignity by virtue of his struggle; he is a bare, forked animal, unredeemed by heroism, who spends his life trying to live up to a lie, trying to perpetuate an illusory conception of himself. All values are equal; neither the self nor its conception has any real existence or importance, and all we can ask of each other is pity and forgiveness. So ends the lifelong day that dawned with O'Neill's searchers in the fog, children of his mother, Mary Tyrone, proceeded with the mad extremists led by his father, James, soared to ecstatic noon with the young Edmund and the finders—before the afternoon fog settled upon the trapped victims of the family fate. (pp. 193-94)

Long Day's Journey Into Night is a tragedy with four heroes. It is tragedy—not melodrama or "slice of life"—because each of its protagonists is partly responsible for his own destruction and partly a victim of the family fate. This, I think, is the chief distinction between tragedy as a genre and other plays in which the protagonist suffers a change of fortune from good to bad. (pp. 194-95)

O'Neill is at his best when he acknowledges the personal, esoteric nature of the struggle and leaves the audience to make the application to itself. (p. 197)

But in his eagerness to make some of his dramas tragic, rather than merely "pessimistic," O'Neill has attempted to explain the inexplicable, to bring home to the audience the meaning of tragic affirmation—a mysterious term whose real significance is implied in the moral order and in the heroism of the action. The plays with weakest conclusions end in paeans of praise for tragic struggle, and the paean usually expresses a mystical insight. It is, in a sense, just what O'Neill was trying to avoid, a kind of happy ending, an explanation to the audience of the positive value of the struggle, which the audience should feel in the action itself. O'Neill's greatest tragedies are those in which the protagonist is brought to his knees by fate, unredeemed by any revelation except that recognition of his own responsibility which follows as a logical consequence of the action. (pp. 197-98)

In the last plays O'Neill walked in the valley not of death alone, but of nothingness in which all values are illusions and all meaning fades before the terror of ambiguity. Like Poe, Melville, and Dostoevsky, O'Neill was driven to dedicate a lifetime of work to the celebration of the dreadful journey. His heroes, like theirs, are doomed to assert their humanity by a struggle with ghosts in the dark night of the soul. The opponent is that most vicious and evasive of all enemies, the self. By him alone can the hero be vanquished, and this is at once his destruction and his triumph, his fall and his resurrection. In the magnificent futility of the struggle is a fragment, at least, of the history of humanity. (p. 201)

Doris V. Falk, in her Eugene O'Neill and the Tragic Tension: An Interpretive Study of the Plays *(copyright © 1958 by Rutgers, The State University; reprinted by permission of Rutgers University Press), Rutgers, 1958, 211 p.*

JOHN HENRY RALEIGH (essay date 1965)

O'Neill was not a cosmologist in the proper sense of the word. Consciously and intellectually, he usually thought of the world, when he could bear to think of it, as a meaningless chaos. . . . There were periods in his life, however, when he was a God-seeker; also as a playwright he created dramatic universes in which there are cosmologies, sometimes theistic, sometimes scientific. . . . Underneath the mood of doubt or the intermittent attempts at belief, however, there is in the plays a cosmological principle—. . . the principle of polarity; the universe and human existence conceived of as an endless series of polarities, oppositions, antitheses, antinomies; the world as a kind of perpetual dialectic without synthesis, or the world as a perpetual alternation between opposites, which are both separate and inseparable. The scientific phenomenon that captured his imagination was electricity, and the attraction resided precisely in the fact that electricity was a polar force, a mysterious—for the layman—power that was both unified and dual. (p. 3)

O'Neill's universe is a disorderly place, sometimes teleological, more often blind and purposeless, and is never a static conception from play to play. As in most other respects, there is a sharp distinction between his cosmological conceptions in his first career as a playwright and those of his second career. Up through *Days Without End*, the last play of the first period, some kind of cosmology, God-filled or God-less, purposeful or Hardyesque, is generally assumed to exist and to have some relationship to and bearing upon human life. This cosmos can be, and is, apprehended in either theistic or scientific or intuitive terms. . . . But in the world of the last masterpieces the curtain drops on the cosmos, and human life is seen as self-contained, except in the imaginations of women like Mary Tyrone in *Long Day's Journey Into Night* and Nora Melody in *A Touch of the Poet*, both of whom believe in God. For most of the other characters in these plays, however, "God is dead," in the Nietzschean phrase quoted by Edmund Tyrone in *Long Day's Journey.* The longing for a universal design to things that O'Neill dramatized over and over again from different perspectives in his first career disappears, and the ambiguities and perplexities of human existence which in the earlier plays were given at least a partial explanation by reason of the fact that they are tied to cosmological processes become in the late, dark masterpieces uniquely and solely human. . . . (p. 5)

In the plays of the first career, however, the universe looms large, and explanations for, or guesses at, its ways and purposes occupy the minds of the characters and are woven into the fabric of the dialogue. At this stage O'Neill and God were like Tolstoi and God, who, according to Gorki, had a most uneasy relationship, like two bears in the same den. Like Tolstoi, O'Neill could neither take Him nor leave Him alone. (pp. 5-6)

In most of the early O'Neill plays, God does and does not exist and does and does not rule the cosmos. Moreover, there is not one God but a whole pantheon of Gods, each with a different set of attributes, which lurks in the wings and is praised, damned, exhorted, regretted by the various characters in the plays. In *Beyond the Horizon*, O'Neill's first, successful, full-length

tragedy, there are in the minds of the characters at least three Gods. One is the traditional Calvinist God of nineteenth-century New England who is simultaneously and paradoxically the implacable Deity who visits mankind with punishment for his sins and the Eternal Referee who merely watches over his free subjects. . . .

But it seems, finally, in this play there is a God, only He is the limited deity of the Manichaean religion and of John Stuart Mill's *Theism,* the posthumous work in which Mill admitted the statistical probability that a deity may, in fact, exist. This God participates in part in the wrongdoings of mankind but He also allows some individuals to create freely their own particular Hells. Like the Calvinist God, He is paradoxical, both determining and undetermining. (p. 7)

[There evolved in O'Neill's early] plays two other cosmological outlooks, the Pascalian nightmare and the polar universe. What I have called the Pascalian nightmare is a conception of human existence as made up of separate individuals existing in soundless solitude in infinite time and space in a boundless and meaningless universe. (p. 9)

But for the majority of the more sentient characters in these plays, . . . the Pascalian nightmare is insupportable. So for them there is the polar universe and a kind of religion of repetition, a refuge in the certainties of the basic "rhythms" of human existence, either repetitions or alternations or both. The classic O'Neill speech on the meaningfulness of repetitive rhythms is Cybel's benediction at the end of *The Great God Brown*. . . . This vision of human existence as alternating between opposites and yet being circularly repetitive, abstract as it is, is about as close as, in his plays anyway, O'Neill came to seeing a consistent meaning and design to the universe. "Rhythm" was his name for these basic dialectical and repetitive movements and, side by side with the speculations on God and existential loneliness in the plays of his first career, there was also developing a kind of poetic mythology concerning the "religion of rhythm," particularly in *Welded, Lazarus Laughed, Strange Interlude,* and especially in *Dynamo,* in which the dance of polarities, in its manifestation in the physical phenomenon of electricity, is made explicitly into a religion. The characters in these plays are always talking about "light years," "splitting cells," "electrical displays," "positive and negative poles," and so on, in short in the language of the layman's version of the modern physical sciences, which are then propitiated in place of the lost God. (pp. 10-11)

The "religion of rhythm" and the attempt to make science a religion reached an ambiguous climax and came to an end with *Dynamo*. But O'Neill's encounters with God were not yet terminated; these were to come to an end, a bad one, in *Days Without End*, his only Catholic play wherein for the last time he tried to get back to the simple, comprehensible, and benign God of his fathers. . . . O'Neill later admitted that he had botched the ending . . . and the play; and it was to be his last religious play, his last play about modernity, and his final attempt in the plays to find a meaningful universe.

From now on in O'Neill's subsequent plays God is dead and the cosmos, whose mysteries once haunted his plays, dims and fades away, while man as man occupies the whole stage, absorbs all meanings, and embodies all mysteries and complexities; henceforth man is to be the measure of all. . . . From this time on his plays would be set in the past and would let the universe go its mystifying ways. He would begin the American history cycle-plays and, of course, would finally come to write *The Iceman Cometh, A Long Day's Journey, Hughie,* and *A Moon for the Misbegotten.* The only generalization that remained was the principle of polarity, for he could never see human experience except in terms of antinomies, alternations, and repetitions. (pp. 16-17)

[The] great natural metaphor for the principle of polarity was the cosmological process itself, the diurnal turn from night to day and the nocturnal return; hence the high incidence of sunsets and sunrises in O'Neill's plays. . . . [The] passage of day to night, and vice versa, in O'Neill's plays verge from effects which are pure theatricality to a blend in which the theatricality suggests a moral mood or even a metaphysic as well. An early one-act play, *The Rope,* takes place at sundown, and the deepening scarlet of the evening is meant to provide a sinister backdrop for the sinister events of the play wherein at the end one man is preparing to torture another man by holding a red-hot file against the soles of his feet. At other times these risings and settings are purely spectacular. . . . Or they are meant to signify a human discovery, as in *The Fountain* when the discovery of land by Columbus' ship coincides with sunrise . . . , or, as in *Days Without End,* when the light of the rising sun strikes the gigantic representation of the crucifixion simultaneously with the regaining of his faith by John Loving. Again the very transitory or indefinable character of a sunrise or a sunset may be used to suggest a kind of moral murk in the human events that are being enacted. . . . [There is also] the conventional notion that dawn, the light of dawn, brings the truth. (pp. 17-18)

O'Neill's most Aristotelian plays are *Long Day's Journey Into Night* and *A Touch of the Poet.* Sure here of his own powers, he used the morning to post-midnight cycle but forewent any spectacular sunrise or sunset. In both plays the journey into night is a journey into the hell of "truth," and each reaches its tragic climax when its tortured protagonist, deep into night, has lost his or her own identity. . . . Night then is a backward journey, the inescapable past become alive once more. If dawn is reality, sunset is memory: both are insupportable, and only alcohol, dope, or a loss of identity can make them so.

If the human imagination first experienced cosmic terror at the electrical displays of God the Father, it probably conceived its first sense of the almost inexhaustible plentitude and variety of terrestrial existence in the polarity between land and sea. Thus it was that O'Neill's imagination, always partially archaic, instinctively seized upon this elementary and primordial antithesis for the background of so many of his plays. . . . (pp. 18-20)

The sea in O'Neill's plays is employed in two ways: first, as a world in itself, with its own meanings, beauties, and defects, and, second, as a place that provides a general contrast to the land and its way of life. . . . [The] sound of the sea itself was inherently rhythmical and was often used by O'Neill as background music in the early plays. (p. 21)

But the sea also has negative rhythms, mostly made by man the mechanic, as, for example, that oppressive, insistent foghorn that sounds the crack of doom for the haunted Tyrones during the last part of *Long Day's Journey,* or the periodic blast of the ship's whistle that announces the impending death of Yank in *Bound East for Cardiff.* Thus the sea really has two great contrasting rhythms, the "natural" movements and sounds of the sea and of sailing vessels, and the "mechanical" movements and sounds of steam vessels and other modern man-made devices. . . . [The] change in the rhythm of the sea from

the natural to the mechanical underlies *Beyond the Horizon,* which spans that era in history when on the sea the sailing ship began to give way to the steamer and on land the horse-drawn carriage was displaced by the automobile. These symptomatic changes are meant to underline the steadily deepening tragedy of the lives of the principals, who fall from Eden into Hell.

In the land-sea antithesis the principal movement or rhythm is embodied in the alternation between the two. It is difficult to say what the sea finally means in O'Neill's plays, for, as in *Moby Dick,* it means everything: rapture, beauty, terror, danger, adventure, isolation, renewal, immolation, union, death, peace, boredom, and so on. . . . Actually, in the plays as a whole there is no single, simple antithesis between the land and the sea, although it can always be confidently asserted that whatever the sea means—and it means different things in different plays—the land has hardly anything, ever, to recommend it. (pp. 21-2)

Always associated with the sea is the fog, that gray nothingness that envelopes everything and blurs all distinctions, even the basic ones between night and day and land and sea. Fog for O'Neill had something mystifying and supernatural about it. . . . (pp. 23-4)

The most powerful and somber evocation of fog and its spell occurs, as with so many other of O'Neill's devices, in *Long Day's Journey Into Night,* where fog is a palpable ambiguity. On the one hand fog, in *Long Day's Journey,* is a profound, brooding, and steadily deepening, natural backdrop for the various tragedies of the Tyrones. . . . On the other hand, fog also represents that blessed loss of identity for which all the main characters, the father excepted, are seeking. . . . [In] the final act of O'Neill's finest tragedy the great antithesis between land and sea and day and night, which underlay so many of his plays, become dissolved into fog whose only rhythm is the repetitive moan of the foghorn and the occasional tinkle of ships' bells. (pp. 24-5)

As immemorial as the antithesis between land and sea is the one between city and country, which constitutes yet another fundamental geographical polarity in O'Neill's plays. As in the biblical legend, where Cain, the fratricide, is reckoned the founder of cities, the city in O'Neill's plays is the place of corruption, evil, despair, loneliness, and heartlessness. In one sense the city is the dead end of life. (p. 25)

The only group of decent big-city people in O'Neill's world are the whores and the down-and-outers, in short, characters such as those of *The Iceman Cometh.* As with all other O'Neill themes, the evil of the city receives its most powerful evocation in the late plays, especially *Long Day's Journey, A Moon for the Misbegotten,* and, above all, *Hughie.* (p. 27)

The most concrete and somber picture of the city is in *Hughie,* which, strangely enough, is in its totality one of the most optimistic plays that O'Neill ever wrote. *Hughie* is Night and the City, one of the most powerful brief evocations of the loneliness, boredom, and despair of the bottom-dog in the modern city in the language. Only Melville's *Bartleby* is comparable. All rhythms are mechanical and repetitive, each harsh sound indicating the alexandrine crawl of time, dragging its snaky length slowly along. As Erie Smith, small-time Broadway "sport," carries on his monologue in a shabby hotel on the West Side of Manhattan at three o'clock of a hot and humid morning in the summer of 1928, we are, by a series of stage directions that amount to a stream of consciousness, allowed into the "consciousness," if it can be called that, of the night clerk, with his greasy, pimply face, and his aching feet. Except for some Walter Mitty-esque overtones and urges, the inner "life" of the night clerk is a stream of nothingness, beyond and below despair. It is all described by O'Neill with great wit, irony, and power. (p. 28)

If city life is usually inhuman, its antithesis, farm life, is by no means paradisical, and comes equipped with its own horrors. Only in the opening part of *Beyond the Horizon* do we get a glimpse of an orderly, well-run, handsome New England farm, with the commanding father, the obedient family, the freshly plowed fields, the checkerboard hills and valleys divided by neat stone walls, the distant hills rimmed by the setting sun. But after this in the play, and in O'Neill's plays as a whole, farm life means narrowness of outlook, or moral degeneracy, or financial ruin, or brutality, or back-breaking work, or sexual repression, in short, a distinctively unlovely way of life. (p. 30)

[The] life of man in O'Neill's world on land or on sea, in the city or on the farm, or in the suburb—is not a happy one. (p. 33)

> John Henry Raleigh, in his The Plays of Eugene O'Neill *(copyright © 1965 by Southern Illinois University Press; reprinted by permission of Southern Illinois University Press), Southern Illinois University Press, 1965, 304 p.*

STEPHEN FENDER   (essay date 1981)

Eugene O'Neill wrote poems before he wrote plays, but not many, and those mainly limited—not only to certain periods of his life, but also in range and (to be frank) in interest. . . .

[O'Neill's poems are collected in *Poems 1912-1944*.]

What do they say? Not a lot. The journalistic pieces, which O'Neill called "laconics", are imitations or parodies of Kipling, Longfellow, Rossetti's version of Villon's "Ballade des dames du temps jadis" (the one about "Where are the snows of yesteryear?"), John Masefield and James Whitcomb Riley. The jokey application of "serious" formulae to current events or other ephemera was an old staple of American newspaper humour, and the *Oxford Book of American Light Verse* supplies dozens of examples in the vein of O'Neill's twist on *Hiawatha*:

> O the bulling and the conning!
> Those three golden days of summer,
> When the Waterways Convention
> Came at last to Old New London.
> Chieftains from far distant regions
> Came to test our festal welcome,
> Came and spoke, and then departed.
> Spoke of what they knew, and often—
> Wisely spoke of that they knew not.

Of his "laconics" O'Neill's judgement was both modest and accurate. He thought them trivial occasional pieces written to order for a provincial newspaper. . . .

The case must have been different with the love poems written for Beatrice Ashe in 1914 and 1915. These still depend heavily on literary models, from rambling Whitmanesque to elaborate stanzaic confections like ballades, rondeaux, villanelles and triolets, but the emotional range widens with the formal variety. Even so, there is a certain coy excitement, as though the conjunction of Renaissance lyrical conventions and unconventional American lovers was too daring to be taken seriously. One of

the poems is entitled **"Villanelle To His Ladye In Which Ye Poore Scribe Complaineth Sorely Because the Cursed Memory of the Thousand Others Doth Poison His Dreams of His Beatrice"**. Another chides Dante for "That soft poetic bull" he wrote about another lady of the same name. . . .

In 1940, while working on *Long Day's Journey,* O'Neill turned again to poetry, only this time without the skittish ambivalence over literary allusions and the use of elaborate verse-forms. . . . [He] began to revise some early experiments in free verse, altering line divisions so as to break up the sense units. Finally, in 1942, he wrote five **"Fragments"** and . . . a **"Song in Chaos"**. In these poems the more relaxed form allows public and private to meet through the anecdotal:

> 'Yes, Doctor, I lie awake
> There is no sleep
> I suffer torments'
> 'Here's a prescription,
> A harmless barbiturate.
> Your trouble is common enough:
> It's the war.
> Everyone has the jitters.'
> Exit, bearing pills.

The reason why this is more satisfactory than any of the earlier verse is that here O'Neill has at last allowed his dialectical skills as a dramatist to invade the special territory of the poetry. The doctor's weariness qualifies the patient's self-pity, and both are caught up in a public context that makes light of their troubles. Or does it? Jamie's self-indulgent, shallow irony works well enough in the play, where it has to contend with blarney of almost equal force from Tyrone, Mary and even Edmund. Without this peculiarly Irish balancing of opposites, however, the mood of the early poems looms as callow, unvaried and (worst of all) exemplary. Everyone has heard of shallow optimism. Pessimism too can be unearned, unjustified by experience.

> Stephen Fender, "Lightly Laconic," in The Times Literary Supplement *(© Times Newspapers Ltd. (London) 1981; reproduced from* The Times Literary Supplement *by permission), No. 4,068, March 20, 1981, p. 306.*

ADDITIONAL BIBLIOGRAPHY

Clark, Barrett. *Eugene O'Neill.* New York: R. M. McBride, 1926, 110 p.
    Valuable for Clark's transcription of O'Neill's comments on his plays, although the biographical detail is unreliable and the criticism overly enthusiastic.

Engel, Edwin A. *The Haunted Heroes of Eugene O'Neill.* Cambridge: Harvard University Press, 1953, 310 p.
    Detailed discussion of the influences upon O'Neill's work and the development of themes which recurred throughout his dramatic career.

Miller, Jordan Y. *Eugene O'Neill and the American Critic.* Rev. ed. Hamden, Conn.: Archon Books, 1973, 553 p.
    Most complete annotated bibliography.

Sheaffer, Louis. *O'Neill: Son and Playwright.* Boston: Little, Brown, 1968, 543 p.
    Definitive biography. This, the first volume of a two-volume work, covers O'Neill's life to 1920.

Sheaffer, Louis. *O'Neill: Son and Artist*. Boston: Little, Brown, 1973, 750 p.

The second volume of Sheaffer's biography, covering O'Neill's life from 1920 until his death.

Winther, Sophus Keith. *Eugene O'Neill: A Critical Study*. Rev. ed. New York: Russell & Russell, 1961, 319 p.

First full-length critical study of O'Neill, originally published in 1934. Winther examines O'Neill as a social critic and as a tragedian who portrays his characters' "heroic will to live." The 1961 edition includes a chapter on O'Neill's later tragedies.

George Orwell

1903-1950

(Pseudonym of Eric Arthur Blair) English novelist, essayist, critic, and journalist.

Orwell is significant for his unwavering commitment, both as a man and as an artist, to personal freedom and social justice. His unpretentious self-examination and his ability to perceive the social effects of political theories inspired Irving Howe to call him "the greatest moral force in English letters during the last several decades." Foremost among Orwell's work is his novel *Nineteen Eighty-Four;* the society it presents has become an archetype for modern political repression.

Orwell was born into a lower-middle-class family that struggled to provide him a decent education. His mother managed to find him a place, at reduced rates, in a well-known preparatory school where, despite his intellectual accomplishments, he felt demeaned because of his low social standing and semicharitable position. In his essay "Such, Such Were the Joys" Orwell explained the guilt and shame he felt throughout his school years and how those experiences fostered his extreme sensitivity to social victimization. After attending Eton on scholarship, Orwell enlisted in the Indian Imperial Police. Stationed in Burma, he encountered the harsh realities of colonial rule: his reactions are vividly evoked in the essays "Shooting an Elephant" and "A Hanging," and in the novel *Burmese Days.* Although *Burmese Days* has often been criticized for its awkward attempts at descriptive writing, it has also been called an excellent study of the guilt, hypocrisy, and loneliness that infects the rulers of a subject population.

Disgusted with colonial life, Orwell left the police after five years, determined to become a writer. His first novel, *Down and Out in Paris and London,* which was based on a year he spent in self-imposed poverty, sympathetically examines the life of the poor. While writing this book Orwell discovered that the lower classes of society are exploited much like colonial subjects. His indignation over this fact is reflected throughout his subsequent work. Orwell's next four novels deal with victimization: his protagonists are confused individuals, preyed upon by society and their own weaknesses, who attempt to rebel against their lot and fail. *Coming Up for Air* is generally considered the best novel of this period, although critics point out that in all of his novels Orwell's characterization is weak and his plot devices contrived.

During the thirties Orwell also wrote two books of autobiography and social criticism. In *The Road to Wigan Pier,* commissioned by the socialist Left Book Club, Orwell described the life of English coal miners, but enraged his sponsors by examining at length the failure of socialists to address the needs of England's poor. After fighting with the loyalists in the Spanish civil war, he wrote *Homage to Catalonia,* a book which depicts the absurdities of war, the duplicity of every ideology, and the decency of ordinary people caught up in events beyond their control. Orwell stated that while writing *Homage to Catalonia* he committed himself to making an art of political writing. Most critics agree that he accomplished this with *Animal Farm.* In this fable about a barnyard revolt Orwell created a satire that specifically attacked the consequences of the

Russian Revolution while suggesting the reasons for the failure of most revolutionary ideals. *Animal Farm* brought Orwell worldwide fame, though the book was often narrowly read as a cold war indictment of the Soviet Union, rather than as a general study of the corrupting effects of power.

Orwell's next and last novel, *Nineteen Eighty-Four,* is one of the most influential books of the century. An attack on totalitarianism, it warns that absolute power in the hands of any government can deprive a people of all basic freedoms. The novel is based in part on the Soviet example, but it also points out the dangers of unchecked power that Orwell perceived in many Western democracies. The language of the book has made terms such as "Newspeak," "Double-think," and "Big Brother" part of our political vocabulary.

Orwell's prose style, especially that of his essays, has become a model for students of writing because of its precision, clarity, and vividness. Many of the essays, which combine observation and reminiscence with literary and social criticism, are considered modern masterpieces. Irving Howe reflected the critical consensus when he called Orwell "the best English essayist since Hazlitt." And V. S. Pritchett succinctly summed up Orwell's position in contemporary literature when he designated him "the conscience of his generation."

(See also *TCLC*, Vol. 2.)

PRINCIPAL WORKS

Down and Out in Paris and London   (novel)   1933
Burmese Days   (novel)   1934
A Clergyman's Daughter   (novel)   1935
Keep the Aspidistra Flying   (novel)   1936
The Road to Wigan Pier   (autobiography and social
 criticism)   1937
Homage to Catalonia   (autobiography and social criticism)
 1938
Coming Up for Air   (novel)   1939
Inside the Whale, and Other Essays   (essays)   1940
Animal Farm   (novel)   1945
Dickens, Dali, & Others   (criticism)   1946; published in
 England as *Critical Essays,* 1946
The English People   (essays)   1947
Nineteen Eighty-Four   (novel)   1949
Shooting an Elephant, and Other Essays   (essays)   1950
Such, Such Were the Joys   (essays)   1953
*The Collected Essays, Journalism and Letters of George
 Orwell.* 4 vols.   (essays, letters, and diaries)   1968

PHILIP RAHV   (essay date 1949)

[*Nineteen Eighty-Four*] is far and away the best of Orwell's books. As a narrative it has tension and actuality to a terrifying degree; still it will not do to judge it primarily as a literary work of art. Like all Utopian literature, from Sir Thomas More and Campanella to William Morris, Bellamy, and Huxley, its inspiration is scarcely such as to be aesthetically productive of ultimate or positive significance; this seems to be true of Utopian writings regardless of the viewpoint from which the author approaches his theme. *Nineteen Eighty-Four* chiefly appeals to us as a work of the political imagination, and the appeal is exercised with gravity and power. It documents the crisis of socialism with greater finality than Koestler's *Darkness at Noon,* to which it will be inevitably compared, since it belongs, on one side of it, to the same genre, the melancholy mid-century genre of lost illusions and Utopia betrayed.

While in Koestler's novel there are still lingering traces of nostalgia for the Soviet Utopia, at least in its early heroic phase, and fleeting tenderness for its protagonists, . . . in Orwell's narrative the further stage of terror that has been reached no longer permits even the slightest sympathy for the revolutionaries turned totalitarian. Here Utopia is presented, with the fearful simplicity of a trauma, as the abyss into which the future falls. The traditional notion of Utopia as the future good is thus turned inside out, inverted—nullified. It is now sheer mockery to speak of its future. Far more accurate it is to speak of its *unfuture.* (pp. 743-44)

The prospect of the future drawn in this novel can on no account be taken as a phantasy. . . . Ingsoc, the system established in Oceania, the totalitarian super-State that unites the English-speaking peoples, is substantially little more than an extension into the near future of the present structure and policy of Stalinism, an extension as ingenious as it is logical, predicated upon conditions of permanent war and the development of the technical means of espionage and surveillance to the point of

the complete extinction of private life. Big Brother, the supreme dictator of Oceania, is obviously modeled on Stalin, both in his physical features and in his literary style. . . . One of Orwell's best strokes is his analysis of the technique of "double-think," drilled into the Party members, which consists of the willingness to assert that black is white when the Party demands it, and even to believe that black is white, while at the same time knowing very well that nothing of the sort can be true. Now what is "doublethink," actually, if not the technique continually practiced by the Communists and their liberal collaborators, dupes, and apologists. . . . (pp. 744-45)

The diagnosis of the totalitarian perversion of socialism that Orwell makes in this book is far more remarkable than the prognosis it contains. This is not to deny that the book is prophetic; but its importance is mainly in its powerful engagement with the present. Through the invention of a society of which he can be imaginatively in full command, Orwell is enabled all the more effectively to probe the consequences for the human soul of the system of oligarchic collectivism. . . . Hence to read this novel simply as a flat prediction of what is to come is to misread it. . . . [Orwell's] intention, rather, is to prod the Western world into a more conscious and militant resistance to the totalitarian virus to which it is now exposed.

As in [Koestler's] *Darkness at Noon,* so in *Nineteen Eighty-Four* one of the major themes is the psychology of capitulation. Winston Smith, the hero of the novel, is shown arming himself with ideas against the Party and defying it by forming a sexual relationship with Julia; but from the first we know that he will not escape the secret police, and after he is caught we see him undergoing a dreadful metamorphosis which burns out his human essence, leaving him a wreck who can go on living only by becoming one of "them." . . . The truth is that the modern totalitarians have devised a methodology of terror that enables them to break human beings by getting inside them. They explode the human character from within, exhibiting the pieces as the irrefutable proof of their own might and virtue. Thus Winston Smith begins with the notion that even if nothing else in the world was his own, still there were a few cubic centimeters inside his skull that belonged to him alone. But O'Brien, with his torture instruments and ruthless dialectic of power, soon teaches him that even these few cubic centimeters can never belong to him, only to the Party. What is so implacable about the despotisms of the twentieth century is that they have abolished martyrdom. . . . The victim crawls before his torturer, he identifies himself with him and grows to love him. That is the ultimate horror. (pp. 746-47)

This novel is the best antidote to the totalitarian disease that any writer has so far produced. Everyone should read it; and I recommend it particularly to those liberals who still cannot get over the political superstition that while absolute power is bad when exercised by the Right, it is in its very nature good and a boon to humanity once the Left, that is to say "our own people," takes hold of it. (p. 749)

Philip Rahv, "The Unfuture of Utopia," in Partisan Review *(copyright © 1949, copyright renewed © 1976, by Partisan Review, Inc.), Vol. XVI, No. 7, July, 1949, pp. 743-49.*

E. M. FORSTER   (essay date 1950)

[That] Orwell was a bit of a nagger cannot be denied. He found much to discomfort him in his world and desired to transmit it, and in *Nineteen Eighty-Four* he extended discomfort into agony. There is not a monster in that hateful apocalypse which does not exist in embryo today. . . . Orwell spent his life in foreseeing transformations and in stamping upon embryos. His strength went that way. *Nineteen Eighty-Four* crowned his work, and it is understandably a crown of thorns.

While he stamped he looked around him, and tried to ameliorate a world which is bound to be unhappy. A true liberal, he hoped to help through small things. (p. 61)

[No] one can embrace Orwell's works who hopes for ease. Just as one is nestling against them, they prickle. They encourage no slovenly trust in a future where all will come right, dear comrades, though we shall not be there to see. They do not even provide a mystic vision. No wonder that he could not hit it off with H. G. Wells. What he does provide, what does commend him to some temperaments, is his belief in little immediate things and in kindness, good-temper and accuracy. He also believes in "the people," who, with their beefy arms akimbo and their cabbage-stalk soup, may survive when higher growths are cut down. He does not explain how "the people" are to make good, and perhaps he is here confusing belief with compassion.

He was passionate over the purity of prose, and in another essay he tears to bits some passages of contemporary writing. It is a dangerous game—the contemporaries can always retort— but it ought to be played, for if prose decays, thought decays and all the finer roads of communication are broken. Liberty, he argues, is connected with prose, and bureaucrats who want to destroy liberty tend to write and speak badly, and to use pompous or woolly or portmanteau phrases in which their true meaning or any meaning disappears. It is the duty of the citizen, and particularly of the practising journalist, to be on the lookout for such phrases or words and to rend them to pieces. . . . Many critics besides Orwell are fighting for the purity of prose and deriding officialese, but they usually do so in a joking offhand way, and from the esthetic standpoint. He is unique in being immensely serious, and in connecting good prose with liberty. (pp. 62-3)

> *E. M. Forster, "George Orwell" (1950), in his* Two Cheers for Democracy *(copyright 1951 by E. M. Forster; copyright 1979 by Donald Parry; reprinted by permission of Harcourt Brace Jovanovich, Inc.; in Canada by Edward Arnold Ltd.), Harcourt, 1951, pp. 60-3.*

JOHN ATKINS (essay date 1954)

The common element in all George Orwell's writing was a sense of decency. Decency itself is one of the vaguest terms in the English language yet most of us have little hesitation in recognising 'decent' behavior. It is behaviour which takes into account the feelings and personality of the other person. . . . Orwell's uniqueness lay in his having the mind of an intellectual and the feelings of a common man. In the conflict between intellect and sentiment the latter usually won. . . . In Orwell the conflict usually took the shape of realising that our civilisation is based on intellect but perceiving that intellect unrefined by sentiment (or decency) may well destroy the culture based on it and eventually itself. He waged a running battle with other intellectuals on this score alone. Towards the end the menace became an obsession and his last book, *1984,* was based on a sense of defeat. The intellectuals would not revert to a sense of decency. (p. 1)

Orwell's heart was in his own past and particularly in the literature of his past. His models were the novelists and storytellers and popular ballad-writers of his boyhood. He felt that in their works, even in those of the imperialist Kipling, there was a human warmth that was lacking in most of the publications that followed the first World War. (p. 3)

At first sight this is a very unpromising starting point for a modern writer. Some people are frightened of 'modern' literature because it seems to revel in the wretchedness of our own time. . . . Orwell also rubbed our noses in the dirt but he did not regard it as a healthy occupation. It was a kind of therapy. It is this quality that distinguished him from the popular writers on the one hand and the more conventional intellectuals on the other. It was never far from his mind that in the not very distant past serious writers actually regarded the simple human virtues of decent behaviour, tender feeling, sentiment and family love as being admirable. It is the basis of his excellent appreciation of Dickens (*Critical Essays*). (p. 5)

1984 is the story of a society in which decency had been destroyed. The terrifying thing is that this society had been established by men who claimed that they were the champions of the oppressed. Because they thought decency did not matter they created a worse oppression than the world had ever known before. Decency is based on respect for the other person, and respect derives from love—not sexual passion, of course, but the quieter passion, or conviction, that all men are brothers and that unless we keep this in mind we will slip into a belief that all men are enemies, with the inevitable results. (p. 6)

If Orwell saw a victim he would drop whatever he was doing to go to his assistance. It must have been an instinct.

Sir Richard Rees points out that all the characters in his novels are victims like himself. The leading characters are guinea-pigs on which life is experimenting. Dorothy, the clergyman's daughter, is a victim of her narrow upbringing. Gordon Comstock is a victim of poverty. Tubby Bowling is a victim of a society running mad. Winston Smith is a victim of the complete totalitarian state. There is no happy or fulfilled character in these novels. There is nothing unusual in this, of course, for there are few happy or fulfilled characters in any modern novel. When we come across them we tend to distrust them. But there is an intensity in Orwell's work which differentiates it from most contemporary fiction. His novels are studies of victimisation pure and simple. In most others the victimisation is incidental, often implied but frequently ignored on the surface. Even the successful characters in Orwell's novels are to be pitied. (p. 119)

In my opinion (not shared by everyone) most of the writing in his first book [*Down and Out in Paris and London*] is excellent. He is attempting to make us see, feel and smell and I think he succeeds to a very great extent. There is amateurishness here and there, but it is in the presentation rather than the expression. He finds it necessary now and again to tell us why he is writing the book, but I doubt if anyone who reads it needs to be told. . . . Orwell had not yet realised that a writer writes because he has to and not for an overt reason—or it would probably be more true to say that he did realise it but did not realise it was safe to leave the reader unappeased. At school one writes essays for very palpable reasons.

Much of the conversation is stilted—exact, grammatical and without colloquial abbreviations. . . . In view of Orwell's love of exact description this may be surprising, until it is remembered that literary conversation is a knack and requires practice before it can be successfully caputred. But in other ways he exhibits that plodding vein of exactness that runs through most of his descriptive work (though not to the same degree through his opinionative work), as when he counted the number of times he was called *maquereau* during one day, and found it was thirty-nine. His justly famous literary integrity expressed itself in this book in his refusal to compromise with the tastes of the public. Such 'refusal' is not uncommon today—in fact, it has become fashionable and some writers have strained themselves to the utmost to shock their readers. But here lies the difference between true and false 'refusal'—Orwell gives the impression of writing down exactly what he saw without exaggeration. He did not compromise but nor did he distort. We appreciated Orwell because he had found a very delicate point of balance which few writers attain and fewer maintain. (pp. 257-58)

Honesty was his chief literary virtue. There were few fireworks in his style, though he could turn a phrase very neatly. Recognising honesty is largely an intuitive matter and it is normally impossible to give any proof. When we can offer proof it is usually circumstantial, while literary honesty is a reflection of psychological integrity. Sometimes he tells us things that hardly any other writer would tell us because it might reflect on his honesty. (pp. 259-60)

There was a coolness and nonchalance about Orwell that made a respect for truth natural to him. It is rather trite to call his attitude scientific but I think it is the term that comes nearest. . . . Part of this aspect of Orwell's literary personality derives from his tendency to under-statement. . . .

Yet fidelity to fact can be a literary vice as well as a virtue. We like to feel that our author is describing things truthfully, but we soon get tired of an excess of fact. One reason why Orwell's novels are not successful is because he cannot resist the temptation to put in all he knows or feels about a particular person or situation. *Coming Up For Air,* the most popular of his novels, is a particularly bad offender in this respect. We never stop hearing new things about Tubby Bowling, and he is not the kind of character one likes to have detailed knowledge of. (p. 260)

I doubt if even [Orwell's] best friends would have called him a novelist. (p. 266)

There are individual parts of the novels which are extremely well done, but usually they are good outside the fictional canon. The Trafalgar Square episode in *A Clergyman's Daughter,* for instance, is a vignette which would be better by itself, preferably making its first appearance in a literary magazine. *Down and Out* masqueraded as fiction—Orwell had to cheat the public to get it published, presumably, or at least to find readers. But viewed as fiction it contains most of the available faults. (*Burmese Days* is the best, and every year scores of novels just as good appear, many of them by unknown writers.) They do not move, the atmosphere is as depressive as a fog, the characters go on repeating themselves, and there is a lack of ease in transition. A novelist needs a quality which I can best call fluidity—the power to persuade the reader that time is actually moving at its accustomed pace, not progressing in leaps and bounds, now jumping like a kangaroo, now hopping like a flea. Orwell did not possess this gift. (pp. 266-67)

In all Orwell's fiction there is one attractive character. I do not mean by this that there is only one person whom we can like but only one whom we can feel interest in. This is not an ethical judgment, it is a question of literary vitality. Rosemary in *Keep the Aspidistra Flying* is the only person we might be tempted to follow beyond the last page of the book. She is a cut above the normal ineffectual, conventional Orwell female. He intended her to be conventional (he was mainly interested in the ordinary, rarely in the extraordinary) and she *is* conventional, but she can surprise us as even the most conventional person can. (It is a mistake, and Orwell makes it, to imagine that conventionality is ever absolute.) Rosemary possesses sufficient understanding and sympathy to rise occasionally above her class and to enter into the processes of a deliberate failure like Gordon. . . . With better chances Rosemary might have been a delightfully fulfilled character, but her loyalty to Gordon makes this impossible. She is the only character in Orwell whom we can feel developing.

His literary models were chiefly Victorian. We know this not only from his own confession but also from his method of writing a novel. He plods, and chronology is sacred. There is an unnatural correctness about the conversations which is characteristic of Victorian fiction. His admiration for Dickens even goes so far in *Burmese Days* as to sum up the subsequent histories of the leading characters in the last chapter, very much in the manner of *David Copperfield*. There is nothing essentially wrong in this, but it is a convention that has fallen out of use and cannot be revived creatively except for a humorous purpose. I doubt if he had sufficient patience to be a novelist. He had a curious habit of ending a conversational outburst with the words 'etc., etc.' Perhaps the etceteras were not worth giving in full but by this device the author intrudes himself and destroys the illusion. When a novelist arises who will not pretend he does not exist this will be allowable, but there was nothing *avant-garde* about Orwell. Very often, instead of finding the exact word, he uses an inexact word in inverted commas, leaving the reader to discover what he really intended. One page in *Keep the Aspidistra Flying* has five examples of this usage. He tries to give specialised meanings to words like 'education' and 'manage' without attempting to define the quality he is searching for.

He was a fluent writer but in his fiction could not always control his fluency. Sometimes this led to an *embarras de richesses* which really did embarrass. . . . Orwell often obtained a good effect by understatement, but that was usually in an account of his own feelings. It was in his imagery that he sometimes tended to say too much. (pp. 268-70)

In his article **'Why I Write'** [Orwell] admitted that a book is often the result of vanity but when it lacked political purpose it was lifeless. During Orwell's lifetime any purpose had become political because the organisation of life had become totalitarian. This had nothing to do with the principles or desires of the government. Circumstances had related every single act of every single individual inextricably and it was useless pretending that one could live outside the network. It was this belief and the practice that followed from it that made *1984* and also *Coming Up For Air,* another product of his maturity, such unsatisfactory novels. Both were much too slow-moving to be good fiction. In each his main purpose had been the diagnosis of society or a section of society and the fictional values had been thrown overboard. (pp. 276-77)

Orwell is the most outstanding example of common sense in modern English literature. It is not so remarkable as it seems that his common sense sometimes led him to what appear to be extreme and even crankish conclusions. This may have been because we have lost sight of common sense in our social and political lives and are astonished by common sense when we meet with it. Like most of the apostles of common sense, he thought in terms of psychological types and wished to legislate for blank faces rather than for organic men and women. This again helps to explain the weakness of his fiction. He knew much less about what human beings were like than about what they ought to be like. (p. 278)

> *John Atkins, in his* George Orwell: A Literary Study *(© John Atkins, 1954, 1971), John Calder (Publishers) Limited, 1954 (and reprinted by Calder & Boyars, 1971, 394 p.).*

JOHN WAIN (essay date 1963)

It is impossible to criticise an author's work adequately until you have understood what kind of books he was writing; there was a time, in fact, when the art of criticism pivoted largely on the doctrine of the 'kinds'. . . . If Orwell's work has been grotesquely misjudged, and I think it has, the explanation is simple: it lies in the complete withering-away of the notion of literary kinds—so complete that we have abandoned the very word, and now speak of *genres,* as the Duchess told Alice to speak in French if she couldn't think of the English for a thing.

The 'kind' to which Orwell's work belongs is the polemic. All of it, in whatever form—novels, essays, descriptive sketches, volumes of autobiography—has the same object: to implant in the reader's mind a point of view, often about some definite, limited topic (the Spanish Civil War, the treatment of tramps in casual wards, the element of reactionary propaganda in boys' fiction) but in any case about an issue over which he felt it was wrong not to take sides. (p. 180)

If we consider Orwell as a writer of polemic, then, it will at least help to guide us past the initial paradox—the fact that his work, with so many and such crippling faults, contrives to be so valuable and interesting. He was a novelist who never wrote a satisfactory novel, a literary critic who never bothered to learn his trade properly, a social historian whose history was full of gaps. Yet he matters. For *as polemic* his work is never anything less than magnificent; and the virtues which the polemic kind demands—urgency, incisiveness, clarity and humour—he possessed in exactly the right combination. (p. 181)

Of course Orwell was in no sense an abstruse thinker. His political ideas were of the simplest. They were, in character, undisguisedly ethical; he believed in the necessity of being frank and honest, and he believed in freedom for everyone, with no authoritarian rule and no tyrannising, economic or otherwise. These were the twin pillars on which all his ideas rested, and, while it may be convenient to take them one at a time for the purposes of rough-and-ready analysis, it is not possible to separate them for long. In his eyes they were one and the same. With the direct clear-sightedness that was his greatest intellectual gift, he saw that modern tyranny works *by means of* dishonesty and evasion. . . . *Homo sapiens* naturally wishes to be free to do as he likes, not enslaved, not caged. Very well, the dictators answer, we will destroy the appetite for freedom; no one will fight for something he is not aware of lacking. Hence the Ministry of Truth, hence Doublethink, Newspeak, and the other devices for preventing people from grasping what is happening to them. It is a curious fact that Orwell's picture of the future is not particularly terrifying from the material point of view. . . . [His] vision of 1984 does not include extinction weapons. . . . He is not interested in extinction weapons because, fundamentally, they do not frighten him as much as spiritual ones; the death of his body is a

misfortune for a man, but it is not as bad as the death of his spirit. . . . Killing people is not likely to remain unnoticed, for their absence will sooner or later be remarked on; but killing their instinct for freedom, degrading their status as human beings, can remain unnoticed almost indefinitely. . . . So he made it his business to point at the very heart of the situation—the power of a totalitarian state to erase the past, by tampering with the records, until any trace of dissent becomes as if it had never been. (pp. 184-85)

That . . . was the prospect that frightened him more than bombs, which accounts for the relative absence of bombs from his nightmare of the future. High explosive was unpopular already. He felt the need to indicate the more deadly danger, and to follow this up by pointing out how easily any of us might unconsciously help to increase that danger. Anyone who talked or wrote in vague, woolly language, for instance—language which tended to veil the issues it claimed to be discussing—he denounced as an enemy. The language of free men must, he held, be vivid, candid, *truthful.* Those who took refuge in vagueness did so because they had something to hide. (p. 186)

The relationship between style and character, always familiar from the adage *Le style, c'est l'homme même,* seemed to Orwell one of the most important truths; and it all came circling back to his conviction that the price of freedom is candour. Why is Orwell himself a model of English prose style? *Because he was not frightened.* He had a relatively simple subject-matter to express, it is true, and his famous clarity may be admitted to arise partly from that fact; but, after all, the great majority of people who write have no very complex subject-matter, and one rarely finds clarity and forthrightness that would pass the Orwellian test. . . . But Orwell carried the argument one stage further. He noticed that large numbers of modern people, uneasy in a world that seemed to be drifting, had attached themselves to the anchorage of some form of orthodoxy. It might be Roman Catholicism, it might be Communism, it might be anarchism or pacifism. For most practical purposes he lumped them together. Any word ending with 'ism' was enough to draw his ridicule. (p. 187)

Orwell believed that an author who sacrificed his intellectual freedom was finished as an author. The ability to create, to imagine story and character, depended, in his view, on the free and wide-ranging use of the mind. And this is exactly what an orthodoxy, of any kind, is designed to prevent. Anyone who accepts a system of beliefs, who declares himself in favour of this or that Ism, lock, stock and barrel, is bound to commit himself to a certain amount of hypocrisy, conscious or otherwise. No intelligent person ever lived who could swallow *all* the details of some overarching dogma such as Marxism or Roman Catholicism. People who embrace these beliefs do so, in the main, for reasons which are not, strictly, intellectual. Many Christians, for example, believe that everything that is best and noblest in the European tradition is rooted in Christianity, that if Christianity goes it will not be long before all values, all sanctions, go too. Consequently they give their support to the Church because they feel that it is more important for the Church to survive than for them to be one hundred per cent clear of intellectual hypocrisy. . . . It is human, understandable and consistent that people should do this. And if they are grocers or gravediggers, there is not much harm done. They can still go about their work efficiently, even though they have accepted a certain amount of built-in censorship. But if they are writers, they are finished. That is Orwell's point, and I have never seen it refuted. The key essay in which he expressed this view is **'The Prevention of Literature'**, reprinted in *Shooting an Elephant.* (pp. 188-89)

I should like to turn, next, to his work as a literary critic. Now, obviously this has serious faults. It is, in fact, 'amateur' in both the good and the bad senses. He thought of his literary criticism as merely an extension of his everyday activities. . . . Unfortunately, it is true that literary criticism is a trade you have to learn; it *is* specialised, just as the writing of history is specialised; and the reader of Orwell's soon learns that he must overlook flaws which are the result of not having thought deeply enough about the nature of criticism. His amateurism permitted him to talk only about what caught his attention, and brush the rest aside; he had the amateur's untroubled assumption that what matters about a work of art is what he thinks about it, rather than what it is. His essay on Tolstoy's criticism of *King Lear,* for instance, is in many ways superb; apart from the fact that it contains a number of acute remarks about both Shakespeare and Tolstoy, it serves as a vehicle for some of Orwell's most moving and impressive utterances about human life. . . . But, all the same, it does contain some misstatements, even absurdities, which arise from his characteristic lack of care over literary *nuances.* . . . What [Orwell] has seen, as usual, is the broad general 'message' of the play, and how it meshes in with life. . . . It is an essay that will keep its relevance as long as human beings have moral problems; but, as a strictly 'literary' essay, it was, in many ways, doomed before it started. Compare it, for instance, with the famous essay on *Boys' Weeklies.* Orwell's treatment of *King Lear* and his treatment of *The Magnet* (a boys' paper that ran for about thirty years) are both brilliant, but they are not different enough. He treats them both as documents, expressing a certain attitude to life; and while it is true that he rather admires the attitude to life he finds in *King Lear,* and doesn't think much of the one he finds in *The Magnet,* this doesn't set them sufficiently far apart. If all the texts of these works were lost, and we had nothing but Orwell's essay to go on, we should never be able to tell, from reading it, that Shakespeare was as far superior to the amiable author of *The Magnet* as, in fact, he is.

So it isn't for 'literary criticism', in the real sense, that one reads Orwell's essays on books, any more than one reads his novels as 'imaginative work' in the real sense. It is all the same thing; a blunt, honest presentation of the important issues as he saw them, usually with a strong 'practical' bias. But it must be said, before we leave his criticism, that in a few instances this limitation actually operates as a strength. The essay on Kipling is perhaps the best example. Kipling is not an author of subtle shades or recondite effects; his work presents no technical problems, even simple ones like that of the relationship of plot and sub-plot in *King Lear;* it was possible for Orwell to arrive at a valid estimate of him merely by being clear-sighted about his subject-matter. (pp. 189-91)

All his life, one of [Orwell's] favourite butts was the 'progressive' who cares more that his ideas should be 'advanced' than that they should be realistic and workable. (p. 192)

[What] interests him is not the theoretically tidy or impressive solution, but the one that *works*—and works here and now. And this brings us back to the point about his 'kind' as a polemic writer. All the strengths and weaknesses of his work come out of this centre. For instance, it will seem to some people staggering and even culpable that Orwell should have steadfastly refused to tackle, in his work, the problem that he constantly acknowledged to be the most urgent of all—that of

faith. As early as *A Clergyman's Daughter,* there is a remarkable outburst on the futility of human life if it is not sustained by faith. And as late as the essay on Arthur Koestler (1944) we find him saying, 'The real problem is how to restore the religious attitude while accepting death as final'. If this was 'the real problem', some will ask, why didn't he address himself to it? Because—and we will give him his own voice again— 'privation and brute labour have to be abolished before the real problems of humanity can be tackled. The major problem of our time is the decay of the belief in personal immortality, and it cannot be dealt with while the average human being is either drudging like an ox or shivering in fear of the secret police.' (*Looking Back on the Spanish War*). So Orwell postponed the ultimate task and laboured at the one nearest at hand. And when we come to weigh up his achievements, it may be that we shall count this sacrifice as one of them. For, to a writer, it *is* a sacrifice to admit that so many other things matter more urgently than writing. Orwell put the claim of his fellow-man consistently before his own, and the paradox is that it is this spirit, rather than any specifically literary quality, that will keep his work alive. (pp. 192-93)

> John Wain, ''George Orwell (I),'' in his Essays on Literature and Ideas *(reprinted by kind permission of Curtis Brown Ltd. on behalf of John Wain), Macmillan and Co Ltd., 1963, pp. 180-93.*

GEORGE P. ELLIOTT   (essay date 1964)

[Despite] the fame of *1984* and the enormous respect in which Orwell is held, I propose that he is a failed prophet. . . .

Not that Orwell was, or claimed to be, a prophet in the full sense. A prophet is one who speaks poetically from divine inspiration, and Orwell was a prose atheist; furthermore, a prophet is one whose audience (and a prophet must have an audience) *believes* that he speaks from divine inspiration, and almost none of the Anglo-American audience to whom Orwell addressed himself will credit a man with speaking God's word. Orwell strove, at his best, to speak directly from his own conscious experience, and blunt prose is the proper instrument for such speech; a true prophet does not deal chiefly with the sorts of truth that fit into prose. (p. 162)

Yet he is a sort of prophet—at least he is viewed as one, the secular prophet of socialism. Secularism can have no analogues to saints, for good men, of whom Orwell was surely one, men who are splendidly virtuous, honorable, upright, courageous, honest, and concerned with right behavior, are not necessarily in a special connection with God as saints are; but it has its analogues to prophets, who speak, and are thought of as speaking, the truth, experienced and reasoned-upon moral and political truth, the truth behind the shifting confusion and lies of events, the steady truth. Prophets do not systematize, are no theologians, no philosophers even; Orwell sticks to his experience as faithfully as any Jeremiah to the word of God, and if it leads him into anti-socialistic or self-contradictory statements he is unconcerned, as are his readers. Prophets use satire as one of their scourges, and Orwell is excellent at satire; indeed, had he been more systematizing and inventive, like his admired Swift, he might have composed satires of a high order; but his chief satire, *Animal Farm,* sticks to (is stuck with) the political facts too nearly. Prophets tell the people, especially the mighty and chosen, what they ought to have done and ought to do, and boldly promise actual punishments for their transgressions and dreamlike rewards for their obedience to the right; all this Orwell does. Prophets want you to hear the word, not their delivery of it; in Orwell's plain, public prose, you never detect a murmur of vanity even when his own experiences are his subject. Prophets want to change the way you think and act; and I am sure that politically, we, his readers, now think and act as we do in some measure because of what Orwell wrote. (p. 163)

Even as a secular prophet, though Orwell was the best of our age, he failed at last. His profound and enduring message, adumbrated in earlier essays, is finally summed up and given its strongest images in *1984,* which was intended to reveal not only the direction of our political drift but also, prophetically, man's inmost nature. Politically, he says, men are interested in power, and the ideals they profess only whitewash this true motive. The aim of the modern totalitarian state is to "reduce consciousness," to obliterate personality and the exercise of the spirit. Now these are the sorts of strictures we need and want prophets to make; in them we can recognize aspects of reality; they are true. However, Orwell, like many another provincial from the Enlightenment, was so shocked at discovering that men are not innately perfectible and good that he decided they are more corruptible than they actually are. He goes on: because of technological progress, greater social organization, more effective methods of propaganda (in sum, because of scientific advances and analytical ways of thinking), rulers are now free to exert their power more and more undisguisedly and will finally be able consciously to exert power just for its own sake. But with this distortion he loses his readers; it belongs to an artificiality like that of a horror-movie. (*1984* was turned into a very bad horror movie.) This, of all the insights he claims the most profound, is untrue, and its untruth darkens his other insights. . . . Those who are conscious of their impulse to power and try to exert power only for their own satisfaction are merely cruel; and cruelty is not so potent a force as love of a cause, however bad, for cruelty has limits and is satiable but perverted love never has enough. The tormentor's speech, in *1984,* setting forth the rationale of the rulers of that society, is a distorting mirror which is intended to show us the very core of ourselves. Because Orwell has previously told us so much about ourselves and our time which we have recognized as true, we approach this revelation with excitement; but the excitement is transformed into a simply nervous excitement, such as one gets from a mad-scientist movie. What do we learn from the tormentor's speech? That George Orwell thought cruelty, when divorced from love, can become the strongest human impulse. In so particular a distortion it is not so much ourselves we see as a curious pathology. Swift is like a man with cancer who says men are wholly disgusting vessels of disease, and because sometimes we feel so we say yes, we are; but Orwell is like a man with cancer who says everyone else has cancer too, and we say no, only some men have cancer, most are not so sick as that, as for me I have asthma and a slipped disc. (pp. 164-65)

Why his failure as a prophet? For one thing, a great or even a successful prophet must be a forceful artist, preferably a good poet, and Orwell was a slight artist. His poetry is rhyming notions; even his judgments on poetry are of value only when he is treating it as a social symptom; he is far more sensitive to bad prose than to good poetry. His novels have the merit of containing descriptions which might have been incorporated in essays or books of reportage, but as novels they are not very good. His one allegory is accomplished and entertaining, but it does not penetrate far beyond the local politics that occasioned it; still, its satire, while slight, is pure and intense; I would guess that if any fiction of Orwell's is much read a

century from now it will be *Animal Farm.* He was a master of the miniature art of the conscious essay, along with Edmund Wilson, Julian Huxley, Aldous Huxley, V. S. Pritchett, T. S. Eliot, Yvor Winters, Virginia Woolf . . . ; such writers are sophisticated and intelligent and say something worth saying . . . ; but they are not prophetic. Imagine Isaiah chopping his vision up and parceling it into essays. Of the humble art of reporting, too, Orwell is a master, one with few peers. . . . [Yet] Orwell is not an artist of the first rank because he succeeded only in the lesser arts of essay-writing and reporting. . . . (pp. 165-66)

Psychologically, the root of Orwell's failure was, no doubt, his extreme sensitivity to cruelty and to the unjust exercise of authority. . . . [He] himself was conscious that civilization demands rulers and that the suffering that results from being exploited was as likely to obliterate men as to fill them with love (see his **"Marrakech"**); more important, though his sensitivity to cruelty and suffering was part of what drove him to write and to become a socialist, it does not begin to explain his limitations. And his limitations, I think, distorted his views more than his illness did; it was because of his limitations that he could suppose, as Swift did not, that all men suffered from his own malady. (pp. 166-67)

His greatest limitation was his rationalistic view of things, his materialism. Some of his minor limitations, of course, were strengths. His Britishness, for example, was total, but he knew it and some of his best insights derive from this very knowledge; he was stuck with the facts of his experience, but from his experience he wrote what must be the best book likely to be written on the Spanish Civil War; he looked mostly for the social function of works of literature, but he served as a sort of corrective to the esoterics who have been overrunning literary criticism. But other of his minor limitations enfeebled him. One of the most startling was his fitful historical imagination; though he understood such important recent changes in the West as the loss of popular belief in immortality, yet he displayed an abysmal ignorance of the Middle Ages, about which he often repeated the eighteenth-century clichés. He believed politics and social problems are, at least nowadays, more important than all the rest of life together and pollute all of it, a belief that is possible only to one who denies, among other things, the validity of religious experience. He had a weakness for generalizing; he sometimes wrote as though all civilized men were London-dwelling materialists with an atavistic love of flowers. He took a rather quantitative view of excellence, when he happened not to be thinking of a given man or act; so that he could suggest that poetry, just because its true audience is limited to the speakers of one language, is inferior to prose, which can be translated for all men. But most damaging, he put his trust in conscious reason as the measure of all things, and he wanted to look only at that which can be seen by the plain light of day. . . . Thus limited, he was hostile to, denied, or was indifferently skeptical about matters of the greatest importance, God, the unconscious, sin and evil; he was inadequate to deal with poetry, love, religious emotions and rituals; and he could not imagine that human suffering might be more than a matter of endurance, sado-masochism, and willed destruction. The materialist rationalism which has been the binding spirit and philosophy of the age of science has at no time or place been stronger than during Orwell's generation in England; as a prophet he knew it was partial and often false, but as a creature of the age he could not break its bonds. (pp. 168-69)

George P. Elliott, "George Orwell" (originally pub-

lished in a slightly different form as "A Failed Prophet," in The Hudson Review, *Vol. X, No. 1, Spring, 1957), in his* A Piece of Lettuce *(© copyright, 1957, 1959, 1960, 1961, 1962, 1963, 1964, by George P. Elliott; reprinted by permission of the Estate of George P. Elliott), Random House, 1964, pp. 161-70.*

WAYNE WARNCKE (essay date 1968)

Whether [George Orwell] was any more conscious of the political crisis that the Western world has faced during the past several decades than many other writers have been is doubtful, but his own involvement in the struggle for human freedom and decency is unquestionable; and it is the most important single factor influencing his essays on literature from the briefest reviews to the more extended and better known studies of writers like Dickens and Henry Miller. Orwell's literary criticism at the very outset is a reaction against the practice of doctrinaire criticism—against the blatant shouting of creeds, the intellectual coercion and falsification of truth that Orwell found especially evident in the left-wing writing of his time. His response to this particular moral failure developed, however, into more than an appeal for honest literary criticism on the part of the orthodox Left. It extended to a general attack on the narrowness of all orthodoxy, political or religious, and undoubtedly made it difficult for him to find a position in his own literary criticism that would allow him the broadest critical point of view, yet allow too a *modus operandi* and a standard of judgment compatible with his attitude toward literature as a sociopolitical and thus moral force. (p. 484)

Orwell's initial problem as a critic of literature is clear enough: the pull toward an acknowledgement of any world view as a source of "good" literature met the counterpull toward acceptance of only a world view that was politically conscious and preferably liberal. . . . Though he stressed the importance of the writer's individuality and freedom, and the validity of one's own truth ("the imaginative writer is unfree when he has to falsify his subjective feelings, which from his point of view are facts"), he took many a writer to task for omitting in his work consideration of the social or political conditions of the life he was depicting. (p. 485)

Orwell suggests a solution to the problem of the writer's responsibility by a repeated emphasis on the importance of a writer's sincerity: his being able to care, his really believing in his beliefs; and by equating literary talent with conviction. . . . Yet even the application of this assertion became problematical when, for example, he evaluated the work of Yeats—a writer whose political and moral tendencies were, from Orwell's point of view, irresponsible. One suspects that Orwell reluctantly gave his concept of sincerity an altered emphasis in order to acknowledge (perhaps less unwillingly) his recognition of a great talent. . . . Despite the inconsistencies that are suggested by his all too brief theoretical commentary concerning literature, his practical criticism shows invariably and without confusion that the writer's responsibility is first to certain basic human values (indeed, including sincerity), which go unchanged whatever political or religious ideology makes claims for the infallibility of its doctrines. The general result in Orwell's criticism is an analysis of the quality of human response expressed in a writer's work. (pp. 485-86)

Orwell's attitude toward literature is essentially pragmatic; literature is a force in the world for good or evil. Though Orwell is very much concerned with literature as a reflection of man and society, the concern itself derives from a belief that the significance of literature is the effect it has had or will have on the quality of human life. In this characteristic, Orwell is much closer to Dr. Johnson than to John Crowe Ransom; his attitude is more closely in line with a traditional view that goes back at least to Horace than it is with contemporary objective theories of art that have dominated literary criticism in the first half of this century. Nowhere does Orwell overtly state that instruction should take precedence over enjoyment or that enlightenment should precede entertainment, but this is an attitude that underlies his criticism; and it is evident that he sees the importance of literature as a means to an end, and that the end is the place where a responsible and significant literature will be discovered.

Yet Orwell's critical approach to literature differs at important points from both traditional literary pragmatism as practiced, for example, by the dominant neoclassical critics of the eighteenth century, and the special variety of pragmatic criticism illustrated by contemporary Marxist critics. (pp. 486-87)

Like both the Marxist and the traditional pragmatic critic, he emphasizes the responsibility of the artist to the reader and sees the aim of the artist in relation to the well-being of man in society, but he differs in his idea of precisely what that relationship is. Whereas the typical Marxist values literature insofar as it promotes the proletariat or the classless society, and the traditional pragmatic critic has tended to evaluate according to the degree that literature reaches the happy balance of both delighting and inducing "virtue" (a now dubious, if not impossible concept), Orwell values literature insofar as it is a free and sincere expression of a human truth, the only prescription being that artistic truth be verifiable in the daily life of humankind—that it have traceable roots in reality. (p. 487)

Orwell's criticism is distinguished from the traditional, though not so much from the contemporary, pragmatic approach in another important respect. Orwell is very much concerned with the source of literature. Although in this characteristic he is close to the Marxist critic in having a vital concern for the mind of the writer and the subject matter of his work, he differs again by not being restricted to an exclusive economic or class accounting for the derivation of the character of literature. . . . Orwell quite naturally would and, indeed, does concern himself chiefly with both source and effect, and less with form; his procedure as a critic is a combined analysis and evaluation of both the source and end of creative literary works. (pp. 487-88)

Orwell's dual critical concerns for both the source and the effect of art make up the heart of his criticism and are perhaps most clearly illustrated in his essays on the traditional English writers, Dickens, Kipling, and Swift. An idea of his fundamental critical approach, however, can be gained by examining in broad outline his general procedure as a critic and the basic premise which underlines his critical point of view. All of Orwell's major criticism follows roughly the same pattern of description and evaluation; in the first instance, through the use of historical, sociological, and psychological methods, literature supports the development of an analysis of the writer's world view; in the second instance literature becomes the subject of an evaluation of the writer's specific literary qualities. (p. 490)

With an approach that places so great an emphasis on a writer's human orientation, it is not strange that the central concept of

Orwell's criticism is the writer's "world view," a term used interchangeably with "tendency," "message," and "purpose" in Orwell's phraseology. Orwell is one of the chief representatives of a critical point of view which attaches most importance to the writer's attitude toward life. At the core of every writer's work is a fundamental vision of life, something analogous to the soul of the writer's being, and Orwell's major criticism centers in this unifying element of both the author and his art.

In Dickens, Orwell finds central a generosity of mind, a quasi-instinctive siding with the oppressed against the oppressors, a sound moral sense, but a narrow intellectual and imaginative vision of human progress; in Kipling, a sense of responsibility to England's ruling power which acted and made necessary decisions; in Swift, a simple refusal of life, a refusal to see anything in human life except dirt, folly, and wickedness, and a disbelief in the possibility of human happiness or the capability of improving earthly existence. . . . Orwell's major critical essays are neither more nor less than an elaboration upon these central concepts, and his critical procedure is to clarify and to evaluate each world view in its pertinent manifestations: as each is expressed through certain categories of the writer's life and as each is translated into certain characteristics of his art. (pp. 490-91)

What is important to note in all of these classifications is that they are not mechanically made, and that Orwell is not simply applying a narrow and absolute category that rules out the recognition of distinctly individual characteristics or even contradictory political tendencies. For example, Orwell observes that Swift shows a progressive strain which is not congruous with his central reactionary orientation. There are moments when he is constructive and advanced, and while he sees utopia as a strongly centralized society, he can also attack totalitarianism. . . . Orwell is not merely labelling, but pointing out the nuances of each writer's political views; and his awareness of relativity and inconsistency, illustrated by his analysis within a category, is equally apparent in the variety of descriptive categories he applies. Other classifications that Orwell uses at different times and with different emphasis to bring out a writer's world view are the social, intellectual, and religious.

What such an analysis amounts to is a revelation of the writer's mind in terms of his attitudes, opinions, alignments, and beliefs, developed from biographical and historical facts, and by examining the writer's social, economic, geographical and psychological origins—all reflected in and supported by the writer's work. But the effect of the analysis and description is more than a clarification of the writer's world view; it is a judgment of that view as well. . . . In a sense this phase of Orwell's criticism is an arraignment, a calling to account, from Orwell's point of view, of the extent and quality of the writer's humanity as it is expressed in his work. . . . (pp. 492-93)

What matters . . . even more than "truth" in Orwell's approach to the specific aesthetic effectiveness of . . . any writer's work is Orwell's sense that the writer has honestly confronted his material. Thus, any world view, freely and sincerely held and not insane in a medical sense, as Orwell phrased it, can produce a genuine work of art. Orwell's ultimate aesthetic criterion is the intellectual and emotional validity of the writer's work, measured in large part by the intensity with which the writer has lived the content of his work; and this criterion saved Orwell most of the time from the blunders of doctrinaire critics he repeatedly condemned throughout his writing career.

Where Orwell's critical approach to literature shows particular strength is in a kind of hard core, relentless exposing of a writer's total human response. Perhaps Swift has never received such an unveiling as Orwell gives him, nor has Dickens been so sharply scrutinized and at the same time so sympathetically understood. Kipling is revealed in all his commonness and impalatable glorifying of a now defunct British military ideal, yet Orwell's essay is one of the most just and perceptive discussions of Kipling's mind and the large ramifications of his work that have been written. Fortunately, Orwell usually chose to write extendedly on authors into whom he had a special insight. Jack London, for example, is a contemporary writer Orwell seems to have understood completely. His analysis of London's dual strains: an intellectual bent toward the common man's struggle for survival and a temperamental or instinctual tendency toward a glorification of brutality and strength, is particularly pointed, especially when he shows that London's best work comes out of an interaction of both strains, as in certain of his short stories. (pp. 495-96)

At times Orwell's revelations are overdrawn and often disconcerting to the reader who is looking for a more aesthetically oriented criticism, but they are to a large degree valid, perhaps disconcerting because of their validity. Where Orwell fails is in the sin of omission, in an overemphasis on the political, social, and moral implications of literature that deprives his criticism of a sense that literature is something in itself, whose purposes are often wholly expressive, self-contained and not less valuable for being so.

The essential quality of such a criticism depends on what the critic conceives of as being explicitly human; how broad and far-reaching his own mind is in his attitude toward humanity and art; how openminded and tolerant he himself is toward his fellow beings; how fully he realizes the variousness and complexity of human experience. Orwell's criticism is adequate within the limited boundaries he sets, the standards he applies, and the distance he goes with them; but by its very nature his criticism denies the efficacy in literature of what one might describe as mythic vision—what E. M. Forster calls "prophecy"—and it is indifferent to the power Yeats' mystical philosophy had in forming his verse and the comparable effect the Christian faith had on Eliot's work after 1930. In emphasizing the reality of man's "points of attachment to the physical world," the "day-to-day struggle," Orwell was led to underrate the modern literature that has explored other realities, other problems than social and political. From Orwell's point of view, the most responsible and therefore valuable literature expresses the author's emotional and intellectual perception of the objective world and the individual's physical struggle for life rather than the author's introspection of a subjective world and the dark night of the human soul. The realities of the former world take precedence in Orwell's mind over the realities of the latter world; indeed, without freedom from political tyranny and social oppression, literature itself might cease to exist. . . . Despite his limitations, the direction of his criticism was necessary in the time of crisis; perhaps there will always be a place for it—at least the threat to human freedom has not abated. (pp. 496-97)

Wayne Warncke, "George Orwell's Critical Approach to Literature," in The Southern Humanities Review *(copyright 1968 by Auburn University), Vol. II, No. 4, Fall, 1968, pp. 484-98.*

RAYMOND WILLIAMS   (essay date 1971)

It would be easy to say that almost all Orwell's important writing is about someone who gets away from an oppressive normality. From the central characters of *The Clergyman's Daughter* and *Keep the Aspidistra Flying* to those of *Coming Up for Air* and *Nineteen Eighty-Four,* this experience of awareness, rejection, and flight is repeatedly enacted. Yet it would be truer to say that most of Orwell's important writing is about someone who tries to get away but fails. That failure, that reabsorption, happens, in the end, in all the novels mentioned, though of course the experience of awareness, rejection, and flight has made its important mark. (p. 36)

Animal Farm is unique in Orwell's writing by the absence of an Orwell figure [his typical character described above]. It is in this sense a more complete projection of his way of seeing the world than anything else he wrote. Yet the terms of the projection limited the consciousness with which the Orwell figure had been invented to deal. It is a work of simplification, in both the good and bad senses.

Orwell described it once as a squib, but it was always more serious than that. He wrote in the preface to the Ukrainian edition:

> Nothing has contributed so much to the corruption of the original idea of Socialism as the belief that Russia is a Socialist country and that every act of its rulers must be excused, if not imitated. And so for the past ten years I have been convinced that the destruction of the Soviet myth was essential if we wanted a revival of the Socialist movement. On my return from Spain I thought of exposing the Soviet myth in a story that could be easily understood by almost anyone and which could be easily translated into other languages.

The precision of his political aim, and yet the search for simplicity and generality, carry some inevitable contradictions. . . . [Contradictions would have appeared] in any work conceived and executed as a general fable. Indeed, by the time the specific situation had been so generally translated, it was always possible, even likely, that not only the myth of Soviet socialism, but also the myth of revolution, would in fact be "destroyed."

Certainly *Animal Farm* has been widely interpreted in this way. Orwell is produced as "evidence" against a new revolutionary generation. . . . But something deeper has to be faced: the real consciousness of the fable itself. Past the easy exploitation and the equally easy rejection, the fable in *Animal Farm* offers positive and negative evidence of a permanently interesting kind.

Orwell got the germ of the fable from seeing

> a little boy, perhaps ten years old, driving a huge cart-horse along a narrow path, whipping it whenever it tried to turn. It struck me that if only such animals became aware of their strength we should have no power over them, and that men exploit animals in much the same way as the rich exploit the proletariat.

This insight is already of a rather different kind from the eventual projection. The speed of his figurative transition from animals to the proletariat is interesting, showing as it does a residue of thinking of the poor as animals, powerful but stupid.

Men, of course, here and in the story, are seen as exploiters. And the worst thing about the Bolshevik pigs, in the story, is that they become indistinguishable from drunken, greedy, and cruel men. The noble beast is the workhorse Boxer. (pp. 70-2)

The powerful but stupid horses of *Animal Farm* are looked on with great respect and pity. The men and the pigs are intelligent, calculating, greedy, and cruel. This is surely more than a simple operative analogy. It is a substantial, even physical, response.

The other element of the analogy is exploitation. If *they* became aware of their strength, *we* should have no power over them. Orwell here is thinking about something more than a political event, about a range of relations in man's use of animals and of nature. . . . The true struggle between animals and humans: is that the real theme of *Animal Farm?* It is difficult to say so, without most of the surface of the story collapsing. What really happens, I think, is that the very deep identification between the laboring and exploited animals and the laboring and exploited poor is retained, almost unnoticed, as a base for the exposure of that "pure illusion . . . of a class struggle between humans"—humans, now, being capitalists and revolutionaries, the old ruling class and the new, who, whatever their differences and their conflicts, can be depended upon to go on exploiting the creatures on whose backs they live, and even, as at the end of the story, to unite against them. Orwell is opposing here more than the Soviet or Stalinist experience. Both the consciousness of the workers and the possibility of authentic revolution are denied.

These denials, I would say, are inhuman. But it is part of the paradox of Orwell that from this despairing base he is able to generate an immediate and practical humanity: the comradeship of the suffering which he feels very deeply, and also, more actively, the critical skepticism of the exploited, an unexpected kind of consciousness that informs the story. I have said that *Animal Farm* is unique among Orwell's books because it contains no Orwell figure, no isolated man who breaks from conformity but is then defeated and reabsorbed. This figure is, rather, projected into a collective action: this is what happens to the animals who free themselves and then, through violence and fraud, are again enslaved.

The collective projection has a further effect. What happens is a common rather than an isolated experience, for all its bitterness. . . . "All animals are equal . . . but some are more equal than others." It is not surprising that this phrase has passed into ordinary language with a meaning much stronger than that of simple satire on revolutionary betrayal. It is one of those permanent statements about the gap between pretense and actuality, profession and practice, that covers a very wide range. In many places throughout *Animal Farm,* this strong and liberating intelligence transforms a bitter perception into an active and stimulating critique. Beyond the details of the local analogy, and paradoxically beyond the more fundamental despair, this lively awareness connects and informs. Even the last sad scene, where the excluded animals look from man to pig and pig to man and cannot tell which is which, carries a feeling that is more than disillusion and defeat. Seeing that they are the same because they act the same, never mind the labels and the formalities—that is a moment of gained consciousness, a potentially liberating discovery. In its small scale and within its limited terms, *Animal Farm* has a radical energy that goes far beyond its occasion and has its own kind of permanence. (pp. 72-5)

Raymond Williams, in his George Orwell *(copyright © 1971 by Raymond Williams; reprinted by permission of Viking Penguin Inc.), Viking Penguin, 1971, 102 p.*

FREDERICK R. KARL (essay date 1972)

The novel was for [Orwell] a way to discuss the issues of his day while providing a maximum of instruction for a large audience. (p. 148)

Orwell does frequently fail us, however, in not clearly indicating what belongs to literature and what is proper to history. History demands, among other things, blinding clarity, while literature can be impressionistic, frenzied, symbolic, romantic. Between the two, as Aristotle remarked in his *Poetics,* there is bound to be a clash, for the intention of one differs crucially from that of the other. Thus, we often feel that Orwell as a topical writer has not integrated the two elements sufficiently, so that one frequently gains at the expense of the other. There is no "conscious sacrifice" on Orwell's part, but there is an evident lack of imagination, the synthetic process capable of wedding dissimilars. Having accepted Naturalism as *the* mode for his type of novel, Orwell forsakes those techniques that might have projected his political ideas into deeply felt literary experiences. Lacking Zola's tremendous intensity, he cannot compensate for what he loses through unadventurous methods.

Nevertheless, because Orwell so cherishes middle-class comforts—although he can forgo them and survive—he conveys, within his limitations, the pathos and terror involved in a man caught between what he wants for himself and what the political system has to offer him. The prison life of *1984* merges with the enclosed life of the private school he attended as a young boy, both visions of what life offers. If the reader recognizes that for Orwell, as for Kafka, the nightmare is an inner one, then he can see the political matter as secondary to the personal content. This is not to relegate Orwell's politics to a less important position, but to retain perspective on the man's talents. Less able than Kafka to project a fully rounded inner vision, Orwell nevertheless sees much that is internal even while seeming to be a reporter.

He is a great reporter simply because he reports impressionistically and does not attempt false objectivity. At his best, he merges history with literature. He reports as he sees, but he recognizes that what he sees is tinged by what he is and by what he chooses to look at. Yet despite the subjectivity of much of Orwell's reporting, we are struck by the compelling clarity of his vision and the sharpness of his images. (pp. 149-50)

[The quality of an Orwell "hero"] is measured by his ability to strike through cant: his own and society's. Orwell is not particularly troubled by what his protagonist is or what he tries to do; he is, however, much concerned with what society prevents him from doing. As in the naturalistic novels of the nineteenth century in which the "hero" is caught in a trap of cause and effect, so here, the "hero" is caught by forces which reduce his desires and needs to those of an animal. He is brought to subsistence level, and few elements of civilization can do him good, for to have enough to eat is the sole luxury in which he can indulge. (pp. 150-51)

[The] quality of an Orwell protagonist is his ability to perceive the hypocrisy of the world and to react to it so that his own aims become clouded. An Orwell "hero" rarely has any hope

for the future—except perhaps for his next meal. He has few ambitions, and his chief emotion, when not hungry, is the sexual itch. Thus, in **Burmese Days** . . . , Flory pursues Elizabeth, the sole available white woman in the area, despite the fact that he and she have nothing in common. Flory fails to see her as she is, and this lack of clarity on his part is a measure of his agony. Everything Flory believes in is vitiated by his feeling for Elizabeth, but nevertheless because of his own weakness he becomes a fool of love.

Consequently, when hypocrisy does appear, it results from a character's need for something that scorns his true feelings. Were Orwell a comic writer, this grim irony would be a subject for social comedy in the manner of Evelyn Waugh, or for playful banter in the style of Henry Green. Flory's ordeal—one that he cannot possibly sustain—is to discover the depth of his self-deception and to lose Elizabeth in the bargain. An honest man is unable to survive self-deceived, and Flory commits suicide. Like one of Conrad's solitaries, Flory cannot exist outside the community of men, although to exist inside would be self-corrupting, for the community itself is rotten. (pp. 152-53)

As a social novelist, Orwell is less interested in man than he is in the society that has infected him. He has shifted emphasis from *the* man to the social group. Like a good naturalist, Orwell "gets" at people through the accumulation of social detail and external phenomena. This method defines both his success and failure. As a way of realizing a particular milieu, such a method has proven successful; as a way of developing people, the method leaves much to chance.

Unfortunately, Orwell's chief characters frequently exist only as social animals. They are indicated in terms of status, race, caste, tradition; and their place in this scheme is more important than what they are. (p. 153)

Orwell was caught in the difficult position of standing strongly behind the individual and yet trying to create through his novels a mold in which individuality is frustrated. He never clearly resolves the conflict between his point of view—individualistic and atomistic—and the naturalistic bent of his technique. . . . [Orwell] starts with the premise that the system traps the individual, and although he may want the individual to succeed, the latter . . . is cursed from birth. This type of frustration has of course been the stuff of great literature, from Cain on, but only when the author has been able to project and intensify his material imaginatively. Otherwise, the novel becomes merely another demonstration of society's attempt to crush its dissenters.

Even Orwell's ability to evoke disgusting sights and smells suggests his need to root everything in definite time and space. And yet this man whose novels seem based so solidly in modern rot is nostalgic for an irrecoverable Eden. . . . [He] tries to recapture the idylls of the past, a golden age that he is too realistic to believe ever really existed. (pp. 157-58)

[Orwell] presents the paradox of a heroic figure who tries to face every major moral decision that the age offers, and yet remains a man with a wistful nostalgia for the days when life was better, or less obviously bad. Even in **Homage to Catalonia,** that cataloguing of deceit and treachery during the Spanish Civil War, Orwell glances back at the time when alliances were just that, and a man at least knew whom he was fighting for before he died. Now, although men continue to fight for what they believe in, they find that their heroics are hopeless and that they are being undermined at the very moment they are dying for what they think is a worthy cause. In *Homage,* Orwell might have had the tragic theme which eluded him in his other works. But here, where he had perhaps the strongest material of any of his books, he turned to journalism, albeit of a superior kind, which precluded characterization and drama. The human drama of the Civil War was partially lost in the urgency of the experience and the necessity to transmit a political message. (pp. 158-59)

In Orwell's earlier work, all society was a prison, whether the prison of Flory's Burma, the prison of London and Paris, the prison of living on a pound a week in *Keep the Aspidistra Flying,* the prison of working in the coal mines in *The Road to Wigan Pier*. . . . *1984* seems a logical outgrowth of these books, the work of a man more interested in analyzing crushed human beings than in placing the individual in conflict with other people. Orwell's characters are generally in struggle against a system, sometimes against themselves, but rarely against other people. One thinks of Orwell's having thrown his characters into a circular machine and then noting their struggle against the machine, their attempts to escape it or compromise themselves with it.

The loss in mature contact is great. Perhaps the thinness apparent in all of Orwell's fiction is the author's failure to provide dramatic confrontation for his chief characters, so that the latter would seem to move in a world of people as well as of events. Since Orwell makes events predominate, people always appear less than what they actually are. The result suggests the same faults contained in the naturalistic novel—the system catches and drains the individual so that his own actions become ultimately meaningless. (pp. 160-61)

Orwell's vision has always been connected to the humanistic and romantic tradition. His books suggest a kind of civilized pastoral in which man fulfills himself through work and sex without regard for money, competition, and self-seeking. Like William Morris's Utopia, Orwell's socialistic state is tinged with this nostalgia for a past that the latter is surely too astute to believe ever existed outside of man's imagination. Orwell argues what seems a tough brand of socialism, but actually his socialism, once the economic machine is controlled, insists on the possibilities of man's goodness. . . . Orwell's Utopia, tinged by its author's optimism, is too permissive to seem possible, too idyllic to make sense in an industrialized society. (pp. 164-65)

[Orwell wished that the world could be] a private place where a man can realize his own aims with decency and propriety.

This ideal is what the reader comes away with after going through Orwell's writing. No single work predominates, no single idea is clearly remembered, no theory has been set up for future expansion or discussion. What cannot be doubted is the sense of decency of this man who was often wrong, often unjustifiably opinionated, but who in his anger tried to become the moral conscience of his generation. Orwell lived through one of the most chaotic periods in history, and he saw radical changes occurring in the world, unprecedented ones, but he chose to retain hard-gained truths and human dignity. Perhaps more than any of his contemporaries, Orwell has to be read as a whole, or else the keenness of a mind which saw through the falsity of his day will ultimately be forgotten, or at best remembered by overpraised works like *Animal Farm* and *1984*. Possibly, he was better as a man than as a novelist. (pp. 165-66)

Frederick R. Karl, "George Orwell: The White Man's Burden," in his A Reader's Guide to the Contem-

porary English Novel *(reprinted by permission of Farrar, Straus & Giroux, Inc.; copyright © 1961, 1962, 1971, 1972 by Frederick R. Karl), revised edition, Farrar, Straus & Giroux, 1972, pp. 148-66.*

JEFFREY MEYERS (essay date 1975)

All Orwell's books are autobiographical and spring from his psychological need to work out the pattern and meaning of his personal experience; his great triumph is his ability to transform his early guilt and awareness of what it means to be a victim, described in 'Such, Such Were the Joys', into a compassionate ethic of responsibility, a compulsive sharing in the suffering and degradation of others. (p. 10)

Orwell's books deal with two dominant themes—poverty and politics—or, as he put it, 'the twin nightmares that beset nearly every modern man, the nightmare of unemployment and the nightmare of State interference'. . . . There is a continuity, consistency (and repetition) of Orwell's major ideas; and a unity, pattern and development in all his books, which are closely related to each other and to the essays. (p. 13)

Orwell writes in 'Such, Such Were the Joys' . . . , which depicts the loss of innocence during the agonizing years of adolescence, that even while at home his early childhood was not altogether happy. (p. 20)

[But he] states that at eight years old he was suddenly separated from his family and . . . 'flung into a world of force and fraud and secrecy, like a gold-fish into a tank full of pike'; and the echo of Milton's Satan ('by fraud or guile/What force effected not') emphasizes the hellish aspect of St Cyprian's school in Eastbourne. (p. 21)

Orwell's reaction to this nightmare, a self-destructive expression of protest and fear, is recorded in his startling opening sentence: 'Soon after I arrived at St Cyprian's . . . I began wetting my bed.' The result of this shameful practice was two beatings which caused that deeper grief which is peculiar to childhood: 'a sense of desolate loneliness and helplessness, of being locked up not only in a hostile world but in a world of good and evil where the rules were such that it was actually not possible for me to keep them. . . . I had a conviction of sin and folly and weakness, such as I do not remember to have felt before. . . . This acceptance of guilt lay unnoticed in my memory for twenty or thirty years,' that is, during the whole course of his life, from schooldays until he tried to purge this guilt by writing the essay in the 1940s.

The bed-wetting was only the first of endless episodes that made Orwell feel guilty: he was poor, he was lazy and a failure, ungrateful and unhealthy, disgusting and dirty-minded, 'weak, ugly, cowardly, smelly'. (pp. 22-3)

These disturbing passages suggest the confusion and anxiety, the guilt and absurdity, of a Kafkaesque world in which the child—who is credulous, weak and vulnerable—is the ready and constant victim. For he lacks any sense of proportion or probability, and is forced to live with the anxious 'dread of offending against mysterious, terrible laws'. The most poignant moments in 'Such, Such' come from Orwell's realization of his own disloyalty, mendacity and hypocrisy, and a major theme in the essay is his retrospective horror at the kind of person he was. He seems to be saying, 'Look what they made me into. I was a foul little coward—but I was goaded by deprivation, insecurity and lack of love.' Orwell may have been a horrid though pitiful and confused child, but the school authorities, who knew precisely what they were doing to the children, were far worse. (pp. 23-4)

'Such, Such', Orwell's most poignant and, after *Animal Farm,* his most perfect work, is of the greatest value for an understanding of his character, life and books, for Orwell's self-portrayal as a vulnerable child-victim is the autobiographical archetype for his fictional anti-heroes. Just as *1984* is a final synthesis of all Orwell's major themes, so 'Such, Such', which was written at the same time, reveals the genesis and impetus of these ideas. Its central themes—poverty, fear, guilt, masochism and sickness—are developed in all his books and manifested in the pattern of his life. (p. 27)

The central political principle in *Burmese Days* derives from Montesquieu, who wrote in *The Spirit of the Laws* . . . , 'If a democratic republic subdues a nation in order to govern them as subjects, it exposes its own liberty.' The truth of this principle is illustrated by the Burmese judge U Po Kyin. . . . U Po is the *primum mobile* of all events in the novel, an underling who has the most actual power in the English outpost of progress and who, through devious machinations, controls even his rulers. . . . U Po has advanced himself by thievery, bribery, blackmail and betrayal, and his corrupt career is a serious criticism of both the English rule that permits his success and his English superiors who so disastrously misjudge his character. (p. 67)

Burmese Days was strongly influenced by [E. M. Forster's] *A Passage to India,* which was published in 1924 when Orwell was serving in Burma. Both novels concern an Englishman's friendship with an Indian doctor, and a girl who goes out to the colonies, gets engaged and then breaks it off. Both use the Club scenes to reveal a cross-section of colonial society, and both measure the personality and value of the characters by their racial attitudes. The themes of lack of understanding and the difficulties of friendship between English and natives, the physical deterioration and spiritual corruption of the whites in the tropics, are sounded by Forster and echo through Orwell's novel. But *Burmese Days* is a far more pessimistic book than *A Passage to India,* because official failures are not redeemed by successful personal relations. There are no characters like Fielding and Mrs Moore, who are able to prevail against the overwhelming cruelty of the English and maintain a civilized standard of behaviour. (pp. 68-9)

The moral conflicts of *A Passage to India* are presented in Flory's everlasting argument with his friend Dr Veraswami, a loyal British subject who always defends imperialism and who also aspires to Club membership for prestige and as protection against his enemies. Flory reveals his moral weakness first by refusing to support his friend's nomination and then by allowing himself to be coerced into signing a statement against native members. Like Orwell, Flory hates to see the English humiliating the Asians, and is ashamed of the imperialistic exploitation and class distinctions. But he recognizes, in an ironic paraphrase of Kipling, that 'even friendship can hardly exist when every white man is a cog in the wheels of despotism'.

This connection between political oppression and private guilt has been acutely described by Nietzsche, who writes that 'Political superiority without any real human superiority is most harmful. One must seek to make amends for political superiority. To be *ashamed* of one's power.' Flory, of course, is ashamed, but his failure to come to terms with the intolerable colonial situation is symbolized by his hideous birthmark—as much a sign of guilt, a mark of Cain, as an indication of his

isolation and alienation. He is unable to mediate between the three worlds of Burma: the English, the 'native' and the natural world of the jungle. (pp. 69-70)

Orwell is concerned with how his characters face responsibility, and Flory's inability to meet responsibility under the pressure of an overwhelming guilt is shown in his relationships with Dr Veraswami, whom he proposes to the Club only when it is too late; and with his Burmese mistress, May Hla, whom he abandons and then bribes after a mutually destructive liaison . . . , and finally with Elizabeth herself, whom he can neither enlighten nor engage. His suicide, a violent yet appropriate gesture of physical courage and moral cowardice, is his terrible protest against these failures. Flory's suicide is a way of concluding the novel, but it is an essentially weak device that resolves neither the themes of the book nor the problems inherent in the colonial experience. (pp. 70-1)

['We all live in terror of poverty'], writes Orwell, and its psychological and social effects are one of his dominant themes. Though almost all of his books treat this question in a significant way (the exploited natives in *Burmese Days,* the plight of the common soldier in *Homage to Catalonia* and of the dehumanized proles in *1984*), Orwell's four books of the depressed mid-thirties—[*Down and Out in Paris and London, A Clergyman's Daughter, Keep the Aspidistra Flying* and *The Road to Wigan Pier*] . . .—are completely devoted to the exploration of this theme. (pp. 74-5)

The theme of class exploitation is dramatized most vividly in *Down and Out* amidst the luxury and squalor of the grand hotel where the splendid customers sit just a few feet away from the disgusting filth of the kitchen workers. The only connection between these two worlds is the food prepared by one for the other, which often contains the cook's spit and the waiter's hair grease. (p. 77)

Perhaps the most interesting aspect of the book, apart from the revelation of Orwell's character, is his description of the psychology of poverty, as he discovered it in the hotels, hospitals, pawnshops and parks of the mean and degenerate Paris. . . . (pp. 77-8)

He speaks of the eccentric freedom from the normal and the decent, the mindless acceptance when you reach destitution after anticipating it for so long, the animal contentment of the simple rhythm of work and sleep. But in the long run, of course, the degrading human effects are disastrous. Hunger reduces men to a spineless, brainless condition and malnutrition destroys their manhood, while extreme poverty cuts men off from contact with women: 'The evil of poverty is not so much that it makes a man suffer as that it rots him physically and spiritually.'

Orwell's suggestions for the alleviation of poverty are both pragmatic and politic, and he hopes to improve conditions by clarifying common misconceptions in the light of first-hand experience. . . . Like Dickens, who tried to persuade his middle-class audience that the poor were not evil and were not to be blamed for their poverty, Orwell explodes a number of common prejudices by explaining them. . . . Orwell, middle-class by birth and working-class by experience, contrasts the two classes in order to reveal how hatred and fear force them into opposition. (p. 78)

Both *A Clergyman's Daughter* and *Keep the Aspidistra Flying* concern the unsuccessful attempt to escape from the boredom and triviality of a middle-class existence. Both Dorothy and

Gordon, after experiences with meanness and poverty similar to those Orwell described in *Down and Out,* return to the economic security of their former lives and (somewhat unconvincingly) reaffirm its values: religious, for Dorothy; familial, for Gordon. (p. 79)

Orwell raises the central critical questions about [*A Clergyman's Daughter*] in his rather harsh comments about his weakest book. He was ashamed of the novel, called it 'bollox' and 'tripe' and, when he finished it in late 1934, wrote to his agent: 'I am not at all pleased with it. It was a good idea, but I am afraid I have made a muck of it—however, it is as good as I can do for the present. There are bits of it that I don't dislike, but I am afraid it is very disconnected as a whole, and rather unreal'. . . . This severe but honest letter identifies the two main faults of the novel: its weak structure and unconvincing plot. (pp. 79-80)

[The] real failure of *A Clergyman's Daughter* is Orwell's inability to find the correct form to embrace his experience and embody his ideas. As he realized, the novel's divergent and disconnected episodes—in the rectory, with hop-pickers and tramps, and at the school—are essentially autobiographical and linked by the weakest transitions. Dorothy is transported into the squalid and boring world of the tramp by an unexplained loss of memory (Orwell's use of psychology is extremely weak), and he omits the most potentially interesting part of the book by ignoring what happened to the heroine during the first eight days between Suffolk and London. (p. 80)

Although *A Clergyman's Daughter* fails as a novel, its parts, considered separately, are individually successful. Orwell could have solved the problem of how to write about his personal experience by using most of it in non-fictional books, for he is never comfortable or convincing in the *persona* of Dorothy. In a 1948 letter he confesses his inability to assimilate and transform this personal experience into fiction: 'One difficulty I have never solved is that one has masses of experience which one passionately wants to write about . . . and no way of using them up except by disguising them as a novel'. . . . In this novel, the experience is 'disguised' too transparently and is reported rather than rendered. (p. 84)

Keep the Aspidistra Flying, like *Down and Out,* has a balanced structure. . . . (p. 85)

Despite Orwell's evident care with the form of the novel, the mechanical plot has some serious weaknesses. . . .

Nor is Orwell in full control of his style in this novel, which is repetitive to the point of boredom and exasperation ('Money, money, always money!') and liberally sprinkled with poetic allusions (Gordon is, or was, a poet) which are rather forced and banal. . . . (p. 86)

The third major flaw in the novel is the character of the hero, Gordon, who lacks integrity and honour, and whose envy and self-pity tend to alienate the reader's interest. . . . But Gordon is more ridiculous and weak than wicked, for Orwell intends him to be an essentially sympathetic hero and suggests that these traits stem less from personality defects than from poverty. (p. 87)

In spite of these weaknesses in plot, style and characterization, there is undoubtedly a poignant and moving quality about the novel that comes from Orwell's perceptive portrayal of the alienation and loneliness of poverty, and from Rosemary's tender response to Gordon's mean misery. His final affirmation of ordinary life is achieved through her selfless acts: the thrust-

ing of cigarettes in his pocket and her sacrificial sexual surrender. Her love vindicates his self-respect. . . . (pp. 87-8)

A number of important ideas from *Keep the Aspidistra Flying* reappear in Orwell's *reportage* of the following year. Gordon's beliefs that poverty kills thought, and that cleanness and decency cost money, are reaffirmed; and the same sense of despair (which culminates in *1984*) is manifest in *Wigan Pier:* 'We live, admittedly, among the wreck of a civilisation.' (pp. 90-1)

In the 1930s coal 'was by far the largest single industry, the only one employing more than a million workers. It had always been the symbol of class struggle.' Orwell's immersion in the reality of this struggle was his very deliberate attempt to overcome what he considered 'the tragic failure of theoretical Socialism, to make contact with the normal working classes'. Orwell believes it is both his duty and his responsibility to have first-hand experience in the slums and mines. . . . Orwell's acute observations on coal mining leave a vivid impression, for his farmer's knowledge of the earth and his Swiftian ability to isolate the significant detail of the grazing cows make you see mining in a new and memorable way: 'You have a tolerable sized mountain on top of you; hundreds of yards of solid rock, bones of extinct beasts, subsoil, flints, roots of growing things, green grass and cows grazing on it—all this suspended over your head and held back only by wooden props as thick as the calf of your leg.' (p. 93)

Orwell's approach is documentary, empirical and pragmatic, filled with statistics, essential information and useful suggestions, and his view is, as far as possible, an 'insider's' view. . . . Orwell constantly refers to his own practical knowledge. . . . The result of this approach is twofold: as in *Down and Out* he questions common assumptions, discredits the illusion and shows the reality; and he also describes the most serious injustices as he has lived through them himself. He has a deep loathing of the ugliness, emptiness and cruelty of what he sees, but is not merely content to describe it—he wants to make people feel morally responsible so that they will radically change it. (p. 94)

The great strength of *Wigan Pier* (and *Down and Out*) is that the economic injustices are always described in human terms. . . . Orwell's moving theme is a fervent plea for human dignity and compassion, and against 'The frightful doom of a decent working man suddenly thrown on the streets after a lifetime of steady work, his agonized struggles against economic laws which he does not understand, the disintegration of families, the corroding sense of shame.' (p. 95)

[*Coming Up For Air*], Orwell's central transitional work, is at once synthetic and seminal, gathering the themes that had been explored in the poverty books of the thirties and anticipating the cultural essays and political satires of the next decade. The location and central symbol of the novel appear as early as *Down and Out* when Orwell describes tramping in Lower Binfield and fishing in the Seine; but the novel has much closer affinities with *Keep the Aspidistra Flying,* for Gordon Comstock's belief that our civilization is dying and the whole world will soon be blown up is very like Bowling's. (p. 100)

Coming Up For Air is about an apocalyptic vision that destroys a nostalgic dream of childhood. For Bowling is in a prophetic mood in which he foresees the end of the world and can feel things cracking and collapsing under his feet. The war that will decide the destiny of Europe is due in 1941, and it seems to Bowling (as it did to Orwell at the end of *Homage*) that he 'could see the whole of England, and all the people in it, and all the things that will happen to all of them'. Bowling, caught in a brief intense moment between the destructive future and the nostalgic past, seeks, like Winston Smith, to escape the painful modern realities by recapturing his idealized childhood memories. Orwell's metaphor of escape in both works (people trapped in a sinking ship is the symbol of man's fate in *1984*) is 'coming up for air'. . . . But escape is impossible for Bowling, who has the archetypal experience of returning home to discover that the lost Eden of childhood is irrecoverable: 'What's the good of trying to revisit the scenes of your boyhood? They don't exist. Coming up for air! But there isn't any air. The dustbin we're in reaches up to the stratosphere.' (pp. 102-03)

[*Homage to Catalonia*], which contains autobiography, military history, political analysis and propaganda, is problematical . . . and seems a mixture of 'kinds', for the structure of the book is determined by Orwell's motivations and psychological needs as well as by the pattern of historical events. The *genre* of *Homage* is war memoir and its model those classic accounts of the Great War, narrated from the victim's viewpoint, which Orwell discusses in **'Inside the Whale'**. Hugh Thomas, writing from a historian's viewpoint, warns that Orwell's account 'should be read with reservations. It is more accurate about war itself than about the Spanish War.' This statement emphasizes Orwell's affinity to the novelists of the Great War and also suggests that he wrote his best books about real, and not fictional, experience.

Critics have frequently noted that Orwell's war experience in Spain provided the original impetus for his late political satires, but they have not observed that *Homage* is closely related to his early life and personal narratives, and that its central theme of comradeship and human solidarity, the main support of the victim in war, is an expression of his intense need to be accepted by and 'involved in mankind'. *Homage* is written with the directness and immediacy of a personal vision, and portrays not only an eye-witness account of what happened in Spain, but also the story of a man's growth in personal and political awareness. The central tension between politics and war, reflection and action, disenchantment and idealism, creates the dominant form of *Homage* and reflects the poignant opposition of victimization and comradeship. (p. 114)

Orwell believes that 'The business of making people *conscious* of what is happening outside their own small circle is one of the major problems of our time, and a new literary technique will have to be evolved to meet it'. . . . His choice of a satiric beast fable for *Animal Farm* . . . was exactly what he needed, for his creation of characters was always rather weak, and the flat symbolic animals of the fable did not have to be portrayed in depth. The familiar and affectionate tone of the story and its careful attention to detail allowed the unpopular theme to be pleasantly convincing, and the Soviet myth was exposed in a subtle fashion that could still be readily understood. It was written in clear and simple language that could be easily translated, and was short so that it could be sold cheaply and read quickly. The gay *genre* was a final attempt to deflect his profound pessimism, which dominated his final realistic vision of decency trampled on and destroyed in *1984*. (p. 130)

Though critics have often interpreted the book in terms of Soviet history, they have never sufficiently recognized that it is extremely subtle and sophisticated, and brilliantly presents a satiric allegory of Communist Russia in which virtually every detail has political significance. (p. 133)

Thus, the human beings are capitalists, the animals are Communists, the wild creatures who could not be tamed and 'con-

tinued to behave very much as before' are the *muzhiks* or peasants, the pigs are the Bolsheviks, the Rebellion is the October Revolution, the neighbouring farmers are the western armies who attempted to support the Czarists against the Reds, the wave of rebelliousness that ran through the countryside afterwards is the abortive revolutions in Hungary and Germany in 1919 and 1923, the hoof and horn is the hammer and sickle, the Spontaneous Demonstration is the May Day celebration, the Order of the Green Banner is the Order of Lenin, the special pig committee presided over by Napoleon is the Politbureau, the revolt of the hens—the *first* rebellion since the expulsion of Jones (the Czar)—is the sailors' rebellion at the Kronstadt naval base in 1921, and Napoleon's dealings with Whymper and the Willingdon markets represent the Treaty of Rapallo, signed with Germany in 1922, which ended the capitalists' boycott of Soviet Russia.

The carefully chosen names are both realistic and highly suggestive of their owners' personalities and roles in the fable. (p. 135)

The most important animals are Napoleon (Stalin) and Snowball (Trotsky), whose personalities are antithetical and who are never in agreement. Both characters are drawn fully and accurately, though with simple strokes, and reflect almost all the dominant characteristics of their historical models. (p. 136)

The three main Russian political events that are most extensively allegorized in *Animal Farm* are the disastrous results of Stalin's forced collectivization (1929-33), the Great Purge Trials (1936-38) and the diplomacy with Germany that terminated with Hitler's invasion in 1941. (p. 139)

Though subtle and compressed, *Animal Farm* shares the serious theme of *Nostromo*: that once in power, the revolutionary becomes as tyrannical as his oppressor. (p. 143)

The most common cliché of Orwell criticism is that *1984* . . . is a 'nightmare vision' of the future. I believe, on the contrary, that it is a very concrete and naturalistic portrayal of the present and the past, and that its great originality results more from a realistic synthesis and rearrangement of familiar materials than from any prophetic or imaginary speculations. *1984* is not only a paradigm of the history of Europe for the previous twenty years, but also a culmination of all the characteristic beliefs and ideas expressed in Orwell's works from the Depression to the cold war. (p. 144)

Like the novels of Malraux and Sartre, *1984* expresses man's fears of isolation and disintegration, cruelty and dehumanization. . . . Orwell's repetition of obsessive ideas is an apocalyptic lamentation for the fate of modern man. His expression of the political experience of an entire generation gives *1984* a veritably mythic power and makes it one of the most influential books of the age, even for those who have never read it. As Harold Rosenberg states, 'The tone of the post-war imagination was set by Orwell's *1984:* since the appearance of that work, [the theme of] the ''dehumanized collective'' haunts our thoughts.' Orwell's unique contribution to English literature is a passionate commitment, a radical sincerity and an ethic of responsibility that ultimately transcends his defeated heroes. (p. 154)

> *Jeffrey Meyers, in his* A Reader's Guide to George Orwell *(© 1975 Thames and Hudson Ltd), Thames and Hudson, 1975, 192 p.*

MURRAY SPERBER　(essay date 1980)

Most critics have focused on *1984*'s politics, how the book reflects certain political concerns of its author, its time, and the entire modern age. Many writers have also connected the work to Orwell's previous writings as well as the genre of dystopian fiction, and a few have discussed it in terms of its author's physical and psychological condition when he wrote it. No writer, however, has connected Orwell's plan for the book to his lifelong psychological feelings, especially his responses to authority and control. . . . (p. 213)

When Orwell was working on *1984*, his only other major piece of writing was his memoir of childhood and adolescence, **"Such, Such, Were the Joys. . . ."** Orwell relates how, as a child, he was obsessively aware of his body and its awkwardness; Winston mirrors this concern. In both works, Orwell describes the brutality of children and the fear that they can generate. The Brotherhood, the secret organization, seems to connect to schoolboy fantasies and fears: is it real, how widespread is its membership and power? Its very name, as well as the litany that Winston and Julia swear on its behalf, echo the world of fearfulness and cruelty in **"Such, Such Were the Joys. . . ."**

The analogies between the memoir and the fiction are numerous and extend to the way that Winston is taught by O'Brien: if we substitute for O'Brien's dial and his electric torture machine, the silver pencil and the riding crop with which the headmaster hit Orwell at school when he did not recite his lessons absolutely correctly, we can see Winston's reeducation as a mirror of Orwell's own education. And O'Brien is described as having "the air of a teacher taking pains with [Winston] a wayward but promising child." . . . Winston's reeducation, where time becomes elastic and oppresive, fits Orwell's description of his time at St. Cyprian's/Crossgates, especially when he was being primed to win a scholarship to Eton (which he won). Winston is a scholarship boy of Oceania. (pp. 218-19)

Orwell was fascinated by schooling. *1984* is an education for its hero and reader; its course title is the possibilities of betrayal: political, the Party and its former and present members; familial, children turning in parents and vice versa; sexual, Julia and Winston; and personal, Winston's self-betrayal. **"Such, Such"** contains the same theme: schoolmates betraying each other and the system betraying the individual. In Orwell's world, with schooling comes punishment: for Winston's stupidity, Room 101; for ours, the disappointment at the denouement.

To say, however, that what Orwell "did in *1984* was to send everybody in England to an enormous Crossgates to be as miserable as he had been," as Anthony West charges, is to minimize the point of Orwell's fiction. His plan is much grander than an attack on his old school. Orwell transforms his experiences—some based on adolescence but most from earlier childhood and later adult events—into a world of fears and fantasies that will encompass all people, during all periods of their lives, for all of history. (p. 219)

Like most artists, Orwell explored and expressed his emotions, but in *1984,* because of his circumstances while writing the book, he worked more deeply and thoroughly than ever before. . . . *1984* is ostensibly about the future, but much of the psychological intensity comes from the author's past, not only his feelings about school but much earlier experiences as well.

Winston is in search of his past: O'Brien, the apparently good father, has the key. "'We shall meet in the place where there is no darkness'." . . . , he tells Winston in a dream—the Thought Police can control dreams—and he helps launch Winston's exploration. The "place" seems to indicate a time and a place where Winston was—and might be again—at peace.

As Winston wanders, a certain smell sends him "back in the half-forgotten world of his childhood." . . . Winston also explores the past in his job: if he can rediscover human history, he might find a clue to his own history. Winston dreams about his mother and being violently separated from her. His dreams as well as his memories of his mother and sister are filled with guilt and self-hate (his father is only a shadowy figure). His desire to rediscover and repair the past impels him, in part, to Charrington's and to his inevitable destruction.

Family love, human love, is impossible in the *1984* world. Because the past does not exist, neither does a childhood of pleasure and growth. . . . Winston has made a brave attempt to become sane—to understand his past and to change his present—but in an insane world, his attempt is doomed. In Oceania, the psyche has permanently fragmented: the Party is super-ego; the proles, id; and all ego functions—what Winston seeks—have been destroyed.

Winston's search for loving parents is futile. The only permitted parents are the Party. Throughout *1984,* there is an implied equation between the Party's control over people and parental control over children. Frequently we can substitute the word *parent* for Party: "she [Julia] had grasped the inner meaning of the Party's [the parents'] sexual puritanism . . . the sex instinct created a world of its own which was outside the Party's [the parents'] control and which therefore had to be destroyed if possible." . . . If one has sexual relations, one might love an outsider, esteem oneself, break out of the insane family, and develop autonomy. (pp. 222-23)

In *1984,* Orwell captures well the return to the source of all fears and fantasies, including paranoid ones, the time when parents are omnipotent and children powerless: "A wave of admiration, almost of worship, flowed out from Winston toward O'Brien . . . it was impossible to believe that he [O'Brien] could be defeated. There was no strategem that he was not equal to, no danger that he could not foresee." . . . Under torture, Winston regresses until he is a whimpering infant; "he clung to O'Brien like a baby, curiously comforted by the heavy arm round his shoulders." . . . Winston must be born anew: "Even after his eyes were open he took in his surroundings only gradually. He had the impression of swimming up into this room from some quite different world, a sort of underwater far beneath." . . . (pp. 224-25)

The reindoctrination process is a means for Winston to learn his lessons correctly this time, to internalize the Party/parental control so that no outside force is needed. The process is successful. . . . "Two gin-scented tears trickled down the sides of his nose. But it was all right, everything was all right, the struggle was finished. He had won the victory over himself. He loved Big Brother." . . . Like a child, he cries and then is comforted—it was all right, everything is all right—and he is reunited at last with the omnipotent parent.

This is a chilling end, a world where no one attains autonomous, rational adulthood, where we are always the victim of brutal parents. Apparently, this was George Orwell's greatest fear; this is the bottom stratum of *1984.* (p. 225)

Murray Sperber, "'Gazing into the Glass Paperweight': The Structure and Psychology of Orwell's '1984,'" in Modern Fiction Studies *(© 1980 by Purdue Research Foundation, West Lafayette, Indiana 47907, U.S.A.), Vol. 26, No. 2, Summer, 1980, pp. 213-26.*

ADDITIONAL BIBLIOGRAPHY

Crick, Bernard. *George Orwell: A Life*. Boston: Atlantic-Little, Brown, 1980, 456 p.

    The most comprehensive biography to date. Crick is the only biographer who has been granted unrestricted access to private papers held by Mrs. Orwell.

Gross, Miriam, ed. *The World of George Orwell*. New York: Simon and Schuster, 1972, 182 p.

    Eighteen brief biocritical essays, the most interesting of which are reminiscences by William Empson and Malcolm Muggeridge.

Lee, Robert A. *Orwell's Fiction*. Notre Dame, Ind.: University of Notre Dame Press, 1969, 188 p.

    Important examination of Orwell's novels as works of fiction, not as fictionalized autobiographies or social criticism.

Meyers, Jeffrey. *George Orwell: The Critical Heritage*. London: Routledge & Kegan Paul, 1975, 392 p.

    Collection of reviews and critical studies with an excellent introduction by Meyers discussing Orwell's career and the dominant themes of Orwell criticism.

Meyers, Jeffrey, and Meyers, Valerie. *George Orwell: An Annotated Bibliography of Criticism*. New York: Garland Publishing, 1977, 132 p.

    Most thorough bibliography to date.

Smyer, Richard I. *Primal Dream and Primal Crime: Orwell's Development as a Psychological Novelist*. Columbia: University of Missouri Press, 1979, 187 p.

    Discusses Orwell's novels as manifestations of sexual guilt.

Stansky, Peter, and Abrahams, William. *The Unknown Orwell*. New York: Alfred A. Knopf, 1972, 316 p.

    A biography of Orwell's first thirty years. This is the first book of a proposed three-volume biography.

Stansky, Peter, and Abrahams, William. *Orwell: The Transformation*. New York: Alfred A. Knopf, 1980, 302 p.

    Biography of Orwell from the publication of his first novel to his involvement in the Spanish civil war. This is the second book of a proposed three-volume biography.

Rainer Maria Rilke

1875-1926

German poet, novelist, biographer, and short story writer.

Rilke stands with Paul Valery and W. B. Yeats as one of the twentieth century's greatest lyric poets. His *Duineser Elegien (Duino Elegies)* is recognized as one of world literature's most important poetic cycles.

Rilke's poetry is characterized by its rich imagery and its mystical introspection and prophecy. All his life Rilke sought, as his translator J. B. Leishman wrote, "symbolic or 'external' equivalents for experiences that were becoming ever more 'inward' and incommunicable, and which when he tried to communicate them, were continually bringing him up against the limitations of language." Rilke's verse receives much critical analysis because of the complexity of his symbolism.

Rilke's career was one of struggle and progressive discovery, and can be divided into three periods. Born into a rigidly conventional family in Prague, then part of the German empire, Rilke was enrolled at the age of eleven in a military school. There, subjected to physical and psychological rigors beyond his endurance, Rilke repudiated the bourgeois values of his youth, seeking to attain a sense of spiritual solitude. In the early 1890s he began writing and publishing verse, mixing in Prague literary circles, and endorsing the Czech independence movement. These nationalist sympathies were expressed in *Larenopher*, his first important cycle. Rilke's early poetry, written in the tradition of the German folk song and reminiscent in its romanticism of Heinrich Heine, revealed the author's obsessive interest in probing his subjects, attempting to discern the essence of love, fear, ecstasy, pain, nature, and death. In 1897 he was introduced to the works of Nietzsche and Jens Peter Jacobsen. Their writings and Rilke's own travels in Russia were essential in the poet's growing philosophy of existential materialism and art as religion. Retaining the style of his earlier poetry, Rilke's work became more religious, and was filled with traditional Christian imagery and concepts, presenting art as the world's only redeemer. *Von liebe Gott und Anderes (Stories of God)* and *Das Stundenbuch (Poems from the Book of Hours)* represent this mystical trend, the latter marking the end of Rilke's poetic apprenticeship.

Dissatisfied with his early work, Rilke strove to endow his writings with the plasticity of the visual arts, to dispense with ideas and treat his poems as carefully crafted objects. He succeeded in *Neue Gedichte (New Poems)* after associating for several years with the Worpswede art colony and, more importantly, with Auguste Rodin. Rilke worked as Rodin's secretary for eight months, and the sculptor's influence in shaping the younger man's attitudes toward poetry proved immense; the second volume of *New Poems* contains Rilke's first recognizable mature verse, showing the transformation of his aesthetic vision into sculptural, interpretive symbols. Regarding the poetry of this period, W. H. Auden has remarked, "Rilke is almost the first poet since the seventeenth century to find a fresh solution of how to express abstract ideas in concrete terms." Two years after completing *New Poems* Rilke published his most accomplished prose work, *Die Aufzeichnungen de Malte Laurids Brigge (The Notebooks of Malte Laurids*

Courtesy of German Information Center

Brigge), a loosely autobiographical novel exploring the angst-filled life of a hypersensitive man in Paris.

After a creative drought of ten years, due in great measure to his anxiety over World War I, Rilke completed the *Duino Elegies* in 1922. Each of the cycle's ten laments explores humanity's plight in an increasingly inhuman world, in which traditional beliefs seem unable to provide meaning to love, nature, death, and language. The Nietzschean *Die Sonette an Orpheus (Sonnets to Orpheus)* answers the *Elegies*, voicing affirmation and joy in the acceptance of humanity's lot. Together, these volumes brought Rilke international recognition as a major artist, and are the pinnacle of his career.

Throughout his development, Rilke was concerned with the same subjects: the importance of the poet's role, the essence of religious faith, and the nature of life and how it should be experienced. Rilke's career is often considered symbolic of the condition of the modern poet: his lifework represents a quest to confirm the need for poetry in an age that seems to deny importance to poetic accomplishments.

(See also *TCLC*, Vol. 1.)

PRINCIPAL WORKS

Larenopfer (poetry) 1896

Traumgekrönt (poetry) 1898

Vom liebe Gott und Anderes (short stories) 1900
[*Stories of God*, 1932]

Auguste Rodin (biography) 1903
[*Auguste Rodin*, 1919]

Das Stundenbuch (poetry) 1905
[*Poems from the Book of Hours*, 1941]

Die Weise von Liebe und Tod des Cornets Christoph Rilke (prose poem) 1906
[*The Tale of the Love and Death of Cornet Christopher Rilke*, 1932; published in England as *The Lay of Love and Death of Cornet Christopher Rilke*, 1948]

Neue Gedichte. 2 vols. (poetry) 1907-08
[*New Poems*, 1964]

Requiem (poetry) 1909
[*Requiem, and Other Poems*, 1935]

Die Aufzeichnungen des Malte Laurids Brigge (novel) 1910
[*The Notebooks of Malte Laurids Brigge*, 1930; published in the United States as *The Journal of My Other Self*, 1930]

Die Sonette an Orpheus (poetry) 1922
[*Sonnets to Orpheus*, 1936]

Duineser Elegien (poetry) 1923
[*Duineser Elegien: Elegies from the Castle of Duino*, 1931; published in the United States as *Duino Elegies*, 1939]

Briefe an einen jungen Dichter (letters) 1929
[*Letters to a Young Poet*, 1934]

PERCIVAL POLLARD (essay date 1911)

In Rainer Maria Rilke the stylistic attitude of modern German poetry reaches its most perfect form. (p. 186)

Rilke sounds the monastic, mystically religious note as well as the aristocratic and the intentionally obscure. You may find in him the German equivalent to much in the mystic and monastic tone that has appeared in many Catholic countries, and to what Francis Thompson did in England. His view of life turns always into himself. The artist, he declares, is only he who has within himself something deep and rare that he cannot share with the world. He avoids the obvious as a nun avoids the world and its pleasures. There is eroticism in Rilke, but it is the eroticism of a cloistered garden where Parsifal walks in white silk, and where tall lilies listen to the annunciation of Mary. I recall single poems of his printed in *Jugend* in the last few years, that were as if some of the most blasphemous ideas of the late Francis Saltus had been treated by a monk whose asceticism had the gorgeous hues of an old missal. There is a prose book of his that bears the title: **"Of the Almighty, and others." (Vom lieben Gott, und andres.)** The conclusion of his poem **"Fate o' Women" (Frauenschicksal)** runs thus: "She simply grew old and went blind, and was not precious and was never rare." . . . Even these lines may give you a notion of the strange remoteness of this poetry. (pp. 187-88)

The titles of Rilke's books tell the story of the ecclesiasticism that distinguishes him as poet. He has never seen life save through stained glass. Note this, for instance: **"The Book of Hours; of monastic life, of pilgrimage, of poverty and of death."** In his earlier verses the symbolism of Romish doctrine appears as an influence; gradually comes sympathy with older mysticisms, and even with such emotionalists as Chopin and Schumann; eventually he reaches his individual, personal note of monistic pantheism. In his **"Book of Pictures" (Buch der Bilder)** the Rodin influence can be found. That book is perhaps his highest achievement.

For sheer technical skill, modern German verse has gone no farther than Rainer Maria Rilke. His poetry remains noteworthy if we would understand the various facets of the modern German soul. (pp. 189-90)

> *Percival Pollard, "A Few Formalists," in his* Masks and Minstrels of New Germany, *John W. Luce and Company, 1911, pp. 178-91.**

HESTER PICKMAN (essay date 1931)

Lyric poetry belongs only to those in whose language it is written. Keats, Shelley, Blake and many others have never been given to the un-English world. They escape translation as taste and perfume escape vocabulary.

Now Rilke is such a poet as they, and as such it is folly to think of him in another language. We can get neither the music nor the mood nor the precision of emotion that lie in his words. Even if we read him in German a great deal must escape us unless we understand all its nuance of overtone and idiom. . . . It is only the qualities of thought that we can study in him, the material out of which that thought is made and what it helps us to see. Rilke divested of his magic is still important because he was one of those rare people who follow thought as far as it will lead them. He was still able to perceive at a point of inner experience where most men lose their bearings and come back to the surface. His poetry takes us carefully and surely through well defined curtains of illusion to a reality that is as unmistakable as daylight. (pp. 325-26)

It is said that a painter of genius must have some imperfection of sight that makes it hard for him to adjust his consciousness to the visible world. Perhaps poets have some such defect in their inner eye; it is certainly Rilke's case. He was incapable of getting used to life. He had no short cuts, no mathematical formulae for the handling of his sensibilities. However much appearance absorbed him—and none has ever described it with more precision—he always remained aware of the inner predicament and it is this that is always to be found at the exact center of his subject. His contemplation unfolded the surfaces of life layer after layer to reach the dark kernel that was seed and sense. (p. 326)

This position and attitude of Rilke's mind has much in common with Christian mysticism. He was looking with the same singleness of purpose for the essence of life. His purpose, like theirs, was to know and serve, but he did not reach the unifying love of God that made all things clear to them. It was a darker thing that remained individualized in his perception. To actualize this perception was the aim of his poetry. (pp. 326-27)

[Rilke spoke] in praise of transposing the essentials of human life into an object, a creation either in form or sound. In this Rilke placed the inherent dignity of man, a dignity dependent on fixing and holding some fragment of the eternal flux:—an aim of artists, and possibly of artisans. What he thought of any more active and worldly life, however unselfish, can be seen by his constant reference to its unreality. To him stones and plants and animals seem nearer to the truth than any man, for man cannot escape the false standards. It is our intricate consciousness that causes their falsity. (p. 328)

It is a point of view that lacks dramatic sense. The blending of many lives, many durations, into a reasoned whole is something he did not think of. He never wrote a passable play. His stories are all allegories or autobiography. The *Elegies of Duino* come nearer to building a philosophy but even that would have required "organization" and taken from their immediacy. He would not take up the cross of organic life, for organisms must be anti-spiritual. Hence his distaste for religions and for all forms of civic life that impose ready-made, inaccurate standards. His God was relegated to darkness that he might not have any part in this mechanical side of life, for light is a part of the machinery. The physical organization of the body impedes the soul, and inanimate things come nearer to true being.

This love of a passive dark is an important part of Rilke's thought. He wrote many things about the blind because their infirmity brings them nearer to truth. They are

> a dark entrance to the Under-world
> among a race who live upon its rind.

In fact all imperfections of the body seem valuable to Rilke, because they constitute a liberation from the ready-made ways in which souls must be cramped and tortured. (p. 329)

It is the healthy body he most fears. And so his books are filled with the old and the sick, the insane and the dying, and always their troubles seem to him so many rifts in the curtain of illusion. Children occupy him also because they have been only partly absorbed. Their pathos is that they must be drawn more and more away from reality until they are so trained that they can do nothing else but act in the senseless play. And death occupies him, which is the core of every life, the object of all fruition and the final liberation from illusion.

His attitude is always one of wondering and compassionate observation. . . . [Its faults are] obscurity and inconclusion. He is obscure out of choice because he mistrusted light; inconclusive because the solutions he offers apply only to his own problem. But though neither the world nor the saints may find comfort in Rilke, it is precisely this that makes him a poet of our time. Whatever his faults are, they are those of all contemporary art—an art of darkness and inconclusion. Only, Rilke has gone further than any one else. He has taken the burden of our life into his, into the architecture of an all-inclusive pattern. This is his defect as an artist. (pp. 330-32)

His own experience alone was real.

The Oxford Dictionary defines lyric poetry as that "which describes the author's own thoughts and sentiments." Rilke, as we have already said, was essentially a lyric poet. He had no faith and little interest in the thoughts of others. In his journey through contemplation he could use nobody's map. (p. 332)

Rilke began writing poetry as a child; his first volume, published when he was nineteen, received a certain notice, but three years later he destroyed the edition and never allowed it to be reprinted. The first volumes to appear for good were *Larenopfer* and *Traumgekrönt* in 1898. His German critics say that the metre of these early poems is borrowed from the rhythm of Bohemian songs. Their music has the unmistakable accent

of talent, but the material in them is slight and pervaded with a spiritual nostalgia that is immature.

Perhaps it was in Russia that he first found substance that could nourish him. . . . "It is a land," he wrote to [a] friend, "where men are solitary." The sense of civic organization so natural to the Germanic race is not a Russian trait, and the Soviets had not yet begun to foster it artificially. In its place there is, judging by almost any character in the novels and plays that have been translated, a sheer sense of reality that leads them to ignore the mechanics of life under the pressure of the inner predicament. It was this inner life that Rilke made the subject of all his work, and the *Book of Hours,* begun after his journey to Russia and finished four years later, is the first consecutive statement of his experience of it. A volume of short poems, the *Book of Pictures,* appeared before it was published, and there already are many beautiful things in this. To consider them too, however, would only confuse us: it is so much easier to measure his development by the sustained effort of a long poem. (pp. 334-35)

The *Book of Hours* is a long collection of prayers in irregular rhyming stanzas. It is divided into three parts. The first is called "Of the Monastic Life," the second "Of the Pilgrimage," the third, "Of Poverty and Death." In the **"Requiem of Karl von Kalckreuth"** he names the three attributes essential to a poet. They are "space around his feelings," a "contemplation that desires naught" and "a well-wrought death." The *Requiem* was written at about the same time, and one can imagine that the *Book of Hours* fell naturally into these divisions. (p. 336)

[Although] there are many passages in the *Book of Hours* that might have fallen out of the writings of Christian contemplatives, the essential pattern is an inversion of theirs. God is not light but darkness—not a father, but a son, not the creator but the created. He and not man is our neighbor for men are infinitely far from each other. They must seek God, not where one or two are gathered in His name, but alone. The search is also inverted. The young monk [of the first part] begins by experiencing the presence of God; then he seeks Him and seeking Him finds not His Kingdom and His Justice, but Poverty and Death that are not only a way of life but life itself. Even this inversion might be Christian—for darkness, isolation and negation are all commonplaces of the mystic experience—if it did not clearly form a part of the antagonism to Christianity that one finds in all Rilke's writing. There is a warm and living piety in these poems that implies a sense of God's immediate presence. Yet . . . Rilke minimizes the possibility of divine intercourse. Prayer for him lay not in a conscious union with God, but in man's creative activity. (pp. 346-47)

The *Book of Hours* is essential to the understanding of what comes afterwards because it fixes the direction of all his future journeys and describes a road which is so familiar to him that he will later refer to it as if we too must know every turn it takes. . . . But in spite of much that is very beautiful the *Book of Hours* remains too constantly abstract. It lacks the solid reality of great poetry. (p. 347)

[In the first volume of the *New Poems,* written shortly after the end of Rilke's association with Rodin, the] nostalgic prettiness of his early poems, still often found in the *Book of Pictures,* has disappeared, and the despairing mysticism of the *Book of Hours* has been given a solid medium. They are almost all short poems of twenty lines or less and in each we find a compactness that recalls French mediaeval sculpture. Reality looks out at us as from the capitals of those Romanesque columns that Rilke loved—a flower, an old man, a statue, an ancient story retold, a procession of children. There are so many excellent poems that it is impossible to choose. . . . It is as if his meditations on Rodin had forced him to isolate each subject in a consciousness of its three dimensions. The inner unapparent life that remains Rilke's essential subject acquired thereby a definiteness that is almost tangible. His tenderness is no longer a mere longing; it has developed into the sense not only of infinitely varied surface, but also of infinitely varied color. For it is not only Rodin's influence that can be traced in them. Judging by his letters of 1907 the effect on him of French painting and especially of Cézanne's work was of even greater importance. . . . [The influence of Paris] changed the music of Rilke's verse into something much severer than that of his earlier period. For even in the *Book of Hours* music still seems to play around the thought, dazzling our understanding of it. This is now no longer true. In these *New Poems* the music and meaning are woven so closely that they are indistinguishable. Perhaps it was in order to escape for a time from the temptation and distraction of metre that he turned next to prose. (pp. 350-52)

[The *Notebooks of Malte Laurids Brigge*] purport to be the memories and reflections of a young Dane. The English translation has been called **"The Journal of My Other Self"** which is accurate enough, though I think Rilke would rather have it uncertain whether he and Malte are really identical. (pp. 352-53)

The subject of the *Book of Hours* still lies at the base of it. It is a search for God—but the search is no longer confined to his own consciousness; we travel with him through a world peopled with men and women, contemporary or long since dead, whose reality he lays bare through a minute scrutiny of appearance and gesture. It has been compared to Proust. Both delve below the surface with the same precise knowledge of what is happening there, and in both the characters remain essentially alone; but *Le Temps Perdu* is a worldly picture of man. Proust is absorbed by the bodily and social peculiarities of his characters, whereas Rilke can never forget their ultimate problems. His accurate descriptions have a pathos, a sense of nightmare and a fantastic humor very different from the clear Latin irony of Proust—Rilke's knife exposes the disparity of body and soul, the disparity of man's insignificant actions and the vastness of his consciousness. Then Proust makes nothing more than a statement of what he has observed, whereas Rilke, as some one has very rightly said, turns everything into a parable. One might call this book "A parable of masks." . . . [He] tries to pierce these masks—and what he finds behind them is always that terror of death that he describes in the *Book of Hours,* and, growing out of that, a fear of showing one's self to the world as one really is. He finds that pure love is the only reality that can tear off this mask and transform those fears into a still greater reality, and yet at the same time he finds that love almost impossible. (pp. 353-54)

The book ends with the parable of the Prodigal Son who left home to escape the affection of his family and who returned to it, not as they interpreted it, to ask forgiveness, but to implore them not to love him. . . .

> What did they know of him? He was now terribly difficult to love, and he felt that One alone was capable of loving him. But he was not yet willing. . . .

Are these last words a cry of despair? Rilke has reached the centre of his consciousness and found a great longing there that is the love of God. But who is this God? He has stripped him of those attributes of love and mercy that make Him accessible. He has removed Him not only out of Time and Space but out of human consciousness. He grants no communication with Him. (p. 364)

That was the isolation that seems here to reach the pitch of despair. The isolation of the artist with a work that has become to him a universe reflecting the one his sense perceives but independent of it. (pp. 364-65)

It is a defect in Rilke that he began by trying to make what he found appear complete. His piety, as we see it in the *Book of Hours,* is a cloudy thing. And it is not such a cloud as could bring forth the hard stone tables of a law—when Rilke speaks as a prophet he is not convincing. The transformation he describes in Malte is his realization of this. The *Notebooks* are a definition of his own incapacity. He must remain an observer who can transform his observations into poetry and forget his longing for a divine communion; for God is not yet ready to love him and moreover he is also not yet ready to love God. (p. 365)

> *Hester Pickman, "Rainer Maria Rilke," in* The Hound & Horn, *Vol. IV, No. 3, April-June, 1931, pp. 325-65.*

W. H. AUDEN (essay date 1939)

It is presumptuous to pretend that one can ever really judge poetry written in a foreign language: one can only define the impression it makes upon oneself. With the appearance of [the] translation of the **"Duino Elegies,"** which, with the Orpheus Sonnets, form the final flower of his work, the bulk of Rilke's poetry is now available in English, and it is possible to attempt such a definition.

Rilke's most immediate and obvious influence has been upon diction and imagery. One of the constant problems of the poet is how to express abstract ideas in concrete terms. The Elizabethans solved it for their generation by an anthropomorphic identification. . . . With the exception of Blake, the poets of the succeeding . . . centuries found no fitting solution: in consequence they are weakest whenever they attempt to deal with abstractions. They were content to state the latter abstractly, with the result that their poetry too often degenerates into preaching.

Rilke is almost the first poet since the seventeenth century to find a fresh solution. His method is the direct opposite to that of the Elizabethans but, like them and unlike the Metaphysicals, he thinks in physical rather than intellectual symbols. While Shakespeare, for example, thought of the non-human world in terms of the human, Rilke thinks of the human in terms of the non-human, of what he calls Things (*Dinge*), a way of thought which, as he himself pointed out, is more characteristic of the child than of the adult. . . . Thus one of Rilke's most characteristic devices is the expression of human life in terms of landscape. . . .

But Rilke's influence is not confined to certain technical tricks. It is, I believe, no accident that as the international crisis becomes more and more acute, the poet to whom writers are becoming increasingly drawn should be one who felt that it was pride and presumption to interfere with the lives of others (for each is unique and the apparent misfortunes of each may be his very way of salvation). . . . (p. 135)

This tendency is not to be dismissed with the cheery cry "defeatism." It implies not a denial of the importance of political action, but rather the realization that if the writer is not to harm both others and himself, he must consider, and very much more humbly and patiently than he has been doing, what kind of person he is, and what may be his real function. When the ship catches fire, it seems only natural to rush importantly to the pumps, but perhaps one is only adding to the general confusion and panic: to sit still and pray seems selfish and unheroic, but it may be the wisest and most helpful course.

A review is not the place to discuss Rilke's ideas in detail. There are curious similarities between them and those of D. H. Lawrence. Both envied the undivided consciousness of the animals, both were obsessed by the idea of Death (*cf.* Lawrence's "Ship of Death" with the **"Tenth Elegy"**), both, to use terms common to Lawrence and Rilke's friend [Rudolph] Kassner, looked back to the physical aristocratic world of the Father rather than forward to the spiritual democratic world of the Son, and were consequently hostile to Christianity, both even were excited by the same Etruscan tombs. But what is important for us and future writers is not the truth or falsehood of their conclusions, but their conception of the writer's real task and the lifelong and humble devotion which they brought to it. (pp. 135-36)

> W. H. Auden, "Rilke in English," in The New Republic, *Vol. 100, No. 1292, September 6, 1939, pp. 135-36.*

E. M. BUTLER (essay date 1941)

The most conspicuous feature of *Duino Elegies* is Rilke's attitude to his own poetry, which underlies the whole cycle, an intensely personal point of view revealing a dangerously isolated mind. Deserted by inspiration during the long period which preceded the inception of *Duino Elegies,* he was to meet the same fate again and again during the following decade. The cycle is the battle-ground of his desperate efforts to win over a fierce and radiant foe; and the scene of a darker conflict, a long, grim struggle with the demon of doubt. Misgivings as to his own poetical mission, dark suspicions of the validity and power of poetry itself in life and the universe often assailed his mind. . . . This spiritual uncertainty has left its mark on *Duino Elegies*. Hardly less harrowing, if on a less exalted plane, was the problem of his human existence, the utter isolation of his genius, the loneliness of his mind, accompanied by sharp stabs of fear that he, and not the world, might be in the wrong. He found some measure of relief in equating his tragic lot in life as a poet with man's position in the universe, which he represented as completely isolated and divorced from nature too. This analogy between his own sufferings and the cosmic desolation of mankind gives to *Duino Elegies* what human significance this strange cycle has. . . . He used the pronoun 'we' in the main as a royal plural for Rilke; but sometimes too for poets in general and occasionally for human beings, as members of the same tragic race.

He saw the world we inhabit as Bunyan saw Vanity Fair, as a city of sorrow situated in the great land of grief. This beautiful, mysterious and glamorous country was inhabited by the noble race of lamentations, once all-powerful throughout the land, but now fallen from their high estate and shunned by the inhabitants of the city who congregate in the garish and strident consolation-market, jostling each other before the gaudy booths, drinking the popular 'deathless' beer and chewing cheap distractions. Just outside the city walls, lovers, children and dogs approach nearer to reality and nature; and it may even happen that some young man from the town meets with a girlish lamentation and follows her through the meadows. But only the youthfully dead realise the full extent of her beauty and charm, and are guided by her into the heart of the mighty, dreaming land. . . . (pp. 316-18)

The contrast between the blatant vulgarity of the city and the serene loveliness of the ancient land surrounding it, given up to the cult of the dead and inhabited by a race of mourners, is not only a glorification of sorrow and pain as greater and more beautiful than joy, but also an affirmation of death as a better and more enlightened state than life, an echo from many and many a poem in the past. The extreme beauty of the vision (which even the ingenuity of the allegory cannot hide) and the literally hypnotic quality of the verse arouse the species of emotion described by a brother-poet as 'being half in love with easeful Death', an effect which Rilke's more proselytising pronouncements do not produce. (p. 318)

The city of sorrow certainly deserves its name; and the inhabitants are to be pitied rather than blamed, for the hand of fate is heavy on them. They are out of tune with the finite and out of touch with the infinite except during their pathetically brief childhood; the dark inheritance in their blood endangers their loves; and only those can be called happy who vanish away early from their death-ridden lives into the soundless realms of outer darkness and primeval pain. This, in so far as Rilke considered his fellow human beings sympathetically, was how he regarded them. . . . Against this sombre background the drama of *Duino Elegies* was played out in the poet's mind, a conflict with a threefold aspect. The first reflected Rilke's lifelong doubt as to 'whether the highest kind of activity is creating works of art or being in love'; the second revealed his tormenting search for his poetical destiny or mission; and the third, closely connected with it, his homeric struggle to win a foothold for himself as a poet in the universe and to stake out a claim for the cosmic significance of poetry. All three aspects helped to inspire the vision of the angels in *Duino Elegies* and to determine Rilke's relationship with them.

Like nearly every other symbol in the cycle, the angels had a long and chequered history behind them. (pp. 322-23)

At the outset of Rilke's poetical career angels had offered the passive resistance of radiance to the dark, tumultuous forces of life. The instinctive and primitive symbolism which had shaped them endowed them with dynamic life, so that they became active antagonists to all that is unworthy in man. Glorious and menacing, they challenged him to mortal combat, from which they emerged victorious, whilst he was defeated, but greater than before. The myth of Jacob wrestling with the angel inspired Rilke with gathering intensity as the desire for the 'blessing' grew. Expanded into a cosmic conflict, it moulded the internal structure of *Duino Elegies*. . . . It perfectly symbolised his own most vital experience, the incalculable nature of inspiration, its dangers, its glories, its inexorability. Rilke's defeats and victories in the struggle, one of the intensest of human conflicts, were given universal proportions in the cycle; so that the whole is essentially a mystery play even down to the allegorical element, so conspicuously present in the tenth elegy. Rilke's angels were the protagonists in a drama which had gradually shifted from the human to the superhuman plane. Behind it was the fierce resolve to force the angels' blessing, to attract their notice, to enter into their consciousness, to be recognised and accepted as belonging to the same sphere and contributing something to the absolute beauty which they represented as well as the forces of spiritual inspiration. For the Duino angels are too truly a poetical creation to be completely susceptible of rational interpretation, and too complex to stand for any one idea. Rilke's idolatry of art as the supreme creative power became incarnate in them; a more mysterious and less ambiguous piece of symbolism than his previous use of the word God to represent an emergent aesthetic creator. These angels had none of the protean nature of the God of *The Book of Hours;* they were far more arresting and terrible in their utter aloofness, and self-sufficiency, as befitted beings who were not in a state of becoming but of eternal and immortal existence. Their absolute beauty annihilated human standards; and Rilke could only avert his personal destruction as a poet by accepting the challenge implicit in their very being. This is the drama inherent in *Duino Elegies.*

Although the angels have a structural part in the elegies, this is poetically less important than the fact of their presence, which drenches the cycle with radiance, giving it greater proportions and a deeper rhythm. They are exciting, dangerous, forbidding; informed with a vitality which discharges itself upon the reader like an electric shock. Whenever the sound of their wings is heard, life becomes intensified, sometimes almost to the limits of endurance. For these dazzling beings are terrible and unnerving. They seem to deny, if not the existence, then the validity of human life, love, suffering and endeavour. They are utterly remote and completely self-absorbed. (pp. 325-27)

The first elegy forms as it were the exposition of the action about to be engaged between Rilke and the angels, whose passive manifestation was absolute art, but whose active aspect, if they could be prevailed upon to show it, would be a mighty whirlwind of inspiration. . . . [Rilke confessed] after the poem was written that the inspiration which had produced it was such a terrible experience that he feared its recurrence. This is strongly brought out in the opening lines, where the poet partly despairs of attracting the angels to him and partly fears his immediate annihilation if they should approach him; coming to the conclusion that he could not use them poetically any more than he could use human beings. For his utter isolation in the world of men was the second subject of the poem, concentrated in the central fact that he was incapable of love. (pp. 327-28)

This first elegy is in fact a bitter confession of poetical and emotional bankruptcy, the inexhaustible theme of his contemporary letters. Were it not for the presence of the angels at the beginning of the poem, one would almost be ready to give him up.

But the vital, magnetic power radiating from them came from Rilke himself and was more clearly manifest in the second poem. Human love shrank almost to nothingness when he surveyed that dazzling host; for love was tragically ephemeral, and they were beyond all time. Heroically he set himself to establish the one possible connection with them; that of contrast between their absolute beauty, glory, intensity and might and the feeble, evanescent nature of mortal emotions and aspirations. Perpetually evaporating into the universe and vanishing, might not all this nevertheless have some almost imperceptible effect upon it? Those shining angelic mirrors, eternally reflecting their own glory might, without meaning to and certainly without noticing it, catch something emanating from us on the way; so that we might be present in their features. . . . This

was barely conceivable; but the angels in the whirlwind of their return to themselves would be totally unaware of it.

If Rilke did not actually reject love in favour of art in this poem, he showed more clearly than in the first elegy his dissatisfaction with it as a poetical subject, and his willingness to relinquish it. . . . [He] turned to his interpretation of sex in the third elegy, representing it as an elemental, dangerous, subversive force which had nothing to do with art, at the very antipodes from the radiant angels of his desire; yet paradoxically enough it was a force which inspired him here with some of the finest poetry he ever wrote, and heralded his later phallus-worship rooted in the creative power of sex. (pp. 329-30)

The crisis in his conflict with the angel occurred in the fourth elegy, in which poem he braced himself to coerce by sheer will-power the austere and reluctant daimon of poetical inspiration. It is a hard poem in more senses than one; hard to like, even when the intellectual difficulties it presents have been partially overcome, on account of its hard tone of contempt for all human values and its convulsive efforts to transcend them. It came from an atrophied heart and an arrogant mind, rigidly determined to divorce life from art at any cost, and there is something grotesque about the endeavour. Yet, for all its grimness, it has tragic proportions; since the violent effort to constrain inspiration met with no apparent success, and the poet reached the nadir of despair. After a bleak and wintry survey of the false position of man in the world and of the pitiful inadequacy and hostility of his human relationships, Rilke hissed him off the stage, irritably and impatiently rejecting himself as an actor in the theatre of life, and as a poet of such dramas. Far better to replace man by a puppet which, however lifeless, was at least solid and full, whereas the human actor was flabby. . . . Rilke, past-master in ambiguity, used *Puppe* at times, and notably in this poem, to convey his dual attitude towards art, a deep-seated discord, never quite resolved and particularly strident in this poem. For although art, or the puppet, seemed preferable by far to life, nevertheless its disillusioning nature, its apparent impotence to act on life, was also represented. The puppet created by man stood, not for absolute art, but for human approximations to it, and in particular for Rilke's own poetry. . . . Hence his insistence that the puppet was filled with sawdust, that its face was completely inexpressive, and the wires all too visible. Having dismissed his fellow human beings from his life, this was what he was faced with, and he had to face it out in utter isolation from his own kind. . . . [In the fourth elegy] love was replaced by external inspiration. There was no love, either human or aesthetic, but desperate anxiety in the gaze Rilke directed at the inanimate puppet whilst he waited tensely in the empty theatre before the grey, deserted, draughty stage. There was not a soul beside him; he had banished his friends and lovers, and even those of his blood and in his blood had left him to practise his magic alone. Self-dedicated, he watched and waited for the miracle which was to reward his utmost effort. He would and must compel the angel to descend at last and manipulate the strings of the seemingly lifeless marionette. . . . The disturbing human element having been eliminated, art and inspiration would perform a real drama, a cosmic event, leaving mortals to their botch-work. This ultimate triumph took place in an uncanny silence and in his mind's eye. There was no motion on the stage, no sound of whirring wings, and nothing whatever happened. Then an anguished voice was heard, Rilke's voice crying out to the hours of his childhood, the magic interlude fit for pure creation. . . . Whether this interpretation is correct or not, the desperate appeal to childhood would seem to prove conclusively that the angel of inspiration had not accepted the burnt offering of human love Rilke had made in the poem.

The fifth elegy still leaves the matter in doubt, although it illuminates it vividly. For here the marionettes came to violent, indeed to galvanic life and performed an amazing *danse macabre,* in dramatic contrast with the inert and motionless puppet of the preceding poem. . . . There was some strange compulsion behind their actions, some eternally unsatisfied will, but certainly not the angel who had tarried in the fourth elegy. Nevertheless, he seemed to be watching them, or at least to be aware of them out of the corner of his eye; for these bewildering and tragic figures were artists of a sort, achieving the utmost it is possible to achieve without real inspiration and true love. Rilke, having rejected love for art's sake in the fourth elegy, now represented art without love in the fifth as the most tragically evanescent and unstable manifestation of life. . . . Metrically as well as imaginatively the poem is a *tour de force,* being a representation of virtuosity and skill gone almost mad, taking one's breath away as such performances are meant to do. The rush, the strain, the fever and the fret of these hectic and agile performers is so verily a dance of death, that the final merging and re-composition of the group into a tableau of love fulfilled after death is almost demanded by the dynamics of the poem. (pp. 330-33)

[Rilke's] tormenting doubts as to his own personal rightness in choosing a poet's life and as to the greatness of poetry altogether . . . account for his hymn to heroes in the sixth elegy, where they are exalted above the rest of mankind, because they live dangerously, pressing onwards towards fruition in death, whereas we linger merely to bloom. This poem, like his early *Cornet,* was written under the compulsion of that lifelong love for those who died young. . . . (p. 335)

The fifth and sixth elegies mark that pause in the conflict between Rilke and his great antagonist which often comes after a crisis has been reached; a pause in which waverings and doubts beset his mind for having made his great refusal in the fourth elegy in the name of art. Art seemed less attainable and less desirable than it had done before the sacrifice, and heroes of a different kind from himself more greatly admirable. Human values reasserted themselves and the heroism of human endeavour. But in the seventh elegy Rilke turned away from them finally. . . . [The] lesson of the seventh elegy [is] that the only real world is within us, and that life is one long transformation. Rilke had at last found the formula for his cosmic mission and a connecting link between himself and the angel. He still dreaded that awful being unutterably, he still called 'Come' and 'Avaunt' in the same breath; he still wished to keep him at a great distance; but during the course of the poem Rilke brought into the consciousness of the angel the mighty achievements of human art. That world of towering cathedrals and soaring columns was vanishing away from sight. The rushing spirit of the age which cared more for power than form was destroying the monuments and temples of the past. And where they still stood, they were already partly invisible, altogether overlooked by many who neither saw them with their bodily eyes nor transformed them with the eyes of the mind. Rilke displayed them to the angel, whose eyes received them; and there, upright and saved in his gaze, they remained. More, the angel was challenged to confess his astonishment, to glorify those works, and to proclaim the miracle that man, encompassed by an incomprehensible fate, had peopled space with such magnificent monuments, which were great, even when measured against his own stature. (pp. 335-36)

In the fluctuating rise and fall which marks the movement of the cycle, the eighth elegy goes subsiding into the depths after the triumph in the preceding poem. This hymn to the brute creation is tragic in the extreme, a bitter contrast between the beautiful unconsciousness of death which marks out the beasts that perish, and man's incessant and despairing awareness of it. One is therefore prepared in the ninth elegy for Rilke's flat denial of the eternal value and significance of human emotions, pain and even love, which had still counted in the seventh elegy. But all our spiritual experiences shrink to nothingness beneath the eternal stars and are not worth uttering either there or here. What then remained for the poet to do? The same task he had undertaken in the seventh elegy, but now contemplated under a more universal aspect. His mission, the only valid poetical mission, was to the world of things, animate and inanimate, which belong to the here and now and not elsewhere. It was they who needed the poet in order to become immortal, and it could only be done here. Let him transform bridges, wells, gateways, pitchers, fruit-trees, windows, houses, at the most towers and columns, in his inmost heart; nay, let him thus transform the whole earth which was demanding to rise again invisibly within him, and thus to be translated into the angelic sphere. Then the angels, who can only apprehend what is invisible, will marvel at this hymn of praise to humble, simple things. They will receive them and rescue them from oblivion. We, whoever we may be, are here simply and solely for this.

Nietzsche said in *The Birth of Tragedy* that the world was justified, but only as an aesthetic phenomenon. Rilke came to the more extremist conclusion that existence was justified only in so far as it was aesthetically active; and he narrowed the sphere of art to include only visible phenomena, expressly stating that emotions such as sorrow and love should be left to the angels to utter, since their power of feeling immeasurably transcends ours. (pp. 336-37)

If beauty was absolute, eternal and unattainable, all that was imperfect and temporal could be translated into that angelic sphere by the magic of poetry; and the poet who could do this might well uplift his voice in a paean of praise and exultation to the assenting choir of angels; he had at last attained the farther end of his grim insight into life.

The tenth elegy opened with this statement; the last in a cycle in which humanity as a whole, and especially lovers, heroes, children, beasts and things, had all been seen in their tragic aspect. For even the beasts who know not death obscurely long to return to the darkness of the womb; even the greatest works of art fade away and vanish from mortal ken. Whilst man himself, cruelly compassed round about by death, at the mercy of sinister antenatal forces, helpless to arrest the descending course of his existence, wanes ineffectively away. In spite of the poet's triumph, this world is one of sorrow; and for this reason, if for no other, it is outside the angels' ken. (pp. 337-38)

But the cycle is not nearly so simple and unambiguous as this reading of it claims. On the contrary, it is one of those baffling and controversial works, so often written by poets who have passed their creative prime, in which poetry is subordinated to the philosophical content and to the didactic aim; in which beauty is not enough unless vouched for by truth. Obscurely aware of treachery to their art, such writers wrap up their meaning in veils of obscurity and offer intellectual puzzles instead of mystery itself. In spite of its intricate symphonic structure, its creative language, the pure magic of some of the poetry, and the simple beauty of some of the thoughts, the strongest impression produced by *Duino Elegies* is an unquiet feeling of treacherous depth, a sensation so vivid and so unremitting that one is justified in concluding that Rilke had experienced it too, and had realised that the attempt to sublimate his emotional and aesthetic experiences on to an astral plane was a desperate and dangerous venture. . . . The poem, in fact, is not only susceptible of philosophical interpretation, but actually seems to demand it. (p. 339)

> *E. M. Butler, in her* Rainer Maria Rilke *(reprinted with permission of Macmillan Publishing Co., Inc.), Macmillan, 1941, 437 p.*

H. F. PETERS   (essay date 1960)

Rilke's style has often been analyzed. Even those who are irritated by some of his mannerisms—a tendency toward preciosity, particularly in his early verse—agree that it is unique. "Any reader," says [Hans Egon] Holthusen,

> who, familiar with other kinds of poetry, comes across a line or stanza of Rilke's for the first time, cannot fail to be fascinated by the purely and unmistakably individual character of his language, by its partiality, self-containedness and self-sufficiency, by the intensely personal and idiomatic, even, in a sense, idiopathic quality of his lyricism.
>
> (pp. 22-3)

"Exposed on the hills of his heart," Rilke struggled to reach "the last hamlet of words" only to find that higher there was "yet one remaining farmstead of feeling." Again and again he tried to reach it, forcing himself up on the "bare rock under his hands" and again and again he reached the realm of the "unsayable," encountered the resistence of language. He strained at these limitations and tried to overcome them by ingenious verbal and syntactical innovations that frequently startle the reader and seem incoherent. But as one gets used to Rilke's style these incoherences fall into a pattern. . . .

Like erratic blocks in a familiar landscape Rilke's images stand out in German poetry. Every sensation, every impression, even the most subtle shift in feeling, he turned into a visual image. At times of great poetic tension a veritable tumult of images poured out of him. (p. 23)

No other poet, says Gundolf, not Shakespeare and no Oriental, has transformed his feeling so fervently into metaphors; "no word occurs more frequently with him than the word 'as.'" Rilke's flight into the image betrays a fundamental aspect of his mind: his deep awareness of the interrelatedness of life, his tendency to be lost in a kaleidoscopic universe of constantly changing patterns, colors, sensations, impressions. "Staying is nowhere" in Rilke's world. Everything is flow and counterflow of great cosmic forces that are utterly indifferent to man. The most he can do is to accept them, let himself be carried by them, enter into a rhythmic relation to them. This is the message Rilke tries to convey in image after image: reject nothing—not even death. (p. 24)

Related to the visual nature of Rilke's imagery is the predominance of the noun in his style. The noun dominates everything: it is color and contour in the ebb and flow of his thought; even the verb frequently appears in substantivized form. . . . [This] combination of the static and dynamic elements of language, which produces an effect of balance between movement and

rest, is very well suited to Rilke's thought. Hence even such unusual noun forms as "the not-knowing-whither" or "this no-longer-grasping," or "this never-being-able-to-give" must be considered legitimate means of his style. But many of the nouns Rilke prefers—and, according to Baudelaire, such key words show the direction of a poet's inner compulsion—are not unusual at all. The way in which he uses them is unusual and often gives them a striking novelty and freshness.

Among such typically Rilkean nouns are "thing," "space," "inwardness," "contradiction," "relation," "center," "circle," "island," "mask," "mirror," "praise," "lament," "being," and "death." For an understanding of Rilke's existential dilemma his use of the words "mask," "island," and "mirror" is particularly significant.

Take the word "mask." A good example of it occurs in the last stanza of the poem *The Death of the Poet*. . . . (pp. 25-6)

Death has torn off the poet's face . . . and all that now remains is a decaying mask. But even when he was alive people did not know his true face . . .—they knew his countenance . . . , i.e., his "life mask," which now "lies propped-up, pale and denying above the silent cover." . . .

Behind these two masks—his life mask and his death mask—the poet had remained hidden, anonymous like running water. What death had torn off was but the outer life, the day-by-day events, the movement on the surface—not the real face. For the real face is indestructible. (p. 26)

Thus all we see are masks. Life, the real life, the life that matters, is invisible, "unmastered and unknown." If, in moments of exaltation, we catch a glimpse of it, it threatens to overwhelm us with its radiance. Hence we need masks. . . .

The mask serves a dual purpose: it conceals and it reveals. . . .

[Another] attribute of the mask must be mentioned: its transforming power. Every actor knows how much he is affected by the part he is playing. Made up as a king, he *is* a king; he lives his part. Rilke also knew "the immense influence of a disguise." (p. 27)

From the frequent mention he makes of it, it is evident that the mask theme held a particular fascination for Rilke. He seems to have both invited and dreaded the loss of identity which every masquerade entails. (p. 28)

"Every profound spirit needs a mask," says Nietzsche, "indeed, a mask grows continuously around every profound spirit, because of the false, i.e., shallow, interpretation of every word, every step, every sign of life he gives." Rilke also knew that. When he was asked about himself, he referred people to "that figure which I am building beyond myself, outside, more valid and more permanent . . . For: Who knows who I am? I am constantly changing." He resented all attempts to penetrate his privacy; he longed for anonymity. He wanted to lose his self in his work. (pp. 28-9)

The key to an understanding of the tragic dichotomy in Rilke's life is that he was an artist who knew the "ancient enmity" that exists between art and life and wanted to transcend it. He knew it was his fate to lose his identity, to spend himself, "pour himself out," but he also knew that this outpouring was an act of purification which prepared the way for the inrush of inspiration, the Dionysiac frenzy which possessed him when he wrote his greatest poetry. . . . "A poet," Keats told his friend Woodhouse, "has no identity, he is continuously in for and filling some other body. . . . It is a wretched thing to confess, but it is a very fact, that no word I utter can be taken for granted as an opinion growing out of my identical nature—how can it, when I have no nature?''

With Rilke this dissolution of the ego went to dangerous extremes because he bestowed the energy belonging to positive thinking upon feeling-sensation, which amounts to a reversal of the introverted type. (p. 29)

This tendency, always present in Rilke, increased in the course of his life and, while it gave incomparable insights to the poet, it caused the suffering of the man. In *An Experience* he tells how, walking in the castle garden of Duino one day at the time when the first *Elegies* began stirring in him, he leaned against the fork of a low tree and felt immediately so pleasantly supported that he gave up reading and surrendered completely to the sensation of being absorbed by nature. He felt as if from the interior of the tree ''almost unnoticeable vibrations passed over to him.'' Gentle movements penetrated his body, which seemed to lose all sense of heaviness, and he felt like a revenant who returns once more to the world that formerly had been indispensable to him. Looking back over his shoulders to the objects around him he experienced the sweet taste of their complete existence. (p. 30)

Rilke realized that by entering such states of ''pure being'' which gave him a deep awareness of the unity of existence, he risked becoming entirely alienated from his self and not being able to communicate at all. Hence his constant desire—even while he longed to enter such states—to be ''himself'' again, to live a normal life with normal human relationships. Besides, there was always the danger of self-deception, the possibility that he mistook for genuine transformation what, in reality, was nothing but play acting, that he pretended to be inspired when he was only disguising his inner emptiness. (p. 31)

The mask theme symbolizes the will to transformation which Rilke considered to be the basic principle of existence. (p. 32)

If, on its highest level of interpretation, the mask symbolizes the Dionysiac power of transformation which dissolves the self and forces men to become mouthpieces of a suprapersonal power: *vates*—the mirror symbol has a converse meaning: that of narcissistic self-love. The frequency with which both symbols occur in Rilke points once more to the tragic split in his personality: his longing for self-surrender and his opposite longing for self-absorption. Torn between Dionysus and Narcissus, his life was one of constant conflict. (pp. 34-5)

To a mind withdrawn into itself and trying to find verbal equivalents for the flood of images that rise up in the soul, the problem of communication becomes of paramount importance. The poet realizes that language is a very blunt instrument, that it is quite unfit to render the subtle variations, tremors and raptures within; therefore he tries to fashion it anew, to break through the established forms of grammar and syntax, only to find that the closer he gets to his goal the more obscure he becomes. In the end he despairs of being understood at all and writes mainly for himself. Rilke's indifference to the reader stems from this insight. He knew that he could not explain how he arrived at his ''lyrical sums'' and that nothing would be gained by subjecting them to a critical analysis. . . . All he can suggest is for the reader to get ''similarly focused''; i.e., to search his soul for meaning—not his intellect. If the reader will but try to catch the images reflected in his soul, he may become aware that they are signals, indicating presences in space which to the mind seems empty. (pp. 37-8)

Another aspect of Rilke's existential dilemma, though complementary to that expressed by the mask and mirror theme, is shown by his preference for the ''island'' situation. . . . Primarily, the island is a symbol of isolation; a piece of land cut off from the main, it reflects the situation of the isolated individual. But, since the water that surrounds an island acts like a mirror, it is a narcissistic symbol as well. Rilke often uses it in this dual meaning. (p. 39)

> *H. F. Peters, in his* Rainer Maria Rilke: Masks and the Man *(copyright © 1960 by the University of Washington Press), University of Washington Press, 1960, 226 p.*

EUDO C. MASON (essay date 1960)

[Rilke] dated his true beginnings as a responsible poet from the great revolution in the direction of discipline, objectivity, concreteness and deliberate craftsmanship which first fully manifests itself in the *New Poems* of 1907. . . . His entire, very voluminous body of writings anterior to this great revolution the later Rilke disowned as immature, 'inexact' (*ungenau*) and marred by a 'cheap lyrical *à peu près*', with the one important exception of the *Book of Hours*. (p. 21)

What above all conferred a unique value on the *Book of Hours* in Rilke's own eyes, so that he could say that 'although it belongs to the works of my youth, it is undatable', is the circumstance that in writing it he had an extraordinary experience of inspiration. . . . In autumn 1899, [Rilke] . . . continued for over three weeks, from 20 September to 14 October, in a remarkable kind of trance, and it was during these weeks that he wrote the first part of the *Book of Hours* (later known as the *Book of Monastic Life*), or rather, as he himself preferred to declare, that it was 'given' or 'dictated' to him. (p. 22)

[In September 1901] he was visited again by another such spell of trance-like inspiration as two years previously, though this time it continued only for eight days, from 18 to 25 September. Then it was that he produced the second cycle of 'Prayers', which was later to receive the title **'The Book of Pilgrimage'**. . . . [After an interval of another year another visitation came upon him] lasting this time again eight days, from 13 to 20 April 1903, and resulting in the third cycle of 'Prayers', later entitled **'The Book of Poverty and Death'**. . . . [The *Book of Hours*] established Rilke's reputation. It soon became and still remains more widely popular than anything else of Rilke's, except the *Lay of Love and Death of Cornet Christoph Rilke*. (pp. 23-4)

The great body of devoted readers that Rilke won for himself in 1906 with the *Book of Hours* were much disappointed, indeed shocked by his *New Poems* . . . and the strange pathological prose work, *Malte Laurids Brigge*. . . . It seemed to them that Rilke with this austere, restrained, impersonal and sometimes even apparently cynical or pessimistic art was taking away from them again what he had just given to them—and that was nothing less than a new religion. There always have since then been many readers for whom Rilke is in the first place the author of the *Book of Hours*, who see in that book not a work of art, but a unique and absolutely valid religious revelation. (p. 24)

[The question is] whether these verses of Rilke's indeed are authentic 'prayers' or 'communings with God'. . . . One of the chief issues involved here is what really happens to Rilke in such extreme experiences of inspiration as those which engendered the *Book of Hours,* or, more precisely, what mysterious power it is that 'dictates' his poetry to him in such moments. This is a topic on which Rilke himself has an immense amount to say—it might almost be asserted that it interested him more than any other topic in the world. He recurs frequently to such conceptions as that his poetry is 'more than of me' and that some mysterious 'power', 'voice' or 'meaning' makes use of him in his moments of inspiration as a mouthpiece through which to manifest itself. Amongst the various names which he gives to this mysterious force that of 'God' sometimes occurs. These declarations of Rilke's are often interpreted quite literally [by critics]. . . . In reality, however, Rilke's experience of inspiration is nothing like so unique as he imagined it to be. . . . The true source of Rilke's inspiration—reluctant though he usually is to admit it—is *his own unconscious mind,* which, in its turn, is the repository of all his own previous highly conscious intellectual processes, of all that he has read, heard, thought, spoken, written, striven after and endured. (pp. 28-9)

The most obvious problem about the *Book of Hours* is: what does Rilke believe about God, and what does the word God mean altogether in his vocabulary? (p. 31)

The view here maintained that Rilke's God, alike in the *Book of Hours* and in everything else he writes, always remains something subjective, is indignantly rejected by many readers. They appeal to the frequent occasions on which Rilke speaks of God as though he really did exist objectively—but that, of course, proves nothing at all in the case of a man demonstrably accustomed to using the name of God as a figure of speech. . . . [Rilke] refuses ever to say unambiguously that God does exist, and he also postulates that it does not in the least matter whether God exists or not, indicating that his own sympathies are far more with those who say he does not exist than with those who say he does. The *Book of Hours* is an experiment in leading a very intense life of devotion and prayer on these unusual assumptions. But what those who maintain that Rilke *must* believe in the objective existence of God most appeal to is the intrinsic fervour and power of his utterances. Surely, they argue, words of such immense evocative force and vitality cannot arise just out of the void—something real must exist that corresponds to them. Nobody wishes to deny this—though some allowance must be made for the extraordinary hallucinatory power of great art, of which Yeats says: 'If I succeed, then I must make men mad'. The reality is always there, but it is not always necessarily identical at all points with what the naive reader takes it to be. It is in the first place Rilke's consciousness of *himself,* of *his own* existence, of the vividness of his own moods, of the intensity of his own emotions. How this works out we can see from a passage in his diary . . . :

> And often I see from their faces that I have
> been speaking too grandiosely. O that what I
> am saying might not be pride, that it might
> sound like humility and gratitude. But there are
> days on which I cannot speak about myself
> without naming God, the solitary God in whose
> shadow my words darken and glisten.

That is the real theme of the *Book of Hours:* Rilke's own inner life, the vibrations and oscillations of a hovering, dithyrambic soul, the sinking and soaring of his aspirations and, above all, his sense of his own uniqueness, of that which distinguishes him as a kind of uncrowned king from everybody else, of his vocation, his creative powers and also his perils *as a poet.* Those are the things he cannot—at least at this stage—express

without using the supreme figure of speech—*God.* (Later, indeed, he was to use other images and symbols for the same purpose, particularly the angel of the *Elegies* and the Orpheus of the *Sonnets.*)

Something else arises here. The Russian monk of the first part of the *Book of Hours* is supposed to be a painter of icons in the ancient tradition of the Eastern Church, and he devotes many of his meditations to the bolder, more individualistic art of the Italian Renaissance. . . . [Throughout] the first two parts of the *Book of Hours* there are frequent references to painting, sculpture, architecture, music, poetry and art in general, and it might at first be supposed that all this is but symbolical for the religious experience, or at least parallel to it, as another variety of religious experience. In reality, however, it is just what is said about *art* here that is meant and should be understood more literally, while religion and all the concepts of religion, particularly God, are symbolical for art, for the artist's sense of vocation, for his exaltations and his humiliations, for his wonderful privileges and his terrible perils and deprivations, and for the great redeeming cosmic function which falls to him and to him alone amongst mankind. Thus Rilke had written . . . :

> Religion is the art of those who are uncreative.
> In prayer they become productive . . . The non-
> artist must have a religion—in the profoundly
> inward sense—even if it only be one reposing
> on collective and historical convention. To be
> an atheist in *his* sense is to be a barbarian.
>
> (pp. 34-6)

Some who have recognised how much the *Book of Hours* is really concerned with the apotheosis of art have dismissed it as at bottom after all nothing but aestheticism. To this judgement I cannot assent. It certainly is aestheticism, but it is not *mere* aestheticism. Rilke is very much concerned with overcoming aestheticism, with in some way extending or deepening the doctrine of art for art's sake (which he—in his own terminology—often enough proclaims) so as to give it, if possible, a genuinely religious character. The conception at which he had arrived some time before he began writing the *Book of Hours,* and which he restates with increasingly subtle variations and with frequent shifting of emphasis throughout his life, is that of the *salvation of the world through art.* (p. 37)

The most striking form which the idea of the salvation of the world through art assumes in the *Book of Hours* is that of the 'Future God'. The conception is that God does *not yet* exist, but that he is being brought into existence, and that the leading, the essential role in thus bringing him into existence is being played by the artists. . . . Something else is involved here, besides Rilke's sense of the vast and unique power of art, for which no claims could be too great. Christianity, he assumes, is completely moribund, and he would not revive it if he could, because there is too much in it that he abhors. But it has left a comfortless void, the void of the soulless, mechanical world revealed by natural science, and he sees it as the function of art to fill this void, to succeed where Christianity has failed, to put back a soul—but a better soul—into the universe, in the place of the soul which departed from it when science killed the Christian God. Extending the idea of evolution, and inspired probably also in some measure by Nietzsche's idea of the Superman, Rilke arrives at the paradoxical conception of God as the final result instead of the first cause of the cosmic process, and of art as the decisive agent in bringing him into existence—all of which is, of course, very remote from any authentic kind of mysticism. (pp. 37-8)

Such conceptions postulate, in addition to the 'Future God', some unconscious and inarticulate force underlying the whole cosmic process and coming to consciousness of itself in individuals of genius who are called upon to carry out its groping purposes—a Life Force or *élan vital*—and this too has its place in Rilke's tentative speculations and can also be designated by him as 'God'. . . . [In a] vague pantheistic sense he can at times call 'Life', or nature, or the sum of things 'God', or anything at all—that is the theme of one of the *Stories of God,* 'that anything can be the dear God'. So it comes about that the word 'God' can have for Rilke a multitude of the most varied meanings, without his ever admitting any necessity for bringing them into harmony with one another or choosing between them. Rilke himself calls this 'trying one's hand productively on God', and speaks contemptuously of all other more traditional forms of devoutness, which, instead of doing this, merely 'accept God as a given fact'.

It is constantly asserted that in all the mysterious things Rilke says about death in the *Book of Hours,* particularly in the third part with its doctrine of 'dying one's own death', he is simply in his own peculiar terminology proclaiming his belief in the immortality of the soul, or at least testifying that he has totally and permanently triumphed over every kind of uneasiness, uncertainty or fear where death is concerned. Against this generally accepted interpretation it may be pointed out that Rilke in all he has to say about the problem of death, . . . meticulously avoids making any explicit, unambiguous statement about the survival of personal identity, and that he is to the last unmistakably haunted by the acutest and most invincible uneasiness and fear in the face of death. All his mysterious formulae are, I would maintain, specially designed to prevent the question of survival after death being so much as fairly asked, still more answered, as though that question were taboo, as though there were something unlucky about it. . . . He is concerned rather to present unconditional acceptance of the mystery of death as the one true solution of the death problem: so long as death is felt to be indeed a vast mystery, and not merely a bald, unmysterious, physical fact, we have all we can expect, all we need. All possibilities, ranging from total extinction through metempsychosis to personal immortality, must be left open, but only as possibilities, not as certainties. To demand certainty here one way or the other is a monstrous error. . . . That, I would maintain, is Rilke's attitude towards death not only in the *Book of Hours,* but even earlier and throughout his entire development. (pp. 38-40)

It is from this angle that Rilke's esoteric doctrine or rather formula of 'dying one's own death' can alone be adequately interpreted. . . . Even in the final second of death, whatever death may be, the individual is not to abdicate—then, more than at any other moment, he is to belong to himself, to make his very death part of himself. How fundamentally Rilke was animated here by hostility to Christian tradition appears above all in the mysterious notion of the 'Death-Bearer' evoked in the third part of the *Book of Hours* to proclaim this doctrine of dying one's own death. The point of this Death-Bearer is that he is the antithesis of Christ, the proclaimer of Eternal Life and of the Resurrection of the Dead—in fact, he is a kind of Anti-Christ. The one point that clearly arises out of the otherwise so obscure passage, in which the engendering of this Death-Bearer is described with so much anatomical detail, is that it is to be the exact opposite of the engendering of Christ:

not a virgin birth of an immaculately conceived mother, but a physical begetting with all the circumstances of sexual intercourse. Here, as all along the line, it is the other-worldliness of Christianity against which Rilke protests. (pp. 40-1)

In most of what he has to say about death both there and in the earlier poem Rilke is less concerned with setting up any genuine new doctrine on the subject than with challenging and discrediting the Christian belief in the life to come, just as in most of what he has to say about God he is less concerned with setting up any definite new doctrine on the subject than with challenging and discrediting the accepted Christian idea of the existence and nature of God.

All attempts at interpretation lead us back, however, to Rilke himself and to the ceaseless ebb and flow of his inner life which, bearing all ideological speculations and visions along with it, remains the ultimate theme of the *Book of Hours* and the secret of its beauty, its force and its magic. (p. 42)

> *Eudo C. Mason, "Introduction" (1960), in* The Book of Hours: Comprising the Three Books, Of the Monastic Life, Of Pilgrimage, Of Poverty and Death *by Rainer Maria Rilke, translated by A. L. Peck (translation copyright © The Hogarth Press Ltd. 1961), Hogarth Press, 1961, pp. 21-44.*

THEODORE ZIOLKOWSKI (essay date 1969)

The story of Nikolai Kusmitsch is one of the longest episodes [in Rilke's novel *The Notebooks of Malte Laurids Brigge*]. As if to underline its importance, Malte concludes: "I remember this story in such detail because it consoled me uncommonly." At this point the reader asks himself why this should be so. In technique the story does not differ from many other episodes in the notebooks. Rilke has taken an abstract topic, time, and treated it with a technical vocabulary borrowed from the area of banking and commerce. This produces the same weirdly comic effect that he achieves elsewhere, for instance, by describing death in terms taken from the jargon of tailors and clothing manufacturers. . . . In the second part of the episode Rilke achieves an equally grotesque effect by describing the reaction of a hypersensitive temperament when it reduces the abstractions of science—the ether and the revolution of the earth—to its own subjective experience.

It is the ending of the anecdote, rather than its technique, that strikes us as important. For despite his anguish over the passing of time, Nikolai Kusmitsch finds tranquillity when he recites poetry to himself. This aesthetic refutation of temporality consoles Malte. The arrow of time is halted by the power of art. When Nikolai Kusmitsch intones the cadences of Pushkin, time is suspended and he is no longer tormented by its flow. In a letter written fifteen years after the publication of *The Notebooks,* Rilke remarked that the many figures evoked in the novel represent "vocables of [Malte's] anguish." . . . Malte seeks in the timelessness of art a refuge from his own temporal existence. If we examine the novel as a whole from this point of view, we find that the tension between the temporality of existence and the timelessness of art does indeed constitute one of the main themes—if not the principal one!—of the whole work and that, further, it determines in large measure the structure of the book.

Time, and especially this conflict between the temporality of life and the timelessness of art, emerges as an increasingly dominant theme throughout Rilke's works. In a poem celebrating **"L'Ange du Méridien"** . . . Rilke explicitly contrasts the clock time of mortals with the eternity of art, for the angel on the cathedral at Chartres is impervious to the hours that flow across the sundial that he holds in his arms. (pp. 4-6)

[In *The Notebooks*] Rilke explicitly and repeatedly refers to time; the story of Nikolai Kusmitsch is simply the most elaborate example. Elsewhere we hear of people whose lives "run down like a clock in an empty room." A voice is said to have "the even, indifferent cadence of a clock." In another description Malte observes that a person's life, in the intervals between real action, "jerks along like the hand of a clock, like the shadow of its hands, like time." In all of these instances the clock is a negative image symbolizing the mechanical movement of temporality. In one notable passage Malte remarks that his own daily life, "which nothing interrupts, is like a clock-face without hands." The only good clock, in other words, is a broken clock, for this observation occurs in one of the scenes during which Malte manages to forget his present temporality by succumbing to his memories of the past. Such textual hints as these alert us to the fact that Malte's struggle for identity, fought out on the battleground of his notebooks, must constantly be viewed in terms of the tension between temporality and timelessness. (pp. 6-7)

[In the first entry in his notebooks, the] fact of isolation is intensified to an almost unbearable pitch by the diction: style and meaning complement each other perfectly and establish one of the central themes of the work. For Malte is always isolated from the group. We see him alone among a frolicking carnival crowd, alone among the readers in the Bibliothèque Nationale. In fact, several of his entries, as when he speaks of Beethoven and Ibsen ("the loneliest one"), are hymns to solitude.

The world that Malte encounters as he looks around is strangely dehumanized. . . . This creeping dehumanization . . . is reflected in the style of the narrative. Hands, for instance, are mentioned with notable frequency, but they are always hands that are somehow detached from the human body; they have become independent things, unrelated objects. "Somewhere a withered, flecked hand crept forward and trembled." . . . The human body has lost its integrity. In a hospital Malte sees, beneath the bandages, "a single eye that belonged to no one" and "a leg in a cast that protruded from the row on the bench, as large as a whole person."

As death and the human body lose their dignity, things become increasingly personalized and dominant. "Electric trains tear, clanging, through my room. Automobiles roll over me. A door falls to. Somewhere a window pane clatters down, I hear its big pieces laugh, the little slivers giggle." (pp. 8-10)

In a world where people are dehumanized and things personalized, man finds himself wholly at the mercy of the objects surrounding him. Twenty-five years before Sartre's *La Nausée*, Malte is oppressed by a sensation closely akin to the existential "viscousness" of things. We hear of "balconies, onto which one is forced by a little door." A little piece of lace can "fence off our sight, as though we were monasteries or prisons." (p. 10)

This, then, is the situation in which Malte finds himself when he begins to write his notebooks. Alienated from the world about him, threatened in the integrity of his own personality, menaced by the intrusion of hostile and powerful objects, Malte has reached the zero point. He is, as he calls himself, "this Nothing"—a terrified Nothing in a world without order or meaning. When he has been in Paris for three weeks, Malte

starts to write a letter, but it occurs to him that his experiences have altered him so radically as to make him a wholly new and different person. (p. 11)

Malte's dilemma prefigures that of the heroes of many modern novels: cut off from his family, his friends, his past, he is rootless, a foreigner, a "stranger" in a hostile city. A new group of images characterizing his situation crowds his mind. He notices, for instance, that he seems to attract beggars and other "rejects" . . . of life—those "peelings, husks of men that fate has spit out." Although his suit is frayed, his shoes scuffed, and his beard neglected, Malte insists at first that he has nothing in common with that band of outcasts. But finally, when his illness drives him to the clinic, he finds that the doctors treat him as one of the "rejects." This exterior change that takes place during his first six months in Paris reflects the total alienation of his inner being. Reduced to a "Nothing," to one of life's "rejects," Malte must find a way out of his dilemma, or perish.

Malte's anguish, and ultimately his redemption, stem directly from the experience that he calls "learning to see." Piercing through the deceptive veil of accepted conceptions, he encounters reality directly and without the mediation of conventional notions. . . . But this new reality is so unaccustomed that he is frightened by each fresh perception. "I am afraid" echoes like a refrain through the opening pages of the book. For Malte's vision has also revealed to him that the conceptions which formerly gave men faith, which formerly held the world together, have also disintegrated, becoming as discrete and random as the dissociated limbs in the hospital. (pp. 11-12)

The trouble, Malte gradually concludes, is that man has analyzed all meaning to pieces. In his blind search for categories and systems, man has overlooked the essentials. . . . Things liberated from the controlling restraints of conventional beliefs float freely, in a chaos, like the parts of bodies that Malte sees about him, and assume that threatening aspect that characterizes the external world in his eyes. Malte's fear, then, is directly related to the breakdown of established order, to his inability to accept conventional patterns of reality any longer. In order to escape his anguish, Malte must find a new possibility of order, one within which the things will once again have a place. And this order, in his mind, is linked to the problem of time.

In the first of his *Duino Elegies* . . . Rilke noted that mortals make the mistake of distinguishing too sharply between things, whereas angels are often unaware whether they are walking among the living or the dead. . . . Yet even in this world it is possible to live like the angels, aware of the "eternal streaming" that unites all realms of being. . . . People who have attained the level of awareness of the angels—or of Grandfather Brahe [in *The Notebooks*]—never feel threatened by reality, for everything exists in an eternal order of simultaneity. Unlike ordinary men, they have not broken down the patterns of being by making ever greater distinctions and articulations until no meaningful whole is left. For such men even death poses no threat, since it too is absorbed into the whole as a meaningful part.

In the course of his notebooks Malte slowly works his way toward this goal of simultaneous experience of totality, which alone produces true freedom from fear and death. But he begins more modestly. His first response to his anguish, like that of Nikolai Kusmitsch, is an aesthetic one. "I have done something against my fear. I have sat up the whole night and written." Here we see the true instigation for Malte's notebooks. They represent, at first, an attempt to combat his fear of reality as it has been exposed to him through his new sense of seeing, by organizing his sensations into meaningful aesthetic patterns that will replace the disintegrated patterns of conventional belief. If he can succeed in giving an aesthetic meaning to the things and sensations that rush in upon him, he can halt the flow of temporality by suspending it in an aesthetic whole.

The entirety of *The Notebooks,* in the last analysis, gains its structure through Malte's attempts to come to grips, progressively, with different areas of his experience. For the material is organized roughly, though not in any rigorously systematic way, into three successive groups. First, he is obsessed with the immediate present reality of his life in Paris. Gradually he moves back, through interpolated memories that are usually catalyzed by experiences in the present, to the reexperiencing of his own family and of his childhood. Finally, in the second part of the novel, his focus expands to embrace the historical past. Malte's quest for meaning, in other words, leads him to search for his identity in three areas: as an individual, within the group, and in the light of history. Ultimately, as we shall see, this progression leads him to search for a new definition of God: his own identity against the background of eternity. Near the end of his notebooks Malte remarks: "Even before we have begun God, we pray to him: let us survive the night. And then illness. And then love." The night, illness, love, and God—these are the stages of Malte's development. The first half of the book reflects his attempts to survive the first terrible nights in Paris and the illness, a hereditary nervous disorder, that drives him into the very hospitals he fears. In the second part he has recovered sufficiently to think about the problem of love, which leads, in the last pages, to his meditations on God.

Up to this point we have talked about *The Notebooks* as though it constituted a novel in the conventional sense of the word. It does not, of course. Even though many novelistic elements are included, they must be reconstructed from the work as a whole. We learn, for instance, a great many details of Malte's life before his arrival in Paris, but these facts are not arranged in any narrative or causal sequence; they are scattered seemingly at random through the notebooks and must be reassembled into a chronological pattern. It is this discrepancy that first alerts us to the fact that Rilke's "prose-book," as he customarily designates it, cannot be grasped according to the structural principles of conventional fiction. (pp. 12-16)

Ripping the events of his past out of their context (even the sequence of deaths in the family is altered), Malte seeks to build up his life into a new pattern. This dissolution of sequential time, moreover, has a deeper, more existential significance for Malte. By freeing his past from any causal nexus, he at the same time asserts his own freedom of identity and liberates himself from temporality. (p. 19)

[Malte's notebooks contain notes] in contrast to systematic journal entries or organized autobiographical reminiscences. Although the first entry is dated and although there are enough hints for us to establish the sequence of early fall, winter, spring, and summer, external time plays no role at all for Malte. The notes themselves are independent blocks of prose, ranging in length from a paragraph to several pages and tied together by no causal links. (p. 20)

[Whether] Malte is concerned with a tableau in the streets glimpsed from his window, . . . or with memories of his childhood, or with episodes from the historical past, in every case

he shapes the raw material into a coherent and meaningful image. It would be a mistake to look for the significance of these scenes in their content. This is, rather, a quest for meaning through form, for a purely aesthetic meaning. Individually, each of the "notes" represents an attempt to transcend temporality by fashioning reality into a timeless pattern in which things take on a new meaning and hence are no longer free to threaten Malte.

When we move from the separate notes to their arrangement in the pattern of the whole novel, we see that Malte is trying to suspend the events of his own life aesthetically in such a way that they become meaningful. When he turns from experience of the present to recovery of the past, Malte writes: "I have prayed for my childhood, and it has come back, and I feel that it is still as difficult as it was then and that it has not done any good to become older." His own childhood gains a meaningful place in his eyes only after he has succeeded in shaping it aesthetically in precisely the same way he shapes the events of his everyday life in Paris. By arranging the events of past, present, and even future into a pattern, Malte is viewing reality as a whole, like the angels and like his grandfather. (p. 24)

The sequence of the notes, each of which constitutes in itself an aesthetic whole, is determined by very subtle principles of association. (p. 27)

The links between the separate tableaux—there are seventy-one altogether—as well as the principle of organization governing each one become quickly evident to anyone who reads the notes carefully. Beyond the law of association that controls the opening sections, however, another factor comes into play: the same principle of complementarity that governs Rilke's poetic cycles, such as the *New Poems* and the *Duino Elegies*. . . . In his poetry the theme of equilibrium—the moment of delicate balance between opposing forces—is conspicuous, and explains, for instance, his frequent use of acrobats as a metaphor for human existence (e.g., in the fifth elegy).

This principle of complementarity, which implies a resolution of opposites, not only underlies individual poems and whole poetic cycles; it also determines the sequence of many of the tableaux in *The Notebooks.* Especially the complementarity of temporal levels fascinates Malte. . . . But the ultimate effect of this radical juxtaposition of various levels of time, for Malte as well as for the reader, is to efface the differences, to suspend time in a continuum. We become acutely conscious of the duration underlying the temporal phenomena as patterns repeat themselves, complementing or contrasting with one another.

In the first third of the book, where Malte is concerned primarily with his own existence in Paris, the principles of association and complementarity that determine the organization of the notes operate largely in the present tense. As he delves back into his own childhood in the second section, these principles are complicated, as we have seen, by different levels of time. Toward the end of the book, however, Malte has grown so accustomed to thinking by association and complementarity that he can afford, repeatedly, to suppress half of the process: his own present existence. Figures from the historical past are simply invoked, without reference to himself, as pure metaphors for his own existence, as "vocables of his anguish." It is quite mistaken to assume that the meaning of these episodes lies in their content. . . . Their significance lies in the "tension of these anonymities," which reflects Malte's state of mind metaphorically.

Through the historical figures Malte's own emotions are generalized in the form of a parable. But as soon as the parabolic significance of the historical life becomes evident through its aesthetic telling in the notebooks, his own life assumes a higher meaning. He *is*, metaphorically, John XXII, Charles VI, and all the other figures that he evokes. Through the historical past Malte is rescued again from the threat of temporality: his own experience is externalized and eternalized in the figures whose stories he narrates. He can stand apart and look at his life objectively, just as he can look objectively at the objects captured in his tableaux.

This process of externalization and objectification of his own life is reflected, in turn, in the style of the narrative. We observed above that the notebooks begin with a radical juxtaposition of self and other. The first-person singular that insistently dominates the first part of the book, as though Malte had to assert his own existence grammatically in the face of the threatening world, gradually gives way to third-person narrative, until, at the end, Malte has been absorbed wholly by the metaphors of his own self. It is characteristic that the work, which begins in the first person, should end with the parable of the Prodigal Son. By the end of his notebooks, in other words, Malte has vanished behind the projections of himself. His own private temporal existence has been subsumed in the supratemporal existence of the parable. (pp. 28-31)

This progression from lyric to epic constitutes stylistic evidence of the fact that Malte has liberated himself sufficiently from the frightening obsessions of the first pages to write objectively about reality. (pp. 32-3)

> Theodore Ziolkowski, *"Rainer Maria Rilke: 'The Notebooks of Malte Laurids Brigge',"* in his Dimensions of the Modern Novel: German Texts and European Contexts *(copyright © 1969 by Theodore Ziolkowski; reprinted by permission of the author), Princeton University Press, 1969, pp. 3-36.*

KLAUS PHILLIPS (essay date 1979)

[Rainer Maria Rilke] perhaps best known for his *Sonnets to Orpheus* and *Duino Elegies* and acclaimed as the century's foremost German-language poet, wrote more than twenty plays between 1894 and 1904. (p. ix)

[Rilke's earliest dramatic attempt was] written during the summer of 1894 and destroyed in a fire. Later in the same year, Rilke turned toward the psychodrama: plays in which there is only one actor. Richard von Meerheimb, a popular writer of psychodramas during the late nineteenth century, became an example for young Rilke. Rilke's *Murillo,* based on the life of the Spanish painter, adheres to von Meerheim's principles, although he clearly adapts these principles to his own purpose. For example, in contrast to the self-centered histrionics that characterize von Meerheimb's personages in a comparable situation, the death scene is dominated by an impassioned and yet restrained description of Christ upon the cross. Thus attention is shifted from the plight of Murillo's impending death to his attempt at rendering the passion of Christ. . . . The psychodrama kindled in Rilke the idea of seeking to represent inner life versus outer experience, an idea that was to remain with Rilke throughout all of his future works.

By the following year, 1895, Rilke had already begun to be interested in the subject matter of naturalism, as is evident in much of the poetry he wrote at that time. . . . Rilke was particularly taken with the pessimistic determinism of [Rudolph

Christoph] Jenny's plays and decided to write such dramas himself. A year later, Rilke's *"Now and in the Hour of Our Death . . ."* was staged in Prague. . . . The play contains a variety of standard naturalistic elements, but lacks the conciliatory tone so characteristic of Jenny's plays. A family encounters difficulties due to illness, lack of money, and villainy; the landlord will allow the family to stay if the elder daughter consents to let him have his way with her. A suggestion of Greek fate permeates the play as the sins of the mother are passed on to the daughter. Yet this drama of seduction and incest constitutes a curious fusion of naturalism and melodrama; it is filled with surprising revelations but ultimately is overshadowed by a sense of inevitable doom.

The next play, *Early Frost,* appears to be a companion piece, yet it stands in closer conformity with the postulates of naturalism. In both plays, a family is threatened by economic demands, and, although not figuring directly in these demands, the daughter is persuaded by a villain that sexual submission is the only recourse. In a traditionally naturalistic play, the protagonist is likely to struggle against circumstances; Eva, in *Early Frost,* remains passive. She represents a higher consciousness trapped in a wicked world, and is destroyed by this world, largely because of her perceptions.

As far as sheer length is concerned, *Early Frost* is Rilke's most extended dramatic work. Principally as a result of his insistence on full presentation of background, motivation, and detail, Rilke was able to accomplish the creation of one of the most towering mother figures in modern German drama. Although essentially repulsive, Clementine is not a totally villainous character. She is steadfast in her beliefs and pursues her goal with indomitable perseverance. She is completely immersed in the material world and has come to terms with it. (pp. ix-x)

Around June 1897, Rilke became deeply fascinated by the writings of the Belgian playwright Maurice Maeterlinck. In a series of essays entitled *Treasure of the Humble (Trésor des humbles)* Maeterlinck claimed that the domain of drama should be the inner processes of the soul and not the outer action of realism. Rilke found himself in agreement with many of Maeterlinck's tenets: outer silence must be maintained if the quiet, inner action of the soul is to be perceived, and thus it is necessary that good drama permit its actors to perform during lengthy pauses in speech; women are closer to the mystical truth of the soul, but all people possess an inner beauty and goodness; minor events are frequently sufficient to facilitate realization of the inner life; since our greatest events are inner actions that require no outer stimuli, the contemporary stage with its emphasis upon externals is an anachronism.

Air at High Altitude, Rilke's next play, heralds his transition from naturalistic to symbolistic drama. . . . The personalities of Max and Anna are developed subtly and ironically. The cast of characters lists Max with his surname, Stark (which in German means "strong"), while his sister's name, Anna, stands alone. The play's title refers to the physical location of Anna's apartment as well as to her spiritual state. Upon the relative strengths of the two main characters is built a series of contrasts. Anna has found inner peace, while Max is an ex-officer and a lover without responsibilities and involvement in everyday realities: a soldier who has never fought and a lover who has never loved. Anna is engaged in life and can still know joy as she anticipates the opportunity to rejoin her parents and help her son; Max is bored, his laughter infused with cynicism. The symbolic mood pervades the action and succeeds in encompassing and suggesting all that Rilke intended. (pp. xi-xii)

The control of mood is also central to *Vigils,* an unconventional little play not so much because it leads the audience to a symbolic level (as does *Air at High Altitude*), but rather because of the oscillation between amusement and confusion that culminates in horror. Throughout the play, the stage is kept in almost total darkness. Only the outlines of certain objects, especially an armchair, are visible. There are many comic moments as the bumbling students and their girlfriends attempt to orient themselves—making this Rilke's only play to contain extended humor.

Details of the students' lives are irrelevant to Rilke's single purpose: to illustrate the experience of death in the midst of happy life. To that end, Rilke manipulates his audience: frequent pauses are used as a means of decelerating the action and giving the audience additional time to contemplate the developments—a device endorsed by Maeterlinck. From this play on, "*pause*" becomes a common item in Rilke's dramas. (p. xii)

Similar in technique and theme to Gerhart Hauptmann's *Michael Kramer,* Rilke's *Everyday Life* . . . fuses lyrical intent with realistic form. According to the play's central theme, every experience has a certain rhythm in which it must be measured, and wisdom is the ability to find the rhythm for each individual situation. Instead of looking for moments of intense rapture in everything, one should find gentler rhythms for everyday experiences, rhythms that permit one to enjoy these everyday experiences to their limited fullness. (p. xiii)

With his play *Orphans,* Rilke explores the psychology of children, juxtaposing their innocence and cruelty. Again reality stands in contrast with fantasy, as *Orphans* uncovers a dichotomous universe within the microcosm of the orphanage. The children's reaction to the death of little Betty is virtually void of emotion. Sympathy is replaced by curiosity and fear. Sensory impulses link the corpse with candles and cheese, since the children are unable to transcend the horizons of the material world. Jerome, the smallest boy in the group, is convinced that the little girl is not dead at all; he associates death with his mother's suicidal plunge from the top of a building. Because of this revelation, Jerome is ostracized from the group. As the old gardener removes the dead girl's coffin, Jerome pursues him. The play ends on an ambiguous note. . . . It is not clear what will happen to Jerome; he may watch the gardener bury the little girl; he may or may not come to understand that she really has died; he may attempt suicide in order to join his mother. Ending the play in this fashion, Rilke forces the audience to enter the "theater of the mind."

Rilke's final attempt at drama resulted in *The White Princess,* his best-known play today. (p. xiv)

A first version of the play was completed in 1899. It is more a lyrical poem than a drama and seems to illustrate Rilke's suggestion that drama and poetry should have a common aim. The substantially revised and expanded version . . . was written in 1904. . . .

Despite the continued predominance of rhymed pentameter, the orchestral potential of language seems extended in the revised play; but it is rather that limitation of language that gives this play its character. As words become increasingly dull and useless tools, *The White Princess* culminates in total silence. The figures assume marionette-like qualities, embodying not only Maeterlinck's dogmas, but also those of Heinrich von Kleist, with whose works Rilke had by then become familiar. Thus, *The White Princess* completes Rilke's curiously circular path back to principles first stated in the psychodramas. (p. xv)

> *Klaus Phillips, in his introduction to* Nine Plays *by Rainer Maria Rilke, translated by Klaus Phillips and John Locke (copyright © 1979 by Frederick Ungar Publishing Co., Inc.), Ungar, 1979, pp. ix-xv.*

ADDITIONAL BIBLIOGRAPHY

Baron, Frank; Dick, Ernst S.; and Maurer, Warren R., eds. *Rilke: The Alchemy of Alienation.* Lawrence: The Regents Press of Kansas, 1980, 268 p.
> A collection of essays, most of which deal with individual works or specific themes of Rilke's. Included are Dana Rothe on the poetic cycle "Die Zaren," Lev Kopelev on Rilke's relationship to Russia, and Erich Simenauer on Rilke's exploration of dream states.

Guardini, Romano. *Rilke's Duino Elegies: An Interpretation.* Translated by K. G. Knight. Chicago: Henry Regnery, 1961, 306 p.
> Detailed reading of the *Duino Elegies.*

Heerikhuizen, F. W. Van. *Ranier Maria Rilke: His Life and Work.* Translated by Fernand G. Renier and Anne Cliff. London: Routledge and Kegan Paul, 1951, 396 p.
> An excellent biographical and critical study of Rilke, providing specific discussions of influences on Rilke's work, and containing many extracts from his letters. The critic believes that *The Notebooks of Malte Laurids Brigge, Sonnets to Orpheus,* and *Duino Elegies* form a modern *Divine Comedy.*

Wood, Frank. *Ranier Maria Rilke: The Ring of Form.* Minneapolis: University of Minnesota Press, 1958, 240 p.
> A study of Rilke's work which seeks "by analyzing persistent themes and motifs in their original context, to give a broader idea of how a great poet can be, at one and the same time, one of the most 'paradoxical' and yet most 'consistent' personalities of our time."

Edmond (Eugène Alexis) Rostand

1868-1918

French dramatist and poet.

Rostand is noted for briefly reviving romantic verse drama at a time when naturalist and symbolist drama dominated the European stage. He has been called the last great romanticist of the French theater, and although he added no new dimension to dramatic art, audiences weary of the comparatively drab realism of the day welcomed his colorful, witty, and rhetorical plays.

While he is known primarily as a dramatist, Rostand began his career as a poet. He first published his poems in *Mireille*, a small Marseilles magazine, but remained little known until the publication of his first collection, *Les musardises*. Although this volume provided some exposure for the young writer, its light romantic verses were considered adolescent and received nominal critical attention. Rostand later published two volumes of patriotic verse, *Le cantique de l'aile* and *Le vol de la Marseillaise*, but these collections, like *Les musardises*, have attracted little notice outside France.

Rostand's first significant drama, *Les romanesques* (*The Romancers*), is a variation of the Romeo and Juliet theme satirizing the romantic naiveté of adolescent love. Encouraged by its relative success, Rostand began *La princesse lointaine* (*The Princess Far-away*), whose title role he wrote for the actress Sarah Bernhardt, the principal interpreter of his works. A more serious and profound attempt than his previous drama, *The Princess Far-away* builds upon the theme of the quest for the unattainable ideal. The influence of Victor Hugo and Alfred de Musset, whose works Rostand had discovered while studying at the College Stanislas in Paris, is evident throughout his early plays. They also demonstrate the beginnings of the verbal precision and rich lyricism so finely expressed in *Cyrano de Bergerac*.

Because it was so different from the contemporary realist and symbolist dramas, the opening performance of *Cyrano de Bergerac* caused a tremendous stir in the French theater. An unequivocal success in France, *Cyrano de Bergerac* quickly developed an international reputation. Critics and public alike praised Rostand's "heroic comedy" for its action, wit, and poetry. Inspired by the life and personality of the seventeenth-century poet Cyrano, the play is based on the simple theme of the conflict between love and friendship. The dialogue, vocabulary, and background, in addition to the theme, derive from standard romantic subjects and settings of the early nineteenth century.

The polish and brilliance of *Cyrano de Bergerac* aroused expectations which were largely disappointed by Rostand's last two completed plays, *L'aiglon* (*The Eaglet*) and *Chantecler*. The life of the Duke of Reichstadt, son of Napoleon I, is the subject of *The Eaglet*, whose title role was also written for Sarah Bernhardt. Although the play enjoyed considerable success in France, it has been criticized for its lack of spontaneity and obvious construction. Because of its patriotic subject, *The Eaglet* never held the international appeal of *Cyrano de Bergerac*. The allegorical *Chantecler*, Rostand's most original play, has been judged variously. While some critics find the play

too lengthy, obscure, and contrived, many praise it as Rostand's most ambitious and profound drama.

Rostand's works, aside from *Cyrano de Bergerac*, have not been greatly influential. They do stand apart, however, from the literature of Rostand's day as a reaction against the naturalism of Ibsen and the symbolism of Maeterlinck. Although some critics argue that *Cyrano de Bergerac* is Rostand's only great work, his unfinished play, *La dernière nuit de Don Juan* (*The Last Night of Don Juan*), indicates a new direction in Rostand's drama and provokes speculation on Rostand's unfulfilled potential.

PRINCIPAL WORKS

Le gant rouge (drama) 1888
Les musardises (poetry) 1890
Les romanesques (drama) 1894
  [*The Romancers*, 1899]
La princesse lointaine (drama) 1895
  [*The Princess Far-away*, 1899]
Cyrano de Bergerac (drama) 1897
  [*Cyrano de Bergerac*, 1898]

La Samaritaine (drama) 1897
   [*The Woman of Samaria* published in *Plays of Edmond
      Rostand*, 1921]
L'aiglon (drama) 1900
   [*L'Aiglon*, 1900; also published as *The Eaglet* in *Plays of
      Edmond Rostand*, 1921]
Le cantique de l'aile (poetry) 1910
Chantecler (drama) 1910
   [*Chantecler*, 1910]
Le vol de la Marseillaise (poetry) 1919
La dernière nuit de Don Juan (drama) 1922
   [*The Last Night of Don Juan*, 1929]

G. B[ERNARD] S[HAW] (essay date 1895)

The romance of chivalry has its good points; but it always dies
of the Unwomanly Woman. And M. Rostand's **"Princess Far
Away"** will die of Melissinde. A first act in which the men
do nothing but describe their hysterical visions of a wonderful
goddess-princess whom they have never seen is bad enough;
but it is pardonable, because men do make fools of themselves
about women, sometimes in an interesting and poetic fashion.
But when the woman appears and plays up to the height of
their folly, intoning her speeches to an accompaniment of harps
and horns, distributing lilies and languors to pilgrims, and roses
and raptures to troubadours, always in the character which their
ravings have ascribed to her, what can one feel except that an
excellent opportunity for a good comedy is being thrown away?
If Melissinde would only eat something, or speak in prose, or
only swear in it, or do anything human—were it even smoking
a cigarette—to bring these silly Argonauts to their senses for
a moment, one could forgive her. But she remains an unredeemed humbug from one end of the play to the other; and
when, at the climax of one of her most deliberately piled-up
theatrical entrances, a poor green mariner exclaims, with open-
mouthed awe, "The Blessed Virgin!" it sends a twinge of
frightful blasphemous irony down one's spine. . . .

It is a pity that the part of M. Rostand's play which deals with
the shipful of enthusiasts did not get over the footlights better;
for it is touched here and there with a certain modern freedom
of spirit, and has some grace, youth, and imagination in it.
But it lacks the force which comes from wisdom and originality. (p. 828)

> G. B[ernard] S[haw], "La Princesse Lointaine" (re-
> printed by permission of The Society of Authors
> on Behalf of the Bernard Shaw Estate), in The
> Saturday Review, *London, Vol. 79, No. 2069, June 22,
> 1895, pp. 828-30.*

MAX BEERBOHM (essay date 1898)

M. Rostand is not a great original genius like (for example)
M. Maeterlinck. He comes to us with no marvelous revelation,
but he is a gifted, adroit artist, who does with freshness and
great force things that have been done before; and he is, at
least, a monstrous fine fellow. His literary instinct is almost
as remarkable as his instinct for the *technique*—the *pyrotech-
nique*—of the theatre, insomuch that I can read **"Cyrano"**
almost as often, with almost as much pleasure, as I could see
it played. . . . It is rather silly to chide M. Rostand for creating
a character and situations which are unreal if one examines

them from a non-romantic standpoint. It is silly to insist, as
one or two critics have insisted, that Cyrano was a fool and a
blackguard, in that he entrapped the lady of his heart into
marriage with a vapid impostor. The important and obvious
point is that Cyrano, as created by M. Rostand, is a splendid
hero of romance. If you have any sensibility to romance, you
admire him so immensely as to be sure that whatever he may
have done was for the best. All the characters and all the
incidents in the play have been devised for the glorification of
Cyrano, and are but, as who should say, so many rays of lime-
light converging upon him alone. And that is as it should be.
The romantic play which survives the pressure of time is always
that which contains some one central figure, to which everything is subordinate—a one-part play, in other words. . . .
Cyrano is, in fact, as inevitably a fixture in romance as Don
Quixote or Don Juan, Punch or Pierrot. Like them, he will
never be out of date. But prophecy is dangerous? Of course it
is. That is the whole secret of its fascination. Besides, I have
a certain amount of reason in prophesying on this point. Realistic figures perish necessarily with the generation in which
they were created, and their place is taken by figures typical
of the generation which supervenes. But romantic figures belong to no period, and time does not dissolve them. . . . Cyrano
will survive because he is practically a new type in drama. I
know that the motives of self-sacrifice-in-love and of beauty-
adored-by-a-grotesque are as old, and as effective, as the hills,
and have been used in literature again and again. I know that
self-sacrifice is the motive of most successful plays. But, so
far as I know, beauty-adored-by-a-grotesque has never been
used with the grotesque as stage-hero. At any rate it has never
been used so finely and so tenderly as by M. Rostand, whose
hideous swashbuckler with the heart of gold and the talent for
improvising witty or beautiful verses . . . is far too novel, I
think, and too convincing, and too attractive, not to be permanent. (pp. 5-6)

> Max Beerbohm, "'Cyrano de Bergerac'" (1898), in
> his Around Theatres (reprinted with permission of
> Mrs. Eva Reichmann), *Rupert Hart-Davis, 1953, pp.
> 4-7.*

POET LORE (essay date 1899)

I suspect, nay, I believe, that nothing could be æsthetically
funnier than [M. Rostand's *Cyrano de Bergerac*] . . . is, save
the sentiment, *au grand sérieux*, that has been lavished upon
it as if it were a real drama instead of a satirical extravaganza.
(p. 118)

The rollicking hyperbole, the color far too high for reality with
which M. Rostand has heightened the effectiveness of all [the]
historic part of his material is alone enough to release him from
the imputation of having himself taken his Cyrano as seriously
as his public has. He has employed his historic sense in the
rehabilitation of seventeenth century Paris; but neither merely
as a savant nor merely as a poet, nor even as a dextrous playwright, but rather as all three combined, plus the most important factor of all in the work—namely, as a satirist, has he
permeated the whole story with irony. This irony peeping out
in his clever manipulation of the historical part of his framework is revealed in all its poignant intentionalness in the invented parts. (p. 119)

It is precisely in these invented parts, which are absolutely
unsuited to the seventeenth century character of the real Cyrano, of course, that the design of the playwright can be un-

questionably traced. In the balcony scene the sentimentality of the artificial lover of the old school and the exacting whims of a *précieuse* are exquisitely ridiculed. The poses of antiquated romance are recalled to mind and they are re-staged here so as to lay bare before the modern eye their archaic quality. The irony is developed to the point of rendering this lapsed sentimentality not merely comical but at times almost farcical—the levity of the treatment, despite a cleverly contrasting instant or two when Cyrano betrays his own earnestness, being at the opposite pole from the impassioned seriousness of the Shakespearian scene it recalls. To break the fair unity of such a love-passage as the balcony scene in 'Romeo and Juliet,' to cut in two the physical beauty of the youth in Romeo, and the spiritual beauty lent his speeches by the ripe poet, and to personify each of these, is virtually what the French poet has done. He has made of the one half, Christian, the clumsy-tongued, fair and lusty animal, and of the other half, Cyrano, ugly, but mature of phrase if not of mind. Still, further, he has made a Juliet of the Hotel Rambouillet, a *précieuse* enamored not of the artist but of art, hankering rather for the wit which love incites than for love itself. The humor this situation involves is tickling to the last degree. Shall we spoil the comedy by taking it in dead earnest? When Christian utters his bald "I love you!" and on encouragement can but reiterate this trite simplicity, and Roxane, with closed eyes, expecting thrills from the rhapsody that halts, cries out impatiently, "That is the subject, work it up, work it up!" and when she bursts scornfully upon his stammering attempts with her, "Oh! Do labyrinthinize your feelings!" are we not to laugh? Again, when Cyrano, acting as Christian's proxy, pours out his dextrously be-rhymed emotions too successfully, till Roxane, mollified, deceived, makes the proposition to descend to him or for him to ascend to her, and throws him into a panic lest she behold him and his nose, are we not to laugh? And when he is made to ask for a kiss, thanks to Christian's crude desires, interjected in the cooing duet with an unpoetical rushing to the point that again almost threatens to unmask them both and spoil their game, so that Cyrano is forced to ward it off in vain, with outrageous quirks and conceits about a kiss being the rosy dot on the *i* of the verb *aimer,* are we to take this petty prettiness, . . . are we to take this burlesque as poetry meant to be genuinely admired? And, finally, when all these fopperies of verse have frittered themselves out to the purpose both of deterring and goading the deluded Roxane till she bids her gallant up to her to take the kiss she never would have given either one of the precious pair without the assistance of the other, and when the acute Cyrano is made to urge the obtuse Christian to climb up, with his "Get up, get up, *animal!*" are we to believe that the playwright did not choose this most appropriate epithet with malice prepense? In a word, is it really meant that we should be so naïve as to take such double-edged fooling as all this for unvarnished tenderness and fresh-born romance?

If so, and this spectacle-bouffe, circling about a nose as its sole dramatic *raison d' être,* is to be shorn of its irony, it will be left bare of any literary distinction worth mentioning. If it is to be considered as a serious dramatic or poetic work, it must be perceived that its structure is of the slightest and most casual. It has neither motive, progression nor climax, and but little of the most elementary surprise of situation—the general effect being rather that of light opera than of actual comedy. Its acts are not acts, but a succession of well-chosen, effective, spectacular stage-settings loosely incorporating a string of incidents linked together in the most external way. Its characters are not characters having any inherent individuality or capacity

for development, or any relationships with one another save of the most accidental sort. Its poetry, as to either imagery or emotional power, is only far-fetched and superficial. . . . If, on the other hand, it makes no pretension to high art, but rather to art semi-cynical, all these defects as to depth become effective; on that lower plane its buffoonery gains sparkle and significance. (pp. 120-22)

[Instead] of being hailed as this play has been by certain old-fashioned critics as a palpable evidence of the departure of what they call, with reproach, modern "Realism" and the rebirth of the good old "Romanticism" to smother the world in cakes and ale, and crowd out all new æsthetic forces forever, it is rather a token of the shutting of the door of modern life upon a certain phase of Romanticism, as henceforth impossible to be enjoyed quite in the old-world mood or without the assistance of a cultured historic sense—such a sign of the natural close of an epoch in literature and life as 'Don Quixote' was of the close of the epoch of the dominance of chivalry in life and in literature. (p. 123)

> *"'Cyrano de Bergerac': What It Is and Is Not,"* in Poet Lore *(copyright, 1899, by Poet Lore, Inc.), Vol. XI, No. 1, Winter, 1899, pp. 118-24.*

VIRGINIA M. CRAWFORD (essay date 1899)

[Cyrano de Bergerac] is, in a sense, a recapitulation of everything that has inspired the French stage from its first inception; it has affinities with the work of every playwright from Corneille to the elder Dumas. . . . With the plot every one is familiar. It rests on an antithesis—on the nobility of Cyrano's soul contrasted with the plainness of his person, on the delicacy of his passion counterbalanced by the abnormal length of his nose. Even here M. Rostand cannot claim to originality of conception, for in making use of startling contradictions in the character of his hero as the pivot of his drama he is merely following in the footsteps of Victor Hugo.

From the very outset of the play it becomes clear that the spectator has been borne aloft into the realms of etherealised romance. The piece is rightly described as a heroic comedy, for its marks the very acme of the sentimental heroism of the early years of the seventeenth century. . . . [Nothing] could be more noble and beautiful, nothing more *attendrissant* than Cyrano's love for his cousin Roxane. It seems brutal to suggest that a little honest common-sense could have put an end, at a stroke, to the heartrending situation, and that Cyrano and his cousin might have enjoyed fourteen years of conjugal happiness with a perfectly clear conscience. For then we should have lost the dying Alexandrines, and the final wave of *mon panache,* in which the artificial *motif* of the drama finds its supreme expression. (pp. 32-4)

The whole *motif* of the play is to me radically false, and consequently lacking in any permanent interest. Yet it were unfair to deny that Rostand himself has realised the complex character of his hero thoroughly, and has drawn him in vigorous and unmistakable lines. His heroism may frequently verge on the ridiculous; but, at least, he is a personage of flesh and blood. . . . To conclude, however, from the definiteness with which Cyrano stands before us, that the author can lay claim to skill as a delineator of character, would be a very grave mistake. There is no characterisation in any of M. Rostand's earlier work; and putting aside Cyrano, there is none in the play by which he has made his reputation. . . . [Amid] the din and the bustle and the fighting which make up the first four acts of the comedy, there is neither time nor space for gazing into the human soul, for penetrating the mysteries of the human heart. M. Rostand has not attempted the task; all his energies have been concentrated on the outward adornment of his central figure.

Yet in spite of this very serious lack, M. Rostand possesses many qualifications for writing a play of the type of *Cyrano de Bergerac,* steeped as it is in seventeenth century romanticism. For the first time his talents have full scope, and his very defects are not without their value. M. Rostand is not a great poet; there is not a line that will live either in *La Princesse Lointaine* or in *La Samaritaine.* But he possesses in a high degree a capacity for facile versification, the talent for expressing anything and everything in rhyme. He is full of buoyant spirits; he has the southern gift for florid expansiveness of expression. . . . The characters positively chatter in twelve-syllable verse. As a poet he has always been tinged with 'preciosity'—in *La Samaritaine* it jars upon the reader almost in every line—but in the present instance to be 'precious' in his choice of language is to be in harmony with his subject. His ingenious conceits and exaggerated metaphors . . . run riot on every page. Cyrano's famous tirade to de Guiche on his own nose is a *tour de force* in audacious repartee and long-drawn-out humour, which entitles the author to a foremost place as a writer—not of poetry—but of mock heroics. . . . But when we come to the passages in the play on which M. Rostand's claims as a serious poet would naturally rest—the dying lines spoken by Cyrano, the long-drawn-out balcony episode, the last scene between Roxane and de Neuvillette on the battle-field—the artificiality both of sentiment and language excludes the author from any right to a place in the front rank. I fail to discern either depth, or grandeur, or passion in his verse. (pp. 34-9)

[Is *Cyrano de Bergerac*] of the literature that will live permanently in the history of a nation? Here, I think, the answer is in the negative. . . . I believe that to a future generation . . . the plays of M. Rostand in France, will be interesting, not as illustrative of the Art of the century, but as exemplifying the fascination exercised over the public mind by those who have the good fortune to interpret the transitory emotions of their time and their country. (pp. 47-8)

> *Virginia M. Crawford, "'Cyrano de Bergerac'," in her* Studies in Foreign Literature, *Duckworth and Co., 1899, pp. 27-48.*

THE EDINBURGH REVIEW   (essay date 1900)

['**La Samaritaine**'] is an extraordinarily interesting example of the working of the dramatic instinct about an old and worn theme. There is, perhaps, some far-off echo of Russian mysticism, some reminiscence of the humble, ardent, *illuminated* heroines of Tolstoy and of Dostoëvsky, in M. Rostand's conception of Photine; at moments in her impassioned and pathetic faith we seem to hear speaking the mystical sister of the Sonia of 'Crime and Punishment,' but with what a distinguishing sense of beauty has he not marked as his own, and rescued even the most hazardous passages of his work! That a few— a very few—of his verses should seem to our ears to border perilously upon the irreverently grotesque and the ridiculous was inevitable, considering his theme. . . . But, apart from these slight incongruities, how admirable is the handling of '**La Samaritaine**'. With what precision is the situation put before us! Done with how few words, and yet how definitely, is the characterisation of the individual disciples; the arch-priest;

the merchants; how swiftly and unconsciously we find ourselves informed of the political situation, the warring interests, all the complicated policy of the little inconspicuous mountain town! (pp. 311-12)

[The] student interested in our author's methods should not fail to note how, in this early work, we find all the leading characteristics of his later and more ambitious writings. The construction, the peculiar breaking-up of his verse, are already here. The long scenes during which a single word is repeated and reiterated with ever-increasing effect have already been invented. . . . This deliberate insistence upon the culminative value of a single word—a mere exclamation—struck upon again and again, as upon a bell, by the same actor, and under circumstances which change before the spectator's eyes, is a very striking example of M. Rostand's admirable stage-craft. . . . His verse is of a consistent and really amazing flexibility. We know of nothing like it. In his hands the old, classic, buck-rammed alexandrine of Corneille or Racine has become fluent, epigrammatic, and supple as the most fluid prose. It is not too much to say that he delights in difficulty; he plays with technical problems, and invents complications only to solve them with a light heart. For scene after scene he limits his actors' 'lines' to speeches of two, three, half a dozen, words. He breaks his verse into fragments, which he polishes until they scintillate like diamond dust; until it requires an effort of the hearer's memory to realise that this flashing, hurrying sword-play of dialogue is yet submitted to all the stringent rules and conditions of poetic composition. Never since Victor Hugo wrote 'Les Misérables' has the French language given us such an example of astonishing abundance of words, of wit, of dexterity, and of richness of epithet. It is well-nigh a debauch of epithet. . . . It would be almost impossible to conceive anything more apparently easy and untrammelled, or to find anything which, on examination, showed more evidence of a scrupulous art. . . . [And yet] it is precisely in this exuberant mastery of his material, in this richness of invention, in the extraordinary *vision* that he has of the remotest dramatic possibilities of any incident, that Rostand's danger lies.

This is not the case in '**La Princesse Lointaine**'—that latest version of the story of Rudel and the Lady of Tripoli—which is, to us, the most daring, as it is the most perfect, of M. Rostand's experiments. (pp. 313-14)

In '**La Princesse Lointaine**' M. Rostand seems to us to touch the high-water mark of his literary achievement. In '**Cyrano de Bergerac**,' the best known of his plays, and the first to be translated into English, it is possible already to foresee how his manner of composition may, unless he be aware and watchful, decline into mannerism. All the opening scenes of '**Cyrano**' are more intelligible to read than to see acted. . . . [To] say of '**Cyrano**' that it is too elaborate is like objecting to some vigorous forest tree that its leafage is confusing. And the comparison holds good on this point—that '**Cyrano de Bergerac**' is as structural and organic as a noble tree. In France, it is necessary to go back to Molière and to Beaumarchais to find anything of equal dramatic fulness of conception, of equal reach and lightness of touch. (pp. 316-17)

M. Rostand has not lacked for candid critics. They reproach him with being abundant—superabundant, they call it; of at times losing sense and grasp of the body of his dramatic action in the multiplicity, the ingeniousness of its turns and twists and windings. This is undoubtedly the threatening fault of his quality; it is only fair to remember this; but it is wise to remind ourselves that the quality is there as well as the fault. . . .

Certainly, to look at the mere enumeration of the persons of the play in a drama like **'Cyrano,'** to recount the famous fifty-eight speaking 'parts,' and to reperuse the catalogue of the author's stage directions . . . may well give one a tingling sense of intellectual richness and adventure. And observe that these characters, even the smallest of them, are there for a purpose; are created and responsible. At his best, M. Rostand gives us to a singular degree the sensation of that capacity to see and handle a crowd which only belongs to the highest type of creative vision. We feel that, were he interested in their coming, a score or a hundred more figures could troop upon his stage through the open doors and from the great hospitable antechambers of his imagination. (pp. 317-18)

Essentially a romantic by temperament, it is [M. Rostand's] distinction that his treatment of his material is always classic treatment. He feels, and he obeys the rules. How far he has solved the great problem of writing plays alive and imbued with the literary spirit, which yet are primarily acting plays for us; remains to be seen. (p. 320)

> *"M. Edmond Rostand and the Literary Prospects of the Drama,"* in The Edinburgh Review, *Vol. CXCI, No. CCCXCIV, October, 1900, pp. 307-21.*

HENRY JAMES (essay date 1901)

If there be a quality of M. Rostand's own idiom, the bristling bravery of his verse, the general frolic of his vocabulary, especially under the happy crack of the whip of rhyme, it is that, surely, of resisting simplification to the death. . . .

The explanation, the solution of everything, and, with this, the supreme sign of our author, is just that he is inordinately romantic. . . . The edge of M. Rostand's gift is sharp and hard, and breaks short off; its connections are, so to speak, all within it, only deepening the glitter. So far as he has given us his measure, he hangs, in other words, thoroughly together: he offers us our finest, freshest occasion for studying the possibilities, for watching the development, of the temperament at its best. (p. 439)

He lays [romance] on thick, and gives it a splendid polish; the work he has hitherto done shines and twinkles with it in his clear morning of youth. We are infinitely amused, we are well-nigh dazzled, by the show; we are so drawn and beguiled that we ask ourselves, with appetite, with curiosity, how much more of the sovereign compound, so lavishly spent, he still has on hand—together with other wonderments as to how it will wear and "wash," how far it will go, what may be its further connections with life. I may seem, with all this, to be taking our author very hard; but, obviously, if such questions are interesting at all, they are interesting with intensity; and I can only, personally, confess to positive suspense as to what will absolutely *become* of the potent principle under the particular impetus he has given and will presumably again give it. As no one, anywhere, has recently expressed it with anything like his art, the case, one must repeat, is practically in his hands; they carry Cæsar and his fortunes. But whither? (p. 440)

["**Les Romanesques**" is] as charming an examination of the nature of the romantic, as pleasant a contribution to any discussion, as can be imagined. The small action takes place in that happy land of nowhere—the land of poetry, comedy, drollery, delicacy, profuse literary association—which the French theatre has so often and so enviably—notably with Alfred de Musset, unsurpassed for the right touch—made its hunting-ground; and if the whole thing is the frankest of fantasies, an excursion into the *pays bleu*, it is the work of a man already conscious of all the values involved. Percinet and Sylvette love each other over the garden wall because they believe in the ferocious mutual enmity of their respective fathers—a situation that makes their snatched and stolen interviews dangerous and wonderful. Their resemblance to Romeo and Juliet is complete, and their appetite for such developments as shall recall the fortunes of the immortal pair constant and exalted. . . . The thing is really too much made up of ribbons and flowers, of masks and mantles, to be rehandled, with whatever fingertips; but we note as its especial charm the ease with which the author's fancy moves in his rococo world.

This it is that in each of his productions makes M. Rostand so enviable, because it makes him, apparently at least, so happy; his rococo world spreads about him in an extraordinarily furnished and appointed, painted and gilded way, and he shows it to us as the master of the house shows the state apartments, knowing their order and relation and name, guiding us among crowded objects and "up" in their history and quality. (pp. 440-41)

[The romantic in "**La Princesse Lointaine**"], instead of being in any degree mocked at or "given away," is taken for granted in all its length and breadth. It is exactly the play in which Percinet and Sylvette themselves would have found their ideal. The poetic picture, as in "**Les Romanesques**," as in "**Cyrano**," is a thing all of consistent tone—tone ever so adroitly arrived at and artfully sustained. M. Rostand knows the special preparation in which his subject must steep itself, as a musical ear knows shades of sound and properties of time, and he can take every sort of liberty of form, of rhyme, of reference, without fear of taking any with the essence. (p. 441)

The finest thing in "**La Princesse Lointaine**"—as also the finest in "**Cyrano**"—is the author's gallantry under fire of the extravagance involved in his subject; as to which, in each instance—and not less, in fact, in "**L'Aiglon**"—we can easily see that it would have been fatal to him to be timid. The pathos, the poetry, or the successive situations, move arm-in-arm with their latent absurdity—the too-much that keeps rising to the brim and that would easily overflow at a wrong touch; and I find a charm the more, I confess, in the dramatist's affinity with such dangers. . . . If his spirit requires, for exhilaration, the acrobatic tight-rope, we are willing enough to sit and watch, it being the acrobatic tight-rope, exactly, that he stretches from one end of each of his productions to the other. The tight-rope in "**La Princesse**" is the high fantasy of the common upliftedness between the distant lady and the dying pilgrim, who *have never met*, over their penetrating relation all the more that their failure to meet is prolonged, is represented, through a large part of the play, and that the amount of communication that might have served instead has been of the slightest. The tight-rope in "**Cyrano**" is, visibly enough, the question of the hero's facial misfortune, doubly great as opposed to his grand imagination, grand manners, and grand soul, the soul that leads his boisterous personality to run riot, for love and for friendship, in self-suppression, in sentimental suicide. The tight-rope in "**L'Aiglon**" is—well, what is it? One is tempted to say that it is simply everything. It is in particular, we surmise, just the challenged, the accepted peril of dealing scenically with the subject at all, and especially of dealing with it on the scale required; the subject being essentially that of the *attitude*, imposed, fixed, of the hapless young man—a young man whose main mark it is that mere attitude is his only life, that anything like action is forbidden him. The rope is here thus stretched higher and tighter than elsewhere; it becomes, in its appeal to the author's agility, a veritable trapeze. For I mean, emphatically, that the extravagant—that extravagant in which, for M. Rostand, the romantic mainly resides—is all there. (pp. 442-43)

Dazzling as [Rostand's] command of the fantastic, both in humor and in pathos, makes him, I confess I am struck with the amount of poetry that he has fairly succeeded in saving from the consequences of his adventure. His freely figurative, his boldly maccaronic style, his verbal gymnastics and pictorial somersaults, his general romp through the unexpected—which is largely his hunt for rhyme through not only the past and present but the future of the language—all represent the elements of toughness and good humor required for so much exposure and such a pitch of reverberation. (p. 444)

I wouldn't, individually, part with an inch of Cyrano's nose. Too much is involved, too much for premature protest, in all the author has made depend on it—more for fame and fortune than ever depended on a nose before. The value of it in the plan, naturally, is that it is liberally symbolic—that it stands for the evil star in the wider sense, the whole body and office of natural affliction on the part of the afflicted. Cyrano is one of the worst afflicted; his nose happens to be only the accident; he might have been displeasing in some other way, for there are but too many ways; and the poet happily caught at the drama that would reside in his being *most* formed to suffer. There we get immediately the romantic formula, the short cut of antithesis, the vital spark, for a conspicuous example, of the theatre of Victor Hugo. The antithesis is a short cut because it ignores shades and lives on high contrasts. Differences are simply successions of shades; but shades are thus transitions and links; and, transitions and links being comparatively quiet things, the deep joy of the close observer, the romantic effect will have none of them. This is what makes one extreme seek another—what made M. Rostand intensely see that his afflicted person should be in every other respect his most showily organized. Cyrano, for a romantic use, had not only to be sensitive, to be conscious, but to be magnificent and imperial; and the brilliancy of the creation is in the author's expression of this.

That is the romantic formula, which obviously deals in a different poetry from the poetry of the "quiet," and which is extremely dependent for success on a certain aggressiveness of style. M. Rostand's vehicle is half his victory: it performs such prodigies on its own account—by which I mean is so perpetually ingenious and amusing that we never quite focus, nor even want to, what he asks us to accept as his human truth. . . . The end is properly as romantic as the beginning and the middle, the perfect art of romance being that it shall, at every point, surpass itself. . . . It is not that M. Rostand's verse has, precisely, wings—these are rather what, considering its quantity of movement, it lacks; but it has legs of abnormal agility, legs that fly about in a manner to forbid our calling it pedestrian. Eloquence can go on legs as well as on wings—perhaps, in fact, better; and our author is easily and admirably eloquent. (pp. 445-46)

Henry James, "Edmond Rostand," in The Critic *(© The Critic 1901), Vol. 29, No. 5, November, 1901, pp. 437-50.*

MAX BEERBOHM (essay date 1901)

Were we Frenchmen, probably we should enjoy **"L'Aiglon"** very much. For this probability there are two reasons. Firstly,

Frenchmen can listen with pleasure to reams of rhetoric in theatres. If the rhetoric be good in itself, they care not at all whether it be or be not dramatically to the point. Secondly, Frenchmen have an enthusiastic cult for Napoleon. Now, **"L'Aiglon"** is composed chiefly of reams of excellent but irrelevant rhetoric about Napoleon, and reams of details about him. Little wonder, then, that Paris took kindly to it. But how should London follow suit? Unless it be dramatic, rhetoric, however good, bores us: such is our fallen nature. (pp. 151-52)

Big plays must have themes proportionally big; and, since for us the little Duc is not merely the ostensible theme but also the actual theme, **"L'Aiglon"** wearies us beyond measure. Had M. Rostand curtailed his play by (say) one half, we could delight in it. In a play written to last from (say) nine to eleven o'clock, the little Duc, so tenderly delineated by M. Rostand (yes! the excuse has been concocted very elaborately), would throughout hold our sympathies. But from eight o'clock to midnight! In a play of such vast structure, with a cast of more than fifty persons! The little Duc fades, evaporates, under such tremendous pressure. He becomes simply a little bore, whose oxymoronically belated-premature death we hail (if we have not already hailed a hansom and been driven home to well-earned rest) as a merciful release for all concerned in his brief-inordinate life. . . . To the pretty little heart of M. Rostand's Duc we are quite indifferent by reason of the enormous circumstances in which it is shown to us. To M. Rostand's technical skill in handling enormous circumstances we are quite indifferent because there is no reason why they should be handled here at all. . . . From five acts of him Heaven defend us! (pp. 153-54)

Max Beerbohm, "The Tame Eaglet" (1901), in his Around Theatres *(reprinted by permission of Mrs. Eva Reichmann), Rupert Hart-Davis, 1953, pp. 151-54.*

EDWARD EVERETT HALE, JR. (essay date 1911)

In M. Rostand's first work for the stage, **"Les Romanesques,"** he was surely attractive, but not very much more. A writer who thinks that in that charming little play we have M. Rostand "tout entier" . . . seems to miss so much suggested by the later plays. . . . **"Les Romanesques"** is not what might be expected of the author of **"Cyrano de Bergerac."** Not because it is slight, nor because it is little more than attractive, but because it is a delicate satire upon the tribe of romancers in general. (pp. 16-17)

M. Rostand's great triumph was in romance. Is it to be said that to begin with a burlesque on romance and to succeed with a romantic triumph shows a lack of sincerity?

That is not just the way to put it. Men do not often jest at what they deem great. But they do jest (and often very bitterly, as Rostand does not) at the world's perversions of what they deem great. Rostand believes in romance, let us say, but he has his laugh at the romancers. (pp. 17-18)

[The] Realists and the Naturalists . . . had laughed at the old romance and its costumes and properties, its phrases and attitudes. They themselves presented truth. Now Rostand is by no means a naturalist, still he loves truth, only he would present truth differently: the realists presented truth by its ever-varying myriad circumstance, Rostand would present it by its essence, its idea, its type. Hence **"La Princesse Lointaine."** . . .

In **"La Princesse Lointaine"** we have the idealist, the ultra-romantic Rudel, faithful to the very door of death to the Princess whom he has never seen. But we also have the Princess, too, and she is not faithful. She fondles the idea of an absent lover devoted to her image, and when she hears from the redoubtable Bertrand that her lover is at hand sick to death, awaiting her on his mattress laid on deck, she will not go to him. And why? (p. 19)

[It] is not really the contrast of the visionary love and the haggard fact that moves her. It is the contrast between the imaginary love and the actuality of the passion that she feels for the messenger. Sorismonde tells her that she passes from a dream into real life. She says herself that she denies the pale flower of the dream for the flower of love. But when the experiment is made it appears that the flower of love, that the actuality of life, has been bought at too high a price, that there was something even more real in the imagination, in the dream, in the romance. (p. 20)

There is much that is beautiful in **"La Princesse Lointaine."** The indomitable hero, the faithful sailors, the audacious quest, the intensity of the moment of action, and a very exquisite reconciliation to the tragic end remain in one's mind and may well outweigh a lightness and over-refinement of handling. (p. 21)

Cyrano de Bergerac is, and will remain, one of the great figures which the French literature of our time offers the world. (p. 22)

Cyrano might, by an enemy, be called a bully and a braggart, but that possibility is quite lost in our general sympathy. We do not think of that any more than of his nose; we feel only that he is a noble figure. (pp. 24-5)

Cyrano is in fact a type—a type of the largest class of people in the world (for it includes every one), namely those who do not get what they know they deserve, who find no chance to do what they know they could do, who are so much greater to themselves than to the cold world. He is also the type of a much smaller class who do not make a fuss about the matter, but carry it all off so gaily and finely that no one has any consciousness of complaint, murmuring, repining. (p. 28)

[With the appearance of **"L'Aiglon,"** many] thought that M. Rostand had bettered his masterpiece. This tragedy, with its poor, weak little hero, with all its frivolity, all its decadent circumstance, made a stronger effect than its wonderful predecessor—stronger, if less obvious.

As before, we have under very special conditions a figure of general appeal. (pp. 30-1)

M. Rostand is not merely a Romanticist in the sense that he gives us rattling sword-and-mantle plays, in which things happen, according to the saying of the day. He is that sort of neo-Romanticist whose figures are types—a romancer, we may think, of the school of Hawthorne. And his figures generally typify the same thing. (p. 32)

"Chantecler," though taken as a whole it was not so fine a piece nor so great a success as its two great predecessors, was certainly a play of very great beauty. In some respects it was extravagant, and it was not so readily suited to the stage, but in other ways it was easily superior. It may be doubted whether the judgment of time will not pronounce it Rostand's greatest play.

It would appear at first that no poetry and no significance could render tolerable a play in which all the actors strove to give the appearance of birds. . . . What possibilities of sympathy, tenderness, love could there be in the relations of a man dressed as a cock and a lady clad as a golden pheasant? (pp. 38-9)

[Rostand's] cocks and pheasants, his blackbird and watchdog, his ducks, bees, frogs, owls, nightingale, are as in the fable types of humanity and his play presents forms and phases of human life. And here he has the fabulist's advantage, namely, that having merely the typical forms,—the simple-hearted, beautiful poet, the wild gipsy of the woods,—he can keep his attention close to the main idea without being diverted to personalities and circumstances. . . . Chantecler himself is felt first and last to be the poet who rejoices in the influence of his song, the pheasant hen is the eternal feminine who has at this moment acquired the brilliant garb of the male, the blackbird in the cage is the satirical cynical man of the world, the dog is the rough and faithful friend, the guinea-hen is the fussy, empty-headed woman of society, and so on. Each figure bears its part in the general extravagance, but each is also an element in the fable of the Poet and the world.

Here Rostand shows himself to be an interpreter of life as well as a poet. . . . At least he presents a man who believes that the world is called to life by his song. Through all temptations—the attacks of the world, the assaults of love—he remains true to his conviction. Finally tempted out of himself by a beauty beyond what he has himself dreamed, he finds that in his own forgetfulness of his mission the world has gone on its own way without his help. What he thought was Life responding to his song, appears to have been a course of events rising from other, far greater causes. (pp. 40-2)

It is in this situation that Rostand shows himself somewhat different from the dramatist of **"Cyrano"** and **"L'Aiglon."** So far as power and poetry are concerned the three plays are on the same plane. Probably the superiority in beauty and brilliancy will in time, if it be not already, be awarded to **"Cyrano de Bergerac."** But **"Cyrano,"** as well as **"L'Aiglon,"** suffers . . . from a sort of inconclusive character. . . . Chantecler is at the end finer than at the beginning. Like Cyrano he is brought to see that the ideal cannot conquer the world at a stroke, like the Duc de Reichstadt before the mirror he sees that he is not to be the master of the world. But Cyrano passes quickly out of the world of achievement, and the unhappy Duke is broken if not bent. Chantecler is neither. If at first his ideal was overweening, there is still something for him to do. The last we hear of him is a victorious "Cocorico," as he goes back from the seclusion of the forest to the realisms of his little world. (p. 43)

Edward Everett Hale, Jr., "Rostand," in his Dramatists of Today: Rostand, Hauptmann, Sudermann, Pinero, Shaw, Phillips, Maeterlinck, *revised edition, Henry Holt and Company, 1911, pp. 12-43.*

G. JEAN-AUBRY (essay date 1919)

Apart from *La Samaritain,* which was, so to speak, a work the writing of which depended on circumstances, there are three distinct periods in the works of Rostand: that of his début, ignored with *Le Gant Rouge* and recognised with *Les Romanesques,* that of his recognition (I mean by this literary recognition and not merely dramatic success) with *La Princesse Lointaine, Cyrano,* and certain parts of *L'Aiglon;* and that of his decadence, with *L'Aiglon* as a whole and *Chantecler,* in spite of certain qualities in this last work. (p. 125)

In studying *Les Romanesques* there will be found in it the germ of all that is best and least good in Rostand; a very great technical cleverness, a facility for making his personages live and move, a tendency to complicate the simplest situations by play of words, and a real charm and address in making his rhymes "sing," rendering them turn by turn suave or piercing. Already he writes verses that are supple, natural, unforced, and others that are tortured and wrung out with difficulty; at moments he shows himself in possession of his *métier* to such a degree as to discourage any poetical aspirant, and at others he is capable of inconceivable negligences. He can be touching, pleasing, and show himself in possession of measure and the rarest tact, and then turns his back on all, losing his treasures in dullness and passing from the most exquisite style to the most insane or to none at all. Rostand is a mass of such contrasts which exist already in *Les Romanesques,* just as in the portraits of Sylvette is to be found the sketch of Roxane and all those touches of preciosity which are to appear almost without relief, not only in Roxane, but in all the characters of *La Samaritaine,* of *La Princesse Lointaine,* in Marie-Louise in *L'Aiglon,* and in the Guinea Fowl and the Pheasant in *Chantecler.* These are Rostand's "eternal feminine," romantic, seductive, cultivated to excess, superficial, *coquette* to such a point that sometimes one is doubtful she has a soul, an apparition rather than a real human being, for the whole charm of these women lies in their grace and manners, in the elegance of their dresses, and their language. But their hearts are hard. . . . (pp. 125-26)

As Sylvette is the forerunner of Roxane, so Straforel in *Les Romanesques* is the forerunner of Cyrano. If Rostand has only one feminine figure in his plays, perhaps also he has only one man, but this man, it must be admitted, certainly lives.

Straforel will also be found more or less in Jeofroy Rudel in *La Princesse Lointaine,* but in full strength in *Cyrano;* we meet him somewhat attenuated in *L'Aiglon,* in which play he takes on turn by turn the character of the Duc de Reichstadt and that of Flambeau, and his last appearance as Chantecler. . . . [He] is, so to speak, the "grand premier" of the melodramas, the Don Quixote of the serial novel, the avenger of social wrongs, the protector of the widow and orphan, and the "everyday visionary," who, having adopted the resolution to do good for its own sake, maintains it almost without effort, attempting the impossible under the conviction that it is not more unreal than that which the crowd considers as real, and who, by dint of talking, creates the belief that he has acted. (pp. 126-27)

Rostand has found in *Cyrano* his veritable subject; he was a man of one idea, of one character, and before *Cyrano* he had been feeling his way little by little to his subject; after *Cyrano* he almost parodied himself, but in *Cyrano* he succeeded, for here his qualities and defects found their frame with a singular perfection. His taste for theatrical exaggeration, his sense of picturesque language and of the theatre, his inclination towards literary preciosity, have all been enabled to find place in this play, and his meridional exuberance of expression, in other places insupportable is, on the lips of Cyrano, amusing and even touching. (p. 128)

After *Cyrano* the falling-off sets in. Heroic failure, which was Rostand's favourite theme, and which he was to again adopt in *Chantecler,* could hardly find a better frame than in the Napoleonic legend dear to so many theatre-goers. Could Rostand have found a more moving figure than that of the King

of Rome become Duc de Reichstadt? But neither the frame nor the figure sufficed, and Rostand was wrong in believing that they would. A poet is not an historian, and Rostand had every right to take liberties with history (as he did in *Cyrano*) provided that he creates an impression of life, but in *L'Aiglon* himself he has unfortunately too much intermingled his two stock characters, the seduction of his woman, or rather of his woman's *dramatis persona,* and the lyrical effusion of his male characters. (p. 129)

There is little action in *L'Aiglon,* and unfortunately the poet has placed that little almost entirely in the third act. This act, it must be admitted, is amongst the best that Rostand ever wrote. . . . This act alone is perfect, but it seems as if in it Rostand exhausted the essence of his subject and that nothing remained for the others.

Rostand's extreme facility, even when using a cultivated and difficult vocabulary, tended already in *L'Aiglon* towards wordiness. This fault was accentuated in *Chantecler.* The theatrical and artificial qualities in *Cyrano* were legitimate, but in *Chantecler* artificiality reigns supreme; the author is witty, not in order to describe or emphasise, but merely to be witty; there is a continuous flow of puns and jests. (pp. 130-31)

In *Chantecler* one is conscious of the despairing efforts of an inspiration which seeks to keep itself alive, but no longer succeeds. What a tragedy when a writer finds a fine subject which he has no longer the strength to do justice to! (p. 132)

> *G. Jean-Aubry, "Edmond Rostand," in* The Fortnightly Review *(reprinted by permission of Contemporary Review Company Limited), n.s. Vol. CV, No. DCXXV, January 1, 1919, pp. 122-32.*

T. S. E[LIOT] (essay date 1919)

What is very rare in modern drama, either verse or prose, is the dramatic sense on the part of the characters in the play themselves. We are given plays of realism in which the parts are never allowed to be consciously dramatic, for fear, perhaps, of their appearing less real. But in actual life, or in those situations in our actual life which we enjoy consciously and keenly, we are, at times, aware of ourselves in this way, and these moments are of very great usefulness to dramatic verse. The employment of this dramatic self-consciousness on the part of the figures in the play is an important cause of the success, and of the merit, of Rostand as a dramatist. It gives his characters a vitality, a gusto in living, which is very uncommon on the modern stage. No doubt they play up to this public rôle too steadily; they often fail of any other existence than this in which they are aware of their own rôle. One is conscious of that in the love scenes of Cyrano in the garden, while in "Romeo and Juliet" the profounder or intenser poet shows his lovers melting into incoherent unconsciousness of their isolated selves, shows the human soul in the process of forgetting itself. Rostand could not do that; but the thing he could do he could do very well, and in the peculiar case of Cyrano on Noses the character, the situation, the occasion, were perfectly suited and combined. The tirade generated by this combination is not only genuinely and highly dramatic; it is possibly poetry also. If a writer is incapable of composing such a scene as this, he is probably incapable of composing a poetic drama.

"Cyrano" satisfies, at least as far as scenes like this can satisfy, the requirements for poetic drama. Poetic drama must take genuine and substantial human emotions, such emotions as observation can verify, typical emotions, and give them æsthetic form; the degree of abstraction reached is a question for the method of each writer separately. In Shakespeare the æsthetic form is determined in the unity of the whole, as well as in isolated scenes; it is something to attain this unity, as Rostand does, in scenes if not in the whole play. Not only as a dramatist, but as a writer of poetic drama, he is superior to Maeterlinck, whose drama, in failing to be dramatic, fails also to be poetic. Maeterlinck has a literary perception of the dramatic, and a literary perception of the poetic, and he joins the two components; but they are not, as sometimes in the work of Rostand, fused. His characters take no conscious delight in their dramatic-poetic rôle—they are sentimental; while Rostand's characters, enjoying awareness, are thereby preserved from sentimentality. The centre of gravity is in the expression of the emotion, not, as with Maeterlinck, in the emotion which cannot be expressed. Rostand is not afraid to be "rhetorical," because he believes that emotion can be expressed; unlike many modern writers, who sometimes disingenuously hide their emotions behind obscure simplicities, because they believe that they will gain in intensity by suppression. Perhaps the emotions are not significant enough to endure full daylight. Whatever the value of anything Rostand had to expose, at least he did not shrink from exposure. (pp. 665-66)

> *T. S. E[liot], "Whether Rostand Had Something about Him" (copyright Mrs. Valerie Eliot; reprinted by permission of Mrs. Valerie Eliot and Faber and Faber Limited), in The Athenaeum, No. 4656, July 25, 1919, pp. 665-66.*

HUGH ALLISON SMITH   (essay date 1925)

In the attempt to evaluate the qualities and permanent worth of Rostand's poetic drama . . . it is fairly clear that all the important problems of this investigation are to be found in one play, *Cyrano de Bergerac*. His other pieces are most significant in tracing the source and destination of evolutionary tendencies, in showing the final lapse of certain leanings, and in underlining and amplifying the more fundamental articles of the poet's faith and experience so as to make them stand out before our eyes as a coherent and fixed philosophy of life, but the summit of his achievement is *Cyrano*. To state the problems of Rostand's position, then, in French drama, one has only to consider *Cyrano;* to solve them, all of his plays are not too much. (p. 76)

[The] philosophy of love, placing its supreme merit and power in idealism and renunciation, is a fixed faith with Rostand and a corner stone of his dramas. (p. 79)

It is interesting to compare this philosophy with that of the early Romanticists, such as Musset. With them also, love is a supreme power, but their love is passion. . . . [In] Rostand it is etherealized into a pure ideal. (p. 80)

[*Cyrano de Bergerac*] is, first of all, a Romantic drama. If it had appeared a half-century earlier, its evolution and place in dramatic development would have seemed easy to fix—at first sight. (p. 93)

The Romantic elements of *Cyrano* are unmistakable. In it Rostand conforms to practically all the theory of the Romanticists—but he also excels most of them in practice.

One of the important features of Romantic drama was local color—in historic drama this color should be the evocation of

the spirit and atmosphere of the age represented. In this respect, the play is superior to any of the Romantic productions. . . . We are back in the seventeenth century, with its heroism and bombast . . . , with all the brave show of the most brilliant city, court and country of the epoch. And this color and history are not on the surface but come from the heart of the work. The plot of the play is made to depend on the preciosity, or super-refinement, of Roxane, and whether or not Rostand has brought to life the real historic Cyrano—a matter of absolutely no importance—he has placed him, as conceived, in the only atmosphere he could breathe and against a background that is both real and artistic. In doing this, he has much surpassed the usual Romantic practice. He does not choose some famous figure and deform it, as Hugo and Dumas often did, but he takes a comparatively obscure one and illuminates it, and at the same time lights up a whole page of interesting history. (pp. 94-5)

Cyrano is primarily a drama of elevated motives and this serious quality forms its lasting appeal. It is, above all, a play based on a single character and the chief motives of this character are honor, independence, and self-sacrifice, all factors of serious drama, and all most fundamental. (p. 95)

Cyrano's independence is as strongly drawn as his honor, with which, moreover, it is closely united. Also, it is this quality which gives him his chief dramatic strength and differentiates him absolutely from the traditional Romantic hero, who is the pawn of fate and events. (p. 96)

Cyrano's self-sacrifice in his love for Roxane is no less a motive in the drama [than his code of honor and independence] and furnishes occasion for most of the emotion of the play. . . . This sacrifice and the idealization of an impossible love . . . is a favorite theme with Rostand. (p. 97)

It is very largely the lyrical passages in *Cyrano* that should decide one of the most disputed questions in Rostand's poetry, his ability to evoke deep and sincere feeling, love or passion. No one denies him the gift to express graceful and agreeable sentiment and emotion, but it is often claimed that he does not have the deeper power. No doubt the highly etherealized and idealistic love that Rostand portrays by preference has contributed to form this opinion. Also, in *Cyrano* there is much intentional super-refinement. However, it is precisely in this play that Rostand has himself invited this test of his ability. In the well-known balcony scene, where Cyrano forgets Christian and speaks his own love to Roxane, the poet explicitly disavows, in sincere love, the elaboration of exquisite similes and highly alembicated sentiment. Here then, if anywhere, his words should express real feeling. (pp. 98-9)

[In the final act of *Cyrano*] where Rostand has thrown the idealistic net of time, of nature and of religion over the stage, to soften before our eyes the more cruel lines of grief and terror in this tragedy of sacrifice and death, we have an almost perfect piece of sustained dramatic artistry. The quiet of the convent, the religious music and the autumn setting combine perfectly in a scene that is thoroughly dramatic and always appropriate. Such little touches as that of the falling leaves, symbolizing the imminent death of Cyrano, fit perfectly into a harmonious whole. (pp. 100-01)

Cyrano is a consistent character, acting in every crisis in accordance with dominating motives, and coming to the end which we should expect the sum total of these qualities to produce. With his Quixotic honor, his keenly sensitive spirit of independence, which prevents his accepting the slightest favor or help, and with his exalted ideal of sacrifice, we anticipate his lack of worldly success, his death in poverty and his failure to win the woman he loves. Also, it is most important to note that in putting the real drama in the soul of Cyrano, developed by motives contained in this character, Rostand returns to the Classic practice initiated by Corneille of making drama interior, and creating dramatic heroes who are masters of their own fate. (pp. 101-02)

There is, to be sure, antithesis in Cyrano's character . . . but it is not the author's basic conception. It is not *because* Cyrano is a poetic genius that he is a failure; it is not *because* he is made grotesque by a large nose that he is a tender and spiritual lover. . . . Rostand has made him a poetic lover and a genuine hero, and has used his wit to keep sentiment from becoming sentimentality, and his sense of humor and irony to prevent Quixotic bravery from appearing as pure boasting and bravado. . . . And it is precisely this conception of the character of Cyrano that makes him most national and offers him the greatest promise of being immortal among French heroes. (p. 102)

Rostand's drama belongs to idealistic literature—the only kind exactly suited to verse. To this extent it does not deal with real life—or rather with everyday physical life, for it is just as real to think, to imagine, to have aspirations, ideals and enthusiasms as it is to eat, to make money, to marry and to be divorced. However, it is not Realistic literature in the accepted sense and hence it can not be judged entirely by realistic criterions. It is more proper to ask if it is artistic, beautiful, noble or poetic than it is to determine if it is practical, probable, typical or informative. (pp. 104-05)

In final analysis, Cyrano's philosophy is a practical one; it is moral contentment and riches. He does not give a code for material existence but he offers a moral philosophy that is complete, and that is not unaware of the struggle in what we call real life. The sadness of realism has touched this philosophy, and we see here the influence of Rostand's age. (pp. 105-06)

And this doctrine of moral contentment, in refusing to be carried away by the rage for material riches and worldly success, is not only practical, but is the only one that is in the reach of all. . . .

In Rostand is found the most recent prominent representative of poetic drama, and his work is clearly a development from the Romantic movement, and is perhaps its most perfect achievement. (p. 106)

> *Hugh Allison Smith, "Edmond Rostand," in his* Main Currents of Modern French Drama *(copyright © 1925 by Henry Holt and Company), Holt, 1925, pp. 76-106.*

JOSEPH CHIARI (essay date 1958)

Edmond Rostand is not a major writer, yet somehow he is an important one. His importance lies in the fact that he is not only a kind of reaction to symbolist poetry, but a combination of the two strains—idealism and realism—which at the end of the nineteenth century were contending for pre-eminence, and also the representative of a great tradition in French poetry, the tradition of rhetorical poetry. (p. 32)

Rostand's rhetoric is above all the rhetoric of a burlesque poet, a poet who is making fun of others, as well as of himself.

Although he is much less brilliant than either of them, his is the rhetoric of Pope or of Byron. . . .

Rostand's passions are thoroughly intellectual. They come not from the heart but from the head; they are not forces which can wrench the human soul as storms can wrench minds or trees, they are thought out, although at times mentally felt and expounded with great skill. We have here a kind of rhetoric of passions reminiscent of that of Corneille and sometimes very successful, for like Corneille—though not to the same degree—Rostand was a master of words. But he did not write, he never wrote with his whole being; he wrote from a divided or rather complex, non-integrated personality. If he shared in the romanticism of his time, his Attic salt, his Mediterranean scepticism prevented him from taking himself too seriously and from striking humourless poses. He has his limitations, and they are very great, for he did not have the supreme quality of the poet, imagination, which can make great poetry; but he had equilibrium, and a sound grasp of realities. When that equilibrium is broken, when the balance leans towards the tragic, as in *La Princesse lointaine* or in *La Samaritaine,* Rostand is at his worst, for he is not a tragic poet; but when, as in *Cyrano,* he can temper the most serious situation with self-criticism and laughter—which forestalls laughter at himself—he is at his best, and he achieves a kind of elevation quasi-unique in his genre in France and very reminiscent of Byron. (p. 34)

Rostand combines some of the technical skill of [Augustin] Scribe with some of the exuberance of language of Victor Hugo. Besides that, he is both a realist and an idealist. His idealism is akin to that of Victor Hugo; like him, he believes in violent contrasts and in the supremacy of the spiritual over the physical. . . . Like Victor Hugo, Rostand can unfold brilliant metaphors and coin striking antitheses, and even his most lyrical outbursts, such as Cyrano's words to Roxane in Act III, have that kind of rhetorical brilliance and verbal lusciousness which we find in Victor Hugo. There is no doubt that with regard to rhetoric and themes, Rostand is the most Hugoesque of contemporary French poets. (p. 36)

Rostand did not believe, as Hugo did, in imagination, and his wit springs from that loss of belief. Hugo believed in his visions, in his apocalyptic dreams; Rostand also could dream, but he knew that dreams could not be realized, and he resolved the contrasts between dreams and reality into mockery, as when Cyrano, in Act I scene V, confesses his love for Roxane to his friend Le Bret. . . . The whole scene, which oscillates between the sentimental dream and the dramatic self-mockery of the main character, is wholly integrated and shows the progressive creation of Cyrano's character.

That power to see himself as he really is, and to laugh instead of crying over what is unchangeable, gives the character a new dimension and increases his dramatic range; it is, if one wishes to call it so, a kind of humour, a quality which is wholly absent from the great romantics like Wordsworth, Shelley or Victor Hugo, who generally wrote on one single plane. . . . Cyrano believes in love but, man of the world as he is, distrusts feelings and fears that other men may laugh at him, so he forestalls them by laughing first. The important thing is that, however shallow Rostand's philosophy may be, he looks at experience not from one single vantage-point, as the great romantics generally did, but from various directions. He may lack depth, but he has complexity and range; he does not attempt to reach for a transcendental order, he deals with reality as he sees it, and Nature, when he describes it, has none of the immanence conferred upon it by Wordsworth or Victor Hugo. (pp. 37-9)

In spite of certain weaknesses, *Cyrano* is Rostand's major dramatic and poetic achievement. Rostand has often enough been dismissed as a mere writer of verse, or a kind of rhetorical poet who was not in fact a poet. Such opinions seem to me to imply a very narrow view of poetry. Granted, Rostand's poetry is different in quality and in degree from that of Shakespeare or Coleridge, or from that of Racine or Baudelaire; still, there are surely various kinds of poetry which can range from that of Shakespeare to that of Rostand.

Cyrano is a heroic comedy in verse, and therefore we cannot expect to find in it the kind of revelatory poetry which we find in *Othello, King Lear* or *Phèdre.* The aims of the poet are here very limited, but they are clear; he does not attempt to confront us with unsolved mysteries, but with the everyday dualism of human nature within definitely human situations. (pp. 40-1)

> Joseph Chiari, "Edmond Rostand," in his The Contemporary French Theatre: The Flight from Naturalism (© 1958 by Joseph Chiari; reprinted by permission of the author), Rockliff, 1958, pp. 32-46.

ALBA della FAZIA AMOIA   (essay date 1978)

Rostand's collections of poetry reflect three definite periods in his life: his unperturbed childhood and adolescence *(Les Musardises),* his "classical" period *(The Canticle of the Wing),* and the war years with their accompanying hardship and horror *(The Flight of the Marseillaise).* (p. 22)

In the first part [of *Les Musardises*] ("**The Student's Room**"), the poems most worthy of note are the three dedicated to Pif Luisant, an ugly and grotesque figure to behold, but possessed of a beautiful and noble soul. Pif was the monitor at Rostand's school in Paris. . . . [Pif was a poet] and the protector of the young, budding poet Edmond—which made them fast friends. Moreover, Pif openly defied standard society. He refused to conform, and in him Rostand found the symbol of his protest against all that is mediocre and vulgar. In the dreamer Pif, whose poetic language captivated the young Edmond, Rostand recognized his true master. (pp. 22-3)

Pif was a failure in life, but a source of inspiration to other poets. The dedicatory poem which opens *Les Musardises* is, in fact, Rostand's declaration of love for "les ratés" (failures in life), whom the public scorns and insults because it cannot understand the dreams and ideals of the great poet's struggle for beauty and perfection. (p. 24)

The second part of *Les Musardises,* entitled "**Uncertainties,**" contains a large number of poems revealing Rostand's introversion and melancholy. Inveighing against lethargy, insisting that we must *will* to be constantly active, the poet nevertheless falls occasionally into a state of boredom and passivity. (p. 26)

"**Home in the Pyrenees,**" the third part of *Les Musardises,* takes us back to the poet's childhood, to the happy days spent at the family's vacation home in Cambo—a place of study, music, mystery, and love. (p. 27)

Rostand's deep, almost religious sensitivity to nature is best revealed in this collection of poems. (p. 28)

Les Musardises contains a certain number of poems worthy of recommendation, especially those containing nature descriptions, but the collection falls far short of *The Canticle of the Wing,* published twenty years later.

The Canticle of the Wing is Rostand's best collection of verses, and contains the poem that may be considered the key to his versification technique. . . . (p. 30)

The five long poems concluding *The Canticle of the Wing* are far superior to the other poems in the collection, and offer the best examples of the poet's verbal alchemy. Rostand was in love with words, with each letter in each word. On them, he performed delicate vivisections to know and love them better. "Words" . . . is a long poem divided into nine parts. The first three parts contain the image of a closet—a sort of Pandora's box—in which are locked all the words of all books that have ever been printed. An uprising takes place in the closet, and we hear the complaints and sobs of the personified words, who are suffering on the page where assassinations, massacres, and other cruel acts are described. . . . The fourth part of the poem dwells on the double esthetic of words: sight and sound. Words are beautiful on the printed page as well as falling from lips, and their two forms of beauty are inseparable. . . . The fifth part groups the "ugly duckling" words, who speak out to protest orthographic changes imposed on them, which mar their beauty. . . . The sixth part, on the other hand, groups words which demonstrate the imperturbable artistry of their composition. . . . In the seventh and eighth parts, language "reform" is protested by words who see themselves transformed into monsters and pygmies, and sense that their end is approaching. . . . (pp. 32-3)

The last scene sees the poet waking from his nightmare, running to the closet, relieved to see that all his words are still there. The poem ends in an exalted declaration of love by Rostand for all French words, wherever they may be. (p. 33)

The weakest of the three collections of Rostand's poetry [is] *The Flight of the Marseillaise.* (p. 37)

The various poems in the collection contain numerous personifications of La Marseillaise (France) which never seem to take flight because they are encumbered by a plethora of literary, mythological, and historic names and references. Bitterly protesting the war, firmly asserting Franco-German incommunicability, and deploring his own sense of despair, Rostand overreacts by singing France's praises too loudly. (pp. 37-8)

On the positive side, *The Flight of the Marseillaise* must be appreciated for its poems in praise of action, for the expressions of Rostand's compassion for the families of soldiers missing in action, and his humanitarian reactions to the cold newspaper announcements of the horrors perpetrated during the years 1914-1918. He heaps shame on the coward and bestows nobility on the humblest foot soldier. The suffering of others becomes his own, and acts of courage fill him with justified pride.

On the whole, however, *The Flight of the Marseillaise* does not succeed in rising above mediocrity to the desired poetic heights, and the increasing irrelevancy of patriotism in our times has assigned it an unhappy destiny. (p. 38)

[*Cyrano of Bergerac*] is an heroic comedy, which is very close to tragedy. (p. 67)

Cyrano may be considered first as an able and clever man with a temperament that, once aroused, can manifest itself sweetly and paternally—but only in intimacy or in a deeply sincere relationship. Usually he is extremely violent. The most important external aspect of his character is the cult of the gesture, of which there are two kinds. First, there is the splendid gesture, the theatrical gesture, the execution of a duel while composing an improvised ballad, or marching at the head of a motley procession to fight single-handed against one hundred men. These are bravuras inspired by Cyrano's grotesque external appearance, but he executes them because he is full of life, energy and goodness—and is timid inside. He is a poet and a creator, but he senses his own ugliness and has lost his love for his own life. This explains the splendor of his verses. (p. 68)

In addition to the splendid gestures, there are Cyrano's heroic gestures, which render his soul so noble and great: the letters he writes for Roxane on behalf of Christian; the balcony scene, in which he directs the unfolding of the lovers' exchange all for his friend's benefit. These magnanimous gestures are so much more beautiful than the others because they are completely gratuitous. They are born of Cyrano's own personal pride and of his heroism. (p. 69)

In the heroic gesture may be seen the tragedy of the man of genius: Cyrano is a poet, a philosopher, an indomitable fencer and an idealist; but he is not successful *because* he is heroic, *because* he is idealistic, and *because* he fears ridicule. . . . The genuine Cyrano is the Cyrano of the *panache*. He desires to be "admirable in all"—and only for his own satisfaction. This is the explanation of his profound sincerity. Even though he may reiterate many times that it is beauty which he loves, Cyrano loves sincerity and courage above all. (p. 72)

As for Roxane, she is affected, very light, with little spiritual depth. She is romantic, but without the youthful simplicity of Sylvette in *Romantics*. Her beauty is legendary, like the far-off princess Melissinde's, and her lace handkerchief inspires the starving garrison at the siege of Arras just as the vision of the princess far away encouraged the feverish sailors to continue rowing. Roxane further resembles Melissinde in that neither would ever consider committing a great crime of love. Roxane seeks only an excessively refined sort of love. Little by little, however, the influence of Cyrano's idealism has an impact on her concept of life's values, giving rise to a deep spiritual evolution within her. Ultimately, she is able to say to Christian: "At last I love thee for thy soul alone!" (p. 73)

Rostand's *Cyrano of Bergerac* will continue to have meaning throughout the ages, will continue to move audiences everywhere, and probably will remain identified with the name of Edmond Rostand long after his other works have sunk into complete oblivion. (p. 75)

An historic drama in six acts, [*The Eaglet*] may be considered a masterpiece of lyricism rather than a masterpiece of drama. It is difficult to say whether it is a psychological drama or a kind of dramatized epic poem. Love is relegated to a secondary level, yet the work breathes a certain sentimentality because Rostand simply wanted to bring "the story of a poor child" to the stage. . . .

As for the dramatic construction of *The Eaglet*, . . . its acts are really tableaus, and each is evocative of the eagle symbol. The entire work may be considered as a sequence of events rather than the evolution of a character. (p. 81)

[The Duke] is nothing but the son of Napoleon. He is a dying soul possessed of a grandiose dream, a figure whose action is entirely inner, whereas the actions of those who have created

their own life make themselves felt beyond their inner life. The action of the drama does not develop as an outgrowth of the Duke's behavior; he acts only when everything has been prepared for him by others. . . . The psychological study of the Eaglet is excellent, but the manner of presentation spoils the effect and produces an atmosphere of melodrama. (p. 87)

As with all of Rostand's plays, the reader is left with a feeling of insufficient psychological development of the characters. The author's genius reveals itself rather in the memorable pictures that capture a state of being or a particular gesture. Rostand is, above all, a love poet; in *The Eaglet,* he was constrained to put love on a secondary level. Even though love is always very close to an inner, sentimental dream, Rostand nevertheless uses it to accentuate the weakness and uselessness in the character of the Duke. (pp. 89-90)

The world of *Chanticleer* is a human world . . . where men live under the guise of animals. The play is a thesis work and the plot is of the simplest. . . . (p. 93)

Can the bizarre animal figures in *Chanticleer* be taken seriously? Rostand had to make a choice between two approaches: either try to reconstruct an animal psychology, have his beasts speak as such, not have them say anything that would go beyond the limits of their assumed intelligence—an almost impossible task; or else treat his animals as symbols and have them speak as men. Having set out along the lines of the first approach, he perhaps was not able to resist the temptation of the second, and he went even beyond. Not content with giving his animals human sentiments, he endowed them with incredible literary knowledge. By so doing, he naturally put himself into a vulnerable position that facilitated attacks from the critics. The animals Rostand created are, indeed, too knowledgeable. To accept them and understand them, however, it is necessary to play the game. (p. 102)

The main defects of the work are found in the weak exposure of ideas. The play is too contrived, too far-fetched for presentation as a serious thesis work; and the language and style are too exaggerated. The plays on words—foreign and popular—and the affected metaphors are often disturbing when they lack taste and purpose. At the same time, however, there is much sincere and poetic lyricism in *Chanticleer* The sonnets at the beginning of each act contain little jewels of expression. The invocation to the Sun, the ballads, and the dramatic, fast-paced dialogue of the Night Birds constitute examples of outstanding verse. (p. 106)

Rostand, the would-be poet-philosopher . . . , is always more of a poet than a philosopher. He interprets the human experience and conceives his dramatic *oeuvre* from a lyrical and spiritual rather than from a rational point of view. (p. 112)

The reality of life for Rostand, the poet, is the dream. (p. 113)

Earthly love is the foundation of the Rostandian dream. Love must be taken seriously. Romantic, affected love, however, does not last; the only real, true love is based on free will, which inspires great sacrifices; it is the love that lends heroic warmth to the dream. If it is the dream that renders the hero's life meaningful, it is his own zeal that renders it sacred, love renders it noble, and poetry renders it beautiful and good. . . . Rostand's poetry is certainly affected, but his sincerity saves it from artificiality. It is sincerity as one of the most important human values that the author attempts to communicate through his plays. (p. 114)

[Rostand's] is a style made up of images—images of heroic action, of things poetic, of color, music, and even perfumes. Somewhat affected and exaggerated at times, the images are nevertheless highly original and unforgettably Rostandian. (p. 116)

Rostand, as a man of the theater, used all kinds of stage effects and, as a background for the action, added the "gesture" in the form of a painting or a color to awaken the senses, with music as a poetic accompaniment. First, there is the music and sound of the descriptive images, then the music of the verses, and, finally, the use of pleasing and diverting sound effects. (p. 118)

There is, however, an element in Rostand's theater that is not typical of the Romantic school: preciosity. Two kinds of preciosity—sincere and ridiculous—are present in all of his works. The latter kind is noticeable in **Romantics, Cyrano of Bergerac,** and **Chanticleer.** The former is noticeable everywhere. It is a preciosity of dramatic images and therefore not seventeenth-century preciosity which is cerebral and of a porcelain beauty. What is most interesting, however, is that in Rostand's precious poetry, the accent falls neither on the idea nor on the beautiful, but rather on the action. Rostandian preciosity is a means of expressing what for him is important in life—that is, zealous action. (p. 122)

Rostand's greatness lies in his mood descriptions, and he has an exceptional capacity for inviting us to meditate on certain phrases that sound like prayers so that we may learn to give *feeling* its just value, to topple *reason* off its pedestal—or, at least, to re-dimension it with respect to the total meaning of life. Serenity, if not happiness, might reign. Let us be iconoclasts by rejecting selfishness as our idol. Perhaps this is Rostand's dedicatory message to us all. (p. 125)

> *Alba della Fazia Amoia, in his* Edmond Rostand *(copyright © 1978 by Twayne Publishers, Inc.; reprinted with the permission of Twayne Publishers, a Division of G. K. Hall & Co., Boston), Twayne, 1978, 141 p.*

ADDITIONAL BIBLIOGRAPHY

Brenner, Clarence D. "Rostand's *Cyrano de Bergerac:* An Interpretation." *Studies in Philology* XLVI, No. 4 (October 1949): 603-11.
Details the similarities between Cyrano de Bergerac and various romantic heroes in French literature.

Chesterton, G. K. "Rostand." In his *Twelve Types*, pp. 79-92. London: Arthur L. Humphreys, 1906.
Discussion of the heroic, comic, and tragic elements in *Cyrano de Bergerac* and *L'aiglon.*

Clark, Barrett H. "Edmond Rostand." In his *Contemporary French Dramatists*, pp. 102-20. Cincinnati: Stewart & Kidd Co., 1915.
Discussion of Rostand's literary career and dramatic style, including an explicative rendering of his major plays.

Hapgood, Norman. "Rostand." In his *The Stage in America 1897-1900*, pp. 249-78. London: Macmillan & Co., 1901.
Critique of the various early productions of *Cyrano de Bergerac* and *L'aiglon*, concentrating on staging and actors' performances.

Henderson, Archibald. "The Theater of Edmond Rostand." *The Arena* XXXIV, No. 190 (September 1905): 225-34.
Brief study of Rostand's drama and its effect on the theater of his day.

Kilker, J. A. "Cyrano without Rostand: An Appraisal." *The Canadian Modern Language Review* XXI, No. 3 (Spring 1965): 21-5.
Biographical sketch of the real Cyrano de Bergerac. Kilker attempts to dispel the legend surrounding Cyrano and present his life and work as they actually were.

Parsons, Coleman O. "The Nose of Cyrano de Bergerac." *The Romanic Review* XXV, No. 3 (July-September 1934): 225-35.
Traces the legend of Cyrano de Bergerac's nose as it developed up until Rostand's *Cyrano de Bergerac.*

Williams, Patricia Elliott. "Some Classical Aspects of *Cyrano de Bergerac.*" *Nineteenth-Century French Studies* I, No. 2 (February 1973): 112-24.
Aristotelian analysis of *Cyrano de Bergerac.*

Duncan Campbell Scott

1862-1947

Canadian poet, short story writer, novelist, biographer, essayist, and dramatist.

Scott is best remembered as one of the leading poets of the "Confederation group." Writing in an era following the formation of the Dominion of Canada, Scott, along with poets Bliss Carman, Archibald Lampman, and Charles G.D. Roberts, helped create and cultivate a sense of national identity. Early cast as a regional writer of the northern wilderness, especially its Indian life, Scott is being reappraised in our time as a writer of great diversity with a complex, though unified, vision and a distinctly Canadian spirit.

Scott's lifelong interest in the American Indian began in his childhood when, with his missionary father, his family spent several years among the Indians. He later entered the civil service in Ottawa's Department of Indian Affairs, spending fifty-two years in a successful administrative career which culminated with his position as Deputy Superintendent General. On his frequent trips in this service, Scott became acquainted with the Canadian wilds and visited many Indian tribes, gaining insight into their customs and life. From these experiences came the material for his narrative poems of Indian life such as "At Gull Lake, 1810" and "The Forsaken." Scott's first poetry writing, however, was prompted by his close friendship with an associate in the civil service, the young poet Archibald Lampman. Together they collaborated with Wilfrid Campbell on a weekly literary column, "At the Mermaid Inn," which appeared in the *Toronto Globe* from 1892-93 and served as a guide to prevailing tastes.

Scott has been alternately praised as a lyric and as a dramatic poet. His best lyric poems are found in the collections *The Magic House, and Other Poems, Beauty and Life,* and *The Green Cloister*. Nature, its moods and seasons, are often the subject of these lyrics, and critics are unfailing in noting Scott's mastery at painting vivid, colorful descriptions and creating a mysterious and compelling atmosphere. Scott's dramatic poems are also highly regarded, especially the narrative pieces on Indian life. Violence emerges as an important theme in many of these narrative studies as well as in Scott's lyric poems. The dialectic of tension and resolution is, in fact, central to Scott's vision—from these conflicts, in nature and between people, issue beauty and peace. An outstanding example of such a dialectic is "The Piper of Arll," called by some Scott's masterpiece, which portrays the role of the artist and the nature of artistic experience. Filled with the tensions of contrasts (secluded bay and wild ocean, rustic shepherd and traveled sailors) and paradoxes (life in death, fulfillment in self-sacrifice), the poem culminates in a transcendent peace.

In the past decade Scott's stories, long neglected by critics, have begun to receive recognition. His two volumes of short stories, *In the Village of Viger* and *The Witching of Elspie,* are often contrasted with each other: the first, a prose counterpart to *The Magic House,* is light and pleasurable; the second, wild and bloody stories of the lonely fur-trade areas, is stark and harsh. Recent publication of Scott's only novel, *Untitled Novel, ca. 1905,* sheds new light on his prose, proving Scott an early

Public Archives Canada / C 3187

innovator in the portrayal of the modern antihero. Some critics now conjecture that Scott may be remembered for his prose rather than his poetry.

Despite a long career as a civil servant, Scott received many awards in his lifetime that were a tribute to his literary artistry, including the Lorne Pierce Medal, which honors Canadians for significant achievements in imaginative or critical literature. He was elected a Fellow of the Royal Society of Canada in 1899 and became its President in 1921. Scott is recognized as a commanding poet of distinct Canadian sensibility. As Desmond Pacey has said, "Is it too much to suggest that in these quietly powerful poems . . . we catch an authentic glimpse of the Canadian spirit at its finest?"

PRINCIPAL WORKS

The Magic House, and Other Poems (poetry) 1893
In the Village of Viger (short stories) 1896
Labor and the Angel (poetry) 1898
John Graves Simcoe (biography) 1905
New World Lyrics and Ballads (poetry) 1905
Lundy's Lane, and Other Poems (poetry) 1916

Beauty and Life   (poetry)   1921
Pierre   (drama)   1923
The Witching of Elspie   (short stories)   1923
The Poems of Duncan Campbell Scott   (poetry)   1926
The Green Cloister   (poetry)   1935
The Circle of Affection and Other Pieces in Prose and Verse
    (poetry, travel essays, short stories, and essays)   1947
Walter J. Phillips   (biography)   1947
Some Letters of Duncan Campbell Scott   (letters)   1959
Untitled Novel, ca. 1905   (unfinished novel)   1979

THE CRITIC   (essay date 1894)

[A number of the poems in **"The Magic House,"**] by Mr. Duncan Campbell Scott, have already appeared in *Scribner's.* Brought together, they make a creditable volume, and the best of them—some of the shorter lyrics—are very good indeed. One notices a few flaws in the workmanship, here and there, and it is evident that Mr. Scott's ear is not always sure of the rhythm of his lines; but, generally speaking, the work is finished, spontaneous, delicate, melodious and individual. Like his brother singers, [William Wilfred Campbell and Charles G. D. Roberts], he is much given to descriptive writing, and in some instances, such as **"At Scarboro Beach," "A Summer Storm"** and **"A Flock of Sheep,"** the mere cataloguing of impressions has a tiring effect upon the reader. His sonnets, too, resemble theirs in kind, although he is less successful than either as a sonnet-writer. Where he succeeds best, and where he excels, is in such a bit of stirring narrative as **"At the Cedars."** . . .

We extend to Mr. Scott a hearty welcome. His **"Magic House"** is stocked with many delights, sweet with charming music and gay with bright pictures.

> *"Canadian Poetry and Verse: 'The Magic House, and Other Poems',"* in The Critic, *Vol. XXI, No. 533, April 7, 1894, p. 236.*

WILLIAM MORTON PAYNE   (essay date 1896)

Mr. Douglas Campbell Scott's volume [*The Magic House and Other Poems*] deserves far more attention than our space permits upon the present occasion, and a few words of emphatic and cordial praise must stand for the detailed examination of its beauties that it would be a pleasure to make. Mr. Scott's poems are mainly nature-lyrics, and often attain to marked nobility of imaginative diction. . . .

> *William Morton Payne, "Recent Books of American Poetry: 'The Magic House and Other Poems',"* in The Dial, *Vol. XX, No. 232, February 16, 1896, p. 116.*

WILLIAM ARCHER   (essay date 1902)

In Mr. Campbell Scott both [observation and imagination] are present in liberal measure. He is above everything a poet of climate and atmosphere, employing with a nimble, graphic touch the clear, pure, transparent colours of a richly-furnished palette. He leaves unrecorded no single phase in the pageant of the northern year, from the odorous heat of June to the ice-bound silence of December. His work abounds in magically luminous phrases and stanzas. (p. 386)

There is scarcely a poem of Mr. Scott's from which one could not cull some memorable descriptive passage. (p. 388)

[It] must not be understood that his talent is merely descriptive. There is a philosophic and also a romantic strain in it. I confess to finding a little vague the philosophy symbolically set forth in *Labor and the Angel,* which nevertheless contains many admirable lines and passages. *The Harvest* is an impressive chant of the earth-hunger of the disinherited multitudes. Even here, however, Mr. Scott's talent seems to me stronger on the pictorial than on the reflective side. . . . Of all Mr. Scott's philosophic utterances, however, the finest is the poem entitled *In the Country Churchyard: To the Memory of my Father.* This is admirable in form, serene and elevated in thought. (pp. 390-91)

Mr. Scott's purely romantic poems are not numerous, but contain some delightful writing. The suave couplets of *By the Willow Spring* tell the story of a "fragile daughter of the earth" who naiad-like, haunted a pool in the woods, and was at last found dead upon its verge. . . . There is a haunting beauty in *The Magic House;* but a still finer, more clear-cut piece of pure imagination is *In the House of Dream. . . . The Piper of Arll,* though its symbolism, if it has any, escapes me, is a singularly beautiful fantasy, full of jewel-like colour and tenuous, unearthly melody. (pp. 391-92)

There is also a purely lyric vein in Mr. Scott's talent represented by such charming pieces as *At the Lattice, Youth and Time,* and *A Little Song.* He is a poet of many gifts, and of few vices—incapable of harshness, incapable of vulgarity. He is not incapable of an occasional touch of commonplace, nor can he be held guiltless of now and then letting pass a piece of makeshift workmanship, a line or two of padding, a word or phrase imposed by the rhyme rather than by the idea. . . . Such flaws, however, are not really characteristic. As a rule, Mr. Scott's workmanship is careful and highly finished. He is before everything a colourist. He paints in hues of a peculiar and vivid translucency. But he is also a metrist of no mean skill, and an imaginative thinker of no common capacity. (p. 393)

> *William Archer, "Duncan Campbell Scott," in his* Poets of the Younger Generation, *John Lane, 1902 (and reprinted by Scholarly Press, 1969), pp. 385-95.*

RAYMOND KNISTER   (essay date 1927)

The newly published volume of the collected *Poems of Duncan Campbell Scott* presents an opportunity to estimate the character and tendency of his work as a whole. Though Scott has shown for something like thirty years an accomplishment distinguished in our poetry, it is somewhat surprising to find how little of his earlier work has been discarded in this book and how all of it gains by the careful arrangement found here, which gives the effect of a unity through variety unusual in such collections. The book is as readable as most novels.

This impression is owing to notable balance of qualities, a unity of perception and mood, an intellectual clarity seldom absent and seldom permitted to dull pure feeling. There is less of the preacher and propagandist than in almost any other poet of comparable power of thought, and there is a clearer singing than would have seemed possible to detached afterthought. . . . Though everything has been experienced, and in so far as the soul is infinite found wanting, there is no mockery here, no bitterness, and but little regret, only an unfailing reflective enjoyment. . . . [There] is a mood of detachment which made for clear vision and sure rendering even in the poet's early work. [*The Magic House, Labor and the Angel, New World Lyrics and Ballads,* and *Spring on Mattagami*] . . . show a more typical or constant Scott than *Lundy's Lane and Other Poems.* . . . (p. 66)

The latter volume is, comparatively speaking at least, a failure, with surprisingly ill-considered inclusions. The title poem has an easy, too easy, and powerful swing, like a burlesque of the newspaper war-ballad. Genuine feeling in the circumstances only spoils it. **"The Height of Land"** avoids a mincing measure, but it presents swamps and wilds in a way which does not allow the reader to forget that it is a cultivated and critical intelligence which views these expanses. Rather commonplace thoughts upon the nature of things may be found in **"Meditation at Perugia."** . . . Altogether it is a book whose moments of insight, not to say inspiration, are rare, save for an occasional lyric like the perfect **"The Closed Door"** and the lines introducing **"A Mystery Play,"** which are hard, clear, and objective.

Yet there is a measure always, which . . . would make one believe Scott incapable of really bad verse. The **"Fragment of an Ode to Canada"** begins with stale afflatus like the copy for a special advertisement to be illustrated in full color, but reality and happy description creep into it. Again and again the reader is astonished by an alchemy which transmutes that old bane of the poets, the set subject, into something of authentic and personal feeling. (p. 67)

[The little volume *Beauty and Life*] is one of the most even and finest in our literature. . . . Several of the lyrics are well-nigh matchless in their way, and there is in the **"Ode for the Keats Centenary"** a contribution hardly to be surpassed in English literature. Here is a sustained conception which never falters from beauty and relevance—and of how many ''odes'' can that be said? Though it flows into magnificent lyric interludes, the indispensable generalities are always based on reality. . . . And **"The Flight,"** a dramatic scene, contains admirable dialogue in the form of poetry—civilized, whimsical, restrained, with a delicate emphasis on fancy and emotion. In such poems as these the rationalizing faculty of the poet has a legitimate artistic place; and in how many others there are lines, passages, in which thought and poetry melt into one, tranquil, reflective feeling. It is not surprising that some show a tendency to keep on writing, letting whimsy follow fancy, and phrase be added to thought, until the poem might well be endless. (pp. 68-9)

The subject-matter upon which these faculties of restraint and fancy are exercised is varied. There are the nature pieces, without which no book of Canadian poetry is complete; but here they do not smack so much as usual of the catalogue. There are poems about Indians and their life, which are based upon long knowledge and observation and yet avoid anything approaching photographic realism. (p. 69)

And there are numerous child-poems of delicate and sure perception. Charmingly turned, well-nigh flawless lyrics abound, and their choice will be a matter of the taste of the reader. . . . These have a delicacy of expression, a strength of feeling, and an inevitable natural flow, freshness, and spontaneity which makes them ever to be valued.

Ballads like **"The Piper of Arll,"** such stories as that of Dominique de Gourgues and his revenge for the Spanish atrocities

perpetrated upon the Huguenot settlement planted on the coast of Florida, Indian tales like **"The Mission of the Trees,"** folk superstition like **"Catnip Jack,"** are vivid and inspiriting and form a link between the other poetry of Duncan Campbell Scott and his prose stories, [*In the Village of Viger* and *The Witching of Elspie*]. . . . These stories, mainly historical, show a knowledge of the north country and a faithfulness to the knowledge, which the novels of this locale, not to mention the movies, have not yet attained. They are honest and sure-footed works, in pleasing style, but they do not show the combination of qualities which makes this writer's poetry unique.

Much of such work, prose and verse, might have been written anywhere in the English-speaking world, by a man cultured, urbane, of keen observation and delicate imagination. But there is enough that could have been conceived only in Canada by a son of Canada to give the work an indigenous value independent of the fact that on purely literary bases it ranks among the highest which has been produced here.

Similarly with comparatively youthful matters of technique which have become accepted as traditional: pain and passion and longing, lonely love and longed-for death, snowflakes and rose leaves, high desire and laughter and tears, flutters of hope and false fancies thronging—perhaps he had gone as far as may be by invoking these things by name and reasoning about them, rather than invoking them, more poignantly, in memorable picture, song, or story. Yet he has done that too, many times, in poems which are almost completely objective, or which even convey themselves solely by inference. (pp. 69-71)

There is variety enough within a charm which is always actual to make this volume interesting to all lovers of poetry and qualities which make it a contribution important and permanent as human reckonings go, to Canadian literature. (p. 71)

Raymond Knister, ''Duncan Campbell Scott'' (originally published in Willison's Monthly, *Vol. II, 1927), in* Duncan Campbell Scott: A Book of Criticism, *edited by S. L. Dragland, The Tecumseh Press Ltd., 1974, pp. 66-73.*

PELHAM EDGAR (essay date 1927)

[Dr. Scott's] methods of composition are interesting from their variety. He rarely writes under any compulsion other than his mood, and of occasional poems—in the sense of poems written for an occasion—there are but a few examples in the present volume. *Lundy's Lane* was written for a prize; and meritorious though it is, we feel that it is not a natural utterance. The *Fragment of an Ode to Canada* bears also the marks of an assigned task. He once asked me to suggest some ballad theme. I referred him to Parkman's account of Dominque de Gourgues. Here his imagination caught fire, and an impressive poem was the result. I congratulate myself more on having asked him to produce an ode for the centenary of Keats's death. He has never surpassed the poem he wrote for that occasion. There are marked affinities between the younger and the older poet, and his noble verses are a revelation at once of Keats and of himself. Some of his poems have had a long germination in his mind. Two of these, that reveal much to us of his attitude towards life, are *The Height of Land* and *Fragment of a Letter*. The suggestion for these poems came during a long summer journey made in 1906 through our remote north country. The first was written nine years and the second thirteen years after the prompting occasion. That summer trip was fruitful of poetic result, but impulse and execution were usually simultaneous. . . . *Fantasia,* that most delightful specimen of the poetry of escape, is our Canadian *Kubla Khan,* the transcription of a vision of sleep, the musical rendering of a dream whose images came stamped with the revealing words. Scores of his lyrics must have come in this unpremeditated way—they lay hidden in consciousness to await there the favouring mood—the releasing phrase or cadence. Their origin and their execution are as much a mystery to their creator as to us who read. (pp. 41-2)

Many of his pieces are carefully wrought and as carefully revised, but whether spontaneous or slowly elaborated they rarely fail to convey the vivid impulse that engendered them. He does not deny his moods, but he never manufactures them.

In some phases of his work Dr. Scott is unique among the poets of his day. Poetry that strikes to the roots of our primitive instincts creates its own value by its rarity. Sophistication and naiveté are an ill-assorted pair; and when a highly civilized poet goes a-fishing for the elemental in the troubled waters of his atavistic memories, he does not usually bring much that is valuable to the surface. The elemental must be encountered by the way, and so Dr. Scott has found it, and has been stirred to a response that is refreshingly spontaneous and unforced. *The Forsaken* is an unforgettable poem for its commingled grimness and tenderness, but he is even closer to the wild heart of pagan superstition in the impressive *Powassan's Drum.* Indian passages abound in the *Lines in Memory of Edmund Morris.* "The Death of Akoose" is a superbly executed narrative fragment, in which, however, the reader's mind is not permitted to dwell on the episode alone, but is led through it to reflect on the mysteries of death and duration which are the major theme of the great poem of which it forms a part. The conception of these Indian poems is always satisfying, and we are never disturbed by slackness in the form. The idea rarely fails of its appropriate rhythm, for musical thought compels musical utterance. With him too we can take for granted that the Nature setting will be adequate. He finds values in Nature that correspond with every human mood, and he establishes his harmonies without drenching us with description. (pp. 42-3)

It was the accident of circumstance that gave him access to his Indian material, and it is also the fortuitous conjunction in him of musical and poetic impulse that gives their characteristic form to some of his longer poems. Milton and Browning were students and lovers of music, and the latter especially has written poems that have their source in a musical idea. Dr. Scott has never endeavoured like Browning to philosophise his music, but he has done something perhaps as ambitious and as interesting. He has written several poems that simulate the movement of a musical sonata. His *Variations on a Seventeenth Century Theme* is his most systematic and successful challenge to musical method. The variations are on two lines of [Henry] Vaughan:

> It was high spring, and all the way
> Primrosed, and hung with shade.

The theme is developed from the contrast of light and shadow, joy and sorrow, life and death, youth and age. A tender, unbiblical myth of Adam and Eve, conveyed in sufficient middle English, serves as prelude. A May-time pedlar interlude follows, and then five grave, symbolic stanzas lead up to a lyric that is the very breathing of the spirit of music,—shadow and light again its delicate motive. . . . The fifth section is a tense,

dramatic variation on the same dominant theme, and is followed by a lyric on the passing of youth, which is assured of permanence as confidently as anything that has come from a Canadian pen. . . . Section Seven is a delicate Herrick-like interlude, *A Fairy Funeral,* and is followed by a grotesque primrose piece. Pots of these flowers in a shop window bring to the mind of a blear-eyed old woman images of English lanes, as the Wood Street thrush reminded Wordsworth's Susan of her country meadows—and Susan, too, if we may trust the excerpted verses, was no paragon of virtue. Light and shadow dance through the next lyric, the dainty *Ecossaise,* and "a few chords" bring the poem to a sad but peaceful close with Adam and Eve at the end of days in their frozen garden.

The *Lines in Memory of Edmund Morris* are developed in similar fashion, with death and immortality as the dominant theme, and with episodic variations that flow naturally and powerfully from the main conception. The *Ode for the Keats Centenary* has also marked affinities with the mode of music. I do not know where to look in poetry for a more penetrating presentation of the great poet's spiritual identity. The theme is built round a phrase from the letters where Keats speaks of the power given to the poet of "seeing great things in loneliness"; and though the cloistral side of his nature is the more fully developed, Scott does not omit to reveal the human quality in Keats which, never wholly alien from his genius, gave promise of such ample development in the years of his failing strength. It is the alternation of these two aspects of Keats as the tremulous lover of beauty and the ardent searcher after truth that makes this poem so interesting and true.

The poem *On the Death of Claude Debussy* is a free fine rendering of the imaginative reactions which music engenders in the consenting mind. With these poems, if we add the interesting *At the Piano,* I have named all that relate themselves closely to the world of music, though everywhere one notes our poet's thrilling response to Nature's unorganized music—the wind in the trees, the voices of birds, the intermittent roar of rapids at night.

I have been concerned with finding elements in Dr. Scott's work that give him identity. All poets who discover the depths of their own nature, if depths they truly are, encounter mystery by the way. Scott, an inheritor of the romantic tradition, is naturally aware of the value of imaginative suggestion. Poems that make their appeal from this source have been common enough for a century, but *The Piper of Arll* is more than a belated echo. It is as fresh and original as if it were the first of its type. . . . As Canadians, we must congratulate ourselves that so fine a volume is soon to represent to English readers the measure of our advance in poetry. (pp. 44-6)

Pelham Edgar, "Duncan Campbell Scott," in The Dalhousie Review, *Vol. 7, No. 1, April, 1927, pp. 38-46.*

W. J. SYKES   (essay date 1939)

Ever since the appearance of Duncan Campbell Scott's Collected Poems [*The Poems of Duncan Campbell Scott*] I have felt that his work has not received the appreciation that it deserves. . . . While it cannot be said that his work is popular or that it has ever aimed to become so, even from poetry-lovers it has received rather less attention than its due. This essay seeks to point out some of its merits. (p. 51)

[About half of the poems in Campbell's first volume of verse, *The Magic House,* are] included in the **Collected Poems**. It contains many delicately drawn pictures, much melodious verse, and a number of tenuous fancies, "irised hours of gossamer', in particular passages of great promise, and some poems of marked achievement. *The End of the Day,* with its imitative echo of the 'antiphonal bells of Hull'; *At the Cedars,* with its swift strong movement exactly suited to the dramatic tale; *Off Riviere du Loup,* with its vigorous opening, . . . and its quiet ending, . . . these and some others are among the most treasured of Canadian poems. (pp. 51-2)

[The second volume, *Labour and the Angel*] shows a further working of the veins of poetic ore revealed in *The Magic House,* as well as the uncovering of new ones. Here are more descriptive lyrics and melodious songs, and here again are vague fanciful verses such as *Avis* and *The Piper of Arll,* where the author is concerned rather with richness of description and beauty of phrase than with any concrete meaning. But in *Harvest* and the title-poem a new note is struck when the poet contemplates with emotion some problems of suffering humanity; in two sonnets he introduces a theme, Indian Life, that plays no small part in his later work; while in a vigorous satire, *The Dame Regnant,* he castigates malignant gossip. On the whole, however, this second volume is notable mainly for the number and excellence of its lyrics. (p. 52)

[The appearance of the third volume, *New World Lyrics and Ballads*] marked an advance in range of subject, in power of treatment, and in freedom of style. Here are found such impressive poems of Indian life as *Forsaken* and *On the Way to the Mission;* the spirited ballad, *Dominique de Gourgues;* a few more lyrics, among which *The Wood Peewee* stands out in its simple beauty; and some philosophical verses. (pp. 52-3)

[In his next volume *Lundy's Lane*] Scott was heard in the full maturity of his powers. As in his earlier books, we find here attractive songs and lyrics, though other kinds of verse are more prominent; the homely dramatic ballad that gives its name to the volume; the noble *Fragment of an Ode to Canada,* the first of the war poems; the group under the heading, *The Closed Door,* in commemoration of his little daughter Elizabeth; and meditative poems in which he speculates on the problem of existence or expresses his convictions about the poet's calling. . . .

[*Beauty and Life*] may be regarded as the most distinguished single volume of Scott's verse. It contains nearly all of his poems called forth by the Great War, the *Ode for the Keats Centenary,* and a number of compositions that, despite one or two of vague fancy, exhibit such a happy union of thought, emotion and felicitous expression as to arouse that pleasurable excitement induced by looking at a painting of genius or hearing noble music. . . .

[When] the Collected Poems appeared even those who had kept in touch with Scott's work were surprised at the range of subject-matter and the variety and mastery of his art that the volume showed. (p. 53)

[His latest volume is] *The Green Cloister*. It shows no diminution in poetic power; it contains poems of types familiar to readers of the earlier volumes—songs and lyrics, descriptions and interpretations of nature, tales of Indian life, meditations on life and art—and ends with a humorous poem, something rare in Scott's work.

Scott is probably the leading conscious artist among Canadian poets. Even in his first volume he showed a mastery of technique which, if then not complete, was to be perfected in later compositions, and shows the thought that even then he had given to his art. This does not detract from his spontaneity; spontaneity and technique go together in the act of creation, or if spontaneity comes first technique follows close after. (pp. 53-4)

If we try to analyse Scott's skill in the poetic art we shall find that it rests on these well-known elements: a wide and aptly chosen vocabulary; a happy invention of phrases; numerous, pleasing and novel comparisons; melody, harmony, and a command of various metres and stanza forms. It may be that at times he seems partial to rare and obscure words, and that this has been a stumbling-block to some of his readers. This peculiarity, however, forces itself on our notice chiefly in his first two volumes and practically disappears in the poems of his maturity. Rhyme he uses or dispenses with according to subject or mood. Sometimes, as in the *Ode for the Keats Centenary,* he varies blank verse and rhymed stanza with fine effect, the rhymed stanza accompanying a surge of feeling. There is some free verse in his poetry, usually marked by rhythm and elevation of thought. Melody there is in abundance, especially in the numerous songs and lyrics. Harmony, a more subtle poetic grace, is found in many places: in poems like *The End of the Day,* with its refrain

The day is done, done, done. The day is done,

suggesting evening bells. . . . (p. 54)

Considering Scott's poems from the earliest volume to the latest, we find his genius predominantly lyric. To be sure, his work includes dramatic strains—poems and passages of effective dialogue—and telling narrative, especially in the Indian poems; yet it is the songs and other lyrics that bulk most largely. The common attitude of his mind is subjective; the poet expresses his wonder, delight, sadness, or despair at this or that aspect of nature or human life.

The songs, each expressing one idea, fancy, or emotion, vary widely. There are love songs of longing, of passion, of disappointment songs written for music, songs of gladness, songs of sorrow, songs of courage. (p. 55)

Among the nature-poems there are purely descriptive pieces, sensitive word pictures, which by selection of detail and delicate phrasing show how the scene affected the poet. . . . Birds, flowers, moods of the day or night, the changes of seasons, bits of landscape or seashore, are the themes of these nature lyrics. Birds especially are dear to the poet: the thrush, the robin, the vireo, the song sparrow, the oriole are the objects of his observation and fancy. In several lyrics he sets words to the robin's tune. *The Wood Peewee* would grace any anthology of bird poems. There are few moods of nature in the four seasons, or types of landscape from the mountains to the sea, that Scott has not reproduced for us in the tone of his emotion. (pp. 56-7)

The most significant, though not the largest, group of Scott's poems is made up of those based on Indian life. . . . His observations and the stories and legends told him are treated imaginatively in a number of poems different from anything else in Canadian literature. (p. 57)

The most striking thing about these poems is the poet's insight into the consciousness of the Indian: the shadowy dreams in the divided mind of the half-breed girl; the mingled traditional superstition and dim Christian faith of the Indian woman who had lost her son; the savage hatred of the old medicine man,

Powassan, who by his magic, to the beating of his drum, called up to sight the headless body of his long-slain foe. No one can rightly appraise Scott's poetry till he has read these poems of Indian life.

Another group of poems gives expression to thoughts and emotions aroused in the poet by events of the Great War. Some of these commemorate the fallen, their heroism, the ideals for which they fought; in others the poet attempts to bring such consolation as he can to the bereaved at home. There is no word of hate, of the fear or the joy of battle, and no boasting of victory. These poems are simple and dignified in thought and expression. . . . Sometimes there is a tender intimate touch, as in *To the Canadian Mothers*. Other poems express the thrill of pride in the courage of men faithful to the end, as in *Lines on a Monument*. Though comparatively few in number, this group of war poems is important. They illustrate a side of Scott's work seen also in *Dominique De Gourgues*, in the Indian poems, and in the early *At the Ferry*—an appreciation of action, of heroism, of endurance—a side that finds direct expression in the two sonnets *To the Heroic Soul*.

Of his varied kinds of poems those about his little daughter Elizabeth are deeply moving. The father's joy in the companionship of the little girl and his profound grief when she died need not be dwelt upon. Not in any long poem is her memory kept green or her loss lamented, but in short "swallow flights of song", or even in a brief allusion. In an early poem, *The Lesson*, there is a tender passage describing the little girl's trust in her father as she falls asleep, and in other poems their merry companionship is pictured. But she fell silent, and in the touching lines, *The Closed Door*, his hopeless grief finds words. (pp. 58-9)

There are some of Scott's poems with which the writer confesses that he has imperfect sympathy; those such as *The Magic House, Avis,* and *The Piper of Arll*. They may be called fanciful or dream poems; remote from actual human life, mysterious, their incidents or ideas constitute but a fragile framework for rich decoration. (p. 60)

The great influence music has had on Scott's life is reflected in his poetry. An obvious instance is the choice of titles such as, *Adagio, Variations on a Seventeenth Century Theme, Improvisation on an Old Song*. In *Adagio*, where the real subject is a sketch of a personality, the title calls attention to the slow movement of the verse. In other poems there are allusions unlikely to be made except by one familiar with music. . . . In his poem, *On the Death of Claude Debussy*, he puts into words felicitously the impression made on him by the great French master's music. The effect of music on one sensitive to its appeal is well described in lines from *At the Piano*. . . . (p. 61)

Many of Scott's poems reveal him in a speculative or meditative mood. Both in his earlier and in his later verse he affirms the permanence of beauty. . . . Whatever one may think of the doctrine there is no doubt about the poetry. In *Meditation at Perugia* he compares the simple faith of St. Francis with our 'views' troubled by science that "leaves us half with doubts and half with fears". In *The Height of Land* he again meditates on "all the welter of the life of men". From his lofty northern camp, in the clear air far from the confusion of the crowded cities, he sees life resolve itself into the simple ideal of noble thought and noble deed. . . . (p. 62)

It might be objected that the poet's views are not always consistent, that in one place he seems grimly fatalistic, while in another he urges man to build his own soul like a fair minster. This means only that at different times he expresses different moods. There is some reason to think that his inclination toward determinism, as seen in *The Cup* and *The Happy Fatalist,* was an attitude of his early manhood, which, as he grew older, gave way to a conviction that man may to a considerable extent shape his own destiny.

Of special interest to us is that part of a poet's philosophy that deals with his own art. What is his conception of it? What are his ideals? These questions Scott answers in *The Woodspring to the Poet*. As the spring feeds rill and brook bringing refreshment and life to the plain, so the poet must give. To all classes of men he brings his message of wonder and hope; to the child, the maiden and youth, the mothers, the oppressed, those who suffer for the truth, those who have lost hope, those who mourn. (pp. 62-3)

[Considering] the amount of his poetry, its variety in theme and treatment, its technical excellence, the balance between intellect and emotion, and the constant service of beauty everywhere evident in it, we may at least conjecture whether in the years to come Duncan Campbell Scott will not be regarded as the foremost Canadian poet of his time. (p. 64)

W. J. Sykes, "The Poetry of Duncan Campbell Scott," in Queen's Quarterly, *Vol. XLVI, No. 1, Spring, 1939, pp. 51-64.*

E. K. BROWN (essay date 1944)

[In Scott's first collection *The Magic House and Other Poems*] there is a mixture of restraint and intensity which grasps at one and will not let one go. As one reads the collection through today, it is to be struck by the predominance of the dark and the powerful—night, storm, the wilderness, the angry sea. The nature he depicts and evokes is a harsh and violent nature. . . . Lampman, Carman and Roberts have in the main presented the more or less cultivated parts of Canada, or those marginal to settlement, Scott, above all those that are untouched or scarcely touched by the hand of man, for example, "the lonely loon-haunted Nipigon reaches" and "the enormous targe of Hudson Bay." By his choice of the wilds he has won an immense advantage over his contemporaries . . . The path to originality is wide before Scott. His problem is to find a form suitable and adequate for his novel matter. It will not be supposed that he succeeded in finding that form at the very outset of his career.

Indeed, the nature-pieces in his first collection are not as satisfying as the dream-pieces. These are definitely *fin de siècle*. They introduce one to a nightmarish world, in which not only are logical relations suspended as they are in symbolist verse, in much of Carman's early work to take a Canadian example, but the relation even between images is extremely loose, exactly as in vivid dreams . . . In general, even in **"The Piper of Arll,"** the thought does not elude, but is a mass of suggestions which do indeed lack definiteness. (pp. 122-24)

Restrained intensity is . . . sought in a very simple narrative, one of Scott's very earliest compositions, called **"At the Cedars,"** something miles removed from the kind of verse that has just been considered. This is a narrative essentially akin to his prose tales. . . . It tells of a log-jam on the Ottawa, in which a man is caught and killed in the presence of his girl, who sets out for the jam in a canoe only to be caught and killed as quickly and brutally as her lover . . . It is significant that in such a subject, new to Scott and treated in such a bald and simple fashion, the same fundamental quality is evident. It is significant because it appears to point to something permanent and instinctive in his practice, permanent and instinctive in himself. We shall see that the appearance is not deceptive.

A search for the adequate theme and the adequate form in which restrained intensity may express itself—here is the emotional centre of Scott's work, in the two collections that followed his first, [*Labour and the Angel* and *New World Lyrics and Ballads*] . . . , there are many failures and a larger number of approaches to success. Most of the failures are similar in theme and form to poems that were being written by the general run of Scott's contemporaries in Canada and in the United States. It was an age in which only bold experimenters and original temperaments went beyond the gentle feeling, the gentle word, the gentle landscape. . . . When [Scott] wrote in the gentle manner he was not as winning, because not as genuine, as Lampman or Carman: it was not his manner and he wrote in it only because he was not yet in sure possession of a manner of his own, and highly sensitive to the winds of taste.

It will be more interesting to consider the approaches to success, in which there is something more original. Sometimes he hits upon a theme which is proper to him, but is impeded by his choice of form. A striking instance is his **"Mission of the Trees."** . . . How can one explain the amazing discrepancy between form and substance? The substance was to give the intensity, the form the restraint. Scott was here satisfied with a balance that is mechanical. . . . For the greatest effects the balance must be organic: the intensity and the restraint must fuse. This they do not often do in Scott's early or intermediate volumes.

When they do his poetry is not to be equalled, I think, by any of the Canadian poets of his generation. **"The Forsaken,"** another Indian narrative, is an admirable example of his success. (pp. 125-28)

Not a few of the poems in which he achieves this peculiar kind of perfection have to do with the Indians. Of all Canadian poets, indeed of all Canadian imaginative writers, he has best succeeded in making great literature out of such distinctively Canadian material as our aborigines supply. . . . His poetry presents [Indians] not as noble savages, whose emotions run in courses unknown to us, surprising us by their strangeness, but as complex yet intelligible persons. What is the real theme of **"The Forsaken"**? It is nothing less than a universal tragedy, the tragedy of Lear and Goriot. Those who once were strong became weak; their value dwindles and those whom they reared from helpless weakness to strength discard them as costly superfluities. (pp. 130-31)

Throughout almost all of the Indian poems the fusion of intensity and restraint is notable. It comes to its perfection in a piece longer than any that have been mentioned, **"Powassan's Drum."** To the end of a poem almost one hundred and fifty lines in length, Scott maintains his spell. There is no monotony of effect. The poem begins quietly. At a safe psychological distance, as vagrant tourists, we watch the old medicine man, Powassan, beating his drum with a fierce steadiness; he impresses us with just the idle curiosity that any anachronism might provoke. Slowly the drum begins to drown all other impressions; from our safe distance we have been pulled within the range where the beat seems to be nothing short of the "pulse of Being"; we cannot remember a time when the beat did not dominate our world or conceive a time when it will not. . . .

The threatening beat is sharply broken at the close of the poem: a storm breaks upon the world, and at its climax seems like the prolongation of the beat of Powassan's drum.

The height of Scott's power in dealing with Indian material is reached in this poem. . . . (pp. 132-33)

The perfection of his best Indian pieces is matched in his best nature-verse, and seldom anywhere else in his work. . . . Scott has found in a multitude of [nature's] explicit or suggested activities an enormous intensity—in the loud beat of partridge wings, the wild laughter of loons, the violent colours of sunrise and sunset and their scarcely less violent reflection in the lakes, the exciting maze of fireflies whose trajectories cross and re-cross. . . . For [Scott] it is only the mass of surface aspects that is violent. But how violent the surface is! So violent that in **"Spring on Mattagami"**—a poem for which he himself does not much care—with perfect appropriateness the response to nature is fused with an intensity of sexual feeling not elsewhere to be found in his work. It is worth noting that this poem is modelled closely and carefully on Meredith's "Love in the Valley." It seems wholly in keeping that he should pass from stanzas which smoulder with the colours and scents of the landscape to stanzas which flame with his longing for some ideal woman, whom he pictures in the midst of wild nature, drawing from it a liberation from her hesitations so that she yields to his passion. (pp. 137-38)

In **"Spring on Mattagami"** he did not appear aware of calm as an aspect of nature: he excluded it. In **"The Height of Land"** he includes it in a broader conception. . . . Scott here shows himself in his formulation of the Being that lies within nature and lends to it its deepest meaning. This Something is neither calm nor violence. As the poem proceeds Scott finds difficulty in maintaining in fusion elements of calm and elements of something else which is more intense. . . . It is one of Scott's greatest accomplishments to have remained sensitive to all his intellectual scruples, to have continued a modern man, and yet to have written, in this poem, with an intensity and depth of emotion which is normally the privilege of assured faith.

The dialectical habit of thought which added a note of distinction to **"The Height of Land"** is a characteristic in many of Scott's later poems. A curious and powerful instance of dialectical thinking which is also highly poetical is the **"Variations on a Seventeenth Century Theme."** . . . The term "variations" suggests very clearly how it is that Scott has turned a method of thought into a poetic approach to life: the analogy with music is evident. . . . But the confession is not to be taken literally; in this final poem the architecture is very careful—it comes to crown the whole. The **"Variations"** put us in touch with a mind with a rich sense of the diversity of experience and with a power to sort it into emotionally significant categories. (pp. 138-41)

E. K. Brown, "The Masters: Duncan Campbell Scott," in his On Canadian Poetry *(reprinted by permission of McGraw-Hill Ryerson Limited and Mrs. E. K. Brown), revised edition, Ryerson Press, 1944 (and reprinted by The Tecumseh Press, 1973), pp. 118-43.*

A. J. M. SMITH (essay date 1958)

[Duncan Campbell Scott], who has much to gain from . . . a re-examination, has not yet, in spite of the Memoir of E. K. Brown and the more recent essay by Desmond Pacey [see excerpt above], been seen as the remarkably original, if not impeccable, poet he really is. I shall do no more in this essay then present some of the evidence drawn from particular poems and specific passages that have led me to this conclusion and try to indicate, however sketchily, the nature of the sensibility that breathes significance into his poetry. (p. 73)

I believe we shall discover that Duncan Campbell Scott is a more complex poet than has generally been realized; that his merits have a greater diversity than those of any of his famous contemporaries; and finally that there is a much greater proportion of the work of Scott that can appeal to a modern taste—as there is much also that attains to the universal. (p. 74)

I cannot do better, perhaps, than begin with Scott's first book. I shall try to discover there the peculiar nature of the poet's sensibility, and then trace it if possible in later poems of various sorts. We shall note the curious fascination that certain aspects of night and dream exercised upon him, and this will lead us to an examination of what may be called his metaphysic of love and to a discussion of his ambivalent attitude to nature and passion that finds expression in two distinct, if not actually conflicting styles—a tremulous, colourful, sensuous one and a calmer, more tightly controlled, and possibly more mature one. (p. 75)

[In the first poem of *The Magic House*], where we find such puerilities as "rosy west," "dreamy lawn," and poppies that begin to yawn, we suddenly come upon an intense and accurate image: "A shore-lark fell like a stone." And on the second page in the midst of a flowery and insipid pastoral we are startled to find a hard, clear, sharply etched picture that shows in its most concentrated form the union of intensity and clarity that distinguishes genuine poetry from pretty verses. It is only a moment, but it is a fine one—just the picture of "the little sharp-lipped pools, / Shrunken with the summer sun," but not even Lampman has excelled that.

As we read further into the book, the vividness and intensity increase. The literary clichés drop away, and more and more poems appear that are almost completely satisfying or that at least can stand as homogeneous and individual works. The nature, at least of their originality, can be discerned in their imagery, and this in turn is a reflection of the poet's individual sensibility. (pp. 76-7)

[The] juxtaposition of light and shade, of colours and sounds, of sense impressions and emotional responses, all are characteristic of what is most original in Scott. His is the poetry of a musician and of a man enraptured and enthralled by the song and the sight of birds and by the flash of colours in nature. (p. 78)

Scott was fascinated by dusk, evening, and night. Of the forty-seven poems in *The Magic House,* sixteen, or more than a third, are nocturnes—evocations of the world after sunset. And nearly all of them illustrate the peculiar power of his sensibility. Darkness is filled with tension and suspense, and the poet chooses those scenes and situations that allow him to deal with nature dramatically and sensuously. In **"A Night in June"** there is a wonderful evocation of the coming of a nocturnal storm when the oppressive heat of summer seems about to break, and a sudden flash of lightning shows the hidden animal life that suffers also in the darkness. . . . All is movement in the intense warm blackness, and all is hushed and breathless, so that the slightest sounds have an almost unnatural and shattering force: "The beetles *clattered* at the blind"—"The hawks fell *twanging* from the sky." When at last the rain comes, it is

with a roar like fire, and after the lightning, thunder *rips* the shattered gloom. (pp. 78-9)

In **"Night and the Pines,"** which I think is the finest of all Scott's nocturnes, the darkness is intensified by the darkness of the pine woods. . . . [After] the half-heard thunder of a lonely fall and the eerie cry of the loon—"that cry of light despair, / As if a demon laughed upon the air," the croak of a raven, and the sound of a pine cone dropping in the dark, we come at the end to the invocation of a Sibyl. . . . (p. 79)

[The association] of love with sorrow, night, dream, mystery, and power may lead us into a consideration of a group of poems even more remarkable than those that deal with the nocturnal aspects of nature—the divided and often ambiguous love poems that bulk large in the body of Scott's collected poetry.

Duncan Campbell Scott's love poems are the product of the clash between a fervid and indeed passionate sensibility and a courtly, gentle, and rather nobly archaic—but very firmly held—conviction about the nature of love as a school of ideals. According to this conviction, love is an act of adoration and the Beloved is the object of a truly religious worship, of a service which paradoxically involves an act of desecration, both real and symbolic, as its central mystery and its culminating hope. As a result, many of the love poems express, or betray, an ambivalence that gives them a curious intensity and interest. It is hard to describe, but they seem to have a mercurial and doubtful sensitivity. They are tremulous and a little feverish. They hang in the balance, as it were, and we don't quite know which way they are going to fall. What contributes to this effect is the simultaneous presence of two opposing forces. T. S. Eliot has named them rightly in a famous passage describing the quality of sensibility in one of the lesser known Elizabethan dramatists as *fascination* and *repulsion*. (pp. 79-80)

[A] dramatic poem called **"By the Seashore"** . . . might have been written by Hardy or Lawrence. At dusk on the sands a man lights a fire of driftwood "as the tide and the sunlight are ebbing away." He is a lover, and he is burning old letters (he promised to burn them)—the image of faith and a sacrificial ritual is clear, and . . . we have the touch of fire and the symbol of a scar—"The desire of the heart leaves sorrow that lives in a scar." The most powerful moment in this rather subdued and elegiac drama grows out of the restraint with which the poet pictures the ironic destruction by fire of the love-words of the letters. . . . (p. 81)

[**"By the Seashore,"**] because of the restraint, the irony, and the controlled passion is a . . . mature and satisfying poem. . . . It is a song of experience, not of innocence; and if it lacks the tremulous nervous excitement of the divided poems in which there is a clash between pleasure and pain, or between duty and desire, or between the dream and the reality, it has something better—a more universal humanity.

Yet it is the tremulous excitement that provides even some of the less successful of Scott's love poems with a glamour which, if a little fortuitous, is nevertheless significant—for it lights up an important aspect of the poet's metaphysic of love—his chivalric and courtly worship of maidenhood, at the worst destroyed and at the best transfigured by desire and passion. (p. 82)

[**"The Water Lily"**] impresses itself on the mind as a symbolist poem akin to Mallarmé's evocation of the snowy swan or Yeats's of the rose upon the rood of time. There is an exotic, almost oriental luxury about the imagery and atmosphere of the poem that recalls Coleridge and again the early Tennyson. There is a strange and very powerful fusion of whiteness and coldness with passionate, almost tropical, ardours and odours that serves to dramatize what I feel is the hidden theme of the poem—the presentation of an ambivalent attitude towards virginity. . . . The end of the poem is ecstatic joy, consummation, release, and rest. Nothing in D. H. Lawrence is deeper, more accurate, or more unmistakable than this.

"The Water Lily" is a symbolist poem and as such it possesses a universality that lifts it above the limitations of the personal. Another of Scott's poems in which the sexual theme is treated with equal frankness is the remarkable "Spring on Mattagami." (pp. 83-5)

The poem is clearly a dramatic presentation of division, and the two impulses of attraction and repulsion . . . are here central to the drama. The beautiful and virginal Beloved in the scented rose garden and the passionate Lover in the rank effulgence of the forest are the opposing poles around which whirl clusters of powerful but uncertain emotions. The drama is presented in two contrasting pictures—the first a garden scene and a gesture of refusal. . . . The second picture is of the forest wilderness, and all is enflamed and heightened by desire. . . . Everything in nature in this season of northern spring teaches the lesson of surrender and acceptance—the partridge drumming, the laughter of the loons, the "shy moose fawn nestling by its mother," the orient perfume of the marsh flowers, the water-spray weaving iridescent fountains, and at night fireflies and stars tangled in the forest branches. (pp. 85-6)

[The] protagonist of the poem . . . begins to indulge his fancy and entertain the pleasures of hope. . . . But this is followed by an awakening and a withering into the truth: "Vain is the dream. . . . Fate is stern and hard—fair and false and vain"— and the poem ends with renunciation and submission to a greater law than the law of personal desire. . . . (pp. 86-7)

From the beginning, of course, there had been present in Duncan Campbell Scott's work another and very different strain from the tremulous and feverish one that pulses through the love poems. From love and from certain aspects of nature, particularly from those associated with night and storm and the hours and seasons of change come the impulses that kindle. But there were also the impulses that restrain. These are derived from the poet's traditions—partly artistic and partly social and religious. (p. 87)

Let us consider for a moment how Lampman and how Scott see nature. As I wrote in The Book of Canadian Poetry, "Lampman is an impressionist. Sensation rather than idea is what he derives from landscape. . . . Details of shape and colour, seen in the light of a precise minute and valued for their own sake are what give a special significance to Lampman's portrayal of nature." I think this is true of Scott also; but while it serves to define almost the whole of Lampman's originality, it is only a part of Scott's. And in Scott nature is usually less exclusively presented as a picture: more often it is a picture and an idea. (p. 88)

[The] characteristic virtue of Duncan Campbell Scott as an interpreter of nature and the real mark of his originality is the glowing fusion in his poetry of keenness of observation with clarity of thought so that the thing and the idea seem to be struck out together.

When we have the happy combination of this kind of sensibility with a classical precision and conciseness of style, we have

work of a major excellence. This excellence can be illustrated in all of his books, and in the latest more effectively than in the first. . . . [This] is how the poet describes a harrow being driven by the farmer up a dry and dusty ploughed slope somewhere on the prairie:

> Up the long slope six horses toil. . . .
> Where a disc-harrow tears the soil,
> Up the long slope six horses toil. . . .
> . . . as they go a cloud of dust
> Comes like a spirit out of earth
> And follows where they go.
>
> (p. 89)

It is the intimate interplay of light and shade and the delicate half-states of twilight and mist together with the magnification and slight distortions of sound that seem intensely to Scott and set him apart from the other poets of his generation in Canada. He is as sensitive and intense as Carman, and far more accurate; as accurate as Lampman or Roberts, and more truly passionate than either. It is this love of the intermediate stage, the moment of change, when things and qualities are intermingled and partake of one another's characteristics that contributes much of the movement and drama to Scott's nature poetry. His most vivid and characteristic scenes are pictures of change, flow, and conflict. The times that fascinate him are times of change—sunset, dawn, or spring—and it is movement and change that make even his descriptive pieces dramatic—they are filled with images of storm, of melting, of thawing, of burgeoning or dying: colours are intermingled; sounds, sights and odours are fused with the emotional overtones that generate or accompany them. (pp. 90-1)

What use does the poet make of his perceptions and impressions? To answer it, let me [describe] what the poet saw from [a] train window. He looks at the foreground . . .

> Traces there are of wild things in the snow—
> Partridge at play, tracks of the foxes' paws
> That broke a path to sun them in the trees.
> They're going fast where all impressions go
> On a frail substance—images like these,
> Vagaries the unconscious mind receives
> From nowhere, and lets go to nothingness
> With the lost flush of last year's autumn leaves.

The theme of the poem, we see, is psychological—the way fleeting impressions fasten on the mind; and it is traditional as well—the great classical commonplace of the impermanence of all things. But the triumph of the poem depends not so much upon the subtlety and precision of the observation as upon the casualness and informality of the occasion. The homeliest and most ordinary experience can be made both unique and universally significant—when it happens to a true poet.

And when we read it and take it in we ourselves become true poets, and our eyes are opened to the possibilities of enrichment in the sensuous world of phenomena. That is why poems like this have a value—I needn't hesitate to call it a usefulness— that is incalculable. But quite apart from this, I would cite these lines as characteristic of a new clarity and simplicity that Scott attains to in the poetry of his last years. It is a poetry that one might well call modern, if it were not timeless. . . . It is both traditional and original. This is high praise indeed, but not unjust praise. (pp. 91-2)

A.J.M. Smith, "Duncan Campbell Scott" (originally a lecture delivered at Carleton University in 1958), in Our Living Tradition, second and third series, *edited by Robert L. McDougall (copyright © 1959, by University of Toronto Press), University of Toronto Press, 1959, pp. 73-94.*

DESMOND PACEY (essay date 1958)

[There are] three types of poetry in which Scott excels: lyrical and descriptive pieces in which his training in music and the visual arts is used to advantage; the relatively austere, restrained but intense ballads of Indian or of other forms of primitive life; and, best of all, the poems of mystery, fantasy, or dream in which the music and colour of the first group combine with the weird and terrible effects of the second. Any adequate appraisal of Scott's work must take account of all three types. (p. 141)

The Magic House is a first volume of surprisingly high quality. There is not a really bad poem in the book, and there are a number of extremely good ones—notably **"The Voice and the Dusk,"** a very colourful descriptive lyric diffused with soft music and tender feeling, **"The Fifteenth of April,"** an exercise in seasonal description which equals Lampman in detailed observation of natural landscape and atmosphere, **"A Summer Storm,"** in which we see for the first time Scott's interest in the contrast of storm and calm, **"In the Country Churchyard,"** an elegy for his father which combines quiet dignity, sincere feeling, and descriptive accuracy, and **"The Reed-Player,"** a poem dedicated to Bliss Carman which evokes the lure of a magical tune at twilight and suggests the later **"Piper of Arll."** On a slightly lower level than these, but still of high quality, are the title poem, which concerns a medieval lady in a turreted castle and is pleasing in spite of its obvious echoes of Tennyson's "Lady of Shallot," **"In the House of Dreams,"** a visionary poem about an enchanted garden, and several short descriptive lyrics such as **"The River Town," "At Les Eboulements," "The First Snow," "In November," "A Night in June," "Night and the Pines,"** and **"A Night in March."** The most frequently anthologized poem in this first book, however, has been **"At the Cedars,"** the story of a double drowning during a logging drive. Written in short, jerky lines, and altogether devoid of decoration, the poem is an interesting experiment; but it is far from being the best poem in the book, and only a critic ignorant of or insensitive to the subtle melodies, suggestive atmosphere, and vivid colouring of most of the volume could possibly prefer it.

The fact is that **"At the Cedars"** is quite atypical of this first volume. The basic pattern of the book is that of natural description of an intensely colourful sort touched here and there with magic and mystery. It is a good book of late romantic verse, influenced to some extent by Coleridge, Keats, and Tennyson, but above all by the Pre-Raphaelite school. It has the Pre-Praphaelite air of melancholy and mystery, the same delight in vivid, detailed word-painting, and in contrasts of colour and shadow, storm and calm, tranquillity and terror, familiarity and strangeness. It is soft, gentle verse, written mainly in quatrains but also in other stanza forms, in the sonnet, and occasionally in free verse. An analysis of the diction shows that rich words with the maximum aura of romantic suggestiveness predominate—words such as golden, silver, rosy, shadowy, gentle, tender, purple. Effects of light and shade are prominent both in the diction—there are many words such as sparkling, shining, twinkling, gleaming, burnished, glimmering, burning—and in the imagery. . . . (pp. 145-47)

Labour and the Angel, like most second books of verse, is something of a disappointment. Rather than a stronger, it is a considerably weaker book than its predecessor. It is dominated by four long poems—the title poem, **"The Harvest," "Dame Regnant,"** and **"The Piper of Arll"**—of which the first three are of negligible value. Indeed **"The Piper of Arll"** is the only really satisfying poem in the whole book. It is obvious that Scott's confidence in the value of purely descriptive poetry was waning—the poems of that sort in this book are much inferior—and that he was trying out various alternatives. One such alternative was poetry of Indian life and character. . . . There are two such Indian poems in the book—**"The Onondaga Madonna"** and **"Watkwenies"**—and though both of them have been praised by other critics (Masefield even going so far as to call **"Watkwenies"** the most perfect of Scott's portraits of Indians) I cannot see them as a successful alternative at this stage. To me, they are both unreal, unconvincing finger exercises which fall far short of the dramatic immediacy of such a later Indian poem as **"The Forsaken."**

Another and more dangerous alternative approach which Scott was apparently trying out at this time was that of explicit didacticism. This temptation to don the surplice of the preacher had already beset Charles G. D. Roberts, and it was never henceforth to be entirely absent from Scott's mind. It betrayed him at this stage into writing **"Labour and the Angel,"** a series of platitudes about the holiness of work, **"The Dame Regnant,"** a long poem whose laboured point is that gossip is a bad thing, and **"The Lesson,"** one of those horrible Victorian album pieces about the wisdom to be learned from a child. It seems that we may blame Browning for these unfortunate lapses on Scott's part: the title poem especially bears strong marks of Browning's influence in both style and thought. . . . (pp. 148-49)

A third alternative to the descriptive verse of *The Magic House* which Scott tried in the second volume was an expression of gay fatalism. The two poems of this sort—**"The Cup"** and **"The Happy Fatalist"**—are much more successful than the didactic pieces, and they reveal a side of Scott's nature to which he too seldom gave expression. There was in his nature a streak of healthy scepticism which is apparent here, occasionally in his prose, but above all in his privately printed *Byron on Wordsworth,* composed for the Byron Centenary in 1924.

None of these alternatives, however, seriously rivalled the mixture of colourful description and mysterious atmosphere which was Scott's most successful formula in *The Magic House.* The two best poems in *Labour and the Angel*—**"The Piper of Arll"** and **"Avis"**—would have fitted very well into the first volume. **"The Piper of Arll"** has in full measure all of Scott's best qualities. It is rich and colourful in diction, striking in imagery, musical in sound, and instinct with a strange and mysterious fascination. **"Avis"** is not quite so memorable, but it too is full of rich word-pictures and of a strange enchantment. (pp. 149-50)

[*New World Lyrics and Ballads*] came as reassuring proof that Scott's poetic inspiration was far from exhausted. There is a new vitality in the more purely descriptive pieces, and such poems as **"The Sea by the Wood"** and its companion piece **"The Wood by the Sea," "Twin-Flowers on the Portage," "Night Hymns on Lake Nipigon," "A Nest of Hepaticas,"** and **"Rapids at Night"** have all the colour, music, brilliance, and restrained intensity of the best poems in *The Magic House.* The distinctive quality of this third volume, however, is provided by the ballads of Indian life, and especially by **"On the Way to the Mission," "The Forsaken,"** and **"The Mission of the Trees." "The Forsaken"** in particular is a haunting poem which rivals "**The Piper of Arll**" for the title of the finest single poem from Scott's pen. The volume, however, is not without its dross, and this again takes the form of poems which are too explicitly didactic and which merely utter platitudes in a solemn voice.

The diction in this third volume remains characteristically rich, although in the Indian ballads it is considerably toned down to suit their more sombre subjects. . . . [The] readiness to experiment with verse-forms, together with the experiments with Indian subject-matter, indicate that Scott's poetic powers were far from dormant in the first years of the new century.

Further evidence of this continued vitality was provided in 1906, when Scott issued *Via Borealis,* a brochure containing seven poems written during an official journey he made that year into the hinterland of northwestern Ontario. . . . These seven poems, as was perhaps to be expected from the circumstances of their composition and rapid publication, are unequal and somewhat lacking in finish, but they share a dynamic intensity which makes even the worst of them interesting. (pp. 150-52)

[*Lundy's Lane and Other Poems*] was given some substance by the republication in it of the seven poems which had appeared in the brochure *Via Borealis,* but the rest of the book is weak. Two of the new poems—"**Night**" and "**The Sailor's Sweetheart**"—are fairly good lyrics, but most of the others are embarrassingly bad. The title poem is almost a parody of sentimental patriotism at its worst, "**Fragment of an Ode to Canada**" is sheer bombast, "**Madonna with Two Angels**" is a sickly Victorian album-piece, "**The Beggar and the Angel**" is humour in the worst possible taste, and so on. Even the poems which E. K. Brown singles out for special praise—"**Meditation at Perugia**," "**The Height of Land**," and "**Lines in Memory of Edmund Morris**"—strike me as mediocre moralizing at best. (pp. 153-54)

Lundy's Lane, then, marked a decline in Scott's poetic artistry. The volume contains some piquant imagery, some brilliant description, some lovely musical lines . . . , and a large amount of technical experimentation with various metrical effects, but these things are largely wasted because they are mixed with a diffuse didacticism.

Fortunately for Canadian poetry, and for Scott's reputation, his next volume, *Beauty and Life,* . . . was much better than its predecessor. Scott's own favourite among his books of verse, it is his finest single volume. It opens with an "**Ode for the Keats Centenary**," a very good elegy in free verse. Marred by occasional archaisms such as "what boots it," it is nevertheless on the whole dignified, eloquent, and thoughtful without being ponderous or pompous. As is usual in Scott's work, the descriptive passages of the poem are the strongest, the didactic sections the weakest. The relatively high level of this ode is maintained throughout most of the poem which follows it, "**Variations on a Seventeenth Century Theme**." . . . The fourth, sixth, and ninth lyrics in the sequence are especially successful. The poem illustrates once more the fascination exerted for Scott by contrasts, especially contrasts of light and shade.

Not all the poems in *Beauty and Life* are of the quality of these first two, but of the thirty-nine poems in the book seventeen are very good, and only half a dozen are really weak. The best poems combine Scott's gifts of colourful description and compelling atmosphere; the worst are those which are either sentimental or didactic or both. The chief trend discernible in the

volume is towards greater brevity and conciseness. One suspects that at about this time Scott had been reading Imagist verse, for many of the lyrics have the sparse, epigrammatic quality of that type of poem. Lyrics such as "**Lilacs and Humming Birds**," "**Afterwards**," "**The Enigma**," "**In Grenada**," "**Impromptu**" and "**In Winter**" are short, clear, and finely chiselled. These lyrics give the volume its distinctive quality, but there are two good longer poems in Scott's more familiar narrative style: "**Senza Fine**," a monologue by a murderer which displays Scott's eeriness near its best, and "**The Eagle Speaks**," in which an eagle describes its manner of killing a man. (pp. 155-56)

Evidence of [Scott's] travel is clearly visible in *The Green Cloister,* many of the poems in which have European settings. The general level of this book is quite high. The great majority of the poems are descriptive or contemplative lyrics, full of colour, atmosphere and exact observation. Of this group, perhaps the most interesting are "**A Blackbird Rhapsody**," a decorative, ecstatic, but somewhat diffuse poem celebrating the song of the blackbird which seems to Scott to express the simple love of life, "**Como**," a piece of straight landscape painting, "**Evening at Ravello**," which achieves a fine sense of twilight tranquillity, and "**Chiostro Verde**," a lovely soft suggestive description of the "green cloister." There are two Indian poems in his stark and violent manner: "**A Scene at Lake Manitou**" and the well-known "**At Gull Lake: August, 1810**." Both of these poems are barely saved from melodrama by the quiet, peaceful endings which Scott imposes upon them. In this respect, if in this respect only, these Indian poems are typical of the volume: the dominant tone is of quietness discovered after much turmoil, a kind of disciplined poise, an achieved serenity. (p. 160)

The Circle of Affection [is] a miscellany which brings together four new short stories and a group of later poems, five essays, nine early but uncollected poems, and six early short stories. Several of the new poems indicate that Scott's poetic talent endured to the end of his life. "**Old Olives at Bordighera**," "**A Song**" and "**The Cascades of the Gatineau**" are late examples of his dominant manner of atmospheric description. The last-named, a poem of only four lines, is in itself a brief epitome of his chief poetic interest: the contrast of rush and calm, of storm and silence. . . . Two other poems in the book— "**Veronique Fraser**" and "**Amanda**"—illustrate his continuing interest in tales of primitive ferocity. Finally, the sonnet sequence entitled "**Twelfth Anniversary**" is a splendid tribute to his second wife. None of the early poems reprinted in the book, with the possible exception of the lush but intermittently pleasing "**The Orchard in Moonlight**," rival these late compositions. (p. 161)

The general conception of Scott's poetry, I believe, is that it is relatively drab and colourless. The critics have emphasized his restraint, his austerity, his discipline, to the point where a quite distorted view of him has been given. This is the result of suggesting that the sombre ballads of Indian life, undoubtedly an important and unique element in the Scott canon, are all of his work that matters. The fact is, as I began this essay by pointing out, that there are three areas in which Scott is successful as a poet—in colourful description, in violent narrative, and in vivid dream—and that only in the narratives, and there only in a qualified sense, are such adjectives as austere and sombre appropriate.

If we look at Scott's most successful descriptive pieces, such as "**A Night in June**" and "**Night and the Pines**" in *The Magic*

House, "**Rapids at Night**" in *New World Lyrics and Ballads,* "**Leaves**" and "**Lilacs and Humming Birds**" in *Beauty and Life,* or "**Como**" and "**Chiostro Verde**" in *The Green Cloister,* we find that they are far from austere or sombre. On the contrary, they are ecstatic, colourful, even at times ornate. (pp. 161-62)

There is, of course, far less bright colour in the Indian ballads. "**The Forsaken,**" as suits its sombre theme of desertion and death, is a study in grey and white; "**On the Way to the Mission,**" similarly, is a study in white, silver, and ivory. But the factors which above all unite these ballads with the fantasies and the descriptive poems, and give a single effect to Scott's work as a whole, are his fascination with contrast and his belief that beauty and peace are the inevitable aftermath of storm and conflict. (p. 163)

As for the dream poems, "**The Piper of Arll**" is a tissue of contrasts—contrast between the secluded bay and the wild ocean, between the rustic shepherd and the travelled sailors, between the peaceful setting and the violence suggested by such images as the three pines "like three warriors reaving home / The plunder of a burning town." (pp. 163-64)

These contrasts are in themselves a form of conflict, but in almost all of Scott's poems there is conflict of a more direct sort. The essence of Scott's view of the world seems to be a vision of a battle-ground where nature is in conflict with itself, man in conflict with nature, and man in conflict with man. But he does not leave it at that. Out of the conflict emerges, whether soon or later, peace and beauty. He has faith in the ultimate rightness of things, in a presiding spirit which in the long run has a beneficent purpose, and in man's capacity to endure. The final note of Scott's work is not that of the storm but of the silence which follows the storm, is not despair but serenity. But it is not an easy nor a complacent serenity; it is a serenity achieved after much effort. His long career, his steady application to the task of poetry, the message of that poetry—all bear quiet witness to the strength of the human will. (p. 164)

> *Desmond Pacey, "Duncan Campbell Scott," in his* Ten Canadian Poets: A Group of Biographical and Critical Essays *(copyright © McGraw-Hill Ryerson Limited, 1958; reprinted by permission), Ryerson Press, 1958, pp. 141-64.*

GARY GEDDES (essay date 1968)

If evaluation of his poetry is to have any meaning, Scott must be re-classified; he must be seen alongside not his temporal but his spiritual mentors—Coleridge, Tennyson and Arnold. In what follows, then, I have tried to approach Scott's poetry through the medium of his published letters, with a view to dispelling a number of misconceptions concerning his aims and achievement; at the same time, I have been tempted to look freshly at some old favourites, especially "**The Piper of Arll**".

To re-classify Scott as a nineteenth-century poet is less seriously limiting than one might think. "Give me some credit for logic as applied to aesthetics", he wrote in 1905, "for I declare that I value brain power at the bottom of everything. If you call *me* a nature poet you will have to forget some of my best work". These are not the words of a man denying his artistic destiny, but rather the sincere expression of a desire to be seen in the right perspective. Scott fully understood the place of nature in his poetry, but he believed that some of his best work derived its stimulus from elsewhere—from man and from the life of the imagination itself. I would like to discuss his poetry

from these three points of view—nature, man, and the life of the imagination. (pp. 15-16)

Scott responded to nature in the best traditions of romanticism—appreciation without prostration. . . . "The life of nature", he declared, "is as varied and complex as the life of the spirit and it is for this reason that man finds in nature infinite correspondences with his spiritual states." Fundamental to this impressionism, however, is the understanding that nature is not a repository of "truth", but rather the means by which man's own important sensations are elicited and activated. (p. 16)

In "**The Height of Land**", his most philosophical poem, nature becomes an incentive to reminiscence and reflection. The poet stands on the uplands in the serenity of evening, brooding about the lives and ideals of men. His senses sharpen to the hush of wind and the play of moths around a low fire, so that he can almost hear the "gathering of rivers in their sources". As he surveys the land in this hyper-sensitive state, a mysterious "Something comes by flashes / Deeper than peace," as unexpectedly quiet and intriguing as the calm at the eye of a hurricane. At that moment the state of the land may be said to reflect exactly the state of the poet's mind. The symbiosis is prelusive to finding a "deeper meaning" than is written on the surface of things. The poet's emphasis is centred not on the details of the physical scene, but on the impression which it fixes on his mind; thus, it may be seen, his reflections on life constitute a somewhat higher level of participation in nature—that is, a philosophical rather than a purely descriptive involvement.

Scott's insistence, that nature can only provide correspondence to man's spiritual states, is perhaps more rigorous than his practice justifies. In the same poem, for example, a significant change of pace occurs. Suddenly the smell of charred ground transports the poet back in time to a bush-fire he has experienced. . . . There is something more instinctive than rational in the way this image is presented. Although the landscape is technically a state of soul, the image of the predatory bush-fire seems rather to have been dragged up involuntarily from the poet's subconscious than to have resulted from a conscious search for secondary correspondences. The sheer force and immediacy of the experience clearly indicates that Scott's response to nature was, at times, stronger than his theory suggests. (p. 17)

Scott was pleasantly surprised to have pointed out to him by E. K. Brown the "intensity and restraint" in his poetry [see excerpt above]. Consciously or unconsciously, Scott had long been pursuing this elusive goal. . . . Scott's respect for the guiding and restraining influence of traditional forms and metres parallels Coleridge's claim that metre originates psychologically, "to hold in check the workings of passion". Control is the standard for both art and life. (p. 19)

While admitting the influence of nature in his poetry, Scott hoped to make clear that his main interest and stimulus was in man. . . . Even his impressionism, which asserts the superiority of the impression to the object, reflects Scott's humanism. Similarly, he despised all types of artistic escapism and obscurantism as much as he despised the mindless veneration of nature, because both led away from the proper study of mankind. . . .

Scott lamented the loss of beauty from life—"Beauty has taken refuge from our life, / That grew too loud and wounding"—but his Indian and habitant poems reveal that he discovered beauty again in the very noise and wounds he had lamented, in the beauty of human suffering. In **"The Height of Land"**, Scott paused to "Brood on the welter of the lives of men", but he did not pause long; he plunged beneath the surface of beaver-skins and tail-feathers into the dark recesses of the human heart. And the raw life he found there is quite distinct from anything outside of Pratt in anthologies of Canadian poetry. The tragic killing of Keejigo in **"At Gull Lake: August, 1810"** is a dramatic *tour de force.* . . . The strength here is not descriptive but dramatic; Scott combines the economy of the ballad, the human interest of the drama, and the suspense of both. (p. 20)

The difficulty Scott had in subduing his subjective and descriptive impulses was largely dispelled when he embraced the human drama. In **"At the Cedars"**, a fascinating dramatic monologue, the narrative is exceedingly stark—boiled right down to the skeleton. Bones, at any time, are provocative, and these are no exception; consequently, the temptation to find allegory in the suggestive names—Isaac, Baptiste and Virginie—and the *diabolus ex machina,* is subdued only by the rapid pace and intensity of the narrative. As in the ballad, much of the success of **"At the Cedars"** depends on what is left unsaid; the poem gains considerably by the indefiniteness of the motives in the suicide of the nameless sister of Virginie. . . . To call Scott a poet of nature in these poems can only be justified if one means what Dr. Johnson meant when he applied the same label to Shakespeare—*human nature.*

While responding creatively to man and nature, Scott also rejoiced in the fervid life of his imagination. "The life of poetry is in the imagination," he insisted, "there lies the ground of true adventure and though the poet's mind may be starved and parched by the lack of variety in life, he persists nevertheless to make poetry out of its dust and ashes." Much of his poetry finds its life not in external stimuli but in an internal compulsion, in the "volcano", as Scott called the imagination. And it is there—in the heat of imagination—that one of Scott's finest poems arose, Phoenix-like from the ashes. (p. 21)

"The Piper" has had a poor press; critics seldom fail to mention it, but always for the wrong reasons. (p. 22)

Criticism of **"The Piper"** seems based on the mistaken assumption that meaning and indefiniteness are mutually exclusive. That the poem is intentionally vague and mysterious there can be little doubt. "At the root of everything is mystery," Scott wrote. "Poetry illuminates this mass of knowledge and by inspiration will eventually reach the core of the mystery." He preferred the poetry of Maeterlinck, who was "endeavouring to awaken the wonder-element in a modern way, constantly expressing the almost unknowable things we all feel." . . . Scott laboured, of set artistic purpose, to leave **"The Piper"** indefinite and suggestive; he aimed at a fusion of form and content. "He may not care for the mystical," Scott said of his critic, Sykes [see excerpt above], "but there is more in 'The Piper of Arll' than he seems to have discovered."

"The Piper" may be seen on one level as an allegory of the artist. Living in harmony with his idyllic environment, the artist is confronted with a vision of loneliness to which he responds creatively. When the vision passes and inspiration dies, his remorse drives him to such distraction that he abuses his powers of compassion and communication. . . . Through conscious self-renunciation the artist begins to heal and he resurrects out of the ashes his initial heart-felt response tò the vision. When this is accomplished, in a burst of selfless energy he pours out

his soul in perfect harmony with the world and is reunited with his dream-vision in a beautiful immortality.

The nature of the poetic experience, thus oversimplified, is essentially religious, and it is almost certain that Scott intended the parallel to run throughout the poem. (pp. 22-3)

The poem does support a religious interpretation of the image of the three pines. The piper responds to God as the bay responds to the ocean's tides. The vision-ship comes with an angel at the bows, who departs just as the piper achieves his immortality. The piper's broken will corresponds, of course, to the Christian paradoxes of life in death, fulfillment in self-sacrifice and knowledge through child-like faith. At the moment of his mastery over passion and power, the piper is standing at the foot of the three pines, "Immortal for a happy hour" (p. 24)

The *Tempest*-like sea change implies a concept of art as stasis. Life, in Scott's poetry, is a movement towards eternal rest, a rest which is common to all men—the poet, the religious and the oppressed of every kind. . . . [The] piper achieves his rest; first his will and then his body merge with the harmonious cosmos.

So much for the lack of meaning in **"The Piper"**. (p. 25)

Scott's many-sidedness stems not so much from his wide areas of interest as from his conception of the function of poetry.

The responsibilities of the poet are outlined in **"The Woodspring to the Poet"**, Scott's poetic manifesto. The woodspring presents himself as an exacting master. He counsels the poet to cultivate flexibility (a good Canadian virtue!), to be all things to all men, a sort of general practitioner whose task it is "To charm, to comfort, to illume." To fill this colossal order the poet must write poems of every kind: he must write those which will guide and inspire youth, "Till over his spirit shall roll / The vast wave of control"; he must nurture the creative spirit with poems like **"The Piper of Arll"** . . . ; and, finally, he must administer to the dead souls of academe and the marketplace a particularly metaphysical cure. . . . This broad view of the function of poetry beggars the notion that Scott was only a nature poet. Whatever his creative stimulus—whether nature, man, or the life of the imagination—Scott directed his various melodies to the needs of the human heart; and if his poetry has a wide-spread appeal, it is because Scott was a piper of many tunes. (pp. 25-6)

Gary Geddes, "Piper of Many Tunes" (reprinted by permission of the author), in Canadian Literature, *No. 37, Summer, 1968, pp. 15-27.*

BERNARD MUDDIMAN (essay date 1974)

Poetry had always interested [Duncan Scott], but music was his first love. His prose work came last of all; and it is there, in the short story form, to my mind, as I shall endeavour to show, Mr. Scott works best. . . . (p. 32)

"The Magic House" was a modest enough volume, without pretention, just the garnered up songs of a young man possessed of a delicate fancy. Immaturity is written over every line of it; but, it is a charming and fresh immaturity that has promise in its quiet restraint. There is no riot here of roses and wine and dancing girls, no poses or startling and dazzling ideas. The poet is not quite yet master of his material; and, sometimes, it has a crudely broken-up music; but, it is never a discord of thought, only of sound. For occasionally a patch of prose in the text retards its small pellucid rill of verse. But the thought is always there. Save for two poems, I would almost call it a volume of delightful minor verse.

It is imitative, to a certain extent like the work of all young poets. Their fancies and dreams are naturally shot through with the magnificent colour tones of the greater poets, who have intoxicated their brains and impregnated the ivory cells of gray matter with the unheard melody of vision. Here and there we notice a touch of Tennyson as in the title poem. **"Above St. Irénée"** is a study of Wordsworthian mode. A Pre-Raphaelite note rings through **"In the House of Dreams."** His meditation in one of the little countryside church-yards of Ontario is a study after the manner of Gray's immortal elegy tuned in the key of Matthew Arnold's wistfulness without the latter's doubt. Death is the eternal leveller of everything, and this hackneyed idea is wrought out in rather tame purple phrases. But it must not be thought that Duncan Scott is merely an imitator. These echoes are really not worth a second consideration. He is, when at his best, purely himself.

Again, another influence, I seem to trace at work in his early poetry, is that of his friend and fellow civil servant Archibald Lampman. (pp. 32-3)

The tedious descriptive quality of Lampman's heavy Dutch landscapes, however, was not to be the métier of Duncan Scott. Even in this volume he shakes himself free of the seductive sweetness of his friend's work. For he has agreed "to choose a beauty puritan and stern." As a contrast, indeed, with Lampman, his creed, it must be admitted, is more active, less drugged with narcotic thoughts, more nimble and aesthetic. . . . (p. 33)

For Scott seizes on human interest of life and is unlulled by the heavy murmur of the bees and heady flower-scents. Like an athlete, his verse at its best carries no superfluous weight, and in this little volume we find him at his best in **"At the Cedars"** and **"The Reed Player."** The latter poem is a most splendid piece of music. . . .

In **"At the Cedars,"** in short, irregular, abrupt, lithe verse, which he affects, Scott chronicles an incident at a log-jam on a river—an incident peculiarly Canadian. This is the first occasion on which he treats of French-Canadian themes, that, afterwards, with the Indian, form the body of his best work.

Five years after **"The Magic House"** Duncan Scott issued in Boston **"Labour and the Angel"**. This second volume reveals a marked growth, a larger vocabulary, a firmer and stronger grip on life and a deliberate study of Meredith and Browning. The poet's mind has developed, has studied the psychology of a young man's day dreams and gone down to the market-places of life. He has suffered. He has rejoiced. Life has taught him something of her cruel lessons, her mystic secrets and hidden raptures. Above all, the philosophy of Browning and his method seem to move the poet in this volume. Perhaps this is in no wise strange. The passage of a soul from the dream-wrapt palaces of the poets of beauty to the jostling throng of Browning's men and women is a natural evolution. Many souls have found this way.

The technic, too, of this volume is more varied, more self-reliant than his first timid verses. The influence of Browning is here also very evident in this poetic expansion. (p. 34)

[This volume] contains an extraordinary excursion, absolutely unique for the restrained verse of Duncan Scott into the sardonic world of Pope and Swift. I refer to the poem entitled **"The Dame Regnant"**. This is nothing more than a savage onset against what the French call *bavardage;* in other words, Lady Tittle-Tattle—Scandal. It flames with almost rabid rage. It sweeps on like the pent-up fury of a man who has suffered a wrong. No other poem of Duncan Scott has this spirit of *saeva indignatio*, of Juvenalian flash. Its style is strongly reminiscent of Browning; but it has a lurid light that is Swift's. . . . (p. 36)

Personally, I consider this mental writhing alien to Scott's work; but the poet himself, strangely enough, considers it "One of the best things I have ever done"

[The third volume of Scott's poetry is] **"New World Lyric and Ballads"**. The whole volume demonstrates that Scott is purely a lyrical and not a dramatic poet. The Indian theme has now become predominant. The ballads relate mainly to incidents in the Far North and are strictly not ballads at all. The old ballad note cannot be recreated. (p. 37)

We can never succeed in forgetting this as we turn over the pages. For example, take the piece entitled **"The Mission of the Trees"**. A small northern tribe suffer much from famine. The witch doctor ascribes this to the fact that one of their number and his son are Christians. The little boy is sick and he tells his father he will never be well again until he hears the Mission bell. So the father binds on his snowshoes and with the child on his back starts on his way to **"The Mission of the Trees"**. Of course, he never attains it. A snow blizzard and danger overwhelm them. The whole is cast in the ballad quatrain; but it is a legend, not a ballad. Again in those irregular ballads **"On the Way to the Mission"** and **"The Forsaken"**, we have two little brutal incidents of Indian life that are essentially dramatic and consequently marred by a lyrical singer. In a harsh way he strains himself to be dramatic in the *vers libre* form he employs; but, the result is unconvincing, and blurred like a smudged charcoal drawing. While a third poem of this style, **"Catnip Jack"**, is possibly the worst poem he has written since maturity. It is horror overdone. The whole atmosphere is as impossible as it is ridiculously repulsive. **"The Forgers,"** on the other hand, is watered-down Schiller. Again he falls back into the fatal rut of the Ontario poets' endless yards of description and reflection in a few poems like **"The Rapids at Night"** and **"A Nest of Hepaticas"**.

However, the volume is saved by a few lyrics which have a beauty in them that Duncan Scott never before attained. It is here we note the poet's increased power, otherwise we might be forced to hail the volume as a temporary relapse. The prelude and epilogue are furnished by two exceptionally beautiful little outbursts of lyrical song. Vague and bizarre almost like the early poems of Maeterlinck, they have a strange, ethereal music. In **"The Sea by the Wood"** we have a strange, out-of-the-world atmosphere of weariness. It is the sea beyond the world and the poet touches a fanciful lute above its spirit waters. In **"The Wood by the Sea"** we are in a magic land of unimagined bird and flower where stray the dreamers of all day-dreams.

His last volume of verse [**"Via Borealis"**] is a kind of glorified Christmas card. . . . The longest of [the poems], **"Spring on Mattagami,"** is in some respects the sweetest poem Duncan Scott has written. It should be called "Love in a Wilderness", for it is clearly modelled after George Meredith's "Love in a Valley". The poet fares by canoe to the northern wilderness, the land of quintessential passion. He ponders the ways of his maid as poets only do, yearns for her presence, and finally pours out his whole heart's tale. . . . (pp. 37-8)

The highly sensuous imagery of the verse rushes on at a fine pace. There is a fuller elation, a wider ecstasy, a happier buoyancy here than one finds in Duncan Scott's other work. Every now and then gushes forth pure music. . . . (p. 39)

> *Bernard Muddiman, "Duncan Campbell Scott" (originally published in a different form in* The Canadian Magazine, *Vol. XLIII, No. 1, May, 1914), in* Duncan Campbell Scott: A Book of Criticism, *edited by S. L. Dragland (© The Tecumseh Press Ltd. and S. L. Dragland, 1974; reprinted by permission of The Tecumseh Press), Tecumseh Press, 1974, pp. 31-42.*

GLENN CLEVER (essay date 1975)

Duncan Campbell Scott's poetry receives more comment than does his fiction, yet his many stories . . . , distinctively Canadian and distinguished by quiet power, deserve attention. A versatile writer, Scott ranges widely. Against the typical village setting in the Quebec of the last half of the nineteenth century, he contrasts logging scenes on the Ottawa, colonial days in Montreal, Indian life on the prairies and in the forests, fur trading adventure in the north, even ghostly drama in a Spanish inn. Against the typical conservative villager, he contrasts children, heroes, lovers, the genteel impoverished, animal life, the blind, the aged, even the crazed. Against the typical tone of tolerance and restraint, he contrasts the tidal force of tragedy, the ripple of humour. Out of this variety themes recur, such as the growth of self-knowledge, the effects of emotion and time, the devotion and tensions of family life, the commitment to one's fellows. (p. ix)

With few exceptions Scott evokes settings that draw us in. Often these are almost pastoral, yet vivid with sense appeal. . . . But he is also adept at conveying wild and lonely panoramic vistas which have equally engrossing appeal. . . . (p. x)

Scott vivifies his description with imagery. . . . Yet constantly Scott sketches an outline, provided by acute perception, which provokes the imagination, for example: "The damp fields commenced to exhale a moist haze that spread, gauze-like, across the woods"; "In spaces of sky as delicately blue as blanched violets, small stars flashed clearly." (**"The Wooing of Monsieur Cuerrier"**).

Most of Scott's characters are alive with psychological actuality, though he seldom paints a full portrait. When he describes directly, he is effective. . . . His characters live close, and in relation to, nature. Paul Farlotte, for example, is to his fellow villagers almost a part of his renowned rose garden. (pp. x-xi)

We usually apprehend Scott's characters by action and speech, their own and others', and see them from the outside, or, at best, learn their moods by overhearing them, as though they were speaking aloud. The closest approach to stream-of-consciousness comes in **"An Adventure of Mrs. Mackenzie's."** . . . (p. xi)

Scott in the main gives us plain and simple folk. He concentrates more on widows, bachelors, orphans, and other "loners" than on full family life. Many of his heroes are middle-aged, even when cast in romantic roles. . . . His antagonists tend to be busy-bodies, bullies, and other social undesirables, rather than figures symbolic or suggestive of a real, malevolent evil. Protagonists and antagonists move in plots which range from

the tight inevitability of **"Expiation"** to the loosely episodic sequences of **"The Circle of Affection."**

Scott varies his narrative technique. He tells **"Paul Farlotte"** in the traditional way of a narrator explaining to his audience about Paul. In **"Labrie's Wife,"** however, he adopts a first person journal form; in **"Charcoal"** he relates largely from Charcoal's own point of view, though in third person; he uses first person for **"The Witching of Elspie"** and the "frame" of a first person fishing tale for **"At Plangeant's Locks,"** and presents **"The Little Milliner"** from the point of view of the busy-body antagonist. He generally effaces himself. Where he is present as narrator, his interpositions are sometimes relatively unobstrusive. . . . However, he can be much more obtrusive; for example, in **"An Adventure of Mrs. Mackenzie's,"** the narrator's interjections are so frequent and overt that they interfere with the flow of the story. . . . (pp. xi-xii)

Scott uses dialogue with variety and effectiveness. . . . The dialogue occasionally approaches the melodramatic but in the main is appropriate and highly functional in its principal effects of drama and humour. (p. xii)

Scott uses French Canadian settings, names, and phrases but fuses them organically into the stories. . . .

The stories are told with simple diction, imagery, and syntax but most distinctive about Scott's style are the rhythm and the tone. His prose rolls easily in long swells of an almost anaepestic flow, the cadence generally running in groups, each of four to five main stresses, spread over some twelve to thirteen relatively unstressed syllables. He uses contrast and parallels as a technique. For example, in **"The Flashlight"** he juxtaposes alcoholic husbands, one with a sympathetic, one with an antipathetic, wife. . . .

Scott typically opens a story with a descriptive setting, as in **"Paul Farlotte,"** following which he introduces the characters and their conflicts. He usually resolves the conflicts by rather quiet narrative, though some stories, for example the unveiling in **"The Pedlar,"** or the stabbing in **"The Tragedy of the Seigniory,"** jump with dramatic action. Mostly the resolution of conflict spreads over considerable time. . . . [He] keeps a constant unity of action. In some instances the sequence shifts abruptly without transition, leaving the reader to bridge the gap. . . . (p. xiii)

A few of Scott's stories are atypical. **"A Night in Cordoba,"** for example, with an exotic Spanish setting, supernatural action, and absence of human conflict, constitutes a pageant more than a short story. **"The Rose of Hope"** reflects, with its dreamy poetic symbolism, more of the Pre-Raphaelite and Celtic twilight auras than Scott's usual Canadian milieu. Similarly, the sledge-hammer duel in **"At Plangeant's Locks,"** the pistol duel and the sexual intrigue in **"An Adventure of Mrs. Mackenzie's,"** and the aristocratic characterization in both these stories, set them apart, as does the escaped murder theme and its handling in **"The Escapade of the Rev. Joshua Geer."**

Good variation in sentence and paragraph structure and length, as well as the variable relationship of rhythm to idea, give variety to Scott's style. . . .

Scott's general tone of objectivity and quiet intensity is frequently underscored with quiet humour, often with a sadness, sometimes with a sombre sorrow towards the inevitably traumatic effect of life on man. His tolerance is everywhere apparent. . . . (p. xiv)

Out of these stories emerges Scott's outlook on life. In **"Tete-Jaune"** the reappearance of the dead Tete in the new generation symbolically expresses Scott's belief in a cyclical life force. In **"An Adventure of Mrs. Mackenzie's"** the comment: "So are our affairs inextricably involved, warp and woof, making the pattern called life, and through all flies the cackling shuttle of gossip," expresses Scott's sense of the interrelationship and interdependence of man. This outlook, of natural renewal, and of the positives of love and sympathy and the negatives ranging from illusion and indifference to deliberate cruelty and hate, runs through Scott's stories. Man prospers in his stories when motivated by positives, suffers when not. This is a literature of reality, a literature, as Samuel Johnson advocates, "rooted in Nature, and manured by Art"; it is, as well, tended and nurtured by Scott's understanding and tolerance. (pp. xiv-xv)

> *Glenn Clever, in his introduction to* Selected Stories of Duncan Campbell Scott *by Duncan Campbell Scott, edited by Glenn Clever (© All rights reserved: The University of Ottawa Press, 1975), second edition, University of Ottawa Press, 1975, pp. ix-xv.*

FRED COGSWELL   (essay date 1979)

The tradition to which Duncan Campbell Scott's **"The Piper of Arll"** belongs is essentially that of the pastoral elegiac, which had in British literature produced such masterpieces as Milton's "Lycidas," Grey's "Elegy," Shelley's "Adonais," and Matthew Arnold's "Thyrsis." In this tradition, which dates back to the Alexandrian phase of Greek literature, poets are portrayed as shepherds; writing poetry is either playing one's pipes or tending one's sheep, and the setting in which these events occur is rural and highly artificial, thus giving the poet great scope to invent a suitably exotic landscape and adorn it with appropriately decorative language. The death of the poet, the "elegiac" element, moreover gives the writer an opportunity to pronounce upon those aspects of the human condition which lie closest to his heart. The success or failure of the pastoral-elegiac depends essentially upon the skill with which the poet combines the decorative elements with the "message" that is the poem's *raison d'être*—and, of course, the worth of that message.

Unlike almost all other pastoral elegies, **"The Piper of Arll"** is written not as a formal ode but as a ballad. It is a ballad, moreover, that is patently modelled after Samuel Taylor Coleridge's "The Rime of the Ancient Mariner." In "The Rime of the Ancient Mariner," Coleridge used his fanciful landscapes primarily for their decorative appeal. The "meat" of his message was conveyed directly by his use of a variant of a well-known medieval legend, that of the Wandering Jew. Like Coleridge in "The Rime of the Ancient Mariner," Duncan Campbell Scott in **"The Piper of Arll"** has adapted to his purposes a medieval legend, the legend of the Ship of Fools. (pp. 47-8)

[In] **"The Piper of Arll"** the rustic setting, Arll, represents the poet's physical universe; the sea becomes eternity; the ship represents an anthology, the repository of the poets and their works that affects the poet at an early stage in his career and to which he and his work are added at the close. (p. 48)

The ballad is essentially a means of telling a story concerned with action and dramatic encounter. Had Duncan Campbell Scott simply described in a ballad a poet's encounter with the craft of other writers in a book, his joy in so meeting others of his kind, his own attempts to compose similar poetry, his

despair when the book was taken from him, and his desperate destruction of his own instrument as a result, the demands of symbolism would have been well served, but the result would have been a very tame ballad. What **"The Piper of Arll"** needed on a narrative level was exactly what Scott provided: pictorial vividness and psychological interest provided by the encounter with an actual ship bearing real poets. The introduction of the ship gives Scott an opportunity to introduce description *à la* "The Rime of the Ancient Mariner" into his poem, and the peopling of the ship with real poets rather than merely poems enables him to have his piper-poet go through the stages of a genuine two-way communion. . . . (p. 51)

"The Piper of Arll" might well be subtitled "The Poet's Progress." . . .

It is as strange a psychic journey as that which Coleridge's Ancient Mariner is forced to undergo, and it ends in as bizarre a psychic landscape. That is where, I believe, it is inferior to Coleridge's masterpiece. By being able to anchor his Mariner in a serio-comic situation, from which he only departs to recount the details of a purely symbolic adventure, and by modulating the form of his verse to suit modification in the subject matter, Coleridge is able to give his poem a variety of tone and mood which Scott's poem lacks. He is able, by separating it strictly from the narrative frame, to deal with the symbolism with less confusion or conflict concerning the demands of the narrative form. At the same time, it may be argued fairly that what Duncan Campbell Scott is trying to convey is more complex and that it is extremely well conveyed. (p. 53)

> *Fred Cogswell, "Symbol and Decoration: 'The Piper of Arll'" (originally a paper delivered at the Duncan Campbell Scott Symposium at the University of Ottawa on April 28, 1979), in* The Duncan Campbell Scott Symposium, *edited by K. P. Stich, University of Ottawa Press, 1980, pp. 47-54.*

MARTIN WARE   (essay date 1979)

I see **"Spring on Mattagami"** as belonging (like **"Veronique Fraser"**) to a group of poems which have not received much of the right kind of critical attention. These are essentially dramatic poems which deal with the adventures of the troubled white soul: adventures which are in significant ways the obverse of those presented in Scott's well-known and much studied Indian poems. The questions which I would like to raise in the context of a consideration of **"Spring on Mattagami"** include questions related to the *personal* or *dramatic* nature of monologues of this kind, and to the general ethos of Scott's poetry. (p. 62)

If we are to take the fervent, if sometimes hectic, passion of the lover [in **"Spring on Mattagami"**] not as a reflection of Scott's own nature, at however great a remove, but as, in Shelley's phrase, a reflection of a nature "not his own", then the poem may well appear in a different perspective. We may be meant to regard the lover's passion as hectic and feverish, and to take the lover's transcendent resignation at the end of the poem as a false resolution.

In the light of this, Scott's assertion that he was a poet not of "nature" but of "human nature" will take on a new force. . . .

In **"Spring on Mattagami"** the naive and ingenuous lover who takes his Pre-Raphaelite longings into the forest can scarcely be said to speak for Scott. He may be constantly drawn back eastwards to the ideal "Beatrice" figure of his dreams, as Scott was drawn back to the European poetic tradition. He entirely lacks, however, Scott's osprey-eyed and rejoicing view of the magnificent energy and defeated ferocity of the Indian homeland. As he gazes eastwards "over the long haggard hills" to the city of his dreams, his eye is caught by a fiendish storm. It is as if the whole primitive and savage environment of northern North America stand between him and the refinement of his European ideal. His idealized vision of the fatal woman of his dreams insulates him from the vitality and power of the New World. He is so possessed by his dream that he is temperamentally incapable of recognizing the means that the Indians, Potan and Silver Lightning, offer him of coming to terms with his new environment. He can derive neither rest nor comfort either from the fragrant balsam bed heaped by Potan, or from the fire which has been gathered and lain by Silver Lightning. (p. 63)

[His beloved] is then some archetypal figure arising from the depths of the European imagination (like Venus who rose from the foam, and was the patroness of the city and the garden); and in the context of this poem she is undoubtedly a siren symbol.

She perpetually tortures the protagonist with unappeasable longings. His most vivid memory reflects something of the cruel light in which he sees her. He remembers her in a perceptibly sinister symbolist twilight: —with his principal metaphors suggesting both hard and exotic beauty and sharp menace. (p. 64)

Her influence over him, however, is so powerful that his most important perceptions are formed in the light of her refining presence. He sees his Indian companions, Potan and Silver Lightning, in the same idyllic light that he perceives nature; as voyagers of innocence ("who break with their slender blades the long clear hush"). Similarly he sees their Western World as illuminated by the mild glow of Venus and the young Moon. For all its newborn appeal, this world of innocence is one in which the protagonist can scarcely participate for his vision of it is generated and insulated on the "reservation" of his impossible love.

The protagonist's sense of the surge and energy of the primitive life force in his new world arises only when his hopeless passion is kindled. There is a haunting irony—discernibly tragic—in the lovely images which his deluded obsession calls forth. (pp. 64-5)

For him the ancient European metaphor of love, with all its dignity and beauty, has in a new world context become a siren symbol, and carries with it symbolic associations of death. (p. 65)

Hard, unsympathetic fatalism is the sublunar side of soaring idealism. Scott's poem is surely to be read in an ironic light. His assertion that he is a poet of human nature is to be taken seriously. (p. 66)

> Martin Ware, "'Spring on Mattagami' in a Dramatic Context" (originally a paper delivered at the Duncan Campbell Scott Symposium at the University of Ottawa on April 29, 1979), in The Duncan Campbell Scott Symposium, edited by K. P. Stich, University of Ottawa Press, 1980, pp. 62-6.

GLENN CLEVER (essay date 1979)

[My] contention is that now, in 1979, we should have the past of English literature in Canada adequately enough in perspec-

tive to state without further hedging that Duncan Campbell Scott is a primary author of the consciousness of Canada and a watershed author between the old ways and the new in our literature, and that his fiction by itself shows his innovative qualities in matter and manner as well as his part in helping to establish the northern western frontier realities in the Canadian sensibility. (p. 85)

In [*Untitled Novel, ca. 1905,* Scott] tries to put into practice his principles of revolt against tradition and of literature as expressing "the age in terms of age." Disregarding photographic realism and not much concerned with reportial realism in either setting or character, he tries for moral realism—to express that kind of life that a world of free personalities, morally unconstrained, gives rise to, a realism of the Callaghan kind and with even a touch of Proust's. Dragland comments that "the publication of Scott's novel would have done little for his reputation." But it does show Scott's innovative qualities. It focuses on the idea that people live their own lives and that no outside influence ultimately alters the course that individual character follows. Scott fleshes this idea with six young main characters, three men and three women, in an interlocking tangle. . . . (p. 88)

In technique Scott can hardly be called innovative. He uses language conventionally and with nothing like the poetic quality that inspirits so many of his stories. Indeed, his stories often open with carefully written emotive settings that reflect the mood of the ensuing action. The novel has little of such descriptive writing, functional or otherwise. Scott concentrates on characters, especially the male characters, to the exclusion of setting. The novel opens in a village . . . called "Ashville," and its environs; but Scott does not particularize with the details of either time or place. Similarly, the lower-town of Ottawa of the main story exists only by street names and sparsely drawn home interiors, plus a few sketchy adjacent localities; and the final scene on a liner taking Barbara and her father down the St. Lawrence en route to England also blurs out.

Nature, in the sense of the Maple Leaf School, scarcely functions. Scott stages more than a dozen dramatic scenes in gardens or fields in or about Ottawa but in only one uses the scene functionally. . . . [In] the longest nature scene in the novel, the natural scenery serves principally as a back-drop rather than being integral to the action as it is in some short stories. . . . For the main part it is an urban world, but expresses no interest, nor sense of mystique; it merely serves as the setting for human interaction. (pp. 91-2)

Time functions even less than setting. . . . Scott makes no particular use of the 1880s period of the main action. Set shortly after Confederation, the novel is silent about political and philosophical issues of the times. . . . [Time] as passage serves no consequential role. It is in the moral milieu that Scott deals with his view that "the desire of creative minds everywhere is to express the age in terms of the age."

As in his shorter fiction, Scott makes much of music. . . . [It] serves mainly to colour character . . . , or it serves to trip the plot. . . .

The novel is low-keyed. Scott does not indulge in purple passage or rhetorical heightening, and limits the major dramatic scenes to four only: Robin's confronting his nominal father about his true identity; Purcell's attempt to blackmail John Applegarth; the climax of the breakdown in the relationship between Barbara and Purcell; and Robin's physical attack on Purcell to prevent his seducing Cornelia. The concentration of these peaks of action in the fourth section of the five narrative phases of the novel (Scott divides it into thirty-eight chapters) structures the dramatic trajectory but fails to save the novel from narrative tedium. Its opening jerks in pace, the main action likewise; and the closing section drags, like Pope's line, its tedious length along to the kind of transcendental resolution with which Scott closes many of his narrative poems. . . . (p. 92)

Scott tells his story in matter-of-fact tone, neutral, enlivened by some touches of humour . . . , but the general voice of the narrator is serious. Unlike the constant authorial intrusion of most of the novelists of this period, Scott keeps relatively distant from his material and his characters, makes no attempt to induce either sympathy or antipathy in the reader but rather a deliberate balancing out, as he does in his shorter fiction; so that an inclination to sympathize with the admirable traits of a figure such as John Applegarth is soon abraded by the revelation that he has fathered Robin illegitimately and uses his wealth and power to try to intrude into and shape Robin's life. Nor does Scott satirize or preach obliquely except by the use of characternyms. . . . (p. 93)

Whereas in technique, then, the novel shows some departures from Scott's received tradition but also many conventional features, its moral climate, relative to other Canadian novels of the period, does mark the novel as distinctly innovative. Scott gives us, for instance, no religious focus. . . . Human love gets thwarted at every turn. . . . [The] peculiar relationship [generates] the strongest kinds of affection and those normally treated in the fiction of the day as strongest, here, fail to hold. In the area of social order even the hero . . . acts negatively by striking down a policeman who is attempting to do his duty. Similarly, Scott gives us an ambiguous commercial world: farming, working as a mill-hand, or piano teaching he presents neutrally, but usury and entrepreneurship negatively. Also, for its day, he treats the relationship between the sexes in *risqué* fashion: we see sex outside marriage, breakdown within marriage, male adultery—at least Scott keeps the Victorian double standard—even a veiled allusion to an Ottawa brothel. No family unity appears; the families live taut with tension and discord. . . . (pp. 93-4)

To sum up the novel, then, Scott was writing fiction in about 1905 that was, for the Canadian scene, ahead of its time in several features: absence of religious tone, amoral fictional world, negative and defeating interpersonal relationship, antiheroic stance, labour and other social disorder, sexual and family malaise, as well as effaced author and psychological cause-effect sequence. (p. 94)

> *Glenn Clever, "Duncan Campbell Scott's Fiction:*
> *Moral Realism and Canadian Identity" (originally a*
> *paper delivered at the Duncan Campbell Scott Symposium at the University of Ottawa on April 29, 1979),*
> *in* The Duncan Campbell Scott Symposium, *edited*
> *by K. P. Stich, University of Ottawa Press, 1980,*
> *pp. 85-100.*

ADDITIONAL BIBLIOGRAPHY

Brown, E. K. "Memoir of Duncan Campbell Scott." In *Selected Poems of Duncan Campbell Scott,* by Duncan Campbell Scott, pp. xi-xlii. Toronto: The Ryerson Press, 1951.

Important biographical account of Scott's life and works.

Burrell, Martin. "A Canadian Poet." In his *Betwixt Heaven and Charing Cross,* pp. 253-61. Toronto: Macmillan Co. of Canada, 1968.

A review of *The Collected Poems of Duncan Campbell Scott* noting the influence of music and of the poets Milton, Tennyson, Browning, and Keats on Scott's work.

Daniells, Roy. "Crawford, Carman, and D. C. Scott." In *Literary History of Canada: Canadian Literature in English, Vol. I,* 2d ed., edited by Carl F. Klinck, pp. 432-37. Toronto: University of Toronto Press, 1976.*

An overview of Scott and his work within the comprehensive scope of a reference book on Canadian literary history.

Davies, Barrie. Introduction to *At the Mermaid Inn: Wilfred Campbell, Archibald Lampman, Duncan Campbell Scott in "The Globe" 1892-93,* pp. vii-xxi. Toronto: University of Toronto Press, 1979.*

A factual account of the column on which Scott, Charles G. D. Roberts, and Archibald Lampman collaborated, and its attempt to encourage literary life in Canada.

Dragland, S. L., ed. *Duncan Campbell Scott: A Book of Criticism.* Ottawa: Tecumseh Press, 1974, 199 p.

Collection of perceptive criticism, covering several decades, on Scott's poetry. Critics included are Milton Wilson, Melvin H. Dagg, and A.J.M. Smith, among others, with an introduction by Dragland before each essay.

Gerson, Carole. "The Piper's Forgotten Tune: Notes on the Stories of D. C. Scott and a Bibliography." *Journal of Canadian Fiction* IV, No. 4 (1976): 138-43.

Illustrates the modern aspects of Scott's short stories such as his detached narrative style and discusses several of his uncollected stories.

Jones, D. G. "The Problem of Job." In his *Butterfly on Rock: A Study of Themes and Images in Canadian Literature,* pp. 83-110. Toronto: University of Toronto Press, 1970.*

A study of the darkness and destruction in Scott's poems as well as the serenity that characterizes his work when taken as a whole.

Marshall, Tom. "Half-Breeds: Duncan Campbell Scott." In his *Harsh and Lovely Land: The Major Canadian Poets and the Makings of a Canadian Tradition,* pp. 23-33. Vancouver: University of British Columbia Press, 1979.

Concludes that Scott's conception of the Canadian half-breed, concomitant with a clash of two cultures, illustrates his view of nature as a duality encompassing both peace and terror.

Pacey, Desmond. "The Poetry of Duncan Campbell Scott." *The Canadian Forum* XXVIII, No. 331 (August 1948): 107-09.

Portrays Scott's concept of nature as violent in contrast to the conceptions of nature by other poets of the "Confederation group" as a refuge, a benefactor, a comfort.

Stich, K. P., ed. *The Duncan Campbell Scott Symposium.* Re-Appraisals: Canadian Writers, edited by Lorraine McMullen, no. 6. Ottawa: University of Ottawa Press, 1980, 155 p.

Reappraisal of Scott's poetry and fiction, as well as new material on his public and private life by various writers including Glenn Clever, C. M. Armitage, and Stan Dragland, among others.

Waterston, Elizabeth. "The Missing Face: Five Short Stories by Duncan Campbell Scott." *Studies in Canadian Literature* I, No. 2 (Summer 1976): 223-29.

Examination of five stories from *The Witching of Elspie.*

Gertrude Stein

1874-1956

American novelist, poet, critic, and dramatist.

Called the mother of modern literature, Stein is an outstanding force both as a daring experimentalist and as a patron of avant-garde artists and writers. Through her various linguistic experiments, she moved toward increasing abstraction in her work, mirroring the movement in the pictorial arts from impressionism to abstract representation. Her desire to break things into pieces in order to discover their essence created a fragmenting effect in her writing which foreshadowed the fragmentation of our modern era and the corresponding interest in the individual—the part instead of the whole.

Born into a wealthy family of German-Jewish origin, Stein had a privileged childhood. Later, she studied psychology under William James at Radcliffe College, where she conducted important experiments with automatic writing. B. F. Skinner, in a celebrated article in the *Atlantic,* identified Stein's stylistic innovations, especially those of *Tender Buttons* and *The Making of Americans,* with the automatic writing of her earlier days. After giving up her studies at Radcliffe and at Johns Hopkins, where she had pursued medicine, Stein moved to France with her secretary, lifelong friend, and companion, Alice B. Toklas. In Paris at 27 rue de fleurus she became the center of modern art for more than a generation with her home serving as a salon for artists and writers. Along with her brother Leo, a gifted art critic, Stein became one of the earliest patrons of avant-garde painters such as Matisse, Picasso, Bracque, and Cézanne. She immersed herself in their theories, especially those of her friend, Picasso, and attempted to accomplish in literature the abstraction characteristic of some of his work. For this reason, her prose poem collection *Tender Buttons* has been likened to literary "cubism."

For the scores of writers who frequented her home during the 1920s, Stein was a model of daring innovation and her home a center of intellectual stimulation. Among these were Sherwood Anderson, Scott Fitzgerald, and Ernest Hemingway, American expatriates whom Stein dubbed the "lost generation." For a later generation, the soldiers of World War II, Stein served as a mother figure. A patriotic American who chose to remain in France during the German occupation, Stein opened her home to young soldiers and listened to their stories. *Brewser and Willie* was her attempt to capture the life of common soldiers, which she hoped to convey through the rhythm of their speech.

Stein's writings show a progressive experimentation with language. In *Three Lives,* her first published work, her manner is straightforward and the use of repetition in words and phrases, for which she became well known, is still subtle. Evident also in the portraits in *Three Lives* is Stein's obsession with the inner lives of her characters—the essence of their personality. *With Tender Buttons* Stein departs dramatically from ordinary logic. Taking normal household objects as the still life subjects of these poems, she describes them by a free association technique, not unlike automatic writing. Though some critics believed her technique removed meaning from words, others saw her purpose as one of greater depth—to convey an almost

religious attitude toward objects that would reveal their essence. Stein's experiments with language—which included simplification of syntax, intricate repetition, and absence of conventional punctuation,—reached new heights in *The Making of Americans,* which Stein considered her greatest achievement and "the beginning really the beginning of modern writing." Abandoning normal presentation of scene and development of character, *The Making of Americans* recounts the history of two families for three generations. Her tireless repetition of nearly identical statements in very long paragraphs using only the present tense carried the novel slowly forward and forced attention on the metaphysical aspects of her writing. Though Stein continued her technical explorations in her portraits and plays, she adopted a more readable style in her witty autobiography of her life in Paris, *The Autobiography of Alice B. Toklas.* In both this and in her later autobiographical work, *Everybody's Autobiography,* which was chiefly an account of her lecture tour in America in 1934, she conveys her strong beliefs about modern art, literature, and life.

Stein has been the subject of prolonged controversy. Some early critics derided her stylistic experiments, pointing to a lack of meaning in both words and design and calling her style nonsensical manipulation. Others extolled her work for emphasizing words in a manner which demanded attentive reading and yielded new depths of meaning. Many critics continue to find fault with the repetitive, often flat style of much of her writing. But some modern critics bemoan the neglect of Stein's extraordinary experimental works. Richard Kostelantetz for example, considers her "among the first imaginative writers to represent the modern awareness of discontinuous experience."

Stein's indefatigable ego survived all critical arguments as well as an inability to find a publisher during most of her career. To the end she considered herself a giant in twentieth-century literature and the center of modern art. In the *Autobiography,* Stein has Alice recount that she knew three geniuses in her lifetime: Picasso, Alfred North Whitehead, and Gertrude Stein. If this estimate of Stein is not shared universally, her influence upon modern writers from Hemingway to Joyce and E. E. Cummings is beyond question.

(See also *TCLC*, Vol. 1, and *Dictionary of Literary Biography*, Vol. 4: *American Writers in Paris, 1920-1939*.)

PRINCIPAL WORKS

Three Lives   (novellas)   1909
Tender Buttons   (prose poems)   1914
The Making of Americans   (novel)   1925
Composition as Explanation   (essay)   1926
Lucy Church, Amiably   (novel)   1930
The Autobiography of Alice B. Toklas   (autobiography)   1933
Four Saints in Three Acts   (play)   1934
Lectures in America   (essay)   1935
Narration   (essay)   1935
Everybody's Autobiography   (autobiography)   1937
Ida   (novel)   1941
Wars I Have Seen   (essays)   1945
Brewser and Willie   (essays)   1946
Things As They Are   (novel)   1950

EDITH SITWELL   (essay date 1923)

[Miss Stein's] work appears to have a certain amount of real virtue, but to understand or apprehend that virtue a reader would have to study Miss Stein's methods for years, and intimately; whereas this is the first book of hers that I have read. Her virtues and faults are in exact contradiction of each other. I think it is indisputable that Miss Stein has a definite aim in her work, and that she is perfectly, relentlessly, and bravely sincere. She is trying to pull language out of the meaningless state into which it has fallen, and to give it fresh life and new significance. For this purpose she uses comparatively few words; and turns them into ever-varying and new patterns till they often do, definitely, surprise us with their meaning. . . . [*Geography and Plays,*] at first sight, appears to be a collection of heterogeneous words, thrown together without any respect for meaning, but only a respect for the shape and rhythm of sentences. I hope I shall not be regarded as a reactionary, but I am bound to say that I prefer words, when collected into a sentence, to convey some sense. And Miss Stein's sentences do not always convey any sense—not even a new one. It is

her habit to open her mind and let words float in and out regardless of each other. . . .

To sum up the book as far as is possible, I find in it an almost insuperable amount of silliness, an irritating ceaseless rattle like that of American sightseers talking in a boarding-house (this being, I imagine, a deliberate effect), great bravery, a certain real originality, and a few flashes of exquisite beauty. One feels, too, that there is a real foundation for Miss Stein's mind, somewhere deep under the earth, but that it is too deep for her to dig down to, and that she herself is not capable of building upon this hidden foundation. She is, however, doing valuable pioneer work, and I should like to take this opportunity of begging *les Jeunes* not to hamper her by imitating her, but to leave her to work out her own literary destiny.

> Edith Sitwell, "Miss Stein's Stories," *in* The Nation & The Athenaeum, *Vol. XXXIII, No. 15, July 14, 1923, p. 492.*

DESMOND MacCARTHY   (essay date 1932)

Among the Second Series of the Hogarth Press Essays you will find one by Miss Gertrude Stein. It bears the title **Composition as Explanation;** but if the word "explanation" raises hopes, you will be disappointed. The first part of the pamphlet is a lecture on her own work, which Miss Stein delivered at Oxford and other places; the latter half contains four specimen compositions of her own, bearing the titles, **"Preciosilla," "A Saint in Seven"** (not in "Heaven" but in "Seven," which has the advantage of meaning nothing), **"Sitwell Edith Sitwell," "Jean Cocteau," "G. Stein."** (p. 260)

Personally, I prefer Miss Stein in her less austere, less repetitive moods. For instance, in a little piece called **"Tails,"** which opens with a word suggested, as often happens in her writings, by rhyme: "Tails: Cold pails, cold with joy no joy. A tiny seat that means meadows and a lapse of cuddles with cheese and nearly bats, all this went messed. The post placed a loud loose sprain. A rest is no better. It is better yet. All the time." I cannot help preferring this to her austerer later work (*Useful Knowledge* . . .), in which the words "and one" are repeated a hundred times on a page, and "yes and yes" considerably more than a hundred times on another.

"Are There Six or Another Question?" she asks in a title to a poem in that book:

> One—Are there six?
> Two—Or another question?
> One—Are there six?
> Two—Or another question?
> Two—Are there six?
> One—Or another question?
> Two—Are there six?
> Two—Or another question?

This is the first poem I have ever read which consisted entirely of the repetition of its title.

I may be misjudging the labour of the artist, but it looks as though it would be easy to write like this if one abandoned one's mind to it. I hope I shall never be tempted to make fun of Miss Stein; I would far rather make fun of those who encourage her to write. (pp. 261-62)

[Her lecture consists] of three commonplaces obscurely expressed; finally she reaches her own work. . . .

We seem to be listening to a little girl who has been taught that she was a genius, and encouraged to talk about "grown-up things." We can almost see her fumbling with her frock and fixing her candid eyes upon her admiring parents. (p. 264)

Alas, the stuff *was* all "so nearly alike." Alas, the idea that the repetition of the same words *must* be different, and that beginning the same sentence again and again led anywhere, was her fatal delusion. It is either very malicious or very asinine of other people to encourage her in it. (pp. 264-65)

The only significant statement in her lecture is that her work would have been "outlawed" in any other generation than this post-war one. That is horribly true, and in that fact alone resides the importance of Miss Gertrude Stein. (p. 265)

She wrote a good many years ago, a good many, many, many, a good many, a good many ago, she, she wrote a good many years ago, a little book called **Tender Buttons,** and more recently a much larger book. I have lost my **Tender Buttons,** and into her last book I only glanced, seeing it was in the same form and only cut up into different lengths. Of course, if you start with a form which can convey no meaning, which ignores syntax, and consists in repeating either the same word or the next that suggests itself while the intelligence is completely in abeyance, it is impossible to develop; and her work has shown no development. (p. 266)

Desmond MacCarthy, "Gertrude Stein," in his Criticism, *Putnam, 1932, pp. 260-72.*

EDMUND WILSON   (essay date 1933)

The Autobiography of Alice B. Toklas has something of the character and charm of a novel—a novel of which the subject is the life that Miss Stein and Miss Toklas have made for themselves in Paris, the salon over which they have presided, the whole complex of ideas and events of which they became the center: a social-artistic-intellectual organism.

It is an instructive and most entertaining book. The chapters which deal with the period before the European War are perhaps the most interesting part: here Miss Stein tells about her discovery of Picasso and Matisse, what they were like in their early phases, the gradual taking-shape as a movement of the tendencies of isolated artists, the development of her own literary methods. There is a good deal of wisdom about art and artists, literature and writers. . . . (pp. 575-76)

The later chapters of the book are less exciting. The painters have all arrived; the writers are all arriving. (p. 577)

The Autobiography of Alice B. Toklas, though not Gertrude Stein's most important book, is likely to prove her most popular. It is the only thing she has published since *Three Lives* which, from the ordinary point of view, is very easily readable. And she explains here, or makes Alice B. Toklas explain, in simpler language than heretofore, what she has subsequently been trying to do in the experiments that, beginning with **Tender Buttons,** have stimulated and troubled the literary world.

Let us hope that the *Autobiography,* with its wisdom, its distinction and its charm, may persuade the general public to recognize Gertrude Stein for what she is: one of the remarkable women of her time and, if not "in english literature the only one," at least one of the original ones. (pp. 579-80)

Edmund Wilson, "Gertrude Stein Old and Young: 27, rue de fleurus" (1933), in his The Shores of Light: A Literary Chronicle of the Twenties and Thir-

ties *(reprinted by permission of Farrar, Straus & Giroux, Inc.; copyright 1952 by Edmund Wilson; copyright renewed © 1980 by Helen Miranda Wilson), Farrar, Straus & Giroux, 1952, pp. 575-80.*

B. F. SKINNER   (essay date 1934)

In the *Autobiography of Alice B. Toklas* Gertrude Stein tells in the following way of some psychological experiments made by her at Harvard:

> She was one of a group of Harvard men and Radcliffe women and they all lived very closely and very interestingly together. One of them, a young philosopher and mathematician who was doing research work in psychology, left a definite mark on her life. She and he together worked out a series of experiments in automatic writing under the direction of Münsterberg. The result of her own experiments, which Gertrude Stein wrote down and which was printed in the *Harvard Psychological Review,* was the first writing of hers ever to be printed. It is very interesting to read because the method of writing to be afterwards developed in *Three Lives* and *The Making of Americans* already shows itself.

There is a great deal more in this early paper than Miss Stein points out. It is, as she says, an anticipation of the prose style of *Three Lives* and is unmistakably the work of Gertrude Stein in spite of the conventional subject matter with which it deals. Many turns of speech, often commonplace, which she had since then in some subtle way made her own are already to be found. But there is much more than this. The paper is concerned with an early interest of Miss Stein's that must have been very important in her later development, and the work that it describes cannot reasonably be overlooked by anyone trying to understand this remarkable person.

Since the paper is hard to obtain, I shall summarize it briefly. It was published in the *Psychological Review* for September 1896 under the title, 'Normal Motor Automatism,' by Leon M. Solomons and Gertrude Stein, and it attempted to show to what extent the elements of a 'second personality' (of the sort to be observed in certain cases of hysteria) were to be found in a normal being. In their experiments the authors investigated the limits of their own normal motor automatism; that is to say, they undertook to see how far they could 'split' their own personalities in a deliberate and purely artificial way. They were successful to the extent of being able to perform many acts (such as writing or reading aloud) in an automatic manner, while carrying on at the same time some other activity such as reading an interesting story. (p. 50)

I shall let Miss Stein describe the result.

> *Spontaneous automatic writing.*—This became quite easy after a little practice. We had now gained so much control over our habits of attention that distraction by reading was almost unnecessary. Miss Stein found it sufficient distraction often to simply read what her arm wrote, but following three or four words behind her pencil. . . .
>
> A phrase would seem to get into the head and keep repeating itself at every opportunity, and

hang over from day to day even. The stuff written was grammatical, and the words and phrases fitted together all right, but there was not much connected thought. The unconsciousness was broken into every six or seven words by flashes of consciousness, so that one cannot be sure but what the slight element of connected thought which occasionally appeared was due to these flashes of consciousness. But the ability to write stuff that sounds all right, without consciousness, was fairly well demonstrated by the experiments. Here are a few specimens:

'Hence there is no possible way of avoiding what I have spoken of, and if this is not believed by the people of whom you have spoken, then it is not possible to prevent the people of whom you have spoken so glibly. . . .'

Here is a bit more poetical than intelligible:

'When he could not be the longest and thus to be, and thus to be, the strongest.'

And here is one that is neither:

'This long time when he did this best time, and he could thus have been bound, and in this long time, when he could be this to first use of this long time. . . .'

Here is obviously an important document. No one who has read *Tender Buttons* or the later work in the same vein can fail to recognize a familiar note in these examples of automatic writing. They are quite genuinely in the manner that has so commonly been taken as characteristic of Gertrude Stein. Miss Stein's description of her experimental result is exactly that of the average reader confronted with *Tender Buttons* for the first time: 'The stuff is grammatical, and the words and phrases fit together all right, but there is not much connected thought.' In short, the case is so good, simply on the grounds of style, that we are brought to the swift conclusion that the two products have a common origin, and that the work of Gertrude Stein in the *Tender Buttons* manner is written automatically and unconsciously in some such way as that described in this early paper.

This conclusion grows more plausible as we consider the case. It is necessary, of course, to distinguish between the Gertrude Stein of *Three Lives* and the *Autobiography* and the Gertrude Stein of *Tender Buttons,* a distinction that is fairly easily made, even though, as we shall see in a moment, there is some of the first Gertrude Stein in the latter work. If we confine ourselves for the present to the second of these two persons, it is clear that the hypothetical author who might be inferred from the writing itself possesses just those characteristics that we should expect to find if a theory of automatic writing were the right answer. Thus there is very little intellectual content discoverable. The reader—the ordinary reader, at least—cannot infer from the writing that its author possesses any consistent point of view. There is seldom any intelligible expression of opinion, and there are enough capricious reversals to destroy the effect of whatever there may be. There are even fewer emotional prejudices. The writing is cold. Strong phrases are almost wholly lacking, and it is so difficult to find a well-rounded emotional complex that if one is found it may as easily be attributed to the ingenuity of the seeker. Similarly, our hypothetical author shows no sign of a personal history or of

a cultural background; *Tender Buttons* is the stream of consciousness of a woman without a past. The writing springs from no literary sources. In contrast with the work of Joyce, to whom a superficial resemblance may be found, the borrowed phrase is practically lacking. (pp. 51-2)

Grammar is ever present—that is the main thing. We are presented with sentences ('sentences and always sentences'), but we often recognize them as such only because they show an accepted order of article, substantive, verb, split infinitive, article, substantive, connective, and so on. The framework of a sentence is there, but the words tacked upon it are an odd company. In the simplest type of case we have a nearly intelligible sentence modified by the substitution for a single word of one sounding much the same. This sort of substitution was reported by Miss Stein in connection with her experiments in automatic reading: 'Absurd mistakes are occasionally made in the reading of words—substitutions similar in sound but utterly different in sense.' The reader will recognize it as the sort of slip that is made when one is very tired. In more complex cases it cannot, of course, be shown that the unintelligibility is due to substitution: if most of the words are replaced, we have nothing to show that a word is a slip. We must be content to characterize it, as Miss Stein herself has done: 'We have made excess return to rambling.'

From this brief analysis it is apparent that, although it is quite plausible that the work is due to a second personality successfully split off from Miss Stein's conscious self, it is a very flimsy sort of personality indeed. It is intellectually unopinionated, is emotionally cold, and has no past. It is unread and unlearned beyond grammar school. It is as easily influenced as a child; a heard word may force itself into whatever sentence may be under construction at the moment, or it may break the sentence up altogether and irremediably. Its literary materials are the sensory things nearest at hand—objects, sounds, tastes, smells, and so on. The reader may compare, for the sake of the strong contrast, the materials of **'Melanctha'** in *Three Lives,* a piece of writing of quite another sort. In her experimental work it was Miss Stein's intention to avoid the production of a true second personality, and she considered herself to be successful. The automatism she was able to demonstrate possessed the 'elements' of a second personality, it was able to do anything that a second personality could do, but it never became the organized *alter ego* of the hysteric. The superficial character of the inferential author of *Tender Buttons* consequently adds credibility to the theory of automatic authorship.

The Gertrude Stein enthusiast may feel that I am being cruelly unjust in this estimate. I admit that there are passages in *Tender Buttons* that elude the foregoing analysis. But it must be made clear that the two Gertrude Steins we are considering are not kept apart by the covers of books. There is a good deal of the Gertrude Stein of the *Autobiography* in *Tender Buttons,* in the form of relatively intelligible comment, often parenthetical in spirit. . . . But, far from damaging our theory, this occasional appearance of Miss Stein herself is precisely what the theory demands. In her paper in the *Psychological Review* she deals at length with the inevitable alternation of conscious and automatic selves, and in the quotation we have given it will be remembered that she comments upon these 'flashes of consciousness.' Even though the greater part of *Tender Buttons* is automatic, we should expect an 'element of connected thought,' and our only problem is that which Miss Stein herself has considered—namely, are we to attribute to conscious flashes all the connected thought that is present?

There is a certain logical difficulty here. It may be argued that, since we dispense with all the intelligible sentences by calling them conscious flashes, we should not be surprised to find that what is left is thin and meaningless. We must therefore restate our theory, in a way that will avoid this criticism. We first divide the writings of Gertrude Stein into two parts on the basis of their ordinary intelligibility. I do not contend that this is a hard and fast line, but it is a sufficiently real one for most persons. It does not, it is to be understood, follow the outlines of her works. We then show that the unintelligible part has the characteristics of the automatic writing produced by Miss Stein in her early psychological experiments, and from this and many other considerations we conclude that our division of the work into two parts is real and valid and that one part is automatic in nature.

I cannot find anything in the *Autobiography* or the other works I have read that will stand against this interpretation. On the contrary, there are many bits of evidence, none of which would be very convincing in itself, that support it. Thus (1) *Tender Buttons* was written on scraps of paper, and no scrap was ever thrown away; (2) Miss Stein likes to write in the presence of distracting noises; (3) her handwriting is often more legible to Miss Toklas than to herself (that is, her writing is 'cold' as soon as it is produced); and (4) she is 'fond of writing the letter *m*,' with which, the reader will recall, the automatic procedure often began. (pp. 53-4)

Miss Stein has not, however, freed herself from the problem of the meaning of the things she writes. She is not above being bothered by criticism on the score of unintelligibility. She often characterizes her work in this vein as experimental, but that is in no sense an explanation. Beyond this her answer seems to be that the writing is its own justification. (p. 55)

The final test of whether it is right is whether anyone likes it. But a literary composition is not 'an event just by itself,' and the answer to Miss Stein's query is that there certainly *are* questions, of a critical sort, that may legitimately be raised. Meaning is one of them. . . .

[The] evidence here offered in support of a theory of automatic writing makes it *more probable* that meanings are not present, and that we need not bother to look for them. A theory of automatic writing does not, of course, necessarily exclude meanings. It is possible to set up a second personality that will possess all the attributes of a conscious self and whose writings will be equally meaningful. But in the present case it is clear that, as Miss Stein originally intended, a true second personality does not exist. This part of her work is, as she has characterized her experimental result, little more than 'what her arm wrote.' And it is an arm that has very little to say. This is, I believe, the main importance of the present theory for literary criticism. It enables one to assign an origin to the unintelligible part of Gertrude Stein that puts one at ease about its meanings. (p. 56)

[In *Composition As Explanation*], there is an intimate fusion of the two styles, and the conscious passages are imitative of the automatic style. This is also probably true of parts of the *Autobiography*. It is perhaps impossible to tell at present whether the effect upon her conscious prose is anything more than a loss of discipline. The compensating gain is often very great.

We have no reason, of course, to estimate the literary value of this part of Miss Stein's work. It might be considerable, even if our theory is correct. It is apparent that Miss Stein believes it to be important and has accordingly published it.

If she is right, if this part of her work is to become historically as significant as she has contended, then the importance of the document with which we began is enormous. For the first time we should then have an account by the author herself of how a literary second personality has been set up.

I do not believe this importance exists, however, because I do not believe in the importance of the part of Miss Stein's writing that does not make sense. On the contrary, I regret the unfortunate effect it has had in obscuring the finer work of a very fine mind. I welcome the present theory because it gives one the freedom to dismiss one part of Gertrude Stein's writing as a probably ill-advised experiment and to enjoy the other and very great part without puzzlement. (p. 57)

B. F. Skinner, "Has Gertrude Stein a Secret?" in The Atlantic Monthly, *Vol. 153, No. 1, January, 1934, pp. 50-7.*

CONRAD AIKEN (essay date 1934)

In an article in the January *Atlantic Monthly* Mr. B. F. Skinner contributes an analysis of Miss Gertrude Stein's work—or, rather, of that part of it which has made her famous, the Gertrude Stein of *Tender Buttons, Geography,* and *The Making of Americans*—which, one suspects, Miss Stein must find somewhat embarrassing. (p. 364)

Whether we agree with him or not, the discovery is certainly an awkward one. For nearly twenty years we have been sedulously taught, by the highbrow critics, the literary left-wingers, and all the masters of the subtler schools that in Miss Stein's work we were witnessing a bold and intricate and revolutionary and always *consciously* radical experiment in style, of which the results were to be of incalculable importance for English literature. Like the splitting of the atom, or the theory of relativity, Miss Stein's destruction of meaning was inevitably going to change, if not the world, at any rate the word. By a systematic dislocation of "affects," we were to get a revivification of word, rhythm, style and meaning. From the Paris laboratory came breathless rumors of the work in progress. Distinguished authors attended the experiments and came away impressed: the influence began to spread: Mr. Van Vechten praised, Mr. Anderson and Mr. Hemingway imitated, the Sitwells took notes. Mr. Joyce was attentive—even the cautious Mr. Eliot opened the pages of *The Criterion* to this new phenomenon, though he as quickly closed them again. In short, the thing was the very finest sort of literary Inside Tip. Not to believe was simply not to belong.

In the light of which, Mr. Skinner's article makes of the whole thing a very cruel joke. What becomes of all this precise and detached and scientific experimentation with rhythm and meaning if, after all, it has been nothing on earth but automatic writing? Is it merely one more instance of the emperor's new clothes? Have we been duped, and has Miss Stein herself, perhaps, been duped? It looks very like it—though of course it is not impossible that Miss Stein has been pulling our legs. That she can write well, even brilliantly, when she wants to, she has amply proved. *Melanctha,* an early story, is a little masterpiece, but perfectly orthodox. The *Autobiography* is a witty and delightful book, again perfectly orthodox—which makes one speculate slyly as to why, at this late date, in giving us her self-portrait, she should thus abruptly abandon the subtler communicativeness of her mature "style" for a method simpler and—shall we say—more effective. Is it a concession? Is it a confession?

There remains, however, the unpleasant little problem of the more purely "automatic" books, of which *The Making of Americans* is a very good example. . . . [Despite] a considerable charm in the opening pages (which were written when Miss Stein was an undergraduate, and for a course in composition), and a clear enough emergence, here and there, of scene and character (notably the two dressmakers), the book can only be described as a fantastic sort of disaster. . . . In an attempt to restrict herself to the use of only the simplest words (for no matter how complicated a psychological statement), Miss Stein falls into a tireless and inert repetitiveness which becomes as stupefying as it is unintelligible. The famous "subtlety of rhythm" simply is not there: one could better find it in a tom-tom. The phrasing is almost completely unsensory, flat and colorless—or, as Mr. Skinner admirably puts it, cold. The abuse of the present participle, in a direct but perhaps simple-minded assault on "presentness," amounts in the end to linguistic murder.

In short, the book is a complete aesthetic miscalculation: it is dull; and although what it seeks to communicate is interesting, the cumbersomeness of the method defeats its own end. The analysis of human types is sometimes exceedingly acute—if one has the patience to worry it out—but as here presented it sounds as if someone had attempted to paraphrase Jung's *Psychological Types* in basic English. The attempt sometimes leads Miss Stein into unintentional comedy. She is presumably making merely a *psychological* statement when she says, "She had very little bottom to her, she had a little sensitive bottom to her enough to give a pleasant sweetness to her."

It remains to say that the book is a miracle of proofreading. How the compositor could keep his eye on the right word, the right phrase, in the gradually mounting whirlwind of repetition, or the proofreader keep accurate count of the interminable series of identical statements, without falling asleep, or, on waking, find his way to the bright particular word again, transcends understanding. Merely to think of it is almost to die of exhaustion. (pp. 365-67)

> *Conrad Aiken, "Gertrude Stein" (originally published as "We Ask for Bread," in* New Republic, *Vol. 78, No. 1009, April 4, 1934), in his* Collected Criticism *(copyright © 1935, 1939, 1940, 1942, 1951, 1958 by Conrad Aiken; reprinted by permission of Brandt & Brandt Literary Agents, Inc.), Oxford University Press, New York, 1968, pp. 364-67.*

SHERWOOD ANDERSON   (essay date 1934)

An article about Gertrude Stein, by B. F. Skinner, appeared in the *Atlantic* [see excerpt above]. Hers is automatic writing. That was the conclusion. A pretty good case was made for the conclusion, but if you think the same result can be accomplished by any one trying automatic writing, try it. If you happen to be a person of real talent, with a feeling for words, word relationships, word color, you may get something that will surprise and please you. Otherwise, you will get pure drivel. (p. 81)

This matter of writing, the use of words in writing, is an odd affair. How much Miss Stein has taught all of us! Let us admit, at the beginning, that there is a confusion here. Words are used to convey thought, but there is for the prose man, as for the poet, such a thing as pure and beautiful prose. At least this may be said for the arts of painting or for music. (p. 82)

This nonsense about automatic writing. All good writing is, in a sense, automatic. It is and it isn't. When I am really writing, not doing as I am doing now, thinking the words out as I go, making an argument, but am really writing, it is always half automatic. There is something stored within that flows out. (p. 83)

Stein is great because she is a releaser of talent. She is a pathfinder. She has been a great, a tremendous influence among writers because she has dared, in the face of ridicule and misunderstanding, to try to awaken in all of us who write a new feeling for words. She has done it.

"Take the word outside so-called 'sense' for the time if you please," she has said. "Let the word man in you come forth, dance for a time." (pp. 84-5)

Stein is a revolutionist. If we ever get again a world that knows what pure writing is, the sense and form in Stein's work will come through. She also will stand as a restorer of "the word." (p. 85)

> *Sherwood Anderson, "Gertrude Stein," in his* No Swank, *The Centaur Press, 1934, pp. 81-5.*

DONALD SUTHERLAND   (essay date 1951)

The early works of Gertrude Stein, *Three Lives* and *The Making of Americans,* though the vocabulary and composition are unusual, do make a perfectly average comprehensible sense. For many critics these are her great and essential works. But the principle objections to them, that they are cold or dead or clumsy or inhuman, are impressions which unhappily kept her from being read seriously by any but a small fraction of the American public. The demands of the educated American public were for precisely the things her work was meant to destroy, biographical or historical emotion, vaguenesses of feeling and slurred ideas, all essential to the average educated American literary taste. . . . With so little in Gertrude Stein's work to appeal to the biographical sense, the familiar personal emotions, it is no wonder her work looked dead or inhuman. The excitement of it was mental, but the intellect was, popularly and to the educated, dead. To Henry James and to Gertrude Stein the consciousness was very much alive, more brilliantly alive than human nature with all its biographies. (p. 20)

To make roughly an anatomy of *Three Lives,* from the broadest elements down, and beginning with narrative structure. Not only does *Three Lives* make a profitable exercise in literary anatomy but it contains already many principles which will stay for the later work of Gertrude Stein. (p. 22)

In *Three Lives* she deals with the poor, whom she had known as servants and patients in Baltimore, but there is very little if any political meaning to it. They are primarily human and not social types. She had what was then not a sentimental or programmatic but a natural democratic feeling that any human being was important just as that, as a human being. This feeling was no doubt reinforced and made confident by her philosophical and medical training, but it was, to start with, a native and direct curiosity about everybody. . . .

So "the good Anna" is first of all a human type, living and dying as that type does. She is presented first not as a child or a young girl but in her full development, in a situation which gives full expression to her typical kind of force, which is incessant managing will. The first chapter gives her as the type of that, the second chapter gives her life, and the third chapter her death. (p. 29)

Now while the situations and episodes in **"The Good Anna"** are chosen and arranged to show the character of the subject in various relationships, the qualities of the character are not primarily moral. The word "good," which is repeated as constantly as a Homeric epithet before the name Anna, does not indicate an evaluation of the character or a conclusion about it but the constantly present essence of the character which is there as a fact and not as a value. Like the word "poor" which is used of Anna, Melanctha, and Lena, it gives a rather perfunctory general shape to the character, like the terribly simple shape of a Cézanne head or apple. . . . [The] good Anna gets weight and existence, almost as a physical consistency, from her relationships within the account. (p. 30)

If the character then is defined by its relationships and its consistency of force, there is the question of presentation. The narrative becomes episodic . . . and there are plenty of flat statements, generalities, and discourses. That is, the *presentation* does still rely on demonstration and even on explanation. But the really extraordinary thing about the good Anna is that the character is thought of also as a musical continuity. Already in Radcliffe Gertrude Stein had described the conflict between the conscious and the automatic parts of her subjects in experiments as being like two themes going on together in music, one and the other dominating alternately. . . . She used to call this "the rhythm of a personality." . . . The means for registering this was inevitably the language as spoken or as written. In *Three Lives* this is conveyed clearly enough in the dialogue parts. (p. 35)

In **"The Good Anna"** she tries numerous other methods for presenting the characters alive, besides direct dialogue. One attempt is to run Anna's abrupt rhythm across the dialogue into the narrative. . . . The quality of incessant strain and pressure, Anna's particular quality, pervades nearly everything in the story, from the structure and transitions to the least matters of style. It is, like the work of Flaubert, exhaustively coordinated. It seems all to be written on the signature as it were of one of the earliest sentences: "Anna led an arduous and troubled life."

Whatever this analysis may make it look like, **"The Good Anna"** is not merely an exercise in technique, though certainly very brilliant as an exercise. (pp. 39-40)

But the impact and influence of *Three Lives* were mainly by its verbal novelty. It destroyed the extenuated rhetoric of the late 19th century. (p. 40)

Three Lives, more radically than any other work of the time in English, brought the language back to life. . . . Gertrude Stein in this work tried to coordinate the composition of the language with the process of consciousness, which, we have seen, was to her a close reflex of the total living personality. If this was to be done at least two serious things had to happen to the language:

First the word had to have not its romantic or literary meaning but the immediate meaning it had to the contemporary using it, a literal axiomatic meaning confined to the simple situations of the average life. The heroines of *Three Lives,* two German women and a Negress, have no connection whatever with the literary past of the language. (pp. 40-1)

The second necessity was to destroy 19th century syntax and word order, which could not follow the movement of a con-

sciousness moving naturally, this movement being, in the early 20th century, of the utmost importance. . . .

As Whitman for example had destroyed 19th century metrics and verse forms, Gertrude Stein destroyed 19th century syntax and word order. (p. 41)

The third story of *Three Lives*, **"The Gentle Lena,"** contains no great novelty beyond **"The Good Anna."** It is in a way a pendant to the first story in that Lena is a study of a soft and fluid and even absent consciousness and character as against the emphatic and hard presence of Anna. . . .

But according to the general agreement the big thing in *Three Lives* is the middle story, **"Melanctha."** It is a tragic love story ending in death from consumption, so that it is available to the traditional literary taste and the educated emotions. . . .

Where **"The Good Anna"** and **"The Gentle Lena"** are composed as the presentation of a single type in illustrative incidents, Melanctha is composed on the dramatic trajectory of a passion. (p. 44)

[**"Melanctha"** is] a time continuum less of events than of considerations of their meaning. The events considered in **"Melanctha"** are mostly the movements of the passion, how Jeff and Melanctha feel differently toward each other from moment to moment. . . .

Gertrude Stein uses the simplest possible words, the common words used by everybody, and a version of the most popular phrasing, to express the very complicated thing. . . . Gertrude Stein uses repetition and dislocation to make the word bear all the meaning it has, but actually one has to give her work word by word the deliberate attention one gives to something written in italics. It has been said that her work means more when one reads it in proof or very slowly, and that is certainly true, the work has to be read word by word, as a succession of single meanings accumulating into a larger meaning, as for example the words in the stanza of a song being sung. (p. 48)

"Melanctha" is more than an exact chart of the passions. The conjugation or play of the abstractions proceeds according to the vital rhythm or tempo of the characters. In this way the essential quality of the characters is not only described but presented immediately. As Emma Bovary is *seen* against the rake Rodolphe and then against the pusillanimous Léon, and is thereby defined, so Melanctha is, in her quick tempo, *played* against the slow Jeff Campbell and then against the very fast "dashing" Jem Richards. (p. 51)

The difference between a prolonged and a continuous present may be defined as this, that a prolonged present assumes a situation or a theme and dwells on it and develops it or keeps it recurring, as in much opera, and Bach, for example. The continuous present would take each successive moment or passage as a completely new thing essentially, as with Mozart or Scarlatti or, later, Satie. This Gertrude Stein calls beginning again. But the problem is really one of the dimensions of the present as much as of the artist's way with it. . . . For the composer this space of time can be the measure, or whatever unit can be made to express something without dependence on succession as the condition of its interest. For the writer it can be the sentence or the paragraph or the chapter or the scene or the page or the stanza or whatever. Gertrude Stein experimented with all these units in the course of her work, but in the early work the struggle was mainly with the sentence and the paragraph. (pp. 51-2)

Compared with *Three Lives*, [*The Making of Americans*] is far more disembodied, both from physical description and from dramatic story. Where the abstracted interiority of Melanctha was seen in dramatic relation to the interiority of Jeff Campbell, the people in *The Making of Americans* are seen as an enormous collection of separate units with almost no active relation to each other. They are fathers, mothers, sons, and daughters well enough, but this is, *to themselves inside them* and to the presentation, a fairly adventitious situation or quality to their separate interior existences. They are always young men and women to themselves, not children or old people; the quality of being a son or an uncle does not depend at all on the specific parents or nephews and nieces who objectively create the position. The individual people in the book go on and on as themselves, schematically situated in family relationships which do or do not have meaning to them. (pp. 52-3)

All these separate individuals are related mainly to a few essential classifications developed by Gertrude Stein—the attacking type and the resisting type, the *dependent independent* type and the *independent dependent* type. These final types serve as coordinates for the exact charting of particular characters, or as absolute black and white can serve to measure the tone of any color. Every possible character can be placed within these coordinates. They give the external coherence and the scope to a book which was projected as the history of "everyone who ever was or is or will be living." (p. 53)

The Making of Americans, being a history of people and not of events, very rarely uses events, even to demonstrate character. The characters are not, as in most traditional history, situated in relation to external events, to war and peace, to progress and reaction, to the formation and decline of national cultures (in spite of the title), or just the ambience of contemporary gossip, but to their ultimate ways of being alive in and to the universe —attacking or resisting, dependence or independence. . . .

Proust is the clearest demonstration of biography written in subjective, not objective, time. *The Making of Americans* is a history written in subjective time. It is not the sequence of events and years but, if you like, the stream of consciousness. (p. 54)

[The] presented continuity in Proust is a continuity of perception, of registration, like the surface of an impressionist painting; while in *The Making of Americans* the continuity is one of conception, of constant activity in terms of the mind and not the senses and emotions, like the surface of a cubist painting. This stream of thought is naturally the stream of Gertrude Stein's thought, and is very simply assumed as the final reality. (pp. 54-5)

However, it should be said that the subjectivity of Gertrude Stein in this work is very nearly anonymous—it approximates being pure undifferentiated subjectivity, or simply the human mind. She was concerned much later with identity, or biographical human nature, as against the human mind, but here already the stream of thought is scarcely at all qualified by biographical feeling, as it is in Proust for example. (p. 55)

At any rate, allowing that *The Making of Americans* is written in a subjective time free of a sequence of events, it is, as Gertrude Stein said, written in a continuous present. This does not make history impossible, insofar as "everyone always is repeating the whole of them." Insofar as the whole subjectivity of an individual is there in any moment of its assertion, and since there is virtually no change in that subjectivity from childhood to old age, any formulation or demonstration of the individual character is a complete account of the essential life of that individual and also of the lives of thousands and thousands like him, past, present, and future. . . . We are complicated rather than profound, and we have almost no connection with anything, with the earth or the past or with each other. We do try connections and we treat ourselves to debauches of depth, but as ourselves we are complicated and disconnected.

At least there is every reason to think so. But if the reality, the essence of the personality, is disconnected and self-contained, how is it to be expressed directly, that is without simply describing its circumstances and exteriors in the naturalist manner, or even the Proustian manner? Gertrude Stein solves the problem by reproducing its rhythm and telling its final relationships, its ultimate kind. Although the book may seem at first to be an impoverishment of human life, the personal and biographical life, it is rather a heroic insistence that something of the present person does exist in itself, independent of the flux of personal history and the adventitious contents of the consciousness. The isolation of this something is desperately difficult, and its articulation into expression still more so, but I think the book does it. At least it should be recognized that far from lacking a sense of life and personality, as it may seem to at first, the book is based on a closer and really a more loving sense of people than anyone of this century has had, with the possible exception of Sherwood Anderson. . . . She was determined to express the essential being, the final mode of existence in people, as a thing in itself and sufficient in itself, independent of their historical and social conditions. This has to be said, because she has been accused often enough and even by her friends, of an inhuman treatment of the human subject. The trouble is that the accusation comes from people who do not understand, as she certainly did, what is properly human and what is not, and that the intelligence—even the scientific intelligence at the time of this book—is a serious human resource, though not more. (pp. 56-7)

While *The Making of Americans* is a description of American people and properly treats them as disembodied and disconnected, the types described do resume, if not all, most possible human beings, as kinds of subjectivity. It is an interior history of all human beings. Or as she might have said, the inside story of the insides. (p. 58)

As to its form, *The Making of Americans,* being so intensely of an interior time, must articulate that time as its primary dimension, not the dimensions of external narrative. It cannot rely on the conventional sequences or the habitual interest of external events and received ideas to sustain the expression. All the beginnings and endings, transitions and elaborations and accents, are not conventionally predetermined but have to be constantly determined afresh by the immediate appetite and impulse of the mind deeply engaged with its subject and its medium. (p. 59)

The form of *The Making of Americans* being temporal, the subject matter is seen and presented as a process in time. . . . The time is of course articulated by rhythm, but also in units which are the paragraphs. These are conceived not merely as a rhetorical problem but, something like a passage in music, as the registration of a space of time, as a habitable and operable and continuous present. Naturally any one paragraph can be short or long, depending on the time it takes for the impulse of the writer to reach the culmination or saturation of what it has to do with the subject matter. Since the business of Gertrude

Stein in this work is not remarking things and their qualities and sequences only but presenting them in time, it is often a very long business. She has to dwell not so much on the subject as with it. The paragraph is made complete, as any natural activity is made complete, by satisfaction, or having enough. This sense of adequacy, of fullness, of everything being accounted for, depends, as in music that is music and not musicology, not on simply exhausting the subject but on a balance of relationships and a rhythm of succession within the paragraph—something like the rhetorical balance and the completion of the rhyme scheme in a stanza of poetry. When the full organic balance is reached, that is that, until the next time. The going on to the next time and the next led Gertrude Stein to compositions by series and lists and the like—corresponding for interior time to the episodic treatment of exterior events. This construction, which became one of her favorites . . . , is already present in *The Making of Americans,* where each paragraph is made to be a complete interior event. (pp. 60-1)

History aside, *The Making of Americans* has the essential quality of a masterpiece, the continuous presence of active mind applied to something alive. (p. 65)

As the problem of time and narrative is always there in literature, to be solved another way each time, so is the problem of space and physical description. Or, to use the plainer terminology of Gertrude Stein, there is the outside to be described as well as the inside. (p. 66)

The logic of her work brought Gertrude Stein rather abruptly against this problem of the physical world. *Three Lives,* it is true, had treated the physical world very expertly, but rather as an accompaniment to character, not as a radically different reality. But *The Making of Americans* had suppressed the physical world almost entirely, in order to disengage the simple persistence of the character in time. (p. 67)

[Her] commitment to the final being of the mind and to the final being of the physical world made her writing less and less historical, or scientific, or moral—that is, less relational, and more and more metaphysical or religious. William James remarked that any total and final attitude toward life could as well be called a religion, and in that sense the work of Gertrude Stein is religious, it is forever concerned with finalities.

The great welter of what seem to be particularities and trivialities in *Tender Buttons* comes from a ''religious'' attitude toward everything as simple existence. She said the change at this time was from feeling that everything was simply alike to feeling that everything was simply different, and that ''simply different'' was the constant intention of these works. (p. 73)

Gertrude Stein, consuming problems and periods as fast as Picasso, did leave *Tender Buttons* well behind her. She decided that the proper subject of literature was man, not objects, and she also felt there had to be more movement. Nevertheless the question of what literary sense a writer is to make of objects in space, indeed what conceptual sense anyone is to make of them beyond naming them, is still and always a fundamental question, and *Tender Buttons* may stand for a long while as one of the most wonderful answers we have ever had. (p. 87)

> *Donald Sutherland, in his* Gertrude Stein: A Biography of Her Work *(copyright, 1951, by Yale University Press; copyright renewed © 1979 by Donald Sutherland), Yale University Press, 1951, 218 p.*

FRANCIS RUSSELL (essay date 1954)

The final significance of Gertrude Stein lies, not in her work, but in the fact that she was the first writer in English to express

fully the disintegrative tendencies that have been the hall-mark of advanced western art movements from the latter part of the nineteenth century. Whether or not her writings in themselves have any permanent or even transient value they are nevertheless representative of the intellectual history of the times, and to that extent she was justified in calling herself the first twentieth-century author. (p. 66)

Things As They Are [her first book], written when Gertrude Stein was in her thirtieth year, is an account of a triangular love affair between three young American women, one of whom is obviously the author. Such a book, possibly the first study of female inversion in English, could not be considered publishable at the time, and there is no evidence that Gertrude Stein made any effort to have it printed.

It is a book written under the compulsive influence of an emotional crisis, and the author in groping to express herself is not concerned with the problem of style. *Things As They Are* has the hothouse atmosphere that one finds in [Radcliffe Hall's] *The Well of Loneliness,* the trembling on the edge of hysteria without adequate motivation, a veiled allusiveness that makes one uncertain whether the author is describing mental or physical states. Only a few times is the veil dropped and the flesh laid bare.

On the whole the effect of *Things As They Are* is flat, yet nevertheless for all its flatness this small book is the most directly felt piece that Gertrude Stein ever wrote. From this point it was as if she turned her back on herself, deliberately thrust her feelings behind her and chose to develop her writing not as an emotional re-creation of past experience but as a form of experimentation akin to the post-impressionistic tendencies in painting with which, thanks to her brother, she was coming in contact. Between *Things As They Are,* written in 1903, and *The Autobiography of Alice B. Toklas,* written thirty years later, the body of her work is characterized by a deliberate and extraordinary absence of feeling. (pp. 70-1)

She approached her next book with a firm determination to achieve greatness. But after *Things As They Are* she had shut off the direct sources of her inspiration, and until she fixed on style, until she went back, not to her feelings, but to [linguistic experiment] . . . , her approach was uncertain. *Three Lives* is her transitional piece. (p. 72)

Only in the story, *Melanctha,* does Gertrude Stein establish her characteristic mode of expression. As she herself later wrote, *Melanctha* is the beginning of her revolutionary work, and if looked at from the point of view of language distortion her remark that it was the first definite step away from the nineteenth and into the twentieth century in literature is also true, for it is one of the source documents of the twentieth-century reaction against form and meaning. (p. 73)

Having rejected her emotions as literary source material, and being deficient in inventiveness, Gertrude Stein, beginning with *Melanctha* and expanding to the word-mass of *The Making of Americans,* evolved her particular consciously unconscious method of writing. Although automatically conceived it was still subordinate to her conscious mind, a species of controlled spontaneity. She wrote *The Making of Americans* from carefully elaborated notes. Subsequently in *Tender Buttons* she described household objects directly in front of her. In both cases her method was the same. With pen in hand she would concentrate on the immediate fact facing her, whether note or object, letting the impulse take its free course from the given stimulus and writing down whatever thoughts occurred to her without making any effort to control or subjugate them. What she wrote she left unchanged. It was not automatic writing—for at the moment of composition she was aware of what her pen was producing—but a kind of literary contemplation. . . . (pp. 76-7)

Gertrude Stein considered *The Making of Americans* her highest achievement, as she herself proclaimed, 'the monumental work which was the beginning, really the beginning of modern writing.' With the monolithic self-assurance integral to her and which she developed increasingly through the years she ranked it with *A la Recherche du Temps Perdu* and *Ulysses* as the most important work of the century. (p. 77)

From the notes and charts of her various relatives and friends that Gertrude Stein prepared for *The Making of Americans* there might have come an extended two or three-generation family chronicle such as *Buddenbrooks*. Her underlying structure is the history of the Hersland (Stein) and Dehring families, the arrival in America of the European grandparents and the gradual Americanization of their descendants. It has been a common theme, but in the case of *The Making of Americans* the author has used her material in accordance with her previously developed theory of spontaneous composition. Instead of controlled development, her collated notes served as points of reference for the uncontrolled reflections to which she gave free rein and which followed one another inexhaustibly. Such constant repetitions with their slight shifts of balance were, she claimed, a replica of human existence. (pp. 78-9)

Gertrude Stein has described people by removing most of their characteristic features, leaving only generalities behind that might be considered as all people because they are equally no people. They become shadows without colour or depth, recurring endlessly—sometimes under one name, sometimes under another—as phantoms of the author's brain beneath which lie buried her emotions. (p. 79)

The Making of Americans from cover to cover is unrelieved by any spark of creative vitality. It is an amorphous and infertile growth, the product of a trivial mind held in suspension. Only later when that mind chose to reveal itself in a series of autobiographies was its essential triviality clearly underscored. (p. 84)

[Stein] explained *Tender Buttons* as cubism applied to writing. . . . The things dealt with are the still-life impedimenta of her own home, arranged under the headings of Objects, Food and Rooms. She wrote these descriptions at odd moments on scraps of paper as the random thoughts came to her. (pp. 84-5)

It has been asserted that through this process of transferring haphazard sequences of words to paper, Gertrude Stein has revivified a moribund language, shaken it out of its stale and outworn mould, refurbished it, removed the associative verdigris and restored the word to its original new-minted brightness. (p. 85)

The elementary fact to understand about Gertrude Stein is that she is incomprehensible because there is nothing to comprehend. It is no use for the reader to puzzle over definitions like the 'elephant beaten with candy' or 'a color in shaving'. There may have been psychological reasons for the author's using these particular phrases, but in themselves they mean nothing. (p. 88)

Twenty years later, looking back on their two careers, Leo Stein maintained that his sister had turned to writing jargon because she could not express herself effectively in English. She, however, and her apologists asserted that she had evolved a method of direct apprehension of reality, that in her portraits she had reached out to the essence of a person stripped of all accidental accretions and had achieved a four-dimensional portrait independent even of time. (p. 92)

Although Gertrude Stein was always to maintain that *The Making of Americans* was her greatest piece of work, the manner of *Tender Buttons* was the one she preferred in her middle period, in the portraits and what she called her plays and landscapes. There were echoes of her earlier repetitive style in a few of the portraits and a continuation of it in the posthumously published *Two*, but this method necessitated following a fairly rigid outline that she now found irksome, as she herself said 'one had to be remembering'. It was easier to adopt the free word-play manner of *Tender Buttons* that could be scribbled down at odd moments without regard for sequence. Her plays were written in this manner, although except for the gratuitous use of the directives 'Scene' and 'Act' they are not plays at all but merely random offshoots of her indifferent fancy. (p. 96)

Where she had divided the fragments of *Tender Buttons* under the headings of Objects, Food and Rooms, she divided her plays into conventionally labelled scenes and acts. There, however, the convention ended, for these play fragments contained no dialogue and lacked any time sequence. Two short paragraphs, for example, became the fifth act of *What Happened*. . . . (p. 97)

According to her own explanation, Gertrude Stein by writing plays stripped of dialogue, action, suspense and characterization uncovered their primal quality. This quality, she maintained, was best typified by a landscape. As she wrote in her autobiography, 'a landscape is such a natural arrangement for a battlefield or a play that one must write plays'. As with most of her theories, when they are applied to the matter at hand they result in no further clarification, nor—as the untoward reference to the battlefield suggests—was there any such intention on the author's part. She defined her most widely-known play, *Four Saints in Three Acts,* in a similar manner:

'In *Four Saints* I made the Saints the landscape. All the saints that I made and I made a number of them because after all a great many pieces of things are in a landscape all these saints together made my landscape.' (p. 98)

One of the idiosyncracies of Gertrude Stein's work, of which there are innumerable examples in *Four Saints,* is the use of internal rhyme in progressions of jingles such as children use, where one word suggests another almost ad infinitum. Sometimes again an actual counting out rhyme is used, as in the second act. . . . (p. 102)

There are in Gertrude Stein's middle writings no clues to her personality. Long ago she had revealed herself and she did not intend to do so again. So consistently did she bar the door to her own feelings that she 'forgot' about her first book, nor when it came to light did she allow it to be published. The rhymes without reason of the Lucy Lilies and the dead-wedleds are a magical gesture, a banning of the active thought beneath the surface of her mind. (p. 103)

With that touch of clairvoyance she possessed and that made her originally sense the currents of anti-reason on which she had built up her reputation, she now sensed—as in the more violent patterns of the surrealists—that she might become eclipsed and outmoded. So after a lapse of thirty years she took up her pen with conscious intent and in six weeks wrote the volume of reminiscences to which she gave the ingenuous title of *The Autobiography of Alice B. Toklas.* (pp. 105-06)

Writing of herself in the third person, through the fiction of Miss Toklas, she came out from behind the barricade of words she had erected. These gossipy sometimes jejune recollections, in spite of their carried-over repetitions and false-naïve manner, have a sprightliness about them that is a welcome relief to what has gone before. *Alice B. Toklas* is easy to read. Time does move, events occur, now and then the author pays off old scores—often amusingly enough as in the cases of Hemingway and Matisse. It is as straight a kind of writing as she could muster. Beneath its surface ripples it gives her away, exposes her shallowness, her flaccid impervious mind.

What is apparent here, what becomes even more apparent in her later autobiographical volumes, is her isolation from the world she lived in. Wars and depressions, the cataclysms of our times, never penetrated into the comfortable isolated existence she had contrived for herself. (p. 106)

Although *Alice B. Toklas* has interest . . . , neither persons nor events really become alive. One does not relive imaginatively Gertrude Stein's experiences, there is no moving sense of continuity with the past such as one finds for example in the autobiographical volumes of Osbert Sitwell. (p. 107)

In Gertrude Stein's second autobiographical volume, *Everybody's Autobiography,* . . . she discarded the fictive Miss Toklas and wrote in the first person, she gave an account of her American tour. The lionizing aspects of it had delighted her. (p. 111)

Everybody's Autobiography is in a sense a summing up of the author's beliefs, habits and tastes. By now the reader is almost used to finding her describing herself and Einstein as the two creative minds of the century. (p. 113)

She remained in the country during the war years, moving from Bilignin to Belley, keeping a record from month to month that was afterward published as *Wars I Have Seen.* . . .

In the incidental details of the German occupation, *Wars I Have Seen* often has considerable interest, particularly in the final section when the American troops appear. Yet against the sweep of world events and the devastation of Europe her pre-occupations with food and dental floss, her garulous crotchety thinkings-aloud, take on for the reader an infuriating quality. She can prattle on about the war as inconsequentially as she did about sentences and paragraphs. (p. 114)

As a result of her contact with the troops she wrote a short book, *Brewsie and Willie,* about American soldiers as she imagined she understood them. It is the most intensely felt piece she had wrritten since *Things As They Are.* What she wanted to do was to grasp the speech of the common soldier and through it transmit a message to her fellow countrymen that she felt was in a sense her summing up.

What she succeeded in doing was merely to express the sterility of her own mind. *Brewsie and Willie* in its message is an inconsequent little tract against industrialism. (p. 118)

Her soldiers are phantoms. She understood neither their thoughts nor their talk. Her Brewsie is an illiterate Werther rather than an infantryman. (p. 119)

She wished to capture the essence of these uniformed men who flocked to see her. But she was locked within herself. The soldiers were incomprehensible to her. She could not even catch the rhythm of their speech, and her final message was no more than the superficial reflections of a rentier. When she spoke in her own person, as she did at the end of *Brewsie and Willie,* her last words were merely a series of commonplaces on the American way.

There have been several books of Gertrude Stein's published since her death, most of them consisting of material left over from her pre-autobiographical period. However, in the posthumous *Last Operas and Plays,* among the brief word sequences she called plays, there is one actual short play written in conventional stage form, called *Yes Is For A Very Young Man.* Though of no particular interest in itself, it has considerable interest in the way it reflects on the author. As in the autobiographies, Gertrude Stein by returning to a discarded convention has subjected herself to conventional criticism. And as the meaning becomes clear so do the limitations of the mind behind the piece. *Four Saints* and the other landscape plays were written deliberately out of focus. The characters in *Yes Is For A Very Young Man* speak comprehensibly enough—though in the rambling manner of *Alice B. Toklas*—and the action is focussed on the French resistance movement.

The play was written under the impact of the liberation of France, but its basic inspiration goes back to the author's childhood and to the melodramas of the 'eighties like *Ben Hur* and *Way Down East.* (pp. 119-20)

As in the Victorian melodramas there are no nuances to this little play, no character development. The love scenes are incredible. It is obviously a juvenile performance. That fact brings one again to the core of Gertrude Stein. What is implicit in all her writings is her insistence on reacting as a child. In the plays and portraits it is the infantile repetitions, the echoes of counting-out rhymes, the stringing of words together the way a four-year-old strings wooden beads. In her autobiographies and war reflections the style and thought currents and general attitude are those of a wide-eyed child. Her inspiration turned back, not like Proust's to remembered childhood but to childhood itself. From what one can gather her views of American history, particularly about the Civil War, were still those of her schooldays. Her retreat into the atmosphere of childhood finally reached the extreme form of her *First Reader* where she tried to re-create the very form of the nineteenth-century McGuffey Readers. It is this stance that accounts for her genial and uncritical egotism, the natural egotism of the child who is the centre of his own solar system.

Gertrude Stein's rejection of the adult world that began tentatively with *Three Lives* became enforced in the automatism of her middle period and externally apparent in her autobiographies, was—however consciously motivated—a necessity to her. In her maturity she could apparently not manage or organize her world except on a juvenile level. She was the child that brooked no contradictions. Whereas there was another calculating side of her nature that could assess the publicity value of her position, it was an inner need that made her retreat into the shell of childhood, maintaining all the time in this retreat that she was one of the great figures of the age. (pp. 121-22)

Francis Russell, "Gertrude Stein," in his Three Studies in Twentieth Century Obscurity *(copyright 1954 by The Hand and Flower Press; permission granted by Dufour Editions, Inc.), Hand and Flower Press (and reprinted by Dufour Editions, 1961), 1954, pp. 66-122.*

JANE RULE (essay date 1975)

For a woman famous for obscuring and eschewing meaning through a great part of her writing life, experimenting in codes and riddles and verbal still-lifes, the flat clarity and relentless honesty of *Q.E.D.* [Gertrude Stein's first novel published under the title *Things As They Are*] come as a contradiction to all those "rose is a rose is a rose" jokes about her. (p. 62)

Q.E.D. is probably the only book about lesbian relationship which confronts its characters with the raw war between desire and morality and reveals the psychological geometry of the human heart without false romanticizing or easy judgment. Recent biographers have scrupulously identified the three characters in the novel with their counterparts in real life and documented many of the events in Gertrude Stein's own life, suggesting that she failed in her last year in medical school not because, as she has so often been quoted as saying to her friend Marion Walker, "You don't know what it is to be bored," but because she was miserably involved in a triangular affair she later described in *Q.E.D.*, a book written as a desperate attempt to understand and, by that means, to survive what had happened to her.

What Gertrude Stein came to terms with in *Q.E.D.* out of her own experience, she later transformed into the novella "Melanctha," published early in her career as the middle piece in *Three Lives,* and in many of her other books the hard knowledge of the part power plays in human relationships surfaces again, based on the model of the three characters in *Q.E.D.*.... Aside from protecting herself from the scorn and moral disapproval of large audiences, she may also have felt that *Q.E.D.* was aesthetically faulty because it was too close to her own experience, too uncertain and pedantic in the sentence rhythms which later became one of her chief preoccupations as a writer. Though "Melanctha" is the story of a black woman in love with a black doctor and therefore does not raise either the question of lesbian love or the power struggles involved in a triangle, it does use great passages of *Q.E.D.* nearly verbatim, Helen of *Q.E.D.* becoming Melanctha, Adele becoming the doctor. In this later work the struggle to understand, trust, love is written in a language of far greater tragic power than it is in *Q.E.D.* The one difficulty in "Melanctha" is that occasionally the transformation is not complete, the psychological tension arbitrary since the heterosexual possibility of marriage is entirely ignored. But it is a minor flaw in a piece of work which otherwise solves many of the stylistic problems that make *Q.E.D.* sometimes clumsy and flatfooted when it should be moving. "Melanctha" embodies the basic separateness of human beings which was to remain Gertrude Stein's view of the nature and limitation of human relationship. It does not, however, offer the insight into relationships between women so remarkable in *Q.E.D.* If honesty is a selfish virtue which Gertrude Stein herself struggled to leave behind, one can feel only gratitude that Adele, the character in *Q.E.D.* who is the mouthpiece for the young Gertrude, has survived the later monumental Gertrude not to overthrow her or to diminish her real achievements but to make her remarkable way clearer and warmer and more humane.

Adele is described in the beginning of *Q.E.D.* as a bright and innocent moralist, making friends with a couple of women, Helen Thomas and Mabel Neathe, who are far more sophisticated than she. (pp. 62-4)

The moments of quiet intimacy between [Helen and Adele] stir Adele's curiosity more than her emotions. There are things she

wants to understand which she doesn't know how to articulate or explore with Helen.... (p. 65)

When Mabel comments on the growing friendship between Adele and Helen, Adele [becomes defensive].... (p. 66)

Adele is relentless in her examination of Helen's character.... She is no less hard on and inconsistent about herself, sometimes believing that she is interested in "the mere machinery" of their complex relationships, sometimes revolted by her own need, sometimes sure she is really learning to love Helen. Each time she bursts out in judgment of any of them, she is immediately contrite. Through this whole process, Adele has not actually consummated the relationship with Helen. (pp. 66-7)

Helen goes off for a European holiday with Mabel. Adele, now ardent and determined to prove her love for Helen, joins them, asking nothing more of Helen than that she allow Adele to help her in any way she can. Mabel is at first fiercely and openly jealous, but gradually, as Helen submits to her demands, she relaxes a little. "Adele's domination was on the wane and Mabel was becoming the controlling power."... The book ends with Adele's understanding that there is no resolution, Helen unable to see things as they are but only as she wishes they were, but it is a despair, a terrible suffering of defeat, for the impetuous and at the same time slow-minded student has finally learned to feel, and it is all pain. (pp. 67-8)

Richard Bridgman, in *Gertrude Stein in Pieces,* suggests that her departure from the clarity of her early work may be due, in part, to her realization that she could not go on being honest in her preoccupation with lesbian experience. "By selecting general nouns and verbs and replacing nouns with pronouns that lacked distinct referents and if possible gender—'one' and 'some', she moved steadily toward abstraction." As she went on writing more and more obscurely, only occasional random references show that she at least sometimes grew weary of disguise. "It is better to name it naturally than to have it changed from Jack to Jaqueline or from Henry to Henrietta." For a person as committed to process writing, to spinning a web of words out of her own experience, the inability to name naturally forced her often into grotesquely private solutions. In *Lifting Belly,* she was reduced to coy code games to tease at rather than explore her domestic and erotic relationship with Alice B. Toklas. About all the insight that can be gained is that Gertrude thought of herself as a man in the relationship, referred to Alice as her wife, that they both played the intimate, inane sexual games in which most people indulge, fortunately without the temptation to record them and claim literary value for them. *Tender Buttons* is probably not code at all, though certainly some words have private and charged sexual meaning for Gertrude Stein. It is more likely that this is a serious if not altogether satisfying experiment to dislodge words from any meaning, personal or public, to create arbitrary aesthetic pleasure from their being grouped together. (pp. 68-9)

Gertrude Stein wanted to be a middle-class, ordinary, honest genius, and at her very best she probably was, teaching, through her own extremes, generations of writers after her what the limits of language are. Whether her whole body of work would have been greater or less interesting if she had lived either in a climate of more acceptance or in a personal style more continuously open is impossible to say. (p. 73)

Jane Rule, "Gertrude Stein," in her Lesbian Images
(copyright © 1975 by Jane Rule; reprinted by per-

mission of Doubleday & Company, Inc.), Doubleday, 1975, pp. 62-73.

RICHARD KOSTELANETZ (essay date 1980)

What distinguishes Gertrude Stein . . . from her chronological contemporaries in American literature (e.g., Dreiser, Stephen Crane, Vachel Lindsay, and others) is that even today most of her works are commonly misunderstood. The principal reason for such continued incomprehension is that her experiments in writing were conducted apart from the major developments in modern literature. Neither a naturalist nor a surrealist, she had no interest in either the representation of social reality or the weaving of symbols, no interest at all in myth, metaphor, allegory, literary allusions, uncommon vocabulary, synoptic cultural critiques, shifts in point of view, or much else that preoccupied writers such as James Joyce, Thomas Mann, and Marcel Proust. Unlike them, she was an empiricist, who preferred to write about observable realities and personally familiar subjects; the titles of her books were typically declarative and descriptive, rather than symbolic and allusive. Not unlike other modern writers, she was influenced by developments in the nonliterary arts; but Stein feasted upon a fertile aesthetic idea that her literary colleagues neglected—to emphasize properties peculiar to one's chosen medium and it alone. As her art was writing, rather than painting, Stein's primary interest was language—more specifically, American English and how *else* its words might be used. Indicatively, the same aesthetic idea that became so quickly acceptable in modernist painting and music was for so long heretical, if not unthinkable, in literature.

From nearly the beginnings of her creative career, Stein experimented with language in several ways. Starting from scratch, she neglects the arsenal of devices that authors had traditionally used to enhance their prose. Though she was personally literate, her language is kept intentionally unliterary and unconnotative. Her diction is mundane, though her sentence structure is not, for it was her particular achievement to build a complex style out of purposely limited vocabulary. An early device, already evident in *Three Lives* (drafted in 1904), is the shifting of syntax, so that parts of a sentence appear in unusual places. Adverbs that customarily come before a verb now follow it, and what might normally be the object of a sentence either becomes its subject or precedes it. These shifts not only repudiate the conventions of syntactical causality, but they also introduce dimensions of subtlety and accuracy. Instead of saying "someone is alive," Stein writes, "Anyone can be a living one." . . . Some parts of speech are omitted, while others are duplicated; and nouns, say, are used in ways that obscure their traditional functions within the structure of a sentence.

Especially in *The Making of Americans,* which was begun in 1902 and revised in 1908-11, Stein inserts extra gerunds into otherwise normal clauses. Around this time she also began to remove adjectives, adverbs, and internal punctuation, thereby increasing the suggestions of ambiguity. (pp. xiii-xiv)

The subjects of Stein's books tended to be personally familiar—that of *The Making of Americans,* say, is the saga of her own family in America; for instead of "making up" plots and characters, she concentrated on inventing linguistic structures.

In that 925-page milestone, her longest single book, Stein broached what subsequently became her initial notorious device—the use of linguistic repetition. To be precise, she repeats certain key words or phrases within otherwise different clauses and sentences; so that even though the repetitions are never exact, this repeated material comes to dominate the entire paragraph or section. The effect is initially wearisome—the reader's eye wants to leap ahead to something else, because he can quickly discern, by looking at the entire paragraph, which words will be emphasized. (And experienced readers, like experienced hikers, invariably short-cut by instinct.) However, it would be wise to linger, or even to read the passage aloud, because what makes Stein's repetitions so interesting is precisely the varying relationships that the repeated elements have to their surrounding frames. As phrases are rarely repeated exactly, what initially seems identical is, upon closer inspection, seen to be quite various, for one theme of Stein's repetitions (and near-repetitions) is the endless differences amid recurring sameness.

By dominating the reader's attention, repetitions become a device for focusing and emphasis; a passage is remembered in terms of this repeated material. (p. xv)

In reading Stein, one finds that the reapplication of attention, especially after a lapse or rebuff, can produce a range of unusual effects, because the reader's mind is forced out of its customary perceptual procedures. While talking about something else, the composer John Cage once suggested, perspicaciously, "In Zen they say: If something is boring after two minutes, try it for four. If still boring, try it for eight, sixteen, thirty-two and so on. Eventually one discovers that it's not boring but very interesting." A similar experience is possible reading Stein. (p. xvi)

Because of its audacious exploration of repetition as a device, not only of style but of understanding, *The Making of Americans* seems "contemporary" and "innovative" and "incredible" long after it was written. Originally drafted in the first decade of this century, well before the innovative novels of James Joyce and William Faulkner, it represents the first giant step beyond nineteenth-century fiction. . . . Stein's biggest book also stands as an epitome of that colossal, uneven, digressive, excessive, eccentric masterpiece that every great American innovative artist seems to produce at least once. Its peers in this respect are Walt Whitman's *Leaves of Grass,* Ezra Pound's *Cantos,* Faulkner's *Absalom, Absalom!,* and Charles Ives's Fourth Symphony. Not unlike other American geniuses, Stein walked the swampy field between brilliance and looniness; and even today, as in her own time, her works are perceived as extraordinary or mad or, more precisely, both.

In addition to defining emphasis, Stein's linguistic repetitions also serve as a structural device, for the repeated word becomes the primary cohering force within a passage. Consequently, expository units, such as the paragraph, are reorganized. Instead of proceeding from a topic sentence through various examples, the paragraph is now filled with clauses that have equal weight within the whole. . . . In Stein's view, the repetition of a single word can also evoke connotations, not only by assuming different meanings in varying contexts but also through the suggestions of secondary qualities. In explaining her most famous repetition of "rose is a rose is a rose is a rose," she once told a university audience: "I'm no fool. I know that in daily life we don't go around saying [that], but I think that in that line the rose is red for the first time in English poetry for a hundred years." Readers struck by the simplicities of much Stein prose tend to forget how intelligent, conscious, and literate she actually was, for only an assuredly smart author would risk such semblances of stupidity. (pp. xvi-xviii)

These innovations, simple at base, had radical and complex effects. As she neglected subject, setting, anecdote, conflict, analysis, and many other conventional elements, *style* became the dominant factor in Stein's writing. It became more important than "theme" or "character"; so that from *The Making of Americans* onward, her books could be characterized as a succession of experiments in particular styles, other dimensions being merely incidental. (Even within *Americans,* her style becomes progressively more experimental.) Secondly, since language is primary, climactic structures become secondary; thus, narrative elements tend to be as flat and uninflected as Stein's language. To put it differently, the kind of structural flattening to which Stein subjected the paragraph was extended to longer forms in her exposition and narrative; so that even in the family history of *The Making of Americans,* no event is more important than any other. In this respect in particular, Stein clearly precedes the formally uninflected, counter-hierarchical prose of, say, Samuel Beckett and Alain Robbe-Grillet.

This emphasis upon style also diminishes the importance of representational concerns, and that in turn contributes to an entirely different kind of flattening—the elimination of both temporal and spatial perspectives. Stein defined this effect when she said that her books take place in the "continuous present." All these changes brought the abolition of linear causality in the portrayal of character and activity; they also enabled Stein to introduce an event at one point of *The Making of Americans* and then postpone further consideration of it for several hundred pages. Historically, we can see that the use of such forms placed her among the first imaginative writers to represent the modern awareness of discontinuous experience. (pp. xviii-xix)

All of these experiments in style progressively freed Stein from the restrictions of conventional syntax (and the Aristotelian assumptions informing it); so that in future works she was able to explore the possibilities of not just one but several kinds of alternative language. Having worked with accretion and explicitness, as well as syntactical transposition, she then experimented with ellipses and economy; having written about something with many more words than usual, she also tried to write with far, far fewer. In *Tender Buttons, . . .* her aim was the creation of texts that described a thing without mentioning it by name. She would approach a subject from various perspectives, just as a cubist painter would; and like them she was interested in discovering the limits of reorganized representation. Each of the prose sections of that early book has a subtitle or opening words that provide a context for otherwise unexplicit language. (p. xix)

[In] Stein, words become autonomous objects, rather than symbols of something else, for they are themselves, rather than windows onto other terrain. They cohere in terms of stressed sounds, rhythms, alliterations, rhymes, textures, and consistencies in diction—linguistic qualities other than subject and syntax; and even when entirely divorced from semantics, these dimensions of prose have their own powers of effect. She also discovered that disconnection enhances language, precisely because the process of transcending mundane sentences makes every word important. (p. xxi)

There are few, if any, purposely ulterior subjects in her writing after 1910. What you read is most of what there is. (p. xxiii)

Stylistic ideas, coupled with her immediate experience, were the root inspirations of her most extraordinary works. "Language as a real thing," she wrote in *Lectures in America,* "is not imitation either of sounds or colors or emotions it is an intellectual recreation." All her experimenting with the tech-

nology of language produced not just one original style but several, some of which are quite different from the others, all of which seem, nonetheless, to be distinctly Steinian. Perhaps the most extraordinary quality of these inventions is their continuing contemporaneity. . . . (p. xxiv)

She frequently claimed that in writing she was "telling what she knew," but most of her knowledge concerned writing. It is probably significant that the principal theme of her essays, reiterated as much by example as by explanation, is the autonomy of language. It was, I think, her greatest ambition to be as inventive and fecund in her arts as Picasso was in his. (p. xxvii)

The enterprise of American literary criticism has scarcely noticed Stein's work, and too many literary professionals honor and teach the simpler books, such as *Three Lives* and *The Autobiography of Alice B. Toklas,* to the neglect of the more extraordinary ones—those whose special qualities have never been exceeded. . . . Remarkably little perceptive criticism of her work appeared during her lifetime, and prior to Donald Sutherland in 1951 [see excerpt above] her best "critics" were other writers. Indeed, this default with Stein is an index of the more general failure of American criticism to acknowledge its native experimental tradition. . . . Furthermore, this failure partly accounts for why Stein never felt obliged to make more precise statements about her purposes. Her essays and speeches on her own work tended to be suggestive and formally interesting but, by critical standards, evasive and incomplete; and I am scarcely alone in regarding *How to Write . . .* as misleadingly labeled. This elusiveness in turn accounts for the sense that I have in 1980: I think I know what she was doing—the techniques and qualities defined in this essay—because I am familiar with the history of experimental literature since Stein (and see her thus as a precursor of contemporary concerns); but I am not at all sure what she ultimately thought she was doing.

Though her work as a whole was commonly dismissed, we can see, by now, that no other twentieth-century American author had as much influence as Stein; and none influenced his or her successors in as many ways. There are echoes of Stein's writings in her friends Sherwood Anderson, Thornton Wilder, and Ernest Hemingway, as well as in William Faulkner's extended sentences, E. E. Cummings's syntactical playfulness, John Dos Passos's ellipses, Allen Ginsberg's attempt to use mantra-like language to escalate into unusual mental states, and any narrative that is structurally uninflected, as well as much else—for current examples, the indefinite poetry of John Ashbery's middle period (the 1960s) and the nonsyntactic writing of Clark Coolidge, John Cage, bp Nichol, and myself. (pp. xxix)

What is more extraordinary is that this influence continues, not only through her imitators but directly through her own works—not only with her experiments in literary alternatives but in her general attitudes toward language and literary art. (p. xxxi)

> *Richard Kostelanetz, "Gertrude Stein: The New Literature," in* The Hollins Critic *(copyright© 1975 by Hollins College), Vol. XII, No. 3, June, 1975 (and reprinted in a slightly different form as the introduction to* The Yale Gertrude Stein *by Richard Kostelanetz, Yale University Press, 1980, pp. xiii-xxxi).*

MARIANNE DeKOVEN (essay date 1981)

Gertrude Stein's writing was undoubtedly influenced by the modes of modern painting she helped to discover and promulgate, particularly cubism. (p. 81)

[The] greatest, or at any rate most interesting influence of modern painting on Stein's work lies in the way its relatively loose strictures on meaning, on the range and significance of content, expanded the possibilities of literature for a writer of her radical propensities. Stein went beyond any other major early modern writer in English: she continues to be the least read giant of twentieth-century literature, primarily because her radical work cannot be read in the normal way. It subverts the kind of coherent, referential meaning we are trained to expect in literature; hence it resists the standard critical method of interpretation, or thematic synthesis. (p. 82)

[In her experimental period] Stein substitutes for coherent meaning and referentiality the primacy of surface—the ascendency of the signifier—and also an order of meaning between conventional coherence and utter unintelligibility: meaning multiplied, fragmented, dedefined, unresolved. . . .

"Unintelligible" connotes the utter absence of readable meaning, while "incoherent" suggests meaning which is present and readable, but incapable of resolution into conventional order or sense. Stein's experimental writing, or the ideal instance of it, is incoherent rather than unintelligible. Meaning is present, but it is multiplied, fragmented, unresolved. . . . (p. 83)

[Unlike] words, painted shapes are not necessarily signs, and therein lies the danger of calling Stein's experimental writing literary cubism. . . . Part of a cubist painting fragments and multiplies its subject (a person, a still life, a landscape); the rest is abstract. Stein's writing is never abstract, and its multiplied, fragmented signification generally ignores its nominal subject. A reader unfamiliar with Stein criticism might be in the best position to recognize that fact: a first reading of *Tender Buttons* seldom suggests any immediate connection between the actual writing and its ostensible subject, while it is clear at first glance that cubist compositions are structured around the fragmentation of their representational elements. . . . (pp. 85-6)

Meaning in cubist painting has very much to do with representation; meaning in Stein's experimental writing does not. Instead, it has to do with language, with writing. Not only the effect of Stein's work on the reader and its linguistic structures, but also its larger significance as an alternative literature can best be understood by referring it to theories of writing.

In *Of Grammatology*, Jacques Derrida describes and dismantles the cultural hegemony of sense, order, and coherence in writing that Stein's work overthrows. He attacks this hegemony as logocentrism. (p. 87)

For Derrida, experimental writing like Stein's points toward a cultural order beyond logocentrism. As the characteristic writing of logocentric culture, the conventional text is "linear," not only in its treatment of time, but, quite literally, in its structure of successive lines. . . . This linearity is not innocent. It has been instituted at the expense of repressing what Derrida calls "pluridimensionality," which is . . . the central feature of Steinian experimental writing. (pp. 87-8)

What for Derrida is a suppressed cultural/historical past of nonlinear writing is for [psychoanalyst Jacques Lacan] a repressed psychological past of presymbolic language. Symbolic language is simply language as we commonly conceive it: primarily a way to make and order communicable meaning. . . . Presymbolic language, like experimental writing and in opposition to symbolic language, is characterized by the ascendancy of the signifier: the play of intonation, rhythm, repetition, sound association. Symbolic language is similar to Derrida's logocentric writing: both encompass the ascendancy of hierarchical order, sense, reason, and the signified. (p. 89)

The acquisition of culture, in human society as we know it, is the institution of what Lacan calls the "Rule of the Father," or patriarchy. To enter or acquire culture is to embrace simultaneously the symbolic order of language and the "Rule of the Father." For Lacan, the two are inseparable, and both come at the cost of repressing, again simultaneously, presymbolic language and the omnipotent, magical unity of the self with the outer world of which presymbolic language is the expression. (pp. 89-90)

For [the French feminist critic] Julia Kristeva, the restoration of the repressed female unconscious, a goal hardly restricted to women, is already accomplished in the experimental writing of the avant-garde. Kristeva's work demonstrates the clear connection between Lacan's symbolic language and Derrida's logocentrism, and, inversely, between Lacan's repressed presymbolic language and Derrida's suppressed past of nonlinear, pluridimensional writing, a supp-repressed past which is both cultural/historical and psychological. (p. 90)

Though cubism also subverts hierarchical order, sense, and coherence, and though . . . Stein and Picasso share and express a common vision, the revolution in painting, unlike that in writing, was able to flourish well within the boundaries of patriarchal/logocentric culture. Painted shapes are not signs: they are not at the core of symbolic thought as words are. Pluridimensionality or incoherence in painting does not threaten hierarchical, linear thought as incoherence in writing inevitably does.

Nonetheless, the relative unimportance of content in modern painting did liberate Stein as literature itself never could from the compulsion of conventional (patriarchal, logocentric) writing to make coherent sense. (p. 92)

To call Stein's writing "literary cubism," to accommodate it to a critical vocabulary developed for painting, is to overlook that central, defining difference: unlike paintings, Stein's experimental work is neither representational nor abstract. If a painting has readable meaning, that meaning is referential, representational. If a painting does not have representational meaning, it is abstract; it has no strictly readable meaning. Stein's writing has readable meaning, and therefore is not abstract, but since it is seldom "about something"—it generally has no coherent thematic content—it is not referential, or representational. Its meaning consists rather of the connections among the lexical meanings of its words. Painting has nothing in its semantic repertoire comparable to lexical meaning, and it is precisely at that level that Stein's experimental writing operates. Because it has lexical meaning, it is able to challenge patriarchal/logocentric thought as pictorial radicalism cannot do. (pp. 94-5)

Marianne DeKoven, "Gertrude Stein and Modern Painting: Beyond Literary Cubism," in Contemporary Literature *(©1981 by the Board of Regents of the University of Wisconsin System), Vol. 22, No. 1, Winter, 1981, pp. 81-95.*

ADDITIONAL BIBLIOGRAPHY

Allen, Mary. "Gertrude Stein's Sense of Oneness." *Southwest Review* 65, No. 1 (Winter 1981): 1-10.
Points to Stein's consistent style of examining the individual, the object, and the word for its essence and meaning. She "tenderly breaks the world into pieces" in order to see things in a fresh way.

Copeland, Carolyn Faunce. *Language and Time and Gertrude Stein.* Iowa City: University of Iowa Press, 1975, 183 p.
An interesting study of Stein which considers her career in three periods: her early years which include her ties with nineteenth-century literature and her initial experiments; her middle years which include her experiments with the nonrepresentational use of language; and her later years marked by a return to narrative form and a closer examination of time.

Van Vechten, Carl. "A Stein Song." In *Selected Writings of Gertrude Stein,* by Gertrude Stein, edited by Carl Van Vechten, pp. ix-xv. New York: Random House, 1946.
Defense of Stein's various techniques of abstraction in literature as comparable to those of Pablo Picasso in art and Arnold Schoenberg in music.

Wilder, Thornton. Introduction to *Four in America,* by Gertrude Stein, pp. v-xxvii. New Haven: Yale University Press, 1947.
Perceives Stein's goal in writing not to be art, but a formulation of a "theory of knowledge, a theory of time, and a theory of passions."

Alfred Sutro

1863-1933

English dramatist and translator.

The best works of Sutro, a popular writer of the well-made play, are well constructed, clever, and filled with amusing dialogue. However, they have been criticized for their contrived plots, artificial themes, and superficial characterization. Sutro also translated a number of Maurice Maeterlinck's works, and some critics feel that these translations constitute Sutro's most noteworthy contribution to literature.

Although he had early literary ambitions, Sutro decided to first make his fortune in business. After becoming quite prosperous, he retired, set himself up in a luxurious London apartment, and wrote steadily until his death. Following in the tradition of the French dramatist Victorien Sardou, Sutro remained dedicated throughout his career to meticulous construction in drama. He was also influenced by the styles of his contemporaries Henry Arthur Jones and Arthur Wing Pinero, though Sutro's was considered a lesser talent.

A relatively early play, *The Walls of Jericho,* brought Sutro recognition and success. Sutro objected to critical interpretation of the play as an attack on society, however, calling it a study of the "new woman" who was discovering and reckoning with her individuality for the first time. Although *The Walls of Jericho* is considered by most to be Sutro's best work, others have called *The Builder of Bridges* his finest, praising its graceful dialogue, wit, and technical finesse.

Always fearful of endangering his financial security, Sutro never risked innovation. He believed that a good play is one that succeeds financially, and once said: "The dramatist should keep one eye raised to heaven and the other on the box-office." This conception of drama, cited by numerous critics as Sutro's downfall, bred a style limited by tradition and inconsequential themes. Although Sutro produced many commercial successes and was popular in his own day, his dramas have failed to endure.

PRINCIPAL WORKS

The Chili Widow [with Arthur Bourchier, adapted from a
   play by Alexandre Bisson]   (drama)   1895
*The Cave of Illusion   (drama)   1900
The Walls of Jericho   (drama)   1904
Mollentrave on Women   (drama)   1905
The Fascinating Mr. Vanderveldt   (drama)   1906
The Builder of Bridges   (drama)   1908
The Perplexed Husband   (drama)   1911
The Two Virtues   (drama)   1914
The Great Well   (drama)   1922
The Laughing Lady   (drama)   1922
Living Together   (drama)   1929
Celebrities and Simple Souls   (memoirs)   1933

*This is the date of first publication rather than first performance.

THE ATHENAEUM   (essay date 1900)

Mr. Sutro's play [*The Cave of Illusion: A Play in Four Acts*] singularly enough, betrays the influence of his master [Maurice Maeterlinck] only in the most general way, and not at all in style of writing, order of subject, or way of construction. It is a problem-play, and the problem is left very significantly unsolved at the end. The problem is really the problem of duty, in all its forms: one's duty to oneself, to one's art, to one's passion, to one's responsibilities. . . . It is a glimpse into a very ordinary and very miserable world, in which men live on illusions, and the illusions fade one after another and leave them without even that sustenance. A large part of our happiness, no doubt, lies in our illusions; the moment we pause and look some pleasant certainty in the face, the pleasure begins to go out of the certainty and the certainty out of the pleasure. Is it better not to pause and not to look? Is it possible?

Such are the questions which this play raises, and it gives no answer to them, being a work of art and not a treatise on ethics. The play is written very quietly, almost commonly; there is not what is called a good phrase, there is not a touch of imaginative language, in the whole of the dialogue. But it is very close to life; it is human in a thoughtful way. . . . It would be interesting to see it on the stage. . . . [The] bareness, the brevity of the language would probably tell for more than it does at present. Mr. Sutro has followed Ibsen rather than Maeterlinck in the character of his dialogue. In the dialogue of Maeterlinck, simple, banal even, as it almost always is, there is an undercurrent of poetry which transfigures the language, giving it a constant quality of suggestion. But in the dialogue of Ibsen, as in this play, the language is frankly the ordinary speech of ordinary people, without the relief of one beautiful phrase, of one illuminating image. Suggestion of another kind there indeed is; an ingenious multiplicity of suggestion, knitting the action closer and closer together, but not concerned with anything beyond the mere psychology of the action.

"Drama: 'The Cave of Illusion: A Play in Four Acts',"
in The Athenaeum, No. 3792, June 30, 1900, p. 827.

THE BOOKMAN (London)   (essay date 1900)

[Alfred Sutro's **"The Cave of Illusion"**] has excellent points. There is careful and artistic work in it. The dialogue is good—infinitely better than we are accustomed to in the plays of the hour. The characterisation—for the first three acts—is clear and interesting. We feel that three-fourths of it is well adapted for the stage—that it would "go." Till the last act began, we had read with admiration, though with increasing wonder how Mr. Sutro could deal with a situation rendered peculiarly complicated by certain excellencies in the character of his chief personages. After all the end is the test of a play, especially of a play that has no pretensions to be pretty, that offers nothing lyrical, nothing even scenically attractive. And the last act here is incredible. In the light of what has gone before, it is false and impossible. . . . If Mr. Sutro had meant to represent the greatest cad and coward that ever lived, he could not have bettered David. But we doubt if this is his intention. . . . Mr. Sutro's thesis seems to be that we must choose between the elementary duties of life and "the kennel." An excellent motive for a play. But a man like the David of the first three acts does not sink into the kennel quite so suddenly, even if he outrages social law, in the company of a woman such as Gabrielle. If she was utterly bad, Mr. Sutro has failed to convince us of it. And as for his David, he is only a disturbing element in the particular problem of this drama. He should have been reserved for a play that would be an exposure of a cad.

There is nothing for it but to rewrite that last act, or the first three. (pp. 186-87)

"'The Cave of Illusion'," in The Bookman, London,
Vol. XVIII, No. 108, September, 1900, pp. 186-87.

MAX BEERBOHM   (essay date 1905)

"A Comedy" Mr. Sutro calls [**"Mollentrave on Women"**]. But it is not really that. "A Philosophic Farce" would be a much better description of it. In a comedy the characters presented are taken from real life without sharp exaggeration, and the incidents are just such as might quite likely be experienced in real life. Mollentrave is a very sharp exaggeration of a type. There's no fool like an old fool, but not even the eldest fool in real life would pretend to such formal and final omniscience in psychology as is pretended to by Mollentrave. Nor is the course of events in the play at all natural or credible. . . . The whole play is founded on an impossibility, and its details are worked out with a conscious disregard of likelihood—with a conscious straining after sheer absurdity. In fact, the play is a farce. I have no objection to that. The scientific expert in affairs of the heart might be well satirised through comedy. But comedy is not the only good means of satirising him. Farce is in itself an equally good medium. All that matters is whether Mr. Sutro has the instinct for satirical farce. Offhand, I should have supposed that he had not the requisite high-spirits. . . . Into **"Mollentrave on Women"**, again, he may not have infused his true soul. Farce may not be his true bent. But no matter. Enough that he seems to have a very real spontaneous instinct for farce. His high-spirits seem quite unforced, and he has an unflagging inventiveness in absurdities. **"Mollentrave on Women"** is great fun, from first to last. It would be well worth seeing even if it had no serious satire in it. But the fact that it is a serious satire, and that every part of it is carefully correlated to the satirical idea, does not make it the less a farce. . . .

In writing farce he has . . . an advantage that he would not have in writing comedy: he can give full rein to his talent for writing. . . . **"Mollentrave on Women"** is distinguished by real grace and charm of dialogue. It is not merely the work of a man who knows our language thoroughly, . . . It is the work of a man who knows how to use our language, and who is revelling in an opportunity for using it. (p. 204)

Max Beerbohm, "Mr. Sutro's New Play," (reprinted
by permission of Mrs. Eva Reichmann), in The Sat-
urday Review, London, Vol. 99, No. 2,573, Feb-
ruary 18, 1905, pp. 204-05.

THE NEW YORK TIMES   (essay date 1905)

It is not very agreeable society to which Alfred Sutro introduces us in **"The Walls of Jericho,"** his smart set being for the most part an assemblage of about as conscienceless a set of prigs, male and female, as one could well imagine. Whether this play really reflects English society—as it purports to do—is, of course, a matter at which the mere outsider may only guess. . . .

It seems just possible [however] that Mr. Sutro in pointing his moral has adorned his tale, the adornment in this case being somewhat in the nature of exaggeration. . . .

One may gather some sort of idea of the kind of society to which Mr. Sutro introduces us from the delight which a party of married women have in recalling the fact that one of their number had arranged to elope, but stopped to play bridge; so fascinating was the game that they played rubber after rubber with the result that the pair missed their train. Lady-Althea's young sister has no compunctions at the thought of marrying her brother-in-law's best friend for his money, even though she has to throw over her cousin, who loves her and whom she loves. . . .

Viewed solely as an exposé of so-called fashionable life, Mr. Sutro's play is not to be accepted as amazingly original or of vast importance. Its sociological questions are not of the kind that can be satisfactorily thrashed out in the course of an evening's entertainment. But its scenes for the most part follow each other in a natural manner with consistently cumulative interest. The characters of Jack Frobisher and his wife are admirable drawn, the woman, however, being the better of the two. Mr. Sutro has a comprehensive grasp of the feminine point of view, and the result is agreeable characterization throughout and several very diverting scenes.

"Sutro Points a Moral and Adorns a Tale," in The
New York Times (© 1905 by The New York Times

Company; reprinted by permission), September 26, 1905, p. 6.

MAX BEERBOHM (essay date 1906)

Mr. Sutro has two manners, for two moods, in dramaturgy. Sometimes life is real, life is earnest to him, and must be strenuously preached about. At other times life appears to him as a trifle in itself, to which he owes no duty except a graceful attitude. It is in this mood that I admire him the more. His sermons do not greatly stir me: they seem too much informed by the desire to say what the congregation expects. But Mr. Sutro's grace in writing, like his humour, is a thing that comes directly from his own inner self. He is, since Mr. Oscar Wilde, the most "literary" of our playwrights—has, more than any other, a fine sense of words, and a delicate ear for cadences. In calling him "literary", I do not mean that he makes his characters talk "like books". In realistic plays of modern life, it is, of course, essential that the characters shall talk with apparent naturalness. . . . Like most of our playwrights, Mr. Sutro casts his lines among the leisured classes. To make them talk with real naturalness, he would have to jettison his literary classicism as surely as he would in reproducing the exact manner of a costermonger. But only apparent naturalness is needed. And because the "barbarians" have, as a rule, pretty manners, and pleasing appearance, it is no strain on us to invest them with other graces also. Much of Mr. Sutro's new play ["**The Fascinating Mr. Vanderveldt**"] consists of a contest of wit between the hero and a Lady Clarice Howland. Neither he nor she uses any phrase or construction that would be pedantic in a talker in real life. But I have rarely heard in real life anyone use the English Language so tastefully. What matter? The words do not sound unnatural. We merely feel that we are listening to a lady and gentleman who happen to be accomplished talkers. And in listening to this dialogue we have as much pleasure as had Mr. Sutro in composing it.

The actual scheme of the play is according to the formula that Mr. Henry Arthur Jones has often used. . . . Mr. Sutro conducts the story with much skill; and, if we are not much excited by it, the fault is not his, but its. We know it so well—know so exactly how it must end. Lady Clarice must be reinstated in the world's favour, and the exact means of her re-instatement can evoke but a technical interest. . . . [The] lady's defiant attitude seems to me not in keeping with her character and with the circumstances of the case. Having disappeared in the afternoon with a gentleman of lax principles and not having returned before the following morning, she would surely not resent the anxiety of her friends and relations to hear some sort of explanation. A strongminded, Ibsenesque heroine, with a contempt for social conventions, might, perhaps, draw herself up to her full height, and snub her interrogators, as does Lady Clarice. But is it natural for Lady Clarice to do so? She is a perfectly conventional woman, who has undoubtedly compromised herself; and she would, in the natural course of things, welcome the opportunities she has of explaining things satisfactorily. (pp. 552-53)

Max Beerbohm, "'The Fascinating Mr. Vanderveldt'" (reprinted by permission of Mrs. Eva Reichmann), in The Saturday Review, London, Vol. 101, No. 2636, May 5, 1906, pp. 552-53.

CLAYTON HAMILTON (essay date 1909)

Considered in the clear light of criticism, *The Builder of Bridges,* by Mr. Alfred Sutro, is seen to be the best of all his plays—

better even than that powerful and popular work, *The Walls of Jericho.* The present piece is strong in story, well-studied and consistent in characterization, neat and firm in structure, and written in dialogue that is fluent, graceful, and often deft and witty. As a representation of life, it has the ring of reality; and as an instance of theatric art, it is an admirable technical achievement, and may be recommended heartily to students of the stage. Yet it was reviewed adversely by nearly all the newspapers of New York, and has also failed to make money with the public. (p. 576)

It will be noticed that this story is motivated entirely by the heroine [Dorothy Faringay], who is the initial, and at all points the central, figure in the plot. It will be noticed also that she is essentially what is called in the theatre an "unsympathetic" character. The audience cannot like her; it cannot, therefore, believe that the apparent happy ending of the piece will be lasting in result; and it leaves the theatre with a feeling of sorry sympathy for Thursfield. This one point is sufficient to account for the popular failure of the play. But if we look upon the matter critically, we shall discern that Mr. Sutro has presented, in the heroine, a very sound and searching study of feminine inconsistency in the sense of right and wrong. Her motives and emotions are always right; her plans and acts are usually wrong. In life, the things she does would be unpardonable if they were done by any man; but they are done every day by many women who are intrinsically fine and wholesome. Of business honor, as it is conceived intellectually by the average man, the average woman has very little sense; confronted with business difficulties, she follows only her emotions, and if these be basically wholesome, she sweeps away all purely masculine considerations of integrity, which to her appear merely formal and secondary. This is a subtle point, and may easily fly over the head of a theatre audience; but it is strange that the point should have been overlooked by the newspaper reviewers. Several of them said that the play was insincere, whereas the truth is, rather, that it presented a sincere study of a familiar type of feminine insincerity. It was surely uncritical to decree that the sins of the heroine should be visited upon the author. (pp. 577-78)

Clayton Hamilton, "The Happy Ending in the Theatre: 'The Builder of Bridges'," in The Forum (copyright, 1909, by The Forum Publishing Company), Vol. XLII, No. 6, December, 1909, pp. 576-79.

CLAYTON HAMILTON (essay date 1912)

In *The Perplexed Husband,* that witty writer, Mr. Alfred Sutro, has set out to satirise the feminist movement that is making so militant a march in the England of today. Thomas Pelling returns from an extended business-trip to discover that his simple-minded wife has fallen a victim to "advanced" ideas. . . . She has welcomed into Mr. Pelling's household, apparently as permanent guests, a Mrs. Dulcie Elstead, . . . and a certain Clarence Woodhouse, an impecunious wind-bag who gives drawing-room lectures on the rights (and wrongs) of women, and is referred to by the wives of solid men who lend him money, as The Master.

The sensible sister of the perplexed husband advised him to fight fire with fire by seeming to accept The Master's teachings and introducing still another woman into the household, with the pretended object of converting her to "the cause." For this purpose Mr. Pelling selects a roseate young girl [Kalleia] whom lately he has dismissed from his office for inefficiency as a typist. . . .

But Mr. Sutro, at his third curtain-fall, makes the mistake of mixing his moods. He allows his hero to grow afraid that he is getting seriously fond of Kalleia, and introduces a scene of sentiment which is out of key with the satirical intention of the comedy. (p. 171)

[The last act] exhibits even more emphatically a mixture of moods. . . . Woodhouse is handled in the key of satire and Kalleia is handled in the key of sincere sentiment; and the result is a discord of two tones that makes it difficult for the auditor to determine how to take the scene.

The trouble with the whole play seems to be that the character of Kalleia is out of keeping with the mood in which the other characters are conceived; but, except for this infirmity of purpose on the author's part, the comedy is clever. . . . The lines are written deftly, and there is a pleasing atmosphere of distinction in the play and the performance. (pp. 171-72)

> Clayton Hamilton, *"Infirmity of Purpose in the Drama: 'The Perplexed Husband',"* in The Bookman, *New York (copyright, 1912, by George H. Doran Company), Vol. XXXVI, No. 2, October 2, 1912, pp. 171-72.*

THE NATION   (essay date 1915)

[Mr. Alfred Sutro] has put new wine into old bottles. And though this may often be done on the stage with impunity, Mr. Sutro has not escaped a certain amount of disaster. His theme, or framework [in **"The Clever Ones"**] is the absurd figure cut by pretentious intellectuals and especially the bother which they make in a household. For one act the author by the brightness of his dialogue is able to give the impression of freshness to the time-honored subject, but as the play progresses it is evident that the types chosen are neither vital nor picturesque enough to hold the interest. Nor has Mr. Sutro helped matters by adopting in the second and third acts that last resort of an embarrassed dramatist—broad farce. It is manifestly incongruous beside the rather careful study attempted in the first act.

> F., *"Drama: 'The Clever Ones',"* in The Nation *(copyright 1915 The Nation magazine, The Nation Associates, Inc.), Vol. 100, No. 2588, February 4, 1915, p. 151.*

THE NATION AND THE ATHENAEUM   (essay date 1922)

The morality Mr. Sutro inculcates [in his **"The Laughing Lady"**] is certainly unexceptionable; his criticisms on the divorce-habit are shrewd as well as witty. But for all that, he doesn't convince us; it is as frigid as a Disraelian love scene. Since nothing is impossible, we suppose a woman might be found to act as does Mrs. Farr, who surrenders her husband to Lady Marjorie without a struggle, only pleading that there shall be no divorce, because that would be bad for the career of a barrister just achieving celebrity. Altruism of this kind takes a good deal of preparing for; when it is sprung on you in the third act of a piece that has hitherto been cynical rather than "uplifting" it strikes chill and incredible. Incredible, too, Lady Marjorie's heroics when she sends her K.C. back to his business. It may be a maliciously fine piece of psychology that makes her give a sharp sermon to the man whom she has tempted to the edge of ruin; but evidently we are not intended to smile just here. . . . Having unloaded our grievance, we should be ungrateful not

to acknowledge the amusement of a score or so of glittering epigrams scattered through the three acts, as well as some character sketches which it is a pity Mr. Sutro's canvas did not allow him to fill in with more detail. The sardonic and pungent war-profiteer, Sir Harrison Peters, to take a single instance, is a sufficiently original rascal to make us want to know more of him and his philosophy.

> D.L.M., *"The Drama: 'The Laughing Lady',"* in The Nation and The Athenaeum, *No. 4831, December 2, 1922, p. 368.*

GRAHAM SUTTON   (essay date 1923)

To read a dramatist *en masse* is always interesting and often instructive; it brings out his private tastes and public method; in Mr. Sutro's case it throws much light on the concensus of critical opinion about his two latest plays [**"The Laughing Lady"** and **"The Great Well"**]. "Well made," "construction," "technical skill"—these are the critical chorus: as they well may be. For Mr. Sutro served his apprenticeship in a strict school. Twenty odd years ago, when he began play-making, the first requisite of drama was that it should be well constructed, as Sardou had defined construction. Young Sutro took the lesson to heart; technique came first with him, and the rest nowhere. Read **"Women in Love,"** a volume of one-act plays . . . , if you would see the manner of his apprenticeship— cold, clockwork little things they are, constructed quite obviously as a mere exercise in making the wheels go round; then turn to a later volume of one-acters—**"Little Plays,"**—and note the development. . . . [The] mechanical apprenticeship is over; the foundation has been truly laid; the dry bones begin to live. . . .

[**"The Walls of Jericho"**] had a curiously old-fashioned flavour; "but of course, it is old stuff," one told oneself—and then remembered other plays of the same age that still seem dateless; the trouble being, I fancy, that when Mr. Sutro wrote **"The Walls of Jericho"** he was still thinking more in stage-technique than in human emotions. But he was also on the verge of a more dangerous pitfall—that very death-trap to all witty English dramatists, the comedy of manners. And here I must digress to Congreve. . . . [While] he wrote, the English theatre was run by and for a highly cultured clique, who were content to take wit like snuff, as an end in itself without moral associations; thus nurtured, comedy sparkled into a perfection that has been the ideal of all later wits—and their despair. For the English audience is no longer responsive to this kind of comedy; it is no longer capable of separating wit from morality; its imagination is like the villas it lives in—only semi-detached; it must have righteousness dragged in by the ears, or the play is damned. So that the modern playwright with an admiration for comedy of manners is like a man boxing with a broken thumb, he can't put his heart into the job—or rather, he has to put too much "heart" into it, at the expense of head. . . . Mr. Sutro, as early as **"The Walls of Jericho,"** shows signs of falling under [this] fatal spell. By fits and starts the play reads like comedy of manners. (p. 231)

But the old lure of comedy of manners had not done with Mr. Sutro yet. He embarked presently upon a comedy period, in which he seemed to be tending quite definitely to the more frivolous mode. After solemn Jack Frobisher [of **"The Walls of Jericho"**], Mr. Vanderveldt [of **"The Fascinating Mr. Vanderveldt"**] was both fascinating and full of promise; yet there was heavy artillery even here—to be precise, our old friend the honest man, who should have stopped in Jericho rather than turn up to balk Mr. Vanderveldt of the heroine, and the whole play of fulfilling its proper function. Mr. Vanderveldt, with his delightfully tinsel wickedness and preposterous tons of granite, cried out for comedy-of-manners treatment. You may object that the honest man's solemn virtue threw Mr. Vanderveldt into higher relief; so it did, of course; but that did not justify its intrusion, still less its ultimate triumph. . . . Even so, the breeze of Mr. Vanderveldt blew through the play disinfecting its stuffiness. There had been no such breeze in Jericho—no breeze at all, save the prolonged blast of sentiment's trumpet; and it still seemed that Mr. Sutro might find his way out of the maze into pure comedy of manners. . . . But it was not to be. . . . [At] the end of this comic period Mr. Sutro, whether from personal inclination or because he feared to scare away his growing public, turned his back on comedy of manners for good and all. True, he retained all his wit, and even increased it, [**"John Glayde's Honour"** and **"The Builder of Bridges"**] . . . being wittier than either of the two predecessors to which I have referred. But wit had ceased to be an end in itself; and a good deal of it was bent to the task of tickling a public taste which liked to be amused and edified at the same time. For these two (like **"The Walls of Jericho"**) were "plays" again—*anglice,* light-comedy with a romantic-moralistic background; or what the French critic would call light-comedy spoiled. Perhaps not even light-comedy: light-drama, one would rather say. Wit became subservient to strong situations and carefully planned effects. Yet in that comedy period Mr. Sutro had kicked up his heels to some purpose, and had worked off the stiffness induced by too much devotion to technique. Just as, in his one-act plays, a series of technical exercises was followed by a series of living folk, so in **"John Glayde"** and **"The Builder of Bridges"** did the cold artifice of "Jericho" come to life. Dialogue grew more natural; more intricate plots moved swiftly and easily; type-characters blossomed into individuals. Here again, the time of apprenticeship was over, and the craftsman arrived.

His two last plays follow the same line of development. **"The Great Well"** is the more "theatrical" (none the worse for that: I will confess an actor's partiality for the "theatrical" play, and protest against the degradation of that adjective into a term of abuse). . . . **"The Laughing Lady"** is in lighter vein, and its first act betrays Mr. Sutro's old affection for comedy of manners. But in each case the plot twists and gleams in Mr. Sutro's practised hands like a silk hat in those of a conjurer; like a good conjurer, he extracts from it an inexhaustible variety of effects, comic and sensational; like a good conjurer again, he takes care that each trick shall be more exciting than the one before. Not till next morning, when the playhouse glamour has paled into the light of day, does one begin to wonder whether these bright, glancing, nimble-witted folk were ever quite so alive as they seemed at the moment: whether they live on in the imagination as they lived in the scene: whether the soul of them, if their body had jigged less nimbly, would not have betrayed itself as unreal and theatrical as its tinselled shell. But these are cold-blooded, matutinal reflections. Such plays aim rather to provide an evening's entertainment than to draw from life; and this Mr. Sutro has twice more done admirably. For their brief three hours' traffic his marionettes are kept alive and kicking; and although at curtain-fall tucked up in the marriage-bed as puppets into a box, they relapse into nothingness, yet they have served their turn. For the prime need of a successful piece is that it should act at night, not that it should grip next morning. Let the superior stallite (if he still survives) deplore this Philistinism: pit and gallery know it to be true. So

do the business managers. So, above all, does Mr. Sutro. (pp. 231-32)

Graham Sutton, "Some Plays of Alfred Sutro" (reprinted by permission of Mildred Sutton), in The Bookman, *London, Vol. LXIII, No. 377, February, 1923, pp. 231-32.*

IVOR BROWN (essay date 1925)

What a casual, trivial affair . . . is [Mr. Sutro's] **'A Man With a Heart.'** There is nothing in it but a slak-fibred rotter and his three women; a few reach-me-down theatre types fill up the scene, but no more is demanded of the audience than that it should observe the embarrassment and the escape of an empty philanderer from the results of his affectionate loitering. I sought without success for some spice of character, some elements of criticism or a creed. Plain story-telling will do very well, it may be answered, without sermons as a by-product. But the narrative quality of Mr. Sutro's play was middling work. . . . (pp. 300-01)

Ivor Brown, "The Theatre: Loiterers and Malcontents," in The Saturday Review, *London, Vol. 139, No. 3621, March 21, 1925, pp. 300-01.**

FRANCIS BIRRELL (essay date 1929)

Mr. Sutro has not had a very good Press for his **"Living Together."** All the brilliant old men have dubbed him out of date. Mr. Sutro, is trying to be advanced, has not been nearly advanced enough, and has given a description of modern *liaisons* in terms not of the stable. This is very shocking, and **"Living Together"** has been given away with a pound of tea. As a matter of fact, this is, in many ways, very unfair. Mr. Sutro puts a play together very well; his dialogue is slick and amusing; he knows what people are like, and why they get into difficulties. . . .

Yet the brilliant old men are right, up to a point. For all its merits, there *is* something wrong with **"Living Together."** Mr. Sutro has tried to put too much new wine into his old bottles. He has tried to sing songs of Cowardice in the tempo of [Victorien] Sardou. . . . The shapelessness of modern life, the chaos of its moral standards cannot be jammed into a neat Sardou box.

Francis Birrell, "The Drama: A Well-Made Play and the Reverse," in The Nation and the Athenaeum, *No. 19, February 9, 1929, p. 652.**

THE SATURDAY REVIEW (London) (essay date 1933)

Alfred Sutro had a varied if not an adventurous life. Starting in the city with a brother—at first shakily and through rough water to prosperity—he found at last the chance to follow his real star and write plays. "The Walls of Jericho" may not have been really the best of these plays. But when it was produced . . . it gave Sutro fame, money, and an endless opportunity. It made him free of the company of all the people he wanted to meet and to know.

And here in [his autobiography, *Celebrities and Simple Souls,*] he wanders among his memories of people and events. He is in some sort autobiographical because one cannot dig among memories without turning over one's own life. But the charm of the book is in the illumination of the characters of others—

Maeterlinck, Shaw, George Moore, Barrie, Wells, Kipling, Lord Reading, all the persons of literature and most of the actors and actresses of the pre-war stage. He is never malicious and yet he is very seldom dull. When he has a hero-worship— and he had many— . . . his praise and admiration are splendidly unstinted. He shows his generosity of spirit not only in his tribute to others but in his acutely critical estimate of his own work. And this generosity is so infectious that his book becomes not only very readable but most lovable.

> *"Joyous Rememberings," in* The Saturday Review, *London, Vol. 4066, No. 156, September 30, 1933, p. 351.*

HUGH ROSS WILLIAMSON   (essay date 1933)

The name of Alfred Sutro, who died last month at the age of seventy, may possibly survive as that of the translator of Maeterlinck's "Life of the Bee"—a great translation of a great book. It is hardly surprising to learn that he rewrote it seven times before he was satisfied with it, so easy and apparently effortless is the result. . . .

Though **"The Walls of Jericho"** had a great success, his plays are uniformly worthless. The reason for his failure (though he did not put it like that) he gave in one sentence in one of his lectures: "The dramatist should keep one eye raised to heaven and the other on the box-office." This is an infallible recipe for bad work. The dramatist (or any other artist) should keep both eyes fixed either on heaven or on the box-office—which only means writing either for a future audience or for a present one. Genuine work will result in each case. The result of Sutro's method was to produce, merely from the box-office standpoint, more failures than successes, and to write nothing that survived even his lifetime.

> *Hugh Ross Williamson, "Notes at Random: Alfred Sutro" (reprinted by permission of Hodder & Stoughton Limited as publishers for Hugh Ross Williamson), in* The Bookman, *London, Vol. LXXXV, No. 505, October, 1933, p. 7.*

ADDITIONAL BIBLIOGRAPHY

"Drama." *The Athenaeum*, No. 3542 (14 September 1895): 363-64.*
  Review of *The Chili Widow*, Sutro's adaptation of Alexandre Bisson's *Monsieur le directeur*.

Beerbohm, Max. "Mr. Sutro, Strategist." *The Saturday Review* (London) 100, No. 2610 (4 November 1904): 586-87.
  Review of *The Perfect Lover*.

Mais, S.P.B. "Alfred Sutro." In his *Some Modern Authors*, pp. 318-24. London: Grant Richards, 1923.
  Criticizes Sutro's commercialism, stating that he "has nothing to say that matters, but his stagecraft is good."

(Edmund) John Millington Synge

1871-1909

Irish dramatist, essayist, poet, journalist, and translator.

Even though he wrote only six plays, critics consider Synge the greatest dramatist of the Irish Literary Renaissance. His unique contribution to Irish literature is his unsentimental but compassionate portrayal of Irish peasants, tinkers, and tramps and his highly imaginative and poetic dialogue patterned after the Irish vernacular. His language, capable of expressing both tragic despair and knock-about farce, is said to capture the essence of the Irish national character. Synge aimed for a realistic rendering of character and speech in his dramas. In contrast to the spiritualism of Yeats and the sentimentality of Lady Gregory, Synge brought vigor, ironic humor, and dramatic pathos to the Irish stage.

Born to a middle-class Protestant Ascendancy, Synge early broke from his strict religious upbringing. He traveled and studied extensively in Germany, France, and Italy, intent on a career in music. After judging himself unfit for that profession, he moved to Paris and devoted himself to criticism of French literature. A chance encounter with Yeats, a leader of the Irish Renaissance in literature, changed Synge's life. Yeats urged him to return to Ireland and to write about the peasants of the Aran Islands—advice which immediately appealed to Synge. Thereafter, he spent many summers among the peasants of Wicklow, Kerry, and the Aran Islands, observing their folkways and dialect. His first published work, a collection of essays called *The Aran Islands*, and his subsequent plays reflect this careful study.

Critics agree that one of Synge's greatest gifts is his invigorating depiction of figures from Irish folklife: the romantic poet-tramp with his penchant for fine talk; the sly, bawdy tinker; and the violent, frustrated peasant. Loneliness, boredom, and poverty plague many of the characters of Synge's comedies, providing, despite robust humor and biting dialogue, an undertone of tragedy and futility. He frequently examines his characters' desire to soften harsh reality with their illusions, their compulsion to live life at its fullest (even in the face of physical hardship and public censure), and their obsessive dread of old age and death. Thus, in *In the Shadow of the Glen*, the poetic eloquence of a tramp persuades a young housewife to leave her unaffectionate, aging husband for the freedom of the open road; in *The Well of the Saints* two blind beggars would sooner remain sightless than confront the truth about the shabbiness of their existence; and in *The Tinker's Wedding* a woman's fear of a lonely and comfortless old age motivates her to foil her son's marriage plans.

Synge's greatest comedy, indeed his masterpiece, is *The Playboy of the Western World*. In this ironic commentary on the Irish peasantry, Christy Mahon, a cloddish weakling, is accepted as a hero by the country folk when he claims that he has just killed his tyrannical father. A propensity for exaggeration, hatred of traditional authority, and exquisite lyrical expression (often cited as peculiarly Irish characteristics), have made this comedy a classic in Irish literature. The play was not always so well received, however. The theme of parricide and what was thought to be coarse language outraged early

audiences in Dublin and the United States, and performances were often cut short by rioting. Disliked by Irish Nationalists because he refused to idealize the peasantry and because he sometimes depicted Irish women as less than completely virtuous, Synge's plays were not accepted in his homeland until many years after his death.

In addition to his more famous comedies, Synge wrote two lyrical tragedies: *Riders to the Sea* and *Deirdre of the Sorrows*. *Riders to the Sea*, Synge's first attempt at tragedy, is considered nearly perfect in its structure and for its true rendering of dialect. Many critics remark on the affinity of *Riders to the Sea* to classical Greek tragedy, and some have called it the greatest short tragedy in modern drama. *Deirdre of the Sorrows* is his last drama and marks a new departure in his work. After years of depicting the peasant, he turned to the ancient legends of Ireland for his inspiration. This drama, left complete but unrevised at his death, echoes many themes from his earlier work, such as obsession with old age and death, but with more restraint in imagery and language.

Although Synge also wrote poetry and essays, it is as a dramatist that he is remembered today. His creation of a stylized language incorporating poetic imagery and vernacular speech patterns had a profound effect on such writers as Yeats, Sean O'Casey, Samuel Beckett, and Brendan Behan; and his plays, which demonstrated that the classical genres of comedy and tragedy were still vital forms in the twentieth century, had a great influence on modern drama.

PRINCIPAL WORKS

In the Shadow of the Glen   (drama)   1903
Riders to the Sea   (drama)   1904
The Well of the Saints   (drama)   1905
The Aran Islands   (essays)   1907
The Playboy of the Western World   (drama)   1907
Poems and Translations   (poetry)   1909
The Tinker's Wedding   (drama)   1909
Deirdre of the Sorrows   (drama)   1910
Collected Works. 4 vols.   (dramas, essays, and poetry)   1962-68

MAX BEERBOHM   (essay date 1904)

There is plenty of poetry in **"Riders to the Sea,"** modern peasants though the characters are. The theme is much the same as in [Herman] Heijermans' play "The Good Hope"— a mother whose youngest son is drowned, as all her other sons have been drowned, at sea. Mr. Synge, being an Irishman, is content to show us the pathos of his theme: he does not, as did Heijermans, try to rouse any indignation. "So it is, and so it must be" is his tone. It is the tone of the mother herself. . . . She submits not merely because it were vain to rebel. To rebel is not in her nature. She has the deep fatalism of her race; and for her, the things that actually happen, for evil as for good, are blurred through the dreams that are within her. (p. 318)

> Max Beerbohm, ''Some Irish Plays and Players'' (originally published in The Saturday Review, London, Vol 97, No. 2528, April 9, 1904), in his Around Theatres (copyright © 1930 by Max Beerbohm; reprinted by permission of Simon & Schuster, a Division of Gulf & Western Corporation), Simon & Schuster, 1954, pp. 314-19.*

W. B. YEATS   (essay date 1905)

Six years ago I was staying in a students' hotel in the Latin Quarter, and somebody, whose name I cannot recollect, introduced me to an Irishman, who, even poorer than myself, had taken a room at the top of the house. It was J. M. Synge, and I, who thought I knew the name of every Irishman who was working at literature, had never heard of him. . . . He told me that he had been living in France and Germany, reading French and German literature, and that he wished to become a writer. He had, however, nothing to show but one or two poems and impressionistic essays, full of that kind of morbidity that has its root in too much brooding over methods of expression, and ways of looking upon life, which come, not out of life, but out of literature, images reflected from mirror to mirror. . . . I said: 'Give up Paris. You will never create anything by reading Racine, and Arthur Symons will always be a better critic of French literature. Go to the Aran Islands. Live there as if you were one of the people themselves; express a life that has

never found expression.' I had just come from Aran, and my imagination was full of those grey islands where men must reap with knives because of the stones.

He went to Aran and became a part of its life, living upon salt fish and eggs, talking Irish for the most part, but listening also to the beautiful English which has grown up in Irish-speaking districts, and takes its vocabulary from the time of Malory and of the translators of the Bible, but its idiom and its vivid metaphor from Irish. . . . [He] made word and phrase dance to a very strange rhythm, which will always, till his plays have created their own tradition, be difficult to actors who have not learned it from his lips. It is essential, for it perfectly fits the drifting emotion, the dreaminess, the vague yet measureless desire, for which he would create a dramatic form. It blurs definition, clear edges, everything that comes from the will, it turns imagination from all that is of the present, like a gold background in a religious picture, and it strengthens in every emotion whatever comes to it from far off, from brooding memory and dangerous hope. (pp. 298-300)

Whether he write of old beggars by the roadside, lamenting over the misery and ugliness of life, or of an old Aran woman mourning her drowned sons, or of a young wife married to an old husband, he has no wish to change anything, to reform anything; all these people pass by as before an open window, murmuring strange, exciting words. (p. 300)

Mr. Synge has in common with the great theatre of the world, with that of Greece and that of India, with the creator of Falstaff, with Racine, a delight in language, a preoccupation with individual life. He resembles them also by a preoccupation with what is lasting and noble, that came to him, not, as I think, from books, but while he listened to old stories in the cottages, and contrasted what they remembered with reality. . . . Every writer, even every small writer, who has belonged to the great tradition, has had his dream of an impossibly noble life, and the greater he is, the more does it seem to plunge him into some beautiful or bitter reverie. . . . [Mr. Synge] sets before us ugly, deformed or sinful people, but his people, moved by no practical ambition, are driven by a dream of that impossible life. That we may feel how intensely his Woman of the Glen dreams of days that shall be entirely alive, she that is 'a hard woman to please' must spend her days between a sour-faced old husband, a man who goes mad upon the hills, a craven lad and a drunken tramp; and those two blind people of *The Well of the Saints* are so transformed by the dream that they choose blindness rather than reality. He tells us of realities, but he knows that art has never taken more than its symbols from anything that the eye can see or the hand measure.

It is the preoccupation of his characters with their dream that gives his plays their drifting movement, their emotional subtlety. (pp. 303-04)

> W. B. Yeats in his preface to The Well of Saints by John Millington Synge, A. H. Bullen, 1905 (and reprinted as ''Preface to the First Edition of 'The Well of Saints','' in his Essays and Introductions, The Macmillan Company, 1961, pp. 298-305).

GEORGE A. BIRMINGHAM   (essay date 1907)

By far the boldest and most original of our Irish dramatists is Mr. Synge. It is unfortunate that two of his plays—*The Shadow of the Glen* and *The Playboy of the Western World*—have excited fierce controversy in Ireland. The only work of his which has been received with real popular approval is the intensely moving one-act play, *Riders to the Sea.* It is creditable to the Irish public that this play should be appreciated as it has been. It is a tragedy, not relieved but intensified by grim touches of the commonplace. It is severe and restrained, not at all what a popular audience might be expected to appreciate. It is less creditable to the Irish people that they wrangled about *The Shadow of the Glen,* and worked themselves up to actual frenzy over *The Playboy of the Western World.* Yet they were not wholly without excuse. The latter play is very difficult to understand, as difficult as Ibsen was at first to English audiences. After a while we shall get to know Mr. Synge better, and pay to his genius the tribute of enthusiastic admiration which it deserves. In the meanwhile it must be his consolation that men do not become fanatics for the sake of the commonplace, and that no work without merit ever earned the distinction of columns of abuse in the daily Press, or had resolutions passed condemning it by Boards of Guardians. It is prophets, not charlatans, whom the multitude stones. (pp. 954-55)

> George A. Birmingham, "The Literary Movement in Ireland," in The Fortnightly Review, n.s. Vol. LXXXII, December 2, 1907, pp. 947-57.*

C. E. MONTAGUE (essay date 1911)

Synge in **"Riders to the Sea"** takes you straight into black tragedy; you step through one door into darkness. The play in a few moments thrills whole theatres to the kind of hush that comes when Othello approaches the sleeping Desdemona. Synge, from the first, is as terse, as exacting, as strange as he likes; yet everyone sees what he means, and all of his people have always the tragic importance. . . . Synge has the touch that works in you that change of optics in a minute; and not at a climax only, or in some picked passages; you tingle with it from the start, as you do in "Macbeth," and you cannot tell why, except that virtue goes out of the artist and into you.

One of Synge's means to this end is a rhythm unlike any other yet used. No doubt it is so far like what Lady Gregory uses and what Mr. Yeats sometimes uses that all three are things of the mouth, and the Irish mouth; all use the common notation of syllables stressed and unstressed, without metre, to fix some audible qualities of Irish country speech. But Synge, within these limits, found or shaped a rhythm of his own . . . far beyond the commoner music of this speech. . . . This rhythm, no doubt, or the rhythm it came of, was caught from the voices of fishers in Aran, shaken by fear or bereavement. But there is, pretty surely, much in it of Synge's own bringing. The tones of a person who tells you a story say not only what someone did and how someone else looked when he did it, but how it all struck the narrator. So you have, in the rising and falling of old Maurya's voice in the play, not only the way some old woman in Connaught lamented a lost son, with Synge and his notebook near by, but also how Synge viewed the world, as a whole, in which people are given such lives.

All this without any prancing about on the tragic high horse; rather, at each turn, some effect of understatement, almost of miscarriage—effects that tragic life commonly has when you see it lived, though it seldom has them in books. . . . (pp. 2-4)

In some ways the best English spoken is spoken in rural Ireland now; the Wicklow peasant's toothsome, idiomatic use of short words is nearer to the English tongue's clean youth than anything you hear in England—even in Northamptonshire—to-

day; and in Synge's plays the English of Elizabeth comes back to us from Ireland as fresh as the Elizabethan settlers left it there. Moment by moment as you hear his **"Shadow of the Glen,"** your ear is caught by some such turn of speech as modern English gives you mere smudged copies of: "Hearing the wind crying and you not knowing on what thing your mind would stay"; "he'd run from this to the city of Dublin and never catch for breath." . . . (p. 5)

In this English of the English Bible Synge presents a way of receiving life, ideas of what is worth having and doing, as far from those of Englishmen as those of Russians or Japanese. In the **"Shadow of the Glen"** the harsh crab-apple tang of peasant cruelty has its own difference from the same taste extracted from other earth. . . . (p. 6)

In Synge's comedies the Authorized Version vocabulary serves an Irish popular gift and passion for a special quality of highly figured speech. . . . (p. 7)

In all countries persons who know what is what, and have read wisely, revel in apt and picturesque diction; most of them come at the feast by the bookman's route; Synge's people come by the child's; they seem to be exploring, make experiments with similes, warm up and go on, rollickingly outdoing their own ventures, in a fever of inventive glee, as if the use of speech were a wonderful continent newly landed upon.

Synge had studied the mechanics of drama in good schools, and when he went to work for himself his genius was not hampered by technical unhandiness. **"Riders to the Sea"** is built as tight and spare as a barrel; no loose ends of verbiage stick out; not a touch in it but is organic; almost every speech earns its position thrice over—explains something past, expresses somebody's character, and helps the action on. To achieve lucidity in a short one-act tragedy is like carving the Commandments on a threepenny-bit; by Synge the little material aids to clearness are picked and used with the demonic acuteness of French experts at the game. . . . There is no amateurish drifting of characters on and off the stage in fortuitous looking floes; when they come in or go out they could, to your sense, do nothing else. (pp. 8-9)

In everything that Synge did there was a touch of harshness, in the good sense, an astringency like the spare suggestion of green that there is in perfect light blue glaze on a vase, a minute admixture of something stingingly sane and hard—not sourness, but just an antiseptic against sugariness and the "sweetly pretty." In some of the things he wrote in the twelve months during which he knew he was dying, the harshness was overforced. He wrote then like a sentenced man, with an invalid's craving for life at its rudest, for full-blooded curses, for drunken men fighting at fairs, for all the things that drovers and poachers value so moderately and sick men of letters so highly. (p. 12)

But it seems as if, after this malady of the temperament was spent, the moribund Synge, like the dying Don Quixote, had ridden at last into a kind sunshine and tranquil waters. In his [**"Deirdre of the Sorrows"**] he not merely won back his balance; he perfected it, and was able, while keeping as fiercely clear of sentimentalism as ever, to achieve a tenderness and radiancy of beauty that he had not before reached. The ecstasy of the two lovers over their life together in exile, "waking with the smell of June in the tops of the grasses," has a loveliness and exaltation quite unembittered, and so has the whole expression of their mood of surrender to the general consignment of lovers to dust. . . . All that was Synge, from first to last, is expressed in this play—the sure ear, the instinct for idiom, the brooding joy in hard, strong lines of character, the disdain for artistic compromise, the energy of tragic imagination, and also a new serenity of beauty.

No such gift has been made to modern Ireland by any of her children as Synge's disengagement of the essence, the differentiating virtue of the native imagination in Irish country folk. . . . [The] august and quiet sadness of **"Riders to the Sea"** has made the word ''tragedy'' mean something yet more stirring and cleansing to the spirit than it did. In his harsh, sane, earthen humour, biting as carbolic acid to slight minds, they find a disinfectant well worth having, at the lowest, in an ailing theatre. (pp. 13-15)

> *C. E. Montague, "The Plays of J. M. Synge," in his* Dramatic Values, *Methuen & Co., Ltd., 1911 (and reprinted by Doubleday, Page & Company, 1925, pp. 1-15).*

CHARLES A. BENNETT   (essay date 1912)

[John M.] Synge was one of that little group of writers, the best known of whom are Mr. W. B. Yeats and Lady Gregory, who in recent years have drawn their inspiration from the people and the soil of Ireland. But with the common love for Ireland the resemblance between Synge and his contemporaries ceases. His work rises to a higher region of attainment. It has the quality of greatness, and it is great because it has strength. Some primitive vigor has here found expression. Synge grasps reality. His peasants are creatures of passion and joy. He gives us a fearless picture of their lives. He is often terrible, most terrible perhaps in his humor; often savage, even to brutality; but the same fierce energy gives an unknown depth to his tragedy and lights up, with an almost unnatural brightness, places of beauty in his work. For his plays are drenched in beauty, a beauty not alone of language but of emotion and thought. In comparison with it, the beauties of Celtic mysticism are as the rain-washed spaces of evening beside a splash of hot sunlight on the gorse. There is nothing wan and exquisite in Synge; he is too close to life. It is his power of presenting what he sees without disguise and without criticism that stamps his work. He is a realist not in the sense that he shuts his eyes to all but the dirt in life and then, pointing, says ''Behold the dung-heap,'' but in that he is a man with a strong, passionate nature who is in love with life and the richness of it. Somehow criticism becomes meaningless: it is enough to share his vision and his joy. (pp. 192-93)

[In Synge's plays we] are among a people who are still close to earth, with something savage and untamed in their natures, running to violence, quick to change from reckless joy to a hopeless despair, or to a melancholy that has in it some of the grayness of their own skies. Life has not yet become artificial and complex; but if it is without the virtues of refinement, it is also without its weaknesses; and if it is simple, it has the vigor of strong blood. (p. 193)

"The Playboy of the Western World" is [Synge's] most characteristic work. It is riotous with the quick rush of life, a tempest of the passions with the glare of laughter at its heart. (p. 194)

It is hard to convey anything of the reckless movement of the play. One has to feel its riotous exuberance. But in spite of the lack of restraint, the frank brutality, and the fierce joy of this peasant life, there is no unsureness of artistic treatment. The characters of Christy and Pegeen are splendidly conceived.

The very violence of their natures, set off so strangely by the gentle in them, makes them great figures. Pegeen, a wild, superb girl, with ''torment in the splendor of her like,'' ''fitted to be handling merchandise in the heavens above,'' yet ''the fright of seven town-lands for her biting tongue,'' moves through the play as a queen in her own right. . . . [The Playboy] is as remarkable a creation. He is a strange mixture of hero and poltroon: in ''his own place . . . drinking, waking, eating, sleeping, a quiet, simple, poor fellow with no man giving me heed,'' and yet he has ''a mighty spirit in him and a gamy heart,'' so that he carries us away with his excitement and ''the blind rages tearing him within.'' (pp. 194-95)

The wildness at the heart of these two has an almost terrifying counterpart in some of the other characters. The picture of Michael, Pegeen's father, who, coming in drunk from a wake, sets his blessing on the union of his daughter with Christy, is a thing of fear. His coarse, frank words fall like blows that bruise. There is something dark and sinister in the man, something lurking in the sullen depths of a nature which is still savage. This quality is in many of the peasants, and Synge has shown it here and elsewhere. . . . (p. 195)

This is the hidden, unknown strength which my issue in any brutality of word or deed. Its effect is to produce a sense of dread and uneasiness. The presence of something incalculable warns us that we are among a people where the forces of life have not been subdued.

Some feeling akin to this is roused by Synge's humor. It is a strange, wild laughter that runs through these plays: laughter that leaps out like a red stab in the darkness and by contrast makes the darkness more terrifying. As it sounds in **"The Playboy"** or **"The Tinker's Wedding,"** it leaves us baffled, on the borderland between mirth and dismay. At the end of these plays we are left with the sense that suddenly this fierce humor has become real, and that here is the very substance of life shot through with pain. (p. 196)

"The Tinker's Wedding" ends with a like stroke of sudden and terrible significance. At first the play seems but a dirty quarrel: two tinkers of the glen, vagabond creatures with the mud and dust of the road on their feet and the ditch words on their tongue, disputing with the priest who must be wheedled into marrying the loose-living pair. When the priest refuses they set upon him, knock him down, and tie him up in a sack. (pp. 196-97)

This is delicious, but the sequel is in a different tone. They release him when he promises not to tell about the affair. (p. 197)

But this laughter has nothing Satanic in it; reflection has not yet come to make it cynical or to refine it away into the subtleties of the Comic Spirit. If it is cruel, if like fire it scorches, like fire it is clean and fierce. It is Synge's use of it that is so striking. He was a man who loved vivid contrasts, and again and again he awakens this mirth in scenes of infinite pathos. **"The Well of the Saints"** is the story of two old blind beggars, husband and wife. They are weather-beaten and ugly, but they will not believe the people who tell them so, and they are always thinking of their fine looks. (pp. 197-98)

The strength of earth is cruel, but it begets also flowers of tenderness and beauty. It is nature's way to rejoice in startling contrasts. It was Synge's way, too. . . .

Side by side with scenes of fierce vigor are others musical as it were with the voices of the wild things, scenes which have in them the fine essence of whatever is gentle. When we come upon them it is as though all men had for a moment become soft-voiced and had touched things no longer roughly but with a caress born of vision and sympathy. They are sudden hushes in a storm, and the thought of what has been and what may follow deepens the stillness. There comes to mind the love scene between the Playboy and Pegeen. The rich and sensuous imagery, the great, deep-colored phrases take nothing from its freshness and youth. It has about it a strange, intense beauty such as comes in a blue gap of sky after heavy rain, so intense that its radiance may not endure. (p. 199)

It is because such moments cannot last, because we know that the clouds will come up again and harsh sounds break the calm, that they have such magic. This is the dominant impression left by **"Deirdre of the Sorrows."** In none of his work was Synge master of such a spell of breathless beauty. The play moves from anger and despair through the joy of woodland love to "a tale of broken bodies and the filth of the grave," but from beginning to end there is only Deirdre—Deirdre with the great stillness in her soul and beauty shining from her. . . . (p. 200)

In the setting forth of such effects of contrast, beauty heightened by despair, tenderness by brutality, joy by gloom, Synge is using no mechanics of art; he is faithful to the life of the people and has caught the movement of their mind. Those who know the quality of the Irish imagination, so subtly influenced by nature, and who know, too, the swift alternations of the Irish climate will see here neither exaggeration nor distortion. For the mind of the peasant but reflects the character of the Irish weather. It is as changeable; it, too, has its brief periods of sunshine and its sad gray days. The peasant may live close to earth, but if he lacks imagination he will take from his surroundings only what is heavy and dull; the soil will stick about his thoughts as about his boots, and he will be dense to the world about him. But these people of whom Synge writes are awake to the magic of all the sights and sounds and smells. Some subtle bond makes them responsive to every mood of nature. (pp. 201-02)

[Here] is to be found the key to the understanding of that strain of plaintive melancholy, never far off in any Irish peasant, which sounds again and again in these plays. In it is all the sadness of Ireland. It is as if we heard the lonely cry of the plover over the bogs. (pp. 202-03)

The sea holds a deeper melancholy than that of the hills, and it fashions to its own sadness those who dwell within sight and sound of it. All that Synge thought and felt when he lived among the natives of the Aran Isles he has conveyed in **"Riders to the Sea."** It is not one of his later plays but it is, without doubt, his greatest achievement. It is not so ambitious as **"Deirdre"**; it lacks the richness of **"The Playboy"**; but within its limits—it is a brief play of one act—it is perfect. Synge has here exercised a restraint such as he brought to no other play. It seems as if the terror and the sublimity of the sea had cast a shadow upon him and made him simple of tongue in the presence of tragedy. It is the never-ending tragedy of fine men claimed by the sea with the women left desolate to keen for them. All that sense of the dark fate brooding over the waters, the fear and the hatred of it, has here found expression. Like some steady monotone beating in one's ears, the presence of the sea is all about the play. . . . Fittingly in this place of sorrow, lonely and grand as the sea itself, rises the figure of Maurya, the old mother. The very majesty of it is only made greater by her loneliness. For her daughters can understand

nothing of the dread at her heart that would make her hold back the last of her six sons from the sea. (pp. 203-04)

It is right that they should not understand, for she is alone in the great places of the soul. (p. 204)

No attempt has been made here to "place" Synge or to assign him to some "school." He scarcely invites such treatment. For he had no "ideas" to impart and he did not set out to teach anything. . . . For him the end of the drama was reality and joy, and he found both in the life of the peasants of whom he wrote. . . . [One] thinks of him always as close to earth, even as they are, close to the sources of vigor and of beauty and—shall it be said?—of life. For if his plays live it will be because they are the work of a man who sought his materials in the primitive and the simple and the strong, in laughter and sorrow, passion and joy. And these are the things that endure. (p. 205)

> *Charles A. Bennett, "The Plays of John M. Synge,"*
> *in* The Yale Review, *n.s. Vol. I, No. 2, January,*
> *1912, pp. 192-205.*

P. P. HOWE (essay date 1912)

In all the English drama, from Sheridan and Goldsmith to Mr. Shaw, there is only one name that will go up amongst the greatest, and that is the name of another Irishman, J. M. Synge. (p. 19)

There is nothing experimental in *The Well of the Saints*. . . . Synge's blind people are the "happy and blind"; not the poor imperfect things dependent upon one who can see, tragic in themselves and overwhelmed by tragedy so soon as his support is withdrawn from them; fit symbols, if you so choose to make them, of a generation of men moving feebly in the dark and stretching out hands for the hand that is denied them. There is nothing for the symbolists in *The Well of the Saints*. (pp. 39-40)

What we shall be better employed in finding in this first play is evidence of Synge's astonishingly certain sense of the theatre; his command of a dialogue apt and pointed for comedy, and capable at the same time of every effect of increased tensity; the racy clearness of the characterization, and the form and finish and personality of the whole work. . . . We may notice too how Mary Doul is clearly distinguished from Martin Doul. . . . Impossible now to speak of them as "two blind, weather-beaten beggars"; they are Martin Doul and Mary Doul, with the great sense of individuality of the Irish peasant, and of all Synge's people.

At the back of all the play hangs that extraordinary atmosphere of reality, imparted, made palpable almost, through the sense of *sound*—of the lambs and hens stirring, little sticks breaking, and the grass moving, not for their own sakes merely, but together creating an illusion of real life behind, of the life of the village, and of the whole of life behind that. Partly this illusion comes to us in this play with the particularity of the blind; but we shall find it in all the work of Synge. A "queerness," if you will; but followed a little further, we shall find this power of Synge's used always in the service of reality. (pp. 40-2)

There is no one-act play in the language for compression, for humanity, and for perfection of form, to put near *In the Shadow of the Glen*. From the moment of the rise of the curtain on that little Wicklow interior, to its fall—about half an hour—we are let into the lives of three people, and the life and death of a fourth. It is a selected half-hour, that marches moment by moment with true occurrence, and yet opens out into years that have passed and years that are to come. (pp. 47-8)

Synge's people do not appear unnaturally strange and solemn, like Maeterlinck's, only extraordinarily arresting and important; and Synge . . . has only a few lines, and not four acts, in which to resume their past. Every line, therefore, must speak of their past. Every line, therefore, must speak of their past, must reveal their character in the present, and must point us forward; and all this with perfect deference to reality. (pp. 48-9)

Riders to the Sea, the most Greek of Synge's plays, in the immensity of its issues, in the high tableland chosen for their presentment, makes [a universal] appeal, despite its own localization. . . . (p. 57)

And yet *Riders to the Sea* is not so perfect a masterpiece in one-act as [*In The Shadow of the Glen*]. . . . The progress is swifter, partly for the reason that there is less to be revealed by the dialogue. Nora's tragedy was rather that of a particular woman left to think thoughts in the dark mist; here the tragedy is the common lot, and is less dependent, therefore, upon character. It is given swiftness also by the marvellous intensity Synge has given it; the temper of the play is like a white flame, in which everything that is irrelevant, or ordinarily below this terrible significance, has been burned up. (pp. 57-8)

It is this very swiftness which is the cause of the structural defect in *Riders to the Sea;* its action does not succeed, like that of the former play, in advancing step by step with reality, for in its half hour's occupation of the stage we are asked to suppose that Bartley should be knocked over into the sea, and washed out where there is a great surf on the white rocks, and his body recovered, and brought back again; when he himself allows for half an hour to ride down only. This unreality is an undeniable difficulty in the theatre; and the keening women, serving at once as messengers and chorus on a Greek convention a little difficult to us of acceptability, are another. A tragic intensity which on the printed page is sublime somehow does not, without reduction, bear this visual embodiment. It may even be that here we are up against the natural limitations of the theatre. At all events, if *Riders to the Sea,* beautiful and moving play as it is, be better in the library than the theatre, then, by that very fact, its readier popularity notwithstanding, it is not the most perfect of Synge's plays. (pp. 59-60)

The Playboy of the Western World brought to the contemporary stage the most rich and copious store of character since Shakespeare. (p. 61)

With *The Playboy of the Western World,* Synge placed himself amongst the masters. There are weaknesses in its design, but none in its composition; he employed a canvas larger by very much than he chose before or after; when he came to attempt high tragedy—high but no higher, because its subject was a queen, than the love and sorrows of Pegeen Mike—he failed to work all in because of death. *The Playboy* remains, rich and copious in speech and character; and yet with none of the faults of copiousness. Through it all runs the firm clear strand of tragedy; each with fine qualities goes his and her way; the tragedy, for Pegeen, is that the ways are not together. The stimulus of fine tragedy is in it, because each has got self-realization in the end of all. The assumption of the commonplace people, as they settle to their drinks, is that all is as it was; but it is not so; we—and they—have seen a tragedy en-

acted, and are the richer by the experience that has deepened two human souls. (pp. 69-70)

We may notice in *The Playboy* a good deal more as to Synge's method. [In particular] the characterization: the people are drawn fully rounded; the comfortable stomach of Michael James, with thumbs in waistcoat, is in every word he says, drunk or sober. They are complete living people every one of them. (p. 71)

The Tinker's Wedding is a small play, because it is, for Synge, unusually simple. The people are jolly souls; but there are no fine people, sensitive to deep sorrows and wild joys and aspirations beyond the usual; there is no tragedy in Sarah's going in the end unmarried, nor poignancy in old Mary's lonesomeness that can be eased by a glass: they are figures of comedy only. Synge's work at its greatest has a way of evading definitions, as life evades the measuring-scale. *The Tinker's Wedding* is comedy, rich and genial and humorous; but there is little in it of that deeper richness that comes when life is viewed with tenderness as well as humorous understanding. There is fire in it, but it burns with a paler flame, leaping a little hungrily. Curious to note the absence of those strokes of natural intensity, which give to the other plays a fullness and depth beyond their own; the bats may squeak in the trees maybe, but there is none of the breathing stillness of life in all its mystery and order, at the back of these few trampers in a ditch. (p. 83)

If Synge's plays had come to us, like Shakespeare's, out of a past insufficiently illumined, there would, one thinks, be little difficulty in naming *The Tinker's Wedding* for a smaller early play taken up again, like *All's Well that Ends Well,* and worked over; and as little difficulty in naming *Deirdre of the Sorrows* for the latest of the plays, like *The Tempest,* for its beautiful serenity, and in addition marked once or twice by an imperfectness in phrase—an imperfectness that, in the eyes of a loving workman like Synge, nothing save death's interposition would excuse. (p. 84)

[Synge's] splendid simplification of the old brave story [of Deirdre] is the first to make it truly and strongly dramatic; never was his sense of the dramatic so clear and so unfailing; and while he simplified and heightened, he elaborated also, so that in none of the other plays, not in the *Playboy* even, do we find the action arising out of, and expressing, so many twists and turns of character. If *Deirdre of the Sorrows* was not worked upon as Synge would have chosen to work upon it—it was his habit, as it was Ibsen's, to go over and over his plays—there is nothing that is not finished in essential character or action. (p. 92)

For [his characters'] loves and hates and aspirations Synge has secured a background here of curious orderliness and serenity, by sending all through the play a feeling that whatever happens is foretold, a feeling of inevitability almost Greek—Deirdre does but what it is ordained for her to do, as Electra did, and when she gets her little grave we have our rest and ease because what has been foretold is accomplished. (pp. 92-3)

[There] are no opinions in Synge's plays, but only men and women passionately speaking out their nature. (p. 161)

The women of the plays are a more wide and wonderful gallery than the men. (p. 162)

Pegeen Mike is one of the most beautiful and living figures in all drama. Twenty and more years of age, she is (in her own opinion) the fright of seven townlands for her biting tongue. . . . [We] may see that Pegeen has her full share of the passion for children which, Synge states, is powerful in all women who are "permanently and profoundly attractive." (pp. 168-69)

Nature never framed a woman's heart of prouder stuff than that of Pegeen Mike. . . . It is characteristic of her proud heart, that when her playboy proves not to be all he had claimed and she had thought him, he should at once be nothing. (p. 171)

Free of her tongue and ready with her hands, ardent in her loves and her sorrows, "fiery and magnificent and tender," Pegeen is the living embodiment of all that Synge loved in life. (p. 172)

[The language of Synge's characters] is generally forcible, often splendid; to them, as to Mr. Hardy's peasantry, "unholy exclamations is a necessity of life." There is a spirit in Synge's diction, free and ardent and ungovernable, that has not its equal outside the best plays of the Restoration. (p. 188)

All Synge's people, indeed, are, in their moments of crisis, on a place where their tongues often take them, the "ridge of the world." We think of the "utter loneliness and desolation" that seemed to Synge to give to the little group of men and girls on a Kerry cliff-top, as to all these people of the West, their finest and clearest qualities; and again of the sense of loneliness that had no equal that came to him in the glen in Wicklow, and intensified the birdsong so that it seemed to fill the valley with sound. We have found this utter intensity in all his art.

His people's love of distinction gives us the type motive in Synge's drama. It is in essence a simple enough antagonism; and yet, since it takes its rise in character rather than circumstance, it is sometimes buried deep. It is always, in its own way, a tragic motive. (p. 192)

With some such definition of true tragic drama, all Synge's work complies. The motive to his drama is in the resolute individuality of his people, their wish to achieve distinction. None in his plays, if we except Conchubor the High King, are born great; none, save in the purest spirit of comedy, have greatness thrust upon them; each is for himself, winning an easy or a cruel end. All the fine people are "lonesome" people, and the antagonism is between their will to be "a wonder," and the "lonesomeness" of life; between the ambition for self-realization and the nullity of circumstance. . . . The passing of life without fulfilment, the ceaseless fading of beauty, the elusive quality of happiness, the agony of disillusion—these are the tragic undercurrents of the plays. A minor tragedy, if you will; product of a tragic mood taking some part of its origin directly in the life Synge found, a little sad and depleted, in the West of Ireland; but who will say that its truth is not universal? (pp. 194-95)

Synge's is a brave and passionate drama, giving admiration to all that is strong and full of its own life; filled with tenderness also for young lives, with their little ways that none can equal, and for the old with their sorrow of lonesomeness that has no end; giving but a short shrift to fools. "The earth itself is a silly place, maybe," says Deirdre, "when a man's a fool and a talker," and the Playboy speaks the brave clear tone of all the plays, when he looks round on the vehement rabble of the inappreciative, and chooses the supreme tragedy of lonesomeness rather; for "It's better to be lonesome than go mixing with the fools of earth." (pp. 197-98)

P. P. Howe, in his J. M. Synge: A Critical Study, *Martin Secker, 1912, 215 p.*

HENRY SEIDEL CANBY (essay date 1913)

[J. M. Synge's] plays range from the farce of **"The Tinker's Wedding"** to the mournful tragedy of **"Deirdre of the Sorrows,"** and yet they do not fit easily into the categories of comedy and tragedy, for pathos is always close behind his humor, and the humor of rich humanity supples his serious drama and keeps it from over-intensity. Peasant drama we might call them, for all but one are made from the fresh and vivid life of the folk by the sea and on the hills in the west of Ireland, were it not that **"Deirdre,"** in which the theme is high romance, differs only in this respect from the other plays. Studies of rich and passionate human nature sought where it expresses itself most freely, that is what they are. (pp. 767-68)

Synge was essentially a dramatist, who put, so far as he was able, not himself but human nature into his plays, and was far more interested in Christy Mahon or in Naisi than in any philosophy of life whatsoever. (p. 768)

I do not mean to deny that Synge's characters reveal a point of view on the part of their author. The seer who turns outward reality into art must shape it in some measure of course. Indeed, his plays are full of a quality which we have been taught to call Celtic—a preference for the ideal over what the material world calls the real—and we must believe that he sought consciously for what was most Celtic in Ireland. Therefore his heroes and his heroines choose many things before prosperity. . . . But Synge's Celticism, even if it limits his genius, is more practical than the otherworldliness to which Yeats has accustomed us. It was hard to recognize the poet's dreamy, fairy-loving Irishman in the race that keeps our kitchens, builds our apartment houses, and rules our American cities. In Synge, however, one begins to see a resemblance. The Playboy who will keep his hard-gained self-respect even if he has to re-kill his father to do so, is only a humorous version of the politician who makes loyalty to his friends a practical consideration above efficiency and right. And it was a melancholy satisfaction to see the turbulent galleries, as they hissed **"The Playboy"** because it did not represent the sentimental and untrue Ireland of the romantic drama, mirrored on the stage in Christy Mahon's passion for distinction no matter what might be the source. (p. 769)

The tramp and the outcast, restless under even the rudimentary civilization of the West, appear again and again in the plays. Undoubtedly this is a symptom of romanticism, a recurrence . . . of that love for the supposedly primitive emotion which Chateaubriand fathered. . . . [This] search for the unsophisticated emotion is, like the Celticism of these plays,—a cause of their charm, not a condition of their greatness. They are great plays, but not because of their romantic vagabonds, nor because they voice far more convincingly than the dreamy poetry of Yeats or the satire of Shaw, the Celtic distrust of the gods of the market place. They are great because, like the novelists and unlike the dramatists of the nineteenth century, Synge has presented types of universal human nature which though rich and deep require no annotation of philosophy or symbolism in order to leap to recognition in the heart.

It is the effective presentation of universal human emotions which, if these plays are great, makes them so:—Old Maurya in the **"Riders to the Sea"** exulting when her last son is drowned: "They're all gone now, and there isn't anything more the sea can do to me . . . I'll have no call now to be up crying and praying when the wind breaks from the south, and you can hear the surf is on the east, and the surf is on the west"; Nora in **"The Shadow of the Glen"** following the tramp to the ditch where she'll hear no talk of growing old and losing the light of her eyes. These emotions, simply put, beautifully put, ringing true as Hermione's speeches in **"A Winter's Tale,"** make the validity and the greatness of this unambitious drama. It does not need the evidence of Synge's prefaces or of his preliminary studies in **"The Aran Islands"** to prove that his model was the heart. (pp. 769-70)

I will not say that Synge's plays have no underlying significance, for that would be to call them untrue to life. But the message, or the philosophy, or the moral, is implicit, not explicit. It is not because youth and with it love decays that Deirdre of the Sorrows touches one's heart when after seven years of perfect joy she leads her lover back to death; it is because she is Deirdre that "the lightning itself wouldn't let down its flame to singe the beauty of her like."

It is not necessary to rank Synge with Shakespeare and Sophocles. His praisers have not hesitated to do so; and indeed the brief **"Riders to the Sea"**—the most moving example of intense pathos which our generation has imagined—tempts one to follow them. But over-statement is worse than inappreciation. Synge's gallery is small. His depth is greater than his breadth. He is master of simple comedy and simple tragedy; but neither the heroic romance of the Elizabethans nor the complex intensities of modern civilization enter into his range. Only once does he step beyond the borders of peasant life, and in **"Deirdre of the Sorrows"** the ancient kings and queens of Ireland are only simple folk freed from homeliness. He is reported to have wearied of peasant drama, and to have been seeking a play in the slums of Dublin.

Genius is unaccountable—but at least there is no evidence that this great writer would have been great in the study of the effects of civilization upon the race. There is more than coincidence in the fact that until he found an unsophisticated people rich in the exhibition of the primitive emotions, his art gave no results. (pp. 770-71)

> *Henry Seidel Canby, "Book Reviews: 'The Works of John M. Synge'," in* The Yale Review, *n.s. Vol. II, No. 4, July, 1913, pp. 767-72.*

THOMAS O'HAGAN   (essay date 1916)

Yeats and Synge found, or thought they found, certain dramatic stuff among the peasantry of Ireland and forthwith proceeded to build up Irish dramas representative of Ireland of today. Both went to London and Paris for their ideals of drama, and then went to Ireland to find the elements of character and incidents upon which to construct their dramas; and when they could not find the characters they wanted they invented them. (pp. 63-4)

Now the work of the dramatist is to represent life, idealized if you will, but full of truth. Synge's purpose in building up or creating his Irish dramas should be to represent Irish life, idealized if you will also, but full of truth. How . . . can this be done if Synge departs so far from truth as to create an unchaste Irish woman [as in **"In the Shadow of the Glen"**] in a country where feminine chastity is supreme, and then hold such a woman up—represent her on the stage as typical of the women of Ireland? (pp. 64-5)

Unfortunately, John Millington Synge lacked the spiritual constitution of a great dramatist. Yet he had many gifts, and not the least of these was his excellent dramatic technique. His

knowledge of Gaelic, too, gave him that splendid command of Irish dialect which fills his lines with a certain rich Irish flavor and savor not found in the work of any other Irish dramatist. . . . Synge, too, was quick to catch the accent of the Irish heart in its deepest and saddest tragedies. His humor at times is as bewildering as that of Cervantes. He has left the **"Playboy of the Western World"** as an enigma to mankind. He who would interpret the significance of this drama must needs enter the inner chamber of the genius of John Millington Synge. To my mind, while it is well constructed, it is of all Synge's plays the least happy as a portrayal of Irish character. There are many successful elements in it, but Synge has put into this creation too much of the improbable and fictitious. Sometimes, too, some of its lines approach blasphemy, and this synthesis of irreverence, to use a mild expression, is so marked a characteristic of the whole drama that after witnessing its performance a feeling of disgust, mingled with anger, fills the mind. (pp. 66-7)

One thing Synge often forgets . . . as a playwright, and that is that the abnormal element alone will not yield us a great drama. Side by side with it we must have the normal. Shakespeare never forgets this. There is not a play of the great dramatist in which the abnormal is not set off by the normal. The **"Playboy of the Western World"** is a very rioting of the abnormal. How joy can issue out of it, though keyed as a comedy, I cannot see. It is altogether too preposterously abnormal.

It is easy to discern the strength and defects of Synge in his drama. Wherever it is a question of the primitive passions of the Celt and the psychology of his ancient racial beliefs surviving in even the slightest form in the Ireland of today, Synge as a creator and portrayer is strong and master of his work. Witness for instance his marvelous one-act tragedy, **"Riders to the Sea."** Here our playwright is dealing with two elements that are entirely, dramatically speaking, in harmony with his genius: the ruthless and all-devouring element of the sea and that wistful "second sight" of the Celt which lies on the borderland between prophecy and predestination. (pp. 68-9)

The trouble with Synge was that in his study and portraiture of Irish character he emphasized certain qualities that are either absent altogether in the Irish or are but minor attributes. In every instance he stressed the abnormal, with no thought of its normal accompaniment. As a result of this we have savagery, irreverence and blasphemy and a flouting of the sacrament of marriage as characteristic of the Ireland of today. Is it any wonder, then, that every self-respecting Irishman holds such a drama as the **"Playboy of the Western World"** as a parody and perversion of Irish peasant life, a libel on Irish national character, and immoral both in language and plot? (p. 70)

> *Thomas O'Hagan, "The Irish Dramatic Movement," in his* Essays on Catholic Life, *John Murphy Company, 1916 (and reprinted by Books for Libraries Press, 1965; distributed by Arno Press, Inc.), pp. 57-73.**

ROBERT LYND   (essay date 1919)

Synge was an extraordinary man of genius, but he was not an extraordinarily great man of genius. He is not the peer of Shakespeare: he is not the peer of Shelley: he is the peer, say, of Stevenson. His was a byway, not a high-road, of genius. (pp. 94-5)

Once and once only Synge achieved a piece of art that was universal in its appeal, satisfying equally the artistic formula of Pater and the artistic formula of Tolstoi. This was *Riders to the Sea*. *Riders to the Sea*, a lyrical pageant of pity made out of the destinies of fisher-folk, is a play that would have been understood in ancient Athens or in Elizabethan London, as well as by an audience of Irish peasants to-day.

Here, incidentally, we get a foretaste of that preoccupation with death which heightens the tensity in so much of Synge's work. There is a corpse on the stage in *Riders to the Sea*, and a man laid out as a corpse in *In the Shadow of the Glen*, and there is a funeral party in *The Playboy of the Western World*. Synge's imagination dwelt much among the tombs. Even in his comedies, his laughter does not spring from an exuberant joy in life so much as from excitement among the incongruities of a world that is due to death. Hence he cannot be summed up either as a tragic or a comic writer. He is rather a tragic satirist with the soul of a lyric poet.

If he is at his greatest in *Riders to the Sea*, he is at his most personal in *The Well of the Saints,* and this is essentially a tragic satire. (p. 95)

Mr. Howe says that "there is nothing for the symbolists in *The Well of the Saints*," but that is because he is anxious to prove that Synge was a great creator of men and women [see excerpt above]. Synge, in my opinion at least, was nothing of the sort. His genius was a genius of decoration, not of psychology. One might compare it to firelight in a dark room, throwing fantastic shapes on the walls. He loved the fantastic, and he was held by the darkness. Both in speech and in character, it was the bizarre and even the freakish that attracted him. In *Riders to the Sea* he wrote as one who had been touched by the simple tragedy of human life. But, as he went on writing and working, he came to look on life more and more as a pattern of extravagances, and he exchanged the noble style of *Riders to the Sea* for the gauded and overwrought style of *The Playboy*. (pp. 95-6)

But, after all, it is not Synge's characters or his plots, but his language, which is his great contribution to literature. . . . [It] is worth noting that he wrote most beautifully in the first enthusiasm of his discovery of the wonders of Irish peasant speech. His first plays express, as it were, the delight of first love. He was always a shaping artist, of course, in search of figures and patterns; but he kept his passion for these things subordinate to reality in the early plays. In *The Playboy* he seemed to be determined to write riotously, like a man straining after vitality. He exaggerated everything. He emptied bagfuls of wild phrases— the collections of years—into the conversations of a few minutes. His style became, in a literary sense, vicious, a thing of tricks and conventions: blank-verse rhythms—I am sure there are a hundred blank-verse lines in the play—and otiose adjectives crept in and spoilt it as prose. It became like a parody of the beautiful English Synge wrote in the noon of his genius. (pp. 96-7)

With all its faults, however, [*The Playboy*] is written by the hand of genius, and the first hearing or reading of it must come as a revelation to those who do not know *Riders to the Sea* or *The Well of the Saints*. . . . *The Playboy* is a marvellous confection, but it is to *Riders to the Sea* one turns in search of Synge the immortal poet. (p. 97)

> Robert Lynd, "The Fame of J. M. Synge," in his
> Old and New Masters, *T. Fisher Unwin Ltd, 1919,*
> *pp. 94-7.*

DANIEL CORKERY   (essay date 1931)

As an artist Synge went about his work, searching always for the character of things, animate, inanimate; and not only with his mind but with his heart, for character is to be felt as well as seen, trickles into the refining chambers of our mind through the very pores of the body. . . . Because Synge had let the mists and the tides, the rocks, the seas, the stars of Aran make him his own in some such way as they had all the long years been making the islanders their own, he had thought himself more deeply into the island consciousness than one could have hoped for: the lounging in the sun, the dreaming beneath the stars had indeed helped him towards considerable riches. (pp. 111-12)

In the recollection of all this is the right approach to [the essays in *The Aran Islands* and *In Wicklow and West Kerry*]. So come upon, they yield us all they have; we perceive at once what separates them from other such studies, with their slickness and their woodenness, written by people who had never dreamt of thinking themselves into the life of the region they dealt with. And portion of what they yield us when so approached is an apprehension more intimate than any study of the plays alone could induce in us. Such passages in these books as give us direct, actual information about the islands themselves or their inhabitants, are so rare that they seem to have found entry into them only by chance. But surely far more valuable than mere information is the feeling we attain to of acquaintanceship with the consciousness of the island people. . . . (pp. 112-13)

[Synge] was a colourist; he was even a sensationist. He noted how ravenously the people, while engaged in their daily work, would snatch at the excitement incidental to it, enlarging it, intensifying it by gesture, outcry and the flashing of the eyes. . . . Even when no excitement is incidental to the work, he notes how they induce it, and all who know those people will remember similar instances. (p. 115)

[These papers] are valuable for their own sake as descriptive of the consciousness of the people. They are perhaps more valuable still for the insight they give us into Synge's own consciousness, his fundamentally emotional nature, his awareness only of whatever would stimulate that nature—colour, violence, dramatic incident. We find in them also, hinted rather than said, his quest for a fatherland, a spiritual home, whether he himself ever fully realised it or not. But those essays are, of course, also the note books where we may find the raw material on which the dramatist was afterwards to try his creative powers. Because of what we discover in these papers, we come to feel how sterling were those creative powers of his, sterling even when they fail sufficiently to chasten the materials with which they would deal, as in the case of *The Tinker's Wedding* and perhaps *The Playboy of the Western World*. . . . [We cannot read these] papers without learning that he knew the necessity of drenching himself with all the influences of the place—the folk-lore; the weather; the home life; life on the sea, in the fields; the nights; the winds; the stars—all those influences, especially such of them as were purely natural,—which have been time out of mind working their will on the consciousness of the people. The spiritual influences which escaped him—at moments he felt that they were escaping him: and for one with such antecedents this was not little.

These papers, then, are valuable in many ways. Sometimes I have the idea that the book on the Aran Islands will outlive all else that came from Synge's pen. (pp. 121-22)

[*The Shadow of the Glen*] is as truly a piece of [Synge] as anything he was afterwards to write. The theme is as old as the hills: an old husband, a young wife; and Synge came by the story in the Aran Islands; but there is no peasant community in the world where it is not to be found. . . . In the tale the elderly husband lets on to be dead that he may discover the unfaithfulness of his youthful wife. (p. 123)

What is likely to happen then if the playwright, one truly under the spell of the folk mind, cannot rightly settle for himself whether his play, based on such a story, is to be comedy or tragedy? As one might have expected, the happy-go-lucky comedy in the folk-tale breaks to the surface again and again in Synge's drama; when all is said, those parts of it which make the audience laugh the loudest—the 'dead' man sitting up in the bed, the lovers, certain he is dead, discussing their affairs in his presence—these are really the best things in it whatever 'poetry' has been written about the young wife and her desire for a fuller life. In his elaboration of the character of the woman, Nora Burke, Synge introduced so many elements that were contrary to the spirit of the comedy that one scarcely knows whether to call his play tragic or comic. . . . If Synge had succeeded in harmonising a fine and sensitive creature with a story so integrally rough and comic, he would indeed have achieved a miracle. His woman is dark and melancholy. . . . [Synge] made no effort to create a fine and sensitive woman: in his folk-lore mood such people had no appeal for him. What he created was a piece of naturalistic flesh and blood, wearing her lusts upon her sleeve, a being all appetite and no faculty, a woman after his own literary fancy, full of physical courage, daring and bold. And being such, she retains in her much of the feeling in the old tale, the spirit of which is frankly naturalistic, as is the way with folk-lore. On the other hand the melancholy that is in her, conflicts with the mood of the tale; and it is this incongruity that keeps the play swinging between comedy and tragedy. (pp. 124-25)

The play is too small for such changes of mood as occur in it; and, to use a musical term, there are no bridges between mood and mood. Nora Burke's disparate character is the reason of this uncertainty. (p. 126)

[Synge] had not yet acquired certainty of touch. The play is a sketch, with some passages as good as any he was afterwards to write; but all of it has the mark of not having been sufficiently thought through. (p. 127)

The outstanding weakness of the play, however, is the aforesaid too rapid transitions from mood to mood that occur in it, no single mood being given the chance thoroughly to infect the mind with its own colour. The play rocks all the time upon its base; and we do nothing but wait for the rocking to cease. (p. 128)

The Shadow of the Glen shows us therefore a playwright unhappy in his theme, inasmuch as the body of his thoughts at that period had a movement in it that was both too slow and too vast for the rhythm this theme demanded. *Riders to the Sea,* his next play, on the other hand shows us that same playwright not only happy (inasmuch as the provenance of thought and theme was identical) but inspired, wrought upon so deeply, so intensely, that such wilful human frailties as were in the way of nature his, solemnly quieted, ceased for the time to show themselves. He had happened on a theme that came in four square with all that he himself was at his best. He had become free enough of the consciousness of the islanders to feel within his bones, almost as they felt it, the immemorial malignity of the sea towards them. (pp. 135-36)

Of itself the play is sufficient evidence of [Synge's] gift of impassioned contemplation: it was that gift that enabled him to make use of such daily happenings as we ordinarily do not notice, to interpret the humanity of his characters. That gift, we may learn, is the be-all of the thaumaturgy the creative artist practises. . . . Those little incidents in the play not only keep it alive; they are in truth so many such kinetic particles, charged with significance, and therefore symbolic; for the true artist cannot help but make use of symbols: almost unconsciously he does so. . . . It was Synge's thorough immersion in the matter he dealt with, his feeling for it, the surrender of himself to its genius, that in this case enabled him to create a piece of art that is at once local and universal in its appeal.

The play is in one act, the story as simple as possible. From time to time the father and five sons of the one household have all been drowned. Nine days before the play opens the fifth son, Michael, was drowned; his body has not yet been recovered from the sea. But a bundle of clothes has arrived at the hut—'got off a drowned man in Donegal.' This bundle is Michael's clothes. (pp. 138-39)

The play, as a play, is almost perfect, unless one maintains a very rigid idea of what a piece of dramatic work should be. All the way through there is a succession of those little happenings that make for life, every one of them charged with significance. We may note how the bundle of clothes is used. At the beginning, our attention is concentrated on it; unopened, its contents guessed at however, it is hidden away from us. When at last it does come to be untied our eyes strain to see what is in it; for we have since become one with those whose fingers tremble to open it. We may note by what simple means we are made aware how great have been the old woman's sufferings: before she enters at all, one daughter says: "Where is she?" and the other answers: "She's lying down, God help her, and maybe sleeping, if she's able." Simpler the words could not be, yet how effective! (pp. 142-43)

[The] touch is perfect. Here and there a passage strikes one as being a little too rounded, a sentence as being too carefully balanced: "He went down to see would there be another boat sailing in the week, and I'm thinking it won't be long till he's here now, for the tide's turning at the green head, and the hooker's tacking from the east." In such cases, if one has a feeling for the fall of a sentence, one almost forgets to gather the meaning; and in such a play this is a defect.

But such defects are too slight and too rare to take from the greatness of the play, which, deeply emotional in its nature, demanded that delicacy of touch of which the intellectual playwright who discards emotion, as if it were beneath him, has no need, it seems. (pp. 143-44)

Synge made always for the fundamental; and in this play, at least, went near achieving it. He had happened, as has been said, on a theme which moved himself so profoundly that it left him freed of that tendency towards the overstatement, the flashy, towards bad taste, indeed, which the imaginative artist is always prone to. In none of the other plays do we come on quite the same writer: in them all he is always less. . . . (p. 145)

[In the two-act comedy *The Tinker's Wedding*] we have only four characters: Michael Byrne, tinker; Sarah Casey, his doxy; Mary Byrne, his mother; and a Priest. We learn that Sarah Casey and Michael Byrne have been living together for many years, but that Sarah is now minded to be married to him properly in a church by a priest. (p. 147)

[The] play is scarcely worth considering either as a piece of stagecraft or as a piece of literature. (p. 149)

In the preface to the play Synge, with a lack of proportion not common with him, wrote that on the stage one must have both reality and joy. Either word, no matter how meagre a signification we give it, is too big, for there is no reality in the play, and such knockabout fun as is in it, is so obviously contrived that it has even a depressing effect. Reality does not need defence, neither does joy if reality be its foundation, even such joy as may be found in a play that laughs at those priests who stray so ludicrously from the normal as to become comic variations. The old woman in the play—the 'ever thirsty Mary'—is the one character that has a trace of roundness in her, of such abundancy as we find in Martin Doul in *The Well of the Saints*. The others are the merest puppets. Lacking reality, the play is barren of such joy as is deepened by our recollections of life: and as an element in drama joy must be assessed by the selfsame tests we apply to terror in a play: we are to be moved by it in the totality of our being, toughened as we have been by living among men and women. Only a coarse-grained hobbledehoy could relish either the character-drawing of the priest or the general shindy in which *The Tinker's Wedding* ends. There is hardly a note of poetry in the play, which is tantamount to saying there is scarcely a trace of John Synge in it. . . . (pp. 149-50)

The quintessence of the original [legend of Deirdre] for us moderns is not to prophecy that Deirdre would bring sorrow to Ulster, but the love of Conchubor for Deirdre, and the love of Deirdre for Naisi. And it was with this quintessence that Synge chose to deal. He worked so earnestly in this spirit, gave himself so whole-heartedly to what was eternally human in the legend, that he may be counted as one of that small band of writers who began the movement to restore the note of intensity to English literature. (p. 209)

It is Synge's recapture of this note of intensity that makes his early death entirely regrettable. Entirely regrettable from the Irish point of view, for if Irish life differs from English life, and it differs everyway, that difference is due to a quality of intenseness in Irish mind, there racially or else induced by whole centuries of suffering, for the expression of which, current modes of English literature offer but little opportunity. Had Synge lived,—but to say this is to bring us to a more personal point of view. His mastery of this note in certain passages in *Deirdre of the Sorrows* marks the end of his first phase, or rather of what would, had he lived, come to be regarded as his first phase. It would also have marked the beginning of his next phase: *Deirdre of the Sorrows* would have been the first of a number of plays more serious than those he had previously written (and if we keep this play in mind we feel how shallow was his own interpretation of that word *Serious*) for the note of intensity is not ever achieved by triflers or by those who are merely clever. (p. 212)

Naturally it is towards the end of the drama where the tragedy is being consummated that we find the better examples of this note of intensity. "Let you not break the thing I've set my life on, and you giving yourself up to sorrow, when it's joy and sorrow do burn out like straw blazing in an east wind." . . . "It was a clean death was your share, Naisi; and it is not I will quit your head, when it's many a dark night among the snipe and plover that you and I were whispering together." (p. 213)

These passages, which illustrate the bleakness of spirit that is in the whole play, are surely very far removed from the lux-uriant verbiage of *The Playboy*. The words in them, it may be noted, are, for the most part, monosyllabic, and always homely; and one is right in describing them as examples of intensity in literature, for, in all cases, it is the feeling behind the words and not the words themselves that seems to invade the mind. A passage that is literary fails to do this. (pp. 213-14)

Where Synge's other plays are lyric, *Deirdre of the Sorrows* is intense, and intensity should be the chief note in tragedy. The dramatist was triumphing over the lyric poet. Indeed it is only in *Deirdre of the Sorrows* that Synge is purely dramatist. (p. 214)

In *Deirdre of the Sorrows* we find everywhere a ripened artistry; we find also a more serious outlook; on any more subtle insight into human motives we, however, do not come; yet we feel that that refinement would not much longer be denied to one whose nature was earnest and not flashy or clever. But then he died. (p. 227)

> *Daniel Corkery, in his* Synge and Anglo-Irish Literature *(© The Mercier Press Ltd.), Mercier, 1931, 247 p.*

V.S. PRITCHETT (essay date 1942)

The return of Synge from Paris to Ireland is a dramatic moment in Anglo-Irish literature. In significance that journey is equalled only by the one made in the other direction by Joyce when he broke with Dublin for ever and went angrily to the Continent. . . . Such migrations, exile and return, are a master rhythm in Irish life. And yet, when one thinks about these journeys in connection with the work of Synge and Joyce, their destinations are not effectively so different after all. Both writers are sedulous linguists and lovers of a phrase who sport like dolphins in the riotous oceans of an English language which has something of the fabulous air of a foreign tongue for them. . . . [A] passion for the bamboozling and baroque of rhetoric leaves both Synge and Joyce with a common emotion: an exhausted feeling of the evanescence of outward things, which is philosophical in Synge and, in Joyce, the very description of human consciousness. The sense of a drunken interpenetration of myth or legend (or should we call it imagination and the inner life) with outer reality is common to them. Where modern Europeans analysed, Synge and Joyce, heirs of an earlier culture, substituted metaphor and image. Again and again, in almost any page you turn to in Joyce and Synge, the tragedy or comedy of life is felt to be the tragedy or comedy of memory and the imagination. It is their imagination which transforms Christy, Pegeen, Deirdre, and Nora in *The Shadow of the Glen;* but when, "the fine talk they have on them" is done, they are aware that time is writing on like a ledger clerk, that the beautiful girls will become old hags like the Widow Quin or Mrs. Bloom grunting among her memories on the chamber-pot. Time dissolves the lonely legendary mind of man, killing the spells of the heart, draining the eloquence of the body—that seems to be not only the subject of Synge's *Deirdre* and all his plays, but the fundamental subject of Anglo-Irish literature.

Reading Synge again one feels all the old excitment of his genius. Nothing has faded. He reads as well as an Elizabethan. In his short creative period all Synge's qualities were brought to a high pitch of intensity and richness and his work stands inviolable in a world apart. It is unaffected by the passing of the fashion for peasant drama, for behind the peasant addict with his ear to the chink in the wall is the intellect of the European tradition, someting of Jonson's grain and gusto. Synge was a master who came to his material at what is perhaps the ripest moment for an artist—the brink of decadence. The Gaelic world was sinking like a ship; and there was an enlightened desperation in the way the Anglo-Irish caught at that last moment, before their own extinction too. That, anyway, is how it looks now. The preoccupation with the solitude of man, with illusion and with the evanescence of life in Synge and Joyce is one of the signs that the old age of a culture has come, and Synge gives to the death of the Gaelic world the nobility and richness of a ritual. It is not, as in the Aran journal, a ritual of sparse sad words, but the festive blaze of life.

It is common in the eulogies of Synge to say that the unfinished *Deirdre of the Sorrows* hints at heights to which Synge's genius might have attained [see Corkery excerpt above]. For me *Deirdre* marks a dubious phase in his development. Even when I allow for the blind spot which English taste has in the matter of legendary or mythological subjects, I cannot help feeling that, in attempting *Deirdre* Synge put himself into a literary straitjacket and went back on the sound opinions he gave in his prefaces to the plays and poems. (pp. 155-57)

Riders to the Sea seems to me genuinely tragic tragedy, but *Deirdre* to be simply poetic material for tragedy where Synge's genius moves stiffly.

Like the Russians in the 'seventies, Synge "returned to the people" when he went to Aran. Unlike the Russians he does not seem to have felt any mystical faith in doing this, and knew quite well that the heroic, primitive life of the West was doomed. There is always the sensation in Synge's work of being one of the last men on earth, the survivor of a dying family. One feels the loneliness of men and women in a lonely scene, and one is also made to feel the personal, inaccessible loneliness of Synge himself. At the back of the plays there is, for all his insistence on the necessity of joy and feasting in the theatre, a dark and rather *fin de siècle* shadow, and there is more than a hint, in the character of the Playboy, of the art-for-art's-sake artist of the 'nineties who lives only in words and illusions. (p. 158)

In one obvious way Synge does belong to an earlier world than ours, and that is in his humour. It is the strong, sculptured, corporeal and baroque humour of knavery, tricks and cunning. We have almost entirely lost the literature of roguery, the life of which has been prolonged in Ireland by the tradition of disrespect for foreign law. To his handling of roguery, Synge brought all the subtlety he had learned from Molière. This has, of course, often been said and it stands out a mile in his handling of the dramatist's use of continual contrast, whereby almost every speech creates a new situation or farcically reverses its predecessor. There is no falsity in his farces; one does not feel that the situation is an artificial one. How easily *The Playboy* could have become Aldwych knockabout; and yet how easily Synge makes us accept his preposterous idea, by trying it first upon the main character before our eyes. The texture of his drama is a continous interweaving of challenge and riposte, a continuous changing of the threads in a single motif; so that we are involved in far more than a mere anecdote which has a jerk of astonishment in the beginning and a sting in the tail at the end. At the height of farce we may instantly, by a quick shift of focus, be faced by that sense of the evanescence of life which is Synge's especially, or we may be jogged by the sharp elbow of mortality. (p. 159)

V.S. Pritchett, "The End of the Gael," in his In My Good Books *(reprinted by permission of A D Peters*

& Co Ltd), Chatto & Windus, 1942 (and reprinted by Kennikat Press, 1970), pp. 155-60.

ROBERT FARREN (essay date 1947)

[John Synge's] original poems are not above a score, yet they must have a word, being strokes of an art very few of whose strokes have not told.

> It may almost be said that before verse can be
> human again it must learn to be brutal.

This dictum occurs in the preface to Synge's *Poems and Translations;* and although in a flowing sentence the author warns us that the poems were written "before the views just stated came into my head", nonetheless it seems plain that, if the views did not generate or form the poems, then the poems prompted or produced the views. In a somewhat forced disclaimer Synge avers that the poems have little to do with the views. I think they have much. Here, from the opening poem in the book, a poem called *Queens,* are lines no other Irishman—except it were [James] Stephens—either could or would have written at the time. . . . :

> Queens whose fingers once did stir men,
> Queens were eaten of fleas and vermin. . .
>
> Yet these are rotten—I ask their pardon—
> And we've the sun on rock and garden.

No Gaelic poet would have batted an eyelid at lines like these; many of their company wrote in that very style, and the medieval bite and *danse macabre* were still in their entrails as much they were in [François] Villon's. But Synge's own company, those who poetized around him, were in different case; *they* can hardly have received this *danse macabre,* this God's Acre wit and doss-house waggery, too civilly: "that meditative man John Synge" made strange meditations. Bringing the Gaelic League, the Gaelic Athletic Association and the Dublin Metropolitan Police to the temples of art, the first two strangers to blaspheme, the third to arrest the blasphemers—working this wonder by writing the play of *The Playboy* was right and decent; but *Queens were eaten of fleas and vermin* were not quite vestal virgins for the temples of art. Synge did his singing a bit crudely!

When he turned his hand to the country ballad it was just the same; his sort of ballad was to those of [William] Allingham and Yeats what an all-in wrestler is to a ballerina. *They* had favoured refined lamentations, allegorical lilts of The Silk of the Kine; but Synge's were more like jute bags stuffed with clayey spuds: murderous action-ballads all about men, and not the one half of a dreamy eye among them. (pp. 124-25)

This poetry of bitch and ditch and rotten queens was part of Synge; a true part; but not all of him. He pitched, when translating, most often on Petrarch and Villon; and the choice tells enough, even forgetting the Notebooks and the nettle-and-nosegay phrases of his plays. Edges and deep lustres he loved, and aimed at making. At first they came separately, but, after a while, together. . . .

It is one of the best-known facts of our literary movement that Synge was the crest of our wave of popular idiom; "Syngesong" is written and parodied in Ireland and elsewhere. To call his elaborate dialogue synthetic is another way of calling it art; the writer, to borrow a radio image, is the man at the controls, mixing his various "intakes": he is not just a microphone, letting words through as they come. Synge, like

Hopkins, and every other writer who finds a forgotten wine-cellar, poured us the wine too eagerly, without decanting; both of them pulled themselves up and cleared the wine, just before dying. To put it plainly, they both were learning plainness. (p. 127)

> Robert Farren, "Synge: Revolt against Tapestry Po-etry, 'Verse Must Learn to Be Brutal.', Synge's Ra-mifying Influence," in his The Course of Irish Verse in English (copyright, 1947, by Sheed & Ward, Inc.; reprinted with permission from Andrews and Mc-Meel, Inc.), Sheed and Ward, Inc., 1947, pp. 123-38.

NORMAN PODHORETZ (essay date 1953)

Synge's *The Playboy of the Western World* is a dramatic masterpiece. . . . But the critics have not been very helpful in explaining what makes the play a masterpiece. . . . [That] there is something to interpret should be obvious from even a casual glance at the plot, which clearly has the myth of rebellion against the father at its basis.

Christy, we are told, "kills" his father for two reasons: he is tired of being goaded on the score of his physical and sexual timidity, and, more immediately, he refuses to marry the old woman who had nursed him as a baby. The primitive people of Mayo (with whom Christy has taken refuge) not only refuse to give him up to the police, but make a hero of him instead. Encouraged by their admiration, Christy begins growing into manhood with full command of his physical and sexual powers. (p. 68)

It is no accident, then, that Christy who is, as will be seen, the undeveloped poet coming to consciousness of himself as man and as artist, should be accepted with such fervour [by the Mayoites]. This was no ordinary, everyday murder he had committed, but an act of great "daring" such as the Mayoites have never had before their very eyes until this day. Moreover, they recognize that there was something herioc, something *necessary* about the deed, which makes the question of crime irrelevant. . . . Consciousness, maturity, self-realization were bound up with revolt against the father, and Pegeen, with her sure earthy instinct, senses this. (p. 69)

The results of Christy's revolt are what we should expect them to be: sexual assertion and a new awareness of self. . . . And Christy's soliloquy at the end of Act I, when the forces have all been set in motion, is exact evidence of Synge's comic genius:

> Well, it's a clean bed and soft with it, and it's
> great luck and company I've won me in the
> end of time—two fine women fighting for the
> likes of me—till I'm thinking this night wasn't
> I a foolish fellow not to kill my father in the
> years gone by.

If we stop to analyse the humour of this passage, we see that it derives from an absurd moral position, and indeed, what Synge has grasped here is nothing less than the paradox on which civilization (according to the myth, at any rate) seems to rest—individual achievement and communal progress depend on murder. The moral consciousness has found a way out of the dilemma for civilized man: he commits a *symbolic* act of murder in place of physical violence by rejecting the father and his values, but in the primitive world of Act I there is as yet no sign of morality. Synge will begin to draw it into

his play slowly in Act II, and it becomes so important to the dénouement that I will have to return to a discussion of the whole problem later. We cannot understand the climax of the play without appreciating Synge's profound sense of the relation between symbolism and morality.

The second reason for Christy's success in Mayo is, of course, his greatness as a poet. . . . "I've heard all times," Pegeen says rhapsodically, "it's the poets are your like—fine, fiery fellows with great rages when their temper's roused." . . . Synge's dialogue, we may note in passing, is never irrelevantly lyrical: the quality of the language itself is organic to the play's meaning. Language is the very being of these people, and so they naturally pay tribute to the great master of language who has come among them. Moreover, it is the poetic, the symbolic deed which has set their imaginations afire: the murder has for them the reality of fitness and beauty but never the reality of fact. Christy, who is taken in by the poetic glory of what he has done no less than Pegeen, neglects to remember the harsh details. . . . Christy has no notion of what he has done to his father; he cannot see the suffering his act has caused and he is not aware of its brutality, which is only a way of saying that he has no moral consciousness. And so with Pegeen; she will not allow Shawn to call Christy a "bloody handed murderer." That there should have been blood cannot occur to her, because the murder is "a gallous story," a symbolic event, an expression of what is fine in the human spirit. Christy had a right to kill his father; and more, it was necessary and good that he should do so.

They all regard the murder essentially in terms of its symbolic and imaginative overtones, and indeed, symbolic is precisely what the first murder turns out to be. The "old man of the tribe" has not been killed, and the fact that his appearance terrifies Christy tells us that the first murder was not so emancipating as it seemed. Still another act of violence is necessary if Christy is to triumph over his father, over, that is, those forces which have prevented the full emergence of his identity. And here the moral paradox of which I spoke above asserts itself most strongly. The original act represented the instinctive stirrings of manhood in Christy, while for the people of Mayo it was "a gallous story" rather than "a dirty deed." Christy, however, murders again not instinctively but deliberately, out of a desire to protect his newly-found independence. . . . This, of course, is a moral act, the result of a choice, and partly for that reason, the Mayoites now turn on Christy. The sight of blood makes them aware of the realities of suffering and murder, and Pegeen, at least, realizes how great a gap there is "between a gallous story and a dirty deed." From the point of view of society, the second murder is certainly a dirty deed. . . . [Christy] makes a choice, but it remains to be noticed that he does so without knowledge of the consequences: Synge is careful to show that Christy had not believed his admirers would turn on him; his immediate motive for killing his father again is that they have taunted him with a lie. His absurd and magnificent willingness, however, to kill his father yet a third time ("Are you coming to be killed a third time, or what ails you now?") is the product of a full moral consciousness. He knows that they will hang him if he raises the loy once more, but the necessity of ultimate triumph is more important, is absolute. This finally establishes Christy as the Hero who has the courage to face up to that paradox on which civilization rests, who will commit the act of violence which all feel to be necessary and which society cannot afford to condone. And it is beautifully proper that Christy's triumph does not entail self-destruction. For Synge is telling us, I think, that the Hero, the poet who does in fact challenge morality with its own contradictions will not be destroyed, that he will be saved by a kind of Grace. There is, unfortunately, no other word (unless it be "luck") for the power which saves Christy and which resolves the dilemma lying at the heart of the play. And we should not be surprised at the invocation of the idea of Grace in a work so saturated with religious awareness. Synge's religion is not Father Reilly's, but it is a religion nonetheless. He believes (to borrow a phrase from Henry James) in the salubrity of genius: Christy is the poet, the playboy, triumphant in games, who will spend his life "romancing" and "telling stories" now that he has been made "a likely gaffer in the end of all." Society has not been able to countenance him and all he represents, and in the name of order and peace they have driven him out into "the lonesome west." . . . But nothing can heal Christy's "vicious bite" as far as Pegeen is concerned. She realizes when Christy leaves declaring that he is "master of all fights now" what she has lost, what the meaning of his strange salvation is, and she knows that she is consigned to a life in society with the likes of Shawn Keogh: "Oh, my grief, I've lost him surely. I've lost the only Playboy of the Western World."

A few remarks are necessary, finally, to clarify Synge's attitude towards society and the Hero. . . . The Hero and society are incompatible in the sense that they pursue different objectives, but the relation between them must be understood as one of reciprocal benefit no less than of antagonism. Christy develops into a Hero only when the superior instinct of society approves what he had done in ignorance and bewilderment, and the Mayoites, on the other hand, move from a primitive state of consciousness to a sense of civilization and its values through their contact with him. The West is a lonesome place, Synge tells us early in the play, but Christy has made his choice: "If it's a poor thing to be lonesome, it's worse, maybe, go mixing with the fools of earth." What he has to do, Christy must do alone. Synge, then, is alive both to the possibilities of the Shawns and the Michael Jameses, and to the worth of the Christies, and his sympathy is patently divided between those two extremes. His pity, however, Synge reserves for Pegeen, who—to paraphrase Eliot—has been visited by the vision of greatness for a few days and will for ever after be a haunted woman. The tragic implications of *The Playboy of the Western World* are that the type represented by Pegeen—those who can perceive greatness but cannot rise to it, who are weighed down by the "society" within them—can neither live in the lonesome west playing out their days, nor be happy in the little world of daily preoccupations. The Christies are somehow taken care of, and so are the Shawns; it is the Pegeens who suffer most from the radical incompatibility of Hero and society. (pp. 70-4)

Norman Podhoretz, "Synge's 'Playboy': Morality and the Hero" (reprinted by permission of the author and Georges Borchardt, Inc.), in Essays in Criticism, Vol. III, No. 3, July, 1953 and reprinted in Twentieth Century Interpretations of "The Playboy of the Western World": A Collection of Critical Essays, edited by Thomas R. Whitaker, Prentice-Hall, Inc., 1969, pp. 68-74).

HUGH N. MACLEAN (essay date 1954)

[*The Playboy of the Western World*] is a rendering into Christian terminology of the scapegoat-theme, a clever parody of the orthodox Christian story, and a special example of the "ad-

venture" which Joseph Campbell, in *The Hero With the Thousand Faces,* finds common to accounts of mythological story. These patterns give *The Playboy* a significance in Western literature which has not been sufficiently emphasized. (p. 9)

It is clear, to begin with, that the scapegoat theme lies at the center of the play, which reproduces those features separately enumerated by [Sir James George] Frazer in his catalogue of scapegoat-ceremonials throughout the world [in *The Golden Bough*]. The pattern of ritual is generically the same: a sin-ridden community selects one particularly handsome, or gifted—or possessed—individual as its representative, pays extravagant homage to him for a season, and then puts him to death. The sins of the community, having been transferred to the victim, are expiated by his death, enabling the community to live in peace until next year. . . .

Synge's use of this formula is developed in Christian terms. It is reasonable that he should have adopted as a vehicle the forms of his religious upbringing—even if his interpretation of Christian story differed considerably from that of his audience. Christy is, in fact, a Christian scapegoat. His name has not been chosen at random. Coming to a world of darkness and sin, which lives in fear of a law it regards as alien, he is soon hailed as savior and protector. He is tempted by material riches and by a devil (the Widow Quin). Shawn Keogh, who epitomizes men under the Law, snarls, "If I wasn't so God-fearing, I'd near have courage to come behind him and run a pike into his side." Christy is repudiated three times by Pegeen, his most faithful follower. . . . (p. 10)

Yet Synge's *Playboy* is not a Christiad. The community, though "left in peace," is not purged of its sin, but sinks back luxuriously into its customary round. Pegeen does not accept the Playboy's departure, but keens in agony for his eternal loss. Christy does not repudiate his tempters, but succumbs at once to their offers. Until the end, Christy is vain, self-pitying, boastful, weak-sprited. Somewhat unexpectedly, Christy at length appears to have found himself: he is at the end of the play in full command of the situation. "Master of all fights from now," he no longer fears his father, whom he calls "a heathen slave," but with whom he willingly leaves Mayo; and he forgives his blind persecutors. . . .

These apparently contradictory factors may be reconciled by a tentative hypothesis, which can be tested by recourse to the text of the play. Synge is concerned not with the hero as warrior or priest, but with the hero as playboy, i.e., the hero as "hoaxer, humbugger . . . one who does sham things." The play reflects Synge's love of mankind, his respect for myth, and his scorn for the Roman Catholic effort to institutionalize religion, and (in his view) deprive it of its natural roots. (p. 11)

[*The Playboy*] is positive. Man must save himself; he is to look within for rescue, not from without. To present this idea, Synge accepts the framework of Christian story, but posits a Christ who fails to take into account the power of evil; a complacent Christ, who assumes for a time that words and formulas will ensure his triumph, and, until he grasps what is required of him, a weak and even craven Christ, who nearly disposes altogether of his birthright as the Son of God. At one point in the play, in fact, he compares himself to Esau. This Christ cannot save the world; he can only, by a determined effort, save himself. But he still has a mission: to demonstrate to men, by his example, the fatuity of seeking salvation through an external agency. Mankind, so long as it depends on such illusory hopes, is lost. "Oh my grief," wails Pegeen, "I've lost

him surely; I've lost the only Playboy of the Western World.''
It is Synge's intention that these last moments of the drama
should entirely abjure burlesque, and that they should partake
of comedy only in the sense that Chaucer's *Troilus and Cri-
seyde* is comic; Christy, like Troilus at the close, can laugh at
human woe. This apotheosis is his alone, and unlike the Gospel
story, it means that men are not saved, but abandoned. (pp.
11-12)

The Playboy at first reproduces the outlines of the Gospel story,
and then gradually diverges from that story—as this Christ
betrays himself—conveying the impression of parody to a perceptive audience. Of course, to an audience predominantly
conventional in a narrow way, and perhaps especially to one
of Roman Catholic faith, the element of parody may be interpreted as an apology for immorality, ''paganism,'' and materialism, although Synge (I believe) intended the play to be
a prolonged keen over the triumph of these forces in man, and
the consequent impossibility of his salvation by a rescue from
without.

Act I begins by introducing the audience to the Mayo-world
of darkness, fear, and imperfection. It is ''a dark, lonesome
place,'' totally surrounded by ''the darkness of the night.''
Shawn Keogh, the only eligible young male available for Pegeen's hand, is ridden and possessed by fears of all kinds: fear
of the darkness, fear of Father Reilly, fear of ''the peelers,''
and fear of public opinion. (p. 12)

The stage would seem to be set for an Irish version of the
Gospel story but for one or two disturbing aspects of Christy's
character, and the first entrance of his earthly opponent, the
Widow Quin. Christy's apparent humility has gradually been
shown by Synge, in dialogue and directions both, to veil self-
pity, vanity, and a fear of authority. . . . At the end of the
act, two things especially appeal to him, and neither is faith.
He boasts exultantly of his ''luck,'' and of ''the company I've
won me,'' by which he means earthly love. He has not yet
betrayed his mission—he is still Christ and not yet Esau—but
the seeds of doubt have been sown in the audience's mind. . . .

Act II makes clear Synge's intention. Christy, tempted by the
material riches of earth, the riches of men, and the love of
women, yields to all three; but only the last shows how completely he is in the hands of the devil-widow. The village girls
who offer him gifts each have symbolic significance. . . . The
girls are servant-friends to the widow, who quickly asserts her
mastery as she sets them to wait on Christy and herself. At a
suggestion that Christy should marry the Widow (''she with a
great yearning to be wedded, though all dread her here''), the
women cluster about Christy and propose a toast to the powers
of evil. . . . (p. 14)

The nearly complete corruption of Christy becomes increasingly clear. He calls his father ''that ghost of hell,'' and ''a
kind of carcass you'd fling upon the sea''; he prays for ''a
high wave to wash him from the world.'' These sea-images
are significant, for the sea, salt, barren, and wild, connotes
evil and the Fall. Eden's life-springs dry up; the sea swallows
Jonah; and not until the Book of Revelation, when ''there shall
be no more sea,'' do the sweet rivers of life return to Scripture.
Christy's oaths are better suited to the Widow Quin; and in his
mouth they are inappropriate and terrific, for Old Mahon is,
after all, God. . . .

As Act III opens, therefore, Christy has all but sold himself
to the devil by becoming enmeshed in earth's attractions and
betraying his mission to men (or the positive part of that mis-

sion); those who awaited a savior have placed their faith in a
charlatan; God seems to be thwarted in his effort to remind
Christ of an almost blunted purpose. (p. 15)

There follows the most ironical and revealing scene of the play,
as Shawn Keogh makes a final effort to win Pegeen. The
dialogue is a key to the meaning of the drama. . . . The golden
calf and the sacrificed bullocks and heifers of the Old Testament
are placed in clear contrast with the lilies and roses of the New.
Shawn's preoccupation with rams, heifers, and bullocks is part
of his role as the man who loves the law and his chains too,
and consequently as one who resents any move toward
change. . . . Pegeen's selection of this moment to speak of
lilies and roses, in view of Christy's defection, is of course
designed to emphasize the terrible mistake she has made. It is
here, too, that she swears she'll ''not renege,'' and here that
her lover boasts for the last time of being ''mounted on the
spring-tide of the stars of luck.''

The nearly-completed marriage, however, is disrupted by Old
Mahon's forceful reminder to Christy of his forgotten mission.
There is, of course, no question of a rescue here; Christy must
save himself. The girl and the Playboy react in significant ways.
Pegeen recalls early doubts and bitterly reproaches Christy—
thus ''reneging'' once—for having misled her. Ironically, she
calls him ''the fool of men.'' Christy's first reaction is to
repudiate his father: ''He's not my father'' . . . ''It's himself
was a liar.'' He turns desperately to the Widow Quin for aid,
but evil is powerless. . . . (p. 15-16)

The Widow's futility is emphasized by the failure of her attempt
to persuade Christy to escape in female attire, i.e., to deny his
manhood. Her plan is irrelevant, for Christy is shaking off his
manhood in any case, and is steadily becoming a god once
more. Earthly love alone continues to hold him, and this is
about to drop away. As he mumbles about his ''luck,'' the
others creep up behind, and Pegeen—the second ''reneging''—
herself puts the rope on his neck. She has relapsed into fear
of the law. . . . The third ''reneging'' follows, as Pegeen brands
Christy; but even before this, he has assumed the role of Chorus, succeeding his father. ''You'll have a gallous jaunt, I'm
saying, coaching out through limbo with my father's ghost.''
Here too, witnessed by Old Mahon, comes the second cry,
''Oh, glory be to God!,'' which announces the final break
between human and divine in Christy. Old Mahon, appropriately, unties the last knots binding his son, and the two depart
together, though their relationship has been reversed. The Mayo
fiasco has at least prepared Christy to succeed to power: ''Go
with you, is it? I will then, like a gallant captain with his
heathen slave . . . I'm master of all fights from now.'' The
gods depart, leaving mortals weltering in their sin or, at best,
mourning what might have been. Christ is saved, but the world
which thought itself easily saved through him is lost—until it
too is willing to understand and follow the dolorous way of
Christy. (pp. 16-17)

> *Hugh N. Maclean, ''The Hero as Playboy,'' in The
> University of Kansas City Review, Vol. XXI, No. 1,
> Autumn, 1954, pp. 9-19.*

UNA ELLIS-FERMOR (essay date 1954)

Synge is the only great poetic dramatist of the [Irish literary]
movement; the only one, that is, for whom poetry and drama
were inseparable, in whose work dramatic intensity invariably
finds poetic expression and the poetic mood its only full expression in dramatic form. All the other playwrights of the

movement seem, in the last analysis, to have been either dramatists in whom the instinct for dramatic expression sometimes brought with it the poetry of diction, imagery, or cadence, or poets who turned for a time to the dramatic form, returning, sooner or later, again to other forms. But it is hard to imagine this separation in Synge; poetic and dramatic expression in him are one and simultaneous, as they appear to have been with Shakespeare and with Webster, in whom the presence of a high degree of one mood meant the presence of a high degree of the other, whether the form were prose or verse, the matter comedy or tragedy.

Yet there is a paradox in Synge's genius, a dualism of a different and a rarer kind. For while he is essentially a dramatic poet, one of the roots of his poetry is mysticism, such as he recognized, in the mountain and sea-faring Irish peasants living far enough out of reach of civilization to respond to and reflect the nature about them. And mystical experience, particularly the extreme form of nature-mysticism that we find in Synge, is in itself as nearly as possible incompatible with dramatic expression. Yet the presence of nature is as strongly felt in the plays as in *The Aran Islands* and *In Wicklow and West Kerry* and it is not there as a digression, irrelevant or undramatic. Nature is a protagonist in *The Shadow of the Glen* and *Riders to the Sea,* so filling the minds of the characters as to shape their actions, moods and fates; it is the ever-present setting, genially familiar, of *The Well of the Saints* and *The Tinker's Wedding;* it remains as a continual and surprising source of imagery and incidental reference throughout *The Playboy* and becomes again a poetic protagonist in *Deirdre.* . . .

[Synge], through affinity of spirit, [seems] to carry on unbroken the tradition of ancient Irish nature poetry. In that poetry a distinctive quality is the sense of intimacy between man and nature about him; animals, birds, trees, and flowers are not only a source of delight but almost a part of man himself. (pp. 35-6)

[In] Synge natural beauty is not merely one of many forms of beauty that he loves or reveres, and nature is not merely a background in harmony with the play, a kind of setting kept before our eyes by allusions coming naturally out of the poet's own affection. It is an actor recognized by the other human actors, sometimes (as in the *Well of the Saints*) as a constant, familiar companion, sometimes (as in the *Shadow of the Glen* and *Riders to the Sea*) as a presence or even an agent who forms their moods or draws down their fates. Very few Irish cities are big enough, even now, to breed men ignorant of country life, and most Irishmen, to this day, are at heart countrymen, responsive to the familiar miracle of their own mountains, rivers, islands, and seas. But in Synge himself, as in A.E., and in the peasants with whom Synge was in natural sympathy, there is a reach of experience beyond this, and animals and birds, even the stranger powers of hills, mists, storms, and seas are accepted as part of the same creation as man himself, experiencing the same moods as he does and drawing him into their spirit. (pp. 37-8)

> *Una Ellis-Fermor, "John Millington Synge," in her* The Irish Dramatic Movement, *(reprinted by permission of Associated Book Publishers Ltd), revised edition, Methuen & Company, 1954 (and reprinted as "Synge's Poetic Drama," in* Twentieth Century Interpretations of "The Playboy of the Western World": A Collection of Critical Essays, *edited by Thomas R. Whitaker, Prentice-Hall, Inc., 1969, pp. 35-43).*

ROBIN SKELTON (essay date 1971)

[Synge's first published work] *The Aran Islands* is told in the first person, and . . . is in journal form. It consists of four sections, each devoted to one visit to the area. The narrator is a sensitive man receptive to beauty, and easily impressed by the grotesque and the vivid. The opening pages of the first section . . . present, like an overture, the various themes which go to make up the whole. The mysterious isolation of the island is shown by the way in which its shoreline, at first visible, is then lost in mist, and then reappears as a 'dreary rock'. It is as if a veil between one world and the next has been pierced. The second theme, that of the humble nature of Aran society, and the simplicity of the islanders' lives, is introduced with an image of the narrator's fellow passengers, the girls with their heads twisted in shawls, and the 'young pigs tied loosely in sacking'.

The theme of desolation, allied to the theme of constant awareness of death, is then introduced. The narrator tells us 'I have seen nothing so desolate'. . . . This mood of desolation, however, is broken into by an awareness of humour and vitality, as the narrator meets a group of girls who hurry past him 'with eager laughter and great talking in Gaelic'.

The theme of untidy confusion, of careless muddle, then emerges as we are told of the broken panes of the public-house and the pigs playing untended in the surf. (p. 29)

These are the main themes, expressed here simply and easily, and with a rhythmic recurrence that is characteristic of the shape of the whole book as well as of the prose style. The narrator is not the protagonist of the work, in that he is largely only receptive to impressions, and only occasionally stimulates activity or event. . . . [As] the book develops, the narrator's feelings about the islands intensify, and his language becomes more vivid and more assured. The book itself, also, becomes more fragmentary and the narrative less connected, as if the narrator no longer found it necessary to explain his emotions to himself, but had grown to accept his insight as being, of necessity, fragmentary and occasional. The book thus shows, as far as the developing character of the narrator goes, a movement from a rather low-key meditative coherence to a much more vivid fragmentation. . . .

The Aran Islands is not, however, the self-portrait of its narrator; the narrator is used to show the way in which the islands impress themselves upon a receptive sensibility and give its owner an understanding of a system of values alien to all his previous experience, and a perspective upon the nature of cultural inheritance. (p. 30)

The narrator's involvement in his own interpretations is such that the whole book becomes much less the account of a series of visits to strange islands than an account of an introspective myth-making which feeds upon any evidence that supports it. The myth itself only forms gradually, and is brought to completion by the outpouring of the three final ramshackle poems that combine wildness of imagination with half recollected learning and an intuitive feeling for heroic values which are now decayed and mutilated as the consequence of isolation.

The islanders, then, have virtues which are not of civilization. Though intensely passionate they are also reserved except at moments of grief and pain when they are proud of betraying excessive emotion. When young, the women are beautiful, filled with awareness of universal myth and natural forces, and, when old, figures of terrible power and decision. (p. 35)

'Grandeur', 'distinction', 'individuality', 'innocence', 'wildness', 'passion', 'despair', are a few of the words most frequently used to describe the islanders. The smallest events are given extravagant dignity and beauty. We see the islands as a fallen paradise, where all the ancient knowledge, innocence and dignity remain, though sometimes in vestigial condition, and where awareness of a lost understanding of the powers of nature and super nature, gives the approach to death a more than usual intensity. The myths of the islanders are now garbled, but show in their fusion of Christian and pagan themes a half recollection of the all-embracing truth which unifies all story. The mist which separates Aran from the mainland is a barrier between the world of commonplace materialist life and the last remaining outpost of the life of the spirit in Europe. (p. 38)

The Aran Islands is not a character study of its narrator; it is a pursuit of a vision of fallen man trapped halfway between earth and heaven. It shows how man will satisfy spiritual and emotional needs by transforming reality and selecting food for his imagination. It shows too how the creative imagination may, from peasants, rock and desolation, create a myth of startling intensity and power. (pp. 38-9)

[The value-system created in this book] gives us an indication of the attitude we must have in reading the later drama. In Inishmaan [Synge] found 'spiritual treasure' and this treasure remained 'a magnet' to his soul. He found in the Aran Islands that 'every symbol' was 'of the cosmos' . . . , in that the whole pattern of man as spirit, as animal, as social being, was there displayed in images as timeless and fundamental as those of universal myth. (p. 39)

The Aran Islands is, like Yeats' *The Celtic Twilight,* not merely an attempt to report upon the persistence of ancient culture and beliefs among the Irish peasantry, but a construction of images and values which have validity in themselves, and which point towards the importance of reviving, and maintaining, a particular sensibility in order to make sense of the predicament of humanity. If *The Aran Islands* is the rock upon which Synge's œuvre is founded, it is not the rock of newly recovered fact but that of fact transformed by the imagination into a vision of universal significance and creative utility. (p. 40)

The very title [of Synge's play *Riders to the Sea*] emphasizes the mythic or supernatural element for there are only two riders in the play, one the doomed Bartley and the other his spectral brother. We are all, Maurya tells us, doomed to death, for 'no man can be living for ever'. We are all, sooner or later, called to destruction. It is one of the messages of Greek tragedy, and the form of the play has much in common with Greek theatre. The climactic action takes place off-stage and is commented upon by Maurya, who returns, distraught with her forebodings, as the Greek chorus returns similarly distraught in so many plays. The old women keening just before the news of Bartley's death is told, function like a Greek chorus, as also do the two women who describe Bartley's death. (p. 49)

The dramatic irony in the play is also similar to that found in Greek tragedy. Nora reports the priest's words thus: 'she'll be getting her death' says he 'with crying and lamenting' . . . : it is, indeed, Maurya's lamenting Bartley's going down to the ship that prevents her from giving her blessing and thus causes his death. . . . The pathos and dignity of Maurya's speech on taking Michael's stick to assist her steps as she goes to the spring to give her blessing to Bartley is not unlike many of the laments in Aeschylus, Sophocles, and Euripides. . . . The

emphasis in this speech upon the way in which the world of Maurya differs from the 'big world' appears to set the island community apart from all other communities. Moreover, while in Greek tragedy and story the suffering of the protagonists is the consequence of the sins they or their kin have committed, intentionally or otherwise, in *Riders to the Sea* there appears to be no reason for Maurya's tribulation. The deaths of her sons are not, as are the deaths of Niobe's children, or Medea's, the consequence of acts of blasphemy or evil. In this, *Riders to the Sea* is closer to the world of Sophocles than Euripides; there is an arbitrary quality about the fates of the characters that reminds one of the world of Oedipus. Even here, however, one can find some historical justification for the cruelty of the fates. In *Riders to the Sea,* however, there is no justification. This is not a place in which there is any kind of justice, or mercy. The priest may say that 'the Almighty God won't leave her [Maurya] destitute with no son living' . . . , but Maurya tells us, 'It's little the like of him knows of the sea'. . . . The sea is, indeed, the 'Almighty God' of the play, an older and more formidable spiritual power than that represented by the priest who, it is emphasized, is 'young'. The priest never enters the action of the play. He is absent physically from the cottage of Maurya just as he is, spiritually, a stranger to her world. His reported words are all comforting, but they do not comfort. (pp. 49-50)

The fusion of pre-Christian and Christian belief is characteristic, of course, of many peasant communities. Synge was not playing fast and loose with the facts. He was, however, portraying a world in which people, insecure and desperate for help against the forces of death and the tyranny of the natural world, seized upon any belief or superstition that might give them comfort and hope. That Maurya finds no comfort or hope for all her observances is the dark message of the play, which ends as a cry, not against God, but against the principle of Mortality. 'No man can be living for ever and we must be satisfied'. . . . (p. 51)

The island of *Riders to the Sea* is Ireland, but more than Ireland. Its predicaments are those of the Irish peasant, but also those of all men subject to the tyranny of forces they do not understand. Its beliefs are those of the Irish peasant, but they are also those of all people who combine superstition with Christian belief, or who are troubled by thoughts of spiritual realities beyond their ability to understand and control. *Riders to the Sea* is not naturalistic theatre; it is poetic theatre, and it is epic. The figure of man placed against the power of the gods who destroy him is a main theme of epic and of heroic tragedy. Maurya, like Oedipus, bows to the will of the gods, and, like Job, finds at last in humilty and endurance a dignity and greatness of spirit, turning down the empty cup of Holy Water in a last symbolic gesture, and asking for mercy upon the souls of all mortal kind. (p. 52)

Although [*The Shadow of the Glen*] was the first of Synge's plays to be staged, it has, as yet, received much less critical attention than its companion, and the reasons for this comparative neglect are easy to understand. In the first place, it might appear on the surface to be little more than a dramatized anecdote whose main interest is the vitality and richness of the dialect in which it is written. In the second place, it does not have the mythic universality of *Riders to the Sea;* and nor, in the third place, does it achieve the vitality of Synge's later comedies. It is, however, in reality, a subtle and complex construction in which Synge for the first time develops that ironic ambiguity of tone which makes the later and rightly celebrated *Playboy of the Western World* so fascinating. (p. 53)

During [the summer of 1902 Synge] drafted three plays, *Riders to the Sea, The Shadow of the Glen,* and *The Tinker's Wedding.* Each of these plays is so constructed as to echo story-patterns which have long existed in Western culture: the death of Bartley in *Riders to the Sea* echoes the story of Hippolitus; the plot of *The Shadow of the Glen* utilizes the Widow of Ephesus pattern; and the story of *The Tinker's Wedding* has a generic similarity to the type of folk material utilized by Boccaccio and Chaucer. Each play, also, is based upon material given Synge by the Irish peasantry.

Indeed, it would hardly be wrenching the facts to describe these three plays as forming a trilogy. . . . [The] central themes of all three plays can be related to each other. In all three there is the conflict between folk belief and conventional Christian attitudes. In all three we are shown a woman trapped by circumstances, and in each one we are presented with a different aspect of her predicament. In *Riders to the Sea* the old woman, the mother figure, broods over the solitude to which she has come at the death of her menfolk. In *The Shadow of the Glen* the still young wife is trapped by the solitude of the glens and by her loveless marriage, and is stirred by a desire for freedom. In *The Tinker's Wedding* Sarah Casey, the young tinker woman, desires to become a bride and to join the ranks of accepted wives, in spite of the advice of old Mary Byrne who stands for the traditionally anarchic freedom of her pagan breed. In all three cases conventional ideas of the 'big world' are challenged, and the play's central figure feels herself the victim of forces she cannot control. The priest in *Riders to the Sea* is regarded as knowing little of the ways of the sea-torn world. The convention of marriage in *The Shadow of the Glen* is opposed to the lyricism of the human heart and the needs of the human spirit. And in *The Tinker's Wedding* the priest proves to be shallow and imperceptive.

Not only do these three plays have thematic links, they also form a kind of progression. As we proceed from *Riders to the Sea,* through *The Shadow of the Glen* to *The Tinker's Wedding,* the age of the central female character diminishes and the psychological complexity of the drama increases. In *Riders to the Sea* the characters are simple, each dominated by a single emotional attitude. In *The Shadow of the Glen* Nora and the Tramp are more varied in their emotional reactions to events. In *The Tinker's Wedding* the two female characters are more complex still and the subsidiary characters less predicatable. The fourth of these plays of the Irish countryside, the plays which I like to label collectively as 'the shanachie plays', is *The Playboy of the Western World,* in which the majority of the characters are fully individuated.

There is also in these three plays a mounting tide of rebellion. The four shanachie plays all have in common their use of a central female character who is the voice of the play's energy. The conflict is centred in her words and her confusions. In *Riders to the Sea* the woman, Maurya, becomes resigned to her fate, and the epic mood of the play prevents niceties of psychological shading. *The Shadow of the Glen,* however, gives us, in Nora Burke, a more complex character hovering upon the edge of outright rebellion, while Sarah Casey in *The Tinker's Wedding* is the passionate protagonist of the play's action and outspoken in her rejection of her condition. The Christian ethos, dismissed as irrelevant in *Riders to the Sea,* is faced and opposed in *The Shadow of the Glen,* and ridiculed outrageously in *The Tinker's Wedding.* Religious beliefs, moral standards, and conventional social attitudes are tackled with increasing vigour and insistence as the plays proceed. In addition, as these

first three shanachie plays progress they become more humorous: the first is tragic, the second tragi-comic, and the third farcical.

If we look at the shanachie plays in these various ways it becomes apparent that *The Shadow of the Glen* is a transitional play involving crucial artistic decisions. It is in this play that the main themes of Synge's drama are first effectively, though perhaps summarily, displayed, and the main varieties of his characterization suggested. As has already been pointed out, *The Shadow of the Glen* is dominated by the personality of a woman, Nora Burke. The three men are no more than her foils, and two of them are stock figures. Dan Burke, the old husband, is a possessive man who cannot bear his young wife even to speak to other men, and who is derisive of her expressions of emotion. Michael Dara is a superstitious and timid youth interested in Nora only for her land and money. Only when he is assured that she can bring him material wealth does he put his arm round her and say, 'It's a fine life you'll have now with a young man, a fine life surely'. . . . These two represent the complacent male materialism against which Synge set restless female idealism in several of his plays. It is not, indeed, Irish womanhood that is being attacked here, but Irish manhood. . . . The third male character, the tramp, is more complex than the others, partly because it is he who attempts to justify impulse and passion. He is also more observant; he registers the 'queer look' . . . of the dead man, and notices immediately that the corpse has not been properly laid out. He gently hints at his own sexual vitality by telling Nora that many a woman would be 'afeard of the like of me in the dark night'. . . . (pp. 55-8)

Nora herself is a complex character. Alone with a corpse, she shows courage and even humour, though she also reveals her belief in the efficacy of curses. She is candid about her unhappiness and unafraid of admitting her sexual frustration to a stranger, saying of her husband, 'he was always cold, every day since I knew him—and every night . . .'. . . . (p. 59)

Her sexual frustration is not the only source of her confusion and despair. She also feels herself trapped by time itself.

It is here that one of Synge's central motifs appears clearly for the first time in his mature drama. In all the completed plays from this time onward he presented a central character animated by a desire for the zestful enjoyment of life's pleasures and anxious at the passing of time and the inevitable approach of death. These characters are afflicted by an inability to avoid taking the long view even while emphasizing the possible delights of the present. The beggars in *The Well of the Saints* look towards an ideal future as desperately and as yearningly as Pegeen Mike in *The Playboy of the Western World,* and yet in all their talk of the future they implicitly deny the possibility of present laughter and offer an amulet to the face of death. In *The Shadow of the Glen* this predicament is presented with harsh clarity and with inescapable logic. The only pleasure possible in the present is, Nora realizes, a dream of the future, and that is simply a fantasy to ward off dread of what the future must finally bring.

Synge was mortality-conscious and time-haunted, and his characters present that double standard with which we deal with our unique human awareness of temporality. Nora may be the most obvious vehicle for this theme in the whole of Synge's drama, largely because she has for so long denied herself dreams and toughened herself by a steady contemplation of the cramping facts. . . . She is, more than any other of Synge's heroines, a trapped and bitter figure, and the ironic note upon which the play ends is itself a tribute to that turbulence of spirit which gives her heroic stature even while it may also underline her moral frailty. The final words of the play, indeed, are an attack upon the poorness of spirit of the society in which she has spent her days, and an indication that there should be more to living than 'quiet' and 'good health'. (pp. 61-2)

In *The Shadow of the Glen* Synge, far from mocking Irish problems, gave them dignity. The lyricism and bitterness of this play do indeed establish it as one of the most original works of the Irish Renaissance, the precursor of much black comedy, and the true forerunner of *Juno and the Paycock* and *Waiting for Godot*. (p. 63)

[One of the protagonists of *The Well of the Saints,* Martin, suggests that it is the right] of every man to choose his own way of life, however odd it may appear to others. He has a right not to bow down to conventional notions of the real or the important. He has a right to avoid 'tormenting' his 'soul'. Martin's view of the soul may not be theologically profound, but Synge's view is interesting. From *The Well of the Saints,* as from *The Shadow of the Glen* and *The Tinker's Wedding,* it would seem that he took what we would now label an existentialist view. Existence precedes essence; it is the life-experience, including the experience of living traditions however flawed and gross, that gives each soul its individual character and its individual road to travel. The saint is an idealist, as are the priests in *The Tinker's Wedding* and *Riders to the Sea,* and as is the husband in *The Shadow of the Glen:* they believe that all must be forced into conformity with the Idea, the established order, the rule of morality and belief which pre-exists us all. Martin is not of this persuasion; nor is Synge. In every play he completed, with the possible exception of the first, he shows individuals asserting their 'right' to be 'blind' to realities that torment them and to protect and defend the vision that sustains their belief in their own human dignity, and in the perfectibility of their world. . . . *The Well of Saints* is, of course, a fable and, like all fables, it preaches. It is also, however, so varied in mood, and so energetic in expression, that we find tragedy, comedy, and lyricism combining to give us a play with all the light and shade of the human condition. It expresses more distinctly than any other of Synge's plays his belief in individualism, his distrust of conventional idealism, his relish of those that stand up for their right to their vision. It may be no accident that Mary Doul calls herself the wonder of the western world, for she is, in her struggle to assert her dignity and in her fantasies of pride, kin to the playboy of the western world who also had a vision of his dignity and found it conflicting with the actual. (100-02)

Robin Skelton, in his The Writings of J. M. Synge *(copyright © 1971 by Robin Skelton), Thames and Hudson, 1971, 190 p.*

ROGER ROSENBLATT (essay date 1975)

It's a good thing that Synge did not wait for one play to be produced before starting another. The critical reception given *In the Shadow of the Glen* was angry enough to have discouraged most writers. Later, in the *Playboy* riots, when Synge would look back upon mere hostile criticism as the halcyon days, he could also be sufficiently secure in the judgment of his own worth to let public condemnation go with scorn. . . .

In The Shadow of the Glen is a story based on a Wicklow "hearth-tale" about Nora Burke, whose husband pretends to

be dead in order to check her fidelity. The idea that an Irish country wife would ever run off with a tramp, as Nora does at the end of the play, was according to the *Irish Times* "a slur on Irish womanhood." Arthur Griffith, editor of the nationalist *United Irishman,* called the *Shadow* "decadent," and compared Synge to "any Englishman who has yet dissected us for the enlightenment of his countrymen." (p. 31)

[Criticism of *The Playboy*] ranged from Synge's use of the word "shift," a small shock to the audience's sensibilities, to what many saw in the play as yet another gross caricature of the stock Irishman. The most outrageous insult was the plot itself: an Irish village glorifying and protecting a young man who had killed his "da" and assaulted society; that, and the implication that there was such a thing as a deliberately loveless marriage in Ireland. (p. 32)

Things that were important to reviewers and politicos, however, were not on Synge's mind, either when he wrote the *Playboy* or any of his work, since it is all of a piece. The key to Synge lies not in violations of taste, but rather in the massive solitude from which he viewed the world, and within which he saw man's proper and lamentable place. His most important term was "desolate." The word appears continually in his works, meaning not merely the absence of life, but the absence of life where life had once been strong. "Desolation" was caused by an establishment or hardened order, such as external nature itself. The more people resembled external nature in appearance or action, the less human, vital, they became, and the more submissive to death-in-life.

Yet there could be "splendour" in the submission if it were fought. Nora Burke goes off with the tramp so as not to resign herself to "a lonesome place." Maurya *(Riders)* gives in only when the sea has taken every man in her family. Deirdre gives in only when the legend to which she is bound prevails. Pegeen's tragedy is the prospect of a dead life with the pipsqueak Shawn. When Christie goes, she has not only lost "the only Playboy of the Western World," but the fight against custom.

Synge knew that this fight could be terribly funny, and could drive one to do strange things. In *The Well of the Saints* the Douls strive for their former blindness because they groped in the light. Nothing is as crazy as it first appears, and the comedy of the plays, often so hilarious, is a way of mocking and surviving an implacable universe. Man at his best *is* comedy standing in relief from desolation. And he is also part of the desolation with which he contends making both more beautiful. It ought to be added, however, that this universe of Synge's was not presided over. Synge believed in God, but also believed as he said in an early unpublished play, that He cares "as little for us as we care for the sorrows of an anthill." Perhaps the Dublin audiences perceived this as well. It would explain the longevity of their hatred of the man. (pp. 32-3)

Roger Rosenblatt, "J. M. Synge (Part Two)," in The New Republic *(reprinted by permission of* The New Republic; © *1975 The New Republic, Inc.), Vol. 173, No. 15, October 11, 1975, pp. 31-3.*

ADDITIONAL BIBLIOGRAPHY

Bourgeois, Maurice. *John Millington Synge and the Irish Theatre.* London: Constable & Co., 1913, 338 p.

Important study of the works of Synge. Bourgeois provides the reader with factual information on every aspect of the publication and performance of Synge's work, primary and secondary bibliographies, a geneology of his family, notes on first performances, and list of portraits of Synge.

Clark, David R., ed. *John Millington Synge: "Riders to the Sea."* Columbus, Ohio: Charles E. Merrill Publishing Co., 1970, 136 p.
> Collection of thirteen critical essays on *Riders to the Sea,* including studies by Denis Donoghue, Alan Price, Richard Ellmann, and Robin Skelton.

Davie, Donald A. "The Poetic Diction of John M. Synge." *The Dublin Magazine* n.s. 27, No. 1 (January-March 1952): 32-8.
> Comments on Synge's assertion in the preface to his *Poems and Translations* that eighteenth-century poetry is too restricted by the rules of poetic diction. Davie contends that in his poetry Synge is not "avoiding poetic diction altogether, but only substituting one sort of diction for another," that is by choosing common or ugly words in place of "the words of romantic glamour."

Fackler, Herbert V. "J. M. Synge's *Deirdre of the Sorrows:* Beauty Only." *Modern Drama* XI, No. 4 (February 1969): 404-09.
> Discussion of the characters of *Deirdre of the Sorrows* that examines their closeness to nature and their view of death as victory over old age. Fackler also examines Synge's distinctive treatment of dialect and the drama's similarity to classical Greek tragedy.

Flood, Jeanne. "The Pre-Aran Writings of J. M. Synge." *Éire* 5, No. 3 (Autumn 1970): 63-80.
> Examination of three early works of Synge, the "Autobiography," the "Vita Vecchia," and the "Étude Morbide," which were written before *The Aran Islands* and published for the first time in 1966. The critic contends that "these early works are essential to an understanding of Synge's aesthetic development."

Greene, David H. *"The Shadow of the Glen* and *The Widow of Ephesus." PMLA* LVII, No. 1, Part 1 (March 1947): 233-38.
> States that *In the Shadow of the Glen* is a combination of the realistic and the symbolic: Synge turns a sombre portrait of an unhappy marriage into a symbolic quest for freedom.

Greene, David H., and Stephens, Edward M. *J. M. Synge: 1871-1909.* New York: Macmillan Co., 1959, 321 p.
> Biography of Synge interspersed with criticism of his work. The authors include a discussion of the riots over *The Playboy of the Western World* and critical reception and reviews of his plays both from Dublin and abroad.

Grene, Nicholas. *Synge: A Critical Study of the Plays.* Totowa, N.J.: Rowman and Littlefield, 1975, 202 p.
> Detailed discussion of each play, viewing the prose work as source material.

Gutierrez, Donald. "Coming of Age in Mayo: Synge's *The Playboy of the Western World* as a Rite of Passage." *Hartford Studies in Literature* 6, No. 2 (1974); 159-66.
> Describes Christy's growth from boyhood to manhood as an archetypal "puberty rite of passage."

Harmon, Maurice, ed. *J. M. Synge Centenary Papers, 1971.* Dublin: Dolmen, 1972, 215 p.
> Eleven critical essays on Synge's work including discussion of the dramas, poetry, and prose works.

Johnston, Denis. *John Millington Synge.* New York, London: Columbia University Press, 1965, 48 p.
> Introductory overview of Synge's work.

Kain, Richard M. "The Image of Synge: New Light and Deeper Shadows." *The Sewanee Review* LXXXIV, No. 1 (January-March 1976): 174-85.
> Charges that Yeats's romantic image of Synge became generally accepted "with the result that criticism remained static for fifty years after his death."

Krutch, Joseph Wood. "Synge and the Irish Protest." In his *'Modernism' in Modern Drama: A Definition and an Estimate,* pp. 88-103. New York: Russell & Russell, 1962.
> Describes Synge's work as "antimodernist." Krutch also contrasts Synge's drama to that of Sean O'Casey.

Levitt, Paul M. "The Structural Craftsmanship of J. M. Synge's *Riders to the Sea." Éire* IV, No. 1 (Spring 1969): 53-61.
> Discussion of the compact structure and biblical imagery in *Riders to the Sea* that contribute to its "extraordinary intensity."

O'Casey, Sean. "John Millington Synge." In his *Blasts and Benedictions: Articles and Stories,* pp. 35-41. London, Melbourne, Toronto: Macmillan; New York: St. Martin's Press, 1967.
> Evaluation of Synge's dramas and discussion of their reception in Dublin.

Price, Alan. *Synge and Anglo-Irish Drama.* London: Methuen & Co., 1961, 236 p.
> Excellent introduction to Synge. In addition to discussing all of Synge's work in detail, Price includes much background material, such as the relationship between Synge and Yeats, and the disturbances in the Abbey Theatre.

Salmon, Eric. "J. M. Synge's *Playboy:* A Necessary Reassessment." *Modern Drama* XIII, No. 2 (September 1970): 111-28.
> Examines themes the critic thinks have been ignored or underrated in Synge criticism, such as the centrality of the theme of illusion versus reality in *The Playboy of the Western World.*

Stephens, James. "Reminiscenes of J. M. Synge." In *James, Seumas & Jacques: Unpublished Writings of James Stephens,* by James Stephens, edited by Lloyd Frankenberg, pp. 54-60. London, New York: Macmillan, 1964.
> Reprint of a 1928 BBC broadcast. Stephens discusses Synge's meticulous methods of composition and his love for nature.

Yeats, William Butler. "The Death of Synge, and Other Pages from an Old Diary." *The Dial* 84, No. 4 (April 1928): 271-88.
> Highly personal notes on Synge, which are frequently cited as having molded the world's view of Synge the man.

Wallace Thurman

(1902-1934)

(Also wrote under pseudonyms of Patrick Casey and Ethel Belle Mandrake) American novelist, critic, dramatist, editor, short story writer, and poet.

Thurman, one of the first effective black satirists, was a central figure in the Harlem Renaissance and one of its severest critics. Regarded as something of a maverick by his contemporaries, Thurman lampooned the prejudices and hypocrisies of blacks as well as whites and vigilantly examined the course of what was called the "new Negro movement." His work is noted for its controversial subject matter and for its vivid depiction of Harlem's "low life" (a motif first popularized by Carl Van Vechten in *Nigger Heaven*). Though his novels and dramas are frequently heavy-handed and superficial in their approach, they afford a rare, behind-the-scenes view of Harlem during the 1920s.

Thurman was born in Salt Lake City and educated at the University of Southern California. He first learned of the Harlem Renaissance while working as a columnist in Los Angeles. Inspired by the critical interest accorded New York's black artists, Thurman tried to generate a similar movement on the west coast. Failing this, he migrated to Harlem in 1925, at the height of the Renaissance. There he furthered his career, serving as editor for several influential black magazines and at Macaulay Publishing Company. In addition, Thurman co-founded two short-lived, esoteric journals, *Fire* and *Harlem*, devoted to publishing only the best of the new black literature.

Famous for his self-described "erotic, Bohemian" lifestyle and esteemed for his dedication to individual artistic excellence, Thurman was a favored and enthusiastic member of the Harlem literati. But his faith and zeal gave way to disillusionment and pessimism. The Renaissance, he argued, had not produced a single literary genius, a writer who could compare with Mann or Tolstoy. Black writers were not committed to art and its perfection, he charged; they had become too race conscious, self-indulgent, and pretentious. White critics had fostered this by patronizing Harlem's artists and by ignoring traditional critical standards when reviewing their works.

Thurman realized that his own writings, though they offer distinct and often compelling sketches of black life, fell short of the literary excellence he demanded. The largely autobiographical novel *Infants of the Spring* is Thurman's legacy to the Renaissance. The whole of Harlem's artistic coterie—the bohemian fringe, patronizing whites, and major writers, such as Alain Locke—is bitterly satirized. Critics find that the novel is more protest and criticism than fiction. They object to its excessively harsh tone, reproving Thurman for his lack of perspective and objectivity. The play *Harlem*, some reviewers maintain, is exploitive in that it overemphasizes the vice and squalor of ghetto life. Yet others view the work as an honest, albeit melodramatic, depiction of the problems of unemployment, racial bias, and overcrowded housing. Thurman's most thematically important novel, *The Blacker the Berry*, has been praised for the candor and irony with which it approaches the issues of intraracial prejudice and self-acceptance. But again Thurman was criticized for focusing on the sordid aspects of

black society. Readers have found that the novel sacrifices subtlety and development for sensationalism.

The Interne, Thurman's last novel, appeared two years before his death. A fictional exposé of the corrupt conditions in a metropolitan hospital, it signified the author's final break with the Renaissance. After its publication Thurman left for Hollywood and a brief screenwriting career. He returned to Harlem in 1934, aware of his tubercular condition and impending death.

There is little argument concerning Thurman's status as an author. Critics conclude that his creative achievement was slight, but they readily acknowledge his satiric ability and critical prowess. Thurman's reputation lies in the shadow of Langston Hughes, Jean Toomer, and other luminaries of the period. Nevertheless, his life and work furnish unique insight into the Harlem Renaissance.

PRINCIPAL WORKS

The Blacker the Berry (novel) 1929
Harlem [with William Jourdan Rapp] (drama) 1929
Infants of the Spring (novel) 1932

The Interne [with A. L. Furman]   (novel)   1932

R. DANA SKINNER (essay date 1929)

The new Negro play, **Harlem**, written by William Jourdan [Rapp] and Wallace Thurman, and subtitled "an episode of life in New York's Black Belt," has plenty of action, plenty of shooting, plenty of raucous passion and plenty of comedy of a distinctly low order. A few critics admitted that certain scenes needed toning down. . . . But none of them, so far as I know, raised a voice to protest against the particular way in which this melodrama exploits the worst features of the Negro and depends for its effects solely on the explosions of lust and sensuality. The "good" characters are hopelessly ineffectual, and all the rest are either worthless hypocrites, like the father who uses his home as a centre for debauched parties in order to pay the rent, or criminals of the worst type. Anyone given to prejudice or haphazard judgments would come away from this play with the impression that Harlem is a den of black filth where animal passions run riot and where the few Negroes with higher ideas or ideals are hopelessly snowed under by black flakes from a sodden sky. . . .

[Just] as producers seem to relish a Chinese or other exotic setting as a means of putting across material which would not be tolerated in domestic drama, so, in **Harlem**, the life of the lower classes of Negroes is treated as something exotic and therefore specially licensed. The party staged in Pa Williams's flat is nothing more than a deliberate display of animalism. Presumably it would be justified in print as "authentic atmosphere," but I do not see that this plea avoids in any way the fact that it is pure animal display, as damaging to the general good name of the Negro as it is unnecessary to the dramatic action of the play. . . .

The story of **Harlem** concerns itself with the rebellious spirit of Cordelia Williams, who involves herself promiscuously with various low characters, causing the death of two of them and the disgrace of her own home—such as it is. There is a redeeming hint that the cause of all this is the migration of the Williams family from a peaceful existence in the South to the hell hole of Harlem, but that is rather a slender thread on which to hang a moral. The chief desire of the authors seems to be to show crime and lust in as much realistic detail as the law permits—gambling, drunkenness, sordid dancing, shooting and the amours of Cordelia. Obviously this goes to make good theatre in the technical sense—plenteous action and tense situations. But it does not constitute either an honest portrayal of Negro character (in the sense of giving a proper balance) nor drama that is free from meretriciousness.

> R. Dana Skinner, "The Play: 'Harlem'," in Commonweal, *Vol. IX, No. 18, March 6, 1929, p. 514.*

THE NEW YORK TIMES (essay date 1929)

This novel of Harlem ["**The Blacker the Berry**"] and the problem of color distinctions within the black world derives its chief interest from the fact that Mr. Thurman is a negro. Better novels of negro life have been written before, and written, ironically enough, by white people. If one excludes the question of authorship, "**The Blacker the Berry**" stands out as a merely competent, somewhat amorphous story. For rhythm and pun-

gency, Claude McKay's "Home to Harlem"—the work of a West Indian negro—still remains at the crest.

There are no passages in "**The Blacker the Berry**" to indicate that Mr. Thurman is out to astound people. He makes no effort to display the swiftly acquired erudition of a [Carl] Van Vechten, but sticks to his main thesis. That thesis is the conflict a "coal-black nigger" is subjected to now that color prejudice has crossed the line into the black belts. . . .

Mr. Thurman takes [the main character, Emma Lou,] through three unhappy years of college in Los Angeles, where she was looked upon askance by the light-hued negroes of the Greek letter society. . . . He takes her to Harlem, where she shows a deplorable lack of will and a deplorable amount of self-commiseration. Sensitive beyond the point of other coal-blacks, she lets every reference to color scrape her nerves. . . .

[This] might have made a poignant story. As it is, Mr. Thurman writes prose in imitation of the white "genteel" tradition without ever making you certain that he is composing his novel from within the vantage point of Emma Lou's "genteel" brain. He gives the effect of objectivity where subjectivity is demanded, chiefly because he reports where he should be dramatizing the world as it appeared to Emma Lou.

> *"Latest Works of Fiction: 'The Blacker the Berry'," in* The New York Times *(© 1929 by The New York Times Company; reprinted by permission), March 17, 1929, p. 6.*

THEOPHILUS LEWIS (essay date 1929)

"**Harlem**," a spirited melodrama by William Jourdan Rapp and Wallace Thurman, introduces an innovation in the treatment of Negro character on the American stage, and if it turns out to be a box office success its influence on the trend of Negro drama will be of far greater significance than its intrinsic merit as a play. Before the production of "**Harlem**," all the so-called Negro plays, except "The Emperor Jones" and "Lulu Belle," show that their authors went to exceptional pains to discover unusual and quaint types for dramatic representation. Their quest has not been for authentic Negro character but for "colorful" types. It is true that only selected types are suitable for dramatic treatment; but they should be selected for their virility, not for their oddity. . . .

"**Harlem**," because it emphasizes "I will" character instead of the gypsy type of Negro, is a wholesome swing toward dramatic normalcy. Its characters are not abnormal people presented in an appealing light but everyday people exaggerated and pointed up for the purposes of melodrama. This is a sound orthodox theatrical practice, and if "**Harlem**" proves to be as profitable as it is entertaining other playwrights will be encouraged to adopt its methods with the result that Negro drama will be changed from an aberrant to a normal form. . . .

[The] character portrayed in "**Harlem**" is superior to the types pictured in any preceding Negro play. . . . What is of more importance to the Negro sociologist as well as the dramatist is the higher type of women presented in "**Harlem**." For example compare Cordelia with Bess, the most vividly portrayed female character in "Porgy." In Bess we have the woman who wants to be good but who is unable to follow her better impulses. . . . In Cordelia we have a purposeful woman who is determined to have her way regardless of the havoc that follows in her wake. She is not a victim of men; men are her victims. She is an immoral woman while Bess, strictly speaking, is unmoral.

Bess, to state the matter in concrete terms, is first cousin to a boar's bride while Cordelia, Lady Macbeth and Hedda Gabbler are sisters under the skin.

As a specimen of theatrical craftsmanship, aside from its portrayal of character, "Harlem" is a well made play which shows very few flaws of construction. The authors had to strain a bit to make the second act long enough but they met the problem in a way that does not result in any conspicuous sagging of suspense. The background and atmosphere are genuine and are so logically interwoven with the plot that only one character is a superfluous loose end.

> *Theophilus Lewis, "If This Be Puritanism," in Opportunity, Vol. VII, No. 4, April, 1929, p. 132.*

EUNICE HUNTON CARTER   (essay date 1929)

[With *Harlem* and *The Blacker the Berry*] Wallace Thurman, a young Negro, who has recently come out of the West, apparently has joined the ranks of the successful. And yet one wonders whether it is a success of artistic achievement or a success consummated because Mr. Thurman has become a devotee of the most fashionable of American literary cults, that dedicated to the exploitation of the vices of the Negro of the lowest stratum of society and to the mental debauching of Negroes in general. . . .

[Emmy Lou Morgan in *The Blacker the Berry* is] an incredibly stupid character. The moral that evidently is intended to adorn this tale is to the effect that young women who are black are doomed to a rather difficult existence should they aspire to anything but life in its most humdrum and sordid forms. But somehow it seems that were she as fair as a lily, a young woman, at once so dominated by the urge of sex and so stupid, would succeed in being exploited by the gentlemen of her acquaintance in one way or another. . . .

Mr. Thurman has painted a vivid picture of Alva, the good looking male, who works spasmodically, lives by his wits and when opportunity offers, on the bounty of women. One gets to know him very well before the tale is ended. His god is pleasure. His master is gin. His credo is Alva first, last and always. Under his gaiety he is vain, petty and unscrupulous. One expects nothing of him beyond the cavalier treatment which he accords Emmy Lou from beginning to end. And though the latter from her first glimpse of him pursues him and for several years lavishes herself upon him, one never acquires any conviction that she really loves him. . . .

With the rest of his characters the author has dealt variedly. In the portrayal of some of them he shows flashes of real genius. Others he handles clumsily and with too great detail for their importance in the story. He spends a great deal of time describing scenes and persons at the University of Southern California without giving any sense of reality to the picture. While the story of Emmy Lou's life there is as necessary to a complete understanding of her as is the description of her family and early home life, yet the background of her University life is as stilted and unreal as a poorly executed stage setting. It is only when the scenes are laid in Harlem that the author seems sure of himself and glides easily through his descriptions. And yet even there there is too much that is purely descriptive, not enough that is creative, too much that is hackneyed, not enough that is new. McKay has done it better. Thurman, like McKay, has seen much, but unlike McKay, he has not yet assimilated his experiences. He is yet lost and fumbling in the morass of them. He suffers a bit from both emotional and intellectual indigestion. Van Vechten's Harlem, though a different and less pleasant Harlem, is much more real. . . .

[The] story of Emmy Lou Morgan as the author presents it in *Blacker the Berry* is short story material strung out into novel length by undue emphasis on the affairs of unimportant characters and a great deal of tiresome repetition, by digressions into other possible short stories, such as that of the love affairs of Braxton, Alva'a roommate. (p. 162)

The more quickly the novelty of the Negro theme wears off and publishers and critics begin to exact from Negro writers that same high standard which they do from others, the more quickly may we expect something better from writers like Wallace Thurman who are capable of things infinitely better than they give. (p. 163)

> *Eunice Hunton Carter, "Our Book Shelf: 'The Blacker the Berry'," in Opportunity, Vol. VII, No. 5, May, 1929, pp. 162-63.*

W. E. BURGHARDT DuBOIS   (essay date 1929)

It is a little difficult to judge fairly Wallace Thurman's "The Blacker the Berry". Its theme [of intraracial prejudice] is one of the most moving and tragic of our day. . . .

[It] is the plight of a soul who suffers not alone from the color line, as we usually conceive it, but from the additional evil prejudice, which the dominant ideals of a white world create within the Negro world itself. (p. 249)

This is the theme, but excellent as is the thought and statement, the author does not rise to its full development. The experience of this black girl at the University is well done, but when she gets to Harlem she fades into the background and becomes a string upon which to hang an almost trite description of black Harlem.

The story of Emma Lou calls for genius to develop it. It needs deep psychological knowledge and pulsing sympathy. And above all, the author must believe in black folk, and in the beauty of black as a color of human skin. I may be wrong, but it does not seem to me that this is true of Wallace Thurman. He seems to me himself to deride blackness; he speaks of Emma's color as a "splotch" on the "pale purity" of her white fellow students and as mocking that purity "with her dark outlandish difference". He says, "It would be painted red—Negroes always bedeck themselves and their belongings in ridiculously unbecoming clothes and ornaments."

It seems to me that this inner self-despising of the very thing that he is defending, makes the author's defense less complete and less sincere, and keeps the story from developing as it should. Indeed, there seems to be no real development in Emma's character; her sex life never becomes nasty and commercial, and yet nothing in her seems to develop beyond sex.

Despite all this, the ending is not bad, and there is a gleam of something finer and deeper than the main part of the novel has furnished. One judges such a book, as I have said, with difficulty and perhaps with some prejudice because of the unpleasant work in the past to which the author has set his hand. Yet this book may be promise and pledge of something better, for it certainly frankly faces a problem which most colored people especially have shrunk from, and almost hated to face. (pp. 249-50)

W. E. Burghardt DuBois, "The Browsing Reader: 'The Blacker the Berry'," in The Crisis, Vol. 36, No. 7, July, 1929, pp. 249-50.

THE NEW YORK TIMES BOOK REVIEW (essay date 1932)

"Infants of the Spring" is a pretty inept book. It is clumsily written. Its dialogue, which ranges from elephantine witticisms to ponderous philosophizing, is often incredibly bad. Its characters, men and women who rotate giddily and senselessly through the mazes of Harlem's Bohemia, are ciphers. For all its earnestness and its obvious sincerity, the book is merely a tedious dramatization of various phases of the Negro problem, full of endless arguments endlessly prolonged.

These arguments occur chiefly in Niggeratti Manor—the name ironically given to their boarding house by a group of artists and writers who have banded together under one roof. . . . Unproductive artistically, frustrated and warped in one way or another by their race consciousness, these tormented Bohemians reel from one gin party to another in search of a workable solution which they never quite find. Only Raymond, the strongest and most intelligent of the lot, has any real prospect of ever achieving fulfillment.

This, then, is the general theme of the novel. It is not, to be sure, wholly without merit. Some of the discussions are challenging. Some of the scenes—such as that of the orgy at which blacks and whites mingle, and of the attempted "salon"—are shrewdly observed. On the whole, however, it lacks life and fails to awake in the reader the necessary emotional response. It is a more pretentious but less successful book than Mr. Thurman's earlier novel, **"The Blacker the Berry."**

"Harlem's Bohemia," in The New York Times Book Review (© 1932 by The New York Times Company; reprinted by permission), February 28, 1932, p. 22.

MARTHA GRUENING (essay date 1932)

There is no mistaking the grimness of [Thurman's] attitude toward artistic and literary Harlem, the Negro Renaissance, and those on both sides of the color line who have made it possible. [In *Infants of the Spring*] Mr. Thurman has written an ironic, mordant, and deeply honest book. I know of no other story of Negro life, unless it is Claude McKay's "Banjo," which reflects with such authenticity the clash of views among Colored People themselves as to the function and achievements of Negro artists in a white world. If one excepts George Schuyler, Thurman is the only Negro writer who has made any attempt to debunk the Negro Renaissance. There is need of such debunking. The Negro Renaissance has produced some first-rate work. It has also produced a great deal which is mediocre and pretentious and which has been almost ludicrously overpraised and ballyhooed. . . .

The narrative framework of the story is slight, a series of episodes in the life of a group of artists and dilettantes who, for a while, occupy the same house in Harlem and who all, in one way or another, find frustration. Their experiences are revealed to a large extent in the give and take of conversation and it is in these conversations that the virtue of the book largely resides. . . .

"Infants of the Spring" is not a great book but it is an important one. Like Mr. Thurman's earlier **"The Blacker the Berry,"** and unlike much of the output of contemporary Harlem, it is written with no weather eye on a possible white audience. There have been a few other books equally honest in their description of certain phases of Negro life—Langston Hughes's "Not Without Laughter" and Claude McKay's "Home to Harlem" come to mind in this connection—but no other Negro writer has so unflinchingly told the truth about color snobbery within the color line, the ins and outs of "passing" and other vagaries of prejudice. . . . [He] tells the world what all intelligent Negroes know but generally admit only among themselves. It is a bitter and extreme statement and, like all such statements, inevitably only a partial one, but its quota of truth is just that which Negro writers, under the stress of propaganda and counter-propaganda, have generally and quite understandably omitted from their picture. By its inclusion Thurman has taken an important step away from mere racial self-consciousness toward self-realization.

Martha Gruening, "Two Ways to Harlem," in The Saturday Review of Literature, Vol. VIII, No. 34, March 12, 1932, p. 585.*

STERLING BROWN (essay date 1937)

[Wallace Thurman is] the "devil's advocate" in his two novels. . . . [Thurman] puts his finger upon one of the sorest points of the Negro bourgeoisie [in *The Blacker the Berry*], its color snobbishness, "its blue vein circle," "aspiring to be whiter and whiter every generation." His descriptions of Harlem rent parties and the like are of Van Vechten's school, but the theme of his novel deserves attention. Unfortunately the writing is slipshod, and the steady decline of his central character is less tragic than depressing. His heroine is as morbidly sensitive about color as any tragic octoroon, and shows as little fight. . . .

[*The Infants of The Spring*] shows Thurman taking less seriously his coterie of Harlem artists. Young in years and achievement, they flatter themselves as "a lost generation," and like Van Vechten's Byron, seek escape in dissipation. (p. 146)

Debunking the Bohemian futility of the intellectuals, Thurman is just as severe on the bourgeois idealists and the various race-messiahs. *Infants of The Spring* is at times peevish, at times angry, crudely written, and not always well thought out. But like Thurman's first novel, it had something to say. (pp. 146-47)

Sterling Brown, "The Urban Scene," in his The Negro in American Fiction, The Associates in Negro Folk Education, 1937 (and reprinted by Kennikat Press, Inc., 1968), pp. 131-50.*

LANGSTON HUGHES (essay date 1940)

The summer of 1926, I lived in a rooming house on 137th Street, where Wallace Thurman and Harcourt Tynes also lived. Thurman was then managing editor of the *Messenger*, a Negro magazine that had a curious career. It began by being very radical, racial, and socialistic, just after the war. . . . Then it later became a kind of Negro society magazine and a plugger for Negro business, with photographs of prominent colored ladies and their nice homes in it. . . . I asked Thurman what kind of magazine the *Messenger* was, and he said it reflected the policy of whoever paid off best at the time.

Anyway, the *Messenger* bought my first short stories. They paid me ten dollars a story. Wallace Thurman wrote me that they were very bad stories, but better than any others they could find, so he published them.

Thurman had recently come from California to New York. He was a strangely brilliant black boy, who had read everything, and whose critical mind could find something wrong with everything he read. (pp. 233-34)

Thurman had read so many books because he could read eleven lines at a time. He would get from the library a great pile of volumes that would have taken me a year to read. But he would go through them in less than a week, and be able to discuss each one at great length with anybody. That was why, I suppose, he was later given a job as a reader at Macaulay's—the only Negro reader, so far as I know, to be employed by any of the larger publishing firms.

Later Thurman became a ghost writer for *True Story,* and other publications, writing under all sorts of fantastic names, like Ethel Belle Mandrake or Patrick Casey. He did Irish and Jewish and Catholic "true confessions." He collaborated with William Jordan Rapp on plays and novels. Later he ghosted books. In fact, this quite dark young Negro is said to have written *Men, Women, and Checks.*

Wallace Thurman wanted to be a great writer, but none of his own work ever made him happy. *The Blacker the Berry,* his first book, was an important novel on a subject little dwelt upon in Negro fiction—the plight of the very dark Negro woman, who encounters in some communities a double wall of color prejudice within and without the race. His play, *Harlem,* considerably distorted for box office purposes, was, nevertheless, a compelling study—and the only one in the theater—of the impact of Harlem on a Negro family fresh from the South. And his *Infants of the Spring,* a superb and bitter study of the bohemian fringe of Harlem's literary and artistic life, is a compelling book.

But none of these things pleased Wallace Thurman. He wanted to be a *very* great writer, like Gorki or Thomas Mann, and he felt that he was merely a journalistic writer. His critical mind, comparing his pages to the thousands of other pages he had read, by Proust, Melville, Tolstoy, Galsworthy, Dostoyevski, Henry James, Sainte-Beauve, Taine, Anatole France, found his own pages vastly wanting. So he contented himself by writing a great deal for money, laughing bitterly at his fabulously concocted "true stories," creating two bad motion pictures of the "Adults Only" type for Hollywood, drinking more and more gin, and then threatening to jump out of windows at people's parties and kill himself. (pp. 234-35)

About the future of Negro literature Thurman was very pessimistic. He thought the Negro vogue had made us all too conscious of ourselves, had flattered and spoiled us, and had provided too many easy opportunities for some of us to drink gin and more gin, on which he thought we would always be drunk. With his bitter sense of humor, he called the Harlem literati, the "niggerati." (p. 238)

> *Langston Hughes, "Harlem Literati," in his* The Big Sea: An Autobiography *(reprinted by permission of Hill & Wang, a division of Farrar, Straus & Giroux, Inc; copyright 1940 by Langston Hughes; copyright renewed © 1968 by Arna Bontemps and George Houston Bass), Knopf, 1940 (and reprinted by Hill and Wang, 1963), pp. 233-41.**

HUGH M. GLOSTER (essay date 1948)

[*The Blacker the Berry*], Wallace Thurman's first novel, is a study of intraracial color prejudice operating upon Emma Lou

Morgan, black daughter of a light-skinned mother whose family motto was "whiter and whiter every generation" until their "grandchildren could easily go over into the white race and become assimilated so that problems of race would plague them no more." (p. 168)

The thesis of *The Blacker the Berry* is that a black woman— unless unusually talented, attractive, or wealthy—faces insurmountable social barriers within her race in the United States. A dark skin handicaps Emma Lou, who is distinctly an ordinary character, in adjusting herself in a metropolitan university, acquiring desirable social contacts, obtaining white-collar employment, and holding the affection of men she would have liked to marry.

The Blacker the Berry imitates [Carl Van Vechten's] *Nigger Heaven* in its treatment of Harlem. The usual pictures are painted of cabaret life, speakeasies, rent parties, midnight vaudeville shows, and ballroom dances. Two "sugar daddies," Alva and Braxton, are among the principal characters. Emma Lou shows incontinent tendencies in a group largely obsessed with sex, drinking, dancing, and gambling. At a rent party she meets such Renascence satellites as Tony Crews (Langston Hughes?) and Cora Thurston (Zora Neale Hurston?), and hears biting explanations of color snobbishness within the Negro group by Truman Walter (the author?). (p. 169)

[In his second novel, *Infants of the Spring,*] Thurman castigates the younger debauchees among the Harlem intelligentsia and satirizes participants in the Negro Renascence. The focal point of the action is Niggeratti Manor, a spacious residence converted into studios for Negro artists and writers by Euphoria Blake, who believes that artistic achievement can bring her people greater freedom. In operation, however, the Manor becomes, to borrow Euphoria's words, "a miscegenated bawdy house" inhabited by comparatively unproductive artists and their mistresses, parasites, and white associates, most of whom are engrossed in drunkenness and venery. (p. 170)

Perhaps the most interesting sections of *Infants of the Spring* are those containing satirical comments on the Negro Renascence. Though the so-called "New Negro" was acclaimed and patronized throughout the United States as a phenomenon in art, Thurman observes that very little "was being done to substantiate the current fad, to make it the foundation for something truly epochal." Through [his protagonist Raymond Taylor] he protests "that the average Negro intellectual and artist has no goal, no standards, no elasticity, no pregnant germ plasm." (pp. 170-71)

To make his satire of the Negro Renascence more personal, Thurman assembles the leading writers—Sweetie Mae Carr (Zora Neale Hurston?), Tony Crews (Langston Hughes?), DeWitt Clinton (Countee Cullen?), . . . and others—at Niggeratti Manor upon the request of Dr. Parkes (Alain Locke?) to establish a salon and a concerted artistic movement. The purpose of the meeting is lost, however, in a heated debate concerning whether the "New Negro" should cultivate his African heritage, espouse full rights of citizenship, join the proletariat in an effort to overthrow capitalism, or strive for individual self-expression. Through Taylor, Thurman recommends the last-named course. . . . (p. 171)

In *Infants of the Spring* Thurman had an unusual opportunity to produce a competent satire upon the young libertines of upper Manhattan and the participants in the Negro Renascence. . . . [However,] Thurman showed himself unable to master this rich literary material. *Infants of the Spring* reveals an author morbid in outlook, diffuse in thinking, and destructive in purpose. . . . Every indication suggests that Thurman had not settled in his own mind the many issues that he introduces helter-skelter in the book. (pp. 171-72)

> *Hugh M. Gloster, "The Van Vechten Vogue," in his* Negro Voices in American Fiction *(copyright, 1948, by The University of North Carolina Press; copyright renewed © 1975 by Hugh Morris Gloster), University of North Carolina Press, 1948, pp. 157-73.**

ROBERT BONE (essay date 1965)

"The blacker the berry, the sweeter the juice"—so runs the Negro folk saying. In a mood of bitter irony, Thurman borrows this phrase for the title of his novel about a dark girl who is the victim of intraracial prejudice. From the moment that Emma Lou enters the world—a black child rejected by her own parents—her pigmentation is a constant source of pain. (p. 92)

Emma Lou's real tragedy is that she accepts the values of the system which torments her. Her use of bleaching agents, for example, betrays her unconscious belief in the magical power of a fair complexion. As the novel unfolds, she outgrows this crippling frame of reference and comes to recognize that her main enemy is within: "What she needed now was to accept her black skin as being real and unchangeable." This theme of self-acceptance is typically Renaissance: to be one's dark-skinned self and not a bleached-out imitation is the essence of emancipation. But Thurman's hard-won victory (the conflict he is acting out, through Emma Lou, is clear enough) does not prove to be decisive. His second novel shows him to be incapable of holding his feelings toward the race in stable equilibrium.

Infants of the Spring is a neurotic novel, in which Thurman broods introspectively on the "failure" of the Negro Renaissance. (pp. 92-3)

[The] canker of Bohemianism, in Thurman's eyes, . . . threatened to nip the New Negro Movement in the bud. The symbolic setting of his novel is Niggeratti Manor, where colored artists, writers, and musicians live in various stages of decadence and sterility. The central characters are Paul, a symbol of dissipated genius, and Ray, a young writer who struggles to free himself from an obsessive race-consciousness. Much of the "action" consists merely of dialogue, which serves to convey the author's impressions of the Negro Renaissance.

After a series of satirical sketches of leading Renaissance personalities, the novel draws to a depressing close. Paul commits suicide in such a manner that his masterpiece is destroyed. A drawing on the title page of the ruined manuscript pictures Niggeratti Manor with a foundation of crumbling stone. . . . The dream of the Negro Renaissance was, for Thurman, to end thus in disillusion and despair. The tone of the novel is too bitter, however, and Thurman's sense of personal failure too acute, to accept his critique of the Renaissance at face value.

It was appropriate enough that Thurman should seek to become the undertaker of the Negro Renaissance; at the time, he was busy digging his own grave with bad gin. His self-hatred, and the suicidal impulses which in engendered, were the central facts of his later years. No one who has read *The Blacker the Berry* will doubt that the source of this self-hatred was his dark complexion. The old struggle for self-acceptance, which Thurman had apparently won through Emma Lou, is reopened and

finally abandoned through the character of Ray. "Eventually," Ray remarks, "I'm going to renounce Harlem and all it stands for." This mood of renunciation pervades *Infants of the Spring*. In his wholesale indictment of the Renaissance generation, Thurman was simply working out his self-destructive impulses on the level of a literary movement. (pp. 93-4)

> *Robert Bone, "The Harlem School," in his* The Negro Novel in America *(© 1965 Yale University), revised edition, Yale University Press, 1965, pp. 65-94.**

DORIS E. ABRAMSON (essay date 1969)

[Wallace Thurman] had written novels and plays that, for all their commercial bias, were amazingly truthful pictures of Negroes and their environment. (p. 32)

Black Belt [the play on which Wallace Thurman and William Jourdan Rapp collaborated] was eventually entitled *Harlem: A Melodrama of Negro Life in Harlem*. . . . The story, the details, the dialogue of *Harlem* were all Wallace Thurman's. William Rapp shaped the play, and both men made penciled revisions. (p. 33)

[Wallace Thurman] moved in circles that thought of Harlem as Nigger Heaven. Carl Van Vechten was his friend and mentor. It was clear to Thurman that to be successful he should address himself to the white audience that was titillated by the subject matter of Van Vechten's novel. Another side of this Negro writer, however, wanted to tell [honestly] the story of a Southern family in Harlem. . . . (p. 34)

The first act of *Harlem* is set in a five-room railroad flat in Harlem. There are a mother, father, at least two sons, two daughters, and three boarders living in the five rooms. Times are bad. To pay the rent the family gives rent parties, a common phenomenon in Harlem during poor times. (p. 35)

The father's dialogue in *Harlem* is a reminder that prejudice is often the result of competition for social and economic security. . . .

There is no real action until the rent party, but from then on there is plenty of it—all melodramatic. (p. 36)

Most of the reviewers in the white press praised *Harlem* as a play representing Negroes honestly though melodramatically. In the Negro press critics were divided; some felt the sordid had been overemphasized, but others found the atmosphere and background genuine. (pp. 37-8)

Wallace Thurman was the first Negro playwright who deliberately set out to write for Broadway about Negro life as only a Negro can know it. How well he succeeded depends really on how much is expected of him at this point in his career, writing in what was a new medium for him. . . . (p. 40)

Wallace Thurman risked being damned by members of his own race for showing the sordid side of their lives.

What was new about *Harlem* was the author's attempt to let sensational melodrama grow out of the *real problems* of Harlem: overcrowded apartment living, prejudices among men of color, the numbers racket, transplanted and unemployed Southern Negroes. (p. 41)

Wallace Thurman was one of the New Negroes who, suffering the indignities of being a Negro in America, wanted to record Negro life honestly, but who usually settled for capitalizing on its exotic-erotic elements in order to succeed. Ironically, he probably never experienced either the financial or the social success of which he dreamed. As a Negro he met discrimination everywhere. He wrote to William Rapp that he had tried five times to buy center seats for **Harlem.** Each time he was put at the side with other Negroes. (p. 42)

One may guess that Wallace Thurman was "entirely the slave" of white values of the twenties, those that emphasized getting rich quick and living for the moment. But neither *post facto* psychosocial analysis of this complex young man nor a value judgment of his attitude toward his people is intended here. . . . Wallace Thurman exhausted himself trying to please the public while at the same time trying to write with a New Negro honesty. He was far from the last Negro playwright to be caught on the horns of the dilemma which had . . . limited the honesty with which the dramatist could portray his race and its problems and still retain an audience. (p. 43)

> *Doris E. Abramson, "The Twenties," in her* Negro Playwrights in the American Theatre 1925-1959 *(copyright © 1967, 1969 Columbia University Press; reprinted by permission of the publisher), Columbia University Press, 1969, pp. 22-43.**

ARTHUR P. DAVIS   (essay date 1974)

[In his first novel, *The Blacker the Berry*,] Thurman launched a frontal attack on a wrong which had been perpetrated on dark-skinned Negro women, not by whites but by Negroes themselves. In much of the folk literature and in a great deal of the street-corner-type joking among black men, the dark-skinned girl was the butt of a great deal of coarse, vulgar, and humiliating humor aimed at her color. (p. 109)

Thurman, writing in the twenties, was one of a very small number of Negro writers brave enough to make a dark-skinned girl a central figure in a novel. . . . Negro heroines, most black novelists felt, had to approximate white heroines. Black was not considered beautiful, except by the Garveyites, until about 1960. And one notes that even Thurman never insisted that his principal character was beautiful or that blackness was a desirable physical feature. In the color-conscious atmosphere of the 1920's this would have been unrealistic. (p. 110)

The trouble with *Blacker the Berry* is that it lacks subtlety in its delineation of Emma Lou and her problem. Surely, no Negro was ever as color-struck as Emma is depicted, no one quite so foolish. The whole matter of color prejudice within the group is far more intricate, complex, and tenuous than Thurman makes it out to be in this novel. He seems to write almost as though he were an outsider, seeing the situation only in terms of black and white, whereas, as every Negro knows, the presentation of this problem must be done in many shades of grey. Thurman knew this, but sacrificed nuance for sensationalism. His main thesis, of course, is valid. The dark-skinned Negro girl, until recently, has borne a double brunt of the cruelty inflicted by American color prejudice. Although he used a sledgehammer to do so, Thurman certainly drove home this point. Emma Lou, of course, is more than just a character. In her split allegiance and overemphasis on certain white values, she symbolizes the majority Negro attitude of the Renaissance years. (pp. 110-11)

Infants of the Spring is a biting commentary on the failure (in Thurman's opinion) of the New Negro Movement. The action of the novel takes place largely in a house for artists and writers called Niggerati Manor (*nigger* plus *literati*)—a house that functioned very much like Thurman's own residence. . . .

What little action there is in the novel serves as interlude to the continuing dialogue that goes on among the residents of Niggerati Manor, particularly the colloquy between Raymond (who probably represents the author) and Stephen. Both are honest and intelligent observers, and their appraisal of the Renaissance is not flattering. (p. 111)

Several critics have said that Thurman tried to tear down the beliefs held by other New Negro writers, yet offered nothing constructive in their stead. Others have said that he was hopelessly confused in his own mind on the issues raised by *Infants of the Spring.* It seems to the present writer, however, that Thurman is saying *inter alia* two very definite things. One is that there was too much phoniness in many aspects of the New Negro Movement, especially the "African survival" gambit; and, second, that the artist should resist with Emersonian firmness any capitulation to "badges and names, to large societies and dead institutions," that he must be first, last, and always a free and individual spirit. Thurman, in all probability, would be appalled by the present-day Black Esthetes who insist that all art become a weapon in the fight for liberation.

Infants of the Spring is more criticism than fiction. It therefore fails as a novel. It is, however, a valuable work for those who are interested in the New Negro years. It will serve as a good control for those who tend to find certain origins in the Renaissance that were not there. (p. 113)

> *Arthur P. Davis, "Wallace Thurman," in his* From the Dark Tower: Afro-American Writers 1900 to 1960 *(copyright © 1974 by Arthur P. Davis; reprinted by permission of Howard University Press), Howard University Press, 1974, pp. 108-13.*

AMRITJIT SINGH   (essay date 1976)

Many Harlem Renaissance writers who led active lives past the twenties talked and wrote about the period, but Wallace Thurman provided the only detailed contemporary account of the movement. *Infants of the Spring* was published in 1932 toward the end of the Renaissance, a little before Thurman's untimely death. . . . (p. 32)

Infants of the Spring presents mediocre artists lost in a web of frivolity and recalcitrance without purpose or privacy, unable to achieve anything worthwhile. (p. 33)

Although it is not necessary to fully agree with Thurman's cripplingly self-conscious judgment on individual writers, including himself, *Infants of the Spring* represents a coming-of-age of the Harlem Renaissance *literati.* It demonstrates the ability of the movement to evaluate and possibly modify its direction. Unfortunately, there was little opportunity for Thurman's criticisms to be absorbed. Two years earlier, the stock market had crashed, and white America's ability to sustain and enjoy the Negro fad had been severely hampered. (p. 36)

> *Amritjit Singh, "'When the Negro Was in Vogue': The Harlem Renaissance and Black America in the Twenties," in his* The Novels of the Harlem Renaissance: Twelve Black Writers 1923-1933 *(copyright © 1976 by The Pennsylvania State University), The Pennsylvania State University Press, University Park, 1976, pp. 1-40.**

FRANCIS X. BARRETT   (essay date 1979)

[Many passages in *Infants of the Spring*] read like excerpts from a high school literary magazine. There is no real in-depth development of the main characters. Too much time is spent describing the parties and the incidents surrounding them. Indeed, the overriding impression is of a continuous party. References to black-white tensions are so poorly developed they fail to catch reader's interest. Indeed, even the hints of both heterosexual and homosexual relationships cause a ho-hum reaction.

The value of the book lies not in its intrinsic worth as a novel, but in the description it provides of the literary scene for blacks in the 20's and specifically in Harlem. . . . The book was chosen for publication as the latest title in the Lost American Fiction series. This is an effort to bring back titles at least 25 years old which illuminated the literary or social history of its time. Considered within this framework, *Infants of the Spring* should be included.

There is an afterword which provides an interesting commentary on the social structure, Mr. Thurman, and the efforts of black artists prior to the depression. If this were placed before the novel, the reader might approach it more positively. Left to stand on its own, *Infants of the Spring* doesn't. (p. 123)

> *Francis X. Barrett, "Fiction: 'Infants of the Spring',"*
> in Best Sellers *(copyright © 1979 Helen Dwight Reid*
> *Educational Foundation), Vol. 39, No. 4, July, 1979,*
> *pp. 122-23.*

ADDITIONAL BIBLIOGRAPHY

Haslam, Gerald. "Wallace Thurman: A Western Renaissance Man." *Western American Literature* VI, No. 1 (Spring 1971): 53-9.
Synopses of novels with summaries of their critical reception.

Henderson, Mae Gwendolyn. "Portrait of Wallace Thurman." In *The Harlem Renaissance Remembered,* edited by Arna Bontemps, pp. 147-70. New York: Dodd, Mead & Co., 1972.
Overview of Thurman's life and work.

Huggins, Nathan Irving. "Art: The Ethnic Province." In his *Harlem Renaissance,* pp. 190-243. New York: Oxford University Press, 1971.
Brief discussion of Thurman's purpose in writing *Infants of the Spring,* which Huggins calls "one of the best written and most readable novels" of the Harlem Renaissance.

Perkins, Huel D. "Renaissance 'Renegade'?: Wallace Thurman." *Black World* XXV, No. 4 (February 1976): 29-35.
Examines Thurman's criticism of the Harlem Renaissance. Perkins maintains that the author was a significant and constructive critic of the movement and not, as some have charged, a disloyal and rebellious member.

West, Dorothy. "A Memoir of Wallace Thurman: Elephants Dance." *Black World* XX, No. 1 (November 1970): 77-85.
Biographical sketch that details Thurman's Harlem years, bringing into focus his early enthusiasm for the Renaissance and the reasons behind his later skepticism and disillusionment.

Young, James O. "Black Reality and Beyond." In his *Black Writers of the Thirties,* pp. 203-36. Baton Rouge: Louisiana State University Press, 1973.*
Comparative essay in which Young argues that Thurman's novels fail as satire when set against the efforts of Countee Cullen, Claude McKay, and other black writers of the period.

Mark Twain

1835-1910

(Pseudonym of Samuel Langhorne Clemens; also wrote under pseudonyms of Thomas Jefferson Snodgrass, Josh, Muggins, Grumbler, and Sieur Louis de Conte) American novelist, short story writer, journalist, essayist, memoirist, and autobiographer.

Twain, considered the father of modern American literature, broke with the genteel traditions of the nineteenth century by endowing his characters and narratives with the natural speech patterns of the common person, and by writing of subjects hitherto considered vulgar. At the peak of his powers Twain contributed America's first novel to international literature— *The Adventures of Huckleberry Finn.* Twain is often regarded as a humorist and children's writer, though very serious subjects are treated in such perennially popular books as *The Adventures of Tom Sawyer* and *A Connecticut Yankee in King Arthur's Court.*

Initially a clowning humorist, Twain matured into the role of the seemingly naive Wise Fool whose caustic sense of humor forced his audience to recognize humanity's foolishness and society's myriad injustices. Later, crushed by personal tragedy, economic hardship, and ill health, Twain turned on "the damned human race," portraying it as the totally corrupt plaything of a cruel God.

Clemens grew up in the Mississippi River town of Hannibal, Missouri, whose landmarks and people later served as models for the settings and characters of many of his novels, particularly *The Adventures of Tom Sawyer.* At age twelve Clemens quit school and became a journeyman printer; by the time he was seventeen his first sketches were appearing in the newspapers he typeset. During the late 1850s Clemens piloted steamboats on the Mississippi, work he enjoyed until the Civil War closed the river to commercial traffic. After brief service in the Confederate militia, Clemens traveled west, working as a silver miner and reporter in Nevada and California. During this period he began writing under the byline of Mark Twain, a navigational term indicating two fathoms of water. In 1865 he published his first important sketch, "Jim Smiley and His Jumping Frog," in a New York periodical. The story was widely popular and was reprinted two years later in Twain's first book, *The Celebrated Jumping Frog of Calaveras County, and Other Sketches,* a collection which appeared just as the author set out on a cruise to southern Europe and the Middle East. The letters Twain wrote to two American newspapers detailing the clash of New and Old World cultures proved immensely popular and two years later were collected as *The Innocents Abroad; or, The New Pilgrim's Progress.* The success of this book and Twain's growing fame as a comic lecturer established him as America's leading humorist, although some readers considered his frontier wit uncouth. Twain published several other collections of sketches in his life, the most notable being *Roughing It* and *A Tramp Abroad.*

In 1870 Twain married Olivia Langdon, and, after settling in Hartford, Connecticut, he published his first novel, *The Gilded Age,* written in collaboration with Charles Dudley Warner. The novel's title became a commonly used term to describe

America's post-Civil War industrial boom. The popular children's book *The Adventures of Tom Sawyer,* the first of four novels set in Twain's native Mississippi Valley, appeared in 1876. Immediately afterward he began work on *Tom Sawyer*'s sequel, a novel concerning young Tom's friend, Huckleberry Finn. This novel was written in three intermittent bursts of inspiration during the next eight years. Though critically misunderstood and banned from public libraries upon its appearance in 1885, *The Adventures of Huckleberry Finn* came to be recognized by later critics as a masterpiece. The meaning of the book, which details a young boy's encounters with the barbarities of civilization, has been debated for more than a century, most notably by Lionel Trilling, T. S. Eliot, and Henry Nash Smith. Twain never again wrote a book equal in power to *Huckleberry Finn.*

Several bad investments plunged Twain into bankruptcy during the next decade. In a few years he had paid off his tremendous debts, and in so doing had published several important books, including *The Tragedy of Pudd'nhead Wilson, and the Comedy Those Extraordinary Twins* and the biographical novel *Personal Recollections of Joan of Arc,* the latter published under the pseudonym Sieur Louis de Conte to test his readers' response, hence, his own skill. Out of the hardships of the

1890s and the tragedies of the 1900s, which included the death of his wife and two of his three daughters, Twain's natural sarcasm deepened into a fatalistic despair over the nature of God and humanity and his work became more introspective and polemical. His growing pessimism had been evident as early as the novel *A Connecticut Yankee in King Arthur's Court*, and dominated his finest short story, "The Man That Corrupted Hadleyburg," which presented evil as a necessary adjunct of good. In the years just before his death he worked on his "gospel" of determinism, *What Is Man?* and the fragments assembled posthumously as *The Mysterious Stranger*, which presents life as "a grotesque and foolish dream." The first of several editions of Twain's autobiography appeared in 1924.

Scholars recognize in Twain a man divided in outlook between comic and tragic perceptions of existence. Throughout his career Twain looked back yearningly to his happy youthful days on the Mississippi, finding in his memories spiritual rejuvenation and inspiration. At the same time he was deeply pessimistic about the future. His longing for an idealized past as a haven from an increasingly hostile present is evident in most of his major works of fiction. Critics have sought to explain this fatalistic division in outlook, and two major theories have risen from the debate. The first, expounded by Van Wyck Brooks in *The Ordeal of Mark Twain,* sees in Twain a genius beset from childhood with a deep guilt complex, stifled by America's crude frontier atmosphere, his writings edited into prettified respectability through the efforts of his wife and his friend William Dean Howells. The influence of Olivia Clemens and Howells has been greatly discounted by Bernard DeVoto, whose *Mark Twain's America* and *Mark Twain at Work* demonstrate the positive effects of frontier life on Twain's development and attribute his pessimism to the many personal tragedies he suffered during the last decades of his life.

As DeVoto and other critics have noted, Twain can be found on both sides of every issue: immortality, war, and the social problems of the South, to name but three. His importance to world literature lies not in the power of his ideas, but in the universality of his characters' dilemmas and his accessibility to readers of all ages.

PRINCIPAL WORKS

The Celebrated Jumping Frog of Calaveras County, and Other Sketches (sketches) 1867
The Innocents Abroad; or, The New Pilgrim's Progress (travel sketches) 1869
Roughing It (travel sketches) 1872
The Gilded Age [with Charles Dudley Warner] (novel) 1874
The Adventures of Tom Sawyer (novel) 1876
A Tramp Abroad (travel sketches) 1880
The Prince and the Pauper (novel) 1882
Life on the Mississippi (autobiographical novel) 1883
The Adventures of Huckleberry Finn (novel) 1884
A Connecticut Yankee in King Arthur's Court (novel) 1889
The Tragedy of Pudd'nhead Wilson, and the Comedy Those Extraordinary Twins (novel and sketch) 1894
Personal Recollections of Joan of Arc [as Sieur Louis de Conte] (novel) 1896
The Man That Corrupted Hadleyburg and Other Stories and Essays (short stories and essays) 1900
What Is Man? (essay) 1906

Extract from Captain Stormfield's Visit to Heaven (novella) 1909
The Mysterious Stranger (novel) 1916
Mark Twain's Autobiography (autobiography) 1924

CHARLES HENRY WEBB (essay date 1867)

"Mark Twain" is too well known to the public to require a formal introduction at my hands. By his story of the Frog, he scaled the heights of popularity at a single jump, and won for himself the *sobriquet* of The Wild Humorist of the Pacific Slope. He is also known to fame as The Moralist of the Main: and it is not unlikely that as such he will go down to posterity. It is in his secondary character, as humorist, however, rather than in his primal one of moralist, that I aim to present him in [*The Celebrated Jumping Frog of Calaveras County*]. And here a ready explanation will be found for the somewhat fragmentary character of many of these sketches; for it was necessary to snatch threads of humor wherever they could be found—very often detaching them from serious articles and moral essays with which they were woven and entangled. Originally written for newspaper publication, many of the articles referred to events of the day, the interest of which has now passed away, and contained local allusions which the general reader would fail to understand; in such cases excision became imperative. Further than this, remark or comment is unnecessary. Mark Twain never resorts to tricks of spelling nor rhetorical buffoonery for the purpose of provoking a laugh; the vein of his humor runs too rich and deep to make surface-gilding necessary. But there are few who can resist the quaint similes, keen satire, and hard good sense which form the staple of his writings.

> *Charles Henry Webb, "Advertisement," in* The Celebrated Jumping Frog of Calaveras County, and Other Sketches *by Mark Twain, C. H. Webb, 1867 (and reprinted in* Mark Twain: Selected Criticism, *edited by Arthur L. Scott, Southern Methodist University Press, 1955, p. 12).*

BRET HARTE (essay date 1870)

[Unless] he has already made "Mark Twain's" acquaintance through the press, [the reader] will not probably meet him until, belated in the rural districts, he takes from the parlor table of a country farm-house an illustrated Bible, Greeley's *American Conflict*, Mr. Parton's apocryphal *Biographies*, successively and listlessly, and so comes at last upon "Mark Twain's" [*The Innocents Abroad*] like a joyous revelation—an Indian spring in an alkaline literary desert. For the book has that intrinsic worth of bigness and durability which commends itself to the rural economist, who likes to get a material return for his money. It is about the size of *The Family Physician,* for which it will doubtless be often mistaken—with great advantage to the patient.

The entire six hundred and fifty pages are devoted to an account of the "steamship *Quaker City*'s excursion to Europe and the Holy Land," with a description of certain famous localities of which a great many six hundred and fifty pages have been, at various times, written by various tourists. Yet there is hardly a line of Mr. Clemens' account that is not readable; and none the less, certainly, from the fact that he pokes fun at other tourists, and that the reader becomes dimly conscious that Mr. Clemens' fellow-passengers would have probably estopped this gentle satirist from going with them could they have forecast his book. The very title—*The Innocents Abroad*—is a suggestive hint of the lawlessness and audacity in which the trip is treated. (p. 1)

And so, with an irreverence for his fellow pilgrims which was equaled only by his scorn for what they admired, this hilarious image-breaker started upon his mission. The situation was felicitous, the condition perfect for the indulgence of an humor that seems to have had very little moral or aesthetic limitation. The whole affair was a huge practical joke, of which not the least amusing feature was the fact that "Mark Twain" had embarked in it. Before the *Quaker City* reached Fayal, the first stopping-place, he had worked himself into a grotesque rage at everything and everybody. In this mock assumption of a righteous indignation lies, we think, the real power of the book, and the decided originality of Mr. Clemens' humor. It enables him to say his most deliberately funny things with all the haste and exaggeration of rage; it gives him an opportunity to invent such epithets as "animated outrage," and "spider-legged gorilla," and apply them, with no sense of personal responsibility on the part of reader or writer. And the rage is always ludicrously disproportionate to the cause. . . . [When] "Mark Twain" is not simulating indignation, he is *really* sentimental. He shows it in fine writing—in really admirable rhetoric, vigorous and picturesque—but too apt, at times, to suggest the lecturing attitude, or the reporter's flourish. Yet it is so much better than what one had any right to expect, and is such an agreeable relief to long passages of extravagant humor, that the reader is very apt to overlook the real fact, that it is often quite as extravagant.

Yet, with all his independence, "Mark Twain" seems to have followed his guide and guide-books with a simple, unconscious fidelity. He was quite content to see only that which everybody else sees, even if he was not content to see it with the same eyes. His record contains no new facts or features of the countries visited. (pp. 1-2)

Most of the criticism is just in spirit, although extravagant, and often too positive in style. But it should be remembered that the style itself is a professional exaggeration, and that the irascible pilgrim, "Mark Twain," is a very eccentric creation of Mr. Clemens'. (p. 2)

To subject Mr. Clemens to any of those delicate tests by which we are supposed to detect the true humorist, might not be either fair or convincing. He has caught, with great appreciation and skill, that ungathered humor and extravagance which belong to pioneer communities—which have been current in bar-rooms, on railways, and in stages—and which sometimes get crudely into literature, as "a fellow out West says." A good deal of this is that picturesque Western talk which we call "slang," in default of a better term for inchoate epigram. His characters speak naturally, and in their own tongue. If he has not that balance of pathos which we deem essential to complete humor, he has something very like it in that serious eloquence to which we have before alluded. Like all materialists, he is an honest hater of all cant—except, of course, the cant of materialism—which, it is presumed, is perfectly right and proper. (pp. 2-3)

> Bret Harte, "Review of 'The Innocents Abroad'" (originally published in *The Overland Monthly, Vol. IV, No. 1, January, 1870), in* Discussions of Mark Twain, *edited by Guy A. Cardwell, D. C. Heath and Company, 1963, pp. 1-3.*

THE BOSTON TRANSCRIPT   (essay date 1885)

The Concord (Mass.) Public Library committee has decided to exclude Mark Twain's latest book from the library. One member of the committee says that, while he does not wish to call it immoral, he thinks [*The Adventures of Huckleberry Finn*] contains but little humor, and that of a very coarse type. He regards it as the veriest trash. The librarian and the other members of the committee entertain similar views, characterizing it as rough, coarse and inelegant, dealing with a series of experiences not elevating, the whole book being more suited to the slums than to intelligent, respectable people.

> "'The Adventures of Huckleberry Finn'," in The Boston Transcript, *March 17, 1885 (and reprinted as part of "The Clash of Issues," in* Huckleberry Finn *by Mark Twain, edited by Barry A. Marks, D. C. Heath and Company, 1959).*

S. L. CLEMENS   (essay date 1889)

The little child is permitted to label its drawings "This is a cow—this is a horse," and so on. This protects the child. It saves it from the sorrow and wrong of hearing its cows and its horses criticized as kangaroos and workbenches. A man who is white-washing a fence is doing a useful thing, so also is the man who is adorning a rich man's house with costly frescoes; and all of us are sane enough to judge these performances by standards proper to each. Now, then, to be fair, an author ought to be allowed to put upon his book an explanatory line: "This is written for the Head"; "This is written for the Belly and the Members." And the critic ought to hold himself in honor bound to put away from him his ancient habit of judging all books by one standard, and thenceforth follow a fairer course. (pp. 525-26)

I have been misjudged, from the very first. I have never tried in even one single instance, to help cultivate the cultivated classes. I was not equipped for it, either by native gifts or training. And I never had any ambition in that direction, but always hunted for bigger game—the masses. I have seldom deliberately tried to instruct them, but have done my best to entertain them. To simply amuse them would have satisfied my dearest ambition at any time; for they could get instruction elsewhere, and I had two chances to help to the teacher's one: for amusement is a good preparation for study and a good healer of fatigue after it. My audience is dumb, it has no voice in print, and so I cannot know whether I have won its approbation or only got its censure. (pp. 527-28)

Yes, you see, I have always catered for the Belly and the Members, but have been served like the others—criticized from the culture-standard—to my sorrow and pain; because, honestly, I never cared what became of the cultured classes; they could go to the theatre and the opera; they had no use for me and the melodeon. (pp. 527-28)

> *S. L. Clemens, in an extract from his letter to Andrew Lang in 1889, in his* Mark Twain's Letters, Vol. II, *edited by Albert Bigelow Paine (copyright 1917 by The Mark Twain Company; reprinted by permission of Harper & Row, Publishers, Inc.), Harper, 1917, pp. 525-28.*

BRANDER MATTHEWS   (essay date 1898)

A humorist is often without honor in his own country. . . . [The] fact is indisputable that the humorist must pay the penalty of his humor, he must run the risk of being tolerated as a mere fun-maker, not to be taken seriously, and not worthy of critical consideration. This penalty has been paid by Mark Twain. In many of the discussions of American literature he has been dismist as tho he were only a competitor of his predecessors, Artemus Ward and John Phœnix, instead of being, what he is really, a writer who is to be classed—at whatever interval only time may decide—rather with Cervantes and Molière.

Like the heroines of the problem-plays of the modern theater, Mark Twain has had to live down his past. His earlier writing gave but little promise of the enduring qualities obvious enough in his later works. . . . The sketches in the '**Jumping Frog**' and the letters which made up the '**Innocents Abroad**' are "comic copy," as the phrase is in newspaper offices—comic copy not altogether unlike what John Phœnix had written and Artemus Ward. . . . (pp. 149-50)

No doubt, a few of his earlier sketches were inexpensive in their elements; made of materials worn threadbare by generations of earlier funny men, they were sometimes cut in the pattern of his predecessors. No doubt, some of the earliest of all were crude and highly colored, and may even be called forced, not to say violent. No doubt, also, they did not suggest the seriousness and the melancholy which always must underlie the deepest humor, as we find it in Cervantes and Molière, in Swift and in Lowell. But even a careless reader, skipping thru the book in idle amusement, ought to have been able to see in the '**Innocents Abroad**,' that the writer of this liveliest of books of travel was no mere merry-andrew, grinning thru a horse-collar to make sport for the groundlings; but a sincere observer of life, seeing thru his own eyes and setting down what he saw with abundant humor, of course, but also with profound respect for the eternal verities. (pp. 151-52)

'**A Tramp Abroad**' is a better book than the '**Innocents Abroad**'; it is quite as laughter-provoking, and its manner is far more restrained. Mark Twain was then master of his method, sure of himself, secure of his popularity; and he could do his best and spare no pains to be certain that it was his best. Perhaps there is a slight falling off in '**Following the Equator**'; a trace of fatigue, of weariness, of disenchantment. But the last book of travels has passages as broadly humorous as any of the first; and it proves the author's possession of a pithy shrewdness not to be suspected from a perusal of its earliest predecessor. The first book was the work of a young fellow rejoicing in his own fun and resolved to make his readers laugh with him or at him; the latest book is the work of an older man, who has found that life is not all laughter, but whose eye is as clear as ever and whose tongue is as plain-spoken.

These three books of travel are like all other books of travel in that they relate in the first person what the author went forth to see. Autobiographic also are '**Roughing It**' and '**Life on the Mississippi**,' and they have always seemed to me better books than the more widely circulated travels. They are better because they are the result of a more intimate knowledge of the material dealt with. . . . There is in both these books a fidelity to the inner truth, a certainty of touch, a sweep of vision, not to be found in the three books of travels. For my own part I have long thought that Mark Twain could securely rest his right to survive as an author on those opening chapters in '**Life on the Mississippi**' in which he makes clear the difficulties, the seeming impossibilities, that fronted those who wisht to learn the river. These chapters are bold and brilliant; and they picture for us forever a period and a set of conditions, singularly interesting and splendidly varied, that otherwise would have had to forego all adequate record.

It is highly probable that when an author reveals the power of evoking views of places and of calling up portraits of people such as Mark Twain showed in '**Life on the Mississippi**,' and when he has the masculine grasp of reality Mark Twain made evident in '**Roughing It**,' he must needs sooner or later turn from mere fact to avowed fiction and become a story-teller. The long stories which Mark Twain has written fall into two divisions,—first, those of which the scene is laid in the present, in reality, and mostly in the Mississippi Valley, and second, those of which the scene is laid in the past, in fantasy mostly, and in Europe. (pp. 152-55)

In writing [the] tales of the past Mark Twain was making up stories in his head; personally I prefer the tales of his in which he has his foot firm on reality. The '**Prince and the Pauper**' has the essence of boyhood in it; it has variety and vigor; it has abundant humor and plentiful pathos; and yet I for one would give the whole of it for the single chapter in which Tom Sawyer lets the contract for white-washing his aunt's fence. (p. 155)

["**A Connecticut Yankee in King Arthur's Court**"] is a humorous romance overflowing with stalwart fun; and it is not irreverent but iconoclastic, in that it breaks not a few disestablished idols. It is intensely American and intensely nineteenth century and intensely democratic—in the best sense of that abused adjective. The British critics were greatly displeased with the book. . . .

But no critic, British or American, has ventured to discover any irreverence in '**Joan of Arc**,' wherein indeed the tone is almost devout and the humor almost too much subdued. Perhaps it is my own distrust of the so-called historical novel, my own disbelief that it can ever be anything but an inferior form of art, which makes me care less for this worthy effort to honor a noble figure. And elevated and dignified as is the '**Joan of Arc**,' I do not think that it shows us Mark Twain at his best; altho it has many a passage that only he could have written, it is perhaps the least characteristic of his works. Yet it may well be that the certain measure of success he has achieved in handling a subject so lofty and so serious, helped to open the eyes of the public to see the solid merits of his other stories, in which his humor has fuller play and in which his natural gifts are more abundantly displayed.

Of these other stories three are "real novels," to use Mr. Howells's phrase; they are novels as real as any in any literature. '**Tom Sawyer**' and '**Huckleberry Finn**' and '**Pudd'nhead Wilson**' are invaluable contributions to American literature—for American literature is nothing if it is not a true picture of American life and if it does not help us to understand ourselves. '**Huckleberry Finn**' is a very amusing volume, and a generation has read its pages and laughed over it immoderately; but it is very much more than a funny book; it is a marvelously accurate portrayal of a whole civilization. Mr. Ormsby, in an essay which accompanies his translation of 'Don Quixote,' has pointed out that for a full century after its publication that greatest of novels was enjoyed chiefly as a tale of humorous misadventure, and that three generations had laughed over it before anybody suspected that it was more than a mere funny book. It is perhaps rather with the picaresque romances of Spain that '**Huckleberry Finn**' is to be compared than with the masterpiece of Cervantes; but I do not think that it will be a century or that it will take three generations before we Americans generally discover how great a book 'Huckleberry Finn' really is, how keen its vision of character, how close its observation of life, how sound its philosophy, and how it records for us once and for all certain phases of southwestern society which it is most important for us to perceive and to understand. (pp. 156-58)

'Huckleberry Finn,' in its art, for one thing, and also in its broader range, is superior to 'Tom Sawyer' and to 'Pudd'nhead Wilson,' fine as both these are in their several ways. In no book in our language, to my mind, has the boy, simply as a boy, been better realized than in 'Tom Sawyer.' In some respects 'Pudd'nhead Wilson' is the most dramatic of Mark Twain's longer stories, and also the most ingenious; like 'Tom Sawyer' and 'Huckleberry Finn,' it has the full flavor of the Mississippi River, on which its author spent his own boyhood, and from contact with the soil of which he has always risen reinvigorated.

It is by these three stories, and especially by 'Huckleberry Finn,' that Mark Twain is likely to live longest. Nowhere else is the life of the Mississippi Valley so truthfully recorded. Nowhere else can we find a gallery of southwestern characters as varied and as veracious as those Huck Finn met in his wanderings. The histories of literature all praise the 'Gil Blas' of Le Sage for its amusing adventures, its natural characters, its pleasant humor, and its insight into human frailty; and the praise is deserved. But in every one of these qualities 'Huckleberry Finn' is superior to 'Gil Blas.' Le Sage set the model of the picaresque novel, and Mark Twain followed his example; but the American book is richer than the French—deeper, finer, stronger. It would be hard to find in any language better specimens of pure narrative, better examples of the power of telling a story and of calling up action so that the reader cannot help but see it, than Mark Twain's account of the Shepardson-Grangerford feud, and his description of the shooting of Boggs by Sherburn and of the foiled attempt to lynch Sherburn afterward.

These scenes, fine as they are, vivid, powerful, and most artistic in their restraint, can be matched in the two other books. In 'Tom Sawyer' they can be paralleled by the chapter in which the boy and the girl are lost in the cave, and Tom, seeing a gleam of light in the distance, discovers that it is a candle carried by Indian Joe, the one enemy he has in the world. In 'Pudd'nhead Wilson' the great passages of 'Huckleberry Finn' are rivaled by that most pathetic account of the weak son willing to sell his own mother as a slave "down the river." Altho no one of the books is sustained thruout on this high level, and altho, in truth, there are in each of them passages here and there that we could wish away (because they are not worthy of the association in which we find them), I have no hesitation in expressing here my own conviction that the man who has given us four scenes like these is to be compared with the masters of literature; and that he can abide the comparison with equanimity. (pp. 158-60)

It would be doing Mark Twain a disservice to compare him to Molière, the greatest comic dramatist of all time; and yet there is more than one point of similarity. . . . [Like Molière,] Mark Twain has kept solid hold of the material world; his doctrine is not of the earth earthy, but it is never sublimated into sentimentality. He sympathizes with the spiritual side of humanity, while never ignoring the sensual. Like Molière, Mark Twain takes his stand on common-sense and thinks scorn of affectation of every sort. He understands sinners and strugglers and weaklings; and he is not harsh with them, reserving his scorching hatred for hypocrites and pretenders and frauds.

At how long an interval Mark Twain shall be rated after Molière and Cervantes it is for the future to declare. All that we can see clearly now is that it is with them that he is to be classed,—with Molière and Cervantes, with Chaucer and Fielding, humorists all of them, and all of them manly men. (pp. 165-66)

Brander Matthews "Introduction" (1898), in The Innocents Abroad; or, The New Pilgrim's Progress, Vol. I by Mark Twain, American Publishing Company, 1899 (and reprinted in his Inquiries and Opinions, Charles Scribner's Sons, 1907, pp. 139-66).

W. D. HOWELLS (essay date 1901)

So far as I know, Mr. Clemens is the first writer to use in extended writing the fashion we all use in thinking, and to set down the thing that comes into his mind without fear or favor of the thing that went before or the thing that may be about to follow. . . . In other words, Mr. Clemens uses in work on the larger scale the method of the elder essayists, and you know no more where you are going to bring up in *The Innocents Abroad* or *Following the Equator* than in an essay of Montaigne. The end you arrive at is the end of the book, and you reach it amused but edified, and sorry for nothing but to be there. You have noted the author's thoughts, but not his order of thinking; he has not attempted to trace the threads of association between the things that have followed one another; his reason, not his logic, has convinced you, or, rather, it has persuaded you, for you have not been brought under conviction. . . . [What] finally remains with the reader, after all the joking and laughing, is not merely the feeling of having had a mighty good time, but the conviction that he has got the worth of his money. He has not gone through the six hundred pages of *The Innocents Abroad,* or *Following the Equator,* without having learned more of the world as the writer saw it than any but the rarest traveller is able to show for his travel; and possibly, with his average practical American public, which was his first tribunal, and must always be his court of final appeal, Mark Twain justified himself for being so delightful by being so instructive. If this bold notion is admissible, it seems the moment to say that no writer ever imparted information more inoffensively.

But his great charm is his absolute freedom in a region where most of us are fettered and shackled by immemorial convention. He saunters out into the trim world of letters, and lounges across its neatly kept paths, and walks about on the grass at will, in spite of all the signs that have been put up from the beginning of literature, warning people of dangers and penalties for the slightest trespass.

One of the characteristics I observe in him is his single-minded use of words, which he employs . . . to express the plain, straight meaning their common acceptance has given them with no regard to their structural significance or their philological implications. He writes English as if it were a primitive and not a derivative language, without Gothic or Latin or Greek behind it, or German and French beside it. The result is the English in which the most vital works of English literature are cast, rather than the English of Milton and Thackeray and Mr. Henry James. I do not say that the English of the authors last named is less vital, but only that it is not the most vital. It is scholarly and conscious; it knows who its grandfather was; it has the refinement and subtlety of an old patriciate. You will not have with it the widest suggestion, the largest human feeling, or perhaps the loftiest reach of imagination, but you will have the keen joy that exquisite artistry in words can alone impart, and that you will not have in Mark Twain. What you will have in him is a style which is as personal, as biographical as the style of any one who has written, and expresses a civilization whose courage of the chances, the preferences, the duties, is not the measure of its essential modesty. It has a thing to say, and it says it in the word that may be the first or second or third choice, but will not be the instrument of the most fastidious ear, the most delicate and exacting sense, though it will be the word that surely and strongly conveys intention from the author's mind to the reader's. It is the Abraham Lincolnian word, not the Charles Sumnerian; it is American, Western.

Now that Mark Twain has become a fame so worldwide, we should be in some danger of forgetting, but for his help, how entirely American he is, and we have already forgotten, perhaps, how truly Western he is, though his work, from first to last, is always reminding us of the fact. But here I should like to distinguish. It is not alone in its generous humor, with more honest laughter in it than humor ever had in the world till now, that his work is so Western. Any one who has really known the West (and really to know it one must have lived it) is aware of the profoundly serious, the almost tragical strain which is the fundamental tone in the movement of such music as it has. Up to a certain point, in the presence of the mystery which we call life, it trusts and hopes and laughs; beyond that it doubts and fears, but it does not cry. It is more likely to laugh again, and in the work of Mark Twain there is little of the pathos which is supposed to be the ally of humor, little suffusion of apt tears from the smiling eyes. It is too sincere for that sort of play; and if after the doubting and the fearing it laughs again, it is with a suggestion of that resentment which youth feels when the disillusion from its trust and hope comes, and which is the grim second-mind of the West in the presence of the mystery. . . . Such, or somewhat like this, was the genesis and evolution of Mark Twain.

Missouri was Western, but it was also Southern, not only in the institution of slavery, to the custom and acceptance of which Mark Twain was born and bred without any applied doubt of its divinity, but in the peculiar social civilization of the older South from which his native State was settled. . . . No Northerner could have come so close to the heart of a Kentucky feud, and revealed it so perfectly, with the whimsicality playing through its carnage, or could have so brought us into the presence of the sardonic comi-tragedy of the squalid little river town where the store-keeping magnate shoots down his drunken tormentor in the arms of the drunkard's daughter, and then cows with bitter mockery the mob that comes to lynch him. The strict religiosity compatible in the Southwest with savage precepts of conduct is something that could make itself known in its amusing contrast only to the native Southwesterner, and the revolt against it is as constant in Mark Twain as the enmity to New England orthodoxy is in Doctor Holmes. But he does not take it with such serious resentment as Doctor Holmes is apt to take his inherited Puritanism, and it may be therefore that he is able to do it more perfect justice, and impart it more absolutely. At any rate, there are no more vital passages in his fiction than those which embody character as it is affected for good as well as evil by the severity of the local Sunday-schooling and church-going. (pp. 166-72)

We owe to *The Gilded Age* a type in Colonel Mulberry Sellers which is as likely to endure as any fictitious character of our time. It embodies the sort of Americanism which survived through the Civil War, and characterized in its boundlessly credulous, fearlessly adventurous, unconsciously burlesque excess the period of political and economic expansion which followed the war. Colonel Sellers was, in some rough sort, the American of that day, which already seems so remote, and is best imaginable through him. Yet the story itself was of the fortuitous structure of what may be called the autobiographical books, such as *The Innocents Abroad* and *Roughing It.* Its desultory and accidental character was heightened by the co-operation of Mr. Clemens's fellow-humorist, Charles Dudley Warner, and such coherence as it had was weakened by the diverse qualities of their minds and their irreconcilable ideals in literature. These never combined to a sole effect or to any variety of effects that left the reader very clear what the story was all about; and yet from the cloudy solution was precipitated at least one character which, as I have said, seems of as lasting substance and lasting significance as any which the American imagination has evolved from the American environment.

If Colonel Sellers is Mr. Clemens's supreme invention, as it seems to me, I think that his *Connecticut Yankee* is his highest achievement in the way of a greatly imagined and symmetrically developed romance. Of all the fanciful schemes in fiction, it pleases me most, and I give myself with absolute delight to its notion of a keen East Hartford Yankee finding himself, by a retroactionary spell, at the court of King Arthur of Britain, and becoming part of the sixth century with all the customs and ideas of the nineteenth in him and about him. (pp. 173-74)

[*Connecticut Yankee*] is a great fancy, transcending in aesthetic beauty the invention in *The Prince and the Pauper,* with all the delightful and affecting implications of that charming fable, and excelling the heartrending story [*Personal Recollections of Joan of Arc*] in which Joan of Arc lives and prophesies and triumphs and suffers. She is, indeed, realized to the modern sense as few figures of the past have been realized in fiction; and is none the less of her time and of all time because her supposititious historian is so recurrently of ours. After Sellers, and Huck Finn, and Tom Sawyer, and the Connecticut Yankee, she is the author's finest creation; and if he had succeeded in portraying no other woman-nature, he would have approved himself its fit interpreter in her. I do not think he succeeds so often with that nature as with the boy-nature or the man-nature, apparently because it does not interest him so much. He will not trouble himself to make women talk like women at all times; oftentimes they talk too much like him, though the simple, homely sort express themselves after their kind; and Mark Twain does not always write men's dialogue so well as he might. He is apt to burlesque the lighter colloquiality, and it is only in the more serious and most tragical junctures that his people utter themselves with veracious simplicity and dignity. That great, burly fancy of his is always tempting him to the exaggeration which is the condition of so much of his personal humor, but which when it invades the drama spoils the illusion. The illusion renews itself in the great moments, but I wish it could be kept intact in the small, and I blame him that he does not rule his fancy better. His imagination is always dramatic in its conceptions, but not always in its expressions; the talk of his people is often inadequate caricature in the ordinary exigencies, and his art contents itself with makeshift in the minor action. Even in *Huck Finn,* so admirably proportioned and honestly studied, you find a piece of lawless extravagance hurled in, like the episode of the two strolling actors in the flatboat; their broad burlesque is redeemed by their final tragedy—a prodigiously real and moving passage— but the friend of the book cannot help wishing the burlesque was not there. One laughs, and then despises one's self for laughing, and this is not what Mark Twain often makes you do. There are things in him that shock, and more things that we think shocking, but this may not be so much because of their nature as because of our want of naturalness; they wound our conventions rather than our convictions. (pp. 174-76)

Mark Twain was born to the common necessity of looking out for himself, and, while making himself practically of another order of things, he felt whatever was fine in the old and could regard whatever was ugly and absurd more tolerantly, more humorously than those who bequeathed him their enmity to it. Fortunately for him, and for us who were to enjoy his humor, he came to his intellectual consciousness in a world so large and free and safe that he could be fair to any wrong while seeing the right so unfailingly; and nothing is finer in him than his gentleness with the error which is simply passive and negative. He gets fun out of it, of course, but he deals almost tenderly with it, and hoards his violence for the superstitions and traditions which are arrogant and active. His pictures of that old river-town, Southwestern life, with its faded and tattered aristocratic ideals and its squalid democratic realities, are pathetic, while they are so unsparingly true and so inapologetically and unaffectedly faithful. (p. 177)

He is deeply and essentially romantic in his literary conceptions, but when it comes to working them out he is helplessly literal and real; he is the impassioned lover, the helpless slave of the concrete. For this reason, for his wish, his necessity, first to ascertain his facts, his logic is as irresistible as his laugh.

All life seems, when he began to find it out, to have the look of a vast joke, whether the joke was on him or on his fellow-beings, or if it may be expressed without irreverence, on their common creator. But it was never wholly a joke, and it was not long before his literature began to own its pathos. The sense of this is not very apparent in *The Innocents Abroad,* but in *Roughing It* we began to be distinctly aware of it, and in the successive books it is constantly imminent, not as a clutch at the heartstrings, but as a demand of common justice, common sense, the feeling of proportion. It is not sympathy with the under dog merely as under dog that moves Mark Twain; for the under dog is sometimes rightfully under. But the probability is that it is wrongfully under, and has a claim to your inquiry into the case which you cannot ignore without atrocity. Mark Twain never ignores it. . . . He always gives his help, even when he seems to leave the pity to others, and it may be safely said that no writer has dealt with so many phases of life with more unfailing justice. . . . His indignation relieves itself as often as not in a laugh; injustice is the most ridiculous thing in the world, after all, and indignation with it feels its own absurdity. (pp. 179-180)

[The] earliest form of Mark Twain's work is characteristic of the greater part of it. The method used in *The Innocents Abroad* and in *Roughing It* is the method used in *Life on the Mississippi,* in *A Tramp Abroad,* and in *Following the Equator,* which constitute in bulk a good half of all his writings, as they express his dominant aesthetics. If he had written the fictions alone, we should have had to recognize a rare inventive talent, a great imagination and dramatic force; but I think it must be allowed that the personal books named overshadow the fictions. They have the qualities that give character to the fictions, and they have advantages that the fictions have not and that no fiction can have. In them, under cover of his pseudonym, we come directly into the presence of the author, which is what the reader

is always longing and seeking to do; but unless the novelist is a conscienceless and tasteless recreant to the terms of his art, he cannot admit the reader to his intimacy. The personal books of Mark Twain have not only the charm of the essay's inconsequent and desultory method, in which invention, fact, reflection, and philosophy wander after one another in any following that happens, but they are of an immediate and most informal hospitality which admits you at once to the author's confidence, and makes you frankly welcome not only to his thought but to his way of thinking. (pp. 180-81)

In the case of the fictions, he conceives that his first affair is to tell a story, and a story when you are once launched upon it does not admit of deviation without some hurt to itself. In Mark Twain's novels, whether they are for boys or for men, the episodes are only those that illustrate the main narrative or relate to it, though he might have allowed himself somewhat larger latitude in the old-fashioned tradition which he has oftenest observed in them. When it comes to the critical writings, which again are personal, and which, whether they are criticisms of literature or of life, are always so striking, he is quite relentlessly logical and coherent. Here there is no lounging or sauntering, with entertaining or edifying digressions. The object is in view from the first, and the reasoning is straightforwardly to it throughout. . . . The facts are first ascertained with a conscience uncommon in critical writing of any kind, and then they are handled with vigor and precision till the polemic is over. It does not so much matter whether you agree with the critic or not; what you have to own is that here is a man of strong convictions, clear ideas, and ardent sentiments, based mainly upon common sense of extraordinary depth and breadth.

In fact, what finally appeals to you in Mark Twain, and what may hereafter be his peril with his readers, is his common sense. (pp. 181-82)

But it would be rather awful if the general recognition of his prophetic function should implicate the renunciation of the humor that has endeared him to mankind. . . . What we all should wish to do is to keep Mark Twain what he has always been: a comic force unique in the power of charming us out of our cares and troubles, united with as potent an ethic sense of the duties, public and private, which no man denies in himself without being false to other men. I think we may hope for the best he can do to help us deserve our self-respect, without forming Mark Twain societies to read philanthropic meanings into his jokes, or studying the Jumping Frog as the allegory of an imperializing republic. I trust the time may be far distant when the Meditation at the Tomb of Adam shall be memorized and declaimed by ingenuous youth as a mystical appeal for human solidarity. (p. 185)

W. D. Howells, ''Mark Twain: An Inquiry'' (originally published in The North American Review, *Vol. CLXXII, No. 531, February, 1901), in his* My Mark Twain: Reminiscences and Criticisms *(copyright © 1910 by Harper & Brothers; reprinted by permission of Harper & Row, Publishers, Inc.), Harper, 1910, pp. 165-85.*

ARCHIBALD HENDERSON   (essay date 1909)

If one would lay his finger upon the secret of Mark Twain's world-wide popularity as a humorist, he must find that secret primarily in the universality and humanity of his humor. Mark Twain is a master in the art of broad contrast; incongruity lurks on the surface of his humor; and there is about it a staggering and cyclopean surprise. But these are mere surface qualities, more or less common, though at lower power, to all forms of humor. Nor is Mark Twain's international reputation as a humorist to be attributed to any tricks of style, to any breadth of knowledge, or even to any depth of intellectuality. His hold upon the world is due to qualities not of the head, but of the heart. I once heard Mr. Clemens say that humor is the key to the hearts of men, for it springs from the heart; and worthy of record is his dictum that there is far more of feeling than of thought in genuine humor.

Mark Twain has a remarkable feeling for words and their uses; and the merit of his style is its admirable adaptation to the theme. And though Mr. Henry James may have said that one must be a very rudimentary person to enjoy Mark Twain, there is unimpeachable virtue in a rudimentary style in treatment of rudimentary—or, as I should prefer to phrase it, fundamental— things. Mark Twain has always written with utter individuality, untrammelled by the limitations of any particular sect of art. Style bears translation ill; in fact, translation is not infrequently impossible. But, as Mr. Clemens once pointed out to me, *humor has nothing to do with style*. Mark Twain's humor has international range, since, constructed out of a deep comprehension of human nature and a profound sympathy for human relationships and human failings, it successfully surmounts the difficulties of translation into alien tongues. . . .

Lafcadio Hearn best succeeded in interpreting poetry to his Japanese students by freeing it from all artificial and local restraints, and using as examples the simplest lyrics which go straight to the heart and soul of man. . . . In the same way Mark Twain as humorist has sought the highest common factor of all nations. "My secret, if there is any secret," Mr. Clemens said to me, "is to create humor independent of local conditions. Though studying humanity as exhibited in the people and localities I best knew and understood, I have sought to winnow out the encumbrance of the local. *Humor, like morality, has its eternal verities*. Most American humorists have not been widely famous because they have failed to create humor independent of local conditions not found or realized elsewhere." (p. 952)

Mark Twain is a great humorist—more genial than grim, more good-humored than ironic, more given to imaginative exaggeration than to intellectual sophistication, more inclined to pathos than to melancholy. He is a great story-teller; and he has enriched the literature of the world with a gallery of portraits so human in their veracious likeness as to rank them with the great figures of classic comedy. He is a remarkable observer and faithful reporter, never allowing himself, in Ibsen's phrase, to be "frightened by the venerableness of the institution"; and his sublimated journalism reveals a mastery of the naïvely comic thoroughly human and democratic. He is the most eminent product of our American democracy. . . . Throughout his long life he has been a factor of high ethical influence in our civilization; and the philosopher and the humanitarian look out from the twinkling eyes of the humorist.

But, after all, Mark Twain's supremest title to distinction as a great writer inheres in his mastery in that highest sphere of thought, embracing religion, philosophy, morality, and even humor, which we call sociology. Mr. Bernard Shaw once remarked to me that he regarded Poe and Mark Twain as America's greatest achievements in literature; and that he thought of Mark Twain primarily, not as humorist, but as sociologist. "Of course," he added, "Mark Twain is in much the same position as myself: he has to put matters in such a way as to make people who would otherwise hang him believe he is joking!" (pp. 954-55)

Archibald Henderson, "Mark Twain," in Harper's Monthly Magazine *(copyright © 1909, copyright renewed © 1936, by* Harper's Magazine; *all rights reserved; reprinted from the May, 1909 issue by special permission), Vol. CXVIII, No. 708, May, 1909, pp. 948-55.*

SHERWOOD ANDERSON   (essay date 1918)

As far as Twain is concerned, we have to remember the influences about him. Remember how he came into literature— the crude buffoon of the early days in the mining camps, the terrible cheap and second-rate humor of much of *Innocents Abroad*. It seems to me that when he began he addressed an audience that gets a big laugh out of the braying of a jackass and without a doubt Mark often brayed at them. He knew that later. There was tenderness and subtility in Mark when he grew older.

You get the picture of him . . .—the river man who could write going East and getting in with that New England crowd—the fellows from barren hills and barren towns. The best he got out of the bunch was Howells and Howells did Twain no good. (p. 32)

The cultural fellows got hold of Mark. They couldn't hold him. He was too big and too strong. He brushed their hands aside.

But their words got into his mind. In the effort to get out beyond that he became a pessimist. . . .

[A] man cannot be a pessimist who lives near a brook or a cornfield. When the brook chatters or at night when the moon comes up and the wind plays in the corn, a man hears the whispering of the gods.

Mark got to that once—when he wrote *Huck Finn*. He forgot Howells and the good wife and everyone. Again he was the half savage, tender, god-worshiping, believing boy. He had proud conscious innocence.

I believe he wrote that book in a little hut on a hill on his farm. It poured out of him. I fancy that at night he came down from his hill stepping like a king—a splendid playboy playing with rivers and men, riding on the Mississippi, on the broad river that is the great artery flowing out of the heart of the land. (p. 33)

Sherwood Anderson, in his letter to Van Wyck Brooks in 1918, in Letters of Sherwood Anderson, *edited by Howard Mumford Jones with Walter B. Rideout (reprinted by permission of Harold Ober Associates Incorporated; copyright © 1953 by Eleanor Copenhaven Anderson), Little, Brown, 1953, pp. 32-3.*

H. L. MENCKEN   (essay date 1919)

The older I grow the more I am convinced that Mark was, by long odds, the largest figure that ever reared itself out of the flat, damp prairie of American literature. He was great absolutely, but one must consider him relatively to get at the measure of his true greatness. Put him beside Emerson, or Whitman, or Hawthorne, or even Poe; he was palpably the superior of all of them. (p. 183)

Mark was the first of our great national artists to be whole-heartedly and enthusiastically American. He was the first to immerse himself willingly and with gusto in the infinitely picturesque and brilliant life of his time and country. He was the first to understand the common man of his race, and to interpret him fairly, honestly and accurately. He was the first to project brilliantly, for the information and entertainment of all the world, the American point of view, the American philosophy of life, the American character, the American soul. He would have been a great artist, I believe, even on the high-flung plane of Emerson or Hawthorne. He would have been *konzertmeister* even among the *umbilicarii*. But being what he was, his greatness was enormously augmented. He stands today at the head of the line. He is the one indubitable glory of American letters.

The bitter, of course, goes with the sweet. To be an American is, unquestionably, to be the noblest, the grandest, the proudest mammal that ever hoofed the verdure of God's green footstool. . . . But, as I have said, there is no perfection under heaven, and so even an American has his small blemishes, his scarcely discernible weaknesses, his minute traces of vice and depravity. Mark, alas, had them: he was as thoroughly American as a Knight of Pythias, a Wheeling stogie or Prohibition. . . . And what were these stigmata that betrayed him? In chief, they were two in number, and both lay at the very foundation of his character. On the one hand, there was his immovable moral certainty, his firm belief that he knew what was right from what was wrong, and that all who differed from him were, in some obscure way, men of an inferior and sinister order. And on the other hand, there was his profound intellectual timorousness, his abiding fear of his own ideas, his incurable cowardice in the face of public disapproval. These two characteristics colored his whole thinking; they showed themselves in his every attitude and gesture. They were the visible signs of his limitation as an Emersonian Man Thinking, and they were the bright symbols of his nationality. He was great in every way that an American could be great, but when he came to the border of his Americanism he came to the end of his greatness. (pp. 185-86)

With more courage, he would have gone a great deal further, and left a far deeper mark upon the intellectual history of his time. Not, perhaps, intrinsically as artist. He got as far in that direction as it is possible for a man of his training to go. *Huckleberry Finn* is a truly stupendous piece of work—perhaps the greatest novel ever written in English. And it would be difficult to surpass the sheer artistry of such things as *A Connecticut Yankee, Captain Stormfield, Joan of Arc* and parts of *A Tramp Abroad*. But there is more to the making of literature than the mere depiction of human beings at their obscene follies; there is also the play of ideas. Mark had ideas that were clear, that were vigorous, and that had an immediate appositeness. True enough, most of them were not quite original. As Prof. Schoenemann, of Harvard, has lately demonstrated, he got the notion of **"The Mysterious Stranger"** from Adolf Wilbrandt's *Der Meister von Palmyra;* much of *What Is Man?* you will find in the forgotten harangues of Ingersoll; in other directions he borrowed right and left. But is is only necessary to read either of the books I have just mentioned to see how thoroughly he recast everything he wrote; how brilliantly it came to be marked by the charm of his own personality; how he got his own peculiar and unmatchable eloquence into the merest statement of it. When, entering these regions of his true faith, he yielded to a puerile timidity—when he sacrificed his conscience and his self-respect to the idiotic popularity that so often more than half dishonored him—then he not only did a

cruel disservice to his own permanent fame, but inflicted genuine damage upon the national literature. He was greater than all the others because he was more American, but in this one way, at least, he was less than them for the same reason. . . .

Well, there he stands—a bit concealed, a bit false, but still a colossus. As I said at the start, I am inclined year by year to rate his achievement higher. In such a work as *Huckleberry Finn* there is something that vastly transcends the merit of all ordinary books. It has a merit that is special and extraordinary; it lifts itself above all hollow standards and criteria; it seems greater every time I read it. The books that gave Mark his first celebrity do not hold up so well. **"The Jumping Frog"** still wrings snickers, but, after all, it is commonplace at bottom. . . . *The Innocents Abroad*, re-read today, is largely tedious. Its humors are artificial; its audacities are stale; its eloquence belongs to the fancy journalism of a past generation. Even *Tom Sawyer* and *A Tramp Abroad* have long stretches of flatness. But in *Huckleberry Finn,* though he didn't know it at the time and never quite realized it, Mark found himself. There, working against the grain, heartily sick of the book before it was done, always putting it off until tomorrow, he hacked out a masterpiece that expands as year chases year. There, if I am not wrong, he produced the greatest work of the imagination that These States have yet seen. (pp. 188-89)

> *H. L. Mencken, "Final Estimate" (originally published as "The Man Within," in* The Smart Set, *Vol. LX, No. 3, October, 1919), in his* H. L. Mencken's "Smart Set" Criticism, *edited by William H. Nolte, Cornell University Press, 1968, pp. 182-89.*

LEONARD WOOLF   (essay date 1924)

[**"Mark Twain's Autobiography"**] was produced sporadically by dictation, and its production, broken by considerable intervals, lasted from 1870 to 1906. Mark Twain stipulated that it should not be published until after his death, for he wished to be able to speak without reserve, or "from the grave," as he said himself. There were very few things about which he did not have very definite, clearcut, and highly personal opinions, and he knew exactly what, in his own opinion, an autobiography should be. "*The thing uppermost in a person's mind* is the thing to talk about or write about," he says; and so, every morning when his stenographer appeared, he began to talk to him about what was uppermost in his mind, something which he had seen in a newspaper or talked about to someone else. His autobiography begins afresh, therefore, every day, in jerks, as a kind of diary which slips back gradually into reminiscence, and breaks off with some suddenness to begin again in the same way next morning. There is no continuity or chronological sequence; it is a disorderly, untidy, ramshackle book; but this conception of autobiography, like most of Mark Twain's ideas, is shown to have in it a broad vein of common sense streaked by genius.

The book is not quite so unreserved as one might be led to expect from the Preface. Indeed, Mark Twain, who was himself singularly free from delusions, says somewhere in the autobiography that he knows that he cannot write, even from the grave, with absolute freedom. This question of reserve in connection with his autobiography is to me rather interesting. In one sense, he is absolutely candid; he says whatever comes into his mind, and he gives his views about people, dead or living, with trenchant outspokenness. He writes about his mother, his wife, and his children, and about his feelings for them without reserve. And yet there is a layer of personal mental existence, which lies below this, which every human being, I imagine, possesses, and must sometimes be aware of, but into which Mark Twain never for one moment ventures. . . . Human personality seems to me to be like a series of cells one behind the other, and with doors leading from one to the other. When you are making a speech, or are at an evening party, you open the first door into the first compartment and are careful to keep the others locked and barred. When you are alone with your family or a few of your most intimate friends, you may open the doors into the second, or even the third, compartment. The door into the fourth compartment is only opened when you are by yourself, and there is a fifth and innermost compartment into which the bravest fears to look. . . .

The peculiarity about this autobiography of Mark Twain is that, although you feel him to be quite frank and unreserved, he never takes you beyond the second compartment, and never gives you a hint that there are, or that he is aware that there are, others behind it. Up to a point it is a very intimate book, but beyond that point it could not be more unintimate. Perhaps this is partly the result of dictating one's reminiscences to a stenographer. You cannot really be speaking from the grave and to a shorthand writer at the same moment.

Given these limitations, the book is remarkably interesting. Mark Twain was a great character, and his character leaves its own mark upon every page of the autobiography. In this country most people, if asked "What was Mark Twain?" would reply: "A humorist." . . . But Mark Twain was many other things besides a mere humorist. It is a considerable time since I have read any of his books, but many of the reminiscences here, particularly those of his childhood, in the first volume, and of early days, in the second, recalled **"Tom Sawyer"** and **"Huckleberry Finn."** No writing could be more vivid and alive than this. But the book showed me that Mark Twain had other qualities which I had certainly not previously appreciated. The first is his literary craftsmanship. The greater part of these two volumes bears the marks of having been dictated, of the voice rather than the pen; yet the words are nearly always deliberately, almost lovingly, chosen, the sentences shaped. The form may be loose; the writing is never slovenly. "I like the exact word and clarity of statement," he says in one place; that is a good foundation for any writer to build on, and it is clear that he took a great deal of trouble to attain it. But behind the clarity and exactness of style was something more—a very good brain. Mark Twain's humour is often very much on the surface; it covers an intense seriousness and a highly intellectual interest in things and ideas. Read, for instance, the curiously bitter, unpublished article on **"The Character of Man,"** in the first of these volumes, or the dissertation on the difference between news and history in the second. Only a man of shrewd, hard, and original intelligence could have written them.

> Leonard Woolf, *"Mark Twain,"* in The Nation & The Athenaeum, *Vol. XXXVI, No. 6, November 8, 1924, p. 217.*

VAN WYCK BROOKS (essay date 1933)

At the circus, no doubt, you have watched some trained lion going through the sad motions of a career to which the tyrannical curiosity of men has constrained him. At times he seems to be playing his part with a certain zest; he has acquired a new set of superficial habits, and you would say that he finds them easy and pleasant. Under the surface, however, he remains the wild, exuberant creature of the jungle. (p. 219)

So it was with Mark Twain. . . . [He] conformed to a moral régime in which the profoundest of his instincts could not function: the artist had been submerged in the bourgeois gentleman, the man of business, the respectable Presbyterian citizen. To play his part, therefore, he had to depend upon the cues his wife and his friends gave him. Here we have the explanation of his statement: "Outside influences, outside circumstances, wind the man and regulate him. Left to himself, he wouldn't get regulated at all, and the sort of time he would keep would not be valuable." We can see from this how completely his conscious self had accepted the point of view of his trainers, how fully he had concurred in their desire to repress that unmanageable creative instinct of his, how ashamed, in short, he was of it. Nevertheless, that instinct, while repressed, continued to live and manifest itself just the same. . . . [In] the end, never having been able to develop, to express itself, to fulfill itself, to air itself in the sun and the wind of the world, it turned as it were black and malignant, like some monstrous, morbid inner growth, poisoning Mark Twain's whole spiritual system. (pp. 219-20)

[Is] it not plain that Mark Twain's books are shot through with all sorts of unconscious revelations of this internal conflict? According to the psychoanalysts, the dream is an expression of a suppressed wish. In dreams we do what our inner selves desire to do but have been prevented from doing either by the exigencies of our daily routine, or by the obstacles of convention, or by some other form of censorship which has been imposed upon us, or which we ourselves, actuated by some contrary desire, have willingly accepted. Many other dreams, however, are not so simple: they are often incoherent, nonsensical, absurd. In such cases it is because two opposed wishes, neither of which is fully satisfied, have met one another and resulted in a "compromise"—a compromise that is often as apparently chaotic as the collision of two railway trains running at full speed. These mechanisms, the mechanisms of the "wish-fulfillment" and the "wish-conflict," are evident, as Freud has shown, in many of the phenomena of everyday life. Whenever, for any reason, the censorship is relaxed and the censor is off guard, whenever we are day-dreaming and give way to our idle thoughts, then the unconscious bestirs itself and rises to the surface, gives utterance to those embarrassing slips of the tongue, those "tender playfulnesses," that express our covert intentions, slays our adversaries, sets our fancies wandering in pursuit of all the ideals and all the satisfactions upon which our customary life has stamped its veto. In Mark Twain's books, or rather in a certain group of them, his "fantasies," we can see this process at work. Certain significant obsessions reveal themselves there, certain fixed ideas; the same themes recur again and again. "I am writing from the grave," he notes in later life, regarding some manuscripts that are not to be published until after his death. "On these terms only can a man be approximately frank. He cannot be straitly and unqualifiedly frank either in the grave or out of it." When he wrote *Captain Stormfield's Visit to Heaven, Pudd'nhead Wilson, The American Claimant, Those Extraordinary Twins,* he was frank without knowing it. He, the unconscious artist, who, when he wrote his autobiography, found that he was unable to tell the truth about himself, has conducted us unawares in these writings into the penetralia of his soul.

Let us note, prefatorily, that in each case Mark Twain was peculiarly, for the time being, free of his censorship. That he wrote at least the first draft of *Captain Stormfield* in reckless disregard of it is proved by the fact that for forty years he did not dare to publish the book at all but kept it locked away in his safe. As for *The American Claimant, Pudd'nhead Wilson,* and *Those Extraordinary Twins,* he wrote them at the time of the failure of the Paige Typesetting Machine. . . . [So] disturbed were his affairs, so disordered was everything, we are told, "that sometimes he felt himself as one walking amid unrealities." At such times, we know, the bars of the spirit fall down; people commit all sorts of aberrations, "go off the handle," as we say; the moral habits of a lifetime give way and man becomes more or less an irresponsible animal. In Mark Twain's case, at least, the result was a violent effort on the part of his suppressed self to assert its supremacy in a propitious moment when that other self, the business man, had proved abysmally weak. Is not that why these books that marked his return to literature appear to have the quality of nightmares? He has told us in the preface to *Those Extraordinary Twins* that the story had originally been a part of *Pudd'nhead Wilson:* he had seen a picture of an Italian monstrosity like the Siamese Twins and had meant to write an extravagant farce about it; but, he adds, "the story changed itself from a farce to a tragedy while I was going along with it—a most embarrassing circumstance." Eventually, he realized that it was "not one story but two stories tangled together" that he was trying to tell, so he removed the twins from *Pudd'nhead Wilson* and printed the two tales separately. That alone shows us the confusion of his mind, the confusion revealed further in *The American Claimant* and in *Pudd'nhead Wilson* as it stands. They are, I say, like nightmares, these books: full of passionate conviction that turns into a burlesque of itself, angry satire, hysterical humour. They are triple-headed chimeras, in short, that leave the reader's mind in tumult and dismay. The censor has so far relaxed its hold that the unconscious has risen to the surface: the battle of the two Mark Twains takes place almost in the open, under our very eyes.

Glance now, among these dreams, at a simple example of "wish-fulfillment." When Captain Stormfield arrives in heaven, he is surprised to find that all sorts of people are esteemed among the celestials who have had no esteem at all on earth. Among them is Edward J. Billings of Tennessee. He was a poet during his lifetime, but the Tennessee village folk scoffed at him; they would have none of him, they made cruel sport of him. In heaven things are different; there the celestials recognize the divinity of his spirit, and in token of this Shakespeare and Homer walk backward before him.

Here, as we see, Mark Twain is unconsciously describing the actual fate of his own spirit and that ample other fate his spirit desires. It is the story of Cinderella, the despised step-sister who is vindicated by the prince's favour, rewritten in terms personal to the author. (pp. 228-32)

Observe, now, the deadly temperamental earnestness of *The Man That Corrupted Hadleyburg,* a story written late in life when Mark Twain's great fame and position enabled him to override the censorship and speak with more or less candour. "The temptation and the downfall of a whole town," says Mr. [Albert Bigelow] Paine, "was a colossal idea, a sardonic idea, and it is colossally and sardonically worked out. Human weakness and rotten moral force were never stripped so bare or so mercilessly jeered at in the marketplace. For once Mark Twain could hug himself with glee in derision of self-righteousness, knowing that the world would laugh with him, and that none would be so bold as to gainsay his mockery. Probably no one but Mark Twain ever conceived the idea of demoralizing a whole community—of making its 'nineteen leading citizens' ridiculous by leading them into a cheap, glittering temptation,

and having them yield and openly perjure themselves at the very moment when their boasted incorruptibility was to amaze the world." It was the "leading citizens," the pillars of society with whom Mark Twain had himself been hobnobbing all those years, the very people in deference to whom he had suppressed his true desires, who admired him only for the success he had won in spite of what he was—it was these people, his friends, who had, in so actual a sense, imposed upon him, that he attacks in this terrible story of the passing stranger who took such a vitriolic joy in exposing their pretensions and their hypocrisy. "I passed through your town at a certain time, and received a deep offense which I had not earned. . . . I wanted to damage every man in the place, and every woman." Is not that the unmistakable voice of the misprized poet and philosopher in Mark Twain, the worm that has turned, the angel that has grown diabolic in a world that has refused to recognize its divinity?

Here, I say, in these two or three instances, we have the "wish-fulfillment" in its clearest form. Elsewhere we find the wish, the desire of the suppressed poet for self-effectuation, expressing itself in many vague hopes and vague regrets. . . . [Consider] the unfinished tale of *The Mysterious Chamber,* "the story," as Mr. Paine describes it, "of a young lover who is accidentally locked behind a secret door in an old castle and cannot announce himself. He wanders at last down into subterranean passages beneath the castle, and he lives in this isolation for twenty years." There is something inescapably personal about that. As for the character of the Colonel Sellers of *The American Claimant*—so different from the Colonel Sellers of *The Gilded Age* who is supposed to be the same man and whom Mark Twain had drawn after one of his uncles—every one has noted that it is a burlesque upon his own preposterous business life. But is it not more than this? That rightful claimant to the great title of nobility, living in exile among those fantastic dreams of wealth that always deceive him—is he not the obscure projection of the lost heir in Mark Twain himself, inept in the business life he is living, incapable of substantiating his claim, and yet forever beguiled by the hope that some day he is going to win his true rank and live the life for which he was intended? (pp. 233-35)

Just before Mark Twain's death, he recalled, says Mr. Paine, "one of his old subjects, Dual Personality, and discussed various instances that flitted through his mind—Jekyll and Hyde phases in literature and fact." One of his old subjects, dual personality! Could he ever have been aware of the extent to which his writings revealed that conflict in himself? Why was he so obsessed by journalistic facts like the Siamese Twins and the Tichborne case, with its theme of the lost heir and the usurper? Why is it that the idea of changelings in the cradle perpetually haunted his mind, as we can see from *Pudd'nhead Wilson* and *The Gilded Age* and the variation of it that constitutes *The Prince and the Pauper*? The prince who has submerged himself in the rôle of the beggar-boy—Mark Twain has drawn himself there, just as he has drawn himself in the *William Wilson* theme of *The Facts Concerning the Recent Carnival of Crime in Connecticut,* where he ends by dramatically slaying the conscience that torments him. And as for that pair of incompatibles bound together in one flesh—the Extraordinary Twins, the "good" boy who has followed the injunctions of his mother and the "bad" boy of whom society disapproves—how many of Mark Twain's stories and anecdotes turn upon that same theme, that same juxtaposition!—does he not reveal there, in all its nakedness, the true history of his life?

We have observed that in Pudd'nhead's aphorisms Mark Twain was expressing his true opinions, the opinions of the cynic he had become owing to the suppression and the constant curdling as it were of the poet in him. . . . But he does so, we perceive, only by taking cover behind a device that enables him to save his face and make good his retreat. . . . As long as he never hit below the belt by speaking in his own person, in short, he was perfectly secure. And Mark Twain, the humorist, who held the public in the hollow of his hand, knew it.

It is only after some such explanation as this that we can understand the supremacy among all Mark Twain's writings of *Huckleberry Finn*. Through the character of Huck, that disreputable, illiterate little boy, as Mrs. Clemens no doubt thought him, he was licensed to let himself go. . . . That Mark Twain was almost, if not quite conscious of his opportunity we can see from his introductory note to the book: "Persons attempting to find a motive in this narrative will be prosecuted; persons attempting to find a moral in it will be banished; persons attempting to find a plot in it will be shot." He feels so secure of himself that he can actually challenge the censor to accuse him of having a motive. Huck's illiteracy, Huck's disreputableness and general outrageousness are so many shields behind which Mark Twain can let all the cats out of the bag with impunity. He must, I say, have had a certain sense of his unusual security when he wrote some of the more frankly satirical passages of the book, when he permitted Colonel Sherburn to taunt the mob, when he drew that picture of the audience who had been taken in by the Duke proceeding to sell the rest of their townspeople, when he made the King put up the notice, "Ladies and Children not Admitted," adding: "There, if that line don't fetch them, I don't know Arkansaw!" The withering contempt for humankind expressed in these episodes was of the sort that Mark Twain expressed more and more openly, as time went on, in his own person; but he was not indulging in that costly kind of cynicism in the days when he wrote *Huckleberry Finn*. He must, therefore, have appreciated the license that little vagabond, like the puppet in the lap of a ventriloquist, afforded him. . . . Mark Twain himself was free at last—that raft and that river to him were something more than mere material facts. His whole unconscious life, the pent-up river of his own soul, had burst its bonds and rushed forth, a joyous torrent! Do we need any other explanation of the abandon, the beauty, the eternal freshness of *Huckleberry Finn*? Perhaps we can say that a lifetime of moral slavery and repression was not too much to pay for it. Certainly, if it flies like a gay, bright, shining arrow through the rather lukewarm atmosphere of American literature, it is because of the straining of the bow, the tautness of the string, that gave it its momentum. (pp. 236-40)

Van Wyck Brooks, "Those Extraordinary Twins," in his The Ordeal of Mark Twain *(copyright, 1920, E. P. Dutton & Company; copyright renewed © 1947 by Van Wyck Brooks; reprinted by permission of the publisher, E. P. Dutton), revised edition, Dutton, 1933 (and reprinted by AMS Press, 1977), pp. 219-41.*

ERNEST HEMINGWAY (essay date 1935)

All modern American literature comes from one book by Mark Twain Called *Huckleberry Finn*. If you read it you must stop where the Nigger Jim is stolen from the boys. That is the real end. The rest is just cheating. But it's the best book we've had. All American writing comes from that. There was nothing before. There has been nothing as good since. (p. 22)

Ernest Hemingway, "Pursuit and Conversation," in his Green Hills of Africa *(copyright 1935 by Charles Scribner's Sons; copyright renewed 1963 by Mary Hemingway; reprinted with the permission of Charles Scribner's Sons), Charles Scribner's Sons, 1935, pp. 2-34.**

WALTER BLAIR (essay date 1939)

The Adventures of Tom Sawyer . . . attacked earlier juvenile literature in something roughly like the way *Joseph Andrews* attacked *Pamela*. . . .

Notable in earlier juvenile fictional works had been their characters, their preachments, and their plots. The children portrayed had been, for the most part, characterized with extraordinary simplicity: they had been good or bad, and that had been an end of it. (p. 75)

During the years before *Tom Sawyer* appeared, such good-bad-child tales, with their preachments and predetermined conclusions, had suggested incongruities between fiction and life useful to many American humorists. (p. 77)

One who turns to *Tom Sawyer* with the conventional literature and the humorous attacks on that literature by various writers including Twain in mind may see some important achievements of Clemens' novel. These were suggested by a contemporary critic who said:

> This literary wag has performed some services which entitle him to the gratitude of his generation. He has run the traditional Sunday-school boy through his literary mangle and turned him out washed and ironed into a proper state of collapse. That whining, canting, early-dying, anaemic creature was held up to mischievous lads as worthy of imitation. He poured his religious hypocrisy over every honest pleasure a boy had. He whined his lachrymous warnings on every playground. He vexed their lives. So when Mark grew old enough, he went gunning for him, and lo, wherever his soul may be, the skin of the strumous young pietist is now neatly tacked up to view on the Sunday-school door of to-day as a warning.

That the attack thus suggested may have been responsible in part for the organization of the narrative becomes clear if the story is restated in the way it would have been handled in the literature attacked. The opening chapter of Clemens' novel reveals a character who, in terms of moralizing juvenile literature, has the indubitable earmarks of a Bad Boy. (pp. 80-1)

Up to the last page of chapter x, he piles up enough horrible deeds to spur the average Sunday school author to write pages of admonitions. His actions are of a sort to show that he is—in the language of such an author—thievish, guileful, untruthful, vengeful, vainglorious, selfish, frivolous, self-pitying, dirty, lazy, irreverrent, superstitious and cowardly.

What a chance for sermonizing! But Clemens makes nothing of his opportunity: he indicates not the least concern about his hero's mendacity. In fact, his preaching (such as it is) is of a perverse sort. Instead of clucking to show his horror, he writes of Tom's sins with a gusto which earlier authors had reserved for the deeds of Good Boys, and on occasion (as when he tells about the whitewashing trick), he actually commends the youth for his chicanery. A ragged ruffian named Huckleberry Finn who smokes and swears is set up as an ideal figure. . . . (p. 81)

The ending of the book departs as determinedly from the patterns of juvenile fiction. It staggers the imagination to guess the sort of punishment which would have been deigned fitting for such a monster as Tom by fictionists who had felt hanging in adulthood was an appropriate result of youthful truancy. From their standpoint, the author of *Tom Sawyer* must have outraged poetic justice to the point of being hideously immoral. Here were Tom and his companions, who had run away, played truant, and smoked to boot; actually lionized because they returned from Jackson's Island. . . . More shocking, here was even the unregenerate Huck dramatically saving the life of the Widow Douglas. And to top it all, these boys were allowed at the end to accumulate a fortune of the size exclusively awarded to only the best of the Alger heroes.

Thus the characterization, the perverse preaching, the unconventional ending of the book, which gave the volume in its day a comic appeal now all but irrecoverable, also, it is possible, did much to mold the form of the narrative. The simplest explanation of the arrangement of happenings in Clemens' book is that it represented a fictional working-out of the author's antipathy to the conventional plot structure of juvenile tales. Here, in other words, is a repetition of the plot so broadly developed in "The story of a bad little boy who didn't come to grief"—a more serious handling of a reversed moralizing narrative. (pp. 82-3)

In attacking in other than a burlesque fashion fictional representations of boys who were unreal, Clemens was faced with the problem of depicting, through characterization and plot, boys who were real. What a real boy was was suggested by the very terms of the attack: he was not simply good or bad but a mixture of virtue and mischievousness. And he could play pranks at the same time he was developing qualities which would make him a normal adult.

This concept allowed elements of incongruity which an author might develop humorously. . . . But the incongruities of boy nature not only had humorous possibilities; they also had potentialities—far beyond those in good-bad-boy books—for plot structures closely linked with developing characters. . . . Less and less, [the boy] would behave like an irresponsible and ignorant savage; more and more he would act like a responsible and intelligent adult.

If *Tom Sawyer* is regarded as a working out in fictional form of this notion of a boy's maturing, the book will reveal, I believe, a structure on the whole quite well adapted to its purpose. My suggestion, in other words, is that Clemens' divergence from the older pattern of juvenile fiction and his concept of the normal history of boyhood led him to a way of characterizing and a patterning of action which showed a boy developing toward manhood.

That this was the unifying theme of the story will be indicated, perhaps, by a consideration of the units of narrative, the lines of action, in the novel, There are four of these—the story of Tom and Becky, the story of Tom and Muff Potter, the Jackson's Island episode, and the series of happenings (which might be called the Injun Joe story) leading to the discovery of the treasure. Each one of these is initiated by a characteristic and typically boyish action. The love story begins with Tom's chil-

dishly fickle desertion of his fiancée, Amy Lawrence; the Potter narrative with the superstitious trip to the graveyard; the Jackson's Island episode with the adolescent revolt of the boy against Aunt Polly, and Tom's youthful ambition to be a pirate; the Injun Joe story with the juvenile search for buried treasure. Three of these narrative strands, however, are climaxed by a chracteristic and mature sort of action, a sort of action, moreover, directly opposed to the initial action. Tom chivalrously takes Becky's punishment and faithfully helps her in the cave; he defies boyish superstition and courageously testifies for Muff Potter; he forgets a childish antipathy and shows mature concern for his aunt's uneasiness about him. The Injun Joe story, though it is the least useful of the four so far as showing Tom's maturing is concerned, by showing Huck conquering fear to rescue the widow, has value as a repetition—with variations—of the motif of the book.

That these actions are regarded by the older folk of St. Petersburg as evidences of mature virtue is suggested in each instance by their reactions. Every subplot in the book eventuates in an expression of adult approval. Sometimes this is private, like Aunt Polly's discovery that Tom has come from the island to tell her of his safety, or like Judge Thatcher's enthusiastic comments upon Tom's chivalry at school. Sometimes it is public, like the adulation lavished on the hero after the trial and after the rescue of Becky, or like the widow's party honoring Huck Finn.

The book contains various episodes extraneous to these lines of action—episodes whose only value in the scheme is variation in the display of the incongruities of boy nature from which the actions arise, but it is notable how much of the novel is concerned with these four threads. Only four of the thirty-five chapters are not in some way concerned with the development of at least one of them. Hence a large share of the book is concerned with actions which show the kind of development suggested.

More important is the fact that, if the novel is regarded as one narrative including the alternately treated lines of action and the episodes as well, as the story progresses, wholly boylike actions become more infrequent while adult actions increase. No such simple and melodramatic a device as a complete reformation is employed: late in the book, Tom is still capable of treasure hunts and fantasies about robber gangs. . . . But actions which are credible late in the story—actions such as Tom's taking Becky's punishment . . . or testifying for Potter . . . would, I think, seem improbable early in the book. One of a few slips Clemens makes strengthens this point: in chapter xxiv, Tom tells Huck that when he is rich he is "going to buy a new drum, and sure 'nough sword, and a red necktie and a bull pup, and get married.". . . It is jarring in chapter xxiv, to be sure, but at any point in the first five chapters of the book, say, it would be highly appropriate.

There is perhaps, then, reason for believing that the theme, the main action, and the character portrayal in the novel are one—the developing of Tom's character in a series of crucial situations. Studying the progress of the novel with this in mind, the reader will see, I believe, that though the earlier chapters emphasize Tom's mischievousness, and though a Sunday school fictionist would therefore call him a Bad Boy, there are potentialities in these chapters for his later behavior. To put the matter negatively, his motives are never vicious; to put it positively, he has a good heart. . . . An appeal to his sympathy, he himself indicates in chapter ii, is more efficacious than physical punishment or scolding "She talks awful," he says of Aunt Polly, "but talk don't hurt—any ways it don't if she don't cry." Inevitably then, when at the end of chapter x, his aunt weeps over him, "this was worse than a thousand whippings." And a chapter later, tender-hearted Tom is ministering to poor Muff Potter as he languishes in jail.

Significant, too, is Tom's acceptance, in times of stress in the early chapters, of the adult code of the particularly godly folk of idyllic St. Petersburg. His feeling that it would be pleasant to die disappears when he remembers that he does not have "a clean Sunday school record," . . . and the howling dog's prophecy of his death brings regret that he has been "playing hookey and doing everything a feller's told *not* to do." "But if I ever get off this time," he promises, "I lay I'll just *waller* in Sunday-schools!". . . He wants to be a soldier, or a plainsman, or a pirate chiefly in order that he may stroll into the drowsy little St. Petersburg church some Sunday morning and bask in the respect of the village. . . . And his impelling desire for a place of honor in the community is a key to his initiating three of the four lines of action; hence the plot strands are closely linked with his character.

Beginning with the final pages of chapter x, these potentialities for something more mature than inconsiderate childhood begin to develop. Tom is touched by his aunt's appeal to his sympathy; his conscience hurts because of his silence about Potter's innocence; he suffers pangs because he realizes he has sinned in running away; he worries about his aunt's concern for his safety, and so on. And well in the second half of the book, in a series of chapters—xx, xxiii, xxix, xxxii—come those crucial situations in which he acts more like a grownup than like an irresponsible boy.

There are some indications that Clemens was aware of the pattern I have suggested. He was aware, undoubtedly, of the divergence from the older fictional models patently burlesqued in his "Bad boy" and "Good boy" travesties. Did he perceive, however, that deliberate divergence from older patterns had led him to create a new structure of his own, nearer to the history of boyhood as he and others conceived it? It is impossible to be sure, but some facts may have a bearing on the problem.

In Clemens' "Conclusion" to *Tom Sawyer* (the italics are his) he wrote: "So endeth this chronicle. It being strictly a history of a *boy*, it must stop here; the story could not go much further without becoming the history of a *man*." (pp. 83-7)

> *Walter Blair, "On the Structure of 'Tom Sawyer',"*
> *in* Modern Philology, *Vol. XXXVII, No. 1, August, 1939, pp. 75-88.*

BERNARD DeVOTO (essay date 1946)

The philosophy which [Mark Twain] spent years refining and supposed he had perfected is a sophomoric determinism. Even so, it is less a philosophy than a symbol or a rationalization; the perceptions it stood for are expressed at the level of genius in his fiction—not as idea but in terms of human life. Most of the nineteenth century's optimisms were his also. He fiercely championed the democratic axioms; they are the ether of his fiction and the fulcrum of his satire. He thought too that the nineteenth century, especially as Progress, and more especially as Progress in the United States, was the happiest estate of man; he believed that it was bringing on a future of greater freedom and greater happiness. This was basic and spontaneous in his mind, but at the same time he felt something profoundly

wrong. There seemed to be some limitation to freedom, some frustration of happiness. He never really came to grips with the conflict. Only in the last fifteen years of his life did he ascribe any part of what might be wrong to any but superficial injustices in American life or any but slight dislocations in our system. By the time he became aware of serious threats to freedom they did not seem to matter much: he was so absorbed in the natural depravity of man that the collapse or frustration of democracy, which he was by then taking for granted, seemed only an unimportant detail. Ideally, his last years would have been spent in more rigorous analysis—if not of the objective data, then of his intuitive awareness of them. They were not and so his judgments remained confused—and his principal importance in our literature belongs to his middle years, the period when his mind and feelings are in healthy equilibrium. It is an importance of his perceptions, not his thinking, and it exists primarily in his fiction, most purely in *Huckleberry Finn*. The best of Mark Twain's fiction is, historically, the first mature realization in our literature of a conflict between the assumptions of democracy and the limitations on democracy. Between the ideal of freedom and the nature of man.

Not less important is the fact that there is a reconciliation, even an affirmation. Detachment could be no greater but it is still somehow compassionate; condemnation could be no more complete, but it is somehow magnanimous. The damned human race is displayed with derision and abhorrence, yet this is on the ground that it has fallen short of its own decencies. Moreover at least *Huckleberry Finn* has a hero, the only heroic character (apart from Joan of Arc, a debauch of gyneolatry) he ever drew, and it is the essence of what Mark Twain had to say that the hero is a Negro slave. It has also a vindication not only of freedom, but of loyalty and decency, kindness and courage; and it is the essence of Mark Twain that this vindication is made by means of a boy who is a spokesman of the folk mind and whom experience has taught wariness and skepticism. Like all great novels *Huckleberry Finn* moves on many levels of significance, but it describes a flight and a struggle for freedom, and the question it turns on is a moral question.

Mark found zest and gusto—nouns that do not describe very much American literature of the first rank—in whatsoever was alive. He liked few novels except those of his intimate friends. What he praised in the ones he did like was reality of behavior, speech, or motive; his notebooks are sulphurous with comments on merely literary, that is false, characters. His taste was for biography, autobiography, history—life direct, men revealing themselves. No doubt the race was damned but it was fascinating. And that was proper for if his fiction is the best of his work, his most salient talent as a novelist is the life giving power. It is a careless and prodigal fecundity, but nevertheless remarkably concentrated. Old Man Finn, for instance, is greatly imagined and he seems to fill the first half of the book, yet he appears in only a few pages. . . . Nor is this fecundity confined to Mark's fiction, for the framework of all his books is anecdotal and all the people in them are dramatized. The whole population of his principal books, nine-tenths of the population of all his books, has the same vividness. Boys, villagers, the rivermen, the Negroes, Colonel Sellers, the two great vagabonds—there is nothing quite like the Mark Twain gallery elsewhere in American literature.

But there is a striking limitation: nowhere in that gallery are there women of marriageable age. No white women, that is, for the slave Roxana in *Pudd'nhead Wilson* lives as vividly as Old Man Finn himself. It must be significant that the only credible woman of an age that might sanction desire is withdrawn from desire behind the barrier of race. None of Mark Twain's nubile girls, young women, or young matrons are believable; they are all bisque, saccharine, or tears. He will do girl children in the romantic convention of boys' books and he is magnificent with the sisterhood of worn frontier wives whom Aunt Polly climaxes, but something like a taboo drains reality from any woman who might trouble the heart or the flesh. There is no love story in Mark Twain, there is no love at all beyond an occasional admission, for purposes of plot only, that someone is married or is going to be. Women seldom have husbands and men seldom have wives unless they are beyond middle age. Mark's endless absorption in human motives did not, for literary purposes at least, extend to sexual motives. Sex seems to be forbidden unless it can be treated mawkishly, and this writer of great prose who habitually flouted the genteel proprieties of language was more prudish than the most tremulous of his friends in regard to language that might suggest either desire or its gratification. So there is a sizable gap in the world he created. That gap has never been accounted for. (pp. 15-18)

Few Americans have written as much as Mark Twain. His published works are not much greater in bulk than his unpublished manuscripts, the books he finished fewer than the ones he broke off and abandoned. He wrote on impulse and enthusiasm and while they lasted he wrote easily, but he wrote as needs must, for he had little faculty of self-criticism and but small ability to sustain or elaborate an idea. (p. 18)

Furthermore, he lacked the attribute of the artist—whatever it may be—that enables him to think a novel through till its content has found its own inherent form. Of his novels only *Joan of Arc, The Prince and the Pauper,* and *Tom Sawyer* have structures that have developed from within; significantly, all are simple and only one is first-rate. Mark lived with his material for a long time, sometimes for many years, but not consciously, not with critical or searching dissatisfaction. A book must come of its own momentum from the unconscious impulse, be it as a whole, as a fragment, or as something that hardly got started before it broke off. This is to say that he had no conscious esthetic. He stood at the opposite pole from Henry James, with the other great contemporary of both, Howells, in between but nearer to James. Yet he had as large a share as either of them in creating the modern American novel. (pp. 19-20)

As the [nineteenth] century neared its end there was a good deal of pessimism and disenchantment in the United States. A wave of doubt and questioning swept many minds. The people who began an imperialistic adventure in the Pacific with the same naïve enthusiasm that had taken Mark Twain into the industrial life were widely, at the very time they stepped out on the world stage, beginning to be troubled about themselves. The nineteenth century, looking back on its course, found cause to be dismayed. (p. 23)

However deep or shallow this *fin de siècle* weariness may have been in the United States at large, Mark Twain's last fifteen years must be seen as related to it, if only distantly. During this period he wrote as much as in any similar length of time in his life, perhaps more, but most of it is fragmentary, unfinished. Almost all of it deals with the nature of man, man's fate, and man's conceptions of honor and morality. There are fables, dialogues, diatribes—sometimes cold, sometimes passionate, derisive, withering, savage. Mark sees the American republic perishing, like republics before it, through the in-

eradicable cowardice, corruption, and mere baseness of mankind. He elaborates theories, which he embodies in imaginary histories of the world (and sometimes of extra-mundane societies) to support his prophecy, and yet he cannot be much troubled by the going-down of this western land, for year by year he is writing a general apocalypse. The Old Testament fables had always served him for humorous derision of man's gullibility, but now he uses them as missiles in a ferocious attack on human stupidity and cruelty. Man is compact of malignity, cowardice, weakness, and absurdity, a diseased organism, a parasite on nature, a foolish but murderous animal much lower than the swine.

Yet *What Is Man?* (published anonymously in 1906 but written before the turn of the century), the fullest of many developments of these themes, cannot be seen solely as a document in anthropophobia. It is also in complex ways a justification, even a self-justification. Its fixed universe, with an endless chain of cause and effect from the beginning of time, permits Mark to compose many variations on the theme of human pettiness, but also it serves to free man of blame—and thus satisfies a need deeply buried in Mark's personal remorse. . . . But a much truer release and a fulfillment as well came, as always, when Mark turned from reasoning to the instinctual portions of his mind. The highest reach of his last period is *The Mysterious Stranger.* It is an almost perfect book—perfect in expression of his final drive, in imaginative projection of himself, in tone and tune, in final judgment on the nature of man and the experience of Mark Twain. It is on a humbler level than his great books. More than any of them it is Mark Twain somewhat in disregard of America. It is not, finally, a major work; but in its small way it is a masterpiece. Those who know and love Mark Twain will always find it as revealing as *Huckleberry Finn.* (pp. 23-5)

No doubt [Mark Twain's] first importance in [American] literature is the democratizing effect of his work. It is a concretely liberating effect, and therefore different in kind from Whitman's vision of democracy, which can hardly be said to have been understood by or to have found a response among any considerable number of Americans. Mark Twain was the first great American writer who was also a popular writer, and that in itself is important. Much more important is the implicit and explicit democracy of his books. They are the first American literature of the highest rank which portrays the ordinary bulk of Americans, expresses them, accepts their values, and delineates their hopes, fears, decencies, and indecencies as from within. (pp. 25-6)

The nature of his writing is hardly less important. Mark Twain wrote one of the great styles of American literature, he helped develop the modern American style, he was the first writer who ever used the American vernacular at the level of art. There has been some failure to understand this achievement. Shortly before this Introduction was written, the most pontifical American critic guessed that Mark must have turned to the vernacular of *Huckleberry Finn* because he lacked education, was unacquainted with literary traditions, and therefore wrote thin or awkward prose. That absurdity disregards Mark's life and his books as well. The reader may determine herein whether the style of *The Mysterious Stranger* lacks strength or subtlety, lacks any quality whatever for the effects required of it, or if that represents too late a period, may turn to **"Old Times on the Mississippi,"** which was written before *Huckleberry Finn,* or "**The Private History of a Campaign That Failed,"** which was written while *Huck* was still half finished. Mark Twain wrote English of a remarkable simplicity and clarity, and of singular sensitiveness, flexibility, and beauty as well. Its simplicity might deceive a patronizing reader for the sentence structure is not involved, usually consisting of short elements in natural sequence, and in order to understand without analysis how much art has gone into it one must have an ear for the tones and accents of speech as well as some feeling for the vigor of words. It is so lucid that it seems effortless—but just what is style?

Now, it is important that Mark made the American vernacular the medium of a great novel. Even before that he had used local, class, and racial dialects with immeasurably greater skill than anyone before him in our literature. **"The Jumping Frog"** raised such dialects above the merely humorous use which was the only one they had previously had and gave them a function in the writing of fiction. And the first two chapters of *The Gilded Age* bring to American literature genuine Negro speech and a rural dialect that are both genuine and an instrument of art—literally for the first time. In the rendition of Negro speech he may have had one equal, though there are those who will not grant that Harris is an equal; but it is doubtful if anyone has used the dialects of the middle South, or for that matter any other American dialect, as well as he. This on the basis of *The Gilded Age* and its immediate successors: the achievement of *Huckleberry Finn* is greater still. Huck's style, which is the spoken language of the untutored American of his place and time, differentiates the most subtle meanings and emphases and proves capable on the most difficult psychological effects. In a single step it made a literary medium of the American language the liberating effect on American writing could hardly be overstated. (pp. 25-8)

Nevertheless, Mark's principal service to the American language was not Huck's vernacular: it lay within the recognized limits of literary prose. Within those limits he was a radical innovator, a prime mover who changed the medium by incorporating in it the syntax the idioms, and especially the vocabulary of the common life. The vigor of his pros comes directly from the speech of the Great Valley and the Far West. A superlative may be ventured: that Mark Twain had a greater effect than any other writer on the evolution of American prose. (p. 28)

Bernard DeVoto, "Introduction" (copyright 1946 by The Viking Press, Inc.; copyright © renewed 1974 by The Viking Press, Inc.; reprinted by permission of Viking Penguin Inc.), in The Portable Mark Twain, *by Samuel Langhorne Clemens, edited by Bernard DeVoto, Viking Penguin, 1946, pp. 1-32.*

LESLIE A. FIEDLER (essay date 1948)

The situations of the Negro and the homosexual in our society pose quite opposite problems, or at least problems suggesting quite opposite solutions. Our laws on homosexuality and the context of prejudice they objectify must apparently be changed to accord with a stubborn social fact; whereas it is the social fact, our overt behavior toward the negro, that must be modified to accord with our laws and the, at least official, morality they objectify. It is not, of course, quite so simple. There is another sense in which the fact of homosexual passion contradicts a national myth of masculine love, just as our real relationship with the Negro contradicts a myth of that relationship; and those two myths with their betrayals are, as we shall see, one.

The existence of overt homosexuality threatens to compromise an essential aspect of American sentimental life: the camaraderie of the locker room and ball park, the good fellowship of the poker game and fishing trip, a kind of passionless passion, at once gross and delicate, homoerotic in the boy's sense, possessing an innocence above suspicion. To doubt for a moment this innocence, which can survive only as *assumed*, would destroy our stubborn belief in a relationship simple, utterly satisfying, yet immune to lust; physical as the handshake is physical, this side of copulation. . . . It is this self-congratulatory buddy-buddiness, its astonishing naïveté that breed at once endless opportunities for inversion and the terrible reluctance to admit its existence, to surrender the last believed-in strong-hold of love without passion.

It is, after all, what we know from a hundred other sources that is here verified: the regressiveness, in a technical sense, of American life, its implacable nostalgia for the infantile, at once wrong-headed and somehow admirable. The mythic America is boyhood—and who would dare be startled to realize that the two most popular, most *absorbed*, I am sure, of the handful of great books in our native heritage are customarily to be found, illustrated, on the shelves of the children's library. I am referring, of course, to *Moby Dick* and *Huckleberry Finn,* so different in technique and language, but alike children's books or, more precisely, *boys'* books. (pp. 143-44)

What, then, do . . . these books have in common? As boys' books we should expect them shyly, guiltlessly as it were, to proffer a chaste male love as the ultimate emotional experience—and this is spectacularly the case. . . . [In Melville it is] Ishmael's love for Queequeg; in Twain, Huck's feeling for Nigger Jim. At the focus of emotion, where we are accustomed to find in the world's great novels some heterosexual passion, be it "platonic" love or adultery, seduction, rape, or long-drawn-out flirtation, we came instead on the fugitive slave and the no-account boy lying side by side on a raft borne by the endless river toward an impossible escape, or the pariah sailor waking in the tattooed arms of the brown harpooner on the verge of their impossible quest. (pp. 144-45)

Even in the *Vita Nuova* of Dante, there is no vision of love less offensively, more unremittingly chaste; that it is not adult seems beside the point. Ishmael's sensations as he wakes under the pressure of Queequeg's arm, the tenderness of Huck's repeated loss and refinding of Jim. . .—these shape us from childhood: we have no sense of first discovering them or of having been once without them.

Of the infantile, the homoerotic aspects of these stories we are, though vaguely, aware; but it is only with an effort that we can wake to a consciousness of how, among us who at the level of adulthood find a difference in color sufficient provocation for distrust and hatred, they celebrate, all of them, the mutual love of *a white man and a colored*. So buried at a level of acceptance which does not touch reason, so desperately repressed from overt recognition, so contrary to what is usually thought of as our ultimate level of taboo—the sense of that love can survive only in the obliquity of a symbol, persistent, obsessive, in short, an archetype: the boy's homoerotic crush, the love of the black fused at this level into a single thing.

I hope I have been using here a hopelessly abused word with some precision; by "archetype" I mean a coherent pattern of beliefs and feelings so widely shared at a level beneath consciousness that there exists no abstract vocabulary for representing it, and so "sacred" that unexamined, irrational restraints inhibit any explicit analysis. Such a complex finds a formula or pattern story, which serves both to embody it, and, at first at least, to conceal its full implications. Later, the secret may be revealed, the archetype "analyzed" or "allegorically" interpreted according to the language of the day.

I find the complex we have been examining genuinely mythic; certainly it has the invisible character of the true archetype, eluding the wary pounce of Howells or Mrs. Twain, who excised from *Huckleberry Finn* the cussing as unfit for children, but who left, unperceived, a conventionally abhorrent doctrine of ideal love. . . . The felt difference between *Huckleberry Finn* and Twain's other books must lie in part in the release from conscious restraint inherent in the author's assumption of the character of Huck; the passage in and out of darkness and river mist, the constant confusion of identities (Huck's ten or twelve names; the question of who is the real uncle, who the true Tom), the sudden intrusions into alien violences without past or future, give the whole work, for all its carefully observed detail, the texture of a dream. (pp. 146-47)

I do not recall ever having seen in the commentaries of the social anthropologist or psychologist an awareness of the role of this profound child's dream of love in our relation to the Negro. . . . Trapped in what have by now became shackling clichés—the concept of the white man's sexual envy of the Negro male, the ambivalent horror of miscegenation—they do not sufficiently note the complementary factor of physical attraction, the archetypal love of white male and black. But either the horror or the attraction is meaningless alone; only together do they make sense. Just as the pure love of man and man is in general set off against the ignoble passion of man for woman, so more specifically (and more vividly) the dark desire which leads to miscegenation is contrasted with the ennobling love of a white man and a colored one. James Fenimore Cooper is our first poet of this ambivalence; indeed, miscegenation is the secret theme of the Leatherstocking novels, especially of *The Last of the Mohicans*. (pp. 147-48)

Nature undefiled—this is the inevitable setting of the Sacred Marriage of males. Ishmael and Queequeg, arm in arm, about to ship out, Huck and Jim swimming beside the raft in the peaceful flux of the Mississippi—here it is the motion of water which completes the syndrome, the American dream of isolation afloat. The notion of the Negro as the unblemished bride blends with the myth of running away to sea, of running the great river down to the sea. The immensity of water defines a loneliness that demands love; its strangeness symbolizes the disavowal of the conventional that makes possible all versions of love. In *Two Years Before the Mast*, in *Moby Dick*, in *Huckleberry Finn* the water is there, is the very texture of the novel. . . . (p. 148)

[There] is a context in which the legend of the sea as escape and solace, the fixated sexuality of boys, the myth of the dark beloved, are dark beloved, are one. In Melville and Twain at the center of our tradition, in the lesser writers at the periphery, the archetype is at once formalized and perpetuated. Nigger Jim and Queequeg make concrete for us what was without them a vague pressure on the threshold of our consciousness; the proper existence of the archetype is in the realized character, who waits, as it were, only to be asked his secret. Think of Oedipus biding in silence from Sophocles to Freud! (p. 149)

In the myth, one notes finally, it is typically in the role of outcast, ragged woodsman, or despised sailor ("Call me Ishmael!"), or unregenerate boy (Huck before the prospect of

being "sivilized" cries out, "I been there before!") that we turn to the love of a colored man. But how, we cannot help asking, does the vision of the white American as a pariah correspond with our long-held public status: the world's beloved, the success? It is perhaps only the artist's portrayal of *himself,* the notoriously alienated writer in America, at home with such images, child of the town drunk, the hapless survivor. But no, Ishamel is in all of us, our unconfessed universal fear objectified in the writer's status as in the outcast sailor's: that compelling anxiety, which every foreigner notes, that we may not be loved, that we are loved for our possessions and not ourselves, that we are really—*alone*. It is that underlying terror which explains our incredulity in the face of adulation or favor, what is called (once more the happy adjective) our "boyish modesty."

Our dark-skinned beloved will take us in, we assure ourselves, when we have been cut off, or have cut ourselves off, from all others, without rancor or the insult of forgiveness. He will fold us in his arms saying, "Honey" or "Aikane"; he will comfort us, as if our offense against him were long ago remitted, were never truly *real*. And yet we cannot ever really forget our guilt; the stories that embody the myth dramatize as if compulsively the role of the colored man as the victim. . . . The immense gulf of guilt must not be mitigated any more than the disparity of color . . . , so that the final reconciliation may seem more unbelievable and tender. The archetype makes no attempts to deny our outrage as fact; it portrays it as meaningless in the face of love.

There would be something insufferable, I think, in that final vision of remission if it were not for the presence of a motivating anxiety, the sense always of a last chance. Behind the white American's nightmare that someday, no longer tourist, inheritor, of liberator, he will be rejected, refused, he dreams of his acceptance at the breast he has most utterly offended. It is a dream so sentimental, so outrageous, so desperate, that it redeems our concept of boyhood from nostalgia to tragedy. (pp. 150-51)

> Leslie A. Fiedler, *"Come Back to the Raft Ag'in, Huck Honey!"* (originally published in Partisan Review, *Vol. XV, No. 6, June, 1948), in his* The Collected Essays of Leslie Fiedler, Vol. I *(copyright © 1971 by Leslie A. Fiedler; reprinted with permission of Stein and Day Publishers), Stein and Day, 1971, pp. 142-51.*

T. S. ELIOT (essay date 1950)

The Adventures of Huckleberry Finn is the only one of Mark Twain's various books which can be called a masterpiece. I do not suggest that it is his only book of permanent interest; but it is the only one in which his genius is completely realized, and the only one which creates its own category. There are pages in *Tom Sawyer* and in *Life on the Mississippi* which are, within their limits, as good as anything with which one can compare them in *Huckleberry Finn;* and in other books there are drolleries just as good of their kind. But when we find one book by a prolific author which is very much superior to all the rest, we look for the peculiar accident or concourse of accidents which made that book possible. In the writing of *Huckleberry Finn* Mark Twain had two elements which, when treated with his sensibility and his experience, formed a great book: these two are the Boy and the River. (p. vii)

[It] was only a few years ago that I read for the first time, and in that order, *Tom Sawyer* and *Huckleberry Finn*.

Tom Sawyer did not prepare me for what I was to find its sequel to be. *Tom Sawyer* seems to me to be a boys' book, and a very good one. The River and *the* Boy make their appearance in it; the narrative is good; and there is also a very good picture of society in a small mid-Western river town (for St. Petersburg is more Western than Southern) a hundred years ago. But the point of view of the narrator is that of an adult observing a boy. And Tom is the ordinary boy, though of quicker wits, and livelier imagination, than most. Tom is, I suppose, very much the boy that Mark Twain had been: he is remembered and described as he seemed to his elders, rather than created. Huck Finn, on the other hand, is the boy that Mark Twain still was, at the time of writing his adventures. We look at Tom as the smiling adult does: Huck we do not look at—we see the world through his eyes. The two boys are not merely different types; they were brought into existence by different processes. Hence in the second book their roles are altered. In the first book Huck is merely the humble friend—almost a variant of the traditional valet of comedy; and we see him as he is seen by the conventional respectable society to which Tom belongs, and of which, we feel sure, Tom will one day become an eminently respectable and conventional member. In the second book their nominal relationship remains the same; but here it is Tom who has the secondary role. The author was probably not conscious of this, when he wrote the first two chapters: *Huckleberry Finn* is not the kind of story in which the author knows, from the beginning, what is going to happen. Tom then disappears from our view; and when he returns, he has only two functions. The first is to provide a foil for Huck. Huck's persisting admiration for Tom only exhibits more clearly to our eyes the unique qualities of the former and the commonplaceness of the latter. Tom has the imagination of a lively boy who has read a good deal of romantic fiction: he might, of course, become a writer—he might become Mark Twain. Or rather, he might become the more commonplace aspect of Mark Twain. Huck has not imagination, in the sense in which Tom has it: he has, instead, vision. He sees the real world; and he does not judge it—he allows it to judge itself.

Tom Sawyer is an orphan. But he has his aunt; he has, as we learn later, other relatives; and he has the environment into which he fits. He is wholly a social being. When there is a secret band to be formed, it is Tom who organizes it and prescribes the rules. Huck Finn is alone: there is no more solitary character in fiction. The fact that he has a father only emphasizes his loneliness; and he views his father with a terrifying detachment. So we come to see Huck himself in the end as one of the permanent symbolic figures of fiction; not unworthy to take a place with Ulysses, Faust, Don Quixote, Don Juan, Hamlet and other great discoveries that man has made about himself.

It would seem that Mark Twain was a man who—perhaps like most of us—never became in all respects mature. We might even say that the adult side of him was boyish, and that only the boy in him, that was Huck Finn, was adult. As Tom Sawyer grown up, he wanted success and applause (Tom himself always needs an audience). He wanted prosperity, a happy domestic life of a conventional kind, universal approval, and fame. All of these things he obtained. As Huck Finn he was indifferent to all these things; and being composite of the two, Mark Twain both strove for them, and resented their violation of his integrity. Hence he became the humorist and even clown:

with his gifts, a certain way to success, for everyone could enjoy his writings without the slightest feeling of discomfort, self-consciousness or self-criticism. And hence, on the other hand, his pessimism and misanthropy. To be a misanthrope is to be in some way divided; or it is a sign of an uneasy conscience. The pessimism which Mark Twain discharged into *The Man That Corrupted Hadleyburg* and *What is Man?* springs less from observation of society, than from his hatred of himself for allowing society to tempt and corrupt him and give him what he wanted. (pp. vii-ix)

You cannot say that Huck himself is either a humorist or a misanthrope. He is the impassive observer: he does not interfere, and, as I have said, he does not judge. Many of the episodes that occur on the voyage down the river, after he is joined by the Duke and the King (whose fancies about themselves are akin to the kind of fancy that Tom Sawyer enjoys) are in themselves farcical; and if it were not for the presence of Huck as the reporter of them, they would be no more than farce. But, seen through the eyes of Huck, there is a deep human pathos in these scoundrels. On the other hand, the story of the feud between the Grangerfords and the Shepherdsons is a masterpiece in itself: yet Mark Twain could not have written it so, with that economy and restraint, with just the right details and no more, and leaving to the reader to make his own moral reflections, unless he had been writing in the person of Huck. And the *style* of the book, which is the style of Huck, is what makes it a far more convincing indictment of slavery than the sensationalist propaganda of *Uncle Tom's Cabin*. Huck is passive and impassive, apparently always the victim of events; and yet, in his acceptance of his world and of what it does to him and others, he is more powerful than his world, because he is more *aware* than any other person in it.

Repeated readings of the book only confirm and deepen one's admiration of the consistency and perfect adaptation of the writing. This is a style which at the period, whether in America or in England, was an innovation, a new discovery in the English language. Other authors had achieved natural speech in relation to particular characters—Scott with characters talking Lowland Scots, Dickens with cockneys: but no one else had kept it up through the whole of a book. Thackeray's Yellowplush, impressive as he is, is an obvious artifice in comparison. In *Huckleberry Finn* there is no exaggeration of grammar or spelling or speech, there is no sentence or phrase to destroy the illusion that these are Huck's own words. It is not only in the way in which he tells his story, but in the details he remembers, that Huck is true to himself. There is, for instance, . . . the list of the objects which Huck and Jim salvaged from the derelict house. . . . [It] is the sort of list that a boy reader should pore over with delight; but the paragraph performs other functions of which the boy reader would be unaware. It provides the right counterpoise to the horror of the wrecked house and the corpse; it has a grim precision which tells the reader all he needs to know about the way of life of the human derelicts who had used the house; and (especially the wooden leg, and the fruitless search for its mate) reminds us at the right moment of the kinship of mind and the sympathy between the boy outcast from society and the negro fugitive from the injustice of society.

Huck in fact would be incomplete without Jim, who is almost as notable a creation as Huck himself. Huck is the passive observer of men and events, Jim the submissive sufferer from them; and they are equal in dignity. There is no passage in which their relationship is brought out more clearly than the conclusion of the chapter in which, after the two have become separated in the fog, Huck in the canoe and Jim on the raft, Huck, in his impulse of boyish mischief, persuades Jim for a time that the latter had dreamt the whole episode. . . . What is obvious in [the passage] is the pathos and dignity of Jim [as he reproaches Huck for fooling him] and this is moving enough; but what I find still more disturbing, and still more unusual in literature, is the pathos and dignity of the boy, when reminded so humbly and humiliatingly, that his position in the world is not that of other boys, entitled from time to time to a practical joke; but that he must bear, and bear alone, the responsibility of a man.

It is Huck who gives the book style. The River gives the book its form. But for the River, the book might be only a sequence of adventures with a happy ending. A river, a very big and powerful river, is the only natural force that can wholly determine the course of human peregrination. (pp. ix-xii)

It is the River that controls the voyage of Huck and Jim; that will not let them land at Cairo, where Jim could have reached freedom; it is the River that separates them and deposits Huck for a time in the Grangerford household; the River that reunites them, and then compels upon them the unwelcome company of the King and the Duke. Recurrently we are reminded of its presence and its power. . . . We come to understand the River by seeing it through the eyes of the Boy; but the Boy is also the spirit of the River. *Huckleberry Finn,* like other great works of imagination, can give to every reader whatever he is capable of taking from it. On the most superficial level of observation, Huck is convincing as a boy. On the same level, the picture of social life on the shores of the Mississippi a hundred years ago is, I feel sure, accurate. On any level, Mark Twain makes you see the River, as it is and was and always will be, more clearly than the author of any other description of a river known to me. But you do not merely see the River, you do not merely become acquainted with it through the senses: you experience the River. Mark Twain, in his later years of success and fame, referred to his early life as a steamboat pilot as the happiest he had known. . . . Certainly, but for his having practised that calling, earned his living by that profession, he would never have gained the understanding which his genius for expression communicates in this book. . . . There are, perhaps, only two ways in which a writer can acquire the understanding of environment which he can later turn to account: by having spent his childhood in that environment—that is, living in it at a period of life in which one experiences much more than one is aware of; and by having had to struggle for a livelihood in that environment—a livelihood bearing no direct relation to any intention of writing about it, of *using* it as literary material. . . . Mark Twain knew the Mississippi in both ways: he had spent his childhood on its banks, and he had earned his living matching his wits against its currents.

Thus the River makes the book a great book. As with Conrad, we are continually reminded of the power and terror of Nature, and the isolation and feebleness of Man. Conrad remains always the European observer of the tropics, the white man's eye contemplating the Congo and its black gods. But Mark Twain is a native, and the River God is his God. It is as a native that he accepts the River God, and it is the subjection of Man that gives to Man his dignity. For without some kind of God, Man is not even very interesting.

Readers sometimes deplore the fact that the story descends to the level of *Tom Sawyer* from the moment that Tom himself re-appears. Such readers protest that the escapades invented

by Tom, in the attempted "rescue" of Jim, are only a tedious development of themes with which we were already too familiar—even while admitting that the escapades themselves are very amusing, and some of the incidental observations memorable. But it is right that the mood of the end of the book should bring us back to that of the beginning. Or, if this was not the right ending for the book, what ending would have been right?

In *Huckleberry Finn* Mark Twain wrote a much greater book than he could have known he was writing. Perhaps all great works of art mean much more than the author could have been aware of meaning: certainly, *Huckleberry Finn* is the one book of Mark Twain's which, as a whole has this unconsciousness. So what seems to be the rightness, of reverting at the end of the book to the mood of *Tom Sawyer,* was perhaps unconscious art. For Huckleberry Finn, neither a tragic nor a happy ending would be suitable. No worldly success or social satisfaction, no domestic consummation would be worthy of him; a tragic end also would reduce him to the level of those whom we pity. Huck Finn must come from nowhere and be bound for nowhere. His is not the independence of the typical or symbolic American Pioneer, but the independence of the vagabond. His existence questions the values of America as much as the values of Europe; he is as much an affront to the "pioneer spirit" as he is to "business enterprise"; he is in a state of nature as detached as the state of the saint. In a busy world, he represents the loafer; in an acquisitive and competitive world, he insists on living from hand to mouth. He could not be exhibited in any amorous encounters or engagements, in any of the juvenile affections which are appropriate to Tom Sawyer. He belongs neither to the Sunday School nor to the Reformatory. He has no beginning and no end. Hence, he can only disappear; and his disappearance can only be accomplished by bringing forward another performer to obscure the disappearance in a cloud of whimsicalities.

Like Huckleberry Finn, the River itself has no beginning or end. In its beginning, it is not yet the River; in its end, it is no longer the River. . . . Things must merely happen, here and there, to the people who live along its shore or who commit themselves to its current. And it is as impossible for Huck as for the River to have a beginning or end—a *career.* So the book has the right, the only possible concluding sentence. I do not think that any book ever written ends more certainly with the right words:

> But I reckon I got to light out for the Territory
> ahead of the rest, because Aunt Sally she's
> going to adopt me and civilize me, and I can't
> stand it. I been there before.

(pp. xiii-xvi)

T. S. Eliot, "Introduction" (reprinted by permission of Mrs. Valerie Eliot and Faber and Faber Ltd.), in The Adventures of Huckleberry Finn *by Samuel L. Clemens (Mark Twain), The Cresset Press, 1950, pp. vii-xvi.*

HENRY SEIDEL CANBY (essay date 1951)

[Mark Twain's] art, such as it was, and at its best it is a great art, is essentially oral. He was not only a born storyteller and wisecracker, but he early learned how to transfer to the written word the overtones, the color (to mix my figure) of conversation, how to select the words which lift narrative, no matter how rapid, above a mere record of events. . . . It is not accurate to say that Mark wrote as he talked; he learned to write so that his words sounded as if he were talking. His written dialogue speaks itself, and presents a flesh-and-blood, personally seen-and-heard speaker to the imagination of the reader. (pp. 37-8)

[Mark's] style is subtly his own, the "tune of it," and you could pick out a speech of Huck's from a Dictionary of Quotations and write his name after it. Well adapted to the lecture platform, where the prime necessity was an immediate response in applause or laughter, this great talent of his was subject to corruption. On the stage he had to exaggerate to get his effects, and include a little acting. There, as Dickens added the effects of excellent acting to a text already written for print, and stirred his audience to tears and shouts so Mark preparing his lectures added his props, his overemphases, his wisecracks and exaggerations, and acquired habits which he carried over into writing and from which he never escaped. To appreciate Mark's genius in his great books you must think of them as oral. (p. 38)

Mark had only one discipline to which he had rigorously and successfully submitted himself—language. Mark's English is superb, his taste in diction impeccable. He boasted of it, and was right. His terse, simple, effective style, his words chosen with a lively sense of values, his accuracy and his force, never fail except in an occasional purple passage when he strains after an artificial beauty which was not his forte. He writes . . . better English than Henry James, both by word and by rhythm, though with far less assistance from a flowing vocabulary. He would, I think, have been incapable of using *aggravated* where he means *irritated*, as James does too often. His cello is a better instrument than James' violin, though realms of expression were admittedly closed to it.

Mark had art enough when his theme was right. But his theme had to be Mark the Innocent; the Innocent for whom he invented the term, the American Innocent as Henry James again and again used the word, with only a shift of emphasis in the meaning. The Innocent was the shrewd, warmhearted, self-confident American, who was also unsophisticated, uncorrupted in faith in humanity, in hope, and in charity, though tough enough in other respects. . . . Mark filled *The Quaker City* with such compatriots, of whom he was the best critic and observer because he was an Innocent himself. (p. 119)

> *Henry Seidel Canby, in his* Turn West, Turn East: Mark Twain and Henry James *(copyright 1951 by Henry Seidel Canby; copyright renewed © 1979 by Edward T. Canby; reprinted by permission of Houghton Mifflin Company), Houghton, 1951, 318 p.**

WILLIAM FAULKNER (essay date 1956)

In my opinion, Mark Twain was the first truly American writer, and all of us since are his heirs, we descended from him. Before him the writers who were considered American were not, really; their tradition, their culture was European culture. It was only with Twain, Walt Whitman, there became a true indigenous American culture. . . . Of course, Whitman was in chronology the first, but Whitman was an experimenter with the notion there might be an American literature. Twain was the first that grew up in the belief that there is an American literature and he found himself producing it. So I call him the father of American literature though he is not the first one. (p. 88)

> *William Faulkner, "Colloquies at Nagano Seminar," in* Faulkner at Nagano, *edited by Robert A. Jelliffe (© 1956 by Kenkyusha Ltd.), Kenkyusha, 1956, pp. 27-132.**

ALBERT E. STONE, JR. (essay date 1959)

Few men in his generation were as widely read in the lore of Joan of Arc as Twain himself.

The chief reason for Clemens's unusual breadth of knowledge was that the story of the Maid of Orleans touched him deeply. The image he constructed of her in his novel was the result of much thought; it answered not only to his intellectual interests but also to his personal emotional needs. Intellectually, Joan of Arc attracted Twain because she epitomized an age-old struggle of common folk against the twin institutions of cruelty and oppression, the Crown and the Church. In this respect, *Joan of Arc* repeats themes of *The Prince and the Pauper* and *A Connecticut Yankee*. Emotionally, the pull was even stronger. In Twain's eyes Joan was the incarnation of youth and purity and power. She was the unique instance in history of the young girl whose innocence not merely *existed* but *acted* in the gross world of adult affairs. She was the peerless human being, and it was of the utmost importance that she remain eternally a young girl. (pp. 4-5)

There is, for example, no hint of sexual development in his growing heroine. . . . Anyone familiar with Clemens' skittishness about sex in his books, not to mention the social attitudes of his day, will not be surprised at his silence on this score. Still, it is a detail that throws light upon Joan's strictly childish appeal for Twain. The notion that the Maid was believed to have remained a child in body as well as in spirit must have pleased him and added force to his iterations of her immaculate girlishness.

Similar sentiments about girlhood animate the whole of *Joan of Arc*, in which the aged narrator, Sieur Louis de Conte, in addition to being an actual historical personage, is the most transparent of personae. Twain discovered the "young man of noble birth" with the convenient initials in Michelet's history and translated a minor figure into the central intelligence around which his story is structured. By so doing the novelist introduced himself and his private feelings into the stream of history.

One of the characteristic features of Mark Twain's fiction is his dramatic use of a narrator. *Joan of Arc* derives much of its power from the character who tells the story. Although it is not clear from the early Domremy chapters, Louis de Conte bears a striking resemblance to the narrators Twain created many years earlier both for *Roughing It* and "Old Times on the Mississippi": that is, he is two people at once. Louis is both the fifteen-year-old boy who leaves Domremy to follow Joan and the old cynic who relates the tale many years later. (p. 9)

It is as if a middle-aged Mark Twain were looking back at himself, the thirteen-year-old boy, Sam Clemens, and commenting on his own naïveté. In this sense *Joan of Arc* is a double initiation. At the same time that a saint is being made of an innocent village maiden her page is becoming an embittered old man.

One reason, however, for the weakness of *Joan of Arc* as a novel is that Twain does not sufficiently dramatize these two narrators or the process by which "the boy" (as Clemens identified him in early marginal notes in his reading) is transformed into the misanthrope. Louis's initiation is already over when he records Joan's career. As a result, the novel, already somewhat desiccated by historical fact and occasional footnotes, loses that freshness which Huck Finn, for example, was able to give to the account of his initiation.

In the opening chapters these effects of the page's disenchantment are less apparent, and this section is in many respects the most successful part of the novel. Certainly it is most completely of Twain's own manufacture. . . . His narrator becomes almost a believable boy and Joan a real girl as the history of their life in the woods and fields is told. The specifically pastoral quality of these chapters is likewise Twain's own idea. Ignoring those sources which point out that the D'Arc family were not simple farmers but prosperous villagers, and that Joan was not often afield, Twain casts Joan almost exclusively in the role of shepherdess. In so doing Twain draws a distinct line between her life in the open fields, where all is idyllic peace beneath the Fairy Tree, and that of the village, where violence and evil can and do occur. (pp. 10-11)

De Conte's account of Joan's childhood is a mixture of pastoral idyll and realistic, even gruesome, picture of medieval village life. But as saint and secretary leave Domremy to fulfill their fates at Orléans, Rheims, and Rouen, the balanced tone of Twain's romance changes. The credulous, boyish side of the narrator's mask is discarded and with it the depiction of outdoors life as innocence. The unhappy old man takes over the story. At the same time the pastoral idyll gives way to blatant melodrama. Whereas Joan and her companions are pictured in the village with considerable individuality (especially in their speech), in later scenes all the characters tend to be projected as stereotypes. Joan herself, of course, is the virtuous heroine. The Paladin is her comic bodyguard with the heart of gold. Cauchon and Loyseleur, the Bishop and Priest who control the trial at Rouen, are the arch-villains. (pp. 11-12)

The tensions between Twain's intellectual aims and his emotional predilections, the pull of "truthfulness" against the image of Joan as his "platonic sweetheart," as it were, are everywhere evident in *Joan of Arc*. The sentimental innocence of the boy, though more palpable in the Domremy chapters, runs all through the narrative; we see it particularly in the melodramatic touches. Side by side with this maudlin sentiment, however, exists the mocking laughter of the old secretary, whose cynicism is directed not at Joan but at himself and at all men. Sieur Louis de Conte, being so thoroughly of two minds about Joan's life, is indeed an ambiguous interpreter of its meaning. (pp. 12-13)

[In his review of *Joan of Arc,* William Dean Howells] could see that Joan was more to Twain than the expression of French nationalism, but he could not tell, judging from the novel alone, whether her power came from a divine source or from the girl's own soul.

At this level of "meaning," *Joan of Arc* is indeed a perplexing mixture. A devotional exercise for a Roman Catholic girl couched in profoundly Protestant terms, it is also a celebration of the world's most perfect human by an oldish man who has lost his faith in mankind. The novel is, moreover, a case history of a religious mystic whose puissance seems to emanate from her own intuition rather than from the temporary indwelling of holy Voices. These ambiguities are implicit in the structure of *Joan of Arc* not simply because the historical Joan was, and is, an enigma, but also because Sieur Louis de Conte cannot resolve his own doubts. (pp. 13-14)

[Joan's] power is not intellectual—it defies rational explanation by the best university minds; nor is it social—the people is a great beast, the Church simply a group of people. Her supernatural deeds must, then, emanate from some mysterious source anterior to reason and to human institutions. That this source

is mysterious is everywhere insisted upon by Twain's commentator. . . .

But has the novel not already suggested one source? If the church or the people cannot, may not the Fairy Tree "explain" Joan of Arc? This Tree is the central symbolic vehicle for Mark Twain's pastorale. (p. 15)

The Tree is the talisman of Joan's oneness with nature; it asserts that she is "born child of the sun, natural comrade of the birds and of all happy free creatures." . . . It gives her the "seeing eye," "the creating mouth," those innate, mysterious qualities which neither the Doctors, nor the soldiers, nor Joan's own page can otherwise account for. A vision of the Tree appears to Joan in prison and aids her as much as the Holy Voices to meet death. For the Fairy Tree is the sign of Paradise. It is a pagan sign, not specifically Christian, being associated with children, fairies, open fields, and animals of the forest rather than with Saint Catherine and Saint Margaret. Furthermore, it signifies a Paradise existing eternally in the past, not a future Christian heaven. (p. 17)

The Fairy Tree is the comprehensive symbol through which Joan's life approximates for Twain the pattern of myth. Her sacrificial death (so like Christ's) completes the cycle of the nature goddess begun by a pastoral childhood, continued through an heroic, miraculous career, and climaxed by the Passion at Rouen. Through her death—and clearly this is the significance of her life to Louis de Conte—Joan of Arc escapes from time, old age, from loss of faith. The vision of the Fairy Tree redeems life.

This interpretation of his heroine clearly fitted Mark Twain's own spiritual condition which, in the 1890's, was in many respects identical in its pessimism and nostalgia with that of his spokesman. That he could represent Joan simultaneously as Christian, democrat, and nature goddess, and yet not exclusively as any of these, argues a spiritual ambivalence, a tension among skepticism, determinism, and faith which was, by 1896, far from being resolved.

Joan of Arc both exemplifies this dilemma and offers a way out. Sieur Louis, with his mixture of irony, resignation, and rage at the human race, is the literary spokesman for the philosophical contradictions (if one may so grace the simplicities of Clemens' thought) of *What Is Man?* More significant, however, is Joan of Arc herself. The Maid embodies and transcends all contradictions. Depicted as girlishly human in speech and manner, Joan escapes the stain of depraved humanity by her indestructible innocence. A devout Catholic, Joan's loyalty to her Voices places her in righteous opposition to that fallible institution, the Church. Her bond with the Fairy Tree, on the other hand, establishes a link with nature, with a prerational source of knowledge, with a pre-institutional source of piety, with an eternal world of values not subject to the pains, disappointments, doubts, and contradictions of adult life. For it is *adult* life which creates ambiguities for Sieur Louis de Conte. *Joan of Arc,* though it culminates in the victimization of childhood, affirms that state as the only form of life worth living—and dying—for. (pp. 17-18)

Albert E. Stone, Jr., "Mark Twain's 'Joan of Arc': The Child As Goddess," in American Literature *(reprinted by permission of the Publisher; copyright 1959 by Duke University Press, Durham, North Carolina), Vol. XXXI, No. 1, March, 1959, pp. 1-20.*

LOUIS J. BUDD (essay date 1959)

Like other great novels, *The Adventures of Huckleberry Finn* has been reinterpreted whenever fashions in ideas have changed. Today many critics search it for Mark Twain's subconscious motives; others claim that it is a reworking of fundamental myths about river gods or initiation rites. Although Twain certainly had psychic tensions and although he liked to speculate—in an eighteenth-century way—about generic man, his interest in going problems was also strong. Perhaps no analysis of *Huckleberry Finn* can fix its proportions of escape, abstract moralizing, basic human warmth, nostalgia, clowning, and social commentary. The debate over the course of the New South, however was an important factor in the novel's genesis. (p. 222)

In *Huckleberry Finn* Twain attacked slavery with strategies worthy of his friend and close neighbor in Hartford, Harriet Beecher Stowe. Through the famous remark about the steamboat explosion he diagnosed the dulling of sensitivity that afflicted even the decent whites like Aunt Sally; through Huck's genuine shock at Tom helping a runaway and therefore becoming a "nigger-stealer" he satirized the tie between chattel slavery and respectability. The sorrows of the chattel himself were highlighted in Jim's longing for his divided family. More forcefully than [George Washington] Cable's fiction, Twain's novel challenged the memory of the old regime. In addition, by questioning the myth of the happy slave Twain cast suspicion, by a weak but common linkage, on any later move that the Deep South might make concerning the Negro. To readers in a country in which there were now no slaves, the novel took on fresh meaning as a judgment of the South's conduct after the withdrawal of federal troops had paroled it to its own conscience. Literary critics who ignore the historical context in which Twain wrote cannot fully explain the adventures of Huck and Jim.

Even before he had Huck and Jim leave the outskirts of St. Petersburg, Missouri, Twain drew Huck's father with a uniqueness beyond the needs of the plot. Pap Finn was more than a supernumerary to his creator, whom a friend recalled as "assured . . . of the social truths behind Pap's diatribe on negro suffrage"; Pap stood for a group excoriated by name in *A Connecticut Yankee* . . . and in Twain's later comment that slavery had a "hardly less baleful influence upon the poor white." (p. 227)

Contradicting the sentimental fiction that was rising to the poor white defense, Pap showed noisomely the meanest qualities of his class. Superstitious, alcoholic, and shiftless, on his first appearance he raged against the "hifalut'n foolishness" of his son's learning to read and write in defiance of family tradition. After taking Huck's dollar and leaving, he stuck his head in the window to remind Huck "about that school, because he was going to lay for me and lick me if I didn't drop that." The only other time that Huck quoted him at length, Pap was angry about what had happened when he was on his way to vote—"if I wan't too drunk to get there." He had seen a Negro who "was a p'fessor in a college" in Ohio, "and could talk all kinds of languages, and knowed everything." On hearing that the well-dressed mulatto—who "wouldn't'a' give me the road if I hadn't shoved him out o' the way"—could vote at home, boozy Pap had sworn never to touch a ballot again. His outrage because this "prowling, thieving, infernal, white-shirted free nigger" could not be seized and sold led back to his favorite tirade. Although Huck reported that "whenever his liquor begun to work he most always went for the govment," this time he outdid himself in criticizing a meddlesome "govment" that even kept him from grabbing Huck's pile. In his words and actions, Pap loudly demonstrated how the poor whites served the Redemptionists by opposing education, by violently insisting on white supremacy, and by holding a larger hostility to "governmental interference of any kind."

To the reader's sorrow, Pap never again growled his magisterial opinions. By getting killed in a brawl, however, he swelled the heavy tone of violence that has often been noticed in *Huckleberry Finn*. In putting together a conventional plot, Twain almost always used mayhem, and *The Adventures of Tom Sawyer* had its share. But he deliberately multiplied the gory episodes in its sequel. The handiest illustration of his increasing concern over southerners' resort to violence is seen in *Life on the Mississippi*, finished less than a year before *Huckleberry Finn*. Talking about the country below Memphis, Twain's account of a killing over a small matter was prefaced with, "Piece of history illustrative of the violent style of some of the people down along here." . . . This aside was expanded in the long footnote which—Twain told his publisher—described "some Southern assassinations"; covering well over a page, it comprised many newspaper reports of homicide or assault. *Huckleberry Finn* continued this emphasis on the proneness of some southerners to shoot or stab or to take the law into their own hands. (pp. 228-29)

To see this emphasis on violence as a demonstration of Twain's neuroses, as some have done, is to ignore his sensitivity to current events. As early as 1869, in an editorial titled **"Only a Nigger,"** he fulminated against southern mob-law and the swashbuckling habits built on pseudo-chivalry. (p. 229)

Twain's abhorrence of southern violence found its fullest outlet in the Sherburn-Boggs scene, the point of which echoed a passage omitted from *Life on the Mississippi*. Noting that many thought of the South as "one vast and gory murder-field" where "every man goes armed, and has at one time or another taken a neighbor's life," Twain had charged that its citizens, while mostly law-abiding, failed to insist on convictions "even in the clearest cases of homicide" and that, therefore, "one hot head defies the hamlet." Such a hothead was Colonel Sherburn, who publicly killed an unarmed, drunken heckler. (pp. 231-32)

Colonel Sherburn, whose airs suggest a former plantation owner, obeyed a cruel, hypersensitive code. As for the community, it enjoyed the break in routine; no one called for the sheriff, no servant of the law stepped forward; when a mob gathered impulsively and swirled out to the murderer's house, it melted before his defiance. And there the matter ended, to the injury of the South. . . . Without rigidly equating lawlessness and the "Solid South," Twain subscribed to the general feeling that they were connected.

Violence was not the only fault that Twain charged against the Redeemed South. He fumed about the related problem of its resistance to intellectual and material progress. Although the folklorist admires *Huckleberry Finn* as a treasury of popular superstitions, it is unlikely that Twain used them merely for realistic detail or for warm humor. . . . His notebook for 1882 tautly complained that "human nature" makes "superstitions and priests necessary," and *A Connecticut Yankee* bludgeoned any notion of witchcraft or of charms like the cross of nails in Pap's left boot heel. Like other freethinkers, Twain was also critical of the camp meetings and the shouting fundamentalists that luxuriated in the South. Remarking that Silas Phelps "never charged nothing for his preaching, and it was worth it," Huck further observed: "There was plenty other farmer-preachers like that . . . down South." . . . The social history in *Huckleberry Finn* was sometimes nostalgic and sometimes reeking with Twain's latent contempt for man everywhere; but much of it emphasized the darker half of the contrast that *Life on the Mississippi* drew between the lower and upper river regions. (pp. 232-33)

The main attack on backwardness, however, had already been made with the pointed attention given to Arkansas. Celebrated unkindly by the native humorists, it was a likely target because it had faltered like the other former rebel states while lacking their traditional glamor. . . . In *Huckleberry Finn,* Pokeville, with its degraded camp meeting, apparently belonged to Arkansas; at Bricksville came the trenchant vignette of a rural slum, the shooting of Boggs, and the swarming to the Royal Nonesuch. Several asides in his later *Connecticut Yankee,* like the quip that Guinevere's glances at Lancelot "would have got him shot in Arkansas, to a dead certainty," echoed Twain's belief that Arkansas, the only southern state Huck named, was the archetype of vicious ignorance. (p. 234)

Since he was supplying, for commercial reasons, a sequel to *Tom Sawyer,* Twain necessarily carried over its ante-bellum setting, but he infused it with opinions and judgments which reflected issues of the 1880's. In other works as well he demonstrated a shrewd skill in relating the past about which he wrote to the present which he keenly felt. By sniping at the protective tariff, *Tom Sawyer Abroad* show that he could give up-to-date purposes to the surrogates for his boyhood. Works like *A Connecticut Yankee* prove that he commanded also the subtlely of treating past event and current question together; in fact, models for fusing history with contemporary argument were much more familiar to Twain than the mythic patterns some wish on him. . . . Contrasting significantly with *Pudd'nhead Wilson* . . . which came much closer to an ante-bellum flavor, *Huckleberry Finn* wasted no time on the field hand writhing under the overseer's lash. It stressed the Negro's basic humanity and created a shrewd, loyal, generous Jim who deserved more respect than perhaps any Negro preceding him in American fiction. Intentionally or not, when Twain made Huck and his black comrade share bed and grub with growing mutual trust, he resisted the tide of Jim Crowism. (pp. 235-36)

Unfortunately, Twain did not maintain the climactic emphasis on Jim's claims to fairer treatment: he had another complaint burning for expression. Although his attitude toward the chivalric legend was changeable, *Huckleberry Finn,* standing between the anti-Scott diatribe in *Life on the Mississippi* and the ragings of Hank Morgan, showed no wavering. Among interpreters of the routine in the rescue of Jim, DeVoto comes nearest the truth by observing that it burlesqued "Scott and Dumas and the phantasies of the Southern gentry." To this must be added Twain's belief that the lingering strength of the chivalric tradition supported the notion of caste and the weakness for personal violence. If we have the least confidence in Twain, we must feel that the length to which he stretched his burlesque measured its urgency. Not that it was successful. Its inadequacy increased with each stab at comedy that also vitiated our image of the self-respecting and respect-worthy Jim, whom we had come to admire rather than just tolerate as a "good nigger."

This relapse was possible because, despite his aroused humaneness, Twain leaned toward crude nineteenth-century er-

rors about race. A number of anecdotes in *Life on the Mississippi* rest on white chauvinism . . . . Because Twain's sympathy had a condescending base, in satirizing the chivalric ideal he could mistreat Jim so crudely that some NAACP leaders have objected to his novel for school use. Still, most of us would rather travel with Jim on a stray raft than with Uncle Tom on a steamboat.

No one has given a convincing reason why *Huckleberry Finn* easily outdistances *Tom Sawyer* as well as their several sequels or, to put the question more narrowly, why "from the arrival of Pap on the mood is clear" in Twain's masterpiece. At least part of its power resulted from topical urgencies, and for its day *Huckleberry Finn* was unmistakably a commentary on the southern question. Brander Matthews found in it facets of postbellum society "important for us to perceive and understand": "The influence of slavery, the prevalence of feuds, the conditions and circumstances that make lynching possible—all these things are set before us clearly." To believe that this effect was accidental is to be naïve in Twain's behalf. The famous raft floated down the currents of a churning debate, and despite our axiom about how art and politics flow in two unrelated channels the enduring drive of *Huckleberry Finn* depends heavily on the skill with which Twain navigated both on the same trip. (pp. 236-37)

> *Louis J. Budd, "The Southward Currents under Huck Finn's Raft,"* in The Mississippi Valley Historical Review, *Vol. XLVI, No. 2, September, 1959, pp. 222-37.*

LANGSTON HUGHES   (essay date 1959)

Mark Twain's ironic little novel, *Pudd'nhead Wilson*, is laid on the banks of the Mississippi in the first half of the 1800's. It concerns itself with, among other things, the use of fingerprinting to solve the mystery of a murder. But *Pudd'nhead Wilson* is not a mystery novel. The reader knows from the beginning who committed the murder and has more than an inkling of how it will be solved. (p. vii)

Although introduced early, it is not until near the end of the book that Wilson becomes a major figure in the tale. The novel is rather the story of another young man's mistaken identity— a young man who thinks he is white but is in reality colored; who is heir to wealth without knowing his claim is false; who lives as a free man, but is legally a slave; and who, when he learns the true facts about himself, comes to ruin not through the temporarily shattering knowledge of his physical status, but because of weaknesses common to white or colored, slave or free. (pp. vii-viii)

Puddn'head Wilson is the man, who, in the end, sets things to rights. But for whom? Seemingly for the spectators only, not for the principals involved, for by that time to them right is wrong, wrong is right, and happiness has gone by the board. The slave system has taken its toll of all three concerned— mother, mammy, ward and child—for the mother and mammy, Roxana, matriarch and slave, are one. Roxy is a puppet whose at first successful deceits cause her to think herself a free agent. She is undone at the climax by the former laughing stock of the town, Pudd'nhead Wilson. . . . (p. viii)

Years before he published *Pudd'nhead Wilson* Mark Twain had been hailed as America's greatest humorist. . . . But in this work of his middle years (Twain was 59) he did not write a humorous novel. Except for a few hilarious village scenes, and a phonetic description of a baby's tantrums, the out-loud laughs to be found in *Tom Sawyer* or *Huckleberry Finn* are not a part of *Pudd'nhead*. In this book the basic theme is slavery, seriously treated, and its main thread concerns the absurdity of man-made differentials, whether of caste or "race." The word *race* might properly be placed in quotes for both of Mark Twain's central Negroes are largely white in blood and physiognomy, slaves only by circumstance, and each only "by a fiction of law and custom, a Negro." The white boy who is mistakenly raised as a slave in the end finds himself "rich and free, but in a most embarrassing situation. He could neither read nor write, and his speech was the basest dialect of Negro quarter. His gait, his attitudes, his gestures, his bearing, his laugh—all were vulgar and uncouth; his manners were the manners of a slave. Money and fine clothes could not mend these defeats or cover them up, they only made them the more glaring and pathetic." (pp. vii-ix)

On the other hand, the young dandy who thought his name was Thomas à Becket, studied at Yale. He then came home to Dawson's Landing bedecked in Eastern finery to lord it over black and white alike. As Pudd'nhead Wilson, who had the habit of penning little musings beneath the dates in his calendar, wrote, "Training is everything. The peach was once a bitter almond; cauliflower is nothing but cabbage with a college education." It took a foreigner with no regard for frontier aristocracy of Old Virginia lineage to kick Thomas à Becket right square in his sit-downer at a public meeting. In the ensuing free-for-all that breaks out, the hall is set afire. Here the sparkle of Twain's traditional humor bursts into hilarious flame, too, as the members of the nearby fire department—"who never stirred officially in unofficial costume"—donned their uniforms to drench the hall with enough water to "annihilate forty times as much fire as there was there; for a village fire company does not often get a chance to show off." Twain wryly concludes, "Citizens of that village . . . did not insure against fire; they insured against the fire-company."

Against fire and water in the slave states there was insurance, but none against the devious dangers of slavery itself. Not even a fine old gentleman like Judge Driscoll "of the best blood of the Old Dominion" could find insurance against the self-protective schemes of his brother's bond servant, Roxy, who did not like being a slave, but was willing to be one for her son's sake. Roxy was also willing to commit a grievous sin for her son's sake, palliating her conscience a little by saying, "white folks has done it." With "an unfair show in the battle of life,"as Twain puts it, Roxy, as an "heir of two centuries of unatoned insult and outrage," is yet not of as evil nature. Her crimes grow out of the greater crimes of the slave system. (pp. ix-x)

In *Pudd'nhead Wilson* Mark Twain wrote what at a later period might have been called in the first sense of the term, "a novel of social significance." Had Twain been a contemporary of Harriet Beecher Stowe, and this novel published before the War between the States, it might have been a minor *Uncle Tom's Cabin*. Twain minces no words describing the unfortunate effects of slavery upon the behavior of both Negroes and whites, even upon children. (p. x)

Mark Twain, in his presentation of Negroes as human beings, stands head and shoulders above the other Southern writers of his times, even such distinguished ones as Joel Chandler Harris, F. Hopkins Smith, and Thomas Nelson Page. It was a period when most writers who included Negro characters in their work at all, were given to presenting the slave as igorant and happy,

the freed men of color as ignorant and miserable, and all Negroes as either comic servants on the one hand or dangerous brutes on the other. That Mark Twain's characters in *Pudd'nhead Wilson* fall into none of these categories is a tribute to his discernment. And that he makes them neither heroes nor villains is a tribute to his understanding of human character. "Color is only skin deep." In this novel Twain shows how more than anything else environment shapes the man. Yet in his day behavioristic psychology was in its infancy. Likewise the science of fingerprinting. In 1894 *Pudd'nhead Wilson* was a "modern" novel indeed. And it still may be so classified. (p. xi)

Curiously enough, as modern as *Pudd'nhead Wilson* is, its format is that of an old-fashioned melodrama, as if its structure were borrowed from the plays performed on the riverboat theatres of that period. Perhaps deliberately, Twain selected this popular formula in which to tell a very serious story. Moving from climax to climax, every chapter ends with a teaser that makes the reader wonder what is coming next while, as in Greek tradegy, the fates keep closing in on the central protagonists. And here the fates have no regard whatsoever for color lines. It is this treatment of race that makes *Pudd'nhead Wilson* as contemporary as Little Rock, and Mark Twain as modern as Faulkner, although Twain died when Faulkner was in knee pants. (p. xii)

> Langston Hughes, "Introduction" (copyright © 1959 by Bantam Books, Inc.; reprinted by permission of Bantam Books, Inc.; all rights reserved), in Pudd'nhead Wilson by Mark Twain, Bantam Books, 1959 (and reprinted by Bantam Books, 1981), pp. vii-xiii.

LEWIS LEARY (essay date 1960)

[Shortly after] the publication of his first book, *The Celebrated Jumping Frog of Calaveras County and Other Sketches,* [Samuel Clemens set out] on an excursion to the Mediterranean and Near East on the steamship *Quaker City*. The letters which he sent back then, to the California paper [*Alta California*] and also to Horace Greeley's *Tribune* in New York, reached a public ripe for appreciation of his confident assumption that many hallowed shrines of the Old World did not measure to American standards. And such was public reponses to what he wrote that, when he returned to New York a few months later, the wild mustang of the western plains discovered himself a literary lion. . . . (p. 18)

[When] *The Innocents Abroad; or, The New Pilgrim's Progress* appeared in 1869, revised from the *Quaker City* letters . . . , reviewers found it "fresh, racy, and sparkling as a glass of champagne." The satire was alert, informed, sophisticated, and sidesplittingly funny. The accent was of western humor, but the subject, a favorite among men of good will since the Enlightenment of the century before, spoke of the decay of transatlantic institutions and their shoddiness beside the energetic freshness of the New World. Traveling American innocents haggled through native bazaars, delightedly conscious that every language but their own was ridiculous, and unconscious completely of their own outlandishness. . . .Because he was clever or because he was by nurture one of them, Clemens touched attitudes shared by many of his countrymen, even to admitting preference for copies of masterpieces because they were brighter than the originals. (pp. 18-19)

As if anticipating Henry James, [*The Innocents Abroad*] takes a fresh look at the transatlantic world and the stature of Americans when measured against its requirements. Without James's subtlety, conscious art, or depth of penetration, it discovers faults on both sides so that it becomes a book which cosmopolites and chauvinists can equally admire.

[*Roughing It*] was also greatly successful, suited, said one commentator, "to the wants of the rich, the poor, the sad, the gay." and a sure recipe for laughter. Again it was a book of traveling, the kind that Mark Twain was always to write best, in which one story after another was strung along a journey overland or on water. Every ingredient was here—the tall tale, the straight-faced shocker, melodrama in adventure, insight into raw life among men unrestrained by convention, folklore and animal lore. The effect was of improvisation, for narrative must flow, Clemens later said, as a stream flows, diverted by every boulder, but proceeding briskly, interestingly, on its course.

Such motion did not characterize **The Gilded Age,** published in 1873, which he wrote in collaboration with his Hartford neighbor, Charles Dudley Warner. For the opening chapters Clemens drew on recollections of frontier life to produce situations not unlike those we associate with *Tobacco Road* or *Li'l Abner,* where back-country people dream expansively of fortunes they have neither energy nor ability to acquire. Colonel Beriah Sellers is a hill-town Mr. Micawber, but drawn from memory of people, even relatives, whom Samuel Clemens had known. Some of the river scenes are beautifully realized. And as the locale shifts to Washington and New York, the novel touches with satirical humor on political corruption, the American jury system, and the mania for speculation, so that it became a best seller and gave title to the age which it reviewed. But artistically it was not a success, for the narrative finally collapses under the weight of plot and counterplot, and is not remembered as one of Mark Twain's best. (p. 20)

Probably no more continuingly popular book has ever appeared in the United States [than **The Adventures of Tom Sawyer**]. On first reading it seems loose and shambling—as Mark Twain was loose and shambling. Episodes designed "to pleasantly remind adults of what they once were themselves" often remain longer in memory than the plot of murder and pursuit which must have been intended to hold younger readers. But there is artistry in it also beyond the artistry of the raconteur who engraved minor realisms about provincial society for all time. Perhaps because he worked long over it, this first independent novel, published when its author was forty, is better constructed than any he was to write again. And its structure reveals levels of meaning which Mark Twain may not have known were there.

The story is divided into three almost exactly equal parts. There are ten chapters in the first part, ten in the second, and thirteen in the climactic third. The first part is separated from the second and the second from the third, each by an interchapter. Within each of the three parts events are detailed carefully, time moves slowly, incident by incident, day by day. In the interchapters time is accelerated, and weeks go by within a few pages. Each of the parts is different from the others in tone, in the kind of adventures in which Tom involves himself, and in the relationship of these adventures to the unifying theme of the whole.

The first ten chapters reveal boys engaged in characteristic play, stealing jam, playing hookey, swapping treasured belongings, until finally they visit a graveyard at midnight and there inadvertently witness a murder. Time has been chronicled exactly, from Friday afternoon to Monday night, but then in the first interchapter, Muff Potter is arrested for the crime which

the boys know he did not commit, and two weeks pass. The second part, Chapters 12 through 21, is divided into two major episodes, the Jackson Island adventure and the last day at school. Again time slows down, the boys are again at play, but no longer at simple play of boys among themselves for their own ends: it is directed now against adults, as if in revolt against what the world holds for boys who grew, as Tom has grown, beyond simple innocence to knowledge and, indirectly, participation in evil. After the second interchapter in which summer days are quickened by the boy's guilty knowledge of Muff's innocence, the plot moves to a cluttered climax.

In the last thirteen chapters the boys begin to act tentatively as adults act. Tom gives evidence in court, he and Huck stalk Injun Joe in a serious, common-sense manner, and they search for treasure which is real and not an imagined product of boyish play. But then Tom shucks off reponsibility and goes to a picnic, leaving matter-of-fact Huck to watch for the murderer. And Huck does discover him but only to frighten him into hiding from which he may emerge to strike again. No adult or even adult-like action succeeds in **The Adventures of Tom Sawyer.** In the first part, Aunt Polly is foiled in efforts to have Tom whitewash a fence. In the second part, grownups arrange a funeral for boys who are not dead and the schoolmaster loses his toupee. Now, as the story draws to an end, bumbling adult planning goes astray, and Tom and Becky are lost in the cave for hours before search for them begins. But adult search does not find them, any more than adult efforts do away with the evil which is Injun Joe. Tom's imaginative exploration at the end of a string brings them to safety. Even when adults seal the mouth of the cave, it is not to capture the murderer, but to prevent a recurrence of Tom's kind of adventuring. This notion of the excellence of simple innocence, imaginative and irrepressible, and superior to adult methods of confronting the world, was one to which Mark Twain would often return.

After several years of miscellaneous publication, which included the popular, now forgotten, **Punch, Brothers, Punch and Other Sketches** . . . and a second account of European travel, **A Tramp Abroad,** . . . Clemens turned to the theme again in **The Prince and the Pauper,** . . . but with less success. The account of Tom Canty's adventures in the court of Edward VI was again addressed to boys and girls . . . but it was addressed also to adults as an expression of its author's continuing assurance that, for all its shortcomings, democracy as practiced in the United States was superior to any other manner of living anywhere. It is the kind of melodramatic story which Tom Sawyer might have told, of a poor boy who became heir to a king and of a prince who learned humility through mixing with common men.

"My idea," Clemens told one of his friends, "is to afford a realistic sense of the severity of the laws of that day by inflicting some of their penalties upon the king himself." Poverty which brutalizes and restrictive statutes which force men to thievery are ridiculed, as well as superstition and meaningless ritual. The language of old England, with which Mark Twain had experimented in the surreptitiously printed, mildly ribald *1601, or Conversation as It Was by the Fireside in the Time of the Tudors,* . . . comes in for a full share of burlesque. . . . Hardly any of the kinds of humor which the public had come to expect from Mark Twain or of sagacious insight into the frailties of man, is left out of **The Prince and the Pauper.** (pp. 22-5)

The Adventures of Huckleberry Finn is the story of a boy who will not accept the kinds of freedom the world is able to offer, and so flees from them, one after another, to become to many readers a symbol of man's inevitable, restless flight. (p. 27)

Huckleberry Finn's solution of the problem of freedom is direct and unworldly: having tested society, he will have none of it, for civilization finally makes culprits of all men. (p. 28)

Boyish Tom, however, seems to have been Samuel Clemens' favorite. He wrote of him again in *Tom Sawyer Abroad* . . . and in *Tom Sawyer Detective* . . . , contrived books, imitative of earlier successes, and crowded with imagined adventure rather than experience. (p. 31)

Among the most persistently anthologized of Clemens' short pieces is the humorously perceptive dissection of **"Fenimore Cooper's Literary Offenses"** in which he finds that "in the restricted space of two-thirds of a page, Cooper has scored 114 offenses against literary art out of a possible 115." He speaks of Cooper's "crass stupidities," his lack of attention to details, and his curious box of stage properties. . . . Surely, Clemens reasoned, history could be presented without such twaddle.

So Clemens wrote of the adventures of a sturdy, practical nineteenth-century mechanic who is knocked unconscious by a blow on the head and awakes to find himself under a tree near Camelot, amid a landscape "as lovely as a dream and as lonesome as Sunday." (pp. 31-2)

[*A Connecticut Yankee in King Arthur's Court*] has been called Mark Twain's finest possibility, combining satire, the tall tale, humor, democracy, religion, and the damned human race. Loosely picaresque and brightly anecdotal, it was an attempt, Clemens explained, "to imagine and after a fashion set forth, the hard condition of life for the laboring and defenseless poor in bygone times in England, and incidentally contrast those conditions with those under which civil and ecclesiastical pets of privilege and high fortune lived in those times." But what finally emerges from beneath the contrast between Yankee ingenuity and medieval superstition is the portrait of an American. He is unlearned, with "neither the refinement nor the weakness of a college education," but quick-witted and completely, even devastatingly successful. Consciously created or not, it is the image of Samuel Clemens and of many of his friends. And it explains something of the nature of the literature which he and his fellows produced. (pp. 32-3)

The Tragedy of Pudd'nhead Wilson is filled with familiar failings, false starts, and rambling excursions. The title makes us wonder why it is Pudd'nhead's tragedy. But it contains excellencies also, of a kind which Sherwood Anderson was to use in writing about village people, and which have earned for it a reputation as "the most extraordinary book in American literature," filled with intolerable insights into evil. Even distorted by drollery, it penetrates toward recognition of social ills not unlike those which William Faulkner was later to probe. Beneath the burlesque which peoples the sleeply village of Dawson's Landing with representatives of decayed gentry bearing such exuberant names as Percy Northumberland Driscoll and Cecil Burleigh Essex runs a vein of satire which allows recognition of these people as ancestors of the Sartorises and Compsons. (pp. 35-6)

Its failure is literary, the failure of words, not of ideas. Mark Twain is telling a story according to a familiar pattern, incident strung on incident as if they might go on forever. Humor, pathos, sentiment, anger, and burlesque rub shoulders with intimacy bred of long acquaintance. *Pudd'nhead Wilson* is serious in intention, for all its belly-laughs and tears. It faces up

to problems made by the venality of man. Seldom is it plainly evident that Mark Twain's eyes rarely twinkle when he laughs. A social conscience here is plainly showing. Scorn looks boldly out from behind the burlesque. But the words do not come true, as Huck's words did or as Clemens' did when he remembered apprentice days on the river. He is saying what he wants to say, but in accents which ring false because they speak now as people expected him to speak. (p. 36)

Readers who found Tom Sawyer silly or Huck Finn finally a profitless model were moved to wry approval of *The Man That Corrupted Hadleyburg* which . . . presented Clemens' most trenchant testimony to the fundamental dishonesty of man. Piercing the shell of respectability which traditionally had made each small town seem inhabited by kindly hearts and gentle people, he demonstrated how easily even prominently moral citizens could be led beyond temptation when confronted with opportunity to acquire wealth dishonestly but undetected. None were exempt, for every contest was rigged. No more astringent or cynical condemnation of contemporary mores had been issued by an American. . . . [In] *A Person Sitting in Darkness,* he struck savagely at the militant morality of missionaries, and in *King Leopold's Soliloquy,* . . . scornfully denounced pious exploitation of underdeveloped countries. *Extracts from Adam's Diary* . . . and *Eve's Diary* . . . were whimsical accounts of the dependence of even the first man on the superior management of women, and spoke feelingly by indirection of the loneliness of life without connubial and familial affection. (pp. 38-9)

In 1906 [Twain] issued privately and anonymously what he called his "wicked book," *What Is Man?* which contains his most astringent diagnosis of man as a mechanism, the plaything of chance, his brain "so constructed that it can originate nothing." (p. 39)

The book is not wicked, but it is tired, like the posthumous *Letters from the Earth.* Its words speak forthrightly, despairingly, echoing the words of other men who testified to man's slavery to forces beyond himself. They are palliative as well as condemnatory, as if their writer were explaining to himself as much as to other men why it was necessary for all men to do what he and they perforce had done. Resolution is not lacking, nor is anger. On its level, the book argues well. It presents its case. What is no longer there is the power of the inevitable word which is in so intimate a relation to the thing of which it speaks that meaning spills over to intimations which ordinary words can never reach. Once Clemens' words had clung thus close to things, but now they gestured and had less to say.

Six months before his death Clemens released an *Extract from Captain Stormfield's Visit to Heaven,* a favorite tale over which he had been puttering for many years. In it almost every contrivance of humor, sentiment, or dissection of human frailty that Mark Twain had ever used was expanded again on the adventure of a crusty, matter-of-fact mariner who went flashing through the air like a bird toward paradise, racing a comet on the way as steamboat pilots used to race on the Mississippi. (p. 40)

As a philosophical humorist [Mark Twain] spoke on two levels, now one, now the other, seldom blending them to unity of tone or consistency of insight.

Convictions he had in plenty, and courage also; but he had a place to preserve and boyhood visions to sustain. His miseries were subtilely compounded and his sense of sin extended as young dreams exploded to recriminatory nightmares at last. (p. 41)

Samuel Clemens created or became Mark Twain who boundlessly created laughter, but he was more than a buffoon. As comic realist he applies for place beside Laurence Sterne, Dickens, Joyce, Faulkner, and Camus, for his eyes like theirs have seen beyond locality to qualities which men universally, sometimes shamefully, share. To remember him only as a creator of boyhood adventure or as a relic of an American frontier or the voice of native idiosyncrasy is to do him disservice. His accomplishment finally contradicts his thinking, thus certifying his literary achievement. Much that is excellent in American literature *did* begin with him, and Lionel Trilling is correct when he says "that almost every contemporary American writer who deals conscientiously with the problems and possibilities of prose must feels, directly or indirectly, the influence of . . . [his] style which escapes the fixity of the printed page, that sounds in our ears with the immediacy of the heard voice, the very voice of unpretentious truth." (p. 43)

Lewis Leary, in his Mark Twain *(American Writers Pamphlet No. 5; © 1960, University of Minnesota), University of Minnesota Press, Minnneapolis, 1960, 47 p.*

HENRY NASH SMITH (essay date 1962)

[*Huckleberry Finn*] contains three main elements. The most conspicuous is the story of Huck's and Jim's adventures in their flight toward freedom. Jim is running away from actual slavery, Huck from the cruelty of his father, from the well-intentioned "sivilizing" efforts of Miss Watson and the Widow Douglas, from respectability and routine in general. The second element in the novel is social satire of the towns along the river. The satire is often transcendently funny, especially in episodes involving the rascally Duke and King, but it can also deal in appalling violence, as in the Grangerford-Shepherdson feud or Colonel Sherburn's murder of the helpless Boggs. The third major element in the book is the developing characterization of Huck.

All three elements must have been present to Mark Twain's mind in some sense from the beginning, for much of the book's greatness lies in its basic coherence, the complete interrelation of its parts. (p. 114)

The narrative tends to increase in depth as it moves from the adventure story of the early chapters into the social satire of the long middle section, and thence to the ultimate psychological penetration of Huck's character in the moral crisis of Chapter 31. Since the crisis is brought on by the shock of the definitive failure of Huck's effort to help Jim, it marks the real end of the quest for freedom. The perplexing final sequence on the Phelps plantation is best regarded as a maneuver by which Mark Twain beats his way back from incipient tragedy to the cosmic resolution called for by the original conception of the story.

Huck's and Jim's flight from St. Petersburg obviously translates into action the theme of vernacular protest. The fact that they have no means of fighting back against the forces that threaten them but can only run away is accounted for in part by the conventions of backwoods humor, in which the inferior social status of the vernacular character placed him in an ostensibly weak position. But it also reflects Mark Twain's

awareness of his own lack of firm ground to stand on in challenging the established system of values.

Huck's and Jim's defenselessness foreshadows the outcome of their efforts to escape. They cannot finally succeed. To be sure, in a superficial sense they do succeed; at the end of the book Jim is technically free and Huck still has the power to light out for the Territory. But Jim's freedom has been brought about by such an implausible device that we do not believe in it. Who can imagine the scene in which Miss Watson decides to liberate him? What were her motives? Mark Twain finesses the problem by placing this crucial event far offstage and telling us nothing about it beyond the bare fact he needs to resolve his plot. And the notion that a fourteen-year-old boy could make good his escape beyond the frontier is equally unconvincing. (pp. 114-15)

The difficulty of imagining a successful outcome for Huck's and Jim's quest had troubled Mark Twain almost from the beginning of his work on the book. (p. 115)

[After writing the first section he] decided upon a different plan for the narrative. Instead of concentrating on the story of Huck's and Jim's escape, he now launched into a satiric description of the society of the prewar South. Huck was essential to this purpose, for Mark Twain meant to view his subject ironically through Huck's eyes. But Jim was more or less superfluous. During Chapters 17 and 18, devoted to the Grangerford household and the feud, Jim has disappeared from the story. Mark Twain had apparently not yet found a way to combine social satire with the narrative scheme of Huck's and Jim's journey on the raft.

While he was writing his chapter about the feud, however, he thought of a plausible device to keep Huck and Jim floating southward while he continued his panoramic survey of the towns along the river. The device was the introduction of the Duke and the King. . . . In this fashion the narrative can preserve the overall form of a journey down the river while providing ample opportunity for satire when Huck accompanies the two rascals on their forays ashore. But only the outward form of the journey is retained. Its meaning has changed, for Huck's and Jim's quest for freedom has in effect come to an end. Jim is physically present but he assumes an entirely passive role, and is hidden with the raft for considerable periods. Huck is also essentially passive; his function now is that of an observer. Mark Twain postpones acknowledging that the quest for freedom has failed, but the issue will have to be faced eventually.

The satire of the towns along the banks insists again and again that the dominant culture is decadent and perverted. Traditional values have gone to seed. The inhabitants can hardly be said to live a conscious life of their own; their actions, their thoughts, even their emotions are controlled by an outworn and debased Calvinism, and by a residue of the eighteenth-century cult of sensibility. With few exceptions they are mere bundles of tropisms, at the mercy of scoundrels like the Duke and the King who know how to exploit their prejudices and delusions.

The falseness of the prevalent values finds expression in an almost universal tendency of the townspeople to make spurious claims to status through self-dramatization. (pp. 116-17)

The Duke and the King personify the theme of fradulent role-taking. These rogues are not even given names apart from the wildly improbable identities they assume in order to dominate Huck and Jim. The Duke's poses have a literary cast, perhaps because of the scraps of bombast he remembers from his experience as an actor. The illiterate King has "done considerable in the doctoring way," but when we see him at work it is mainly at preaching, "workin' camp-meetin's, and missionaryin' around." Pretended or misguided piety and other perversions of Christianity obviously head the list of counts in Mark Twain's indictment of the prewar South. . . . His revulsion, expressed through Huck, reaches its highest pitch in the scene where the King delivers his masterpiece of "soul-butter and hogwash" for the benefit of the late Peter Wilks's fellow townsmen. (p. 118)

Huck is revolted by the King's hypocrisy: "I never see anything so disgusting." He has had a similar reaction to the brutality of the feud: "It made me so sick I almost fell out of the tree." In describing such scenes he speaks as moral man viewing an immoral society, an observer who is himself free of the vices and even the weaknesses he describes. Mark Twain's satiric method requires that Huck be a mask for the writer, not a fully developed character. The method has great ironic force, and is in itself a technical landmark in the history of American fiction, but it prevents Mark Twain from doing full justice to Huck as a person in his own right, capable of mistakes in perception and judgment, troubled by doubts and conflicting impulses. (pp. 118-19)

Huck is shown to have depths and complexities not relevant to the immediate context. Huck's and Jim's journey down the river begins simply as a flight from physical danger; and the first episodes of the voyage have little bearing on the novelistic possibilities in the strange comradeship between outcast boy and escaped slave. But in Chapter 15, when Huck plays a prank on Jim by persuading him that the separation in the fog was only a dream, Jim's dignified and moving rebuke suddenly opens up a new dimension in the relation. Huck's humble apology is striking evidence of growth in moral insight. It leads naturally to the next chapter in which Mark Twain causes Huck to face up for the first time to the fact that he is helping a slave to escape. It is as if the writer himself were discovering unsuspected meanings in what he had thought of as a story of picaresque adventure. . . .

The introduction of the Duke and the King not only took care of the awkwardness in the plot but also allowed Mark Twain to postpone the exploration of Huck's moral dilemma. If Huck is not a free agent he is not responsible for what happens and is spared the agonies of choice. Throughout the long middle section, while he is primarily an observer, he is free of inner conflict because he is endowed by implication with Mark Twain's own unambiguous attitude toward the fraud and folly he witnesses.

In Chapter 31, however, Huck escapes from his captors and faces once again the responsibility for deciding on a course of action. His situation is much more desperate than it had been at the time of his first struggle with his conscience. The raft has borne Jim hundreds of miles downstream from the pathway of escape and the King has turned him over to Silas Phelps as a runaway slave. The quest for freedom has "all come to nothing, everything all busted up and ruined." Huck thinks of notifying Miss Watson where Jim is. . . . (p. 119)

The account of Huck's mental struggle in the next two or three pages is the emotional climax of the story. It draws together the theme of flight from bondage and the social satire of the middle section, for Huck is trying to work himself clear of the perverted value system of St. Petersburg. Both adventure story

and satire, however, are now subordinate to an exploration of Huck's psyche which is the ultimate achievement of the book. The issue is identical with that of the first moral crisis, but the later passage is much more intense and richer in implication. The differences appear clearly if the two crises are compared in detail.

In Chapter 16 Huck is startled into a realization of his predicament when he hears Jim, on the lookout for Cairo at the mouth of the Ohio, declare that "he'd be a free man the minute he seen it, but if he missed it he'd be in a slave country again and no more show for freedom." Huck says: "I begun to get it through my head that he *was* most free—and who was to blame for it? Why, *me*. I couldn't get that out of my conscience, no how nor no way." He dramatizes his inner debate by quoting the words in which his conscience denounces him. . . . The counterargument is provided by Jim, who seems to guess what is passing through Huck's mind and does what he can to invoke the force of friendship and gratitude. . . . Huck nevertheless sets out for the shore in the canoe "all in a sweat to tell on" Jim, but when he is intercepted by the two slave hunters in a skiff he suddenly contrives a cunning device to ward them off. We are given no details about how his inner conflict was resolved.

In the later crisis Huck provides a much more circumstantial account of what passes through his mind. He is now quite alone; the outcome of the debate is not affected by any stimulus from the outside. It is the memory of Jim's kindness and goodness rather than Jim's actual voice that impels Huck to defy his conscience. . . . The most striking feature of this later crisis is the fact that Huck's conscience, which formerly had employed only secular arguments, now deals heavily in religious cant. . . . (pp. 120-21)

In the earlier debate the voice of Huck's conscience is quoted directly, but the bulk of the later exhortation is reported in indirect discourse. This apparently simple change in method has remarkable consequences. According to the conventions of first-person narrative, the narrator functions as a neutral medium in reporting dialogue. He remembers the speeches of other characters but they pass through his mind without affecting him. When Huck's conscience speaks within quotation marks it is in effect a character in the story, and he is not responsible for what it says. But when he paraphrases the admonitions of his conscience they are incorporated into his own discourse. Thus although Huck is obviously remembering the bits of theological jargon from sermons justifying slavery, they have become a part of his vocabulary.

The device of having Huck paraphrase rather than quote the voice of conscience may have been suggested to Mark Twain by a discovery he made in revising Huck's report of the King's address to the mourners in the Wilks parlor. . . . The manuscript version of the passage shows that the King's remarks were composed as a direct quotation, but in the published text they have been put, with a minimum of verbal change, into indirect discourse. The removal of the barrier of quotation marks brings Huck into much more intimate contact with the King's "rot and slush" despite the fact that the paraphrase quivers with disapproval. The voice of conscience speaks in the precise accents of the King but Huck is now completely uncritical. He does not question its moral authority; it is morality personified. The greater subtlety of the later passage illustrates the difference between the necessarily shallow characterization of Huck while he was being used merely as a narrative persona, and the profound insight which Mark Twain eventually brought to bear on his protagonist.

The recognition of complexity in Huck's character enabled Mark Twain to do full justice to the conflict between vernacular values and the dominant culture. By situating in a single consciousness both the perverted moral code of a society built on slavery and the vernacular commitment to freedom and spontaneity, he was able to represent the opposed perspectives as alternative modes of experience for the same character. In this way he gets rid of the confusions surrounding the pronoun "I" in the earlier books, where it sometimes designates the author speaking in his own person, sometimes an entirely distinct fictional character. Furthermore, the insight that enabled him to recognize the conflict between accepted values and vernacular protest as a struggle within a single mind does injustice to its moral depth. . . . The satire of a decadent slaveholding society gains immensely in force when Mark Twain demonstrates that even the outcast Huck has been in part perverted by it. Huck's conscience is simply the attitudes he has taken over from his environment. What is still sound in him is an impulse from the deepest level of his personality that struggles against the overlay of prejudice and false valuation imposed on all members of the society in the name of religion, morality, law, and refinement.

Finally, it should be pointed out that the conflict in Huck between generous impulse and false belief is depicted by means of a contrast between colloquial and exalted styles. In moments of crisis his conscience addresses him in the language of the dominant culture, a tawdry and faded effort at a high style that is the rhetorical equivalent of the ornaments in the Grangerford parlor. Yet speaking in dialect does not in itself imply moral authority. By every external criterion the King is as much a vernacular character as Huck. The conflict in which Huck is involved is not that of a lower against an upper class or of an alienated fringe of outcasts against a cultivated elite. It is not the issue of frontier West versus genteel East, or of backwoods versus metropolis, but of fidelity to the uncoerced self versus the blurring of attitudes caused by social conformity, by the effort to achieve status or power through exhibiting the approved forms of sensibility.

The exploration of Huck's personality carried Mark Twain beyond satire and even beyond his statement of a vernacular protest against the dominant culture into essentially novelistic modes of writing. Some of the passages he composed when he got out beyond his polemic framework challenge comparison with the greatest achievements in the world's fiction.

The most obvious of Mark Twain's discoveries on the deeper levels of Huck's psyche is the boy's capacity for love. The quality of the emotion is defined in action by his decision to sacrifice himself for Jim, just as Jim attains an impressive dignity when he refuses to escape at the cost of deserting the wounded Tom. Projected into the natural setting, the love of the protagonists for each other becomes the unforgettable beauty of the river when they are allowed to be alone together. . . . Huck's description of [the thunderstorm over Jackson's island] is only less poetic than his description of the dawn which he and Jim witness as they sit half-submerged on the sandy bottom.

Yet if Mark Twain had allowed these passages to stand without qualification as a symbolic account of Huck's emotions he would have undercut the complexity of characterization implied in his recognition of Huck's inner conflict of loyalties. Instead,

he uses the natural setting to render a wide range of feelings and motives. The fog that separates the boy from Jim for a time is an externalization of his impulse to deceive Jim by a Tom Sawyerish practical joke. (pp. 121-22)

Still darker aspects of Huck's inner life are projected into the natural setting in the form of ghosts, omens, portents of disaster—the body of superstition that is so conspicuous in Huck's and Jim's world. At the end of Chapter I Huck is sitting alone at night by his open window in the Widow Douglas' house, [imagining portents of death in the nighttime sounds of the nearby woods]. . . (p. 123)

The whimpering ghost with something incommunicable on its mind and Huck's cold shivers suggest a burden of guilt and anxiety that is perhaps the punishment he inflicts on himself for defying the mores of St. Petersburg. Whatever the source of these sinister images, they develop the characterization of Huck beyond the needs of the plot. The narrator whose stream of consciousness is recorded here is much more than the innocent protagonist of the pastoral idyl of the raft, more than an ignorant boy who resists being civilized. The vernacular persona is an essentially comic figure; the character we glimpse in Huck's meditation is potentially tragic. Mark Twain's discoveries in the buried strata of Huck's mind point in the same direction as does his intuitive recognition that Huck's and Jim's quest for freedom must end in failure. (p. 124)

Henry Nash Smith, in his Mark Twain: The Development of a Writer *(© copyright 1962 by the President and Fellows of Harvard College), The Belknap Press of Harvard University Press, 1962, 212 p.*

ROBERT PENN WARREN (essay date 1972)

In *The Prince and the Pauper,* a children's book laid in Tudor England, Mark Twain had . . . taken his first excursion into historical fiction. This work, which interrupted the composition of *Huckleberry Finn,* was nothing more than a piece of sentimental junk cynically devised to captivate his own children, clergymen of literary inclinations, nervous parents, and genteel reviewers, but it broke ground for *A Connecticut Yankee.* That work, however, was on the direct line of Mark Twain's inspiration; it was connected with the grinding issues of his nature, and it drew deeply on earlier work. Laid in the sixth century, in Arthurian England, it put the new American mind in contrast with feudal Europe, the remains of which the "Innocents" of the *Quaker City,* and their chronicler, had had to face on their tour. But *A Connecticut Yankee* also harks back to the contrast between the "feudal" South and the "modern" North that looms so large in *Life on the Mississippi;* it embodies not only the spirit of social criticism found in *Huckleberry Finn,* but something of Huck's pragmatic mind that always wanted to start things "fresh"; and in a paradoxical way, after it celebrates the new Yankee order of industry, big business, and finance capitalism, it also returns to the Edenic vision of Hannibal and the river found in *Tom Sawyer* and *Huckleberry Finn.*

Most deeply, however, *A Connecticut Yankee* draws on the social and personal contexts of the moment in which it was composed. At this time Mark Twain was totally bemused by one James W. Paige, the inventor of a typesetting machine which Twain was trying to organize a company to manufacture, and by which he dreamed of becoming a financial titan. Behind Hank Morgan, the Yankee, stands Paige. And, we may add, stands Twain himself, for if Hank (a superintendent in the Colt Arms Company) is an inventor (he claims that he can "invent, contrive, create'' anything), he quickly becomes the ''Boss''—a titan of business such as Twain dreamed of becoming.

The medieval values that Hank confronts were not confined to Arthurian Britain. For one thing, there was also present-day England, for whatever remnants had remained of an Anglophilia once cherished by Twain were now totally demolished by Matthew Arnold who, after a visit to America, had declared, in ''Civilization in the United States,'' that the idea of ''distinction'' in this country could not survive the ''glorification of 'the average man' and the addiction to the 'funny man.''' In his outraged patriotism and outraged *amour propre*, Twain, a ''funny man,'' tended to merge the England of Arthur with that of Victoria.

In addition, the Romantic movement had discovered—or created—the Middle Ages, and made them current in nineteenth-century thought and art. (pp. 485-86)

This cult of medievalism had a strongly marked class element; usually it was cultivated by persons of aristocratic background or pretensions, often with an overlay of sentimental Catholicism. It was also associated with wealth, but with inherited wealth as contrasted with that, usually greater, of the new kind of capitalist; for inherited wealth, untainted by immediate contact with the crude world of business, was ''genteel.'' It was only natural, then, that a poem like Sidney Lanier's ''Symphony'' and the early novels attacking business should use the aristocratic feudal virtues as the thongs with which to scourge the business man. So when Hank guns down Malory's knights in armor with his six-shooters, he is also gunning down Tennyson, Ruskin, Lowell, Lanier, *et al. A Connecticut Yankee* is, in fact, the first fictional glorification of the business man.

But Hank is arrayed not only against Sir Sagramar le Desirious and Alfred Lord Tennyson and their ilk, but also against the spectral legions of Lee, abetted by the ghost of Sir Walter Scott. (pp. 486-87)

If the anachronistically slaveholding society of Britain is an image of the Old South and if Hank's military masterpiece, the Battle of the Sand Belt, in which, after the explosion of Hank's mines, the air is filled with the ghastly drizzle of the atomized remains of men and horses, is an image of the Civil War (the first ''modern'' war), then Hank's programs for Britain is a fable of the Reconstruction of the South and the pacification of that undeveloped country. Furthermore, in being a fable of that colonial project, this is also a fable of colonialism in general and of the great modern period of colonialism in particular, which was now well under way from the Ganges to the Congo; thus to Hank, Britain is simply something to develop in economic terms—with, of course, as a paternalistic benefit to the natives, the by-product of a rational modern society. In this context *A Connecticut Yankee* is to be set alongside Conrad's *Nostromo* and *The Heart of Darkness* and the works of Kipling.

There is, however, another and more inclusive context in which to regard it. More and more in our century we have seen a special variety of millenialism—the variety in which bliss (in the form of a ''rational'' society) is distributed at gunpoint or inculcated in concentration camps. So in this context, *A Connecticut Yankee* is to be set alongside historical accounts of Fascist Italy, Nazi Germany, or Communist Russia. This novel was prophetic. (pp. 487-88)

The body of the work has to do with Hank's operations from the moment when he decides that he is ''just another Robinson

Crusoe,'' and has to ''invent, contrive, create, reorganize things.'' The narrative proceeds in a two-edged fashion: there is the satirical exposure of the inhuman and stultifying life in Arthur's kingdom, with the mission for modernization and humanitarian improvement, but there is also the development of Hank's scheme for his economic and political aggrandizement, his way of becoming the ''Boss.'' By and large, it seems that the humanitarian and selfish interests coincide; what is good for Hank is good for the people of Britain, and this would imply a simple fable of progress, with the reading that technology in a laissez faire order automatically confers the good life on all. There is no hint, certainly, that Twain is writing in a period of titanic struggle between labor and capital, a struggle consequent upon the advent of big technology. In the new order in Britain there are no labor problems. The boys whom Hank had secretly recruited and instructed in technology are completely loyal to him, and as his Janissaries, will fight for him in the great Armageddon to come, enraptured by their own godlike proficiency; if they represent ''labor'' they have no parallel in the nineteenth-century America of the Homestead strike and the Haymarket riot.

In the fable there are, indeed, many lags and incoherences that, upon the slightest analysis, are visible. Twain had not systematically thought through the issues in his world, or his own attitudes, and he did not grasp, or did not wish to grasp, the implications of his own tale. During the course of composition he had written—in a letter of either cynical deception or confusion of mind—that he had no intention of degrading any of the ''great and beautiful characters'' found in Malory, and that Arthur would keep his ''sweetness and purity,'' but this scarcely squares with the finished product. . . . And most telling of all, though *A Connecticut Yankee* was rapturously received, even by such discerning readers as Howells, as a great document of the democratic faith, and though Twain himself, sometimes at least, took it as such, Hank is not ethically superior to Jay Gould or Diamond Jim Brady in many of his manipulations. What Hank turns out to be is merely the ''Boss,'' more of a boss than even Boss Tweed ever was, something like a cross between a Carnegie and a commissar.

There are various other logical confusions in *A Connecticut Yankee,* but one is fundamental. If the original idea of the book had been a celebration of nineteenth-century technology, something happened to that happy inspiration, and in the end progress appears a delusion, Hank's modernization winds up in a bloody farce, and Hank himself can think of the people whom he had undertaken to liberate as merely ''human muck.'' In the end Hank hates life, and all he can do is to look nostalgically back on the beauty of pre-modern Britain as what he calls his ''Lost World,'' and on the love of his lost wife Sandy, just as Twain could look back on his vision of boyhood Hannibal.

What emerges here is not only the deep tension in Twain, but that in the period. There was in America a tension concerning the Edenic vision, a tension between two aspects of it: some men had hoped to achieve it in a natural world—as had Jefferson—but some had hoped to achieve it by the conquest of nature. The tension, in its objective terms, was, then, between an agrarian and an industrial order; but in subjective terms the tension existed, too, and in a deep, complex way it conditioned the American sensibility from *Snow-Bound* through *A Connecticut Yankee* and Henry Adams' idea of the Virgin versus the dynamo, on through the poetry of T. S. Eliot and John Crowe Ransom, to the debased Rousseauism of a hippie commune.

The notion of the Edenic vision reminds us of *Huckleberry Finn,* for thematically *A Connecticut Yankee* is a development of that work—and the parallel in the very names of the heroes suggests the relation: *Huck/Hank.* Huck journeys through the barbarous South, Hank through barbarous Britain, both mythic journeys into a land where mania and brutality are masked by pretensions of chivalry, humanity, and Christianity. After each encounter with a shocking fact of the land-world, Huck returns to his private Eden on the river and in the end contemplates flight to an Edenic West. In other words, Huck belongs to the world of Jefferson's dream, in which man finds harmony with man in an overarching harmony of man in nature. Hank, however, is of sterner stuff. When he encounters a shocking fact he undertakes to change it—to conquer both nature and human nature in order to create a rational society.

Both Huck and Hank come to a desperate collision with reality, Huck on the Phelps farm and Hank at the Battle of the Sand Belt; but the end of the project of regeneration through technology and know-how is more blankly horrible than life on the Phelps farm, with not even a façade of humor but only the manic glee of the victors exalted by their expertise of destruction. The "human muck" has refused the rule of reason—and the prophet of reason has done little more than provide magnificently lethal instruments by which man may vent his mania.

When the book was finished, Twain wrote to Howells: "Well, my book is written—let it go. But if it were only to write over again there wouldn't be so many things left out. They burn in me. . . . They would require a library—and a pen warmed up in hell." But the pen had already been warmed enough to declare that dark forces were afoot in history and in the human soul to betray all aspiration, and with this we find, at the visceral level of fable, the same view of history later to be learnedly, abstractly, and pitilessly proclaimed by Henry Adams and dramatized in (to date) two world wars. (pp. 488-91)

> *Robert Penn Warren, "Mark Twain" (copyright 1972, by Robert Penn Warren), in* The Southern Review, *Vol. VIII, No. 3, Summer, 1972, pp. 459-92.*

KURT VONNEGUT, JR.   (essay date 1976)

Although he was raised in what has been called the country's "Bible Belt," Twain found church services, especially the praying, to be downright comical. Why? Because, in an age of steam engines and dynamos and the telegraph and so on, praying seemed so *impractical,* I think.

Twain himself had had tremendously satisfying adventures with the most glamorous conglomerations of machinery imaginable, which were riverboats. So praying, as opposed to inventing and engineering, was bound to seem to him, and to so many like him, as the silliest possible way to get things done.

He was what would later be called "a technocrat."

He wished to sweep away superstitions and romantic illusions with laughter—because they were so *useless.* Connecticut Yankees should run the world, because they kept up with scientific discoveries and they had no illusions. They knew what would *really* work. They knew what was *really* going on. (p. xxi)

I have heard it said that the ending of *A Connecticut Yankee* was a prophecy of the World Wars Twain did not live to see. Superstitious knights fight technocrats, and both armies become parts of a pestilential mulch of corpses. This seems to me a better description of the war between the Confederacy and the Union than of the World Wars, which pitted technocrats against technocrats, and in which no one could have any illusions any more.

It is my belief that Twain was less interested in prophecy than ending his tale some way—almost any *which* way. So he did what Herman Melville did in *Moby Dick.* He killed everybody, except for one survivor to tell the tale.

It is such a clumsy ending, in my opinion, that it destroys the balance of the author himself. It causes him to suggest some things about himself which he would have preferred not to see the light of day.

For instance: Merlin, the personification of contemptible superstitions, is present at the end. All through the book, Merlin has been a transparent fraud. But then he casts a spell which is more astonishing than anything the Connecticut Yankee has done. Merlin puts the Yankee to sleep for thirteen centuries. He can work miracles after all.

Not only that, but Merlin comes on his wicked errand *disguised as a woman.*

Imagine that.

Is it possible that Twain, the clear-eyed technocrat, could not help believing in magic after all? I think maybe so.

Is it possible that he suspected that women and their praying, from whom Huck Finn fled in such a frenzy, had mysterious powers superior to those of scientists and engineers? I think maybe so. (pp. xxi-xiii)

I do not mean to raise Freudian questions about Twain. I am not particularly respectful of the sorts of answers they can bring.

Sigmund Freud himself *did* write about Twain, incidentally—after Twain was dead. He set a refreshingly unFreudian example by saying little about Twain's relationships to women, or any of that. He did what we should do, too, which was to celebrate how cunningly Twain's best jokes were made. (p. xiii)

> *Kurt Vonnegut, Jr., "Opening Remarks," in* The Unabridged Mark Twain *by Mark Twain, edited by Lawrence Teacher (copyright © 1976 Running Press), Running Press, 1976, pp. xi-xv.*

KENNETH S. LYNN   (essay date 1977)

By all odds, the most insinuating, the most seductive, of American novels is *Huckleberry Finn*—partly because of the enormous influence the book has had on our twentieth-century writers. . . . But the main reason why the book has come to play such a major role in the life of the mind in America is that students repeatedly run into it in the course of their formal education. (p. 338)

What's wrong with a literary masterpiece being popular? The lonesome poetry of the novel's vernacular style, the beautifully tender relationship that develops between the boy and the black man, Huck's unforgettable description of a sunrise on the river, the tall-tale humor of the episodes involving the King and the Duke, the piercing insights into the seamy aspects of antebellum southern life—why am I upset because American students are repeatedly being exposed to these marvelous things? The trouble lies not in the novel, but in its interpreters. . . . In the classrooms of this country, students are being seduced—perhaps "poisoned" is a better word—by an antisocial vision of human relations that Mark Twain himself did not formulate. How this corrupt redirection of desire and purpose affects youthful minds ought to concern us all.

The misinterpretation of *Huckleberry Finn* originated in the 1950s, largely as a result of the misreadings of its famous final sentences: "But I reckon I got to light out for the Territory ahead of the rest, because Aunt Sally she's going to adopt me and sivilize me and I can't stand it. I been there before." By 1958, the situation had become so bad that Professor Henry Nash Smith, the nation's foremost authority on Mark Twain, was moved to write an essay pointing out how completely we were distorting the author's intentions. . . .

> But when [at the end of the book] the Evasion from the Phelps plantation under Tom Sawyer's leadership restores the mood of the opening chapters, Huck's desire to escape is stripped of the meaning it had acquired in the middle section of the book. We are brought back to the situation at the end of *Tom Sawyer.* Even the robber gang reappears, for Tom's imagination peoples the territory with robbers in his "nonnamous letters" of warning. It is Tom, again, who conceives the plan to "go for howling adventures amongst the Injuns, over in the Territory, for a couple of weeks or two." When Huck says he means to set out ahead of the others, there is nothing in the text to indicate that his intention is more serious than Tom's.

> This reading of Huck's last sentence contradicts a view that has been gaining in popularity among critics, a view which sees a portentuous meaning in Huck's final escape on the theory that he has become disgusted with a society that tolerates slavery and is making a drastic, final gesture of alienation and rejection. . . .

For almost twenty years now, what might be termed the Dropoutsville interpretation of *Huckleberry Finn* has been rammed into the minds of American students.

Yet, as Professor Smith tried in vain to tell us, Huck Finn at the end of the novel is most emphatically *not* planning to exile himself from organized society. In lighting out for the Territory he is merely going along with Tom Sawyer's latest disappearance-reappearance act. (pp. 338-40)

At the end of *Huckleberry Finn,* therefore, students should be asked what sort of life Huck will lead when he returns to St. Petersburg, rather than encouraged to conjure up misleading fantasies about a young boy's continuing search for freedom and self-realization in the tabula rasa of the Territory. Since the question takes us beyond the limits of the story, the severe holistic standards of some literary critics might forbid it. In reality, though, the question takes us directly back into *Huckleberry Finn*, and into *Tom Sawyer* as well. Moreover, it spotlights the curiously overlooked character of the Widow Douglas, and thereby throws into even higher relief the antiinstitutional ideas that teachers of American literature are preaching to students.

Potentially, the Widow Douglas, "fair, smart, and forty," is the most interesting female character Mark Twain ever created. We meet her for the first time in *Tom Sawyer.* The house she occupies atop beautiful Cardiff Hill, "the only palace in town," symbolizes her social position in the St. Petersburg community.

As hospitable as she is intelligent, this aristocratic lady gives parties that are "the most lavish . . . that St. Petersburg could boast." Her generosities, furthermore, are not limited to her gentry friends or to people of her own age. So far as we know, the Widow herself is childless, but she likes and understands boys and girls all the same, and encourages them to come see her . . . Even Huckleberry Finn, the juvenile pariah of the village, son of the town drunkard and an illiterate woman long since dead, with whom the middle-class mothers of St. Petersburg have forbidden their children to associate, has "more than once" been befriended by the Widow. (pp. 340-41)

One dark night, on the edge of the Widow's estate, Huck overhears the dreaded Injun Joe vow to a criminal companion that before leaving St. Petersburg for good he is going to slit the Widow's nostrils and notch her ears like a sow, in revenge for being jugged as a vagrant and publicly horsewhipped by order of the Widow's late husband, who had been the town's justice of the peace. Although Huck fears he will be murdered if Injun Joe should discover who has informed on him, he immediately plunges down the hillside to warn a sturdy townsman and his sons that the Widow is in peril. All Huck asks for himself is that his own role in the affair be kept secret from everyone, including the Widow. . . .

Thus it is out of no special feeling of gratitude to Huck that the Widow Douglas volunteers to nurse the homeless boy when, a short time later, he falls deliriously ill with fever. . . . In contrast to the disdainful attitudes of the other women of St. Petersburg, the Widow's feeling about Huck is that "whether he was good, bad, or indifferent, he was the Lord's, and nothing that was the Lord's was a thing to be neglected." Her Christianity, in other words, is a living faith, not an ossified piety.

In towns the size of St. Petersburg, secrets do not keep for long. Eventually, the Widow learns who had saved her from the Indian's revenge. From this revelation flows her decision "to give Huck a home under her roof and have him educated; and . . . when she could spare the money she would start him in business in a modest way." Huck accepts the Widow's offer—but with a deep sense of unease. (p. 341)

In the last episode of *Tom Sawyer,* we witness this child being "introduced . . . no, dragged" into society. . . . After three weeks of misery, he runs off. Finally Tom Sawyer locates him, stretched at ease in an empty hogshead down behind an abandoned slaughterhouse, smoking a pipe, clad in rags, and superbly uncombed. Tom understands the feelings of his friend— and yet loves him enough to give him advice he knows Huck doesn't want to hear. Go back to the Widow's, Tom urges him; "if you'll try this thing just a while longer you'll come to like it." Huck adamantly refuses.

In the long run, however, Huck is no match for the master manipulator. . . . Thinking fast, Tom tells Huck he is going to form a "high-toned" robber gang, of the sort that in most Eurpean countries is made up of "dukes and such." In order to keep up the tone of his gang, Tom will restrict its membership to respectable boys. Returning to the Widow is the price Huck will have to pay for belonging. Upon hearing this, Huck's resistance collapses. "I'll stick to the widder till I rot," Huck declares, as *The Adventures of Tom Sawyer* draws to a close, "and if I git to be a reg'lar ripper of a robber, and everybody talking 'bout it, I reckon she'll be proud she snaked me in out of the wet."

With that sentence Mark Twain set the stage for a follow-up novel that could have become one of the most extraordinary studies of acculturation in modern literature, centering on a psychological contest between an emotionally deprived juvenile outcast and a smart, attractive, still youthful woman. Somewhere along the line, though, Mark Twain decided he had a better idea. The sequel to *Tom Sawyer* became a story about a runaway boy and a runaway slave, rafting down the big river on the June rise.

It was a marvelous idea. Yet by making Huck Finn his runaway hero, Mark Twain created certain problems for himself. The conventional wisdom about the *Adventures of Huckleberry Finn* is that the novel lets its readers down only in the long final episode at the Phelps plantation, when Tom Sawyer reenters the story and, with his romantic schemes, effectively destroys the emotional connection between Huck and Jim. . . . [As bad] however, are the incidents that occur at the outset of the story, in the chapters dealing with Huck's life at the Widow's.

The first problem Mark Twain confronted was how to blur his readers' awareness that Huck and the Widow are bound together by mutual feelings of gratitude, that they both are warmhearted, and that their experiment in living as symbolic son and mother has a chance of succeeding. Since *Huckleberry Finn* was to be a story of rafting on the river, the author had to spring Huck free from his ties to the Widow. Mark Twain solved this problem—if one can call a travesty a solution—by introducing, on page two, the cartoon character of Miss Watson. . . . It is altogether incredible that the Widow would surrender the bulk of her parental responsibilities to this two-dimensional caricature of old-maid prissiness and henpecking tyranny, but that is exactly what Mark Twain was forced to ask us to believe. The richly interesting psychological drama that seemed to be promised to us at the end of *Tom Sawyer* is reduced in the first three chapters of *Huckleberry Finn* to a series of farcical confrontations between Huck and old Goggle Eyes, with the gentle, understanding Widow coming on stage only now and again.

As if embarrassed by the baldness of this stratagem, Mark Twain admits at the beginning of chapter 4 that after four months in the same household Huck and the Widow have grown somewhat closer together, and that Huck is "getting sort of used" to her ways, albeit he still prefers his former habits. For her part, the Widow believes that Huck is coming along slowly but surely and is doing very satisfactorily, thank you. Almost immediately, however, the reason why Mark Twain could afford this outburst of literary candor is revealed: he had hit upon a legalistic means of removing Huck from the Widow's jurisdiction, once and for all. No matter tha in the course of executing this maneuver the author would have to resort to a few "stretchers," as Huck would say.

Pap Finn has been missing from town for more than a year. Now, suddenly, he returns. He has heard about Huck's and Tom's discovery (in *Tom Sawyer*) of a buried treasure of golden coins. Huck's share, which comes to six thousand dollars, has been banked for him by the Widow at 6 percent interest. Pap claims that as Huck's father he should be given control of the six thousand dollars, and swears he will go to court about it. In the face of this threat, the Widow and the influential Judge Thatcher ask the court to take Huck away from his father and appoint one of them the boy's legal guardian. (pp. 342-44)

St. Petersburg is a small southern town, whose power structure stands before the judge in the persons of the Widow and Judge Thatcher. The power structure's adversary is the trashiest white for miles around, a man totally without influence. How will the judge rule? Mark Twain knows damned well, yet he has no choice but to lie to us. "It was a new judge," the novel lamely explains, "that had just come, and he didn't know. . . ." (p. 344)

Consequently, when Pap snatches Huck one day in the spring, takes him across the river to the Illinois shore, and locks him up in an old log hut, the Widow has no legal right to recover him. Some weeks later, Pap comes storming into the cabin on one of his irregular visits and reports that there are rumors floating around St. Petersburg that the Widow is about to make a second effort in the court. But by this time Huck has completely reverted to his old ways, and doesn't want to be "cramped up and sivilized" any more. He has also long since decided that he has no desire to go on living with his nightmarish Pap. Thus, on the day he breaks out of the cabin and makes for the river, Huck is fleeing first of all from his father, which is entirely understandable. But much less understandable is that he is also fleeing from all his boyhood friends, including the woman who had befriended him off and on throughout his childhood, and nursed him through a dangerous illness, had invested his money for him rather than mulcting him out of it, had supplied him with bed and board and loving understanding for four months, and had sent him to school so that he could learn to read and write. Can it be that we have been wrong in thinking that Huck Finn is a warmhearted boy—that in fact he is a cold-blooded little bastard who doesn't really care about the people who care about him? Of course not. It is simply that Mark Twain had to turn Huck into a runaway, and he could not do so without temporarily violating the consistency of his hero's character.

The point of this analysis is not to downgrade Mark Twain's literary reputation by exposing the social and psychological implausibilities in the early chapters of his masterpiece. Implausibilities, after all, were Mark Twain's stock in trade, in every book he ever wrote. The point, rather, is that teachers of *Huckleberry Finn* read every detail in the early chapters with a deadly literal-mindedness. Partly this is becuase a lot of professional interpreters of literature lack a sense of humor. But mainly they misread the beginning of *Huckleberry Finn* because of what appears to be their desire to denigrate American family life. Instead of showing students that the account of Huck's life at the Widow's is not to be taken seriously—that it is simply a series of chess moves designed to get Huck onto that raft with Nigger Jim as rapidly as possible, and that it most certainly does not reflect Mark Twain's real opinion of the Widow Douglas—they take the account at face value, in preparation for their Dropoutsville misreading of the novel's final sentences. (pp. 344-45)

Back in the 1950s, when this whole mess started, literary critics were moved to misread *Huckleberry Finn* for a variety of reasons. To its everlasting credit, American society in the postwar period gradually came to the conclusion—first in the area of sports, but raying out from there into other aspects of our national life—that the ancient pattern of discrimination against Negroes was morally and legally indefensible. This conclusion precipitated numerous misinterpretations of *Huckleberry Finn*. Critics wanted to believe that Huck was renouncing his membership in a society that condoned slavery because they themselves did not wish to live in a segregationist America. A less palatable concomitant of this truth is that some misreaders were as strongly motivated by a distaste for southern whites as by a sympathy for southern blacks. "Anti-southernism is the anti-Semitism of the liberals.". . . (p. 345)

Still another reason why the Dropoutsville interpretation of *Huckleberry Finn* became popular when it did was that the suddenly affluent America of the postwar era was interested above all else in the instant gratification of its desires. We had suffered through years of economic depression and global war, and now we wanted all restraints on our pleasure seeking to be removed at once. As a result, we experienced a particularly grave case of Freudian discomfort at having to continue to live in a framework of civilized repressions, and kicked violently against it. Our drive to escape responsibility was revealed in our extravagant enthusiasm for runaway novels like Salinger's *Catcher in the Rye,* Kerouac's *On the Road,* and Updike's *Rabbit, Run.* . . .

That *Huckleberry Finn* continues to be misinterpreted in the classrooms of this country is a sign that the antisocial values of the postwar era still flourish in the mid-1970s. (p. 346)

Mark Twain would be very uncomfortable if he knew this. In private life he was a devoted parent who not only believed in the importance of close family ties, but delighted in them. As the author of *Huckleberry Finn,* to be sure, he showed another side of his personality, the side that wanted to kick free of all social restraints. Yet at the end of the book, he not only tried to tell us that Huck was planning to return to St. Petersburg, but he showed signs of feeling ashamed of himself for relegating the strong and admirable Widow Douglas to a minor role in her own household. In the final chapters, as the loose threads of the story are hastily being gathered up, we learn that Miss Watson, the erstwhile owner of Nigger Jim and persecutor of small white boys, is dead. We also learn that Pap Finn is dead. But what about the Widow Douglas? Amidst all the questions and answers that are flying about, she is never once mentioned. Even in the final sentences, in which Huck says he had tried being adopted and civilized once before, he does not pronounce the name of the woman who had done so much for him throughout his life.

The best face I can put on this strange—indeed disgraceful—literary lapse is that Mark Twain could not bear to summon up the memory of the Widow because he felt guilty about her. Mark Twain, a tortured man, often felt guilty, and on this occasion, I would argue, he had good reason, even though the exigencies of his story left him with no other choice than to mistreat the lady.

Students in this country ought to be told more about the Widow Douglas than they now know. They also ought to be told that at the end of the book Huck is planning to go back home, and that the raft is only a memory. For novels are modes of prediction that insinuate visions of human relations not to be found in official rules or precepts or admonitions. As such, they exert an incalculable social influence, especially on young people. Some day soon, I hope, teachers of *Huckleberry Finn* will decide to tear up their yellowing lecture notes and read the book, along with their students, with fresh eyes. (pp. 346-47)

Kenneth S. Lynn, "Welcome Back from the Raft, Huck Honey!" in The American Scholar *(copyright ©1977 by the United Chapters of Phi Beta Kappa; reprinted by permission of the publishers), Vol. 46, No. 3, Summer, 1977, pp. 338-47.*

BRUCE MICHELSON (essay date 1980)

Knowing more than ever now about the gloom of Mark Twain's final years, we can imagine his miseries driving him into an artistic senility, a senility in which he spent year after year,

ream after ream of manuscript "proving" to nobody that nothing and nobody are of any consequence, that life is meaningless, reality a lie. We cannot pretend that the last fables, chief among them the three variations on the Mysterious Stranger tale, reveal any reconciliation with life, or that the theology in these stories will hold water, or that as stories they are without serious flaw. (p. 44)

Throughout the *Letters from the Earth, What is Man?,* and the numerous short pieces that Twain worked on after 1895, the same paradoxical truths assert themselves again and again: first, that even in his most agnostic moments, Mark Twain usually managed to keep his pen "warmed up" for the only God he could sensibly vilify: the finite conception of God that man develops out of his own stupidity; and second, that whenever God and the human condition are Twain's targets, he runs into both structural and stylistic trouble. Those most admirable qualities in his storytelling and his prose, his economy, his grace, his playfulness, drift out of his reach, and his late writings all too frequently deteriorate into mechanical fables or mere rant. Most readers of these works seem to agree that before the Mysterious Stranger experiment, Twain the storyteller and Twain the accuser of mankind's God have not mixed well at all. This is the common way now of explaining the challenge which all three versions of the Stranger tale try to face: to tell a good story somehow, a Mark-Twain story with vitality, wit, and grace, and still speak Twain's piece on God, fate, and mankind's muddled theistic imagination. But we can get a good deal farther in understanding the method of these tales if we can describe this general challenge in a somewhat different way.

Critics have commonly noticed that Mark Twain's masterworks are filled with people who go on holidays and play games: happy tourists, romantic greenhorns, pre-adolescent pranksters, giddy young recruits, Connecticut tinkers—the list is a long one. Play, games, make-believe, these are constant themes in the major fiction and constant obsessions in the man. Twain was himself a notorious game-player and practical joker, the greatest of our writers, perhaps, in recreating the make-believe of children and childlike adults; and very early on he had comprehended that any God who would bother with the petty affairs of mankind must do so as a cosmic Tom Sawyer, an all-powerful Player who amuses Himself recklessly at the world's expense. (p. 45)

No one seems to doubt Tom Sawyer's total involvement in his make-believe, thoughtless and ill-timed as it often is; and when Twain as the young tourist or the cub pilot sets out to have "ever such a fine time," to turn his fictive imagination loose on some dusty, unenchanted reality and make magic out of it, the spell he casts on himself is cast over the reader at the same time. But what a different matter it is to enchant with the play of gods. So much seems to stand in the way: the deadening solemnity that commonly surrounds the Divine, the damage that omnipotence necessarily wreaks on the tension and challenge of any make-believe, the mortal threat that such an unavoidably didactic arrangement poses to the life of fiction. And finally, there is this about play: that by nature it is an affirmative act when it is true, an act of celebration which, according to [Johan] Huizinga, brings joy, promotes mystery, stirs wonder. The true player is happy in his play, not detached and cool; the player charms us much more than he instructs. And so we can come upon a central problem of the Stranger story from another angle: how are these essential attributes of true play, which reveal themselves to such advantage in the works of

Mark Twain's major phase, to be reconciled with Mark Twain's case against life?

Bearing in mind the problems that play and cosmic fables can cause each other, one needs to go a step further, to recollect the special influence that play has upon the shape and tone of Mark Twain's earlier works, and what play commonly signifies when it turns up there. Not simply play and mood, but play and structure have had much to do with each other. When Twain sets a character loose to amuse himself in the world, the festivity has a way of reverberating in the narrative stance. The energy, the exuberant looseness of Twain's best writings have been accounted for variously; but most readers seem to agree that there is some sort of connection between this free-wheeling, improvisatory storytelling and the play and games in the story told. Twain's own fun on tour, or Tom Sawyer's as master of local revels, or Hank Morgan's as master of a nation, finds its way into the language and structure of the novel. Narrative voices may come and go, scenes, anecdotes and whole plotlines may drift in and out of the pages, jokes and sideline issues pop up unexpectedly, sometimes to get out of hand—all reinforcing *our* sense of the pleasure someone has in simply telling the story. How often it is that loose plot structures, false leads, and altered purposes show us Mark Twain in full genius and high spirits—his genius and his high spirits being perhaps inseparable. In contrast, the controlled, linear, single-minded Mark Twain is the Twain of *Tom Sawyer Abroad* and *Personal Recollections of Joan of Arc,* the tidier mind-set of decidedly minor works. The point is not that flawed books are better than tidy ones, but rather that Twain's major fiction shows a kind of faith *in* fiction, a willingness to give himself over to the story the way a child gives all to a game of make-believe. And signs of that strange faith, when they show themselves in these final writings, should be taken seriously by anyone trying to understand Mark Twain's meaning and mind. (pp. 46-7)

Among the work notes to the "Eseldorf manuscript," the first version of the Stranger story, . . . we find these lines, copied from Mary Baker Eddy's *Science and Health,* a book Twain had led the country in laughing at:

> Finite belief can never do justice to truth in any direction. It limits all things and would compress Mind, which is infinite, into a skullbone.

Finite, banal belief: this is the central theme of every version of *The Mysterious Stranger,* and it is never clearer than here in the first manuscript. . . . This is Twain's first attempt to build a story around the notion of Deus as Deus Ludens, around God as a divine, omnipotent, playful Tom Sawyer. The story's failure, apparently provided him with a late education in reconciling games, gods, and literary necessities. (p. 47)

Philip Traum, angel, alias Satan, nephew to the Prince of Darkness, is one of the Heavenly Host; the name is meant to do what the name of Satan is always meant for in Twain's stories, letters and humorous speeches: to thumb a nose at tidy theistic arrangements of the universe, the clean division of the world into Miss Watson's Heaven and everyone else's hell. There is really no question whom Philip is meant to represent here. Seeking playmates and amusements in Eseldorf, leading the others and deciding the game, Satan is a caricature of a personal God; he is an omnipotent Tom Sawyer on a permanent holiday, and those who have prayed for God's intervention in their mortal lives now get much more than they bargained for. The world is of course Philip's playground; nothing to him is

"for keeps," or of any consequence at all. And just as obvious and familiar are the themes of Eseldorf: the utter inconsequence of humanity in the divine perspective, and the trivial game that human life must seem to any infinite Being who might bother with it.

But this is precisely the paradox which spoils the story: Satan comes to mankind as a playful child, spreading "rapture" among his mortal playmates; yet there is no rapture at all in Philip himself. His tranquil indifference is ruinously out of keeping with the spirit of true play. (p. 48)

This, then, is the hollow ring one hears in the first version of *The Mysterious Stranger;* and this gives us some idea why Mark Twain abandoned Philip Traum, whose spoil-sport coolness and spiritless, lesson-teaching mock play is paralleled by a spiritlessness in Mark Twain's telling of the tale. . . . In contrast to the works of Twain's major phase, "Eseldorf" is oddly linear, monochromatic in tone. Satan never escapes from Mark Twain's didactic nets the way Huck does, the way Hank Morgan does, the way Mark Twain the narrator does in the earliest of his book-length triumphs. (pp. 49-50)

[There] is more whim, more improvisation in "Schoolhouse Hill" [the second version of the Stranger story], even though the piece is doomed by a rigidity that Twain still has not shaken off. There is real progress here: the lecturing unsatisfactory boy-sage of "Eseldorf" has dropped away, yet in his place now is a simple, unsatisfactory mechanical reversal of Christian convention. The son of Satan, straight from Hell, is kind, helpful, respectful; his red demons are models of politeness and efficiency; he is on a Christlike quest to set the world right, and so on. Conventional theism stood neatly on its head—a fine source of true comedy at least, but what hope is there yet for a full, rich story? Mark Twain's own play impulse has broken out of its confinement. It is clashing now with the fixedness of the tale's basic arrangements. For good or ill, a more festive mood is making itself felt in his storytelling, and the Stranger tale had to change again to accommodate it, if the story was to make a genuine escape from tract.

But there may be one more recognition, more important than any structural or aesthetic discovery behind the last and best of the Stranger stories—an ontological recognition, growing straight out of both his own despair and his unextinguishable play-impulse: if man's God, as man has conceived him, is truly a gamester and practical joker, then a story about the antics of this Tom Sawyer-God, a story meant to dispel banal imaginings and confront man with the mystery *behind* the Gamester, should *itself* be an act of celebration of that mystery. To put it another way, a story about a playful God must serve two ends: the play must reveal the essential foolishness of the God we imagine, and it must celebrate the God we cannot imagine—the Unknown, the "God beyond God" to borrow the famous phrase from Paul Tillich. True play and the sacred always have much to do with each other, and so the potential in the story was enormous for solving its own greatest problem. The divine Improvisor, and Twain's own talent and love for improvisation, may have offered him more than the intense, momentary pleasures of yarn-spinning. A truly playful Stranger would be truly mysterious, as well as more effectively satiric. And there is reason to think that it *was* mystery that Mark Twain sought for in his last version of the tale—not mere nihilism and misanthropy. Only that last manuscript was titled **"The Mysterious Stranger,"** suggesting that Mark Twain had fully recognized that without mystery the teleological farce made no sense at all. The problem he faced now was this: how to balance his rejection of theological theism with an affirmation, however dim, of the possibility of something greater than the limited, man-conceived, theistic God? There is no pretending that ''No. 44, The Mysterious Stranger'' is a perfect answer. But in understanding how this tale works in comparison to its predecessors, we can marvel at how close Mark Twain finally came.

The Stranger who comes in now is younger, psychologically, as well as more mysterious. His bloodlines are perfectly obscure, and without even a shirttail connection to God or Satan, he arrives in Stein's print shop as a vulnerable innocent, more capricious and more needful of companionship than any of his surrogates. . . . There are no practical jokes, no games from him—yet. He is the first magic-working Stranger we are cajoled into both liking and pitying.

All this, of course, turns out to be the set-up for one long practical joke. That, finally, is the structure the tale follows: that of one great practical joke. In Chapter Fifteen, the rug is pulled out from beneath us. Forty-Four seems to be under a sentence of death from the magician Balthasar Hoffman—we have as yet no reason to suspect that Forty-Four is the real worker of the magic—and August resolves to give himself to the ''rescuing of this endangered soul.'' A little serious theology is all it takes to spring the trap: mention God and the Divine order of things, and suddenly our meek and suffering servant is capering on the ceiling. . . . (pp. 51-3)

From this point on the circus is in town, the Feast of Fools is declared, and prayer and pity are banished. The suffering little Christ-figure has been swept away by the Supreme joker, Showoff, Thrillseeker—and the play of this new Stranger is both convincing and infectious. Forty-Four can truly lose himself in his fun; August, by the sheer rambling run of his narration in the above paragraph, is certainly caught up too. And what of Mark Twain? The exuberance that sweeps into the prose at this point, the variety of jests and sports and whatnot that heap into the story hereafter, and most importantly the sheer affection Mark Twain shows for the fun-loving, childlike Forty-Four, all demonstrate that Twain has begun to delight in this playful Stranger rather than merely to use him. (p. 53)

For the first time in the Stranger experiments, for the first time in ten years, Twain is trusting his tale to a child who ingeniously plays, plays more wildly and capriciously and truly, in fact, than Tom Sawyer ever did. (p. 54)

What difference does all this make, that on the third try, the divine Player becomes a real player and the play real play, wild and exuberant enough to tie the story itself in knots? Indeed it makes a great difference. . . . [A] certain boisterousness, an air of celebration, has come back to Twain's prose after long absence, back into the tone and fabric of his fiction; but there is something further, and still more important to notice. To recognize what Twain has achieved with his playful stranger is to have a vital clue—perhaps the only textual clue—to making any sense of the ending of the tale. . . . (p. 55)

Many of the interpretators—and they are not scarce—of the famous ''dream conclusion'' overlook one or another important contradiction in those last hundred-odd lines, some ontological short-circuit which damages any attempt at a solipsistic, or nihilistic or cautiously theistic reading. We shall never understand that conclusion any better unless we recognize how it grows out of and completes the particular story it ends—and what Forty-Four's previous antics have to do with it. Forty-Four's genuine, convincing, playful rampage has disrupted everything else, wrecking the sentimental melodrama that the

first dozen chapters set up, boggling all our expectations and logical plot developments, confounding our sense of individual characters, our sense of place and time, and upsetting any effort by anybody in the story to be logical and serious. The world of logic, the tidy imagination confined by the skull-bone, the very human faculties which create the banal theistic God, all these are put to rout—and it is Forty-Four's play that does the job. As readers, we are left, even before the concluding chapter, in a kind of vertigo, with every structural and thematic rug pulled out from under us. Vertigo is precisely one of the conditions sought for in true play. With our sense of reality thrown off balance, the player is left open to new perceptions, new possibilities. The end of the story is the confirmation of the story: the disruptive player's final blow at anyone's complacent notion of the real and of man's place in it. It is very possible that Forty-Four's object remains, to the very end, quite the same—not to instruct, but to astound us, to dizzy us, as countless readers have been astounded before drawing back from the story and rationalizing its irrational last pages. What is August left with, what are we left with but a kind of thematic empty space through which to reach out to better dreams? Through play, the world we have trusted has been set reeling; through play, the absurdities of the theistic God have been driven home. But the marvelous paradox in that sustained negation is this: that through play, a vital, enduring hopeful festivity and life have been restored to Mark Twain's fiction. Through play the world we cannot understand is celebrated in and by the very act of overthrowing the world we thought we knew. At the last, Mark Twain has dreamed a better dream out of the Stranger idea. The argument may go on forever about just how nihilistic Twain really was in his final years, but as it does so, one needs to bear in mind that in the last and best version of the Stranger tale, Twain's fiction does recover that mysterious power of great fiction to celebrate even as it denies, to say even as Forty-Four says to August very near the story's end: ''Sit down. Keep your head. There's no hurry. Things are working; I think we can have a good time.'' . . . (pp. 55-6)

Bruce Michelson, ''Deus Ludens: The Shaping of Mark Twain's 'Mysterious Stranger','' in Novel: A Forum on Fiction *(copyright © Novel Corp., 1980), Vol. 14, No. 1, Fall, 1980, pp. 44-56.*

ADDITIONAL BIBLIOGRAPHY

Blair, Walter. ''When Was *Huckleberry Finn* Written?'' *American Literature* XXX, No. 1 (March 1958): 1-25.
> Offers convincing evidence that *Huckleberry Finn* was written in three periods, during 1876, 1880, and 1883.

Brashear, Minnie M. *Mark Twain: Son of Missouri.* 1934. Reprint. New York: Russell & Russell, 1964, 294 p.
> Emphasizes the positive influence on Twain of eighteenth-century European literature and his childhood in Hannibal.

Brazil, John R. ''Perception and Structure in Mark Twain's Art and Mind: *Life on the Mississippi.*'' *The Mississippi Quarterly* XXXIV, No. 2 (Spring 1981): 91-112.
> Explains the difference between the ''Old Times on the Mississippi'' and the appended sections of *Life on the Mississippi* in terms of Twain's struggle to find a common language that would reflect both his boyish romanticism and his mature practicality.

DeVoto, Bernard. *''Mark Twain's America'' and ''Mark Twain at Work.''* Boston: Houghton Mifflin Co., 1967, 491 p.

Combines two of DeVoto's important critical works in one volume. The first, written in response to Van Wyck Brooks's *The Ordeal of Mark Twain,* presents a portrait of American frontier life and humor of the mid-nineteenth century, showing this background to have been beneficial to Twain's development. The second book, written after scrutiny of Twain's manuscripts, examines the composition of *Tom Sawyer* and *Huckleberry Finn.* The last chapter outlines the personal tragedies that shaped Twain's final writings.

Fuller, Daniel J. "Mark Twain and Hamlin Garland: Contrarieties in Regionalism." *Mark Twain Journal* XVII, No. 1 (Winter 1973-74): 14-18.*

A short study of the widely different uses made by Twain and Garland of their midwestern backgrounds.

Hill, Hamlin. *Mark Twain: God's Fool.* New York: Harper & Row, 1973, 308 p.

Detailed biography of the last decade of Twain's life based on unpublished material from the papers of Mark Twain. Hill portrays Twain's last years as a tragedy of declining artistic powers and growing bitterness.

Jones, Alexander E. "Mark Twain and the Determinism of *What Is Man?*" *American Literature* XXIX, No. 1 (March 1957): 1-17.

Traces Twain's evolving philosophy and its culmination in *What Is Man?* Jones finds the work to be Twain's gospel of hope rather than pessimism.

Jones, Howard Mumford. "The Pessimism of Mark Twain." In his *Belief and Disbelief in American Literature,* pp. 94-115. Chicago, London: The University of Chicago Press, 1967.

An explication of Twain's beliefs regarding the nature of God and humanity, finding Twain's pessimism representative of a late nineteenth-century trend in philosophy and religion.

Kaplan, Justin. *Mr. Clemens and Mark Twain: A Biography.* New York: Simon and Schuster, 1966, 424 p.

A well researched biography, emphasizing conflicting aspects of Twain's personality.

Kipling, Rudyard. "An Interview with Mark Twain." In his *From Sea to Sea, Vol. II,* pp. 304-18. Leipzig: Bernhard Tauchnitz, 1900.

A lively interview covering a wide variety of subjects.

Krause, Sydney J. "Twain's Method and Theory of Composition." *Modern Philology* LVI, No. 3 (February 1959): 167-77.

A short study of Twain's seemingly haphazard techniques of composition, focusing on his practices of "spontaneous writing" and extensive revision.

Neider, Charles. *Mark Twain and the Russians: An Exchange of Views.* New York: Hill and Wang, 1960, 32 p.

An exchange of letters between Neider and Russian journalist Y. Bereznitsky, the latter charging that Mark Twain's writings are subject to official suppression in the United States.

Paine, Albert Bigelow. *Mark Twain: A Biography; The Personal and Literary Life of Samuel Langhorne Clemens.* 4 vols. New York, London: Harper & Brothers Publishers, 1912.

The authorized biography, containing much valuable material on Twain, though criticized by some scholars as idealized.

Rubin, Louis D., Jr. "*Tom Sawyer* and the Use of Novels." in his *The Curious Death of the Novel: Essays in American Literature,* pp. 88-99. Baton Rouge: Louisiana State University Press, 1967.

An examination of the literary components of *Tom Sawyer.* The book is used as a model for understanding the construction of novels.

Tenney, Thomas Asa. *Mark Twain: A Reference Guide.* Boston: G. K. Hall, 1977, 443 p.

Annotated bibliography which thoroughly covers criticism on Twain through 1976.

Trilling, Lionel. "*Huckleberry Finn.*" In his *The Liberal Imagination: Essays on Literature and Society,* pp. 104-17. New York: The Viking Press, 1950.

An essay on *Huckleberry Finn,* examining, with acknowledgement to T. S. Eliot, Huck as a servant of the brown river-god, the Mississippi.

Turner, Arlin. *Mark Twain and George W. Cable: The Record of a Literary Friendship.* East Lansing: Michigan State University Press, 1960, 141 p.

Contains "the twins of genius's" opinions of each other and of many other subjects, in letters written during their joint lecture tour of 1884-85.

Wagenknecht, Edward. *Mark Twain: The Man and His Work.* 3d rev. ed. Norman: University of Oklahoma Press, 1967, 302 p.

An essential biographical and critical study of Twain and his outlook, demonstrating extensive knowledge of Twain criticism through 1960, and including valuable footnotes and bibliographies.

Jules (Gabriel) Verne

1828-1905

French novelist, short story writer, and dramatist.

Verne is acknowledged as one of the world's first and most imaginative modern science fiction writers. He is commonly viewed as a children's writer because of the adventure and scientific gadgetry present in the simplest level of his plots. But he wrote primarily for adults, reflecting nineteenth-century concerns with contemporary scientific innovation and its potential for human benefit or destruction.

"At heart," wrote Verne's nephew Maurice, "my uncle had only three passions: freedom, music, and the sea." These three motifs recur throughout Verne's voluminous production, being essential elements in the lives of his principal characters. His development of these themes reached a pinnacle in *Vingt mille lieues sous les mers (Twenty Thousand Leagues under the Sea)* and its sequel *L'île mystérieuse (The Mysterious Island)* in the character of Captain Nemo. A wandering orphan of the world, Nemo epitomized Verne's vision of humanity, vainly attempting, with the dazzling machinery at his command, to create a peaceful world, while encumbered by the base passions of his nature.

As a young man, Verne worked for a short time as a stockbroker before turning his full attention to literature. He struggled as a playwright, sometimes collaborating with Alexandre Dumas *fils,* but with little success. Verne's mediocre fortunes changed with the publication of *Cinq semaines en ballon (Five Weeks in a Balloon)* in 1863. This, the first of his many adventure novels in the series "Les voyages extraordinaires," was highly popular in France, and commenced a long, mutually rewarding working relationship with publisher Jules Hetzel, who provided Verne with much-needed advice and encouragement. Verne saw little but success for the rest of his life. In addition to his first novel, *Voyage au centre de la terre (A Journey to the Centre of the Earth), The Mysterious Island, Maître du monde (The Master of the World)*, and several others are considered classics, while *Twenty Thousand Leagues under the Sea* is regarded as his masterpiece. The jaunty *Le tour du monde en quatre-vingt jours (Around the World in Eighty Days)*, originally serialized, was his most popular book, generating international excitement and speculation about the fortunes of Phileas Fogg and his valet, Passepartout.

Verne's powers waned after *The Mysterious Island,* and as he recognized the destructive potential of the industrial age's technological advances his books became murky and pessimistic in tone and subject matter. Characteristic of this period is "L'eternal Adam," one of Verne's last stories, which plumbed the nadir of his despair. By the time of his death, however, he had been named a Chevalier of the French Legion of Honor and was internationally known and beloved as a highly imaginative adventure writer, although such literary creations as his submarine and spaceship were dismissed as preposterous dreams.

Verne borrowed numerous ideas from Edgar Allen Poe for his own plots, appending one of the American's stories to form *Le sphinx des glaces (The Mystery of Arthur Gordon Pym).* To Poe Verne also owes the fascination with cryptograms appar-

ent in his works. His novels and stories, in clumsily worded English translation, were long consigned to the children's bookshelf by many critics. But recent research is bearing out suspicions that Verne was victimized by an incompetent translator. As evidence of Verne's importance and depth, critics point to his careful research and his allegiance to, and gradual rejection of, the Saint-Simonian ideal of scientific subjugation of nature for humanity's benefit.

Although Verne may seem quaint and dated today, his works inspired many scientists and explorers, including Richard E. Byrd, Guglielmo Marconi, and Wernher von Braun. He predicted the advent of television, helicopters, neon lights, air-conditioning, and other twentieth-century inventions, and, with H. G. Wells, was one of the progenitors of modern science fiction.

PRINCIPAL WORKS

Les pailles rompues (drama) 1850
*Cinq semaines en ballon (novel) 1863
  [*Five Weeks in a Balloon,* 1870]

Voyage au centre de la terre (novel) 1864
  [*A Journey to the Centre of the Earth,* 1872]
De la terre à la lune, trajet direct en 97 heures. 2 vols.
  (novel) 1865-69
  [*From the Earth to the Moon Direct in 97 Hours 20
  Minutes: And a Trip around It,* 1873]
Les aventures du Capitaine Hatteras. 2 vols. (novel)
  1866
  [*The Adventures of Captain Hatteras,* 1876]
Les enfants du Capitaine Grant. 3 vols. (novel) 1867-68
  [*A Voyage round the World,* 1876-77; also published as
  Captain Grant's Children, 1964]
Vingt mille lieues sous les mers (novel) 1870
  [*Twenty Thousand Leagues under the Seas,* 1873; also
  published as *Twenty Thousand Leagues under the Sea,*
  1876]
Une ville flottante suivi de les forceurs de blocus (novel
  and short story) 1871
  [*A Floating City, and the Blockade Runners,* 1876]
Le pays des fourrures. 2 vols. (novel) 1873
  [*The Fur Country; or, Seventy Degrees North Latitude,*
  1873]
Le tour du monde en quatre-vingt jours (novel) 1873
  [*Around the World in Eighty Days,* 1874; also translated
  as *Round the World in Eighty Days,* 1879]
*Le docteur Ox; Maître Zacharias; Un hivernage dans les
  glaces; Un drame dans les airs* (short stories) 1874
  [*Dr. Ox's Experiment,* 1874]
L'ile mystérieuse. 3 vols. (novel) 1874-75
  [*The Mysterious Island,* 1875]
Michel Strogoff. 2 vols. (novel) 1876
  [*Michael Strogoff, the Courier of the Czar,* 1876-77]
Hector Servadac. 2 vols. (novel) 1877
  [*Hector Servadac,* 1878; also translated as *To the Sun?*
  and *Off on a Comet!,* 1878]
*Les cinq cents millions de la Begúm, suivi de les revoltés
  de la "Bounty"* (novel and short story) 1878
  [*The Begum's Fortune,* 1880]
Robur le conquérant (novel) 1886
  [*The Clipper of the Clouds,* 1887]
L'ile à hélice. 2 vols. (novel) 1895
  [*The Floating Island,* 1896; also translated as *Propellor
  Island,* 1961]
Face au drapeau (novel) 1896
  [*For the Flag,* 1897]
Le sphinx des glaces. 2 vols. (novel) 1897
  [*An Antarctic Mystery,* 1898; also translated as *The
  Mystery of Arthur Gordon Pym,* 1960]
Maître du monde (novel) 1904
  [*The Master of the World,* 1914]
Le phare du bout du monde (novel) 1905
  [*The Lighthouse at the End of the World,* 1923]
Les naufragés du Jonathan. 2 vols. (novel) 1909
  [*The Survivors of the "Jonathan,"* 1962]
Hier et demain (short stories) 1910
  [*Yesterday and Tomorrow,* 1965]
L'etonnante aventure de la mission Barsac. 2 vols.
  (novel) 1919
  [*Into the Niger Bend and City in the Sahara,* 1965]

*These volumes comprise the series "Les voyages extraordinaires."

NATURE (essay date 1878)

[In Jules Verne] we have a science teacher of a new kind. He
has forsaken the beaten track, *bien entendu;* but acknowledging
in him a travelled Frenchman with a keen eye and vivid imagination—and no slight knowledge of the elements of science—
we do not see how he could have more usefully employed his
talents. He will at once forgive us for saying that when we
compare his romances of the ordinary type, such as **"Martin
Paz,"** with [his science fiction stories], we think that he, as
well as his readers, is to be congratulated upon the new line
he has opened out.

There have been many books before his time in which the
interest has centred in some vast convulsion of nature, or in
nature generally being put out of joint, but in these there has
been no attempt made to reach the *vraisemblable;* indeed in
most cases there has not been sufficient knowledge on the part
of the author to connect his catastrophe either with any law or
the breaking of one. But with Jules Verne for once grant the
possibility of his chief incident, and all the surroundings are
secundem artem. The time at which the projectile was to be
shot out of the Columbiad towards the moon was correctly
fixed on true astronomical grounds, and the boy who follows
its flight will have a more concrete idea of, and interest in,
what gravity is and does, possibly, than if he were to read half-
a-dozen text-books in the ordinary way. Once grant the submarine vessel and the use made of electricity, and the various
scenes through which the strange ship passes are sketched by
no 'prentice hand. To take the most extreme case, if it be
possible to imagine one in such a connection—Algeria torn
from the earth by a comet and started on an orbit of its own;
the astronomical phenomena have been most carefully thought
out, and children of larger growth will, if they choose, find
much to learn as well as to amuse them. Indeed it is very rare
that one finds our author tripping in such matters, although he
does sometimes. One case that occurs to us is when, in the
"Fur Country," he refers to the midnight sun touching the
edges of the *western* horizon without dipping beneath it, and
even this may be due to the translator, for we have not the
original French edition to refer to. (pp. 197-98)

> *"Jules Verne," in* Nature, *Vol. XVII, No. 428, Jan-
> uary 10, 1878, pp. 197-99.*

JULES VERNE (essay date 1894)

My object has been to depict the earth, and not the earth alone,
but the universe, for I have sometimes taken my readers away
from the earth, in the novel. And I have tried at the same time
to realize a very high ideal of beauty of style. It is said that
there can't be any style in a novel of adventure, but that isn't
true; though I admit that it is very much more difficult to write
such a novel in a good literary form than the studies of character
which are so in vogue to-day. . . .

Dumas used to say to me, when I complained that my place
in French literature was not recognized, 'You ought to have
been an American or an English author. Then your books,
translated into French, would have gained you enormous popularity in France, and you would have been considered by your
countrymen as one of the greatest masters of fiction.' But as
it is, I am considered of no account in French literature. (p. 121)

I am not and never have been a money-getting man. I am a
man of letters and an artist, living in the pursuit of the ideal,

running wild over an idea, and glowing with enthusiasm over my work. (p. 124)

> *Jules Verne, "Jules Verne at Home: His Own Account of His Life and Work," in an interview with R. H. Sherard, in* McClure's Magazine, *Vol. II, No. 2, January, 1894, pp. 115-24.*

H. G. WELLS (essay date 1933)

[My scientific romances] have been compared with the work of Jules Verne and there was a disposition on the part of literary journalists at one time to call me the English Jules Verne. As a matter of fact there is no literary resemblance whatever between the anticipatory inventions of the great Frenchman and [my science] fantasies. His work dealt almost always with actual possibilities of invention and discovery, and he made some remarkable forecasts. The interest he invoked was a practical one; he wrote and believed and told that this thing or that thing could be done, which was not at that time done. He helped his reader to imagine it done and to realise what fun, excitement or mischief would ensue. Many of his inventions have "come true". But [my stories] . . . do not pretend to deal with possible things; they are exercises of the imagination in a quite different field. (p. 262)

> *H. G. Wells, in an extract from his introduction to his* The Scientific Romances of H. G. Wells *(reprinted by permission of the Estate of the late H. G. Wells), V. Gollancz, Ltd., 1933 (and reprinted in "The Future of a Sentiment," in* Jules Verne *by Kenneth Allott, Kennikat Press, 1970, p. 262).*

GEORGE ORWELL (essay date 1941)

Although later he was to have misgivings—he was not altogether easy about the theory of evolution, for instance—Verne belongs to the early scientific period, the period of the Great Eastern and the Hyde Park Exhibition of 1851, when the key-phrase was "Command over Nature" rather than, as now, "Mysterious Universe." The mechanical sciences were advancing at tremendous speed and their sinister possibilities were seldom foreseen. . . . The modern wars of extermination had not only not started, but, no doubt, would have been difficult to imagine. Later, however, Verne watched with disgust the rise of modern imperialism and the scramble for Africa. One result of this was the disappearance from his books of the sympathetic Englishman. In his earlier work this character appears over and over again—a queer figure, as in most nineteenth-century French novels, given to wearing check suits and breaking long silences with cries of "Hip, hip, hurrah!" but symbolising the pragmatism and inventiveness which Verne admired in the English-speaking races.

It is difficult not to couple Verne's name with that of H. G. Wells. . . . Wells, even more than Verne, has made himself the apostle of Science, but he belongs to a less confident period in which the smallness of man against the background of the spiral nebulae is more obvious than his mastery over Nature. Wells's early romances are less scientific than Verne's—that is, less close to the established knowledge of the time—but there is far more feeling of *wonder* in them. If one compares *A Journey to the Moon* with *The First Men in the Moon*, one sees the advantage, at any rate from a purely literary point of view, of a less anthropocentric standpoint. Verne's story is scientific, or very nearly so. Granted that one could fire a projectile out of the earth's gravitational pull, and that the

human beings inside it could survive the shock, the thing might have happened as it is recorded. Wells's story is pure speculation, based on nothing except a predilection for thinking that the moon and the planets are inhabited. But it creates a universe of its own, which one remembers in detail years after reading it. The most memorable incident in Verne's book is the time when the oxygen cylinder sprang a leak and produced symptoms of drunkenness in the explorers—precisely the incident that tethers the story to the earth. . . . [It] seems doubtful whether Verne will be read much longer, except by schoolchildren "doing" *A Journey to the Centre of the Earth* as an alternative to *Tartarin of Tarascon*. He set out to combine instruction with entertainment, and he succeeded, but only so long as his scientific theories were more or less up to date. He does, however, enjoy a sort of anonymous immortality because of a controversy that has sprung out of one of his books. In *Round the World in Eighty Days*—itself based . . . on a short story of Poe's—he makes play with the fact that if one travels round the world eastward one gains a day in the passage. And this has given rise to the question, "What will happen when an aeroplane can fly round the world in twenty-four hours?", which is much debated by imaginative boys, readers of the *Wizard* and the *Hotspur*, who have probably never heard Verne's name.

> *George Orwell, "Two Glimpses of the Moon," in* The New Statesman & Nation *(© 1941 The Statesman & Nation Publishing Co. Ltd.), Vol. XXI, No. 517, January 18, 1941, p. 64.*

ROLAND BARTHES (essay date 1957)

Verne has built a kind of self-sufficient cosmogony, which has its own categories, its own time, space, fulfilment and even existential principle.

This principle, it seems to me, is the ceaseless action of secluding oneself. Imagination about travel corresponds in Verne to an exploration of closure, and the compatibility between Verne and childhood does not stem from a banal mystique of adventure, but on the contrary from a common delight in the finite, which one also finds in children's passion for huts and tents: to enclose oneself and to settle, such is the existential dream of childhood and of Verne. The archetype of this dream is this almost perfect novel: *L'Ile mystérieuse,* in which the man-child re-invents the world, fills it, closes it, shuts himself up in it, and crowns this encyclopaedic effort with the bourgeois posture of appropriation: slippers, pipe and fireside, while outside the storm, that is, the infinite, rages in vain.

Verne had an obsession for plenitude: he never stopped putting a last touch to the world and furnishing it, making it full with an egg-like fullness. . . . Verne belongs to the progressive lineage of the bourgeoisie: his work proclaims that nothing can escape man, that the world, even its most distant part, is like an object in his hand, and that, all told, property is but a dialectical moment in the general enslavement of Nature. Verne in no way sought to enlarge the world by romantic ways of escape or mystical plans to reach the infinite: he constantly sought to shrink it, to populate it, to reduce it to a known and enclosed space, where man could subsequently live in comfort: the world can draw everything from itself; it needs, in order to exist, no one else but man.

Beyond the innumerable resources of science, Verne invented an excellent novelistic device in order to make more vivid this appropriation of the world: to pledge space by means of time, constantly to unite these two categories, to stake them on a single throw of the dice or a single impulse, which always come off. Even vicissitudes have the function of conferring on the world a sort of elastic state, making its limits more distant, then closer, blithely playing with cosmic distances, and mischievously testing the power of man over space and schedules. And on this planet which is triumphantly eaten by the Vernian hero, like a sort of bourgeois Antaeus whose nights are innocent and 'restoring', there often loiters some desperado, a prey to remorse and spleen, a relic from an extinct Romantic age, who strikingly shows up by contrast the health of the true owners of the world, who have no other concern but to adapt as perfectly as possible to situations whose complexity, in no way metaphysical nor even ethical, quite simply springs from some provocative whim of geography.

The basic activity in Jules Verne, then, is unquestionably that of appropriation. The image of the ship, so important in his mythology, in no way contradicts this. Quite the contrary: the ship may well be a symbol for departure; it is, at a deeper level, the emblem of closure. An inclination for ships always means the joy of perfectly enclosing oneself, of having at hand the greatest possible number of objects, and having at one's disposal an absolutely finite space. To like ships is first and foremost to like a house, a superlative one since it is unremittingly closed, and not at all vague sailings into the unknown: a ship is a habitat before being a means of transport. And sure enough, all the ships in Jules Verne are perfect cubby-holes, and the vastness of their circumnavigation further increases the bliss of their closure, the perfection of their inner humanity. The *Nautilus,* in this regard, is the most desirable of all caves: the enjoyment of being enclosed reaches its paroxysm when, from the bosom of this unbroken inwardness, it is possible to watch, through a large window-pane, the outside vagueness of the waters, and thus define, in a single act, the inside by means of its opposite.

Most ships in legend or fiction are, from this point of view, like the *Nautilus,* the theme of a cherished seclusion, for it is enough to present the ship as the habitat of man, for man immediately to organize there the enjoyment of a round, smooth universe, of which, in addition, a whole nautical morality makes him at once the god, the master and the owner (*sole master on board,* etc.). (pp. 65-7)

> *Roland Barthes, "The 'Nautilus' and the Drunken Boat," in his* Mythologies, *edited and translated by Annette Lavers (reprinted by permission of Hill & Wang, a division of Farrar, Strauss & Giroux, Inc.; translation copyright © 1972 by Jonathan Cape Ltd.; originally published as* Mythologies *(© 1957 by Editions du Seuil), Editions du Seuil, 1957), Hill and Wang, 1972, pp. 65-7.*

ARTHUR C. CLARKE   (essay date 1959)

During our last fifty years, scientific progress has been so enormous that one might think that any work of science fiction written during the Nineteenth Century would be hopelessly out of date. But Verne's stories do not depend on their science alone to make them interesting; if they did, they would have been forgotten except by a few specialists and collectors. The reason Verne is still read by millions today is simply that he was one of the best storytellers who have ever lived; and *A Journey to the Centre of the Earth* is a particularly flawless specimen of his art. (pp. v-vi)

The leading character, Professor Hardwigg (Lidenbrock in the original French version) is one of Verne's most memorable creations, in the same tradition as Captain Nemo of the *Nautilus,* and Michael Arden of *From the Earth to the Moon,* or Phileas Fogg of *Around the World in Eighty Days.* All these Verne heroes are implacably (one might even say demoniacally) determined individuals who will let nothing—and nobody—stand in the way of their ambition, whether it is to race round the world for a wager or to uncover some new secret of science. They usually lack a sense of humor, but the author more than makes up for this with his sly asides. Verne derived a great deal of amusement in his books by poking good-natured fun at national characteristics. In this volume, the contrast between the erudite German professor, the imperturbable Icelandic guide and the easy-going English narrator provides all the variation of characters that is needed. It is something of a feat to write an entire book about three people; Verne brings it off perfectly.

But perhaps his greatest achievement is the absolute plausibility he maintains; it looks simple, but few later writers of scientific romances have been able to manage it. How did Verne succeed? Chiefly by a strict attention to detail. Every book involved an enormous amount of research—probably quite as much as would be required to write a serious factual work on the same subject. Not that Verne always avoided errors; in Chapter II he refers to Galileo when he should have said Huygens, and in the dream sequence in Chapter XL, he repeats the old fallacy that a shark has to turn on its back to bite. Yet such slips are trivial, and do little to detract from the merit of the book.

Verne was not a great writer by the standards of such literary giants as Melville, Dickens, Poe, Scott, Dumas and the other titans of the nineteenth century. But he was one of the most influential writers who ever lived, for he inspired literally hundreds of inventors and explorers. (pp. vi-vii)

[He] was the first writer to welcome change and to proclaim that scientific discovery could be the most wonderful of all adventures. For this reason he will never grow out of date; though he died in 1905 his spirit was never more alive than it is at this moment, when his greatest dream—that of space-travel—is about to become reality. (p. viii)

> *Arthur C. Clarke, "Introduction" (reprinted by permission of Dodd, Mead & Company, Inc.; copyright © 1959 by Dodd, Mead & Company, Inc.), in A* Journey to the Centre of the Earth *by Jules Verne, Dodd, Mead & Company, 1959, pp. v-viii.*

WILLIAM GOLDING   (essay date 1961)

A child's ignorant eye can make a Western out of a Dumas tapestry. (p. 111)

If we revisit our childhood's reading, we are likely to discover that we missed the satire of *Gulliver,* the evangelism of *Pilgrim's Progress,* and the loneliness of *Robinson Crusoe.*

But when we revisit some books in this way, we find that the iridescent film has burst, to leave nothing behind but a wet mark. Henty, Ballantyne, Burroughs, require an innocence of approach which, while it is natural enough to a child, would be a mark of puerility in an adult. I declare this with some feeling, since during the last week or so I have undertaken a long course of Jules Verne, and suffer at the moment, not from indigestion so much as hunger.

Yet once [his] books satisfied me. They held me rapt, I dived with the *Nautilus,* was shot round the moon, . . . drifted in the South Atlantic, dying of thirst, and tasted—oh rapture! It always sent me indoors for a drink—the fresh waters of the Amazon. And now?

Of course the books have not vanished wholly. They have the saving grace of gusto. Verne had his generation's appetite for facts, and he serves them up in *grande cuisine:* 'How amazing . . . were the microscopical jellyfish observed by Scoresby in the Greenland seas, which he estimated at 23,898,000,000,000,000,000 in area of two square miles!' But a diet of such creatures palls, for Verne's verbal surface lacks the slickness of the professional; it is turgid and slack by turns. Only the brio of his enthusiasm carries us forward from one adventure to another. What is left for the adult is off-beat; something so specialized that to enjoy it is about as eccentric as collecting the vocal chords of prima donnas. For Verne attracts today, not so much by his adventures as by the charm of his nineteenth-century interiors. . . . Here live the savants, and a savant is related to a scientist as an antiquary is to an archaeologist. He is a learned enthusiast, a man of boundless absurdity, energy and stubbornness. At any moment he may leap from his hip-bath, sell his Consols and buy 1,866 gallons of suphuric acid, 16,050 pounds of iron and 11,600 square feet of twilled Lyons silk coated with gutta-percha. His oath is 'A thousand thunders!' Cross him, and he will dash his smoking-cap into the grate. Take leave to doubt his wisdom and he will attempt to assault you. Held back by force, he will wager a fortune on the outcome of his adventure. Without knowing it, he passes a large part of his life under the influence of alcohol, for at the touch of success he will dash off, or drain off, or toss off, a bumper of brandy, which he follows with an endless succession of toasts. This half-gallon or so of brandy has as little effect on him as whisky has on the tough hero of a television serial. Indeed, his euphoria has always been indistinguishable from intoxication. (pp. 111-12)

This typification is moderated but not destroyed by national distinction. Verne reserved, as was perhaps natural, his greatest *élan* for the French, or at least, the Europeans. He divided sang-froid between the English and the American. All these qualities, and others, are laid on with the trowel of farce. Indeed, the sang-froid of his Englishman, Mr. Phileas Fogg, is at times indistinguishable from advanced schizophrenia. But when his characters let themselves go—here is Captain Nemo expressing his sense of displeasure:

'Captain Nemo was before me but I could hardly recognize him. His face was transfigured. His eyes flashed sullenly; his teeth were set; his taut body, clenched fists, and head hunched between his shoulders, betrayed the violent agitation that pervaded his whole frame. He did not move. My telescope, fallen from his hands, had rolled at his feet.'

I must remember that these jerky cut-outs once convinced me, moved me, excited me, as they still move children. (pp. 112-13)

What the child misses most in these books—if I am anything to go by—is the fact that Verne was a heavy-handed satirist. The organization which fires its shot at the moon is the Gun Club of Baltimore. These were the savants who engaged in the arms race of the American Civil War.

'Their military weapons attained colossal proportions, and their projectiles, exceeding the prescribed limits, unfortunately occasionally cut in two some unoffending bystanders. These in-

ventions, in fact, left far in the rear the timid instruments of European artillery.' (p. 113)

Throughout the seventeen books there is an almost total absence of women. Verne was honester here than some of his SF descendants who lug in a blonde for the look of the thing. His male world was probably all he could manage. You cannot hack out a woman's face with an axe; he could not, or would not, write about women. He remains the only French writer who could get his hero right round the world without meeting more than one woman while he was doing it.

Verne's talent was not spurred by a love of what we should now call pure science, but by technology. His books are the imaginative counterpart of the Great Eastern, the Tay Bridge, or the Great Steam Flying Machine. It is this which accounts for his continued appeal to sub-adolescent boyhood. For the science sides of our schools are crammed to bursting with boys who have confused a genial enjoyment in watching wheels go round with the pursuit of knowledge. His heroes, too, are a pattern of what the twelve-year-old boy considers a proper adult pattern—they are tough, sexless, casually brave, resourceful, and *making something big*. Compared with the Sheriff of Dumb Valley, or the Private Eye, they constitute no mean ideal; to the adult, their appeal is wholly nostalgic. Apart from the odd touch that convinces—the pleasures of Professor Aronnax when, after years of groping for fish, he observes them through the windows of *Nautilus;* the willingness of the Frenchman to go to the moon with no prospect of coming back—apart from this they are a dead loss.

A study of Verne makes me uncomfortable. It seems that on the level of engineering, predictions can be made that will come true. So the soberer SF is no more than a blueprint for tomorrow. . . . This prospect would not dismay me, had one of Verne's characters not suggested that the heating of a colossal boiler to three million degrees would one day destroy the world.

Nevertheless, Verne's nineteenth-century technology and mania for size sometimes result in a combination which has a charm to be found nowhere else. He was excited with arc lighting and gives us a picture with all the fascination of an early lantern slide. Light itself, sheer brilliance, is an enchantment to him, when it is produced by man. (pp. 114-15)

Perhaps the best moment comes when we get a mixture of the fantastic, but future and possible, with the ordinary paraphernalia of nineteenth-century living. In ***Round the Moon,*** the three voyagers move about their spaceship, peering delightedly at this and that. In the shadow of the earth all is dark; but as they move into the sun's rays, they find them shining *up* through the base of the ship—and are able to turn off the light, in order to save gas. (p. 115)

William Golding, "Astronaut by Gaslight," in The Spectator (© 1961 by The Spectator; reprinted by permission of The Spectator), Vol. 206, No. 6937, June 9, 1961 (and reprinted in his The Hot Gates and Other Occasional Pieces, Faber and Faber, 1965, pp. 111-15).

KINGSLEY AMIS (essay date 1963)

The year 1963 should not be allowed to pass without some salute to [Jules Verne] . . . who, a century ago, brought out [*Five Weeks in a Balloon,*] a novel that initiated a new literary form. . . . [It] was Jules Verne who set science fiction going.

The physical context and the scale of gadgetry were to be widely varied in his later books, but in other respects *Five Weeks in a Balloon* shows Verne's method already firmly settled. He introduces his favourite trio of intrepid adventure types. In this instance they are Dr Fergusson, the eccentric, obstinate, absurdly omniscient and resourceful scientist who designs, builds and skippers the dirigible; Kennedy, the honourable but hot-tempered man of action with his rifles and pistols; and Joe, the brave, loyal servant who is allowed to provide some comic relief, though never of a sort that might threaten Fergusson's dignity (or raise much more than an indulgent smile). Girls are soppy and don't come into it: this is a boy's world: To say so is not to denigrate it, for an adult's world that was not also a boy's world here and there, now and then, would be a chilly place.

The airborne voyage across Africa with which the story mainly deals is preceded by a short scene at a London Geographical Society meeting. . . . Kenneth Allott, in his excellent biography suggests that this mundane opening, a favourite device of Verne's, was aimed at reassuring Parisian sophisticates who might have balked at unleavened romance.

However this may be, anything so ambitious is dropped with the balloon's first load of ballast, and all the way across the Dark Continent enthusiastic earnestness flourishes unchecked. In the intervals between Fergusson's lectures on history, geography and science the travellers incur adventures, described with innocent energy, see remarkable sights, decked out in profuse but largely unevocative detail, and deliver volubly wooden harangues. . . . It is hard to imagine any sort of equivalent to these verbal postures in mid-twentieth-century idiom, nor should we feel happy with them, I think, if they could be devised. Verne's flavour is of the later nineteenth century and, to a great degree, of his original Victorian translators. (pp. 33-5)

One settles down to read or re-read Verne with an eagerness based on ruminating about him, rather than on any notion of what he is actually like to read. He displays that curious property—shared perhaps with Dickens?—of making his effect not so much when the book is open as after it is shut and put away, so that each novel starts to improve in retrospect the moment one starts to forget it. At any rate, he arouses an expectation that is never properly fulfilled. It is not that the style and narrative method are a barrier; they are part of the fun. And although Verne had no interest in character, his people always endear themselves, so much so as to cast doubt on the first clause of this sentence. The trouble is partly that the adventures, which sound all right in summary and feel all right in memory— a typhoon, an attack on the gas envelope by gyrfalcons, the rescue of a French missionary from the sacrificial stake—are never brought to the pitch of real suspense. We know much too certainly that if Fergusson hasn't got the answer, Kennedy or Joe will come up with it rather too soon.

The most obvious chances of drama and excitement are missed. When Joe, imprisoned by tribesmen in a town on an island in Lake Chad, wakes up to find that a cataclysm has submerged tribesmen, town and island, he might have been pardoned a momentary sense of puzzlement, even alarm. *Mais non!* In a trice the worthy fellow has taken his courage in his hands and seized a sort of boat, roughly hewn out of a tree-trunk, that chances to be drifting past!

This kind of insensitivity is connected with a rather deadening scrupulousness about probability and fact. The Africa seen by the Fergusson expedition is altogether too much the Africa of reliable contemporary report, of Livingstone and Burton and Speke. (pp. 35-6)

Again, Verne's balloon travelled four thousand miles, but a real one had gone eight hundred miles four years earlier, and a straight multiplication factor of five is hardly enough for a tale of wonder. (The immediate source of the novel, Poe's *Balloon-Hoax* of 1844, featured a non-stop flip from North Wales to South Carolina.) A similar conservatism saw to it that that supposed marvel, Captain Nemo's *Nautilus,* was behind the submarine technology of its era in every respect but its electrical power supply; and a voyage to the Moon that omits a landing on the Moon is a dud, never mind the author's excuses about the impracticability of returning to Earth.

All this might matter less if Verne's science were consistently real science. But it is not. The account of the cruise of the *Nautilus* is riddled with errors and contradictions of fact and principle, all of which could have been put right by a session with an encyclopaedia of the day or even half an hour's chat with a reasonably informed schoolmaster. The Moon projectile was fired from a gun at an initial acceleration which would have instantly killed its occupants. (p. 36)

Verne got his fingertips on to some of the great myths of our time—the wonderful submarine, the ship so huge that it becomes a floating island, the moon voyage, the monstrous explosion—without ever showing the ability to grasp them. And yet, in more than one sense, this inability hardly matters. . . . [Up] to a point a myth works without the intervention of style and treatment and . . . is more durable than these in the memory.

But only up to a point. An author who cannot be read without continuous disappointment is only half an author, however much the larger that half may be. It is tempting to urge of Verne, as others have urged of Dickens, that he should be swallowed whole; but how do you do that? (p. 37)

Kingsley Amis, "Founding Father" (1963), in his What Became of Jane Austen? and Other Questions *(copyright © 1970 by Kingsley Amis; reprinted by permission of Harcourt Brace Jovanovich, Inc.; in Canada by Jonathan Clowes Limited), Jonathan Cape, 1970 (and reprinted by Harcourt, 1971), pp. 33-7.*

I. O. EVANS (essay date 1966)

It would take one of Verne's compatriots to judge his position among the literary figures of France. One critic has compared him with Corneille, and another, describing his style as typically Breton, with such authors as Chateaubriand and Renan. It may well be that he achieved his ambition and became the Dumas of science fiction, aiming not at classical correctness but at 'lived and living scenes'. But though like Dumas he wrote historical stories these were never so popular as those with a scientific basis.

Among Verne's faults was a tendency to slur over his endings, as though his mind were already more concerned with his next book. Occasionally, too, he skipped an episode that seemed to call for full treatment. Phileas Fogg sets out to rescue Passepartout, taken prisoner by the Indians; and after a time he brings him back in triumph—and that is all. How the rescue was accomplished we are not told.

Verne also had some rather curious mannerisms, sometimes copied by his translators and sometimes omitted. Instead of saying, for example, 'The captain did so-and-so', he has a trick of putting it 'As for the captain, he did so-and-so', though nothing is gained by this oblique construction.

A few books have no titles for the chapters; for many the titles are short but explicit. But for some the titles are an inordinate length, extending to two or three lines perhaps, and begin in the rather archaic style 'In which . . .' so-and-so happens. I get the impression that Verne used this needless verbiage when he was not really gripped by his story, when 'words would not come' to him—and I find it significant that this applies to his brilliant idea, so disappointingly worked out, *The Clipper of the Clouds*.

Verne's work is so obviously didactic that he might be regarded less as a story-teller than as a geographer and a popularizer of science, using the fictional form simply because that was his only way in conveying information to the public.

It was not that he regarded the factual detail in his narrative as the pill in a spoonful of jam; to his mind the pill was part of the jam. So great was his interest in geography and general science that he may well have taken it for granted that his readers shared it. (pp. 149-50)

Though Verne always had his youthful readers in mind, he seldom wrote expressly for them. The widespread impression that he did . . . may be largely due to his works having first appeared in Britain serialized in the *Boy's Own Paper*. Yet is it not unreasonable: young readers will accept uncritically statements which thoughtful adults would question.

A boy, lost in the excitement of the story, will fail to reflect that if an outlaw-gang take a prisoner they are hardly likely to supply him with unlimited writing-material, and still less likely to leave his writings unread; nor that in such circumstances the captive would hardly be so naïve as to confide to paper his inmost thoughts, including his schemes for sending out an appeal for help!

Nor is a young reader likely to be as sceptical as an adult when Verne yields to one of his weaknesses, a shameless use of coincidence. A speleologist, lost and panic-stricken in the bowels of the earth, drops exhausted at the one point where his voice will reach his comrades along a natural whispering-gallery; a boat-load of castaways on the verge of starvation drifts through the uncharted polar wastes within sight of a rescue expedition. Though he may suppress his doubts in the excitement of the narrative, such incidents startle an adult, but the boy takes them in his stride.

Akin to this is Verne's predilection for 'last moment' rescues—how many of his characters are saved just as all help seems lost? He uses the same technique even when no question of peril is involved as when Captain Nemo is able to 'pin-point' the South Pole by shooting the sun only as it is about to sink below the horizon for the long polar night.

This may be deliberate. A religious man, Verne may have regarded chance occurrences as providential and have felt fully justified in making use of them. (pp. 150-51)

Not all Verne's characters are so wooden as has been made out: in *A Family Without a Name,* for example, they are clearly and sympathetically drawn, and even in his science fiction and adventure stories they may develop in response to life. The growing mental instability of Captain Hatteras is depicted as clearly as his mate's gradual descent from determination to irresolution and thence to open mutiny; Hatteras and his Amer-

ican rival are transformed from bitter enmity into frank comradeship; Captain Nemo's unavailing remorse reduces him from a Byronic hero into a fugitive from his own conscience.

On the whole, however, Verne's characterization tends to be 'in black and white', another feature which appeals less to adults than to young readers, who like to know where they are. His heroes are stalwart and idealistic, resourceful, self-sacrificing, regardless of hardship and peril while pursuing worth-while ends, the sort of people that most of us would like to be. Similarly, his villains are satisfyingly bad, and nobody is likely to shed any tears over them when they meet their doom.

Yet—and this helped to endear his books to parents—his villains are 'nicely' bad. Except in the posthumous *Barsac Mission,* written when Verne—or his editor—was influenced by the tendencies of the age, they may threaten a woman with death, but not with 'a fate worse than death'.

Even in that book, however, Verne shows a typical reticence. Its villain's inveterate baseless hatred for the noble family he had entered into is explained, rather unconvincingly, as due to his being not the son, but only the stepson, of its head. A modern author would much more plausibly have made him the nobleman's illegitimate son, enraged at having no claim on his father's rank and wealth.

Verne protested against the idea that women appeared but little in his work. 'Whenever they are necessary,' he declared, 'they will be found.' True, and wherever they are not necessary, as in most of his science fiction, they are left out. His heroines, he claimed, were 'adorable girls'; and his heroes, too, are clean-living. He always sought to avoid anything which could not be placed without hesitation in the hands of youth, anything which a boy—of Victorian times, of course—'would not like to see in his sister's hands'. (pp. 151-52)

There was no place in Verne's work for passionate or sensual love, desire, or jealousy, or eternal triangle nonsense, but that from his point of view was an advantage. 'Maybe the widespread diffusion of my works', he said, 'is chiefly due to my doing what I have always set out to do, not to publish a page or a phrase which could not be read by the young people whom I write for and love.'

In Verne characterization is always subsidiary to the plot, usually the record of some worthwhile achievement. Freed from excessive technical matter, his narratives are full of exciting action, enlivened by humour and with unexpected turns leading up to his favourite literary device, in which he forestalled O. Henry, the Vernian surprise ending. Very seldom throughout his work does he repeat an incident, and only once, I think, does he repeat it twice, in the geographical location with the missing longitude (and only his most inveterate readers would notice the repetition). For the most part, though he recurs time and again to his favourite scenes, the jungle, the icefields, or the desert island, he always finds something new to say about them, some unexpected episode of which they form the background.

Subordinate to plot as they are, however, his characters are memorable. Dr Fergusson and his companions; Hatteras and Dr Clawbonny; Lidenbrock and his nephew and Hans the guide; the three pioneer astronauts; Captain Nemo and Aronnax; Phileas Fogg and Passepartout; Michael Strogoff—they may be wildly improbable, but they do stick in the memory, and most of them are great fun.

It was in other fields for the imagination that Verne excelled. Scenes never beheld by man become almost visible in his pages, the most fantastic creatures seem alive. The African jungle as seen from the air; the fantastic shapes, like the architecture of some dreamland city, of the icebergs; . . . the coral forests that clothe the sea-floor and the ruins of lost Atlantis—all these are described with vivid realism. (pp. 152-53)

Jules Verne did not actually 'create' science fiction, which is the modern development of an art-form older than written literature, the wonder story. (p. 155)

In spite of its title, Poe's *The Balloon Hoax* . . . is probably the earliest example of 'straight' science fiction; it describes plausibly, and with reassuring technical detail, the flight of a dirigible balloon across the Atlantic.

In this, as in his *Hans Pfall* story, Poe made it clear that he was only romancing, and that he had completely failed to foresee the possibilities of science fiction. Verne was the first to realize them clearly, take them seriously, and exploit them systematically. It is in this sense that he can be regarded as the founder of science fiction.

Sheer romancing figures little in his work, and satire and utopianization play only a minor part in it. His great aim was to impart information through the medium of an exciting story, and to this end he described his heroes' achievements with almost a documentary precision; he always sought to be able to give 'chapter and verse' for the conditions they encounter and the methods they use.

Here he contrasts sharply with H. G. Wells, of whom it might be said that he would have founded science fiction had not Verne forestalled him. Wells gave his imagination much freer range and was not so scrupulous about the factual basis. (pp. 155-56)

In his treatment of technical detail Wells is much less documentary than Verne, seeking to get his effects not by matter-of-fact description but by imaginative boldness. (p. 156)

On the other hand, when it comes to real flights of the imagination, it is Verne who is vague and Wells who goes into detail. When Verne's super-speleologists meet a prehistoric giant, their one desire, reasonably enough, is to get away from him. When Wells's heroes are able to study unearthly creatures, they describe them graphically and at some length.

The contrast between the two authors is even more strikingly shown in the ideas which they were the first to give to science fiction. These make it obvious that they were thinking on different mental 'wave-lengths'.

Those of Verne include journeys into the bowels of the earth, into the depths of the sea, and into outer space; aircraft and submarines of extraordinary efficiency, . . . weather control; the use of attractive and repulsive rays; and the devastation of the whole earth. Though not the first to imagine the possibility of an artificial satellite, he popularized the idea; and though he did not foresee the atomic bomb as such, he had an inkling of something almost as dreadful.

Even some of his minor ideas, which he put forward facetiously, have been shown by his successors as amenable to serious treatment. Dr Ox, influencing a community's thoughts, is suggestive of Big Brother in fiction and Dr Goebbels in real life. Gil Braltar leading the apes of 'the Rock' to attack its garrison has been excelled in science fiction by experts training

a variety of animals to wage super-scientific warfare. More seriously, the failure of the time-keepers of Master Zacharius is the first example of what in some modern science fiction stories has been called the 'death of metal'.

Wells's contributions to science fiction include time travel: the 'fourth dimension', the conversion of animals, by vivisection, into humanoid beings; human invisibility; invasion from outer space; giantism in plant, animal, and man; . . . tanks, anti-tank flame-throwers, tank-trapping slime-pits, and the atomic bomb.

The contrast is still clearer when they discuss similar themes. The *Nautilus* is attacked by gigantic squids; Wells's prototype bathyscaph, by humanoid fish. Verne's future world is ruled by an arbitrary but benevolent journalist, that of Wells by a grim financial oligarchy overthrown by a ruthless dictator. (pp. 156-58)

That Verne's ideas should seem so matter-of-fact compared with those of later science fiction authors is because he had not less imagination than they, but more. He did not need to turn to other worlds to find strange surroundings or strange creatures; there were plenty of both on our own earth. (p. 158)

Apart from the method and the themes he gave science fiction, he had also endowed it with humour, idealism, and vivid, if rather improbable, characterization. In other hands, though certainly not in those of Wells, it might have been repulsively dull.

One other service Verne performed for science fiction: he made it austere. There is neither vulgarity nor undue violence in his writings, and though the lack of a love-interest may be regarded as a merit or otherwise, it is certainly well that there should be a complete absence of lust. (pp. 159-60)

Personally courageous, [Verne] disliked brutality and violence and never dwelt upon them: where fist-fights, murder, torture, or battles come into his stories he usually deals with them very briefly. Even the heroic last stand of the French Separatists in *A Family Without a Name* is not described as fully as one might expect.

Verne was too patriotic to make any of his French characters villains, though some of them are eccentric beyond all reason. Those who serve as his heroes are less burdened with information, and less fanatically single-minded, than those of the other nationalities; they are courageous, devoted to duty and at the same time debonair. As might be expected, for Verne had had more experience of Frenchmen than of foreigners, they are more like human beings than most of his other heroes.

His villains and other objectionable characters vary in their nationality, but even here Verne never ceases to be objective. Herr Schultz, in *The Begum's Fortune,* an exponent of total war and frightfulness, might well have been a Nazi Gauleiter. . . . (p. 168)

But though Verne makes this scoundrel not only appalling but ludicrous, he pays tribute to his countrymen's virtues by extolling his brilliance as an inventor and by giving him a more-than-Teutonic efficiency as an organizer, dealing single-handed with the complex commercial and financial affairs of a great industrial city!

As was then the tendency among the French, Verne had a great admiration for the Russians, and he managed to reconcile this with his love of freedom by representing the Tsar as benevolent and merciful, always ready to grant an amnesty to political exiles and refugees.

Though Verne has been 'vehemently accused' of being too hard on the Anglo-Saxons, his attitude towards them was strangely ambivalent. He scorned the 'Barnum' aspect, and was sardonically amused at some of the vagaries, of the American character, but he did full justice to its enterprise, its audacity, its ability to 'think large'.

His dislike of the English governing and official classes, of what is now called our 'Establishment' was so marked that I am tempted, though, I must admit, without any direct evidence, to suspect some unfortunate personal incident that rankled all his life. On the other hand he honoured the adventurers of our nation, our explorers and seamen. (pp. 168-69)

Verne's early enthusiasm for science was damped by a growing realization of its possibilities, in unscrupulous hands, for evil. The technicians of the Gun Club seek to reach the moon, again to quote the words of Mallory, 'because it's there', and work openly in the sight of all the world; but later, when they want to move the earth's axis for financial profit, they act in hiding, as callously disregardful of the possible results of their activities as any refugee physicist striving to produce a newer and nastier bomb. . . .

As has been seen, he did not agree with the views of Darwin, but it was only the theory of Natural Selection that he rejected, not the general idea of Evolution. His views on this, as expressed in *The Eternal Adam,* might read almost like an anticipation of the modern suggestion that atomic radiations might produce remarkable transformations in living creatures—except that in Verne's story there are no such radiations! (p. 169)

Towards the end Verne's attitude mellowed, as is shown by the three narratives each of which might well be regarded as conveying a farewell message to the world. His scientists in *The Eternal Adam* are wise and benevolent, seeking only to transmit the achievements of their age to posterity.

The Barsac Mission suggests that he had even overcome his quarrel with the English aristocracy for Lord Blazon of Glenor is noble not only by title but by character. The hero of *The Survivors of the 'Jonathan',* an atheist and anarchist—hardly a character likely to appeal to a French Catholic with some experience of politics—is shown as devoting his life to his fellow-men and finally as retiring, as though to the secular equivalent of a monastery, from the world. (p. 171)

> *I. O. Evans, in his* Jules Verne and His Work *(copyright © I. O. Evans 1966; reprinted with the permission of Twayne Publishers, a Division of G. K. Hall & Co., Boston), Twayne, 1966, 188 p.*

BRIAN W. ALDISS (essay date 1973)

[The] writings of Poe in Baudelaire's translation had a stimulating effect [on Verne]; one of Verne's earliest stories, *Cinq Semaines en Balloon (Five Weeks in a Balloon)* . . . bears a clear relationship to Poe's *The Balloon-Hoax* of 1844.

Poe's use of scientific detail must have attracted Verne; he would have liked, too, the way in which the Poeian protagonist stands outside society, as do Verne's great heroes. But where Poe is the doomed poet of the Inward, Verne is the supreme celebrant of the Outward; the subterranean chamber gives way to the sea, the elements. (p. 94)

One of Verne's critics, Marcel Moré, has argued that behind Verne's industrious and bourgeois façade lay a more anguished personality, the key to which is the way the novels concern only masculine relationships and where women, the few there are, are mere cyphers. In the words of a British biographer, Verne "never sullied his pages by descending to scenes of lust."

Michel Butor, a novelist and critic to be respected, has another view of Verne, seeing him as "a cryptologist of the universe," composing imaginative variations on the themes of the four elements, earth, air, fire, and water, with electricity as a pure form of fire. His characters forever oppose the unruliness of the world with logic; the poles are sacred places because they form still points in a turning world.

Such theories illuminate some aspects of the novels. More centrally, it needs to be said that *Les Voyages Extraordinaires* (the collective title of Verne's novels) span the last four decades of the last century, and cover the globe, moving from one place to another in which struggles for liberty were being waged. He wrote in the great imperialist age; like Wells, he is not on the side of the imperialists. Unlike later sf writers such as Robert Heinlein and Poul Anderson, Verne is quietly against conquest. His typical hero is a rebel or outcast from society, the most notable example being Captain Nemo, the nationless figure at the centre of *Twenty Thousand Leagues Under the Sea.* . . . (pp. 95-6)

In the early novels, detailing tremendous voyages to the centre of the Earth, to the bottom of the sea, to the Moon, or off on a comet, Verne celebrates man's progress. Everything works like mad. Both machines and machine-builders exist apart from society as a whole. But society comes creeping up. The tone of the novels changes, the atmosphere darkens with time. The later novels clog with satanic cities instead of super-subs, with Stahlstadt, Blackland, Milliard City. Even the brave scientists show signs of deterioration, eccentricity, blindness. The heroic age of the engine is done. Things fall apart, the centre will not hold.

Verne's great land of the future, America—setting of twenty-three of his sixty-four novels—develops increasingly negative aspects. Dollar diplomacy enters, expansionism takes over, the machine-mentality triumphs. Robur, benevolent hero of 1886's *Robur le Conquérant* (generally translated as *Clipper of the Clouds*) returns in a 1904 sequel as a destroyer (*Maître du Monde—Master of the World*). Men and societies are going down into eclipse, driving and driven by their dark angels, the machines. Sam Smiles has moved over to make room for Nietzsche.

The poverty of English translations of Verne has not diminished his popularity, merely his chance of better critical appraisal. His tone is flat, his characters are thin, and he pauses all too frequently for lectures; his is a non-sensual world. These are his negative features, and very damaging they are, even if his books are regarded as fit merely for boys. (pp. 96-7)

Verne, who preached a sermon of work and militant liberty, seems fusty now; but a good translation of his best novels might effect a revaluation of his vast *oeuvre*. (p. 99)

> *Brian W. Aldiss, "The Gas-Enlightened Race: Victorian Visions," in his* Billion Year Spree: The True History of Science Fiction *(copyright © 1973 by Brian W. Aldiss; reprinted by permission of Doubleday & Company, Inc.; in Canada by the author), Double-*

*day, 1973 (and reprinted by Schocken Books, 1974),
pp. 81-112.***

WALTER JAMES MILLER   (essay date 1976)

[This new, annotated edition of *Twenty Thousand Leagues under the Sea* is presented so that] we can understand why adults on the Continent admire Verne and why Anglo-Americans disparage him as "fit merely for boys." Our reconstruction of Verne's masterpiece shows that European critics know precisely whereof they speak. As the German-born scientist Wernher von Braun puts it, Verne does do his scientific homework "so carefully." He is perfectly able to develop flesh-and-blood characters, although he may prefer to accent some of them as mythic archetypes. He is capable of creating mood and atmosphere, convincing motivation, and authentic dream states. He is mature in his ideological message, seeing science as intertwined with social and political circumstances. That is the real Verne, enjoyed by sea captains in Murmansk and social philosophers in Paris, and a perennial challenge to critics all over Europe.

The false "English" Verne proves to be a cynical creation of his early translators. One of those, the Reverend Lewis Page Mercier, master of arts from Oxford, working under the name of Mercier Lewis, cut 23 percent of Verne's text and committed hundreds of errors in translation. Many of his cuts seem ideologically motivated. Such tendentious carelessness has subjected a great man to generations of neglect by adult readers and to unmerited scorn by Anglo-American critics. Surely [an examination of the annotated text] bears out Brian W. Aldiss's two hunches that "the poverty of English translations" has diminished Verne's chance of decent critical appraisal, and "a good translation . . . might effect a revaluation of his vast *oeuvre*" [see excerpt above].

Looking back over our restorations, corrections, and annotations, we see that Verne never failed to provide scientific underpinning for his story. T. L. Thomas to the contrary, Verne actually did meet head-on his responsibility for explaining how Nemo powered his *Nautilus*. Verne created an ingenious, humorous scene to teach the reader painlessly how scientists classify fishes. He explained the origin of pearls, the controversy over the nature of sponges, the basic assumptions of the modern scientific method, how life develops on an islet of naked rock, and the way scientists from Archimedes to Maury have shaped our views of Nature. But Anglo-American critics couldn't even begin to sense the scientific integrity in Verne because Lewis had cut all these passages and many others just as important. What he didn't cut he blurred, confusing bell with clock, manometer with compass, channel with canal, degree with date.

Again, our reconstituted story shows the mathematics in Verne's text to be accurate about 99 percent of the time. This was as much as an author of his day could hope for when herding hand-written technical materials into print. But almost every time that Verne's story swiveled on mathematics, or even on a single numerical value like the specific gravity of iron, Lewis muffed it. This gave rise to such sneering criticism as, "Verne can get away with almost anything, and he does."

Our restorations also enlarge our knowledge of Verne's gifts as prophet. (pp. 356-57)

So much in summary for the desecration of the science in Verne's science fiction. Now for the violation of the fiction.

Our restorations and corrections demonstrate that Verne was a master at plotting a story, creating suspense, and pacing his action. For example, he heightened the significance of the collision between the *Nautilus* and the *Scotia* by reviewing the safety record of the Cunard Line. By making Aronnax the kind of thinker who obsessively rehearses all the possibilities, Verne keeps us in a perpetual state of expectation. Regularly he plants ordinary seeds that later blossom into extraordinary circumstances; for example, Aronnax's early remark about his annoyance over Conseil's penchant for the third person. Mercier Lewis managed time and time again to botch Verne's artistry. For example, he emasculated the third-person joke; he cut the Cunard background; he omitted many of Aronnax's suspense-building hypotheses; he left out Aronnax's discovery of Nemo's gallery of heroes, so essential to understanding the captain's behavior. Lewis cut so much that the ebb and flow of the narrative—the very biorhythms of the fictional organism—are destroyed. As a consequence adult readers in English have regarded Verne's narration as "jerky," uneven, often amateurish.

Perhaps worst of all, Verne's characterization has been downgraded in translations like Lewis's. We simply cannot know the complexity of Aronnax's personality unless we are privy to his interior monologues about his shifting loyalties, his hypotheses about Nemo's intentions, his strategies to discover Nemo's nationality, and his fears of sharks and of Nemo's "madness." Yet Lewis considerably reduced or entirely omitted many such passages. We simply cannot feel as sympathetic toward Nemo as Verne was, if we do not know such crucial facts as who his heroes are and what the "law of the *Nautilus*" is. Lewis even cut the speech in which Nemo reveals the international character of his education.

Ned, too, is a much fuller person than most English readers could ever imagine. He is a passionate believer in civil rights and personal dignity; his behavior is powered equally by idealism and practical intelligence. Yet when Lewis is finished with Ned, the harpooner is all stomach and mouth, and there is little real motivation or build-up for his "tempers." In the reconstructed novel, we can see that while Conseil was intended only as a stock comic character, he is still a consistently successful one. In the original, for example, Conseil raises his head above the waves and asks the swimming Arronax: "Did monsieur ring for me?" The grim parson translated that as "Did master call me?" Lewis either muffs or omits many of Conseil's jokes as well as the big joke that fate plays on Conseil when he is forced to call for help in the second person.

Our restorations and corrections make it clear that Verne knew well the separate artistic advantages of "developing" a character as opposed to using him as a type. With Conseil, for example, it is clear that Verne knew that some people want to be typed. They try hard to type themselves. Conseil deliberately takes refuge in the social stereotype of "the gentleman's gentleman." And Nemo, too, to the extent that he is a type, deliberately strikes the pose of the Romantic exile, the misunderstood Byronic hero fighting for Greek independence. Nemo serves also as the archetypal "perfect father" for the professor. Both Conseil and Nemo are further justified as types because they are seen as such through Aronnax's eyes, in both cases to satisfy his own psychological needs.

But Nemo also grows as a personality. He struggles with the contradictions between his love of absolute freedom and his passionate need for revenge. He actually binds himself to his ugly enemy by his need for retaliation, then yields to remorse, loses control, goes down in the moral maelstrom and, as Verne will show in *The Mysterious Island,* experiences the classic death-and-rebirth in the whirlpool. And Aronnax suffers through a full-blown identity crisis: He retreats like Jonah from world affairs into the whale's belly, switches loyalties from friend to friend's enemy, and finally tears himself away from the illusion of the ''perfect father'' to emerge as a stronger man.

Verne, at least in the reconstructed novel, proves to be talented in characterizing group mood and group behavior. Think of how little we would know of the three companions without their long man-to-man bull sessions over pearls and whales and that long scene in which, irritable and hungry, they probe each other's psyches. Mercier Lewis chose precisely those scenes for his biggest excisions. When Lewis finished, there was much less blood in Verne. I think this was why the critics could accuse Verne of ''weak characterization,'' as Sam Moskowitz sums it up, and why Aldiss could say, ''his characters are thin.'' Weakened and thinned, we now know, by translators like Mercier Lewis and Louis Mercier.

The restored novel shows that Verne's talent for metaphor and symbolism took him even into the realms of depth psychology. He describes Ned with exuberant phallic imagery: ''powerful telescope that could double as a cannon always . . . ready to fire.'' He reveals Aronnax's perseveration about sharks through slips of the tongue. He explores Arronax's unconscious desire to retreat to the womb in four separate analogies: his yearning to meet Jonah's whale, his happiness living like a snail in its shell, his happiness sleeping in a cave, and his dream of himself as a mollusk with now the cave as his shell. But alas, this dimension of Verne is almost entirely dynamited by Lewis who cut both the phallic imagery, the scene with the Freudian slips, and the cave scene with the dream. No wonder that Aldiss, unfamiliar with the full ebb and flow of Verne's action, his moody bull sessions, his dream symbolism, should say of Verne's writing, ''His tone is flat.''

Finally, the complete novel proves to be much richer in ideas than the ''standard translation'' had allowed us to think. Verne was not limited to expounding the concepts of Darwin and Maury. He was also concerned with such questions as the chance of reconciling Genesis with geological theory, the evils of imperialist treatment of aborigines, the nature of the so-called primitive peoples, and dishonesty in business. Mercier Lewis simply omitted most of Verne's crucial passages that explore these concerns. (pp. 357-59)

After a century of stultification in the Anglo-American world, Jules Verne now emerges vindicated. (p. 359)

Walter James Miller, ''Jules Verne, Rehabilitated,'' in his The Annotated Jules Verne: ''Twenty Thousand Leagues under the Sea'' (copyright © 1976 by Walter James Miller; reprinted by permission of Harper & Row, Publishers, Inc.), Thomas Y. Crowell Co., Inc., 1976, pp. 356-59.

PETER COSTELLO (essay date 1978)

[*Five Weeks in a Balloon*] was published in time for the New Year of 1863, and was a present to many children, the first of a long series. . . . 'An unknown writer,' [Verne's friend] Duquesnel comments, 'had created the scientific novel.' (pp. 72-3)

Five Weeks in a Balloon provides a good example of just how Verne was to use contemporary science for his own fictional purposes during his long career. In this novel he adroitly combines mechanics and geography, balloons and African exploration. (p. 75)

'The scientific romance': this was the genre that Verne can justly claim to have invented. The elements had existed in writers before him, but in his long series of novels beginning with *Five Weeks in a Balloon* he bridged the gap between the romantics and the modern movement, between the age of balloons and the aeroplane, and helped to establish science fiction as a major form of fiction in the twentieth century. (p. 80)

[In his next book,] *A Journey to the Centre of the Earth,* Verne set out to explore a realm of pure imagination, a poetic elaboration of the prosaic facts of scientific geology. (p. 81)

The book was planned as a geological epic. From our point of view this seems a strange interest for Verne. For many religious people at the time, Catholic as well as Protestant, the findings of modern geology which questioned the account of the Creation of the World in *Genesis* were anathema. Verne seems to have had few qualms about this. . . . As Bishop Wilberforce had expressed it a few years before, one was either on the side of the apes or the angels. Verne, it seems, was on the side of the apes.

The novel was right up to date. For the new illustrated edition published in 1867, Verne included the very latest details about the discovery of fossil men. (p. 83)

From the Earth to the Moon was set in post-bellum America. The Gun Club of Baltimore, a group of irascible enthusiasts and retired artillery men, most of them lacking limbs, have grown bored with peace. Their president Impey Barbicane suggests that they attempt something altogether new: shooting a projectile at the moon. Greeted with enthusiasm, the scheme rapidly gets under way. . . .

When all the preparations for the firing are nearly complete, the Gun Club receives a strange telegram. From Paris an adventurer wires his offer to travel in the shell. His name is Michel Ardan. . . . (p. 88)

The shell is redesigned as a spacecraft with padded walls, in which Ardan will travel to the moon with Barbicane and his rival in gunnery expertise, Nicholl. The book ends with the firing of the gun and the attempts to track its flight with a giant telescope, whose twenty-inch mirror rivalled that of Mount Palomar. Would the three space travellers be heard from again? Would they be able to communicate with the earth?

Verne's readers had to wait until the publication of the sequel, *Autour de la Lune* (*Around the Moon*) in 1870. This novel described the experiences of the three adventurers in the capsule, including the strange weightless conditions of outer space but neglecting, unfortunately, the initial shock of the firing, the sudden acceleration of which would certainly have crushed them to pulp. Much of the book is taken up with mathematical and astronomical speculations. (p. 89)

[In these two novels] Verne created the idea of space travel as a real possibility in many people's minds. And he rightly emphasised that the problem was basically one of reaching the right escape velocity. (pp. 89-90)

These were then, for all their errors and naïveties, prophetic novels of the first order. Already Verne had seen one clear function of science fiction, the creation of possible futures. (p. 90)

In his novels Verne also explored more mundane areas than the interior of the earth or the dark side of the moon. His first novels had been science fiction of a recognisable kind. But geographical adventure and the romance of the real world was to be his main forte in the years to come. Two early novels were good examples of this other kind of fiction he wrote. In *Voyages et Aventures du Capitaine Hatteras* and *Les Enfants du Capitaine Grant* he explored two contrasting parts of the real world which fascinated him: the North Pole and the Antipodes. (p. 91)

[*The Adventures of Captain Hatteras*] in which the determined Hatteras leads his reluctant crew towards the North Pole came at an opportune time. Verne was able to rehearse much of what [Arctic explorers] had already . . . discovered and to make use of some of the popular Polar theories. These included not only the idea of an open sea at the Pole, but also Captain Symmes's notion of a large opening there into the interiors of the earth. Mount Hatteras, the volcano they discover at the Pole, reflects this idea. For the details of his book he relied on Sir John Ross, on Edward Parry who had tried to reach the Pole overland in 1827 and on the American Kane who had tried to make his way into the 'open sea' in 1853-55. (p. 92)

'My story,' says Captain Grant, 'is that of all Robinsons thrown up on an island who . . . feel the struggle for existence pressing on them.' The use of this Darwinian phrase is striking, making it clear that [in *The Children of Captain Grant*] Verne was influenced by the current debate about evolution at a very basic level. (p. 94)

Verne's [next major] novel is an imaginative extension of man's knowledge of the oceans a century ago, and so little have we progressed that *Twenty Thousand Leagues Under the Sea* still remains his most prophetic book. (p. 106)

[*Pays des Fourrures* translated as *The Fur Country*] was set in the Canadian wilderness on the edge of the Polar seas in the year 1859. The novel was an escape from the more pressing events of 1870 perhaps, the story of a Hudson Bay Company trading post which is thought to be built on solid ground, but is in fact standing on part of the ice-cap. The ice-cap calves and, perched on a shrinking iceberg, the post is carried away to the south through the Bering Strait to melt in the warm waters of the Pacific. The novel might almost be a parable of how precarious civilisation really is. (p. 113)

In a passage in *Around the Moon*, after the astronauts have recovered from the toxic effects of breathing in pure oxygen by error, Verne had speculated on the social effects which an oxygen *regime* might have. If a whole nation could be saturated with the gas 'what a supplement of life it would receive'.

This was the idea he developed a little later in *Dr. Ox.* A sleepy Flemish town has new lighting installed by the mysterious doctor and his assistant Ygene. As the pipes spread through the town curious things begin to happen. The whole population changes over night, and is suffused with energy. While they are preparing for a war, the gas works explodes, and things return to normal. Dr. Ox vanishes.

The mystery is explained: instead of gas, Dr. Ox was pumping oxygen into the houses and streets of the town. And, although pure oxygen would have been fatal in the long run, at the start it exalted and excited the citizens.

These ideas about the physiological action of oxygen Verne derived from the recent researches of Paul Bert, a stout Burgundian anti-clerical. . . . 'Are virtue, courage, talent, wit,

imagination—are all these qualities or faculties only a question of oxygen?' That was Dr. Ox's theory, and also the theory of Paul Bert. 'For ourselves, we utterly reject it,' says Verne. But the doubt was there. Were personal qualities, the moral views his father admired, merely a matter of organic physiology? Verne was perplexed. (pp. 115-16)

[Verne's] masterpiece was *The Mysterious Island.* . . . [In] many ways this 'scientific Robinsonade' was the epitome of Verne's life's work.

The book begins in America, for Verne a country of infinite possibilities. Five Union prisoners escape from Richmond during the last months of the Civil War by balloon (echoes here of the escapes from Paris in 1870). A storm carries them across the American continent to be wrecked on a desert island in the Pacific. Equipped only with the barest of essentials, they set about colonising Lincoln Island, as they call it, building a new life for themselves. . . . The novel was planned by Verne as the ultimate version of the island theme as used by Defoe and Wyss: from one stray seed they are able to grow an entire crop of corn. Slowly they recreate man's discovery of all the arts and sciences. The book is a parable of man's resourcefulness in the face of adversity, and is optimistic about man's future. (p. 126)

[After *The Mysterious Island*] Verne's novels show a falling off in quality. Quantity was well maintained according to his contract, and a book or two a year continued to appear right up to the time of his death. But rarely did they rise to the great imaginative heights of the earlier books. For the most part their titles are unfamiliar, and some of the later ones were not even translated. . . . (p. 145)

Hector Servadac was originally to have been called *A Journey Round the Solar System*, which would have been a better title. In translation it appeared as *Off on a Comet.* A comet strikes the earth and carries away part of Algeria into space. The alterations of gravity and climate are amusingly described. As a reflection of contemporary knowledge the book is of great interest. Verne's novel was a fictional counterpart to the more sober works of an astronomer such as his friend Camille Flammarion. As a scientific fantasy it was a return to the spirit of his first triumphs. (pp. 146-47)

Black Diamonds is the strange story of a coal mine under Loch Katrine, the biggest in the world, and of the child who lives in its depths, unaware of daylight. As a parable of the new industrial age and its consequences, the book is chilling. . . .

[*A Captain at Fifteen*, a] Marryat-like tale of a boy who takes command of a party of survivors after a shipwreck on the Angolan coast and leads them to safety, is a somewhat tedious story, interesting however for Verne's views on the effects of slavery, white traders and alcohol in undermining the morale of the Africans. Verne's hatred of slavery is made explicit.

The Tribulations of a Chinaman in China . . . is a light-hearted affair centring around the arrangements by Kin-Fo to have himself murdered in the hopes of adding some excitement to his life, as well as providing for the widow he plans to marry. Verne had a touching habit of providing his heroes with young widows whenever some love interest was needed. . . .

Far more serious in its intentions was . . . *The Begum's Fortune.* (p. 147)

Clearly influenced by the events of the Franco-Prussian war, the novel forecast the fascist manifestations of the present century only too clearly. Whether Verne was being too optimistic in his hopes for the eventual triumph of good over evil is another question. (p. 148)

But the great masterpiece of [Verne's later] period, which rises above [the others] in both plot and imaginative quality, was *Robur the Conqueror* . . . , a visionary novel of aerial adventure. (p. 150)

Robur is a peculiar figure. He lacks something of the mystery and romance that surrounded Captain Nemo. But in his ruthless pursuit of his own ends, he does indeed foreshadow the popular idea of the scientist in the twentieth century, toiling to perfect the radiation bomb or biological weapons. Robur identifies himself with the science of the future. If so, one feels, God help the future. (p. 152)

Verne's more sombre mood in his later years was increasingly reflected in his writings, even though these dealt with similar ranges of subjects, themes and places. (p. 175)

History and the struggle for freedom were still dominant subjects. In *North Against South* . . . he dealt again with the American Civil War, siding with the enslaved Negroes of the South. *The Road to France* . . . was an historical novel set at the time (1792) of the triumph of the French revolutionary army over the Prussian troops at the battle of Valmy, of which a vivid description is given. The theme of French nationalism was a new one for Verne, reflecting perhaps his increasing interest in real politics. A novel dealing with the revolt of the French in Canada, *Family Without A Name* . . . dealt with the harsh treatment meted out by the British after the rising of 1837 failed. . . . The theme of British imperialism also provided the background to a novel set in Ireland, *Foundling Mick*. . . . Beginning realistically enough with scenes of the land war and eviction, the novel soon becomes a straightforward success story. (pp. 175-76)

Geographical adventures still formed a large part of his output. *Two Years Holiday* . . . was the only story Verne wrote which was specifically for children. One of the characters called Briant is said to be based on the young Aristide Briand, later Prime Minister of France, whom Verne met in Nantes a few years before writing it. A Robinsonade involving shipwreck and survival, the book also includes what the critic Kenneth Allott calls 'school-boy politics', these being largely a reflection of Verne's own political experiences in Amiens. . . . Verne's limitations as a novelist are pointed up by contrasting this book with William Golding's *Lord of the Flies,* where the same desert-island material is given a far more subtle and sombre treatment. (p. 176)

The Narrative of Arthur Gordon Pym [was] a strange narrative of bizarre adventures in the Antarctic, which had strong autobiographical elements. Verne, writing about Poe in 1863, had claimed that the novel was incomplete and hoped that some day a writer would finish it off. In 1895 he took up his own challenge. Starting from a new beginning with the narrative of an American naturalist, and skilfully incorporating details and hints from Poe's original tale, Verne provided a typically extraordinary explanation of the 'sphinx of the ice-fields', the great white figure which suddenly looms up before Pym at the end of Poe's story.

Verne made the sphinx literally 'a lodestone mountain', a magnetic mass which attracted all the iron in the area to itself. This was an old legend. Worked into Poe's novel and Verne's con-

clusion were elements taken from the idea of Captain Symmes, to whom he owed notions in earlier novels. (pp. 193-94)

[In *The Master of the World*] the sinister Robur returns to terrorise the world. This book had a curious development, as originally it was to have been rather blandly entitled *The Adventures of an American Detective*. This period was of course the era of Sherlock Holmes and his rivals, and Verne may well have wanted to try and write a really popular novel once again by catching at the latest vogue. But as he worked on the book, it changed into something else, a science fiction novel of his old sort. (pp. 201-02)

In 1886 Robur had been represented as the science of the future. Now he returned as an embodiment of what that science might really mean. Written in the form of a detective story with John Strock of the Federal Police as the hero, the book is immensely superior to *Robur the Conqueror.* The dramatic climaxes are well developed, especially the scenes over Niagara Falls and in the thunderstorm which destroys *The Terror,* as Robur calls his futuristic flying machine which also doubles as the fastest racing car in the world and a miniature submarine. (p. 202)

[The short story '**The Eternal Adam,**' written shortly before his death,] is one of Verne's almost forgotten masterpieces. In the story Verne develops the idea of an eternal cycle of events continuously repeating themselves. This deterministic idea had already been elaborated by Nietzsche. . . . (pp. 218-19)

'**The Eternal Adam**' is a bleak denial of the eternal god. At the time of his death Verne's intellect had broken completely at last with the stern god of his father's faith. (p. 219)

> *Peter Costello, in his* Jules Verne: Inventor of Science Fiction *(copyright © 1978 by Peter Costello; reprinted with the permission of Charles Scribner's Sons; in Canada by permission of Hodder and Stoughton Limited), Hodder and Stoughton, 1978, Charles Scribner's Sons, 1978, 239p.*

MARC ANGENOT   (essay date 1979)

Verne wrote eighty novels or so and, although he reached the peak of his career in the 1870s, there are only a few of his later works that are decidedly uninteresting. In this essay, I shall attempt to circumscribe a specific world-view that in my opinion underlies all his books: not only the actual 'scientific romances'—which would leave us with a balance of travelogues, fantasy tales, and adventure stories that are usually labelled as 'less interesting' by critics of SF—but his opus as a whole.

Let us begin with something obvious on the surface of the text: all the narratives of Jules Verne, or almost all, are narratives of circulation and even—as Michel Serres has pointed out—of circular circulation. All his practically minded characters are bodies in motion; but one can also see that this mobility does not apply to the actors alone. Other things circulate also: desires, information, money, machines, celestial bodies. Everything circulates—*mobilis in mobili:* what can be more suitable than to use Captain Nemo's own motto as the *leitmotif* of the entire opus?

It has often been noted that Verne's most significant characters are people with fixations: Lidenbrock in *Journey to the Centre of the Earth,* Hatteras in *English at the North Pole* . . . , Phileas Fogg in *Around the World in Eighty Days* . . . and, to the point of being ridiculous, Jos Merritt in *Mistress Branican* . . . who goes all the way to Australia in search of a hat worn by Queen

Victoria. Yet, paradoxically, all these fixations are ambulatory fixations.

What of the 'supreme point' towards which the characters tend . . . ? No doubt it exists, but it is always a question, not of remaining there, but of *attaining* it. In fact, by virtue of its being a fixed point, it cannot be occupied: the geographic pole is an erupting volcano, while the centre of the earth is never reached by Professor Lidenbrock and his nephew. The 'American' qualities of the characters—energy, tenacity, steadiness, insensitivity—are qualities of an object bound to a periplus or circumnavigatory voyage, the trajectory of which ought to be accelerated, but cannot be bent inwards. 'This gentleman asked for nothing. He did not travel, he described a circumference', says Verne very accurately of Phileas Fogg.

In *Captain Antifer* . . . , the hunt for treasure, determined by geographic coordinates, results in the tracing of a 'circle of circles', but the treasure (the fixed point, meaning or value) has been swallowed up by the sea. Equally, Verne's frequent cryptogram is a machine which causes meaning to circulate: it has a key but no referent; circulation comes to a halt with the last message. The entire *oeuvre* is a 'cycle of cyclical voyages', says Michel Serres, who returns to Hegel, but could just as easily refer to Marx's concept of the commodity circuit (commodity→money→commodity). To add a Freudian element, the theme of 'triangulation' can be interpreted as analogous to the Oedipus triangle, in a work where the Oedipus myth is present through a number of avatars. (p. 19)

[Since] mythological interpretations have a good time with Jules Verne, it remains to be noted that Verne uses only the *ambulatory* myths which are, in effect, transposed, and very systematically, in his work: Ulysses being the model for *Mathias Sandorf* . . . ; Orpheus, the ancestor of Franz de Telek in *Castle of the Carpathians* . . . ; Icarus, the ancestor of Robur in *Clipper of the Clouds* . . . ; Oedipus being reversed in *Michael Strogoff*. . . . These myths, of which Verne retains the general configuration, are superficial features; to look here for the essence of the work, as the archetypal critics do, would be a mistake. It is the 'theme' of circulation (for lack of a more appropriate expression) which gives unity to the work, and which permits the bringing together of the scientific romances and the 'simple' travel narratives such as *Michael Strogoff, Eight Hundred Leagues on the Amazon* . . . , and *Cesar Cascabel*. . . .

Verne reactivates in his work *all* the fictional models of the voyage. *Around the World in Eighty Days* revives the picaresque model of flight and pursuit stories: Fix behind Fogg, policeman and thief. Fogg is accused of having invented his extravagant bet to cover a bank robbery. Fogg is the movable body and Fix's is fixed, an obstacle to circulation, attempting to head back the circulating gold to the 'fixed capital' of the Bank of England, the victim of the theft. This confusion of Phileas Fogg with a *gold thief* is worth emphasizing. In the economic image that I shall describe, gold is an imaginary equivalent for capitalization, i.e. sedentariness, as opposed to the circulation of commodities in the axiomatic paradox of the capitalist system. (p. 20)

There are other epics of *release* and *circulation*. *L'Invasion de la Mer* . . . predicts that the Sahara Desert, travelled by wretched and culturally stagnant people, will become an ocean, open to commercial ventures, if a canal can be dug between the Gulf of Gabes and the Tunisian Schotts. *The Underground City* . . . is likewise the story of a struggle between the engineer, Starr,

who wants to reopen the Aberfoyle coal mine, and Silfax, the Hermit of the mine and the superstitious guardian of stagnation and autistic obscurity. In *Off on a Comet!* Gibraltar, symbol of imperialist protectionism and blockading, is sucked away by the comet Gallia, so that its obtuse garrison begins to circulate within the solar system. The same goes for the 'polar' novels, narratives of the struggle against entropy and 'zero degree': 'I do not believe in uninhabitable areas', Captain Hatteras had said. . . .

It has often been noted that all Verne's imaginary machines are machines meant to circulate more rapidly: the Steam House, the Albatross, the *Nautilus,* the Épouvante, the Columbiad rocket, Propeller Island; and even (minus the machinery) the giant raft of la Jangada, and the gypsy wagon of Cesar Cascabel. (p. 21)

These circulating machines finally permit a dialectical transcendence of values attached to sedentariness: the vehicles are homely and comfortable, deterritorialized territories. Hence, the paradoxes of the Steam House, the Floating City, and the Propellor Island. What is meant by this means of travelling which carries its shelter along with it? By the hero who is both a sedentary bourgeois and a stateless person, like Captain Nemo in the rococo stateroom of the *Nautilus,* with its opulent pictures and tapestries, its marble statues and its magnificent organ? (p. 22)

Why does one circulate? One circulates in order to circulate, and one gains no profit from it, except a 'capital' of knowledge (but science is an immanent accelerator). Circulation is an end in itself; the only thing to do is to speed it up, and the highest moral quality is haste which is always valued.

All the narratives are bound to this principle of acceleration: Lidenbrock and his companions are thrown forth by the Stromboli, while Phileas Fogg moves more and more rapidly in spite of the obstacles. A ludicrous variant of this is to be found in *Dr Ox's Experiment*. . . . The experiment consists of exposing a placid Flemish village to the effects of pure oxygen. Over a period of several hours, the normally phlegmatic behaviour of these people becomes more and more frantic, but finally everything goes back to normal. That's all: the narrative has no other interest than to stage this incongruous acceleration.

The paradox is that this accelerated circulation takes place in a closed circuit, in a limited universe, a world without transcendence, where science is identified with an integrated and accrued acceleration. (p. 23)

From the eighteenth century to the end of the nineteenth, we progress from the ideological figure of the Island to that of the accelerated Voyage, from the appropriation of nature to the economy of consumption. Movement is measured in time and energy; progress is a drive having neither limit nor backlash. As Lewis Mumford writes in *Technics and Civilization,* 'Progress was motion toward infinity, motion without completion or end, motion for motion's sake. One could not have too much progress, it could not come too rapidly, it could not spread too widely and it could not destroy the "unprogressive" elements in society too swiftly and ruthlessly.'

In this hypothesis, capitalism, as an ideological form, is perceived as the paradoxical coexistence of sedentary capital and circulating abundance (technical progress, consumption). The necessity for increased circulation leads to the valorization of science as a solvent of social contradictions, an immanent anticipative apparatus, a Utopia without rupture or setback, constantly producing divergences and integration. In a society which is torn apart by its transformation, Vernian fiction produces an imaginative synthesis of the contradictions of sedentariness and circulation. (p. 25)

This circulation is tied to a generalized accountability—energy is measurable. Phileas Fogg is a neurotic of accountable time. Verne disregards the fact that circulation is tied to a sedentary pole, *Capital*. Everything is seen as accelerated fluidity; all unproductive accumulation (of meaning, knowledge, riches) is condemned in the story itself. For instance, his condemnation of permanent capital is illustrated in the character of Isaac Hakkabut, a merchant and usurer, in *Off on a Comet!* Carried away through the solar system, Hakkabut thinks only of centralizing the economic exchanges on Gallia in order to increase his small hoard of money. What the parable shows is that capital, once made 'unsedentary', no longer has any value. First because the comet itself is made of gold—which never more merited the name of a 'dirt cheap metal'! Second, because in orbit around Saturn, gold no longer weighs what it weighed on earth. The novel is a metaphorical critique of capitalist 'fetishism'.

There is no encoding which resists mobility, which is to say that capitalism destroys itself, not through crises, but in the very process of its reproduction. Private property is not a major element in modern society, it is an archaism, a contradiction. All of Verne's imaginative art puts this mobility and its liberating effects on stage. Science opposes fixed Capital: they are the positive and negative aspects of modernity. On this level, we already see Verne's ideological paradox: a utopia without rupture for a capitalism without capital. Verne portrays expense, not accumulation; circulation, not surplus value.

If capitalism tends to become, in economic terms, undifferentiated circulation, it is also undifferentiated circulation in its *lateral* effects. Here Verne sometimes expresses most directly the presuppositions which we ascribe to his world-view. The political effect of industrial capitalism is an effect of deterritorializing and anonymizing. In suppressing by force the archaic axioms dependent on territorial investments, it creates a universe of stateless persons and orphans, in which everybody can be called a *Nemo*.

The capitalist market, and the apparatus of political expansion that it relies on, pitilessly eliminates particularisms, local traditions, old cultures which interfere with its expansion, and subverts the closed social nuclei—families, tribes—to mix up everything in the insignificance of exchange. Imperialist mobilization involves alienation, but equally the liberation from traditional bonds: the peasant uprooted from the soil becomes a proletarian, and the Hindu prince brutally expelled from his feudal world becomes Captain Nemo (Latin: nobody), the anonymous avenger, builder of a submarine, the *Nautilus*, which circulates more rapidly than the fleets of the imperialist powers pursuing him. Nemo does not try to reconstitute what 'inevitable progress' has crushed. He haunts a non-territory which no one will appropriate, the Ocean, with its inexhaustible abundance. He is the figure of the Wandering Jew, the Romantic image of the man without a territory.

Let us consider the ideological elements which Nemo's case transposes:

1. His motto *mobilis in mobili* is at once ambiguously Romantic theme ('Homme libre, toujours, tu chériras la mer!') and the epitome of circulation and technological modernity.

2. The *Nautilus,* a machine which produces no surplus value, makes for the coexistence of deterritorialization and territorial nostalgia; it is a closed whole, a museum and an encyclopaedia.

3. For Nemo to become an anarchist rebel who seeks to avenge himself on the imperialist powers, imperialism had to tear him from his static and condemned feudal world and to strip him of his identity as the former Prince Dakkan, a leader of the Sepoys in the Indian Mutiny of 1857. (Nemo's past is not revealed in *Twenty Thousand Leagues under the Sea,* but is established retrospectively in *The Mysterious Island.*) Nemo is both a new Prometheus and a Frankenstein's monster; he is at once the Creature dehumanized by progress, and the Creator who makes use of progress in accelerating it. His mobility is a fate which he transforms into a Romantic choice, and this is why the Saint-Simonian hero Cyrus Smith (Cyrus Harding in the English translation) must both admire and condemn him: 'Your error lay in supposing that the past could be resuscitated and in contending against inevitable progress'. . . . It should be noted that 'inevitable progress' includes the genocide of the Sepoys and that Verne is perfectly conscious of this.

4. Nemo intervenes politically by financing the Cretans' liberation movement against the English imperialists, but he draws the money from the unproductive treasure of the Spanish galleons sunk in the Bay of Vigo. In other words, here again he places in circulation 'sedentary' capital.

5. His voyage, zigzagging without a goal, a case of conspicuous consumption in undersea lands, is deterritorialized circulation, thus reproducing the capitalist axiom.

6. Imperialism, by stripping Nemo of his name, his property, and his flag made of him a 'free' man, a negative liberty that he changes into a positive one. Is Nemo a father figure, as Marcel Moré would have it? An odd father whose name is no-one! He is an orphan rather, like many Vernian heroes, born of a 'family without a name', in the violent midwifery of Capital made History. This outcast is not in reaction against, but rather ahead of history—he struggles against 'inevitable progress', but it must be said that in doing so, he passes beyond it. In the last chapters of *Twenty Thousand Leagues under the Sea,* when a British frigate blocks him up in an estuary, he can avenge himself, because he has, in the circumstances, the ultimate value of circulation against blockage.

7. This is also clearly stated in *The Mysterious Island.* Verne is forced to admire the power of imperialism to place things in circulation, at the very time when he tries to vindicate the right. Of the crushing of the Sepoys he says: 'Right, once again, had succumbed in the face of might. But civilization never recedes and it seems that it borrows all its rights from necessity.' This is an ambiguous and frightening phrase to which no one has paid sufficient attention. (pp. 25-7)

Science, for Verne, is at the same time exterior to social vicissitudes, innocent of society's contradictions and completely understood in its effects. In the place of need and labour it is the transcendental subject of history, whose inscription in the social body is called *progress*. Exterior to social relations but the agent of their transformations, it is the *alibi*, in the etymological sense, of the dominant class. It cannot be enslaved. It does not, then, have an institutional dimension: there are isolated scientists, but there is no technostructure; the rocket to the moon is launched by a private society supported by gifts. With isolated scientists as heroes, the passage from knowledge to praxis is made in the same person.

But science is not described for its own sake, and never does the narrative focus on isolated gadgets. The referent of Vernian discourse is the *effect* of science, as the successive projection of discrete inventions on the social body. This effect is essentially a quantifiable acceleration. Science is thus at once the guardian of the social *status quo,* and the means of its immanent transcendence.

Verne is far from manifesting the futurological fantasy of Rosny the Elder or Albert Robida, as his ideological project lies elsewhere: to show the social and historical effect of the introduction of new techniques into a state of society—his own. (Although Verne has for a long time been seen as the 'prophet of the twentieth century', it has been discovered that there is scarcely an 'invention' in his work which did not already exist in blueprint form.) His works are a portrayal of the influence of science in history. It is a one-way effect: science accelerates general circulation, but it is not influenced by the conflicts or the interests which were pre-existent. This lack of realism is proportional to Verne's optimism. Science cannot progress, however, without freedom (free criticism, free diffusion): it demands an unbounded and fluid society which it, in turn, contributes to produce; a dialectical harmony to which Verne holds.

Identifying Progress and Growth—an idea which our century has learned to distrust—Verne sees science taking the place of the immediate means of manual industry. 'They *knew*', he says of the colonists of Lincoln Island, comparing their progress to the failure of other, more primitive colonists. Progress is a continual process, unequivocal: its contradictions are only archaic resistances, reminders of a former order which will erode. It is fully positive. Does Verne write *science fiction*? Yes, as fiction about science in its global, historical effect, not in its scattering in specific discoveries. (p. 29)

Verne is paradoxically a utopianist without an alternative society; he is the last SF writer who believes in industrialist euphoria, even if some pessimism overshadows his last books. H. G. Wells or Rosny the Elder are of another generation, prey to a cataclysmic world-view counterbalanced by a quest for mutations and radical changes. At the cost of some oversimplifications, Verne is able to harmonize most of the social ideas of his time.

Rather than a precursor of the twentieth century, he is the last 'happy' SF writer. Hence his everlasting seduction. Nostalgically the reader sees this world-view which is neither critical, nor tragic, nor clouded with resentment, and is free from the paranoia that invades conjectural fiction after him. Verne is a great writer, whose profundity and aesthetic richness were discovered only recently. Far from anticipating the twentieth century, he only marks the end of certain illusions. (pp. 31-2)

> *Marc Angenot, "Jules Verne: The Last Happy Uto-*
> *pianist" (© Marc Angenot 1979), in* Science Fiction:
> A Critical Guide, *edited by Patrick Parrinder, Long-*
> *man Group Limited, 1979, pp. 18-33.*

MARK ROSE   (essay date 1981)

[Science fiction] can be understood in the context of 19th and 20th-century spiritual loneliness as a manifestation of our culture's longing to escape the prison-house of the merely human. It might be considered as an attempt to reestablish, in some way that will sustain conviction even in our technological and

post-Christian culture, the channels of communication with the non-human world. (p. 53)

The *voyages extraordinaires* explore worlds known and unknown: the interior of Africa, the interior of the Earth, the deeps of the sea, the deeps of space. Characteristically, Verne's voyagers travel in vehicles that are themselves closed worlds—his imagination projects itself in terms of "inside" and "outside"—from which the immensity of nature can be appreciated in upholstered comfort. The *Nautilus* is the most familiar of these comfortable, mobile worlds; inside all is cozy elegance, the epitome of the civilized and human, while outside the oceans gleam or rage in inhuman beauty or mystery.

The basic activity in Verne is the construction of closed and safe spaces, the enslavement and appropriation of nature to make a place for man to live in comfort. (pp. 53-54)

[*Journey to the Center of the Earth*] is just such an exploration of "insideness," except that here the interior world is the non-human world, a realm of subterranean galleries, caverns, and seas, and here rather than being the place of enclosed safety the interior world becomes an immensity, a fearful abyss. Abysses dominate the novel. Even before Professor Lidenbrock and his nephew, Axel, begin their journey into the interior, Axel, the story's narrator, has nightmares in which he finds himself "hurtling into bottomless abysses with the increasing velocity of bodies dropping through space." The idea of the abyss is continually kept before us, and always the danger is as much psychic as physical. Standing on the edge of the first real chasm, Axel speaks of the "fascination of the void" taking hold of him: "I felt my centre of gravity moving, and vertigo rising to my head like intoxication. There is nothing more overwhelming than this attraction of the abyss." . . . The danger, evidently, is of losing one's sense of self and of disappearing, intoxicated, into the infinite void.

The abyss in this novel is a version of the cosmic void, but the geometry of the earthly chasm differs from that of the astronomical infinity, for the Earth is round and therefore has both poles and a center. Poles and center are magical loci, the three still places on the turning globe. . . . To reach and explore the poles is to achieve the completion of the human sphere by defining the Earth in its entirety. (This is the meaning that seems to generate the 19th and early 20th-century obsession with polar exploration.) To reach the center of the globe also means to achieve completion, except that now the Earth itself has become the imagined immensity and the attainment of the center means the penetration of the essence, the achievement of the heart of the mystery. The liminal poles are frigid; the mystical center is generally imagined as hot, as the fluid, living core of the globe. The earthly chasm thus opens onto a different kind of imaginative space from the astronomical void; at the bottom of the bottomless abyss is the region not of transcendence but of immanence, the locus in which all knowledge, all being, all power are immediately present. To attain the center of the Earth, then, means to penetrate the heart of nature, to possess nature absolutely. This is the object of Professor Lidenbrock and his nephew Axel's quest.

Extremes meet and magical opposites are always, in a sense, identical. At the time Verne was writing *Journey to the Center of the Earth,* he was also writing *Captain Hatteras* . . . , in which an obsessed adventurer reaches the North Pole. The pole itself turns out to be an erupting volcano—magical heat in the center of the regions of cold—and standing on the lip of the polar crater, the margin of the space in which heat and cold, life and death, inside and outside, immanence and transcendence interpenetrate, Hatteras goes mad. Significantly, in *Journey to the Center of the Earth* Lidenbrock and Axel gain access to the interior by travelling north to the cold and barren arctic limits of the habitable world, Iceland, where they enter the subterranean regions through the cone of the extinct volcano Sneffels. (pp. 54-56)

[In] their descent Lidenbrock and Axel must in effect read nature backwards as they pass through the strata of successively earlier and earlier periods of natural history, eventually finding themselves in a marvelous underground world filled with plants from the era of the giant ferns. Here, too, they discover long extinct animals. . . . Finally, they have a brief glimpse of a giant prehistoric man guarding a herd of mastodons. . . .

This journey to the Earth's center is thus also a journey into the abyss of evolutionary time, and the fusion of the spatial and temporal modes is one of the novel's sources of power. Temporally projected, the quest for the center, the heart of the mystery, becomes the pursuit of origins, the quest for an ultimate moment of beginning. (p. 57)

The process of decoding, of learning to read nature, is in this fiction essentially an action of naming. Like many of Verne's protagonists—think, for instance, of Aronnax and Conseil in *Twenty Thousand Leagues Under the Sea* . . .—Lidenbrock and Axel are obsessive categorizers concerned to find the exact name for each geological stratum, the exact botanical and zoological classification for each underground species of plant or animal. As they descend they are concerned, too, with being able to name their precise position in relation to the surface, the exact number of vertical and lateral feet that they have travelled at each point. Moreover, since they are penetrating an unknown world, Lidenbrock and Axel are obliged not only to discover but at times to create names: the "Hansback" for the underground stream that guides tham part of their way, "Port Gräuben," "Axel Island," "Cape Saknussemm." The imposition of human names on the non-human world is obviously an act of appropriation and conquest, for to be able to decipher and read nature is here to possess it, to drain it of its mysterious otherness and make it part of the human world. (p. 58)

From the beginning, Lidenbrock is a figure of heroic will engaged in mortal combat with the non-human world. Arriving at the base of Sneffels, he is described as "gesticulating as if he were challenging" the volcano. "So that is the giant I am going to defeat!" . . . he announces in a phrase that sustains this aspect of the fiction. Nothing daunts the professor. Obsessively, he presses forward through every difficulty that lies in the way of the total conquest of nature. . . .

The narrative establishes the professor's significance in part by placing him in opposition to Hans, the phlegmatic Icelandic peasant who acts as guide. By trade an eiderdown hunter—an occupation that significantly involves no struggle with nature since the "hunter" merely collects the feathers from the eider's readily accessible nest—Hans is clever and resourceful but utterly without will. . . . The principal thing that Hans cares about is his salary; he insists upon having three rix-dollars doled out to him each Saturday evening no matter what the exploring party's situation or location. This mechanical action becomes a comic leitmotif in the novel, but it also suggests the peasant's absolute unconcern about his surroundings, his obliviousness to nature's marvels. (p. 60)

Both Hans' passivity and Lidenbrock's will to conquer nature are opposed to Axel's romanticism. In a characteristic ex-

change, the professor and his nephew discuss the fact that the subterranean sea has tides like those on the surface. Axel is amazed and delighted; his uncle, however, finds nothing marvelous in the discovery, pointing out that a subterranean sea will be as subject to the Sun and Moon's gravitation as any other. . . . Axel and his uncle live in different mental universes, Axel embodying the spiritualistic response to the non-human ("That's wonderful!"), Lidenbrock embodying bourgeois materialism ("No, it's perfectly natural"). Not surprisingly, each at various points in the story believes that the other has gone mad.

Near the end of the novel, however, Axel undergoes a conversion. Confronted with what appears to be an insurmountable obstacle to further descent—a huge boulder has sealed the gallery through which they must pass—the youth is suddenly seized by his uncle's demon of heroic conquest. Now it is Axel who is impatient with delay and who insists that they must immediately blow up the rock with explosive gun-cotton. "The Professor's soul had passed straight into me, and the spirit of discovery inspired me. I forgot the past and scorned the future." . . . Nothing matters for him now except the imperative of penetration to the center. Daemonically possessed, Axel has become like his uncle a "hero." His journey, then, has become an initiation into the bourgeois-heroic attitude toward nature, a "going in" in a social as well as a physical sense, and the story ultimately ratifies his new status as an adult male by granting him the hand of the professor's beautiful goddaughter, Gräuben. Nevertheless, as the comic ironies persistently directed against Professor Lidenbrock's limited vision suggest, in the youth's passage something has been lost as well as gained. Caring neither for past nor future, imprisoned in the narrow cage of his own will to dominate, Axel can no longer confront nature except as an antagonist, something utterly apart from himself.

Axel and his uncle never do reach the Earth's mysterious center. . . . [The] point of furthest penetration, the journey's true climax, is reached, significantly, not by the professor but by his romantic nephew and not in literal reality but in a vision.

Before his conversion, Axel, reflecting upon "the wonderful hypotheses of paleontology," has an extended daydream in which, first, he supposes the subterranean world filling with long extinct creatures. . . . As his dream continues, however, the great animals disappear, the Earth grows steadily warmer, and he finds himself in a still earlier age, the period of gigantic vegetation. Even here the dream does not end. Sweeping backward into the abyss of time in quest of the center, the point of origin, Axel finds the heat becoming more and more intense until the Earth's granite liquifies and finally the planet itself dissolves into its original white-hot gaseous mass. . . . Climactically, Axel himself disappears, becoming part of the cosmic infinity. At the ecstatic center, the boundary between man and nature, the human and the non-human, melts and the explorer merges with the world being explored.

Axel's dream represents, of course, both a romantic alternative to the professor's treatment of nature as an antagonist to be conquered and a fusion of spiritualistic and materialistic world views. Moreover, in Axel's dream, the text calls attention to its own status as a fiction, an imaginary voyage. This kind of fictive self-consciousness was perhaps implicit in such earlier passages as Axel's rhetorical question, "Who could ever have imagined that inside the earth's crust there was a real ocean, with ebbing and flowing tides, winds and storms?" Now, however, in the description of the fossil world coming to life in

Axel's imagination—these events are shortly to occur in the narrative proper as the explorers begin to encounter extinct animals and plants—the text's play with its own fictionality is particularly emphatic and we can hardly miss seeing Axel as momentarily a version of Verne.

Expelled from the interior, the explorers emerge in an eruption of Mt. Stromboli in Sicily. . . . Like the interior, the surface is a realm of infinities, but here the "infinity" is one of welcoming, protective vegetation. Since, in this novel, the interior space has become the void, the exterior world becomes the known and safe space. In reaching Sicily, Lidenbrock and Axel have, ironically, reached the Earth's center, the primitive heart not of nature but of the human sphere. (pp. 61-65)

> *Mark Rose, "Space" (originally published as "Filling the Void: Verne, Wells, and Lem," in* Science-Fiction Studies, *Vol. 8, No. 24, July, 1981), in his* Alien Encounters: Anatomy of Science Fiction *(copyright © 1981 by the President and Fellows of Harvard College; excerpted by permission), Cambridge, Mass.: Harvard University Press, 1981, pp. 50-95.**

ADDITIONAL BIBLIOGRAPHY

Allot, Kenneth. *Jules Verne.* 1954. Reprint. Port Washington, N.Y.: Kennikat Press, 1970, 283 p.
 A Verne biography.

Amis, Kingsley. "Starting Points." In his *New Maps of Hell: A Survey of Science Fiction,* pp. 15-41. New York: Harcourt, Brace & Co., 1960.*
 Identifies Verne as "the first great progenitor of modern science fiction." Amis provides a brief survey of Verne's canon.

Bishop, Claire Huchet. "Children and Science-Fiction." *Commonweal* LXIII, No. 7 (18 November 1955): 172-74.
 Contends that Verne's universal appeal among young readers is due not only to his ability at spinning well-told tales, but to his use of scientific technology in quest of freedom from war, slavery, and other age-old nemeses of humanity.

Butor, Michel. "The Golden Age in Jules Verne." In his *Inventory: Essays,* by Michel Butor, edited by Richard Howard, pp. 114-45. New York: Simon and Schuster, 1968.
 An essay examining several recurring themes and elements in Verne's "Extraordinary Voyages."

Clarke, Arthur C. Introduction to *"From the Earth to the Moon" and "Round the Moon,"* by Jules Verne, pp. v-viii. New York: Dodd, Mead & Co., 1962.
 Contains appraisals of the varying scientific accuracy of Verne's books.

Jules-Verne, Jean. *Jules Verne: A Biography.* Taplinger Publishing Co., 1976, 245 p.
 An insightful biography by Verne's grandson.

Kent, George. "Mister Imagination." *The Saturday Review* (New York) XXXVII, No. 23 (5 June 1954): 9-10, 39-40.
 A concise biographical sketch, emphasizing Verne's role as a prophet of twentieth-century technology.

[Lang, Andrew]. "Jules Verne." *Living Age* 245, No. 3174 (April-June 1905): 377-79.
 A general essay on Verne's work, of interest because of the critic's dismissive attitude toward such "impossible" scientific developments as space travel and submarine warfare.

Portuondo, José Antonio. "Jules Verne's America." *Américas* 9, No. 10 (October 1957): 30-5.
 A discussion of Verne's portrayal of the Americas in his novels and stories.

Serres, Michel. "Jules Verne's 'Strange Journeys'," *Yale French Studies, Special Issue,* No. 52 (1975): 174-88.
 A rambling essay in which elements of Verne's novels are related to mythology and psychology.

Sprout, Monique. "The Influence of Poe on Jules Verne." *Revue de Litterature Comparée* 41, No. 1 (January-March 1967): 37-53.
 Traces similarities between certain plots of Verne and Poe.

Suvin, Darko. "Communication in Quantified Space: The Utopian Liberalism of Jules Verne's Science Fiction." *Clio* IV, No. 1 (October 1974): 51-71.
 Relates Verne's scientific vision to the nineteenth century's Saint-simonian model of utopia.

Winandy, André. "The Twilight Zone: Imagination and Reality in Jules Verne's *Strange Journeys.*" *Yale French Studies,* No. 43 (1969): 97-110.
 A cogent essay on Verne's work.

Jakob Wassermann

1873-1934

German novelist, short story writer, autobiographer, essayist, biographer, dramatist, journalist, librettist, and poet.

Known primarily as a novelist, Wassermann was preoccupied with the problem of ethical conduct in a modern industrialized world. His heroes are often spiritually tormented nonconformists with messianic qualities, who are pitted against a society devoid of justice and indifferent to human suffering. Because of the moral earnestness, psychological realism, and sensationalism of his writings, Wassermann is often called "the German Dostoyevsky."

The themes in Wassermann's work reflect his troubled youth. His father, a poor Jewish merchant, was scornful of his son's literary aspirations, and sent him to work in a relative's factory in Vienna. A failure at business, Wassermann entered the army, where he became a victim of anti-Semitism. Later, after losing an ill-paid clerical job because he was Jewish, he wandered penniless for many weeks, and nearly starved. He began to write for newspapers, and, finally, won an editorial position with a new literary journal, *Simplicissimus*, which subsequently published some of his short stories and poems.

The motifs Wassermann developed in his first well-known novel, *Die Juden von Zirndorf* (*The Dark Pilgrimage*)—man's longing for a messianic savior, religious bigotry, the conflict between generations, visionary experiences, human toleration of social injustice—permeate his entire *oeuvre*. In *Caspar Hauser; oder, Die Trägheit des Herzens* (*Caspar Hauser*), Wassermann's version of the famous legend of Baden's outcast prince, he portrays the tragedy of an innocent foundling suddenly thrust into a pitiless community. *Caspar Hauser* brought Wassermann international acclaim, and, until the Second World War, his books enjoyed wide readership both in Germany and abroad.

While the protagonist of *Caspar Hauser* was deprived of human contact and education, the hero of *Christian Wahnschaffe* (*The World's Illusion*) is a young man of great charm and sophistication who rejects his parents' wealth in order to experience poverty, in the hope of gaining spiritual redemption. In *The World's Illusion* Wassermann depicts a broad panorama of social life from the wealthiest citizens of industrialized Germany to the most exploited poor. Wassermann draws a realistic picture of prison life in *Der Fall Maurizius* (*The Maurizius Case*), his best known work. In this classic detective novel, he examines the psychology of criminal behavior and the incomprehensibility of human conduct and character. But the theme of justice, as in all Wassermann's work, dominates this story of an idealistic boy's efforts to free a man wrongfully condemned by the boy's father, a corrupt and slothful judge.

Although Wassermann is best known for his novels, he also wrote an important autobiography, *Mein Weg als Deutscher und Jude* (*My Life as German and Jew*), in which he describes the plight of being Jewish in a country governed by hostile Aryans. In demand as a lecturer throughout Europe, Wassermann spoke out for the ideals of democratic liberalism; consequently, he was dropped from membership in the Prussian Academy of Letters, and, eventually, his books were banned by the Nazis.

Wide World Photos

While critics praise Wassermann for the sweeping, epical qualities of his work, they criticize his tendency toward sensationalism and suspenseful melodrama. And, indeed, the heavy plotting and obvious exhortation in many of his novels may seem dated today. Nevertheless, he is remembered for his often skillful presentation of timeless and universal themes.

PRINCIPAL WORKS

Melusine (novel) 1896
Die Juden von Zirndorf (novel) 1897
  [*The Dark Pilgrimage,* 1933; published in England as *The Jews of Zirndorf,* 1933]
Die Geschichte der jungen Renate Fuchs (novel) 1900
Caspar Hauser; oder, Die Trägheit des Herzens (novel) 1908
  [*Caspar Hauser,* 1928]
Der goldene Spiegel (short stories) 1911
Das Gänsemännchen (novel) 1915
  [*The Goose Man,* 1922]
Christian Wahnschaffe (novel) 1918
  [*The World's Illusion,* 1920]

Der unbekannte Gast (short stories) 1920
  [*World's Ends*, 1927]
Mein Weg als Deutscher und Jude (autobiography) 1921
  [*My Life as German and Jew*, 1933]
Oberlins drei Stufen und Sturreganz (novel and novella)
  1922
  [*Oberlin's Three Stages*, 1925]
Ulrike Woytich (novel) 1923
  [*Gold*, 1924]
Faber; oder, Die verlorenen Jahre (novel) 1924
  [*Faber; or, The Lost Years*, 1925]
Laudin und die Seinen (novel) 1925
  [*Wedlock*, 1926]
Der Aufruhr um den Junker Ernst (novel) 1926
  [*The Triumph of Youth*, 1927]
Der Fall Maurizius (novel) 1928
  [*The Maurizius Case*, 1929]
Christoph Columbus, der Don Quichote des Ozeans
  (biography) 1929
  [*Columbus, Don Quixote of the Seas*, 1930]
Etzel Andergast (novel) 1931
  [*Doctor Kerkhoven*, 1932]
Joseph Kerkhovens dritte Existenz (novel) 1934
  [*Kerkhoven's Third Existence*, 1934]

THE NEW YORK TIMES (essay date 1920)

Those whose mental digestion is not too squeamish will admit that [**"The World's Illusion"**] is a book one cannot ignore or even treat as of minor import. Wassermann is tremendously in earnest, and there is nothing tawdry about his purpose. Like his hero, he is striving to pierce the great "illusions" and to become constructive. Whether he has succeeded in doing this is another question, but, at the least he is struggling valiantly.

Simply as a story **"The World's Illusion"** would have gained by condensation. There is repetition, a putting on of additional detail and incident that is perhaps unnecessary though intended for cumulative effect and skillfully managed. The history of the hero's disillusion and long search for an outward path is planned upon a grandiose scale; he needs elbow room, but he might have moved more rapidly.

The book's chief values lie in its interpretation of modern industrial society as Wassermann sees it—aristocrat, bourgeois, peasant and proletarian. It is not a pleasant summation: a presentation of one monstrosity after another, a parade of creatures, male and female, that at first, seem scarcely credible as human beings. But they grow upon one as authentic realities: convincingly, livingly real. Therein lies the power—and the horror—of the book. There is hardly a character of importance among the score or so who will seem quite static or normal to an English reader. The hero's father, a substantial, intelligent multi-millionaire steel magnate, is perhaps the one exception to this, and he is little more than a sketch. All the rest have a touch of morbidity, ranging from what alienists would classify as insanity down to eccentricity. Yet, one believes in them, to the last line. And nearly the whole inferno of the book is stated primarily, in terms of sex and widely spreading psychopathia. . . .

[There] can be no doubt whatever of the graphic power of Wassermann's infernal scenes. The account of the murder of Ruth given by Niels, the murderer himself can hardly be matched for significant minute detail or lightning like flashes of color. There is no sense of any unreal striving for an effect in the picture. Neither does the writer gloat over the horror he depicts. He simply sees it in its stark hideousness and makes the reader see it. . . .

Doubtless it is faithful to what the author sees. But surely not all European society is degenerate, not every aristocrat a sybaritic monster, not every merchant or manufacturer a slave driver nor every proletarian bestial. Humanity as a whole is not portrayed in **"The World's Illusion"** although the reader is apt to gain the unfortunate impression that the book aims to give a complete picture of twentieth century civilization.

> *"Latest Works of Fiction: 'The World's Illusion',"*
> in The New York Times (© 1920 by The New York
> Times Company; copyright renewed © 1948 by The
> New York Times Company; reprinted by permission),
> November 28, 1920, p. 16.

J. W. KRUTCH (essay date 1922)

Wassermann's name may be mentioned without too much apology with the names of some of the greater Russians. It is true that neither **"The World's Illusion"** nor **"The Goose Man"** is the equal of "Crime and Punishment" or "The Idiot," but there is enough similarity to suggest the comparison and not enough disparity of merit to make it ridiculous. Like Dostoevski, Wassermann belongs with those men who have descended into the hell of poverty and want and who have brought back with them a vision of life which is as fascinating as it is terrible. The form of his novels with their enormous scope and rapidly changing scene is striking, but it is not this form so much as it is the intensity of his spiritual ardor which makes him remarkable. Few contemporary novelists are capable of giving the reader an emotional experience equally powerful.

"The Goose Man" like **"The World's Illusion"** is the story of a suffering Titan—this time a musician—and the end is again renunciation and a sort of absorption into the vile mass of humanity which Wassermann clasps to his breast with the paradoxical loathing-love of the Russians. Daniel Nothaff, born in destitution, belongs to the race of Brand and Zarathustra in his devotion to impossible perfection. (pp. 625-26)

The world through which Daniel moves is the nightmare world of the Russians, with avarice, baseness, stupidity, and pure malice the leading motives in the universal symphony. The Anglo-Saxon does not readily accept so hellish a vision but he can understand the circumstances which produced it and feel its horrible power. Like Dostoevski, Wassermann sees things with a sort of insane intensity. . . . Characters and incidents detach themselves with incredible emphasis and trail gigantic shadows behind them, forming a world more intense than any which we ordinarily see, but none the less real. . . .

The philosophy as well as the vision of Wassermann needs its explanation, but it too must be accepted as a characteristic phenomenon. The idea of redemption through degradation which runs through Russian fiction and is the keynote of Wassermann as well, has to our minds an element of the grotesque, and it seems to us a sort of perversity to search for one's idealism in the gutter. Yet there certain mystics who have given the tone to a whole school of modern fiction have found it, and sneer as the apostles of healthy-mindedness may, their philosophy has a spiritual reality. Wassermann must be put down as another who has gone the paradoxical way and learned the lesson of love in the contemplation of human depravity. (p. 626)

J. W. Krutch, ''Two Major Novelists,'' in The Nation *(copyright 1922 The Nation magazine, The Nation Associates, Inc.), Vol. 115, No. 2996, December 6, 1922, pp. 625-27.**

ALBERT W. ARON (essay date 1928)

Throughout the great diversity of his very voluminous literary output [Jakob Wassermann] has always remained true to a peculiar social vision, which has developed but not changed. It is in his social vision perhaps more than in any other phase that we may find a key to the understanding of Wassermann. (pp. 46-7)

The great literary importance of Wassermann consists in his having come nearer to realizing the ideal of the expressionistic writers, a group to which he does not ostensibly belong, than any of the iconoclastic expressionists themselves. He stands in a somewhat similar relation to absolute consistent expressionism as did Gerhart Hauptmann to consistent naturalism. Certain social views may be called directly programmatic for the expressionists; Wassermann has been actuated from the very beginning of his literary career by a social vision closely akin to that of the expressionists though he antedates their movement by a number of years. (p. 47)

Wassermann's social vision . . . is the antipode to the socialistic goal of the naturalistic period. It may be briefly characterized as a primitive Christian ideal or, in other words, as the social order set forth in the Beatitudes. Its realization is to be attained by individuals who feel in themselves a Messianic urge. There is hardly a novel in the long list of Wassermann's published works in which this is not increasingly true. (p. 48)

His very first novel, *Die Juden von Zirndorf*, plays in a more or less narrowly Jewish world. The prelude contains the story of a false Messiah of the 17th century, the second part the story of a genuine redeemer, a young Jew of the 19th century. (p. 49)

As has been mentioned above, in almost every one of his following novels we find some such person with the Messianic urge. As Wassermann's art grows finer, these heroes grow less articulate, at the same time that the sphere of their activity is transferred from the narrow confines of Jewish life . . . to the very pinnacle of modern European civilization in *Christian Wahnschaffe*. (pp. 49-50)

Wassermann in his capacity as a German Jew has constantly suffered from man's inhumanity to man. He has suffered alike from Jew and Christian and he has longed for some Messiah to lead humanity out of the desert. Long before the World War he has seen the emptiness and futility of contemporary European civilization. He opposes to it the social human relations of the primitive Christians, the social creed of the Beatitudes. He does not believe in an outward overthrow of established powers and established social relations, but in a new attitude toward them. The form is nothing, the spirit is everything. He does not believe in new social organizations except as brought about by the redeeming power of a heart filled with love. Almost all of his novels contain some person, usually the central character, who follows the urge of his heart in this direction. (p. 54)

Albert W. Aron, ''A Key to Jakob Wassermann,'' in The Germanic Review *(copyright 1928 by Helen Dwight Reed Foundation), Vol. III, No. 1, January, 1928, pp. 46-54.*

WILLIAM A. DRAKE (essay date 1928)

Like Heine, [Wassermann] was a Jew and a German, the keenest spirit, yet the most remote, in the mêlée of modernity; the type closest to the heart of our changing culture, yet the least a part of it. . . . Slowly a new world-conception, which is as old as Nature itself, was forming in his mind—the idea of the common identity of all things in Nature, of man's individual responsibility for the whole of humanity. One can observe this idea, coloring and directing all his thought, gradually taking form through the long procession of his early novels and tales: in *Die Schwestern, Caspar Hauser, Die Masken Erwin Reiners, Der Goldene Spiegel,* and his first great success, *Das Gänsemännchen,* before it comes to its first complete and mystical expression in *Christian Wahnschaffe.*

This idea, which reacts upon the art of Jakob Wassermann with the force of an obsession, is the pure conception of Christ, which perhaps only Saint Francis of Assisi and Dostoevsky have perfectly understood and communicated in action. It is a doctrine at once humble and proud: that man, as an inseparable part of the universe, bears within himself, with tragic glory, the whole sad blight of the world's sin; that the virtue of the brother whom he has never seen is his virtue, and his guilt his guilt; that it is his obligation to utilize for good the terrible creative force of evil; that, being the universe itself within the miserable particle of the universe which he is, he has no being save in the whole which makes him noble, and no worthy employment save in the humble service of the fellow-men who are more a part of him than he is of himself. (pp. 217-18)

One has found this conception, expressed with transcendental conviction, in the novels of Dostoevsky. But Dostoevsky, while he conveys this sentiment of the mystical unity of humanity with greater art than Wassermann—he could not do so with greater conviction and passion—was a sufferer from the holy malady, seeking his consummations in blacker hearts and amid deeper depravity and more malignant evil than Wassermann dares to describe or than any but the most unimaginable dregs of the earth can produce for the accusation of life.

Wassermann is closer to life in his conceptions than Dostoevsky, but infinitely farther removed from it in art and fact. His characters, like Dostoevsky's, are at once individuals and symbols. But Christian Wahnschaffe never lives and breathes, as Myshkin; nor Niels Heinrich, as Rogojin. Nor do his carefully constructed plots bear the conviction of reality. His figures, for the most part, move like puppets in a fantastic show, dense with symbolical meanings of terrific significance. They move, they talk; they seek, they suffer, and achieve: but only now and again do they breathe, like a sick Pierrot taking his farewell to love, or a marionette touched to life for a magical instant while it heaves a sigh and wishes it were dead again. And this is where the pure, spontaneous, undisciplined art of Dostoevsky rises above the magnificently harmonious prose, the careful poise, the diligently constructed plots, and the finished dexterity of his German disciple. With all his haste and prolixity, with all his melodrama and his disorganization, he accomplishes a transcendent greatness which Wassermann will never be able to approach.

Wassermann's deficiency is hard to specify, but it undoubtedly exists. . . . It is obviously not a question of Wassermann's sincerity, of the vigor of his conception, the capacity of his art, or the passion of its execution. In all of these qualities, Jacob Wassermann stands beyond challenge. It is rather the indecision which apparently still remains in Wassermann's mind between the art of Balzac and that of Dostoevsky, and as well the question . . . of his own inherent spiritual capacity for absorbing and utilizing such a conception as that which he has set forth in *Christian Wahnschaffe.*

Stefan Zweig calls Wassermann the Balzac of German literature. The influence of Balzac, in fact, has been and remains stronger in Wassermann's art than that of Dostoevsky, which has decisively inspired only his finest book and lent color to the rest. The design of *Der Wendekreis,* which he plans in ten volumes—of which *Der Unbekannte Gast, Oberlin's Drei Stufen, Ulrike Woytich* and *Faber oder die Verlorenen Jahre* have already appeared—bears a curious resemblance to that of *Comédie Humaine.* "I am interested primarily in life, in making a synthesis of life which is based firmly upon my own viable contacts," Wassermann told Pierre Loving in 1924. "I try not to ignore the inner vision; the inner vision is of overwhelming importance, but my objective observation is always at work correcting that inner grasp of reality. My aim is to pack the whole complex modern scene into my books. . . ."

This he is certainly doing, if we can grant, as in this case we do, that Germany, in the thirty years between Wassermann's maturity and the Spartacan Revolution, presents to the novelist a clinical study in which all the cancerous growths of our modern social maladjustment may be profitably scrutinized. Like Balzac, he concentrates the society which he wishes to weigh in suitable groupings of characters, who are at once the fact and the symbols of the reality. In their fortunes, we follow the fortunes of Europe. Wiser than Balzac, he lavishes his power upon the development of these characters, leaving the setting to create itself through their reality. Also like Balzac—and this is his greatest fault—he makes concessions to his aim of reaching the great public. We will grant at once that he does so for a more worthy purpose than Balzac's—Wassermann, despite his success, is, in his art itself, the least commercial and the most messianic of novelists. But all that he has given to the numerical increase of his immediate public, through providing each of his novels with an exciting plot, so contrived as to awaken and sustain interest, he has lost to his characters and to his art; for his plots are constantly tripping his characters up and rudely edging them off the scene. He has, we may say, striven too well to correct, in his own work, the obvious faults of Dostoevsky; and his efforts in this direction have resulted in a disadvantage, rather than in a gain. For they have helped to keep him from the complete, decisive, organic expression which his controlling ideas demand and which his sincerity merits. Perhaps this too will come, for Wassermann's art is a thoroughly self-conscious instrument, critical and sure. But nothing that Wassermann has thus far given us, privileges such a confidence. His talent appears, in reality, to be more conventional and less significant than our admiration for his world conception makes us willing to admit. (pp. 218-21)

William A. Drake, "Jakob Wassermann," in his *Contemporary European Writers (copyright, 1927, by William A. Drake), John Day, 1928, Harrap, 1929, pp. 214-21.*

ARTHUR ELOESSER (essay date 1931)

[Jakob Wassermann's first novel, *Die Juden von Zirndorf (The Jews of Zirndorf),* attracted attention] by the evidence of un-

common talent that it gave, especially in its imaginative prelude, glowing with colour, the scene of which is laid in the seventeenth century, and in its pictures of the misery of the ghetto, against the background of which stands out in brilliant relief the figure of the Jewish Messiah Sabatai Zewi, who became an apostate to Islam. The modern part, connected with the prelude only by the recurrence of certain motives and a certain atmosphere, has as its background the Franconian countryside and a no longer tangible ghetto. From this environment comes forth a prophet and dreamer, typical of almost all of Wassermann's heroes, who is sent out in quest of adventures. Wassermann is the most romantic of German novelists, his particular sphere being that lying between dream and reality, in which the limits of spiritual possibility, untroubled by everyday standards of probability, are considerably extended. (pp. 270-71)

[*Geschichte der jungen Renate Fuchs (The Story of Young Renate Fuchs)*] is a romantic, rambling book, but breathes a music made tender and alluring by the suspense and longing of an age that was seeking to recover its fullness, independence, and inviolability of soul after so much rigorous observation and resigned submission to the sociological and physiological conditions of life. In spite of this penetrating psychologist's understanding of life, this inferno—for such this book is, especially for the women—withdraws into a visionary dream-world, in which one exaggerated improbability neutralizes another and into which a whole generation seems to have breathed its sighs, expectations, and Messianic hopes. All mankind has embarked upon a pilgrimage in search of it knows not what; but those who are predestined for each other are drawn together by secret signs and would manage to come together by force of magnetic attraction even with their eyes shut. Wassermann speaks somewhere of the "law of chance encounters (*Gesetz der Begegnung*)"—but this is the invention of a Romantic novelist with a faith in the miraculous. (p. 272)

In *Renate Fuchs* Jakob Wassermann had gone forth with his charmed lyre into the streets and sung to the people, interpreting their fearful dreams and bringing them fairer ones as a gift. . . . Once more he assumed the writer's most lofty function—that of a secret confidant, profoundly responsible for all that happens, of a judge and priest who measures guilt and expiation and dispenses justice and favour. The first product of this moral solicitude was *Die Masken Erwin Reiners (Erwin Reiners's Masks),* in which a young *viveur,* sportsman; and lady-killer of infamous character lays siege by the aid of his consummate experience and his millions to Virginia, who is betrothed to one of his friends. . . . The attitude of [an] idle, corrupt society, which has nothing to do but watch the pitiless pursuit of Reiners's noble game and even lay wagers on the result, is highly Viennese and reminds us of [Arthur] Schnitzler's society plays. This gradual working up of excitement about a much-discussed sensational event takes place, as often happens with Wassermann, in an artificial hothouse atmosphere. The reader certainly enjoys the thrill as he holds his breath in amazement at the power of evil and, above all, of wealth; and if anybody feels any further doubts of its probability, he is likely to come to the conclusion that the doors have been closed to reality, fresh air, sun, and rain in order to create an atmosphere favourable to the growth of a novel.

Wassermann's masterpiece, *Christian Wahnschaffe,* which in Germany and, above all, in America won him the reputation of a German Dostoyevsky, also starts among the idle, self-indulgent classes of society, with regard to whom we may feel satisfied that they know how to conduct themselves without offending against any of the canons of cosmopolitan high society. . . . Once Christian has passed through the eye of the needle, renouncing family and wealth and shaking off the sluggishness of his sympathies, he succeeds, by a simplicity that reminds us of Dostoyevsky's Idiot, in awakening the human feelings of a wretched prostitute on her very deathbed and in inducing a brutal criminal to relieve his soul by making the confession by which he can find salvation in the only brotherhood—that of human suffering. The legend of his conversion and self-examination is related with great virtuosity and a stateliness which, though somewhat rigid, is carefully calculated, and accompanied by an imposing flow of imagination, which is, however, subordinated to the general plan. (pp. 273-75)

Wassermann also produced an unusually simple and beautiful version of the story of Caspar Hauser and his sufferings [in *Caspar Hauser*] which he himself called "a novel on the sluggishness of human sympathies (*Trägheit des Herzens*)." He returned more than once to this motive, which was, as it were, the distress signal of his work, and intensified it with the most passionate fervour. *Der Fall Maurizius* (*The Maurizius Case*) shows how the heart of a sixteen-year-old boy is inflamed by the desire to fight for the right. . . . With this novel, which had as its sequel *Etzel Andergast*, Wassermann took up the subject of the conflict between fathers and sons, which he had so far left to the younger generation of the expressionists and activists. The sequel develops into a comprehensive picture of the state of Germany and the attitude of mind of the young people of the post-War generation. In it Wassermann wished to set up, as it were, a second "Magic Mountain (*Zauberberg*)" on which should be gathered together all the ills of Europe and their physicians, not to speak of all the quacks and those who tried to exploit these ills for their profit. In this work Wassermann does not approach strictly political questions, but, rising above these, tries to suggest those atmospheric and cosmic upheavals which produce clashes of will, moral disorders, and spiritual plagues. It reveals him as a sort of Paracelsus, relying upon the magic powers of the soul to correct the disturbance in the relations between nature and the intelligence by once more placing these irrational forces at the service of mankind. (pp. 275-76)

> *Arthur Eloesser, "The Novel," in his* Modern German Literature, *translated by Catherine Alison Phillips (copyright 1933 by Alfred A. Knopf, Inc.; Canadian rights by permission of Alfred A. Knopf, Inc.; originally published as* Die Deutsche Literatur vom Barock bis zur Gegenwart, *Bruno Cassirer, 1931), Alfred A. Knopf, Inc., 1933, pp. 211-307.**

EDWARD CRANKSHAW (essay date 1932)

[From] time to time a man appears who bids us regard reality intently, and these are the greatest artists in history; every great artist gives us rare glimpses of reality, but the greatest seem to comprehend it fully. And it is among them that Jakob Wassermann has his place.

Wassermann is a realist as Shakespeare was a realist, Goethe or Dostoievsky; that is to say he is concerned with essential reality, and not with things, except in so far as they reflect or illustrate reality. . . . (p. 104)

The most obvious business of the artist is to widen the onlooker's experience, to help him to comprehend life more fully; the greatest artists go further than this: they justify life it-

self. . . . I do not read novels to discover that human misery is great, but in the hope of being convinced by a greater mind than mine that life for all its misery is beautiful, that the shocking things which happen to individuals are but accidents on the surface of real life. And this is the conviction that comes from reading Wassermann.

That is why it seems to me that Wassermann is the greatest living novelist and one of the greatest novelists who has ever lived. The only men who can be compared with him are Dostoievsky and the Tolstoy of "War and Peace"; and Wassermann has all the intensity of Dostoievsky without any sign of his hysteria; **"The World's Illusion"** has all the immensity of "War and Peace" with none of its cloudiness; it is clear-cut and anchored in rock.

"The World's Illusion" is Wassermann's greatest achievement, but perhaps the best way to come to him is through **"Caspar Hauser."** . . . The sub-title of **"Caspar Hauser"** is **"Die Trägheit des Herzens"** a phrase which has passed into German literature, and which means approximately "The laziness of the heart," or, freely, "The unheeding world." Wassermann's characters are all pitted against society, but not, as in the ordinary pamphleteering novel, against one particular section of society, or against specific conventions or cruelties of society, but against the inertia in the heart of every human being. "Die Trägheit des Herzens" is at the root of all Wassermann's writing; in **"The Maurizius Case"** it is interwoven with several other issues; in **"The World's Illusion"** it forms the ground base of continuity over which is woven a staggering counterpoint of ideas, motives, actions—surely everything that has ever passed through the mind of man; if there were no such word as "universal" it would have to be invented for Wassermann.

"Die Trägheit des Herzens" calls for vitality, clear seeing, lack of prejudice, the will to action, innocence, yet suppleness of mind, in its adversary; and it is no accident that Wassermann's hero is so often a youth, taken before he is permanently twisted to fill society's iron mould. In Caspar Hauser, the wonder child, the rightful heir to the throne of Baden, who as a baby had been smuggled away and for sixteen years kept in utter darkness, seeing nothing, knowing nothing, learning nothing—in this Caspar Hauser who with his sudden, unexplained apparition startled the citizens of Nürnberg, a hero was ready-made. He was at once the human spirit coming nearer to maturity, yet utterly unimpressioned, and the victim of the crass, unheeding world, lazy of heart. Christian Wahnschaffe, who gives his name as title to the original of **"The World's Illusion,"** is a youth of extraordinarily brilliant and sympathetic nature whose spiritual development, in essence, reminds us of that of St. Francis of Assisi; but there the resemblance ends. His background is contemporary life in every aspect, and the characters form a microcosm of the world, and their deeds of the deeds of the world. Etzel Andergast, of **"The Maurizius Case,"** is a boy of fourteen who with all the subtlety of innocence carries out his business by force of his enlightened *naïveté*. . . . Etzel Andergast is an expression of all that is splendid and unwarped in the human spirit; the vessel is of no account.

There is yet another aspect of Wassermann's greatness on view in this book. The prevailing passion of the book might easily be labelled "justice." Yet how remote is Wassermann's approach from that of the typical humanitarian sentimentalist. . . . Although in one section of the book Wassermann says all that there is to say about prisons, through the mouths of prisoner and warders, far more powerfully than it has ever been said before, this book is not a tract for penal reform. It is a book to show the human spirit in action; it is the tale of one who feels strongly, who is convinced, and who proceeds inevitably to justify his conviction. (pp. 104-05)

Even now we have only a lop-sided idea of the man. Nothing has been said about his women, and they require an article to themselves. Perhaps it is enough to say that in a hundred years' time the dancer Eva, the actress Louise Dercum will be as familiar to the world as Ophelia, and because of them we may understand Ophelia more fully. (p. 105)

> Edward Crankshaw, "Jakob Wassermann" (reprinted by permission of A D Peter & Co Ltd), in The Bookman, *London, Vol. LXXXII, No. 488, May, 1932, pp. 104-05.*

HAROLD STRAUSS (essay date 1934)

Merely as a novel, **"Kerkhoven's Third Existence,"** despite its moments of profundity and great power, despite its occasional Dostoievskian penetration to the core of being, is helter-skelter, full of loose ends and digressions, and lacking in any unifying main strand of action. But this book demands consideration not as a novel but as a journal of ideas, for in it Wassermann brought to culmination his life-long absorption in two major trains of thought.

These spring directly from his life. In his autobiography [**"My Life as German and Jew"**] he tells us of his unhappy youth: of maladjustments in his sensitive nature, of the opposition of his family to his career as a writer, and of the lasting conflicts between his inner being and his environment, the most serious of which was the clash between his Jewish origin and his German nationality as an artist. These conflicts destroyed that inner harmony necessary (for him) to positive creation. By hard experience he learned that there was no solution to be found on the plane of what we ordinarily call reality. He was driven steadily toward the escape of mysticism.

He became a dealer in illusions; but he conceived of the actual world of the flesh as the greatest illusion of all, and of reality as resting only in the godhead, faith and eternity. . . . His concept of the godhead was based on biology. To protoplasm, to unicellular organisms multiplying by fission, he attributed, because of the everlastingness of their reproduction, a faith in eternity, immortality, the godhead. . . . The ego develops as the organism becomes more and more complex, until in man its destructive conflict with the inherent life-principle reaches the point of disaster. Dr. Kerkhoven attains his third existence by discovering that his fear of death is but the greatest of all illusions conjured by his temporal ego. Thus he casts it out and serenely unites himself to the life-principle, the faith inherent in protoplasm.

This is the outline of Wassermann's first train of thought. If it seems formidable, the simplicity of his second focus of interest will come as a relief. It too grows out of his life. Because of his own troubles, his attention was called to pathological cases. He began with individual ailments of the soul, but he found them so prevalent that he soon came to view the whole of society as infected with psychological unbalance. . . .

"Kerkhoven's Third Existence" is simply the vehicle for these twin attitudes. In many ways Kerkhoven is Wassermann himself. His first existence, revealed in a related novel, **"Dr. Kerkhoven,"** embraced his tormented youthful struggle to ob-

tain a foothold in the world of actuality. . . . Dr. Kerkhoven became a great psychologist and neurologist, a healer of almost psychic powers. He considered that his impersonal immersion in his work took him beyond suffering, beyond the grasp of his own fate.

At the opening of this book this conviction has been shattered by his discovery of his wife's intimacy with his pupil, Etzel Andergast. . . . He must give up his practice, and he must restore his relationship with her. How he does this is an account of great beauty and magnificent insight. While he turns upon himself the treatments he has for so long practiced upon others, there intervenes the second spiritual interregnum. At last he returns from a voyage to Java, to found a sanatorium in a mountain retreat and to approach his third existence. To this point Wassermann is truly great.

Then the novel turns into a case-book of pathological ailments. In this field Wassermann has been excelled by none save Schnitzler. But though these cases are fascinating, and illustrate Kerkhoven's restored and even magnified powers of healing, they distract us from whatever main thread of action the novel may have. Finally the all-important case of Alexander Herzog turns up. Herzog is a celebrated German writer who has been reduced to a psychic pulp by his relations with his first and now divorced wife Ganna. . . . Wassermann suggests that Ganna is really the symbol of a basic principle the embodiment of the illusions of time and actuality upon this earth. A horrible character, this woman who is a ruthless and frenzied priestess of the ordinary morals and attitudes of bourgeois society! Ganna, in short, is the world of illusion, a heavy, feverish, terror-stricken world, a world of agony, perplexity and supplication. To this Wassermann counterposes the peace and faith and serenity of Kerkhoven's third existence; for he has attained the world of the only reality, of harmony with eternal time and space and destiny.

The liberation of Kerkhoven does not lend itself to logical formulation. It is a vague process, in which Wassermann invokes the doctrines of a fourteenth-century mystic, Tauler. Though the central thesis of this novel is lacking in clarity and directness, it nevertheless cannot be denied that in whole and in part it makes the profoundest impression. It is only the Ganna-Herzog episode that is insufferably dull, being far too detailed in its investigation of characters too hateful and petty. Possibly Wassermann inserted bodily into this book an unused and unfinished draft for another novel. Though it proves his point, it is thoroughly inorganic. And although Herzog is cured by Kerkhoven, the story of his relationship with Ganna is not conclusive.

For the final details of Kerkhoven's transfiguration and death (notice that transfiguration comes before the death) we have nothing but praise. So keenly do we sense Wassermann's conviction of a supernal reality that his description of Kerkhoven's last days have the objectivity, the remoteness and the simplicity of a parable. . . . This novel offers scant diversion, but for those able to digest it, ample food for thought.

> Harold Strauss, "Wassermann's Journal of Ideas," in The New York Times *(© 1934 by The New York Times Company; reprinted by permission), November 11, 1934, p. 9.*

FÉLIX BERTAUX (essay date 1935)

The individual, kept bound in chains by the naturalists, reappeared in Wassermann's work not only as a creature of flesh and blood but as mind, action, caprice. Wassermann conceives of a novel first in terms of a character who overpowers the author—"*die Gestalt*," the individual who is glimpsed in the mass and who fires the imagination of the observer. The author watches through half-closed eyes, and as the character takes on color and relief, begins to move and live, so the novel is born and the plot gets under way. The novelist is carried along by the character he has created, never knows exactly where he is being led, finally discovers that the story has been told by the character rather than by himself. This sort of hallucination probably accounts for the intensity of Wassermann's characters. Even when their actions are banal and the plot is obviously over-complicated or over-ingenious, the story moves astonishingly, seizes the reader's interest, and flaws are overlooked.

This does not mean that Wassermann neglects the effort to achieve psychological unity. The point is that where others would conceive of the novel as a picture of the evolution of an individual, he conceives of it as the history of the spasmodic advances which the individual makes in the course of that evolution. For him the interesting moment in the life of an individual is the moment when "*die Wandlung*" takes place, when there is a sudden metamorphosis in an apparently stable ego behind which abruptly and inexplicably appears a new and different ego. He used this idea of psychological discontinuity in *Ulrike Woytich,* in *Oberlins drei Stufen,* in *Faber,* in *Laudin und die Seinen,* it borrows something from Freud, but is not to be confused with the theory of inhibition. We harbor within us, according to Wassermann, a whole series of coexistent selves, which substitute themselves one for the other under the pressure of events, or which come to the surface through accident. These events, these accidents, become the material of the novel which, instead of containing drab uniformity, deals with the brilliant instant, the momentary evolutionary burst, and consists entirely of clear images.

There is little doubt that Wassermann learned this process of selection from the French novelists, but he does not write as they write. While his novels tend toward a fixed architectural form, their chief virtue lies in the unpredictability of what happens, in a plot which unfolds in arabesques. The author follows his instinct like a hunting-dog set on a scent that he is mad with eagerness to pursue. At the same time, however, Wassermann has a certain formula that he follows. This is to keep his characters purposely cloaked in mystery during the first chapters of the novel in order to hold the reader in suspense, in order to give his hero a romantic halo. It is the technique of "*Entschleierung*," which consists in keeping curiosity aroused by letting the veils of mystery fall slowly one by one. This is a revival of the methods of the cheap newspaper writers, but Jakob Wassermann handles it with a master's hand. He is a story-teller whose chief charm lies in the quickness of his inventive faculties; and it is when he pretends to no more than story-telling that he reaches a certain perfection of his own. (pp. 152-54)

> *Félix Bertaux, "The Novel," in his* A Panorama of German Literature from 1871 to 1931, *translated by John J. Trounstine (copyright 1935 by the McGraw-Hill Book Company, Inc.), Whittlesey House, 1935, pp. 122-59.**

JOHN C. BLANKENAGEL (essay date 1942)

[*Die Juden von Zirndorf*] appeared in 1897. Its prelude, *Sabbatai Zewi,* is written with more sustained artistry than the novel proper. Indeed, the difference is so marked that one might well believe the prelude had been written by a maturer author with greater sureness of touch. (p. 30)

The scene of the prelude is Fürth, near Nuremberg, and the surrounding region; the time is the year 1666 when the coming of Sabbatai Zewi as the great Messiah and ultimate redeemer of the Jews was proclaimed throughout Europe. Zewi, born in Smyrna in 1626, announced himself as the Messiah, was received in triumph in his native city, found fervent followers among Jews, was imprisoned by the Turkish government, and saved his life by embracing the Islamic faith. The prelude has relatively little plot, for the essential element is the portrayal of the boundless enthusiasm, the religious frenzy and the passionate, fanatical zeal with which the alleged coming of the Messiah was greeted in the Jewish community. . . .

With remarkable skill Wassermann portrayed the growing religious zeal of the Jews which flared up into wild, feverish delirium. It manifested itself in mystic expectancy, transports of joy, tense excitement, ecstasy, abandoned eroticism, bacchanalian revelry, and emotional fervor devoid of reason or practical considerations. (p. 32)

Although the opening scene with its peaceful picture of this region is in marked contrast with the frenzied religious upheaval that follows, the subsequent varied aspects of nature are in accord with frequent changes in the temper of personages and events.

Unobstrusively, with genuine poetic beauty, Wassermann here paints nature in ever changing mood as the background and accompaniment of human activity, hopes and aspirations. . . . In no other novel did Wassermann portray nature with the same breadth nor with equal poetic charm and affection. (pp. 33-4)

In spite of the emotional intensity of much of the prelude, its style is direct, relatively simple, and at times in the manner of an old chronicle. It varies to suit the change from calm to animated mood; it is effective and is devoid of the rhetorical extravagance found in some of Wassermann's writings. The limited amount of dialogue is employed largely to mark a higher pitch of intensity.

The relation of *Sabbatai Zewi* and *Die Juden von Zirndorf* is tenuous. Obviously, the founding of Zirndorf by Jews who returned from their unsuccessful expedition to meet the alleged Messiah is but a casual, external link. An outward connection between the prelude and the novel lies in the characterization of the Jew at the end of the former and the portrayal of Jewish persons and life in the latter. In addition, the novel contains an allusion to the prelude. For in *Die Juden von Zirndorf* Agathon discovers an old book in which he reads the story of Sabbatai Zewi. Though he reads it with avid eyes, he distinguishes carefully between truth and falsehood, between capricious phantasy and profundity. As he beholds this impostor, he reads the souls of men that yield to the half-truths of an ostentatious phrasemonger who toys with their enthusiasm and walks heedlessly over their dead bodies. A definite reference to the prologue is made in the statement that "two hundred years do not change human nature, and that they represent but a tiny phase in the process of transformations. It seems as if across the centuries characters or souls must awaken to new life in a new chain of phenomena and events." (pp. 34-5)

Throughout almost two hundred and twenty years which separate *Sabbatai Zewi* from *Die Juden von Zirndorf,* the longing for redemption, liberation and salvation remains; its expression merely undergoes a change with the passing of time. The implication is that Agathon, though he gropes somewhat blindly and achieves but little, has the earnestness, sympathy and good will of a redeemer who may ultimately lead men to a kingdom within them, to a richer inner life. This, rather than a flight to Zion, means genuine liberation. (p. 35)

The novel, *Die Juden von Zirndorf*, has decided weaknesses. Since Wassermann's main concern was with the character and development of Agathon, he neglected plot and structure. The plot is loosely fashioned; various strands run side by side with but little connection, and occasionally the shifting of the narrative from one strand to another in successive chapters seems capricious. There is a wealth of incident which has not been brought to a focus. Though interesting in itself, such incident has not always been carefully integrated in the structure of the novel. . . . At times the motivation is superficial; because of its fancifulness it occasionally imposes too great a strain on the reader's credulity, and fails to carry conviction. (pp. 35-6)

A further weakness lies in the character portrayal. Most of the characters in *Die Juden von Zirndorf* are shadowy creatures, mosaic compositions of qualities or traits without organic, life-like unity. They live primarily in the author's imagination. Some of their comments on life sound like Wassermann's rather than their own. (p. 36)

It is surprising to note the number of motifs, more or less implicit in *Die Juden von Zirndorf*, which recur in Wassermann's later works. Some of the themes which are subsequently developed in detail are "Trägheit des Herzens," human indifference and indolence, as manifest particularly in the cold aloofness of teachers toward their impressionable pupils; the conflict between father and son, based on opposing points of view; the relation of the Jew to the Gentile community in which he lives; the problem of woman and her sex-life in and out of matrimony; the aimless, impractical, visionary idealist with messianic traits; the portrayal of social injustice, human misery and depravity before which Agathon stands aghast and helpless; human greed for gold; and the problem of the young artist as exemplified in Gudstikker. (p. 38)

Wassermann's desire to present singularly striking situations, and to individualize characters that at the same time have symbolical significance is already manifest with all the attendant dangers of overstatement, exaggeration and sentimentality. Certain doubts of Wassermann about his own writings seem to find an echo in Bojesen's criticisms of Gudstikker's novel. For in Gudstikker's narrative Bojesen sees much skillful portrayal and many brilliant details. But he notes also overwrought romanticism in the presentation of emotions, and inability to produce simple effects with becoming naturalness. Bojesen evidently sets forth Wassermann's ideals in literature when he tells Jeanette that all life is but a symbol, and that we are to regard everything that happens to us as symbolical. Consequently, the greatest poets, concludes Bojesen, are those who simplify life as much as possible.

Much of the importance of *Die Juden von Zirndorf* lies in the artistry of the prelude and in the foreshadowing of the development of Wassermann's ideals, interests, technique, and points of strength and weakness. (p. 39)

In *Caspar Hauser oder Die Trägheit des Herzens* Wassermann wrote the first of his maturer novels. . . . The theme announced in the subtitle, namely human indifference to the lot of others, has appeared before in Wassermann's narratives. Here, however, it is no longer an incidental motif, but has become fun-

damental. With greater artistry the author brings out his theme through implication in the unfolding of events rather than by direct pronouncement. . . .

For more than a century the mystery of the origin of Caspar Hauser has defied all efforts at a solution. (p. 84)

[This is not the place] to hazard an opinion as to the foundling's identity. A few details about the controversy may suffice. In the judgment of some, Caspar Hauser was the legitimate heir to the throne of Baden who was smuggled away and replaced by a dying or dead child, thus enabling a scion of another branch of the reigning house to take the throne. . . . Whether Caspar Hauser was a prince who was thrust aside and finally assassinated, or whether he was an impostor who died of self-inflicted wounds is still unknown. What matters to Wassermann in writing this novel is less the question of Caspar's origin than his character and his relation to his environment. (p. 85)

In brief outline the plot of the novel runs as follows: Caspar Hauser, a youth of about seventeen, appears in Nuremberg one day early in the summer of 1828, ignorant of where he came from, scarcely able to walk or talk, and bearing an unsigned letter in which he is described as a foundling of unknown parentage; for about fifteen years he has never set foot out of doors, nor seen a human being. Nobody knows about him, and he knows nobody. In the course of the action Caspar undergoes the belated development of his senses and mind, passes from one tutor and guardian to another, is treated with but occasional kindness and with varying degrees of harshness, cruelty, condescension, skepticism and suspicion. No one in his environment stands the test of human affection, of sacrificial love, moral greatness and enlightenment which would enable him to see and appreciate in Caspar the purity of a human being of pristine innocence, untouched by contacts with mankind. In the end, Caspar is murdered by an assassin, presumably in the hire of those whose dynastic interests are threatened by his existence, yet even in death he is accused of being a deceiver. Mankind has been put to the test and found wanting.

The besetting sin of humanity, "Trägheit des Herzens," is revealed by Wassermann largely as one of omission; it manifests itself in lack of spontaneity, in self-absorption, preoccupation with paltry ambitions and petty interests, selfishness, coldness of heart, indifference to human wants, failure to come to the aid of others, indolence and inertia. Men are caught in the trivialities of life, their vision is dulled, and they are no longer able to see humanity in its essential goodness and promise. *Caspar Hauser* is a wistful commentary rather than a diatribe on human indifference.

In "**Faustina, ein Gespräch über die Liebe,**" . . . Wassermann characterizes "Trägheit des Herzens" as an insidious disease, and as the one deadly sin. It is manifest, says he, in passing by when the voice of concience urges one to stop; in closing one's eyes when one should espouse a cause; in judging and condemning when much depends on silence and magnanimity; in striving for justice while forgetting love; in praising friendship and denying a friend. All such forgetting, all such knowing and not doing constitutes "Trägheit des Herzens." (pp. 88-9)

Wassermann presents the strange situation of a youth of seventeen who has known no childhood, who arrives in this world with the mental age of little more than a toddling babe, and who in a very short period of time passes through the stages of a child's mental development, emotional disturbances and adolescence into early manhood. Much of this portrayal is given through the treatment of Caspar by his guardians. Consequently their attitude, which is carefully presented, must be scrutinized in some detail.

Daumer, the first of these guardians, is actuated less by warm interest in the person of Caspar than by the desire to prove certain theories and to arouse the wonders of the dull, philistine, petty bourgeoisie. . . . Caspar remains for him primarily a most singular phenomenon to be studied for a time with a certain pedantic interest. Consequently he carries on various experiments to test the lad's sense perception and reactions, he studies and disturbs the soundness of his sleep, investigates his susceptibility to hypnosis, and the effect of homeopathic remedies on him; he exhibits and fatigues the poor boy as one might a guinea pig of a higher order. (pp. 91-2)

Baron Tucher's attitude is that of an unimaginative, prosaic realist, who accepts the guardianship of Caspar from a sense of duty and in the belief that a firm, manly hand, simple living, orderliness and judicious severity may bring an errant being back to the right course. A man of firm convictions, he feels compelled to establish distance between himself and Caspar. He shows no emotion, his look is cool, and his face is stern, for his principles demand an unbending attitude. (p. 93)

[The personality of Lord Stanhope, Caspar's next guardian,] is somewhat enigmatic. Here Wassermann has given way to his fondness for portraying involved, complex characters whose thoughts at times are a mystery, perhaps even to themselves. Stanhope is described as a man of the world, with charm, mobile features, and insight into life. For a time the reader is baffled by the nature of his interest in Caspar. He seems so spontaneous and so warmly affectionate that for the first time in his life Caspar is filled with the exultant joy of being loved. Here, as in other narratives, Wassermann occasionally pretends ignorance of the motives that prompt a character of his. Perhaps, says he, Stanhope was in earnest, perhaps he found delight in rousing Caspar's hopes and desires. . . . Now and then Wassermann takes the reader into his confidence sufficiently to lift the veil partially, and to inform him that Stanhope is playing a rôle. Yet he takes pleasure for some time in keeping his readers guessing as to the exact nature of this strange rôle. (pp. 93-4)

Stanhope's checkered career is full of tortuous intrigue in the service of unscrupulous princes. He has orders from Caspar's hidden enemies to remove him to a distant country, or to drown him, or hurl him into an abyss or have him assassinated. But Caspar's affection moves Stanhope whose own innocent youth confronts him in the foundling. Under the spell of Caspar's love he is torn by conflicting emotions, and temporarily allows himself to drift along on the tide of events. The importance of Stanhope lies not merely in the opportunity it gives Wassermann to present the remarkable influence of Caspar's innocence on an unscrupulous man who has been hired to put him out of the way. For in addition, the author is enabled to portray strikingly Caspar's need of kindness, and to give an idea of what genuine affection would have meant in the lad's life. (p. 94)

In its approach to caricature the characterization of Quandt reflects Wassermann's loathing of the meanness and petty pedantry of Caspar's last guardian. . . . [Quandt] is a petty moralizer, as fussy as an old maid, jealous of honors bestowed on others, ever ready to detract from the achievements of his fellows, happy in the detection of their foibles, and exulting in the losses and discomfitures of his neighbors. . . . Commonplace himself, Quandt is unable to see anything extraor-

dinary in Caspar. Watchful as a jailer, he is suspicious of everything his ward does or does not; he interprets all things to Caspar's disadvantage, pronouncing him hard-hearted, ungrateful and defiant, and is so convinced of the youth's mendacity that the very multiplication table from Caspar's lips would sound like a falsehood. He drags Caspar, who is mortally wounded, back to the scene of the attack, denouncing him as a liar and impostor who wounded himself merely to attract attention. Even while Caspar is dying, Quandt tries to worm an alleged secret from him. (p. 96)

[These] characters, well-drawn as they are, do not exist for their own sake, but are designed to bring out in one way or another the underlying theme of human indifference in this unheeding world.

The author is successful in creating and holding the reader's sympathetic interest in Caspar from his first appearance as a helpless, tottering, terrified creature until his death at the hand of a hired assassin. He has drawn an arresting picture of the gradual awakening of Caspar's consciousness, his first recognition of environment, of self and other beings, of dreams and numerous other phenomena of life. (pp. 97-8)

Sympathy for Caspar in a harsh, cold world is aroused without resorting to pathos in the presentation of his varied experiences. (p. 98)

The structure of *Caspar Hauser* is simple and highly unified. Interest centers first and last around the principal figure; other characters, no matter how carefully they are portrayed, are of importance solely through their relation to the hero in the development of the fundamental motif. And this motif is ever before the reader. Events are narrated almost entirely in chronological sequence. The unilinear plot of *Caspar Hauser* is in marked contrast with some of Wassermann's subsequent intricate plots in which separately developed threads are brought together only now and then. (pp. 99-100)

[Wassermann] resorts to the easy device of letters for imparting information. Evidently this is done in order to bring the opinions of various people on Caspar to a sharper focus. But although this device is obviously convenient for the author, its effect on the reader is not altogether pleasing. It entails an added change in the style of the narrative which is already slightly lacking in uniformity. For Wassermann begins his novel in the manner of an old chronicle, but yields at times to a more impassioned, subjective interest in the trials of his hero, and to ironical treatment of the foibles of such men as Daumer, Tucher and Quandt. With considerable frequency he comments directly on characters, ideas and situations. (p. 101)

There are occasional brief, somewhat sententious disquisitions of a moral nature which likewise are not in keeping with the style of an old chronicle. At times Wassermann associates himself playfully with his reader in joint assumptions and declarations. Although the whimsical humor of some comments affords relief, others are felt as unnecessary intrusion on the part of the narrator. . . .

But on the whole, the style and diction of *Caspar Hauser* are restrained. . . . [Exaggerations] and extravagances are rare in this novel whose earnest simplicity carries conviction and inspires profound sympathy. Wassermann's treatment of the theme of *Caspar Hauser* came from his heart. (p. 102)

Christian Wahnschaffe [is] well-known to English and American readers under the title *The World's Illusion*. . . . [The] author states that the fundamental idea of the novel is religious, and that it is based on a modernization of the theme of Francis of Assisi. . . .

Christian, the principal character, is portrayed as a young man of great charm and fascinating personality. As the son of a millionaire manufacturer he lives a life of luxury, is admired by friends, and is able to gratify every desire. In a society of elegance his associates are aristocrats, idlers, men of the world and women of easy virtue. But various experiences gradually open his eyes to the seriousness of life, to human distress and suffering; he gives up his wealth and social position, and lives among wretched social outcasts, sympathizing with them in their need, appealing to the good in them, and bringing it to the fore. Eventually, he takes leave from the vain world of his youth to disappear in the service of sufferers who are in need of kindness and respectful understanding rather than censure and condemnation. This central theme is presented against a varied, colorful, vivid background of great breadth. (p. 157)

The wide range of events, the varied background, the shifting of the stage from country to country, and the large number of characters from different social strata combine to give *Christian Wahnschaffe* an international rather than a German atmosphere. The range of characters extends from titled aristocrats, captains of industry and rich European social idlers to criminals and prostitutes.

Some of these numerous personages have but little bearing on the central theme of the novel. The fundamental unity of the lengthy narrative lies in the principal character Christian, to whom all others stand in some relation at one time or another. In some instances this relation is intimate; in others it is merely through association in the different social strata that he frequents.

The novel is divided into two parts of almost equal length. The first of these bears the name of Eva Sorel, the beautiful dancer and selfish adventuress who toys with the destinies of men and peoples. The second is named after Ruth Hofmann, a lovable, poor Jewish student who serves her fellows with innate kindness. The first half is staged in the atmosphere of vast wealth and luxury; by way of contrast much of the second has a background of squalor, ugliness and vice. Division of chapters into short, numbered sections facilitates transfer from one strand of the broad narrative to another, and a shift of emphasis to other persons or groups. Various strands of the narrative have their own independent existence, but they touch here and there when members of one group come in contact with those of another. (pp. 159-60)

In keeping with the easy breadth of the story, its tempo is, on the whole, somewhat leisurely. Anecdotes are inserted, letters and newspaper reports are interspersed; incidental episodes and lengthy conversations frequently retard the flow of events. Although a tense situation accelerates the tempo now and then, Wassermann, contrary to his practice in some other novels, makes little attempt to build up suspense in this narrative. Because of the limited amount of natural, convincing tension the reader is rarely irked even when the scene shifts suddenly from one country, group or individual to another.

Over against the broad background of characters and happenings the fundamental element is the revelation of Christian's character as it is seen in the process of change. Wassermann has presented his central figure in great detail and from a variety of angles. The reader sees him through the eyes of women who are fascinated by different qualities. . . . Even hostile critics like his brother Wolfgang and ungrateful Amadeus Voss admit

that he has an irresistible, captivating personality. Their disparaging criticisms prove to be false. The worshipful love of his mother, and the respectful affection he inspires in his father, whose views are quite opposed to his own, reveal Christian in another light. . . . Wassermann repeatedly portrays the effect of Christian's radiant personality on the humble and needy, and on those who have been engulfed in a life of vice. (pp. 161-62)

Wassermann again resorts to his favorite device of contrast in the portrayal of character. Christian is contrasted with his father and brother, the successful magnates who think in terms of wealth, position and power; with Crammon, whose only care is to enjoy life to the full; with the petty morbidity and warped personality of Amadeus Voss, and the vain superficiality of the actor Edgar Lorm. In addition, there is sharp contrast between Christian's own attitudes as they are revealed at the beginning and at the end of the novel. The change which takes place in him is presented in great detail through his thoughts, acts, associates and relations to others. Much of the characterization is given by description. (p. 162)

With careful planning, which is obvious enough, Wassermann presents a series of incidents that gradually arouse Christian from his idle indifference to awareness of human suffering, want and degradation. (p. 163)

In *Christian Wahnschaffe* Wassermann drew a broad picture of life that includes various strata of society and touches on numerous problems. (p. 173)

It is apparent that Wassermann was under the influence of the broad panorama of social life found in the novels of Tolstoi and Dostoievski. But in *Christian Wahnschaffe* there are too many traces of conscious creation out of surcharged imagination rather than from a reality in which the author was entirely at home. This accounts for repeated failure to portray incidents in such a manner as to make them a complete experience for others. Much of the portrayal of extravagant social life of the idle rich seems like a mere fiction of the author's fancy and like an attempt at escape from his early poverty. Although he has a remarkable faculty for making unusual situations seem plausible, there are times when he imposes too heavy a strain on the reader's imagination and when visions become vapid. The desire to draw highly individualized characters, far removed from the typical aspects of human behavior, brings him dangerously close to caricature in the portrayal of Amadeus Voss.

Much of the atmosphere of *Christian Wahnschaffe,* the glaring contrasts, violent changes, flaming passions, and turgid diction savor of strained artifice. (pp. 173-74)

Wassermann yields too readily to the temptation to use the devices of the lurid novel with its melodramatic situations, sudden, unforeseen developments, theatrical effects, glaring contrast, incendiarism, the artificial piling up of incident to build up a violent climax, strained situations, exaggerations, characters that are close to caricature, lavish wealth of incident, turgidity of style, perverse eroticism, and sensationalism. Too frequently he uses these devices without refining them. His cardinal weakness is lack of refined taste rather than seriousness of purpose. (p. 175)

In spite of obvious weaknesses *Christian Wahnschaffe* is grand in conception. Although it lacks the compelling warmth of simplicity it was prompted by a spirit of noble humanitarianism. Of significance are the wide range of life and characters, contrasts and numerous gradations in human behavior, acts of generosity in an environment of depravity, social need, responsiveness to a spirit of kindness and understanding, the striving to alleviate human suffering, affirmation of life, and faith in mankind rather than despairing pessimism. . . . Despite a tendency to overdraw, Wassermann has made of Christian an impressive figure whose spirit of self-surrender stands out all the more sharply because his relatives and friends of old are quite unable to understand his changed attitude toward life. (p. 176)

Wassermann regarded his existence as a Jew, and particularly his existence as a German Jew, as the most problematical part of his life. He thought of himself as a German and as a Jew, one as much as the other, and he felt that the two were indissoluble. In writing [*Mein Weg als Deutscher und Jude*] his stated intention was not to indulge in argument, vindication and indictment, but rather to present his own experience. He was impelled to seek an understanding of the discord, the misunderstandings, tragedy, contradictions, strife and sufferings which ran through his life and his activities, and of which, in the course of time, he became ever more painfully conscious. (p. 356)

The problem of the Jew in an Aryan society is so involved and perplexing that it is doubtful whether an Aryan can fully sense and interpret it. (p. 357)

When treated as a creature of a lower order, the youth sought in vain to determine the fundamental difference between Jews and Germans. He was not a believer in the Jewish faith, and, moreover, his ancestors had lived in Germany for centuries. . . . He felt that the German language was the breath of life to him. . . . Was not this, Wassermann asked, more important than a formal confession of faith, than an ingrown prejudice, than a mere entry on a register? There are Jews and Jews, said Wassermann in an argument with a young Gentile of his age, as he pointed out that generalizations are fraught with distorted, perverted, partisan judgments. Why not view the Jews humanly as individuals?

Wassermann subsequently concluded that the tragedy in the life of the Jew is the union in his soul of a sense of superiority and the feeling of being under a stigma of inferiority; his life is spent in conflict between these two emotional currents. Wassermann asserted that from a simple, human standpoint the fact of being a Jew means neither superiority nor inferiority. And the idea of being chosen is justified only within temporal limits. Moreover, he maintained that the individual, but not a people, may be elect. (pp. 358-59)

Germans, according to Wassermann, want to hate the Jews; they want a scapegoat. So it has been for centuries, says he; the menacing embitterment of the masses has always been diverted into the convenient channel of antisemitism. And he holds that a non-German has no conception of the heartbreaking position of the German Jew. His indictment of the Germans is that they lack imagination, freedom and kindness, and that there must be some essential defect if a people so constantly practises injustice, sows discord, and heaps up mountains of hatred. (pp. 360-61)

Despairingly Wassermann states that all efforts on the part of the Jew to effect conciliation and understanding are in vain. Whether he lives or dies for the Germans, the Jew still remains a Jew. Although Wassermann comes very close to indicting a whole nation he admits that there are Germans who disapprove of and revolt at antisemitism. Yet even they, even the best of

them, says he, cannot fully understand the predicament, the suffering and the problem of the Jew. What can they do? he asks. His reply is: Snatch the whip from savage tyrants.

Conversely he asks: What is the Jew to do when sacrifices are disregarded and friendly advances are misconstrued? The only hope lies in endeavoring to open and take possession of men's hearts, and in renouncing ignoble things. (p. 361)

As he beholds the persecution prompted by individuals Wassermann wonders why one individual can work so much evil, whereas one man alone can accomplish so little good.

Wassermann has another, a final word to say . . . by way of reply to those who dispute his essential identification with the country of his birth, those who take the blood in his veins as a pretext for relegating him to an inferior category of mankind. They forget, he says, that the landscape in which a person lives enters into his very being and becomes a part of him. They forget that what race and blood make of us is unfathomable, while the inner influence of climate, landscape, language and environment is demonstrable and palpable.

The dominant idea of his writings, asserts Wassermann, is that of justice; he had revelled in the dream that he might set an example and a precedent which would be natural in a rational and decent world, yet that, he sadly concludes, had proven to be impossible. Justice, social justice, he regards as a distant goal, almost beyond human reach, yet he remains convinced that humanity must continue to strive for it, if mankind is not to perish. His own bitter experience as a German and a Jew served to weld him more closely to those who suffer injustice. (p. 362)

> *John C. Blankenagel, in his* The Writings of Jakob Wassermann *(copyright 1942 by The Christopher Publishing House), The Christopher Publishing House, 1942, 410 p.*

JOHN C. BLANKENAGEL (essay date 1946)

Jakob Wassermann has frequently been sharply criticized because of alleged fondness for portraying singular, erratic, grotesque individuals. In his character drawing he has been charged with violent sensationalism, fantastic exaggeration, unseemly striving for effect, and morbid insistence on irrational, discordant, convulsive, bizarre, and abnormal traits. (p. 3)

Numerous direct pronouncements by Wassermann bear out his strong conviction that human nature is complex, incalculable, and intangible, and that human conduct consequently is bound to seem contradictory and unpredictable. Thus, in attempting to ascertain the motives for Luise Dercum's singular conduct [in *Laudin und die Seinen*] he says that in the last analysis beings like her are unfathomable and incalculable. He regards Baron von Andergast [in *Der Fall Maurizius*] as so strange, so inscrutable and inaccessible, that language no longer serves as a means of communication with him. In *Christoph Columbus* Wasserman refers again and again to the mysteriousness, complexity, and ambiguity of Columbus' unintelligible being. The human soul, says he, in commenting on the discoverer of America, is a dark labyrinth, inhabited by terrifying specters, the very association with other people necessitates constant revision of one's judgments of them. (p. 4)

In view of the large number of such direct comments by Wassermann it is not surprising that his characters make similar pronouncements. . . . In *Das Gänsemännchen* Gertrud Jordan's life is regarded by her father as impenetrable; to Daniel Nothafft, Lenore Jordan seems mysterious, Lenore does not understand Daniel, Philippine Schimmelweis is incomprehensible to Daniel. (p. 5)

This conviction of the mysteriousness and complexity of human nature manifests itself in various ways in Wassermann's narratives. Characters sometimes are baffling and ambiguous because they are revealed bit by bit through incident and situation rather than by detailed, direct description when they are first introduced. Sometimes Wassermann sketches characters with a certain vagueness that suggests mystery. This is true of Renate Fuchs. . . . Renate is baffling because her ignorance of life and of herself, and her vaguely sensed desires make her conduct difficult to predict. Impressionable and responding readily to suggestion, she seems to pass through life like a somnambulist. Much of her conduct and experience is presented by implication rather than in concrete detail. (p. 7)

Wassermann believed there are areas of the soul which cannot be explored, but now and then, as if by a sudden flash, traits hitherto unknown or unnoticed, are revealed. It is then that the necessity for revising judgments about one's fellows becomes imperative. . . . Like Schnitzler, Wassermann occasionally presented characters who have lived side by side for years, taking each other for granted, yet without really knowing each other. But some day a word or deed reveals traits and attitudes hitherto unknown, yet of deep significance. (pp. 9-10)

Wassermann frequently regarded incalculability of conduct as rooted in dual personality which, under certain conditions, may permit a character to do one thing just as well as the opposite. Thus in *Der goldene Spiegel* Borsati says that most people are empty vessels which under certain circumstances can be filled with the basest greed or with fiery zeal for a great cause. In the foreword to *Deutsche Charaktere und Begebenheiten* Wassermann maintains that nobody can be more petty, shallow, and devoid of light than the German when he is dominated by the drab humdrum of everyday routine; but no one can be greater when inexorable necessity confronts him, or when great, stirring events inspire him. Waremme, in *Der Fall Maurizius* says to Etzel that Shakespeare might just as well have become an ingenious robber à la Robin Hood as a dramatist, Lenin might just as well have become a chief of the Czar's secret police as the destroyer of a system, for our outward activity depends upon a profound dualism that is implanted in us like the sense of left and right. (p. 11)

One of the perplexing questions which Wassermann pondered was that of transformation of character and change of identity. It is raised for the first time in *Laudin und die Seinen* by Laudin, who desires to escape from troublesome, defective reality. . . . Laudin feels that, like other professional men, he is pursuing a course which he cannot leave arbitrarily, and that he is moving toward a goal which he can no longer determine. Volition is mere delusion; there is nothing but compulsion. He wonders whether it is impossible to cast off the old, weary, worn-out man and become new. As Laudin looks back on his past, he can no longer remember just when the longing arose in him to be what he is not. But the emotional experience that gave rise to the desire is ever before him: boredom with his own being, with that steely, immutable, abiding something known as character. (pp. 11-12)

But although Wassermann was convinced that character as such is virtually immutable, he asserted that there are new contacts which may exert a determining influence on the life of the individual. They may give life a new direction and new content without, however, entailing fundamental change of character or identity. They serve to call out dormant traits or possibilities which have never before had full chance of realization. (pp. 12-13)

Joseph Kerkhoven says there are meetings which renew men. Commenting directly in *Joseph Kerkhovens dritte Existenz,* Wassermann declared it is a peculiarity of human beings that they need a new contact, if renewal is to take place; they tend to wear each other smooth, and they grow indolent in the intimacy of pleasant association. Even so simple a drudge as Janach is lifted out of the dull lethargy of her routine experience at the sight of a woman to whom she becomes abjectly devoted. Her subsequent desire to do something unprecedented for her idol was an impulse, says Wassermann, a desire whose mystery was deeper than all thinking; no one, he adds, knows enough about human nature to fathom this. (pp. 13-14)

As might be expected, Wassermann's fondness for delving into the mysteries of the subconscious is manifest in his frequent narration of dreams. In *Sara Malcolm* he states that the decisive experiences of human life are not enacted in the world of the concrete and the tangible; the profoundest things to which the souls of mortals are attached are haze and dreams. Cajetan, in *Der goldene Spiegel,* maintains that there are real experiences which are almost like dreams. Lamberg, who agrees with him, adds that most happenings in this world partake of the nature of dreams. One need never recall dreams, and yet one is full of them, says he; indeed, what we call soul is perhaps merely the play of dreams within us, and the thinner the wall is that separates man from his dreams, the more soulful man becomes. (pp. 16-17)

In keeping with his insistence on the mysterious complexity and incomprehensibility of human nature, Wassermann again and again claimed to be ignorant of the motives that prompt his characters. . . . [In] *Der Fall Maurizius* Wassermann asserts that it would be futile to try to disclose the complicated chain of thought which prompted Etzel to disturb his grandmother's peace of mind. He wonders why, on a certain occasion, Etzel is in such good humor, he states that it is not quite clear why Baron von Andergast enters a room at a specific moment, he endeavors to guess why Andergast goes to the penitentiary to see Maurizius, at certain junctures he claims it is not easy to determine what goes on in Maurizius' mind, and what his emotions are. (pp. 17-18)

Such devices serve to place responsibility on the reader for interpreting unusual manifestations of character. The author indulges in conjectures about the motives of his personages as if to demonstrate that he himself is forced to speculate on what goes on in their hearts and minds. (p. 19)

It now becomes apparent that much of the alleged exaggeration, contradictoriness, discordance, and grotesqueness of Wassermann's characters grew out of his conviction of the inherent complexity and infinite variety of human beings. But instead of deliberately striving for melodramatic effect, he was endeavoring to delve into the hidden recesses of man's involved, irrational nature, and to probe more deeply into the mysteries of human conduct and relationships. He used glaring contrasts, striking situations, sensational incidents, violent conflicts between persons, and sudden unforeseen developments as a means of bringing out highly individualized traits of character. . . . Because of Wassermann's emphasis on irrational, unpredictable, and incalculable behavior, his characters sometimes appear to be shadowy figments of the author's imagination. They are often seen through his eyes rather than as vigorous beings who exist independently of him. Frequently they fail to impress the reader as creatures of flesh and blood, products of German soil and tradition, at home in a world of concrete reality. (pp. 19-20)

> *John C. Blankenagel, "Jakob Wassermann's Conception and Treatment of Character," in* Modern Language Quarterly *(© 1946 University of Washington), Vol. 7, No. 1, March, 1946, pp. 3-20.*

HENRY MILLER   (essay date 1959)

[*The Maurizius Case*] is based on a famous miscarriage of justice which, like our own Sacco and Vanzetti case, had repercussions throughout the world.

With that fullness and depth of insight which distinguishes the creative artist, Wassermann expanded the theme to a degree which gives it the magnitude of a Greek tragedy.

Etzel Andergast, a boy of sixteen, plays a singular and most disturbing role in this drama of conflicting passions. It is through his fanatical belief in, and pursuit of, justice that the condemned Maurizius, who has already spent eighteen years in the penitentiary, is released.

The book offers no balm, no solutions. All the characters involved in the affair suffer tragic fates with the exception of Anna Jahn who had committed the murder for which Maurizius was unjustly punished. Etzel, the hero of the book, is definitely blighted by his experience. Maurizius himself, shortly after his release, commits suicide. Etzel's father who as prosecuting attorney was responsible for the injustice done Maurizius, goes completely to pieces.

A grim and grisly story shot through with lurid flashes which reveal the heights and depths of the German soul awaiting the advent of a leader who will bring about its dissolution. (p. 5)

The story opens eighteen years after the famous crime has occurred. We follow the incidents leading up to the shooting of Maurizius' wife through the eyes and lips of the various characters—Maurizius himself, Waremme-Warschauer, old man Maurizius, and others. Everything hinges on the false testimony of Waremme, the close friend of Maurizius. Who did the shooting remains a mystery until almost the end.

The boy Etzel, who is obsessed with Maurizius' innocence, seems to be motivated by a higher sense of duty and justice than his inflexible father who, in his personification of the law, takes on the proportions of a monster. But in reality, though the boy is unaware of it, his chivalrous deed is prompted by a spirit of vengeance: he wants to destroy his father's work. In the back of his mind is the obscure feeling that his father is responsible for everything. Deprived of his mother's affection he turns into an avenger. In seeking the liberation of the innocent victim, Maurizius, he is unconsciously seeking the libration of his mother, who, like the prisoner, has been made to suffer unjustly at the hands of the father.

The theme of the story is not alone the inadequacy of human justice, but the impossibility of ever attaining it. All the characters testify to this, in their own way, even that "Pillar of Justice," Herr Von Andergast himself. Justice, it appears, is merely a pretext for inflicting cruelty upon the weaker one. Justice, divorced from love, becomes revenge.

Around the figure of Maurizius, whose weakness of character precipitates the crime, revolves as in a whirlpool a veritable constellation of figures whose motives, passions and interests are inextricably interwoven. The question of justice, which is the underlying theme, is practically smothered by the wealth of subsidiary drama engendered by what might be called fate. (pp. 5-6)

[As] the story unrolls, as the dark strands in which the crime is knotted are undone, each of the characters involved, from the iron-clad prosecuting attorney down to the weak Maurizius, even to Etzel the deliverer, are seen to be equally guilty. Society itself is arraigned: we are all stained with guilt. That seems to be the author's point of view. And therefore there can be no solution, no end to crime, no end to man's injustice to man except through the tedious and painful increase of understanding, sympathy and forbearance. In trying to fix the responsibility, in searching for the motive and the cause of crime, we sink into a bog from which there seems to be no possibility of extrication. All is illusion and delusion. There is no firm ground on which to stand. Crime and punishment are rooted in the very fibre of man's being. Even the lovers of justice—perhaps especially the lovers of justice—stand condemned before the higher tribunal of love and mercy.

Little Etzel Andergast, whom Wassermann pictures as a David battling against Goliath, and who seems the very incarnation of justice, is a figure worthy of the most serious study. As the sequels to *The Maurizius Case* reveal [*Doctor Kerkhoven* and *Kerkhoven's Third Existence*], the author seems to have been baffled by his own creation. He died before he was able to give us the final book which would expose the full nature of this enigmatic creature. There is something monstrous about Etzel Andergast: he is fascinatingly attractive and repellent at the same time. (pp. 10-11)

In the second volume of the trilogy Wassermann gives a rather spacious summary of *The Maurizius Case* in order to throw further light on the baleful character of young Etzel Andergast. Once again we shudderingly observe the effect upon Etzel of the news that Maurizius was pardoned. "Can they throw him (Maurizius) a wretched alms instead of paying him what they owe?" he screams. At this point the world becomes for Etzel chaos; there is no longer sense to anything. Justice, he believes, demands not that Maurizius be pardoned but that the State, or society, beg forgiveness of Maurizius. What Etzel expected was not only complete exoneration of the innocent victim but the exposure and punishment of all who contributed to the man's needless persecution and suffering. (p. 11)

Why this ingrained, obsessive hatred of injustice in a mere lad of sixteen? Obviously only one reason: the loss of his mother's affection. Who is responsible for this deprivation? Obviously that tyrannical monster, his father. . . . The amputation, then, of the boy's affective nature made him, so to speak, lop-sided. Unable to give expression to the normal instinct to love, he could assert himself only through rebellion. To save Maurizius is tantamount to saving himself. Impossible to live in this world as an amputated, crippled being: the father's crippling influence must be destroyed, injustice must be wiped out.

Needless to point out, we have here the crux of Etzel's dilemma. The fight against injustice, the desire to overthrow the established order, the very instinct to rebel, so fundamental in the human heart, is revealed as ambivalence. What Etzel demands, what the world of suffering million demands, though they know not how to voice it, is not the elimination of injustice nor even the establishment of justice, but the satisfaction of a hunger more imperious still, because it is a positive and a permanent need of the human heart. This is nothing less than the condition of love. Whoever is denied his rightful share of love is crippled and thwarted in the very roots of his being. (pp. 13-14)

Though [the Etzels of this world] pose as the saviours of the innocent, they succeed only in bringing about destruction. They are the self-deluders, and the very passion which wings them on their way is a poison to the world. This seems to be the gist of Wassermann's message. (p. 14)

I made mention earlier of the fact that the author had stressed the connection, in Etzel's mind, between the prisoner Maurizius and the mother whom he had been robbed of. I come back to this again. To liberate the mother! It has only one meaning for me—to liberate his own power to love. To save Maurizius really means nothing. Etzel never knew the man. He is for him, as he was for his father before him, "a case." He is the excuse which Etzel needs in order to revenge himself upon the father. Why does he fly into such a rage when he learns that Maurizius has been released? (The release meant only that he had been "pardoned.") Had the man's freedom been his sole concern, as it would be if one acted from ordinary human motives, he would have been happy, even if not entirely satisfied with his father's actions or motives. But it is not Maurizius he is concerned about—it is this abstract thing, justice. Is it, however? Is it justice he wants in fullest measure, or is it that lost twin of justice—love? It is he, Etzel, who has been cheated, not Maurizius.

It is in the second volume of the trilogy, ***Dr. Kerkhoven***, that we perceive with horror how distorted has become Etzel's love. Here begins the enigma of another triangular affair, one in which Etzel behaves very much like the Maurizius whom he tried to succor. I mean, to use Wassermann's own words when referring to Maurizius, that "he is not man enough to give up one thing or the other." "Renunciation," says Wassermann, "requires a clear recognition; but such half-baked characters (as Maurizius) are seldom clearly aware of their situations or of their secret impulses; they prefer to flounder about in uncertainty."

The difference between the two cases, however, is that Maurizius was merely a "weak" man. Etzel is positively evil. He has not only betrayed himself, he betrays his saviour, Dr. Kerkhoven. It is interesting to note, in this connection, that the woman in the triangle, Marie, the wife of Kerkhoven, is a woman somewhat older than Etzel. Can it be that in his twisted brain she has replaced the mother whose love he was denied? His passion for Marie is uncontrollable. There is something desperate about it, something almost ferocious. Etzel, like Maurizius, is to be pitied, not censured. We know that he does not wish to dishonour the man he reveres, Dr. Kerkhoven. He is compelled to do so by forces beyond him. But he is guilty, we feel, and towards Maurizius we are not inclined to feel thus. His acts are all violations, that is it. He makes us recoil in horror and dismay. He makes even that great, saintly figure, Kerkhoven, lust to murder. And we applaud Kerkhoven. We know that he is justified in wishing Etzel dead. (pp. 21-2)

Henry Miller, in his Maurizius Forever *(copyright 1959 by Henry Miller), Fridtjof-Karla Publications, 1959, 62 p.*

PAUL M. ALLEN (essay date 1972)

For more than a century and a quarter the life-story of Caspar Hauser has touched the humanitarian impulses of people in many parts of the world. This tragic, unforgettable figure of "the Child of Europe," as he was called, now appears to have been the rightful Crown Prince of Baden, son of the Grand Duchess Stephanie Beauharnais, adopted daughter of Napoleon Bonaparte and niece of the Empress Josephine. . . .

However, it is Caspar Hauser's *spiritual significance* which towers above and beyond the multitude of things written about him in many countries and languages during his lifetime and since. And the unusual quality of Wassermann's book [*Caspar Hauser*] is attributable to the fact that something of this spiritual significance of Caspar Hauser has been intuitively grasped by the novelist, forming the life-blood and foundation-impulse of this remarkable work. (p. iii)

This significance was felt almost immediately by a number of men and women when they first came in more or less close contact with him, particularly during the first months after his "entrance" into the world. In varying degrees they were touched by there markable gentleness, the unworldliness, and most of all by what one of them characterized as "the truly sacred feeling for truth" which streamed from his whole nature.

Perhaps Gottlieb Freiherr von Tucher, in whose care Caspar Hauser was placed for a time, came very near a fundamental truth when he wrote: "Everything I have found in him, including his natural piety and freedom from self-consciousness, gives most fully the picture of the first human beings in Paradise before the Fall." (p. iv)

Most impressive of all, however, is the testimony of Caspar Hauser's first teacher, the remarkable philosopher, educator and writer, Georg Friedrich Daumer. . . . Professor Daumer recalled Caspar Hauser's love and sympathy for the sufferings of others, his unearthly innocence, his "unbelievable power of memory." His first sight of a rainbow left him speechless with joy; a sunset, the sight of a night-sky filled with stars, the magic of falling snowflakes—the wonders of nature around him—were subjects for endless hours of contemplation and pleasure. Daumer summed up this aspect of Caspar Hauser's nature: "What the glance, wearied by custom cannot perceive, appears to his eye as though fresh from the hand of God." Disclaiming any exaggeration or romanticism in his words, Daumer recalled Caspar Hauser's nature as "the heavenly appearance of an angelic-beautiful, an angelic-pure soul."

How then did it come about that all this which spoke the language of the incarnation upon earth of a soul so innocent, so pure in nature that it even seemed not to have experienced the Fall of man, began to fade until—even among those persons most well-disposed toward him—grave doubts began to arise as to the true nature of his character?

This development, as Wassermann graphically describes it in his novel, can be understood through an indication Rudolf Steiner once gave when he described earlier stages in the evolution of human consciousness, and the later role of the intellect in weakening the tremendous power of memory formerly possessed by mankind. He referred to Caspar Hauser's extraordinary power of memory, his innocence, his inborn ability to tame savage animals simply through his presence, through what he was, and—most important—his "incredible, entirely inborn truthfulness" which went more and more astray, particularly under the hands of overly-conscientious, one-sided teachers. One of these teachers once expressed himself as "scandalised that apparently Hauser has no understanding for the functional significance of the subjunctive or the rule of three." Armed with logic, Latin grammar and similar materials, these teachers pitted their strength against the obstinate spirit of one who longed ardently for truth, beauty and goodness in himself and in those around him.

The result was that as his innate longing for freedom, his remarkable powers of memory, weakened and faded under the impact of this kind of "teaching," at last "his incredible, entirely inborn truthfulness" became corrupted as well, because as Rudolf Steiner explained, "The more he nibbled, so to say, at intellectuality, the more it vanished."

Thus Caspar Hauser became an innocent victim of the coarse self-seeking, the obtuse, materialistic self-righteousness of those into whose power he had fallen. (pp. iv-vi)

Though a murderer's knife took the life of one who appeared to be simply an innocent young man in a small, Bavarian town, this deed had enormous consequences. For since that time the passing decades have shown that the destiny of Caspar Hauser has become more and more the destiny of mankind. It becomes ever clearer that had Caspar Hauser . . . been able to unfold those spiritual impulses necessary for the progressive development of mankind, the dagger plunged by Hitler into the heart of Middle Europe, with all its catastrophic consequences for humanity, might have been averted.

Nevertheless, despite this apparent failure, Rudolf Steiner pointed out that had Caspar Hauser not experienced what he did at the hands of friend and foe, finally dying a death of sacrifice, the contact between the earth and the spiritual world would have been entirely interrupted. . . .

This supra-human dimension and significance of the figure and mission of Caspar Hauser can be glimpsed through the pages of Jacob Wassermann's novel. One such moment of insight is his impressive description of the cosmic setting, the phenomena which provided the background for Caspar Hauser's funeral: "At that hour the sun and moon were to be seen in the heavens at the same time, the one in the west and the other in the east, and both their discs shone with the same leaden light."

From this one can begin to understand perhaps something of the significance of Rudolf Steiner's remark that "Everyone who connects himself with Caspar Hauser connects himself with the mission of the future." For this reason the reappearance of this novel is of outstanding importance. . . . (pp. vi-vii)

Paul M. Allen, "Foreword" (1972), In "Caspar Hauser": The Enigma of a Century by Jacob Wassermann, translated by Caroline Newton (copyright © 1973 by Rudolf Steiner Publications; reprinted by permission of Rudolf Steiner Publications, Blauvelt, N.Y.), Rudolf Steiner, 1973, pp. iii-vii.

ADDITIONAL BIBLIOGRAPHY

Blankenagel, John C. "Jakob Wassermann's *Christoph Columbus.*" *Monatshefte* XXIX, No. 5 (May 1937): 201-07.
    Examination of Wassermann's biography of Christopher Columbus, which the critic states is a "convincing portrait," but also too moralizing and lacking historical perspective.

Blankenagel, John C. "Human Fears in Jakob Wassermann's Writings." *The Journal of English and Germanic Philology* L, No. 3 (July 1951): 309-19.
    Argues that fear is a recurring motif in Wassermann's work.

Mann, Thomas. *Letters of Thomas Mann: 1889-1955,* edited by Richard and Clara Winston. New York: Alfred A. Knopf, 1971, 690 p.*
    Contains a letter discussing Wassermann's death. Mann remarks that: "A certain empty pomp and solemn verbosity in his work sometimes forced a smile from me, although I recognized that as a fashioner of plots he was far greater than I am."

Porterfield, Allen W. "Behind the Scenes with Wassermann." *The Journal of English and Germanic Philology* L, No. 2 (April 1951): 141-55.
    Textual criticism of the novel *Ulrike Woytich* by one of Wassermann's many translators.

Regensteiner, Henry. "The Obsessive Personality in Jakob Wassermann's Novel *Der Fall Maurizius.*" *Literature and Psychology* XIV, Nos. 3 & 4 (Summer-Fall 1964): 106-15.
    Comparison of the obsessive personalities of many characters in *Der Fall Maurizius* with certain biographical facts of Wassermann's youth.

Schneider, Franz. "Browning's *The Ring and the Book* and Wassermann's *Der Fall Maurizius.*" *Modern Language Notes* XLVIII, No. 1 (January 1933): 16-17.*
    Brief discussion of the similarities in technique and structure between *The Ring and the Book* and *Der Fall Maurizius.*

Steiner, Arpad. "William H. Prescott and Jakob Wassermann." *The Journal of English and Germanic Philology* XXIV, No. 4 (October 1925): 555-59.*
    Accuses Wassermann of plagiarizing Prescott's *Conquest of Peru* in the three short stories making up *Der Geist des Pilgers.*

H(erbert) G(eorge) Wells

1866-1946

(Also wrote under pseudonyms of Sosthenes Smith, Walter Glockenhammer, and Reginald Bliss) English novelist, short story writer, essayist, historian, autobiographer, and critic.

Wells is best known today, along with Jules Verne, as the father of modern science fiction, and as a utopian idealist who correctly foretold an era of chemical warfare, atomic weaponry, and world wars.

Wells was born into a lower middle-class Cockney family in Bromley, Kent, and acquired an interest in literature while lying bedridden with a broken leg at the age of seven. He studied zoology at the Royal College of Science under Thomas H. Huxley, who sparked Wells's beliefs in social as well as biological evolution. After college he wrote a biology textbook and contributed short stories to several magazines. The serialization of *The Time Machine* brought his first substantial critical notice—he was declared a genius by the commentator for the *Review of Reviews*—and launched his career.

As his popularity grew, Wells met Arnold Bennett, Joseph Conrad, and other authors of the day, with whom he exchanged criticism and opinions on the art of writing. Their works and his experience as literary critic under Frank Harris at *The Saturday Review* shaped his own theories of good writing. Wells quarreled with many of his literary friends. For example, when his longtime friend Henry James criticized Wells for his journalistic style, Wells retaliated by caricaturing James in *Boon*.

Wells's works fall into four broad and overlapping categories. The writing of science fiction and science fantasies, such as *The Invisible Man, The Island of Dr. Moreau,* and *The War of the Worlds,* occupied the earliest part of his career and brought him great popular and critical attention. Wells's literary reputation rests on these early works, many of which have since been adapted for television, radio, and the cinema. His humorous Dickensian novels followed those first books; they involve lower middle-class characters living at odds with their constricting cultures, and include *Kipps* and *The History of Mr. Polly.* The publication of the latter in 1910, according to many critics, marked the end of Wells's literary ascension. His novels had by that time taken on a pedantic nature, and many of his subsequent works, such as *Joan and Peter* and *The World of William Clissold,* examined social problems in a didactic way that drew the scorn of major critics of the day. However, *Tono-Bungay,* Wells's ambitious treatment of societal and political decay, stands out among his social novels and serves as a bridge between his character and expository fiction. From the turn of the century until his death, he wrote sociopolitical criticism and prognostications. Of these, *The War That Will End War* gave the world, through its title, a cynical catch-phrase for obstinate naiveté in the face of human corruptness—a criticism of much of Wells's social fiction and nonfiction.

A socialist, Wells joined the Fabian Society but left the group after fighting a long, unsuccessful war of wit and rhetoric over the society's policies with prominent Fabian George Bernard Shaw. World War I and its aftermath upset Wells's optimistic

vision of humankind and coming Utopia. In response he wrote *The Outline of History,* in which he attempted to evidence the commonality of the origins and histories of the world's peoples. Wells wrote and lectured on the betterment of society through education, in which scientific innovation played a key role, but in his last years he grew increasingly despondent about the future. His last book, *Mind at the End of Its Tether,* bleakly foretells the end of all things. Yet Wells's celebrated advocacy of free love and socialism and his attacks on what he considered the stifling constraints of society liberalized Western thought throughout the twentieth century.

For all his concern over the future of the human race, critics remain uncertain as to whether Wells actually believed that humanity itself could be improved. There is evidence that, as the Time Traveller of his first major work suggests, Wells believed that even if life is indeed a meaningless, dualistic struggle, "it remains for us to live as though it were not so."

PRINCIPAL WORKS

The Time Machine   (novel)   1895
The Wonderful Visit   (novel)   1895

522

The Island of Dr. Moreau   (novel) 1896
The Wheels of Chance   (novel) 1896
The Invisible Man   (novel) 1897
The War of the Worlds (novel) 1898
When the Sleeper Wakes   (novel) 1899
Love and Mr. Lewisham   (novel) 1900
Anticipations of the Reaction of Mechanical and Scientific Progress upon Human Life and Thought   (essay) 1901
The First Men in the Moon   (novel) 1901
Mankind in the Making   (essays) 1903
The Food of the Gods, and How It Came to Earth   (novel) 1904
Kipps   (novel) 1905
A Modern Utopia   (essay) 1905
In the Days of the Comet   (novel) 1906
New Worlds for Old   (essay) 1908
The War in the Air and Particularly How Mr. Bert Smallways Fared While It Lasted   (novel) 1908
Ann Veronica   (novel) 1909
Tono-Bungay   (novel) 1909
The History of Mr. Polly   (novel) 1910
The Country of the Blind, and Other Stories   (short stories) 1911
The New Machiavelli   (novel) 1911
Marriage   (novel) 1912
The War That Will End War   (essays) 1914
The Wife of Sir Isaac Harmon   (novel) 1914
The World Set Free   (novel) 1914
Boon [as Reginald Bliss]   (sketches) 1915
The Research Magnificent   (novel) 1915
Mr. Britling Sees It Through   (novel) 1916
The Soul of a Bishop   (novel) 1917
Joan and Peter   (novel) 1918
The Outline of History. 2 vols.   (history)   1919-20
The Undying Fire   (novel) 1919
Men Like Gods   (novel) 1923
The World of William Clissold   (novel) 1926
Mr. Blettsworthy on Rampole Island   (novel) 1928
The Open Conspiracy   (essay) 1928
The Bulpington of Blup   (novel) 1932
The Shape of Things to Come   (essays) 1933
Experiment in Autobiography. 2 vols.   (autobiography) 1934
The Croquet Player   (novel) 1936
Guide to the New World   (essay) 1941
Mind at the End of Its Tether   (essay) 1945

[RICHARD HOLT HUTTON]   (essay date 1895)

[In **"The Time Machine"** a] speculative mechanician is supposed to have discovered that the "fourth dimension," concerning which mathematicians have speculated, is Time, and that with a little ingenuity a man may travel in Time as well as in Space. . . . Mr. Wells supposes his Time-traveller to travel forward from A.D. 1895 to A.D. 802,701, and to make acquaintance with the people inhabiting the valley of the Thames. . . . [He finds that the gentle, pleasure-loving] race of the surface of the earth has improved away all its dangers and embarrassments . . . [while] the race of the underworld,—the race which has originally sprung from the mining popu-

lation,—has developed a great dread of light, and a power of vision which can work and carry on all its great engineering operations with a minimum of light. At the same time, by inheriting a state of servitude it has also inherited a cruel contempt for its former masters, who can now resist its attacks only by congregating in crowds during the hours of darkness, for in the daylight, or even in the bright moonlight, they are safe from the attacks of their former serfs. . . . This is, we take it, the warning which Mr. Wells intends to give:—'Above all things avoid sinking into a condition of satisfied ease; avoid a soft and languid serenity; even evil passions which involve continuous effort, are not so absolutely deadly as the temperament of languid and harmless playfulness.' We have no doubt that, so far as Mr. Wells goes, his warning is wise. But we have little fear that the languid, ease-loving, and serene temperament will ever paralyse the human race after the manner he supposes, even though there may be at present some temporary signs of the growth of the appetite for mere amusement.

In the first place, Mr. Wells assumes, what is well-nigh impossible, that the growth of the pleasure-loving temperament would not itself prevent that victory over physical obstacles to enjoyment on which he founds his dream. (p. 42)

In the next place Mr. Wells's fancy ignores the conspicuous fact that man's nature needs a great deal of hard work to keep it in order at all, and that no class of men or women are so dissatisfied with their own internal condition as those who are least disciplined by the necessity for industry. . . . There would be no tranquility or serenity at all in any population for which there were not hard tasks and great duties. . . . Yet Mr. Wells's fanciful and lively dream is well worth reading, if only because it will draw attention to the great moral and religious factors in human nature which he appears to ignore. (pp. 42-3)

> [Richard Holt Hutton,] "In A.D. 802,701," in The Spectator (© 1895 by The Spectator), Vol. 75, No. 3498, July 13, 1895, pp. 41-3.

JOSEPH CONRAD   (essay date 1898)

[Frankly—**The Invisible Man**] is uncommonly fine. One can always *see* a lot in your work—there is always a "beyond" to your books—but into this (with due regard to theme and length) you've managed to put an amazing quantity of effects. If it just misses being tremendous, it is because you didn't make it so—and if you didn't, there isn't a man in England who could. As to b— furriners they ain't in it at all.

I suppose you'll have the common decency to believe me when I tell you I am always powerfully impressed by your work. . . . And if you want to know what impresses me it is to see how you contrive to give over humanity into the clutches of the Impossible and yet manage to keep it down (or up) to its humanity, to its flesh, blood, sorrow, folly. *That* is the achievement! In this little book you do it with an appalling completeness. I'll not insist on the felicity of incident. This must be obvious even to yourself. Three of us have been reading the book . . . and we have been tracking with delight the cunning method of your logic. It is masterly—it is ironic—it is very relentless—and it is very true. We all three (the two others are no fools) place the *I.M.* above the *War of the Worlds*. Whether we are right—and if so why—I am not sure, and cannot tell. I fancy the book is more strictly human, and thus your diabolical psychology plants its points right into a man's bowels. To me the *W. of the W.* has less of that sinister air of truth that arrests the reader in reflexion at the turn of the page so often in the *I.M.* In reading this last, one is touched by the anguish of it as by something that any day may happen to oneself. It is a great triumph for you. (pp. 259-60)

> *Joseph Conrad, in his letter to H. G. Wells on December 4, 1898, in* Joseph Conrad: Life and Letters, Vol I *by Joseph Conrad, edited by G. Jean-Aubry (copyright © 1926, 1927 by Doubleday, Page & Company; copyright renewed, 1954, by Mme. Jean-Aubry Drovet; reprinted by permission of Hope Leresche & Sayle; as agents for the Estate of Joseph Conrad), Doubleday, 1927, pp. 259-60.*

JULES VERNE (essay date 1904)

There is an author whose work has appealed to me very strongly from an imaginative stand-point, and whose books I have followed with considerable interest. I allude to Mr. H. G. Wells. Some of my friends have suggested to me that his work is on somewhat similar lines to my own, but here, I think, they err. I consider him, as a purely imaginative writer, to be deserving of very high praise, but our methods are entirely different. I have always made a point in my romances of basing my so-called inventions upon a groundwork of actual fact, and of using in their construction methods and materials which are not entirely without the pale of contemporary engineering skill and knowledge.

Take, for instance, the case of the 'Nautilus.' This, when carefully considered, is a submarine mechanism about which there is nothing wholly extraordinary, nor beyond the bounds of actual scientific knowledge. (pp. 669-70)

The creations of Mr. Wells, on the other hand, belong unreservedly to an age and degree of scientific knowledge far removed from the present, though I will not say entirely beyond the limits of the possible. Not only does he evolve his constructions entirely from the realm of imagination, but he also evolves the materials of which he builds them. See, for example, his story **'The First Men in the Moon.'** You will remember that here he introduces an entirely new anti-gravitational substance, to whose mode of preparation or actual chemical composition we are not given the slightest clue, nor does a reference to our present scientific knowledge enable us for a moment to predict a method by which such a result might be achieved. In **'The War of the Worlds,'** again, a work for which I confess I have a great admiration, one is left entirely in the dark as to what kind of creatures the Martians really are, or in what manner they produce the wonderful heat ray with which they work such terrible havoc on their assailants.

[In saying this], I am casting no disparagement on Mr. Wells' methods; on the contrary, I have the highest respect for his imaginative genius. I am merely contrasting our two styles and pointing out the fundamental difference which exists between them, and I wish you clearly to understand that I express no opinion on the superiority of either the one or the other. (p. 670)

> *Jules Verne, "Jules Verne at Home," in an interview with Gordon Jones, in* Temple Bar, *Vol.CXXIX, No. 523, June, 1904, pp. 664-71.*

GILBERT K. CHESTERTON (essay date 1905)

[One] purely modern man has emerged in the strictly modern decades who does carry into our world the clear personal simplicity of the old world of science. One man of genius we have

who is an artist, but who was a man of science, and who seems to be marked above all things with . . . great scientific humility. I mean Mr. H. G. Wells. (p. 73)

The most interesting thing about Mr. H. G. Wells is that he is the only one of his many brilliant contemporaries who has not stopped growing. One can lie awake at night and hear him grow. Of this growth the most evident manifestation is indeed a gradual change of opinions; but it is no mere change of opinions. It is not a perpetual leaping from one position to another like that of Mr. George Moore. It is a quite continuous advance along a quite solid road in a quite definable direction. But the chief proof that it is not a piece of fickleness and vanity is the fact that it has been upon the whole in advance from more startling opinions to more humdrum opinions. It has been even in some sense an advance from unconventional opinions to conventional opinions. This fact fixes Mr. Wells's honesty and proves him to be no *poseur*. . . . He has come to the most dreadful conclusion a literary man can come to, the conclusion that the ordinary view is the right one. It is only the last and wildest kind of courage that can stand on a tower before ten thousand people and tell them that twice two is four.

Mr. H. G. Wells exists at present in a gay and exhilarating progress of conservativism. (pp. 74-6)

[Mr. Wells] is not quite clear enough of the narrower scientific outlook to see that there are some things which actually ought not to be scientific. He is still slightly affected with the great scientific fallacy; I mean the habit of beginning not with the human soul, which is the first thing a man learns about, but with some one such thing as protoplasm, which is about the last. The one defect in his splendid mental equipment is that he does not sufficiently allow for the stuff or material of men. In [**"A Modern Utopia"**] he says, for instance, that a chief point of the Utopia will be a disbelief in original sin. If he had begun with the human soul—that is, if he had begun on himself—he would have found original sin almost the first thing to be believed in. He would have found, to put the matter shortly, that a permanent possibility of selfishness arises from the mere fact of having a self, and not from any accidents of education or ill-treatment. And the weakness of all Utopias is this, that they take the greatest difficulty of man and assume it to be overcome, and then give an elaborate account of the overcoming of the smaller ones. (pp. 78-9)

But I think the main mistake of Mr. Wells's philosophy is a somewhat deeper one, one that he expresses in a very entertaining manner in the introductory part of the new Utopia. His philosophy in some sense amounts to a denial of the possibility of philosophy itself. At least, he maintains that there are no secure and reliable ideas upon which we can rest with a final mental satisfaction. (pp. 80-1)

It *cannot* be true that there is nothing abiding in what we know. For if that were so we should not know it all and should not call it knowledge. Our mental state may be very different from that of somebody else some thousands of years back; but it cannot be entirely different, or else we should not be conscious of a difference. Mr. Wells must surely realize the first and simplest of the paradoxes that sit by the springs of truth. (pp. 81-2)

"The Food of the Gods" is, like Mr. Bernard Shaw's play, in essence a study of the Superman idea. And it lies, I think, even through the veil of a half-pantomimic allegory, open to the same intellectual attack. We cannot be expected to have any regard for a great creature if he does not in any manner conform to our standards. For unless he passes our standard of greatness we cannot even call him great. Nietzsche summed up all that is interesting in the Superman idea when he said, "Man is a thing which has to be surpassed." But the very word "surpass" implies the existence of a standard common to us and the thing surpassing us. (pp. 84-5)

"The Food of the Gods" is the tale of "Jack the Giant-Killer" told from the point of view of the giant. This has not, I think, been done before in literature; but I have little doubt that the psychological substance of it existed in fact. (p. 85)

The old and correct story of Jack the Giant-Killer is simply the whole story of man; if it were understood we should need no Bibles or histories. But the modern world in particular does not seem to understand it at all. The modern world, like Mr. Wells, is on the side of the giants; the safest place, and therefore the meanest and the most prosaic. (p. 87)

I recur for a last word to Jack the Giant-Killer. I have dwelt on this matter of Mr. Wells and the giants, not because it is specially prominent in his mind; I know that the Superman does not bulk so large in his cosmos as in that of Mr. Bernard Shaw. I have dwelt on it for the opposite reason; because this heresy of immoral hero-worship has taken, I think, a slighter hold of him, and may perhaps still be prevented from perverting one of the best thinkers of the day. (p. 89)

> *Gilbert K. Chesterton, "Mr. H. G. Wells and the Giants," in his* Heretics, *(reprinted in Canada by permission of The Bodley Head), John Lane Company, 1905 (and reprinted by Books for Libraries Press, 1970, pp. 68-91).*

HENRY JAMES   (essay date 1905)

Let me tell you . . . simply, that [*A Modern Utopia* and *Kipps*] have left me prostrate with admiration, and that you are, for me, more than ever, the most interesting "literary man" of your generation—in fact, the only interesting one. These things do you, to my sense, the highest honour, and I am lost in amazement at the diversity of your genius. As in everything you do (and especially in [*Anticipations, Mankind in the Making,* and *A Modern Utopia*]), it is the quality of your intellect that primarily (in the Utopia) obsesses me and reduces me—to that degree that even the colossal dimensions of your Cheek (pardon the term that I don't in the least invidiously apply) fails to break the spell. Indeed your Cheek is positively the very sign and stamp of your genius, valuable to-day, as you possess it, beyond any other instrument or vehicle, so that when I say it doesn't break the charm, I probably mean that it largely constitutes it, or constitutes the force: which is the force of an irony that no one else among us begins to have—so that we are starving, in our enormities and fatuities, for a sacred satirist (the satirist *with* irony—as poor dear old Thackeray was the satirist without it,) and you come, admirably, to save us. . . . Cheeky, cheeky, cheeky is *any* young-man-at-Sandgate's offered Plan for the life of Man—but so far from thinking that a disqualification of your book, I think it is positively what makes the performance heroic. I hold, with you, that it is only by our each contributing Utopias (the cheekier the better) that anything will come, and I think there is nothing in the book truer and happier than your speaking of this struggle of the rare yearning individual toward that suggestion as one of the certain assistances of the future. Meantime you set a magnificent example—of *caring*, of feeling, of seeing, above all, and of suffering from, and with, the shockingly sick ac-

tuality of things. Your epilogue tag in italics strikes me as of the highest, of an irresistible and touching beauty. Bravo, bravo, my dear Wells!

And now, coming to *Kipps*, what am I to say about *Kipps* but that I am ready, that I am compelled, utterly to *drivel* about him? He is not so much a masterpiece as a mere born gem—you having, I know not how, taken a header straight down into mysterious depths of observation and knowledge, I know not which and where, and come up again with this rounded pearl of the diver. But of course you know yourself how immitigably the thing is done—it is of such a brilliancy of *true* truth. I really think that you have done, at this time of day, two particular things for the first time of their doing among us. (1) You have written the first closely and intimately, the first intelligently and consistently ironic or satiric novel. In everything else there has always been the sentimental or conventional interference, the interference of which Thackeray is full. (2) You have for the very first time treated the English "lower middle" class, etc., without the picturesque, the grotesque, the fantastic and romantic interference of which Dickens, e.g., is so misleadingly, of which even George Eliot is so deviatingly, full. You have handled its vulgarity in so scientific and historic a spirit, and seen the whole thing all in its *own* strong light. And then the book has throughout such extraordinary life; everyone in it, without exception, and every piece and part of it, is so vivid and sharp and *raw*. Kipps himself is a diamond of the first water, from start to finish, exquisite and radiant; Coote is consummate, Chitterlow magnificent (the whole first evening with Chitterlow perhaps the most brilliant thing in the book—unless that glory be reserved for the way the entire matter of the *shop* is done, including the admirable image of the boss. (pp. 39-40)

> *Henry James, in his letter to H. G. Wells on November 19, 1905, in* The Letters of Henry James, *edited by Percy Lubbock (abridged by permission of Charles Scribner's Sons; copyright © 1920 by Charles Scribner's Sons; copyright renewed 1948 by William James and Margaret James Porter), Scribner's, 1920, pp. 37-41.*

REBECCA WEST   (essay date 1912)

Mr. Wells' mannerisms are more infuriating than ever in *Marriage*. One knows at once that Marjorie is speaking in a crisis of wedded chastity when she says at regular intervals, 'Oh, my dear! . . . Oh, my dear!' or at moments of ecstasy, 'Oh, my *dear!* My *dear!*' For Mr. Wells' heroines who are loving under legal difficulties say 'My man!' or 'Master!' Of course, he is the Old Maid among novelists; even the sex obsession that lay clotted on *Ann Veronica* and *The New Machiavelli* like cold white sauce was merely Old Maids' mania, the reaction towards the flesh of a mind too long absorbed in airships and colloids. The Cranford-like charm of his slow, spinsterish gossip made *Kipps* the delightful book it was; but it palls when, page after page, and chapter after chapter, one is told how to furnish a house. . . .

And then there is Mr. Wells' habit of spluttering at his enemies. He splutters less in *Marriage* than in *The New Machiavelli*, but in the hospital atmosphere of the latter, where a soul-sick man drugged himself with the ether of sex, it seemed less offensive than in this purer, brighter air. Altiora Bailey reappears as Aunt Plessington, and makes a speech that would be perfect but for its omission of the phrase, 'the morass of destitution.' There is a devilishly realistic picture of the English humorist whose parodies have drawn tears from the sentient part of the nation for the last twenty years. It is great fun, but at times it is ill-mannered. It offends one beyond measure in the last impressive pages of the book. (pp. 203-04)

[There] is no author who has a more religious faith; nor one who speaks in gospel with such a tongue of flame. His first sin lies in pretending that Marjorie, that fair, fleshy being who at forty would look rather like a cow—and the resemblance would have a spiritual significance—is the normal woman; and the second lies in his remedy, which Marjorie discovers in a period of spiritual turmoil brought on by debt. 'A woman gives herself to a man out of love, and remains clinging parasitically to him out of necessity. Was there no way of evading that necessity?' she meditates sentimentally. 'Suppose the community kept all its women, suppose all property in homes and furnishings and children vested in them. . . . Then every woman would be a princess to the man she loved.' The cheek of it! (p. 207)

> Rebecca West, '"Marriage'," in Freewoman, *Vol. II, No. 44, September 12, 1912 (and reprinted in* H. G. Wells: The Critical Heritage, *edited by Patrick Parrinder, Routledge & Kegan Paul, 1972, pp. 203-08).*

HENRY JAMES (essay date 1914)

[Mr. Wells,] a novelist very much as Lord Bacon was a philosopher, affects us as taking all knowledge for his province and as inspiring in us to the very highest degree the confidence enjoyed by himself—enjoyed, we feel, with a breadth with which it has been given no one of his fellow-craftsmen to enjoy anything. If confidence alone could lead utterly captive we should all be huddled in a bunch at Mr. Wells's heels—which is indeed where we *are* abjectly gathered so far as that force does operate. It is literally Mr. Wells's own mind, and the experience of his own mind, incessant and extraordinarily various, extraordinarily reflective, even with all sorts of conditions made, of whatever he may expose it to, that forms the reservoir tapped by him, that constitutes his provision of grounds of interest. It is, by our thinking, in his power to name to us, as a preliminary, more of these grounds than all his contemporaries put together, and even to exceed any competitor, without exception, in the way of suggesting that, thick as he may seem to lay them, they remain yet only contributive, are not in themselves full expression but are designed strictly to subserve it, that this extraordinary writer's spell resides. When full expression, the expression of some particular truth, seemed to lapse in this or that of his earlier novels (we speak not here of his shorter things, for the most part delightfully wanton and exempt,) it was but by a hand's breadth, so that if we didn't inveterately quite know what he intended we yet always felt sufficiently that *he* knew. The particular intentions of such matters as **"Kipps,"** as **"Tono-Bungay,"** as **"Ann Veronica,"** so swarmed about us, in their blinding, bluffing vivacity, that the mere sum of them might have been taken for a sense over and above which it was graceless to inquire. The more this author learns and learns, or at any rate knows and knows, however, the greater is this impression of his holding it good enough for us, such as we are, that he shall but turn out his mind and its contents upon us by any free familiar gesture and as from a high window forever open—an entertainment as copious surely as any occasion should demand, at least till we have more intelligibly expressed our title to a better. Such things as **"The New Machiavelli," "Marriage," "The Pas-**

sionate Friends," are so very much more attestations of the presence of material than attestations of an interest in the use of it that we ask ourselves again and again why so fondly neglected a state of leakage comes not to be fatal to *any* provision of quantity, or even to stores more specially selected for the ordeal than Mr. Wells's always strike us as being. Is not the pang of witnessed waste in fact great just in proportion as we are touched by our author's fine offhandedness as to the value of the stores, about which he can for the time make us believe what he will? so that, to take an example susceptible of brief statement, we wince at a certain quite peculiarly gratuitous sacrifice to the casual in **"Marriage"** very much as at seeing some fine and indispensable little part of a mechanism slip through profane fingers and lose itself. Who does not remember what ensues after a little upon the aviational descent of the hero of the fiction just named into the garden occupied, in company with her parents, by the young lady with whom he is to fall in love?—and this even though the whole opening scene so constituted, with all the comedy hares its function appears to be to start, remains with its back squarely turned, esthetically speaking, to the quarter in which the picture develops. The point for our mortification is that by one of the first steps in this development, the first impression on him having been made, the hero accidentally meets the heroine, of a summer eventide, in a leafy lane which supplies them with the happiest occasion to pursue their acquaintance—or in other words supplies the author with the liveliest consciousness (as we at least feel it should have been) that just so the relation between the pair, its seed already sown and the fact of that bringing about all that is still to come, pushes aside whatever veil and steps forth into life. To show it step forth and affirm itself as a relation, what is this but the interesting function of the whole passage, on the performance of which what follows is to hang?—and yet who can say that when the ostensible sequence *is* presented, and our young lady, encountered again by her stirred swain, under cover of night, in a favouring wood, is at once encompassed by his arms and pressed to his lips and heart (for celebration thus of their third meeting) we do not assist at a well-nigh heartbreaking miscarriage of "effect"? We see effect, invoked in vain, simply stand off unconcerned; effect not having been at all consulted in advance she is not to be secured on such terms. And her presence would so have redounded—perfectly punctual creature as she is on a made appointment and a clear understanding—to the advantage of all concerned. The bearing of the young man's act is all in our having begun to conceive it as possible, begun even to desire it, in the light of what has preceded; therefore if the participants have *not* been shown us as on the way to it, nor the question of it made beautifully to tremble for us in the air, its happiest connections fail and we but stare at it mystified. The instance is undoubtedly trifling, but in the infinite complex of such things resides for a work of art the shy virtue, shy at least till wooed forth, of the whole susceptibility. The case of Mr. Wells might take us much further—such remarks as there would be to make, say, on such a question as the due understanding, on the part of **"The Passionate Friends"** (not as associated persons but as a composed picture), of what that composition is specifically *about* and where, for treatment of this interest, it undertakes to find its centre: all of which, we are willing however to grant, falls away before the large assurance and incorrigible levity with which this adventurer carries his lapses— far more of an adventurer as he is than any other of the company. The composition, as we have called it, heaven saving the mark, is simply at any and every moment "about" Mr. Wells's general adventure; which is quite enough while it preserves, as we trust it will long continue to do, its present robust pitch. (pp. 333-35)

Henry James, "The New Novel" (1914), in his Notes on Novelists, with Some Other Notes *(copyright 1914 by Charles Scribner's Sons; copyright renewed 1942 by Henry James; reprinted with the permission of Charles Scribner's Sons), Scribner's, 1914, pp. 314-61.**

VIRGINIA WOOLF   (essay date 1918)

The moralists of the nursery used to denounce a sin which went by the name of "talking at", and was rendered the more expressive by the little stress which always fell upon the "at", as if to signify the stabbing, jabbing, pinpricking nature of the sin itself. . . . This old crime of the nursery is very apt to blossom afresh in people of mature age when they sit down to write a novel. It blossoms often as unconsciously as we may suppose that the pearl blossoms in the breast of the oyster. Unfortunately for art, though providentially for the moralist, the pearl that is produced by this little grain of rancour is almost invariably a sham one.

In the early chapters of *Joan and Peter* there are a great many scenes and characters which seem to have been secreted round some sharp-edged grain which fate has lodged in the sensitive substance of Mr Wells's brain. Lady Charlotte Sydenham had some such origin; so, too, had Miss Phoebe Stubland; the sketch of Arthur Stubland was due to a disturbance of the kind, and certainly the schoolmistresses of St George and the Venerable Bede had no other begetter. We catch ourselves wondering whether Mr Wells is any longer aware of the grotesque aspect of these figures of his, burdened as they are with the most pernicious or typical views of their decade, humped and loaded with them so that they can hardly waddle across the stage without coming painfully to grief. The conscientious reader will try to refer these burlesques to some such abstraction as the Anglican Church, or the vagaries of aimless and impulsive modernism in the eighteen-nineties; but if you are indolent you will be inclined to give up playing your part in the game of illusion, and to trifle with idle speculations as to the idiosyncrasies of Mr Wells. But soon the very crudeness of the satire leads us to make a distinction, and directly we are satisfied of its truth our irritation is spent and our interest aroused. Mr. Wells is not irritated with these people personally, or he would have taken more pains to annoy them; he is irritated with the things they represent. Indeed, he has been so much irritated that he has almost forgotten the individual. He is sore and angry and exaggerated and abusive because the waste, the stupidity, the senility of our educational system have afflicted him as men are, for the most part, afflicted only by their personal calamities. He possesses the queer power of understanding that "the only wrongs that really matter to mankind are the undramatic general wrongs", and of feeling them dramatically, as if they had wronged him individually. Here, he says, we have two children endowed with everything that the world most needs, and let us see what the world will make of them. What education have we to offer them? What are we able to teach them about the three great questions of sex and State and religion? First, he gluts his rage upon Lady Charlotte and Miss Phoebe Stubland, much to the detriment of the book, and then the matter is seriously taken in hand by Mr Oswald Stubland. . . . [As he rages Mr. Wells] throws off the trammels of fiction as lightly as he would throw off a coat in running a race. The ideas come pouring in whether he speaks them in

his own person or lets Oswald have them, or quotes them from real books and living authorities, or invents and derides some who are not altogether imaginary. He does not mind what material he uses so long as it will stick in its place and is roughly of the shape and colour he wants. Fiction, you can imagine him saying, must take care of itself; and to some extent fiction does take care of itself. No one, at any rate, can make an inquiry of this sort so vivid, so pressing, so teeming and sprouting with suggestions and ideas and possibilities as he does; indeed, when he checks himself and exclaims, "But it is high time that Joan and Peter came back into the narrative," we want to cry out, "Don't bother about Joan and Peter. Go on talking about education." We have an uneasy suspicion that Joan and Peter will not be nearly so interesting as Mr Wells's ideas about their education and their destiny. But, after all, we know that Mr Wells is quite right when he says that it is time to bring them in. He would be shirking the most difficult part of his task if he left them out.

Like his own Oswald Stubland, Mr Wells "belongs to that minority of Englishmen who think systematically, whose ideas join on". He has "built up a sort of philosophy for himself", by which he does try his problems and with which he fits in such new ideas as come to him. He is not writing about education, but about the education of Joan and Peter. He is not isolating one of the nerves of our existence and tracing its course separately, but he is trying to give that nerve its place in the whole system and to show us the working of the entire body of human life. That is why his book attains its enormous bulk; and that is why, with all its sketchiness and crudeness and redundancy, its vast soft, billowing mass is united by a kind of coherency and has some relation to a work of art. If you could isolate the seed from which the whole fabric has sprung you would find it, we believe, to consist of a fiery passion for the rights of youth—a passion for courage, vitality, initiative, inventiveness, and all the qualities that Mr Wells likes best. And as Mr Wells can never think without making a picture of his thought, we do not have youth in the abstract, but Joan and Peter, Wilmington and Troop, Huntley and Hetty Reinhart. We have Christmas parties and dressings up and dances and night clubs and Cambridge and London and real people disguised under fictitious names, and very bright covers on the chairs and Post Impressionist pictures on the walls and advanced books upon the tables. This power of visualizing a whole world for his latest idea to grow in is the power that gives these hybrid books their continuity and vitality.

But because Mr Wells's ideas put on flesh and blood so instinctively and admirably we are able to come up close to them and look them in the face; and the result of seeing them near at hand is, as our suspicions assured us that it would be, curiously disappointing. Flesh and blood have been lavished upon them, but in crude lumps and unmodelled masses, as if the creator's hand, after moulding empires and sketching deities, had grown too large and slack and insensitive to shape the fine clay of men and women. It is curious to observe, for example, what play Mr Wells is now constrained to make with the trick of modernity. It is as if he suspected some defect in the constitution of his characters and sought to remedy it with rouge and flaxen wigs and dabs of powder, which he is in too great a hurry nowadays to fix on securely or plaster in the right places. But if Joan and Peter are merely masquerading rather clumsily at being the heirs of the ages, Mr Wells's passion for youth is no make-believe. The sacrifice, if we choose to regard it so, of his career as a novelist has been a sacrifice to the rights of youth, to the needs of the present moment, to the lives of the rising generation. He has run up his buildings to house temporary departments of the Government. But if he is one of those writers who snap their fingers in the face of the future, the roar of genuine applause which salutes every new work of his more than makes up, we are sure, for the dubious silence, and possibly the unconcealed boredom, of posterity. (pp. 90-3)

> *Virginia Woolf, "The Rights of Youth" (originally published in* The Times Literary Supplement, *No. 870, September 19, 1918), in her* Contemporary Writers *(copyright © 1965 by Leonard Woolf; reprinted by permission of Harcourt Brace Jovanovich; in Canada by the Author's Literary Estate and The Hogarth Press), The Hogarth Press, 1965, pp. 90-3.*

H. L. MENCKEN (essay date 1918)

[The] decline of Wells has been as steady as his rise was rapid. Call the roll of his books, and you will discern a progressive and unmistakable falling off. Into **"The Passionate Friends"** there crept the first downright dullness. By this time his readers had become familiar with his machinery and his materials—his elbowing suffragettes, his tea-swilling London uplifters, his smattering of quasi-science, his intellectualized adulteries, his Thackerayan asides, his text-book paragraphs, his journalistic raciness—and all these things had thus begun to lose the blush of their first charm. To help them out he heaved in larger and larger doses of theory—often diverting enough, and sometimes even persuasive, but in the long run a poor substitute for the proper ingredients of character, situation and human passion. Next came **"The Wife of Sir Isaac Harman,"** an attempt to rewrite "A Doll's House" (with a fourth act) in terms of ante-bellum 1914. The result was 500-odd pages of bosh, a flabby and tedious piece of work, Wells for the first time in the rôle of unmistakable bore. And then **"Bealby,"** with its Palais Royal jocosity, its running in and out of doors, its humor of physical collision, its reminiscences of "A Trip to China-town" and "Peck's Bad Boy." And then **"Boon,"** a heavy-witted satire, often incomprehensible, always incommoded by its disguise as a novel. And then **"The Research Magnificent"**: a poor soup from the dry bones of Nietzsche. And then **"Mr. Britling Sees It Through."** . . .

Here, for a happy moment, there seemed to be something better—almost, in fact, a recrudescence of the Wells of 1910. But that seeming was only seeming. What confused the judgment was the enormous popular success of the book. Because it presented a fifth-rate Englishman in an heroic aspect, because it sentimentalized the whole reaction of the English proletariat to the war, it offered a subtle sort of flattery to other fifth-rate Englishmen, and, *per corollary,* to Americans of corresponding degree, to wit, the second. Thus it made a great pother, and was hymned as a masterpiece. . . . But there was in the book, in point of fact, a great hollowness, and that hollowness presently begat an implosion that disposed of the shell. . . . There followed—what? **"The Soul of a Bishop,"** perhaps the worst novel ever written by a serious novelist since novel-writing began. And then—or perhaps a bit before, or simultaneously—an idiotic religious tract—a tract so utterly feeble and preposterous that even the Scotchman, William Archer, could not stomach it. And then, to make an end, came **"Joan and Peter"**—and the collapse of Wells was revealed at last in its true proportions. (pp. 23-5)

[In **"Joan and Peter"**] there is the fault that the Wells of those days, almost beyond any other fictioneer of the time, was incapable of—the fault of dismalness, of tediousness—the witless and contagious coma of the evangelist. Here, for nearly six hundred pages of fine type, he rolls on in an intellectual cloud, boring one abominably with uninteresting people, pointless situations, revelations that reveal nothing, arguments that have no appositeness, expositions that expose naught save an insatiable and torturing garrulity. Where is the old fine address of the man? Where is his sharp eye for the salient and significant in character? Where is his instinct for form, his skill at putting a story together, his hand for making it unwind itself? These things are so far gone that it becomes hard to believe that they ever existed. . . . The book is a botch from end to end, and in that botch there is not even the palliation of an arduous enterprise gallantly attempted. No inherent difficulty is visible. The story is anything but complex, and surely anything but subtle. Its badness lies wholly in the fact that the author made a mess of the writing, that his quondam cunning, once so exhilarating, was gone when he began it. (pp. 25-6)

What has slowly crippled him and perhaps disposed of him is his gradual acceptance of the theory, corrupting to the artist and scarcely less so to the man, that he is one of the Great Thinkers of his era, charged with a pregnant Message to the Younger Generation—that his ideas, rammed into enough skulls, will Save the Empire, not only from the satanic Nietzscheism of the Hindenburgs and post-Hindenburgs, but also from all those inner Weaknesses that taint and flabbergast its vitals, as the tapeworm with nineteen heads devoured Atharippus of Macedon. In brief, he suffers from a messianic delusion—and once a man begins to suffer from a messianic delusion his days as a serious artist are ended. (p. 28)

The man impinged upon us and made his first solid success, not as a merchant and banal pedagogics, not as a hawker of sociological liver-pills, but as a master of brilliant and life-like representation, an evoker of unaccustomed but none the less deep-seated emotions, a dramatist of fine imagination and highly resourceful execution. It was the stupendous drama and spectacle of modern life, and not its dubious and unintelligible lessons, that drew him from his test-tubes and guinea-pigs and made an artist of him, and to the business of that artist, once he had served his apprenticeship, he brought a vision so keen, a point of view so fresh and sane and a talent for exhibition so lively and original that he straightway conquered all of us. Nothing could exceed the sheer radiance of **"Tono-Bungay."** It is a work that glows with reality. It projects a whole epoch with unforgettable effect. It is a moving-picture conceived and arranged, not by the usual ex-bartender or chorus man, but by an extremely civilized and acute observer, alert to every detail of the surface and yet acutely aware of the internal play of forces, the essential springs, the larger, deeper lines of it. In brief, it is a work of art of the soundest merit, for it both represents accurately and interprets convincingly, and under everything is a current of feeling that coordinates and informs the whole. (pp. 29-30)

[But it] was not enough to display the life of his time with accuracy and understanding; it was not even enough to criticize it with a penetrating humor and sagacity. From the depths of his being, like some foul miasma, there arose the old, fatuous yearning to change it, to improve it, to set it right where it was wrong, to make it over according to some pattern superior to the one followed by the Lord God Jehovah. With this sinister impulse, as aberrant in an artist as a taste for legs in an archbishop, the instinct that had created **"Tono-Bungay"** and **"The New Machiavelli"** gave battle, and for a while the issue was in doubt. But with **"Marriage,"** its trend began to be apparent—and before long the evangelist was triumphant, and his bray battered the ear, and in the end there was a quite different Wells before us, and a Wells worth infinitely less than the one driven off. To-day one must put him where he has begun to put himself—not among the literary artists of English, but among the brummagem prophets of England. (pp. 30-1)

Nor are Wells' ideas, as he has so laboriously expounded them, worth the sacrifice of his old lively charm. They are, in fact, second-hand, and he often muddles them in the telling. In **"First and Last Things"** he preaches a flabby Socialism, and then, toward the end, admits frankly that it doesn't work. In **"Boon"** he erects a whole book upon an eighth-rate platitude, to wit, the platitude that English literature, in these latter times, is platitudinous—a three-cornered banality, indeed, for his own argument is a case in point, and so helps to prove what was already obvious. . . . He seems to respond to all the varying crazes and fallacies of the day; he swallows them without digesting them; he tries to substitute mere timeliness for reflection and feeling. And under all the rumble-bumble of bad ideas is the imbecile assumption of the jitney messiah at all times and everywhere: that human beings may be made over by changing the rules under which they live, that progress is a matter of intent and foresight. . . . (pp. 32-3)

What remains of Wells? There remains a little shelf of very excellent books, beginning with **"Tono-Bungay"** and ending with **"Marriage."** It is a shelf flanked on the one side by a long row of extravagant romances in the manner of Jules Verne, and on the other side by an even longer row of puerile tracts. But let us not underestimate it because it is in such uninviting company. There is on it some of the liveliest, most original, most amusing, and withal most respectable fiction that England has produced in our time. In that fiction there is a sufficient memorial to a man who, between two debauches of claptrap, had his day as an artist. (pp. 34-5)

> *H. L. Mencken, "The Late Mr. Wells" (1918), in his* Prejudices: First Series *(copyright 1919 by Alfred A. Knopf, Inc.; renewed 1947 by H. L. Mencken; reprinted by permission of Alfred A. Knopf, Inc.), Knopf, 1919, pp. 22-35.*

D. H. LAWRENCE (essay date 1926)

[*The World of William Clissold*] is simply not good enough to be called a novel. If *Tono-Bungay* is a novel, then this is not one. . . .

This first volume consists of "A Note before the Title-Page," in which we are forbidden to look on this book as anything but a novel, and especially forbidden to . . . identify the characters with any living people such as, for instance, Mr. Winston Churchill or the Countess of Oxford and Asquith; which negative command is very easy to obey, since, in this first volume, at least, there are no created characters at all: it is all words, words, words, about Socialism and Karl Marx, bankers and cave-men, money and the superman. One would welcome any old scarecrow of a character on this dreary, flinty hillside of abstract words.

The next thing is the title-page: **"The World of William Clissold: A Novel from a New Angle"**—whatever that pseudoscientific phrase may mean.

Then comes Book I: "The Frame of the Picture." (p. 346)

The frame consists of William Clissold informing us that he is an elderly gentleman of fifty-nine, and that he is going to tell us all about himself. He is . . . and always has been a somewhat scientific gentleman with an active mind, and . . . his mental activities have been more important than any other activity in his life. In short, he is not a "mere animal," he is an animal with a ferocious appetite for "ideas," and enormous thinking powers. (pp. 346-47)

Mr. Clissold, being somewhat of an amateur at making a self-portrait and framing it, has got bits of the picture stuck on to the frame, and great angular sections of the frame occupying the space where the picture should be. But patience! It is a sort of futuristic interpenetration, perhaps.

The first bit of the story is a little boy at a country house, sitting in a boat and observing the scientific phenomena of refraction and reflection. He also observes some forget-me-nots on the bank, and rather likes the look of them. So, scrambling carefully down through mud and sedges, he clutches a handful of the blue flowers, only to find his legs scratched and showing blood, from the sedges. "Oh! Oh! I cried in profound dismay. . . . Still do I remember most vividly my astonishment at the treachery of that golden, flushed, and sapphire-eyed day.—That it should turn on me!"

This "section" is called "The Treacherous Forget-me-nots." But since, after all, the forget-me-nots had never asked the boy to gather them, wherein lay the treachery?

But they represent poetry. And perhaps William Clissold means to convey that, scrambling after poetry, he scratched his legs, and fell to howling, and called the poetry treacherous.

As for a child thinking that the sapphire-eyed day had turned on him—what a dreary old-boy of a child, if he did! But it is elderly-gentleman psychology, not childish.

The story doesn't get on very fast, and is extremely sketchy. The elderly Mr. Clissold is obviously bored by it himself. (p. 347)

William Clissold, having in "The Frame" written a feeble résumé of Mr. Wells's *God the Invisible King,* proceeds in The Story, Book II, to write a much duller résumé of Mr. Wells's *Outline of History.* . . . Mr. Clissold, who holds forth against "systems," cannot help systematizing us all into a gradual and systematic uplift from the ape. There is also a complete *exposé* of Socialism and Karl Marxism and finance, and a denunciation of Communism. There is a little feeble praise of the pure scientist who does physical research in a laboratory, and a great contempt of professors and dons who lurk in holes and study history. Last, and not least, there is a contemptuous sweeping of the temple, of all financiers, bankers, and money-men: they are all unscientific, untrained semi-idiots monkeying about with things they know nothing of.

And so, rather abruptly, end of Vol. I.

Except, of course, William Clissold has been continually taking a front seat in the picture, aged fifty-nine, in the villa back of Cannes. There is a slim slip of a red-haired Clem, who ruffles the old gentleman's hair. (p. 348)

Clementina, really, sounds rather nice. What a pity *she* didn't herself write *The World of William Clissold*: it would have been a novel, then. But she wouldn't even look at the framework of that world, says Clissold. And we don't blame her.

What is the elderly gentleman doing with her at all? Is it his "racial urge," as he calls it, still going on, rather late in life? We imagine the dear little bounder saying to her: "You are the mere object of my racial urge." To which, no doubt, she murmurs in the approved Clissold style: "My King!"

But it is altogether a poor book: the effusion of a peeved elderly gentleman who has nothing to grumble at, but who peeves at everything, from Clem to the High Finance, and from God, or Mr. G., to Russian Communism. His effective self is disgruntled, his ailment is a peevish, ashy indifference to *everything,* except himself, himself as centre of the universe. There is not one gleam of sympathy with anything in all the book, and not one breath of passionate rebellion. Mr. Clissold is too successful and wealthy to rebel and too hopelessly peeved to sympathize.

What has got him into such a state of peevishness is a problem: unless it is his insistence on the Universal Mind, which he, of course exemplifies. The emotions are to him irritating aberrations. Yet even he admits that even thought must be preceded by some obscure physical happenings, some kind of confused sensation or emotion which is the necessary coarse body of thought and from which thought, living thought, arises or sublimates.

This being so, we wonder that he so insists on the Universal or racial *mind* of man, as the only hope or salvation. If the mind is fed from the obscure sensations, emotions, physical happenings inside us, if the mind is really no more than an exhalation of these, is it not obvious that without a full and subtle emotional life the mind itself must wither: or that it must turn itself into an automatic sort of grind-mill, grinding upon itself?

And in that case the superficial Clementina no doubt knows far more about the "deeps of the pond" of Mr. Clissold than that tiresome gentleman knows himself. He grinds on and on at the stale bones of sociology, while his actual living goes to pieces, falls into a state of irritable peevishness which makes his "mental autobiography" tiresome. (pp. 349-50)

So far, anyhow, this work is not a novel, because it contains none of the passionate and emotional reactions which are at the root of all thought, and which must be conveyed in a novel. This book is all chewed-up newspaper, and chewed-up scientific reports, like a mouse's nest. (p. 350)

> *D. H. Lawrence, "Reviews of Books: 'The World of William Clissold'" (originally published under a different title, in* Calendar of Modern Letters, *Vol. 3, No. 3, October, 1926), in* Phoenix: The Posthumous Papers of D. H. Lawrence, *edited by Edward D. McDonald (copyright 1936 by Frieda Lawrence; copyright renewed © 1964 by the Estate of the late Frieda Lawrence Ravagli; reprinted by permission of Viking Penguin Inc.), Viking Penguin, 1936, pp. 346-50.*

HILAIRE BELLOC (essay date 1926)

At the outset of my task [criticizing Mr. Wells's *Outline of History*] it behoves me to set forth the great talents with which Mr. Wells has been endowed by Almighty God, and especially the talents suitable to the writer of general history. For, indeed, he seemed from his earlier works admirably fitted for writing a general outline of history, and would, by the consent of all, have been thought apt for the task—had he not undertaken it.

First, he writes very clearly; he practises an excellent economy in the use of words. This, for popular exposition, is essential; and he never fails in it. He never lapses into verbosity. He is direct, simple, clear.

Next, he possesses a sense of time. Now in history nothing is more valuable. Within his lights, within the measure of his limited instruction, he does see *time* in right scale; and that is so rare in any historian that one cannot welcome it too warmly.

Next, we should remark that Mr. Wells has (as his works of fiction amply show) a strong power of making the image he has framed in his own mind arise in the mind of his reader. This is, indeed, his chief talent.

It is a talent extremely rare: the very essential of good imaginative writing, but of particular importance in historical writing. For History, as the great Michelet finely put it, should be a resurrection of the flesh. Were I engaged upon a critique of Mr. Wells's more permanent literary claims I would dilate on this: for such a gift is of quite exceptional power in him. None of our contemporaries possesses it in anything like the same degree. But I am not concerned here with his style, and must reluctantly leave it. . . .

But much more important than these advantages which he possesses for a writing of an Outline of History is his sincerity. (p. 2)

I put his sincerity thus last in this category of his advantages for writing History, because it is the chief. He is conspicuously and naively sincere. This good quality is apparent in every line of the work as it first appeared. It is equally apparent in the first part of the new revised edition. He does really believe from the bottom of his heart all that he read in the textbooks of his youth. He does really and from the bottom of his heart believe that the little world he knows is the whole world; and that his doctrines of goodwill, vague thinking, loose loving, and the rest—all soaked in the local atmosphere of his life—may be the salvation of mankind. (pp. 2-3)

Greatly as I admire Mr. Wells's scientific romances, and have always admired them, I am compelled to use exact terms in this criticism. I cannot do otherwise, because the truth of History is a sacred thing—the most sacred next to the truths of Religion. If History is falsely written, the reader not warned of it obtains a distorted view of human action and comes to misunderstand all the most essential things of life, including Religion itself; and Mr. Wells's History is obviously and fatally distorted through Provincialism. (pp. 4-5)

The moment he is on a thing that is not of his own religion and social experience he rejects it or blunders on it. I shall [mention but one example]. . . . This is Mr. Wells's hopelessly provincial attitude towards the fragmentary record of the Gospels. He can only think of the events recorded as though they were taking place in the time and place he himself has known—they took place, as a fact, in the first century and in the Roman Empire. He imagines them taking place in a world where the supernatural elements of the story could only have been introduced gradually and after the death of the founder; whereas, in point of fact, the atmosphere of that time was in every class of society especially apt to the reception of the supernatural. There was scepticism among them—but the scepticism of society in the first century was not like our scepticism and—quite apart from the question whether such a state of mind were wise or unwise—the men of the first century accepted the

Thaumaturge and expected the marvellous in connection with religion.

The next disadvantage which I find in Mr. Wells for the writing of an outline of History is one which he has developed somewhat late in his life, which is more and more warping his writing as a whole, and which is quite fatal to any attempt at History. This is his entertaining unreasoning reactions which one may now without exaggeration term rabid.

These reactions have a common root. They are all provoked by anything *traditional.* It is *Tradition,* its usage and Nobility which irks our author. Lineage offends him, and whatever is venerable and great.

He suffers these reactions against the Gentry—especially the Gentry of his own country—against soldiers, great military characters in history, against certain contemporaries of his, but, most of all, against the Catholic Church. To be thus provoked to action by others—not to direct one's pen of one's own initiative, but to have it jerked into action by the strength of another—is weakening to all authors, but it is death to the historian. For History, of all forms of writing, most demands a general and balanced action of the mind, free from all control save that of a calm, inward judgment. (pp. 5-6)

Now these disadvantages taken together have ruined the book. Had they not done so, I should have taken for Catholic readers a different line. . . . [But as the book stands] I can say to my readers: "Mr. Wells's sketch of History is not insincere in spirit; it is simply out of drawing from lack of common instruction. He has not kept abreast of the modern scientific and historical work. He has not followed the general thought of Europe and America in matter of physical science. While, in history proper, he was never taught to appreciate the part played by Latin and Greek culture, and never even introduced to the history of the early Church. . . ." (p. 8)

> *Hilaire Belloc, in his introduction to his* A Companion to Mr. Wells's "Outline of History" *(reprinted by permission of Sheed & Ward Ltd.) Sheed & Ward, 1926 (and reprinted by Ecclesiastical Supply Association, 1927), pp. 1-8.*

PATRICK BRAYBROOKE   (essay date 1929)

It must not be thought that because Wells is an ardent reformer he is also of necessity a gloomy onlooker at human activities. Life to him has much of amusement in it. His characters can achieve the double cleverness of roaring with laughter and making the reader roar with laughter also. Wells does not make his characters amusing, for they are themselves amusing. It is the truest form of humour. It is this ability to see the funny side of things that has probably prevented the deep pessimism of Hardy from entering into Wells' work. His humour is the leaven which, as it were, keeps the whole thing human. Yet, broadly speaking, the whole modern world appears to Wells as a gigantic mix-up in which no one is able quite to sort himself out. (p. 74)

At the present day Wells almost more than any other living novelist uses the novel for the propagation of a non-academic but nevertheless ambitious philosophy. Very generally speaking his prophetic novels appear to indicate that mankind has no idea of the possibilities of science. He then goes on to formulate the opinion that people are severely cramped by industrial conditions and that many of them, if not most, chafe at the conditions in which they find themselves. His most up

to date fiction has veered between considerations concerning a new kind of theology and gibes and blows at the present political system. As a sociologist Wells is full out for a Utopia. The general lines of it seem to be a kind of socialism with no very marked religious basis. He points the way to the coming of supermen and it seems as though the word super will indicate with almost vulgar straightforwardness that these supermen will be physically bigger than the race that has gone before. Probably this is Wells' essential weakness that he postulates advancement through the combination of size and quality, a combination which seems to me to be founded on a false complementary couple. Wells is more discontented than gloomy; such a position does not indicate a doctrine of despair, for discontent is more often than not potential activity. His interest in humanity is absolutely sincere; he evidently wishes that the fifteen hundred million inhabitants who happen to be alive shall find for themselves fifteen hundred million congenial spheres of existence so that the sum of energy belched forth from these fifteen hundred million people shall be the most efficient in result. Such, in a word, would seem to be his ideal of Utopia. (p. 75)

> *Patrick Braybrooke, "H. G. Wells," in his* Philosophies in Modern Fiction, *The C. W. Daniel Company Ltd., 1929 (and reprinted by Books for Libraries, Inc., 1965), pp. 71-6.*

H. G. WELLS   (essay date 1934)

[In] my hands the Novel proved like a blanket too small for the bed and when I tried to pull it over to cover my tossing conflict of ideas, I found I had to abandon questions of individuation. I never got "all life within the scope of the novel." (What a phrase! Who could?)

In the criticism of [the early twentieth century] there was a certain confusion between this new spreading out of the interest of the novel to issues of custom and political and social change, and the entirely more limited "Novel with a Purpose" of the earlier nineteenth century. . . . A much closer approximation to the spread-out novel I was advocating is the propaganda novel. But I have always resented having my novels called propaganda novels, because it seems to me the word propaganda should be confined to the definite service of some organized party, church or doctrine. It implies direction from outside. If at times I have been inclined to thrust views upon my readers, they were at any rate my own views and put forward without any strategic aim. (p. 417)

[Regarding] *Marriage,* the story tells how masculine intellectual interest met feminine spending and what ensued. Trafford is not so much a solid man as a scientific intelligence caught in the meshes of love, and Marjorie Pope's zest in buying and arrangement is emphasized to the exclusion of any minor tricks and turns. But the argument of the book would not have stood out, if there had been any such tricks and turns. Marjorie's father is an intrusion of character drawing who really had no business in the book at all. Mr. Magnet also is a slightly malicious irrelevance; the humourless speech he makes in London on humour is, for example, transcribed verbatim from a reported speech by a distinguished contemporary.

Indisputably the writing is scamped in places. It could have been just as light and much better done. But that would have taken more time than I could afford. I do not mean by that I could have earned less money and been a more conscientious writer, though that consideration very probably came in, but

I mean that I had very many things to say and that if I could say one of them in such a way as to get my point over to the reader I did not worry much about finish. The fastidious critic might object, but the general reader to whom I addressed myself cared no more for finish and fundamental veracity about the secondary things of behaviour than I. I did not want to sweep under the mat for crumbs of characterization, nor did he want me to do so. What we wanted was a ventilation of the point at issue.

It required some years and a number of such experiments and essays in statement . . . , before I got it really clear in my own mind that I was feeling my way towards something outside any established formula for the novel altogether. In the established novel, objective through and through, the characteristic exterior reactions of the character were everything and the conflicts and changes of ideas within his brain were ignored. . . . But I was becoming more and more interested in the interior conflict, this controversial matter stewing and fermenting in all our brains, and its ventilation in action. There is no satisfactory device I knew for exhibiting a train of reasoning in a character unless a set of ideas similar to those upon which the character thinks exists already in the reader's mind. . . . I could not see how, if we were to grapple with new ideas, a sort of argument with the reader, an explanation of the theory that is being exhibited, could be avoided. I began therefore to make my characters indulge in impossible explicit monologues and duologues. As early as 1902, Chatteris in the *Sea Lady* talks a good deal more than is natural. (pp. 417-19)

By 1919, in *The Undying Fire,* I was at last fully aware of what I was doing and I took a new line. I realized I had been trying to revive the Dialogue in a narrative form. I was not so much expanding the novel as getting right out of it. *The Undying Fire* is that great Hebrew imitation of the Platonic Dialogue, the Book of Job, frankly modernized. The arrangement of the ancient book is followed very closely; the speakers even to their names are recognizably the same. (p. 419)

My experimentation with what I may call the Dialogue Novel, was only one of the directions in which I have wandered away from the uncongenial limitations of the novel proper. The plain fact is that I have never been willing to respect these limitations or to accept the Novel as an art form. *Mr. Britling Sees It Through* is a circumstantial story, but it ends in Dialogue and Monologue. *Joan and Peter* . . . again starts respectably in large novel form and becomes dialogue only towards the end. It is as shamelessly unfinished as a Gothic cathedral. . . . *The World of William Clissold* . . . again is quite unorthodox in shape and approach. It is an attempt to present a thesis upon contemporary life and social development, in the form of a fictitious autobiography. . . . The main strand of the earlier novels reappears in this, the perplexity of the man with general ideas and a strong constructive impulse when he finds that the women he meets do not enter into this stream of motive, but, except for the odd concluding "book," this obsession of so much of my fiction sits lightly here because of the predominance of economic and political questioning. (pp. 420-21)

The Autocracy of Mr. Parham . . . is a rather boisterous caricature not of the personality but of the imaginations of a modern British imperialist of the university type. It might have been dedicated to Mr. L. S. Amery. It amuses me still, but few people share my liking. Reality has outdone fiction since and [Sir Oswald Ernald] Mosley fooling it in the Albert Hall with his black shirts . . . makes Parham's great dream-meeting there seem preposterously sane and sound. *Men Like Gods*

frankly caricatures some prominent contemporaries. Another breach of established literary standards with which, in spite of its very tepid reception, I am mainly content, was *Mr. Blettsworthy on Rampole Island*. . . . The gist of Rampole Island is a caricature-portrait of the whole human world. (pp. 421-22)

Exhaustive character study is an adult occupation, a philosophical occupation. So much of my life has been a prolonged and enlarged adolescence, an encounter with the world in general, that the observation of character began to play a leading part in it only in my later years. It was necessary for me to reconstruct the frame in which individual lives as a whole had to be lived, before I could concentrate upon any of the individual problems of fitting them into this frame. I am taking more interest now in individuality than ever I did before. As mankind settles down into the security of that modern world-state with which contemporary life is in labour, as men's minds escape more and more from the harsh urgencies and feelings of a primary struggle, as the conception of the modern world-state becomes the common basis of their education and the frame of their conduct, the discussion of primary issues will abate and the analysis of individual difference again become a dominating interest. But then surely people will be less round-about in their approach to expression and the subterfuge of fiction will not be so imperative as it is to-day.

Our restraints upon the written discussion of living people are antiquated. Why should David Low say practically what he likes about actual people with his pencil, while I must declare every character in a novel is fictitious? So I am disposed to question whether the Novel will have any great importance in the intellectual life of the future because I believe we are moving towards a greater freedom of truthful comment upon individuals; if it survives I think it will become more frankly caricature-comment upon personalities and social phases than it is at present, but it seems equally probable to me that it will dwindle and die altogether and be replaced by more searching and outspoken biography and autobiography. (p. 422)

[I find this experiment in autobiography so] much more real and interesting and satisfying that I doubt if I shall ever again turn back towards The Novel. I may write a story or so more—a dialogue, an adventure or an anecdote. But I shall never come as near to a deliberate attempt upon The Novel again as I did in *Tono Bungay*. . . .

Even *Tono Bungay* was not much of a concession to Henry James and his conception of an intensified rendering of feeling and characterization as the proper business of the novelist. It was an indisputable Novel, but it was extensive rather than intensive. That is to say it presented characters only as part of a *scene*. It was planned as a social panorama in the vein of Balzac. (p. 423)

H. G. Wells, "Digression about Novels," in his Experiment in Autobiography: Discoveries and Conclusions of a Very Ordinary Brain (since 1866) *(reprinted with permission of the Estate of H. G. Wells; © 1934 by H. G. Wells), The Macmillan Company, 1934, pp. 410-24.*

FORD MADOX FORD (essay date 1937)

Mr. H. G. Wells and I must have been enemies for more years than I care now to think of. And the situation is rendered the more piquant by the fact that one or the other of us must by now be the *doyen* of English novelists—though I prefer not to discover which of us it is. At any rate in the kingdom of letters

Mr. Wells and I have been leaders of opposing forces for nearly the whole of this century. (p. 107)

What we contended was that the world could be saved only by the Arts; Mr. Wells and his followers proclaimed that that trick could only be done by Science. What, secondly, we contended was that if you intended to practice the Arts you had better know something of the mental processes of how works of art are produced; the enemy forces proclaimed, with drums a-beat and banners waving, that to be an artist of any sort you had only to put some vine leaves in your hair, take pen or brush and paper or canvas and dip pen or brush in inkstand or paint pot, and Art would flow from your fingertips. The opposing doctrines were, in short, those of Inspiration and of Conscious Art. (pp. 107-08)

The Mr. Wells that one knew of in those earliest days was the imaginative Scientist—Scientist professedly but imaginer above all things as far as we were concerned. (p. 109)

And we welcomed Science—Mr. Wells's brand of Science—with acclamations. Fairy tales are a prime necessity of the world, and he and Science were going to provide us with a perfectly new brand. And he did. And all Great London lay prostrate at his feet.

Mr. Wells struck the Empire with all the impact of Mr. Kipling. He struck everybody. He delighted the bourgeois profane with his imagination, and we intelligentsia snorted with pleasure at the idea of a Genius whom we could read without intellectual effort. And with immense admiration for his 'technique.' One could ask no more. (pp. 109-10)

And re-reading as I have just done the magnificent volume called *The Country of the Blind* I see how absolutely right we were in our appreciation. It contains all Mr. Wells's short stories. It is a book that is Literature and one that is also delight. It is a book that prophesied so far ahead that it is still modern, and one so instinct with the observations of human nature that he has picked up in the course of his snooping—so full that it is not of any date at all. It has the quality of the Greek idyll of the two women watching a procession, holding up their children and treating themselves to ha'porths of perfume from the slot machine in the temple of the Great God. (pp. 110-11)

One loved his longer books for the arbitrary conceits of *The First Men in the Moon, The Time Machine*—and above all *The Sea Lady,* which united to the conceits, inventions, quips, and brilliant images of the others a certain poetry and regret.

And then gradually one realized that more and more frequently there crept into Mr. Wells's work the note of exasperation at the futility of human life. . . . (pp. 111-12)

But after reading More's *Utopia,* Mr. Wells saw that he, he only and no other, was actually the Man Who Could See in a Country of the Blind. Life at once became clear to him and it was *Utopia* that had showed him the way. (p. 117)

So began Mr. Wells's period of Utopian Romances with their paraphernalia of Daimios and Japanese chivalry, called I think *Bushido,* and the rest of it. I am a little hazy about them because I did not read them. I was rather disgruntled and wished that Mr. Wells would not spend so much time over them. I wanted to know more about the gentlemen who threw each other onto red-hot cones or how, as in *Fear*—which is perhaps Mr. Wells's greatest piece of writing as writing—the candles went out without draughts or human agency. (p. 118)

[Mr. Wells] has had a life of many glories. And fittingly . . . and of many experiences. He was watching the world before Mass Production was so much as an invented word and, during the late era of Prosperity at Any Price, he saw his prophecies come true. And indeed, mayn't he be said to have had a certain hand in bringing about that era of hilarious thoughtlessness? For I doubt if the world would have so unquestionably accepted those irrational speciousnesses if it hadn't been for Mr. Wells with his prophecies of the triumphs of Science and the Machine. We accepted, I mean, million-wise production of everything, universal sterilization, the asphyxiation of tens of thousands, the razing from the earth of whole cities, largely because Mr. Wells had prepared our minds for those horrors. We accepted them as inevitable because that immensely read writer had told us that they were inevitable. Without that a shuddering and hypnotized world might have made a greater effort to shake off these tentacles. (pp. 121-22)

> *Ford Madox Ford, "H. G. Wells," in his* Portraits from Life *(copyright © 1936, 1937 by Ford Madox Ford; reprinted by permission of Janice Biala, as executrix to the Estate of Ford Madox Ford), Houghton Mifflin Company, 1937, pp. 107-23.*

GEORGE ORWELL (essay date 1941)

Only in the English-speaking countries was it fashionable to believe, right up to the outbreak of war, that Hitler was an unimportant lunatic and the German tanks made of cardboard. Mr. Wells, it will be seen [in *Guide to the New World*], believes something of the kind still. I do not suppose that either the bombs or the German campaign in Greece have altered his opinion. A lifelong habit of thought stands between him and an understanding of Hitler's power.

Mr. Wells, like Dickens, belongs to the non-military middle class. . . . If one looks through nearly any book that he has written in the last forty years one finds the same idea constantly recurring: the supposed antithesis between the man of science who is working towards a planned World State and the reactionary who is trying to restore a disorderly past. In novels, Utopias, essays, films, pamphlets, the antithesis crops up, always more or less the same. On the one side science, order, progress, internationalism, aeroplanes, steel, concrete, hygiene: on the other side war, nationalism, religion, monarchy, peasants, Greek professors, poets, horses. History as he sees it is a series of victories won by the scientific man over the romantic man. Now, he is probably right in assuming that a "reasonable", planned form of society, with scientists rather than witch-doctors in control, will prevail sooner or later, but that is a different matter from assuming that it is just round the corner. . . . Hitler is all the war-lords and witch-doctors in history rolled into one. Therefore, argues Wells, he is an absurdity, a ghost from the past, a creature doomed to disappear almost immediately. But unfortunately the equation of science with common sense does not really hold good. . . . Much of what Wells has imagined and worked for is physically there in Nazi Germany. The order, the planning, the State encouragement of science, the steel, the concrete, the aeroplanes, are all there, but all in the service of ideas appropriate to the Stone Age. Science is fighting on the side of superstition. But obviously it is impossible for Wells to accept this. It would contradict the world-view on which his own works are based. (pp. 142-43)

Wells is too sane to understand the modern world. The succession of lower-middle-class novels which are his greatest achievement stopped short at the other war and never really began again, and since 1920 he has squandered his talents in slaying paper dragons. But how much it is, after all, to have any talents to squander. (p. 145)

George Orwell, "Wells, Hitler and the World State" (originally published in The Horizon, Vol. IV, No. 20, August, 1941), in The Collected Essays, Journalism and Letters of George Orwell: My Country Right or Left, 1940-1943, Vol. II, edited by Sonia Orwell and Ian Angus (copyright © 1968 by Sonia Brownell Orwell; reprinted in Canada by permission of the Estate of the late George Orwell), Secker & Warburg, 1968, pp. 139-45.*

V. S. PRITCHETT (essay date 1946)

There are always fist-fights and fires in the early Wells. Above all, there are fires. They occur, as far as I remember, in all the scientific romances except *The Island of Dr. Moreau*—a very pessimistic book—and are an ingredient of the Wellsian optimism, an optimism whose other name, I fear, is ruthlessness. I have lately read all those scientific books from *The Time Machine* to *The War in the Air* and it has been a refreshing experience. There was a time, one realises, when science was fun. For the food of the gods is more entertaining than the prosaic efficacy of vitamins; the tripods of the Martians are more engaging than tanks. And then, here you have Wells at his best, eagerly displaying the inventive imagination, first with the news and at play, with an artist's innocence. Here you see his intoxicated response—a response that was lacking in his contemporaries—to the front-page situation of his time, and here you meet his mastery of the art of story-telling, the bounce and resource of it. Above all, in these early books, you catch Wells in the act, his very characteristic act, of breaking down mean barriers and setting you free. He has burst out himself and he wants everyone else to do the same. (pp. 32-3)

[It] is a suggestive fact that we have to go back to Swift, the Swift of Lilliput and Laputa, before we find another English novelist going to science for his data and material as Wells has done. (The influence of science, in the 150 years that lie between those two writers, is philosophical, not factual.) Wells's eager recognition of the new environment is one of the sources of the sense of freedom we get from him. I make no comparison of the merits of Wells and Swift—though the Beast-Men of *The Island of Dr. Moreau* are derivatives of the Yahoos and are observed with Swift's care for biological detail—but in his best narratives Wells does go back to the literary traditions of the early eighteenth century, the highest traditions of our narrative literature. The ascendancy of Swift is a question of imaginative range and style; above all it is due to a humanity which is denied to Wells because he arrived at the beginning, the crude beginning, of a new enlargement, whereas Swift arrived towards the end of one. None of Wells's narrators, whether they are South Kensington scientists or people, like the awful Bert, who appear to be suffering from an emotional and linguistic toothache, is capable of the philosophical simplicity and sanity of Gulliver; for Wells has only just spotted this new world of agitating chemicals, peculiar glands, and obliterating machines. The sense of wonder has not grown far beyond a sense of copy. He is topical and unstable, swept by eagerness yet visited by nauseas sudden and horrifying. Suppose we evolve into futility or revert to the beast from which we have arisen? Such speculations are alien to the orthodox eyes which were set in Swift's mad head; he had no eye to the future; the eighteenth century believed in a static world. The things Swift sees *have happened*. To Wells—and how typical of an expanding age—the things he sees have *not* happened. They are possibilities. In these scientific romances one catches occasionally the humane and settled note: in *The Time Machine*, in *The Island of Dr. Moreau* and in *The War of the Worlds*, which are the most imaginative stories of the group and are free of the comic Edwardian horseplay. (pp. 33-4)

It is not surprising that the passages of low comedy, which elsewhere are Wells's excellence, should be a failure in the scientific romances. Naturally they break the spell of the illusion with their clumsy realism. And if love is born, Wells is Walt Disney at his worst. The love scenes between the giants in *The Food of the Gods* are the most embarrassing in English fiction, and one wonders that the picture of the awful Princess, goggling in enormous close-up and fanning herself with half a chestnut tree, did not destroy the feminist movement. But except for faint squirms of idyllic petting in *The Time Machine*, none of these aberrations misdirects the narratives of the three books I have mentioned. I cannot include *The War in the Air* among the best; it is an astonishing piece of short-term prophecy and judgment. One remembers the bombing of battleships and the note on the untroubled minds of those who bomb one another's cities; but the book is below Wells's highest level. So, too, is *The Invisible Man*, which is a good thriller, but it develops jerkily and is held up by horseplay and low comedy. Without question *The Time Machine* is the best piece of writing. It will take its place among the great stories of our language. Like all excellent works it has meanings within its meaning and no one who has read the story will forget the dramatic effect of the change of scene in the middle of the book, when the story alters its key, and the Time Traveller reveals the foundation of slime and horror on which the pretty life of his Arcadians is precariously and fearfully resting. I think it is fair to accuse the later Wells of escaping into a dream world of plans, of using science as a magic staircase out of essential social problems. I think the best Wells is the destructive, ruthless, black-eye-dealing and house-burning Wells who foresaw the violence and not the order of our time. However this may be, the early Wells of *The Time Machine* did not escape. . . . Here Wells's images of horror are curious. The slimy, the viscous, the foetal reappear; one sees the sticky, shapeless messes of pond life, preposterous in instinct and frighteningly without mind. One would like to hear a psychologist on these shapes which recall certain surrealist paintings; but perhaps the biologist fishing among the algae, and not the unconscious, is responsible for them. In *The Time Machine*—and also in the other two books—Wells is aware of pain. None of his investigators returns without wounds and bruises to the mind as well as the body, and Dr. Moreau is, of course, a sadist. *The Island* is hard on the nerves and displays a horror more definite and calculated than anything in Wells's other books. Where *The Time Machine* relieves us by its poetic social allegory, *The Island of Dr. Moreau* takes us into an abyss of human nature. . . . This book is a superb piece of story-telling from our first sight of the unpleasant ship and its stinking, mangy menagerie, to the last malign episode where the narrator is left alone on the island with the Beast-Men. . . . The description of the gradual break in the morale of the Beast-Men is a wonderful piece of documented guesswork. It is easy enough to be sensational. It is quite another matter to domesticate the sensational. One notices, too, how Wells's idea comes full circle in his best thrillers. There is the optimistic outward journey, there is the chastened return.

It would be interesting to know more about the origins of *The Island of Dr. Moreau,* for they must instruct us on the pessimism and the anarchy which lie at the heart of Wells's ebullient nature. This is the book of a wounded man who has had a sight of sadism and death. The novelist who believes in the cheerful necessity of evolution is halted by the thought of its disasters and losses. Perhaps man is unteachable. It is exciting and emancipating to believe we are one of nature's latest experiments, but what if the experiment is unsuccessful? . . . The price of progress may be perversion and horror, and Wells is honest enough to accept that. (pp. 34-7)

Wells can be wounded. It is one of his virtues. One is reminded of Kipling, another wounded writer—was Wells satirising Kipling in that chapter of *The Island of Dr. Moreau* where the Beast-Men are seen mumbling their pathetic Law?—and Kipling and Wells are obviously divergent branches of the same tree. Wells the Utopian, Kipling the patriot—they represent the day-dreams of the lower middle class which will either turn to socialism or fascism. Opposed in tendency, Wells and Kipling both have the vision of artists; they foresee the conditions of our time. They both foretell the violence with a certain appetite. Crudity appeals to them. They are indifferent or bad-hearted, in human relations. They understand only personal independence which, from time to time, in their work is swallowed up in mass relationships. In the final count, Kipling—like Wells's man in the sewer in *The War of the Worlds*—falls back on animal cunning. It is the knowing, tricky, crafty animal that survives by lying low and saying nothing. Kipling, for all his admiration of power, believes in the neurotic, the morbid and defeated mind. This strain is in Wells also, but he has more private stoicism than Kipling has, a stoicism which blossoms from time to time into a belief in miracles and huge strokes of luck. Impatient of detail, mysteriously reticent about the immediate practical steps we must take to ensure any of his policies, Wells believes—like Kipling —in magic: a magic induced by impudence or rebellion. Wells and Kipling—these two are light and shadow to each other.

Wells's achievement was that he installed the paraphernalia of our new environment in our imagination; and life does not become visible or tolerable to us until artists have assimilated it. We do not need to read beyond these early scientific works of his to realise what he left out. The recent war, whose conditions he so spryly foresaw, has made that deficiency clear. When we read those prophetic accounts of mechanised warfare and especially of air bombardment, we must be struck by one stupendous misreading of the future. . . . He did not reckon with the nature, the moral resources, the habits of civilised man. Irresponsible himself, he did not attribute anything but an obstructive value to human responsibility. That is a serious deficiency, for it indicates an ignorance of the rooted, inner life of men and women, a jejune belief that we live by events and programmes; but how, in the heyday of a great enlargement of the human environment, could he believe otherwise? We turn back to our Swift and there we see a mad world also; but it is a mad world dominated by the sober figure of the great Gulliver, that plain, humane figure. Not a man of exquisite nor adventurous spirituality; not a great soul; not a man straining all his higher faculties to produce some new mutation; not a man trying to blow himself out like the frog of the fable to the importunate dimensions of his programme; but, quite simply, a man. Endowed with curiosity, indeed, but empowered by reserve. Anarchists like Wells, Kipling, Shaw and the pseudo-orthodox Chesterton, had no conception of such a creature. They were too fascinated by their own bombs. (pp. 37-8)

V. S. Pritchett, "The Scientific Romances," in his The Living Novel *(copyright 1947 © 1964; renewed 1975 by V.S. Pritchett; reprinted by permission of Random House, Inc.; in Canada by Chatto and Windus Ltd), Chatto and Windus, 1946; (and reprinted in* H. G. Wells: A Collection of Critical Essays, *edited by Bernard Bergonzi, Prentice-Hall, Inc., 1976, pp. 32-8).*

MARK SCHORER (essay date 1948)

Technique alone objectifies the materials of art; hence technique alone evaluates those materials. This is the axiom which demonstrates itself so devastatingly whenever a writer declares under the urgent sense of the importance of his materials—whether these are autobiography, or social ideas, or personal passions—whenever such a writer declares that he cannot linger with technical refinements. That art will not tolerate such a writer H. G. Wells handsomely proves. His enormous literary energy included no respect for the techniques of his medium, and his medium takes its revenge upon his bumptiousness. (p. 15)

"Literature," Wells said, "is not jewelry, it has quite other aims than perfection, and the more one thinks of 'how it is done' the less one gets it done. These critical indulgences lead along a fatal path, away from every natural interest towards a preposterous emptiness of technical effort, a monstrous egotism of artistry, of which the later work of Henry James is the monumental warning. 'It,' the subject, the thing or the thought, has long since disappeared in these amazing works; nothing remains but the way it has been manipulated." Seldom has a literary theorist been so totally wrong; for what we learn as James grows for us and Wells disappears is that without what he calls "manipulation," there *is* no "it," no "subject" in art. There is again only social history.

The virtue of the modern novelist—from James and Conrad down—is not only that he pays so much attention to his medium, but that, when he pays most, he discovers through it a new subject matter, and a greater one. Under the "immense artistic preoccupations" of James and Conrad and Joyce, the form of the novel changed, and with the technical change, analogous changes took place in substance, in point of view, in the whole conception of fiction. And the final lesson of the modern novel is that technique is not the secondary thing that it seemed to Wells, some external machination, a mechanical affair, but a deep and primary operation; not only that technique *contains* intellectual and moral implications, but that it *discovers* them. For a writer like Wells, who wished to give us the intellectual and the moral history of our times, the lesson is a hard one; it tells us that the order of intellect and the order of morality do not exist at all, in art, except as they are organized in the order of art.

Wells' ambitions were very large. "Before we have done, we will have all life within the scope of the novel." But that is where life already is, within the scope of the novel; where it needs to be brought is into novels. In Wells we have all the important topics in life, but no good novels. He was not asking too much of art, or asking that it include more than it happily can; he was not asking anything of it—as art, which is all that it can give, and that is everything.

A novel like *Tono Bungay,* generally thought to be Wells' best, is therefore instructive. "I want to tell—*myself,*" says George, the hero, "and my impressions of the thing as a whole"—the thing as a whole being the collapse of traditional British institutions in the twentieth century. George "tells himself" in terms of three stages in his life which have rough equivalents in modern British social history, and this is, to be sure, a plan, a framework; but it is the framework of Wells' abstract thinking, not of his craftsmanship, and the primary demand which one makes of such a book as this—that means be discovered whereby the dimensions of the hero contain the experiences he recounts—is never met. The novelist flounders through a series of literary imitations—from an early Dickensian episode, through a kind of Shavian interlude, through a Conradian episode, to a Jules Verne vision at the end. The significant failure is in that end, and in the way that it defeats not only the entire social analysis of the bulk of the novel, but Well's own ends as a thinker. For at last George finds a purpose in science. "I decided that in power and knowledge lay the salvation of my life; the secret that would fill my need; that to these things I would give myself."

But science, power, and knowledge are summed up at last in a destroyer. As far as one can tell Wells intends no irony, although he may here have come upon the essence of the major irony in modern history. The novel ends in a kind of meditative rhapsody which denies every value that the book had been aiming toward. For all the kinds of social waste which Wells has been describing, this is the most inclusive, the final waste. Thus he gives us in the end not a novel, but a hypothesis; not an individual destiny, but a theory of the future; and not his theory of the future, but a nihilistic vision quite opposite from everything that he meant to represent. With a minimum of attention to the virtues of technique, Wells might still not have written a good novel; but he would at any rate have established a point of view and a tone which would have told us what he meant. (pp. 15-17)

> Mark Schorer, "Technique As Discovery" (copyright © 1948 by The Hudson Review, Inc.; copyright renewed © 1975 by Mark Schorer; reprinted by permission), in The Hudson Review, Vol. I, No. 1, Spring, 1948 (and reprinted in Forms of Modern Fiction: Essays Collected in Honor of Joseph Warren Beach, edited by William Van O'Connor, The University of Minnesota Press, 1948, pp. 9-29.)

FRANK SWINNERTON (essay date 1950)

Concurrently with the scientific romances Wells was writing novels not very much outside the manner of his period, but noteworthy because of their personal humour and increasing richness. They were simple narratives, long and short, of events in the lives of very simple-minded people. The first of them ["**The Wheels of Fortune**"] was the tale of Mr. Hoopdriver, the drapers' assistant with a bicycle, who went for a cycling holiday and became for the time being a knight-errant. There was also the more autobiographical, but still indulgent, story of "**Love and Mr. Lewisham.**" . . . A little later there was "**Kipps.**" Finally, as the supreme example of this sort of book, there was "**Mr. Polly,**" the story of a little shopkeeper who set fire to his shop, ran away from his wife, and found a nice cosy widow who kept an inn to which all sorts of odd visitors came, and lived happily ever after.

All these books belong to the same order. All are fairy stories, and all are about "simple souls." All were written, not merely as relaxations, but because one side of Wells's genius, the happiest side, had kinship with the comic genius of Dickens, his favourite author. Whenever Wells was amused, he was

happy and inventive. The living figures in his books are all comic characters, fantastic, talkative, simple, phonetically colloquial, seen with what used to be called "open pleasantry," but seen none the less with keenness and precision. Teddy Ponderevo, Polly, Chaffery, Kipps, Chitterlow, having amused us as we read, persist in our imaginations. We love them. When Wells was serious, he was expository; he did not create. We lost the character in the exposition; and this, I think, is why, as novels, all but the two best books in the serious and discursive manner must remain unsatisfactory. That is fot to be said of the simple soul novels.

What is to be said of them, and of the early romances, is something else. It is that they were all written in an easy narrative form untrammelled by those shackles to which the rising authority of Henry James presently condemned romancers. . . . [Wells] was allowed, unreproved, to enrich our literature with several artless works of genius which still give delight to all but the aesthetically unco' guid.

As a consequence, Wells never learnt how to write a novel which was a work of art. . . . Wells, charged with being unaesthetic, replied that he never said he was, and alternatively that the aesthetes can't prove it, and anyway, Yah! This seems to me, coming from Wells, to be entirely justifiable. The rules of art need revision, so as to include the work of Wells. . . . The rules of art are not made by edicts; they are developed from the practice of artists; and if they cannot admit of provision for such a book as "**Tono-Bungay**" they ought to be stretched; for "**Tono-Bungay,**" illustrating as it does the form and pressure of the time in which it was written, is one of the great modern novels, and will be so appreciated after a century's variations of aesthetic dogmatism. (pp. 65-6)

Having written the scientific romances, and having begun to write novels, Wells at the turn of the century found himself working in a new field. He had been a young schoolmaster, a young scientist, a journalist, a writer of romances, and a novelist; and now his increasing range of knowledge led him ever farther into speculation. It was speculation directed by the schoolmaster and the scientist in him; for his interests lay in the everyday world of that time and the future. For him the first step in the "New Republicanism" of which he became the champion was "to reject and set aside all abstract, refined, and intellectualized ideas as starting propositions, such ideas as Right, Liberty, Happiness, Duty or Beauty." He was a Darwinian; he knew that the world was to be more and more dominated by inventions and practical ideas; and he wanted to breed good citizens who would create a world in which order replaced present chaos. First of all, therefore, it was imperative that he should make up his mind as to the most probable developments of the near future. He did this, and wrote "**Anticipations.**"

I need not say that many of Wells's anticipations were proved accurate. The book exists to demonstrate the fact. From my point of view it is more interesting to realize that "**Anticipations**" was but a first step in the clarification of Wells's own mind. He went on to imagine what kind of world it was that he and his fellow-reformers were striving to create. He dared to formulate his idea of a practical Utopia. That was much more difficult. It was so difficult that he made a number of false starts in the writing of the book, and at last took refuge in a hybrid literary form—half essay, half tale—that excellently suited his gifts. And as a bridge between "**Anticipations**" and "**A Modern Utopia**" he wrote another book, called "**Mankind**

in the Making," in which he discussed elaborately the problems of Eugenics and Education.

The three books, taken together, represent the character of Wells's interest in the world and the human species. Later books in the same vein—and here I include such works as **"The Outline of History," "The Science of Life,"** and **"The Work, Wealth and Happiness of Mankind"**—were educational. And whatever their positive qualities they were undertaken deliberately as stop-gaps, with no pretence to much more than utilitarian purpose. . . . They concentrate upon inventions, social order, education; they have little concern with aesthetics or what is called the psyche. And they are so simply expressed that any man of ordinary intelligence can read them with understanding. That is a quality due to the journalist in Wells. He is readable. It was made a matter of reproach against him. He was said to have betrayed culture to the Philistines. It should rather be said that he introduced the Philistines to a culture larger than that of the Dons. (pp. 66-8)

[Wells's] vision had its limitations. He did not see what the poet sees and what the musician sees: I do not think he could sit still for long enough to relish the pure contemplation which Shaw considered the highest intellectual state. He must be turning the room, the world, the lazy mind about and about, like a house-proud woman with a vacuum cleaner in her eager hands. His heroes are not military men, nor poets, nor philosophers, but scientists. (p. 68)

[When Wells] talks of beauty he never carries conviction, and his future world, in spite of every persuasive effort of his, and in spite of the fascinating ingenuity of parts of his analysis, remains, as all Utopias do, a place from which one hurries back to one's own fireside with relief.

Why is this? . . . The truth is that Wells, with all his quickness, all his power, all his vivid inventive habits of mind, had no true sense of beauty in art or in life. Even love, in his books, never moves us; every one of his busy scientific heroes, interrupted in full flight of research or political activity by what he terms an "urgency," has an affair with a woman, but as to emotion there is no sign of it, and as to beauty of relation there is so little that we quite coldly estimate the duration of the urgency and the affair. . . . [Save] in so far as it is useful to one or other of [his] ends he was indifferent to beauty. That is the weakness of his "serious" works, which reach out to a greater synthesis than is possible in the world we know. He was a prose writer, at his best in books where he was nearest his own time and his own people. His best novels are **"Tono-Bungay"** and **"Mr. Polly,"** which are both rich with the very texture of life itself. His best expository books are also novels— **"The Undying Fire," "The New Machiavelli,"** and **"The World of William Clissold"**;—and they are the best because the first is passionate and the two others are less expository than exploratory of the author's always original and interesting mind and experience. (p. 69)

[Any] visitor to Wells's library must have noticed one row of books which bore all the signs of constant reading: it was the row of Dickens's novels. There can be no doubt at all that when he began to plan **"Tono-Bungay"** Wells thought "David Copperfield" was a very great novel indeed. He used the form of the pseudo-autobiography with deliberation, as the one in which most freedom was allowed for the introduction of innumerable details of contemporary life, and the one in which such details could best be related to a select group of characters and a *milieu* with which he was thoroughly acquainted. "I

want to show," he said, "a contemporary man in relation to the state and social usage, and the social organism in relation to that man." While we may wish that largeness of conspectus could have been more intimately associated with fineness of concept, we cannot without eccentricity deny to **"Tono-Bungay"** its importance both as a social picture and as a development in the craft of novel-writing. (p. 71)

[But Henry James, writing to Wells about the second great autobiographic novel, **"The New Machiavelli,"** said:] "I make remonstrance . . . bear upon the bad service you have done your cause by riding so hard again that accurst autobiographic form which puts a premium on the loose, the improvised, the cheap and the easy. . . . There is, to my vision, no authentic, and no really interesting and no *beautiful,* report of things on the novelist's, the painter's part unless the great stewpot or crucible of the imagination, of the observant and recording and interpreting mind in short, has intervened and played its part— and this detachment, this chemical transmutation for the aesthetic, the representational, end is terribly wanting in autobiography brought, as the horrible phrase is, up to date."

This criticism—for it must be admitted that James's mind was like the mills of God—sums up all or nearly all the objections to the Wellsian novel. The weakness of the method is better seen when one contemplates the repetitions or variations that followed **"Tono-Bungay."** The stories told in these books were different; and yet the more they differed the more they emphatically remained the same story—the story of the man with a job to do, a marriage, an affair, a flight, the whole involved in a richly and consummately sketched chiaroscuro of the social and intellectual life of England between 1860 and 1930. **"Tono-Bungay"** is the best of these books because it was the first pressing of the grapes. It is a really amazing picture, furthermore, of the change that occurred in English life between the author's childhood and his maturity. It is contemporary history. Its vigour never fails; its detail, both domestic and social, is exact and sufficient. It is absorbingly interesting; it was a genuine attempt to present a modern man at something like full length in spite of every moral convention of the time.

It is also the best, however, because of another feature, not apparent in its successors: it is the only sociological novel of Wells's in which there are comic characters in any way to be compared with those in the humorous novels. Not all the intellectual interest of **"The New Machiavelli"** and **"The World of William Clissold"** can compensate for the loss, the temporary loss, by Wells of his comic genius.

When that comic genius had free play, as in **"Kipps,"** there may be—there is—the air of improvisation to which James objected in **"The New Machiavelli."** But although **"Kipps"** may stumble, it stumbles from point to point, from one comic invention to another, and is a feast of character. Even better is **"Mr. Polly,"** which does not stumble at all (does it falter just once, almost into sentimentality, when Polly talks to the schoolgirl?), but has a poignance not elsewhere to be found in Wells's work. Wells was always most at ease in writing about poor and half-cultured people; he understood and loved the simple souls among them, and understood and loved rather less the cupidity, the inquisitiveness, and the bad manners of the not so simple. They were, so to speak, in the hollow of his hand. He perceived the significance of every gesture they made, and every glance they cast. He could be kind to them—sometimes mercilessly kind,—ribald, indulgent without sentimentality, Dickensian and more than Dickensian because more economical in illustration, beautifully suggestive in phonetics or in phrase. In dealing with poor people he was an artist. Personally, I think that in this field he had no equal. (pp. 71-2)

> *Frank Swinnerton, "Teachers: Shaw and Wells," in his* The Georgian Literary Scene, 1910-1935: A Panorama *(reprinted by permission of Farrar, Straus & Giroux, Inc.; in Canada by Hutchinson Publishing Group Ltd.),* Farrar, Straus and Company, 1950, pp. 39-75.*

BERTRAND RUSSELL   (essay date 1953)

Wells's importance was primarily as a liberator of thought and imagination. He was able to construct pictures of possible societies, both attractive and unattractive, of a sort that encouraged the young to envisage possibilities which otherwise they would not have thought of. Sometimes he does this in a very illuminating way. His *Country of the Blind* is a somewhat pessimistic restatement in modern language of Plato's allegory of the cave. His various utopias, though perhaps not in themselves very solid, are calculated to start trains of thought which may prove fruitful. He is always rational, and avoids various forms of superstition to which modern minds are prone. . . . In spite of some reservations, I think one should regard Wells as having been an important force toward sane and constructive thinking both as regards social systems and as regards personal relations. I hope he may have successors, though I do not at the moment know who they will be. (p. 85)

> *Bertrand Russell, "H. G. Wells" (originally published in* The Listener, *Vol. L, No. 1280, September 10, 1953), in his* Portraits from Memory: And Other Essays *(copyright © 1951, 1952, 1956 by Bertrand Russell; reprinted by permission of Simon & Schuster, a Division of Gulf & Western Corporation; in Canada by George Allen & Unwin (Publishers) Ltd.),* Simon & Schuster, 1956, pp. 81-5.

ANTHONY WEST   (essay date 1957)

[Wells's pessimistic last writings and utterances] were, and still are, being represented as an abandonment of a superficial optimism in the face of those realities of which his coming death was a part. The suggestion is made that they were some kind of final admission that he had been wrong about the nature of things for the greater part of his life. . . . I cannot now agree that his final phase of scolding and complaining at human folly represented any essential change in his views at all. What happened as his powers declined from 1940 onwards was that he reverted to his original profoundly-felt beliefs about the realities of the human situation. He was by nature a pessimist, and he was doing violence to his intuitions and his rational perceptions alike when he asserted in his middle period that mankind could make a better world for itself by an effort of will. (p. 10)

Wells' first serious piece of writing was a paper called **"The Rediscovery of the Unique"** of which he remained proud throughout his career. . . . [It] restates with clarity and force the idea which Hobbes put forward in *Leviathan* . . . when he says that there is "nothing in the World Universal but Names, for the things named are every one of them Individual and Singular."

This is the foundation stone of the mechanistic view according to which the whole world is "nothing but a mere heap of dust, fortuitously agitated" and the universe a similar aggregation.

It is impossible to believe in progress if you believe in a universe in which mind figures as a local accident, and which by its nature cannot support any permanent moral order or indeed any permanent thing.

That Wells was deeply committed to this view is evident from his first novel, *The Time Machine,* which has its climactic scene at a point some thirty million years in the future. . . . A cosmic catastrophe is impending which will finally obliterate the material context in which such concepts as mind, consciousness, and value can possess any meaning. The possibility of such a situation is irreconcilable with the idea of progress, and Wells states his disbelief in it in this book without ambiguity. (pp. 11-12)

[Implicit in the questions raised by this book] is the idea that an evolutionary trend that would make a man a more intellectual animal might also make him a much less humane one. This not only questions the idea of progress, but also suggests that virtue is not innate in the intellect as Victorian moralists were inclined to believe. I stress this point because it seems to me to be an important one if one wants to understand Wells' thinking. . . . This nagging fear of the liberated intellect as something inhumane was to play an important part in Wells' later work, but he raised it in *The Time Machine* only to drop it in favour of an explicit statement about natural selection. The premise is that the nineteenth century layered class society constituted an artificial environment to which man was adapting himself. The donnée for the purpose of *The Time Machine* was that it was going to endure; so the Time Traveller finds, in the year A.D. 802701 that adaptation has divided the human race into two distinct [and degenerate] subspecies. . . . It is with something of a shock that one finds that what has brought about their debasement is precisely the complete success of mankind in establishing a technological society and world order of the kind to which Wells is supposed to have given his unqualified endorsement. (pp. 12-13)

One of the difficulties of writing about Wells is that his mind was undisciplined, and that on any given point he can be found either to contradict himself, or to appear to do so. *The Time Machine* was immediately followed by *The Island of Dr. Moreau,* which Wells discussed much later, in the twenties, as if he had accepted a dualistic picture of human nature while he was writing it. . . . (p. 13)

This would give innate virtue a refuge in the intellect, and would allow for optimism as a possibility. But what happens in *The Island of Dr. Moreau* is a disaster, the liberated intellect in the person of a Darwinian humanitarian arrives on the island and disintegrates its theocratic moral order by making an appeal to reason which assumes that Dr. Moreau's victims are moral creatures with better natures. When they are set free from the Hobbesian régime of terror under which they have been living it is revealed that they are, beneath Dr. Moreau's scar tissue, brutes interested only in the satisfaction of their appetites. So far as a conflict between instinct and injunction goes, it is no contest; order and law are imposed on the brutish inhabitants of the island by an exterior force, and as soon as that is removed the system collapses. What the book in fact expresses is a profound mistrust of human nature, and a doubt about the intellect's ability to contain it. There is even a doubt about the intellect as a possible containing force, since its role in the story is a purely destructive one.

The Island of Dr. Moreau relates closely to two other stories, a short novel and a short story, which deal with the same theme of the liberated intellect as a destructive element. *The Invisible Man* is a parable about the amoral aspects of the scientific outlook, and invisibility figures in it as a symbol of intellectual isolation. **"The Country of the Blind"** is a much more mature version of the same parable. . . . The theme is carried further in *The War of the Worlds* and in *The First Men in the Moon.* The Martians, like the ruling class on the moon, are brain cases with the merest of vestigial bodies, symbols of the intellect triumphant over the animal. The point that technological mastery has given the Martians a sense that they are free from moral responsibility is obscured by the surface action in *The War of the Worlds.* Most readers do not see beyond the fact that the Martians arrive, and treat Europeans as Europeans had been treating native populations and animals in the hey-day of colonialism, to the deeper argument. But there is no possibility of misunderstanding the description of lunar society which appears towards the end of *The First Men in the Moon.* The unfettered intellect rules, and respect for efficiency stands in the place of morality. What has come into being is the worst kind of slave state. . . . In the end, what Wells is saying in *The First Men in the Moon,* is that the basis of operations which Huxley recommended in his famous Romanes lecture, and which he had himself adopted and stated in the concluding paragraphs of *The Time Machine,* is not viable. Because if a mechanistic view of the universe is constructed by the right hand the left will inevitably loose its grip on any ethical system it may have decided to grasp.

It may seem that this is reading something into *The First Men in the Moon* which is not there, but Wells went out of his way to state it in a mundane context in *When the Sleeper Wakes.* . . . It stands as the optimistic and naïvely uncritical forerunner of Aldous Huxley's *Brave New World,* and Orwell's *1984.* . . . The difference between Wells' horrors and those described by Huxley and Orwell reside mainly in points of detail. Wells was writing before the two great wars and the dictatorships had made the State as dangerous an engine as it now seems. For Wells the enemy was monopoly capitalism as it presented itself in the form of the great corporations. But his business State is just as monstrous as the police State of Orwell's imagination, and is perhaps worse in that it does not bother to persecute individuals as individuals, but simply treats people in terms of social categories and utility. (pp. 14-16)

[I think] that the view of human nature taken in these early books accounts for the flaw in the later ones which now makes them seem ill-considered and confused. These are forced in so far as they say things which Wells wishes to believe, and in which he, ultimately, does not believe. What he ultimately does not believe in is the ability of the human animal to live up to its ideals. . . . In mid-career Wells stopped saying this and adopted the progressive line, stating a body of ideas which can be called Wellsian. (p. 17)

Wells' "progressive" writing represents an attempt to straddle irreconciliable positions, and it involved a perpetual conflict of a wasteful character. In all too much of his work he is engaged in shouting down his own better judgment.

The change of front from an explicit pessimism to an apparent optimism dates roughly from 1901 and the publication of *Anticipations.* It coincides with Wells' entry into the sphere of influence of the Fabian society in political matters and of that of William James in philosophy. . . . James invented the idea of operative truth which is supposed to cover the difficulty:

> . . . ideas (which themselves are but parts of
> our experience) become true just in so far as

> they help us to get into satisfactory relations
> with other parts of our experience.

> True ideas are those we can assimilate, validate, corroborate, and verify. False ideas are those we cannot.

> The true, to put it very briefly, is only the expedient in the way of our thinking, just as "the right" is only the expedient in the way of our behaving.
>
> (p. 18)

However much these propositions may have appealed to Wells' humanitarian feelings, they grated on his aesthetic sense and his intelligence fought with them, so that it became an increasing effort to pretend that they "worked." The doubts emerge as early as 1904, in *The Food of The Gods.* This is a progressive parable about the way in which human undertakings have outgrown petty national States and their parochial administrative units. . . . The book is very convincing as long as it is describing how things go wrong and hardly convincing at all when it attempts to say how they will go right. What it effectively describes is the frustration and destruction of a great possibility by inferior human material. The optimism of the conclusion rests on a trick. The food of the Gods has produced a new, larger, nobler breed of human being adequate to the technological possibilities open to it, and the future rests with them. The device is transparent, and it is hard not to feel that the evasion of the real problem, of what can be done with human nature as it is, is not a conscious one. It is the first of a series of such calculated evasions. They are less apparent in the books about people than elsewhere, but they emerge from these too: *Kipps, Tono-Bungay, Ann Veronica, The History of Mr. Polly, The New Machiavelli, Marriage, The Passionate Friends,* and *The Wife of Sir Isaac Harman,* all superficially suggest that Wells is asking the question "what shall we do with our lives" as if the answer could be "whatever we wish." But the line of development followed in the books shows an underlying doubt about this answer. They show a steadily diminishing confidence in the possibility of individual solutions. What emerges at the end of the chain is the idea of the Mind of the Race, a group intellect which will be freed from individual weaknesses, and which will save humanity from its instincts. This group intellect is to be served by semi-religious orders of devotees, the Samurai, who are to surrender their lives to it. But at the back of this conception is an awareness that it is not consistent with human nature that such a surrender should in fact take place. This recognition led to Wells writing a series of catastrophe books, stories in which he imagines that human nature undergoes some fundamental change that will permit the construction of a Utopian society. The ideas of Hobbes play a large part in these fantasies. Fear, generated by a cosmic disaster as *In the Days of the Comet,* or by atomic war in *The World Set Free* . . . , leads men to submit to some kind of central world government modelled on the Common Power described in *Leviathan.* But the idea of a change in human nature itself is the *sine qua non* of his utopias, and in the end Wells conceded that such a change was not within the realm of possibility. His much-parodied *Men Like Gods* is the point of concession, and it is odd that those who have criticized the book as representing the unpracticality and unreality of his idealism in its extreme form have not noticed the fact. The ideal beings which inhabit its Utopia exist in a free zone which is not within the realm of human reality. They are special creations like the giant children in *The Food of The Gods* and like them they are designed to evade the truth about human nature. They live in another universe outside the earth's spatial scheme altogether. . . . (pp. 19-20)

[The] construction has the effect of making the book not a debate between man-as-he-might-be and man-as-he-is, but an essentially sterile clash between reality and an unattainable ideal. At best it is a cry of distress, a plea for things to be other than they are. *Men Like Gods* is in reality an altogether pessimistic book. Read in conjunction with *The Undying Fire*, which prepared the way for it, and which is a violently expressed hymn of loathing of things as they are, it leaves no doubt that in his last writings Wells was only giving a new form to beliefs which he had held all along. *The Undying Fire* is particularly moving, to those who have any sympathy with Wells at all. It shows the pendulum of his mind swinging away from its natural despairing bent over to the side of determination to construct something better out of human opportunities and back, again and again. (p. 21)

The Outline of History was designed to provide a universal history which would serve as the basis for a patriotism of humanity, as national histories serve as a basis for national patriotism. What the book states is, not that progress is inevitable, but that mankind has a common historical background, not a racial or a regional one. It goes on to say that given the will mankind might, by a tremendous concerted effort, establish a world order in which all its energy could be consumed in constructive and creative enterprises, physical, aesthetic, and intellectual. . . .

If I appear to be saying that Wells was inconsistent, it cannot be helped, inconsistency is the natural consequence of an unresolved conflict in a writer's work or thought. (p. 22)

It was, of course, *Boon* with its parody of Henry James, and its harsh criticism of aesthetic values, which finally established his reputation as a Philistine. From *Boon* onwards he made increasingly strident attacks on literary values which are, in my view, only partially explicable by his sense that in the state in which the world found itself aesthetics were a luxury for which there was not enough time. It is my view that these attacks, which went along with his reiterated statements that his own work had no literary value, that it was merely journalism, attached to contemporary issues; which would become meaningless inside a couple of decades, reflected a troubled inner sense that there was something profoundly wrong about his own course of development. In the end I believe, on the strength of conversations which I had with him on the particular subject of what he meant by Dr. Moreau, and on some related topics, that he came to feel that a realization of the truth of the human situation, in all its ultimate hopelessness, was much more likely to stir men to present effort to make life more tolerable than any pretence. . . . He knew in his bones that the aesthetes were right, and that the writer's sole duty is to state the truth which he knows. At the close of his life, from *The Croquet Player* onwards, he was trying to recapture the spirit in which he had written *The Island of Dr. Moreau*, and what haunted him, and made him exceedingly unhappy, was a tragic sense that he had returned to the real source of what could have been his strength too late. (p. 23)

Anthony West, "H. G. Wells," in his Principles and Persuasions: The Literary Essays of Anthony West *(copyright © 1957 by Anthony West; reprinted by permission of Wallace & Sheil Agency, Inc.), Harcourt, 1957 (and reprinted in* H. G. Wells: A Collection of Critical Essays, *edited by Bernard Bergonzi, Prentice-Hall, 1976, pp. 8-24).*

GORDON N. RAY   (essay date 1960)

[In *Tono-Bungay* Wells] drew freely from his early life, as he had in *Love and Mr. Lewisham* and *Kipps,* but his focus was on the world in which he currently lived rather than on these memories. His objective was nothing less than to present in a single novel a comprehensive "view of the contemporary social and political system in Great Britain."

To accomplish this spacious aim Wells presented his story as the autobiography of one of his two principals, George Ponderevo, instead of telling it in his own person as he had in his two earlier novels. Thus he contrived to make acceptable *Tono-Bungay's* loose narrative structure as well as what might otherwise seem an excessive proportion of auctorial commentary. But, as a matter of fact, George is practically Wells's *alter ego.* His childhood, his scientific training, and a large part of his love-involvements parallel Wells's own history. Nor does his skeptical, ironical, generalizing habit of mind, "reaching out into vastly wider issues than our personal affairs," differ from that of his creator.

The "hero" of George's story is his uncle Edward Ponderevo. When the reader first encounters him he is a "little chemist," to all appearances one more ill-educated, ineffectual member of the lower middle class like Kipps or Mr. Polly. But Ponderevo dreams audaciously of "the romance of modern commerce," by which he means vast schemes of monopolistic chicanery made palatable by advertising. (pp. 141-42)

After failing to make any impression in his country retreat, Ponderevo removes to London, where he soon achieves spectacular success. His "open sesame" is "Tono-Bungay," a patent medicine which he has found in an old book of recipes. "The stuff was . . . a mischievous trash," George confesses. . . . Once "Tono-Bungay" has been established, Ponderevo moves on to a group of "subsidiary specialities," branches out into related fields, and finally embarks on large combinations of firms producing domestic conveniences which make him a famous company promoter. (pp. 142-43)

Ponderevo is now "the symbol of the age . . . , the man of luck and advertisement, the current master of the world." He becomes a leader among "that multitude of economically ascendant people who are learning how to spend money." A lively chapter recounts his social rise in terms of the houses in which he successively resides.

These distractions finally involve Ponderevo in financial troubles from which no ingenuity of manipulation can extricate him. When a trial for fraud and forgery impends, George spirits him off by balloon to southern France, where he shortly dies, a frightened and broken man, "his race of glory run and race of shame." He has done society enormous harm, yet the reader finds it difficult to think of him except with forgiving affection. (p. 144)

George's history is presented in counterpoint to his uncle's. He grows up at Bladesover in Kent, a great country estate where his mother is housekeeper. After serving as an assistant in his uncle's chemist's shop, he wins a scholarship to London University. He leaves without a degree to help his uncle in the exploitation of "Tono-Bungay"; but after the success of Ponderevo's enterprises seems assured, he returns to science and engineering, in which he makes a substantial reputation for himself. Meanwhile he has passed through an unsatisfactory marriage and a troubled love affair.

At this point George's story veers into what the reader had come to expect from Wells in his "science fiction." It is surprising enough to find him seeking to make a contribution to the development of lighter-than-air craft through experimentation with balloons. But credence is strained to the breaking point when in a vain effort to save Ponderevo from financial disaster he leads a desperate expedition to a remote island where there are great heaps of "quap," "the most radio-active stuff in the world." In this age of the Geiger counter, when uranium stocks are booming, the "quap" episode has acquired an adventitious realism. Certainly we raise no question when George writes: "Suppose indeed that is to be the end of our planet; no splendid climax and finale, no towering accumulation of achievement but just—atomic decay." But we are still inclined to ask whether Wells would not have done better to rely on quieter plot elements. As the novel ends, George is an engineer for a shipbuilding concern, supervising the construction of destroyers.

The histories of Ponderevo and his nephew are absorbing in themselves, but they acquire far greater interest as the reader is shown how they fit into the "immense process of social disintegration" which is the pattern of contemporary life. (pp. 144-45)

[To George, England has become] the "spectacle of forces running to waste, of people who use and do not replace, . . . a country hectic with a wasting aimless fever of trade and money-making and pleasure-seeking." Once it is understood that the "Bladesover System" is an empty shell, . . . that waste and purposelessness are the leading features of English life, George's experiences and those of Ponderevo assume a thoroughly representative aspect. So George reflects: "All this present commercial civilisation is no more than my poor uncle's career writ large, a swelling, thinning bubble of assurances; . . . its arithmetic is just as unsound, its dividends as ill-advised, its ultimate aim as vague and forgotten; . . . it all drifts on perhaps to some tremendous parallel to his individual disaster." Even the "quap" has its suggestiveness. "It is in matter," George urges, "exactly what the decay of our old culture is in society, a loss of traditions and distinctions and assured reactions."

Wells had concluded *Love and Mr. Lewisham* and *Kipps* with the retreat of his principal characters to an island of domestic content. This solution was not open to George Ponderevo, just as it was not open to Wells himself. Instead George turns to science, as the force that may eventually bring order and purpose into the world, and dedicates himself to this "one enduring thing." But the hope held out for the future by science seems feeble when compared with the tremendous actualities that Wells has described. The dominant impression left by *Tono-Bungay* is that left by Shaw's *Heartbreak House*. It is a picture of a world over which doom impends.

Ranging as it does through past and present and through all levels of English society, *Tono-Bungay* is Wells's supreme effort to embody social forces through individual histories. He considered "A Picture of the World," "One Man's View of England," "The End of an Age," and "Waste," as possible titles, before finally settling on "Tono-Bungay." He was right to choose the thing rather than the abstraction, for the book remains a true novel despite the weight of generalization that it has to bear. One can only agree with Wells's own estimate

that it is "his finest and most finished novel upon the accepted lines." (pp. 147-48)

Gordon N. Ray, "H. G. Wells Tries to Be a Novelist," in Edwardians and Late Victorians, *edited by Richard Ellmann (copyright © 1960 Columbia University Press; reprinted by permission of the publisher), Columbia University Press, 1960, pp. 106-59.*

BERNARD BERGONZI (essay date 1961)

Wells [began] life as a writer in, if not quite of, the eighteen-nineties. If, like his friend Stephen Crane, he had died in 1900 he would already have been established as the author of more than a dozen short novels and collections of stories or essays. Had Wells's career been truncated in this fashion he would be remembered primarily as a literary artist and hardly at all as a publicist and pamphleteer. In 1900 Wells had scarcely embarked on the self-appointed task of educating humanity that was to take up most of his time and energy during the next four decades.

In the course of this study I hope to show why Wells could be considered an artist in the first few years of his career. It must be admitted that he was temperamentally alien to the self-conscious aestheticism that is thought of as a characteristically *fin de siècle* phenomenon, and which is inevitably associated with the names of Oscar Wilde and Aubrey Beardsley, despite the personal antipathy that existed between the two men. There were, however, occasional points of contact between the young Wells and the aesthetic *milieu*. (pp. 1-2)

[The] young Wells, though not an aesthete, was, in essentials, a *fin de siècle* writer. (p. 3)

In its widest sense *fin de siècle* was simply the expression of a prevalent mood: the feeling that the nineteenth century—which had contained more events, more history than any other—had gone on too long, and that sensitive souls were growing weary of it. . . . The *fin de siècle* mood produced, in turn, the feeling of *fin du globe,* the sense that the whole elaborate intellectual and social order of the nineteenth century was trembling on the brink of dissolution. *Fin de siècle* was not confined to art or aesthetics; its wider implications affected moral and social and even political attitudes and behaviour. (pp. 3-4)

Wells drew on ideas and attitudes which can, I think, be called *fin de siècle*. Both *The Island of Dr Moreau* and *The Time Machine,* as I hope to demonstrate, make substantially the same claim as Tille in his interpretation of Nietzsche: that the traditional view of man's place in the universe, and the morality appropriate to that place, is no longer supportable. (pp. 11-12)

Wells has not, on the whole, been taken very seriously as a literary artist; partly, perhaps, because he was at such pains in later years to deny that he was one. (p. 16)

I want to suggest that Wells's romances are something more than the simple entertaining yarns they are generally taken to be—though without, of course, wishing to deny that they *are* admirably entertaining. I refer to them as 'romances' rather than 'scientific romances', since, apart from anything else, the adjective is not always appropriate. There are no 'scientific' elements, for instance, in a novel such as *The Wonderful Visit* or in stories like **'The Country of the Blind'** and **'The Door in the Wall'**. Wells's early novels and tales are romances in the traditional sense, insofar as they contain an element of the marvellous, which may have a scientific—or pseudo-scientific—explanation, but which may equally originate in a supernatural happening, or in some disturbance of the individual consciousness. To stress the scientific component to the exclusion of the other qualities may give a distorted picture. (pp. 16-17)

It is, I think, more helpful to compare Wells not with Verne but with such masters of the romance and the imaginative fable as Hawthorne—whose influence on his earliest work he acknowledged—or Kafka. Romance is more likely to be symbolic—even if not specifically allegorical—than realistic fiction, and this is true of Wells. Some of his critics have already hinted at the symbolic quality of his romances. V. S. Pritchett [see excerpt above], for instance, has remarked of *The Time Machine,* 'Like all excellent works it has meanings within its meaning . . .' while as long ago as 1923 Edward Shanks observed of Wells's romances, 'They are, in their degree, myths; and Mr. Wells is a myth-maker.' Shanks's use of the word 'myth' is particularly suggestive; it has, of course, become a fashionable term in recent criticism, but it has a peculiar applicability to Wells's romances. The word is easier to use than to define accurately, but one can, I suggest, distinguish between major and minor myths as they occur in works of literature. The former are centred on such archetypal figures as Prometheus, Don Quixote, Faust, and Don Juan, whose significance is universal and not confined to a specific phase of cultural development. . . . The major myths, one might say, give a generalized cultural form to certain abiding elements in the pattern of human experience. The minor myths, on the other hand, possess a wide relevance but nevertheless have a particular historical point of departure. (pp. 18-19)

Wells's early romances are minor myths of this kind. As I have suggested, they reflect some of the dominant pre-occupations of the *fin de siècle* period; and it is important to remember that this significance is more than simply historical. If the *fin de siècle* expressed the final convulsions of the nineteenth century, it also marked the birth pangs of the twentieth, and many of the issues that concern mid-twentieth century man first appeared during that period. For that reason its literary myths still have a contemporary relevance. (p. 19)

In addition to their objective *fin de siècle* elements, Wells's romances also contain themes personal to himself, and one could, no doubt, subject them to a fairly detailed search for psychological symbolism: I have resisted the temptation to do so, except in the case of one or two short stories, where such symbolism seems unusually obtrusive. Certainly, the longer romances abound in suggestions of archetypal imagery; this is most apparent, perhaps, in *The Time Machine,* with its division between paradisal and demonic imagery, seeming to symbolize the conflict between a precarious consciousness and the increasingly menacing pressures of the unconscious. Similarly, *The Island of Dr Moreau* has various complex implications, but one can see Moreau as a manifestation of the Super-ego, eventually succumbing to the dark forces he is trying to control. Griffin, in *The Invisible Man,* has affinities with Stevenson's Dr Jekyll, and, like him, suggests the Jungian Shadow or Dark Self. *The War of the Worlds* can be read as an expression of the traditional eschatological preoccupation with the end of the world, which has been the source of so much religious imagery; equally, it expresses the myth of things or creatures falling from the skies, most recently manifested in the form of 'flying saucers'.

However, my interpretation will, in general, be inclined towards history rather than psychology. Apart from certain short

stories, this study will not go beyond 1901. In that year Wells published *The First Men in the Moon,* which I consider his last genuine novel-length romance, and *Anticipations,* his first major non-fictional work, where we see him ceasing to be an artist and beginning his long career as publicist and pamphleteer. . . . While the early romances originated in what J. D. Beresford called 'the effervescence of creative imagination', Wells's later attempts at the form all had a didactic aim, and suffered an according loss of imaginative power. (pp. 20-1)

Wells, at the beginning of his career, was a genuine and original imaginative artist, who wrote several books of considerable literary importance, before dissipating his talents in directions which now seem more or less irrelevant. In considering these works, it will be necessary to modify the customary view of Wells as an optimist, a utopian and a passionate believer in human progress. The dominant note of his early years was rather a kind of fatalistic pessimism, combined with intellectual scepticism, and it is this which the early romances reflect. It is, one need hardly add, a typically *fin de siècle* note. (p. 22)

The central narrative of *The Time Machine* is of a kind common to several of Wells's early romances; a character is transferred to or marooned in a wholly alien environment, and the story arises from his efforts to deal with the situation. This is the case with the Time Traveller, with the Angel in *The Wonderful Visit* and with Prendick in *The Island of Dr Moreau,* while Griffin in *The Invisible Man* becomes the victim of his environment in attempting to control it. In all these novels, themes and motifs frequently recur so that cross-reference is inevitable when discussing them. Though Wells is a writer of symbolic fiction—or a myth-maker—the symbolism is not of the specifically 'heraldic' kind that we associate, for instance with Hawthorne's scarlet letter, Melville's white whale, or James's golden bowl. In Wells the symbolic element is inherent in the total fictional situation and to this extent he is closer to Kafka. When, for instance, we see in *The Time Machine* a paradisal world on the surface of the earth inhabited by beautiful carefree beings leading a wholly aesthetic existence, and a diabolic or demonic world beneath the surface inhabited by brutish creatures who spend most of their time in darkness in underground machine shops, and only appear on the surface at night, and when we are told that these two races are the descendants respectively of the present-day bourgeoisie and proletariat, and that the latter live by cannibalistically preying on the former—then clearly we are faced with a symbolic situation of considerable complexity, where several different 'mythical' interpretations are possible. (pp. 45-6)

[While some of the thematic strands of *The Time Machine*] are peculiarly of their period, others have a more general and perhaps more fundamental human relevance. The opposition of Eloi and Morlocks can be interpreted in terms of the late nineteenth-century class-struggle, but it also reflects an opposition between aestheticism and utilitarianism, pastoralism and technology, contemplation and action, and ultimately, and least specifically, between beauty and ugliness, and light and darkness. The book not only embodies the tensions and dilemmas of its time, but others peculiar to Wells himself, which a few years later were to make him cease to be an artist and become a propagandist. Since the tensions are imaginatively but not intellectually resolved we find that a note of irony becomes increasingly more pronounced as the Traveller persists in his disconcerting exploration of the world in which he has found himself. *The Time Machine* is not only a myth, but an ironic myth, like many other considerable works of modern literature. And despite the complexity of its thematic elements, Wells's art is such that the story is a skilfully wrought imaginative whole, a single image. (p. 61)

The Time Machine is polarized between images of beauty and ugliness, and the Angel takes over and continues the characteristic aestheticism of the Eloi, transposing it to the contemporary world. The Angel, in fact, is the medium for a critique of society that is fundamentally aesthetic in its mode of operation. . . .

Because it has an aesthetic rather than an ideological basis, the satire of *The Wonderful Visit* is of a general kind, attacking the absurdities inherent in the human condition itself, in the manner of Swift, or the late Wyndham Lewis, rather than some specific disorder in the social system. (p. 92)

The satire of *The Wonderful Visit,* though falling far short of Swift in its savagery, is wide-ranging enough to include the kind of faith in physical science with which the later Wells was to be identified. (p. 93)

Though *The Wonderful Visit* was no doubt intended to be a wide-ranging satire on the human condition, and in places succeeds as such, the satire lacks intensity, and one is apt to remember the book rather for its generalized charm and humour. It has never had the reputation of the more 'scientific' romances that immediately preceded and followed it, and it lacks the symbolic or mythical qualities of *The Time Machine* or *The Island of Dr Moreau.* Nevertheless, it provides significant thematic links between these two works, and illustrates certain of Wells's fundamental attitudes. (pp. 96-7)

It is in [the tradition of 'the English Island' myth] that *The Island of Dr Moreau* takes its place; it may even be a demonic parody of another and older island story, *The Tempest,* for Moreau as king of the island, seems to be a perverted image of Prospero, while his drunken assistant, Montgomery, stands for Ariel, and the humanized bear, M'ling, for Caliban. But if Wells's novel takes its place in a long and venerable line of 'island myths', the myth, in this particular instance, is given vitality by the meaning which it conveys. And the meaning of the novel is to be found, I think, in one of the profoundest intellectual preoccupations of the second half of the nineteenth century: the implications of Darwinism. (p. 100)

The Island of Dr Moreau, if my reading of it is correct, is a version of the 'island myth' which conveys a powerful and wholly imaginative response to the implications of Evolution. . . . Wells's book shows us a world in which animals can be changed into men at the command of the quasi-divine scientist, and then, after his power has been removed, can be seen to regress to a distorted version of their original shape. There is no essential difference between man and animal, nothing which cannot be affected by surgical manipulation. (pp. 111-12)

[There] can be no doubt that *The Island of Dr Moreau* is a deeply pessimistic book, and its Swiftian view of human nature is not a mere literary exercise. . . . When we compare this with the relative complacency of Wells's later utopian constructions, we have a measure of the change of attitude he was to undergo in the next few years. . . .

In *The Invisible Man* Wells was to return to the blend of fantasy and everyday detail that he had employed in *The Wonderful Visit* and many of his short stories. (p. 112)

The early chapters of *The Invisible Man,* in my opinion, contain some of Wells's finest social comedy, showing to full advantage his perception of topographical detail and his acute ear for vernacular dialogue: they anticipate such later sustained comedies as *Kipps* and *The History of Mr Polly.* The tramp, Mr Thomas Marvell, though a development of the 'Philosophical Tramp' who appears in *The Wonderful Visit,* is a more genial and fully rounded character, and is one of Wells's most successful neo-Dickensian creations.

The significance of *The Invisible Man* in terms of Wells's fictional development is that, for the first time in his romances, we are shown a recognizable society in being which engages our sympathy and interest for its own sake. Instead of seeing a society, albeit a small one, through the eyes of a strange visitor, as in *The Wonderful Visit,* we see the strange visitor—to begin with—through the eyes of the society. And, as Wells emphasizes, it is a smug, settled and apparently prosperous little community. Later, Griffin is to disturb its peace in the farcical events of Whit Monday when he goes berserk and inflicts widespread—if minor—damage to property and injury to its inhabitants. Thematically, *The Invisible Man* relates those romances in which the interest is centred in the heuristic perceptions of a single figure—the Time Traveller, the Angel, Prendick—to *The War of the Worlds,* where attention is focused on society as a whole as it is subject to the unwelcome attentions of not one but a multitude of alien visitants. (pp. 116-17)

It is certainly possible, as Norman Nicholson has suggested, to take *The Invisible Man* as a simple manifestation of the traditional myth of invisibility, of the fear of 'things that go bump in the night', of that which can be apprehended but not seen. But the story has more particular meanings than this. For instance, it is not difficult to draw an ironic moral from Griffin's adventures. Once he has made himself invisible, he is filled with a sense of power:

> I was invisible, and I was only just beginning
> to realize the extraordinary advantage my in-
> visibility gave me. My head was already teem-
> ing with plans of all the wild and wonderful
> things I had now impunity to do. . . .

But in the event he becomes a helpless creature, naked in January on the streets of London, sniffed at by dogs, with children tracking his footprints, and having to take ignominious refuge in a department store. . . . In this reading, *The Invisible Man* becomes a moral story of hubris and its inevitable downfall.

However, this interpretation needs to be modified—or deepened—by the knowledge that Griffin is not merely a private and isolated individual, but does in some sense stand for the possibilities of scientific achievement, or at least for Wells's romantic apprehension of these possibilities. Thus Griffin's punishment must be seen as a rebuke for the pretensions of science. . . . Wells in his early years was far from being an unquestioning positivist. His attitude to science was, in fact, sceptical where it was not ambiguous. In *Moreau* we are shown the *possibilities* of science without in any way being convinced that these are necessarily beneficial. And something similar is true of *The Invisible Man.* One can take this interpretation further and point out that Griffin is not only Wells's last version of the romantic scientist of the Frankenstein type, but also his most fully realized. In this novel Wells seems to have brought the type to final realization before imaginatively casting him out of his consciousness. Conceived in strictly mythical terms,

Griffin, at the point of his death, has become a scapegoat figure hunted out of society: it is perhaps not altogether fanciful to suppose that what is being 'cast out' is not merely the dangerous pretensions of contemporary science, but also the young Wells's own identification with a highly romanticized kind of scientist-magician, first apparent in the aspirations of Nebogipfel. The point is underlined by the introduction into the story of the calm and pragmatic figure of the 'orthodox' scientist, Dr. Kemp. (pp. 119-21)

The Invisible Man is a fundamentally homogeneous book, despite its superficial variety of moods. Thematically it can be seen as marking the end of the earliest phase of Wells's romances, which embodies in various ways an individualistic preoccupation with the romantic scientist, whether he was seen as Nebogipfel, the Time Traveller, Moreau or Griffin. (pp. 121-22)

In my opinion, *The War of the Worlds* is, after *The Time Machine,* Wells's finest piece of sustained imaginative writing. (p. 123)

Historically, *The War of the Worlds* can be considered as the forerunner of much subsequent science fiction. Yet its central interest comes not from its mere treatment of the theme of interplanetary travel, as others had done before, but from the way in which Wells presents an image of human society as the passive victim of extraterrestrial invaders. (p. 124)

The War of the Worlds lacks the comedy and sense of vivid characterization that mark the first part of *The Invisible Man*, but there is the same tangible sense of place, and the setting for the Martian invasion is rendered with extraordinary topographical detail and solidity. . . . In *The War of the Worlds* the Martians establish the 'Reign of Terror' that the Invisible Man could only dream of—and on an infinitely larger scale. . . . Wells's imagination ran to images of mutilation and violence [with ease,] already evident from *The Island of Dr. Moreau* and *The Time Machine.* (pp. 125-26)

The theme of *The War of the Worlds,* the physical destruction of society, or at least the dissolution of the social order, was one of the dominant preoccupations of the *fin de siècle* period. (p. 131)

[The Martians] embody the kind of 'Superman' ideal that both Moreau and Griffin aspired to. *The War of the Worlds* can be seen, then, as continuing the Darwinian preoccupation of *The Time Machine* and *Moreau,* even though its major stress is sociological. Wells was to return to the theme of dissolution, and the near-destruction of society, in his short story, '**The Star**'.

But there is a further sense in which *The War of the Worlds* is pre-eminently a work of its time. . . .

On the one hand, *The War of the Worlds* can be seen as expressing a certain guilty conscience about imperialism, and on the other as dramatizing the fear of invasion that was an intermittent preoccupation of English society in the final decades of the last century. (p. 134)

Whereas *The Time Machine* is organized poetically, *The War of the Worlds* employs the methods of minute documentary realism; but both have a mythical significance. Before long, however, Wells was to consider fiction not as a means of dramatizing and imaginatively enacting ideas, but simply of discussing them. (pp. 138-39)

When the Sleeper Wakes was not an essay in pure imagination as *The Time Machine* and *The War of the Worlds* had been. It had a perceptible didactic and speculative element, and though the narrative retained some of Wells's earlier vigour, the novel was as much an attempt at systematic prophecy as a work of fiction. . . . Between 1899 and 1901 the split between the artist and the prophet or publicist became overt; from the point of view of the latter, the imaginative achievement of his first few years could be dismissed as 'the result of falling in love with an effect in writing for its own sake'. The unhappy mixture of fiction and prophecy in *When the Sleeper Wakes* was the first clear indication that Wells was ceasing to be primarily an artist, responding in imaginative and mythical terms to the life of his times, and was turning to a more directly intellectual treatment of the problems of the present and the possibilities of the future. (pp. 141-42)

[The] central weakness of *When the Sleeper Wakes* is that it creates its world by directly projecting certain observable tendencies in contemporary society, without subjecting them to any imaginative transmutation or aesthetic distancing. (p. 144)

When the Sleeper Wakes is an incoherent book, not only because of the conflict between fiction and prophecy, or the exhaustion of Wells's imagination, though both these factors are important and must be allowed for, but ultimately because it embodies, without any attempt at resolution, the radical ambiguities of its author's intellectual and imaginative attitudes. . . . During his initial period of creative activity the ambiguity of Wells's dual allegiance both to the past and the future was expressed in imaginative and symbolic terms, which transcended the logical problems involved. But from about 1898 onwards Wells's concern with the future was to be expressed in increasingly intellectual terms and his imagination became increasingly coerced by his intellectual convictions. The most crude and grotesque result of this process can be seen in *The Food of the Gods,* but it is already apparent in *When the Sleeper Wakes.* Although this novel is in one sense in the tradition of the utopias of Bellamy and Morris, it differs from them in one very important respect: both these writers attempted to present an image of the future not only as they thought it would be, but as they hoped it would be. Their utopias, in short, embody their authors' desires. . . . The world of Wells's novel, however, is repulsive rather than desirable: one cannot imagine the London of 2100 as a spur for socialist endeavours to remake society. (pp. 145-46)

[Though] *The First Men in the Moon* possesses much of the imaginative quality of *The Time Machine* or *The War of the Worlds,* one must emphasize that it does not have the mythical note of these novels. In describing the imaginary panic in London following the Martian invasion, Wells was making certain implications about the society he lived in; in describing the equally imaginary blossoming of the lunar flowers, he was simply exercising his imagination for its own sake. Considered as a story, however, *The First Men in the Moon* could not be bettered: the heuristic method, centred in Bedford's consciousness, is brilliantly employed, and the interest is heightened since Bedford has to record his relationship with Cavor, and their shared responses to the lunar world, in addition to his own particular perceptions. The pace of the narrative is gradually increased until one reaches the climax at the end of Chapter 18, with Bedford racing back to the sphere as the lunar night falls, almost succumbing to the unbearable cold.

Yet no discussion of *The First Men in the Moon* would be complete without examining in some detail the society of the Selenites. . . . (pp. 160-61)

It would be wrong to suggest that Wells would have unreservedly approved of Selenite society in all its aspects, but it represented an extreme, and even grotesque, type of the totally organized social order that was increasingly to be the ideal of his utopian speculations. Since the Selenites are drawn with the same imaginative exuberance that characterizes the rest of the novel, we are not conscious of any transition from pure narrative to sociological speculation, and the very grotesqueness of this insect-like race prevents too immediate comparisons between them and recognizable humanity. Yet there can be no doubt that Wells's picture of Selenite society embodies the characteristic ambiguities of his thinking at this period. Like Mr Cavor, confronting the young Selenites confined in jars to become machine minders, he both admires a society that could do such things, and is dismayed by the results in practice.

Within the limits that I have indicated, *The First Men in the Moon* is a successful work, and an unquestionably entertaining one. It can be seen as the final flowering of Wells's initial phase of intense imaginative activity, and so is a suitable work with which to conclude this study. (p. 164)

> *Bernard Bergonzi, in his* The Early H. G. Wells: A Study of the Scientific Romances *(© 1961 Bernard Bergonzi; reprinted by permission of Manchester University Press), Manchester University Press, 1961 (and reprinted by University of Toronto Press, 1961), 226 p.*

JORGE LUIS BORGES   (essay date 1964)

Not only do [Wells's excellent first novels *The Island of Dr. Moreau* and *The Invisible Man*] tell an ingenious story; but they tell a story symbolic of processes that are somehow inherent in all human destinies. The harrassed invisible man who has to sleep as though his eyes were wide open because his eyelids do not exclude light is our solitude and our terror; the conventicle of seated monsters who mouth a servile creed in their night is the Vatican and is Lhasa. Work that endures is always capable of an infinite and plastic ambiguity; it is all things for all men, like the Apostle; it is a mirror that reflects the reader's own traits and it is also a map of the world. And it must be ambiguous in an evanescent and modest way, almost in spite of the author; he must appear to be ignorant of all symbolism. Wells displayed that lucid innocence in his first fantastic exercises, which are to me the most admirable part of his admirable work.

Those who say that art should not propagate doctrines usually refer to doctrines that are opposed to their own. Naturally this is not my own case; I gratefully profess almost all the doctrines of Wells, but I deplore his inserting them into his narratives. An heir of the British nominalists, Wells condemns our custom of speaking of the "tenacity of England" or the "intrigues of Prussia." The arguments against that harmful mythology seem to be irreproachable, but not the fact of interpolating them into the story of Mr. Parham's dream. As long as an author merely relates events or traces the slight deviations of a conscience, we can suppose him to be omniscient, we can confuse him with the universe or with God; but when he descends to the level of pure reason, we know he is fallible. (pp. 87-8)

Like Quevedo, like Voltaire, like Goethe, like some others, Wells is less a man of letters than a literature. He wrote garrulous books in which the gigantic felicity of Charles Dickens somehow reappears; he bestowed sociological parables with a

lavish hand; he constructed encyclopedias, enlarged the possibilities of the novel, rewrote the Book of Job—"that great Hebrew imitation of the Platonic dialogue"; for our time, he wrote a very delightful autobiography without pride and without humility. . . . Of the vast and diversified library he left us, nothing has pleased me more than his narration of some atrocious miracles: *The Time Machine, The Island of Dr. Moreau, The Plattner Story, The First Men in the Moon*. . . .

I think they will be incorporated, like the fables of Theseus or Ahasuerus, into the general memory of the species and even transcend the fame of their creator or the extinction of the language in which they were written. (p. 88)

> *Jorge Luis Borges, "The First Wells," in his* Other Inquisitions: 1937-1952, *translated by Ruth L. C. Simms (copyright © 1964 by the University of Texas Press; reprinted by permission), University of Texas Press, 1964, pp. 86-8.*

ALFRED BORRELLO   (essay date 1972)

Like so many authors before and after him, Wells has suffered the critical neglect which all too often follows on the heels of wild adulation. He is not altogether without blame for this neglect. In a period when the experimental plays so important a role in judging the quality of a work of art, he does not nor cannot fare well. His early prose sounds vaguely Victorian and his later blatantly journalistic; and generally he writes as if Conrad, James, and Joyce, whom he admired, had never existed. But his neglect is not solely the result of changing literary tastes. Wells did not help the matter any. So much of what he wrote mitigates against an appreciation of his work in any age. There are his ideas, often half-formed, which rush at the reader with the speed and deadly results of a machine gun. There is his black, doom-filled negativeness which clouds even the most optimistic of his works. There is his insatiable and insistent polemicism which crowds almost every page. Most of all, there is the vast, bloated mass of his work. . . . He wrote too much and repeated himself too often. To reverse what was said of Dr. Johnson: had he written less and spoken more, he would have been more successful. (p. 108)

There is much in Wells that can be dismissed as journalism, but these pieces are the results of a mind vitally interested in the current affairs of his day. They also reflect an impatience and a despair on his part which grew out of the limitations he discovered in the art he practiced so diligently in the first half of his career. While he never hesitated in giving loud expression to his ideas for the salvation of mankind, he was generally reticent to discuss his art and the theory out of which it was produced. He claimed that he was not an artist. Behind his claim lies not an inability to articulate his theory of esthetics, but rather a sensitivity developed over the years. Critics had far too often and far too consistently demonstrated greater interest in his sociological ideas than the art he practiced. (p. 109)

[Wells] held to the English tradition of the novel: loosely constructed, rambling, discursive, philosophical, argumentative, filled with the sights and sounds of life. It was in this tradition that he produced *Tono-Bungay, Kipps, The History of Mr. Polly*, the other seriocomic novels widely accepted by a public nurtured on Dickens, and ultimately, his long polemic works. Unity, which is the product of a tight structure, might produce art, but never life. "Why should a book have unity?" Wells wrote. "For a picture it's reasonable, because you have to see it all at once. It's like wanting to have a whole country done in one style and period of architecture.''

Wells's insistence on the need for a free and uninhibited structure must not be understood to mean that he believed the novel should be equally free thematically. He believed, rather, that the novel has at the core of its being a vital purpose far beyond that conceived of by any of his contemporaries. The novel, he insisted, must effect "moral consequences." As the population of the world grows, he insisted, and an ever-increasing multitude becomes capable of reading, some common ground must be found on which could be discussed and debated those themes of mutual importance to mankind. Out of these discussions and debates could come the answers to problems and the directions for actions which are the "moral consequences." He understood the novel to be a "social mediator. . . ." (pp. 110-11)

In effect, in defining a role for the novel, Wells pleads for its relevancy in a world changing so rapidly that all of the constants, including the long-established means of communication, are losing or are in the process of losing their validity. (p. 111)

So too, Wells maintains, should there exist a laboratory for testing knowledge far more important to humanity than the preservation of its biological existence, important as that is. There are forces loose in the world, he realized, far more deadly than the most potent of viruses. . . . These forces are man's dark side: his disposition to violence, his hatred, his greed, his hypocrisy, his complacency. . . . It is the very inability of man to perceive the insidious workings of these black forces within himself which is their greatest strength. All the more reason, Wells affirmed, for exposing and destroying them in a laboratory where all their deviousness can be revealed. Wells understood the novel as such a laboratory. . . . In short, the novelist may once again assume the roles of prophet and teacher which the creative artist has long played, and out of whose hands they were torn only in the recent past. The novelist can forecast the future, warn his readers against its dangers, and urge them with all the passion at his command to take the proper course of action, the proper paths which will lead humanity from certain doom to that millennia for which it longs.

Wells attempted to perform such tasks in his own work. . . . What he attempted to do in his own work, he believed, was not duplicated in the work of his contemporaries. For him, James represented a prime example of that isolation produced, ironically, by the artist himself who insists upon relinquishing his vital, contemporary role and withdrawing within the walls of his art by ignoring the swift changes taking place in the real world about him. Wells saw no point in involving oneself in the eternal verities if, in doing so, one overlooks the present, more pressing truths. He was aware that his insistence upon topicality in the novel was condemning much of his work to oblivion. Nevertheless, he continued to demand that the novel must give meaning and direction to the present, even if its value for the future is destroyed in the process.

Paradoxically, despite his insistence upon timeliness, he did produce works which have endured and have held the public's interest long after their first success. None of these, however, live because they carry Wells's messages to the world. They live because they manage to capture and hold attention through their essentially honest statements about the human condition. Among these more lasting works are his science fiction novels which have been often copied but never surpassed. . . . [They have] set the pattern for the themes which control contemporary

science fiction as well as suggest those which permeate almost every form of the contemporary novel. There are those themes which treat of man in search of his identity in a world increasingly dedicated to the mass rather than the individual; man versus the terrible consequences of progress, be it technological or scientific; man and his attempt to control his destiny through a development of his own potentialities. But it is not Wells's science fiction alone which has survived. There are his serio-comic novels, one of which, *Tono-Bungay,* has found its way into the standard college course in the modern British novel. Here, too, Wells touches a theme familiar to the reader of the twentieth-century novel—the individual struggling to establish his identity in a world more comfortable for the conformist rather than the rebel. (pp. 112-15)

It is important to note, however, that much of his plea for the relevancy of the novel, while he was still producing such work, devolves upon the direction he believed must be given the form if it is to result in the required "moral consequences" of which he speaks. He held that this direction must be completely personal and not objective. . . . In involving himself personally, the author becomes one with the reader and the two jointly explore the problem at hand.

Wells suggests further that the author has no emotional or logical right to objectivity. Certainly he has no moral right. For Wells, the author's personal involvement in his novel is a moral obligation. Once he identifies within the events of his own life the sources of the social, moral, or political problems he is to treat, he must realize that they also exist in his readers. As a member of humanity, he cannot divorce himself from the matter discussed in the novel because he is involved by his very nature. In the same way, he cannot divorce himself logically because of the nature of creativity. Wells held, somewhat scientifically, that nothing can be "created" in the strictest sense of the word. Every character, every event, every theme, is fundamentally a "compilation" a "fabrication" frankly or furtively drawn from life. Creativity is essentially a synthesizing process. To attempt to divorce oneself entirely from the process is as illogical as it is impossible. . . . Wells insisted that only by giving of himself—and by this he means the very facts of his life, his thoughts, his opinions—consciously or unconsciously, does the writer breathe the spirit of life into his work.

But Wells does not leave the argument at this point. True, the vital force the author imparts to his work flows from a personal involvement and an intimate relationship with it established out of the fabric of his own life. Another element, nevertheless, is necessary. Logically, if the characters, episodes, themes are drawn from life, they must be fixed in structures which resemble life as closely as it is possible for the written word to do so. To do otherwise is not to confer life on the work, but death. Life is loose, formless, unpatterned, filled with irrelevancies, discursive, lacking completeness. So too, Wells insisted, should be the structure of the novel. If the novel is to effect the all-important "moral consequences" the novelist must convince the reader that what he is reading is true. Balance, unity, finish mitigate against the "trueness" of a work because it is manifest even to the most unsophisticated reader that life is in no way so neat.

Wells held that what is true of character, episode, theme, and structure also must be true of the language employed in the novel. It too must be identified with life. He was not, however, always successful in reaching this ideal in his own work, much of which suffers from the stiffness and awkwardness inherited from the Victorian period. Nevertheless, he makes a valiant attempt. . . . He strove for the uncomplicated sentence, a simple and "instinctive" vocabulary—the happy word rather than a bookish and labored substitute. All this reminds one of the later accomplishments of Hemingway and others who strove to capture the cadences of speech on the written page. Out of discussions with James, Conrad, and later Ford Maddox Hueffer (Ford) came a crystallization of Wells's style. "I write as I walk because I want to get somewhere and I write as straight as I can, because that is the best way to get there."

Obviously, Wells believed that the "there" and the "somewhere" are far more important than the route taken—the importance of the "moral consequences" outweighs the style employed. This theory spelled honesty for Wells. (pp. 115-17)

Wells came at a stifling period in England's history when an age, the Victorian, had long outlived those vital forces which moved men to think and act for the good of their species. He came at a period which was growing more and more content with the lifeless formulas of society and growing more and more impervious to needed changes in those formulas. He came at a period when the masses were growing more and more conscious of the power which was in their numbers. He came when a new age, the Edwardian, and a new century, the twentieth, were waiting expectantly to take their places at the center of the stage. He came when science and technology were beginning to make the first great advances into the ignorance which had clouded humanity for so many centuries. He came when these advances were effecting rapid changes in all aspects of man's life save one, seemingly, the novel. Paradoxically, these effects which were altering life so radically were ignored by an art which prided itself on its close relationship to that life. Wells was one of the first to sense the great need to probe in the realm of the novel the growing social and moral unrest occasioned by the applications of the discoveries of this new science and technology to the long unchanged conditions of man's daily life. In doing so he discovered and discussed many of the major social, psychological, and moral questions which plague us today and are as yet unanswered satisfactorily.

His greatest fault, however, was his fundamental inability to develop his suspicions that these problems are not solely the province of contemporary man, nor solely attributable to scientific and technological advances, nor to a deadening social system, but have plagued man throughout his existence. He failed to understand that these problems rise up out of man's nature. In his failure to come directly to grip with the root cause of humanity's difficulties, he supplied answers that were and are too simple to believe and too idealistic to be completely achieved. As a result, he committed the unpardonable aesthetic sin of misreading human nature and translating this misreading into characters who became merely puppets for their creator to move as he willed. He reduced human nature to rigid, immutable, and predictable patterns. He divided humanity into two camps: the good who espoused Wellsian philosophy without argument, and the evil who rejected it and as a consequence were condemned. Eventually, he failed to see any good in those he considered evil nor any evil in those whom he considered good. But he did all of this for a reason—his love of mankind and his fear for its future. In loving mankind so much, he lost, ironically, a love for man. Like Swift, whom he somewhat resembles, he failed to discern the glory of man which lies behind man's stupidities, his inconsistencies, cantankerousness, and the evil he does. Consequently, Wells failed in the first immutable requirement of the novel—that its creator

love his creatures. Wells paid the full price for his failure—despair in his later years and oblivion for much of his work. (pp. 119-20)

Alfred Borrello, "'I Write as I Walk.' A Critical View of Wells," in his H. G. Wells: Author in Agony, *edited by Harry T. Moore (copyright © 1972 by Southern Illinois University Press; reprinted by permission of Southern Illinois University Press), Southern Illinois University Press, 1972, pp. 108-20.*

KENNETH YOUNG (essay date 1974)

The Time Machine [was] the first and among the best of [Wells's] fantasies. (p. 14)

[Much] of *The Time Machine* is as inconsequential as a dream and that is in part due to hasty, awkward writing. Yet, eighty years on, it grips the reader no less than the centuries older *Revelations* of St John the Divine, with which in some aspects it may be compared.

[*The Wonderful Visit*] is *The Time Machine* run backwards, as it were, though it has no element of even pseudo-science in it. . . . The novel is really an ironical study of life in the English countryside. . . . The satire—on ownership, on the ugliness of people's lives—is gentle, though there is a dark passage on the 'readiness of you Human Beings to inflict pain.' . . . From the point of view of Wells's literary development the novel is a first sketch for some of the purely human characters he was to draw with much greater effect in *Kipps* and *Mr Polly*.

The Island of Dr Moreau is the most horrifying of Wells's fantasies and one of the best written and tautly constructed. It marks the introduction into his fiction of the mad or immoral scientist. (pp. 16-17)

[Here, Wells is] concerned with Huxley's point that suffering is 'the badge of all the tribe of sentient things, attaining its highest level in man.' . . .

The Island of Dr Moreau is not merely a savage attack on science and unethical experiments. . . . It is a broader attack—as in the fourth book of *Gulliver's Travels*—on the nature of humanity itself. (p. 18)

The Wheels of Chance is light, good-natured fun-poking at some diverse sections of English society—not excluding its hero—in the 1890s, a trial run for the greater *Kipps* and *Mr Polly*. One criticism, and it applies to some later novels as well: the narrator is the old-style 'buttonholer', permitting himself too many flourishes and a jocosity that can grate.

[Next], Wells returned to the fantastic genre with *The Invisible Man*. It is a less satisfactory story than *The Time Machine* partly because . . . it lacks the poetry, the multiplication of meanings, of its predecessor. Though it was no less appreciated by its early readers, there is now an air of staleness about it; even the pseudo-scientific explanation of how Griffin made himself invisible seems unconvincingly nebulous. (p. 22)

Griffin is a less effective portrait of the amoral scientist than is Dr Moreau. As a character he exists uneasily between farce and melodrama. He is never quite credible. [However, his] return, dying, to visibility is imaginatively done. (pp. 23-4)

[In] the descriptions of lunar scenery [in *The First Men in the Moon* Wells's] imaginative gifts were at full blast—and remarkably prophetic. . . . There is narrative excitement, too,—

another race against time—yet something is lacking, possibly the multiple meanings [of his previous work]. . . . [It] is entertaining but it is not the equal of *The Time Machine*. (pp. 26-7)

[*Love and Mr. Lewisham*] is an unusual mixture of love's young dream and disillusion. This, along with its depiction of an age so innocently inhibited about sexual relations, at least in the lower and middle middle-classes, and its vivid awareness of London from the point of view of those classes, gives it a unique flavour.

[*Kipps*] was, said Wells himself, 'the complete study of life in relation to England's social condition'. It is not quite that. . . . Where it is strongest and most observant is with its lower middle class and shopkeepers and the genteel and somewhat pretentious middle class.

But to speak thus is to make *Kipps* sound dull, and it never is. (pp. 29-30)

[*Kipps*] comes up, fresh and sparkling, one of the three best novels that Wells wrote.

In the Days of the Comet, which came out . . . a year after *Kipps,* has been variously regarded as the tail-end of his fantasies, a fictionalized version of some of his ideas in *A Modern Utopia,* and a satire on politicians. It is possibly trying to be all of these which would account for its schematic incoherence. (p. 32)

[*Tono-Bungay*] is a jumble, 'an agglomeration' as its narrator calls it. . . . All the same, it is a jumble of genius. . . . Some have seen *Tono-Bungay* as Wells's greatest novel. (p. 33)

[The tone of the novel] bespeaks the brimming vitality of life—however, from the moralist's point of view, misdirected—in these Edwardian years. (pp. 34-5)

[*Boon*] is a curious incident rather than a novel. It is a ragbag of pieces written over a decade. . . . From the literary point of view what remains to interest the general reader today are the parodies, some of them bitter, of such writers as . . . Shaw, Yeats and, most hurtful of all, Henry James, then ill, who died the year after *Boon* appeared.

The parodies *are* funny—as funny as the comedy in *The Wheels of Chance,* in *Kipps* and *Mr Polly*. (p. 38)

Mr Britling is Wells's equivalent of Shaw's *Heartbreak House.* There is scarcely a false note; the argument about the future, of world government—England in the van—fits naturally, not obtrusively; and he expresses English patriotism as few others have done, which was a considerable shock to some of his Socialist friends. . . .

This is his last true novel in the writing of which all his great gifts were fully deployed, though none of the later novels are totally lacking a touch here, a spark there, witty dialogue, sharp observation, not least in *Apropos of Dolores.* . . . *Men Like Gods* . . . is not a return to the manner of the early fantasies; it is a picture of Wellsian Utopia. It is perfectly possible to write propaganda which is also good fiction, e.g. Charles Kingsley's *Alton Locke.* . . . But Wells did not. . . . (pp. 39-40)

Wells was never in the philosophical sense a thinker, nor a discoverer. . . . He was more an Autolycan picker-up of ideas which he absorbed, developed, popularized and scattered to the four winds in the form of journalism, even if the journalism was often book-length. . . .

[There is a] deep strain of pessimism in the famous fantasies of the 1890s. *Anticipations* is notably *optimistic* . . . , and might have taken as its text the sentence quoted above from *Mr Polly:* 'If the world does not please you, you can change it.' . . . It was a short distance from 'can' to 'must'. The world must *be* changed and with it human nature.

How, then, was the world to be changed? By a group of men and women . . . who would 'take the world in hand' and create 'a sane order'. Plato's 'guardians' were no doubt Wells's models. There is no reference to democratic election. Wells was that accursed being of present day Socialist demonology, an élitist. (pp. 41-2)

[What Wells came] to realize—and it made him very unhappy—was that, discounting violent revolution and drastic brainwashing and surgery such as took place in Russia, human nature itself was the greatest stumbling block to the achievement of his objectives. . . .

Was he to write as he saw or as he thought? Here was the crux of his painful dilemma; and it was not merely in the despairing and somewhat incoherent pamphlet, *Mind at the End of Its Tether* . . . that he despaired. As early as *The Undying Fire* . . . , while expressing his loathing of things as they were, he wrote: 'I talk . . . I talk . . . and then a desolating sense of reality blows like a destroying gust through my mind, and my little lamp of hope blows out.' (p. 45)

Kenneth Young, in his H. G. Wells, *edited by Ian Scott-Kilvert (© Kenneth Young 1974; Longman Group Ltd., for the British Council), British Council, 1974, 49 p.*

ROBERT BLOOM (essay date 1977)

The titles of the novels of [Wells's] last period are not likely to be familiar to readers or even students of modern letters. . . . Some [such as *The Bulpington of Blup*] are considerably better than others, and most are more beset by ideas and speculation than our sensibilities will ordinarily allow, unless we are reading Tolstoy, or Dostoevsky, or Mann. But the intelligence, grace, feeling, wit, and truth that is in them deserves a hearing. Their style—Wells's extraordinary naturalness and ease of sentence-making, his acute observation, his deployment of complex comic ironies, and his superb dramatic instinct—is noteworthy, despite the legend of his general haste and carelessness. These novels render and enact life in narrative form—the complexities, impasses, delusions, anxieties, aspirations—with unmistakable Wellsian richness, vitality, and immediacy; and they help us to gauge as well as experience these things with unmistakable Wellsian urgency. He never ceased to be a compelling writer or, as I hope to show, a compelling novelist, even when he no longer compelled, or even won, any serious attention. Decidedly, it is an occasion for redress and amends. My conviction is that Wells the novelist, not merely Wells the scientific romancer, or Wells the prophet, or Wells the educator, or Wells the anti-utopian utopian, or Wells the thinker, or Wells the savior, will have his day. If it be not now, yet it will come. (p. 6)

There are two obsessive foci in Wells's novels: his interest in his own ideas and his interest in his own experience, erotic, social, intellectual, political: [Henry] James was right in perceiving that these obsessions meant that, in a more complete sense than is usual with novelists, Wells's novels were always about himself. Wells's way of seeing this was to say that they were about life—an addendum and aid that afforded relief and ventilation for him, edification and encouragement for others. (p. 33)

The last novels of Wells continue to reflect his two obsessions and the fundamental devotion to himself that is their source. But these books also reveal a willingness to escape from such limitations, to establish a new balance between these matters and other matters, between himself and other people, between his ideas and conflicting ideas, and sometimes between the novel as an unburdening and the novel as a thing of interest quite apart from the writer's personal connection with it, an artifact that may work its way into the lives and apprehension of others, regardless of what subjective habitation and name it began in.

Well's means of moving in this more aesthetic direction consist, for one thing, in his readiness to connect the ideas in his novels more intimately with action, character, scene, form, emotion, and total purport; the ideas gain force and interest from the kind of modulation that the narrative imposes on them while reciprocally the narrative is raised to importance by the quality of thought that it must somehow find itself equal to. There are also modifications of the ideas themselves. They tend to be less abstract and detachedly speculative or less programmatically urged and more closely connected with the situations and psyches in which they purportedly arise, which is to say that they belong more to the characters than to Wells himself. Hence the novel, rather than Wells's intellectual career, becomes the ground of their being. As for the personal element, it is still very much present, with the people drawn from Wells's life still filling his pages. But they are there for a new reason—not to participate in Wells's lifelong activity of vindication and self-justification, but to constitute sources of interest for readers quite unacquainted with Wells, his companions, and his embroilments. That is, they have the reality of figures in a novel, to whom the novel gives such life as they have, not the attested reality of autobiography. It no longer matters whether they have an original or not. Their importance derives more than ever before from their participation in, their contribution to, a work of fiction. (pp. 33-4)

[In *The Bulpington of Blup*] Wells delivered himself of his most profound and elaborate indictment of the aestheticism that had been dogging him all his creative life. . . . Because Theodore is at once an aesthete and a complex being, Wells is able to explore ideas and values in a legitimately novelistic way.

The idea that he wishes most intensely to explore in *Bulpington,* his own more or less settled belief, irony, and satire notwithstanding, is our relation to reality, which tends, of course, to be the preoccupation of all good novels. The particular form that the idea takes in *Bulpington* is that the novel's hero has very little taste for reality and that this disinclination is actively nourished by his interest in the arts. That sounds like indictment enough, but Wells's novelistic skill in devising Bulpington's peculiar aesthetic self-regard gives the work as much the air of a special case as of a general position. And Wells's incomparable intellectual power as he ranges, with the appearance of utter disinterestedness, among alternative, indeed quite opposed views manages to persuade us that something very like justice is being done. When toward the end of the novel we withdraw almost with loathing from Theodore, we are responding to what a character in a fiction has made of his life, not to an argument of his creator's. So it is that in *Bulpington* Wells is able to make his most comprehensive, variegated, and

effective statement against aestheticism, Jamesian and non-Jamesian, with considerable aesthetic success. (pp. 38-9)

Wells extends a certain amount of sympathy to the young Theodore as a victim of his posturing *fin de siècle* parents and their world, but before very long it becomes clear that for Wells Theodore is decidedly an antihero, not in the sense that he is unheroic but in the sense that his creator detests him. One of the triumphs of *Bulpington* is that it succeeds on these terms, that with the relish and penetration of his aversion Wells is able to fashion a figure who is unfailingly interesting and, in a curious way, deserving of the reader's sympathy, even if he has been cut off from his author's.

The book's title is an epitome of these matters. It represents at once Theodore's most cherished daydream and Wells's sense of its absurdity and repulsiveness. . . . [The] fanciful Theodore one day at the beach concludes that the ancient name of Blayport must have been Blup, much as he had learned from his history mistress that Brighton had been Brighthelmstone and London Londinium. Having conjured it up, he is quite taken with it. "*Blup.* It sounded like a great cliff, a 'bluff'; it sounded like the smack of waves; it made him think of a horde of pirates, desperate fellows, harbouring there, Bulpingtons all. And among them a leader, one, head of the clan, spite of his tender years, the best of the breed, *The* Bulpington—himself.". . . So the myth of himself as leader, adventurer, warrior, lover is born, the dream into which he falls from out of the life which Wells would prefer him to face; and as he explores and modulates his fantasy throughout the novel, Theodore is pursued by the phonetic snigger of the name Blup.

A short time later Theodore fashions an ancillary symbolic personage and completes his dream world. . . . Thus while still but a boy, Theodore evolves the phantasm of an ideal self and the phantasm of an ideal beloved which, between them, govern his adult life. They comprise the axes of the little world of romance, perfection, and refuge in which he chiefly lives.

Just as Michelangelo's art supplies Theodore with the image of an ideal woman, so art in general nourishes his inwardness and dreaming, authorizing and even implementing his impulse to fend off reality. (pp. 39-40)

Theodore's romantic, reactionary aestheticism, even at its most distasteful, especially at its most distasteful, is rendered with a fullness, a strange compulsive antagonistic scrupulousness that is impressive. It is as though having determined to exorcise a set of attitudes that he finds monstrous and dangerous to life itself, Wells is bent on setting them down as accurately as he can. Without portraying them fully, without allowing them such power and seductiveness as they have for Theodore, Wells cannot be sure of a meaningful victory, satirically, intellectually, novelistically, over them. One of his enduring attractions as a writer is his ability to realize his detestations vividly in their essence, to destroy them, as it were, by knowing them. His parody of James's late style in *Boon,* for example, remains the best of the many that we have had because his mastery of what he disliked in James was so complete. (pp. 41-2)

In Theodore, Wells achieves a portrait of the modern romantic sensiblity that ranks with Conrad's Jim and Fitzgerald's Gatsby; but where Conrad and Fitzgerald, despite their reservations, admire, Wells, despite his understanding, demurs.

Wells's plan in *Bulpington* is to spawn his romantic-aesthetic shirker of a hero in a suitably turn of the century romantic-aesthetic environment, expose him subsequently to a range of inimical ideas and experience to which he remains impervious, or which drives him deeper into fantasy, and then to bring him, with all his evasions and yearnings upon his head, into and through the First World War. Wells thus obligates himself in some measure to present the reality that Theodore shrinks from, along with alternative ways of construing it. His solution is to push *Bulpington* in the direction of what he came to call the dialogue novel, that is to say, to use it not only as he had always used fiction, to examine "the problems of human life and behaviour as we find them incarnate in persons," but to approach that purer form where novels become "primarily discussions carried on through living characters"—discussions of considerable intellectual depth and suppleness, taking for their model the Platonic dialogue. Wells is quite aware that in order for the speakers in such a fictional dialogue to become "persons" or "living characters" they need to do more than entertain ideas, and in *Bulpington* he takes more care to establish the dramatic force of their experience, feeling, and interaction than he was disposed to take in such rigorously conceived dialogue novels as *The Holy Terror* or *Babes in the Darkling Wood*. Thus in *Bulpington*, Wells provides a number of convincingly incarnate voices and outlooks that conflict with Theodore's, together with an action, a range of experience, for Theodore that Theodore's own outlook cannot quite accommodate.

The first of these alternative possibilities is religion, which threads its way ambiguously in and out of Theodore's romanticism. (pp. 43-4)

For all of the intricacy of theological debate in the novel, Wells clearly wishes us to understand that for Theodore religion, like art and history, is but an adjunct to a realm of private fantasy, founded and ruled by self-absorption, need, and fear. The posture and dynamics are simple and familiar enough, but the conflicts, issues, and ideas that Theodore must traverse on his way to solace and refuge are not. In their complexity, and in Theodore's resourceful and subtle, if self-deluding, manipulation of them, Wells gives us a compelling sense of the ways in which a capable, even sophisticated mind leads itself on childish errands. The pattern of self-delusion, of escapism is universal, but the terms are always particular. Out of those particulars, as Wells is thoroughly aware, come persons, characters, interest, fiction, and life. Out of them comes Theodore, who in the imaginativeness of his withdrawal, the intensity of it, becomes interesting.

The intricacy of a number of the religious, historical, or aesthetic ideas in *Bulpington* and Wells's practice of presenting them in debate also serve to remind us that these ideas, regardless of Theodore's employment or distortion of them, are real for others. Theodore does not discredit religion, art, or history by making them elements of his romance. They remain honorable pursuits for other characters, for Wells, for us as we read. What the novel does is to make them momentarily suspect, or, better, momentarily more difficult to honor. . . . It is a tribute to the intellectual and dramatic validity of *Bulpington* that Wells achieves the same effect with those commitments—science, sex, and social consciousness—which oppose Theodore's romanticism and which come closer to Wells's own view of things. (pp. 51-2)

Wells's whole career is based on the idea that the world can be, must be, changed for the better by the application of intelligence and good will. . . . [Art] and literature figure for him as part of that process. Fruitful change can be projected and achieved in his view only by those who have an adequate apprehension of reality—real needs, real desirabilities, real possibilities, real means—and it is a function of the art of which he approves to inculcate this reality. In addition, because Wells is urgently interested in changing the world, he is passionately interested in the forces that on the one hand resist, and on the other encourage, change. For him these forces are largely incarnate in persons. That is why he continued to write novels; and that is why, as the prospects for salutary change grew dimmer and dimmer late in his life, he wrote novels dominated, for the most part, by characters whose casts of mind and temper oppose change. In Wells's view, James had such a mind; as a pure artist, James's impulse is to keep the world what it is, to get it to hold still long enough so that it may be exquisitely, profoundly, lovingly portrayed. Theodore embodies this impulse in *Bulpington,* but in a thoroughly antiheroic way, for he has none of James's command of even a static reality and none of James's genius. Indeed, he has no genius at all, only a number of pretenses. The Broxteds, on the other hand, for all of their foibles, are receptive to the idea of change; it is inherent in the very discipline of the science to which they subscribe. It is this receptivity, this capacity for discovery and emendation, rather than their biology or methodology, that Wells commends. And on the whole he is less interested in commending it than he is distressed by its utter absence in Theodore. (pp. 57-8)

[Theodore achieves] considerable success in overcoming the more or less theoretical challenges that spiritual, scientific, and historical considerations pose to his retreat from the world. . . . There are, however, two realities with which he fares far less triumphantly. One is the war, and the other is love, particularly love under the conditions imposed by the war. These are matters that he must undergo and cannot evade by means of talk or fantasy. He manages to live them through, but on terms that render him both pathetic and repulsive. They are tests that he fails on all but his own bizarre terms. Wells has carefully shaped the novel so as to make these failures climactic and definitive, the disastrous measure of all the pretense and self-deception that have governed Theodore's life from the beginning. Had there been no war, Theodore might have escaped reckoning; but it is part of the intimation of the novel that given enough Theodores, there had to be a war, and inevitably the war had to call in question much of what Theodore represents.

Wells introduces the war in Chapter Six with observations on the way in which it made the old private life, the indulgent pursuit of one's own ends and pleasures, impossible. Prior to 1914, Theodore and his like might ignore history, politics, business, society, the whole public sphere, with impunity and leave the management of the world to those foolish or ambitious enough to be absorbed with it. . . . But the coming of world war in 1914 ushered in the conditions of inescapable involvement that have since become the basis on which all life in this century must perforce be conducted. Like everyone, Theodore is swept up in the excitement of the conflict.

Surprisingly enough, he responds eagerly. Both his newfound flexibility in the face of change and the essential trivialness of his aesthetic dabbling make him emotionally available. For him the war is not so much the end of productive and serious private labors as it is the offer of a new sphere of operations for his old heroic dreams. Speaking unmistakably in the accents of the Bulpington of Blup, he greets the conflict enthusiastically as an opportunity to restore the soul of England under the discipline of struggle. The honor of his country, he tells the Broxteds, impels it to fight. A great romantic victory is inevitable for dear England, his England. (pp. 64-5)

From this point on action dominates the novel, allowing dream and reality to clash and regroup. The war becomes a context of verification for all that Theodore represents or suggests. Writing with an economy and vividness that recall the imaginative achievement of another noncombatant, Stephen Crane in *The Red Badge of Courage,* Wells traces Theodore's experience in the trenches. At his first sight of blood, dismemberment, and death Theodore goes to pieces, retching and weeping. . . . Along with this hysterical behavior, Theodore is guilty of constant heroic chatter, meant to encourage others and quiet his own anxiety. Its effect, however, is only to make him unbearably obnoxious. . . . Through it all, Theodore manages to sustain the illusion that he is a good soldier. The more cowardly his behavior, the more adroit his pretense and hypocrisy. (p. 67)

The pattern of cowardice, self-delusion, and heroic posturing established in this first segment of Theodore's military service persists throughout the war. (p. 68)

[His] war service comes to its climax in an episode that Wells contrives to make immensely appropriate. . . . Theodore undergoes a furious bombardment, far in excess of anything he had experienced or seen during his earlier tour. He represses his memory of what occurred and what he did almost completely, but it is clear that he fled from the scene and sought safety in the rear, leaving his men to face the danger without him. Yet [a] compassionate medical officer intervenes and designates Theodore a victim of shell shock although he is in fact guilty of total dereliction of duty. Summoning his powers of self-deception, Theodore persuades himself before long that he was actually wounded in the shelling. By the time he is qualified for discharge, he has set his military house in good Bulpingtonian order by totally eradicating the truth. Wells's handling of this entire sequence is a remarkable adumbration of the delicate and arcane modes of self-delusion. (pp. 69-70)

Like all novels, *Bulpington* is centrally occupied with the relation of its characters to reality—to the reality, that is, that Wells defines as reality. As readers we must assess both Theodore's failure to come to grips with the actual circumstances of his time and Wells's success in persuading us that they are the actual circumstances. Wells's delineation of Theodore's shrinking from actualities is clear enough when it occurs on the level of personal action, like Theodore's quite unmistakable cowardice and desertion during the war and his subsequent falsification of it. But the level of ideas is more problematic. In order to see Theodore precisely as Wells does, it is probably necessary for the reader to be more sympathetic to the revolutionary young man's hopes and anticipations of a new world a-coming—and the Broxteds' as well—than the reader might be disposed to be. Yet, because it is a novel, and a very artful one, we need not see Theodore precisely as Wells does. It is quite enough for us to feel not that the young man and his friends are right, but that for one terrible moment Theodore feels that they are. By the same token, it is enough for us to feel not that Theodore is wrong about everything, but that he represents real impulses abroad in the world. The reality of the novel itself is that both attitudes exist and have consequences which the novel traces. (pp. 75-6)

[In *Bulpington*] Wells has devised an intriguing form—the anti-*Bildungsroman*. Instead of growing from an inadequate subjectivity to a mature consciousness of the objective world and his own place in it, the putative hero reverses the process, progressively embracing and inventing illusions, more and more determinedly resisting alternatives and voices that clash with

his own. The reason, Wells keeps insisting, is not in Theodore's stars but in the arts, or in such special and dubious forms of the arts as *fin de siècle* aestheticism, escapist romanticism, and the reactionary poetics of the twenties. The range and depth of the indictment is disconcerting. It is one thing for us to consent to the presense of moral or social irresponsibility in the art of Oscar Wilde, since he was himself quite deliberate about putting it there, or to agree with Wells that on the whole it is better to face life than to run away from it. But it is quite another thing to find Theodore mouthing approximations of such twentieth-century articles of aesthetic faith as Conrad's belief in saving illusions, or Yeats's commendation of war as a glorious and, in any case, perpetually inevitable enterprise. For what *Bulpington* does is to take such assumptions of modern romanticism and set them in a context of personality and events which renders them heinous. It is at this point that Wells makes us wonder . . . if he has not, indeed, hit upon some rudimentary human flaw in the modern artistic sensibility which leads it into strange postures and admirations. One may balk at *Bulpington's* intimation that since an unreality principle governs romantic art, romantic art is largely responsible for sanctioning the lie of World War I, as it will be largely responsible for sanctioning the lie, or the madness, of World Wars II and III; but one balks slowly and thoughtfully. For the book makes its case with persuasive, patient, cumulative power, and that case is authenticated by an adroit, unstated psychology: the sound compensatory link between Theodore's heroic dream and his utter heroic incapacity.

Theodore the antihero, the solipsist and egoist, is the first of a series of extensive portraits in these last novels of precisely what in human personality Wells sees as impeding the coming of a new order. Although he had achieved fame through his power to envision the future, by the time Wells reached his late sixties he had come to a very full recognition indeed of the stubborn, unyielding elements in human nature that stood in the path of any future he could still imagine. The burden of these novels, their common theme, is not Wells's affirmation of a new, and rational, and just world order but, regrettably enough, his sense of the difficulty, the improbability of ever securing it. (pp. 83-4)

The satirical novel—the novel which is genuinely a novel and genuinely satirical—is a difficult form to sustain. The mimetic and empathic tendencies of fiction do not usually sort well with the admonitory, repelling and the heroes of *Decline and Fall, Vile Bodies,* and *A Handful of Dust* are likeable simpletons in a mad world, with none of the intimidating power and responsibility of Theodore. The black comedians of our own era characteristically offer a more general, scattered indictment of things as they are, forgoing the concentration of *Bulpington,* as they forego, as well, its essential rationality.

There is only one *Bulpington of Blup,* and one hopes that it will come to notice in this age that has not yet outlived—nor ever will, if we accept the book's premises—its concerns. (pp. 85-6)

Robert Bloom, in his Anatomies of Egotism: A Reading of the Last Novels of H. G. Wells *(reprinted by permission of University of Nebraska Press; © 1977 by the University of Nebraska Press), University of Nebraska Press, 1977, 196 p.*

JOHN R. REED (essay date 1979)

In 1920 H. G. Wells did mankind the courtesy of telling it the story of its life. The story of *The Outline of History* was familiar in most details, but the general shape was new, for human events were not bound together by the decisions of great men or the accidents of national conflict, but by the increasing self-consciousness of human communities through the development of communications. Wells' purposes in fashioning his narrative of man's history was not to offer a panorama of memory, but to free man from his past and to guide him toward the future. By telling men what they were, he hoped to persuade them to make themselves what they might be.

Long before he wrote *The Outline of History*, Wells had developed the habit of viewing history as mutable and open to rearrangement. Two of his early science fiction successes exploited the most alterable part of history, the future, and he considered himself to be the inventor of futurology with his remarkable *Anticipations* . . . , a book studded with keen predictions about the future. Because he did not view history as a fixed line, he felt no embarrassment in describing it as a continuum including what had been, but also what was yet to be. The present was not, for him, the end of a process or story, but a juncture, hence Wells treated all historical accounts as provisional, though in general he inherited the Victorian assumption, stated to his taste in Winwood Reade's *The Martyrdom of Man* . . . and Thomas Huxley's many essays and lectures, that human history was progressing in an evolutionary, ascending, or improving manner. Nonetheless, like Huxley, he never supposed that his improvement was guaranteed. His many books hint always that the future of man is in man's hands. Consequently, it was important that man should have an accurate picture of where he had been and where he might go. To understand the history of his race, man could begin with the rudimentary proving ground of his own nature. . . . Wells assumed that the life of the individual followed a process of growth and maturity similar to that of the race. If a man could examine his own life and, by will and discipline, shape its course, then mankind could do something similar. The main purpose of Wells' career was to tell men this simple truth and to persuade them to act on it.

Wells felt that his personal history reflected the history of his time. He insisted that his autobiography was an account, open to modification, of a "very ordinary brain," and he pictured his life as representative. (p. 53)

Wells' fictional characters inherit this tendency to see their careers as typical, thereby demonstrating at least two things: that Wells' fiction is powerfully autobiographical, and that these characters are educational devices whose purpose is to liberate Wells and his readers by offering proof that each individual can shape his life into a personal history which helps to shape the larger story of the race. George Ponderevo, in *Tono-Bungay* . . . , says that he is trying to render "nothing more nor less than Life—as one man has found it. I want to tell—myself . . .''. His life is worth recording, he says, because he has had the advantage of transcending the normal patterns; he has not lived "true to the rules of [a] type" but has been jerked out of his stratum and has lived crosswise to various planes of existence. His life is peculiarly indicative of his times. Moreover, his slow acquisition of consciousness about the nature of society parallels, in microcosm, the human race's developing consciousness. Although he claims to be offering not a "constructed tale," but "unmanageable reality," George records a life shaped from disorder and confusion into order and purpose. He calls his guiding purpose Science or Truth. . . . Science teaches George to subordinate his individual life to the larger life of man which "emerges from

life with each year one lives and feels, and generation by generation and age by age, [though] the how and why of it are all beyond the compass of [his] mind . . .''.

That George's incomplete life story is meant to recapitulate a larger history is most evident at the end of the novel when he makes his night journey down the Thames. . . . "We are all things that make and pass," he says, "striving upon a hidden mission, out to the open sea." As he says this he is at the boundary between land and sea, past and future, the provisional point where he can give life a shape because he believes it is open to change.

Tono-Bungay was an early attempt to present a private history as a model for mankind's story. In creating this model, Wells was also inventing his personal history. Through fiction, he offered himself an alternative design for his life. He was to repeat this test time and again in his fiction and in his *Experiment in Autobiography* . . . as well. The practice is apparent in *The New Machiavelli*. . . . (pp. 53-4)

Like the original Machiavelli, Remington wishes to be an architect of history, though he is concerned principally with what history will be, not with what it has been. In telling his story, which resembles Wells', Remington gives his life a shape which is governed, like Ponderevo's, by an abstract ideal. The pattern of his life is similar as well, showing a progress from impulsive disorder to intellectual command. However, Remington's lawless nature conflicts with the conservative regulations of society and he is unable to put his plans for a New Republic into effect. Nonetheless, he discovers that just as he may give his own past life a design by documenting it, he may also compose the future by fixing its outline in print. He believes that he has found his place in the larger destiny of mankind. . . . Remington's book represents the embodied will of man, the forcing into reality of what was only dream.

Remington, like other Wells characters, discovers that any writer is an historian, for he is a recorder of what passes in man. . . . History, Wells said more than once, was the story of man struggling toward comprehension and control. Remington's book, while serving as the history of an individual life, provides at the same time a model for the life of the race. Out of ignorance and power, mankind comes to self-consciousness and purpose by shaping the story of his past and giving a direction to his future.

Like Remington, Wells was devoting himself to a literature designed to create a new picture of human history. He realized that his schemes reflected his own desires and were not necessarily "true." The titles of his books of social commentary indicate that he was more interested in the shape of the future than the record of the past: [*Anticipations, The Discovery of the Future, Mankind in the Making*] . . . and so on. History is the past chaos out of which a design may come into being. But it is man who evokes that design. And it is the writer who is master of that evocation.

Many of Wells' novels from about the time of *Tono-Bungay* to *The Outline of History* concentrate upon the theme of an individual life emerging out of ignorance and chaos to some form of command and focus. . . . [However,] the First World War convinced him that mankind's need to consolidate its racial will toward a coherent social system or World State was more urgent than he had supposed. He became more evangelistic in the writings that followed the war, constantly reminding men to observe the lessons provided by the past and to seize the time to make a better future. (p. 54)

Wells had been concerned with the future from the very outset of his career and had written a diagram for that future in *A Modern Utopia* as early as 1905. *The World Set Free* . . . was another fictional picture of how the future of man might be given a suitable form. After publication of *The Outline of History,* Wells became more insistent in his science-fiction and fantasy tales, reiterating in different ways the contrast between past and present chaos with future design, from the outright oppositions in *Men Like Gods* [and *The Dream*] . . . , to Ruritanian sketches like *The King Who Was a King* [and *The Brothers*] . . . , and the grimmer political projection of *The Holy Terror* . . . , to the variously dark or playful pieces such as [*Mr. Blettsworthy on Rampole Island, The Croquet Player* and *Star-Begotten*]. . . .

These outright departures from realistic portrayal were accompanied by a consistent stream of non-fictional essays and books making the same points in more immediate and practical terms. These works show that Wells was trying to transfer the picture of his personal history, which he believed to be typical of his generation, to mankind at large. . . . Two realistic novels written after the *Outline* illustrate Wells' attitude in a more complicated and intriguing fashion. In *The Secret Places of the Heart* . . . , Wells went out of his way to demonstrate the connection between racial and personal history. Sir Richmond Hardy, seeking a cure for nervous distress, makes a tour of England's most important archeological sites and discovers that "Archeology is very like remembering." . . . During his therapeutic holiday, Sir Richmond has traced man's history and recovered the vision of a future open to modification by man. Unfortunately, he dies while laboring to give that future shape.

The Secret Places of the Heart is a slight attempt compared to the elaborate examination of these same themes in *The World of William Clissold* . . . . Clissold openly acknowledges that while men have made valiant attempts "to impose a coherent and comprehensive story" upon life, there is actually "no plot nor schema nor drama nor pattern in the flow of events as they are apprehended by human minds . . .". Consequently, the design that man gives to history—the story he tells about mankind—is a fabrication, but a fiction with a purpose, for if man can picture a better world, he may be able to live into it. Although Clissold sees his life divided into chapters and says that "Thinking of one's childhood is like opening a great neglected volume haphazard and reading in it," he knows that there is no story to individual or racial history until man wills that there should be one. In telling his story, Clissold gives it form. Likewise, if one tells the story of mankind, one creates a believable shape that mankind may approximate.

In *The Salvaging of Civilization* . . . , Wells said that what modern civilization needs is "a revised and enlarged Bible . . . to restore a common ground of ideas and interpretations . . .". Because science had invalidated the Bible's scheme [of giving humanity a sense of purpose and order], Wells argued, modern man needed a new story of this order. . . .

Behind this conviction is Wells' belief that the true direction of man's progress is from selfish individualism to communal cooperation. This is the sequence he hoped for in himself and described in the *Outline.* (p. 55)

All of Wells' fiction and journalism after *The Outline of History* was designed to create a new Bible, a new cosmogony for modern man. Mankind, he hoped, would imitate the novelist who could imagine an alternative reality and then bring it into being. He urged men to believe that they were capable of this

high endeavor, but they did not seem to comprehend. How this must have baffled Wells. It had all been so simple in his own case. He told the story of his own growth and success time and again in his fiction and even disguised it as the story of the race, but though the race bought the book by millions, they did not get the message. Even in his decline Wells continued to read his own story into that of the race, and as he faded he foresaw in *Mind at the End of its Tether* . . . the *Götterdämmerung* of mankind. (pp. 55-6)

John R. Reed, "The Future According to H. G. Wells," in The North American Review *(reprinted by permission from* The North American Review; *copyright © 1979 by the University of Northern Iowa), Vol. 264, No. 2, Summer, 1979, pp. 53-6.*

ROSLYNN D. HAYNES   (essay date 1980)

[The] chief formative influence on Wells's thought was that of [Thomas H.] Huxley. (p. 16)

[Evolutionary theory] seemed to Wells, and may still be regarded as, the nearest approach to a unifying factor in contemporary thought. Life, and even cosmology, could be seen as an unfolding of the same underlying process so that, although a missing factor might temporarily block one's understanding, all phenomena would ultimately be seen to obey universal laws. No other concept ever made an equivalent impact on Wells—rather the criteria of biology became his yardstick to measure the claims of all other disciplines—astronomy, physics, sociology, politics, even theology and art. Some idea of the extent of this influence may be gained by tracing in broad outline through Wells's work those principles which are also the basic assumptions of the scientific method, particularly of biology.

The first assumption, for Huxley as for all his contemporary scientists was the necessity for an objective viewpoint, and it is clear that in virtually all the scientific romances and novels, with the partial exception of *Kipps, Tono-Bungay* and *Mr. Polly,* Wells's method of looking at the world was almost ruthlessly objective. This is one of the reasons why, although he was capable of expressing that depth of pathos which is the mark of great comedy, he was unable to write anything approaching tragedy; the latter presupposes an element of identification on the part of the audience with the protagonist while comedy depends, for its fullest effect, on the detachment or objectivity of the audience. Van Wyck Brooks has commented that Wells saw men chemically and anatomically, and the world astronomically, all of which terms presuppose an analytical gaze; he might, with equal truth, have said that Wells saw life through a microscope or as stuffed remains. (pp. 16-17)

More subtle, but no less a part of this objective viewing of life, is Wells's general approach to his characters. Rarely, even with sympathetic characters, do we penetrate the wall erected by the narrator's deprecatory humour: if a character is not absolutely the butt of Wellsian wit, like Kipps, Edward Ponderevo, Mr Polly and the other 'little men', he may frequently be distanced by an indulgently avuncular tone which makes him appear significantly smaller-than-life. Lewisham is introduced in this manner and never wholly outgrows the initial diminishing effect. . . . (p. 18)

The chief exceptions to this belittling process of characterisation are Wells's scientists, or those who, like Remington the politician, are seen as the progenitors of his ideal citizens of the future. That is to say, the chief exceptions are those who, in turn, regard the world scientifically and objectively and with a mind to impose order on its chaos.

The most striking manifestation, however, of Wells's objective viewpoint is his preoccupation with the future. His writings about it, far from being escapist in attitude, constitute the first literary experiment in deductive thinking about science. (p. 19)

[Because] we may not know the future in any personal and individual sense, we may experience an intellectual hope for it, but not a deep emotion, not the emotion which can mentally fondle the well-remembered experiences of the past or the intimate sensations of the present. In this sense the phrase 'scientific romance' is often a misleading term in the description of Wells's work, for, traditionally, the romance, which seeks to elicit an emotional involvement on the part of the reader with the events described, has always, for the reasons indicated above, been set in the past or, less often, in the present. . . . [This] suggests one reason why the scientific romances, the future histories and the utopias, have never been regarded as major works of literature or even, by some critics, as literature at all. Their characters are too deficient in human sympathy, precisely because they are credible citizens of a future state and not of our past or present systems. The vistas of the dying world in *The Time Machine* or of the lunar dawn and the awakening of life in *The First Men in the Moon,* are magnificent in scope and descriptive power, but with the possible exception of the last Martian whose death-cries are heard on Primrose Hill, the characters of these stories fail to stir either love or hate. The only sensations we feel are vicarious ones on behalf of the protagonist—the disgust, for example, of the Time Traveller at the Morlocks—but even here the emotion experienced is at one or two removes and thus considerably attenuated.

A second fundamental scientific procedure and again a cornerstone of Huxley's system of education, is the desire to impose some order upon the universe, to collate the immense mass of data indiscriminately recorded by our senses and to evolve a unifying set of 'laws' which will both explain and predict the apparent confusion of phenomena. . . . This was one explanation for the triumph of Darwinian theory over the static and cumbersome Linnaean system—it had provided a model which seemed capable of assimilating whatever variations Nature might produce in the future. . . . [Drawing] together strands from all disciplines and relating them in one unifying theory, [the Darwinian system seemed to Wells] to symbolise order itself. (pp. 20-1)

In his creed, discipline, research and planning are the sole means of saving the world from the insidious destroyer, waste, and hence the leaders of his utopias must display precisely these credentials if society is to be saved.

The principle of order, then, is Wells's remedy for virtually all social maladies but such an ideal might be thought to entail a cost in the sphere of personal life—the imposing of certain restrictions on individual freedom. But here another characteristic of Wells's utopias is important in moderating the regimentation which is usually regarded as inevitable in a highly-ordered society: that is, their non-static quality. The concept of an evolving utopia in which the ideal of perfection is itself changing is effectively a Wellsian innovation in the history of utopian thought, and one which has been largely overlooked by those later writers who have condemned Wells's utopias for the alleged exaction of conformity from all their members. On the contrary, Wells regarded order as itself partaking of a

kinetic quality, not a stasis: order means, for him, ordered change. (pp. 21-2)

Although all these themes may be traced directly to Wells's science studies, the most striking evidence of Huxley's influence is to be seen in his concept of the dual nature of man. As a student of evolution, Wells was fully aware of the 'sub-human' elements in man; indeed Darwin's words at the conclusion of *The Descent of Man,* 'With all his noble qualities . . . with all these exalted powers, man still bears in his bodily frame the indelible stamp of his lowly origin,' remained too controversial and too recent to admit of being forgotten in Wells's life-time. How little Wells was likely to forget man's 'lowly origin', *The Island of Dr. Moreau* shows only too clearly. But neither did he lose hope in the further evolution of man, for it was no inconsiderable triumph that the mind of man had advanced so far as to be capable of formulating an explanation of its own ancestry. *The Island of Dr. Moreau* displays both these aspects of man's nature—Moreau himself is the man endowed with creativity and understanding; the beast-men, with their recurrent regressions to a sub-human state, stand for those debased instincts which delay the progress of civilisation. . . . [The novel] may be considered as a physical Jekyll and Hyde parable. Like Stevenson, Wells does not merely describe the duality of human nature; in both stories the 'beast' is victorious. But whereas Stevenson implies that this was the result of mere chance—because Dr Jekyll happened to drink the transforming potion first at a time when his sentiments were tending towards malevolence so that this side of his nature became exaggerated—Wells makes no such concessions. Reversion to the beast, in his novel, is the norm rather than the exception, as Prendick, like Gulliver, discovers on his return to so-called civilisation. *Dr. Moreau* is Wells's starkest and most sustained treatment of man's dual nature. . . . (pp. 23-4)

At various stages of his career Wells's ideas about the possible outcome of these clashes alternated between hope and despair and frequently combined both to provide a warning and an incentive to action, but it is possible to find a basis in the biological climate of the time for each of these attitudes. Wells's pessimism may have been partly innate, partly influenced by the prevailing *fin de siècle* atmosphere, as Bergonzi has claimed [see except above], but the main source of it was the pessimism of Huxley, who was certainly not blind to the possibility of man's regression or extinction. . . . [The] clearest expression of his pessimism was his famous Romanes lecture, *'Evolution and Ethics'.* (p. 25)

The cosmic process, he declared, is a ferment of incessant struggle and change, inevitably entailing great suffering and death. But precisely because of his understanding of the evolutionary 'jungle', of 'nature red in tooth and claw' and of 'the ape and the tiger' aspects of man's nature, Huxley also strove to see some alternative, some hope for the future of the race. This hope he formulated in his concept of an 'Ethical Process'. Though he believed this to have arisen through the natural mechanism of evolution, he saw as its main function the countering of the hitherto amoral evolutionary process and the substitution of willing cooperation for competitive struggle. . . . Because man is only partially emancipated from nature, he still suffers pain, still struggles against the marks of his lowly origin, and Huxley did not blink from the spectacle of waste and suffering inherent in the natural process:

> I deem it an essential condition of the realization of that hope [that evil may be abated] that we should cast aside the notion that escape

from pain and sorrow is the proper object of
life.

In the Eloi of *The Time Machine* Wells created a literary symbol
of precisely this warning. The Eloi desire above all else to
escape from pain and effort, from seeing the unpleasant reality
of their situation and seek only comfort and ease, the shallow
happiness of an illusion. Their plight and their imminent evolutionary extinction are the natural and inevitable result of
their childish hedonism.

Three years after '*Evolution and Ethics*' Wells published *The
Island of Dr. Moreau* in which the parallels are immediately
obvious. Indeed there is almost nothing in Huxley's lecture
which did not issue in a literary equivalent somewhere in Wells's
work. (pp. 25-6)

[Whereas] Huxley's emphasis on ethics led him at times to
mistrust even the intellect when it was divorced from a moral
education, Wells came increasingly to place his hope for the
future of mankind in intelligence and will as the means of
overcoming the chance and cruelty of the evolutionary process.
This purposive effort is certainly a moral one, but Wells (unlike
Huxley) seems to have believed that it could be inspired by,
and developed from, reason and intellect alone. . . . [Thus]
evolutionary advance appears in his work to result from a better
trained intellect and imagination which inevitably generate a
more highly developed moral consciousness and will. Hence
Wells's undisguised contempt for the 'natural man' who deliberately isolates himself from the social, and particularly the
intellectual advances of utopia. (p. 27)

Moreau, who tries to force his beasts to evolve by non-genetic
means, is fully aware of the three aspects of the process [of
evolution] . . .—chance, waste and pain; indeed he accepts
them with no apparent signs of regret as obvious necessities.
The element of chance in the novel is forced upon our attention
repeatedly. . . . Moreau [in arbitrarily choosing the human
form as his model] certainly sees chance as the very basis of
his 'design'. . . . (p. 30)

[Once] chance is accepted, the implication of waste is inescapable. This was immediately seen to be one of the major
evils of Darwin's scheme and a severe charge against [the long-
held beliefs in] a supposedly benevolent Creator. Moreau is
no loving god; he personifies the insentient, mechanistic process which Tyndall and Huxley had so ruthlessly exposed. . . .
The almost arbitrary succession of beasts which passes through
Moreau's hands re-enacts the idea of the evolutionary process
as Nature's giant experiment, wherein much material must, of
necessity, be lost for the sake of a few 'successes'. Moreau is
as ruthlessly amoral as the Huxleyan view of nature; indeed
his character is virtually a dramatisation of the dangers which
Huxley had warned would result from an 'imitation' of the
'cosmic process', or from the attempt to derive a social ethic
from it. Characteristically, Moreau endeavours to justify his
relentless pursuit by just such an appeal to a 'natural' philosophy. . . . (pp. 31-2)

Waste in any process involving living beings necessarily implies also pain, and pain is one of the most recurrent themes
of the novel. It first assails Prendick through the agonised cries
of the vivisected puma. . . . The contrast between Prendick's
emotional reaction to the cries and Moreau's unemotional acceptance of the necessity of pain epitomises the difference
between the two men: the one cannot bear to know, or be
forced to share in any sense the depths of suffering of living
beings; the other extols suffering and inflicts it with a grim

sense of inevitability. . . . [The] bath of pain through which
the beasts must pass to be made whole, i.e. more human, is
a highly significant symbol, for clearly it is intended to have
overtones of the baptismal ceremony, a washing away of original sin and a passing from death into life, just as it is certainly
intended to be reflected in Moreau's own name, a condensation
of 'water of death'. This is sufficiently emphasised, if emphasis
were needed, when Prendick hears Montgomery calling out
the name as a disyllable—'Mor—eau'.

Moreau is also associated with the deist idea of God and with
several aspects of Judaeo-Christian orthodoxy. Apart from the
oblique reference to the ceremony of baptism, the gatherings
of the Beast-folk are, whatever the similarity to Kipling's *Jungle Book,* intended primarily as religious ceremonies involving
a litany of prohibition, commandments delivered from on high,
and a grovelling acknowledgment of Moreau's omnipotence
and rights over them. . . . Moreau even follows the Genesis
pattern of creation to the extent of 'creating' a serpent-devil:
'It was a limbless thing, with a horrible face that writhed along
the ground in a serpentine fashion.' But the most startling
parallel with Christian orthodoxy is Moreau's mock resurrection. Strangely enough, this episode, which one might suppose
would have been considered highly offensive, if not blasphemous, seems to have passed unnoticed by critics; yet the effect
of this grotesque 'resurrection' cannot but be intended to reflect
upon the authenticity of Christian doctrine. The very language
used is highly reminiscent of the Gospel accounts of the empty
tomb. . . . Moreau, then, represents a nightmarish hybrid, the
logical and inevitable outcome, as Wells saw it, of the desire
to graft on to a deistic belief in an omnipotent Creator, the
postulates of Darwinian theory including the assertion of a
continuum of creation which acknowledged no gap, no essential difference in kind, between man and his forebears. Wells
thus deliberately set out to destroy the hope cherished by liberal
theologians, that some valid, if tacit, compromise was possible
between science and natural theology. But he was not yet
sufficiently interested in the fate of religion to launch out and
devise the outlines of a substitute faith, as he was to do later.
(pp. 32-4)

The scale of reality which Wells has succeeded in portraying
in the handful of characters on his island (and we should not
miss the irony that this island which disposes once for all of
the romantic idea of the 'noble savage' is presumed in the
Introduction to be Noble's Island) shows the extent of his
mythopoeic capacities. Despite the apparent realism of the
novel—and the recoil of his contemporaries from its vivid
pictures of horror testifies to its atmosphere of authenticity and
betokens a mind firmly grounded in facts—Wells's success in
creating the sense of a mythical dimension in the novel, resides
in its very ambiguities. The images do not quite reinforce each
other and the resultant blurred and composite pictures seems
to bespeak a complexity all the more striking because of the
clarity of the surrounding detail. Thus, at one level, the Beast-
People represent the dual nature of man—the bestial instincts
which are his evolutionary inheritance, and the cultural ac-
quirements uneasily and painfully superimposed upon them.
But they also represent the nineteenth-century confusion as to
man's origins. Just as in pre-Darwinian belief man was regarded as a fallen angel, so Prendick at first assumes that
Moreau's grotesques are degenerate and mutilated human beings,
until Moreau shows him that they have in fact been developed
from lower forms.

Even more significant is the reaction that Prendick, like Gulliver, experiences towards his compatriots after returning to

England [where he fears the emergence of the bestial side of the people he encounters, all of whom he suspects of being Beast People.] (p. 35)

Similarly Moreau himself has an ambiguous role in the novel. He seems to be both fully human in that he errs and proceeds by trial and error, and also a parody of the Old Testament Jehovah, in that he is both Creator and Law-Giver. Moreover he is both an individual scientist and an allegory of the evolutionary process. In the coalescence of these suggestions lie the fascination and the subtlety of Wells's modern myth. (p. 36)

> *Roslynn D. Haynes, "Wells's Scientific Background: Scientist or Visionary?" in her* H. G. Wells, Discoverer of the Future: The Influence of Science on His Thought *(reprinted by permission of New York University Press; in Canada by Macmillan, London and Basingstoke; copyright © 1980 by R. D. Haynes), New York University Press, 1980, pp. 9-66.*

ADDITIONAL BIBLIOGRAPHY

Bellamy, William. "H. G. Wells." In his *The Novels of Wells, Bennett, and Galsworthy*, pp. 114-43. New York: Barnes & Noble, 1971.
    A critical study of *In the Days of the Comet, Kipps, Tono-Bungay,* and *The History of Mr. Polly.*

Bergonzi, Bernard, ed. *H. G. Wells: A Collection of Critical Essays.* Englewood Cliffs, N.J.: Prentice-Hall, 1976, 182 p.
    Ten important essays on Wells and his work, several of which are excerpted above. Critics include Bernard Bergonzi, Robert M. Philmus, David Lodge, and others.

Brome, Vincent. *H. G. Wells: A Biography.* London: Longmans, Green and Co., 1952, 255 p.
    A biography containing interesting personal glimpses into Wells's life, and including many examples of the critical reception of his works.

Brome, Vincent. "H. G. Wells as a Controversialist." *The University of Windsor Review* II, No. 2 (Spring 1967): 31-45.
    An account of Wells's quarrels with the Fabians, Stalin, James, and Belloc.

Farrell, John K. A. "H. G. Wells as an Historian." *The University of Windsor Review* II, No. 2 (Spring 1967): 47-57.
    Appraisal of *The Outline of History* and *The Shape of Things to Come,* finding the former suspect as a work of history because of oversimplification and lack of documentation, and the latter a surprisingly prophetic book.

Freeman, John. "H. G. Wells." In his *The Moderns: Essays in Literary Criticism,* pp. 53-101. 1917. Reprint. Freeport, N.Y.: Books for Libraries Press, 1967.
    A critical examination of Wells's canon, emphasizing his social and humorous novels and his nonfiction.

Hynes, Samuel. "H. G. and G.B.S." In his *Edwardian Occasions: Essays on English Writing in the Early Twentieth Century,* pp. 18-23. New York: Oxford University Press, 1972.*
    Comparison of the lives and beliefs of Shaw and Wells, both of whom the critic sees suffering from *"Weltverbesserungswahn—* a rage to better the world."

Mackenzie, Norman, and Mackenzie, Jean. *The Time Traveller: The Life of H. G. Wells.* London: Weidenfeld and Nicolson, 1973, 487 p.
    A detailed and complete biography of Wells.

Macy, John. "H. G. Wells and Utopia." In his *The Critical Game,* pp. 269-76. New York: Boni and Liveright, 1922.
    An essay on Wells's vision of Utopia as set forth in *The World Set Free.*

Parrinder, Patrick, ed. *H. G. Wells: The Critical Heritage.* London: Routledge & Kegan Paul, 1972, 351 p.
    A collection of important reviews and studies of Wells's work.

Shaw, Bernard. "H. G. Wells on the Rest of Us." In his *Pen Portraits and Reviews,* pp. 279-83. London: Constable and Co., 1932.
    A remembrance of Wells as a petulant, childish man of many talents. This essay contains Shaw's wry appraisal: "I never met such a chap. I could not survive such another."

Snow, C. P. "H. G. Wells." In his *Variety of Men,* pp. 63-85. New York: Charles Scribner's Sons, 1967.
    Snow's reminiscences of conversations with Wells, and a brief biography.

Suvin, Darko, and Philmus, Robert M., eds. *H. G. Wells and Modern Science Fiction.* Lewisburg, Pa.: Bucknell University Press, 1977, 277 p.
    A collection of essays concerning Wells's influence on and comparative stature within the modern science fiction world, and containing criticism of his early scientific romances.

Wilson, Harris, ed. *Arnold Bennett and H. G. Wells: A Record of a Personal and a Literary Friendship.* Urbana: University of Illinois Press, 1960, 290 p.*
    An insightful collection of articles and letters by Bennett and Wells.

Woolf, Virginia. "Modern Fiction." In her *The Common Reader,* pp. 207-18. New York: Harcourt, Brace and Co., 1925.*
    An appraisal of Wells as a "materialist" who makes "the trivial and transitory appear the true and the enduring."

Émile Zola

1840-1902

French novelist, short story writer, critic, essayist, dramatist, poet, and journalist.

With Zola, the realism of Balzac, Flaubert, and the Goncourt brothers lost some of its artistic qualities, gained features of the scientific and sociological document, and was reborn as naturalism. In *Le roman experimental (The Experimental Novel)*, Zola defined naturalism as "a corner of nature seen through a temperament." The "Rougon-Macquart" novels, subtitled "The Natural and Social History of a Family under the Second Empire," were designed to dramatize the current theories of hereditary determinism as outlined in such works as Prosper Lucas's *Traité de l'hérédité naturelle*. Through the successive generations of the families in the "Rougon-Macquart" novels, Zola shows various hereditary and environmental factors as they determine the psychology and behavior of his characters. He was a tireless student of human society, and his ambition was to write "the impersonal novel in which the novelist is nothing but a recorder of facts, who has no right to judge or form conclusions." But while Zola did succeed in documenting a historical milieu with great detail and precision, his commentators also find in the novels a highly personal vision expressed with emotion and intensity.

Born in Paris, Zola was raised in Aix-en-Provence, where his father was an engineer. Returning to Paris at the age of eighteen, he took a series of jobs, all the while reading voraciously and beginning to develop his skills in journalism. Zola's earliest fiction appears in *Contes à Ninon*. These short stories have more in common with medieval fables of fantasy than the strict realism of the author's later work. Similarly, Zola's first novel, *La confession de Claude (Claude's Confession)*, relies more on imagination and subjectivity than on an objective rendering of psychological and social types. With *Thérèse Raquin (The Devil's Compact)* and *Madeleine Férat (Magdalen Férat)* Zola began to experiment with techniques of realism that would lead to the naturalism of the "Rougon-Macquart" cycle.

In the "Rougon-Macquart" series Zola applied the methods of science to the novelist's art. "Zola reduced the craft of fiction to a mechanical technique," remarks F.W.J. Hemmings. This technique is visible in the author's *ébauches*: plot outlines, character formulations, and a general thesis to be worked out in each individual novel. He exhaustively researched the background of his works, compiling a dictionary of slang, for instance, to lend verisimilitude to the dialogue of the lower classes in *L'assommoir (Gervaise)*. More than one critic has compared Zola to a bricklayer for his orderly fictional constructions. Modern criticism, however, has come to emphasize the importance of imagination and inspiration in the "Rougon-Macquart" novels. Nevertheless, it was Zola's intention to generate his characters and their destinies according to the most current scientific theories. The families of the "Rougon-Macquart" represent the three major classes of French society: the upper-class Rougons, the middle-class Mourets, and the lower-class Lantiers. Critics generally regard the working-class novels, such as *Gervaise, Nana,* and *Germinal,* as Zola's most important works. These are often

described as anatomies of disease, insanity, and perversion. The misery and degradation depicted in these works earned Zola a reputation among his contemporaries as a pessimistic determinist, if not a pornographer, as many asserted. Eventually he turned from the scientific analysis of the "Rougon-Macquart" cycle to the social pamphleteering of later novels such as *Fécondité (Fruitfulness)*.

Zola's sense of social duty was visibly manifested with his involvement in the notorious Dreyfus case. "J'accuse" ("The Dreyfus Case"), his vehement open letter to the President of the Republic defending Captain Alfred Dreyfus, a Jewish army officer falsely accused of treason, is considered instrumental in the eventual pardon of Dreyfus. As a result of his role in this scandal, Zola was twice tried for libel. He fled to England, returning to Paris only after a general amnesty had been proclaimed.

Although Zola's scientific conception of literature is no longer popular, he served as its most devoted spokesman and articulated a theory of fiction that affected the course of literature throughout the world. His literary theories can be seen as an influence on the naturalistic dramas of Ibsen and Hauptmann, on the Italian *verismo* movement, and on the American realists,

557

among others. The best novels of the "Rougon-Macquart" are regarded as masterpieces of their kind, embodying an extremely important phase in the history of literature.

(See also *TCLC*, Vol. 1.)

PRINCIPAL WORKS

Contes à Ninon   (short stories)   1864
    [*Stories for Ninon*, 1895]
La confession de Claude   (novel)   1865
    [*Claude's Confession*, 1882]
Thérèse Raquin   (novel)   1867
    [*The Devil's Compact*, 1892]
Madeleine Férat   (novel)   1868
    [*Magdalen Férat*, 1880]
*La fortune des Rougon   (novel)   1871
    [*The Rougon-Macquart Family*, 1879]
*La curée   (novel)   1872
    [*In the Whirlpool*, 1882]
*Le ventre de Paris   (novel)   1873
    [*The Markets of Paris*, 1879]
*La conquête de Plassans   (novel)   1874
    [*The Conquest of Plassans*, 1879; also published as *A Mad Love; or, The Abbé and His Court*, 1882]
*La faute de l'abbé Mouret   (novel)   1875
    [*Albine; or, The Abbe's Temptation*, 1882]
*Son excellence Eugène Rougon   (novel)   1876
    [*Eugene Rougon*, 1876]
*L'assommoir   (novel)   1877
    [*Gervaise*, 1879]
*Une page d'amour   (novel)   1878
    [*Hélène*, 1878]
*Nana   (novel)   1880
    [*Nana*, 1880]
Le roman experimental   (criticism)   1880
    [*The Experimental Novel*, 1880]
Les romanciers naturalistes   (criticism)   1881
*Pot-bouille   (novel)   1882
    [*Piping Hot*, 1889]
*Au bonheur des dames   (novel)   1883
    [*The Bonheur des Dames; or, The Shop Girls of Paris*, 1883; published in England as *The Ladies' Paradise*, 1883]
*La joie de vivre   (novel)   1884
    [*Life's Joys*, 1884]
*Germinal   (novel)   1885
    [*Germinal*, 1885]
*L'oeuvre   (novel)   1886
    [*His Masterpiece?*, 1886]
*La terre   (novel)   1886
    [*The Soil*, 1886; also published as *Earth*, 1954]
*La rêve   (novel)   1888
    [*The Dream*, 1888]
*La bête humaine   (novel)   1890
    [*The Human Brutes*, 1890; also published as *The Human Animals*, 1890]
*L'argent   (novel)   1891
    [*Money*, 1891]
*La débâcle   (novel)   1892
    [*The Downfall*, 1892]
*Le docteur Pascal   (novel)   1893
    [*Doctor Pascal*, 1893]
**Lourdes   (novel)   1894
    [*Lourdes*, 1896]

**Rome   (novel)   1896
    [*Rome*, 1896]
"J'accuse"   (letter)   1898
    ["The Dreyfus Case," 1898]
**Paris   (novel)   1898
    [*Paris*, 1898]
***Fécondité   (novel)   1899
    [*Fruitfulness*, 1900]
***Travail   (novel)   1901
    [*Labor*, 1901]
***Vérité   (novel)   1903
    [*Truth*, 1903]

*These volumes comprise the series "Les Rougon-Macquart."

**These volumes comprise the trilogy "Les trois villes."

***These volumes comprise the unfinished tetralogy "Les quatre evangiles."

STÉPHANE MALLARMÉ   (essay date 1877)

[*L'assommoir*] is truly great, and worthy of an age in which truth has become the popular form of beauty. Those who accuse you of not writing for the people are just as wrong, in a way, as those who are sorry to see you abandon certain ideals of the past. Actually, you have simply invented a modern ideal. The essence of the book is your marvelous experiment with language; this enables you to take over many expressions which are often flat when handled by third-rate writers, and recast them in the most beautiful of literary forms. You succeed in making even writers laugh and cry! I find it all tremendously moving. So far, the beginning of the book is the part I like best: is that just my own inclination or the result of a supreme effort on your part? The tremendous simplicity and sincerity in your descriptions of Coupeau at work or of his wife's garret cast a spell over me which even the gloomy ending couldn't break. We turn the pages of your book as quietly as we live our lives from day to day. You have given something absolutely new to Literature. (p. 99)

> *Stéphane Mallarmé, in his letter to Émile Zola on February 3, 1877 in his* Mallarmé: Selected Prose Poems, Essays, & Letters, *translated by Bradford Cook (© 1956, The Johns Hopkins Press), The Johns Hopkins University Press, 1956, p. 99.*

H. SCHÜTZ WILSON   (essay date 1878)

M. Zola possesses emphatically that art which conceals the appearance of art; and it is only great art that can attain to this result. He always seems to narrate, never to invent. He gives evidence; he does not seem to create. No great novel is dependent upon plot; such a work of art, like life itself, has a plan, but no plot. M. Zola cares nothing for plot; his characters develop, his events progress, as they do in the procession of human life itself. M. Zola's talent as a littérateur is—apparently—rendered subservient to his purpose as a philanthropist. Criticism has to look beneath this illusion of realism to find out how subtle and how powerful his art really is.

Although he does not indulge in much real *cochonnerie pure*, M. Zola very frequently revolts us by his unvarnished allusions to things which lie outside the pale of modest decency. There is, however, it must be remembered, in justice to him, a vast difference in their treatment of man as an animal between French and English writers. English authors will not leave a celestial bed to prey on garbage. French writers do not sometimes shun even ordure. French literature knows but little reticence in the mention of such things. English writers avoid, with the reticence of fine shame, all allusion to the ignobler needs and functions of the body. It is not, I think, solely because I am English that I prefer our nobler chastity of imagination, our purer delicacy of thought. M. Zola has but little of the modesty, the measure, the moderation of art; but he has all the energy of his purpose. *J'ai un but.*

There is something in M. Zola's intense realism which obscures the shows of art. He is as one constrained to observe, and compelled to report. He records everything that he sees or hears. He seems quite impartial; he has no leanings, no theories; his function is simply that of intelligent witness. To read *l'Assommoir* is not like reading an ordinary book. We seem to be actually living among actual, living people. M. Zola studies carefully, sees clearly, and depicts graphically. He resembles rather a realistic painter, a Defoe of the canvas, than a writer. He is a singular instance of the almost complete absorption of an author into his theme. In the book there is no humour for its own sake, or for the sake of abstract drollery. Zola merely reports. He sinks his personality as an author; he avoids abstract reflections; he cares only for an intense and vivid picture. To read him is like standing amongst a crowd of the common people; we see much that we would gladly shun seeing, we hear much to which we would gladly shut our ears; but we see and hear clearly, and we learn actual facts. We feel in living contact with humanity and with the working class. We learn to realise their infirmities, temptations, sorrows, sins, struggles. M. Zola scarcely ever allows himself a touch of sarcasm; he never shows indignation. He paints all things with a ruthless rectitude. In the fulfilment of his purpose he is remorseless, relentless. He seems to feel neither pity, love, or fear; and yet he is—perhaps—only cruel to be merciful. His work is a dramatic *morale en action*. He makes no humanitarian professions; and yet, perhaps, behind his fierce restraint beats a heart beating with profoundest sympathy for the people that he paints. He seems to us to remain calm, unmoved, untouched. He hides all evidence of art, aim, or effort; he suppresses all show of his warm humanity. He writes with lips sternly compressed, with a powerful effort at self-repression. He restrains his natural indignation, and paints with a fierce, forced calm. He gives no criticism of life, he simply paints. He will not betray emotion, or suffering—or even sympathy—but yet this strong man feels them all. He poses as a mere spectator; he studies intently and narrates gloomily. His style is vivid with life, vigorous with keen reality, energetic with virile force. Some must watch while others sleep: and it is good for society that it can find such a watchman as M. Zola to tell it how goes the night. A man with all the strength of self-command, he seems unimpassioned while he feels the most. (pp. 745-46)

[*L'Assommoir*] throbs with energy and latent power. Its pictures are vivid and are vital; are clear, yet dark; and very, very intense. His strong points are not nobleness or tenderness, but power and pathos. (p. 748)

The book will live and work. It is unique. It is a portent in literature. It is powerful and terrible. It holds the mind and detains the memory. It has the influence which art has when she becomes the handmaid of humanity. It is a book for the statesman, for the philanthropist, for the social reformer, for the humanitarian, for the critic, for the thinker. He that hath ears to hear, let him hear, as he listens to M. Zola, while this powerful writer speaks so meaningly, so movingly, so memorably, through *l'Assommoir.* (p. 749)

> *H. Schütz Wilson, "L'assommoir," in* The Gentleman's Magazine, *Vol. CCXLIII, No. 1776, December, 1878, pp. 737-49.*

A. LANG (essay date 1882)

[In M. Zola we find] a writer with a method and an aim, a workman conscientious according to his lights; not without poetry, not without a sense of beauty, but more and more disinclined to make use of these qualities. In all his work you see the "joins," and know where the "notes" come in. It is part of his method to abstain from comment; never to show the author's personality, never to turn to the reader for sympathy. He is as cold as a vivisectionist at a lecture. His conception of modern literature, as science in disguise, did much to spoil the later work of George Eliot. His own knowledge of the literature of the world appears to be scanty; his judgments—as when he calls Scot "a clever arranger, whose work is dead"—do not deserve to be discussed. His lack of humour is absolute, a darkness that can be felt. Finally, temperament, or system, or desire of success, or all combined, make several of his stories little better than a Special Reporter's description of things and people that should not be described. (p. 452)

> *A. Lang, "Emile Zola," in* The Fortnightly Review, *(reprinted by permission of Contemporary Review Company Limited), Vol. XXXII, April 1, 1882, pp. 439-52.*

LAFCADIO HEARN (essay date 1883)

A curious report had been vented by the press to the effect that Zola, wearied of writing immoral novels, had in *Au Bonheur des Dames* attempted to retrieve his reputation, and create an "honest" romance,—a novel that might be safely laid upon the drawing-room tables of austerely pious households. The ludicrousness of the report will appear huge to any person who glances even cursorily through the novel—which is simply a continuation of *Pot-Bouille*. Zola has certainly been more disgusting, more insolently foul in other volumes of the *Rougons-Marquart* series; but he has never been—and it may reasonably be doubted whether he could possibly be—much more immoral.

In addition to the microscopical analysis of familiar sins, numerous hints or suggestions of abnormal iniquity are scattered through the volume. The morality of *Au Bonheur des Dames* differs little from the immorality of *Pot-Bouille*, although the outrage upon humanity perpetrated in the last portion of the latter-mentioned work has no parallel in its successor. Nevertheless the mere absence of stercoraceous nastiness from the new volume cannot suffice to justify its claim to superior morality.

Considered as a work of realism, the book is certainly astounding; and the reader is appalled at the idea of that vast labor which must have been consumed in its preparation. It is the history of a dry goods establishment—one of those monster stores in Paris which surpass the wildest dreams of New York or Chicago merchants. . . . Let it be remembered that almost every well-known variety of dry goods is described as to texture, color, and effect; that there are separate specifications of stock for winter, spring, summer and fall trade: that the relations between the great manufacturing firms and their customers are accurately set forth,—and one can acquire some idea of the immense preparation such a book must have demanded. . . . There are passages in the work superior in grace and force to much that Zola had before written;—one cannot always be materially realistic; the mere aspect of dainty and womanly things must sometimes thaw the coldest fancy; and the pages describing feminine *lingerie,* trousseaux, etc. . . . , are almost worthy of Theophile Gautier.

Thus the author envelopes his reader in the life which his characters live,—with its atmosphere of sounds and odors,—with its circumfluence of commercial excitements and jealousies. And as in everyday existence we can judge new acquaintances only by their acts, methods, converse, and that unexplainable repulsion or attraction which is a sort of social instinct-feeling,—so are these characters gradually revealed to us. First, the man or woman is painted for us with the precision of a master-portraitist; then the reader is left to correct or confirm his first impression by the aid of a succession of incidents which reveal the moral character. The purpose of each motion is made manifest; the secret mental organization of every personage laid bare by a marvelous process of physiological analysis. This philosophic positivism of the author's plan, never weakened since the beginning of his enormous series of romances, appears to remarkable advantage in the present book. He interweaves hypotheses of evolution and natural selection with the whole plot of the novel. . . . (pp. 113-17)

The immorality of the story chiefly appears in the scandalous gossip of the establishment, and certain incidents of dissoluteness on the part of employers toward employes. The character of Denise approaches the beautiful more nearly than any other which Zola has drawn; she is as noble and pure a creation as the author is capable of evolving. And, nevertheless, having created her, he refuses her justice,—as though she were an illegitimate literary offspring. Her career is wholly one of kindness, truth and purity; but Zola, who is no believer in free agency, cannot allow himself to praise her. . . . The bad cannot help being bad; the good must be good in spite of themselves. Irrefutable this philosophy may be; but the philosopher-novelist, who affects to consider questions of *influence* so broadly and dispassionately, would seem to have entirely forgotten his own ability to influence the minds of many millions of readers in a better manner than he has been doing; and his colossal work proves in the most terrible and exhaustive manner, how much the French mind of the nineteenth century needs the invigorating and purifying force of that idealism which the Zolaites would banish from the world. (pp. 118-20)

> *Lafcadio Hearn, "Zola's 'Au bonheur des dames'"*
> *(1883), in his* Essays in European and Oriental Literature, *edited by Albert Mordell (reprinted by permission of Dodd, Mead & Company Inc.; copyright 1923 by Dodd, Mead and Company, Inc; copyright renewed 1951 by Albert Mordell), Dodd, Mead and Company, 1923, pp. 113-20.*

HAVELOCK ELLIS (essay date 1898)

The chief service which Zola has rendered to his fellow-artists and successors, the reason of the immense stimulus he supplies, seems to lie in the proofs he has brought of the latent artistic uses of the rough, neglected details of life. The **Rougon-Macquart** series has been to his weaker brethren like that great sheet knit at the four corners, let down from Heaven full of four-footed beasts and creeping things and fowls of the air, and bearing in it the demonstration that to the artist as to the moralist nothing can be called common or unclean. It has henceforth become possible for other novelists to find inspiration where before they could never have turned, to touch life with a vigour and audacity of phrase which, without Zola's example, they would have trembled to use, while they still remain free to bring to their work the simplicity, precision, and inner experience which he has never possessed. Zola has enlarged the field of the novel. He has brought the modern material world into fiction in a more definite and thorough manner than it has ever been brought before, just as Richardson brought the modern emotional world into fiction; such an achievement necessarily marks an epoch. In spite of all his blunders, Zola has given the novel new power and directness, a vigour of fibre which was hard indeed to attain, but which, once attained, we may chasten as we will. And in doing this he has put out of court, perhaps for ever, those unwholesome devotees of the novelist's art who work out of their vacuity, having neither inner nor outer world to tell of. (pp. 143-44)

> *Havelock Ellis, "Zola," in his* Affirmations, *Walter Scott Limited, 1898 (and reprinted by Houghton Mifflin Company, 1922), pp. 131-57.*

GEORGE SAINTSBURY   (essay date 1904)

[Zola] wrote a good deal of criticism; his combative temperament supplying the impulse, and his journalist experience the means.

But of the nearly half-score volumes in which this criticism has been collected, perhaps only one, *Le Roman Expérimental,* is much worth re-reading; at any rate, it will give as quite sufficient "document" here. Issued at the very culminating-point of its author's talent and popularity, in 1880, long after he had come through the struggles of his youth, and long before he had fallen into that condition of a naturalist and anti-theistic *voyant* which we find in *Travail* and *Vérité,* it is thoroughly characteristic, thoroughly equipped. There is no reason, if the author had had the same talent for criticism that he had (after making all allowances) for creation, why it should not display as much power in the one direction as the nearly contemporary *Attaque du Moulin* does in the other.

Not to mince matters (and waste time in the mincing), it does nothing of the sort: but, on the contrary, proves that he had next to no critical aptitude. (pp. 455-56)

[How] can the *writer* experiment? He can observe, he can experience, he can (the ambiguous sense of the word is probably the source of M. Zola's blunder) analyse, as we call it. But he can never experiment, he can only imagine. The check of nature and of the actual, the blow of the quintain if you charge at it and fail, can never be his except in the metaphorical and transformed sense of "literary" success or failure, which brings us back to another region altogether. Now "imagination," "idealism," and the like are M. Zola's abomination, the constant targets of his ineffectual arrows. He does not see that he is himself using them all the time to form his subjects, just as he is using the "rhetoric," which he abominates equally, to convey his expression.

Consult other places to fill out M. Zola's ideas of literature, and they will be found all of a piece. Read his **"Lettre à La Jeunesse,"** with its almost frenzied cry for a literature of *for-*

mula, excluding genius, excluding individuality, though only to smuggle them in again afterwards by a backdoor. Read his account (very well done and producing quite the opposite effect to that which he intends) of the old man of letters, the man of letters *à la* Sainte-Beuve, in **"L'Argent dans la Littérature,"** and the funny details about royalties and centimes which follow. Read him on **"L'expression personnelle"** in the novel—where he is specially interesting, because with all his talent this is exactly what he himself had not got. Read him on the famous **"Human Document,"** where he misses—misses blindly and obstinately, almost ferociously, with the ferocity of the man who *will* not see—the hopeless, the insuperable rejoinder, "Study your documents as much as you like, but *transform* the results of the study before you give them as art." Read the astonishing paralogism entitled **"La Moralité,"** where he excuses the production of *tacenda* in literature because *tacenda* are constantly recurring in life, and even being inserted in the newspapers which object to them in fiction. Read his queer reversal of a truth (certainly not too generally recognised) that Naturalism is only Romanticism "drawn to the dregs." . . . (pp. 456-57)

The truth, I think, of it all is, that M. Zola, though in his way a rather great man of not the best kind of letters, knew nothing critically about literature, and did not even take any real interest in it. I do not know that it has been generally remarked, but I am sure that if any one who is familiar with the enormous stretch of the novels will exert his memory, he will find an almost unexampled absense of literary reference, literary allusion, literary flavour in them. Even Dickens is not to be named in this respect beside Zola. Nay, his very critical works themselves, though they deal with books, have nothing of the book-atmosphere about them. . . . When M. Zola read books it seems generally to have been to coach up his documents and his details: indeed, why should a person who despised poetry and rhetoric read them for anything else? Given this ignorance or this want of appetite, given a consuming desire to philosophise, combined with a very weak logical faculty, an intense belief in one formula or set of formulas, and a highly combative temperament, and you get a set of conditions . . . sufficient to turn out or account for a personage nothing if not *uncritical.* (p. 458)

> *George Saintsbury, "The Successors of Sainte-Beuve," in his* A History of Criticism and Literary Taste in Europe: From the Earliest Texts to the Present Day, *Vol. III,* William Blackwood & Sons Ltd., *1904 (and reprinted by Blackwood & Sons, 1935), pp. 431-71.**

F.W.J. HEMMINGS (essay date 1953)

[*Thérèse Raquin* and *Madeleine Férat*] cannot be fully appreciated except . . . as experiments in a new realism—new, at all events, in the path of Zola's development, but one which leads back to Balzac and the positivist gospel. In these two works the young writer can be observed trying his hand at objective presentation of invented characters, the difficult feat that his other great forerunner, Flaubert, had toiled to achieve. Zola, of course, was far from succeeding at this first attempt. But he seems to have seen where and why he failed, and afterwards to have resolutely recast his method in order to come closer to grips with the problem. *Thérèse Raquin* and *Madeleine Férat* are not blind alleys from which Zola was obliged to retrace his steps; they are stages in the steady progression that led him up to the peaks of attainment, *L'Assommoir* and

Germinal and *La Terre,* where the dispassionate objectivity of the artist is almost perfectly balanced by the passionate sincerity of his art.

The test by which we can most readily judge the objectivity of a work of fiction is a negative one: the reader should be unable, simply by studying the text in front of him, to draw any conclusions about the author's sympathies or antipathies, his creed or his philosophy. Flaubert, just about the time when Zola was meditating *Thérèse Raquin,* formularized this ideal when he wrote: 'A novelist, to my mind, *has no right* to give his opinion about the things of this world. He should, in his calling, imitate God in His, that is, create—and hold his peace (*faire et se taire*).' (pp. 23-4)

Measured against this standard of objectivity, neither *Thérèse Raquin* nor *Madeleine Férat* qualifies fully as a product of the 'new aesthetic'.

For a start, it cannot be said that, in the first of them, Zola 'never reveals himself in the turn of a sentence'. In little question-begging touches which will not escape the sensitive reader, Zola betrays the moral assumptions on which his book is based. The two central characters of *Thérèse Raquin* are a couple of villains; the pity is that they are considered in their villainy rather than in their humanity. Zola cannot conceal the repugnance he feels for them, however scrupulously he analyses the attendant circumstances of their adultery and crime. (pp. 24-5)

What Zola wanted to demonstrate in *Thérèse Raquin*—in the main, that 'crime does not pay'—is, however, a moral truism, to which his readers might, on the whole, be supposed to subscribe without many misgivings. There was, therefore, little need for display of argument to persuade them to arrive at the conclusions Zola wished to lead up to. In *Madeleine Férat,* the case is different. Here Zola set out to wring consent to a belief by no means commonly accepted. *Thérèse Raquin* is a tract against homicide, and against adultery only incidentally. In *Madeleine Férat* . . . the preoccupation with sexual infidelity in woman stands alone. It is abundantly evident that the author is himself preoccupied with the problem, that he interprets it along personal lines, and that, to all intents and purposes, he wrote the novel to phrase this interpretation. (p. 25)

Thérèse Raquin and *Madeleine Férat* are thus not true works of scientific realism as Zola had intended they should be; they are not objective presentations of any recognizable reality. They are, in different degrees, stories with a high content of interpolated subjectivism; and their psychology, thickened into 'physiology', is engineered by unrealistic and unscientific postulates: Fate, and the all-powerful 'temperament', or the irresistible force of 'impregnation'. The books differ from the 'Gothic novel' of the eighteenth century only in that the supernatural, externalized as ghosts and bugaboos by Horace Walpole and Mrs. Radcliffe, is seated by Zola in his characters' nerves, in their blood, in their genital organs. (pp. 32-3)

For sheer determination and purposefulness there had been few events in recorded literature to match the twenty-volume series of *Les Rougon-Macquart,* and subsequently there has been perhaps nothing that can be put beside it except *À la Recherche du Temps perdu.* (pp. 35-6)

The innovation intended in *Les Rougon-Macquart* was to show the successive flowering of three, four, even five interlinked generations, to construct vertically down a genealogical line, not simply horizontally over a social superficies. As he promised his publisher, Lacroix, in the general plan he submitted in 1869, he would not only 'study the whole of the Second Empire, from the *coup d'état* down to the present day', but he would also 'study in a family the questions of common blood and environment'. In the first article, he would still be a historian; in the second, a student of embryology and physiology. (p. 38)

That heredity in some way influences individuality is . . . a truism: 'like father, like son' rates as one of the most commonplace of proverbs. To the artist in Zola, heredity was a substitute for old-fashioned Fate, the Spinner of the Homeric sagas. . . . (p. 40)

The hereditary streak is sometimes of hardly any practical account; environment seems all-powerful. Would Gervaise [Macquart in *L'Assommoir*] have turned into a drunken old harridan without the misery of her life and the example of her husband?—surely the intemperance of her father and mother provided no more than an innate disposition to alcoholism which might just as well not have been there? Would her daughter have turned prostitute without the corrupting influences of the street and especially without the total disorganization of her home? Allowance must, of course, be made for the hereditary freak of exceptional sexual appeal and the hereditary thirst for enjoyment—but to these Zola attributes far less importance, in *L'Assommoir* and in *Nana,* than he does to environmental factors. (pp. 43-4)

The new importance given to environment and experience was the means by which Zola insured himself against the danger of producing, as he had in *Thérèse Raquin* and *Madeleine Férat,* mere fatalist melodramas. Alone in the series, *La Bête humaine* provides an example of a character entirely dominated by atavistic forces beyond his control. In the other novels, the influence of the family is not allowed to show itself too nakedly, its very presence remains shadowy. Each novel is primarily concerned, not with one or the other aspect of the legacy of evil in the Rougon-Macquart stock, but with one or another of the worlds which fit together as a panorama of the Second Empire. (pp. 44-5)

As far as possible, then, Zola reduced the craft of fiction to a mechanical technique; and his extraordinary thoroughness and patience will not fail to dismay many who imagine masterpieces to spring—as sometimes, undoubtedly, they do appear to—all complete from the brain of a great novelist. Through what hole in this tight-woven fabric could the wind of inspiration blow?—or is Zola's example one more piece of evidence in support of Carlyle's view that genius 'means transcendent capacity of taking trouble'? (p. 50)

La Fortune des Rougon is a study in miniature of the passions and interests that conspired to overthrow the Second Republic. (p. 59)

It is an unsavoury story, and Zola's design is obvious: he wishes to show the inglorious origins of imperial rule. He does this firstly by exposing the pettiness, cruelty, and cowardice of the champions of Bonapartism, and secondly by throwing a halo of martyrdom round the heads of the militant republicans doomed to extinction. (p. 60)

On the whole, *La Fortune des Rougon* reads as a satire of man's folly in ever hoping to establish, by violent political and revolutionary action, the ideal society. Save for the heroic but misled exceptions, men are too self-seeking to be effective agents of their own communal betterment.

The first book of the series is not one of the greatest. It has glaring faults of construction, due mainly to the huge amount of preparatory matter Zola felt it necessary to include as an introduction to the succeeding volumes. Like the last volume of all, *Le Docteur Pascal,* it is a wall left unfinished, with the toothings projecting. (pp. 61-2)

Considered, however, as a prologue to the cycle, *La Fortune des Rougon* is sometimes stirring; it is shot through with fitful prophetic gleams, when we seem, with Pascal Rougon, 'to glimpse for a moment, as in a flash of lightning, the future of the Rougon-Macquarts, a pack of ravening beasts unleashed and gorged, in a blaze of blood and gold'. It is a book that contributes to our understanding of the remaining nineteen novels, but it has few rewards to offer in itself. (p. 62)

[*Son Excellence Eugene Rougon* is] the most truly political of [Zola's] novels until we come to [*La Ventre de Paris*]. (p. 69)

After *Son Excellence* Zola began his 'novel of the working class', *L'Assommoir.* Here the fact of social suffering, evaded in the earlier books (except perhaps in *Le Ventre de Paris*), is stated with an emphasis that leaves nothing to be desired. But *L'Assommoir* is not a political novel, because there is no attempt to lay at anyone's door the blame for the degradation of the masses. The book demonstrated that the impartiality of the realist need not exclude a sense of social wrongs; but it also showed that, if the rules of realism were to be observed, and the artist were to refrain indefinitely from intervention and conclusion, then the social formula he reached would always be short of one term or the other. Either the oppressed would be shown without the oppressors, or the exploiters without the classes they exploit.

Zola overcame the difficulty once only in his career: in *Germinal.* There, the formula he evolved to avoid a crude siding against social tyrants was to exonerate them of the intention of tyranny, even though he could not overlook its reality. The *rentiers* in *Germinal* are naïvely unaware that their privileged comfort is founded on the blood and sweat of the miners; the manager class is a powerless agent of the abstract monster 'capital', which Zola relegates carefully to the shadows. By these means no one set of characters is shown to be unjust, though the fact of injustice is painfully evident; and so the appearance of impartiality is maintained, precariously but all the same convincingly.

This juggling feat was not repeated. Zola's logic eventually demanded that a verdict of Guilty should be returned against someone or something, even if only against a social system. Once he took it on himself to act the juryman, however, his artistic integrity was of necessity compromised, he found himself among the politicians, 'at the very bottom, in what is relative among human activities'. This is what happened in *Paris* and in the last three novels of his life; and it partly explains why *Paris* and the *Évangiles* rank increasingly lower as literature. (pp. 71-2)

L'Assommoir was Zola's first unmistakable masterpiece. He was to write two or three books which might be considered more stirring, more moving, or more overwhelming, but he was never to compose a more perfect work of art. Sheer artistic perfection was not something Zola often came within reach of—perhaps he seldom even strove seriously after it; but among all his books *L'Assommoir* alone is practically proof against the acid of purely formal criticism. (p. 94)

L'Assommoir proved that Zola could, at his best, construct a novel as well as Flaubert and better than any other of his predecessors or contemporaries. None of the earlier novels had been to anything like the same degree so purposefully and economically built. By comparison, they sprawl and bulge; they do not sweep up to their culmination, they distract by subsidiary outgrowths. But *L'Assommoir* has a classic simplicity of line which was not incompatible with the complexity and denseness of a work of realism. (p. 95)

There is nothing in the population of *L'Assommoir* but what is redolent of human nature. For the first time Zola vaulted the forbidding walls of the 'prisons of clay'. Admittedly, it was human nature at its least polished and least subtle: this was perhaps why he managed it so well. His unlettered toilers, whose native spontaneity has not been trimmed or refined by any life of the mind or the spirit, were the ideal caryatids of the kind of monumental art which it was in him to construct. (p. 99)

[*Une Page d'Amour, Nana,* and *Au Bonheur des Dames*] all deal, in the last resort, with the same problem: the disruptive force of the passion of love. It was a subject which had hardly concerned Zola up till then. As a literary theme it has, of course, been common property since Helen's face launched the thousand ships, but there is, in Zola's treatment of it, a blend of horror and fascination, which suggests origins in a much nearer, in fact a private, conflict. (p. 138)

[In *Une Page d'Amour*] the intrinsic destructiveness of passion becomes, for the first time, the principal theme of a novel by Zola. . . .

There is a stuffiness in *Une Page d'Amour,* a muffling of echoes, which represents a regression to the period before the *Rougon-Macquart* cycle was started. It is a closet drama of the same sort as *Thérèse Raquin,* with the difference that Zola tried to rise above the 'physiological' portrayal of character which had contented him in 1867. The result was a notable failure, unless Zola was serious in his declared intention of being 'flat and colourless'. (p. 146)

[*Une Page d'Amour* is] remarkable for a suddenly intensified exteriorization of Zola's latent dread of sexual passion, that incalculable and destructive outside force; and with it went, this time, a readiness to sound the alarm, to put his reader—and through him, society at large—on guard against the intruder. These are tendencies of which the first at least arose . . . from the recesses of Zola's personality. They display themselves far more strikingly in the next novel, *Nana.* (pp. 148-49)

Nana, the sequel to *L'Assommoir,* is a coldly austere work, for all the licentiousness of many of the scenes. (p. 150)

To put his intentions beyond any doubt, Zola provided within the text of the novel the key to his symbolism, in the shape of a summarized article supposedly written by a journalist, Fauchery, under the heading **'The Golden Fly'.** Here we read that Nana is the biological product of a diseased ancestral line and the social product of mean streets and stinking hovels. (p. 151)

While we may not doubt that Zola's intention was to issue a solemn warning against licensed prostitution and private vice among the leaders of a nation, we cannot doubt either that *Nana* mercifully exceeds this limited brief. The novel, as it develops, becomes a tremendous phantasmagoria in which an opulent and cultured civilization is shown sinking through vulgarity and debauchery to enervation and ultimate dissolution. (pp. 152-53)

Au Bonheur des Dames, in spite of its far sunnier treatment of the erotic theme, does not really represent any final abatement of this deep-seated disturbance. The story of the taming of Octave Mouret, now a millionaire, by the unambitious and instinctively virtuous Denise Baudu, a story which ends with the ringing of wedding-bells off-stage, has the innocent air of a prim mid-Victorian novel. (p. 160)

Au Bonheur des Dames was a transition novel, inaugurating the series of up-to-date economic or industrial studies which were to include *Germinal, La Terre, La Bête humaine, L'Argent,* and, beyond the *Rougon-Macquart* series, *Paris* and *Travail.* The war between the sexes . . . pales before the death-struggle of a doomed commercial order. (pp. 160-61)

If Zola's novels are read, as he intended they should be read, straight through in the order in which he wrote them, a subtle change of texture will make itself felt somewhere halfway through the *Rougon-Macquart* cycle. Up to *Nana,* the books are *gratuitous,* almost, it might be said, decorative; they reflect, record, not always flatly and seldom unemotionally; but whatever intentions they have (political intentions in *La Fortune des Rougon,* social ones in *L'Assommoir*) are rudimentary, perhaps accidental. In the later phase, the works, while they never descend to pleading causes, are nevertheless *functional;* they serve to bring into prominence certain questions, certain problems: of a moral order in *Nana, Pot-Bouille,* and *Au Bonheur des Dames;* of an economic and social order in *Germinal, La Terre,* and *L'Argent;* of an aesthetic order in *L'Oeuvre,* an international one in *La Débâcle,* a religious one in *Le Docteur Pascal.* This seems to be the characteristic quality and common denominator of the later books in the series. . . . (p. 164)

[As] we continue to consider Zola's literary career in terms of a gradual perfecting of the realist formula, we are bound to place *Germinal* in a class by itself. Here, the impersonal treatment of the theme is unexceptional: Flaubert's principle, *faire et se taire,* was observed to the letter, as it had already been in *L'Assommoir.* But between *L'Assommoir* and *Germinal* the balance tips slightly in favour of the second book. There is, in *L'Assommoir,* a certain chilliness in the relentless march to catastrophe, which in *Germinal* is dissipated by the heat of dramatic friction. Gervaise has to fight her losing battle in desperate isolation and against forces many times too strong for her; Étienne and the miners, at least have the comfort of fellowship and the strength of their numbers, and they do not succumb without inflicting terrible damage on their adversary; their defeat, moreover, is anything but irrevocable. The generous fervour and the final—if deceptive—surge of optimism in *Germinal* humanize the austerely dispassionate handling of the subject. (pp. 175-76)

In another respect *Germinal* may be thought superior to *L'Assommoir.* The merit of a work of art may up to a point be measured by the artist's skill in solving the difficulties set him by his subject. In a sense *L'Assommoir* and *Germinal* deal with the same subject, or at any rate with the same problem—that of social injustice; and for a writer with even the dullest social conscience, the temptation to extract from that theme a momentarily successful but ephemeral *roman à thèse* [novel of ideas] is almost irresistible. In *L'Assommoir,* as we have seen, the danger was met by suppressing the factor of social strife; in *Germinal,* however, Zola had the courage to give this factor full weight. In his preliminary notes he defined his novel as 'the struggle between capital and labour', adding that this question was 'the most important one the twentieth century will have to face'. Both the helots and their lords would be given equal place in the economy of the work, and none of the horrors of the class war would be glossed over. Zola's secret for preserving impartiality was to absolve both parties in the conflict from guilt: the root of the evil was to be left buried, and the author would refuse to point to scapegoats or to venture into any specific dialectical analysis of the situation. (p. 179)

In both *Au Bonheur des Dames* and *Germinal* (and later, in *La Terre* also) the dilemma is the same: the path of free competition is the path of progress; but, since competition is simply the right of the stronger to devour the weaker, there will be stretched by the wayside the bodies of many an innocent victim. In *Au Bonheur des Dames* Zola was able to endorse this process, at least for its ends if not for its means; but, when, turning from a purely internal struggle within the commercial class, he looked at the major clash between the possessors and the dispossessed, his complacency was shattered. (p. 181)

The most that can properly be claimed for *Germinal* is that its picture of social conditions was such that no reader save the most callous could remain complacent.

Yet even when so much is admitted, there remain the figures of Étienne Lantier and Hennebeau which cancel any over-optimistic estimations of the practicability and ultimate value of deliberately engineered social changes. *Germinal*, in short, is neither revolutionary nor counter-revolutionary; it is not primarily a vehicle for extra-literary concerns, and thus ought not to be judged, as too often it has been judged, by its accuracy as a social document, still less by its effectiveness as a piece of propaganda. The only standards of evaluation which can properly be applied are aesthetic ones. (p. 197)

Although Zola understood them well enough for his purpose, he gave rather less place to economic questions in *La Terre* than he had in *Germinal*, in which they are fundamental. (p. 205)

La Terre was not the first novel of Zola's to deal with peasant life: there had been a forerunner, *La Faute de l'Abbé Mouret*. It is true that peasants play only a subsidiary part in this earlier book; but the little that is said of them is enough to show that Zola's conception of country life had changed little in the thirteen years' interval. In both books, the villagers' behaviour knows no moral restraints: rarely is a bride brought to church unless she is pregnant or perhaps already a mother. Their profligacy, however, is simply the brutish satisfaction of periodic appetites, their emotions being reserved for the earth. They farm their land with the passionate tenderness of a lover cherishing his first mistress, or, as Archangias puts it baldly: 'They love their plots of land so much, they would fornicate with them.' They are godless, but retain a certain respect for ministers of religion and a deep reserve of superstition. (pp. 205-06)

The passionate cleaving to the earth, amounting to an erotic frenzy—something that was only hinted at in *L'Abbé Mouret*—is of primary importance in *La Terre* and gives the book its overpowering odour of sweat and manure. In different degrees, the lust for land runs in the veins of most of the main characters in *La Terre*. (p. 206)

Horrifying and yet strangely peaceful, ribald and grave in turns, *La Terre* is a kind of *summa* of all that is characteristic of Zola. For this alone, perhaps, it has a better right to be styled epic than any other of his works. In contrast with *L'Assommoir* and particularly with *Pot-Bouille*, nearly all the action of *La Terre* takes place out of doors. The freshness of the air blows away

much of what would otherwise be sordid in Zola's invention. (pp. 214-15)

Nearer to hand and possessed of a more real existence than the 'god Capital' in *Germinal*, the earth had provided Zola with that impassive, indifferent antagonist which his dramatic instinct craved, to stand aloofly opposed to brawling humanity. He tried, but much less successfully, to use the same formula in *Le Rêve*, where it is religion, in the shape of the cathedral, which fills the part. *La Bête humaine*, his next work and the seventeenth of the series, was based on a similar dichotomy, but although far more impressive than *Le Rêve*, it does not exhibit quite the same mastery as *La Terre*. (p. 215)

La Bête humaine is a good average specimen of Zola's art in its maturity. . . . It qualifies for the title 'epic' by the broad sweep of the author's vision. . . .

In particular, the rudimentary characterization Zola practised is nowhere easier to observe than in *La Bête humaine* in which Zola was determined once more, as the preliminary notes indicate, to show 'psychology yielding to physiology'. He was reverting to his beginnings, in giving Jacques, Séverine, and Roubaud as little cerebral motivation as Thérèse and Laurent in *Thérèse Raquin*. (p. 216)

La Bête humaine, with its theme of the underlying animalism of civilized man, is more rawly disillusioning than ever. (p. 222)

In *Le Docteur Pascal* all the tried principles by the application of which Zola had achieved integrated and lofty works of art are rejected: objectivity, irony, the adherence to logical determinism, the refusal to philosophize and to read a sermon into 'the study of nature, just as it is'. The last novel of *Les Rougon-Macquart* makes a regrettably discordant coda.

It is not too much to say that it ends not only the 'Natural and Social History of a Family under the Second Empire' but also the period of Zola's specifically artistic production. If one reads on through the *Lourdes—Rome—Paris* trilogy, and if one still has the courage to trek through the 'deep desert sand' (the words are Henry James's) of the *Évangiles*, it can only be to mark the melancholy spectacle of an artist in gradual disintegration. (p. 239)

[Zola's] work has a living interest which it owes to the one significant innovation that his vision of the universe contained. Zola was the first writer to show a society in which the aggregate was greater than the separate unit. All through the novels of his maturity and decline runs this one fruitful and fundamental idea. It manifests itself artistically in his characteristic descriptions of crowds in which the individual founders and is lost to view; in the way his imagination was time and time again captivated by huge impersonal entities, factories and mines, bazaars and markets, battlefields and railways; in his evident incapacity to isolate, explore, and expound the self-sufficient character. It declares itself, too, in his thought, in the glorification of human fertility and productive labour, in the rapt fascination with which he brooded over ancestry and progeny; there is always the same idea, that the individual is negligible, that what matters is the whole, and the contribution the individual makes to the whole. . . . Zola was the prophet of a new age of mass-psychology, mass-analysis, mass-education, and mass-entertainment, an age in which the part is never greater than the whole. An age without fineness, almost certainly; without fire and without colour, perhaps; but an age, it may be, of greater strength and broader justice; on that no one can speak yet with finality, for this age that Zola wrote of is, without the least doubt, our own age. (pp. 290-91)

F.W.J. Hemmings, in his Émile Zola *(reprinted by permission of Oxford University Press), Oxford University Press, Oxford, 1953, 308 p.*

GEORGE ROSS RIDGE (essay date 1961)

[Decadent writers] depict Parisians as lunatics, misers, wastrels, perverts, *hystériques,* idiots, psychotics, egomaniacs—human wrecks of the most pitiable kind. Such a portrait of Paris is more devastating in effect than any philosophical denunciation: it shows the great city, concretely, as Babylon.

Perhaps more than any other writer in the French decadence Zola is obsessed with the megalopolis. Indeed his abstraction, Paris as the great city, brings out and magnifies his characters, who often seem real only as they move against the backdrop of Babylon. *Les Rougon-Macquart,* to be sure, is the portrait of a family, but of that family within a particular megalopolitan context. Zola's creatures are unimaginable without Paris.

The Rougon-Macquart swarm into Babylon from their little provincial town, Plassans. Lured by visions of success, they rapidly spread like poison through the arteries of the city. In varying settings they reveal their hereditary ills, the result of *la tare initiale.* Tante Dide is the mother of all illness. The members of the family achieve different stations as cosmopolitans, but they remain a diseased and doomed unit. Paris acts on them like a hothouse on the growth of malignant plants. Such an image recurs throughout Zola, in fact, notably in the love scenes of *La Curée.* It is significant that novels taking place outside Babylon, like *Le Rêve* and *La Faute de l'Abbé Mouret,* are attenuated, more poetic and authentically hopeful, than the passionate and violent struggles occurring in the city. Paris magnifies the very worst in the Rougon-Macquart.

In *La Curée,* for instance, Aristide Saccard arrives from Plassans, in the healthy South determined to gain wealth by any means. . . . After his wife dies he unscrupulously marries Renée Saccard, who is pregnant by a married man, in an effort to get her family fortune. The callous bargain is concluded with his receiving the money for giving his name, such as it is, to Renée's illegitimate child. The novel portrays scenes of fantastic decadence—all documented, Zola believes, by the period itself of the Second Empire. Liaisons are too numerous to mention. (pp. 74-5)

Son Excellence Eugène Rougon is Zola's portrayal of a modern Macbeth, a cosmopolitan athirst with an unquenchable ambition. Paris appears like a jungle where, as in Darwin, only the strongest and cleverest will survive. Rougon is determined to be among them. He is an egomaniac who almost mystically tries to absorb Paris into himself. His ambition knows no bounds.

Zola's great epics of men and movements give a vast panorama of corruption. Indeed the vista, Paris, is the real hero, and men and women act more in relationship to it than to themselves. The megalopolis is, so to speak, the first cause. *L'Assommoir* is notable for the amorality of its men and women—brutish, vicious, drunken. Gervaise Macquart, typically, runs away from Plassans to the city with the conviction that a better life awaits her. Her aspirations are soon dashed. Her destruction takes place in the biologically living city, with its moving masses, twisting streets, personified stores. Gervaise, in spite of her pathetic appeal, is always of secondary interest. The city itself captivates the reader.

It is symbolic that Zola turns to the great department store, Au Bon Marché, to inspire his portrait of the fictional store, Au Bonheur des Dames, in the novel of that name. It is his epic poem to modern activity in commercial Babylon. Though he claims to be singing a hymn to work, happiness, and success, his personification of the store is horrifying, and he has to remind himself in his *ébauche* to the novel to be optimistic. Zola's optimism, as usual, is forced. The picture of the store and of Paris as Babylon is brutal. The callous Octave Mouret, who has made a previous appearance in *Pot-Bouille,* speculates on the artificiality and whimsy of Parisian women. For them the department store is not only a commercial house but also, and more importantly, a temple to modern life. Zola is explicit. He describes it as such, with worshipers filing in and out amid the personified offerings of silks, satins, tapestries. The symbolism is transparent. . . . Zola's ambivalence in depicting the store is evident. While trying to suggest its real beauty, he rather testifies to its horrors. The colossal department store ruthlessly destroys the surrounding shopkeepers, just as Paris drains the provinces. The high priest, Mouret, is vain, smug, greedy, licentious. He is the priest of Baal, not Jehovah. And what purpose does the modern temple fill in the new Babylon? The image of the temple, let it be remembered, is Zola's own idea. The store is a temple to anti-nature. It appeals to modern woman's cult of artificiality. It serves humanity by satisfying greed and the Babylonian frenzy for movement. The joy of work, which Zola claims for the store, is only the happiness of obtaining money by any possible means. Man's goal is to enjoy his vices, wines, women, with the offerings garnered in the new temple. (pp. 76-7)

Zola gives a vividly putrefying portrait of modern Babylon in *Paris.* While he may admire the grandeur of the megalopolis and its possibilities, he abhors its basic artificiality. Zola's condemnation is explicit. The cosmopolitan is not only anti-natural, and hence reprehensible, but repulsive. (p. 79)

Les Rougon-Macquart has two great themes: the city and the city-dweller (the cosmopolitan) reacting to stress. In this case Babylon intensifies the hereditary ills and weaknesses deriving from Tante Dide. Zola's study is of psychological and physiological degeneration, and despite its appended optimism the series is profoundly pessimistic. Paris is destructive and modern man is anti-natural; he will be destroyed for his transgressions against nature. This is his constant theme. The follies of the example, the peculiar foibles of the Rougon-Macquart families, provide another theme. The motifs are of course inextricably related. But by separating them, somewhat artificially, the importance of Paris as Babylon, and of *all* cosmopolitans reacting to the city, becomes much clearer.

Zola may not have realized what an abject picture of Paris he has really drawn. In his notes . . . he is constantly reminding himself to be "optimistic," to show the "real joys of life and work." His efforts seem unconvincing. The weakest link in the *Rougon-Macquart* series is his final novel. *Le Docteur Pascal,* as a dénouement, is neither logically nor artistically satisfying. Dr. Pascal is made into something of a superman so that Zola could verify, he thought, his scientific theories on progress. Pascal's medical discoveries and miraculous cures seem, artistically, like a *deus ex machina.* They are totally unconvincing and obviously forced. Thematically they are incongruent with the tragic vision of Babylon given in his long epic of despair and degeneracy. *Le Docteur Pascal* is jarring. The reader has been prepared for nineteen novels to expect a *Götterdämmerung* the like of which literature has seen neither before nor after. Instead of that he receives a pious sermon on the necessity for hygiene. There is no greater anti-climax in the whole of literature. (p. 80)

George Ross Ridge, "The Decadent: A Cosmopolitan in Babylon," in his The Hero in French Decadent Literature *(reprinted by permission of the University of Georgia Press; © 1961 by The University of Georgia Press), University of Georgia Press, 1961, pp. 67-82.**

HARRY LEVIN   (essay date 1963)

Zola believed as sincerely in naturalism as in science and democracy; and those words, too, still held the untarnished promise of novelty during the opening years of the Third Republic. (p. 306)

Naturalisme has always belonged to the vocabulary of French philosophy, designating any system of thought which accounts for the human condition without recourse to the supernatural and with a consequent emphasis upon the material factors. Where *réalisme,* borrowed from the fine arts, need imply no more than detailed visualization, the philosophical catchword brings with it a further and more limiting implication: the conditioning effect of men's backgrounds upon their lives. (p. 307)

[Zola adopted the assumptions of an up-to-date science], which has badly dated since his day, and more especially the genetic studies of Dr. Prosper Lucas as expanded in his *Traité philosophique de l'hérédité naturelle.* Zola was not really experimenting; he was parroting Lucas' notions, when he showed hereditary weaknesses—such doubtful ones as criminality—being transmitted from parents to children. But it was a good excuse for creating an inordinately large cast of characters who turn out to be remarkably similar to one another. (p. 308)

Surely no comparable man of letters, with the exception of Poe, had tried so hard to grasp the scientific imagination. [Zola's] contemporary, Jules Verne, led the way for writers of science fiction to tinker with imaginary gadgets. Science for them has been an Aladdin's lamp, a magical fulfillment, an easy trick for outstripping the inventors. For Zola it was much tougher than that; it was behavior under pressure; and the literary experimenter was both the witness of the behavior and the gauge of the pressure. "What is a good experiment then?" the mathematician Henri Poincaré would later ask, and would answer: "It is what lets us know more than an isolated fact; it is what enables us to predict—in other words, to generalize." By that broader definition, Zola's art may have something in common with science after all. . . .

[A] formulation, which [Zola] liked to repeat, defines a work of art as "an aspect of nature visualized through a temperament." This gives the artist back almost everything that naturalistic rigor would take away. Both components of that definition were amplified in a letter written at the very outset of his career, shortly before his discovery of Claude Bernard: "I believe that in the study of nature, *just as it is,* there is a great source of poetry; I believe that a poet born with *a certain temperament* will in future centuries be able to discover new effects by addressing himself to exact investigations." Thus behind the experiment looms the experience—or, at any rate, the observation. That, in Zola's case, was less intensive or extensive than his printed avowals or his publicized impact and image may have led us into believing. (p. 309)

To his interviewers he staunchly declared that he invented nothing; while *Le Roman expérimental* proposed to substitute novels of observation for novels of imagination. (p. 310)

Frequently, when observation flags and invention takes over, obsession tips its hand. Certain situations are so peculiar and so recurrent that we may accord to them a thematic significance. Then again Zola speaks explicitly through personages very close to himself such as Sandoz, the burgeoning writer in *L'Oeuvre,* or the eponymous hero of *Le Docteur Pascal.* He walks in and out as an incorruptible journalist through the corrupting sphere of *L'Argent,* or as a novelistic witness in *Paris,* "the man of crowds. . . alone in the midst of everybody." (p. 311)

"It is around a symbol that a book is composed," André Gide has remarked, concluding that any well-composed work must therefore by symbolic, and that a work of art has to be the exaggeration of an idea. Gide's remark is borne out not only by Zola; it is corroborated by the very titles of lesser novels composed in his vein around American institutions—*The Octopus,* Frank Norris on the railroad; *The Jungle,* Upton Sinclair on the stockyards. As Anatole France discerned, concurring in a view which many critics surprised themselves by taking, the view of Zola as poet: "His grand and simple genius creates symbols, and brings to birth new myths."

That is the pith of the paradox: new myths. At a moment when fiction has been swinging away from naturalism, when the interplay of symbols is tending to obscure a primary sense of actuality, we scarcely need encouragement to look for archetypal recurrences amidst the accumulation of particular details. Flaubert struck a proper balance for Zola when he testified, "Nana turns into a myth without ceasing to be real." . . . Where the Flaubertian ironies play off the present against the past, Zola, by making every effort to be timely, somehow breaks through to the semblance of timelessness. Nana was completely designed to be a *demi-mondaine* of the Second Empire; she makes her appearance, singing atrociously, in a parody of an Offenbach burlesque; yet, under the aspect of the Blonde Venus, she is metamorphosed into a sempiternal goddess of love. Similarly in *La Curée,* where the love story is a modernized version of *Phèdre,* the analogy is pointed up when the aberrant wife and son attend Ristori's performance of Racine's tragedy. The mythical component is less explicit in *La Terre;* but there is a clear similarity between Père Fouan, who parcels out his land among three children, and the King Lear of Shakespeare—or of Turgenev. (p. 325)

Zola created "a pessimistic epic of human animality," said Jules Lemaître anent *Germinal,* and went on to say of *La Bête humaine* that the title would serve for the whole of Zola's work. (p. 328)

It is not a long distance from *Le Roman expérimental* to *The Call of the Wild.* The lesson of mute suffering is underlined in Zola's bestiary, as it was in Flaubert's or Vigny's, but even more the stark ferocity that Balzac had discerned in Cooper's Indians. Those carpetbaggers of the Second Empire, the Rougons, are regularly compared to famished wolves. Prostitutes prowl the streets like "beasts in a cage." It may be significant that Zola's best play. *Les Heritiers Rubourdin* was based upon Volpone or The Fox and Zola admits that what he saw in Ben Jonson's satiric beast-fable was "the human beast unleashed with all its appetites." But where the English comic playwright was a traditionalist—like the author of the *Comédie humaine*—holding up beastly conduct to more humane standards, Zola bases his ethic upon the state of nature. "Ancient art deified Nature," he asserted in a sketch, *Aux champs,* "Modern art has humanized her." Where the ancients were pantheists, the moderns are Rousseauists, continuing to look toward the landscape for sympathy. "Nature," as Zola restates it in *Mes Haines,* "is associated with our griefs." He is careful not to commit a pathetic fallacy; nature may also be associated with our joys; but it is we who project the association. And, since we have relegated ourselves to the side of the apes, grief seems likely to prevail over joy.

The contrast between shadow and sunlight in *La Faute de l'abbé Mouret,* between the gloomy church and the teeming barnyard outside, reinforces that basic antithesis between religion and nature which Zola connected with "the eternal struggle of life against death." This conflict is pursued to the very ending, when the priest's imbecile sister, who "cares only for animals," interrupts a burial service to announce that her cow has just calved. Even more crudely, *La Terre* commences with the graphic description of a farm-girl, Françoise Mouche, stoutly assisting the local bull to mate with her cow. Later the accouchement of her sister, Lise, is closely paralleled by that of the cow. The latter's case has obstetrical complications, since one of the twin calves is born alive and one dead, and so the eternal struggle goes on. These touches, which many readers attributed to a congenital low-mindedness, are not bathetic nor even, for Zola, shocking. They are variations on his persistent theme, the cycle of fertility and sterility. (pp. 329-30)

In contradistinction to creative forces, whether carnal or vegetative, the power of destruction works through mechanics, most expressly through the engines of war in *La Débâcle.* Under the surface of the earth, the mining operations of *Germinal* are ill-omened and suspect, enveloped in an almost primitive awe before the violation of nature's underground secrets, and grimly contrasted at the beginning and end with the sprouting beet-fields overhead. The title, signifying germination, was the name of the first month of spring in the revolutionary calendar; and its more orthodox counterpart, April, is noted for both cruelty and potentiality. The seasonal rhythm it sets is the prophecy of an ideological ripening for seeds and roots now crammed beneath the soil. The gesture of a countryman picking up a clod and hurling it at his wayward daughter, in *La Faute de l'abbé Mouret,* might well serve as a signature for the earthy Zola. . . . The good earth, in spite of those fecundating virtues hymned by Zola-Sandoz, is not necessarily a healthy influence; it is whatever man makes of it. "Man makes the earth," runs a proverb from his ancestral Reauce, which Zola cites in *La Terre.* Robert Frost has given Americans a rough equivalent: "The land was ours before we were the land's." (pp. 331-32)

The texture of Zola's writing was inherently coarse-grained; it suffered comparatively when it was printed along with *nouvelles* by more succinct and elegant disciples, notably Maupassant and Huysmans; but he had the perception to make good the virtue of its defect, its unliterary vigor. The gap between academic canons and the norms of *la langue parlée* has been wider in French than in many other languages, certainly much wider than in our own. . . . The resulting narration does not assume any higher tone than the conversation, but mingles, by way of *le style indirect libre,* with the more relaxed syntax and the more pungent diction of vulgar speech. The innovation has subsequently developed into the stock-in-trade of such vernacularists as Charles-Louis Philippe, Louis-Ferdinand Céline, and Raymond Queneau. But it is still a salutary shock to open the book and listen at once to the vivid phraseology of the concierge's lodge and the neighborhood *bistro.* (p. 348)

> *Harry Levin, in his* The Gates of Horn: A Study of Five French Realists *(copyright © 1963 by Harry Levin; reprinted by permission of the author and Oxford University Press, Inc.), Oxford University Press, New York, 1963, 550 p.*

LAWSON A. CARTER (essay date 1963)

Zola's life-long courtship of the stage was inspired by motives which varied with the changes in his literary stature and personal ambitions. After some youthful, tentative exercises in playwriting, of which only *Madeleine* has survived, financial necessity obliged him to approach the theater as an empty-handed adventurer in whom the commercial instinct was uppermost. In this spirit was conceived his first produced play, the hackneyed *Mystères de Marseille* written in collaboration with Marius Roux. The failure of the venture taught him to treat the theater with greater respect and originality, and his next plays, *Thérèse Raquin* and *les Héritiers Rabourdin,* were real efforts to enlarge the horizons of the stage. The inability of critics and public alike to appreciate their worth induced a shift in his perspective. His literary stature was growing with the first novels of the *Rougon-Macquart,* and he was now armed with the powerful weapon of naturalism, derived from his assimilation of scientific methods to literature. As if determined to avenge his own defeats by destroying the forces which had operated against him and to conquer by force of argument a medium which had resisted his creative efforts, Zola began a series of weekly articles in the press, in which for more than four years he laid vigorous siege to theatrical conventions. Early in this campaign, the astounding success of his novel *l'Assommoir* brought him renown and independence, and caused a further shift in his perspective. While continuing to denounce the contemporary theater in a voice resonant with his success as a novelist, he poured all of his naturalist philosophy into his novels, and, for a time, contented himself in the theater with somewhat cynical concessions to the box office. His farce of *le Bouton de Rose,* unobjectionable for a hack writer, was on Zola's part a contemptuous gesture to the theater. His collaborations with Busnach were intended for the most part as popular melodramas, exhibiting some aspects of naturalism in their scenes of every-day life, but generally impregnated with commercial considerations. In refusing to allow his name to appear as co-author of the Busnach adaptations, Zola in effect served notice on the public that he considered them unworthy of his talent, although he defended them stoutly against hostile criticism. He was willing to acknowledge authorship to only one other play of his naturalist period, but *Renée,* built on the most implausible of foundations, was inadequate as a demonstration of his theories, in spite of its well-projected characters. . . . The six librettos which represent his final work for the stage reveal a new Zola, a Zola who, in keeping with his epoch, turned from an objective and scientific examination of life to a symbolic and lyric interpretation of what life is and of what it may be. His unrealized project for a vast cycle of dramas demonstrates that at the time of his death, far from discouraged at his many past frustrations in the theater, he was determined to devote his major effort to this form of expression, and to repeat on the stage his triumphs in the novel.

As a liberating force, Zola exercised considerable influence on the contemporary stage, even though in large measure the influence was intangible. His program of theatrical reform, as to both subject matter and technique, did in fact come to pass, stripped, however, of his scientific pretensions. The scope of the stage was in fact enlarged to include the frank and objective portrayal of disagreeable subjects, of unsympathetic characters, and of all classes of society engaged in scenes of every-day life. Dialogue, stage movement and scenery became more faithful to the speech, gestures and settings of real life, so that actors were increasingly able to convey the illusion of "living", rather than of "play-acting", their rôles. . . . The failure of Zola's own plays detracted from his reputation as a critic. *Thérèse Raquin* appears in retrospect as a minor theatrical landmark. . . . Zola's subsequent plays offered examples of dramatic art which no playwright of genuine talent would have wanted to emulate. In his collaborations with Busnach, particularly in the adaptation of *l'Assommoir*, Zola was able to present successfully some elements of naturalism on the stage, but the value of these contributions was limited to superficial matters of setting and of costume, and to a few isolated scenes foreshadowing the "slice of life" technique. Essentially, however, the Busnach collaborations were so tainted with time-worn theatrical clichés as to disqualify them as models of a new art.

Although Zola's failure in the theater impaired his reputation as critic, his prestige as novelist gave amplitude to his voice. Specially privileged by success to speak of the novel, he cannily extended this privilege into the domain of the theater by drawing a parallel between the two forms. Why, he enquired, did the novel enjoy greater freedom than the stage? The force of his dramatic criticism was derived from this parallel. The indisputable success of the naturalist novel, with its freedom to reveal festering sores of humanity, was a reproach to the theater. Zola's complaint could not be ignored, and the theatrical climate of the 1880s did in fact become more favorable to shocking or repellant plays than it had been before his campaign of reform. . . . It is justifiable to believe that Zola's dramatic criticism was instrumental in creating an atmosphere receptive to new ferments in the theater.

The weakness of Zola's criticism, corroborated by the weakness of his own plays, lay in his inability or unwillingness to distinguish between freedom of subject matter and freedom of technique. He never acknowledged that the stage had a discipline of its own. In his enthusiasm to rid the theater of conventions which hampered a candid portrayal of life, he failed to recognize the necessity of other conventions to replace them. Expert in the free manipulation of prose narrative, he was a theatrical anarchist, hoping to make the stage over into a utopia for novelists. But, as in the case of the social utopias of his last novels, he was unable or unwilling to supply workable disciplines in exchange for those which he sought to destroy. The task of carrying on the theatrical evolution fell to other minds, more sensitive than Zola's to the subtle currents of the stage. Nevertheless, his insensitivity was redeemed by his force. The strident tone of his criticism tolled the knell of outworn theatrical methods. The seeds of his discontent were fertile, and yielded a harvest which, insofar as the theater is concerned, was left for others to gather. (pp. 207-10)

> *Lawson A. Carter, in his summary to his* Zola and the Theater *(a revision of a dissertation presented at Yale University in 1951;* © *1963, Presses Universitaires de France), Presses Universitaires de France, 1963, pp. 207-11.*

JOHN C. LAPP (essay date 1964)

[Zola's *Contes à Ninon* and *Nouveaux Contes à Ninon*] have nothing of the objectivity, concision and geometric structure we have come to expect in the short story. Frequently mere observations, these stories in almost every instance conform to a process of thinking out loud, serious and humorous in turn, in which the author mingles critical speculation with the record of his personal experiences. Only in a very few cases do they contain a plot with a beginning, middle and end, and they are never built upon such carefully planned structures as his best-known tale, **"L'Attaque du moulin."**

Zola's first *contes* possess, however, two dominant characteristics. First, they are deliberately and unabashedly autobiographical, inevitably taking as their subject the author's memories and observations. They even include diary-like fragments entitled baldly: **"Souvenirs"**. . . . Secondly, despite their seeming formlessness, they follow a basic pattern; the "song of do-you-remember" is a lyrical exchange between the author and the imaginary Ninon, a beautiful girl from the Midi. Out of this dialogue emerges a polarity: the age-old opposition of city and country. But this contrast does not merely serve as an outlet for romantic longings, it demonstrates the aesthetic problem which very clearly confronted the young author in the mid-1860's: the nature and role of reality in art. For the Zola of *Les Contes à Ninon*, the Paris from which he writes stands for reality; dull, disillusioning, with its "jour blafard." Provence, and in particular the country around Aix that he knew so well, seen from afar, becomes the situs of dream and fantasy, of limitless horizons, of "les clairs soleils, les midis ardents." Later on, the outskirts of Paris replace the Midi; the pastel tones of Saint-Ouen or Bennecourt crowd out the raucous colours of Pourrières and Le Tholonet.

It is precisely these two characteristics that lend the early *contes,* regardless of their literary merit, a special importance for the student of Zola who attempts to lay bare the permanent qualities of his genius.

The urge to confess, so evident a motive in Zola's early works, produced a conflict, equally evident, in a novelist dedicated to objectivity. The persistence of this urge perhaps explains the persistent survival of certain themes and patterns throughout the *Rougon-Macquart*. The important role of memory, on both the conscious and unconscious levels, of memories never those of the characters but always the author's, results . . . in a fusion of past and present, typical of Zola's work.

The dialogue with Ninon is the first instance of the well-known duality in Zola's work. Any Zola novel mingles documentary truth and imaginative speculation, reality and myth, fact and fantasy: a quality of which he was well aware, since he not infrequently referred to a particular novel as "mon poème." A study of the *contes* should permit us to go deeper into these known facts, to examine certain elements of his work "in the raw," that is, to examine them as they appeared at the precise time when Zola was attempting to determine what their relative importance should be. (pp. 3-5)

Among Zola's later works, those that were the most resolutely realistic were to be precisely those that dealt with social injustice. *L'Assommoir, Germinal,* and *La Terre* lead inevitably to a consideration of socialism as a remedy. In his *contes,* Zola seems already to be fully aware of social injustice and to consider it a fitting subject for literature. But when he treats poverty or social misfortune in these early works he seems unable or unwilling to take the usual realistic path of depicting people in a contemporaneous setting. Far from remaining dispassionate and objective he frequently uses a rather heavy-handed irony, and the only remedy he seems to consider is charity. (pp. 11-12)

[The *contes* in which charity appears as the solution for poverty] belong to the realm of fantasy, of miracles and visitations of the Virgin; to a faraway period of quasi-mediaeval hue. Despite their frequently realistic descriptions and sombre themes, such tales remain within the fairy domain of **"La Fée Amoureuse."** Elsewhere in his *contes,* however, Zola presents poverty and misery unrelieved by sentimentality. One such study is **"Le Chômage,"** an episode in the experience of a worker and his family after a week's unemployment. We first see the employer telling his men that his plant must close. No blame attaches to him, for, like the mine managers in **Germinal,** he is a victim of economic circumstances; no orders for his goods have come and he is forced to close. The men shake his hand in silence and depart. There follow the worker's search for employment, the pawning of every belonging, the temptation to beg, and finally the return, empty-handed, to the desolate room where a starving child is crying out "J'ai faim."

In these stark pages there is no hint of fantasy or sentimentality; no charitable figure appears in the nick of time to succour the destitute family. Zola maintains a rigid objectivity throughout. Yet realism is not fully attained, for the protagonists bear no name: they are "le patron," "les ouvriers," "l'ouvrier," "la femme de l'ouvrier"; the nature of their work is unknown. **"Le Chômage"** is one of the rare *contes* narrated throughout in the present tense, a device which adds to its quality of timelessness. (p. 15)

The theme of the endless cycle of life and death in nature, from the seed in fertile earth to the final burial; the theme of growth and fertility, of the unceasing communion of all things, was to become prominent in the **Rougon-Macquart,** with its most conspicuous examples the luxuriant garden of **La Faute de l'abbé Mouret** and the fertility symbolism of **La Terre.** . . . [This] theme manifested itself in the early *contes,* but it does not assume a position of central importance until **"Les Quatre Journées de Jean Gourdon."**

In its early form this story offers the first example of Zola's preference for the rigorously symmetrical construction later exemplified in such works as **Une Page d'amour** and **La Bête humaine.** Each of the four *journées*—the mediaeval term for one section of a drama Zola undoubtedly chose purposely— falls in one of the four seasons, and each season symbolizes an age of man. Zola's principal subject is growth, marriage and catastrophe in the opulent valley of the Durance, the benevolent river that fertilizes its verdant shores, only to burst its banks savagely during a January thaw, destroying all the family but Jean and his grandchild. (pp. 32-33)

[One characteristic] casts light upon the very nature of the Zola novel and its place in the development of the genre. This is the never quite resolved struggle, in the name of objectivity, to submerge his own person, the I of the narrator, in the character-receptor through whose consciousness the world of *conte* or novel comes into being. This all-seeing character begins by being Zola himself, the first-person narrator of the *contes* and "Souvenirs," who later on appears transparently in the Claude of **La Confession** [*de Claude*]. Even when he becomes a fullfledged character, like the Claude in **L'Oeuvre,** Muffat in **Nana,** Etienne in **Germinal,** he shares with his creator that all-embracing viewpoint that lies somewhere between the stare of the *voyeur* and the gaze of the *voyant,* in Rimbaud's sense of the term. (p. 160)

> *John C. Lapp, in his* Zola before the "Rougon-Macquart" *(copyright, 1964, by University of Toronto Press), University of Toronto Press, 1964, 171 p.*

DEMETRA PALAMARI (essay date 1979)

"A great producer, a creator, has no other function than to eat his century in order to create life from it"—thus Emile Zola thought of himself as "a shark who swallows his epoch." His particular focus in "creating life" was the family, and his fame rests on the series of twenty novels subtitled *The Natural and Social History of a Family of the Second Empire,* in which he traced the fortunes of the Rougon-Macquart family through all levels of French society in the second half of the nineteenth century. In this great work, Zola examined the family closely and realistically, considering its relation to the social and cultural context; moreover he used the family as a metaphor for social evolution, as a vehicle for an explication of natural laws, to set forth the actual unfolding of the principles of Darwin and Comte in their specific, historical, and human manifestations. These ideas, powerful in his time, were selectively interpreted and presented, sometimes deliberately and accurately, at other times unconsciously—reflecting his own peculiarities. . . . His description of himself as a consuming shark illuminates a major theme that is woven in and out of many of the novels: social forms are secondary elaborations, often corrupted and corrupting, in conflict with the amoral repetitiveness of life itself, blind nature living by tooth and claw but ultimately ever renewing itself, hence indestructible. Human institutions, societies, nations, individual personalities, whole historical epochs arise and decay (often brought down by their own blindness, selfishness, and artifice). Humanity continues; the animal world continues; new epochs are born out of the old ones, and they too will decay and die. Zola is fascinated with the interplay of nature and culture, the absorption of the latter by the former, the corruption of the former by the latter: over and over his imagery reconsiders their relatedness, their antagonism and their common basis in the unquenchable amoral rhythms rooted in the imperishability of life itself.

In the center of this set of concerns is the family: an anomalous institution, neither fully cultural nor yet a part of nature. It is the absolutely essential organization without which there is no humanity, yet it becomes the agent for repressive and antinatural forces, thus life-threatening as well as life-sustaining in this capacity. The family is used by Zola to demonstrate the paradoxical nature of the human beast, neither wholly angel nor brute, stranded between nature and culture, subject to the laws of both, which, often contradictory, inevitably generate destructive choices and consequences. Zola illuminates his time, to be sure, but he goes considerably beyond this and draws to our attention some of the genuinely paradoxical features of the family, features that we do well to attend in our studies of any century of society.

Zola makes the family the principal actor in his artistic creation. In the preface to the **Rougon-Macquart** novels, he states his aims:

> I want to explain how a family, a small group of beings, acts in a society. . . . I will show how this group behaves as an actor in a historical epoch. I will create its action in all of its complexity, I will analyze both the sum of the will of each of its members and the general direction of the group.

In this passage Zola reveals conceptions basically inspired by Comte: that social groups, including families, are, like a single organism, made up of interdependent parts whose full mutual functioning is necessary to the survival of the whole. . . . Solidarity of social classes is a fact of life for Zola. None survives if one part is overlooked. Justice is thus part of a natural reciprocity. Insofar as society is a human invention, humanity poisons itself. Indeed it is one of Zola's express purposes to show how the social milieu that mankind has produced makes itself felt. Humanity's invention, culture, has forever set mankind apart from animal nature and so has changed the course of evolution. This is a point which Zola perceives and shows, while he consciously denies it, asserting over and over that the same laws apply to all of life, mankind and nature. He recognizes the differences made by culture, denies them, is ambivalent about them, and this ambivalence is reflected in his views of the family and individuals. (pp. 155-57)

In the lower classes the family is oriented to mere survival, economical and physical, and this it does inadequately and sporadically in Zola's novels. Nothing is left over beyond the survival struggle; socialization of children, the other major task of the family, is out of the question. And those families mercifully freed from the desperate requirements of mere existence—to be found among the bourgeoisie—are no more viable, for there, socialization takes place but is as deadly as the traditional enemies of the poor. The family, imperiled from within and without, is more necessary than ever, and, paradoxically, pressed beyond its capacities by this inordinate necessity. (p. 158)

Of the **Rougon-Macquart** novels, *Germinal, Pot-Bouille,* and *L'Assommoir* contain the most explicit and fully expressed examples of the breakdown of family life, but there are many additional instances in the other novels of the series, covering all levels of society. In almost every treatment of the family, Zola underscores two principal themes: the family is a central and necessary part of the social structure; at the same time it is corrupt and dissolute. (p. 166)

The families of the lower classes are not the only casualties of the social attitudes Zola depicts. Bourgeois and aristocratic families are also menaced morally, if not physically. Just as Zola's society refuses to acknowledge any physical conditions not in harmony with the bourgeois adage of *enrichissez-vous* (get rich), so it condemns any human urge that endangers the facade of rigid morality designed to hold the family together. It is an oppressive morality that condemns the spontaneous and natural, and the family is its vehicle. Ironically, then, the family brings about its own breakdown. In upholding a morality that is false and applied only superficially, the family becomes corrupt. To remain a viable institution morally, the family must avoid extremes, neither encouraging too much restraint nor allowing too much laxity. The nineteenth-century family that Zola portrays fosters both of these extremes by professing a morality that allows for almost no natural urges and tacitly condoning the violation of its own rules. (p. 171)

The picture of the family given by Zola in the **Rougon-Macquart** novels indicates that, in the case of the poor, whether rural or urban, the family gives no protection to the individual against the ills of the social order, while the bourgeois or aristocratic family is so morally repressive in its very nature that it causes its own breakdown. Ideally, the family should serve both the individual and society, for it socializes the individual and at the same time upholds the social moral order. In Zola's view, the French family of the mind-nineteenth century, beset by economic and moral problems, was no longer capable of performing these necessary functions. (p. 172)

> *Demetra Palamari, "The Shark Who Swallowed His Epoch: Family, Nature, and Society in the Novels of Emile Zola," in Changing Images of the Family,*

> *edited by Virginia Tufte and Barbara Myerhoff (copyright © 1979 by Yale University), Yale University Press, 1979, pp. 155-72.*

F.W.J. HEMMINGS   (essay date 1980)

[Zola was] one of the most prolific letter-writers of his period. . . .

As an *épistolier,* however, Zola is not to be compared with Stendhal, or even with Mérimée. . . . Nor is it really possible to say of him what he himself said of Balzac, whose letters he was reading in 1876 in the edition brought out that year by Michel Lévy: "Never did a writer's correspondence show that writer to be so great and so good." For one thing, his letters are almost entirely to other men . . . ; nor did he have, as did Balzac, Flaubert, and Stendhal too, a beloved younger sister to whom he could confide his hopes and ambitions. The nearest equivalent to Laure Surville, to Caroline Flaubert or to Pauline Beyle was Paul Cézanne, to whom he wrote a series of long, affectionate letters when he first came to Paris, aged eighteen, having left his boyhood companion behind in Aix. Their enforced separation seems to have drawn the pair of them closer together; the superscriptions, almost formal in the earliest letters ("Mon cher Cézanne") graduate progressively through "Mon cher ami" and "Mon cher Paul" to "Mon bon vieux."

But one searches in vain through [*Correspondance: Tome 1, 1858-1867; Tome 2, 1868-mai 1877*] for those gossipy details that would allow one to fill in the tantalizing gaps in our knowledge of Zola's life during those crucial *années de bohème* between 1859 and 1862. "If I don't talk to you about my private life", he writes in 1860, "if I don't describe to you how I'm fixed, it's because these material details could neither fan nor cool our friendship, and would have no effect except to make me more depressed." The letters are stuffed instead with nostalgic reminiscences of the good old days, the hunting, shooting, and . . . bathing they indulged in on hot days in Provence, with well-meant advice to Cézanne (all his life, Zola could never resist the temptation to give his friends the benefit of his superior wisdom), and with impractical schemes for his own future, for at this time Zola saw himself as a *doux poète* living on air. But there are no indiscretions.

> *F.W.J. Hemmings, "The Making of a Naturalist," in The Times Literary Supplement (© Times Newspapers Ltd. (London) 1980; reproduced from The Times Literary Supplement by permission), No. 4044, October 3, 1980, p. 1107.*

ADDITIONAL BIBLIOGRAPHY

Barbusse, Henri. *Zola.* Translated by Mary Balairdie Green and Frederick C. Green. New York: E. P. Dutton, 1933, 279 p.
    Documents Zola's research and compositional methods.

Cady, W. W. "Emile Zola." In his *Studies of Paris,* pp. 178-242. New York, London: G. P. Putman's Sons, 1887.
    Laudatory survey describing Zola as "one of the most moral novelists in France."

De Bacourt, Pierre, and Cunliffe, J. W. "Emile Zola (1840-1902)." In their *French Literature During the Last Half Century,* pp. 15-40. New York: The Macmillan Co., 1927.
    Literary career of Zola and outline of the "Rougon-Macquart" novels, explicating Zola's literary theories, themes, and style.

Kanes, Martin. *Zola's "La Bête humaine": A Study in Literary Creation*. Berkeley, Los Angeles: University of California Press, 1962, 138 p.

Critical study designed "to elucidate 'structure' and to explore the complex process by which form and meaning reciprocally determine each other" in *La bête humaine*. The critic analyzes Zola's notes, reference sources, and stages of composition.

Lapp, John C. "The Watcher Betrayed and the Fatal Woman: Some Recurring Patterns in Zola." *PMLA* LXXIV, No. 3 (June 1959): 276-84.

Examines the recurrence in Zola's works of situations in which either "a lover returns to supplant the husband" or an observer "must in some way witness his own ignominy," associating these with the presence of a Fatal Woman and discussing Zola's treatment of this traditional literary theme.

Levin, Harry. "Zola." In his *The Gates of Horn: A Study of Five French Realists*, pp. 305-71. New York: Oxford University Press, 1963.

Analyzes Zola's literary theories and development as a novelist, observing that his "cycle of life and work had revolved . . . from sociological observation to socialistic action."

Pasco, Allan H. "Myth, Metaphor, and Meaning in *Germinal*." *The French Review* XLVI, No. 4 (March 1973): 739-49.

Mythic parallel in *Germinal*.

Smethurst, Colin. *Emile Zola: Germinal*. London: Edward Arnold, 1974, 64 p.

Study of the composition, themes, and theory behind *Germinal*.

Turnell, Martin. "Zola." In his *The Art of French Fiction: Prévost, Stendhal, Zola, Maupassant, Gide, Mauriac, Proust*, pp. 91-194. London: Hamish Hamilton, 1959.

Critical overview of the *Rougon-Macquart* novels, with an analysis of Zola's prose style.

Appendix

THE EXCERPTS IN TCLC, VOLUME 6, WERE REPRINTED FROM THE FOLLOWING PERIODICALS:

The Academy
Accent
American Literary Realism: 1870-1900
American Literature
The American Review of Reviews
The American Scholar
Arizona and the West
The Athenaeum
The Atlantic Monthly
Best Sellers
The Bookman (London)
The Bookman (New York)
The Boston Transcript
Canadian-American Slavic Studies
Canadian Literature
The Canadian Magazine
Catholic World
The Chesterton Review
The Colophon
Commonweal
Comparative Literature
Contemporary Literature
Contemporary Review
The Cornhill Magazine
The Crisis
The Critic
The Dalhousie Review
The Dial
Dissertation Abstracts
The Edinburgh Review
Elementary English
Essays in Criticism
The Fortnightly Review
Forum
The Freeman
Freewoman
The French Review
French Studies
The Gentleman's Magazine
The Germanic Review
Harper's

Hispania
Hollins Critic
Horizon
The Hound & Horn
The Hudson Review
The Journal of Arizona Culture
Journal of Modern Literature
Journal of Popular Culture
The Junior Bookshelf
The Lion and the Unicorn
The Listener
The Literary Review (New York)
Literature and Psychology
The London Mercury
The Markham Review
McClure's Magazine
Midcontinent American Studies
  Journal
The Midwest Quarterly
The Mississippi Valley Historical
  Review
Modern Fiction Studies
The Modern Language Journal
Modern Language Review
Modern Philology
Ms.
The Nation
The Nation and The Athenaeum
National Review
Nature
The New Republic
The New Statesman & Nation
New York Herald Tribune Book Review
The New York Review of Books
The New York Times
The New York Times Book Review
The New Yorker
The North American Review
North Dakota Quarterly
Novel: A Forum on Fiction
The Observer

Opportunity
Outlook
The Overland Monthly
Parnassus: Poetry in Review
Partisan Review
Poet Lore
Queen's Quarterly
Renascence
The Reviewer
Review of English Studies
Review of National Literatures
Romance Notes
The Saturday Review (London)
The Saturday Review of Literature
Scando-Slavica
Science-Fiction Studies
The Sewanee Review
Shenandoah
Slavic and East European Journal
The Slavonic Review
The Smart Set
South Atlantic Quarterly
The Southern Humanities Review
The Southern Review
The Spectator
Studies in Contemporary Satire
Studies in the Novel
Symposium
Temple Bar
Time & Tide
The Times Literary Supplement
Tulane Studies in English
The Twentieth Century
The University of Kansas City Review
Vanity Fair
Virginia Quarterly Review
Western American Literature
Willison's Monthly
World Literature Today
The Yale Review
The Yellow Book

THE EXCERPTS IN TCLC, VOLUME 6, WERE REPRINTED FROM THE FOLLOWING BOOKS:

Abramson, Doris E. Negro Playwrights in the American Theatre, 1925-1959. *Columbia University Press, 1969.*

Aiken, Conrad. Collected Criticism. *Oxford University Press, 1968.*

Alcott, Louisa May. Louisa May Alcott: Her Life, Letters, and Journals. *Edited by Ednah D. Cheney. Roberts Brothers, 1890.*

Aldiss, Brian W. Billion Year Spree: The True History of Science Fiction. *Doubleday, 1973, Schocken Books, 1974.*

Allen, Paul M. *Foreward to* "Caspar Hauser": The Enigma of a Century, *by Jacob Wassermann. Translated by Caroline Newton. Rudolf Steiner, 1973.*

Allott, Kenneth. Jules Verne. *Kennikat Press, 1970.*

Altrocchi, Rudolph. Sleuthing in the Stacks. *Harvard University Press, 1944.*

Amis, Kingsley. What Became of Jane Austen? and Other Questions. *Jonathan Cape, 1970, Harcourt, 1971.*

Amoia, Alba della Fazia. Edmond Rostand. *Twayne, 1978.*

Anderson, Sherwood. No Swank. *The Centaur Press, 1934.*

Anderson, Sherwood. Letters of Sherwood Anderson. *Edited by Howard Mumford Jones with Walter B. Rideout. Little, Brown, 1953.*

Archer, William. Poets of the Younger Generation. *John Lane, 1902, Scholarly Press, 1969.*

Atkins, John. George Orwell: A Literary Study. *John Calder, 1954, Calder & Boyars, 1971.*

Austin, William W., ed. New Looks at Italian Opera: Essays in Honor of Donald J. Grout. *Cornell University Press, 1968.*

Barker, Dudley. G. K. Chesterton: A Centenary Appraisal. *Edited by John Sullivan. Barnes & Noble, 1974.*

Barthes, Roland. Mythologies. *Edited and translated by Annette Lavers. Hill and Wang, 1972.*

Beaumont, E. M., Cocking, J. M., and Cruickshank, J., eds. Order and Adventure in Post-Romantic French Poetry: Essays Presented to C. A. Hackett. *Basil Blackwell, 1973.*

Beerbohm, Max. Around Theatres. *Simon & Schuster, 1954.*

Bell, Aubrey F. G. Contemporary Spanish Literature. *Alfred A. Knopf, 1925.*

Belloc, Hilaire. *Introductin to* A Companion to Mr. Wells's "Outline of History". *Sheed & Ward, 1926.*

Bennett, Arnold. Mark Twain: The Critical Heritage. *Edited by Frederick Anderson and Kenneth M. Sanderson. Rutledge and Kegan Paul Ltd, 1971.*

Bentley, Eric. The Brecht Commentaries. *Grove Press, 1981.*

Bergonzi, Bernard. The Early H. G. Wells: A Study of the Scientific Romances. *Manchester University Press, 1961.*

Bergonzi, Bernard, ed. H. G. Wells: A Collection of Critical Essays. *Prentice-Hall, Inc., 1976.*

Bertaux, Félix. A Panorama of German Literature from 1871 to 1931. *Translated by John J. Trounstine. Whittlesey House, 1935.*

Blankenagel, John C. The Writings of Jakob Wassermann. *The Christopher Publishing House, 1942.*

Bloom, Robert. Anatomies of Egotism: A Reading of the Last Novels of H. G. Wells. *University of Nebraska Press, 1977.*

Bone, Robert. The Negro Novel in America. *Rev. ed. Yale University Press, 1965.*

Borello, Alfred. H. G. Wells: Author in Agony. *Edited by Harry T. Moore. Southern Illinois University Press, 1972.*

Borges, Jorge Luis. Other Inquisitions: 1937-1952. *Translated by Ruth L. C. Simms. University of Texas Press, 1964.*

Boyd, Ernest. Studies from Ten Literatures. *Scribner's, 1925.*

Boyd, Ian. The Novels of G. K. Chesterton: A Study in Art and Propaganda. *Barnes & Noble, 1975.*

Bradbury, Malcolm. Possibilities: Essays on the State of the Novel. *Oxford University Press, 1973.*

Branch, Douglas. The Cowboy and His Interpreters. *Appleton, 1926.*

Braybrooke, Patrick. Philosophies in Modern Fiction. *The C. W. Daniel Company Ltd., 1929.*

Briggs, Julia. Night Visitors: The Rise and Fall of the English Ghost Story. *Faber and Faber, 1977.*

Brooks, Cleanth. A Shaping Joy: Studies in the Writer's Craft. *Methuen, 1971.*

Brooks, Cleanth, Purser, John Thibaut, and Warren, Robert Penn, eds. An Approach to Literature. *3rd. ed. Appleton-Century-Crofts, 1952.*

Brooks, Van Wyck. The Ordeal of Mark Twain. *Rev. ed Dutton, 1933, A.M.S. Press, 1977.*

Brown, Clarence. Introductin to The Prose of Osip Mandelstam: ''The Noise of Time,'' ''Theodosia,'' ''The Egyptian Stamp,'' *by Osip Mandelstam. Translated by Clarence Brown. Princeton University Press, 1965.*

Brown, Clarence. Osip Mandelshtam: Sobranie sochenenii. *Inter-Language Literary Associates, 1967.*

Brown, E. K. On Canadian Poetry. *Rev. ed. Ryerson Press, 1944, The Tecumseh Press, 1973.*

Brown, Sterling. The Negro in American Fiction. *The Associates in Negro Folk Education, 1938, Kennikat Press, Inc., 1968.*

Broyde, Steven. Osip Mandel'stam and His Age. *Harvard University Press, 1975.*

Bryer, Jackson R., ed. F. Scott Fitzgerald: The Critical Reception. *Burt Franklin & Co., Inc., 1978.*

Bunin, Ivan. The Village. *Knopf, 1933.*

Burdett, Osbert. Critical Essays. *Henry Holt and Company, 1925.*

Burnshaw, Stanley, et al, eds. The Poem Itself. *Holt, 1960.*

Butler, E. M.Rainer Maria Rilke. *Macmillan, 1941.*

Canby, Henry Seidel. Turn West, Turn East: Mark Twain and Henry James. *Houghton, 1959.*

Cancalon, Elaine D. Fairy-Tale Structures and Motifs in ''Le grand Meaulnes''. *Herbert Lang, Peter Lang, 1975.*

Canetti, Elias. Kafka's Other Trial: The Letters to Felice. *Translated by Christopher Middleton. Schocken Books, 1974.*

Cardwell, Guy A., ed. Discussions of Mark Twain. *D. C. Heath and Company, 1963.*

Cargill, Oscar. Intellectual America: Ideas on the March. *Macmillan, 1941.*

Cargill, Oscar, & others, eds. O'Neill and His Plays: Four Decades of Criticism. *New York University Press, 1961.*

Carter, Lawson A. Zola and the Theater. *Presses Universitaires de France, 1963.*

Champigny, Robert. Portrait of a Symbolist Hero: An Existential Study Based on the Work of Alain-Fournier. *Indiana University Press, 1954.*

Chiari, Joseph. The Contemporary French Theatre: The Flight from Naturalism. *Rockliff, 1958.*

Chandler, Raymond. The Simple Art of Murder. *Houghton, 1950, Ballantine Books, 1972.*

Chesterton, Gilbert K. Heretics. *John Lane Company, 1905, Books for Libraries Press, 1970.*

Chesterton, G. K. Lunacy and Letters. *Sheed and Ward, 1958.*

Clarke, Arthur C. Introduction to A Journey to the Center of the Earth, *by Jules Verne. Dodd, Mead & Company, 1959.*

Clemens, S. L. Mark Twain's Letters, Vol. II. *Edited by Albert Bigelow Paine. Harper, 1917.*

Colby, Frank Moore. Imaginary Obligations. *Dodd, Mead & Company, 1913.*

Conrad, Joseph. Joseph Conrad: Life and Letters, Vol. I. *Edited by G. Jean-Aubry. Doubleday, 1927.*

Corkery, Daniel. Synge and Anglo-Irish Literature. *Mercier, 1931.*

Corrigan, Mathew. Malcolm Lowry: The Man and His Work. *Edited by George Woodcock. University of British Columbia Press, 1971.*

Corrigan, Robert W. Masterpieces of the Modern Spanish Theatre. *Macmillan/Collier Books, 1967.*

Costa, Richard Hauer. Malcolm Lowry. *Twayne, 1972.*

Costello, Peter. Jules Verne: Inventor of Science Fiction. *Hodder and Stoughton, 1978.*

Crawford, Virginia M. Studies in Foreign Literature. *Duckworth and Co., 1899.*

Cross, Richard K. Malcolm Lowry: A Preface to His Fiction. *The University of Chicago Press, 1980.*

Davis, Arthur P. From the Dark Tower: Afro-American Writers 1900 to 1960. *Howard University Press, 1974.*

Day, Douglas. Preface to Dark as the Grave Wherein My Friend Is Laid, *by Malcolm Lowry. Edited by Douglas Day and Margerie Lowry. The New American Library, 1968.*

Day, Douglas. Malcolm Lowry: A Biography. *Oxford University Press, 1973.*

DeVoto, Bernard. Minority Report. *Little, Brown and Company, 1940.*

DeVoto, Bernard. Introduction to The Portable Mark Twain, *by Samuel Langhorne Clemens. Edited by Bernard DeVoto. Viking Penguin, 1946.*

Dorosz, Kristofer. Malcolm Lowry's Infernal Paradise. *Almqvist Wiksell International, 1976.*

Dragland, S. L., ed. Duncan Campbell Scott: A Book of Criticism. *Tecumseh Press, 1974.*

Drake, William A. Contemporary European Writers. *John Day, 1928, Harrap, 1929.*

Drinkwater, John. The Muse in Council. *Sidgwick and Jackson Limited, 1925.*

Dukes, Ashley. The Youngest Drama: Studies of Fifty Dramatists. *Ernest Benn, Limited, 1923.*

Eliot, T. S. Introduction to The Adventures of Huckleberry Finn, *by Samuel Langhorne Clemens (Mark Twain). The Cresset Press, 1950.*

Ellis, Havelock. Affirmations. *Walter Scott Limited, 1898, Houghton Mifflin Co., 1922.*

Ellis, Havelock. Introductin to The Wanderer, *by Alain Fournier. Translated by Françoise Delisle. Houghton, 1928.*

Ellis-Fermor, Una. The Irish Dramatic Movement. *Rev. ed. Methuen & Company, 1954.*

Ellman, Richard, ed. Edwardians and Late Victorians. *Columbia University Press, 1960.*

Eloesser, Arthur. Modern German Literature. *Translated by Catherine Alison Phillips. Alfred A. Knopf, 1933.*

Epstein, Perle S. The Private Labyrinth of Malcolm Lowry: ''Under the Volcano'' and the Cabbala. *Holt, 1969.*

Evans, I. O. Jules Verne and His Work. *Twayne Publishers, Inc., 1966.*

Fairchild, Hoxie Neale. Religious Trends in English Poetry: 1880-1920, Gods of a Changing Poetry, Vol. V. *Columbia University Press, 1962.*

Falk, Doris V. Eugene O'Neill and the Tragic Tension: An Interpretive Study of the Plays. *Rutgers, 1958.*

Farren, Robert. The Course of Irish Verse in English. *Sheed and Ward, Inc., 1947.*

Faulkner, William. Faulkner at Nagano. *Edited by Robert A. Jelliffe. Kenkyusha, 1956.*

Fiedler, Leslie A. The Collected Essays of Leslie Fiedler, Vol. I. *Stein and Day, 1971.*

Folsom, James K. The American Western Novel. *College & University Press, 1966.*

Ford, Ford Madox. Portraits from Life. *Houghton Mifflin Company, 1937.*

Forster, E. M. Two Cheers for Democracy. *Harcourt, 1951.*

Fowlie, Wallace. Climate of Violence: The French Literary Tradition from Baudelaire to the Present. *Macmillan, 1967.*

French, Warren, ed. The Twenties: Fiction, Poetry, Drama. *Everett/Edwards, Inc., 1975.*

Gagey, Edmond M. Revolution in American Drama. *Columbia University Press, 1947.*

Garland, Hamlin. Hamlin Garland's Diaries. *The Huntington Library, 1968.*

Gass, Willaim H. Fiction and the Figures of Life. *Alfred A. Knopf, 1970.*

Gibson, Robert. The Land without a Name: Alain-Fournier and His World. *Paul Elek, 1975.*

Gloster, Hugh M. Negro Voices in American Fiction. *University of North Carolina Press, 1948.*

Golding, William. The Hot Gates and Other Occasional Pieces. *Faber and Faber, 1965.*

Gray, Ronald D. Brecht the Dramatist. *Cambridge University Press, 1976.*

Gray, Ronald, ed. Kafka: A Collection of Critical Essays. *Prentice-Hall, 1962.*

Grey, Zane. To the Last Man: A Novel. *Harper, 1921.*

Griffiths, Richard, ed. Claudel: A Reappraisal. *Dufour Editions, 1968.*

Grigson, Geoffrey. The Contrary View: Glimpses of Fudge and Gold. *Rowman and Littlefield, 1974.*

Guerard, Albert J. Conrad: The Novelist. *Harvard University Press, 1965.*

Hale, Edward Everett, Jr. Dramatists of Today: Rostand, Hauptmann, Sudermann, Pinero, Shaw, Phillips, Maeterlinck. *Henry Holt and Company, 1911.*

Harkins, William E. Karel Čapek. *Columbia University Press, 1962.*

Haynes, Roslynn D. H. G. Wells, Discoverer of the Future: The Influence of Science on his Thought. *New York University Press, 1980.*

Hearn, Lafcadio. Essays in European and Oriental Literature. *Dodd, Mead and Company, 1923.*

Heller, Erich. Franz Kafka. *Edited by Frank Kermode. Viking Penguin, 1974.*

Hemingway, Ernest. Green Hills of Africa. *Charles Scribner's Sons, 1935.*

Hemingway, Ernest. By-Line, Ernest Hemingway: Selected Articles and Dispatches of Four Decades. *Scribner's, 1967.*

Hemmings, F.W.J. Émile Zola. *Oxford University Press, 1953.*

Hergesheimer, Joseph. Introduction to Tales of My Native Town, *by Gabriele D'Annunzio. Translated by Rafael Mantellini. Doubldeday, Page & Company, 1920, Greenwood Press, 1968.*

Hewitt, Douglas. Conrad: A Reassessment. *3rd. ed. Rowman and Littlefield, 1975.*

Howe, P. P. J. M. Synge: A Critical Study. *Martin Secker, 1912.*

Howells, W. D. My Mark Twain: Reminiscences and Criticisms. *Harper, 1910.*

Hughes, Langston. The Big Sea: An Autobiography. *Knopf, 1940, Hill and Wang, 1963.*

Hughes, Langston. Introduction to Pudd'nhead Wilson, *by Mark Twain, Bantam Books, 1959, 1981.*

Jacob, Max. The Dice Cup: Selected Prose Poems. *Edited by Michael Brownstein. Translated by Zack Rogow. Sun, 1979.*

James, Henry. Notes on Novelists, with Some Other Notes. *Scribner's, 1914.*

James, Henry. The Letters of Henry James. *Edited by Percy Lubbock. Scribner's, 1920.*

James, M. R. Ghost Stories of an Antiquary. *Dover, 1971.*

James, M. R. The Ghost Stories of M. R. James. *2nd. ed. Edward Arnold, 1974.*

Jaye, Michael C., and Watts, Ann C., eds. Literature and the Urban Experience: Essays on the City and Literature. *Rutgers University Press, 1981.*

Jullian, Phillipe. D'Annunzio. *Librairie Artheme Fayard, 1971, Viking Penguin, 1973.*

Kafka, Franz. The Diaries of Franz Kafka: 1910-1913. *Edited by Max Brod. Translated by Joseph Kresh. Schocken Books, 1948.*

Karl, Frederick R. A Reader's Guide to Joseph Conrad. *Rev. ed. Farrar, Straus & Giroux, 1969.*

Karl, Frederick R. A Reader's Guide to the Contemporary English Novel. *Rev. ed. Farrar, Straus & Giroux, 1972.*

Kazin, Alfred. On Native Ground: An Interpretation of Modern American Prose Literature. *Reynal & Hitchcock, 1942.*

Kazin, Alfred. F. Scott Fitzgerald: The Man and His Work. *The World Publishing Company, 1951.*

Knox, Ronald. Introduction to Father Brown: Selected Stories, by G. K. Chesterton. *Oxford University Press, 1955.*

Kostelanetz, Richard. The Yale Gertrude Stein. *Yale University Press, 1980.*

Kuehl, John, and Bryer, Jackson R., eds. Dear Scott/Dear Max: The Fitzgerald-Perkins Correspondence. *Charles Scribner's Sons, 1971.*

Lapp, John C. Zola before the ''Rougon-Macquart.'' *University of Toronto Press, 1964.*

Lawrence, D. H. Phoenix: The Posthumous Papers of D. H. Lawrence. *Edited by Edward D. McDonald. Viking Penguin, 1936.*

Leary, Lewis. Mark Twain. *University of Minnesota Press, Minneapolis, 1960.*

Levin, Harry. The Gates of Harn: A Study of Five French Realists. *Oxford University Press, 1963.*

Lovecraft, H. P. ''Dagon'' and Other Macabre Tales. *Edited by August Derleth. Arkham House, 1965.*

Lowry, Malcolm. Selected Letters of Malcolm Lowry. *Edited by Harvey Breit and Margerie Bonner Lowry. J. B. Lippincott Company, 1965.*

Lynd, Robert. Old and New Masters. *T. Fisher Unwin Ltd, 1919.*

MacCarthy, Desmond. Criticism. *Putnam, 1932.*

Mallarmé, Stéphane. Mallarmé: Selected Prose Poems, Essays, & Letters. *Translated by Bradford Cook. The Johns Hopkins University Press, 1956.*

Mandelstam, Nadezhda. Hope Abandoned. *Translated by Max Hayard. Atheneum, 1974.*

Martínez Sierra, Gregorio. The Cradle Song and Other Plays. *Translated by John Garrett Underhill. E. P. Dutton & Co., Inc., 1922.*

Martínez Sierra, Gregorio. The Kingdom of God and Other Plays. *Translated by Helen Granville-Barker and Harley Granville-Barker. E. P. Dutton & Co., Inc., 1922.*

Martínez Sierra, Gregorio. Sueño de una noche de agosto. *Edited by May Gardner and Arthur L. Owen. Translated by H. Granville-Barker. Holt, 1953.*

Mason, Eudo C. Introduction to The Book of Hours: Comprising the Three Books, Of the Monastic Life, Of Poverty and Death, *by Rainer Maria Rilke. Translated by A. L. Peck. Hogarth Press, 1961.*

Matthews, Brander. Introduction to The Innocents Abroad; or The New Pilgrim's Progress, Vol. I, *by Mark Twain. American Publishing Company, 1899.*

McDougall, Robert L., ed. Our Living Tradition. *University of Toronto Press, 1959.*

Mencken, H. L. Prejudices: First Series. *Knopf, 1919.*

Mencken, H. L. H. L. Mencken's ''Smart Set'' Criticism. *Edited by William H. Nolte. Cornell University Press, 1968.*

Meyers, Jeffrey. A Reader's Guide to George Orwell. *Thames and Hudson, 1975.*

Michaud, Régis. Modern Thought and Literature in France. *Funk & Wagnalls, 1934.*

Miller, Henry. Maurizius Forever. *Fridtjof-Karla Publications, 1959.*

Miller, Walter James, ed. The Annotated Jules Verne: ''Twenty Thousand Leagues under the Sea,'' *by Jules Verne. Thomas Y. Crowell Co., Inc., 1976.*

Milne, A. A. Autobiography. *E. P. Dutton & Co., Inc., 1939.*

Monahan, Michael. Nemesis. *Frank-Maurice Inc., 1926.*

Monas, Sidney. Introduction to Osip Mandelstam: Selected Essays, *by Osip Mandelstam. Translated by Sidney Monas. University of Texas Press, 1977.*

Montague, C. E. Dramatic Values. *Methuen & Co., Ltd., 1911, Doubleday, Page & Company, 1925.*

Moore, Virginia. Distinguished Women Writers. *Dutton, 1934.*

More, Paul Elmer. The Demon of the Absolute. *Princeton University Press, 1928.*

Mott, Frank Luther. Golden Multitudes: The Story of Best Sellers in the United States. *The Macmillan Company, 1947.*

Nabokov, Vladimir. Lectures on Literature. *Edited by Fredson Bowers. Harcourt, 1980.*

Nathan, George Jean. The World in Falseface. *Knopf, 1923.*

Nathan, George Jean. The Theatre Book of the Year, 1948-1949: A Record and an Interpretation. *Alfred A. Knopf, Inc., 1949.*

Nilsson, Nils Ake. Major Soviet Writers: Essays in Criticism. *Edited by Edward J. Brown. Oxford University Press, 1973.*

Nye, Russel. The Unembarrassed Muse: The Popular Arts in America. *Dial, 1970.*

O'Connor, Patricia W. Gregorio and María Martínez Sierra. *Twayne, 1977.*

O'Connor, Patricia Walker. Women in the Theater of Gregorio Martínez Sierra. *The American Press, 1966.*

O'Connor, William Van, ed. Forms of Modern Fiction: Essays Collected in Honor of Joseph Warren Beach. *The University of Minnesota Press, 1948.*

O'Hagen, Thomas. Essays on Catholic Life. *John Murphy Company, 1916, Books for Libraries Press, 1965.*

Olson, Tillie. ''Biographical Interpretation'' *to* Life in the Iron Mills; or The Korl Woman, *by Rebecca Harding Davis. The Feminist Press, 1972.*

Orwell, George. The Collected Essays, Journalism and Letters of George Orwell: My Country Right or Left, 1940-1943, Vol. II. *Edited by Sonia Orwell and Ian Angus. Secker & Warburg, 1968.*

Pacey, Desmond. Ten Canadian Poets: A Group of Biographical and Critical Essays. *Ryerson Press, 1958.*

Parker, H. T. Introduction to The Makropoulos Secret, *by Karel Capek. Edited by Randal C. Burrell. John W. Luce & Company, 1925.*

Parrinder, Patrick, ed. H. G. Wells: The Critical Heritage. *Routledge & Kegan Paul, 1972.*

Parrinder, Patrick, ed. Science Fiction: A Critical Guide. *Longman, 1979.*

Parrington, Vernon Lewis. Main Currents in American Thought, an Interpretation of American Literature from the Beginnings to 1920: The Beginnings of Critical Realism In America, 1860-1920, Vol. 3. *Harcourt, 1958.*

Pattee, Fred Lewis. The Development of the American Short Story: An Historical Survey. *Harper, 1923, Biblo and Tannen, 1966.*

Pellizzi, Camille. English Drama: The Last Great Phase. *Translated by Rowan Williams. Macmillan, 1935.*

Penzoldt, Peter. The Supernatural in Fiction. *P. Nevill, 1952, Humanities Press, 1965.*

Peters, H. F. Rainer Maria Rilke: Masks and the Man. *University of Washington Press, 1960.*

Phillips, Klaus. Introduction to Nine Plays, *by Rainer Maria Rilke. Translated by Klaus Phillips and John Locke. Ungar, 1979.*

Poggioli, Renato. The Phoenix and the Spider: A Book of Essays about Some Russian Writers and Their View of the Self. *Harvard University Press, 1957.*

Pollard, Percival. Masks and Minstrels of New Germany. *John W. Luce and Company, 1911.*

Pritchett, V. S. In My Good Books. *Chatto and Windus, 1942, Kennikat Press, 1970.*

Pritchett, V. S. The Living Novel. *Chatto and Windus, 1946.*

Pryce-Jones, Alan. Introduction to The Lost Domain: ''Le grande Meaulnes'', *by Alain-Fournier. Translated by Frank Davison. Oxford University Press, 1974.*

Quinn, Arthur Hobson. American Fiction: An Historical and Critical Survey. *Appleton-Century-Crofts, 1936.*

Raleigh, John Henry. The Plays of Eugene O'Neill. *Southern Illinois University Press, 1965.*

Rayfield, Donald. Introduction to ''Chapter 42'' by Nadezhda Mandel'shtam and ''The Goldfinch and Other Poems'' by Osip Mandel'shtam. *The Menard Press, 1973.*

Reilly, Joseph J. Dear Prue's Husband and Other People. *The Macmillan Company, 1932.*

Rhodes, Anthony. D'Annunzio: The Poet As Superman. *Astor-Honor, Inc., 1960.*

Ridge, George Ross. The Hero in French Decadent Literature. *University of Georgia Press, 1961.*

Ronald, Ann. Zane Grey. *Boise State University, 1975.*

Rose, Mark. Alien Encounters: Anatomy of Science Fiction. *Harvard University Press, 1981.*

Rule, Jane. Lesbian Images. *Doubleday, 1975.*

Russell, Bertrand. Portraits from Memory: And Other Essays. *Simon & Schuster, 1956.*

Russell, Francis. Three Studies in Twentieth Century Obscurity. *Hand and Flower Press, 1954.*

Saintsbury, George. A History of Criticism and Literary Taste in Europe: From the Earliest Texts to the Present Day, Vol. III. *Blackwood & Sons, 1904, 1935.*

Sale, Roger. Fairy Tales and After: From Snow White to E. B. White. *Harvard University Press, 1978.*

Schlegel, Dorothy B. James Branch Cabell: The Richmond Iconoclast. *The Revisionist Press, 1975.*

Schneider, Judith Morganroth. Clown at the Altar: The Religious Poetry of Max Jacob. *University of North Carolina Department of Romance Languages, 1978.*

Scott, Arthur P., ed. Mark Twain: Selected Criticism. *Southern Methodist University Press, 1955.*

Scott, Duncan Campbell. Selected Stories of Duncan Campbell Scott. *Edited by Glenn Clever. University of Ottawa Press, 1975.*

Seltzer, Alvin J. Chaos in the Novel, the Novel in Chaos. *Schocken Books, 1974.*

Shain, Charles E. F. Scott Fitzgerald. *University of Minnesota Press, 1961.*

Shaw, Bernard. Pen Portraits and Reviews. *Rev. ed. Constable and Company, Ltd, 1932.*

Singh, Amritjit. The Novels of the Harlem Renaissance: Twelve Black Writers 1923-1933. *The Pennsylvania State University Press, University Park, 1976.*

Skelton, Robin. The Writings of J. M. Synge. *The Bobbs-Merrill Company, Inc., 1971.*

Slonim, Marc. Modern Russian Literature: From Chekhov to the Present. *Oxford University Press, 1953.*

Smith, Henry Nash. Mark Twain: The Development of a Writer. *The Belknap Press of Harvard University Press, 1962.*

Smith, Hugh Allison. Main Currents of Modern French Drama. *Holt, 1925.*

Spender, Stephen. Introduction to Under the Volcano, by Malcolm Lowry. *J. B. Lippincott Company, 1965.*

Squire, J. C. Essays on Poetry. *Hodder and Stoughton, 1923.*

Squire, J. C. Sunday Mornings. *William Heinemann Ltd, 1930.*

Stich, K. P., ed. The Duncan Campbell Scott Symposium. *University of Ottawa Press, 1980.*

Strakhovsky, Leonid I. Craftsmen of the Word: Three Poets of Modern Russia, Gumilyov, Akhmatova, Mandelstam. *Harvard University Press, 1949, Greenwood Press, 1969.*

Sullivan, Jack. Elegant Nightmares: The English Ghost Story from Le Fanu to Blackwood. *Ohio University Press, 1978.*

Sutherland, Donald. Gertrude Stein: A Biography of Her Work. *Yale University Press, 1951.*

Sutton, Graham. Some Contemporary Dramatists. *Kennikat Press, Inc., 1925.*

Suvin, Darko. Metamorphoses of Science Fiction: On the Poetics and History of a Literary Genre. *Yale University Press, 1979.*

Swann, Thomas Burnett. A. A. Milne. *Twayne, 1971.*

Swinnerton, Frank. The Georgian Scene: A Literary Panorama, *Farrar & Rinehart, 1934.*

Swinnerton, Frank. The Georgian Literary Scene, 1910-1935: A Panorama. *Farrar, Straus and Company, 1950.*

Symons, Arthur. Introduction to The Child of Pleasure, by Gabriele D'Annunzio. *Translated by Georgina Harding. William Heinemann, Ltd., 1898.*

Synge, John Millington. The Well of Saints. *A. H. Bullen, 1905.*

Szczesny, Gerhard. The Case Against Bertolt Brecht, with Arguments Drawn from His "Life of Galileo." *Translated by Alexander Gode. Ungar, 1969.*

Tarrant, Desmond. James Branch Cabell: The Dream and the Reality. *University of Oklahoma Press, 1967.*

Thau, Annette. Poetry and Antipoetry: A Study of Selected Aspects of Max Jacob's Poetic Style. *University of North Carolina Department of Romance Languages, 1976.*

Thompson, Francis. The Real Robert Louis Stevenson and Other Critical Essays. *Edited by Rev. Terence L. Connolly. S.J. University Publishers, 1959.*

Tuell, Anne Kimball. Mrs. Meynell and Her Literary Generation. *E. P. Dutton & Company, 1925.*

Tufte, Virginia, and Myerhof, Barbara, eds. Changing Images of the Family. *Yale University Press, 1979.*

Turrell, Charles Alfred, ed. Contemporary Spanish Dramatists. *Translated by Charles Alfred Turrell. The Gorham Press, 1919.*

Ullmann, Stephen. The Image in the Modern French Novel: Gide, Alain-Fournier, Proust, Camus. *Cambridge University Press, 1960.*

Van Doren, Carl. Contemporary American Novelists: 1900-1920. *Macmillan, 1922.*

Van Doren, Carl; Mencken, H. L.; and Walpole, Hugh. James Branch Cabell: Three Essays. *Kennikat, 1967.*

Vittorini, Domenico. The Modern Italian Novel. *University of Pennsylvania Press, 1930.*

Völker, Klaus. Brecht: A Biography. *Translated by John Nowell. The Seabury Press, 1978.*

Vonnegut, Kurt Jr. "Opening Remarks" to The Unabridged Mark Twain. *Edited by Lawrence Teacher. Running Press, 1976.*

Wain, John. Essays on Literature and Ideas. *Macmillan and Co., 1963.*

Warren, Austin. Connections. *University of Michigan Press, 1970.*

Warren, L. A. Modern Spanish Literature: A Comprehensive Survey of the Novelists, Poets, Dramatists and Essayists from the Eighteenth Century to the Present Day, Vol. II. *Brentano's, Ltd, 1929.*

Way, Brian. F. Scott Fitzgerald and the Art of Social Fiction. *St. Martin's, 1980.*

Wellek, René. Essays on Czech Literature. *Mouton Publishers, 1963.*

Wells, Arvin R. Jesting Moses: A Study in Cabellian Comedy. *University of Florida Press, 1962.*

Wells, H. G. The Scientific Romances of H. G. Wells. *Gollancz Ltd., 1933.*

Wells, H. G. Experiment in Autobiography: Discoveries and Conclusions of a Very Ordinary Brain (since 1866). *The Macmillan Company, 1934.*

West, Anthony. Principles and Persuasions: The Literary Essays of Anthony West. *Harcourt, 1957.*

Whipple, T. K. Study Out the Land: Essays. *University of California Press. 1943.*

Wilkins, Ernest Hatch. A History of Italian Literature. *Harvard University Press, 1954.*

Williams, Raymond. George Orwell. *Viking Penguin, 1971.*

Wilson, Colin. The Strength to Dream: Literature and the Imagination. *Houghton, 1962.*

Wilson, Edmund. The Shores of Light: A Literary Chronicle of the Twenties and Thirties. *Farrar, Straus & Giroux, 1952.*

Wilson, Edmund. The Bit between My Teeth: A Literary Chronicle of 1950-1965. *The Noonday Press, 1965.*

Wilson, Edmund, ed. The Crack-Up, *by F. Scott Fitzgerald. New Directions, 1945.*

Wilson, Edmund, ed. The Collected Essays of John Peale Bishop. *Charles Scribner's Sons, 1948.*

Woodward, James B. Ivan Bunin: A Study of His Fiction. *University of North Carolina Press, 1980.*

Woolf, Virginia. Contemporary Writers. *The Hogarth Press, 1965.*

Young, Kenneth. H. G. Wells. *Edited by Ian Scott-Kilvert. British Council, 1974.*

Young, Stark. Immortal Shadows: A Book of Dramatic Criticism. *Charles Scribner's Sons, 1948.*

Ziolkowski, Theodore. Dimensions of the Modern Novel: German Texts and European Contexts. *Princeton University Press, 1969.*

Cumulative Index to Authors

Cumulative Index to Nationalities

587

NATIONALITY
INDEX

Cumulative Index to Critics

CRITIC INDEX

Cole, Leo R.
Juan Ramón Jiménez 4:220

Collier, Eugenia W.
James Weldon Johnson 3:242

Collier, S. J.
Max Jacob 6:191

Collins, Joseph
Edna St. Vincent Millay 4:309

Colombo, J. R.
Malcolm Lowry 6:237

Colum, Padraic
A. E. 3:6
Lord Dunsany 2:142
Kahlil Gibran 1:328
Lady Gregory 1:333
Edna St. Vincent Millay 4:306
James Stephens 4:414

Combs, Robert
Hart Crane 2:125

Comerchero, Victor
Nathanael West 1:482

Commager, Henry Steele
Henry Adams 4:6
Willa Cather 1:155
F. Scott Fitzgerald 1:245

Connolly, Cyril
A. E. Housman 1:354
James Joyce 3:276
D. H. Lawrence 2:369
Gertrude Stein 1:434

Connolly, Francis X.
Willa Cather 1:156

Connolly, Julian W.
Ivan Bunin 6:58

Conrad, Joseph
Joseph Conrad 6:112
Henry James 2:245
Hugh Walpole 5:495
H. G Wells 6:523

Cook, Bruce
Raymond Chandler 1:175

Cooper, Frederic Taber
Gertrude Atherton 2:13
Arnold Bennett 5:23
Ellen Glasgow 2:175
Zane Grey 6:176

Cordle, Thomas
André Gide 5:222

Corkery, Daniel
John Millington Synge 6:432

Corrigan, Matthew
Malcolm Lowry 6:244

Corrigan, Robert W.
Bertolt Brecht 1:119
Federico García Lorca 1:324
Henrik Ibsen 2:239
Gregorio Martínez
Sierra and María Martínez
Sierra 6:284

Cortissoz, Royal
Hamlin Garland 3:190

Cosman, Max
Joyce Cary 1:141

Costa, Richard Hauer
Malcolm Lowry 6:246

Costello, Peter
Jules Verne 6:499

Costich, Julia F.
Antonin Artaud 3:62

Coustillas, Pierre
George Gissing 3:236

Coward, Noël
Saki 3:373

Cowley, Malcolm
Sherwood Anderson 1:51
Guillaume Apollinaire 3:33
Henri Barbusse 5:13
A. E. Coppard 5:176
Hart Crane 2:117
F. Scott Fitzgerald 1:238, 272;
6:166
Amy Lowell 1:371, 378
Katherine Mansfield 2:445
Arthur Schnitzler 4:392
Virginia Woolf 1:533

Cox, C. B.
Joseph Conrad 1:218

Cox, James Trammell
Ford Madox Ford 1:286

Coxe, Louis O.
Edith Wharton 3:567

Coxhead, Elizabeth
Lady Gregory 1:335

Craig, G. Dundas
Rubén Darío 4:63

Crane, Hart
Hart Crane 5:184

Crankshaw, Edward
Jakob Wassermann 6:511

Crawford, Virginia M.
Edmond Rostand 6:373

Crews, Frederick
Joseph Conrad 1:216

Croce, Arlene
Eugene O'Neill 1:404

Croce, Benedetto
Émile Zola 1:588

Cross, Richard K.
Malcolm Lowry 6:253

Cross, Wilbur
Arnold Bennett 5:33
John Galsworthy 1:297

Crowley, Aleister
James Branch Cabell 6:65

Cruse, Harold
James Weldon Johnson 3:246

Cullen, Countee
James Weldon Johnson 3:240

Cunliffe, John W.
A. E. Housman 1:354

Cunningham, J. V.
Wallace Stevens 3:454

Currey, R. N.
Alun Lewis 3:289

Curtis, Penelope
Anton Chekhov 3:170

Cushman, Keith
Ernest Dowson 4:93

D., B.
Kahlil Gibran 1:327

Daemmrich, Horst S.
Thomas Mann 2:441

Dahlberg, Edward
Sherwood Anderson 1:56
F. Scott Fitzgerald 1:256

Daiches, David
Willa Cather 1:157
Joseph Conrad 1:211
A. E. Housman 1:355
James Joyce 3:258
Katherine Mansfield 2:449
Wilfred Owen 5:362
Dylan Thomas 1:469
Virginia Woolf 1:539
William Butler Yeats 1:558

Daleski, H. M.
Joseph Conrad 1:220

Dalphin, Marcia
A. A. Milne 6:309

Damon, S. Foster
Amy Lowell 1:374

Dane, Clemence
Hugh Walpole 5:497

Daniel, John
Henri Barbusse 5:16

Daniels, Jonathan
Marjorie Kinnan Rawlings
4:359

Danielson, Larry W.
Selma Lagerlöf 4:242

Damon, S. Foster
Amy Lowell 1:374

Darton, F. J. Harvey
Arnold Bennett 5:25

Dauner, Louise
Joel Chandler Harris 2:212

Davenport, Basil
Lewis Grassic Gibbon 4:120,
121

Daviau, Donald G.
Karl Kraus 5:282

Davidson, Donald
Joseph Conrad 6:114

Davie, Donald
D. H. Lawrence 2:373
Wallace Stevens 3:449

Davies, J. C.
André Gide 5:237

Davies, John
Alun Lewis 3:289

Davies, Margaret
Colette 5:165

Davies, Robertson
Stephen Leacock 2:381

Davies, Ruth
Leonid Andreyev 3:27
Anton Chekhov 3:168

Davis, Arthur P.
Countee Cullen 4:44
Wallace Thurman 6:450

Davis, Cynthia
Dylan Thomas 1:475

Davis, Robert Murray
F. Scott Fitzgerald 6:167

Davis, Oswald H.
Arnold Bennett 5:45

Davison, Edward
Robert Bridges 1:125
Walter de la Mare 4:74
Saki 3:365

Day, Douglas
Malcolm Lowry 6:241, 247

Debicki, Andrew P.
César Vallejo 3:530

de Bosschere, Jean
May Sinclair 3:437

De Castris, A. L.
Luigi Pirandello 4:342

DeKoven, Marianne
Gertrude Stein 6:415

de la Mare, Walter
Rupert Brooke 2:53

de la Selva, Salomón
Rubén Darío 4:55

de Ónis, Harriet
Mariano Azuela 3:80

Derleth, August
H. P. Lovecraft 4:266

De Selincourt, E.
Robert Bridges 1:129

Desmond, Shaw
Lord Dunsany 2:143

Des Pres, Terrence
Bertolt Brecht 6:38

Deutsch, Babette
A. E. Coppard 5:177
Hart Crane 5:186
Countee Cullen 4:40
Edna St. Vincent Millay 4:311
Wilfred Owen 5:365
Edwin Arlington Robinson
5:413
Sara Teasdale 4:426, 427

Deutscher, Isaac
George Orwell 2:500

DeVoto, Bernard
Eugene O'Neill 6:328
Mark Twain 6:465
Thomas Wolfe 4:509

Dick, Kay
Colette 1:192

Dickey, James
Edwin Arlington Robinson
5:414

Dickman, Adolphe-Jacques
André Gide 5:213

Didier, Pierre
Georges Bernanos 3:117

Dimock, Edward C., Jr.
Rabindranath Tagore 3:493

Dobie, Ann B.
Gerhart Hauptmann 4:207

Dobrée Bonamy
D. H. Lawrence 2:345

Dobson, A.
Miguel de Unamuno 2:569

CRITIC INDEX

CRITIC INDEX

Povey, John
Roy Campbell 5:126

Powell, Anthony
George Orwell 2:513

Powell, Lawrence Clark
Gertrude Atherton 2:18
Raymond Chandler 1:172

Powys, John Cowper
Edgar Lee Masters 2:464
Dorothy Richardson 3:350

Praz, Mario
Luigi Pirandello 4:326

Predmore, Michael P.
Juan Ramón Jiménez 4:221,
225

Prescott, Orville
Joyce Cary 1:141

Preston, Harriet Waters
Vernon Lee 5:309

Prevelakis, Pandelis
Nikos Kazantzakis 2:313

Price, Martin
Joyce Cary 1:141

Price, Nancy
Lord Dunsany 2:144

Priestley, J. B.
J. M. Barrie 2:45
Arnold Bennett 5:29
James Bridie 3:137
Walter de la Mare 4:72
Henrik Ibsen 2:231
Stephen Leacock 2:380
Sinclair Lewis 4:255
August Strindberg 1:451
Hugh Walpole 5:495
William Butler Yeats 1:567
Émile Zola 1:594

Primeau, Ronald
Countee Cullen 4:52

Pritchard, William H.
Edwin Arlington Robinson
5:417

Pritchett, V. S.
Arnold Bennett 5:44
Samuel Butler 1:136, 137
Karel Čapek 6:86
Anton Chekhov 3:155
Joseph Conrad 1:203, 206
Ronald Firbank 1:229
George Gissing 3:232
Thomas Hardy 4:165
D. H. Lawrence 2:355
Wyndham Lewis 2:387
Katherine Mansfield 2:451
George Orwell 2:497
Dorothy Richardson 3:358
Saki 3:366
Bruno Schulz 5:425
John Millington Synge 6:434
Giovanni Verga 3:545
H. G. Wells 6:534
Émile Zola 1:594

Proffer, Carl R.
Aleksandr Kuprin 5:301

Proust, Marcel
Leo Tolstoy 4:466

Prusek, Jaroslav
Lu Hsün 3:299

Pryce-Jones, Alan
Alain-Fournier 6:18
Bertolt Brecht 1:107

Purdom, C. B.
Harley Granville-Barker 2:196

Purser, John Thibaut
Ivan Bunin 6:47

Pyatkovsky, A. Ya.
Leo Tolstoy 4:445

Quinn, Arthur Hobson
James Branch Cabell 6:67
Rebecca Harding Davis 6:150
Joel Chandler Harris 2:210
Bret Harte 1:342

Quinn, Vincent
Hart Crane 5:188

Rabinovich, Isaiah
Sholom Aleichem 1:29

Ragussis, Michael
D. H. Lawrence 2:373

Rahv, Philip
Franz Kafka 2:289
George Orwell 6:340
Virginia Woolf 5:509

Raknes, Ola
Jonas Lie 5:325

Raleigh, John Henry
F. Scott Fitzgerald 1:251
Eugene O'Neill 6:335

Ralston, W.R.S.
Leo Tolstoy 4:447

Ramsey, Warren
Guillaume Apollinaire 3:36
Paul Valéry 4:493

Rankin, Daniel S.
Kate Chopin 5:144

Ransom, John Crowe
Thomas Hardy 4:164
Edna St. Vincent Millay 4:314
Edith Wharton 3:563

Raper, J. R.
Ellen Glasgow 2:189

Rascoe, Burton
Zane Grey 6:180

Raven, Simon
Joyce Cary 1:142

Ray, Gordon N.
H. G. Wells 6:540

Ray, Robert J.
Ford Madox Ford 1:285

Rayfield, Donald
Osip Mandelstam 6:266

Read, Herbert
Robert Bridges 1:126

Reck, Rima Drell
Georges Bernanos 3:121

Redding J. Saunders
Charles Waddell Chesnutt
5:132
Countee Cullen 4:42
Paul Laurence Dunbar 2:128
James Weldon Johnson 3:241

Redman, Ben Ray
Georges Bernanos 3:116

Reed, F. A.
Nikos Kazantzakis 5:267

Reed, John R.
H. G. Wells 6:551

Reeve, F. D.
Aleksandr Blok 5:88

Rehder, R. M.
Thomas Hardy 4:177

Reilly, Joseph J.
Kate Chopin 5:146
Alice Meynell 6:300

Reinert, Otto
August Strindberg 1:458

Reiss, H. S.
Arthur Schnitzler 4:394

Repplier, Agnes
Alice Meynell 6:295

Revitt, Paul J.
W. S. Gilbert 3:215

Rexroth, Kenneth
Roy Campbell 5:124
Ford Madox Ford 1:290
Wallace Stevens 3:459

Rhodes, Anthony
Gabriele D'Annunzio 6:137

Rhys, Brian
Henri Barbusse 5:14

Rhys, Ernest
Rabindranath Tagore 3:483

Ribbans, Geoffrey
Miguel de Unamuno 2:564

Richardson, Jack
Eugene O'Neill 1:406

Richardson, Maurice
M. R. James 6:209

Richey, Elinor
Gertrude Atherton 2:18

Riddel, Joseph N.
Wallace Stevens 3:466

Rideout, Walter B.
Sherwood Anderson 1:54

Ridge, George Ross
Émile Zola 6:565

Ridge, Lola
Henri Barbusse 5:13

Riewald, J. G.
Max Beerbohm 1:69

Riley, Anthony W.
Frederick Philip Grove 4:142,
144

Rimanelli, Giose
Cesare Pavese 3:339

Ringe, Donald A.
George Washington Cable 4:35

Ritchie, J. M.
Gottfried Benn 3:113

Rittenhouse, Jessie B.
Edna St. Vincent Millay 4:305
Sara Teasdale 4:425

Rizzo, Gino
Ugo Betti 5:57, 62

Roback, A. A.
Sholem Asch 3:67

Robertson, J. G.
Henry Handel Richardson 4:371

Robinson, Christopher
Kostes Palamas 5:385

Robinson, Henry Morton
James Joyce 3:261

Robinson, Lennox
Lady Gregory 1:333

Robinson, W. R.
Edwin Arlington Robinson
5:416

Robson, W. W.
G. K. Chesterton 1:188

Rodgers, Lise
Hart Crane 5:194

Roditi, Edouard
Oscar Wilde 1:500

Rogers, Timothy
Rupert Brooke 2:57

Rogers, W. G.
Gertrude Stein 1:429

Roggendorf, Joseph
Tōson Shimazaki 5:430

Ronald, Ann
Zane Grey 6:185

Rose, Marilyn Gaddis
Katharine Tynan 3:506

Rose, Mark
Jules Verne 6:504

Rose, Shirley
Dorothy Richardson 3:358

Rosen, Norma
Rebecca Harding Davis 6:154

Rosenbaum, Sidonia Carmen
Gabriela Mistral 2:476
Alfonsina Storni 5:444

Rosenberg, Harold
James Weldon Johnson 3:241

Rosenblatt, Roger
John Millington Synge 6:442

Rosenfeld, Paul
Sherwood Anderson 1:34

Rosenthal, M. L.
César Vallejo 3:529
William Butler Yeats 1:567

Rosenthal, Michael
Joyce Cary 1:147

Rosenthal, Raymond
Leo Tolstoy 4:469
Giovanni Verga 3:544

Ross, Alan
Nathanael West 1:478

Ross, Stephen M.
James Weldon Johnson 3:249

Rostropowicz, Joanna
Bruno Schulz 5:424

Rowse, A. L.
Alun Lewis 3:285

Rozhdestvensky, Vsevolod
Sergei Esenin 4:113

CRITIC INDEX

CRITIC INDEX

CRITIC INDEX